CLASSICS
OF MODERN
POLITICAL
THEORY

CLASSICS OF MODERN POLITICAL THEORY

Machiavelli to Mill

Edited by

STEVEN M. CAHN

New York · Oxford
OXFORD UNIVERSITY PRESS
1997

OXFORD UNIVERSITY PRESS

Oxford   New York
Athens   Auckland   Bangkok   Bogota   Bombay   Buenos Aires
Calcutta   Cape Town   Dar es Salaam   Delhi
Florence   Hong Kong   Istanbul   Karachi
Kuala Lumpur   Madras   Madrid   Melbourne
Mexico City   Nairobi   Paris   Singapore
Taipei   Tokyo   Toronto

and associated companies in
Berlin   Ibadan

Library of Congress Cataloging-in-Publication Data
Classics of modern political theory / edited by Steven M. Cahn.
        p.   cm.
    Includes index.
    ISBN 0-19-510173-1
    1. Political science—History.   2. Political science—History—
Sources. I. Cahn, Steven M.
JA83.C535   1996
320—dc20   95-26515
                                                CIP

Printing (last digit): 9 8 7 6 5 4 3 2

Printed in the United States of America
on acid-free paper.

To my teachers at Columbia College

CONTENTS

PREFACE

This volume contains the complete texts of many of the masterpieces of modern political theory, along with substantial selections from numerous others. An original introduction to each author's writings, contributed by an authority on that subject, includes biographical data, philosophical commentary, and bibliographical guides.

The idea for this collection developed from a conversation with Robert B. Miller, senior editor at Oxford University Press, and I appreciate his continuing encouragement and advice. Karen Shapiro was the able Project Editor, and Ian Gardiner proofread the manuscript with his customary conscientiousness. I am grateful especially to those scholars who provided introductions: Professors Bernard E. Brown (City University of New York/Graduate School), Joshua Cohen (Massachusetts Institute of Technology), Charles L. Griswold, Jr. (Boston University), the late Jean Hampton (University of Arizona), Michael O. Hardimon (University of California/San Diego), Mark Hulliung (Brandeis University), Arthur Kuflik (University of Vermont), Roger D. Masters (Dartmouth College), Richard Miller (Cornell University), Thomas W. Pogge (Columbia University), Gordon Schochet (Rutgers University), Steven B. Smith (Yale University), Jeremy Waldron (University of California/Berkeley), and Burleigh T. Wilkins (University of California, Santa Barbara).

I benefited from advice offered by Professor Masters regarding Machiavelli's *Discourses,* Professor Hampton regarding Hobbes's *Leviathan,* Professor Griswold regarding Smith's *The Wealth of Nations,* Professor Brown regarding *The Federalist,* and Professor Kuflik regarding a variety of strategic and substantive matters. I also received wise counsel from several reviewers selected by Oxford University Press, namely: Larry Arnhart, professor of political science, Northern Illinois University; Donald Becker, assistant professor of philosophy, University of Texas at Austin; Daniel Breazeale, professor of philosophy, University of Kentucky; John Champlin, associate professor of political science, Ohio State University; Jim Curtis; Karen Hanson, professor of philosopy, Indiana University; Diane Jeske, assistant professor of philosophy, The University of Iowa; David Keyt, professor of philosophy, University of Washington; and Alan Mabe, professor of philosophy, Florida State University.

CLASSICS
OF MODERN
POLITICAL
THEORY

NICCOLÒ MACHIAVELLI

Niccolò Machiavelli (1469–1527) was born in Florence during the most brilliant epoch of the Italian Renaissance. A member of an old Florentine family, Machiavelli was trained as a classical humanist. With the fall of Savanorola's puritanical regime in 1498, Machiavelli entered the service of his native city as second chancellor of the Signoria and secretary to the Committee of Ten, the body responsible for foreign and military affairs. Closely connected with Piero Soderini, the Gonfaloniere or head of state, Machiavelli was entrusted with a number of delicate diplomatic missions. During the autumn of 1502, he was at the court of Cesare Borgia. While there, he apparently met Leonardo da Vinci, who was to work with Machiavelli on several projects between 1503 and 1507. Among these was an attempt in 1503 to 1504 to divert the Arno River during the siege of Pisa—a strategy that failed for technical reasons. Machiavelli was also directly active in raising a citizen militia to end Florence's reliance on mercenary troops, only to have the newly formed army defeated by the Spanish at Prato (1512).

As a consequence of this defeat, the Medici overthrew the Florentine republic in 1512. Machiavelli was deprived of his governmental positions and, when his name was found on a list of conspirators, imprisoned and tortured. Released from jail on condition that for one year he neither leave the territory of Florence nor enter the government offices, Machiavelli retired to his home in San Casciano, where he began writing *The Prince* and the *Discourses on Titus Livy*. In subsequent years, Machiavelli wrote in a variety of genres, including *Mandragola* (1518)—sometimes called the greatest comedy in the Italian language; *The Art of War* (1521)—a dialogue on military strategy incorporating ancient practices and his own experience; and *Florentine Histories* (1525)—an account of the history of this native city commissioned by the Medici Pope Leo X. Despite attempts to secure political employment from the Medici, Machiavelli never regained office. He died in 1527, shortly after the Medici were overthrown and a republic restored.

Although Machiavelli is often described as the founder of modern political theory, there is much controversy about his intentions and theories. *The Prince*, Machiavelli's best-known work, circulated in manuscript before his death and was published posthumously in 1532. It is dedicated to Lorenzo de' Medici, ruler of Florence from 1516 to 1519, and seems to espouse the unscrupulous methods of ambitious leaders like Cesare Borgia. His *Discourses on Titus Livy*, also published posthumously (1531), uses Roman political history as the basis for republican political principles. The apparent contradictions between these two works have led many to treat Machiavelli as a teacher of political expediency and immorality, with little concern for fundamental principles. For some, however, he was the proponent of classical or pagan republicanism, opposed to Christianity and feudal monarchy. Others see him as the first to adopt an objective or "scientific" perspective on politics.

Understanding Machiavelli is difficult. One key may be Machiavelli's assertion, in both *The Prince* and *Discourses*, that his understanding of politics is based on a combination of "long experience" of modern things (his responsibilities for the Florentine republic) and a "continuous study of antiquity" (especially such pagan writers as Xenophon and Polybius, as well as Livy). As those who consult Machiavelli's diplomatic dispatches and private correspondence discover, Machiavelli often wrote in code and used obscurity to ensure that his messages were only understood by his addressee. More important, Machiavelli's diplomatic papers prove that the apparent praise of Cesare Borgia in *The Prince* is not to be taken at face value. Rousseau concluded that "*The Prince* of Machiavelli is the book of republicans" because "the mere choice of his execrable hero sufficiently manifests his secret intention; and the opposition of the maxims of his book *The Prince* and those of his *Discourses on Titus Livy* and his *History of Florence* shows that this profound political theorist has had until now only superficial or corrupt readers" (Rousseau, *Of The Social Contract*, Book 3, Chap. 6).

Even those who dispute Rousseau's republican interpretation often agree that Machiavelli does much to introduce a secular, materialistic orientation at odds with traditional Christianity. Aware of Leonardo's use of scientific inquiry to invent weapons and imagine a technologically founded regime, Machiavelli seeks to show how ambitious leaders can "channel" fortune through the "dikes and dams" of good laws and good arms. But perhaps chastened by the failure of his technical and military projects, Machiavelli remained skeptical of the notion, later developed by Bacon, that humans can definitively or permanently "conquer nature" for the "relief of man's estate." As Machiavelli puts it in Chapter 25 of *The Prince*, humans can control "about half" of fortune or chance through a combination of force, intelligence, and impulsiveness.

It is possible to reconcile the diverse interpretations of Machiavelli's works by viewing the ambitious leader of *The Prince* as the legislator or founder of the republican regime favored in the *Discourses*. Such a reading suggests that Machiavelli sought the creation of "new modes and orders" capable of establishing lasting states. To this end, laws must channel the selfish desires and conflicts inherent in political life, while fear ensures obedience to law and those in power. Rejecting "imagined principalities," whether in the form of Plato's *Republic* or Augustine's *City of God*, Machiavelli thus tries to direct the ambitious leader to the task of founding and maintaining "good arms and good laws" (*The Prince*, Chap. 12). In this interpretation, Machiavelli combines views of human nature and prudence derived from pagan antiquity with a conception of secular power and technology that has come to characterize modernity.

There is thus good reason for the widespread opinion that Machiavelli initiated "modern" political thought. In the Preface to Book I of the *Discourses*, Machiavelli says he seeks to open a "new route" and compares this goal to Columbus's discovery of America. In Chapter 15 of *The Prince*, Machiavelli explicitly asserts that he differs from "others"—presumably *all* prior writers on political theory—with regard to the relationship between rulers and ruled. Even his play *Mandragola* opens with a novelty: The personage of the author comes on stage to address the audience directly, and tells them they will see a "new case."

What, however, did Machiavelli mean by the novelty of his teaching? Many commentators focus on his worldly emphasis on the "actual truth" rather than on the "imagined principalities" of the Platonic and Christian tradition, citing Chapter 15 of *The Prince*. But that chapter states Machiavelli's intention quite explicitly as theoretical rather than practical: "[M]y intention is to write something useful for *whoever understands it*" (p. 30). Readers who think that Machiavelli was merely concerned with practical advice to rulers ignore his explicit assertion that the ancients used "covert" images in the education of rulers (*The Prince*, Chap. 18), and therefore fail to see how that work relates to Machiavelli's stated goal of working "for the common benefit of all" (*Discourses*, Preface to Book I).

When read very carefully, Machiavelli's works present a coherent political philosophy. Nurtured by his study of ancient philosophy (there exists a copy of Lucretius' *De Rerum Natura* copied in Machiavelli's own hand), Machiavelli intentionally challenges the Western philosophic tradition. He does not, however, claim there is any novelty in his skeptical view of human nature (men are "ungrateful, fickle pretenders and dissemblers, evaders of danger, eager for gain"; *The Prince*, Chap. 17). On the contrary, Machiavelli explicitly states that "all writers on politics have pointed out . . . [that] it must needs be taken for granted that all men are wicked" (*Discourses*, I, 3). Far from being a novelty, Machiavelli's theory of human nature simply endorses a traditional view, such as the teachings of Xenophon (the classical author suggested as required reading in both *The Prince* and *Discourses*).

The novelty of the Machiavellian teaching is, rather, the use of science and technology to control nature and achieve, by design, consequences hitherto only achieved by good luck (fortune). In pagan antiquity, science or philosophy were limited to understanding nature rather than designing technologies that control it. Modernity, in contrast, is characterized by the continuous development of scientific and technological developments devoted to the Baconian "conquest of nature." Machiavelli marks the transition with his suggestion that humans could control about "half" of history or fortune.

The famous allegory of fortune as a river (*The Prince*, Chap. 25), which symbolizes this view, echoes Machiavelli's experience in the attempt to channel the Arno as a means of defeating Pisa in 1503 to 1504. Leonardo da Vinci, who had gained great expertise in hydraulic engineering during sixteen years as advisor to Ludovico Sforza, Duke of Milan, was the technical advisor who approved the project; Machiavelli supervised it. Along with other evidence of Leonardo's influence, this experience suggests that Machiavelli was the first major thinker to consider the political implications of the integration of theoretical science and technology which became the hallmark of the modern epoch.

The full development of modernity can be associated with Hobbes, who extends the constructive view of science and politics by combining Galileo's new view of physics (inertia as the principle of continuous motion) with Euclidian geometry (mathematics as the model of certain knowledge). For moderns following Hobbes, all humans are equal in the essential respect. As Locke later put it, the human brain is a *tabula rasa* or blank slate, on which experience or nurture engraves all thought. Machiavelli does not go this far, retaining the ancient view that individual natures (intelligence, boldness, caution, and the like) differ in ways that cannot be totally controlled by human will. Because findings in contemporary biology call into question the premises of Hobbes, Locke, and other moderns, Machiavelli's works take on renewed importance as a complex and powerful political philosophy with continued relevance for understanding human life.

The secondary literature on Machiavelli is immense. For biographies, see Roberto Ridolfi, *The Life of Niccolò Machiavelli*, Cecil Grayson, trans. (Chicago: University of Chicago Press, 1963), and Alfred de Grazia, *Machiavelli in Hell* (Princeton: Princeton University Press, 1989). On the pre-modern elements in Machiavelli's thought, J. G. A. Pocock, *The Machiavellian Moment: Florentine Thought and the Atlantic Republican Tradition* (Princeton: Princeton University Press, 1975), and Anthony J. Parel, *The Machiavellian Cosmos* (New Haven: Yale University Press, 1992). On Machiavelli's political career, see Denis Fachard's biography of Machiavelli's assistant, *Biagio Buonaccorsi* (Bologna: Massimiliano Boni, 1976); Felix Gilbert, *Machiavelli and Guiccardini; Politics and History in Sixteenth Century Florence* (Princeton: Princeton University Press, 1965); and John H. Najemy, *Between Friends: Discourses of Power and Desire in the Machiavelli-Vettori Letters of 1513–1515* (Princeton: Princeton University Press, 1993). For the interpretation of Machiavelli as the founder of modernity, see Leonardo Olschlei, *Machiavelli the Scientist* (Berkeley: University of California Press, 1945); Leo Strauss, *Natural Right and History* (Chicago: University of Chicago Press, 1957), as well as *Thoughts on Machiavelli* (Glencoe, IL: Free Press, 1964); and—with special emphasis on the relationship with Leonardo da Vinci—Roger D. Masters, *Machiavelli, Leonardo, and the Science of Power* (Notre Dame: University of Notre Dame Press, 1996).

R. D. M.

THE PRINCE

DEDICATORY PREFACE

Niccolò Machiavelli to Lorenzo de' Medici, the Magnificent

In most instances, it is customary for those who desire to win the favour of a Prince to present themselves to him with those things they value most or which they feel will most please him; thus, we often see princes given horses, arms, vestments of gold cloth, precious stones, and similar ornaments suited to their greatness. Wishing, therefore, to offer myself to Your Magnificence with some evidence of my devotion to you, I have not found among my belongings anything that I might value more or prize so much as the knowledge of the deeds of great men, which I have learned from a long experience in modern affairs and a continuous study of antiquity; having with great care and for a long time thought about and examined these deeds, and now having set them down in a little book, I am sending them to Your Magnificence.

And although I consider this work unworthy of your station, I am sure, nevertheless, that your humanity will move you to accept it, for there could not be a greater gift from me than to give you the means to be able, in a very brief time, to understand all that I, in many years and with many hardships and dangers, have come to understand and to appreciate. I have neither decorated nor filled this work with fancy sentences, with rich and magnificent words, or with any other form of rhetorical or unnecessary ornamentation which many writers normally use in describing and enriching their subject matter; for I wished that nothing should set my work apart or make it pleasing except the variety of its material and the seriousness of its contents. Neither do I wish that it be thought presumptuous if a man of low and inferior station dares to debate and to regulate the rule of princes; for, just as those who paint landscapes place themselves in a low position on the plain in order to consider the nature of the mountains and the high places and place themselves high atop mountains in order to study the plains, in like manner, to know well the nature of the people one must be a prince, and to know well the nature of princes one must be of the people.

Accept, therefore, Your Magnificence, this little gift in the spirit that I send it; if you read and consider it carefully, you will discover in it my most heartfelt desire that you may attain that greatness which fortune and all your own capacities promise you. And if Your Magnificence will turn your eyes at some time from the summit of your high position toward these lowlands, you will realize to what degree I unjustly suffer a great and continuous malevolence of fortune.

CHAPTER I

How Many Kinds of Principalities There Are and the Way They Are Acquired

All states, all dominions that have had and continue to have power over men were and still are either republics or principalities. Principalities are either hereditary, in which instance the family of the prince has ruled for generations, or they are new. The new ones are either completely new, as was Milan for Francesco Sforza, or they are like members added to the hereditary state of the prince who acquires them, as is the Kingdom of Naples for the King of Spain. Dominions taken in this way are either used to living under a prince or are accustomed to being free; and they are gained either by the arms of others or by one's own, either through fortune or through ingenuity.

CHAPTER II

On Hereditary Principalities

I shall set aside any discussion of republics, because I treated them elsewhere at length. I shall consider solely the principality, developing as I go the topics mentioned above; and I shall discuss how these principalities can be governed and maintained.

I say, then, that in hereditary states accustomed to the rule of their prince's family there are far fewer difficulties in maintaining them than in new states; for it suffices simply not to break ancient customs, and then to suit one's actions to unexpected events; in this manner, if such a prince is of ordinary ability, he will always maintain his state, unless some extraordinary and inordinate force deprive him of it; and although it may be taken away from him, he will regain it with the slightest mistake of the usurper.

As an example, we have in Italy the Duke of Ferrara, who withstood the assaults of the Venetians in 1484 and those of Pope Julius in 1510 for no other reason than the tradition of his rule in that dominion. Because a prince by birth has fewer reasons and less need to harm his subjects, it is natural that he should be more loved; and if no unusual vices make him hated, it is reasonable and natural that he be well liked by them. And in the antiquity and continuity of his rule, the records and causes of innovations die out, because one change always leaves space for the construction of another.

CHAPTER III

On Mixed Principalities

But it is the new principality that causes difficulties. In the first place, if it is not completely new but is instead an acquisition (so that the two parts together may be called mixed), its difficulties derive from one natural problem inherent in all new principalities: men gladly change their masters, thinking to better themselves; and this belief causes them to take arms against their ruler; but they fool themselves in this, since with experience they see that things have become worse. This stems from another natural and ordinary necessity, which is that a new prince must always offend his new subjects both through his soldiers and other countless injuries that are involved in his new conquest; thus, you have made enemies of all those you injured in occupying the principality and you are unable to maintain as friends those who helped you to rise to power, since you cannot satisfy them in the way that they had supposed, nor can you use strong measures against them, for you are in their debt; because, although one may have the most powerful of armies, he always needs the support of the inhabitants to seize a province. For these reasons, Louis XII, King of France, quickly occupied Milan and just as quickly lost it; and the first time, the troops of Ludovico alone were needed to retake it from him, because those citizens who had opened the gates of the city to the king, finding themselves deceived in their beliefs and in that future improvement they had anticipated, could not support the offences of the new prince.

It is indeed true that when lands which have rebelled once are taken a second time, it is more difficult to lose them; for the lord, taking advantage of the revolt, is less reticent about punishing offenders, ferreting out suspects, and shoring up weak positions. So that, if only a Duke Ludovico threatening the borders was sufficient for France to lose Milan the first time, the whole world had to oppose her and destroy her armies or chase them from Italy to cause her to lose it the second time; and this happened for the reasons mentioned above. Nevertheless, it was taken from her both the first and the second time.

The general explanations for the first loss have been discussed; now there remains to specify those for the second, and to see what remedies the King of France had, and those that one in the same situation might have, so that he might be able to maintain a stronger grip on his conquest than did France. Therefore, I say that those dominions which, upon being conquered, are added to the long-established state of him who acquires them are either of the same province and language or they are not. When they are, it is easier to hold them, especially when they are unaccustomed to freedom; and to possess them securely, it is only necessary to have extinguished the family line of the prince who ruled them, because in so far as other things are concerned, men live peacefully as long as their old way of life is maintained and there is no change in customs: thus, we have seen what happened in the case of Burgundy, Brittany, Gascony, and Normandy, which have been part of France for such a long time; and although there are some linguistic differences, nevertheless the customs are similar and they have been able to get along together easily. And anyone who acquires these lands and wishes to maintain them must bear two things in mind: first, that the family line of the old prince must be extinguished; second, that neither their laws nor their taxes be altered; as a result they will become in a very brief time one body with the old principality.

But when dominions are acquired in a province that is not similar in language, customs, and laws, it is here that difficulties arise; and it is here that one needs much good fortune and much diligence to hold on to them. And one of the best and most efficacious remedies would be for the person who has taken possession of them to go and live there. This would make that possession more secure and durable, as the Turks did with Greece; for despite all the other precautions they took to retain that dominion, if they had not gone there to live, it would have been impossible for them to hold on to it. Because, by being on the spot, one sees trouble at its birth and one can quickly remedy it; not being there, one hears about it after it has grown and there is no longer any remedy. Moreover, the province would not be plundered by one's own officers; the subjects would be pleased to have direct recourse to their prince; thus, wishing to be good subjects, they have more reason to love him and, wanting to be otherwise, more reason to fear him. Anyone who might wish to invade that dominion from abroad would be more hesitant; so that, living right there, the prince can only with the greatest of difficulties lose it.

The other and better solution is to send colonies into one or two places that will act as supports for your own state; for it is necessary that the prince either do this or maintain a large number of infantry and cavalry. Colonies do not cost much, and with little or no expense a prince can send and maintain them; and in so doing he hurts only those whose fields and houses have been taken and given to the new inhabitants, who are only a small part of that state; and those that he hurts, being dispersed and poor, can never be a threat to him, and all others remain on the one hand unharmed (and because of this, they should remain silent), and on the other afraid of making a mistake, for fear that what happened to those who were dispossessed might happen to them. I conclude that these colonies are not expensive, they are more faithful, and they create fewer difficulties; and those who are hurt cannot pose a threat, since they are poor and scattered, as I have already said. Concerning this, it should be noted that one must either pamper or do away with men, because they will avenge themselves for minor offences while for more serious ones they cannot; so that any harm done to a man must be the kind that removes any fear of revenge. But by maintaining soldiers there instead of colonies, one spends much more, being obliged to consume all the revenues of the state in guarding its borders, so that the profit becomes a loss; and far greater injury is committed, since the entire state is harmed by the army changing quarters from one place to another; everybody resents this inconvenience, and everyone becomes an enemy; and these are enemies that can be harmful, since they remain, although conquered, in their own home. And so, in every respect, this kind of defence is as useless as the other kind, colonization, is useful.

Moreover, anyone who is in a province that is unlike his own in the ways mentioned above should make himself the leader and defender of the less powerful neighbours and do all he can to weaken those who are more powerful, and he should be careful that, for whatever reason, no foreigner equal to himself in strength enter there. And it will always happen that the outsider will be brought in by those who are dissatisfied, either because of too much ambition or because of fear, as was once seen when the Aetolians brought the Romans into Greece, and in every other province that the Romans entered, they were brought in by the inhabitants. What occurs is that as soon as a powerful foreigner enters a province, all who are less powerful cling to him, moved by the envy they have for the one who has ruled over them; so that, concerning these weaker powers, he has no trouble whatsoever in winning them over, since all of them will immediately and willingly become part of the state that he has acquired. He has only to be on his guard that they do not seize too much power and authority; and, with his force and their support, he can very easily put down those who are powerful, and remain complete arbiter of that province. And anyone who does not follow this procedure will quickly lose what he has taken, and while he holds it, he will find it full of infinite difficulties and worries.

In the provinces that they seized, the Romans followed these methods very carefully; they sent colonies, had dealings with the less powerful without increasing their strength, put down the powerful, and did not allow powerful foreigners to gain prestige there. And I shall cite only the province of Greece as an example: the Romans kept the Achaeans and the Aetolians in check; the Macedonian kingdom was put down; Antiochus was driven out; nor were they ever persuaded by the merits of the Achaeans or the Aetolians to allow them any gain of territory; nor did the persuasion of Philip of Macedonia ever convince them to make him their friend without first humbling him; nor could the power of Antiochus force their consent to his having any authority whatsoever in that province. For the Romans did in these instances what all wise princes should do: these princes have not only to watch out for present problems but also for those in the future, and try diligently to avoid them; for once problems are recognized ahead of time, they can be easily cured; but if you wait for them to present themselves, the medicine will be too late, for the disease will have become incurable. And what physicians say about disease is applicable here: that at the beginning a disease is easy to cure but difficult to diagnose; but as time passes, not having been recognized or treated at the outset, it becomes easy to diagnose but difficult to cure. The same thing occurs in affairs of state; for by recognizing from afar the diseases that are spreading in the state (which is a gift given only to the prudent ruler), they can be cured quickly; but when they are not recognized and are left to grow to the extent that everyone recognizes them, there is no longer any cure.

Thus, seeing trouble from afar, the Romans always found a remedy; and they never allowed such trouble to develop unopposed, in order to avoid a war, because they knew that war cannot be avoided but can only be put off to the advantage of others; therefore, they wanted to go to war with Philip and Antiochus in Greece in order not to have to combat them in Italy; and they could have, at the time, avoided both the one and the other, but they did not want to. Nor did they ever like what is always on the tongues of our wise men today, to enjoy the benefits of time, but they enjoyed instead the benefits of their strength and prudence; for time brings with it all things, and it can bring with it the good as well as the bad and the bad as well as the good.

But let us return to France and determine if she did any of the things we have just mentioned; and I shall speak of Louis and not of Charles; and therefore about the one whose progress has been observed better because he held territory in Italy for a longer period, and you will see that he did the contrary of those things that must be done in order to hold one's rule in a foreign province.

King Louis was installed in Italy because of the ambition of the Venetians, who wanted by his coming to gain for themselves half of Lombardy. I will not criticize the enterprise the King undertook; for, wishing to establish a first foothold in Italy and not having any friends in this land and, furthermore, having all the gates closed to him because of the actions of King Charles, he was forced to strike up whatever friendships he could; and this worthy undertaking would have succeeded if he had not erred in his other moves. After having taken Lombardy, then, the King immediately regained the prestige that Charles had lost him: Genoa surrendered; the Florentines became his allies; the Marquis of Mantua, the Duke of Ferrara, the Bentivogli, the Countess of Forlì, the lords of Faenza, Pesaro, Rimini, Camerino, and Piombino, and the people of Lucca, Pisa, and Siena all rushed to gain his friendship. And at that point the Venetians could see the recklessness of the enterprise they had undertaken; in order to acquire a bit of Lombardy, they had made the King the master of a third of Italy.

Consider, now, with what little trouble the King might have maintained his reputation in Italy if he had followed the rules listed above and kept secure and defended all those friends of his who, there being a goodly number of them, both weak and fearful, some of the Church, others of the Venetians, were always forced to be his allies; and through them he could have easily secured himself against the remaining great powers. But no sooner was he in Milan than he did the contrary, giving assistance to Pope Alexander so that he could seize Romagna. Nor did he realize that with this decision he had made himself weaker, abandoning his allies and those who had thrown themselves into his lap, and made the Church stronger by adding to it so much temporal power in addition to the spiritual power from which it derives so much authority. And having made an initial mistake, he was obliged to make others; so that in order to put an end to the ambition of Alexander and to keep him from becoming lord of Tuscany, he was forced to come to Italy. He was not satisfied to have made the Church powerful and to have lost his allies, for, coveting the Kingdom of Naples, he divided it with the King of Spain; and where he first had been the arbiter of Italy, he brought in a partner so that the ambitious and the malcontents of that province had someone else to turn to; and where he could have left a figurehead king to rule that kingdom, he replaced him, establishing one there who could, in turn, drive Louis out.

The desire to acquire is truly a very natural and normal thing; and when men who are able do so, they will always be praised and not condemned; but when they cannot and wish to do so at any cost, herein lies the error and the blame. If France, therefore, could have assaulted Naples with her own troops, she should have done so; if she could not, she should not have shared it. And if the division of Lombardy with the Venetians deserves to be overlooked, since it allowed Louis to gain a foothold in Italy, the other division deserves to be criticized, since it cannot be excused by necessity.

Thus, Louis had made these five mistakes: he had destroyed the weaker powers; he increased the power of another force in Italy; he had brought into that province a powerful foreigner; he did not come there to live; and he did not send colonies there. In spite of this, these mistakes, had he lived, might not have damaged him if he had not made a sixth: that of reducing the Venetians' power; for if he had not made the Church stronger, nor brought Spain into Italy, it would have been most reasonable and necessary to put them down; but, having taken those first initiatives, he should never have agreed to their ruin; for as long as they were powerful they would have always kept the others from trying to seize Lombardy, partly because the Venetians would not have allowed this unless they themselves became the rulers of Lombardy, and partly because the others would not have wanted to take it away from France to give it to the Venetians; and they would not have had the nerve to provoke both of them. And if someone were to say: King Louis relinquished Romagna to Alexander and the Kingdom of Naples to Spain in order to avoid a war, I would reply with the arguments given above: that one should never allow chaos to develop in order to avoid going to war, because one does not avoid a war but instead puts it off to his disadvantage. And if some others were to note the promise that the King had made the Pope to undertake that enterprise in return for the annulment of his marriage and for the Cardinal's hat of Rouen, I should answer with what I shall say further on about the promises of princes and how they should be observed.

King Louis lost Lombardy, therefore, by not following any of the principles observed by others who had taken provinces and who wished to retain them. Nor is this in any sense a miracle, but very ordinary and understandable. And I spoke about this at Nantes with the Cardinal of Rouen when Valentino (for this was what Cesare Borgia, son of Pope Alexander, was commonly called) occupied Romagna; for when the Cardinal of Rouen told me that Italians understood little about war, I replied to him that the French understood little about politics; for if they did understand, they would not permit the Church to gain so much power. And we have learned through experience that the power of the Church and of Spain in Italy has been caused by France, and that her downfall has been brought about by them. From this one can derive a general rule which rarely, if ever, fails: that anyone who is the cause of another's becoming powerful comes to ruin himself, because that power is the result either of cunning or of force, and both these two qualities are suspect to the one who has become powerful.

CHAPTER IV

Why the Kingdom of Darius, Occupied by Alexander, Did Not Rebel Against His Successors after the Death of Alexander

Considering the difficulties one has in maintaining a newly acquired state, one might wonder how it happened that when Alexander the Great, having become lord of Asia in a few years and having hardly occupied it, died—wherefore it would have seemed reasonable for the whole state to revolt—Alexander's successors nevertheless managed to hold on to it; and they had, in keeping it, no other difficulty than that which originated among themselves from their own ambition. Let me reply that all principalities known to us are governed in one of two different ways: either by a prince with the others as his servants, who, as ministers, through his favour and permission, assist in governing that kingdom; or by a prince and barons who hold that position not because of any favour of their master but because of the nobility of their birth. Such barons as these have their own dominions and subjects who recognize them as masters and are naturally fond of them. Those dominions governed by a prince and his ministers hold their prince in greater authority, for in all his province there is no one that may be recognized as superior to him; and if they do obey any other, they do so as his minister and officer, and they do not harbour any special affection for him.

Examples of these two different kinds of governments in our own times are the Turkish Emperor and the King of France. The entire kingdom of the Turk is ruled by one master; the others are his servants; and dividing his kingdom into parts, he sends various administrators there, and he moves them and changes them as he pleases. But the King of France is placed among a group of established nobles who are recognized in that state by their subjects and who are loved by them; they have their hereditary rights; the King cannot remove them without danger to himself. Anyone, therefore, who considers these two states will find that the difficulty lies in taking possession of the Turkish state, but once it has been conquered, it is very simple to retain it. On the other hand, you will find that in some ways it is easier to seize the French state, but it is extremely difficult to hold on to it.

The reasons for the difficulty in being able to occupy the Turkish kingdom are that it is not possible to be summoned there by the rulers of that kingdom, nor to hope to make your enterprise easier with the rebellion of those the ruler has around him. This is because of the reasons mentioned above since they are all slaves and dependent on the ruler, it is more difficult to corrupt them; and even if they were corrupted, you cannot hope that they will be very useful, not being able to attract followers for the reasons already discussed. Therefore, anyone who attacks the Turks must consider that he will find them completely united, and he must rely more on his own strength than on their lack of unity. But once beaten and broken in battle so that they cannot regroup their troops, there is nothing else to be feared but the family of the prince; once it is extinguished, there remains no one else to be feared, for the others have no credit with the people; and just as the victor before the victory could not place hope in them, so he need not fear them afterwards.

The opposite occurs in kingdoms governed like France, because you can enter them with ease once you have won to your side some baron of the kingdom; for you always find malcontents and those who desire a change; these people, for the reasons already given, can open the way to that state and facilitate your victory. However, wishing to hold on to it is accompanied by endless problems, problems with those that have aided you and with those you have suppressed; nor does it suffice to do away with the family of the prince, because the lords who make themselves heads of new factions still remain; and you lose that state at the first occasion, for you are neither able to make them happy nor are you able to do away with them.

Now, if you will consider the type of government Darius established, you will find it similar to the kingdom of the Turks; and therefore Alexander first had to overwhelm it totally and defeat it in battle; after this victory, Darius being dead, that state remained securely in Alexander's hands for the reasons discussed above. And his successors, had they been united, could have enjoyed it with ease; for in that kingdom no disorders arose other than those they themselves had caused. But in states organized like France, it is impossible to hold them with such ease. Because of this, there arose the frequent revolts of Spain, France, and Greece against the Romans, all because of the numerous principalities that were in those states; as long as the memory of them lasted, the Romans were always unsure of their power; but once that memory had been extinguished, because of their long and powerful rule, they became sure possessors. Afterwards, when the Romans fought among themselves, each one was able to draw a following from those provinces, according to the authority he enjoyed there; and since the families of their former rulers had been extinguished, they recognized only the Romans. Taking all these things into account, therefore, no one at all should marvel at the ease with which Alexander retained the state of Asia, or at the problems that others suffered in preserving their acquisition, such as Pyrrhus and many others. This is not caused by the greater or lesser skill of the victor but rather by the difference of the situations.

CHAPTER V

How Cities or Principalities Should be Governed that Lived by Their Own Laws Before They Were Occupied

As I have said, when those states that are acquired are used to living by their own laws and in freedom, there are three methods of holding on to them: the first is to destroy them; the second is to go there in person to live; the third is to allow them to live with their own laws, forcing them to pay a tribute and creating therein a government made up of a few people who will keep the state friendly toward you. For such a government, having been created by that prince, knows it cannot last without his friendship and his power, and it must do everything possible to maintain them; and a city used to living in freedom is more easily maintained through the means of its own citizens than in any other way, if you decide to preserve it.

As examples, there are the Spartans and the Romans. The Spartans held Athens and Thebes by building therein a government consisting of a few people; eventually they lost them both. The Romans, in order to hold Capua, Carthage, and Numantia, destroyed them and did not lose them; they wished to hold Greece in almost the same manner as the Spartans held it, making it free and leaving it under its own laws, and they did not succeed; thus, they were obliged to destroy many of the cities in that province in order to retain it. For, in fact, there is no secure means of holding on to them except by destroying them. And anyone who becomes lord of a city used to living in liberty and does not destroy it may expect to be destroyed by it, because such a city always has as a refuge, in any rebellion, the spirit of liberty and its ancient institutions, neither of which is ever forgotten either because of the passing of time or because of the bestowal of benefits. And it matters little what one does or foresees, since if one does not separate or scatter the inhabitants, they will not forget that spirit or those institutions; and immediately, in every case, they will return to them just as Pisa did after one hundred years of being held in servitude by the Florentines. But when cities or provinces are accustomed to living under a prince and the family of that prince has been extinguished, they, being on the one hand used to obedience and, on the other, not having their old prince and not being able to agree on choosing another from amongst themselves, yet not knowing how to live as free men, are as a result hesitant in taking up arms, and a prince can win them over and assure himself of their support with greater ease. But in republics there is greater vitality, greater hatred, greater desire for revenge; the memory of ancient liberty does not and cannot allow them to submit, so that the most secure course is either to destroy them or to go there to live.

CHAPTER VI

On New Principalities Acquired by One's Own Arms and Skill

No one should marvel if, in speaking of principalities that are totally new as to their prince and organization, I use the most illustrious examples; since men almost always tread the paths made by others and proceed in their affairs by imitation, although they are not completely able to stay on the path of others nor attain the skill of those they imitate, a prudent man should always enter those paths taken by great men and imitate those who have been most excellent, so that if one's own skill does not match theirs, at least it will have the smell of it; and he should proceed like those prudent archers who, aware of the strength of their bow when the target they are aiming at seems too distant, set their sights much higher than the designated target, not in order to reach to such a height with their arrow but rather to be able, with the aid of such a high aim, to strike the target.

I say, therefore, that in completely new principalities, where there is a new prince, one finds in maintaining them more or less difficulty according to the greater or lesser skill of the one who acquires them. And because this act of transition from private citizen to prince presupposes either ingenuity or fortune, it appears that either the one or the other of these two things should, in part, mitigate many of the problems; nevertheless, he who relies upon fortune less maintains his position best. Things are also facilitated when the prince, having no other dominions to govern, is constrained to come to live there in person. But to come to those who, by means of their own skill and not because of fortune, have become princes, I say that the most admirable are Moses, Cyrus, Romulus, Theseus, and the like. And although we should not discuss Moses, since he was a mere executor of things ordered by God, nevertheless he must be admired, if for nothing but that grace which made him worthy of talking with God. But let us consider Cyrus and the others who have acquired or founded kingdoms; you will find them all admirable; and if their deeds and their particular institutions are considered, they will not appear different from those of Moses, who had so great a guide. And examining their deeds and their lives, one can see that they received nothing from fortune except the opportunity, which gave them the material they could mould into whatever form they desired; and without that opportunity the strength of their spirit would have been extinguished, and without that strength the opportunity would have come in vain.

It was therefore necessary for Moses to find the people of Israel in Egypt slaves and oppressed by the Egyptians in order that they might be disposed to follow him to escape this servitude. It was necessary for Romulus not to stay in Alba and to be exposed at birth so that he might become King of Rome and founder of that nation. It was necessary for Cyrus to find the Persians discontented with the empire of the Medes, and the Medes soft and effeminate after a lengthy peace. Theseus could not have shown his skill if he had not found the Athenians scattered. These opportunities, therefore, made these men successful, and their outstanding ingenuity made that opportunity known to them, whereby their nations were ennobled and became prosperous.

Like these men, those who become princes through their skill acquire the principality with difficulty, but they hold on to it easily; and the difficulties they encounter in acquiring the principality grow, in part, out of the new institutions and methods they are obliged to introduce in order to found their state and their security. And one should bear in mind that there is nothing more difficult to execute, nor more dubious of success, nor more dangerous to administer than to introduce a new order of things; for he who introduces it has all those who profit from the old order as his enemies, and he has only lukewarm allies in all those who might profit from the new. This lukewarmness partly stems from fear of their adversaries, who have the law on their side, and partly from the scepticism of men, who do not truly believe in new things unless they have actually had personal experience of them. Therefore, it happens that whenever those who are enemies have the chance to attack, they do so enthusiastically, whereas those others defend hesitantly, so that they, together with the prince, are in danger.

It is necessary, however, if we desire to examine this subject thoroughly, to observe whether these innovators act on their own or are dependent on others: that is, if they are forced to beg or are able to use power in conducting their affairs. In the first case, they always come to a bad end and never accomplish anything; but when they depend on their own resources and can use power, then only seldom do they find themselves in peril. From this comes the fact that all armed prophets were victorious and the unarmed came to ruin. Besides what has been said, people are fickle by nature; and it is simple to convince them of something but difficult to hold them in that conviction; and, therefore, affairs should be managed in such a way that when they no longer believe, they can be made to believe by force. Moses, Cyrus, Theseus, and Romulus could not have made their institutions long respected if they had been unarmed; as in our times happened to Brother Girolamo Savonarola, who was ruined by his new institutions when the populace began no longer to believe in them, since he had no way of holding steady those who had believed nor of making the disbelievers believe. Therefore, such men have great problems in getting ahead, and they meet all their dangers as they proceed, and they must overcome them with their skill; but once they have overcome them and have begun to be respected, having removed those who were envious of their merits, they remain powerful, secure, honoured, and happy.

To such noble examples I should like to add a minor one; but it will have some relation to the others, and I should like it to suffice for all similar cases: and this is Hiero of Syracuse. From a private citizen, this man became the prince of Syracuse; he did not receive anything from fortune except the opportunity, for since the citizens of Syracuse were oppressed, they elected him as their leader; and from that rank he proved himself worthy of becoming their prince. And he was so skillful while still a private citizen that someone who wrote about him said 'that he lacked nothing to reign save a kingdom.' He did away with the old militia and established a new one; he put aside old friendships and made new ones; and since he had allies and soldiers that depended on him, he was able to construct whatever building he wished on such a foundation; so that it cost him great effort to acquire and little to maintain.

CHAPTER VII

On New Principalities Acquired with the Arms of Others and by Fortune

Those private citizens who become princes through fortune alone do so with little effort, but they maintain their position only with a great deal; they meet no obstacles along their way since they fly to success, but all their problems arise when they have arrived. And these are the men who are granted a state either because they have money or because they enjoy the favour of him who grants it: this occurred to many in Greece in the cities of Ionia and the Hellespont, where Darius created princes in order that he might hold these cities for his security and glory; in like manner were set up those emperors who from private citizens came to power by bribing the soldiers. Such men depend solely upon two very uncertain and unstable things; the will and the fortune of him who granted them the state; they do not know how and are not able to maintain their position. They do not know how, since if men are not of great intelligence and ingenuity, it is not reasonable that they know how to rule, having always lived as private citizens; they are not able to, since they do not have forces that are friendly and faithful. Besides, states that rise quickly, just as all the other things of nature that are born and grow rapidly, cannot have roots and ramifications; the first bad weather kills them, unless these men who have suddenly become princes, as I have noted, are of such ability that they know how to prepare themselves quickly and to preserve what fortune has put in their laps, and to construct afterwards those foundations that others have built before becoming princes.

Regarding the two methods just listed for becoming a prince, by skill or by fortune, I should like to offer two recent examples: these are Francesco Sforza and Cesare Borgia. Francesco, through the required means and with a great deal of ingenuity, became Duke of Milan from his station as a private citizen, and that which he had acquired with countless hardships he maintained with little trouble. On the other hand, Cesare Borgia (commonly called Duke Valentino) acquired the state through the favour and help of his father, and when this no longer existed, he lost it, and this despite the fact that he did everything and used every means that a prudent and skilful man ought to use in order to root himself securely in those states that the arms and fortune of others had granted him. Because, as stated above, anyone who does not lay his foundations beforehand could do so later only with great skill, although this would be done with inconvenience to the architect and danger to the building. If, therefore, we consider all the steps taken by the Duke, we shall see that he laid sturdy foundations for his future power; and I do not judge it useless to discuss them, for I would not know of any better precepts to give to a new prince than the example of his deeds; and if he did not succeed in his plans, it was not his fault but was instead the result of an extraordinary and extreme instance of ill fortune.

Alexander VI, in his attempts to advance his son, the Duke, had many problems, both present and future. First, he saw no means of making him master of any state that did not already belong to the Church; and if he attempted to seize anything belonging to the Church, he knew that the Venetians and the Duke of Milan would not agree to it because Faenza and Rimini were already under the protection of the Venetians. Moreover, he saw that the troops of Italy, and especially those he would have to use, were in the hands of those who had reason to fear the Pope's power; and he could not count on them, since they were all Orsini, Colonnesi, and their allies. Therefore, he had to disturb the order of things and cause turmoil among these states in order securely to make himself master of a part of them. This was easy for him to do, for he found that the Venetians, moved by other motives, had decided to bring the French back into Italy; not only did he not oppose this, but he rendered it easier by annulling King Louis' first marriage. The King, therefore, entered Italy with the aid of the Venetians and the consent of Alexander; and no sooner was he in Milan than the Pope procured troops from him for the Romagna campaign; these were granted to him because of the reputation of the King.

Having seized, then, Romagna and having beaten the Colonna, the Duke, wishing to maintain his gain and to advance further, was held back by two things: first, his troops' lack of loyalty; second, the will of France; that is, the troops of the Orsini, which he had been using, might let him down and not only keep him from acquiring more territory but even take away what he had already conquered; and the King, as well, might do the same. He had one experience like this with the Orsini soldiers, when, after the seizure of Faenza, he attacked Bologna and saw them go reluctantly into battle; as for the King, he learned his purpose when he invaded Tuscany after the capture of the Duchy of Urbino; the King forced him to abandon that campaign. As a consequence, the Duke decided to depend no longer upon the arms and favour of others. And his first step was to weaken the Orsini and Colonna factions in Rome; he won over all their followers who were noblemen, making them his own noblemen and giving them huge subsidies; and he honoured them, according to their rank, with military commands and civil appointments; as a result, in a few months their affection for the factions died out in their hearts and all of it was turned towards the Duke. After this, he waited for the opportunity to do away with the Orsini leaders, having already scattered those of the Colonna family; and good opportunity arose and the use he put it to was even better: for when the Orsini later realized that the greatness of the Duke and of the Church meant their ruin, they called together a meeting at Magione, in Perugian territory. From this resulted the rebellion of Urbino and the uprisings in Romagna, and endless dangers for the Duke, all of which he overcame with the aid of the French. And when his reputation had been regained, placing no trust either in France or other outside forces, in order not to have to test them, he turned to deceptive methods. And he knew how to falsify his intentions so well that the Orsini themselves, through Lord Paulo, made peace with him; the Duke did not fail to use all kinds of gracious acts to reassure Paulo, giving him money, clothing, and horses, so that the stupidity of the Orsini brought them to Sinigaglia and into his hands. Having killed these leaders and having changed their allies into his friends, the Duke had laid very good foundations for his power, having all of Romagna along with the Duchy of Urbino, and, more important, it appeared that he had befriended Romagna and had won the support of all of its populace once the people began to taste the beneficial results of his rule.

And because this matter is notable and worthy of imitation by others, I shall not pass it over. After the Duke had taken Romagna and had found it governed by powerless lords who had been more anxious to plunder their subjects than to govern them and had given them reason for disunity rather than unity, so that the entire province was full of thefts, fights, and of every other kind of insolence, he decided that if he wanted to make it peaceful and obedient to the ruler's law it would be necessary to give it good government. Therefore, he put Messer Remirro de Orco, a cruel and able man, in command there and gave him complete authority. This man, in little time, made the province peaceful and united, and in doing this he made for himself a great reputation. Afterwards, the Duke decided that such great authority was no longer required, for he was afraid that it might become odious; and he set up in the middle of the province a civil court with a very distinguished president, wherein each city had its own counsellor. And because he realized that the rigorous measures of the past had generated a certain amount of hatred, he wanted to show, in order to purge men's minds and to win them to his side completely, that if any form of cruelty had arisen, it did not originate from him but from the harsh nature of his minister. And having found the occasion to do this, one morning at Cesena he had Messer Remirro placed on the piazza in two pieces with a block of wood and a bloody sword beside him. The ferocity of such a spectacle left those people satisfied and amazed at the same time.

But let us return to where we digressed. I say that the Duke, finding himself very powerful and partially secured from present dangers, having armed himself the way he wanted to, and having in large measure destroyed those nearby forces that might have harmed him, still had to take into account the King of France if he wished to continue his conquests, for he realized that the King, who had become aware of his error too late, would not support further conquest. And because of this, he began to seek out new allies and to temporize with France during the campaign the French undertook in the Kingdom of Naples against the Spaniards who were besieging Gaeta. His intent was to make himself secure against them; and he would have quickly succeeded in this if Alexander had lived.

And these were his methods concerning present things. But as for future events, he had first to fear that a new successor in control of the Church might not be his friend and might try to take away from him what Alexander had given him. Against this possibility he thought to secure himself in four ways: first, by putting to death all the relatives of those lords that he had dispossessed in order to prevent the Pope from employing that opportunity; second, by gaining the friendship of all the noblemen of Rome, as already mentioned, in order to hold the Pope in check by means of them; third, by making the College of Cardinals as much his own as he could; fourth, by acquiring such a large territory before the Pope died that he would be able to resist an initial attack without need of allies. Of these four things, he had achieved three by the time of Alexander's death; the fourth he had almost achieved, for he killed as many of the dispossessed noblemen as he could seize, and very few saved themselves; and he had won over the Roman noblemen; and he had a great following in the College of Cardinals; and as for the acquisition of new territory, he had planned to become lord of Tuscany and was already in possession of Perugia and Piombino and had taken Pisa under his protection. And as soon as he no longer needed to respect the wishes of France (for he no longer had to, since the French had already been deprived of the kingdom by the Spaniards, so that it was necessary for both of them to purchase his friendship), he would attack Pisa. After this, Lucca and Siena would have immediately surrendered, partly to spite the Florentines and partly out of fear, and the Florentines would have had no means of preventing it. If he had carried out these designs (and he would have brought them to fruition during the same year that Alexander died), he would have gathered together so many forces and such a reputation that he would have been able to stand alone and would no longer have had to rely upon the favour and forces of others, but rather on his own power and ingenuity. But Alexander died five years after he had drawn his sword. He left his son, gravely ill, with only the state of Romagna secured and with all the others up in the air, between two very powerful enemy armies. And there was in the Duke so much ferocity and so much ability, and so well did he understand how men can be won or lost, and so firm were the foundations that he had laid in such a short time, that if he had not had those armies upon him or if he had been healthy, he would have overcome every difficulty. And that his foundations were good is witnessed by the fact that Romagna waited more than a month for him; in Rome, although only half alive, he was safe; and although the Baglioni, the Vitelli, and the Orsini came to Rome, they found none of their allies opposed to him; if he could not set up a Pope he wanted, at least he could act to ensure that it would not be a man he did not want. But if he had been healthy at the time of Alexander's demise, everything would have been simple. And he himself said to me, on the day when Julius II was made Pope, that he had thought of what might happen on his father's death, and he had found a remedy for everything, except he never dreamed that at the time of his father's death he too would be at death's door.

Now, having summarized all of the Duke's actions, I would not know how to censure him; on the contrary, I believe I am correct in proposing that he be imitated by all those who have risen to power through fortune and with the arms of others. Because he, possessing great courage and high aims, could not have conducted himself in any other manner; and his plans were frustrated solely by the brevity of Alexander's life and by his own illness. Anyone, therefore, who determines it necessary in his newly acquired principality to protect himself from his enemies, to win friends, to conquer either by force or by fraud, to make himself loved and feared by the people, to be followed and respected by his soldiers, to put to death those who can or may do him harm, to replace ancient institutions with new ones, to be severe and gracious, magnanimous and generous, to do away with unfaithful soldiers and to select new ones, to maintain the friendship of kings and of princes in such a way that they must assist you gladly or offend you with caution—that person cannot find more recent examples than this man's deeds. One can only censure him for making Julius Pope; in this he made a bad choice, since, as I said before, not being able to elect a Pope of his own, he could have kept anyone he wished from the papacy; and he should have never agreed to raising to the papacy any cardinal he might have offended or who, upon becoming Pope, might have cause to fear him. For men do harm either out of fear or hatred. Those he had injured were, among others, San Pietro ad Vincula, Colonna, San Giorgio, Ascanio; any of the others, upon becoming Pope, would have to fear him, except for Rouen and the Spaniards; the latter because they were related to him and were in his debt, the former because of his power, since he was joined to the kingdom of France. Therefore, the Duke, above all else, should have made a Spaniard Pope; failing in that, he should have agreed to the election of Rouen and not to that of San Pietro ad Vincula. And anyone who believes that new benefits make men of high station forget old injuries is deceiving himself. The Duke, then, erred in this election, and it was the cause of his ultimate downfall.

CHAPTER VIII

On Those Who Have Become Princes Through Wickedness

But because there are yet two more ways one can from an ordinary citizen become prince, which cannot completely be attributed to either fortune or skill, I believe they should not be left unmentioned, although one of them will be discussed at greater length in a treatise on republics. These two are: when one becomes prince through some wicked and nefarious means or when a private citizen becomes prince of his native city through the favour of his fellow citizens. And in discussing the first way, I shall cite two examples, one from classical times and the other from recent days, without otherwise entering into the merits of this method, since I consider them sufficient for anyone forced to imitate them.

Agathocles the Sicilian, not only from being an ordinary citizen but from being of low and abject status, became King of Syracuse. This man, a potter's son, lived a wicked life at every stage of his career; yet he joined to his wickedness such strength of mind and of body that, when he entered upon a military career, he rose through the ranks to become commander of Syracuse. Once placed in such a position, having decided to become prince and to hold with violence and without any obligations to others what had been granted to him by universal consent, and having made an agreement with Hamilcar the Carthaginian, who was waging war with his armies in Sicily, he called together one morning the people and the senate of Syracuse as if he were going to discuss things concerning the state; and with a prearranged signal, he had his troops kill all the senators and the richest citizens; and when they were dead, he seized and held the rule of the city without any opposition from the citizenry. And although he was twice defeated by the Carthaginians and eventually besieged, not only was he able to defend his city but, leaving part of his troops for the defence of the siege, with his other men he attacked Africa, and in a short time he freed Syracuse from the siege and forced the Carthaginians into dire straits: they were obliged to make peace with him and to be content with possession of Africa and to leave Sicily to Agathocles.

Anyone, therefore, who examines the deeds and the life of this man will observe nothing or very little that can be attributed to fortune; since, as was said earlier, not with the aid of others but by rising through the ranks, which involved a thousand hardships and dangers, did he come to rule the principality which he then maintained by many brave and dangerous actions. Still, it cannot be called ingenuity to kill one's fellow citizens, to betray friends, to be without faith, without mercy, without religion; by these means one can acquire power but not glory. For if one were to consider Agathocles's ability in getting into and out of dangers, and his greatness of spirit in supporting and in overcoming adversaries, one can see no reason why he should be judged inferior to any most excellent commander; nevertheless, his vicious cruelty and inhumanity, along with numerous wicked deeds, do not permit us to honour him among the most excellent of men. One cannot, therefore, attribute to either fortune or skill what he accomplished without either the one or the other.

In our own days, during the reign of Alexander VI, Oliverotto of Fermo, who many years before had been left as a child without a father, was brought up by his maternal uncle, Giovanni Fogliani. While still very young he was sent to serve as a soldier under Paulo Vitelli so that, once he was versed in that skill, he might attain some outstanding military position. Then, after Paulo died, he served under his brother, Vitellozzo; and in a very brief time, because of his intelligence and his vigorous body and mind, he became the commander of his troops. But since he felt it was servile to work for others, he decided to seize Fermo with the aid of some citizens of Fermo who preferred servitude to the liberty of their native city, and with the assistance of the followers of Vitellozzo; and he wrote to Giovanni Fogliani that, having been away many years from home, he wished to come to see him and his city and to inspect his own inheritance; and since he had exerted himself for no other reason than to acquire glory, he wanted to arrive in honourable fashion, accompanied by an escort of a hundred horsemen from among his friends and servants so that his fellow citizens might see that he had not spent his time in vain; and he begged his uncle to arrange for an honourable reception from the people of Fermo, one which might bring honour not only to Giovanni but also to himself, being his pupil. Giovanni, therefore, in no way failed in his duty toward his nephew: he had him received in honourable fashion by the people of Fermo, and he gave him rooms in his own house. Oliverotto, after a few days had passed and he had secretly made the preparations necessary for his forthcoming wickedness, gave a magnificent banquet to which he invited Giovanni Fogliani and all of the first citizens of Fermo. And when the meal and all the other entertainment customary at such banquets were completed, Oliverotto, according to plan, began to discuss serious matters, speaking of the greatness of Pope Alexander and his son, Cesare, and of their undertakings. After Giovanni and the others had replied to his comments, he suddenly rose up, announcing that these were matters to be discussed in a more secluded place; and he retired into another room, followed by Giovanni and all the other citizens. No sooner were they seated than from secret places in the room out came soldiers who killed Giovanni and all the others. After this murder, Oliverotto mounted his horse, paraded through the town, and besieged the chief officials in the government palace; so that out of fear they were forced to obey him and to constitute a government of which he made himself prince. And when all those were killed who, because they were discontented, might have harmed him, he strengthened himself by instituting new civil and military institutions; so that, in the space of the year that he held the principality, not only was he secure in the city of Fermo, but he had become feared by all its neighbours. His expulsion would have been as difficult as that of Agathocles if he had not permitted himself to be tricked by Cesare Borgia, when at Sinigaglia, as was noted above, the Duke captured the Orsini and the Vitelli; there he, too, was captured, a year after he committed the parricide, and together with Vitellozzo, who had been his teacher in ingenuity and wickedness, he was strangled.

One might wonder how Agathocles and others like him, after so many betrayals and cruelties, could live for such a long time secure in their cities and defend themselves from outside enemies without being plotted against by their own citizens; many others, using cruel means, were unable even in peaceful times to hold on to their state, not to speak of the uncertain times of war. I believe that this depends on whether cruelty be well or badly used. Well used are those cruelties (if it is permitted to speak well of evil) that are carried out in a single stroke, done out of necessity to protect oneself, and are not continued but are instead converted into the greatest possible benefits for the subjects. Badly used are those cruelties which, although being few at the outset, grow with the passing of time instead of disappearing. Those who follow the first method can remedy their condition with God and with men as Agathocles did; the others cannot possibly survive.

Wherefore it is to be noted that in taking a state its conqueror should weigh all the harmful things he must do and do them all at once so as not to have to repeat them every day, and in not repeating them to be able to make men feel secure and win them over with the benefits he bestows upon them. Anyone who does otherwise, either out of timidity or because of poor advice, is always obliged to keep his knife in his hand; nor can he ever count upon his subjects, who, because of their fresh and continual injuries, cannot feel secure with him. Injuries, therefore, should be inflicted all at the same time, for the less they are tasted; the less they offend; and benefits should be distributed a bit at a time in order that they may be savoured fully. And a prince should, above all, live with his subjects in such a way that no unforeseen event, either good or bad, may make him alter his course; for when emergencies arise in adverse conditions, you are not in time to resort to cruelty, and the good you do will help you little, since it will be judged a forced measure and you will earn from it no thanks whatsoever.

CHAPTER IX

On the Civil Principality

But coming to the second instance, when a private citizen, not through wickedness or any other intolerable violence, but with the favour of his fellow citizens, becomes prince of his native city (this can be called a civil principality, the acquisition of which neither depends completely upon skill nor upon fortune, but instead upon a mixture of shrewdness and luck), I maintain that one reaches this princedom either with the favour of the common people or with that of the nobility. For these two different humours are found in every body politic; and they arise from the fact that the people do not wish to be commanded or oppressed by the nobles, and the nobles desire to command and to oppress the people; and from these two opposed appetites there arises one of three effects: either a principality or liberty or anarchy.

A principality is brought about either by the common people or by the nobility, depending on which of the two parties has the opportunity. For when the nobles see that they cannot resist the populace, they begin to support one among them and make him prince in order to be able, under his protection, to satisfy their appetites. The common people as well, seeing that they cannot resist the nobility, give their support to one man and make him prince in order to have the protection of his authority. He who attains the principality with the aid of the nobility maintains it with more difficulty than he who becomes prince with the assistance of the common people, for he finds himself a prince amidst many who feel themselves to be his equals, and because of this he can neither govern nor manage them as he wishes. But he who attains the principality through popular favour finds himself alone and has around him either no one or very few who are not ready to obey him. Moreover, one cannot honestly satisfy the nobles without harming others, but the common people can certainly be satisfied: their desire is more just than that of the nobles—the former want not to be oppressed and the latter want to oppress. Moreover, a prince can never make himself secure when the people are his enemy because they are so many; he can make himself secure against the nobles because they are so few. The worst that a prince can expect from a hostile people is to be abandoned by them; but with a hostile nobility not only does he have to fear being abandoned but also that they will unite against him; for, being more perceptive and shrewder, they always have time to save themselves, to seek the favours of the side they believe will win. Furthermore, a prince must always live with the same common people; but he can easily do without the same nobles, having the power to create them and to destroy them from day to day and to take away and give back their prestige as he sees fit.

And in order to clarify this point better, I say that the nobles should be considered chiefly in two ways: either they conduct themselves in such a way that they commit themselves completely to your cause or they do not. Those who commit themselves and are not greedy should be honoured and loved; those who do not commit themselves can be analysed in two ways. They act in this manner out of fear and a natural lack of courage, in which case you should make use of them, especially those who are wise advisers, since in prosperous times they will gain you honour and in adverse times you need not fear them. But when, cunningly and influenced by ambition, they refrain from committing themselves to you, this is a sign that they think more of themselves than of you; and the prince should be wary of such men and fear them as if they were open enemies, because they will always, in adverse times, help to bring about his downfall.

However, one who becomes prince with the support of the common people must keep them as his friends; this is easy for him, since the only thing they ask of him is not to be oppressed. But one who, against the will of the common people, becomes prince with the assistance of the nobility should, before all else, seek to win the people's support, which should be easy if he takes them under his protection. And because men, when they are well treated by those from whom they expected harm, are more obliged to their benefactor, the common people quickly become better disposed toward him than if he had become prince with their support. And a prince can gain their favour in various ways, but because they vary according to the situation no fixed rules can be given for them, and therefore I shall not talk about them. I shall conclude by saying only that a prince must have the friendship of the common people; otherwise he will have no support in times of adversity.

Nabis, prince of the Spartans, withstood the attacks of all of Greece and of one of Rome's most victorious armies, and he defended his city and his own rule against them, and when danger was near he needed only to protect himself from a few of his subjects; but if he had had the common people against him, this would not have been sufficient. And let no one dispute my opinion by citing that trite proverb, 'He who builds upon the people builds upon the mud', because that is true when a private citizen lays his foundations and allows himself to believe that the common people will free him if he is oppressed by enemies or by the public officials (in this case a man might often find himself deceived, like the Gracchi of Rome or like Messer Giorgio Scali of Florence); but when the prince who builds his foundations on the people is one who is able to command and is a man of spirit, not bewildered by adversities, and does not lack other necessities, and through his courage and his institutions keeps up the spirits of the populace, he will never find himself deceived by the common people, and he will discover that he has laid sound foundations.

Principalities of this type are usually endangered when they are about to change from a proper civil society to an absolute form of government. For these princes either rule by themselves or by means of public officials; in the latter case their position is weaker and more dangerous since they depend entirely upon the will of those citizens who are appointed to hold the offices; these men, especially in adverse times, can very easily seize the state either by open opposition or by disobedience. And in such times of danger the prince has no time for taking absolute control, for the citizens and subjects who are used to receiving their orders from public officials are, in these crises, not willing to obey his orders; and in doubtful times he will always find a scarcity of men he can trust. Such a prince cannot rely upon what he sees during periods of calm, when the citizens need his rule, because then everyone comes running, makes promises, and each one is willing to die for him—since death is unlikely; but in times of adversity, when the state needs its citizens, then few are to be found. And this experiment is all the more dangerous in that it can be made but once. And, therefore, a wise prince should think of a method by which his citizens, at all times and in every circumstance, will need the assistance of the state and of himself; and then they will always be loyal to him.

CHAPTER X

How the Strength of All Principalities Should be Measured

In analysing the qualities of these principalities, another consideration must be discussed; that is, whether the prince has so much power that he can, if necessary, stand on his own, or whether he always needs the protection of others. And in order to clarify this section, I say that I judge those princes self-sufficient who, either through abundance of troops or of money, are able to gather together a suitable army and fight a good battle against whoever should attack them; and I consider those who always need the protection of others to be those who cannot meet their enemy in the field, but must seek refuge behind their city walls and defend them. The first case has already been treated, and later on I shall say whatever else is necessary on the subject. Nothing more can be added to the second case than to encourage such princes to fortify and provision their cities and not to concern themselves with the surrounding countryside. And anyone who has well fortified his city and has well managed his affairs with his subjects in the manner I detailed above (and discuss below) will be besieged only with great caution; for men are always enemies of undertakings in which they foresee difficulties, and it cannot seem easy to attack someone whose city is well fortified and who is not hated by his people.

The cities of Germany are completely free, they have little surrounding territory, they obey the emperor when they wish, and they fear neither him nor any other nearby power, as they are fortified in such a manner that everyone thinks their capture would be a tedious and difficult affair. For they all have sufficient moats and walls; they have adequate artillery; they always store in their public warehouses enough to drink and to eat and to burn for a year; and besides all this, in order to be able to keep the lower classes fed without exhausting public funds, they always have in reserve a year's supply of raw materials sufficient to give these people work at those trades which are the nerves and the lifeblood of that city and of the industries from which the people earn their living. Moreover, they hold the military arts in high regard, and they have many regulations for maintaining them.

Therefore, a prince who has a strong city and who does not make himself hated cannot be attacked; and even if he were to be attacked, the enemy would have to depart in shame, for human affairs are so changeable that it is almost impossible that one maintain a siege for a year with his troops idle. And if it is objected that if the people have their possessions outside the city and see them destroyed, they will lose patience, and the long siege and self-interest will cause them to forget their prince, I reply that a powerful and spirited prince will always overcome all such difficulties, inspiring his subjects now with the hope that the evil will not last long, now with the fear of the enemy's cruelty, now by protecting himself with clever manoeuvres against those who seem too outspoken. Besides this, the enemy will naturally burn and waste the surrounding country on arrival, just when the spirits of the defenders are still ardent and determined on the city's defence; and thus the prince needs to fear so much the less, because after a few days, when their spirits have cooled down a bit, the damage has already been inflicted and the evils suffered, and there is no means of correcting the matter; and now the people will rally around their prince even more, for it would appear that he is bound to them by obligations, since their homes were burned and their possessions wasted in his defence. And the nature of men is such that they find themselves obligated as much for the benefits they confer as for those they receive. Thus, if everything is taken into consideration, it will not be difficult for a prudent prince to keep high the spirits of his citizens from the beginning to the conclusion of the siege, so long as he does not lack enough food and the means for his defence.

CHAPTER XI

On Ecclesiastical Principalities

There remain now only the ecclesiastical principalities to be discussed: concerning these, all the problems occur before they are acquired; for they are acquired either through ability or through fortune and are maintained without either; they are sustained by the ancient institutions of religion, which are so powerful and of such a kind that they keep their princes in power in whatever manner they act and live their lives. These princes alone have states and do not defend them, subjects and do not rule them; and the states, remaining undefended, are never taken away from them; and the subjects, being ungoverned, show no concern, and they do not think about, nor are they able to sever, their ties with them. These principalities, then, are the only secure and happy ones. But since they are protected by higher causes that the human mind is unable to reach, I shall not discuss them; for, being exalted and maintained by God, it would be the act of a presumptuous and foolhardy man to discuss them. Nevertheless, someone might ask me why it is that the Church, in temporal matters, has arrived at such power when, until the time of Alexander, the Italian powers—not just those who were the established rulers, but every baron and lord, no matter how weak—considered her temporal power as insignificant, and now a King of France trembles before it and it has been able to throw him out of Italy and to ruin the Venetians; although this situation may already be known, it does not seem superfluous to me to recall it in some detail.

Before Charles, King of France, came into Italy, this country was under the rule of the Pope, the Venetians, the King of Naples, the Duke of Milan, and the Florentines. These rulers had to keep two major problems in mind: first, that a foreigner could enter Italy with his armies; second, that no one of them increase his territory. Those whom they needed to watch most closely were the Pope and the Venetians. And to restrain the Venetians the alliance of all the rest was necessary, as was the case in the defence of Ferrara; and to keep the Pope in check they made use of the Roman barons, who, divided into two factions, the Orsini and the Colonna, always had a reason for squabbling amongst themselves; they kept the papacy weak and unstable, standing with their weapons in hand right under the Pope's eyes. And although from time to time there arose a courageous Pope like Pope Sixtus, neither fortune nor his wisdom could ever free him from these inconveniences. And the brevity of the reigns of the popes was the cause; for in ten years, the average life expectancy of a Pope, he might with difficulty put down one of the factions; and if, for example, one Pope had almost extinguished the Colonna, a new Pope who was the enemy of the Orsini would emerge, enabling the Colonna to grow powerful again, and yet he would not have time enough to destroy the Orsini.

As a consequence, the temporal powers of the Pope were little respected in Italy. Then Alexander VI came to power, and he, more than any of the popes who ever reigned, showed how well a Pope, with money and troops, could succeed; and he achieved, with Duke Valentino as his instrument and the French invasion as his opportunity, all those things that I discussed earlier in describing the actions of the Duke. And although his intention was not to make the Church great but rather the Duke, nevertheless what he did resulted in the increase of the power of the Church, which, after his death and once the Duke was destroyed, became the heir of his labours. Then came Pope Julius, and he found the Church strong, possessing all of Romagna, having destroyed the Roman barons, and, by Alexander's blows, having snuffed out their factions; and he also found the way open for the accumulation of wealth by a method never before used by Alexander or his predecessors. These practices Julius not only continued but intensified; and he was determined to take Bologna, to crush the Venetians, and to drive the French from Italy, and he succeeded in all these undertakings; and he is worthy of even more praise, since he did everything for the increased power of the Church and not for any particular individual. He also managed to keep the Orsini and the Colonna factions in the same condition in which he found them; and although there were some leaders among them who wanted to make changes, there were two things which held them back: one, the power of the Church, which frightened them; and, two, not having any of their own family as cardinals, for these were the source of the conflicts among them. These factions will never be at peace as long as they have cardinals, since such men foster factions, both in Rome and outside it, and those barons are compelled to defend them; and thus, from the ambitions of the prelates are born the discords and the tumults among the barons. Therefore, His Holiness Pope Leo has found the papacy very powerful indeed; and it is to be hoped that if his predecessors made it great by feats of arms, he will, through his bounty and his infinite virtues, make it very great and worthy of reverence.

CHAPTER XII

On the Various Kinds of Troops and Mercenary Soldiers

Having treated in detail all the characteristics of those principalities which I proposed to discuss at the beginning, and having considered, to some extent, the reasons for their success or shortcomings, and having demonstrated the ways by which many have tried to acquire them and to maintain them, it remains for me now to speak in general terms of the kinds of offence and defence that can be adopted by each of the previously mentioned principalities. We have said above that a prince must have laid firm foundations; otherwise he will of necessity come to grief. And the principal foundations of all states, the new as well as the old or mixed, are good laws and good armies. And since there cannot exist good laws where there are no good armies, and where there are good armies there must be good laws, I shall leave aside the treatment of laws and discuss the armed forces.

Let me say, therefore, that the armies with which a prince defends his state are made up of his own people, or of mercenaries, or auxiliaries, or of mixed troops. Mercenaries and auxiliaries are useless and dangerous. And if a prince holds on to his state by means of mercenary armies, he will never be stable or secure; for they are disunited, ambitious, without discipline, disloyal; they are brave among friends; among enemies they are cowards; they have no fear of God, they keep no faith with men; and your downfall is deferred only so long as the attack is deferred; and in peace you are plundered by them, in war by your enemies. The reason for this is that they have no other love nor other motive to keep them in the field than a meagre wage, which is not enough to make them want to die for you. They love being your soldiers when you are not making war, but when war comes they either flee or desert. This would require little effort to demonstrate, since the present ruin of Italy is caused by nothing other than her dependence for a long period of time on mercenary forces. These forces did, at times, help some get ahead, and they appeared courageous in combat with other mercenaries; but when the invasion of the foreigner came they showed themselves for what they were; and thus, Charles, King of France, was permitted to take Italy with a piece of chalk. And the man who said that our sins were the cause of this disaster spoke the truth, but they were not at all those that he had in mind, but rather these that I have described; and because they were the sins of princes, the princes in turn have suffered the penalty for them.

I wish to demonstrate more fully the sorry nature of such armies. Mercenary captains are either excellent soldiers or they are not; if they are, you cannot trust them, since they will always aspire to their own greatness either by oppressing you, who are their masters, or by oppressing others against your intent; but if the captain is without skill, he usually ruins you. And if someone were to reply that anyone who bears arms will act in this manner, mercenary or not, I would answer that armies have to be commanded either by a prince or by a republic: the prince must go in person and perform the duties of a captain himself; the republic must send its own citizens; and when they send one who does not turn out to be an able man, they must replace him; if he is capable, they ought to restrain him with laws so that he does not go beyond his authority. And we see from experience that only princes and armed republics make very great advances, and that mercenaries do nothing but harm; and a republic armed with its own citizens is less likely to come under the rule of one of its citizens than a city armed with foreign soldiers.

Rome and Sparta for many centuries stood armed and free. The Swiss are extremely well armed and are completely free. An example from antiquity of the use of mercenary troops is the Cathaginians; they were almost overcome by their own mercenary soldiers after the first war with the Romans, even though the Carthaginians had their own citizens as officers. Philip of Macedonia was made captain of their army by the Thebans after the death of Epaminondas, and after the victory he took their liberty from them. The Milanese, after the death of Duke Philip, employed Francesco Sforza to war against the Venetians; having defeated the enemy at Caravaggio, he joined with them to oppress the Milanese, his employers. Sforza, his father, being in the employ of Queen Giovanna of Naples, all at once left her without defences; hence, in order not to lose her kingdom, she was forced to throw herself into the lap of the King of Aragon. And if the Venetians and the Florentines have in the past increased their possessions with such soldiers, and their captains have not yet made themselves princes but have instead defended them, I answer that the Florentines have been favoured in this matter by luck; for among their able captains whom they could have had reason to fear, some did not win, others met with opposition, and others turned their ambition elsewhere. The one who did not win was John Hawkwood, whose loyalty, since he did not succeed, will never be known; but anyone will admit that had he succeeded, the Florentines would have been at his mercy. Sforza always had the Bracceschi as enemies so that each checked the other. Francesco turned his ambition to Lombardy, Braccio against the Church and the Kingdom of Naples.

But let us come to what has occurred just recently. The Florentines made Paulo Vitelli their captain, a very able man and one who rose from private life to achieve great fame. If this man had taken Pisa, no one would deny that the Florentines would have had to become his ally; for, if he had become employed by their enemies, they would have had no defence, and if they had kept him on, they would have been obliged to obey him. As for the Venetians, if we examine the course they followed, we see that they operated securely and gloriously as long as they fought with their own troops (this was before they started fighting on land); with their nobles and their common people armed, they fought courageously. But when they began to fight on land, they abandoned this successful strategy and followed the usual practices of waging war in Italy. As they first began to expand their territory on the mainland, since they did not have much territory there and enjoyed a high reputation, they had little to fear from their captains; but when their territory increased, which happened under Carmagnola, the Venetians had a taste of this mistake; for, having found him very able, since under his command they had defeated the Duke of Milan, and knowing, on the other hand, that he had lost some of his fighting spirit, they judged that they could no longer conquer under him, for he had no wish to do so, yet they could not dismiss him for fear of losing what they had acquired; so in order to secure themselves against him, they were forced to execute him. Then they had as their captains Bartolomeo da Bergamo, Roberto da San Severino, the Count of Pitigliano, and the like; with such as these they had to fear their losses, not their acquisitions, as occurred later at Vailà, where, in a single day, they lost what had cost them eight hundred years of exhausting effort to acquire. From these soldiers, therefore, come only slow, tardy, and weak conquests and sudden and astonishing losses. And because with these examples I have begun to treat of Italy, which has for many years been ruled by mercenary soldiers, I should like to discuss the matter more thoroughly, in order that once their origin and developments are revealed they can be more easily corrected.

You must, then, understand how in recent times, when the Empire began to be driven out of Italy and the Pope began to win more prestige in temporal affairs, Italy was divided into many states; for many of the large cities took up arms against their nobles, who, at first backed by their Emperor, had kept them under their control; and the Church supported these cities to increase its temporal power; in many other cities citizens became princes. Hence, Italy having come almost entirely into the hands of the Church and of several republics, those priests and other citizens who were not accustomed to bearing arms began to hire foreigners. The first to give prestige to such troops was Alberigo of Conio, a Romagnol. From this man's school emerged, among others, Braccio and Sforza, who in their day were the arbiters of Italy. After them came all the others who, until the present day, have commanded these soldiers. And the result of their ability has been that Italy has been overrun by Charles, plundered by Louis, violated by Ferdinand, and insulted by the Swiss. Their method was first to increase the reputation of their own forces by taking away the prestige of the infantry. They did so because they were men without a state of their own who lived by their profession; a small number of foot soldiers could not give them prestige, and they could not afford to hire a large number of them; and so they relied completely upon cavalry, since for having only a reasonable number of horsemen they were provided for and honoured. And they reduced things to such a state that in an army of twenty thousand troops, one could hardly find two thousand foot soldiers. Besides this, they had used every means to spare themselves and their soldiers hardship and fear, not killing each other in their battles but rather taking each other prisoner without demanding ransom; they would not attack cities at night; and those in the cities would not attack the tents of the besiegers; they built neither stockades nor trenches around their camps; they did not campaign in the winter. And all these things were permitted by their military code and gave them a means of escaping, as was stated, hardships and dangers: so that these condottieri have led Italy into slavery and humiliation.

CHAPTER XIII

On Auxiliary, Mixed, and Citizen Soldiers

Auxiliary troops, the other kind of worthless armies, are those that arrive when you call a powerful man to bring his forces to your aid and defence, as was done in recent times by Pope Julius, who, having witnessed in the campaign of Ferrara the sad showing of his mercenary soldiers, turned to auxiliary soldiers and made an agreement with Ferdinand, King of Spain, that he assist him with his troops and his armies. These soldiers can be useful and good in themselves, but for the man who summons them they are almost always harmful; for, if they lose you are defeated; if they win you end up their prisoner. And although ancient histories are full of such instances, nevertheless I am unwilling to leave unexamined this recent example of Pope Julius II, whose policy could not have been more poorly considered, for, in wanting to take Ferrara, he threw himself completely into the hands of a foreigner. But his good fortune brought about a third development so that he did not gather the fruit of his poor decision: for after his auxiliaries were routed at Ravenna, the Swiss rose up and, to the consternation of Pope Julius as well as everyone else, chased out the victors. Thus, he was neither taken prisoner by his enemies, since they had fled, nor by his auxiliaries, since he triumphed with arms other than theirs. And the Florentines, completely unarmed, hired ten thousand French soldiers to take Pisa; such a plan endangered them more than any of their previous predicaments. The emperor of Constantinople, in order to oppose his neighbours, brought ten thousand Turkish troops into Greece, who, when the war was over, did not want to leave; this was the beginning of Greek servitude under the infidel.

Anyone, therefore, who does not wish to conquer should make use of these soldiers, for they are much more dangerous than mercenary troops. Because with them defeat is certain: they are completely united and all under the command of others; but the mercenaries need more time and a greater opportunity if they are to harm you after they have been victorious, for they are not a united body and are hired and paid by you; a third party whom you may make their leader cannot immediately seize enough authority to harm you. In short, with mercenaries the greatest danger is their cowardice, with auxiliaries their courage.

A wise prince has always avoided these soldiers and has relied upon his own men; and he has chosen to lose with his own troops rather than to conquer with those of others, judging no true victory one gained by means of foreign armies. I shall never hesitate to cite Cesare Borgia and his deeds as an example. This Duke entered Romagna with auxiliary forces, leading an army composed entirely of Frenchmen; and with them he captured Imola and Forlì. But not thinking the troops reliable, he turned to mercenary forces, judging them to be less dangerous, and he hired the Orsini and Vitelli. When he found out that they were unreliable, unfaithful, and treacherous, he destroyed them and turned to his own men. And it is easy to see the difference between these two sorts of troops if we consider the difference between the Duke's reputation when he had only French troops and when he had the Orsini and Vitelli, as opposed to when he was left with his own troops and himself to depend on: we find that his reputation always increased; never was he esteemed more highly than when everyone saw that he was complete master of his own army.

I did not wish to depart from citing recent Italian examples; yet I do not want to omit Hiero of Syracuse, one of those I mentioned above. This man, as I said previously, having been named by the Syracusans captain of their armies, immediately realized that mercenary forces were useless, composed, as they were, of men resembling our own Italian condottieri;

and it seemed to him that he could neither keep them on nor dismiss them, so he had them all cut to pieces: and afterwards he made war with his own troops and not with those of foreigners. I would also like to recall to mind an example from the Old Testament that fits this argument. David offered himself to Saul to battle against Goliath, the Philistine challenger; Saul, in order to give him courage, armed him with his own armour, which David, when he had put it on, cast off, declaring that with it he could not test his true worth; he therefore wished to meet the enemy with his own sling and his own sword.

In short, the arms of another man either slide off your back, weigh you down, or tie you up. Charles VII, father of Louis XI, having freed France from the English by means of his good fortune and his ability, recognized the necessity of arming himself with his own men, and he set up in his kingdom an ordinance to procure cavalry and infantry. Later, his son, King Louis, abolished the ordinance of the infantry and began to hire Swiss troops; this mistake, followed by others as we can now witness, is the cause of the many threats to that kingdom. By giving prestige to the Swiss, he discredited his own troops; for he did away entirely with his foot soldiers and obliged his cavalry to depend upon the soldiers of others; being accustomed to fighting with the Swiss, the French horsemen felt that they could not conquer without them. From this it came about that the French were not strong enough to match the Swiss, and without the Swiss they did not dare to meet others. The armies of France have, therefore, been mixed, partly mercenaries and partly citizen troops; armies combined together in such a fashion are much better than a purely auxiliary force or a purely mercenary army, but are greatly inferior to one's own troops. And the example just cited should suffice, for the kingdom of France would be invincible if Charles's policy had been developed or retained. But man's shortsightedness will initiate a policy that seems good at the outset but does not notice the poison that is concealed underneath, as I said earlier in connection with consumptive fevers.

And thus anyone who does not diagnose the ills when they arise in a principality is not really wise; and this skill is given to few men. And if the primary cause of the downfall of the Roman Empire is examined, one will find it to be only when the Goths began to be hired as mercenaries; because from that beginning the strength of the Roman Empire began to be weakened, and all that strength was drained from it and was given to the Goths.

I conclude, therefore, that without having one's own soldiers, no principality is safe; on the contrary, it is completely subject to fortune, not having the power and the loyalty to defend it in times of adversity. And it was always the opinion and belief of wise men that 'nothing is so unhealthy or unstable as the reputation for power that is not based upon one's own power.' And one's own troops are those which are composed either of subjects or of citizens or your own dependants; all others are either mercenaries or auxiliaries. And the means to organize a citizen army are easily discovered if the methods followed by those four men I have cited above are examined, and if one observes how Philip, father of Alexander the Great, and many republics and princes have armed and organized themselves: in such methods I have full confidence.

CHAPTER XIV

A Prince's Duty Concerning Military Matters

A prince, therefore, must not have any other object nor any other thought, nor must he take anything as his profession but war, its institutions, and its discipline; because that is the only profession which befits one who commands; and it is of such importance that not only does it maintain those who were born princes, but many times it enables men of private station to rise to that position; and, on the other hand, it is evident that when princes have given more thought to personal luxuries than to arms, they have lost their state. And the most important cause of losing it is to neglect this art; and the way to acquire it is to be well versed in this art.

Francesco Sforza became Duke of Milan from being a private citizen because he was armed; his successors, since they avoided the inconveniences of arms, became private citizens after having been dukes. For, among the other bad effects it causes, being unarmed makes you despised; this is one of those infamies a prince should guard himself against, as will be treated below: for between an armed and an unarmed man there is no comparison whatsoever, and it is not reasonable for an armed man to obey an unarmed man willingly, nor that an unarmed man should be safe among armed servants; since, when the former is suspicious and the latter are contemptuous, it is impossible for them to work well together. And therefore, a prince who does not understand military matters, besides the other misfortunes already noted, cannot be esteemed by his own soldiers, nor can he trust them.

He should, therefore, never take his mind from this exercise or war, and in peacetime he must train himself more than in time of war; this can be done in two ways: one by action, the other by the mind. And as far as actions are concerned, besides keeping his soldiers well disciplined and trained, he must always be out hunting, and must accustom his body to hardships in this manner; and he must also learn the nature of the terrain, and know how mountains slope, how valleys open, how plains lie, and understand the nature of rivers and swamps; and he should devote much attention to such activities. Such knowledge is useful in two ways: first, one learns to know one's own country and can better understand how to defend it; second, with the knowledge and experience of the terrain, one can easily comprehend the characteristics of any other terrain that it is necessary to explore for the first time; for the hills, valleys, plains, rivers, and swamps of Tuscany, for instance, have certain similarities to those of other provinces; so that by knowing the lie of the land in one province one can easily understand it in others. And a prince who lacks this ability lacks the most important quality in a leader; because this skill teaches you to find the enemy, choose a campsite, lead troops, organize them for battle, and besiege towns to your own advantage.

Philopoemen, Prince of the Achaeans, among the other praises given to him by writers, is praised because in peacetime he thought of nothing except the means of waging war; and when he was out in the country with his friends, he often stopped and reasoned with them: 'If the enemy were on that hilltop and we were here with our army, which of the two of us would have the advantage? How could we attack them without breaking formation? If we wanted to retreat, how could we do this? If they were to retreat, how could we pursue them?' And he proposed to them, as they rode along, every predicament in which an army may find itself; he heard their opinions, expressed his own, and backed it up with arguments; so that, because of these continuous deliberations, when leading his troops no unforeseen incident could arise for which he did not have the remedy.

But as for the exercise of the mind, the prince must read histories and in them study the deeds of great men; he must see how they conducted themselves in wars; he must examine the reasons for their victories and for their defeats in order to avoid the latter and to imitate the former; and above all else he must do as some distinguished man before him has done, who elected to imitate someone who had been praised and honoured before him, and always keep in mind his deeds and actions; just as it is reported that Alexander the Great imitated Achilles; Caesar, Alexander; Scipio, Cyrus. And anyone who reads the life of Cyrus written by Xenophon will realize how important in the life of Scipio that imitation was for his glory and how much, in purity, goodness, humanity, and generosity, Scipio conformed to those characteristics of Cyrus that Xenophon had written about.

Such methods as these a wise prince must follow, and never in peaceful times must he be idle; but he must turn them diligently to his advantage in order to be able to profit from them in times of adversity, so that, when fortune changes, she will find him prepared to withstand such times.

CHAPTER XV

On Those Things for Which Men, and Particularly Princes, Are Praised or Blamed

Now there remains to be examined what should be the methods and procedures of a prince in dealing with his subjects and friends. And because I know that many have written about this, I am afraid that by writing about it again I shall be thought of as presumptuous, since in discussing this material I depart radically from the procedures of others. But since my intention is to write something useful for anyone who understands it, it seemed more suitable to me to search after the effectual truth of the matter rather than its imagined one. And many writers have imagined for themselves republics and principalities that have never been seen nor known to exist in reality; for there is such a gap between how one lives and how one ought to live that anyone who abandons what is done for what ought to be done learns his ruin rather than his preservation: for a man who wishes to profess goodness at all times will come to ruin among so many who are not good. Hence it is necessary for a prince who wishes to maintain his position to learn how not to be good, and to use this knowledge or not to use it according to necessity.

Leaving aside, therefore, the imagined things concerning a prince, and taking into account those that are true, I say that all men, when they are spoken of, and particularly princes, since they are placed on a higher level, are judged by some of these qualities which bring them either blame or praise. And this is why one is considered generous, another miserly (to use a Tuscan word, since 'avaricious' in our language is still used to mean one who wishes to acquire by means of theft; we call 'miserly' one who excessively avoids using what he has); one is considered a giver, the other rapacious; one cruel, another merciful; one treacherous, another faithful; one effeminate and cowardly, another bold and courageous; one humane, another haughty; one lascivious, another chaste; one trustworthy, another frivolous; one religious, another unbelieving; and the like. And I know that everyone will admit that it would be a very praiseworthy thing to find in a prince, of the qualities mentioned above, those that are held to be good; but since it is neither possible to have them nor to observe them all completely, because the human condition does not permit it, a prince must be prudent enough to know how to escape the bad reputation of those vices that would lose the state for him, and must protect himself from those that will not lose it for him, if this is possible; but if he cannot, he need not concern himself unduly if he ignores these less serious vices. And, moreover, he need not worry about incurring the bad reputation of those vices without which it would be difficult to hold his state; since, carefully taking everything into account, he will discover that something which appears to be a virtue, if pursued, will end in his destruction; while some other thing which seems to be a vice, if pursued, will result in his safety and his well-being.

CHAPTER XVI

On Generosity and Miserliness

Beginning, therefore, with the first of the above-mentioned qualities, I say that it would be good to be considered generous; nevertheless, generosity used in such a manner as to give you a reputation for it will harm you; because if it is employed virtuously and as one should employ it, it will not be recognized and you will not avoid the reproach of its opposite. And so, if a prince wants to maintain his reputation for generosity among men, it is necessary for him not to neglect any possible means of lavish display; in so doing such a prince will always use up all his resources and he will be obliged, eventually, if he wishes to maintain his reputation for generosity, to burden the people with excessive taxes and to do everything possible to raise funds. This will begin to make him hateful to his subjects, and, becoming impoverished, he will not be much esteemed by anyone; so that, as a consequence of his generosity, having offended many and rewarded few, he will feel the effects of any slight unrest and will be ruined at the first sign of danger; recognizing this and wishing to alter his policies, he immediately runs the risk of being reproached as a miser.

A prince, therefore, being unable to use this virtue of generosity in a manner which will not harm himself, if he is known for it, should, if he is wise, not worry about being called a miser; for with time he will come to be considered more generous once it is evident that, as a result of his parsimony, his income is sufficient, he can defend himself from anyone who makes war against him, and he can undertake enterprises without overburdening his people, so that he comes to be generous with all those from whom he takes nothing, who are countless, and miserly with all those to whom he gives nothing, who are few. In our times we have not seen great deeds accomplished except by those who were considered miserly; the others were failures. Pope Julius II, although he made use of his reputation for generosity in order to gain the papacy, then decided not to maintain it in order to be able to wage war; the present King of France has waged many wars without imposing extra taxes on his subjects, only because his habitual parsimony has provided for the additional expenditures; the present King of Spain, if he had been considered generous, would not have engaged in or won so many campaigns.

Therefore, in order not to have to rob his subjects, to be able to defend himself, not to become poor and contemptible, and not to be forced to become rapacious, a prince must consider it of little importance if he incurs the reputation of being a miser, for this is one of those vices that permits him to rule. And if someone were to say: Caesar with his generosity achieved imperial power, and many others, because they were generous and known to be so, achieved very high positions; I would reply: you are either already a prince or you are on the way to becoming one; in the first instance such generosity is damaging; in the second it is very necessary to be thought generous. And Caesar was one of those who wanted to gain the principality of Rome; but if, after obtaining this, he had lived and had not moderated his expenditures, he would have destroyed his rule. And if someone were to reply: there have existed many princes who have accomplished great deeds with their armies who have been reputed to be generous; I would answer you: a prince either spends his own money and that of his subjects or that of others; in the first case he must be economical; in the second he must not restrain any part of his generosity. And for that prince who goes out with his soldiers and lives by looting, sacking, and ransoms, who controls the property of others, such generosity is necessary; otherwise he would not be followed by his troops. And with what does not belong to you or to your subjects you can be a more liberal giver, as were Cyrus, Caesar, and Alexander; for spending the wealth of others does not lessen your reputation but adds to it; only the spending of your own is what harms you. And there is nothing that uses itself up faster than generosity, for as you employ it you lose the means of employing it, and you become either poor and despised or else, in order to escape poverty, you become rapacious and hated. And above all other things a prince must guard himself against being despised and hated; and generosity leads you to both one and the other. So it is wiser to live with the reputation of a miser, which produces reproach without hatred, than to be forced to incur the reputation of rapacity, which produces reproach along with hatred, because you want to be considered generous.

CHAPTER XVII

On Cruelty and Mercy, and Whether It Is Better to Be Loved Than To Be Feared or the Contrary

Proceeding to the other qualities mentioned above, I say that every prince must desire to be considered merciful and not cruel; nevertheless, he must take care not to misuse this mercy. Cesare Borgia was considered cruel; none the less, his cruelty had brought order to Romagna, united it, restored it to peace and obedience. If we examine this carefully, we shall see that he was more merciful than the Florentine people, who, in order to avoid being considered cruel, allowed the destruction of Pistoia. Therefore, a prince must not worry about the reproach of cruelty when it is a matter of keeping his subjects united and loyal; for with a very few examples of cruelty he will be more compassionate than those who, out of excessive mercy, permit disorders to continue, from which arise murders and plundering; for these usually harm the community at large, while the executions that come from the prince harm particular individuals. And the new prince, above all other princes, cannot escape the reputation of being called cruel, since new states are full of dangers. And Virgil, through Dido, states: 'My difficult condition and the newness of my rule make me act in such a manner, and to set guards over my land on all sides.'

Nevertheless, a prince must be cautious in believing and in acting; nor should he be afraid of his own shadow; and he should proceed in such a manner, tempered by prudence and humanity, so that too much trust may not render him imprudent nor too much distrust render him intolerable.

From this arises an argument: whether it is better to be loved than to be feared, or the contrary. I reply that one should like to be both one and the other; but since it is difficult to join them together, it is much safer to be feared than to be loved when one of the two must be lacking. For one can generally say this about men: that they are ungrateful, fickle, simulators and deceivers, avoiders of danger, greedy for gain; and while you work for their good they are completely yours, offering you their blood, their property, their lives, and their sons, as I said earlier, when danger is far away; but when it comes nearer to you they turn away. And that prince who bases his power entirely on their words, finding himself completely without other preparations, comes to ruin; for friendships that are acquired by a price and not by greatness and nobility of character are purchased but are not owned, and at the proper moment they cannot be spent. And men are less hesitant about harming someone who makes himself loved than one who makes himself feared because love is held together by a chain of obligation which, since men are wretched creatures, is broken on every occasion in which their own interests are concerned; but fear is sustained by a dread of punishment which will never abandon you.

A prince must nevertheless make himself feared in such a manner that he will avoid hatred, even if he does not acquire love; since to be feared and not be hated can very well be combined; and this will always be so when he keeps his hands off the property and the women of his citizens and his subjects. And if he must take someone's life, he should do so when there is proper justification and manifest cause; but, above all, he should avoid seizing the property of others; for men forget more quickly the death of their father than the loss of their patrimony. Moreover, reasons for seizing their property are never lacking; and he who begins to live by stealing always finds a reason for taking what belongs to others; on the contrary, reasons for taking a life are rarer and disappear sooner.

But when the prince is with his armies and has under his command a multitude of troops, then it is absolutely necessary that he not worry about being considered cruel; for without that reputation he will never keep an army united or prepared for any combat. Among the praiseworthy deeds of Hannibal is counted this: that, having a very large army, made up of all kinds of men, which he commanded in foreign lands, there never arose the slightest dissension, neither among themselves nor against their leader, both during his good and his bad fortune. This could not have arisen from anything other than his inhuman cruelty, which along with his many other qualities, made him always respected and terrifying in the eyes of his soldiers; and without that, to attain the same effect, his other qualities would not have sufficed. And the writers of history, having considered this matter very little, on the one hand admire these deeds of his and on the other condemn the main cause of them.

And that it is true that his other qualities would not have been sufficient can be seen from the example of Scipio, a most extraordinary man not only in his time but in all recorded history, whose armies in Spain rebelled against him; this came about from nothing other than his excessive compassion, which gave to his soldiers more liberty than military discipline allowed. For this he was censured in the senate by Fabius Maximus, who called him the corruptor of the Roman militia. The Locrians, having been ruined by one of Scipio's officers, were not avenged by him, nor was the arrogance of that officer corrected, all because of his tolerant nature; so that someone in the senate who tried to apologize for him said that there were many men who knew how not to err better than they knew how to correct errors. Such a nature would have, in time, damaged Scipio's fame and glory if he had continued to command armies; but, living under the control of the senate, this harmful characteristic of his not only was concealed but brought him glory.

I conclude, therefore, returning to the problem of being feared and loved, that since men love at their own pleasure and fear at the pleasure of the prince, a wise prince should build his foundation upon that which belongs to him, not upon that which belongs to others: he must strive only to avoid hatred, as has been said.

CHAPTER XVIII

How a Prince Should Keep His Word

How praiseworthy it is for a prince to keep his word and to live by integrity and not by deceit everyone knows; nevertheless, one sees from the experience of our times that the princes who have accomplished great deeds are those who have known how to manipulate the minds of men by shrewdness; and in the end they have surpassed those who laid their foundations upon loyalty.

You must, therefore, know that there are two means of fighting: one according to the laws, the other with force; the first way is proper to man, the second to beasts; but because the first, in many cases is not sufficient, it becomes necessary to have recourse to the second. Therefore, a prince must know how to use wisely the natures of the beast and the man. This policy was taught to princes allegorically by the ancient writers, who described how Achilles and many other ancient princes were given to Chiron the Centaur to be raised and taught under his discipline. This can only mean that, having a half-beast and half-man as a teacher, a prince must know how to employ the nature of the one and the other; and the one without the other cannot endure.

Since, then, a prince must know how to make good use of the nature of the beast, he should choose from among the beasts the fox and the lion; for the lion cannot defend itself from traps and the fox cannot protect itself from wolves. It is therefore necessary to be a fox in order to recognize the traps and a lion in order to frighten the wolves. Those who play only the part of the lion do not understand matters. A wise ruler, therefore, cannot and should not keep his word when such an observance of faith would be to his disadvantage and when the reasons which made him promise are removed. And if men were all good, this rule would not be good; but since men are a contemptible lot and will not keep their promises to you, you likewise need not keep yours to them. A prince never lacks legitimate reasons to break his promise. Of this one could cite an endless number of modern examples to show how many pacts, how many promises have been made null and void because of the infidelity of princes; and he who has known best how to use the fox has come to a better end. But it is necessary to know how to disguise this nature well and to be a great hypocrite and a liar: and men are so simple-minded and so controlled by their present needs that one who deceives will always find another who will allow himself to be deceived.

I do not wish to remain silent about one of these recent instances. Alexander VI did nothing else, he thought about nothing else, except to deceive men, and he always found the occasion to do this. And there never was a man who had more forcefulness in his oaths, who affirmed a thing with more promises, and who honoured his word less; nevertheless, his tricks always succeeded perfectly since he was well acquainted with this aspect of the world.

Therefore, it is not necessary for a prince to have all of the above-mentioned qualities, but it is very necessary for him to appear to have them. Furthermore, I shall be so bold as to assert this: that having them and practising them at all times is harmful; and appearing to have them is useful; for instance, to seem merciful, faithful, humane, trustworthy, religious, and to be so; but his mind should be disposed in such a way that should it become necessary not to be so, he will be able and know how to change to the contrary. And it is essential to understand this: that a prince, and especially a new prince, cannot observe all those things for which men are considered good, for in order to maintain the state he is often obliged to act against his promise, against charity, against humanity, and against religion. And therefore, it is necessary that he have a mind ready to turn itself according to the way the winds of fortune and the changeability of affairs require him; and, as I said above, as long as it is possible, he should not stray from the good, but he should know how to enter into evil when necessity commands.

A prince, therefore, must be very careful never to let anything slip from his lips which is not full of the five qualities mentioned above: he should appear, upon seeing and hearing him, to be all mercy, all faithfulness, all integrity, all kindness, all religion. And there is nothing more necessary than to seem to possess this last quality. And men in general judge more by the eyes than their hands; for everyone can see but few can feel. Everyone sees what you seem to be, few touch upon what you are, and those few who do not dare to contradict the opinion of the many who have the majesty of the state to defend them; and in the actions of all men, and especially of princes, where there is no impartial arbiter, one must consider the final result. Let a prince therefore act to conquer and to maintain the state; his methods will always be judged honourable and will be praised by all; for ordinary people are always deceived by appearances and by the outcome of a thing; and in the world there is nothing but ordinary people; and there is no room for the few, while the many have a place to lean on. A certain prince of the present day, whom I shall refrain from naming, preaches nothing but peace and faith, and to both one and the other he is entirely opposed; and both, if he had put them into practice, would have cost him many times over either his reputation or his state.

CHAPTER XIX

On Avoiding Being Despised and Hated

But now that I have talked about the most important of the qualities mentioned above, I would like to discuss the others briefly in this general manner: that the prince, as was noted above, should concentrate upon avoiding those things which make him hated and despised; and when he has avoided this, he will have carried out his duties and will find no danger whatsoever in other vices. As I have said, what makes him hated above all else is being rapacious and a usurper of the property and the women of his subjects; he must refrain from this; and in most cases, so long as you do not deprive them of either their property or their honour, the majority of men live happily; and you have only to deal with the ambition of a few, who can be restrained without difficulty and by many means. What makes him despised is being considered changeable, frivolous, effeminate, cowardly, irresolute; from these qualities a prince must guard himself as if from a reef, and he must strive to make everyone recognize in his actions greatness, spirit, dignity, and strength; and concerning the private affairs of his subjects, he must insist that his decision be irrevocable; and he should maintain himself in such a way that no man could imagine that he can deceive or cheat him.

That prince who projects such an opinion of himself is greatly esteemed; and it is difficult to conspire against a man with such a reputation and difficult to attack him, provided that he is understood to be of great merit and revered by his subjects. For a prince should have two fears: one, internal, concerning his subjects; the other, external, concerning foreign powers. From the latter he can defend himself by his good troops and friends; and he will always have good friends if he has good troops; and internal affairs will always be stable when external affairs are stable, provided that they are not already disturbed by a conspiracy; and even if external conditions change, if he is properly organized and lives as I have said and does not lose control of himself, he will always be able to withstand every attack, just as I said that Nabis the Spartan did. But concerning his subjects, when external affairs do not change, he has to fear that they may conspire secretly: the prince secures himself from this by avoiding being hated or despised and by keeping the people satisfied with him; this is a necessary accomplishment, as was treated above at length. And one of the most powerful remedies a prince has against conspiracies is not to be hated by the masses; for a man who plans a conspiracy always believes that he will satisfy the people by killing the prince; but when he thinks he might anger them, he cannot work up the courage to undertake such a deed; for the problems on the side of the conspirators are countless. And experience demonstrates that there have been many conspiracies but few have been concluded successfully; for anyone who conspires cannot be alone, nor can he find companions except from amongst those whom he believes to be dissatisfied; and as soon as you have revealed your intention to one malcontent, you give him the means to make himself content, since he can have everything he desires by uncovering the plot; so much is this so that, seeing a sure gain on the one hand and one doubtful and full of danger on the other, if he is to maintain faith with you he has to be either an unusually good friend or a completely determined enemy of the prince. And to repeat the matter briefly, I say that on the part of the conspirator there is nothing but fear, jealousy, and the thought of punishment that terrifies him; but on the part of the prince there is the majesty of the principality, the laws, the defences of friends and the state to protect him; so that, with the good will of the people added to these things, it is impossible for anyone to be so rash as to plot against him. For, where usually a conspirator has to be afraid before he executes his evil deed, in this case he must be afraid even after the crime is performed, having the people as an enemy, nor can he hope to find any refuge because of this.

One could cite countless examples on this subject; but I shall be satisfied with only the one which occurred during the time of our fathers. Messer Annibale Bentivogli, prince of Bologna and grandfather of the present Messer Annibale, was murdered by the Canneschi family, who conspired against him; he left behind no heir except Messer Giovanni, then only a baby. As soon as this murder occurred, the people rose up and killed all the Canneschi. This came about because of the good will that the house of the Bentivogli enjoyed in those days; this good will was so great that with Annibale dead, there being no one of that family left in the city who could rule Bologna, the Bolognese people, having heard that in Florence there was one of the Bentivogli blood who was believed until that time to be the son of a blacksmith, went to Florence to find him, and they gave him the control of that city; it was ruled by him until Messer Giovanni became of age to rule.

I conclude, therefore, that a prince should not be too concerned with conspiracies when the people are well disposed toward him; but when the populace is hostile and regards him with hatred, he must fear everything and everyone. And well-organized states and wise princes have, with great diligence, taken care not to anger the nobles and to satisfy the common people and keep them contented; for this is one of the most important concerns that a prince has.

Among the kingdoms in our times that are well organized and well governed is that of France: in it one finds countless good institutions upon which depend the liberty and the security of the king; of these the foremost is the parliament and its authority. For he who organized that kingdom, recognizing the ambition of the nobles and their insolence, and being aware of the necessity of keeping a bit in their mouths to hold them back, on the one hand, while, on the other, knowing the hatred, based upon fear, of the populace of the nobles, and wanting to reassure them, did not wish this to be the particular obligation of the king. In order to relieve himself of the difficulties he might incur from the nobles if he supported the common people, and from the common people if he supported the nobles, he established a third judicial body that might restrain the nobles and favour the masses without burdening the king. There could be no better nor more prudent an institution than this, nor could there be a better reason for the safety of the king and the kingdom. From this one can extract another notable observation: that princes must delegate distasteful tasks to others; pleasant ones they should keep for themselves. Again I conclude that a prince must respect the nobles but not make himself hated by the common people.

Perhaps it may seem to many who have studied the lives and deaths of some Roman emperors that they afford examples contrary to my point of view; for we find that some of them always lived nobly and demonstrated great strength of character yet nevertheless lost their empire or were killed by their own subjects who plotted against them. Wishing, therefore, to reply to these objections, I shall discuss the traits of several emperors, showing the reasons for their ruin, which are not different from those which I myself have already deduced; and I shall bring forward for consideration those things which are worthy of note for anyone who reads about the history of those times. And I shall let it suffice to choose all those emperors who succeeded to the throne from Marcus the philosopher to Maximinus: these were Marcus, his son Commodus, Pertinax, Julian, Severus, Antoninus Caracalla his son, Macrinus, Heliogabalus, Alexander, and Maximinius. And it is first to be noted that while in other principalities one has only to contend with the ambition of the nobles and the arrogance of the people, the Roman emperors had a third problem: they had to endure the cruelty and the avarice of the soldiers. This created such difficulties that it was the cause of the downfall of many of them, since it was hard to satisfy both the soldiers and the populace; for the people loved peace and quiet and because of this loved modest princes, while the soldiers loved the prince who had a military character and who was arrogant, cruel, and rapacious; they wanted him to practise such qualities on the people so that they might double their pay and give vent to their avarice and cruelty. As a result of this situation, those emperors always came to ruin who by nature or by guile did not have so great a reputation that they could keep both the people and the soldiers in check; and most of them, especially those who came to power as new princes, recognizing the difficulty resulting from these two opposing factions, turned to appeasing the soldiers, caring little about injuring the people. Such a decision was necessary; since princes cannot avoid being hated by somebody, they must first seek not to be hated by the bulk of the populace; and when they cannot achieve this, they must try with every effort to avoid the hatred of the most powerful group. And therefore, those emperors who had need of extraordinary support because of their newness in power allied themselves with the soldiers instead of the people; nevertheless, this proved to their advantage or not, according to whether the prince knew how to maintain his reputation with the soldiers.

For the reasons listed above, it came about that, of Marcus, Pertinax, and Alexander, all of whom lived modest lives, were lovers of justice, enemies of cruelty, humane, and kindly, all except Marcus came to an unhappy end. Marcus alone lived and died with the greatest of honour, for he succeeded to the empire by birthright, and he did not have to recognize any obligation for it either to the soldiers or to the people; then, being endowed with many characteristics which made him revered, he always held, while he was alive, both the one party and the other within their limits, and he was never either hated or despised. But Pertinax was made emperor against the will of the soldiers, who, being used to living licentiously under Commodus, could not tolerate the righteous manner of life to which Pertinax wished to return them; whereupon, having made himself hated, and since to this hatred was added contempt for his old age, he came to ruin at the initial stage of his rule.

And here one must note that hatred is acquired just as much by means of good actions as by bad ones; and so, as I said above, if a prince wishes to maintain the state, he is often obliged not to be good; because whenever that group which you believe you need to support you is corrupted, whether it be the common people, the soldiers, or the nobles, it is to your advantage to follow their inclinations in order to satisfy them; and then good actions are your enemy. But let us come to Alexander. He was of such goodness that among the other laudable deeds attributed to him is this: in the fourteen years that he ruled the empire he never put anyone to death without a trial; nevertheless, since he was considered effeminate and a man who let himself be ruled by his mother, because of this he was despised, and the army plotted against him and murdered him.

Considering now, in contrast, the characteristics of Commodus, Severus, Antoninus Caracalla, and Maximinus, you will find them extremely cruel and greedy: in order to satisfy their troops, they did not hesitate to inflict all kinds of injuries upon the people; and all except Severus came to a sorry end. For in Severus there was so much ability that, keeping the soldiers as his friends even though the people were oppressed by him, he was always able to rule happily; for those qualities of his made him so esteemed in the eyes of both the soldiers and the common people that the former were awestruck and stupefied and the latter were respectful and satisfied.

And since the actions of this man were great and noteworthy for a new prince, I wish to demonstrate briefly how well he knew how to use the masks of the fox and the lion, whose natures, as I say above, a prince must imitate. As soon as Severus learned of the indecisiveness of the emperor Julian, he convinced the army of which he was in command in Slavonia that it would be a good idea to march to Rome to avenge the death of Pertinax, who had been murdered by the Praetorian Guards. And under this pretext, without showing his desire to rule the empire, he moved his army to Rome, and he was in Italy before his departure was known. When he arrived in Rome, the senate, out of fear, elected him emperor, and Julian was killed. After this beginning, there remained two obstacles for Severus if he wanted to make himself master of the whole state: the first in Asia, where Pescennius Niger, commander of the Asiatic armies, had himself named emperor; and the other in the West, where Albinus was, who also aspired to the empire. And since he judged it dangerous to reveal himself as an enemy to both of them, he decided to attack Niger and to deceive Albinus. He wrote to the latter that, having been elected emperor by the senate, he wanted to share that honour with him; and he sent him the title of Caesar and, by decree of the senate, he made him his coequal: these things were accepted by Albinus as the truth. But after Severus had conquered and executed Niger and had pacified affairs in the East, upon returning to Rome, he complained to the senate that Albinus, ungrateful for the benefits received from him, had treacherously sought to kill him, and for this he was obliged to go and punish his ingratitude. Then he went to find him in France and took both his state and his life.

Anyone, therefore, who will carefully examine the actions of this man will find him a very ferocious lion and a very shrewd fox; and he will see him feared and respected by everyone and not hated by his armies; and one should not be amazed that he, a new man, was able to hold so great an empire; for his outstanding reputation always defended him from that hatred which the common people could have had for him on account of his plundering. But Antoninus, his son, was also a man who had excellent abilities which made him greatly admired in the eyes of the people and pleasing to the soldiers, for he was a military man, most able to support any kind of hardship, a despiser of all delicate foods and soft living; this made him loved by all the armies; nevertheless, his ferocity and cruelty were so great and so unusual—since he had, after countless individual killings, put to death a large part of the populace of Rome and all that of Alexandria— that he became most despised all over the world. And he aroused the fears even of those whom he had around him, so that he was murdered by a centurion in the midst of his army. From this it is to be noted that such deaths as these, which result from the deliberation of a determined individual, are unavoidable for princes, since anyone who does not fear death can harm them; but the prince must not be too afraid of such men, for they are very rare. He must only guard against inflicting serious injury on anyone who serves him and anyone he has about him in the administration of the principality: Antoninus had done this, for he had shamefully put to death a brother of that centurion, and he threatened the man every day; yet he kept him as a bodyguard. This was a rash decision, and, as it happened, one which would bring about his downfall.

But let us come to Commodus, who held the empire with great ease, having inherited it by birth, being the son of Marcus; and it would have been enough for him to follow in the footsteps of his father in order to satisfy the soldiers and the common people. But being a cruel and bestial person by nature, in order to practise his greed upon the common people, he turned to pleasing the armies and to making them undisciplined; on the other hand, by not maintaining his dignity, frequently descending into the arenas to fight with the gladiators and doing other degrading things unworthy of the imperial majesty, he became contemptible in the sight of the soldiers. And being hated on the one hand, and despised on the other, he was plotted against and murdered.

The qualities of Maximinus remain to be described. He was a very warlike man; and because the armies were angered by Alexander's softness, which I explained above, after Alexander's death they elected him to the empire. He did not retain it very long, for two things made him hated and despised: the first was his base origin, having herded sheep once in Thrace (this fact was well known everywhere and it caused him to lose considerable dignity in everyone's eyes); the second was that at the beginning of his reign he deferred going to Rome to take possession of the imperial throne, and he had acquired the reputation of being very cruel, having through his prefects, in Rome and in all other parts of the empire, committed many cruelties. As a result, the entire world was moved by disgust for his ignoble birth and by the hatred brought about by fear of his cruelty; first Africa revolted, then the senate with the entire populace of Rome, and finally all of Italy conspired against him. To this was added even his own army; for, while besieging Aquileia and finding the capture difficult, angered by his cruelty and fearing him less, seeing that he had many enemies, they murdered him.

I do not wish to discuss Heliogabalus or Macrinus or Julian, who, since they were universally despised, were immediately disposed of; but I shall come to the conclusion of this discourse. And I say that the princes of our times in their affairs suffer less from this problem of satisfying their soldiers by extraordinary means, for, although they have to consider them to some extent, yet they resolve the question quickly, for none of these princes has standing armies which have evolved along with the government and the administration of the provinces as did the armies of the Roman empire. And therefore, if it was then necessary to satisfy the soldiers more than the common people, it was because the soldiers could do more than the common people; now it is more necessary for all princes, except the Turk and the Sultan, to satisfy the common people more than the soldiers, since the people can do more than the soldiers. I make an exception of the Turk, for he always maintains near him twelve thousand infantrymen and fifteen thousand calvarymen, upon whom depend the safety and the strength of his kingdom, and it is necessary that, setting aside all other concerns, that ruler maintain them as his friends. Likewise, the kingdom of the Sultan being entirely in the hands of the soldiers, it is fitting that he, too, should maintain them as his friends without respect to the people. And you must note that this state of the Sultan is unlike all the other principalities, since it is similar to the Christian pontificate, which cannot be called either a hereditary principality or a new principality; for it is not the sons of the old prince that are the heirs and that remain as lords, but instead the one who is elected to that rank by those who have the authority to do so. And because this system is an ancient one, it cannot be called a new principality, for in it are none of these difficulties that are to be found in new ones, since, although the prince is new, the institutions of that state are old and are organized to receive him as if he were their hereditary ruler.

But let us return to our subject. Let me say that anyone who considers the discourse written above will see how either hatred or contempt has been the cause of the ruin of these previously mentioned emperors; and he will also recognize how it comes to pass that, although some acted in one way and others in a contrary manner, in each of these groups one man had a happy end and the others an unhappy one. Because for Pertinax and Alexander, being new princes, it was useless and damaging to wish to imitate Marcus, who was installed in the principality by hereditary right; and likewise for Caracalla, Commodus, and Maximinus, it was disastrous to imitate Severus, since they did not have enough ability to follow in his footsteps. Therefore, a new prince in a new principality cannot imitate the deeds of Marcus, nor yet does he need to follow those of Severus; instead, he should take from Severus those attributes which are necessary to found his state and from Marcus those which are suitable and glorious in order to conserve a state which is already established and stable.

CHAPTER XX

On Whether Fortresses and Many Things that Princes Employ Every Day Are Useful or Harmful

Some princes have disarmed their subjects in order to hold the state securely; others have kept their conquered lands divided; some have encouraged hostilities against themselves; others have turned to winning the support of those who were suspect at the beginning of their rule; some have built fortresses; others have torn them down and destroyed them. And although one cannot give a definite rule concerning these matters without knowing the particular details of those states wherein one had to take some similar decision, nevertheless I shall speak in as general a manner as the subject matter will allow.

Now there has never been a time when a new prince disarmed his subjects; on the contrary, when he has found them unarmed he has always armed them, because when armed those arms become yours; those whom you suspect become faithful, and those who were faithful remain so, and they become your partisans rather than your subjects. And since all of your subjects cannot be armed, when those you arm are favoured you can deal more securely with the others; and that distinction in treatment which they recognize toward themselves makes them obliged to you; the others excuse you, judging it necessary that those who are in more danger and who hold more responsibility should have more reward. But when you disarm them you begin to offend them; you demonstrate that you have no trust in them, either out of cowardice or from little confidence in them; and both these attitudes generate hatred against you. And since you cannot be unarmed, you will have to turn to mercenary soldiers, who have the characteristics explained above; and even if they were good, they could not be strong enough to defend you from powerful enemies and from unfaithful subjects. Therefore, as I have said, a new prince in a new principality has always instituted an army; and history is full of such examples.

But when a prince acquires a new state that, like a member, is joined to his old one, then it is necessary to disarm that state, except for those who have been your partisans in its acquisition; and they as well, with time and the appropriate opportunity, must be rendered weak and effeminate; and things must be organized in such a fashion that the armed strength of your entire state will be concentrated in your own troops who live near to you in your older state.

Our ancestors, and those who were considered wise, used to say that it was necessary to hold Pistoia by factions and Pisa by fortresses; and because of this they would encourage factional strife in some of their subject towns in order to control them more easily. This advice, during those times when Italy had, to a certain extent, a balance of power, may have been a good policy; but I do not believe that today it can be given as a rule, since I do not think that factions ever did any good. On the contrary, when the enemy approaches, divided cities are, of necessity, always lost; for the weaker factions will always join the external forces and the others will not be able to resist.

The Venetians, moved by the reasons stated above, I believe, encouraged the Guelf and Ghibelline factions in their subject cities; and although they never permitted matters to come to bloodshed, they still fostered these quarrels between them so that those citizens, busy with their own disputes, would not unite against them. This, as we have seen, did not result in their gain; for, having been defeated at Vailà, one faction of these cities immediately took courage and seized the entire territory from them. Methods such as these, moreover, imply weakness in a prince; for in a strong principality such divisions will never be allowed, since they are profitable only in peacetime, allowing the subjects to be more easily controlled by such means; but when war comes such a policy reveals its defects.

Without a doubt, princes become great when they overcome difficulties and obstacles that are imposed on them; and therefore fortune, especially when she wishes to increase the reputation of a new prince, who has a greater need to acquire prestige than a hereditary prince does, creates enemies for him and has them take action against him so that he will have the chance to overcome them and to climb higher up the ladder his enemies have brought him. Therefore many judge that a wise prince must, whenever he has the occasion, foster with cunning some hostility so that in stamping it out his greatness will increase as a result.

Princes, and especially those who are new, have discovered more loyalty and more utility in those men who, at the beginning of their rule, were considered suspect than in those who were at first trusted, Pandolfo Petrucci, prince of Siena, ruled his state more with the assistance of men who had been held in suspicion than by others. But on this issue one cannot speak in generalities, for it varies according to the case. I shall only say this: that the prince will always easily win the support of those men who had been enemies at the start of a principality, the kind who must have support in order to maintain themselves; and they are even more obliged to serve him faithfully inasmuch as they recognize the need, through their actions, to cancel the suspicious opinion that the prince had of them. And thus, the prince will always derive more profit from them than from those who, serving him with too much security, neglect his affairs.

And since the subject requires it, I do not wish to fail to remind princes who have conquered a state recently by means of assistance from its inhabitants to consider carefully what cause may have moved those who have helped him to do so; and if it is not natural affection for him, but simply because they were not happy with the preceding state, he will be able to keep them as his allies only with hard work and the greatest of difficulty, since it will be impossible for him to satisfy them. And considering carefully the reason for this, with the examples taken from antiquity and from modern times, it will be seen that he can more easily win friends for himself from among those men who were content with the preceding state, and therefore were his enemies, than from those who, since they were not satisfied with it, became his allies and helped him to occupy it.

In order to hold their states more securely, princes have been accustomed to build fortresses that may serve as the bridle and bit for those who might plot an attack against them, and to have a secure shelter from a sudden rebellion. I praise this method, because it has been used since ancient times; nevertheless, Messer Niccolò Vitelli, in our own times, was seen to demolish two fortresses in Città di Castello in order to hold that state; Guido Ubaldo, Duke of Urbino, on returning to the rule from which Cesare Borgia had driven him, completely destroyed all the fortresses of that province, and he decided that without them it would be more difficult to recapture that state; the Bentivogli, having returned to power in Bologna, took similar measures. Fortresses, then, are either useful or not, according to the circumstances: if they benefit you in one way they injure you in another. This matter may be dealt with as follows: that prince who is more afraid of his own people than of foreigners should build fortresses; but one who is more afraid of foreigners than of his people should not consider constructing them. The castle of Milan, which Francesco Sforza built there, has caused and will cause more wars against the Sforza family than any other disorder in that state. However, the best fortress that exists is not to be hated by the people; because, although you may have fortresses, they will not save you if the people hate you; for once the people have taken up arms, they never lack for foreigners who will aid them. In our times we have not seen that they have benefited any prince except the Countess of Forlì after her husband, Count Girolamo, was killed; for because of her castle she was able to escape the popular uprising and to wait until help arrived from Milan in order to regain her state. And the times were such at that moment that no foreigner could give assistance to her people. But then fortresses were of little use to her when Cesare Borgia attacked her and when her hostile populace joined with the foreigner. Therefore, then and earlier, it would have been safer for her not to have been hated by her people than to have had the fortresses.

Considering all these matters, therefore, I praise both those princes who build fortresses and those who do not; and I criticize any prince who, trusting in fortresses, considers the hatred of the people to be of little importance.

CHAPTER XXI

How a Prince Should Act to Acquire Esteem

Nothing makes a prince more esteemed than great undertakings and examples of his unusual talents. In our own times we have Ferdinand of Aragon, the present King of Spain. This man can be called almost a new prince, since from being a weak ruler he became, through fame and glory, the first king of Christendom; and if you consider his accomplishments, you will find them all very grand and some even extraordinary. In the beginning of his reign he attacked Granada, and that enterprise was the basis of his state. First, he acted while things were peaceful and when he had no fear of opposition: he kept the minds of the barons of Castile busy with this, and they, concentrating on that war, did not consider changes at home. And he acquired, through that means, reputation and power over them without their noticing it; he was able to maintain armies with money from the Church and the people, and with that long war he laid a basis for his own army, which has since brought him honour. Besides this, in order to be able to undertake greater enterprises, always using religion for his own purposes, he turned to a pious cruelty, hunting down and clearing out the Moors from his kingdom: no example could be more pathetic or more unusual than this. He attacked Africa, under the same cloak of religion; he undertook the invasion of Italy; he finally attacked France. And in such a manner, he has always done and planned great deeds which have always kept the minds of his subjects in suspense and amazed and occupied with their outcome. And one action of his would spring from another in such a way that between one and the other he would never give men enough time to be able to work calmly against him.

It also helps a prince a great deal to display rare examples of his skills in dealing with internal affairs, such as those which are reported about Messer Bernabò Visconti of Milan. When the occasion arises that a person in public life performs some extraordinary act, be it good or evil, he should find a way of rewarding or punishing him that will provoke a great deal of discussion. And above all, a prince should strive in all of his deeds to give the impression of a great man of superior intelligence.

A prince is also respected when he is a true friend and a true enemy; that is, when he declares himself on the side of one prince against another without any reservation. Such a policy will always be more useful than that of neutrality; for if two powerful neighbours of yours come to blows, they will be of the type that, when one has emerged victorious, you will either have cause to fear the victor or you will not. In either of these two cases, it will always be more useful for you to declare yourself and to fight an open war; for, in the first case, if you do not declare your intentions, you will always be the prey of the victor to the delight and satisfaction of the vanquished, and you will have no reason why anyone would come to your assistance; because whoever wins does not want reluctant allies who would not assist him in times of adversity; and whoever loses will not give you refuge since you were unwilling to run the risk of coming to his aid.

Antiochus came into Greece, sent there by the Aeolians to drive out the Romans. Antiochus sent envoys to the Achaeans, who were friends of the Romans, to encourage them to adopt a neutral policy; and, on the other hand, the Romans were urging them to take up arms on their behalf. This matter came up for debate in the council of the Achaeans, where the legate of Antiochus persuaded them to remain neutral; to this the Roman legate replied: 'The counsel these men give you about not entering the war is indeed contrary to your interests; without respect, without dignity, you will be the prey of the victors.'

And it will always happen that he who is not your friend will request your neutrality and he who is your friend will ask you to declare yourself by taking up your arms. And irresolute princes, in order to avoid present dangers, follow the neutral road most of the time, and most of the time they are ruined. But when the prince declares himself vigorously in favour of one side, if the one with whom you have joined wins, although he may be powerful and you may be left to his discretion, he has an obligation to you and there does exist a bond of friendship; and men are never so dishonest that they will crush you with such a show of ingratitude; and then, victories are never so clear-cut that the victor need be completely free of caution, especially when justice is concerned. But if the one with whom you join loses, you will be taken in by him; and while he is able, he will help you, and you will become the comrade of a fortune which can rise up again.

In the second case, when those who fight together are of such a kind that you need not fear the one who wins, it is even more prudent to join his side, since you go to the downfall of a prince with the aid of another prince who should have saved him if he had been wise; and in winning he is at your discretion, and it is impossible for him not to win with your aid.

And here it is to be noted that a prince should avoid ever joining forces with one more powerful than himself against others unless necessity compels it, as was said above; for you remain his prisoner if you win, and princes should avoid, as much as possible, being left at the mercy of others. The Venetians allied themselves with France against the Duke of Milan; and they could have avoided that alliance, which resulted in their ruin. But when such an alliance cannot be avoided (as happened to the Florentines when the Pope and Spain led their armies to attack Lombardy), then a prince should join in, for the reasons given above. Nor should any state ever believe that it can always choose safe courses of action; on the contrary, it should think that they will all be doubtful; for we find this to be in the order of things: that we never try to avoid one disadvantage without running into another; but prudence consists in knowing how to recognize the nature of disadvantages and how to choose the least bad as good.

A prince also should demonstrate that he is a lover of talent by giving recognition to men of ability and by honouring those who excel in a particular field. Furthermore, he should encourage his subjects to be free to pursue their trades in tranquillity, whether in commerce, agriculture, or in any other trade a man may have. And he should act in such a way that a man is not afraid to increase his goods for fear that they will be taken away from him, while another will not be afraid to engage in commerce for fear of taxes; instead, he must set up rewards for those who wish to do these things, and for anyone who seeks in any way to aggrandize his city or state. He should, besides this, at the appropriate times of the year, keep the populace occupied with festivals and spectacles. And because each city is divided into guilds or clans, he should take account of these groups, meet with them on occasion, offer himself as an example of humanity and munificence, always, nevertheless, maintaining firmly the dignity of his position, for this should never be lacking in any way.

CHAPTER XXII

On the Prince's Private Advisers

The choice of advisers is of no little import to a prince; and they are good or not, according to the wisdom of the prince. The first thing one does to evaluate the wisdom of a ruler is to examine the men that he has around him; and when they are capable and faithful one can always consider him wise, for he has known how to recognize their ability and to keep them loyal; but when they are otherwise one can always form a low impression of him; for the first error he makes is made in this choice of advisers.

There was no one who knew Messer Antonio da Venafro, adviser of Pandolfo Petrucci, Prince of Siena, who did not judge Pandolfo to be a very worthy man for having him as his minister. For there are three types of intelligence: one understands on its own, the second discerns what others understand, the third neither understands by itself nor through the intelligence of others; that first kind is most excellent, the second excellent, the third useless; therefore, it was necessary that if Pandolfo's intelligence were not of the first sort it must have been of the second: for, whenever a man has the intelligence to recognize the good or the evil that a man does or says, although he may not have original ideas of his own, he recognizes the bad deeds and the good deeds of the adviser, and he is able to praise the latter and to correct the others; and the adviser cannot hope to deceive him and thus he maintains his good behaviour.

But as to how a prince may know the adviser, there is this way which never fails. When you see that the adviser thinks more about himself than about you, and that in all his deeds he seeks his own interests, such a man as this will never be a good adviser and you will never be able to trust him; for a man who has the state of another in his hand must never think about himself but always about his prince, and he must never be concerned with anything that does not concern his prince. And on the other hand, the prince should think of the adviser in order to keep him good—honouring him, making him wealthy, putting him in his debt, giving him a share of the honours and the responsibilities—so that the adviser sees that he cannot exist without the prince and so his abundant wealth will not make him desire more riches, or his many duties make him fear changes. When, therefore, advisers and princes are of such a nature in their dealings with each other, they can have faith in each other; and when they are otherwise, the outcome will always be harmful either to the one or to the other.

CHAPTER XXIII

On How to Avoid Flatterers

I do not wish to omit an important matter and an error from which princes protect themselves with difficulty if they are not very clever or if they do not have good judgement. And these are the flatterers which fill the courts; for men delight so much in their own concerns, deceiving themselves in this manner, that they protect themselves from this plague with difficulty; and wishing to defend oneself from them brings with it the danger of becoming despised. For there is no other way to guard yourself against flattery than by making men understand that telling you the truth will not offend you; but when each man is able to tell you the truth you lose their respect. Therefore, a wise prince should take a third course, choosing wise men for his state and giving only those free rein to speak the truth to him, and only on such matters as he inquires about and not on others. But he should ask them about everything and should hear their opinions, and afterwards he should deliberate by himself in his own way; and with these counsels and with each of his advisers he should conduct himself in such a manner that all will realize that the more freely they speak the more they will be acceptable to him; besides these things, he should not want to hear any others, he should follow through on the policy decided upon, and he should be firm in his decisions. Anyone who does otherwise is either prey for flatterers or changes his mind often with the variance of opinions: because of this he is not respected.

I wish, in this regard, to cite a modern example. Father Luca, the representative of the present Emperor Maximilian, explained, speaking about His Majesty, how the emperor never sought advice from anyone, nor did he ever do anything in his own way; this came about because of the emperor's secretive nature, a policy contrary to the one discussed above. He communicates his plans to no one, he accepts no advice about them; but as they begin to be recognized and discovered as they are put into effect, they begin to be criticized by those around him; and he, being easily influenced, is drawn away from his plans. From this results the fact that those things he achieves in one day he destroys during the next, and no one ever understands what he wishes or plans to do, and one cannot rely upon his decisions.

A prince, therefore, should always seek counsel, but when he wishes and not when others wish it; on the contrary, he should discourage anyone from giving him counsel unless it is requested. But he should be a great inquisitor and then, concerning the matters inquired about, a patient listener to the truth; furthermore, if he learns that anyone, for any reason, does not tell him the truth, he should become angry. And although many feel that any prince who is considered clever is so reputed not because of his own character but because of the good advisers he has around him, without a doubt they are deceived. For this is a general rule which never fails: that a prince who is not wise in his own right cannot be well advised, unless by chance he has submitted himself to a single person who governs him in everything and who is a very prudent individual. In this case he could well receive good advice, but it would not last long because that adviser would in a brief time take the state away from him. But if he seeks advice from more than one, a prince who is not wise will never have consistent advice, nor will he know how to make it consistent on his own; each of his advisers will think about his own interests; he will not know either how to correct or to understand them. And one cannot find advisers who are otherwise, for men always turn out badly for you unless some necessity makes them good. Therefore, it is to be concluded that good advice, from whomever it may come, must arise from the prudence of the prince and not the prince's prudence from the good advice.

CHAPTER XXIV

Why Italian Princes Have Lost Their States

The things written above, if followed prudently, make a new prince seem well established and render him immediately safer and more established in his state than if he had been in it for some time. For a new prince is far more closely observed in his activities than is a hereditary prince; and when his deeds are recognized to be good actions they attract men much more and bind them to him more strongly than does antiquity of lineage. For men are much more taken by present concerns than by those of the past; and when they find the present satisfactory they enjoy it and seek nothing more; in fact, they will seize every measure to defend the new prince as long as he is not lacking in his other responsibilities. And thus he will have a double glory: that of having given birth to a new principality and of having adorned it and strengthened it with good laws, good arms, and good examples; as he will have double shame who, having been born a prince, loses his principality on account of his lack of prudence.

And if one considers those rulers in Italy that have lost their states in our times, such as the King of Naples, the Duke of Milan, and others, one discovers in them, first, a common defect in so far as arms are concerned, for the reasons that were discussed at length earlier; and then, one sees that some had the people hostile to them, while others had the people well disposed towards them but were unable to control the nobles; for without these defects states are not lost which have enough strength to take an army into battle. Philip of Macedonia—not the father of Alexander but the one who was defeated by Titus Quinctius—did not have much of a state compared to the great power of the Romans and Greeks who attacked him; none the less, because he was a good soldier and knew how to hold the people and to secure himself from the nobility, he was able to wage war against them for many years; and if at the end he lost possession of several cities, he was nevertheless left with his kingdom.

Therefore, these princes of ours who have been in their principalities for many years, and who have then lost them, must not blame fortune but rather their own idleness; for, never having thought in peaceful times that things might change (which is a common defect in men, not to consider in good weather the possibility of a tempest), when adverse times finally arrived they thought about running away and not about defending themselves; and they hoped that the people, angered by the insolence of the victors, would eventually recall them. This policy, when others are lacking, is good; but it is indeed bad to have disregarded all other solutions for this one; for you should never wish to fall, believing that you will find someone else to pick you up; because whether this occurs or not, it does not increase your security, that method being a cowardly defence and one not dependent upon your own resources. And those methods alone are good, are certain, are lasting, that depend on yourself and your own ingenuity.

CHAPTER XXV

On Fortune's Role in Human Affairs and How She Can Be Dealt With

It is now unknown to me that many have held, and still hold, the opinion that the things of this world are, in a manner, controlled by fortune and by God, that men with their wisdom cannot control them, and, on the contrary, that men can have no remedy whatsoever for them; and for this reason they might judge that they need not sweat much over such matters but let them be governed by fate. This opinion has been more strongly held in our own times because of the great variation of affairs that has been observed and that is being observed every day which is beyond human conjecture. Sometimes, as I think about these things, I am inclined to their opinion to a certain extent. Nevertheless, in order that our free will be not extinguished, I judge it to be true that fortune is the arbiter of one half of our actions, but that she still leaves the control of the other half, or almost that, to us. And I compare her to one of those ruinous rivers that, when they become enraged, flood the plains, tear down the trees and buildings, taking up earth from one spot and placing it upon another; everyone flees from them, everyone yields to their onslaught, unable to oppose them in any way. But although they are of such a nature, it does not follow that when the weather is calm we cannot take precautions with embankments and dikes, so that when they rise up again either the waters will be channelled off or their impetus will not be either so unchecked or so damaging. The same things happen where fortune is concerned: she shows her force where there is no organized strength to resist her; and she directs her impact there where she knows that dikes and embankments are not constructed to hold her. And if you consider Italy, the seat of these changes and the nation which has set them in motion, you will see a country without embankments and without a single bastion: for if she were defended by the necessary forces, like Germany, Spain, and France, either this flood would not have produced the great changes that it has or it would not have come upon us at all. And this I consider enough to say about fortune in general terms.

But, limiting myself more to particulars, I say that one sees a prince prosper today and come to ruin tomorrow without having seen him change his character or any of the reasons that have been discussed at length earlier; that is, that a prince who relies completely upon fortune will come to ruin as soon as she changes; I also believe that the man who adapts his course of action to the nature of the times will succeed and, likewise, that the man who sets his course of action out of tune with the times will come to grief. For one can observe that men, in the affairs which lead them to the end that they seek—that is, glory and wealth— proceed in different ways; one by caution, another with impetuousness; one through vio- lence, another with guile; one with patience, another with its opposite; and each one by these various means can attain his goals. And we also see, in the case of two cautious men, that one reaches his goal while the other does not; and, likewise, two men equally succeed using two different means, one being cautious and the other impetuous: this arises from nothing else than the nature of the times that either suit or do not suit their course of action. From this results that which I have said, that two men, working in opposite ways, can produce the same outcome; and of two men working in the same fashion one achieves his goal and the other does not. On this also depends the variation of what is good; for, if a man governs himself with caution and patience, and the times and conditions are turning in such a way that his policy is a good one, he will prosper; but if the times and conditions change, he will be ruined because he does not change his method of procedure. Nor is there to be found a man so prudent that he knows how to adapt himself to this, both because he cannot deviate from that to which he is by nature inclined and also because he cannot be persuaded to depart from a path, having always prospered by following it. And therefore the cautious man, when it is time to act impetuously, does not know how to do so, and he is ruined; but if he had changed his conduct with the times, fortune would not have changed.

Pope Julius II acted impetuously in all his affairs, and he found the times and conditions so apt to this course of action that he always achieved successful results. Consider the first campaign he waged against Bologna while Messer Giovanni Bentivogli was still alive. The Venetians were unhappy about it; so was the King of Spain; Julius still had negotiations going on about it with France; and nevertheless, he started personally on this expedition with his usual ferocity and lack of caution. Such a move kept Spain and the Venetians at bay, the latter out of fear and the former out of a desire to regain the entire Kingdom of Naples; and at the same time it drew the King of France into the affair, for when the King saw that the Pope had already made this move, he judged that he could not deny him the use of his troops without obviously harming him, since he wanted his friendship in order to defeat the Venetians. And therefore Julius achieved with his impetuous action what no other pontiff would ever have achieved with the greatest of human wisdom; for, if he had waited to leave Rome with agreements settled and things in order, as any other pontiff might have done, he would never have succeeded, because the King of France would have found a thousand excuses and the others would have aroused in him a thousand fears. I wish to leave unmentioned his other deeds, which were all similar and which were all successful. And the brevity of his life did not let him experience the opposite, since if times which necessitated caution had come his ruin would have followed from it: for never would he have deviated from those methods to which his nature inclined him.

I conclude, therefore, that since fortune changes and men remain set in their ways, men will succeed when the two are in harmony and fail when they are not in accord. I am certainly convinced of this: that it is better to be impetuous than cautious, because fortune is a woman, and it is necessary, in order to keep her down, to beat her and to struggle with her. And it is seen that she more often allows herself to be taken over by men who are impetuous than by those who make cold advances; and then, being a woman, she is always the friend of young men, for they are less cautious, more aggressive, and they command her with more audacity.

CHAPTER XXVI

An Exhortation to Liberate Italy From the Barbarians

Considering, therefore, all of the things mentioned above, and reflecting as to whether the times are suitable, at present, to honour a new prince in Italy, and if there is the material that might give a skilful and prudent prince the opportunity to introduce a form of government that would bring him honour and good to the people of Italy, it seems to me that so many circumstances are favourable to such a new prince that I know of no other time more appropriate. And if, as I said, it was necessary that the people of Israel be slaves in Egypt in order to recognize Moses' ability, and it was necessary that the Persians be oppressed by the Medes to recognize the greatness of spirit in Cyrus, and it was necessary that the Athenians be dispersed to realize the excellence of Theseus, then, likewise, at the present time, in order to recognize the ability of an Italian spirit, it was necessary that Italy be reduced to her present condition and that she be more enslaved than the Hebrews, more servile than the Persians, more scattered than the Athenians; without a leader, without organization, beaten, despoiled, ripped apart, over-run, and prey to every sort of catastrophe.

And even though before now some glimmer of light may have shown itself in a single individual, so that it was possible to believe that God had ordained him for Italy's redemption, nevertheless it was witnessed afterwards how at the height of his career he was rejected by fortune. So now Italy remains without life and awaits the man who can heal her wounds and put an end to the plundering of Lombardy, the ransoms in the Kingdom of Naples and in Tuscany, and who can cure her of those sores which have been festering for so long. Look how she now prays to God to send someone to redeem her from these barbaric cruelties and insolence; see her still ready and willing to follow a banner, provided that there be someone to raise it up. Nor is there anyone in sight, at present, in whom she can have more hope than in your illustrious house, which, with its fortune and ability, favoured by God and by the Church, of which it is now prince, could make itself the head of this redemption. This will not be very difficult if you keep before you the deeds and the lives of those named above. And although those men were out of the ordi-nary and marvelous, they were nevertheless men; and each of them had less opportunity than the present one; for their enterprises were no more just, nor easier, nor was God more a friend to them than to you. Here justice is great: 'Only those wars that are necessary are just, and arms are sacred when there is no hope except through arms.' Here there is a great willingness; and where there is a great willingness there cannot be great difficulty, if only you will use the institutions of those men I have proposed as your target. Besides this, we now see extraordinary, unprecedented signs brought about by God: the sea has opened up; a cloud has shown you the path; the rock pours forth water; it has rained manna here; everything has converged for your greatness. The rest you must do yourself. God does not wish to do everything, in order not to take from us our free will and that part of the glory which is ours.

And it is no surprise if some of the Italians mentioned previously were not capable of doing what it is hoped may be done by your illustrious house, and if, during the many revolutions in Italy and the many campaigns of war, it always seems that her military abil-ity is spent. This results from the fact that her ancient institutions were not good and that there was no one who knew how to discover new ones; and no other thing brings a new man on the rise such honour as the new laws and the new institutions discovered by him. These things, when they are well founded and have in themselves a certain greatness, make him revered and admirable. And in Italy there is no lack of material to be given a form: here there is great ability in her members, were it not for the lack of it in her lead-ers. Consider how in duels and skirmishes involving just a few men the Italians are supe-rior in strength, dexterity, and cunning; but when it comes to armies they do not match others. And all this comes from the weakness of her leaders; for those who know are not followed; and with each one seeming to know, there has not been to the present day any-one who has known how to set himself above the others, either because of ingenuity or fortune, so that others might yield to him. As a consequence, during so much time, during the many wars fought over the past twenty years, whenever there has been an army made up completely of Italians it has always made a poor showing. As proof of this, there is first Taro, then Alexandria, Capua, Genoa, Vailà, Bologna, and Mestri.

Therefore, if your illustrious house desires to follow these excellent men who redeemed their lands, it is necessary before all else, as a true basis for every undertaking, to provide yourself with your own native troops, for one cannot have either more faithful, more loyal, or better troops. And although each one separately may be brave, all of them united will become even braver when they find themselves commanded, honoured, and well treated by their own prince. It is necessary, therefore, to prepare yourself with such troops as these, so that with Italian strength you will be able to defend yourself from foreigners. And although Swiss and Spanish infantry may be reputed terrifying, nevertheless both have defects, so that a third army could not only oppose them but be confident of defeating them. For the Spanish cannot withstand cavalry and the Swiss have a fear of foot soldiers they meet in combat who are as brave as they are. Therefore, it has been witnessed and experience will demonstrate that the Spanish cannot withstand French cavalry and the Swiss are ruined by Spanish infantrymen. And although this last point has not been completely confirmed by experience, there was nevertheless a hint of it at the battle of Ravenna, when the Spanish infantry met the German battalions, who follow the same order as the Swiss; and the Spanish, with their agile bodies, aided by their spiked shields, entered between and underneath the Germans' long pikes and were safe, without the Germans having any recourse against them; and had it not been for the cavalry charge that broke them, the Spaniards would have slaughtered them all. Therefore, as the defects of both these kinds of troops are recognized, a new type can be instituted which can stand up to cavalry and will have no fear of foot soldiers: this will come about by creating new armies and changing battle formations. And these are among those matters that, when newly organized, give reputation and greatness to a new prince.

This opportunity, therefore, must not be permitted to pass by so that Italy, after so long a time, may behold its redeemer. Nor can I express with what love he will be received in all those provinces that have suffered through these foreign floods; with what thirst for revenge, with what obstinate loyalty, with what compassion, with what tears! What doors will be closed to him? Which people will deny him obedience? What jealousy could oppose him? What Italian would deny him homage? For everyone, this barbarian dominion stinks! Therefore, may your illustrious house take up this mission with the spirit and with that hope in which just undertakings are begun; so that under your banner this country may be ennobled and, under your guidance, those words of Petrarch may come true:

> Ingenuity over rage
> Will take up arms; and the battle will be short.
> For ancient valour
> In Italian hearts is not yet dead.

DISCOURSES

NICCOLÒ MACHIAVELLI TO ZANOBI BUONDELMONTI AND COSIMO RUCELLAI GREETING

I am sending you a present which, if it does not come up to the obligations I owe you, is at any rate the best that Niccolò Machiavelli is able to send you. For in it I have set down all that I know and have learnt from a long experience of, and from constantly reading about, political affairs. And since neither you nor anyone else can well expect more from me than this, you will not be disappointed that I am not sending you more. You may perhaps lament my lack of skill, should these my narratives be thin, and also errors of judgement, should I, in discussing things, have in many places made mistakes. If this be so, I know not which of us is less obliged to the other, I to you, for having forced me to write what I should never have written of my own accord, or you to me, if what I have written fails to satisfy you. Accept it, then, in the manner in which things are accepted amongst friends, by whom the intention of the giver is always more esteemed than the quality of the gift. And believe me when I say that I have in this just one consolation. It is that when I reflect on the many mistakes I may have made in other circumstances, I know that I have made no mistake at any rate in this, that I have chosen to dedicate these my discourses to you in preference to all others; both because, in doing so, I seem to be showing some gratitude for benefits received, and also because I seem in this to be departing from the usual practice of authors, which has always been to dedicate their works to some prince, and, blinded by ambition and avarice, to praise him for all his virtuous qualities when they ought to have blamed him for all manner of shameful deeds.

So, to avoid this mistake, I have chosen not those who are princes, but those who, on account of their innumerable good qualities, deserve to be; not those who might shower on me rank, honours, and riches, but those who, though unable, would like to do so. For, to judge aright, one should esteem men because they are generous, not because they have the power to be generous; and, in like manner, should admire those who know how to govern a kingdom, not those who, without knowing how, actually govern one. There are, indeed, writers who praise Hiero the Syracusan though but a private person, in preference to Perseus the Macedonian though he was a king, because Hiero to become a prince lacked but a principality, whereas the other had no kingly attribute save his kingdom. Entertain yourselves, then, with what you were anxious to get, whether it be good or bad; and, should you be so mistaken as to find my views acceptable, I shall not fail to follow this up with the rest of the history as I promised at the start. Farewell.

Translated by Leslie J. Walker, S.J., revised by Brian Richardson.

Book One

THE PREFACE

Although owing to the envy inherent in man's nature it has always been no less dangerous to discover new ways and methods than to set off in search of new seas and unknown
lands because most men are much more ready to belittle than to praise another's actions,
none the less, impelled by the natural desire I have always had to labour, regardless of anything, on that which I believe to be for the common benefit of all, I have decided to enter
upon a new way, as yet untrodden by anyone else. And, even if it entails a tiresome and
difficult task, it may yet reward me in that there are those who will look kindly on the
purpose of these my labours. And if my poor ability, my limited experience of current
affairs, my feeble knowledge of antiquity, should render my efforts imperfect and of little
worth, they may none the less point the way for another of greater ability, capacity for
analysis, and judgement, who will achieve my ambition; which, if it does not earn me
praise, should not earn me reproaches.

When, therefore, I consider in what honour antiquity is held, and how—to cite but
one instance—a bit of an old statue has fetched a high price that someone may have it by
him to give honour to his house and that it may be possible for it to be copied by those
who are keen on this art; and how the latter then with great industry take pains to reproduce it in all their works; and when, on the other hand, I notice that what history has to say
about the highly virtuous actions performed by ancient kingdoms and republics, by their
kings, their generals, their citizens, their legislators, and by others who have gone to the
trouble of serving their country, is rather admired than imitated; nay, is so shunned by
everybody in each little thing they do, that of the virtue of bygone days there remains no
trace, it cannot but fill me at once with astonishment and grief. The more so when I see
that in the civic disputes which arise between citizens and in the diseases men get, they
always have recourse to decisions laid down by the ancients and to the prescriptions
they drew up. For the civil law is nothing but a collection of decisions, made by jurists of
old, which the jurists of today have tabulated in orderly fashion for our instruction. Nor,
again, is medicine anything but a record of experiments, performed by doctors of old,
upon which the doctors of our day base their prescriptions. In spite of which in constituting republics, in maintaining states, in governing kingdoms, in forming an army or
conducting a war, in dealing with subjects, in extending the empire, one finds neither
prince nor republic who repairs to antiquity for examples.

This is due in my opinion not so much to the weak state to which the religion of today
has brought the world, or to the evil wrought in many provinces and cities of Christendom by ambition conjoined with idleness, as to the lack of a proper appreciation of
history, owing to people failing to realize the significance of what they read, and to their
having no taste for the delicacies it comprises. Hence it comes about that the great bulk
of those who read it take pleasure in hearing of the various incidents which are contained
in it, but never think of imitating them, since they hold them to be not merely difficult
but impossible of imitation, as if the heaven, the sun, the elements and man had in their
motion, their order, and their potency, become different from what they used to be.

Since I want to get men out of this wrong way of thinking, I have thought fit to write
a commentary on all those books of Titus Livy which have not by the malignity of time
had their continuity broken. It will comprise what I have arrived at by comparing ancient
with modern events, and think necessary for the better understanding of them, so that
those who read what I have to say may the more easily draw those practical lessons which

one should seek to obtain from the study of history. Though the enterprise is difficult, yet, with the help of those who have encouraged me to undertake the task, I think I can carry it out in such a way that there shall remain to another but a short road to traverse in order to reach the place assigned.

1. Concerning the Origin of Cities in General and of Rome in Particular

Those who read of the origin of the city of Rome, of its legislators and of its constitution, will not be surprised that in this city such great virtue was maintained for so many centuries, and that later on there came into being the empire into which that republic developed.

Since this first discourse will deal with its origin, I would point out that all cities are built either by natives of the place in which they are built, or by people from elsewhere. The first case comes about when inhabitants, dispersed in many small communities, find that they cannot enjoy security since no one community of itself, owing to its position and to the smallness of its numbers, is strong enough to resist the onslaught of an invader, and, when the enemy arrives, there is no time for them to unite for their defence; or, if there be time, they have to abandon many of their strongholds, and thus at once fall as prey to their enemies. Hence, to escape these dangers, either of their own accord or at the suggestion of someone of greater authority among them, such communities undertake to live together in some place they have chosen in order to live more conveniently and the more easily to defend themselves.

This was the case with Athens and Venice, among many others. Athens was built under the authority of Theseus for reasons such as these by inhabitants who were dispersed; Venice by numerous peoples who had sought refuge in certain islets at the top of the Adriatic Sea that they might escape the wars which daily arose in Italy after the decline of the Roman empire owing to the arrival of a new lot of barbarians. There, without any particular person or prince to give them a constitution, they began to live as a community under laws which seemed to them appropriate for their maintenance. And this happened because of the long repose the situation afforded them in that the sea at their end had no exit and the peoples who were ravaging Italy had no ships in which to infest them. This being so, a beginning, however small, sufficed to bring them to their present greatness.

The second case occurs when a city is built by men of a foreign race. They may either be free men, or men dependent on others, as are the colonies sent out either by a republic or a prince to relieve their towns of some of the population or for the defence of newly acquired territory which they desire to hold securely and without expense. The Romans built a number of such cities, and this throughout the whole of their empire. Others have been built by a prince, not that he may dwell there, but to enhance his reputation, as the city of Alexandria was built by Alexander. And since such cities are not at the outset free, it very seldom happens that they make great progress or that of their own doing they come to be reckoned among the capitals of kingdoms.

It was thus that Florence came to be built; for—whether it was built by the soldiers of Sulla, or was built by chance by inhabitants from the hills of Fiesole who, relying on the long peace which the world enjoyed under Octavian, came to dwell in the plains above the Arno—it was built under the Roman empire, and could at the outset make no addition to its territory save such as was allowed by the courtesy of the emperor.

Free cities are those which are built by peoples who, either under a prince or of their own accord, are driven by pestilence or famine or war to abandon the land of their birth and to look for new habitations. These may be either cities they find in countries they have occupied and in which they go to dwell, as Moses did; or new cities which they build, as Aeneas did. In this case the virtue of the builder is discernible in the fortune of what was built, for the city is more or less remarkable according as he is more or less virtuous who is responsible for the start. This virtue shows itself in two ways: first in the choice of a site, and secondly in the drawing up of laws.

Since men work either of necessity or by choice, and since there is found to be greater virtue where choice has less to say to it, the question arises whether it would not be better to choose a barren place in which to build cities so that men would have to be industrious and less given to idleness, and so would be more united because, owing to the poor situation, there would be less occasion for discord; as happened in Ragusa and in many other cities built in such-like places.

Such a choice would undoubtedly be wiser and more advantageous were men content to earn their own living and not anxious to lord it over others. Since, however, security for man is impossible unless it be conjoined with power, it is necessary to avoid sterile places and for cities to be put in very fertile places where, when expansion has taken place owing to the fruitfulness of the land, it may be possible for them both to defend themselves against attack and to overcome any who stand in the way of the city's greatness. As to the idleness which such a situation may encourage, it must be provided for by laws imposing that need to work which the situation does not impose. It is advisable here to follow the example of those wise folk who have dwelt in most beautiful and fertile lands, i.e. in such lands as tend to produce idleness and ineptitude for training in virtue of any kind, and who, in order to obviate the disasters which the idleness induced by the amenities of the land might cause, have imposed the need for training on those who were to become soldiers, and have made this training such that men there have become better soldiers than those in countries which were rough and sterile by nature.

A case in point is the kingdom of the Egyptians which, not withstanding the amenities of the land, imposed the need to work so successfully by means of laws that it produced most excellent men, whose names, if they had not been lost in antiquity, would be even more celebrated than that of Alexander the Great, and than those of many others whose memory is still fresh. So, too, anyone who has reflected on the kingdom of the Sultan, on the discipline of the Mamelukes, and on that of their troops, before they were wiped out by Selim, the Great Turk, might have noted there the many exercises the troops underwent and might have inferred from this how greatly they feared the idleness to which the beneficence of the country might have led if they had not obviated it by very strict laws.

I maintain, then, that it is more prudent to place a city in a fertile situation, provided its fertility is kept in due bounds by laws. When Alexander the Great was proposing to build a city that should redound to his credit, Deinocrates, the architect, came to him and suggested that he should build it on Mount Athos, for, besides being a strong place, it could be so fashioned as to give the city a human form, which would be a remarkable thing, a rare thing, and worthy of his greatness. And on what, Alexander asked, would the inhabitants live? Deinocrates replied that he had not thought of this. Whereupon Alexander laughed, and, leaving the mountain alone, built Alexandria where inhabitants would be glad to live owing to the richness of the land and to the conveniences afforded by the sea and by the Nile.

For those, then, who, having examined the question how Rome came to be built, hold that Aeneas was its first founder, it will be a city built by foreigners, but for those who prefer Romulus, it will be a city built by natives of the place. But, whichever be the case, both will recognize that it began as a free city, dependent upon no one. They will also recognize, as we shall presently point out, under what strict discipline it was placed by the laws made by Romulus, Numa, and others, and that, in consequence, neither its fertile situation, the convenience afforded by the sea, its frequent victories, nor the greatness of its empire, were for many centuries able to corrupt it, but that these laws kept it so rich in virtue that there has never been any other city or any other republic so well adorned.

Wherefore since what was done by this city, as Titus Livy records it, was done sometimes in accordance with public enactments, sometimes on the initiative of private individuals, and sometimes within the city, sometimes abroad, I shall begin by discussing such of the events due to public decrees as I shall judge to be more worthy of comment, and with the events shall conjoin their consequences to which the discourses of this first book or first part will be restricted.

2. How many Kinds of State there are and of what Kind was that of Rome

I propose to dispense with a discussion of cities which from the outset have been subject to another power, and shall speak only of those which have from the outset been far removed from any kind of external servitude, but, instead, have from the start been governed in accordance with their wishes, whether as republics or principalities. As such cities have had diverse origins, so too they have had diverse laws and institutions. For either at the outset, or before very long, to some of them laws have been given by some one person at some one time, as laws were given to the Spartans by Lycurgus; whereas others have acquired them by chance and at different times as occasion arose. This was the case in Rome.

Happy indeed should we call that state which produces a man so prudent that men can live securely under the laws which he prescribes without having to emend them. Sparta, for instance, observed its laws for more than eight hundred years without corrupting them and without any dangerous disturbance. Unhappy, on the other hand, in some degree is that city to be deemed which, not having chanced to meet with a prudent organizer, has to reorganize itself. And, of such, that is the more unhappy which is the more remote from order; and that is the more remote from order whose institutions have missed altogether the straight road which leads it to its perfect and true destiny. For it is almost impossible that states of this type should by any eventuality be set on the right road again; whereas those which, if their order is not perfect, have made a good beginning and are capable of improvement, may become perfect should something happen which provides the opportunity. It should, however, be noted that they will never introduce order without incurring danger, because few men ever welcome new laws setting up a new order in the state unless necessity makes it clear to them that there is need for such laws; and since such a necessity cannot arise without danger, the state may easily be ruined before the new order has been brought to completion. The republic of Florence bears this out, for owing to what happened at Arezzo in '02 it was reconstituted, and owing to what happened at Prato in '12 its constitution was destroyed.

It being now my intention to discuss what were the institutions of the city of Rome and what events conduced to its perfection, I would remark that those who have written about states say that there are to be found in them one of three forms of government, called by them *Principality*, *Aristocracy* and *Democracy*, and that those who set up a government in any particular state must adopt one of them, as best suits their purpose.

Others—and with better judgement many think—say that there are six types of government, of which three are very bad, and three are good in themselves but easily become corrupt, so that they too must be classed as pernicious. Those that are good are the three above mentioned. Those that are bad are the other three, which depend on them, and each of them is so like the one associated with it that it easily passes from one form to the other. For *Principality* easily becomes *Tyranny*. From *Aristocracy* the transition to *Oligarchy* is an easy one. *Democracy* is without difficulty converted into *Anarchy*. So that if anyone who is organizing a commonwealth sets up one of the three first forms of government, he sets up what will last but for a while, since there are no means whereby to prevent it passing into its contrary, on account of the likeness which in such a case virtue has to vice.

These variations of government among men are due to chance. For in the beginning of the world, when its inhabitants were few, they lived for a time scattered like the beasts. Then, with the multiplication of their offspring, they drew together and, in order the better to be able to defend themselves, began to look about for a man stronger and more courageous than the rest, made him their head, and obeyed him.

It was thus that men learned how to distinguish what is honest and good from what is pernicious and wicked, for the sight of someone injuring his benefactor evoked in them hatred and sympathy and they blamed the ungrateful and respected those who showed gratitude, well aware that the same injuries might have been done to themselves. Hence to prevent evil of this kind they took to making laws and to assigning punishments to those who contravened them. The notion of justice thus came into being.

In this way it came about that, when later on they had to choose a prince, they did not have recourse to the boldest as formerly, but to one who excelled in prudence and justice.

But when at a yet later stage they began to make the prince hereditary instead of electing him, his heirs soon began to degenerate as compared with their ancestors, and, forsaking virtuous deeds, considered that princes have nought else to do but to surpass other men in extravagance, lasciviousness, and every other form of licentiousness. With the result that the prince came to be hated, and, since he was hated, came to be afraid, and from fear soon passed to offensive action, which quickly brought about a tyranny.

From which, before long, was begotten the source of their downhill; for tyranny gave rise to conspiracies and plots against princes, organized not by timid and weak men, but by men conspicuous for their liberality, magnanimity, wealth and ability, for such men could not stand the dishonourable life the prince was leading. The masses, therefore, at the instigation of these powerful leaders, took up arms against the prince, and, when he had been liquidated, submitted to the authority of those whom they looked upon as their liberators. Hence the latter, to whom the very term 'sole head' had become odious, formed themselves into a government. Moreover, in the beginning, mindful of what they had suffered under a tyranny, they ruled in accordance with the laws which they had made, subordinated their own convenience to the common advantage, and, both in private matters and public affairs, governed and preserved order with the utmost diligence.

But when the administration passed to their descendants who had no experience of the changeability of fortune, had not been through bad times, and instead of remaining content with the civic equality then prevailing, reverted to avarice, ambition and to seizing other men's womenfolk, they caused government by an aristocracy to become government by an oligarchy in which civic rights were entirely disregarded; so that in a short time there came to pass in their case the same thing as happened to the tyrant, for the masses, sick of their government, were ready to help anyone who had any sort of plan for attacking their rulers; and so there soon arose someone who with the aid of the masses liquidated them.

Then, since the memory of the prince and of the injuries inflicted by him was still fresh, and since, having got rid of government by the few, they had no desire to return to that of a prince, they turned to a democratic form of government, which they organized in such a way that no sort of authority was vested either in a few powerful men or in a prince.

And, since all forms of government are to some extent respected at the outset, this democratic form of government maintained itself for a while but not for long, especially when the generation that had organized it had passed away. For anarchy quickly supervened, in which no respect was shown either for the individual or for the official, and which was such that, as everyone did what he liked, all sorts of outrages were constantly committed. The outcome was inevitable. Either at the suggestion of some good man or because this anarchy had to be got rid of somehow, principality was once again restored. And from this there was, stage by stage, a return to anarchy, by way of the transitions and for the reasons assigned.

This, then, is the cycle through which all commonwealths pass, whether they govern themselves or are governed. But rarely do they return to the same form of government, for there can scarce be a state of such vitality that it can undergo often such changes and yet remain in being. What usually happens is that, while in a state of commotion in which it lacks both counsel and strength, a state becomes subject to a neighbouring and better organized state. Were it not so, a commonwealth might go on for ever passing through these governmental transitions.

I maintain then, that all the forms of government mentioned above are far from satisfactory, the three good ones because their life is so short, the three bad ones because of their inherent malignity. Hence prudent legislators, aware of their defects, refrained from adopting as such any one of these forms, and chose instead one that shared in them all, since they thought such a government would be stronger and more stable, for if in one and the same state there was principality, aristocracy and democracy each would keep watch over the other.

Lycurgus is one of those who have earned no small measure of praise for constitutions of this kind. For in the laws which he gave to Sparta, he assigned to the kings, to the aristocracy and to the populace each its own function, and thus introduced a form of government which lasted for more than eight hundred years to his every great credit and to the tranquillity of that city.

It was not so in the case of Solon, who drew up laws for Athens, for he set up merely a democratic form of government, which was so short-lived that he saw before his death the birth of a tyranny under Pisistratus; and though, forty years later, Pisistratus' heirs were expelled, and Athens returned to liberty because it again adopted a democratic form of government in accordance with Solon's laws, it did not retain its liberty for more than a hundred years. For, in spite of the fact that many constitutions were made whereby to restrain the arrogance of the upper class and the licentiousness of the general public, for which Solon had made no provision, none the less Athens had a very short life as compared with that of Sparta because with democracy Solon had not blended either princely power or that of the aristocracy.

But let us come to Rome. In spite of the fact that Rome had no Lycurgus to give it at the outset such a constitution as would ensure to it a long life of freedom, yet, owing to friction between the plebs and the senate, so many things happened that chance effected what had not been provided by a law giver. So that, if Rome did not get fortune's first gift, it got its second. For her early institutions, though defective, were not on wrong lines and so might pave the way to perfection. For Romulus and the rest of the kings made many good laws quite compatible with freedom; but, because their aim was to found a kingdom, not a republic, when the city became free, it lacked many institutions essential to the preservation of liberty, which had to be provided, since they had not been provided by the kings. So, when it came to pass that its kings lost their sovereignty, for reasons and in the manner described earlier in this discourse, those who had expelled them at once appointed two consuls to take the place of the king, so that what they expelled was the title of king, not the royal power. In the republic, then, at this stage there were the consuls and the senate, so that as yet it comprised but two of the aforesaid estates, namely, Principality and Aristocracy. It remained to find a place for Democracy. This came about when the Roman nobility became so overbearing for reasons which will be given later— that the populace rose against them, and they were constrained by the fear that they might lose all, to grant the populace a share in the government; the senate and the consuls retaining, however, sufficient authority for them to be able to maintain their position in the republic.

It was in this way that tribunes of the plebs came to be appointed, and their appointment did much to stabilize the form of government in this republic, for in its government all three estates now had a share. And so favoured was it by fortune that, though the transition from Monarchy to Aristocracy and thence to Democracy, took place by the very stages and for the very reasons laid down earlier in this discourse, none the less the granting of authority to the aristocracy did not abolish altogether the royal estate, nor was the authority of the aristocracy wholly removed when the populace was granted a share in it. On the contrary, the blending of these estates made a perfect commonwealth; and since it was friction between the plebs and the senate that brought this perfection about, in the next two chapters we shall show more fully how this came to be.

9. That it is necessary to be the Sole Authority if one would constitute a Republic afresh or would reform it thoroughly regardless of its Ancient Institutions

To some it will appear strange that I have got so far in my discussion of Roman history without having made any mention of the founders of that republic or of either its religious or its military institutions. Hence, that I may not keep the minds of those who are anxious to hear about such things any longer in suspense, let me say that many perchance will think it a bad precedent that the founder of a civic state, such as Romulus, should first have killed his brother, and then have acquiesced in the death of Titus Tatius, the Sabine, whom he had chosen as his colleague in the kingdom. They will urge that, if such actions be justifiable, ambitious citizens who are eager to govern, will follow the example of their prince and use violence against those who are opposed to *their* authority. A view that will hold good provided we leave out of consideration the end which Romulus had in committing these murders.

One should take it as a general rule that rarely, if ever, does it happen that a state, whether it be a republic or a kingdom, is either well-ordered at the outset or radically transformed *vis-à-vis* its old institutions unless this be done by one person. It is likewise essential that there should be but one person upon whose mind and method depends any similar process of organization. Wherefore the prudent organizer of a state whose intention it is to govern not in his own interests but for the common good, and not in the interest of his successors but for the sake of that fatherland which is common to all, should contrive to be alone in his authority. Nor will any reasonable man blame him for taking any action, however extraordinary, which may be of service in the organizing of a kingdom or the constituting of a republic It is a sound maxim that reprehensible actions may be justified by their effects, and that when the effect is good, as it was in the case of

Romulus, it always justifies the action. For it is the man who uses violence to spoil things, not the man who uses it to mend them, that is blameworthy.

The organizer of a state ought further to have sufficient prudence and virtue not to bequeath the authority he has assumed to any other person, for, seeing that men are more prone to evil than to good, his successor might well make ambitious use of that which he had used virtuously. Furthermore, though but one person suffices for the purpose of organization, what he has organized will not last long if it continues to rest on the shoulders of one man, but may well last if many remain in charge and many look to its maintenance. Because, though the many are incompetent to draw up a constitution since diversity of opinion will prevent them from discovering how best to do it, yet when they realize it has been done, they will not agree to abandon it.

That Romulus was a man of this character, that for the death of his brother and of his colleague he deserves to be excused, and that what he did was done for the common good and not to satisfy his personal ambition, is shown by his having at once instituted a senate with which he consulted and with whose views his decisions were in accord. Also, a careful consideration of the authority which Romulus reserved to himself will show that all he reserved to himself was the command of the army in time of war and the convoking of the senate. It is clear, too, that when the Tarquins were expelled and Rome became free, none of its ancient institutions were changed, save that in lieu of a permanent king there were appointed each year two consuls. This shows that the original institutions of this city as a whole were more in conformity with a political and self-governing state than with absolutism or tyranny.

I might adduce in support of what I have just said numberless examples, for example Moses, Lycurgus, Solon and other founders of kingdoms and republics who assumed authority that they might formulate laws to the common good; but this I propose to omit since it is well known. I shall adduce but one further example, not so celebrated but worth considering by those who are contemplating the drawing up of good laws. It is this. Agis, King of Sparta, was considering how to confine the activities of the Spartans to the limits originally set for them by the laws of Lycurgus, because it seemed to him that it was owing to their having deviated from them in part that this city had lost a good deal of its ancient virtue, and, in consequence, a good deal of its power and of its empire. He was, however, while his project was still in the initial stage, killed by the Spartan ephors, who took him to be a man who was out to set up a tyranny. But Cleomenes, his successor in that kingdom, having learned from some records and writings of Agis which he had discovered, what was the latter's true mind and intention, determined to pursue the same plan. He realized, however, that he could not do this for the good of his country unless he became the sole authority there, and, since it seemed to him impossible owing to man's ambition to help the many against the will of the few, he took a suitable opportunity and had all the ephors killed and anybody else who might obstruct him. He then renewed in their entirety the laws of Lycurgus. By so doing he gave fresh life to the Sparta, and his reputation might thereby have become as great as that of Lycurgus if it had not been for the power of the Macedonians and the weakness of other Greek republics. For, after Sparta had thus been reorganized, it was attacked by the Macedonians, and, since its forces proved to be inferior and it could get no outside help, it was defeated, with the result that Cleomenes' plans, however just and praiseworthy, were never brought to completion.

All things considered, therefore, I conclude that it is necessary to be the sole authority if one is to organize a state, and that Romulus' action in regard to the death of Remus and Titus Tatius is excusable, not blameworthy.

10. Those who set up a Tyranny are no less Blameworthy than are
the Founders of a Republic or a Kingdom Praiseworthy.

Of all men that are praised, those are praised most who have played the chief part in founding a religion. Next come those who have founded either republics or kingdoms. After them in the order of celebratees are ranked army commanders who have added to the extent of their own dominions or to that of their country's. With whom may be conjoined men of letters of many different kinds who are each celebrated according to their status. Some modicum of praise is also ascribed to any man who excels in some art and in the practice of it, and of these the number is legion. On the other hand, those are held to be infamous and detestable who extirpate religion, subvert kingdoms and republics, make war on virtue, on letters, and on any art that brings advantage and honour to the human race, i.e. the profane, the violent, the ignorant, the worthless, the idle, the coward. Nor will there ever be anyone, be he foolish or wise, wicked or good, who, if called upon to choose between these two classes of men, will not praise the one that calls for praise and blame the one that calls for blame.

And yet, notwithstanding this, almost all men, deceived by the false semblance of good and the false semblance of renown, allow themselves either wilfully or ignorantly to slip into the ranks of those who deserve blame rather than praise; and, when they might have founded a republic or a kingdom to their immortal honour, turn their thoughts to tyranny, and fail to see what fame, what glory, security, tranquillity, conjoined with peace of mind, they are missing by adopting this course, and what infamy, scorn, abhorrence, danger and disquiet they are incurring.

Nor is it possible for anybody, whether he be but a private citizen living in some republic, or has been fortunate enough or virtuous enough to have become a prince, to read history and to make use of the records of ancient deeds, without preferring, if he be a private citizen, to conduct himself in his fatherland rather as Scipio did than as Caesar did, or, if he be a prince, as did Agesilaus, Timoleon and Dion, rather than as did Nabis, Phalaris and Dionysius, for he could not but see how strongly the latter are dismissed with scorn, and how highly the former are praised. He would also notice that Timoleon and the like had no less authority in their respective countries than had Dionysius or Phalaris in theirs, and would observe that they enjoyed far greater security.

Nor should anyone be deceived by Caesar's renown when he finds writers extolling him before others, for those who praise him have either been corrupted by his fortune or overawed by the long continuance of the empire which, since it was ruled under that name, did not permit writers to speak freely of him. If, however, anyone desires to know what writers would have said, had they been free, he has but to look at what they say of Catiline. For Caesar is the more blameworthy of the two, in that he who has done wrong is more blameworthy than he who has but desired to do wrong. Or, again, let him look at the praise bestowed on Brutus: Caesar they could not find fault with on account of his power, so they cry up his enemy.

Let he who has become a prince in a republic consider, after Rome became an Empire, how much more praise is due to those emperors who acted, like good princes, in accordance with the laws, than to those who acted otherwise. It will be found that Titus, Nerva, Trajan, Hardrian, Antoninus and Marcus, had no need of soldiers to form a praetorian guard, nor of a multitude of legions to protect them, for their defence lay in their habits, the goodwill of the people, and the affection of the senate. It will be seen, too, in the case of Caligula, Nero, Vitellius and other bad emperors, how it availed them little to have armies from the East and from the West to save them from the enemies they had made by their bad habits and their evil life.

If the history of these emperors be pondered well, it should serve as a striking lesson to any prince, and should teach him to distinguish between the ways of renown and of infamy, the ways of security and of fear. For of the twenty-six emperors from Caesar to Maximinus, sixteen were assassinated and only ten died a natural death. And, if some of those who were killed were good men, as Galba and Pertinax were, their death was due to the corruption which their predecessors had introduced among the troops. While, if among those who died ordinary death, there was a wicked man, like Severus, it must be put down to his great good luck and to his 'virtue', two things of which few men enjoy both. It will be seen, too, from a perusal of their history on what principle a good kingdom should rest; for all the emperors who acquired imperial power by inheritance were bad men, with the exception of Titus; those who acquired it through adoption, were all good, like the five counting from Nerva to Marcus; and when it fell to their heirs a period of decadence again ensued.

Let a prince put before himself the period from Nerva to Marcus, and let him compare it with the preceding period and with that which came after, and then let him decide in which he would rather have been born, and during which he would have chosen to be emperor. What he will find when good princes were ruling, is a prince securely reigning among subjects no less secure, a world replete with peace and justice. He will see the senate's authority respected, the magistrates honoured, rich citizens enjoying their wealth, nobility and virtue held in the highest esteem, and everything working smoothly and going well. He will notice, on the other hand, the absence of any rancour, any licentiousness, corruption or ambition, and that in this golden age everyone is free to hold and to defend his own opinion. He will behold, in short, the world triumphant, its prince glorious and respected by all, the people fond of him and secure under his rule.

If he then looks attentively at the times of the other emperors, he will find them distraught with wars, torn by seditions, brutal alike in peace and in war, princes frequently killed by assassins, civil wars and foreign wars constantly occurring, Italy in travail and ever a prey to fresh misfortunes, its cities demolished and pillaged. He will see Rome burnt, its Capitol demolished by its own citizens, ancient temples lying desolate, religious rites grown corrupt, adultery rampant throughout the city. He will find the sea covered with exiles and the rocks stained with blood. In Rome he will see countless atrocities perpetrated; rank, riches, the honours men have won, and, above all, virtue, looked upon as a capital crime. He will find calumniators rewarded, servants suborned to turn against their masters, freed men to turn against their patrons, and those who lack enemies attacked by their friends. He will thus happily learn how much Rome, Italy, and the world owed to Caesar.

There can be no question but that every human being will be afraid to imitate the bad times, and will be imbued with an ardent desire to emulate the good. And, should a good prince seek worldly renown, he should most certainly covet possession of a city that has become corrupt, not, with Caesar, to complete its spoliation, but, with Romulus, to reform it. Nor in very truth can the heavens afford men a better opportunity of acquiring renown; nor can men desire anything better than this. And if in order to reform a city one were obliged to give up the principate, someone who did not reform it in order not to fall from that rank would have some excuse. There is, however, no excuse if one can both keep the principate and reform the city.

In conclusion, then, let those to whom the heavens grant such opportunities reflect that two courses are open to them: either so to behave that in life they rest secure and in death become renowned, or so to behave that in life they are in continual straits, and in death leave behind all imperishable record of their infamy.

Book Two

THE PREFACE

Men always, but not always with good reason, praise bygone days and criticize the present, and so partial are they to the past that they not only admire past ages the knowledge of which has come down to them in written records, but also, when they grow old, what they remember having seen in their youth. And, when this view is wrong, as it usually is, there are, I am convinced, various causes to which the mistake may be due.

The first of them is, I think, this. The whole truth about olden times is not grasped, since what redounds to their discredit is often passed over in silence, whereas what is likely to make them appear glorious is pompously recounted in all its details. For so obsequious are most writers to the fortune of conquerors that, in order to make their victories seem glorious, they not only exaggerate their own valorous deeds, but also magnify the exploits of the enemy, so that anyone born afterwards either in the conquering or in the conquered province may find cause to marvel at such men and such times, and is bound, in short, to admire them and to feel affection for them.

Another reason is that, since it is either through fear or through envy that men come to hate things, in the case of the past the two most powerful incentives for hating it are lacking, since the past cannot hurt you nor give you cause for envy. Whereas it is otherwise with events in which you play a part and which you see with your own eyes, for of these you have an intimate knowledge, are in touch with every detail, and in them find, mingled with the good, also much which displeases you; so that you cannot help thinking them far inferior to the remote past, even though in fact the present may be much more deserving of praise and renown. I am not here referring to what pertains to the arts, for in themselves they have so much lustre that time can scarce take away or add much to the glory which they themselves deserve. I am speaking of things appertaining to human life and human customs, the evidence for whose merit is not so clear to one's eyes.

My answer is, then, that it is true there exists this habit of praising the past and criticizing the present, and not always true that to do so is a mistake, for it must be admitted that sometimes such a judgment is valid because, since human affairs are ever in a state of flux, they move either upwards or downwards. Thus one sees a city or a province that has been endowed with a sound political constitution by some eminent man, thanks to its founder's virtue for a time go on steadily improving. Anyone born in such a state at such a time, is wrong if he gives more praise to the past than to the present, and his mistake will be due to the causes we have mentioned above. But those who are born in this city or province later on, when there has come a time in which it is on the decline and is deteriorating, will not then be in error.

When I reflect that it is in this way that events pursue their course it seems to me that the world has always been in the same condition, and that in it there has been just as much good as there is evil, but that this evil and this good has varied from province to province. This may be seen from the knowledge we have an ancient kingdoms, in which the balance of good and evil changed from one to the other owing to changes in their customs, whereas the world as a whole remained the same. The only difference was that the world's virtue first found a home in Assyria, then flourished in Media and later in Persia, and at length arrived in Italy and Rome. And, if since the Roman empire there has been no other which has lasted, and in which the world's virtue has been centered, one none the less finds it distributed among many nations where men lead virtuous lives. There was, for instance, the kingdom of the Franks; the kingdom of the Turks, [i.e.] that of the Sultan; and today all the peoples of Germany. Earlier still there were the Saracens, who performed such great exploits and occupied so much of the world, since they broke up the Roman empire in the East. Hence, after ruin had overtaken the Romans, there continued to exist in all these provinces and in all these separate units, and still exists in some of them, that virtue which is desired and quite rightly praised. If, then, anyone born there praises the past over and above the present, he may well be mistaken; but anyone born in Italy who has not become at heart an ultramontane, or anyone born in Greece who has not become at heart a Turk, has good reason to criticize his own times and to praise others, since in the latter there are plenty of things to evoke his admiration, whereas in the former he comes across nothing but extreme misery, infamy and contempt, for there is no observance either of religion or of the laws, or of military traditions, but all is besmirched with filth of every kind. And so much the more are these vices detestable when they are more prevalent among those who sit on the judgement seat, prescribe rules for others, and expect from them adoration.

But to return to our main point, I maintain that if man's judgement is biased when he tries to decide which is the better, the present age, or some past age of which he cannot have so perfect a knowledge as he has of his own times precisely because it is long since past, this ought not to bias the judgment of old men when they compare the days of their youth with those of their old age, for of both they have had the same knowledge and experience. Nor would it in point of fact, if during the various phases of their lives men judged always in the same way and had the same appetites. But, as men's appetites change, even though their circumstances remain the same, it is impossible that things should look the same to them seeing that they have other appetites, other interests, other standpoints, from what they had in their youth. For, since, when men grow old, they lack energy but increase in judgement and prudence, it is inevitable that what in their youth appeared to be tolerable and good, in their old age should become intolerable and bad; so that, instead of blaming the times, they should lay the blame on their own judgement.

Furthermore, human appetites are insatiable, for by nature we are so constituted that there is nothing we cannot long for, but by fortune we are such that of these things we can attain but few. The result is that the human mind is perpetually discontented, and of its possessions is apt to grow weary. This makes it find fault with the present, praise the past, and long for the future; though for its doing so no rational cause can be assigned. Hence I am not sure but that I deserve to be reckoned among those who thus deceive themselves if in these my discourses I have praised too much the days of the ancient Romans and have found fault with our own. Indeed, if the virtue which then prevailed and the vices which are prevalent today were not as clear as the sun, I should be more reserved in my statements lest I should fall into the very fault for which I am blaming others. But as the facts are there for any one to see, I shall make so bold as to declare plainly what I think of those days and of our own, so that the minds of young men who read what I have written may turn from the one and prepare to imitate the other whenever fortune provides them with occasion for so doing. For it is the duty of a good man to point out to others what is well done, even though the malignity of the times or of fortune has not permitted you to do it for yourself, to the end that, of the many who have the capacity, some one, more beloved of heaven, may be able to do it.

Having, therefore, in the discourses of the last book spoken of the decisions the Romans came to in regard to the internal affairs of the city, in this we shall speak of the measures the Roman people took to increase their empire.

1. Whether Virtue or Fortune was the Principal Cause of the Empire which Rome acquired

Many are of opinion, and among them Plutarch, a writer of great weight, that the Roman people was indebted for the empire it acquired rather to fortune than to virtue. Among other reasons he adduces he says that the Roman people by their own confession admit this since they ascribed all their victories to fortune, and erected more temples to Fortune than to any other god. It would seem that with this view Livy also agrees, for rarely does he put into the mouth of any Roman a speech in which he tells of virtue without conjoining fortune with it.

With this view I cannot by any means agree, nor do I think it can be upheld. For if there is nowhere to be found a republic so successful as was Rome, this is because there is nowhere to be found a republic so constituted as to be able to make the conquests Rome made. For it was the virtue of her armies that caused Rome to acquire an empire, and it was her constitutional procedure and the peculiar customs which she owed to her first legislator that enabled her to maintain what she had acquired, as will be explained at length in many of the discourses which follow.

The aforesaid writers claim that Rome's never having been engaged in two very big wars at one and the same time was due to the fortune, not to the virtue, of the Roman people; for there was no war with the Latins until Rome had so thoroughly beaten the Samnites that she had to go to war in their defence. Nor did the Romans fight the Tuscans until the Latins had been subjugated and the Samnites were almost entirely exhausted by frequent defeats; yet had two of these powers, while yet intact and vigorous, united together, it is easy to conjecture, nor can one doubt, that it would have meant ruin for the Roman republic. Anyhow, however it came about, it is a fact that the Romans never had two very big wars going on at the same time; on the contrary, one finds that either when one began the other faded out, or that when one faded out the other began. This can easily be seen from the order in which their wars took place. For, setting aside those waged before Rome was taken by the Gauls, we see that, while they were fighting with the Aequi and the Volsci, no other people attacked them so long as the Aequi and Volsci were strong. It was only after they were beaten that the war with the Samnites arose; and although before this war was over the Latin peoples rebelled against the Romans, yet, when this rebellion occurred, the Samnites were already in alliance with Rome and with their armies helped the Romans to subjugate Latin insolence. When they had been subjugated, the war with Samnium flared up again. And when the forces of the Samnites were beaten owing to the many routes inflicted on them, war with the Tuscans broke out; and, when this was settled, the Samnites started a fresh one, owing to the arrival of Pyrrhus in Italy. On Pyrrhus being repulsed and sent back to Greece, they started on their first war with the Carthaginians; and, scarce was this war over, when all the Gauls, both from this and from the other side of the Alps, conspired against the Romans, with the result that they were defeated with immense slaughter between Popolonia and Pisa, where the tower of St. Vincent now stands. When this war ended, they had no war of any importance for the space of twenty years, for they fought with no one except the Ligurians and what remained of the Gauls in Lombardy. Matters stood thus until the second Punic war, which led to Italy's being occupied for sixteen years. When this came to an end amid great glory, the Macedonian war broke out, and, when this was over, there came the war with Antiochus and with Asia. After which victories there remained in the whole world neither princes nor republics which, either alone or all together, could successfully oppose the forces of Rome.

If, before the final victory, we consider well the order in which these wars took place and the Roman method of procedure, it will be seen that in them, mingled with fortune, was virtue and prudence of a very high order. Hence, if one looks for the cause of this fortune, it should be easy to find. For it is quite certain that, when a prince and a people has acquired such repute that each of the neighbouring princes and peoples is afraid to attack it and fears it, no one will ever assault it unless driven thereunto by necessity; so that it will be open, so to speak, to that power to choose the neighbour on which it seems best to make war, and industriously to foster tranquillity among the rest. In this, owing in part to the respect they have for its power, and in part to their being deceived by the means it takes to lull them to sleep, they readily acquiesce. For other powers, which are farther away and have no intercourse with it, look on the affair as remote from their interests and as no concern of theirs; and in this error they remain until the conflagration is at their door. Nor, when it arrives, have they any means of stopping it except by their own forces, which will then be inadequate since the state in question has become very powerful.

I do not propose to deal with the Samnites, who stood by, watching the Roman people overcome the Volsci and the Aequi; and lest I should be too prolix, only the Carthaginians, who were already a great power and in great esteem when the Romans were fighting the Samnites and the Tuscans, for they held the whole of Africa, held Sardinia and Sicily, and had dominion over part of Spain. This their power, conjoined with the fact that they were remote from the confines of the Roman people, accounts for their never having thought of attacking the Romans, or of helping the Samnites and Tuscans. On the contrary, they acted as men do when things seem to be moving rapidly in another's favour, namely, came to terms with her, and sought her friendship. Nor was the mistake thus made at the outset realized until the Romans had conquered all the peoples that lay between them and the Carthaginians and they began to contend with each other for the dominion of Sicily and Spain. The same thing happened to the Gauls, to Philip, king of Macedon, and to Antiochus as happened to the Carthaginians. Whilst Rome was engaged with some other state, each of them thought the other state would beat Rome, and that they had time enough to protect themselves against her either by peaceful or by warlike methods. I am of opinion, therefore, that the fortune which Rome had in these matters, all rulers would have who should emulate Roman methods and should be imbued with the same virtue.

I should point out in this connection how the Romans behaved on entering foreign provinces, had I not spoken of it at length in my treatise on principalities, for I have there discussed the question fully. Here I shall make but this remark in passing. The Romans always took care to have in new provinces some friend to act as a ladder up which to climb or a door by which to enter, or as a means whereby to hold it. Thus we see that with the help of the Capuans they got into Samnium, of the Camertini into Tuscany, of the Mamertini into Sicily, of the Saguntines into Spain, of Masinissa into Africa, of the Aetolians into Greece, of Eumenes and other princes into Asia, of the Massilians and the Aedui into Gaul. Hence they never lacked supporters of this kind to facilitate their enterprise alike in acquiring the province and in holding it. Peoples who observe such customs will be found to have less need of fortune than those who do not observe them well.

That everyone may the better know how much more virtue helped the Romans to acquire their empire than did fortune, we shall in the next chapter discuss the character of the peoples with whom they had to fight, and show how obstinate they were in defending their liberty.

2. Concerning the Kind of People the Romans had to fight, and how obstinately they defended their Freedom

Nothing made it harder for the Romans to conquer the peoples of the central and outlying parts of Italy than the love which in those times many peoples had for liberty. So obstinately did they defend it that only by outstanding virtue could they ever have been subjugated. For numerous instances show to what dangers they exposed themselves in order to maintain or to recover it, and what vendettas they kept up against those who had taken it away. The study of history reveals, too, the harm that servitude has done to peoples and to cities. There is, indeed, in our own times only one country which can be said to have in it free cities, whereas in ancient times quite a number of genuinely free peoples were to be found in all countries. One sees how in the times of which we are speaking at present the peoples of Italy from the Apennines which now divide Tuscany from Lombardy, right down to its toe, were all of them free. The Tuscans, the Romans, the Samnites were, for instance, and so were many other peoples who dwelt in other parts of Italy. One never hears of there being any kings, apart from those who reigned in Rome, and Porsenna, the king of Tuscany, whose stock became extinct, though history does not tell us how. It is quite clear, however, that at the time when the Romans laid siege to Veii, Tuscany was free. Moreover, it enjoyed its freedom so much, and so hated the title of prince, that, when the people of Veii appointed a king in that city for the purpose of defence, and asked the Tuscans to help them against the Romans, the Tuscans after many consultations had been held, decided not to give help to the people of Veii so long as they lived under a king, since they held that they could not well defend a country whose people had already placed themselves in subjection to someone else.

It is easy to see how this affection of peoples for self-government comes about, for experience shows that cities have never increased either in dominion or wealth, unless they have been independent. It is truly remarkable to observe the greatness which Athens attained in the space of a hundred years after it had been liberated from the tyranny of Pisistratus. But most marvellous of all is it to observe the greatness which Rome attained after freeing itself from its kings. The reason is easy to understand; for it is not the well-being of individuals that makes cities great, but the well-being of the community; and it is beyond question that it is only in republics that the common good is looked to properly in that all that promotes it is carried out; and, however much this or that private person may be the loser on this account, there are so many who benefit thereby that the common good can be realized in spite of those few who suffer in consequence.

The opposite happens where there is a prince; for what he does in his own interests usually harms the city, and what is done in the interests of the city harms him. Consequently, as soon as tyranny replaces self-government the least of the evils which this tyranny brings about are that it ceases to make progress and to grow in power and wealth: more often than not, nay always, what happens is that it declines. And should fate decree the rise of an efficient tyrant, so energetic and so proficient in warfare that he enlarges his dominions, no advantage will accrue to the commonwealth, but only to himself, for he cannot bestow honours on the valiant and good citizens over whom he tyrannizes, since he does not want to have any cause to suspect them. Nor yet can he allow the cities he acquires to make their submission to, or to become the tributaries of, the city of which he is the tyrant, for to make it powerful is not to his interest. It is to his interest to keep the state divided so that each town and each district may recognize only him as its ruler. In this way he alone profits by his acquisitions, not his country. Should anyone desire to confirm this view by a host of further arguments, let him read Xenophon's treatise *On Tyrannicide.*

It is no wonder, then, that peoples of old detested tyrants and gave them no peace, or that they were so fond of liberty and held the word itself in such esteem, as happened when Hieronymus, the grandson of Hiero, the Syracusan, was killed in Syracuse, and the news of his death came to his army which was then not very far from Syracuse. At first there was a tumult, and men took up arms against those who had killed him, but when they perceived that in Syracuse the cry was for liberty, they were so delighted to hear the word, that all became quiet, and setting aside their anger against the tyrannicides, they began to consider how self-government could be organized in that city.

Nor is it surprising that peoples are so extraordinarily revengeful towards those who have destroyed their liberty. Of this there are numerous examples, but I propose to give but one, which happened in Corcyra, a city of Greece, during the Peloponnesian war. Greece was then divided into two parties, of which one supported the Athenians, the other the Spartans. The result was that in many cities internal dissensions arose, some advocating an alliance with Sparta, others an alliance with Athens. This happened in Corcyra, where the nobles got the upper hand, and deprived the populace of its liberty. But with the help of the Athenians the populace regained their strength, laid hands on all the nobles, and shut them up in one prison which held them all. Then they took them, eight or ten at a time, on the plea of banishing them to various parts, and then to set an example put them to death with much cruelty. When those who were left heard of this, they considered whether there was any possible way in which they could escape this igno-minious death. So, having armed themselves with anything at hand, they defended the entrance to the prison, and fought with those who tried to get in. The result was that, when rumors of this reached the populace, they came in a crowd, removed the upper storey and roof from the building, and smothered the inmates beneath the ruins. Many well-known instances of a like horrible nature happened later in this country. We thus see how true it is that a liberty which you have actually had taken away is avenged with much greater ferocity than is a liberty which someone has only tried to take away.

If one asks oneself how it comes about that peoples of old were more fond of liberty than they are today, I think the answer is that it is due to the same cause that makes men today less bold than they used to be; and this is due, I think, to the difference between our education and that of bygone times, which is based on the difference between our religion and the religion of those days. For our religion, having taught us the truth and the true way of life, leads us to ascribe less esteem to worldly honour. Hence the gentiles, who held it in high esteem and looked upon it as their highest good, displayed in their actions more ferocity than we do. This is evidenced by many of their institutions. To being with, com-pare the magnificence of their sacrifices with the humility that characterizes ours. The cer-emonial in ours is delicate rather than imposing, and there is no display of ferocity or courage. Their ceremonies lacked neither pomp nor magnificence, but, conjoined with this, were sacrificial acts in which there was much shedding of blood and much ferocity; and in them great numbers of animals were killed. Such spectacles, because terrible, caused men to become like them. Besides, the old religion did not beatify men unless they were replete with worldly glory: army commanders, for instance, and rulers of republics. Our religion has glorified humble and contemplative men, rather than men of action. It has assigned as man's highest good humility, abnegation, and contempt for mundane things, whereas the other identified it with magnanimity, bodily strength, and everything else that conduces to make men very bold. And, if our religion demands that in you there be strength, what it asks for is strength to suffer rather than strength to do bold things.

This pattern of life, therefore, appears to have made the world weak, and to have handed it over as a prey to the wicked, who run it successfully and securely since they are well aware that the generality of men, with paradise for their goal, consider how best to bear, rather than how best to avenge, their injuries. But, though it looks as if the world were become effeminate and as if heaven were powerless, this undoubtedly is due rather to the pusillanimity of those who have interpreted our religion in terms of *laissez faire*, not in terms of *virtù*. For, had they borne in mind that religion permits us to exalt and defend the fatherland, they would have seen that it also wishes us to love and honour it, and to train ourselves to be such that we may defend it.

This kind of education, then, and these grave misinterpretations account for the fact that we see in the world fewer republics than there used to be of old, and that, consequently, in peoples we do not find the same love of liberty as there then was. Yet I can well believe that it was rather the Roman empire, which, with its armed forces and its grandiose ideas, wiped out all republics and all their civic institutions, that was the cause of this. And though, later on, Rome's empire disintegrated, its cities have never been able to pull themselves together nor to set up again a constitutional regime, save in one or two parts of that empire.

Anyhow, however this may be, the Romans encountered in all parts of the world, however small, a combination of well-armed republics, extremely obstinate in the defence of their liberty; which shows that, if the virtue of the Roman people had not been of a rare and very high order, they would never have been able to overcome them. Of instances which bear this out, I shall cite but one case, that of the Samnites. It is a remarkable thing, as Livy admits, that they should have been so powerful and their arms so strong that they were able to withstand the Romans right up to the time of Papirius Cursor, the consul, son of the first Papirius; i.e. to withstand them for the space of forty-six years in spite of many disastrous defeats, the destruction of towns and the slaughter of the inhabitants of their country, a slaughter so great that this country, in which there were formerly seen so many cities and so many inhabitants, was now almost deserted, whereas at one time, it was so well ordered and so strong that it would have been insuperable if it had not been confronted with a virtue such as Rome's.

It is easy, moreover, to see whence arose that order and how this disorder came about. For it is all due to the independence which then was and to the servitude which now is. Because, as has been said before, all towns and all countries that are in all respects free, profit by this enormously. For, wherever increasing populations are found, it is due to the freedom with which marriage is contracted and to its being more desired by men. And this comes about where every man is ready to have children, since he believes that he can rear them and feels sure that his patrimony will not be taken away, and since he knows that not only will they be born free, instead of into slavery, but that, if they have virtue, they will have a chance of becoming rulers. One observes, too, how riches multiply and abound there, alike those that come from agriculture and those that are produced by the trades. For everybody is eager to acquire such things and to obtain property, provided he be convinced that he will enjoy it when it has been acquired. It thus comes about that, in competitions one with the other, men look both to their own advantage and to that of the public; so that in both respects wonderful progress is made. The contrary of this happens in countries which live in servitude; and the harder the servitude the more does the well-being to which they are accustomed dwindle.

Of all forms of servitude, too, that is the hardest which subjects you to a republic. First because it is more lasting, and there is no hope of escape; secondly because the aim of a republic is to deprive all other corporations of their vitality and to weaken them, to the end that its own body corporate may increase. A prince who makes you his subject, does not do this unless he be a barbarian who devastates the country and destroys all that man has done for civilization, as oriental princes do. On the contrary, if his institutions be humane and he behave constitutionally, he will more often than not be equally fond of all the cities that are subject to him, and will leave them in possession of all their trades and all their ancient institutions. So that, if they are unable to increase, as free cities do, they will not be ruined like those that are enslaved. I refer here to the servitude that befalls cities which are subject to a foreigner, for of those that are subject to one of their own citizens I have already spoken.

He who reflects, therefore, on all that has been said, will not wonder at the power the Samnites had when free, or at the weakness that befell them later, when they became a subject state. This Titus Livy attests in several places, particularly in his account of the war with Hannibal, where he shows how the Samnites, when they had been maltreated by a legion which lay at Nola, sent messengers to Hannibal to ask him to come to their aid. In their address they told him that for a hundred years they had been fighting the Romans with their own troops and their own officers, and that often they had held up two consular armies and two consuls, but that now they had come to such a pass that they could scarce hold their own against the small Roman legion that was at Nola.

5. Changes of Religion and of Language, together with such Misfortunes as Floods or Pestilences, obliterate the Records of the Past

To those philosophers who want to make out that the world is eternal, I think the answer might be that, if it really were as old as all this, it would be reasonable to expect there would be records going back further than five thousand years, did we not see how the records of times gone by are obliterated by diverse causes, of which some are due to men and some to heaven. Those which are due to men are changes in religious institutions and in language. For, when a new religious institution comes into being, i.e. a new religion, its first care is, for the sake of its own reputation, to wipe out the old one; and, when the founders of a new religion happen to speak a different tongue, the old one is easily abolished. This becomes clear if we consider the measures which Christianity adopted *vis-à-vis* Paganism; how it abolished all pagan institutions, all pagan rites, and destroyed the records of the theology of the ancients. It is true that Christianity did not succeed in wiping out altogether the record of what outstanding men of the old religion had done; which was due to the retention of the Latin language, for this they had to retain so that they might use it in writing down their new laws. Had they been able to write them in a new tongue, there would, if we bear in mind the way they persecuted in other matters, have been no record of the past left at all.

Whoever reads of the measures taken by Saint Gregory and other heads of the Christian religion, will see what a fuss they made about getting rid of all records of the past, how they burnt the works of poets and historians, destroyed images and spoiled everything else that betokened in any way antiquity. So much so that, if to this persecution there had been conjoined a new language, in a short time one would have found all traces of the past wiped out. One can well believe, therefore, that what Christianity did with regard to Paganism, Paganism did to the religion that preceded it; and, as there have been two or three changes of religion in five or six thousand years, the record of what happened before that has been lost; or, if of it there remains a trace, it is regarded as a fable and no credence is given to it; as has happened with regard to the *History of Diodorus Siculus*, which covers a period of some forty or fifty thousand years, but is looked upon as untrustworthy, as I believe it to be.

The causes due to heaven are those which wipe out a whole generation and reduce the inhabitants in certain parts of the world to but a few. This is brought about by pestilence or by famine or by a flood and of these the most important is the last alike because it is more widespread and because those who survive are all of them rude mountain-dwellers who have no knowledge of antiquity and so cannot hand it down to posterity; and should there be among the survivors anyone who has such knowledge he will conceal it or distort it in his own fashion so as to establish his own reputation and that of his family, with the result that there will remain to this successors just so much as he has chosen to record and nothing more.

That these floods, pestilences and famines happen, I do not think anyone can doubt, for plenty of them are recorded everywhere in history, their effect in obliterating the past is plain to see, and it seems reasonable that it should be so. For, as in the case of simple bodies, when nature has accumulated too much superfluous material, it frequently acts in the same way and by means of a purge restores health to the body. Similarly in the case of that body which comprises a mixture of human races, when every province is replete with inhabitants who can neither obtain a livelihood nor move elsewhere since all other places are occupied and full up, and when the craftiness and malignity of man has gone as far as it can go, the world must needs be purged in one of these three ways so that mankind, being reduced to comparatively few and humbled by adversity, may adopt a more appropriate form of life and grow better.

There was, then, as we have said before, a time when Tuscany was a powerful country, full of religion and of virtue, with its own customs and its own language, all of which we know was wiped out by the power of Rome, so that of it, as has been said, there remains nought but the remembrance of its name.

29. Fortune blinds Men's Minds when she does not wish them to obstruct her Designs

If one ponders well the course of human affairs, it will be seen that many events happen and many misfortunes come about, against which the heavens have not been willing that any provision at all should be made. Since this statement holds good in the case of Rome, which was conspicuous alike for virtue, religion and orderly conduct, it is no wonder that the same thing happens yet more often in cities and provinces which are lacking in these respects. There is a well-known passage in which Titus Livy shows at length and with great force the power that heaven exercises over human affairs. He says that, with a view to making the Romans recognize its power, heaven first caused the Fabii to act wrongly when sent as ambassadors to the Gauls, and by means of what they did excited the Gauls to make war on Rome; then ordained that in Rome nothing worthy of the Roman people should be done to meet their attack; for first it brought about that Camillus, who was the only hope they had in those evil days, should be sent as an exile to Ardea; then that, when the Gauls were marching on Rome, they did not appoint a dictator, as they had done many times to meet the attack of the Volsci and other enemies in the neighborhood. It also caused them to be weak and to take no particular care in calling up troops, who were so slow in taking up arms that they scarce had time to confront the Gauls on the banks of the Allia, which was but ten miles from Rome. There the tribunes set up their camp without their accustomed diligence, since they did not inspect the site beforehand, nor surround it with trenches and stockades, nor take any other precautions, either human or divine; while in preparing for battle they made their ranks thin and weak, and neither troops nor officers behaved as Roman discipline required. No blood was shed during the battle because at the first onslaught the Romans ran away, the greater number going to Veii, and the rest retiring to Rome, where they sought refuge in the Capitol without first going home; whereupon the senate took so little thought for Rome's defence that, for one thing, they omitted to close the gates; and some of its members fled, while others went with the rest into the Capitol. Granted, in their defence of the Capitol they used some sort of discipline, for they did not pack all the useless people inside, and they got in all the corn they could, so as to be able to stand the siege; while of the useless crowd of old men, women and children, most fled to the country round about, and the rest stayed in Rome at the mercy of the Gauls. So that no one who had read of what was done so often in years gone by and were to read what was now being done, would think they were one and the same people.

Having described all the disorders mentioned above, Titus Livy concludes with the remark: 'To such an extent does fortune blind the minds of men when she does not want them to oppose the force she is using.'

Nor can anything be more true than the conclusion Livy draws. Hence men who in this life normally either suffer great adversity or enjoy great prosperity, deserve neither praise nor blame; for one usually finds that they have been driven either to ruin or to greatness by the prospect of some great advantage which the heavens have held out, whereby they have been given the chance, or have been deprived of the chance, of being able to act virtuously. Fortune arranges this quite nicely. For, when it wants a man to take the lead in doing great things, it chooses a man of high spirits and great virtue who will seize the occasion it offers him. And in like manner, when it wants a man to bring about a great disaster, it gives precedence to men who will help to promote it; and, if anyone gets in the way, it either kills him off or deprives him of all power of doing good.

It plainly appears from Livy's evidence that, in order to make Rome greater and to lead it on to its future greatness, fortune decided it was necessary first to chastize it in a way that will be described at length in the beginning of the next book, but did not want to ruin it altogether. Hence we see that it made an exile of Camillus, but did not cause him to die; that it caused Rome to be taken, but not the Capitol; that it arranged matters so that nothing useful was thought of to help Rome, nor anything overlooked that could help in the defence of the Capitol. It brought it about that, since Rome was to be taken, the greater part of the troops which were routed at Allia, should go on to Veii, thus leaving the city without any men to defend it. But in arranging things thus, it also prepared the way for Rome's recovery; for since there was a Roman army at Veii, and Camillus was at Ardea, it became possible to make a more vigorous attempt to deliver the fatherland under a general whose career was free from the stain of defeat and whose reputation was untarnished.

In confirmation of this one might adduce further examples from modern times, but I do not think this necessary, so pass them over, since that I have given should be enough to satisfy anybody. I assert once again as a truth to which history as a whole bears witness that men may second their fortune, but cannot oppose it; that they may weave its warp, but cannot break it. Yet they should never give up, because there is always hope, though they know not the end and move towards it along roads which cross one another and as yet are unexplored; and since there is hope, they should not despair, no matter what fortune brings or in what travail they find themselves.

Book Three

1. In Order that a Religious Institution or a State should long survive it is essential that it should frequently be Restored to its original principles

It is a well-established fact that the life of all mundane things is of finite duration. But things which complete the whole of the course appointed them by heaven are in general those whose bodies do not disintegrate, but maintain themselves in orderly fashion so that if there is no change; or, if there be change, it tends rather to their conservation than to their destruction. Here I am concerned with composite bodies, such as are states and religious institutions, and in their regard I affirm that those changes make for their conservation which lead them back to their origins. Hence those are better constituted and have a longer life whose institutions make frequent renovations possible, or which are brought to such a renovation by some event which has nothing to do with their constitution. For it is clearer than daylight that, without renovation, these bodies do not last.

The way to renovate them, as has been said, is to reduce them to their starting-points. For at the start religious institutions, republics and kingdoms have in all cases some good in them, to which their early reputation and progress is due. But since in process of time this goodness is corrupted, such a body must of necessity die unless something happens which brings it up to the mark. Thus, our medical men, speaking of the human body, say that 'every day it absorbs something which from time to time requires treatment'.

This return to its original principles in the case of a republic, is brought about either by some external event or by its own intrinsic good sense. Thus, as an example of the former, we see how it was necessary that Rome should be taken by the Gauls in order that it should be re-born and in its re-birth take on alike a new vitality and a new virtue, and also take up again the observance of religion and justice, both of which had begun to show blemishes. This plainly appears from Livy's account where he shows how, when the Romans led out their army against the Gauls and created tribunes with consular power, they observed no religious ceremony. And, in like manner, not only did they not punish the three Fabii who had attacked the Gauls 'in contravention of the Law of Nations', but they made them tribunes. Whence it is easy to infer that of the good constitutions established by Romulus and by those other wise princes they had begun to take less account than was reasonable and necessary for the maintenance of a free state. This defeat in a war with outsiders, therefore, came about so that the institutions of this city should be renovated and to show this people that not only is it essential to uphold religion and justice, but also to hold in high esteem good citizens and to look upon their virtue as of greater value than those comforts of which there appeared to them to be a lack owing to what these men had done. This actually came about. For as soon as Rome had been recovered they renewed all the ordinances of their ancient religion and punished the Fabii who had fought 'in contravention of the Law of Nations'. They also set such esteem on the virtue and goodness of Camillus that the senate and the rest, putting envy aside, laid on his shoulders the whole burden of this republic.

It is, therefore, as I have said, essential that men who live together under any constitution should frequently have their attention called to themselves either by some external or by some internal occurrence. When internal, such occurrences are usually due to some law which from time to time causes the members of this body to review their position; or again to some good man who arises in their midst and by his example and his virtuous deeds produces the same effect as does the constitution.

Such benefits, therefore, are conferred on a republic either by the virtue of some individual or by the virtue of an institution. In regard to the latter, the institutions which
caused the Roman republic to return to its start were the introduction of plebeian tribunes, of the censorship, and of all the other laws which put a check on human ambition
and arrogance; to which institutions life must needs be given by some virtuous citizen
who cooperates strenuously in giving them effect despite the power of those who contravene them. Notable among such drastic actions, before the taking of Rome by the Gauls,
were the death of Brutus' sons, the death of the ten citizens, and that of Maelius, the corn-
dealer. After the taking of Rome there was the death of Manlius Capitolinus, the death of
Manlius Torquatus' son, the action taken by Papirius Cursor against Fabius, his master of
horse, and the charge brought against the Scipios. Such events, because of their unwonted
severity and their notoriety, brought men back to the mark every time one of them happened; and when they began to occur less frequently, they also began to provide occasion
for men to practise corruption, and were attended with more danger and more commotion. For between one case of disciplinary action of this type and the next there ought
to elapse at most ten years, because by this time men begin to change their habits and to
break the laws; and, unless something happens which recalls to their minds the penalty
involved and reawakens fear in them, there will soon be so many delinquents that it will
be impossible to punish them without danger.

In regard to this, those who governed the state of Florence from 1434 to 1494 used to
say that it was necessary to reconstitute the government every five years; otherwise it was
difficult to maintain it; where by 'reconstituting the government' they meant instilling
men with that terror and that fear with which they had instilled them when instituting
it—in that at this time they had chastised those who, looked at from the established way
of life, had misbehaved. As, however, the remembrance of this chastisement disappears,
men are emboldened to try something fresh and to talk sedition. Hence provision has of
necessity to be made against this by restoring that government to what it was at its origins.

Such a return to their original principles in republics is sometimes due to the simple
virtue of one man alone, independently of any laws spurring you to action. For of such
effect is a good reputation and good example that men seek to imitate it, and the bad
are ashamed to lead lives which go contrary to it. Those who in Rome are outstanding
examples of this good influence, are Horatius Cocles, Scaevola, Fabricius, the two Decii,
Regulus Attilius, and several others, whose rare and virtuous examples wrought the same
effects in Rome as laws and institutions would have done. If then effective action of the
kind described above, together with this setting of good example, had occurred in that
city at least every ten years, it necessarily follows that it would never have become corrupt. But when both the one and the other began to occur more rarely, corruption began
to spread. For, after the time of Marcus Regulus, there appeared no examples of this kind,
and, though in Rome there arose the two Catos, between them and any prior instance
there was so great an interval, and again between the Catos themselves, and they stood so
alone that their good example could have no good effect; especially in the case of the
younger Cato who found the greater part of the city so corrupt that he could not by his
example effect any improvement among the citizens. So much then for republics.

As to religious institutions one sees here again how necessary these renovations are
from the example of our own religion, which, if it had not been restored to its starting-
point by St Francis and St Dominic, would have become quite extinct. For these men by
their poverty and by their exemplification of the life of Christ revived religion in the
minds of men in whom it was already dead, and so powerful were these new religious

orders that they prevented the depravity of prelates and of religious heads from bringing ruin on religion. They also lived so frugally and had such prestige with the populace as confessors and preachers that they convinced them it is an evil thing to talk evilly of evil doing, and a good thing to live under obedience to such prelates, and that, if they did wrong, it must be left to God to chastise them. And, this being so, the latter behave as badly as they can, because they are not afraid of punishments which they do not see and in which they do not believe. It is, then, this revival which has maintained and continues to maintain this religion.

Kingdoms also need to be renovated and to have their laws brought back to their starting-points. The salutary effect this produces is seen in the kingdom of France, for the conduct of affairs in this kingdom is controlled by more laws and more institutions than it is in any other. These laws and these institutions are maintained by *parlements*, notably by that of Paris, and by it they are renovated whenever it takes action against a prince of this realm or in its judgements condemns the king. Up to now it has maintained its position by the pertinacity with which it has withstood the nobility of this realm. But should it at any time let an offence remain unpunished and should offences begin to multiply, the result would unquestionably be either that they would have to be corrected to the accompaniment of grievous disorders or that the kingdom would disintegrate.

The conclusion we reach, then, is that there is nothing more necessary to a community, whether it be a religious establishment, a kingdom or a republic, than to restore to it the prestige it had at the outset, and to take care that either good institutions or good men shall bring this about rather than that external force should give rise to it. For though this on occasion may be the best remedy, as it was in Rome's case, it is so dangerous that in no case is it what one should desire.

In order to make it clear to all how much the action of particular men contributed to the greatness of Rome and produced in that city so many beneficial results, I shall proceed to narrate and to discuss their doings, and shall confine myself to this topic in this third and last book on this first Decad [of Livy's history]. And, though the actions of the kings were great and noteworthy, since history deals with them at length I shall not mention them here, except where they may have done things with a view to their personal advantage. I begin, then, with Brutus, the father of Rome's liberties.

7. How it comes about that Changes from Liberty to Servitude and from Servitude to Liberty sometimes occur without Bloodshed and sometimes abound in it

Some perchance may wonder how it comes about that of many revolutions involving a change from freedom to tyranny or the other way about, some are accompanied by bloodshed and others not. For it is plain from history that in such revolutions sometimes vast numbers of men get killed, and that in others nobody at all gets hurt, as happened in the change which Rome made from kingship to rule by consult, for in it no one was banished except the Tarquins, and nobody else at all got hurt.

The answer is that it all depends upon whether the change in form of government is or is not brought about by violence; for when it is accompanied by violence it is inevitable that many should get hurt, and then of necessity those who in their downfall have been injured seek revenge, and this desire for vengeance gives rise to bloodshed and loss of life; but when that form of government has been brought into being by the common consent of a whole people which has made it great, there is no reason why, when the said people as a whole meets its downfall, they should harm anyone except its head. This was the case with Rome's government and with the expulsion of the Tarquins. It was also the case with the government of the Medici in Florence, which, when it fell in 1494, harmed nobody but the Medici themselves.

Revolutions of this kind, therefore, are not attended with much danger. Those, on the other hand, are extremely dangerous which are brought about by men who are out for vengeance, and have invariably been of such a kind as to appal those who read of them, to say the least. Since of such revolutions there are plenty of instances in history, I propose to leave it at that.

8. He who would transform a Republic should take Due Note of the Governed

That a bad citizen cannot do much harm in a republic that is not corrupt has been shown in a previous discourse, and, in addition to the reasons there adduced, this conclusion is confirmed by the case of Spurius Cassius and that of Manlius Capitolinus. The former, an ambitious man, desirous of acquiring extraordinary authority in Rome, ingratiated himself with the plebs by conferring on them many benefits, such as dividing among them the lands which the Romans had taken from the Hernici. When the city fathers discovered his ambitious projects and made them known, he became so suspect that, on his addressing the populace and offering to give them the money accruing from the sale of the corn which the public had caused to be brought from Sicily, they refused it outright, since it seemed to them that Spurius was offering it them as the price of their liberty. Whereas, had the populace been corrupt, they would have accepted the money, and would have laid open the way to tyranny instead of closing it.

The example of Manlius Capitolinus is even more remarkable; for from his case it may be seen how the inordinate desire to rule afterwards cancels out virtues of mind and body and services rendered to one's country, however great they may be. This desire, it is clear, was in his case aroused by the envy he felt for Camillus on whom great honours had been bestowed, and in him it begat so great a mental blindness that without pausing to reflect on the mode of life prevailing in the city, or to inquire with what kind of subjects he had to deal and whether they were yet averse to accept a bad form of government, he set about raising tumults in Rome alike against the senate and against his country's laws. This incident shows how perfect the city then was and how good the material of which it was composed; for in his case none of the nobles, who were usually very keen to defend one another, rose to support him, nor did any of his relations make a move on his behalf; nor yet, though it was customary in the case of an accused person for his relations to appear in mourning, clad in black, and all of them sorrowing, so as to evoke sympathy in favour of the accused, did anyone at all appear in Manlius's case. The tribunes of the plebs, who were wont always to look favourably on causes which appeared likely to benefit the populace, and to promote them the more vigorously the more inimical they were to the nobles, in this case joined with the nobles in suppressing a common pest. The Roman populace, looking eagerly to its own interests and sympathetic to projects which might thwart the nobility, in spite of its having been so favourable to Manlius, none the less when the tribunes cited him to appear, and referred his case to the judgement of the populace, this same populace, become now the judge of its defender, paid no attention to this, but condemned him to death.

Hence I do not think that there is any example in the history we are considering, capable of showing more clearly than this, how sound were all the institutions of that republic, in view of the fact that not a soul in that city was disposed to defend a citizen who was replete with virtue of every kind and alike in public and in private had done very many things worthy of commendation. For with all of them love of country weighed more than any other consideration, and they looked upon the present dangers for which he was responsible as of much greater importance than his former merits; with the result that they chose he should die in order that they might remain free. 'Such,' says Titus Livy, 'was the fate of a man who would have been illustrious if he had not been born in a free city.'

There are two things here which should be borne in mind. One is that, in order to obtain glory, a man must use different methods in a city that is corrupt from what he would use in one in which political life is still vigorous. The other, which is almost the same as the first, is that in the way they behave, and especially where deeds of moment are concerned, men should take account of the times, and act accordingly.

Those who owing to bad judgement or to their natural inclinations are out of touch with the times are in most cases unfortunate in their life and unsuccessful in their undertakings. But it is otherwise with those who are in accord with the times. From the words of the historian cited above, it may without hesitation be inferred that, had Manlius been born in the days of Marius or Sulla, when the material was corrupt and it would have been possible to impress on it the form to which his ambition looked, he would have met with the same success that attended the actions of Marius and Sulla and others who, after them, aspired to tyranny. And in the same way, had Sulla and Marius lived in the time of Manlius, they would have been crushed at the very outset of their careers. For a man can easily by his behaviour and his evil devices begin to corrupt the populace in a city, but it is impossible for him to live long enough to corrupt it to such an extent that he himself shall reap the fruits. And, even if it were possible for him to live long enough to do this, it would still be impossible for him to succeed, for men are so impatient in the way they carry on that they cannot restrain their passions for very long. Consequently they make mistakes in handling their affairs, especially when they are too eager; with the result that, either through impatience or through mistakes, they are likely to take premature action and to meet with disaster.

If anyone, then, wants to seize supreme power in a republic and to impose on it a bad form of government, it is essential that he should find there a material which has in course of time become disordered, and that this disorder shall have been introduced little by little and in one generation after another. And this, as we have remarked in a previous discourse, must of necessity come about unless that republic be given fresh life by the example of good men or by fresh legislation be brought back to what it was at the start.

Manlius, therefore, would have been an exceptional and a remarkable man, had he been born in a corrupt city. Hence citizens who in republics take up any enterprise, whether in favour of liberty or with a view to tyranny, should take account of the subjects with which they have to deal and on this should base their estimate of the difficulties their undertaking involves; for it is just as difficult and dangerous to try to free a people that wants to remain servile as it is to enslave a people that wants to remain free.

Since I have remarked above that in human affairs men should study the nature of the times and act accordingly, of this we shall speak at length in the next chapter.

9. *That it behoves one to adapt Oneself to the Times if one wants to enjoy Continued Good Fortune*

I have often thought that the reason why men are sometimes unfortunate, sometimes fortunate, depends upon whether their behaviour is in conformity with the times. For one sees that in what they do some men are impetuous, others look about them and are cautious; and that, since in both cases they go to extremes and are unable to go about things in the right way, in both cases they make mistakes. On the other hand, he is likely to make fewer mistakes and to prosper in his fortune when circumstances accord with his conduct, as I have said, and one always proceeds as the force of nature compels one.

Everybody knows how Fabius Maximus, when in command of the army, proceeded circumspectly and with a caution far removed from the impetuosity and boldness characteristic of the Roman; and by good luck this sort of thing just fitted the circumstances. For Hannibal had arrived in Italy, a young man flushed with success, and had twice routed the Roman people, so that this republic had lost almost all its best troops and was alarmed. Hence it could not have been more fortunate than to have had a general who by his slowness and his caution held the enemy at bay. Nor could Fabius have met with circumstances more suited to his ways; and it is to this that his fame was due.

That in so doing Fabius behaved naturally and not by choice is shown by the fact that, when Scipio wanted to go to Africa with his armies to bring the war to an end, Fabius was much against this, since he could not get out of his ways and habits; so that, if it had been left to him, Hannibal would still be in Italy, for he did not see that times had changed, and that new methods of warfare were called for. So that, if Fabius had been king of Rome, he might easily have lost this war, since he was incapable of altering his methods according as circumstances changed. Since, however, he was born in a republic where there were diverse citizens with diverse dispositions, it came about that, just as it had a Fabius, who was the best man to keep the war going when circumstances required this, so later it had a Scipio at a time suited to its victorious consummation.

For this reason a republic has a fuller life and enjoys good fortune for a longer time than a principality, since it is better able to adapt itself to diverse circumstances owing to the diversity found among its citizens than a prince can do. For a man who is accustomed to act in one particular way, never changes, as we have said. Hence, when times change and no longer suit his ways, he is inevitably ruined.

Piero Soderini, whom we have mentioned several times, conducted all his affairs in his good-natured and patient way. So long as circumstances suited the way in which he carried on, both he and his country prospered. But when afterwards there came a time which required him to drop his patience and his humility, he could not bring himself to it; so that both he and his country were ruined. Pope Julius II during the whole course of his pontificate acted with impetuosity and dash, and, since the times suited him well, he succeeded in all his undertakings; but had other times come which called for other counsels, he would of necessity have been undone, for he could not have changed his ways or his method of handling affairs.

There are two reasons why we cannot change our ways. First, it is impossible to go against what nature inclines us to. Secondly, having got on well by adopting a certain line of conduct, it is impossible to persuade men that they can get on well by acting otherwise. It thus comes about that a man's fortune changes, for she changes his circumstances but he does not change his ways. The downfall of cities also comes about because institutions in republics do not change with the times, as we have shown at length already, but change very slowly because it is more painful to change them since it is necessary to wait until the whole republic is in a state of upheaval; and for this it is not enough that one man alone should change his own procedure.

Since we have mentioned Fabius Maximus who held Hannibal at bay, it seems to me appropriate in the next chapter to discuss whether a general who is determined at all costs to force the enemy to fight, can be prevented by the enemy from doing this.

THOMAS HOBBES

Thomas Hobbes (1588–1679) was born in Malmesbury, England, arriving prematurely because, he claimed, rumors that the Spanish armada was off the coast of England ready to invade scared his mother: "She brought twins to birth, myself and fear at the same time." Ironically, fear of death was the central psychological assumption of his moral and political theorizing as an adult. Hobbes's father was a clergyman, whom some reports describe as prone to drink and violence, and who eventually deserted his family in order to avoid a charge of assault. Educated at the expense of his uncle, Hobbes attended Oxford from 1603 to 1608. Because he was not from a wealthy family, on graduation he got a job as the tutor and companion of William Cavendish, who eventually became the Earl of Devonshire. Thus began his long association with that family; except for a few brief periods, he remained in service to them for nearly seventy years. He also worked briefly for Sir Francis Bacon, serving as his amanuensis and translator.

According to his friend and biographer John Aubrey, Hobbes's philosophical interests owed much to the geometer Euclid, whose proofs he loved because of the way they relied on logical reasoning to derive surprising and sometimes seemingly implausible conclusions from highly plausible and seemingly innocuous premises. However his first full-scale philosophical manuscript was not circulated until 1640. This work, called *The Elements of Laws, Natural and Politic,* advocated the creation of an absolute sovereign in order to secure the peace and stability of the community. Because of the antiroyalist sentiment at this time (which eventually resulted in full-scale civil war and the beheading of King Charles I), many people, including members of Parliament, were outraged by the manuscript, and Hobbes believed he had to flee for his life to Europe (he used to boast that he was one of the "first to flee" from England). Like many prominent royalist sympathizers he spent the rest of the civil war in Paris, where he enjoyed philosophical conversations with French intellectuals (such as Gassendi and Mersenne) and exiled British thinkers. During that time he wrote *De Cive* [*The Citizen*] (1642), a reworked version of his argument in *The Elements of Laws* (written in Latin but later published in English in 1651 under the title *The Philosophical Rudiments of Government*). In 1651 he published his masterpiece *Leviathan,* which contains his mature argument for absolute sovereignty.

Oliver Cromwell was in power when *Leviathan* was completed, and Cromwell supposedly welcomed the book because of the way its arguments could be used to justify any de facto political authority even if it was installed through rebellion. Accordingly, Hobbes was allowed to come home, unlike other royalist exiles (who resented Hobbes's return and considered him to have sold out to the new Puritan regime). On his return, he continued philosophizing in areas other than political philosophy, producing works in philosophy of law, history, metaphysics, and epistemology (including ontology, scientific method, and free will), and topics in science and mathematics (including optics, geometry, and human physiology). After the restoration of King Charles

II, Hobbes enjoyed access to the king because of his wit and intelligence. However, he remained a highly controversial figure throughout the country, both because of his political absolutism and because of his materialist metaphysics and his views on free will and religion, which were viewed by many of the larger population as "atheistic" and heretical. Hobbes finally died at the ripe old age of 91.

Hobbes's argument for absolute sovereignty in all his political writings makes use of the idea of a "social contract," an idea also used by other political thinkers of his day but which Hobbes revolutionized in ways that powerfully influenced the political thinking of subsequent philosophers such as Locke, Rousseau, and Kant. Imagine, says Hobbes, a "state of nature" prior to the creation of all governments. In this state, human behavior would be unchecked by law, and since Hobbes believes that human beings are predominantly self-interested (concerned above all else with their own preservation), he argues that they would inevitably come into conflict with one another, while having little or no other-regarding sentiments or psychological resources to resolve those conflicts. So before long he says, there would be a "war of every one against every one," so that every person's life in this natural state would be "solitary, poor, nasty, brutish and short" (*Leviathan,* chap. 13). To remedy such war and satisfy their desire for self-preservation, people, Hobbes argues, would be rational to contract with one another to create a government run by a sovereign holding absolute power, because only absolute power is sufficient to resolve disputes that otherwise would precipitate conflict dissolving the commonwealth and threatening the lives of all. Such an argument is meant to show the kind of government we contemporary human beings would be rational to create and sustain, lest we descend into a state of war analogous to the one that would exist in the state of nature. Note that Hobbes doesn't require that sovereignty be held only by an absolute monarchy; he also recognizes that sovereignty can be invested in a small number of people, constituting an oligarchy, or in all the people, constituting a democracy. Hobbes explicitly prefers the absolute monarchy, but believes the other two forms of government are also viable. What is not viable, in his view, is some form of "mixed" government with different branches of government holding different components of political authority, or governments in which power is supposed to be limited by a constitution or by a contract made between the government and the people. Such limits or divisions, says Hobbes, will only lead to conflicts that cannot be resolved by self-interested people, who require for peace a unified sovereignty with the power to decide any issue that might lead to conflict in the regime.

Hobbes's use of this social contract argument was occasioned in large part by his rejection of the scholastic philosophizing of many of his contemporaries and his forebears, whom he thought were too inclined to appeal to authority rather than reason, and too inclined to use nonsensical or empty terms (such as *immaterial substance* or *consubstantiation*). Accordingly, Hobbes turned to science, and particularly to geometry, as a guide to constructing a theory of our moral and political life. Starting with what he took to be sound premises, Hobbes sought to construct a social contract argument so as to derive, in geometric fashion, valid conclusions about morals and politics in a way that would command assent even from those reluctant to endorse such conclusions. Hobbes's faith in the power of reason to provide truth in moral and political matters makes him an enlightenment thinker, although, ironically, it is partly because he thinks there will be persistent failures of rationality in any human community that peace must be secured by giving the ruler absolute power.

Does Hobbes's argument work? To create an absolute sovereign, Hobbes says that each person must agree with every other person to "give up" his or her "right to all things" to the sovereign, thereby "authorizing" the sovereign to rule in this community. But can people who are committed to securing their self-preservation above all else rationally risk giving up *all* their rights to another? Hobbes explicitly compares subjects to servants and sovereigns to masters. But is such voluntary political "enslavement" even psychologically possible for people as Hobbes describes them? Observant readers will note qualifications to the alienation of all power to the sovereign in Chapter 21. For example, Hobbes writes:

> The obligation of subjects to the sovereign is understood to last as long, and no longer, than the power lasteth, by which he is able to protect them. For the right men have by nature to protect themselves when none else can protect them can by no covenant be relinquished.

But is such a qualification consistent with the idea that the sovereign has absolute power over his subjects? The ultimate validity of Hobbes's argument has been questioned by generations of readers, who have tended to be both intrigued by its power and alarmed by its conclusions.

For an overview of Hobbes's work, see Tom Sorell, *Hobbes* (London: Routledge & Kegan Paul, 1986). For a view of Hobbes's life by one of his contemporaries, see the discussion of Hobbes in John Aubrey's *Brief Lives,* Oliver Lawson Dick, ed. (Ann Arbor: University of Michigan Press, 1975). For three detailed examinations of the validity of Hobbes's social contract argument, see David Gauthier, *The Logic of Leviathan* (Oxford: Oxford University Press, 1969); Jean Hampton, *Hobbes and the Social Contract Tradition* (Cambridge: Cambridge University Press, 1986); and Gregory Kavka, *Hobbesian Moral and Political Theory* (Princeton: Princeton University Press, 1986). Many of the nonpolitical aspects of Hobbes's thinking are discussed in J. W. N. Watkins, *Hobbes's System of Ideas* (London: Hutchison, 1965). For a discussion of Hobbes's religious arguments in *Leviathan,* see A. P. Martinich, *The Two Gods of Leviathan* (Cambridge: Cambridge University Press, 1992), and S. A. Lloyd, *Ideals as Interest in Hobbes's Leviathan* (Cambridge: Cambridge University Press, 1992). Finally, for a collection of classic interpretive essays on Hobbes's work, see K. C. Brown, *Hobbes Studies* (Oxford: Blackwell, 1965).

J. H.

LEVIATHAN

THE INTRODUCTION

Nature (the art whereby God hath made and governs the world) is by the *art* of man, as in many other things, so in this also imitated, that it can make an artificial animal. For seeing life is but a motion of limbs, the beginning whereof is in some principal part within; why may we not say that all *automata* (engines that move themselves by springs and wheels as doth a watch) have an artificial life? For what is the *heart,* but a *spring;* and the *nerves,* but so many *strings;* and the *joints,* but so many *wheels,* giving motion to the whole body, such as was intended by the artificer? *Art* goes yet further, imitating that rational and most excellent work of nature, *man.* For by art is created that great LEVIATHAN called a COMMONWEALTH, or STATE, (in Latin CIVITAS) which is but an artificial man; though of greater stature and strength than the natural, for whose protection and defence it was intended; and in which, the *sovereignty* is an artificial *soul,* as giving life and motion to the whole body; the *magistrates,* and other *officers* of judicature and execution, artificial *joints; reward* and *punishment* (by which fastened to the seat of the sovereignty every joint and member is moved to perform his duty) are the *nerves,* that do the same in the body natural; the *wealth* and *riches* of all the particular members, are the *strength; salus populi* (the *people's safety*) its *business; counsellors,* by whom all things needful for it to know are suggested unto it, are the *memory; equity,* and *laws,* an artificial *reason* and *will; concord, health; sedition, sickness;* and *civil war, death.* Lastly, the *pacts* and *covenants,* by which the parts of this body politic were at first made, set together, and united, resemble that *fiat,* or the *let us make man,* pronounced by God in the creation.

> To describe the nature of this artificial man, I will consider
> First, the *matter* thereof, and the *artificer;* both which is *man.*
> Secondly, *how,* and by what *covenants* it is made; what are the *rights* and just *power* or *authority* of a sovereign; and what it is that *preserveth* and *dissolveth* it.
> Thirdly, what is a *Christian commonwealth.*
> Lastly, what is the *kingdom of darkness.*

Concerning the first, there is a saying much usurped of late, that *wisdom* is acquired, not by reading of *books,* but of *men.* Consequently whereunto, those persons, that for the most part can give no other proof of being wise, take great delight to show what they think they have read in men, by uncharitable censures of one another behind their backs. But there is another saying not of late understood, by which they might learn truly to read one another, if they would take the pains; and that is, *nosce teipsum, read thyself:* which was not meant, as it is now used, to countenance, either the barbarous state of men in power, towards their inferiors; or to encourage men of low degree, to a saucy behaviour towards their betters; but to teach us, that for the similitude of the thoughts and passions of one man, to the thoughts and passions of another, whosoever looketh into himself, and considereth what he doth, when he does *think, opine, reason, hope, fear,* &c. and upon what grounds; he shall thereby read and know, what are the thoughts and passions of all other men upon the like occasions. I say the similitude of passions, which are the same in all men, *desire, fear, hope,* &c.; not the similitude of the objects of the passions, which are the things *desired, feared, hoped,* &c.; for these the constitution individual, and particular education, do so vary and they are so easy to be kept from our knowledge, that the characters of man's heart, blotted and confounded as they are with dissembling, lying, counterfeiting, and erroneous doctrines, are legible only to him that searcheth hearts. And though by men's actions we do discover their design sometimes; yet to do it without comparing them with our own, and distinguishing all circumstances, by which the case may come to be altered, is to decypher without a key, and be for the most part deceived, by too much trust, or by too much diffidence; as he that reads, is himself a good or evil man.

But let one man read another by his actions never so perfectly, it serves him only with his acquaintance, which are but few. He that is to govern a whole nation, must read in himself, not this or that particular man; but mankind: which though it be hard to do, harder than to learn any language or science; yet when I shall have set down my own reading orderly, and perspicuously, the pains left another, will be only to consider, if he also find not the same in himself. For this kind of doctrine admitteth no other demonstration.

Part 1
Of Man

CHAPTER 1

Of Sense

Concerning the thoughts of man, I will consider them first *singly,* and afterwards in *train,* or dependence upon one another. *Singly,* they are every one a *representation* or *appearance,* of some quality, or other accident of a body without us; which is commonly called an *object.* Which object worketh on the eyes, ears, and other parts of a man's body; and by diversity of working, produceth diversity of appearances.

The original of them all, is that which we call SENSE; (For there is no conception in a man's mind, which hath not at first, totally, or by parts, been begotten upon the organs of sense.) The rest are derived from that original.

To know the natural cause of sense, is not very necessary to the business now in hand; and I have elsewhere written of the same at large. Nevertheless, to fill each part of my present method, I will briefly deliver the same in this place.

The cause of sense, is the external body, or object, which presseth the organ proper to each sense, either immediately, as in the taste and touch; or mediately, as in seeing, hearing, and smelling; which pressure, by the mediation of nerves, and other strings and membranes of the body, continued inwards to the brain and heart, causeth there a resistance, or counter-pressure, or endeavour of the heart, to deliver it self: which endeavour, because *outward,* seemeth to be some matter without. And this *seeming,* or, *fancy,* is that which men call *sense;* and consisteth, as to the eye, in a *light,* or *colour figured;* to the ear, in a *sound;* to the nostril, in an *odour;* to the tongue and palate, in a *savour;* and to the rest of the body, in *heat, cold, hardness, softness,* and such other qualities as we discern by *feeling.* All which qualities called *sensible,* are in the object, that causeth them, but so many several motions of the matter, by which it presseth our organs diversely. Neither in us that are pressed, are they any thing else, but divers motions; (for motion produceth nothing but motion.) But their appearance to us is fancy, the same waking, that dreaming. And as pressing, rubbing, or striking the eye, makes us fancy a light; and pressing the ear, produceth a din; so do the bodies also we see, or hear, produce the same by their strong, though unobserved action. For if those colours and sounds were in the bodies, or objects that cause them, they could not be severed from them, as by glasses, and in echoes by reflection, we see they are; where we know the thing we see, is in one place; the appearance in another. And though at some certain distance, the real and very object seem invested with the fancy it begets in us; yet still the object is one thing, the image or fancy is another. So that sense in all cases, is nothing else but original fancy, caused (as I have said) by the pressure, that is, by the motion, of external things upon our eyes, ears, and other organs thereunto ordained.

But the philosophy-schools, through all the universities of Christendom, grounded upon certain texts of *Aristotle,* teach another doctrine; and say, for the cause of *vision,* that the thing seen, sendeth forth on every side a *visible species* (in English) a *visible show, appari-*

tion, or *aspect,* or *a being seen;* the receiving whereof into the eye, is *seeing.* And for the cause of *hearing,* that the thing heard, sendeth forth an *audible species,* that is, an *audible aspect,* or *audible being seen;* which entering at the ear, maketh *hearing.* Nay for the cause of *understanding* also, they say the thing understood, sendeth forth *intelligible species,* that is, an *intelligible being seen;* which coming into the understanding, makes us understand. I say not this, as disapproving the use of universities; but because I am to speak hereafter of their office in a commonwealth. I must let you see on all occasions by the way, what things would be amended in them; amongst which the frequency of insignificant speech is one.

CHAPTER 2

Of Imagination

That when a thing lies still, unless somewhat else stir it, it will lie still for ever, is a truth that no man doubts of. But that when a thing is in motion, it will eternally be in motion, unless somewhat else stay it, though the reason be the same, (namely, that nothing can change it self,) is not so easily assented to. For men measure, not only other men, but all other things, by themselves: and because they find themselves subject after motion to pain, and lassitude, think every thing else grows weary of motion, and seeks repose of its own accord; little considering, whether it be not some other motion, wherein that desire of rest they find in themselves, consisteth. From hence it is, that the schools say, heavy bodies fall downwards, out of an appetite to rest, and to conserve their nature in that place which is most proper for them; ascribing appetite and knowledge of what is good for their conservation, (which is more than man has) to things inanimate, absurdly.

When a body is once in motion, it moveth (unless something else hinder it) eternally; and whatsoever hindreth it, cannot in an instant, but in time, and by degrees quite extinguish it: And as we see in the water, though the wind cease, the waves give not over rolling for a long time after; so also it happeneth in that motion, which is made in the internal parts of a man, then, when he sees, dreams, &c. For after the object is removed, or the eye shut, we still retain an image of the thing seen, though more obscure than when we see it. And this is it, the Latins call *imagination,* from the image made in seeing; and apply the same, though improperly, to all the other senses. But the Greeks call it *fancy;* which signifies *appearance,* and is as proper to one sense, as to another. IMAGINATION therefore is nothing but *decaying sense;* and is found in men, and many other living creatures, as well sleeping, as waking.

The decay of sense in men waking, is not the decay of the motion made in sense; but an obscuring of it, in such manner as the light of the sun obscureth the light of the stars; which stars do no less exercise their virtue, by which they are visible, in the day, than in the night. But because amongst many strokes, which our eyes, ears, and other organs receive from external bodies, the predominant only is sensible; therefore the light of the sun being predominant, we are not affected with the action of the stars. And any object being removed from our eyes, though the impression it made in us remain; yet other objects more present succeeding, and working on us, the imagination of the past is obscured, and made weak, as the voice of a man is in the noise of the day. From whence it followeth, that the longer the time is, after the sight or sense of any object, the weaker is the imagination. For the continual change of man's body destroys in time the parts which in sense were moved: so that distance of time, and of place, hath one and the same effect in us. For as at a great distance of place, that which we look at appears dim, and without distinction of the smaller parts; and as voices grow weak, and inarticulate: so also, after great distance of time, our imagination for the past is weak; and we lose (for example) of cities we have seen, many particular streets, and of actions, many particular circumstances. This *decaying sense,* when we would express the thing it self, (I mean *fancy* it self,) we call *imagination,* as I said before: but when we would express the *decay,* and signify that the sense is fading, old and past, it is called *memory.* So that *imagination* and *memory* are but one thing, which for divers considerations hath divers names.

Much memory, or memory of many things, is called *experience.* Again, imagination being only of those things which have been formerly perceived by sense, either all at once, or by parts at several times; the former, (which is the imagining the whole object, as it was presented to the sense) is *simple imagination;* as when one imagineth a man, or horse, which he hath seen before. The other is *compounded;* as when from the sight of a man at one time, and of a horse at another, we conceive in our mind a Centaur. So when a man compoundeth the image of his own person with the image of the actions of another man; as when a man imagines himself a *Hercules* or an *Alexander,* (which happeneth often to them that are much taken with reading of romances) it is a compound imagination, and properly but a fiction of the mind. There be also other imaginations that rise in men, (though waking) from the great impression made in sense: as from gazing upon the sun, the impression leaves an image of the sun before our eyes a long time after; and from being long and vehemently attent upon geometrical figures, a man shall in the dark, (though awake) have the images of lines and angles before his eyes: which kind of fancy hath no particular name; as being a thing that doth not commonly fall into men's discourse.

The imaginations of them that sleep are those we call *dreams.* And these also (as all other imaginations) have been before, either totally or by parcels in the sense. And because in sense, the brain and nerves, which are the necessary organs of sense, are so benumbed in sleep, as not easily to be moved by the action of external objects, there can happen in sleep no imagination; and therefore no dream, but what proceeds from the agitation of the inward parts of man's body; which inward parts, for the connexion they have with the brain, and other organs, when they be distempered, do keep the same in motion; whereby the imaginations there formerly made, appear as if a man were waking: saving that the organs of sense being now benumbed, so as there is no new object, which can master and obscure them with a more vigorous impression, a dream must needs be more clear, in this silence of sense, than are our waking thoughts. And hence it cometh to pass, that it is a hard matter, and by many thought impossible to distinguish exactly between sense and dreaming. For my part, when I consider that in dreams, I do not often, nor constantly think of the same persons, places, objects, and actions that I do waking; nor remember so long a train of coherent thoughts, dreaming, as at other times; and because waking I often observe the absurdity of dreams, but never dream of the absurdities of my waking thoughts; I am well satisfied, that being awake, I know I dream not; though when I dream I think myself awake.

And seeing dreams are caused by the distemper of some of the inward parts of the body; divers distempers must needs cause different dreams. And hence it is, that lying cold breedeth dreams of fear, and raiseth the thought and image of some fearful object (the motion from the brain to the inner parts, and from the inner parts to the brain being reciprocal;) and that as anger causeth heat in some parts of the body, when we are awake; so when we sleep the over heating of the same parts causeth anger, and raiseth up in the brain the imagination of an enemy. In the same manner, as natural kindness, when we are awake, causeth desire; and desire makes heat in certain other parts of the body; so also, too much heat in those parts, while we sleep, raiseth in the brain an imagination of some kindness shown. In sum, our dreams are the reverse of our waking imaginations; the motion when we are awake, beginning at one end; and when we dream, at another.

The most difficult discerning of a man's dream, from his waking thoughts, is then, when by some accident we observe not that we have slept: which is easy to happen to a man full of fearful thoughts; and whose conscience is much troubled; and that sleepeth, without the circumstances, of going to bed, or putting off his clothes, as one that noddeth in a chair. For he that taketh pains, and industriously lays himself to sleep, in case any uncouth and exorbitant fancy come unto him, cannot easily think it other than a dream. We read of *Marcus Brutus,* (one that had his life given him by *Julius Caesar,* and was also his favourite, and notwithstanding murdered him), how at *Philippi,* the night before he gave battle to *Augustus Caesar,* he saw a fearful apparition, which is commonly related by historians as a vision; but considering the circumstances, one may easily judge to have been but a short dream. For sitting in his tent, pensive and troubled with the horror of his rash act, it was not hard for him, slumbering in the cold, to dream of that which most affrighted him; which fear, as by degrees it made him wake; so also it must needs make the apparition by degrees to vanish; and having no assurance that he slept, he could have no cause to think it a dream, or any thing but a vision. And this is no very rare accident; for even they that be perfectly awake, if they be timorous, and superstitious, possessed with fearful tales, and alone in the dark, are subject to the like fancies; and believe they see spirits and dead men's ghosts walking in churchyards; whereas it is either their fancy only, or else the knavery of such persons, as make use of such superstitious fear, to pass disguised in the night, to places they would not be known to haunt.

From this ignorance of how to distinguish dreams, and other strong fancies, from vision and sense, did arise the greatest part of the religion of the Gentiles in time past, that worshipped satyrs, fawns, nymphs, and the like; and now-a-days the opinion that rude people have of fairies, ghosts, and goblins, and of the power of witches. For as for witches, I think not that their witchcraft is any real power; but yet that they are justly punished, for the false belief they have, that they can do such mischief, joined with their purpose to do it if they can: their trade being nearer to a new religion than to a craft or science. And for fairies, and walking ghosts, the opinion of them has I think been on purpose, either taught, or not confuted, to keep in credit the use of exorcism, of crosses, of holy water, and other such inventions of ghostly men. Nevertheless, there is no doubt, but God can make unnatural apparitions: But that he does it so often, as men need to fear such things, more than they fear the stay, or change, of the course of nature, which he also can stay, and change, is no point of Christian faith. But evil men under pretext that God can do any thing, are so bold as to say any thing when it serves their turn, though they think it untrue; it is the part of a wise man, to believe them no further, than right reason makes that which they say, appear credible. If this superstitious fear of spirits were taken away, and with it, prognostics from dreams, false prophecies, and many other things depending thereon, by which, crafty ambitious persons abuse the simple people, men would be much more fitted than they are for civil obedience.

And this ought to be the work of the schools: but they rather nourish such doctrine. For (not knowing what imagination, or the senses are), what they receive, they teach: some saying, that imaginations rise of themselves, and have no cause; others, that they rise most commonly from the will; and that good thoughts are blown (inspired) into a man by God, and evil thoughts by the Devil; or that good thoughts are poured (infused) into a man by God, and evil ones by the Devil. Some say the senses receive the species of things, and deliver them to the common sense; and the common sense delivers them over to the fancy, and the fancy to the memory, and the memory to the judgement, like handing of things from one to another, with many words making nothing understood.

The imagination that is raised in man (or any other creature indued with the faculty of imagining) by words, or other voluntary signs, is that we generally call *understanding;* and is common to man and beast. For a dog by custom will understand the call, or the rating of his master; and so will many other beasts. That understanding which is peculiar to man, is the understanding not only his will, but his conceptions and thoughts, by the sequel and contexture of the names of things into affirmations, negations, and other forms of speech; and of this kind of understanding I shall speak hereafter.

CHAPTER 3

Of the Consequence or Train of Imaginations

By *Consequence,* or TRAIN of thoughts, I understand that succession of one thought to another, which is called (to distinguish it from discourse in words) *mental discourse.*

When a man thinketh on any thing whatsoever, his next thought after, is not altogether so casual as it seems to be. Not every thought to every thought succeeds indifferently. But as we have no imagination, whereof we have not formerly had sense, in whole, or in parts; so we have no transition from one imagination to another, whereof we never had the like before in our senses. The reason whereof is this. All fancies are motions within us, relics of those made in the sense: and those motions that immediately succeeded one another in the sense, continue also together after sense: insomuch as the former coming again to take place, and be predominant, the latter followeth, by coherence of the matter moved, in such manner, as water upon a plain table is drawn which way any one part of it is guided by the finger. But because in sense, to one and the same thing perceived, sometimes one thing, sometimes another succeedeth, it comes to pass in time, that in the imagining of any thing, there is no certainty what we shall imagine next; only this is certain, it shall be something that succeeded the same before, at one time or another.

This train of thoughts, or mental discourse, is of two sorts. The first is *unguided, without design,* and inconstant; wherein there is no passionate thought, to govern and direct those that follow, to it self, as the end and scope of some desire, or other passion: in which case the thoughts are said to wander, and seem impertinent one to another, as in a dream. Such are commonly the thoughts of men, that are not only without company, but also without care of any thing; though even then their thoughts are as busy as at other times, but without harmony; as the sound which a lute out of tune would yield to any man; or in tune, to one that could not play. And yet in this wild ranging of the mind, a man may oft-times perceive the way of it, and the dependance of one thought upon another. For in a discourse of our present civil war, what could seem more impertinent, than to ask (as one did) what was the value of a Roman penny? Yet the coherence to me was manifest enough. For the thought of the war, introduced the thought of the delivering up the king to his enemies; the thought of that, brought in the thought of the delivering up of Christ; and that again the thought of the 30 pence, which was the price of that treason; and thence easily followed that malicious question, and all this in a moment of time; for thought is quick.

The second is more constant; as being *regulated* by some desire, and design. For the impression made by such things as we desire, or fear, is strong, and permanent, or, (if it cease for a time,) of quick return; so strong it is sometimes, as to hinder and break our sleep. From desire, ariseth the thought of some means we have seen produce the like of that which we aim at; and from the thought of that, the thought of means to that mean;

and so continually, till we come to some beginning within our own power. And because the end, by the greatness of the impression, comes often to mind, in case our thoughts begin to wander, they are quickly again reduced into the way; which observed by one of the seven wise men, made him give men this precept, which is now worn out, *Respice finem;* that is to say, in all your actions, look often upon what you would have, as the thing that directs all your thoughts in the way to attain it.

The train of regulated thoughts is of two kinds; one, when of an effect imagined, we seek the causes, or means that produce it: and this is common to man and beast. The other is, when imagining any thing whatsoever, we seek all the possible effects, that can by it be produced; that is to say, we imagine what we can do with it, when we have it. Of which I have not at any time seen any sign, but in man only; for this is a curiosity hardly incident to the nature of any living creature that has no other passion but sensual, such as are hunger, thirst, lust, and anger. In sum, the discourse of the mind, when it is governed by design, is nothing but *seeking,* or the faculty of invention, which the Latins called *sagacitas,* and *solertia;* a hunting out of the causes, of some effect, present or past; or of the effects, of some present or past cause. Sometimes a man seeks what he hath lost; and from that place, and time, wherein he misses it, his mind runs back, from place to place, and time to time, to find where, and when he had it; that is to say, to find some certain, and limited time and place, in which to begin a method of seeking. Again, from thence, his thoughts run over the same places and times, to find what action, or other occasion might make him lose it. This we call *remembrance,* or calling to mind: the Latins call it *reminiscentia,* as it were a *re-conning* of our former actions.

Sometimes a man knows a place determinate, within the compass whereof he is to seek; and then his thoughts run over all the parts thereof, in the same manner as one would sweep a room, to find a jewel; or as a spaniel ranges the field, till he find a scent; or as a man should run over the alphabet, to start a rhyme.

Sometime a man desires to know the event of an action; and then he thinketh of some like action past, and the events thereof one after another; supposing like events will follow like actions. As he that foresees what will become of a criminal, recons what he has seen follow on the like crime before; having this order of thoughts, the crime, the officer, the prison, the judge, and the gallows. Which kind of thoughts, is called *foresight,* and *prudence,* or *providence;* and sometimes *wisdom;* though such conjecture, through the difficulty of observing all circumstances, be very fallacious. But this is certain; by how much one man has more experience of things past, than another; by so much also he is more prudent, and his expectations the seldomer fail him. The *present* only has a being in nature; things *past* have a being in the memory only, but things *to come* have no being at all; the *future* being but a fiction of the mind, applying the sequels of actions past, to the actions that are present; which with most certainty is done by him that has most experience; but not with certainty enough. And though it be called prudence, when the event answereth our expectation; yet in its own nature, it is but presumption. For the foresight of things to come, which is providence, belongs only to him by whose will they are to come. From him only, and supernaturally, proceeds prophecy. The best prophet naturally is the best guesser; and the best guesser, he that is most versed and studied in the matters he guesses at: for he hath most *signs* to guess by.

A *sign* is the event antecedent of the consequent; and contrarily, the consequent of the antecedent, when the like consequences have been observed, before: and the oftener they have been observed, the less uncertain is the sign. And therefore he that has most experience in any kind of business, has most signs, whereby to guess at the future time: and consequently is the most prudent: and so much more prudent than he that is new in that kind of business, as not to be equalled by any advantage of natural and extemporary wit: though perhaps many young men think the contrary.

Nevertheless it is not prudence that distinguisheth man from beast. There be beasts, that at a year old observe more, and pursue that which is for their good, more prudently, than a child can do at ten.

As prudence is a *presumption* of the *future*, contracted form the *experience* of time *past;* so there is a presumption of things past taken from other things (not future but) past also. For he that hath seen by what courses and degrees, a flourishing state hath first come into civil war, and then to ruin; upon the sight of the ruins of any other state, will guess, the like war, and the like courses have been there also. But this conjecture, has the same uncertainty almost with the conjecture of the future; both being grounded only upon experience.

There is no other act of man's mind, that I can remember, naturally planted in him, so as to need no other thing, to the exercise of it, but to be born a man, and live with the use of his five senses. Those other faculties, of which I shall speak by and by, and which seem proper to man only, are acquired, and increased by study and industry; and of most men learned by instruction, and discipline; and proceed all from the invention of words, and speech. For besides sense, and thoughts, and the train of thoughts, the mind of man has no other motion: though by the help of speech, and method, the same faculties may be improved to such a height, as to distinguish men from all other living creatures.

Whatsoever we imagine is *finite.* Therefore there is no idea, or conception of any thing we call *infinite.* No man can have in his mind an image of infinite magnitude; nor conceive infinite swiftness, infinite time, or infinite force, or infinite power. When we say any thing is infinite, we signify only, that we are not able to conceive the ends, and bounds of the things named; having no conception of the thing, but of our own inability. And therefore the name of God is used, not to make us conceive him; (for he is *incomprehensible;* and his greatness, and power are unconceivable;) but that we may honour him. Also because whatsoever (as I said before,) we conceive, has been perceived first by sense, either all at once, or by parts; a man can have no thought, representing any thing, not subject to sense. No man therefore can conceive any thing, but he must conceive it in some place; and indued with some determinate magnitude; and which may be divided into parts; nor that any thing is all in this place, and all in another place at the same time; nor that two, or more things can be in one, and the same place at once; for none of these things ever have, or can be incident to sense; but are absurd speeches, taken upon credit (without any signification at all,) from deceived philosophers, and deceived, or deceiving schoolmen.

CHAPTER 4

Of Speech

The invention of *printing,* though ingenious, compared with the invention of *letters,* is no great matter. But who was the first that found the use of letters, is not known. He that first brought them into *Greece,* men say was *Cadmus,* the son of *Agenor,* king of Phoenicia. A profitable invention for continuing the memory of time past, and the conjunction of mankind, dispersed into so many, and distant regions of the earth; and withal difficult, as proceeding from a watchful observation of the divers motions of the tongue, palate, lips, and other organs of speech; whereby to make as many differences of characters, to remember them. But the most noble and profitable invention of all other, was that of SPEECH, consisting of *names* or *appellations,* and their connexion; whereby men register their thoughts; recall them when they are past; and also declare them one to another for mutual utility and conversation; without which, there had been amongst men, neither commonwealth, nor society, nor contract, nor peace, no more than amongst lions, bears, and wolves. The first author of speech was God himself, that instructed Adam how to name such creatures as he presented to his sight; for the Scripture goeth no further in this matter. But this was sufficient to direct him to add more names, as the experience and use of the creatures should give him occasion; and to join them in such manner by degrees, as to make himself understood; and so by succession of time, so much language might be gotten, as he had found use for; though not so copious, as an orator or philosopher has need of. For I do not find any thing in the Scripture, out of which, directly or by consequence can be gathered, that *Adam* was taught the names of all figures, numbers, measures, colours, sounds, fancies, relations; much less the names of words and speech, as *general, special, affirmative, negative, interrogative, optative, infinitive,* all which are useful; and least of all, of *entity, intentionality, quiddity,* and other insignificant words of the school.

But all this language gotten, and augmented by *Adam* and his posterity, was again lost at the tower of *Babel,* when, by the hand of God, every man was stricken, for his rebellion, with an oblivion of his former language. And being hereby forced to disperse themselves into several parts of the world, it must needs be, that the diversity of tongues that now is, proceeded by degrees from them, in such manner as need (the mother of all inventions) taught them; and in tract of time grew every where more copious.

The general use of speech, is to transfer our mental discourse, into verbal; or the train of our thoughts, into a train of words; and that for two commodities, whereof one is the registering of the consequences of our thoughts; which being apt to slip out of our memory, and put us to a new labour, may again be recalled, by such words as they were marked by. So that the first use of names is to serve for *marks, or notes* of remembrance. Another is, when many use the same words, to signify (by their connexion and order,) one to another, what they conceive, or think of each matter; and also what they desire, fear, or have any other passion for. And for this use they are called *signs.* Special uses of speech are these; first, to register, what by cogitation, we find to be the cause of any thing, present or past; and what we find things present or past may produce, or effect: which in sum, is acquiring of arts. Secondly, to show to others that knowledge which we have attained; which is, to counsel and teach one another. Thirdly, to make known to others our wills, and purposes, that we may have the mutual help of one another. Fourthly, to please and delight ourselves and others, by playing with our words, for pleasure or ornament, innocently.

To these uses, there are also four correspondent abuses. First, when men register their thoughts wrong, by the inconstancy of the signification of their words; by which they register for their conceptions, that which they never conceived, and so deceive themselves. Secondly, when they use words metaphorically; that is, in other sense than that they are ordained for; and thereby deceive others. Thirdly, when by words they declare that to be their will, which is not. Fourthly, when they use them to grieve one another: for seeing nature hath armed living creatures, some with teeth, some with horns, and some with hands, to grieve an enemy, it is but an abuse of speech, to grieve him with the tongue, unless it be one whom we are obliged to govern; and then it is not to grieve, but to correct and amend.

The manner how speech serveth to the remembrance of the consequence of causes and effects, consisteth in the imposing of *names,* and the *connexion* of them.

Of names, some are *proper,* and singular to one only thing, as *Peter, John, this man, this tree:* and some are *common* to many things, as *man, horse, tree;* every of which though but one name, is nevertheless the name of divers particular things; in respect of all which together, it is called an *universal;* there being nothing in the world universal but names; for the things named, are every one of them individual and singular.

One universal name is imposed on many things, for their similitude in some quality, or other accident; and whereas a proper name bringeth to mind one thing only, universals recall any one of those many.

And of names universal, some are of more, and some of less extent; the larger comprehending the less large: and some again of equal extent, comprehending each other reciprocally. As for example, the name *body* is of larger signification than the word *man,* and comprehendeth it; and the names *man* and *rational,* are of equal extent, comprehending mutually one another. But here we must take notice, that by a name is not always understood, as in grammar, one only word; but sometimes by circumlocution many words together. For all these words, *he that in his actions observeth the laws of his country,* make but one name, equivalent to this one word, *just.*

By this imposition of names, some of larger, some of stricter signification, we turn the reckoning of the consequences of things imagined in the mind, into a reckoning of the consequences of appellations. For example, a man that hath no use of speech at all, (such as is born and remains perfectly deaf and dumb,) if he set before his eyes a triangle, and by it two right angles, (such as are the corners of a square figure,) he may by meditation compare and find, that the three angles of that triangle, are equal to those two right angles that stand by it. But if another triangle be shown him, different in shape from the former, he cannot know without a new labour, whether the three angles of that also be equal to the same. But he that hath the use of words, when he observes, that such equality was consequent, not to the length of the sides, nor to any other particular thing in his triangle; but only to this, that the sides were straight, and the angles three; and that that was all, for which he named it a triangle; will boldly conclude universally, that such equality of angles is in all triangles whatsoever; and register his invention in these general terms, *every triangle hath its three angles equal to two right angles.* And thus the consequence found in one particular, comes to be registered and remembered, as an universal rule, and discharges our mental reckoning, of time and place, and delivers us from all labour of the mind, saving the first, and makes that which was found true *here,* and *now,* to be true in *all times* and *places.*

But the use of words in registering our thoughts is in nothing so evident as in numbering. A natural fool that could never learn by heart the order of numeral words, as *one, two,* and *three,* may observe every stroke of the clock, and nod to it, or say *one, one, one,* but can never know what hour it strikes. And it seems, there was a time when those names of number were not in use; and men were fain to apply their fingers of one or both hands, to those things they desired to keep account of; and that thence it proceeded, that now our numeral words are but ten, in any nation, and in some but five, and then they begin again. And he that can tell ten, if he recite them out of order, will lose himself, and not know when he has done. Much less will he be able to add, and subtract, and perform all other operations of arithmetic. So that without words there is no possibility of reckoning of numbers; much less of magnitudes, of swiftness, of force, and other things, the reckonings whereof are necessary to the being, or well-being of mankind.

When two names are joined together into a consequence, or affirmation, as thus, *a man is a living creature;* or thus, *if he be a man, he is a living creature,* if the latter name *living creature,* signify all that the former name *man* signifieth, then the affirmation, or consequence is *true;* otherwise *false.* For *true* and *false* are attributes of speech, not of things. And where speech is not, there is neither *truth* nor *falsehood. Error* there may be, as when we expect that which shall not be, or suspect what has not been: but in neither case can a man be charged with untruth.

Seeing then that *truth* consisteth in the right ordering of names in our affirmations, a man that seeketh precise *truth* had need to remember what every name he uses stands for, and to place it accordingly; or else he will find himself entangled in words, as a bird in lime twigs, the more he struggles the more belimed. And therefore in geometry, (which is the only science that it hath pleased God hitherto to bestow on mankind,) men begin at settling the significations of their words; which settling of significations they call *definitions,* and place them in the beginning of their reckoning.

By this it appears how necessary it is for any man that aspires to true knowledge, to examine the definitions of former authors; and either to correct them, where they are negligently set down, or to make them himself. For the errors of definitions multiply themselves according as the reckoning proceeds, and lead men into absurdities, which at last they see, but cannot avoid, without reckoning anew from the beginning, in which lies the foundation of their errors. From whence it happens, that they which trust to books do as they that cast up many little sums into a greater, without considering whether those little sums were rightly cast up or not; and at last finding the error visible, and not mistrusting their first grounds, know not which way to clear themselves, but spend time in fluttering over their books; as birds that entering by the chimney, and finding themselves enclosed in a chamber, flutter at the false light of a glass window, for want of wit to consider which way they came in. So that in the right definition of names lies the first use of speech; which is the acquisition of science: and in wrong, or no definitions, lies the first abuse; from which proceed all false and senseless tenets; which make those men that take their instruction from the authority of books, and not from their own meditation, to be as much below the condition of ignorant men, as men endued with true science are above it. For between true science and erroneous doctrines, ignorance is in the middle. Natural sense and imagination are not subject to absurdity. Nature itself cannot err; and as men abound in copiousness of language, so they become more wise, or more mad than ordinary. Nor is it possible without letters for any man to become either excellently wise, or (unless his memory be hurt by disease or ill constitution of organs) excellently foolish. For words are wise men's counters, they do but reckon by them; but they are the money of fools, that value them by the authority of an *Aristotle,* a *Cicero,* or a *Thomas,* or any other doctor whatsoever, if but a man.

Subject to names, is whatsoever can enter into or be considered in an account, and be added one to another to make a sum, or subtracted one from another and leave a remainder. The Latins called accounts of money *rationes,* and accounting *ratiocinatio;* and that which we in bills or books of account call *items,* they call *nomina,* that is *names;* and thence it seems to proceed, that they extended the word *ratio* to the faculty of reckoning in all other things. The Greeks have but one word, λóγος, for both *speech* and *reason;* not that they thought there was no speech without reason, but no reasoning without speech: and the act of reasoning they called *syllogism,* which signifieth summing up of the consequences of one saying to another. And because the same things may enter into account for divers accidents, their names are (to show that diversity) diversly wrested and diversified. This diversity of names may be reduced to four general heads.

First, a thing may enter into account for *matter* or *body;* as *living, sensible, rational, hot, cold, moved, quiet;* with all which names the word *matter,* or *body,* is understood; all such being names of matter.

Secondly, it may enter into account, or be considered, for some accident or quality, which we conceive to be in it; as for *being moved,* for *being so long,* for *being hot,* &c.; and then, of the name of the thing it self, by a little change or wresting, we make a name for that accident, which we consider; and for *living* put into the account *life;* for *moved, motion;* for *hot, heat;* for *long, length,* and the like: and all such names are the names of the accidents and properties by which one matter and body is distinguished from another. These are called *names abstract,* because severed (not from matter, but) from the account of matter.

Thirdly, we bring into account the properties of our own bodies, whereby we make such distinction; as when any thing is *seen* by us, we reckon not the thing it self, but the *sight,* the *colour,* the *idea* of it in the fancy: and when any thing is *heard,* we reckon it not, but the *hearing* or *sound* only, which is our fancy or conception of it by the ear; and such are names of fancies.

Fourthly, we bring into account, consider, and give names, to *names* themselves, and to *speeches:* For *general, universal, special, equivocal,* are names of names. And *affirmation, inter-rogation, commandment, narration, syllogism, sermon, oration,* and many other such, are names of speeches. And this is all the variety of names *positive;* which are put to mark somewhat which is in nature, or may be feigned by the mind of man, as bodies that are, or may be conceived to be; or of bodies, the properties that are, or may be feigned to be; or words and speech.

There be also other names, called *negative,* which are notes to signify that a word is not the name of the thing in question; as these words *nothing, no man, infinite, indocible, three want four,* and the like; which are nevertheless of use in reckoning, or in correcting of reck-oning, and call to mind our past cogitations, though they be not names of any thing, because they make us refuse to admit of names not rightly used.

All other names are but insignificant sounds; and those of two sorts. One when they are new, and yet their meaning not explained by definition; whereof there have been abundance coined by schoolmen, and puzzled philosophers.

Another, when men make a name of two names, whose significations are contradictory and inconsistent; as this name, an *incorporeal body,* or (which is all one) an *incorporeal substance,* and a great number more. For whensoever any affirmation is false, the two names of which it is composed, put together and made one, signify nothing at all. For example, if it be a false affirmation to say a *quadrangle is round,* the word *round quadrangle* signifies nothing, but is a mere sound. So likewise, if it be false to say that virtue can be poured, or blown up and down, the words *in-poured virtue, in-blown virtue,* are as absurd and insignificant as a *round quadrangle.* And therefore you shall hardly meet with a senseless and insignificant word, that is not made up of some Latin or Greek names. A Frenchman seldom hears our Saviour called by the name of *parole,* but by the name of *verbe* often; yet *verbe* and *parole* differ no more, but that one is Latin, the other French.

When a man, upon the hearing of any speech, hath those thoughts which the words of that speech, and their connexion, were ordained and constituted to signify, then he is said to understand it; *understanding* being nothing else but conception caused by speech. And therefore if speech be peculiar to man (as for aught I know it is,) then is understanding peculiar to him also. And therefore of absurd and false affirmations, in case they be uni-versal, there can be no understanding; though many think they understand then, when they do but repeat the words softly or con them in their mind.

What kinds of speeches signify the appetites, aversions, and passions of man's mind; and of their use and abuse, I shall speak when I have spoken of the passions.

The names of such things as affect us, that is, which please and displease us, because all men be not alike affected with the same thing, nor the same man at all times, are in the common discourses of men of *inconstant* signification. For seeing all names are imposed to signify our conceptions, and all our affections are but conceptions, when we conceive the same things differently, we can hardly avoid different naming of them. For though the nature of that we conceive, be the same yet the diversity of our reception of it, in respect of different constitutions of both and prejudices of opinion, gives every thing a tincture of our different passions. And therefore in reasoning a man must take heed of words; which besides the signification of what we imagine of their nature, have a signification also of the nature, disposition, and interest of the speaker; such as are the names of virtues and vices; for one man calleth *wisdom,* what another calleth *fear;* and one *cruelty,* what another *justice;* one *prodigality,* what another *magnanimity;* and one *gravity,* what another *stupidity,* &c. And therefore such names can never be true grounds of any ratiocination. No more can metaphors, and tropes of speech; but these are less dangerous, because they profess their inconstancy; which the other do not.

CHAPTER 5

Of Reason and Science

When a man *reasoneth,* he does nothing else but conceive a sum total, from *addition* of parcels; or conceive a remainder, from *subtraction* of one sum from another; which (if it be done by words,) is conceiving of the consequence of the names of all the parts, to the name of the whole; or from the names of the whole and one part, to the name of the other part. And though in some things, (as in numbers,) besides *adding* and *subtracting,* men name other operations, as *multiplying* and *dividing,* yet they are the same; for multiplication, is but adding together of things equal; and division, but subtracting of one thing, as often as we can. These operations are not evident to numbers only, but to all manner of things that can be added together, and taken one out of another. For as arithmeticians teach to add and subtract in *numbers;* so the geometricians teach the same in *lines, figures* (solid and superficial,) *angles, proportions, times, degrees of swiftness, force, power,* and the like; the logicians teach the same in *consequences of words;* adding together *two names* to make an *affirmation,* and *two affirmations* to make a *syllogism;* and *many syllogisms* to make a *demonstration;* and from the *sum,* or *conclusion* of a *syllogism,* they subtract one *proposition* to find the other. Writers of politics add together *pactions* to find men's *duties;* and lawyers, *laws* and *facts,* to find what is *right* and *wrong* in the actions of private men. In sum, in what matter soever there is place for *addition* and *subtraction,* there also is place for *reason;* and where these have no place, there *reason* has nothing at all to do.

Out of all which we may define, (that is to say determine,) what that is, which is meant by this word *reason,* when we reckon it amongst the faculties of the mind. For REASON, in this sense, is nothing but *reckoning* (that is, adding and subtracting) of the consequences of general names agreed upon for the *marking* and *signifying* of our thoughts; I say *marking* them when we reckon by ourselves, and *signifying,* when we demonstrate or approve our reckonings to other men.

And as in arithmetic, unpractised men must, and professors themselves may often err, and cast up false; so also in any other subject of reasoning, the ablest, most attentive, and most practised men may deceive themselves, and infer false conclusions; not but that reason itself is always right reason, as well as arithmetic is a certain and infallible art: but no one man's reason, nor the reason of any one number of men, makes the certainty; no more than an account is therefore well cast up, because a great many men have unanimously approved it. And therefore, as when there is a controversy in an account, the parties must by their own accord, set up for right reason, the reason of some arbitrator, or judge, to whose sentence they will both stand, or their controversy must either come to blows, or be undecided, for want of a right reason constituted by nature; so is it also in all debates of what kind soever. And when men that think themselves wiser than all others, clamour and demand right reason for judge, yet seek no more, but that things should be determined by no other men's reason but their own, it is as intolerable in the society of men, as it is in play after trump is turned, to use for trump on every occasion, that suite whereof they have most in their hand. For they do nothing else, that will have every of their passions, as it comes to bear sway in them, to be taken for right reason, and that in their own controversies: bewraying their want of right reason, by the claim they lay to it.

The use and end of reason, is not the finding of the sum and truth of one, or a few consequences, remote from the first definitions, and settled significations of names, but to begin at these, and proceed from one consequence to another. For there can be no certainty of the last conclusion, without a certainty of all those affirmations and negations, on which it was grounded and inferred. As when a master of a family, in taking an account, casteth up the sums of all the bills of expense into one sum, and not regarding how each bill is summed up, by those that give them in account; nor what it is he pays for; he advantages himself no more than if he allowed the account in gross, trusting to every of the accountants' skill and honesty: so also in reasoning of all other things, he that takes up conclusions on the trust of authors, and doth not fetch them from the first items in every reckoning, (which are the significations of names settled by definitions,) loses his labour; and does not know any thing, but only believeth.

When a man reckons without the use of words, which may be done in particular things, (as when upon the sight of any one thing, we conjecture what was likely to have preceded, or is likely to follow upon it;) if that which he thought likely to follow, follows not, or that which he thought likely to have preceded it, hath not preceded it, this is called *error;* to which even the most prudent men are subject. But when we reason in words of general signification, and fall upon a general inference which is false, though it be commonly called error, it is indeed an *absurdity,* or senseless speech. For error is but a deception, in presuming that somewhat is past or to come; of which, though it were not past, or not to come, yet there was no impossibility discoverable. But when we make a general assertion, unless it be a true one, the possibility of it is inconceivable. And words whereby we conceive nothing but the sound, are those we call *absurd, insignificant,* and *nonsense.* And therefore if a man should talk to me of a *round quadrangle;* or, *accidents of bread in cheese;* or *immaterial substances;* or of a *free subject; a free will;* or any *free,* but free from being hindered by opposition, I should not say he were in an error, but that his words were without meaning, that is to say, absurd.

I have said before, (in the second chapter,) that a man did excel all other animals in this faculty, that when he conceived any thing whatsoever, he was apt to inquire the consequences of it, and what effects he could do with it. And now I add this other degree of the same excellence, that he can by words reduce the consequences he finds to general rules, called *theorems,* or *aphorisms;* that is, he can reason, or reckon, not only in number, but in all other things, whereof one may be added unto or subtracted from another.

But this privilege is allayed by another; and that is, by the privilege of absurdity, to which no living creature is subject, but man only. And of men, those are of all most subject to it, that profess philosophy. For it is most true that Cicero saith of them somewhere; that there can be nothing so absurd, but may be found in the books of philosophers. And the reason is manifest. For there is not one of them that begins his ratiocination from the definitions, or explications of the names they are to use; which is a method that hath been used only in geometry; whose conclusions have thereby been made indisputable.

I.   The first cause of absurd conclusions I ascribe to the want of method; in that they begin not their ratiocination from definitions; that is, from settled significations of their words: as if they could cast account, without knowing the value of the numeral words, *one, two,* and *three.*

      And whereas all bodies enter into account upon divers considerations, (which I have mentioned in the precedent chapter;) these considerations being diversely named, divers absurdities proceed from the confusion, and unfit connexion of their names into assertions. And therefore,

II.   The second cause of absurd assertions, I ascribe to the giving of names of *bodies* to *accidents;* or of *accidents* to *bodies;* as they do, that say, *faith is infused,* or *inspired;* when nothing can be *poured,* or *breathed* into any thing, but body; and that, *extension to body;* that *phantasms* are *spirits,* &c.

III.   The third I ascribe to the giving of names of the *accidents* of *bodies without us,* to the *accidents* of our *own bodies;* as they do that say, the *colour is in the body; the sound is in the air,* &c.

IV.   The fourth, to the giving of the names of *bodies* to *names,* or *speeches;* as they do that say, that *there be things universal;* that *a living creature is genus,* or *a general thing,* &c.

V.   The fifth, to the giving of the names of *accidents* to *names* and *speeches;* as they do that say, *the nature of a thing is its definition; a man's command is his will;* and the like.

VI.   The sixth, to the use of metaphors, tropes, and other rhetorical figures, instead of words proper. For though it be lawful to say, (for example) in common speech, *the way goeth, or leadeth hither, or thither; the proverb says this or that* (whereas ways cannot go, nor proverbs speak;) yet in reckoning, and seeking of truth, such speeches are not to be admitted.

VII. The seventh, to names that signify nothing; but are taken up, and learned by rote from the schools, as *hypostatical, transubstantiate, consubstantiate, eternal-now,* and the like canting of schoolmen.

To him that can avoid these things it is not easy to fall into any absurdity, unless it be by the length of an account; wherein he may perhaps forget what went before. For all men by nature reason alike, and well, when they have good principles. For who is so stupid, as both to mistake in geometry, and also to persist in it, when another detects his error to him?

By this it appears that reason is not, as sense and memory, born with us; nor gotten by experience only, as prudence is; but attained by industry; first in apt imposing of names; and secondly by getting a good and orderly method in proceeding from the elements, which are names, to assertions made by connexion of one of them to another; and so to syllogisms, which are the connexions of one assertion to another, till we come to a knowledge of all the consequences of names appertaining to the subject in hand; and that is it, men call SCIENCE. And whereas sense and memory are but knowledge of fact, which is a thing past, and irrevocable; *Science* is the knowledge of consequences, and dependance of one fact upon another: by which, out of that we can presently do, we know how to do something else when we will, or the like, another time; because when we see how any thing comes about, upon what causes, and by what manner; when the like causes come into our power, we see how to make it produce the like effects.

Children therefore are not endued with reason at all, till they have attained the use of speech; but are called reasonable creatures, for the possibility apparent of having the use of reason in time to come. And the most part of men, though they have the use of reasoning a little way, as in numbering to some degree; yet it serves them to little use in common life; in which they govern themselves, some better, some worse, according to their differences of experience, quickness of memory, and inclinations to several ends; but specially according to good or evil fortune, and the errors of one another. For as for *science,* or certain rules of their actions, they are so far from it, that they know not what it is.

Geometry they have thought conjuring but for other sciences, they who have not been taught the beginnings and some progress in them, that they may see how they be acquired and generated, are in this point like children, that having no thought of generation, are made believe by the women that their brothers and sisters are not born, but found in the garden.

But yet they that have no *science*, are in better, and nobler condition, with their natural prudence; than men, that by mis-reasoning, or by trusting them that reason wrong, fall upon false and absurd general rules. For ignorance of causes, and of rules, does not set men so far out of their way, as relying on false rules, and taking for causes of what they aspire to, those that are not so, but rather causes of the contrary.

To conclude, the light of human minds is perspicuous words, but by exact definitions first snuffed, and purged from ambiguity; *reason* is the *pace;* increase of *science* the *way;* and the benefit of mankind, the *end.* And on the contrary, metaphors, and senseless and ambiguous words, are like *ignes fatui;* and reasoning upon them a wandering amongst innumerable absurdities; and their end, contention and sedition, or contempt.

As much experience, is *prudence;* so, is much science *sapience.* For though we usually have one name of wisdom for them both, yet the Latins did always distinguish between *prudentia* and *sapientia;* ascribing the former to experience, the latter to science. But to make their difference appear more clearly, let us suppose one man endued with an excellent natural use and dexterity in handling his arms; and another to have added to that dexterity, an acquired science, of where he can offend, or be offended by his adversary, in every possible posture or guard: the ability of the former, would be to the ability of the latter, as prudence to sapience; both useful but the latter infallible. But they that trusting only to the authority of books, follow the blind blindly, are like him that, trusting to the false rules of a master of fence ventures presumptuously upon an adversary, that either kills or disgraces him.

The signs of science are some, certain and infallible; some, uncertain. Certain when he that pretendeth the science of any thing, can teach the same, that is to say demonstrate the truth thereof perspicuously to another; uncertain, when only some particular events answer to his pretence, and upon many occasions prove so as he said they must. Signs of prudence are all uncertain; because to observe by experience, and remember all circumstances that may alter the success, is impossible. But in any business, whereof a man has not infallible science to proceed by; to forsake his own natural judgment, and be guided by general sentences read in authors, and subject to many exceptions, is a sign of folly, and generally scorned by the name of pedantry. And even of those men themselves, that in councils of the commonwealth love to show their reading of politics and history, very few do it in their domestic affairs, where their particular interest is concerned; having prudence enough for their private affairs; but in public they study more the reputation of their own wit, than the success of another's business.

CHAPTER 6

Of the Interior Beginnings of Voluntary Motions:
Commonly Called the Passions; and the Speeches by Which They Are Expressed

There be in animals, two sorts of *motions* peculiar to them: one called *vital;* begun in generation, and continued without interruption through their whole life; such as are the *course* of the *blood,* the *pulse,* the *breathing,* the *concoction, nutrition, excretion,* &c.; to which motions there needs no help of imagination: the other is *animal motion,* otherwise called *voluntary motion;* as to *go,* to *speak,* to *move* any of our limbs, in such manner as is first fancied in our minds. That sense is motion in the organs and interior parts of man's body, caused by the action of the things we see, hear, &c.; and that fancy is but the relics of the same motion, remaining after sense, has been already said in the first and second chapters. And because *going, speaking,* and the like voluntary motions, depend always upon a precedent thought of *whither, which way,* and *what;* it is evident, that the imagination is the first internal beginning of all voluntary motion. And although unstudied men do not conceive any motion at all to be there, where the thing moved is invisible; or the space it is moved in, is (for the shortness of it) insensible; yet that doth not hinder, but that such motions are. For let a space be never so little, that which is moved over a greater space, whereof that little one is part, must first be moved over that. These small beginnings of motion, within the body of man, before they appear in walking, speaking, striking, and other visible actions, are commonly called ENDEAVOUR.

This endeavour, when it is toward something which causes it, is called APPETITE, or DESIRE; the latter, being the general name; and the other, oftentimes restrained to signify the desire of food, namely *hunger* and *thirst.* And when the endeavour is fromward something, it is generally called AVERSION. These words, *appetite* and *aversion,* we have from the *Latins;* and they both of them signify the motions, one of approaching, the other of retiring. So also do the Greek words for the same, which are ὁρμή and ἀφορμή. For nature itself does often press upon men those truths, which afterwards, when they look for somewhat beyond nature, they stumble at. For the Schools find in mere appetite to go, or move, no actual motion at all: but because some motion they must acknowledge, they call it metaphorical motion; which is but an absurd speech: for though words may be called metaphorical; bodies and motions cannot.

That which men desire, they are also said to LOVE: and to HATE those things for which they have aversion. So that desire and love are the same thing; save that by desire, we always signify the absence of the object; by love, most commonly the presence of the same. So also by aversion, we signify the absence; and by hate, the presence of the object.

Of appetites and aversions, some are born with men; as appetite of food, appetite of excretion and exoneration, (which may also and more properly be called aversions, from somewhat they feel in their bodies;) and some other appetites, not many. The rest, which are appetites of particular things, proceed from experience, and trial of their effects upon themselves or other men. For of things we know not at all, or believe not to be, we can have no further desire, than to taste and try. But aversion we have for things, not only which we know have hurt us, but also that we do not know whether they will hurt us, or not.

Those things which we neither desire, nor hate, we are said to *contemn;* CONTEMPT being nothing else but an immobility, or contumacy of the heart, in resisting the action of certain things; and proceeding from that the heart is already moved otherwise, by other more potent objects; or from want of experience of them.

And because the constitution of a man's body is in continual mutation, it is impossible that all the same things should always cause in him the same appetites, and aversions: much less can all men consent, in the desire of almost any one and the same object.

But whatsoever is the object of any man's appetite or desire, that is it which he for his part calleth *good:* and the object of his hate and aversion, *evil;* and of his contempt, *vile* and *inconsiderable.* For these words of good, evil, and contemptible, are ever used with relation to the person that useth them: there being nothing simply and absolutely so; nor any common rule of good and evil, to be taken from the nature of the objects themselves; but from the person of the man (where there is no commonwealth;) or, (in a commonwealth,) from the person that representeth it; or from an arbitrator or judge, whom men disagreeing shall by consent set up, and make his sentence the rule thereof.

The Latin tongue has two words, whose significations approach to those of good and evil; but are not precisely the same; and those are *pulchrum* and *turpe.* Whereof the former signifies that, which by some apparent signs promiseth good; and the latter, that which promiseth evil. But in our tongue we have not so general names to express them by. But for *pulchrum* we say in some things, *fair;* in others, *beautiful,* or *handsome,* or *gallant,* or *honourable,* or *comely,* or *amiable;* and for *turpe, foul, deformed, ugly, base, nauseous,* and the like, as the subject shall require; all which words, in their proper places, signify nothing else but the *mine,* or countenance, that promiseth good and evil. So that of good there be three kinds; good in the promise, that is *pulchrum;* good in effect, as the end desired, which is called *jucundum, delightful;* and good as the means, which is called *utile, profitable;* and as many of evil: for *evil* in promise, is that they call *turpe;* evil in effect, and end, is *molestum, unpleasant, troublesome;* and evil in the means, *inutile, unprofitable, hurtful.*

As, in sense, that which is really within us, is, (as I have said before,) only motion, caused by the action of external objects, but in apparence; to the sight, light and colour; to the ear, sound; to the nostril, odour, &c.: so, when the action of the same object is continued from the eyes, ears, and other organs to the heart, the real effect there is nothing but motion, or endeavour; which consisteth in appetite, or aversion, to or from the object moving. But the apparence, or sense of that motion is that we either call *delight,* or *trouble of mind.*

This motion, which is called appetite, and for the apparence of it *delight,* and *pleasure,* seemeth to be a corroboration of vital motion, and a help thereunto; and therefore such things as caused delight, were not improperly called *jucunda, (a juvando,)* from healing or forti-fying; and the contrary, *molesta, offensive,* from hindering, and troubling the motion vital.

Pleasure therefore, (or *delight,*) is the apparence, or sense of good; and *molestation* or *dis-pleasure,* the apparence, or sense of evil. And consequently all appetite, desire, and love, is accompanied with some delight more or less; and all hatred and aversion, with more or less displeasure and offence.

Of pleasures or delights, some arise from the sense of an object present; and those may be called *pleasures of sense,* (the word *sensual,* as it is used by those only that condemn them, hav-ing no place till there be laws.) Of this kind are all onerations and exonerations of the body; as also all that is pleasant, in the *sight, hearing, smell, taste, or touch.* Others arise from the ex-pectation, that proceeds from foresight of the end, or consequence of things; whether those things in the sense please or displease. And these are *pleasures of the mind* of him that draweth those consequence, and are generally called JOY. In the like manner, displeasures are some in the sense, and called PAIN; others in the expectation of consequences, and are called GRIEF.

These simple passions called *appetite, desire, love, aversion, hate, joy,* and *grief,* have their names for divers considerations diversified. As first, when they one succeed another, they are diversely called from the opinion men have of the likelihood of attaining what they desire. Secondly, from the object loved or hated. Thirdly, from the consideration of many of them together. Fourthly, from the alteration or succession it self.

· For *appetite,* with an opinion of attaining, is called HOPE.

· The same, without such opinion, DESPAIR.

· *Aversion,* with opinion of *hurt* from the object, FEAR.

· The same, with hope of avoiding that hurt by resistance, COURAGE.

· Sudden *courage,* ANGER.

· Constant *hope,* CONFIDENCE of ourselves.

· Constant *despair,* DIFFIDENCE of ourselves.

· *Anger* for great hurt done to another, when we conceive the same to be done by injury, INDIG-NATION.

· *Desire* of good to another, BENEVOLENCE, GOOD WILL, CHARITY. If to man generally, GOOD NATURE.

· *Desire* of riches, COVETOUSNESS: a name used always in signification of blame; because men contending for them, are displeased with one another's attaining them; though the desire in itself, be to be blamed, or allowed, according to the means by which those riches are sought.

· *Desire* of office, or precedence, AMBITION: a name used also in the worse sense, for the reason before mentioned.

· *Desire* of things that conduce but a little to our ends, and fear of things that are but of little hindrance, PUSILLANIMITY.

· *Contempt* of little helps and hindrances, MAGNANIMITY.

· *Magnanimity,* in danger of death or wounds, VALOUR, FORTITUDE.

· *Magnanimity,* in the use of riches, LIBERALITY.

· *Pusillanimity,* in the same, WRETCHEDNESS, MISERABLENESS, or PARSIMONY; as it is liked or disliked.

· *Love* of persons for society, KINDNESS.

· *Love* of persons for pleasing the sense only, NATURAL LUST.

· *Love* of the same, acquired from rumination, that is, imagination of pleasure past, LUXURY.

· *Love* of one singularly, with desire to be singularly beloved, THE PASSION OF LOVE. The same, with fear that the love is not mutual, JEALOUSY.

· *Desire,* by doing hurt to another, to make him condemn some fact of his own, REVENGEFULNESS.

· *Desire* to know why and how, CURIOSITY; such as is in no living creature but *man;* so that man is distinguished, not only by his reason, but also by this singular passion from other *animals;* in whom the appetite of food, and other pleasures of sense, by predominance, take away the care of knowing causes; which is a lust of the mind, that by a perseverance of delight in the continual and indefatigable generation of knowledge, exceedeth the short vehemence of any carnal pleasure.

· *Fear* of power invisible, feigned by the mind, or imagined from tales publicly allowed, RELIGION; not allowed, SUPERSTITION. And when the power imagined, is truly such as we imagine, TRUE RELIGION.

· *Fear,* without the apprehension of why, or what, PANIC TERROR, called so from the fables, that make *Pan* the author of them; whereas in truth, there is always in him that so feareth, first, some apprehension of the cause, though the rest run away by example, every one supposing his fellow to know why. And therefore this passion happens to none but in a throng, or multitude of people.

· *Joy,* from apprehension of novelty, ADMIRATION; proper to man, because it excites the appetite of knowing the cause.

· *Joy,* arising from imagination of a man's own power and ability, is that exultation of the mind which is called GLORYING: which if grounded upon the experience of his own former actions, is the same with *confidence:* but if grounded on the flattery of others; or only supposed by himself, for delight in the consequences of it, is called VAINGLORY: which name is properly given; because a well grounded *confidence* begetteth attempt; whereas the supposing of power does not, and is therefore rightly called *vain.*

· *Grief,* from opinion of want of power, is called DEJECTION of mind.

· The *vain-glory* which consisteth in the feigning or supposing of abilities in ourselves, which we know are not, is most incident to young men, and nourished by the histories, or fictions of gallant persons; and is corrected oftentimes by age, and employment.

· *Sudden glory,* is the passion which maketh those *grimaces* called LAUGHTER; and is caused either by some sudden act of their own, that pleaseth them; or by the apprehension of some deformed thing in another, by comparison whereof they suddenly applaud themselves. And it is incident most to them, that are conscious of the fewest abilities in themselves; who are forced to keep themselves in their own favour, by observing the imperfections of other men. And therefore much laughter at the defects of others, is a sign of pusillanimity. For of great minds, one of the proper works is, to help and free others from scorn; and compare themselves only with the most able.

· On the contrary, *sudden dejection,* is the passion that causeth WEEPING; and is caused by such accidents, as suddenly take away some vehement hope, or some prop of their power: and they are most subject to it, that rely principally on helps external, such as are women, and children. Therefore some weep for the loss of friends; others for their unkindness; others for the sudden stop made to their thoughts of revenge, by reconciliation. But in all cases, both laughter, and weeping, are sudden motions; custom taking them both away. For no man laughs at old jests; or weeps for an old calamity.

· *Grief,* for the discovery of some defect of ability, is SHAME, or the passion that discovereth itself in BLUSHING; and consisteth in the apprehension of some thing dishonourable; and in young men, is a sign of the love of good reputation, and commendable; in old men it is a sign of the same; but because it comes too late, not commendable.

· The *contempt* of good reputation is called IMPUDENCE.

· *Grief,* of the calamity of another, is PITY; and ariseth from the imagination that the like calamity may befall himself; and therefore is called also COMPASSION, and in the phrase of this present time a FELLOW-FEELING: and therefore for calamity arriving from great wickedness, the best men have the least pity; and for the same calamity, those have least pity, that think themselves least obnoxious to the same.

· *Contempt,* or little sense of the calamity of others, is that which men call CRUELTY; proceeding from security of their own fortune. For, that any man should take pleasure in other men's great harms, without other end of his own, I do not conceive it possible.

· *Grief,* for the success of a competitor in wealth, honour, or other good, if it be joined with endeavour to enforce our own abilities to equal or exceed him, is called EMULATION: but joined with endeavour to supplant, or hinder a competitor, ENVY.

When in the mind of man, appetites, and aversions, hopes, and fears, concerning one and the same thing, arise alternately; and divers good and evil consequences of the doing, or omitting the thing propounded, come successively into our thoughts; so that sometimes we have an appetite to it; sometimes an aversion from it; sometimes hope to be able to do it; sometimes despair, or fear to attempt it; the whole sum of desires, aversions, hopes and fears continued till the thing be either done, or thought impossible, is that we call DELIBERATION.

Therefore of things past, there is no *deliberation;* because manifestly impossible to be changed: nor of things known to be impossible, or thought so; because men know, or think such deliberation vain. But of things impossible, which we think possible, we may deliberate; not knowing it is in vain. And it is called *deliberation;* because it is a putting an end to the *liberty* we had of doing, or omitting, according to our own appetite, or aversion.

This alternate succession of appetites, aversions, hopes and fears, is no less in other living creatures than in man: and therefore beasts also deliberate.

Every *deliberation* is then said to *end,* when that whereof they deliberate is either done, or thought impossible; because till then we retain the liberty of doing, or omitting, according to our appetite, or aversion.

In *deliberation,* the last appetite, or aversion, immediately adhering to the action, or to the omission thereof, is that we call the WILL; the act, (not the faculty,) of *willing.* And beasts that have *deliberation,* must necessarily also have *will.* The definition of the *will,* given commonly by the Schools, that it is a *rational appetite,* is not good. For if it were, then could there be no voluntary act against reason. For a *voluntary act* is that, which proceedeth from the *will,* and no other. But if instead of a rational appetite, we shall say an appetite resulting from a precedent deliberation, then the definition is the same that I have given here. *Will* therefore is *the last appetite in deliberating.* And though we say in common discourse, a man had a will once to do a thing, that nevertheless he forbore to do; yet that is properly but an inclination, which makes no action voluntary; because the action depends not of it, but of the last inclination, or appetite. For if the intervenient appetites, make any action voluntary; then by the same reason all intervenient aversions, should make the same action involuntary; and so one and the same action, should be both voluntary and involuntary.

By this it is manifest, that not only actions that have their beginning from covetousness, ambition, lust, or other appetites to the thing propounded; but also those that have their beginning from aversion, or fear of those consequences that follow the omission, are *voluntary actions*.

The forms of speech by which the passions are expressed, are partly the same, and partly different from those, by which we express our thoughts. And first, generally all passions may be expressed *indicatively*; as *I love, I fear, I joy, I deliberate, I will, I command*: but some of them have particular expressions by themselves, which nevertheless are not affirmations, unless it be when they serve to make other inferences, besides that of the passion they proceed from. Deliberation is expressed *subjunctively*; which is a speech proper to signify suppositions, with their consequences; as, *if this be done, then this will follow*; and differs not from the language of reasoning, save that reasoning is in general words; but deliberation for the most part is of particulars. The language of desire, and aversion, is *imperative*; as *do this, forbear that*; which when the party is obliged to do, or forbear, is *command*; otherwise *prayer*; or else *counsel*. The language of vain-glory, of indignation, pity and revengefulness, *optative*: but of the desire to know, there is a peculiar expression, called *interrogative*; as, *what is it, when shall it, how is it done*, and *why so?* other language of the passions I find none: of cursing, swearing, reviling, and the like, do not signify as speech; but as the actions of a tongue accustomed.

These forms of speech, I say, are expressions, or voluntary significations of our passions: but certain signs they be not; because they may be used arbitrarily, whether they that use them, have such passions or not. The best signs of passions present, are either in the countenance, motions of the body, actions, and ends, or aims, which we otherwise know the man to have.

And because in deliberation, the appetites, and aversions, are raised by foresight of the good and evil consequences, and sequels of the action whereof we deliberate; the good or evil effect thereof dependeth on the foresight of a long chain of consequences, of which very seldom any man is able to see to the end. But for so far as a man seeth, if the good in those consequences be greater than the evil, the whole chain is that which writers call *apparent*, or *seeming good*. And contrarily, when the evil exceedeth the good, the whole is *apparent*, or *seeming evil*: so that he who hath by experience, or reason, the greatest and surest prospect of consequences, deliberates best himself; and is able when he will, to give the best counsel unto others.

Continual success in obtaining those things which a man from time to time desireth, that is to say, continual prospering, is that men call FELICITY; I mean the felicity of this life. For there is no such thing as perpetual tranquillity of mind, while we live here; because life itself is but motion, and can never be without desire, nor without fear, no more than without sense. What kind of felicity God hath ordained to them that devoutly honour Him, a man shall no sooner know, than enjoy; being joys, that now are as incomprehensible, as the word of school-men *beatifical vision* is unintelligible.

The form of speech whereby men signify their opinion of the goodness of any thing, is PRAISE. That whereby they signify the power and greatness of any thing, is MAGNIFYING. And that whereby they signify the opinion they have of a man's felicity, is by the Greeks called μακαρισμός for which we have no name in our tongue. And thus much is sufficient for the present purpose, to have been said of the PASSIONS.

CHAPTER 7

Of the Ends, or Resolutions of Discourse

Of all *discourse,* governed by desire of knowledge, there is at last an *end,* either by attaining, or by giving over. And in the chain of discourse, wheresoever it be interrupted, there is an end for that time.

If the discourse be merely mental, it consisteth of thoughts that the thing will be, and will not be, or that it has been, and has not been, alternately. So that wheresoever you break off the chain of a man's discourse, you leave him in a presumption of *it will be,* or, *it will not be;* or *it has been,* or, *has not been.* All which is *opinion.* And that which is alternate appetite, in deliberating concerning good and evil; the same is alternate opinion, in the enquiry of the truth of *past,* and *future.* And as the last appetite in deliberation is called the *will;* so the last opinion in search of the truth of past, and future, is called the JUDG-MENT, or *resolute* and *final sentence* of him that *discourseth.* And as the whole chain of appetites alternate, in the question of good, or bad, is called *deliberation;* so the whole chain of opinions alternate, in the question of true, or false, is called DOUBT.

No discourse whatsoever, can end in absolute knowledge of fact, past, or to come. For, as for the knowledge of fact, it is originally, sense; and ever after, memory. And for the knowledge of consequence, which I have said before is called science, it is not absolute, but conditional. No man can know by discourse, that this, or that, is, has been, or will be; which is to know absolutely: but only, that if this be, that is; if this has been, that has been; if this shall be, that shall be: which is to know conditionally; and that not the consequence of one thing to another; but of one name of a thing, to another name of the same thing.

And therefore, when the discourse is put into speech, and begins with the definitions of words, and proceeds by connexion of the same into general affirmations, and of these again into syllogisms; the end or last sum is called the conclusion; and the thought of the mind by it signified, is that conditional knowledge, or knowledge of the consequence of words, which is commonly called SCIENCE. But if the first ground of such discourse, be not definitions; or if the definitions be not rightly joined together into syllogisms, then the end or conclusion, is again OPINION, namely of the truth of somewhat said, though sometimes in absurd and senseless words, without possibility of being understood. When two, or more men, know of one and the same fact, they are said to be CONSCIOUS of it one to another; which is as much as to know it together. And because such are fittest wit-nesses of the facts of one another, or of a third; it was, and ever will be reputed a very evil act, for any man to speak against his *conscience:* or to corrupt or force another so to do: inso-much that the plea of conscience, has been always hearkened unto very diligently in all times. Afterwards, men made use of the same word metaphorically, for the knowledge of their own secret facts, and secret thoughts; and therefore it is rhetorically said, that the conscience is a thousand witnesses. And last of all, men, vehemently in love with their own new opinions, (though never so absurd,) and obstinately bent to maintain them, gave those their opinions also that reverenced name of conscience, as if they would have it seem unlawful, to change or speak against them; and so pretend to know they are true, when they know at most, but that they think so.

When a man's discourse beginneth not at definitions, it beginneth either at some other contemplation of his own, and then it is still called opinion; or it beginneth at some say-ing of another, of whose ability to know the truth, and of whose honesty in not deceiving, he doubteth not; and then the discourse is not so much concerning the thing, as the per-son; and the resolution is called BELIEF, and FAITH: *faith, in* the man; *belief,* both *of* the man, and *of* the truth of what he says. So that in belief are two opinions; one of the saying of the man; the other of his virtue. To *have faith in,* or *trust to,* or *believe a man,* signify the same thing; namely, an opinion of the veracity of the man: but to *believe what is said,* signifieth only an opinion of the truth of the saying. But we are to observe that this phrase, *I believe in;* as also the Latin, *credo in;* and the Greek, πιστεύω έις, are never used but in the writings of divines. Instead of them, in other writings are put, *I believe him; I trust him; I have faith in him; I rely on him;* and in Latin, *credo illi: fido illi:* and in Greek, πιστεύω αὐτῶ: and that this singularity of the ecclesiastic use of the word hath raised many disputes about the right object of the Christian faith.

But by *believing in,* as it is in the creed, is meant, not trust in the person; but confession and acknowledgment of the doctrine. For not only Christians, but all manner of men do so believe in God, as to hold all for truth they hear him say, whether they understand it, or not; which is all the faith and trust can possibly be had in any person whatsoever: but they do not all believe the doctrine of the creed.

From whence we may infer, that when we believe any saying whatsoever it be, to be true, from arguments taken, not from the thing it self, or from the principles of natural reason, but from the authority, and good opinion we have, of him that hath said it; then is the speaker, or person we believe in, or trust in, and whose word we take, the object of our faith; and the honour done in believing, is done to him only. And consequently, when we believe that the Scriptures are the word of God, having no immediate revelation from God himself, our belief, faith, and trust is in the church; whose word we take, and acquiesce therein. And they that believe that which a prophet relates unto them in the name of God, take the word of the prophet, do honour to him and in him trust, and believe, touching the truth of what he relateth, whether he be a true, or a false prophet. And so it is also with all other history. For if I should not believe all that is written by historians, of the glorious acts of *Alexander,* or *Caesar;* I do not think the ghost of *Alexander,* or *Caesar,* had any just cause to be offended; or any body else, but the historian. If *Livy* say the Gods made once a cow speak, and we believe it not; we distrust not God therein, but *Livy.* So that it is evident, that whatsoever we believe, upon no other reason, than what is drawn from authority of men only, and their writings; whether they be sent from God or not, is faith in men only.

CHAPTER 10

Of Power, Worth, Dignity, Honour, and Worthiness

The power *of a man,* (to take it universally), is his present means, to obtain some future apparent good; and is either *original* or *instrumental.*

Natural power, is the eminence of the faculties of body, or mind: as extraordinary strength, form, prudence, arts, eloquence, liberality, nobility. *Instrumental* are those powers, which acquired by these, or by fortune, are means and instruments to acquire more: as riches, reputation, friends, and the secret working of God, which men call good luck. For the nature of power, is in this point, like to fame, increasing as it proceeds; or like the motion of heavy bodies, which the further they go, make still the more haste.

The greatest of human powers, is that which is compounded of the powers of most men, united by consent, in one person, natural, or civil, that has the use of all their powers depending on his will; such as is the power of a common-wealth: or depending on the wills of each particular; such as is the power of a faction or of divers factions leagued. Therefore to have servants, is power; to have friends, is power: for they are strengths united.

Also riches joined with liberality, is power; because it procureth friends, and servants: without liberality, not so; because in this case they defend not; but expose men to envy, as a prey.

Reputation of power, is power; because it draweth with it the adherence of those that need protection.

So is reputation of love of a man's country, (called popularity,) for the same reason.

Also, what quality soever maketh a man beloved, or feared of many; of the reputation of such quality, is power; because it is a means to have the assistance, and service of many.

Good success is power; because it maketh reputation of wisdom, or good fortune; which makes men either fear him, or rely on him.

Affability of men already in power, is increase of power; because it gaineth love.

Reputation of prudence in the conduct of peace or war, is power; because to prudent men, we commit the government of ourselves, more willingly than to others.

Nobility is power, not in all places, but only in those commonwealths, where it has privileges: for in such privileges consisteth their power.

Eloquence is power, because it is seeming prudence.

Form is power; because being a promise of good, it recommendeth men to the favour of women and strangers.

The sciences, are small power; because not eminent; and therefore, not acknowledged in any man; nor are at all, but in a few, and in them, but of a few things. For science is of that nature, as none can understand it to be, but such as in a good measure have attained it.

Arts of public use, as fortification, making of engines, and other instruments of war; because they confer to defence, and victory, are power: and though the true mother of them, be science, namely the mathematics; yet, because they are brought into the light, by the hand of the artificer, they be esteemed (the midwife passing with the vulgar for the mother,) as his issue.

The *value,* or WORTH of a man, is as of all other things, his price; that is to say, so much as would be given for the use of his power: and therefore is not absolute; but a thing dependant on the need and judgment of another. An able conductor of soldiers, is of great price in time of war present, or imminent; but in peace not so. A learned and uncorrupt judge, is much worth in time of peace; but not so much in war. And as in other things, so in men, not the seller, but the buyer determines the price. For let a man (as most men do,) rate themselves at the highest value they can; yet their true value is no more than it is esteemed by others.

The manifestation of the value we set on one another, is that which is commonly called honouring, and dishonouring. To value a man at a high rate, is to *honour* him; at a low rate, is to *dishonour* him. But high, and low, in this case, is to be understood by comparison to the rate that each man setteth on himself.

The public worth of a man, which is the value set on him by the commonwealth, is that which men commonly call DIGNITY. And this value of him by the commonwealth, is understood, by offices of command, judicature, public employment; or by names and titles, introduced for distinction of such value.

To pray to another, for aid of any kind, is to HONOUR; because a sign we have an opinion he has power to help; and the more difficult the aid is, the more is the honour.

To obey, is to honour, because no man obeys them, whom they think have no power to help, or hurt them. And consequently to disobey, is to *dishonour*.

To give great gifts to a man, is to honour him; because it is buying of protection, and acknowledging of power. To give little gifts, is to dishonour; because it is but alms, and signifies an opinion of the need of small helps.

To be sedulous in promoting another's good; also to flatter, is to honour; as a sign we seek his protection or aid. To neglect, is to dishonour.

To give way, or place to another, in any commodity, is to honour; being a confession of greater power. To arrogate, is to dishonour.

To show any sign of love, or fear of another, is to honour; for both to love, and to fear, is to value. To contemn, or less to love or fear, than he expects, is to dishonour; for it is undervaluing.

To praise, magnify, or call happy, is to honour; because nothing but goodness, power, and felicity is valued. To revile, mock, or pity, is to dishonour.

To speak to another with consideration, to appear before him with decency, and humility, is to honour him; as signs of fear to offend. To speak to him rashly, to do any thing before him obscenely, slovenly, impudently, is to dishonour.

To believe, to trust, to rely on another, is to honour him; sign of opinion of his virtue and power. To distrust, or not believe, is to dishonour.

To hearken to a man's counsel, or discourse of what kind soever, is to honour; as a sign we think him wise, or eloquent, or witty. To sleep, or go forth, or talk the while, is to dishonour.

To do those things to another, which he takes for signs of honour, or which the law or custom makes so, is to honour; because in approving the honour done by others, he acknowledgeth the power which others acknowledge. To refuse to do them, is to dishonour.

To agree with in opinion, is to honour; as being a sign of approving his judgment, and wisdom. To dissent, is dishonour, and an upbraiding of error; and (if the dissent be in many things) of folly.

To imitate, is to honour; for it is vehemently to approve. To imitate one's enemy, is to dishonour.

To honour those another honours, is to honour him; as a sign of approbation of his judgment. To honour his enemies, is to dishonour him.

To employ in counsel, or in actions of difficulty, is to honour; as a sign of opinion of his wisdom, or other power. To deny employment in the same cases, to those that seek it, is to dishonour.

All these ways of honouring, are natural; and as well within, as without commonwealths. But in commonwealths, where he, or they that have the supreme authority, can make whatsoever they please, to stand for signs of honour, there be other honours.

A sovereign doth honour a subject, with whatsoever title, or office, or employment, or action, that he himself will have taken for a sign of his will to honour him.

The king of *Persia,* honoured *Mordecai,* when he appointed he should be conducted through the streets in the king's garment, upon one of the king's horses, with a crown on his head, and a prince before him, proclaiming, *thus shall it be done to him that the king will honour.* And yet another king of *Persia,* or the same another time, to one that demanded for some great service, to wear one of the king's robes, gave him leave so to do; but with this addition, that he should wear it as the king's fool; and then it was dishonour. So that of civil honour, the fountain is in the person of the commonwealth, and dependeth on the will of the sovereign; and is therefore temporary, and called *civil honour;* such as are magistracy, offices, titles; and in some places coats and scutcheons painted: and men honour such as have them, as having so many signs of favour in the commonwealth; which favour is power.

Honourable is whatsoever possession, action, or quality, is an argument and sign of power.

And therefore to be honoured, loved, or feared of many, is honourable; as arguments of power. To be honoured of few or none, *dishonourable.*

Dominion, and victory is honourable; because acquired by power; and servitude, for need, or fear, is dishonourable.

Good fortune (if lasting,) honourable, as a sign of the favour of God. Ill fortune, and losses, dishonourable. Riches, are honourable; for they are power. Poverty, dishonourable. Magnanimity, liberality, hope, courage, confidence, are honourable; for they proceed from the conscience of power. Pusillanimity, parsimony, fear, diffidence, are dishonourable.

Timely resolution, or determination of what a man is to do, is honourable; as being the contempt of small difficulties, and dangers. And irresolution, dishonourable; as a sign of too much valuing of little impediments, and little advantages: for when a man has weighed things as long as the time permits, and resolves not, the difference of weight is but little; and therefore if he resolve not, he overvalues little things, which is pusillanimity.

All actions, and speeches, that proceed, or seem to proceed from much experience, science, discretion, or wit, are honourable; for all these are powers. Actions, or words that proceed from error, ignorance, or folly, dishonourable.

Gravity, as far forth as it seems to proceed from a mind employed on something else, is honourable; because employment is a sign of power. But if it seem to proceed from a purpose to appear grave, it is dishonourable. For the gravity of the former, is like the steadiness of a ship laden with merchandise; but of the latter, like the steadiness of a ship ballasted with sand, and other trash.

To be conspicuous, that is to say, to be known, for wealth, office, great actions, or any eminent good, is honourable; as a sign of the power for which he is conspicuous. On the contrary, obscurity, is dishonourable.

To be descended from conspicuous parents, is honourable; because they the more easily attain the aids, and friends of their ancestors. On the contrary, to be descended from obscure parentage, is dishonourable.

Actions proceeding from equity, joined with loss, are honourable; as signs of magnanimity: for magnanimity is a sign of power. On the contrary, craft, shifting, neglect of equity, is dishonourable.

Covetousness of great riches, and ambition of great honours, are honourable; as signs of power to obtain them. Covetousness, and ambition, of little gains, or preferments, is dishonourable.

Nor does it alter the case of honour, whether an action (so it be great and difficult, and consequently a sign of much power,) be just or unjust: for honour consisteth only in the opinion of power. Therefore the ancient heathen did not think they dishonoured, but greatly honoured the Gods, when they introduced them in their poems, committing rapes, thefts, and other great, but unjust, or unclean acts: insomuch as nothing is so much celebrated in *Jupiter*, as his adulteries; nor in *Mercury*, as his frauds, and thefts: of whose praises, in a hymn of *Homer*, the greatest is this, that being born in the morning, he had invented music at noon, and before night, stolen away the cattle of *Apollo*, from his herdsmen.

Also amongst men, till there were constituted great commonwealths, it was thought no dishonour to be a pirate, or a highway thief; but rather a lawful trade, not only amongst the Greeks, but also amongst all other nations; as is manifest by the histories of ancient time. And at this day, in this part of the world, private duels are, and always will be honourable, though unlawful, till such time as there shall be honour ordained for them that refuse, and ignominy for them that make the challenge. For duels also are many times effects of courage; and the ground of courage is always strength or skill, which are power; though for the most part they be effects of rash speaking, and of the fear of dishonour, in one, or both the combatants; who engaged by rashness, are driven into the lists to avoid disgrace.

Scutcheons, and coats of arms hereditary, where they have any eminent privileges, are honourable; otherwise not: for their power consisteth either in such privileges, or in riches, or some such things as is equally honoured in other men. This kind of honour, commonly called gentry, has been derived from the ancient Germans. For there never was any such thing known, where the German customs were unknown. Nor is it now any where in use where the Germans have not inhabited. The ancient Greek commanders, when they went to war, had their shields painted with such devices as they pleased; insomuch as an unpainted buckler was a sign of poverty, and of a common soldier; but they transmitted not the inheritance of them. The Romans transmitted the marks of their families: but they were the images, not the devices of their ancestors. Amongst the people of *Asia, Africa,* and *America,* there is not, nor was ever, any such thing. The Germans only had that custom; from whom it has been derived into *England, France, Spain,* and *Italy,* when in great numbers they either aided the Romans, or made their own conquests in these western parts of the world.

For *Germany,* being anciently, as all other countries, in their beginnings, divided amongst an infinite number of little lords, or masters of families, that continually had wars one with another; those masters, or lords, principally to the end they might, when they were covered with arms, be known by their followers; and partly for ornament, both painted their armour, or their scutcheon, or coat, with the picture of some beast, or other thing; and also put some eminent and visible mark upon the crest of their helmets. And this ornament both of the arms, and crest, descended by inheritance to their children; to the eldest pure, and to the rest with some note of diversity, such as the old master, that is to say in Dutch, the *Here-alt* thought fit. But when many such families, joined together, made a greater monarchy, this duty of the Herealt, to distinguish scutcheons, was made a private office apart. And the issues of these lords, is the great and ancient gentry; which for the most part bear living creatures, noted for courage, and rapine; or castles, battlements, belts, weapons, bars, palisadoes, and other notes of war; nothing being then in honour, but military virtue. Afterwards, not only kings, but popular commonwealths, gave divers manners of scutcheons, to such as went forth to the war, or returned from it, for encouragement, or recompense to their service. All which, by an observing reader, may be found in such ancient histories, Greek and Latin, as make mention of the German nation and manners, in their times.

Titles of *honour,* such as are duke, count, marquis, and baron, are honourable; as signifying the value set upon them by the sovereign power of the commonwealth: which titles, were in old time titles of office, and command, derived some from the Romans, some from the Germans and French. Dukes, in Latin *duces,* being generals in war; counts, *comites,* such as bare the general company out of friendship, and were left to govern and defend places conquered, and pacified: marquises, *marchiones,* were counts that governed the marches, or bounds of the empire. Which titles of duke, count, and marquis, came into the empire, about the time of *Constantine* the Great, from the customs of the German *militia.* But baron, seems to have been a title of the Gauls, and signifies a great man; such as were the king's, or prince's men, whom they employed in war about their persons; and seems to be derived from *vir,* to *ber,* and *bar,* that signified the same in the language of the Gauls, that *vir* in Latin; and thence to *bero,* and *baro;* so that such men were called *berones,* and after barones; and (in Spanish) *varones.* But he that would now more particularly the original of titles of honour, may find it, as I have done this, in Mr. Selden's most excellent treatise of that subject. In process of time these offices of honour, by occasion of trouble, and for reasons of good and peaceable government, were turned into mere titles; serving for the most part, to distinguish the precedence, place, and order of subjects in the commonwealth: and men were made dukes, counts, marquises, and barons of places, wherein they had neither possession, nor command: and other titles also, were devised to the same end.

WORTHINESS, is a thing different from the worth, or value of a man; and also from his merit, or desert; and consisteth in a particular power, or ability for that, whereof he is said to be worthy: which particular ability, is usually named FITNESS, or *aptitude.*

For he is worthiest to be a commander, to be a judge, or to have any other charge, that is best fitted, with the qualities required to the well discharging of it; and worthiest of riches, that has the qualities most requisite for the well using of them: any of which qualities being absent, one may nevertheless be a worthy man, and valuable for something else. Again, a man may be worthy of riches, office, and employment, that nevertheless, can plead no right to have it before another; and therefore cannot be said to merit or deserve it. For merit presupposeth a right, and that the thing deserved is due by promise: of which I shall say more hereafter, when I shall speak of contracts.

CHAPTER 11

Of the Difference of Manners

By manners, I mean not here, decency of behaviour; as how one man should salute another, or how a man should wash his mouth, or pick his teeth before company, and such other points of the *small morals;* but those qualities of mankind, that concern their living together in peace, and unity. To which end we are to consider, that the felicity of this life, consisteth not in the repose of a mind satisfied. For there is no such *finus ultimus,* (utmost aim,) nor *summum bonum,* (greatest good,) as is spoken of in the books of the old moral philosophers. Nor can a man any more live, whose desires are at an end, than he, whose senses and imaginations are at a stand. Felicity is a continual progress of the desire, from one object to another; the attaining of the former, being still but the way to the latter. The cause whereof is, that the object of man's desire, is not to enjoy once only, and for one instant of time; but to assure for ever, the way of his future desire. And therefore the voluntary actions, and inclinations of all men, tend, not only to the procuring, but also to the assuring of a contented life; and differ only in the way: which ariseth partly from the diversity of passions, in divers men; and partly from the difference of the knowledge, or opinion each one has of the causes, which produce the effect desired.

So that in the first place, I put for a general inclination of all mankind, a perpetual and restless desire of power after power, that ceaseth only in death. And the cause of this, is not always that a man hopes for a more intensive delight, than he has already attained to; or that he cannot be content with a moderate power: but because he cannot assure the power and means to live well, which he hath present, without the acquisition of more. And from hence it is, that kings, whose power is greatest, turn their endeavors to the assuring it at home by laws, or abroad by wars: and when that is done, there succeedeth a new desire; in some, of fame from new conquest; in others, of ease and sensual pleasure; in others, of admiration, or being flattered for excellence in some art, or other ability of the mind.

Competition of riches, honour, command, or other power, inclineth to contention, enmity, and war: because the way of one competitor, to the attaining of his desire, is to kill, subdue, supplant, or repel the other. Particularly, competition of praise, inclineth to a reverence of antiquity. For men contend with the living, not with the dead; to these ascribing more than due, that they may obscure the glory of the other.

Desire of ease, and sensual delight, disposeth men to obey a common power: because by such desires, a man doth abandon the protection might be hoped for from his own industry, and labour. Fear of death, and wounds, disposeth to the same: and for the same reason. On the contrary, needy men, and hardy, not contented with their present condition; as also, all men that are ambitious of military command, are inclined to continue the causes of war; and to stir up trouble and sedition: for there is no honour military but by war; not any such hope to mend an ill game, as by causing a new shuffle.

Desire of knowledge, and arts of peace, inclineth men to obey a common power: For such desire, containeth a desire of leisure; and consequently protection from some other power than their own.

Desire of praise, disposeth to laudable actions, such as please them whose judgment they value; for of those men whom we contemn, we contemn also the praises. Desire of fame after death does the same. And though after death, there be no sense of the praise given us on earth, as being joys, that are either swallowed up in the unspeakeable joys of Heaven, or extinguished in the extreme torments of hell: yet is not such fame vain; because men have a present delight therein, from the foresight of it, and of the benefit that may redound thereby to their posterity: which though they now see not, yet they imagine; and any thing that is pleasure in the sense, the same also is pleasure in the imagination.

To have received from one, to whom we think ourselves equal, greater benefits than there is hope to requite, disposeth to counterfeit love; but really secret hatred; and puts a man into the estate of a desperate debtor, that in declining the sight of his creditor, tacitly wishes him there, where he might never see him more. For benefits oblige, and obligation is thraldom; and unrequitable obligation, perpetual thraldom: which is to one's equal, hateful. But to have received benefits from one, whom we acknowledge for superior, inclines to love; because the obligation is no new depression: and cheerful acceptation, (which men call *gratitude,*) is such an honour done to the obliger, as is taken generally for retribution. Also to receive benefits, though from an equal, or inferior, as long as there is hope of requital, disposeth to love: for in the intention of the receiver, the obligation is of aid, and service mutual; from whence proceedeth an emulation of who shall exceed in benefiting; the most noble and profitable contention possible; wherein the victor is pleased with his victory, and the other revenged by confessing it.

To have done more hurt to a man, than he can, or is willing to expiate, inclineth the doer to hate the sufferer. For he must expect revenge, or forgiveness; both which are hateful.

Fear of oppression, disposeth a man to anticipate, or to seek aid by society: for there is no other way by which a man can secure his life and liberty.

Men that distrust their own subtlety, are in tumult and sedition, better disposed for victory, than they that suppose themselves wise, or crafty. For these love to consult, the other (fearing to be circumvented,) to strike first. And in sedition, men being always in the precincts of battle, to hold together, and use all advantages of force, is a better strategem, than any that can proceed from subtlety of wit.

Vain-glorious men, such as without being conscious to themselves of great sufficiency, delight in supposing themselves gallant men, are inclined only to ostentation; but not to attempt: because when danger or difficulty appears, they look for nothing but to have their insufficiency discovered.

Vain-glorious men, such as estimate their sufficiency by the flattery of other men, or the fortune of some precedent action, without assured ground of hope from the true knowledge of themselves, are inclined to rash engaging; and in the approach of danger, or difficulty, to retire if they can: because not seeing the way of safety, they will rather hazard their honour, which may be salved with an excuse; than their lives, for which no salve is sufficient.

Men that have a strong opinion of their own wisdom in matter of government, are disposed to ambition. Because without public employment in council or magistracy, the honour of their wisdom is lost. And therefore eloquent speakers are inclined to ambition; for eloquence seemeth wisdom, both to themselves and others.

Pusillanimity disposeth men to irresolution, and consequently to lose the occasions, and fittest opportunities of action. For after men have been in deliberation till the time of action approach, if it be not then manifest what is best to be done, it is a sign, the difference of motives, the one way and the other, are not great: therefore not to resolve then, is to lose the occasion by weighing of trifles; which is pusillanimity.

Frugality, (though in poor men a virtue,) maketh a man unapt to achieve such actions, as require the strength of many men at once: for it weakeneth their endeavor, which is to be nourished and kept in vigour by reward.

Eloquence, with flattery, disposeth men to confide in them that have it; because the former is seeming wisdom, the latter seeming kindness. Add to them military reputation, and it disposeth men to adhere, and subject themselves to those men that have them. The two former, having given them caution against danger from him; the latter gives them caution against danger from others.

Want of science, that is, ignorance of causes, disposeth, or rather constraineth a man to rely on the advice, and authority of others. For all men whom the truth concerns, if they rely not on their own, must rely on the opinion of some other, whom they think wiser than themselves, and see not why he should deceive them.

Ignorance of the signification of words, which is want of understanding, disposeth men to take on trust, not only the truth they know not; but also the errors; and which is more, the non-sense of them they trust: for neither error nor non-sense, can without a perfect understanding of words, be detected.

From the same it proceedeth, that men give different names, to one and the same thing, from the difference of their own passions: as they that approve a private opinion, call it opinion; but they that mislike it, heresy: and yet heresy signifies no more than private opinion; but has only a greater tincture of choler.

From the same also it proceedeth, that men cannot distinguish, without study and great understanding, between the one action of many men, and many actions of one multitude; as for example, between one action of all the senators of *Rome* in killing *Cataline,* and the many actions of a number of senators in killing *Caesar;* and therefore are disposed to take for the action of the people, that which is a multitude of actions done by a multitude of men, led perhaps by the persuasion of one.

Ignorance of the causes, and original constitution of right, equity, law, and justice, disposeth a man to make custom and example the rule of his actions; in such manner, as to think that unjust which it hath been the custom to punish; and that just, of the impunity and approbation whereof they can produce an example, or (as the lawyers which only use this false measure of justice barbarously call it) a precedent; like little children, that have no other rule of good and evil manners, but the correction they receive from their parents and masters; save that children are constant to their rule, whereas, men are not so; because grown strong, and stubborn, they appeal from custom to reason, and from reason to custom, as it serves their turn; receding from custom when their interest requires it, and setting themselves against reason, as oft as reason is against them: which is the cause, that the doctrine of right and wrong, is perpetually disputed, both by the pen and the sword: whereas the doctrine of lines, and figures, is not so; because men care not, in that subject, what be truth, as a thing that crosses no man's ambition, profit or lust. For I doubt not, but if it had been a thing contrary to any man's right of dominion, or to the interest of men that have dominion, *that the three angles of a triangle, should be equal to two angles of a square;* that doctrine should have been, if not disputed, yet by the burning of all books of geometry, suppressed, as far as he whom it concerned was able.

Ignorance of remote causes, disposeth men to attribute all events, to the causes immediate, and instrumental: for these are all the causes they perceive. And hence it comes to pass, that in all places, men that are grieved with payments to the public, discharge their anger upon the publicans, that is to say, farmers, collectors, and other officers of the public revenue; and adhere to such as find fault with the public government; and thereby, when they have engaged themselves beyond hope of justification, fall also upon the supreme authority, for fear of punishment, or shame of receiving pardon.

Ignorance of natural causes disposeth a man to credulity, so as to believe many times impossibilities: for such know nothing to the contrary, but that they may be true; being unable to detect the impossibility. And credulity, because men love to be hearkened unto in company, disposeth them to lying: so that ignorance it self without malice, is able to make a man both to believe lies, and tell them: and sometimes also to invent them.

Anxiety for the future time, disposeth men to inquire into the causes of things: because the knowledge of them, maketh men the better able to order the present to their best advantage.

Curiosity, or love of the knowledge of causes, draws a man from consideration of the effect, to seek the cause; and again, the cause of that cause; till of necessity he must come to this thought at last, that there is some cause, whereof there is no former cause, but is eternal; which is it men call God. So that it is impossible to make any profound inquiry into natural causes, without being inclined thereby to believe there is one God eternal; though they cannot have any idea of him in their mind, answerable to his nature. For as a man that is born blind, hearing men talk of warming themselves by the fire, and being brought to warm himself by the same, may easily conceive, and assure himself, there is somewhat there, which men call *fire,* and is the cause of the heat he feels; but cannot imagine what it is like; nor have an idea of it in his mind, such as they have that see it: so also, by the visible things of this world, and their admirable order, a man may conceive there is a cause of them, which men call God; and yet not have an idea, or image of him in his mind.

And they that make little, or no inquiry into the natural causes of things, yet from the fear that proceeds from the ignorance it self, of what it is that hath the power to do them much good or harm, are inclined to suppose, and feign unto themselves, several kinds of powers invisible; and to stand in awe of their own imaginations; and in time of distress to invoke them; as also in the time of an expected good success, to give them thanks; making the creatures of their own fancy, their gods. By which means it hath come to pass, that from the innumerable variety of fancy, men have created in the world innumerable sorts of gods. And this fear of things invisible, is the natural seed of that, which every one in himself calleth religion; and in them that worship, or fear that power otherwise than they do, superstition.

And this seed of religion, having been observed by many; some of those that have observed it, have been inclined thereby to nourish, dress, and form it into laws; and to add to it of their own invention, any opinion of the causes of future events, by which they thought they should be best able to govern others, and make unto themselves the greatest use of their powers.

CHAPTER 12

Of Religion

Seeing there are no signs, nor fruit of *religion,* but in man only; there is no cause to doubt, but that the seed of *religion,* is also only in man; and consisteth in some peculiar quality, or at least in some eminent degree thereof, not to be found in other living creatures.

And first, it is peculiar to the nature of man, to be inquisitive into the causes of the events they see, some more, some less; but all men so much, as to be curious in the search of the causes of their own good and evil fortune.

Secondly, upon the sight of any thing that hath a beginning, to think also it had a cause, which determined the same to begin, then when it did, rather than sooner or later.

Thirdly, whereas there is no other felicity of beasts, but the enjoying of their quotidian food, ease, and lusts; as having little or no foresight of the time to come, for want of observation, and memory of the order, consequence, and dependence of the things they see; man observeth how one event hath been produced by another; and remembereth in them antecedence and consequence; and when he cannot assure himself of the true causes of things, (for the causes of good and evil fortune for the most part are invisible,) he supposes causes of them, either such as his own fancy suggesteth; or trusteth to the authority of other men, such as he thinks to be his friends, and wiser than himself.

The two first, make anxiety. For being assured that there be causes of all things that have arrived hitherto, or shall arrive hereafter; it is impossible for a man, who continually endeavoureth to secure himself against the evil he fears, and procure the good he desireth, not to be in a perpetual solicitude of the time to come; so that every man, especially those that are over provident, are in an estate like to that of *Prometheus*. For as *Prometheus*, (which interpreted, is, *the prudent man*,) was bound to the hill *Caucasus*, a place of large prospect, where, an eagle feeding on his liver, devoured in the day, as much as was repaired in the night: so that man, which looks too far before him, in the care of future time, hath his heart all the day long, gnawed on by fear of death, poverty, or other calamity; and has no repose, nor pause of his anxiety, but in sleep.

This perpetual fear, always accompanying mankind in the ignorance of causes, as it were in the dark, must needs have for object something. And therefore when there is nothing to be seen, there is nothing to accuse, either of their good, or evil fortune, but some *power*, or agent *invisible*: in which sense perhaps it was, that some of the old poets said, that the gods were at first created by human fear: which spoken of the gods, (that is to say, of the many gods of the Gentiles) is very true. But the acknowledging of one God, eternal, infinite, and omnipotent, may more easily be derived, from the desire men have to know the causes of natural bodies, and their several virtues, and operations; than from the fear of what was to befall them in time to come. For he that from any effect he seeth come to pass, should reason to the next and immediate cause thereof, and from thence to the cause of that cause, and plunge himself profoundly in the pursuit of causes; shall at last come to this, that there must be (as even the heathen philosophers confessed) one first mover; that is, a first, and an eternal cause of all things; which is that which men mean by the name of God: and all this without thought of their fortune; the solicitude whereof, both inclines to fear, and hinders them from the search of the causes of other things; and thereby gives occasion of feigning of as many gods, as there be men that feign them.

And for the matter, or substance of the invisible agents, so fancied; they could not by natural cogitation, fall upon any other conceit, but that it was the same with that of the soul of man; and that the soul of man, was of the same substance, with that which appeareth in a dream, to one that sleepeth; or in a looking-glass, to one that is awake; which, men not knowing that such apparitions are nothing else but creatures of the fancy, think to be real, and external substances; and therefore call them ghosts; as the Latins called them *imagines*, and *umbrae*, and thought them spirits, that is, thin aerial bodies; and those invisible agents, which they feared, to be like them; save that they appear, and vanish when they please. But the opinion that such spirits were incorporeal, or immaterial, could never enter into the mind of any man by nature; because, though men may put together words of contradictory signification, as *spirit*, and *incorporeal*; yet they can never have the imagination of any thing answering to them: and therefore, men that by their own meditation, arrive to the acknowledgment of one infinite, omnipotent, and eternal God, choose rather to confess he is incomprehensible, and above their understanding, than to define his nature by *spirit incorporeal*, and then confess their definition to be unintelligible: or if they give him such a title, it is not *dogmatically*, with intention to make the divine nature understood; but *piously*, to honour him with attributes, of significations, as remote as they can from the grossness of bodies visible.

Then, for the way by which they think these invisible agents wrought their effects; that is to say, what immediate causes they used, in bringing things to pass, men that know not what it is that we call *causing*, (that is, almost all men) have no other rule to guess by, but by observing, and remembering what they have seen to precede the like effect at some other time, or times before, without seeing between the antecedent and subsequent event, any dependence or connexion at all: and therefore from the like things past, they expect the like things to come; and hope for good or evil luck, superstitiously, from things that have no part at all in the causing of it: as the Athenians did for their war at *Lepanto*, demand another *Phormio*; the Pompeian faction for their war in *Africa*, another *Scipio*; and others have done in divers other occasions since. In like manner they attribute their fortune to a stander by, to a lucky or unlucky place, to words spoken, especially if the name of God be amongst them; as charming and conjuring (the liturgy of witches;) insomuch as to believe, they have power to turn a stone into bread, bread into a man, or any thing into any thing.

Thirdly, for the worship which naturally men exhibit to powers invisible, it can be no other, but such expression of their reverence, as they would use towards men; gifts, petitions, thanks, submission of body, considerate addresses, sober behavior, premeditated words, swearing (that is, assuring one another of their promises,) by invoking them. Beyond that reason suggesteth nothing; but leaves them either to rest there; or for further ceremonies, to rely on those they believe to be wiser than themselves.

Lastly, concerning how these invisible powers declare to men the things which shall hereafter come to pass, especially concerning their good or evil fortune in general, or good or ill success in any particular undertaking, men are naturally at a stand; save that using to conjecture of the time to come, by the time past, they are very apt, not only to take casual things, after one or two encounters, for prognostics of the like encounter ever after, but also to believe the like prognostics from other men, of whom they have once conceived a good opinion.

And in these four things, opinion of ghosts, ignorance of second causes, devotion towards what men fear, and taking of things casual for prognostics, consisteth the natural seed of *religion*; which by reason of the different fancies, judgments, and passions of several men, hath grown up into ceremonies so different, that those which are used by one man, are for the most part ridiculous to another.

For these seeds have received culture from two sorts of men. One sort have been they, that have nourished, and ordered them, according to their own invention. The other have done it, by God's commandment, and direction: but both sorts have done it, with a purpose to make those men that relied on them, the more apt to obedience, laws, peace, charity, and civil society. So that the religion of the former sort, is a part of human politics; and teacheth part of the duty which earthly kings require of their subjects. And the religion of the latter sort is divine politics; and containeth precepts to those that have yielded themselves subjects in the kingdom of God. Of the former sort, were all the founders of commonwealths, and the lawgivers of the Gentiles: of the latter sort, were

Abraham, Moses and our *blessed Saviour;* by whom have been derived unto us the laws of the kingdom of God.

And for that part of religion, which consisteth in opinions concerning the nature of powers invisible, there is almost nothing that has a name, that has not been esteemed amongst the Gentiles, in one place or another, a god, or devil; or by their poets feigned to be inanimated, inhabited, or possessed by some spirit or other.

The unformed matter of the world, was a god, by the name of *Chaos.*

The heaven, the ocean, the planets, the fire, the earth, the winds, were so many gods.

Men, women, a bird, a crocodile, a calf, a dog, a snake, an onion, a leek, deified. Besides that, they filled almost all places, with spirits called *demons;* the plains, with *Pan,* and *Panises,* or Satyrs; the woods, with Fawns, and Nymphs; the sea, with Tritons, and other Nymphs; every river, and fountain, with a ghost of his name, and with Nymphs; every house with its *Lares,* or familiars; every man with his *Genius;* hell with ghosts, and spiritual officers, as *Charon, Cerberus,* and the *Furies;* and in the night time, all places with *larvae, lemures,* ghosts of men deceased, and a whole kingdom of fairies and bugbears. They have also ascribed divinity, and built temples to meer accidents, and qualities; such as are time, night, day, peace, concord, love, contention, virtue, honour, health, rust, fever, and the like; which when they prayed for, or against, they prayed to, as if there were ghosts of those names hanging over their heads, and letting fall, or withholding that good, or evil, for, or against which they prayed. They invoked also their own wit, by the name of *Muses;* their own ignorance, by the name of *Fortune;* their own lust, by the name of *Cupid;* their own rage, by the name *Furies;* their own privy members, by the name of *Priapus,* and attributed their pollutions, to *Incubi,* and *Succubae:* insomuch as there was nothing, which a poet could introduce as a person in his poem, which they did not make either a *god,* or a *devil.*

The same authors of the religion of the Gentiles, observing the second ground for religion, which is men's ignorance of causes; and thereby their aptness to attribute their fortune to causes, on which there was no dependence at all apparent, took occasion to obtrude on their ignorance, instead of second causes, a kind of second and ministerial gods; ascribing the cause of fecundity, to *Venus;* the cause of arts, to *Apollo;* of subtlety and craft, to *Mercury;* of tempests and storms, to *Aeolus;* and of other effects, to other gods; insomuch as there was amongst the heathen almost as great variety of gods, as of business.

And to the worship, which naturally men conceived fit to be used towards their gods, namely, oblations, prayers, thanks, and the rest formerly named; the same legislators of the Gentiles have added their images, both in picture, and sculpture; that the more ignorant sort (that is to say, the most part or generality of the people,) thinking the gods for whose representation they were made, were really included, and as it were housed within them, might so much the more stand in fear of them: and endowed them with lands, and houses, and officers, and revenues, set apart from all other human uses; that is, consecrated, and made holy to those their idols; as caverns, groves, woods, mountains, and whole islands; and have attributed to them, not only the shapes, some of men, some of beasts, some of monsters; but also the faculties, and passions of men and beasts; as sense, speech, sex, lust, generation, (and this not only by mixing one with another, to propagate the kind of gods; but also by mixing with men, and women, to beget mongrel gods, and but inmates of heaven, as *Bacchus, Hercules,* and others;) besides anger, revenge, and other passions of living creatures, and the actions proceeding from them, as fraud, theft, adultery, sodomy, and any vice that may be taken for an effect of power, or a cause of pleasure; and all such vices, as amongst men are taken to be against law, rather than against honour.

Lastly, to the prognostics of time to come; which are naturally, but conjectures upon the experience of time past; and supernaturally, divine revelation; the same authors of the religion of the Gentiles, partly upon pretended experience, partly upon pretended revelation, have added innumerable other superstitious ways of divination; and made men believe they should find their fortunes, sometimes in the ambiguous or senseless answers of the priests at *Delphi, Delos, Ammon,* and other famous oracles; which answers, were made ambiguous by design, to own the event both ways; or absurd, by the intoxicating vapour of the place, which is very frequent in sulphurous caverns: sometimes in the leaves of the Sybils; of whose prophecies (like those perhaps of *Nostradamus;* for the fragments now extant seem to be the invention of later times) there were some books in reputation in the time of the Roman republic: sometimes in the insignificant speeches of madmen, supposed to be possessed with a divine spirit, which possession they called enthusiasm; and these kinds of foretelling events, were accounted theomancy, or prophecy: sometimes in the aspect of the stars at their nativity; which was called horoscopy, and esteemed a part of judiciary astrology: sometimes in their own hopes and fears, called thumomancy, or presage: sometimes in the prediction of witches, that pretended conference with the dead; which is called necromancy, conjuring, and witchcraft; and is but juggling and confederate knavery: sometimes in the casual flight, or feeding of birds: called augury: sometimes in the entrails of a sacrificed beast; which was *aruspicina:* sometimes in dreams: sometimes in croaking of ravens, or chattering of birds: sometimes in the lineaments of the face; which was called metoposcopy; or by palmistry in the lines of the hand; in casual words, called *omina:* sometimes in monsters, or unusual accidents; as eclipses, comets, rare meteors, earthquakes, inundations, uncouth birds, and the like, which they called *portenta,* and *ostenta,* because they thought them to portend, or foreshow some great calamity to come; sometimes, in mere lottery, as cross and pile; counting holes in a sieve; dipping of verses in *Homer,* and *Virgil;* and innumerable other such vain conceits. So easy are men to be drawn to believe any thing, from such men as have gotten credit with them; and can with gentleness, and dexterity, take hold of their fear, and ignorance.

And therefore the first founders, and legislators of commonwealths among the Gentiles, whose ends were only to keep the people in obedience, and peace, have in all places taken care; first, to imprint in their minds a belief, that those precepts which they gave concerning religion, might not be thought to proceed from their own device, but from the dictates of some god, or other spirit; or else that they themselves were of a higher nature than mere mortals, that their laws might the more easily be received: so *Numa Pompilius* pretended to receive the ceremonies he instituted amongst the Romans, from the nymph *Egeria:* and the first king and founder of the kingdom of Peru, pretended himself and his wife to be the children of the Sun: and *Mahomet,* to set up his new religion, pretended to have conferences with the Holy Ghost, in form of a dove. Secondly, they have had a care, to make it believed, that the same things were displeasing the gods, which were forbidden by the laws. Thirdly, to prescribe ceremonies, supplications, sacrifices, and festivals, by which they were to believe, the anger of the gods might be appeased; and that ill success in war, great contagions of sickness, earthquakes, and each man's private misery, came from the anger of the gods, and their anger from the neglect of their worship, or the forgetting, or mistaking some point of the ceremonies required. And though amongst the ancient Romans, men were not forbidden to deny, that which in the poets is written of the pains, and pleasures after this life; which divers of great authority, and gravity in that state have in their *harangues* openly derided; yet that belief was always more cherished, than the contrary.

And by these, and such other institutions, they obtained in order to their end, (which was the peace of the commonwealth,) that the common people in their misfortunes, laying the fault on neglect, or error in their ceremonies, or on their own disobedience to the laws, were the less apt to mutiny against their governors. And being entertained with the pomp, and pastime of festivals, and public games, made in honour of the gods, needed nothing else but bread to keep them from discontent, murmuring, and commotion against the state. And therefore the Romans, that had conquered the greatest part of the then known world, made no scruple of tolerating any religion whatsoever in the city of *Rome* itself, unless it had something in it, that could not consist with their civil government; nor do we read, that any religion was there forbidden, but that of the Jews; who (being the peculiar kingdom of God) thought it unlawful to acknowledge subjection to any mortal king or state whatsoever. And thus you see how the religion of the Gentiles was a part of their policy.

But where God himself, by supernatural revelation, planted religion; there he also made to himself a peculiar kingdom; and gave laws, not only of behaviour towards himself, but also towards one another; and thereby in the kingdom of God, the policy, and laws civil, are a part of religion; and therefore the distinction of temporal, and spiritual domination, hath there no place. It is true, that God is king of all the earth: yet may he be king of a peculiar, and chosen nation. For there is no more incongruity therein, than that he hath the general command of the whole army, should have withal a peculiar regiment, or company of his own. God is king of all the earth by his power: but of his chosen people, he is king by covenant. But to speak more largely of the kingdom of God, both by nature, and covenant, I have in the following discourse assigned another place.

From the propagation of religion, it is not hard to understand the causes of the resolution of the same into its first seeds, or principles; which are only an opinion of a deity, and powers invisible, and supernatural; that can never be so abolished out of human nature, but that new religions may again be made to spring out of them, by the culture of such men, as for such purpose are in reputation.

For seeing all formed religion, is founded at first, upon the faith which a multitude hath in some one person, whom they believe not only to be a wise man, and to labour to procure their happiness, but also to be a holy man, to whom God himself vouchsafeth to declare his will supernaturally; it followeth necessarily, when they that have the government of religion, shall come to have either the wisdom of those men, their sincerity, or their love suspected; or that they shall be unable to show any probable token of divine relevation; that the religion which they desire to uphold, must be suspected likewise; and (without the fear of the civil sword) contradicted and rejected.

That which taketh away the reputation of wisdom, in him that formeth a religion, or addeth to it when it is already formed, is the enjoining of a belief of contradictories: for both parts of a contradiction cannot possibly be true: and therefore to enjoin the belief of them, is an argument of ignorance; which detects the author in that; and discredits him in all things else he shall propound as from revelation supernatural: which revelation a man may indeed have of many things above, but of nothing against natural reason.

That which taketh away the reputation of sincerity, is the doing or saying of such things, as appear to be signs, that what they require other men to believe, is not believed by themselves; all which doings, or sayings are therefore called scandalous, because they be stumbling blocks, that make men to fall in the way of religion: as injustice, cruelty, profaneness, avarice, and luxury. For who can believe, that he that doth ordinarily such actions as proceed from any of these roots, believeth there is any such invisible power to be feared, as he affrighteth other men withal, for lesser faults?

That which taketh away the reputation of love, is the being detected of private ends: as when the belief they require of others, conduceth or seemeth to conduce to the acquiring of dominion, riches, dignity, or secure pleasure, to themselves only, or specially. For that which men reap benefit by to themselves, they are thought to do for their own sakes, and not for love of others.

Lastly, the testimony that men can render of divine calling, can be no other, than the operation of miracles; or true prophecy, (which also is a miracle;) or extraordinary felicity. And therefore, to those points of religion, which have been received from them that did such miracles; those that are added by such, as approve not their calling by some miracle, obtain no greater belief, than what the custom and laws of the places, in which they be educated, have wrought into them. For as in natural things, men of judgment require natural signs, and arguments; so in supernatural things, they require signs supernatural, (which are miracles,) before they consent inwardly, and from their hearts.

All which causes of the weakening of men's faith, do manifestly appear in the examples following. First, we have the example of the children of Israel; who when *Moses,* that had approved his calling to them by miracles, and by the happy conduct of them out of *Egypt,* was absent but 40 days, revolted from the worship of the true God, recommended to them by him; and setting up (*Exod.* 32. 1, 2.) a golden calf for their god, relapsed into the idolatry of the Egyptians; from whom they had been so lately delivered. And again, after *Moses, Aaron, Joshua,* and that generation which had seen the great works of God in Israel, (*Judges* 2. 11.) were dead; another generation arose, and served *Baal.* So that miracles failing, faith also failed.

Again, when the sons of *Samuel,* (1 *Sam.* 8. 3.) being constituted by their father judges in *Bersabee,* received bribes, and judged unjustly, the people of Israel refused any more to have God to be their king, in other manner than he was king of other people; and therefore cried out to Samuel, to choose them a king after the manner of the nations. So that justice failing, faith also failed: insomuch, as they deposed their God, from reigning over them.

And whereas in the planting of Christian religion, the oracles ceased in all parts of the Roman empire, and the number of Christians increased wonderfully every day, and in every place, by the preaching of the Apostles, and Evangelists; a great part of that success, may reasonably be attributed, to the contempt, into which the priests of the Gentiles of that time, had brought themselves, by their uncleanness, avarice, and juggling between princes. Also the religion of the church of *Rome,* was partly, for the same cause abolished in *England,* and many other parts of Christendom; insomuch, as the failing of virtue in the pastors, maketh faith fail in the people: and partly from bringing of the philosophy, and doctrine of *Aristotle* into religion, by the Schoolmen; from whence there arose so many contradictions, and absurdities, as brought the clergy into a reputation both of ignorance, and of fraudulent intention; and inclined people to revolt from them, either against the will of their own princes, as in *France* and *Holland;* or with their will, as in *England.*

Lastly, amongst the points by the church of *Rome* declared necessary for salvation, there be so many, manifestly to the advantage of the Pope, and of his spiritual subjects, residing in the territories of other Christian princes, that were it not for the mutual emulation of those princes, they might without war, or trouble, exclude all foreign authority, as easily as it has been excluded in *England.* For who is there that does not see, to whose benefit it conduceth, to have it believed, that a king hath not his authority from Christ, unless a bishop crown him? That a king, if he be a priest, cannot marry? That whether a prince be born in lawful marriage, or not, must be judged by authority from *Rome?* That subjects may be freed from their allegiance, if by the court of *Rome,* the king be judged an heretic? That a king (as *Chilperic* of *France*) may be deposed by a pope (as Pope *Zachary*) for no cause; and his kingdom given to one of his subjects? That the clergy and regulars, in what country soever, shall be exempt from the jurisdiction of their king, in cases criminal? Or who does not see, to whose profit redound the fees of private masses, and vales of purgatory; with other signs of private interest, enough to mortify the most lively faith, if (as I said) the civil magistrate, and custom did not more sustain it, than any opinion they have of the sanctity, wisdom, or probity of their teachers? So that I may attribute all the changes of religion in the world, to one and the same cause; and that is, unpleasing priests; and those not only amongst Catholics, but even in that church that hath presumed most of reformation.

CHAPTER 13

Of the Natural Condition of Mankind as Concerning Their Felicity, and Misery

Nature hath made men so equal, in the faculties of body, and mind; as that though there be found one man sometimes manifestly stronger in body, or of quicker mind than another; yet when all is reckoned together, the difference between man, and man, is not so considerable, as that one man can thereupon claim to himself any benefit, to which another may not pretend, as well as he. For as to the strength of body, the weakest has strength enough to kill the strongest, either by secret machination, or by confederacy with others, that are in the same danger as himself.

And as to the faculties of the mind, (setting aside the arts grounded upon words, and especially that skill of proceeding upon general, and infallible rules, called science; which very few have, and but in few things; as being not a native faculty, born with us; nor attained, (as prudence,) while we look after someone else,) I find yet a greater equality amongst men, than that of strength. For prudence, is but experience; which equal time, equally bestows on all men, in those things they equally apply themselves unto. That which may perhaps make such equality incredible, is but a vain conceit of one's own wisdom, which almost all men think they have in a greater degree, than the vulgar; that is, than all men but themselves, and a few others, whom by fame, or for concurring with themselves, they approve. For such is the nature of men, that howsoever they may acknowledge many others to be more witty, or more eloquent, or more learned; yet they will hardly believe there be many so wise as themselves: For they see their own wit at hand, and other men's at a distance. But this proveth rather that men are in that point equal, than unequal. For there is not ordinarily a greater sign of the equal distribution of any thing, than that every man is contented with his share.

From this equality of ability, ariseth equality of hope in the attaining of our ends. And therefore if any two men desire the same thing, which nevertheless they cannot both enjoy, they become enemies; and in the way to their end, (which is principally their own conservation, and sometimes their delectation only,) endeavour to destroy, or subdue one another. And from hence it comes to pass, that where an invader hath no more to fear, than another man's single power; if one plant, sow, build, or possess a convenient seat, others may probably be expected to come prepared with forces united, to dispossess, and deprive him, not only of the fruit of his labour, but also of his life, or liberty. And the invader again is in the like danger of another.

And from this diffidence of one another, there is no way for any man to secure himself, so reasonable, as anticipation; that is, by force, or wiles, to master the persons of all men he can, so long, till he see no other power great enough to endanger him: and this is no more than his own conservation requireth, and is generally allowed. Also because there be some, that taking pleasure in contemplating their own power in the acts of conquest, which they pursue farther than their security requires; if others, that otherwise would be glad to be at ease within modest bounds, should not by invasion increase their power, they would not be able, long time, by standing only on their defence, to subsist. And by consequence, such augmentation of dominion over men, being necessary to a man's conservation, it ought to be allowed him.

Again, men have no pleasure, (but on the contrary a great deal of grief) in keeping company, where there is no power able to over-awe them all. For every man looketh that his companion should value him, at the same rate he sets upon himself: and upon all signs of contempt, or undervaluing, naturally endeavours, as far as he dares (which amongst them that have no common power to keep them in quiet, is far enough to make them destroy each other,) to extort a greater value from his contemners, by damage; and from others, by the example.

So that in the nature of man, we find three principal causes of quarrel. First, competition; secondly, diffidence; thirdly, glory.

The first, maketh man invade for gain; the second, for safety; and the third, for reputation. The first use violence, to make themselves masters of other men's persons, wives, children, and cattle; the second, to defend them; the third, for trifles, as a word, a smile, a different opinion, and any other sign of undervalue, either direct in their persons, or by reflection in their kindred, their friends, their nation, their profession, or their name.

Hereby it is manifest, that during the time men live without a common power to keep them all in awe, they are in that condition which is called war; and such a war, as is of every man, against every man. For WAR, consisteth not in battle only, or the act of fighting; but in a tract of time, wherein the will to contend by battle is sufficiently known: and therefore the notion of *time,* is to be considered in the nature of war; as it is in the nature of weather. For as the nature of foul weather, lieth not in a shower or two of rain; but in an inclination thereto of many days together: so the nature of war, consisteth not in actual fighting; but in the known disposition thereto, during all the time there is no assurance to the contrary. All other time is PEACE.

Whatsoever therefore is consequent to a time of war, where every man is enemy to every man; the same is consequent to the time, wherein men live without other security, than what their own strength, and their own invention shall furnish them withal. In such condition, there is no place for industry; because the fruit thereof is uncertain: and consequently no culture of the earth; no navigation, nor use of the commodities that may be imported by sea; no commodious building; no instruments of moving, and removing such things as require much force; no knowledge of the face of the earth; no account of time; no arts; no letters; no society; and which is worst of all, continual fear, and danger of violent death; and the life of man, solitary, poor, nasty, brutish, and short.

It may seem strange to some man, that has not well weighed these things; that nature should thus dissociate, and render men apt to invade, and destroy one another: and he may therefore, not trusting to this inference, made from the passions, desire perhaps to have the same confirmed by experience. Let him therefore consider with himself, when taking a journey, he arms himself, and seeks to go well accompanied; when going to sleep, he locks his doors; when even in his house he locks his chests; and this when he knows there be laws, and public officers, armed, to revenge all injuries shall be done him; what opinion he has of his fellow subjects, when he rides armed; of his fellow citizens, when he locks his doors; and of his children, and servants, when he locks his chests. Does he not there as much accuse mankind by his actions, as I do by my words? But neither of us accuse man's nature in it. The desires, and other passions of man, are in themselves no sin. No more are the actions, that proceed from those passions, till they know a law that forbids them: which till laws be made they cannot know: nor can any law be made, till they have agreed upon the person that shall make it.

It may peradventure be thought, there was never such a time, nor condition of war as this; and I believe it was never generally so, over all the world: but there are many places, where they live so now. For the savage people in many places of *America,* except the government of small families, the concord whereof dependeth on natural lust, have no government at all; and live at this day in that brutish manner, as I said before. Howsoever, it may be perceived what manner of life there would be, where there were no common power to fear; by the manner of life, which men that have formerly lived under a peacefull government, use to degenerate into, in a civil war.

But though there had never been any time, wherein particular men were in a condition of war one against another; yet in all times, kings, and persons of sovereign authority, because of their independency, are in continual jealousies, and in the state and posture of gladiators; having their weapons pointing, and their eyes fixed on one another; that is, their forts, garrisons, and guns upon the frontiers of their kingdoms; and continual spies upon their neighbours; which is a posture of war. But because they uphold thereby, the industry of their subjects; there does not follow from it, that misery, which accompanies the liberty of particular men.

To this war of every man against every man, this also is consequent; that nothing can be unjust. The notions of right and wrong, justice and injustice have there no place. Where there is no common power, there is no law: where no law, no injustice. Force, and fraud, are in war the two cardinal virtues. Justice, and injustice are none of the faculties neither of the body, nor mind. If they were, they might be in a man that were alone in the world, as well as his senses, and passions. They are qualities, that relate to men in society, not in solitude. It is consequent also to the same condition, that there be no propriety, no dominion, no *mine* and *thine* distinct; but only that to be every man's, that he can get; and for so long, as he can keep it. And thus much for the ill condition, which many by mere nature is actually placed in; though with a possibility to come out of it, consisting partly in the passions, partly in his reason.

The passions that incline men to peace, are fear of death; desire of such things as are necessary to commodious living; and a hope by their industry to obtain them. And reason suggesteth convenient articles of peace, upon which men may be drawn to agreement. These articles, are they, which otherwise are called the Laws of Nature: whereof I shall speak more particularly, in the two following chapters.

CHAPTER 14

Of the First and Second Natural Laws, and of Contracts

The RIGHT OF NATURE, which writers commonly call *jus naturale,* is the liberty each man hath, to use his own power, as he will himself, for the preservation of his own nature; that is to say, of his own life; and consequently, of doing any thing, which in his own judgment, and reason, he shall conceive to be the aptest means thereunto.

By LIBERTY, is understood, according to the proper signification of the word, the absence of external impediments: which impediments, may oft take away part of a man's power to do what he would; but cannot hinder him from using the power left him, according as his judgment, and reason shall dictate to him.

A LAW OF NATURE, (*lex naturalis,*) is a precept, or general rule, found out by reason, by which a man is forbidden to do that, which is destructive of his life, or taketh away the means of preserving the same; and to omit that, by which he thinketh it may be best preserved. For though they that speak of this subject, use to confound *jus,* and *lex, right* and *law;* yet they ought to be distinguished; because RIGHT, consisteth in liberty to do, or to forbear; whereas LAW, determineth, and bindeth to one of them: so that law, and right, differ as much, as obligation, and liberty; which in one and the same matter are inconsistent.

And because the condition of man, (as hath been declared in the precedent chapter) is a condition of war of every one against every one; in which case every one is governed by his own reason; and there is nothing he can make use of, that may not be a help unto him, in preserving his life against his enemies; it followeth, that in such a condition, every man has a right to every thing: even to one another's body. And therefore, as long as this natural right of every man to every thing endureth, there can be no security to any man, (how strong or wise soever he be,) of living out the time, which nature ordinarily alloweth men to live. And consequently it is a precept, or general rule of reason, *that every man, ought to endeavour peace, as far as he has hope of obtaining it; and when he cannot obtain it, that he may seek, and use, all helps, and advantages of war.* The first branch of which rule, containeth the first, and fundamental law of nature; which is, *to seek peace, and follow it.* The second, the sum of the right of nature; which is, *by all means we can, to defend ourselves.*

From this fundamental law of nature, by which men are commanded to endeavor peace, is derived this second law; *that a man be willing, when others are so too, as farforth, as for peace, and defence of himself he shall think it necessary, to lay down this right to all things; and be contented with so much liberty against other men, as he would allow other men against himself.* For as long as every man holdeth this right, of doing any thing he liketh; so long are all men in the condition of war. But if other men will not lay down their right, as well as he; then there is no reason for any one, to divest himself of his: for that were to expose himself to prey, (which no man is bound to) rather than to dispose himself to peace. This is that law of the Gospel; *whatsoever you require that others should do for you, that do ye to them.* And that law of all men, *quod tibi fieri non vis, alteri ne feceris.*

To *lay down* a man's *right* to any thing, is to *divest* himself of the *liberty,* of hindering another of the benefit of his own right to the same. For he that renounceth, or passeth away his right, giveth not to any other man a right which he had not before; because there is nothing to which every man had not right by nature: but only standeth out of his way, that he may enjoy his own original right, without hindrance from him; not without hindrance from another. So that the effect which redoundeth to one man, by another man's defect of right, is but so much diminution of impediments to the use of his own right original.

Right is laid aside, either by simply renouncing it; or by transferring it to another. By *simply* RENOUNCING; when he cares not to whom the benefit thereof redoundeth. By TRANSFERRING; when he intendeth the benefit thereof to some certain person, or persons. And when a man hath in either manner abandoned, or granted away his right; then is he said to be OBLIGED, or BOUND, not to hinder those, to whom such right is granted, or abandoned, from the benefit of it: and that he *ought,* and it is his DUTY, not to make void that voluntary act of his own: and that such hindrance is INJUSTICE, and INJURY, as being *sine jure;* the right being before renounced, or transferred. So that *injury,* or *injustice,* in the controversies of the world, is somewhat like to that, which in the disputations of scholars is called *absurdity.* For as it is there called an absurdity, to contradict what one maintained in the beginning: so in the world, it is called injustice, and injury, voluntarily to undo that, which from the beginning he had voluntarily done.

The way by which a man either simply renounceth, or transferreth his right, is a declaration, or signification, by some voluntary and sufficient sign, or signs, that he doth so renounce, or transfer; or hath so renounced, or transferred the same, to him that accepteth it. And these signs are either words only, or actions only; or (as it happeneth most often) both words, and actions. And the same are the BONDS, by which men are bound, and obliged: bonds, that have their strength, not from their own nature, (for nothing is more easily broken than a man's word,) but from fear of some evil consequence upon the rupture.

Whensoever a man transferreth his right, or renounceth it; it is either in consideration of some right reciprocally transferred to himself; or for some other good he hopeth for thereby. For it is a voluntary act: and of the voluntary acts of every man, the object is some *good to himself.* And therefore there be some rights, which no man can be understood by any words, or other signs, to have abandoned, or transferred. As first a man cannot lay down the right of resisting them, that assault him by force, to take away his life; because he cannot be understood to aim thereby, at any good to himself. The same may be said of wounds, and chains, and imprisonment; both because there is no benefit consequent to such patience; as there is to the patience of suffering another to be wounded, or imprisoned: as also because a man cannot tell, when he seeth men proceed against him by violence, whether they intend his death or not. And lastly the motive, and end for which this renouncing, and transferring of right is introduced, is nothing else but the security of a man's person, in his life, and in the means of so preserving life, as not to be weary of it. And therefore if a man by words, or other signs, seem to despoil himself of the end, for which those signs were intended; he is not to be understood as if he meant it, or that it was his will; but that he was ignorant of how such words and actions were to be interpreted.

The mutual transferring of right, is that which men call CONTRACT.

There is difference between transferring of right to the thing; and transferring, or tradition, that is, delivery of the thing it self. For the thing may be delivered together with the translation of the right; as in buying and selling with ready money; or exchange of goods, or lands: and it may be delivered some time after.

Again, one of the contractors, may deliver the thing contracted for on his part, and leave the other to perform his part at some determinate time after, and in the mean time be trusted; and then the contract on his part, is called PACT, or COVENANT: or both parts may contract now, to perform hereafter: in which cases, he that is to perform in time to come, being trusted, his performance is called *keeping of promise,* or faith; and the failing of performance (if it be voluntary) *violation of faith.*

When the transferring of right, is not mutual; but one of the parties transferreth, in hope to gain thereby friendship, or service from another, or from his friends; or in hope to gain the reputation of charity, or magnanimity; or to deliver his mind from the pain of compassion; or in hope of reward in heaven; this is not contract, but GIFT, FREE-GIFT, GRACE: which words signify one and the same thing.

Signs of contract, are either *express,* or *by inference.* Express, are words spoken with understanding of what they signify: and such words are either of the time *present,* or *past;* as, *I give, I grant, I have given, I have granted, I will that this be yours:* or of the future; as, *I will give, I will grant:* which words of the future are called PROMISE.

Signs by inference, are sometimes the consequence of words; sometimes the consequence of silence; sometimes the consequence of actions; sometimes the consequence of forbearing an action: and generally a sign by inference, of any contract, in whatsoever sufficiently argues the will of the contractor.

Words alone, if they be of the time to come, and contain a bare promise, are an insufficient sign of a free-gift and therefore not obligatory. For if they be of the time to come, as, *tomorrow I will give,* they are a sign I have not given yet, and consequently that my right is not transferred, but remaineth till I transfer it by some other act. But if the words be of the time present, or past, as, *I have given, or do give to be delivered tomorrow,* then is my tomorrow's right given away to day; and that by the virtue of the words, though there were no other argument of my will. And there is a great difference in the signification of these words, *volo hoc tuum esse cras,* and *cras dabo;* that is, between *I will that this be thine tomorrow,* and, *I will give it thee tomorrow:* for the word *I will,* in the former manner of speech, signifies an act of the will present; but in the latter, it signifies a promise of an act of the will to come: and therefore the former words, being of the present, transfer a future right; the latter, that be of the future, transfer nothing. But if there be other signs of the will to transfer a right, besides words; then, though the gift be free, yet may the right be understood to pass by words of the future: as if a man propound a prize to him that comes first to the end of a race; the gift is free; and though the words be of the future, yet the right passeth: for if he would not have his words so be understood, he should not have let them run.

In contracts, the right passeth, not only where the words are of the time present, or past, but also where they are of the future: because all contract is mutual translation, or change of right; and therefore he that promiseth only, because he hath already received the benefit for which he promiseth, is to be understood as if he intended the right should pass: for unless he had been content to have his words so understood, the other would not have performed his part first. And for that cause, in buying, and selling, and other acts of contract, a promise is equivalent to a covenant; and therefore obligatory.

He that performeth first in the case of a contract, is said to MERIT that which he is to receive by the performance of the other; and he hath it as *due.* Also when a prize is propounded to many, which is to be given to him only that winneth; or money is thrown amongst many, to be enjoyed by them that catch it; though this be a free gift; yet so to win, or so to catch, is to *merit,* and to have it as DUE. For the right is transferred in the propounding of the prize, and in throwing down the money; though it be not determined to whom, but by the event of the contention. But there is between these two sorts of merit, this difference, that in contract, I merit by virtue of my own power, and the contractor's need; but in this case of free gift, I am enabled to merit only by the benignity of the giver: in contract, I merit at the contractor's hand that he should depart with his right; in this case of gift, I merit not that the giver should part with his right; but that when he has parted with it, it should be mine, rather than another's. And this I think to be the meaning of that distinction of the Schools, between *meritum congrui,* and *meritum condigni.* For God Almighty, having promised Paradise to those men (hoodwinked with carnal desires,) that can walk through this world according to the precepts, and limits prescribed by him; they say, he that shall so walk, shall merit Paradise *ex congruo.* But because no man can demand a right to it, by his own righteousness, or any other power in himself, but by the free grace of God only; they say, no man can merit Paradise *ex condigno.* This I say, I think is the meaning of that distinction; but because disputers do not agree upon the signification of their own terms of art, longer than it serves their turn; I will not affirm any thing of their meaning: only this I say; when a gift is given indefinitely, as a prize to be contended for, he that winneth meriteth, and may claim the prize as due.

If a covenant be made, wherein neither of the parties perform presently, but trust one another; in the condition of mere nature, (which is a condition of war of every man against every man,) upon any reasonable suspicion, it is void: but if there be a common power set over them both, with right and force sufficient to compel performance, it is not void. For

he that performeth first, has no assurance the other will perform after; because the bonds
of words are too weak to bridle men's ambition, avarice, anger, and other passions, without the fear of some coercive power; which in the condition of mere nature, where all men
are equal, and judges of the justness of their own fears, cannot possibly be supposed. And
therefore he which performeth first, does but betray himself to his enemy; contrary to the
right (he can never abandon) of defending his life, and means of living.

But in a civil estate, where there is a power set up to constrain those that would otherwise violate their faith, that fear is no more reasonable; and for that cause, he which by the
covenant is to perform first, is obliged so to do.

The cause of fear, which maketh such a covenant invalid, must be always something
arising after the covenant made; as some new fact, or other sign of the will not to perform:
else it cannot make the covenant void. For that which could not hinder a man from
promising, ought not to be admitted as a hindrance of performing.

He that transferreth any right, transferreth the means of enjoying it, as far as lieth in
his power. As he that selleth land, is understood to transfer the herbage, and whatsoever
grows upon it; nor can he that sells a mill turn away the stream that drives it. And they
that give to a man the right of government in sovereignty, are understood to give him
the right of levying money to maintain soldiers; and of appointing magistrates for the
administration of justice.

To make covenants with brute beasts, is impossible; because not understanding our
speech, they understand not, nor accept of any translation of right; not can translate any
right to another: and without mutual acceptation, there is no covenant.

To make covenant with God, is impossible, but by mediation of such as God speaketh
to, either by revelation supernatural, or by his lieutenants that govern under him, and in
his name: for otherwise we know not whether our covenants be accepted, or not. And
therefore they that vow any thing contrary to any law of nature, vow in vain; as being a
thing unjust to pay such vow. And if it be a thing commanded by the law of nature, it is
not the vow, but the law that binds them.

The matter, or subject of a covenant, is always something that falleth under deliberation; (for to covenant, is an act of the will; that is to say an act, and the last act, of deliberation;) and is therefore always understood to be something to come; and which is judged
possible for him that covenanteth, to perform.

And therefore, to promise that which is known to be impossible, is no covenant. But
if that prove impossible afterwards, which before was thought possible, the covenant is
valid, and bindeth, (though not to the thing it self,) yet to the value, or if that also be
impossible, to the unfeigned endeavour of performing as much as is possible: for to more
no man can be obliged.

Men are freed of their covenants two ways; by performing; or by being forgiven. For
performance, is the natural end of obligation; and forgiveness, the restitution of liberty; as
being a retransferring of that right, in which the obligation consisted.

Covenants entered into by fear, in the condition of mere nature, are obligatory. For
example, if I covenant to pay a ransom, or service for my life, to an enemy; I am bound by
it. For it is a contract, wherein one receiveth the benefit of life; the other is to receive
money, or service for it; and consequently, where no other law (as in the condition, of mere
nature) forbiddeth the performance, the covenant is valid. Therefore prisoners of war, if
trusted with the payment of their ransom, are obliged to pay it: and if a weaker prince,
make a disadvantageous peace with a stronger, for fear; he is bound to keep it; unless (as
hath been said before) there ariseth some new, and just cause of fear, to renew the war. And
even in commonwealths, if I be forced to redeem myself from a thief by promising him

money, I am bound to pay it, till the civil law discharge me. For whatsoever I may lawfully do without obligation, the same I may lawfully covenant to do through fear: and what I lawfully covenant, I cannot lawfully break.

A former covenant, makes void a later. For a man that hath passed away his right to one may today, hath it not to pass tomorrow to another: and therefore the later promise passeth no right, but is null.

A covenant not to defend myself from force, by force, is always void. For (as I have showed before) no man can transfer, or lay down his right to save himself from death, wounds, and imprisonment, (the avoiding whereof is the only end of laying down any right, and therefore the promise of not resisting force, in no covenant transferreth any right; nor is obliging. For though a man may covenant thus, *unless I do so, or so, kill me;* he cannot covenant thus, *unless I do so, or so, I will not resist you, when you come to kill me.* For man by nature chooseth the lesser evil, which is danger of death in resisting; rather than the greater, which is certain and present death in not resisting. And this is granted to be true by all men, in that they lead criminals to execution, and prison, with armed men, notwithstanding that such criminals have consented to the law, by which they are condemned.

A covenant to accuse one self, without assurance of pardon, is likewise invalid. For in the condition of nature, where every man is judge, there is no place for accusation: and in the civil state, the accusation is followed with punishment; which being force, a man is not obliged not to resist. The same is also true, of the accusation of those, by whose condemnation a man falls into misery; as of a father, wife, or benefactor. For the testimony of such an accuser, if it be not willingly given, is presumed to be corrupted by nature; and therefore not to be received: and where a man's testimony is not to be credited, he is not bound to give it. Also accusations upon torture, are not to be reputed as testimonies. For torture is to be used but as means of conjecture, and light, in the further examination, and search of truth: and what is in that case confessed, tendeth to the ease of him that is tortured, not to the informing of the torturers: and therefore ought not to have the credit of a sufficient testimony: for whether he deliver himself by true, or false accusation, he does it by the right of preserving his own life.

The force of words, being (as I have formerly noted) too weak to hold men to the performance of their covenants; there are in man's nature, but two imaginable helps to strengthen it. And those are either a fear of the consequence of breaking their word; or a glory, or pride in appearing not to need to break it. This latter is a generosity too rarely found to be presumed on, especially in the pursuers of wealth, command, or sensual pleasure; which are the greatest part of mankind. The passion to be reckoned upon, is fear; whereof there be two very general objects: one, the power of spirits invisible; the other, the power of those men they shall therein offend. Of these two, though the former be the greater power, yet the fear of the latter is commonly the greater fear. The fear of the former is in every man, his own religion: which hath place in the nature of man before civil society. The latter hath not so; at least not place enough, to keep men to their promises; because in the condition of mere nature, the inequality of power is not discerned, but by the event of battle. So that before the time of civil society, or in the interruption thereof by war, there is nothing can strengthen a covenant of peace agreed on, against the temptations of avarice, ambition, lust, or other strong desire, but the fear of that invisible power, which they every one worship as God; and fear as a revenger of their perfidy. All therefore that can be done between two men not subject to civil power, is to put one another to swear by the God he feareth: which *swearing,* or OATH, is a *form of speech, added to a promise; by which he that promiseth, signifieth, that unless he perform, he renounceth the mercy of his God, or calleth to him for vengeance on himself.* Such was the heathen form, *Let* Jupiter *kill me else, as I kill this beast.* So is our form, *I shall do thus, and thus, so help me God.* And this, with the rites and ceremonies, which every one useth in his own religion, that the fear of breaking faith might be the greater.

By this it appears, that an oath taken according to any other form, or rite, than his, that sweareth, is in vain; and no oath: and that there is no swearing by any thing which the swearer thinks not God. For though men have sometimes used to swear by their kings, for fear, or flattery; yet they would have it thereby understood, they attributed to them divine honour. And that swearing unnecessarily by God, is but prophaning of his name: and swearing by other things, as men do in common discourse, is not swearing, but an impious custom, gotten by too much vehemence of talking.

It appears also, that the oath adds nothing to the obligation. For a covenant, if lawful, binds in the sight of God, without the oath, as much as with it: if unlawful, bindeth not at all; though it be confirmed with an oath.

CHAPTER 15

Of Other Laws of Nature

From that law of nature, by which we are obliged to transfer to another, such rights, as being retained, hinder the peace of mankind, there followeth a third; which is this, *that men perform their covenants made:* without which, covenants are in vain, and but empty words; and the right of all men to all things remaining, we are still in the condition of war.

And in this law of nature, consisteth the fountain and original of JUSTICE. For where no covenant hath preceded, there hath no right been transferred, and every man has right to every thing; and consequently, no action can be unjust. But when a covenant is made, then to break it is *unjust;* and the definition of INJUSTICE, is no other than *the not performance of covenant.* And whatsoever is not unjust, is *just.*

But because covenants of mutual trust, where there is fear of not performance on either part, (as hath been said in the former chapter,) are invalid; though the original of justice be the making of covenants; yet injustice actually there can be none, till the cause of such fear be taken away; which while men are in the natural condition of war, cannot be done. Therefore before the names of just, and unjust can have place, there must be some coercive power, to compel men equally to the performance of their covenants, by the terror of some punishment, greater than the benefit they expect by the breach of their covenant; and to make good that propriety, which by mutual contract men acquire, in recompense of the universal right they abandon: and such power there is none before the erection of a commonwealth. And this is also to be gathered out of the ordinary definition of justice in the Schools: for they say, that *justice is the constant will of giving to every man his own.* And therefore where there is no *own,* that is, no propriety, there is no injustice; and where there is no coercive power erected, that is, where there is no commonwealth, there is no propriety; all men having right to all things: therefore where there is no comonwealth, there nothing is unjust. So that the nature of justice, consisteth in keeping of valid covenants: but the validity of covenants begins not but with the constitution of a civil power, sufficient to compel men to keep them: and then it is also that propriety begins.

The fool hath said in his heart, there is no such thing as justice; and sometimes also with his tongue; seriously alleging, that every man's conservation, and contentment, being committed to his own care, there could be no reason, why every man might not do what he thought conduced thereunto: and therefore also to make, or not make; keep, or not keep covenants, was not against reason, when it conduced to one's benefit. He does not therein deny, that there be covenants; and that they are sometimes broken, sometimes kept; and that such breach of them may be called injustice, and the observance of them justice: but he questioneth, whether injustice, taking away the fear of God, (for the same fool hath said in his heart there is no God,) may not sometimes stand with that reason, which dictateth to every man his own good; and particularly then, when it conduceth to such a benefit, as shall put a man in a condition, to neglect not only the dispraise, and revilings, but also the power of other men. The kingdom of God is gotten by violence: but what if it could be gotten by unjust violence? were it against reason so to get it, when it is impossible to receive hurt by it? and if it be not against reason, it is not against justice; or else justice is not to be approved for good. From such reasoning as this, successful wickedness hath obtained the name of virtue: and some that in all other things have disallowed the violation of faith; yet have allowed it, when it is for the getting of a kingdom. And the heathen that believed, that *Saturn* was deposed by his son *Jupiter,* believed nevertheless the same *Jupiter* to be the avenger of injustice: somewhat like to a piece of law in *Coke's Commentaries on Littleton;* where he says, if the right heir of the crown be attainted of treason; yet the crown shall descend to him, and *eo instante* the attainder be void: from which instances a man will be very prone to infer; that when the heir apparent of a kingdom, shall kill him that is in possession, though his father; you may call it injustice, or by what other name you will; yet it can never be against reason, seeing all the voluntary actions of men tend to the benefit of themselves; and those actions are most reasonable, that conduce most to their ends. This specious reasoning is nevertheless false.

For the question is not of promises mutual, where there is no security of performance on either side; as when there is no civil power erected over the parties promising; for such promises are no covenants: but either where one of the parties has performed already; or where there is a power to make him perform; there is the question whether it be against reason, that is, against the benefit of the other to perform, or not. And I say it is not against reason. For the manifestation whereof, we are to consider; first, that when a man doth a thing, which notwithstanding any thing can be foreseen, and reckoned on, tendeth to his own destruction, howsoever some accident which he could not expect, arriving may turn it to his benefit; yet such events do not make it reasonably or wisely done. Secondly, that in a condition of war, wherein every man to every man, for want of a common power to keep them all in awe, is an enemy, there is no man can hope by his own strength, or wit, to defend himself from destruction, without the help of confederates; where every one expects the same defence by the confederation, that any one else does: and therefore he which declares he thinks it reason to deceive those that help him, can in reason expect no other means of safety, than what can be had from his own single power. He therefore that breaketh his covenant, and consequently declareth that he thinks he may with reason do so, cannot be received into any society, that unite themselves for peace and defence, but by the error of them that receive him; nor when he is received, be retained in it, without seeing the danger of their error; which errors a man cannot reasonably reckon upon as the means of his security: and therefore if he be left, or cast out of society, he perisheth; and if he live in society, it is by the errors of other men, which he could not foresee, nor reckon upon; and consequently against the reason of his preservation; and so, as all men that contribute not to his destruction, forbear him only out of ignorance of what is good for themselves.

As for the instance of gaining the secure and perpetual felicity of heaven, by any way; it is frivolous: there being but one way imaginable; and that is not breaking, but keeping of covenant.

And for the other instances of attaining sovereignty by rebellion; it is manifest, that though the event follow, yet because it cannot reasonably be expected, but rather the contrary; and because by gaining it so, others are taught to gain the same in like manner, the attempt thereof is against reason. Justice therefore, that is to say, keeping of covenant, is a rule of reason, by which we are forbidden to do any thing destructive to our life; and consequently a law of nature.

There be some that proceed further; and will not have the law of nature, to be those rules which conduce to the preservation of man's life on earth; but to the attaining of an eternal felicity after death; to which they think the breach of covenant may conduce; and consequently be just and reasonable; (such are they that think it a work of merit to kill, or depose, or rebel against, the sovereign power constituted over them by their own consent.) But because there is no natural knowledge of man's estate after death; much less of the reward that is then to be given to breach of faith; but only a belief grounded upon other men's saying, that they know it supernaturally, or that they know those, that knew them, that knew others, that knew it supernaturally; breach of faith cannot be called a precept of reason, or nature.

Others, that allow for a law of nature, the keeping of faith, do nevertheless make exception of certain persons; as heretics, and such as use not to perform their covenant to others: and this also is against reason. For if any fault of a man, be sufficient to discharge our covenant made; the same ought in reason to have been sufficient to have hindered the making of it.

The names of just, and unjust, when they are attributed to men, signify one thing; and when they are attributed to actions, another. When they are attributed to men, they signify conformity, or inconformity of manners, to reason. But when they are attributed to actions, they signify the conformity, or inconformity to reason, not of manners, or manner of life, but of particular actions. A just man therefore, is he that taketh all the care he can, that his actions may all be just: and an unjust man, is he that neglecteth it. And such men are more often in our language styled by the names of righteous, and unrighteous; than just, and unjust; though the meaning be the same. Therefore a righteous man, does not lose that title, by one, or a few unjust actions, that proceed from sudden passion, or mistake of things, or persons: nor does an unrighteous man, lose his character, for such actions, as he does, or forbears to do, for fear: because his will is not framed by the justice, but by the apparent benefit of what he is to do. That which gives to human actions the relish of justice, is a certain nobleness or gallantness of courage, (rarely found,) by which a man scorns to be beholding for the contentment of his life, to fraud, or breach of promise. This justice of the manners, is that which is meant, where justice is called a virtue; and injustice a vice.

But the justice of actions denominates men, not just, but *guiltless:* and the injustice of the same, (which is also called injury,) gives them but the name of *guilty.*

Again, the injustice of manners, is the disposition, or aptitude to do injury; and is injustice before it proceed to act; and without supposing any individual person injured. But the injustice of an action, (that is to say injury,) supposeth an individual person injured; namely him, to whom the covenant was made: and therefore many times the injury is received by one man, when the damage redoundeth to another. As when the master commandeth his servant to give money to a stranger; if it be not done, the injury is done to the master, whom he had before covenanted to obey; but the damage redoundeth to the stranger, to whom he had no obligation; and therefore could not injure him. And so also in commonwealths, private men may remit to one another their debts; but not robberies or other violences, whereby they are endamaged; because the detaining of debt, is an injury to themselves; but robbery and violence, are injuries to the person of the commonwealth.

Whatsoever is done to a man, conformable to his own will signified to the doer, is no injury to him. For if he that doeth it, hath not passed away his original right to do what he please, by some antecedent covenant, there is no breach of covenant; and therefore no injury done him. And if he have; then his will to have it done being signified, is a release of that covenant: and so again there is no injury done him.

Justice of actions, is by writers divided into *commutative,* and *distributive:* and the former they say consisteth in proportion arithmetical; the latter in proportion geometrical. Commutative therefore, they place in the equality of value of the things contracted for; and distributive, in the distribution of equal benefit, to men of equal merit. As if it were injustice to sell dearer than we buy; or to give more to a man than he merits. The value of all things contracted for, is measured by the appetite of the contractors: and therefore the just value, is that which they be contented to give. And merit, (besides that which is by covenant, where the performance on one part, meriteth the performance of the other part, and falls under justice commutative, not distributive,) is not due by justice; but is rewarded of grace only. And therefore this distinction, in the sense wherein it useth to be expounded, is not right. To speak properly, commutative justice, is the justice of a contractor; that is, a performance of covenant, in buying, and selling; hiring, and letting to hire; lending, and borrowing; exchanging, bartering, and other acts of contract.

And distributive justice, the justice of an arbitrator; that is to say, the act of defining what is just. Wherein, (being trusted by them that make him arbitrator,) if he perform his trust, he is said to distribute to every man his own: and this is indeed just distribution, and may be called, (though improperly,) distributive justice; but more properly equity; which also is a law of nature, as shall be shown in due place.

As justice dependeth on antecedent covenant; so does GRATITUDE depend on antecedent grace; that is to say, antecedent free-gift: and is the fourth law of nature: which may be conceived in this form, *that a man which receiveth benefit from another of mere grace, endeavour that he which giveth it, have no reasonable cause to repent him of his good will.* For no man giveth, but with intention of good to himself; because gift is voluntary; and of all voluntary acts, the object is to every man his own good; of which if men see they shall be frustrated, there will be no beginning of benevolence, or trust; nor consequently of mutual help; nor of reconciliation of one man to another; and therefore they are to remain still in the condition of *war;* which is contrary to the first and fundamental law of nature, which commandeth men to *seek peace.* The breach of this law, is called *ingratitude;* and hath the same relation to grace, that injustice hath to obligation by covenant.

A fifth law of nature, is COMPLAISANCE; that is to say, *that every man strive to accommodate himself to the rest.* For the understanding whereof, we may consider, that there is in men's aptness to society, a diversity of nature, rising from their diversity of affections; not unlike to that we see in stones brought together for the building of an edifice. For as that stone which by the asperity, and irregularity of figure, takes more room from others, than itself fills; and for the hardness, cannot be easily made plain, and thereby hindereth the building, is by the builders cast away as unprofitable, and troublesome: so also, a man that by asperity of nature, will strive to retain those things which to himself are superfluous, and to others necessary; and for the stubbornness of his passions, cannot be corrected, is to be left, or cast out of society, as cumbersome thereunto. For seeing every man, not only by right, but also by necessity of nature, is supposed to endeavour all he can, to obtain that which is necessary for his conservation; he that shall oppose himself against it, for things superfluous, is guilty of the war that thereupon is to follow; and therefore doth that, which is contrary to the fundamental law of nature, which commandeth *to seek peace.* The observers of this law, may be called SOCIABLE, (the Latins call them *commodi;*) the contrary, *stubborn, insociable, froward, intractable.*

A sixth law of nature, is that, *that upon caution of the future time, a man ought to pardon the offences past of them that repenting, desire it.* For PARDON, is nothing but granting of peace; which though granted to them that persevere in their hostility, be not peace, but fear; yet not granted to them that give caution of the future time, is sign of an aversion to peace; and therefore contrary to the law of nature.

A seventh is, *that in revenges,* (that is retribution of evil for evil,) *men look not at the greatness of the evil past, but the greatness of the good to follow.* Whereby we are forbidden to inflict punishment with any other design, than for correction of the offender, or direction to others. For this law is consequent to the next before it, that commandeth pardon, upon security of the future time. Besides, revenge without respect to the example, and profit to come, is a triumph, or glorying in the hurt of another, tending to no end; (for the end is always somewhat to come;) and glorying to no end, is vain-glory, and contrary to reason; and to hurt without reason, tendeth to the introduction of war; which is against the law of nature; and is commonly styled by the name of *cruelty.*

And because all signs of hatred, or contempt, provoke to fight, insomuch as most men choose rather to hazard their life, than not to be revenged; we may in the eighth place, for a law of nature, set down this precept, *that no man by deed, word, countenance, or gesture, declare hatred, or contempt of another.* The breach of which law, is commonly called *contumely.*

The question who is the better man, has no place in the condition of mere nature; where, (as has been shewn before,) all men are equal. The inequality that now is, has been introduced by the laws civil. I know that *Aristotle* in the first book of his *Politics,* for a foundation of his doctrine, maketh men by nature, some more worthy to command, meaning the wiser sort, (such as he thought himself to be for his philosophy;) others to serve, (meaning those that had strong bodies, but were not philosophers as he;) as if master and servant were not introduced by consent of men, but by difference of wit: which is not only against reason; but also against experience. For there are very few so foolish, that had not rather govern themselves, than be governed by others; nor when the wise in their own conceit, contend by force, with them who distrust their own wisdom, do they always, or often, or almost at any time, get the victory. If nature therefore have made men equal, that equality is to be acknowledged: or if nature have made men unequal; yet because men that think themselves equal, will not enter into conditions of peace, but upon equal terms, such equality must be admitted. And therefore for the ninth law of nature, I put this, *that every man acknowledge other for his equal by nature.* The breach of this precept is *pride.*

On this law, dependeth another, *that at the entrance into conditions of peace, no man require to reserve to himself any right, which he is not content should be reserved to every one of the rest.* As it is necessary for all men that seek peace, to lay down certain rights of nature; that is to say, not to have liberty to do all they list: so is it necessary for man's life, to retain some; as right to govern their own bodies; enjoy air, water, motion, ways to go from place to place; and all things else without which a man cannot live, or not live well. If in this case, at the making of peace, men require for themselves, that which they would not have to be granted to others, they do contrary to the precedent law, that commandeth the acknowledgment of natural equality, and therefore also against the law of nature. The observers of this law, are those we call *modest,* and the breakers *arrogant* men. The Greeks call the violation of this law πλεονεξια; that is, a desire of more than their share.

Also if *a man be trusted to judge between man and man,* it is a precept of the law of nature, *that he deal equally between them.* For without that, the controversies of men cannot be determined but by war. He therefore that is partial in judgment, doth what in him lies, to deter men from the use of judges, and arbitrators; and consequently, (against the fundamental law of nature,) is the cause of war.

The observance of this law, from the equal distribution to each man, of that which in reason belongeth to him, is called EQUITY, and (as I have said before) distributive justice: the violation, *acception of persons,* προσωποληψία.

And from this followeth another law, *that such things as cannot be divided, be enjoyed in common, if it can be; and if the quantity of the thing permit, without stint; otherwise proportionably to the number of them that have right.* For otherwise the distribution is unequal, and contrary to equity.

But some things there be, that can neither be divided, nor enjoyed in common. Then, the law of nature, which prescribeth equity, requireth, *that the entire right; or else, (making the use alternate,) the first possession, be determined by lot.* For equal distribution, is of the law of nature; and other means of equal distribution cannot be imagined.

Of *lots* there be two sorts, *arbitrary,* and *natural.* Arbitrary, is that which is agreed on by the competitors: natural, is either *primogeniture,* (which the Greek calls κληρονομία, which signifies, *given by lot;* or *first seizure.*

And therefore those things which cannot be enjoyed in common, nor divided, ought to be adjudged to the first possessor; and in some cases to the first-born, as acquired by lot.

It is also a law of nature, *that all men that mediate peace, be allowed safe conduct.* For the law that commandeth peace, as the *end,* commandeth intercession, as the *means*; and to intercession the means is safe conduct.

And because, though men be never so willing to observe these laws, there may nevertheless arise questions concerning a man's action; first, whether it were done, or not done; secondly, (if done,) whether against the law, or not against the law; the former whereof, is called a question *of fact*; the latter a question *of right*; therefore unless the parties to the question, covenant mutually to stand to the sentence of another, they are as far from peace as ever. This other, to whose sentence they submit, is called an ARBITRATOR. And therefore it is of the law of nature, *that they that are at controversy, submit their right to the judgment of an arbitrator.*

And seeing every man is presumed to do all things in order to his own benefit, no man is a fit arbitrator in his cause: and if he were never so fit; yet equity allowing to each party equal benefit, if one be admitted to be judge, the other is to be admitted also; and so the controversy, that is, the cause of war, remains, against the law of nature.

For the same reason no man in any cause ought to be received for arbitrator, to whom greater profit, or honour, or pleasure apparently ariseth out of the victory of one party, than of the other: for he hath taken (though an unavoidable bribe, yet) a bribe; and no man can be obliged to trust him. And thus also the controversy, and the condition of war remaineth, contrary to the law of nature.

And in a controversy of *fact,* the judge being to give no more credit to one, than to the other, (if there be no other arguments,) must give credit to a third; or to a third and fourth; or more: for else the question is undecided, and left to force, contrary to the law of nature.

These are the laws of nature, dictating peace, for a means of the conservation of men in multitudes; and which only concern the doctrine of civil society. There be other things tending to the destruction of particular men; as drunkenness, and all other parts of intemperance; which may therefore also be reckoned amongst those things which the law of nature hath forbidden; but are not necessary to be mentioned, nor are pertinent enough to this place.

And though this may seem too subtle a deduction of the laws of nature, to be taken notice of by all men; whereof the most part are too busy in getting food, and the rest too negligent to understand; yet to leave all men inexcusable, they have been contracted into one easy sum, intelligible, even to the meanest capacity; and that is, *Do not that to another, which thou wouldest not have done to thyself*; which sheweth him, that he has no more to do in learning the laws of nature, but, when weighing the actions of other men with his own, they seem too heavy, to put them into the other part of the balance, and his own into their place, that his own passions, and self-love, may add nothing to the weight; and then there is none of these laws of nature that will not appear unto him very reasonable.

The laws of nature oblige in *foro interno*; that is to say, they bind to a desire they should take place: but *in foro externo*; that is, to the putting them in act, not always. For he that should be modest, and tractable, and perform all he promises, in such time, and place, where no man else should do so, should but make himself a prey to others, and procure his own certain ruin, contrary to the ground of all laws of nature, which tend to nature's preservation. And again, he that having sufficient security, that others shall observe the same laws towards him, observes them not himself, seeketh not peace, but war; and consequently the destruction of his nature by violence.

And whatsoever laws bind *in foro interno*, may be broken, not only by a fact contrary to the law, but also by a fact according to it, in case a man think it contrary. For though his action in this case, be according to the law; yet his purpose was against the law; which, where the obligation is *in foro interno*, is a breach.

The laws of nature are immutable and eternal; for injustice, ingratitude, arrogance, pride, iniquity, acception of persons, and the rest, can never be made lawful. For it can never be that war shall preserve life, and peace destroy it.

The same laws, because they oblige only to a desire, and endeavour, I mean an unfeigned and constant endeavour, are easy to be observed. For in that they require nothing but endeavour; he that endeavoureth their performance, fulfilleth them; and he that fulfilleth the law, is just.

And the science of them, is the true and only moral philosophy. For moral philosophy is nothing else but the science of what is *good*, and *evil*, in the conversation, and society of mankind. *Good*, and *evil*, are names that signify our appetites, and aversions; which in different tempers, customs, and doctrines of man, are different: and divers men, differ not only in their judgment, on the senses of what is pleasant, and unpleasant to the taste, smell, hearing, touch, and sight; but also of what is comfortable, or disagreeable to reason, in the actions of common life. Nay, the same man, in divers times, differs from himself; and one time praiseth, that is, calleth good, what another time he dispraiseth, and calleth evil: from whence arise disputes, controversies, and at last war. And therefore so long a man is in the condition of mere nature, (which is a condition of war,) as private appetite is the measure of good, and evil: and consequently all men agree on this, that peace is good, and therefore also the way, or means of peace, which, (as I have shewed before) are *justice, gratitude, modesty, equity, mercy*, and the rest of the laws of nature, are good; that is to say, *moral virtues*; and their contrary *vices*; evil. Now the science of virtue and vice, is moral philosophy; and therefore the true doctrine of the laws of nature, is the true moral philosophy. But the writers of moral philosophy, though they acknowledge the same virtues and vices; yet not seeing wherein consisted their goodness; nor that they come to be praised, as the means of peaceable, sociable, and comfortable living; place them in a mediocrity of passions: as if not the cause, but the degree of daring, made fortitude; or not the cause, but the quantity of a gift, made liberality.

These dictates of reason, men use to call by the name of laws; but improperly: for they are but conclusions, or theorems concerning what conduceth to the conservation and defence of themselves; whereas law, properly, is the word of him, that by right hath command over others. But yet if we consider the same theorems, as delivered in the word of God, that by right commandeth all things; then are they properly called laws.

CHAPTER 16

Of Persons, Authors, and Things Personated

A person, is he, *whose words or actions are considered, either as his own, or as representing the words or actions of another man, or of any other thing to whom they are attributed, whether truly or by fiction.*

When they are considered as his own, then is he called a *natural person;* and when they are considered as representing the words and actions of another, then is he a *feigned* or *artificial person.*

The word person is Latin: instead whereof the Greeks have πρόσωπον, which signifies the *face,* as *persona* in Latin signifies the *disguise,* or *outward appearance* of a man, counterfeited on the stage; and sometimes more particularly that part of it, which disguiseth the face, as a mask or vizard: and from the stage, hath been translated to any representer of speech and action, as well in tribunals, as theatres. So that a *person,* is the same that an *actor* is, both on the stage and in common conversation; and to *personate,* is to *act,* or *represent* himself, or another; and he that acteth another, is said to bear his person, or act in his name; (in which sense Cicero useth it where he says, *Unus sustineo tres personas; mei, adversarii, et judicis,* I bear three persons; my own, my adversary's, and the judge's;) and is called in divers occasions, diversly; as a *representer,* or *representative,* a *lieutenant,* a *vicar,* an *attorney,* a *deputy,* a *procurator,* an *actor,* and the like.

Of persons artificial, some have their words and actions *owned* by those whom they represent. And then the person is the *actor;* and he that owneth his words and actions, is the AUTHOR: in which case the actor acteth by authority. For that which in speaking of goods and possessions, is called an *owner,* and in Latin *dominus,* in Greek κύριος; speaking of actions, is called author. And as the right of possession, is called dominion; so the right of doing any action, is called AUTHORITY. So that by authority, is always understood a right of doing any act: and *done by authority,* done by commission, or licence from him whose right it is.

From hence it followeth, that when the actor maketh a covenant by authority, he bindeth thereby the author, no less than if he had made it himself; and no less subjecteth him to all the consequences of the same. And therefore all that hath been said formerly, (*chap.* 14) of the nature of covenants between man and man in their natural capacity, is true also when they are made by their actors, representers, or procurators, that have authority from them, so far forth as is in their commission, but no farther.

And therefore he that maketh a covenant with the actor, or representer, not knowing the authority he hath, doth it at his own peril. For no man is obliged by a covenant, whereof he is not author; nor consequently by a covenant made against, or beside the authority he gave.

When the actor doth any thing against the law of nature by command of the author, if he be obliged by former covenant to obey him, not he, but the author breaketh the law of nature: for though the action be against the law of nature; yet it is not his: but contrarily, to refuse to do it, is against the law of nature, that forbiddeth breach of covenant.

And he that maketh a covenant with the author, by mediation of the actor, not knowing what authority he hath, but only takes his word; in case such authority be not made manifest unto him upon demand, is no longer obliged: for the covenant made with the author, is not valid, without his counter-assurance. But if he that so covenanteth, knew beforehand he was to expect no other assurance, than the actor's word; then is the covenant valid; because the actor in this case maketh himself the author. And therefore, as when the authority is evident, the covenant obligeth the author, not the actor; so when the authority is feigned, it obligeth the actor only; there being no author but himself.

There are few things, that are incapable of being represented by fiction. Inanimate things, as a church, an hospital, a bridge, may be personated by a rector, master, or overseer. But things inanimate, cannot be authors, nor therefore give authority to their actors: yet the actors may have authority to procure their maintenance, given them by those that are owners, or governors of those things. And therefore, such things cannot be personated, before there be some state of civil government.

Likewise children, fools, and madmen that have no use of reason, may be personated by guardians, or curators; but can be no authors, (during that time) of any action done by them, longer than (when they shall recover the use of reason) they shall judge the same reasonable. Yet during the folly, he that hath right of governing them, may give authority to the guardian. But this again has no place but in a state civil, because before such estate, there is no dominion of persons.

An idol, or mere figment of the brain, may be personated; as were the gods of the heathen; which by such officers as the state appointed, were personated, and held possessions, and other goods, and rights, which men from time to time dedicated, and consecrated unto them. But idols cannot be authors: for an idol is nothing. The authority proceeded from the state: and therefore before introduction of civil government, the gods of the heathens could not be personated.

The true God may be personated. As he was; first, by Moses; who governed the Israelites, (that were not his, but God's people,) not in his own name, with *hoc dicit Moses;* but in God's name, with *hoc dicit Dominus.* Secondly, by the Son of man, his own Son, our blessed Saviour Jesus Christ, that came to reduce the Jews, and induce all nations into the kingdom of his father; not as of himself, but as sent from his father. And thirdly, by the Holy Ghost, or Comforter, speaking, and working in the Apostles: which Holy Ghost, was a Comforter that came not of himself; but was sent, and proceeded from them both.

A multitude of men, are made *one* person, when they are by one man, or one person, represented; so that it be done with the consent of every one of that multitude in particular. For it is the *unity* of the representer, not the *unity* of the represented, that maketh the person *one*. And it is the representer that beareth the person, and but one person: and *unity,* cannot otherwise be understood in multitude.

And because the multitude naturally is not *one,* but *many;* they cannot be understood for one; but many authors, of every thing their representative saith, or doth in their name; every man giving their common representer, authority from himself in particular; and owning all the actions the representer doth, in case they give him authority without stint: otherwise, when they limit him in what, and how far he shall represent them, none of them owneth more, than they gave him commission to act.

And if the representative consist of many men, the voice of the greater number, must be considered as the voice of them all. For if the lesser number pronounce (for example) in the affirmative, and the greater in the negative, there will be negatives more than enough to destroy the affirmatives; and thereby the excess of negatives, standing uncontradicted, are the only voice the representative hath.

And a representative of even number, especially when the number is not great, whereby the contradictory voices are oftentimes equal, is therefore oftentimes mute, and incapable of action. Yet in some cases contradictory voices equal in number, may determine a question; as in condemning, or absolving, equality of votes, even in that they condemn not, do absolve; but not on the contrary condemn, in that they absolve not. For when a cause is heard; not to condemn, is to absolve: but on the contrary, to say that not absolving, is condemning, is not true. The like it is in a deliberation of executing presently, or deferring till another time: for when the voices are equal, the not decreeing execution, is a decree of dilation.

Or if the number bo odd, as three, or more, (men, or assemblies;) whereof every one has by a negative voice, authority to take away the effects of all the affirmative voices of the rest, this number is no representative; because by the diversity of opinions, and interests of men, it becomes oftentimes, and in cases of the greatest consequence, a mute person, and unapt, as for many things else, so for the government of a multitude, especially in time of war.

Of authors there be two sorts. The first simply so called; which I have before defined to be him, that owneth the action of another simply. The second is he, that owneth an action, or covenant of another conditionally; this is to say, he undertaketh to do it, if the other doth it not, at, or before a certain time. And these authors conditional, are generally called SURETIES, in Latin *fidejussores,* and *sponsores;* and particularly for debt, *praedes;* and for appearance before a judge, or magistrate, *vades.*

PART 2
OF COMMONWEALTH

CHAPTER 17

Of the Causes, Generation, and Definition of a Commonwealth

The final cause, end, or design of men, (who naturally love liberty, and dominion over others,) in the introduction of that restraint upon themselves, (in which we see them live in commonwealths,) is the foresight of their own preservation, and of a more contented life thereby; that is to say, of getting themselves out from that miserable condition of war, which is necessarily consequent (as hath been shown), to, the natural passions of men, when there is no visible power to keep them in awe, and tie them by fear of punishment to the performance of their covenants, and observation of those laws of nature set down in the fourteenth and fifteenth chapters.

For the laws of nature (as *justice, equity, modesty, mercy,* and (in sum) *doing to others, as we would be done to,)* of themselves, without the terror of some power, to cause them to be observed, are contrary to our natural passions, that carry us to partiality, pride, revenge, and the like. And covenants, without the sword, are but words, and of no strength to secure a man at all. Therefore notwithstanding the laws of nature, (which every one hath then kept, when he has the will to keep them, when he can do it safely,) if there be no power erected, or not great enough for our security; every man will, and may lawfully rely on his own strength and art, for caution against all other men. And in all places, where men have lived by small families, to rob and spoil one another, has been a trade, and so far from being reputed against the law of nature, that the greater spoils they gained, the greater was their honour; and men observed no other laws therein, but the laws of honour; that is, to abstain from cruelty, leaving to men their lives, and instruments of husbandry. And as small families did then; so now do cities and kingdoms which are but greater families (for their own security) enlarge their dominions, upon all pretences of danger, and fear of invasion, or assistance that may be given to invaders, endeavour as much as they can, to subdue, or weaken their neighbours, by open force, and secret arts, for want of other caution, justly; and are remembered for it in after ages with honour.

Nor is it the joining together of a small number of men, that gives them this security; because in small numbers, small additions on the one side or the other, make the advantage of strength so great, as is sufficient to carry the victory; and therefore gives encouragement to an invasion. The multitude sufficient to confide in for our security, is not determined by any certain number, but by comparison with the enemy we fear; and is then sufficient, when the odds of the enemy is not of so visible and conspicuous moment, to determine the event of war, as to move him to attempt.

And be there never so great a multitude; yet if their actions be directed according to their particular judgments, and particular appetites, they can expect thereby no defence, nor protection, neither against a common enemy, nor against the injuries of one another. For being distracted in opinions concerning the best use and application of their strength, they do not help, but hinder one another; and reduce their strength by mutual opposition to nothing: whereby they are easily, not only subdued by a very few that agree together; but also when there is no common enemy, they make war upon each other, for their particular interests. For if we could suppose a great multitude of men to consent in the observation of justice, and other laws of nature, without a common power to keep them all in awe; we might as well suppose all mankind to do the same; and then there neither would be, nor need to be any civil government, or commonwealth at all; because there would be peace without subjection.

Nor is it enough for the security, which men desire should last all the time of their life, that they be governed, and directed by one judgment, for a limited time; as in one battle, or one war. For though they obtain a victory by their unanimous endeavour against a foreign enemy; yet afterwards, when either they have no common enemy, or he that by one part is held for an enemy, is by another part held for a friend, they must needs by the difference of their interests dissolve, and fall again into a war amongst themselves.

It is true, that certain living creatures, as bees, and ants, live sociably one with another, (which are therefore by *Aristotle* numbered amongst political creatures;) and yet have no other direction, than their particular judgments and appetites; nor speech, whereby one of them can signify to another, what he thinks expedient for the common benefit: and therefore some man may perhaps desire to know, why mankind cannot do the same. To which I answer,

First, that men are continually in competition for honour and dignity, which these creatures are not; and consequently amongst men there ariseth on that ground, envy and hatred, and finally war; but amongst these not so.

Secondly, that amongst these creatures, the common good differeth not from the private; and being by nature inclined to their private, they procure thereby the common benefit. But man, whose joy consisteth in comparing himself with other men, can relish nothing but what is eminent.

Thirdly, that these creatures, having not, (as man) the use of reason, do not see, nor think they see any fault, in the administration of their common business; whereas amongst men, there are very many, that think themselves wiser, and abler to govern the public, better than the rest; and these strive to reform and innovate, one this way, another that way; and thereby bring it into distraction and civil war.

Fourthly, that these creatures, though they have some use of voice, in making known to one another their desires, and other affections; yet they want that art of words, by which some men can represent to others, that which is good, in the likeness of evil; and evil, in the likeness of good; and augment, or diminish the apparent greatness of good and evil; discontenting men, and troubling their peace at their pleasure.

Fifthly, irrational creatures cannot distinguish between *injury,* and *damage;* and therefore as long as they be at ease, they are not offended with their fellows: whereas man is then most troublesome, when he is most at ease: for then it is that he loves to shew his wisdom, and control the actions of them that govern the commonwealth.

Lastly, the agreement of these creatures is natural; that of men, is by covenant only, which is artificial: and therefore it is no wonder if there be somewhat else required (besides covenant) to make their agreement constant and lasting; which is a common power, to keep them in awe, and to direct their actions to the common benefit.

The only way to erect such a common power, as may be able to defend them from the invasion of foreigners, and the injuries of one another, and thereby to secure them in such sort, as that by their own industry, and by the fruits of the earth, they may nourish themselves and live contentedly; is, to confer all their power and strength upon one man, or upon one assembly of men, that may reduce all their wills, by plurality of voices, unto one will: which is as much as to say, to appoint one man, or assembly of men, to bear their person; and even one to own, and acknowledge himself to be author of whatsoever he that so beareth their person, shall act, or cause to be acted, in those things which concern the common peace and safety; and therein to submit their wills, every one to his will, and their judgments, to his judgment. This is more than consent, or concord; it is a real unity of them all, in one and the same person, made by covenant of every man with every man, in such manner, as if every man should say to every man, *I authorise and give up my right of governing myself, to this man, or to this assembly of men, on this condition, that thou give up thy right to him, and authorize all his actions in like manner.* This done, the multitude so united in one person, is called a COMMONWEALTH, in Latin CIVITAS. This is the generation of that great LEVIATHAN, or rather (to speak more reverently) of that *mortal god,* to which we owe under the *immortal God,* our peace and defence. For by this authority, given him by every particular man in the commonwealth, he hath the use of so much power and strength conferred on him, that by terror thereof, he is enabled to form the wills of them all, to peace at home, and mutual aid against their enemies abroad. And in him consisteth the essence of the commonwealth; which (to define it,) is *one person, of whose acts a great multitude, by mutual covenants one with another, have made themselves every one the author, to the end he may use the strength and means of them all, as he shall think expedient, for their peace and common defence.*

And he that carrieth this person, is called SOVEREIGN, and said to have sovereign power; and every one besides, his SUBJECT.

The attaining to this sovereign power, is by two ways. One, by natural force; as when a man maketh his children, to submit themselves, and their children to his government, as being able to destroy them if they refuse; or by war subdueth his enemies to his will, giving them their lives on that condition. The other, is when men agree amongst themselves, to submit to some man, or assembly of men, voluntarily, on confidence to be protected by him against all others. This latter, may be called a political commonwealth, or commonwealth by *institution;* and the former, a commonwealth by *acquisition.* And first, I shall speak of a commonwealth by institution.

CHAPTER 18

Of the Rights of Sovereigns by Institution

A *commonwealth* is said to be *instituted,* when a *multitude* of men do agree, and *covenant, every one, with every one,* that to whatsoever *man,* or *assembly of men,* shall be given by the major part, the *right to present* the person of them all, (that is to say, to be their *representative;*) every one, as well he that *voted for it,* as he that *voted against it,* shall *authorize* all the actions and judgments, of that man, or assembly of men, in the same manner, as if they were his own, to the end, to live peaceably amongst themselves, and be protected against other men.

From this institution of a commonwealth are derived all the *rights,* and *faculties* of him, or them, on whom the sovereign power is conferred by the consent of the people assembled.

First, because they covenant, it is to be understood, they are not obliged by former covenant to any thing repugnant hereunto. And consequently they that have already instituted a commonwealth, being thereby bound by covenant, to own the actions, and judgments of one, cannot lawfully make a new covenant, amongst themselves, to be obedient to any other, in any thing whatsoever, without his permission. And therefore, they that are subjects to a monarch, cannot without his leave cast off monarchy, and return to the confusion of a disunited multitude; nor transfer their person from him that beareth it, to another man, or other assembly of men: for they are bound, every man to every man, to own, and be reputed author of all, that he that already is their sovereign, shall do, and judge fit to be done: so that any one man dissenting, all the rest should break their covenant made to that man, which is injustice: and they have also every man given the sovereignty to him that beareth their person; and therefore if they depose him, they take from him that which is his own, and so again it is injustice. Besides, if he that attempteth to depose his sovereign, be killed, or punished by him for such attempt, he is author of his own punishment, as being by the institution, author of all his sovereign shall do: and because it is injustice for a man to do any thing, for which he may be punished by his own authority, he is also upon that title, unjust. And whereas some men have pretended for their disobedience to their sovereign, a new covenant, made, not with men, but with God; this also is unjust: for there is no covenant with God, but by mediation of somebody that representeth God's person; which none doth but God's lieutenant, who hath the sovereignty under God. But this pretence of covenant with God, is so evident a lie, even in the pretender's own consciences, that it is not only an act of an unjust, but also of a vile, and unmanly disposition.

Secondly, because the right of bearing the person of them all, is given to him they make sovereign, by covenant only of one to another, and not of him to any of them; there can happen no breach of covenant on the part of the sovereign; and consequently none of his subjects, by any pretence of forfeiture, can be freed from his subjection. That he which is made sovereign maketh no covenant with his subjects beforehand, is manifest; because either he must make it with the whole multitude, as one party to the covenant; or he must make a several covenant with every man. With the whole, as one party, it is impossible; because as yet they are not one person: and if he make so many several covenants as there be men, those covenants after he hath the sovereignty are void, because what act soever can be pretended by any one of them for breach thereof, is the act both of himself, and of all the rest, because done in the person, and by the right of every one of them in particular. Besides, if any one, or more of them, pretend a breach of the covenant made by the sovereign at his institution; and others, or one other of his subjects, or himself alone, pretend there was no such breach, there is in this case, no judge to decide the controversy; it returns therefore to the sword again; and every man recovereth the right of protecting himself by his own strength, contrary to the design they had in the institution. It is therefore in vain to grant sovereignty by way of precedent covenant. The opinion that any monarch receiveth his power by covenant, that is to say, on condition, proceedeth from want of understanding this easy truth, that covenants being but words and breath, have no force to oblige, contain, constrain, or protect any man, but what it has from the public sword; that is, from the untied hands of that man, or assembly of men that hath the sovereignty, and whose actions are avouched by them all, and performed by the strength of them all, in him united. But when an assembly of men is made sovereign; then no man imagineth any such covenant to have passed in the institution; for no man is so dull as to say, for example, the people of Rome made a covenant with the Romans, to hold the sovereignty on such or such conditions; which not performed, the Romans might lawfully depose the Roman people. That men see not the reason to be alike in a monarchy, and in a popular government, proceedeth from the ambition of some, that are kinder to the government of an assembly, whereof they may hope to participate, than of monarchy, which they despair to enjoy.

Thirdly, because the major part hath by consenting voices declared a sovereign; he that dissented must now consent with the rest; that is, be contented to avow all the actions he shall do, or else justly be destroyed by the rest. For if he voluntarily entered into the congregation of them that were assembled, he sufficiently declared thereby his will, (and therefore tacitly covenanted) to stand to what the major part should ordain: and therefore if he refuse to stand thereto, or make protestation against any of their decrees, he does contrary to his covenant, and therefore unjustly. And whether he be of the congregation, or not; and whether his consent be asked, or not, he must either submit to their decrees, or be left in the condition of war he was in before; wherein he might without injustice be destroyed by any man whatsoever.

Fourthly, because every subject is by this institution author of all the actions, and judgments of the sovereign instituted; it follows, that whatsoever he doth, it can be no injury to any of his subjects; nor ought he to be by any of them accused of injustice. For he that doth any thing by authority from another, doth therein no injury to him by whose authority he acteth; but by this institution of a commonwealth, every particular man is author of all the sovereign doth; and consequently he that complaineth of injury from his sovereign, complaineth of that whereof he himself is author; and therefore ought not to accuse any man but himself; no nor himself of injury; because to do injury to one's self, is impossible. It is true that they that have sovereign power, may commit iniquity; but not injustice, or injury in the proper signification.

Fifthly, and consequently to that which was said last, no man that hath sovereign power can justly be put to death, or otherwise in any manner by his subjects punished. For seeing every subject is author of the actions of his sovereign; he punisheth another, for the actions committed by himself.

And because the end of this institution, is the peace and defence of them all; and whosoever has right to the end, has right to the means; it belongeth of right, to whatsoever man, or assembly that hath the sovereignty, to be judge both of the means of peace and defence; and also of the hindrances, and disturbances of the same; and to do whatsoever he shall think necessary to be done, both beforehand, for the preserving of peace and security, by prevention of discord at home, and hostility from abroad; and, when peace and security are lost, for the recovery of the same. And therefore,

Sixthly, it is annexed to the sovereignty, to be judge of what opinions and doctrines are averse, and what conducing to peace; and consequently, on what occasions, how far, and what, men are to be trusted withal, in speaking to multitudes of people; and who shall examine the doctrines of all books before they be published. For the actions of men proceed from their opinions; and in the well-governing of opinions, consisteth the well-governing of men's actions, in order to their peace, and concord. And though in matter of doctrine, nothing ought to be regarded but the truth; yet this is not repugnant to regulating of the same by peace. For doctrine repugnant to peace, can no more be true, than peace and concord can be against the law of nature. It is true, that in a commonwealth, where by the negligence, or unskillfulness of governors, and teachers, false doctrines are by time generally received; the contrary truths may be generally offensive: Yet the most sudden, and rough busling in of a new truth, that can be, does never break the peace, but only sometimes awake the war. For those men that are so remissly governed, that they dare take up arms, to defend, or introduce an opinion, are still in war; and their condition not peace, but only a cessation of arms for fear of one another; and they live as it were, in the precincts of battle continually. It belongeth therefore to him that hath the sovereign power, to be judge, or constitute all judges of opinions and doctrines, as a thing necessary to peace; thereby to prevent discord and civil war.

Seventhly, is annexed to the sovereignty, the whole power of prescribing the rules, whereby every man may know, what goods he may enjoy, and what actions he may do, without being molested by any of his fellow-subjects; and this is it men call *propriety*. For before constitution of sovereign power (as hath already been shown) all men had right to all things; which necessarily causeth war: and therefore this propriety, being necessary to peace, and depending on sovereign power, is the act of that power, in order to the public peace. These rules of propriety (or *meum* and *tuum*) and of *good, evil, lawful,* and *unlawful* in the actions of subjects, are the civil laws; that is to say, the laws of each commonwealth in particular; though the name of civil law be now restrained to the ancient civil laws of the city of *Rome;* which being the head of a great part of the world, her laws at that time were in these parts the civil law.

Eighthly, is annexed to the sovereignty, the right of judicature; that is to say, of hearing and deciding all controversies, which may arise concerning law, either civil, or natural; or concerning fact. For without the decision of controversies, there is no protection of one subject, against the injuries of another; the laws concerning *meum* and *tuum* are in vain; and to every man remaineth, from the natural and necessary appetite of his own conservation, the right of protecting himself by his private strength, which is the condition of war; and contrary to the end for which every commonwealth is instituted.

Ninthly, is annexed to the sovereignty, the right of making war and peace with other nations, and commonwealths; that is to say, of judging when it is for the public good, and how great forces are to be assembled, armed, and paid for that end; and to levy money upon the subjects, to defray the expenses thereof. For the power by which the people are to be defended, consisteth in their armies; and the strength of an army, in the union of their strength under one command; which command the sovereign instituted, therefore hath; because the command of the *militia,* without other institution, maketh him that hath it sovereign. And therefore whosoever is made general of an army, he that hath the sovereign power is always generalissimo.

Tenthly, is annexed to the sovereignty, the choosing of all counsellors, ministers, magistrates, and officers, both in peace, and war. For seeing the sovereign is charged with the end, which is the common peace and defence, he is understood to have power to use such means, as he shall think most fit for his discharge.

Eleventhly, to the sovereign is committed the power of rewarding with riches, or honour; and of punishing with corporal, or pecuniary punishment, or with ignominy every subject according to the law he hath formerly made; or if there be no law made, according as he shall judge most to conduce to the encouraging of men to serve the commonwealth, or deterring of them from doing disservice to the same.

Lastly, considering what values men are naturally apt to set upon themselves; what respect they look for from others; and how little they value other men; from whence continually arise amongst them, emulation, quarrels, factions, and at last war, to the destroying of one another, and diminution of their strength against a common enemy; it is necessary that there be laws of honour, and a public rate of the worth of such men as have deserved, or are able to deserve well of the commonwealth; and that there be force in the hands of some or other, to put those laws in execution. But it hath already been shown, that not only the whole *militia*, or forces of the commonwealth; but also the judicature of all controversies, is annexed to the sovereignty. To the sovereign therefore it belongeth also to give titles of honour; and to appoint what order of place, and dignity, each man shall hold; and what signs of respect, in public or private meetings, they shall give to one another.

These are the rights, which make the essence of sovereignty; and which are the marks, whereby a man may discern in what man, or assembly of men, the sovereign power is placed, and resideth. For these are incommunicable, and inseparable. The power to coin money; to dispose of the estate and persons of infant heirs; to have praeemption in markets; and all other statute prerogatives, may be transferred by the sovereign; and yet the power to protect his subjects be retained. But if he transfer the *militia,* he retains the judicature in vain, for want of execution of the laws: or if he grant away the power of raising money; the *militia* is in vain: or if he give away the government of doctrines, men will be frighted into rebellion with the fear of spirits. And so if we consider any one of the said rights, we shall presently see, that the holding of all the rest will produce no effect, in the conservation of peace and justice, the end for which all commonwealths are instituted. And this division is it, whereof it is said, *a kingdom divided in itself cannot stand;* for unless this division precede, division into opposite armies can never happen. If there had not first been an opinion received of the greatest part of England, that these powers were divided between the King, and the Lords, and the House of Commons, the people had never been divided and fallen into this civil war; first between those that disagreed in politics; and after between the dissenters about the liberty of religion; which have so instructed men in this point of sovereign right, that there be few now (in *England,*) that do not see, that these rights are inseparable, and will be so generally acknowledged at the next return of peace; and so continue, till their miseries are forgotten; and no longer, except the vulgar be better taught than they have hitherto been.

And because they are essential and inseparable rights, it follows necessarily, that in whatsoever words any of them seem to be granted away, yet if the sovereign power itself be not in direct terms renounced, and the name of sovereign no more given by the grantees to him that grants them, the grant is void: for when he has granted all he can, if we grant back the sovereignty, all is restored, as inseparably annexed thereunto.

This great authority being indivisible, and inseparably annexed to the sovereignty, there is little ground for the opinion of them, that say of sovereign kings, though they be *singulis majores,* of greater power than every one of their subjects, yet they be *universis minores,* of less power than them all together. For if by *all together,* they mean not the collective body as one person, then *all together,* and *every one,* signify the same; and the speech is absurd. But if by *all together,* they understand them as one person, (which person the sovereign bears,) then the power of all together, is the same with the sovereign's power; and so again the speech is absurd: which absurdity they see well enough, when the sovereignty is in an assembly of the people; but in a monarch they see it not; and yet the power of sovereignty is the same in whomsoever it be placed.

And as the power, so also the honour of the sovereign, ought to be greater, than that of any, or all the subjects. For in the sovereignty is the fountain of honour. The dignities of lord, earl, duke, and prince are his creatures. As in the presence of the master, the servants are equal, and without any honour at all; so are the subjects, in the presence of the sovereign. And though they shine some more, some less, when they are out of his sight; yet in his presence, they shine no more than the stars in presence of the sun.

But a man may here object, that the condition of subjects is very miserable; as being obnoxious to the lusts, and other irregular passions of him, or them that have so unlimited a power in their hands. And commonly that they live under a monarch, think it the fault of monarchy; and they that live under the government of democracy, or other sovereign assembly, attribute all the inconvenience to that form of commonwealth; whereas the power in all forms, if they be perfect enough to protect them, is the same; not considering that the estate of man can never be without some incommodity or other; and that the greatest, that in any form of government can possibly happen to the people in general, is scarce sensible, in respect to the miseries, and horrible calamities, that accompany a civil war, or that dissolute condition of masterless men, without subjection to laws, and a coercive power to tie their hands from rapine and revenge: nor considering that the greatest pressure of sovereign governors, proceedeth not from any delight, or profit they can expect in the damage or weakening of their subjects, in whose vigour, consisteth their own strength and glory; but in the restiveness of themselves, that unwillingly contributing to their own defence, make it necessary for their governors to draw from them what they can in time of peace, that they may have means on any emergent occasion, or sudden need, to resist, or take advantage on their enemies. For all men are by nature provided of notable multiplying glasses, (that is their passions and self-love,) through which, every little payment appeareth a great grievance; but are destitute of those propsective glasses, (namely moral and civil science,) to see afar off the miseries that hang over them, and cannot without such payments be avoided.

CHAPTER 19

Of the Several Kinds of Commonwealth by Institution,
and of Succession to the Sovereign Power

The difference of commonwealths, consisteth in the difference of the sovereign, or the person representative of all and every one of the multitude. And because the sovereignty is either in one man, or in an assembly of more than one; and into that assembly either every man hath right to enter, or not every one, but certain men distinguished from the rest; it is manifest, there can be but three kinds of commonwealth. For the representative must needs be one man, or more: and if more, then it is the assembly of all, or but of a part. When the representative is one man, then is the commonwealth a MONARCHY: when an assembly of all that will come together, then it is a DEMOCRACY, or popular commonwealth: when an assembly of a part only, then it is called an ARISTOCRACY. Other kind of commonwealth there can be none: for either one, or more, or all, must have the sovereign power (which I have shown to be indivisible) entire.

There be other names of government, in the histories, and books of policy; as *tyranny*, and *oligarchy*: But they are not the names of other forms of government, but of the same forms misliked. For they that are discontented under *monarchy*, call it *tyranny*; and they that are displeased with *aristocracy*, call it *oligarchy*: so also, they which find themselves grieved under a *democracy*, call it *anarchy*, (which signifies want of government;) and yet I think no man believes, that want of government, is any new kind of government: nor by the same reason ought they to believe, that the government is of one kind, when they like it, and another, when they mislike it, or are oppressed by the governors.

It is manifest, that men who are in absolute liberty, may, if they please, give authority to one man, to represent them every one; as well as give such authority to any assembly of men whatsoever; and consequently may subject themselves, if they think good, to a monarch, as absolutely, as to any other representative. Therefore, where there is already erected a sovereign power, there can be no other representative of the same people, but only to certain particular ends, by the sovereign limited. For that were to erect two sovereigns; and every man to have his person represented by two actors, that by opposing one another, must needs divide that power, which (if men will live in peace) is indivisible; and thereby reduce the multitude into the condition of war, contrary to the end for which all sovereignty is instituted. And therefore as it is absurd, to think that a sovereign assembly, inviting the people of their dominion, to send up their deputies, with power to make known their advice, or desires, should therefore hold such deputies, rather than themselves, for the absolute representative of the people: so it is absurd also, to think the same in a monarchy. And I know not how this so manifest a truth, should of late be so little observed; that in a monarchy, he that had the sovereignty from a descent of 600 years, was alone called sovereign, had the title of Majesty from every one of his subjects, and was unquestionably taken by them for their king, was notwithstanding never considered as their representative; that name without contradiction passing for the title of those men, which at his command were sent up by the people to carry their petitions, and give him (if he permitted it) their advice. Which may serve as an admonition, for those that are the true, and absolute representative of a people, to instruct men in the nature of that office, and to take heed how they admit of any other general representation upon any occasion whatsoever, if they mean to discharge the trust committed to them.

The difference between these three kinds of commonwealth, consisteth not in the difference of power; but in the difference of convenience, or aptitude to produce the peace, and security of the people; for which end they were instituted. And to compare monarchy with the other two, we may observe; first, that whosoever beareth the person of the people, or is one of that assembly that bears it, beareth also his own natural person. And though he be careful in his politic person to procure the common interest; yet he is more, or no less careful to procure the private good of himself, his family, kindred and friends; and for the most part, if the public interest chance to cross the private, he prefers the private: for the passions of men, are commonly more potent than their reason. From whence it follows, that where the public and private interest are most closely united, there is the public most advanced. Now in monarchy, the private interest is the same with the public. The riches, power, and honour of a monarch arise only from the riches, strength and reputation of his subjects. For no king can be rich, nor glorious, nor secure, whose subjects are either poor, or contemptible, or too weak through want, or dissention, to maintain a war against their enemies: whereas in a democracy, or aristocracy, the public prosperity confers not so much to the private fortune of one that is corrupt, or ambitious, as doth many times a perfidious advice, a treacherous action, or a civil war.

Secondly, that a monarch receiveth counsel of whom, when, and where he pleaseth; and consequently may hear the opinion of men versed in the matter about which he deliberates, of what rank or quality soever, and as long before the time of action, and with as much secrecy, as he will. But when a sovereign assembly has need of counsel, none are admitted but such as have a right thereto from the beginning; which for the most part are of those who have been versed more in the acquisition of wealth than of knowledge; and are to give their advice in long discourses, which may, and do commonly excite men to action, but not govern them in it. For the *understanding* is by the flame of the passions, never enlightened, but dazzled: Nor is there any place, or time, wherein an assembly can receive counsel with secrecy, because of their own multitude.

Thirdly, that the resolutions of a monarch, are subject to no other inconstancy, than that of human nature; but in assemblies, besides that of nature, there ariseth an inconstancy from the number. For the absence of a few, that would have the resolution once taken, continue firm, (which may happen by security, negligence, or private impediments,) or the diligent appearance of a few of the contrary opinion, undoes to day, all that was concluded yesterday.

Fourthly, that a monarch cannot disagree with himself, out of envy, or interest; but an assembly may; and that to such a height, as may produce a civil war.

Fifthly, that in monarchy there is this inconvenience; that any subject, by the power of one man, for the enriching of a favourite or flatterer, may be deprived of all he possesseth; which I confess is a great and inevitable inconvenience. But the same may as well happen, where the sovereign power is in an assembly: for their power is the same; and they are as subject to evil counsel, and to be seduced by orators, as a monarch by flatterers; and becoming one another's flatterers, serve one another's covetousness and ambition by turns. And whereas the favourites of monarchs, are few, and they have none else to advance but their own kindred; the favourites of an assembly, are many; and the kindred much more numerous, than of any monarch. Besides, there is no favourite of a monarch, which cannot as well succour his friends, as hurt his enemies: but orators, that is to say, favourites of sovereign assemblies, though they have great power to hurt, have little to save. For to accuse, requires less eloquence (such is man's nature) than to excuse; and condemnation, than absolution more resembles justice.

Sixthly, that it is an inconvenience in monarchy, that the sovereignty may descend upon an infant, or one that cannot discern between good and evil: and consisteth in this, that the use of his power, must be in the hand of another man, or of some assembly of men, which are to govern by his right, and in his name; as curators, and protectors of his person, and authority. But to say there is inconvenience, in putting the use of the sovereign power, into the hand of a man, or an assembly of men; is to say that all government is more inconvenient, than confusion, and civil war. And therefore all the danger that can be pretended, must arise from the contention of those, that for an office of so great honour, and profit, may become competitors. To make it appear, that this inconvenience, proceedeth not from that form of government we call monarchy, we are to consider, that the precedent monarch, hath appointed who shall have the tuition of his infant successor, either expressly by testament, or tacitly, by not controlling the custom in that case received: and then such inconvenience, (if it happen) is to be attributed, not to the monarchy, but to the ambition, and injustice of the subjects; which in all kinds of government, where the people are not well instructed in their duty, and the rights of sovereignty, is the same. Or else the precedent monarch hath not at all taken order for such tuition; and then the law of nature hath provided this sufficient rule, that the tuition shall be in him, that hath by nature most interest in the preservation of the authority of the infant, and to whom least benefit can accrue by his death, or diminution. For seeing every man by nature seeketh his own benefit, and promotion; to put an infant into the power of those, that can promote themselves by his destruction, or damage, is not tuition, but treachery. So that sufficient provision being taken, against all just quarrel, about the government under a child, if any contention arise to the disturbance of the public peace, it is not to be attributed to the form of monarchy, but to the amibition of subjects, and ignorance of their duty. On the other side, there is no great commonwealth, the sovereignty whereof is in a great assembly, which is not, as to consultations of peace, and war, and making of laws, in the same condition, as if the government were in a child. For as a child wants the judgment to dissent from counsel given him, and is thereby necessitated to take the advice of them, or him, to whom he is committed: so an assembly wanteth the liberty, to dissent from the counsel of the major part, be it good, or bad. And as a child has need of a tutor, or protector, to preserve his person and author-ity: so also (in great commonwealths,) the sovereign assembly, in all great dangers and troubles, have need of *custodes libertatis*; that is of dictators, or protectors of their authority; which are as much as temporary monarchs; to whom for a time, they may commit the entire exercise of their power; and have (at the end of that time) been oftener deprived thereof, than infant kings, by their protectors, regents, or any other tutors.

Though the kinds of sovereignty be, as I have now shown, but three; that is to say, monarchy, where one man has it; or democracy, where the general assembly of subjects hath it; or aristocracy, where it is in an assembly of certain persons nominated, or otherwise dis-tinguished from the rest: yet he that shall consider the particular commonwealths that have been, and are in the world, will not perhaps easily reduce them to three, and may thereby be inclined to think there be other forms, arising from these mingled together. As for example, elective kingdoms; where kings have the sovereign power put into their hands for a time; or kingdoms, wherein the king hath a power limited: which governments, are nev-ertheless by most writers called monarchy. Likewise if a popular, or aristocratical com-monwealth, subdue an enemy's country, and govern the same, by a president, procurator, or other magistrate; this may seem perhaps at first sight, to be a democratical, or aristo-cratical government. But it is not so. For elective kings, are not sovereigns, but ministers of the sovereign; nor limited kings sovereigns, but ministers of them that have the sover-eign power: nor are those provinces which are in subjection to a democracy, or aristocracy of another commonwealth, democratically, or aristocratically governed, but monarchically.

And first, concerning an elective king, whose power is limited to his life, as it is in many places of Christendom at this day; or to certain years or months, as the dictator's power amongst the Romans; if he have right to appoint his successor, he is no more elec-tive but hereditary. But if he have no power to elect his successor, then there is some other man, or assembly known, which after his decrease may elect anew, or else the common-wealth dieth, and dissolveth with him, and returneth to the condition of war. If it be known who have the power to give the sovereignty after his death, it is known also that the sovereignty was in them before: for none have right to give that which they have not right to possess, and keep to themselves, if they think good. But if there be none that can give the sovereignty, after the decease of him that was first elected; then has he power, nay he is obliged by the law of nature, to provide, by establishing his successor, to keep those that had trusted him with the government, from relapsing into the miserable condition of civil war. And consequently he was, when elected, a sovereign absolute.

Secondly, that king whose power is limited, is not superior to him, or them that have the power to limit it; and he that is not superior, is not supreme; that is to say not sover-eign. The sovereignty therefore was always in that assembly which had the right to limit him; and by consequence the government not monarchy, but either democracy, or aristoc-racy; as of old time in *Sparta*; where the kings had a privilege to lead their armies; but the sovereignty was in the *Ephori*.

Thirdly, whereas heretofore the Roman people governed the land of *Judea* (for ex-ample) by a president; yet was not *Judea* therefore a democracy; because they were not governed by any assembly, into which, any of them, had right to enter; nor by an aris-tocracy; because they were not governed by any assembly, into which, any man could enter by their election: but they were governed by one person, which though as to the people of *Rome* was an assembly of the people, or democracy; yet as to people of *Judea*, which had no right at all of participating in the government, was a monarch. For though where the people are governed by an assembly, chosen by themselves out of their own number, the government is called a democracy, or aristocracy; yet when they are governed by an assembly, not of their own choosing, it is a monarchy; not of *one* man, over another man; but of one people, over another people.

Of all these forms of government, the matter being mortal, so that not only monarchs, but also whole assemblies die, it is necessary for the conservation of the peace of men, that as there was order taken for an artificial man, so there be order also taken, for an artificial eternity of life; without which, men that are governed by an assembly, should return into the condition of war in every age; and they that are governed by one man, as soon as their governor dieth. This artificial eternity, is that which men call the right of *succession*.

There is no perfect form of government, where the disposing of the succession is not in the present sovereign. For if it be in any other particular man, or private assembly, it is in a person subject, and may be assumed by the sovereign at his pleasure; and consequently the right is in himself. And if it be in no particular man, but left to a new choice; then is the commonwealth dissolved; and the right is in him that can get it; contrary to the intention of them that did institute the commonwealth, for their perpetual, and not temporary security.

In a democracy, the whole assembly cannot fail, unless the multitude that are to be governed fail. And therefore questions of the right of succession, have in that form of government no place at all.

In an aristocracy, when any of the assembly dieth, the election of another into his room belongeth to the assembly, as the sovereign, to whom belongeth the choosing of all counsellors and officers. For that which the representative doth, as actor, every one of the subjects doth, as author. And though the sovereign assembly may give power to others, to elect new men, for supply of their court; yet it is still by their authority, that the election is made; and by the same it may (when the public shall require it) be recalled.

The greatest difficulty about the right of succession, is in monarchy: and the difficulty ariseth from this, that at first sight, it is not manifest who is to appoint the successor; nor many times, who it is whom he hath appointed. For in both these cases, there is required a more exact ratiocination, than every man is accustomed to use. As to the question, who shall appoint the successor, of a monarch that hath the sovereign authority; that is to say, who shall determine of the right of inheritance, (for elective kings and princes have not the sovereign power in propriety, but in use only,) we are to consider, that either he that is in possession, has right to dispose of the succession, or else that right is again in the dissolved multitude. For the death of him that hath the sovereign power in propriety, leaves the multitude without any sovereign at all; that is, without any representative in whom they should be united, and be capable of doing any one action at all: and therefore they are incapable of election of any new monarch; every man having equal right to submit himself to such as he thinks best able to protect him; or if he can, protect himself by his own sword, which is a return to confusion, and to the condition of a war of every man against every man, contrary to the end for which monarchy had its first institution. Therefore it is manifest, that by the institution of monarchy, the disposing of the successor, is always left to the judgment and will of the present possessor.

And for the question (which may arise sometimes) who it is that the monarch in possession, hath designed to the succession and inheritance of his power; it is determined by his express words, and testament; or by other tacit signs sufficient.

By express words, or testament, when it is declared by him in his lifetime, *viva voce*, or by writing; as the first emperors of *Rome* declared who should be their heirs. For the word heir does not of itself imply the children, or nearest kindred of a man; but whomsoever a man shall any way declare, he would have to succeed him in his estate. If therefore a monarch declare expressly, that such a man shall be his heir, either by word or writing, then is that man immediately after the decease of his predecessor, invested in the right of being monarch.

But where testament, and express words are wanting, other natural signs of the will are to be followed: whereof the one is custom. And therefore where the custom is that the next of kindred absolutely succeedeth, there also the next of kindred hath right to the succession; for that, if the will of him that was in possession had been otherwise, he might easily have declared the same in his life time. And likewise where the custom is, that the next of the male kindred succeedeth, there also the right of succession is in the next of the kindred male, for the same reason. And so it is if the custom were to advance the female. For whatsoever custom a man may by a word control, and does not, it is a natural sign he would have that custom stand.

But where neither custom, nor testament hath preceded, there it is to be understood, first, that a monarch's will is, that the government remain monarchical; because he hath approved that government in himself. Secondly, that a child of his own, male, or female, be preferred before any other; because men are presumed to be more inclined by nature, to advance their own children, than the children of other men; and of their own, rather a male than a female; because men, are naturally fitter than women, for actions of labour and danger. Thirdly, where his own issue faileth, rather a brother than a stranger; and so still the nearer in blood, rather than the more remote; because it is always presumed that the nearer of kin, is the nearer in affection; and it is evident that a man receives always, by reflection, the most honour from the greatness of his nearest kindred.

But if it be lawful for a monarch to dispose of the succession by words of contract, or testament, men may perhaps object a great inconvenience: for he may sell, or give his right of governing to a stranger; which, because strangers (that is, men not used to live under the same government, nor speaking the same language) do commonly undervalue one another, many turn to the oppression of his subjects; which is indeed a great inconvenience: but it proceedeth not necessarily from the subjection to a stranger's government, but from the unskilfulness of the governors, ignorant of the true rules of politics. And therefore the Romans when they had subdued many nations, to make their government digestible, were wont to take away that grievance, as much as they thought necessary, by giving sometimes to whole nations, and sometimes to principal men of every nation they conquered, not only the privileges, but also the name of Romans; and took many of them into the senate, and offices of charge, even in the Roman city. And this was it our most wise king, king *James*, aimed at, in endeavouring the union of his two realms of *England* and *Scotland*. Which if he could have obtained, had in all likelihood prevented the civil wars, which make both those kingdoms, at this present, miserable. It is not therefore any injury to the people, for a monarch to dispose of the succession by will; though by the fault of many princes, it hath been sometimes found inconvenient. Of the lawfulness of it, this also is an argument, that whatsoever inconvenience can arrive by giving a kingdom to a stranger, may arrive also by so marrying with strangers, as the right of succession may descend upon them: yet this by all men is accounted lawful.

CHAPTER 20

Of Dominion Paternal, and Despotical

A *commonwealth by acquisition*, is that, where the sovereign power is acquired by force; and it is acquired by force, when men singly, or many together by plurality of voices, for fear of death, or bonds, do authorize all the actions of that man, or assembly, that hath their lives and liberty in his power.

And this kind of dominion, or sovereignty, differeth from sovereignty by institution, only in this, that men who choose their sovereign, do it for fear of one another, and not of him whom they institute: but in this case, they subject themselves, to him they are afraid of. In both cases they do it for fear: which is to be noted by them, that hold all such covenants, as proceed from fear of death, or violence, void: which if it were true, no man, in any kind of commonwealth, could be obliged to obedience. It is true, that in a commonwealth once instituted, or acquired, promises proceeding from fear of death or violence, are no covenants, nor obliging, when the thing promised is contrary to the laws; but the reason is not, because it was made upon fear, but because he that promiseth, hath no right in the thing promised. Also, when he may lawfully perform, and doth not, it is not the invalidity of the covenant, that absolveth him, but the sentence of the sovereign. Otherwise, whensoever a man lawfully promiseth, he unlawfully breaketh: but when the sovereign, who is the actor, acquitteth him, then he is acquitted by him that extorted the promise, as by the author of such absolution.

But the rights, and consequences of sovereignty, are the same in both. His power cannot, without his consent, be transferred to another: he cannot forfeit it: he cannot be accused by any of his subjects, of injury: he cannot be punished by them: he is judge of what is necessary for peace; and judge of doctrines: he is sole legislator; and supreme judge of controversies; and of the times, and occasions of war, and peace: to him it belongeth to choose magistrates, counsellors, commanders, and all other officers, and ministers; and to determine of rewards, and punishments, honour, and order. The reasons whereof, are the same which are alleged in the precedent chapter, for the same rights, and consequences of sovereignty by institution.

Dominion is acquired two ways; by generation, and by conquest. The right of dominion by generation, is that, which the parent hath over his children; and is called PATERNAL. And is not so derived from the generation, as if therefore the parent had dominion over his child because be begat him; but from the child's consent, either express, or by other sufficient arguments declared. For as to the generation, God hath ordained to man a helper; and there be always two that are equally parents: the dominion therefore over the child, should belong equally to both; and he be equally subject to both, which is impossible; for no man can obey two masters. And whereas some have attributed the dominion to the man only, as being of the more excellent sex; they misreckon in it. For there is not always that difference of strength, or prudence between the man and the woman, as that the right can be determined without war. In commonwealths, this controversy is decided by the civil law: and for the most part, (but not always) the sentence is in favour of the father; because for the most part commonwealths have been erected by the fathers, not by the mothers of families. But the question lieth now in the state of mere nature; where there are supposed no laws of matrimony; no laws for the education of children; but the law of nature, and the natural inclination of the sexes, one to another, and to their children. In this condition of mere nature, either the parents between themselves dispose of the dominion over the child by contract; or do not dispose thereof at all. If they dispose thereof, the right passeth according to the contract. We find in history that the *Amazons* contracted with the men of the neighbouring countries, to whom they had recourse for issue, that the issue male should be sent back, but the female remain with themselves: so that the dominion of the females was in the mother.

If there be no contract, the dominion is in the mother. For in the condition of mere nature, where there are no matrimonial laws, it cannot be known who is the father, unless it be declared by the mother: and therefore the right of dominion over the child dependeth on her will, and is consequently hers. Again, seeing the infant is first in the power of the mother, so as she may either nourish, or expose it; if she nourish it, it oweth its life to the mother; and is therefore obliged to obey her, rather than any other; and by consequence the dominion over it is hers. But if she expose it, and another find and nourish it, the dominion is in him that nourisheth it. For it ought to obey him by whom it is preserved; because preservation of life being the end, for which one man becomes subject to another, every man is supposed to promise obedience, to him, in whose power it is to save, or destroy him.

If the mother be the father's subject, the child, is in the father's power: and if the father be the mother's subject, (as when a sovereign queen marrieth one of her subjects,) the child is subject to the mother; because the father also is her subject.

If a man and woman, monarchs of two several kingdoms, have a child, and contract concerning who shall have the dominion of him, the right of the dominion passeth by the contract. If they contract not, the dominion followeth the dominion of the place of his residence. For the sovereign of each country hath dominion over all that reside therein.

He that hath the dominion over the child, hath dominion also over the children of the child; and over their children's children. For he that hath dominion over the person of a man, hath dominion over all that is his; without which, dominion were but a title, without the effect.

The right of succession to paternal dominion, proceedeth in the same manner, as doth the right of succession to monarchy; of which I have already sufficiently spoken in the precedent chapter.

Dominion acquired by conquest, or victory in war, is that which some writers call DESPOTICAL, from $\Delta\epsilon\sigma\pi\acute{o}\eta s$, which signifieth a *lord*, or *master*; and is the dominion of the master over his servant. And this dominion is then acquired to the victor, when the vanquished, to avoid the present stroke of death, convenanteth either in express words, or by other sufficient signs of the will, that so long as his life, and the liberty of his body is allowed him, the victor shall have the use thereof, at his pleasure. And after such covenant made, the vanquished is a SERVANT, and not before: for by the word *servant*, (whether it be derived from *servire*, to serve, or from *servare*, to save, which I leave to grammarians to dispute) is not meant a captive, which is kept in prison, or bonds, till the owner of him that took him, or bought him of one that did, shall consider what to do with him: (for such men, (commonly called slaves,) have no obligation at all; but may break their bonds, or the prison; and kill, or carry away captive their master, justly:) but one, that being taken, hath corporal liberty allowed him; and upon promise not to run away, nor to do violence to his master, is trusted by him.

It is not therefore the victory, that giveth the right of dominion over the vanquished, but his own covenant. Nor is he obliged because he is conquered; that is to say, beaten, and taken, or put to flight; but because he cometh in, and submitteth to the victor; nor is the victor obliged by an enemy's rendering himself, (without promise of life,) to spare him for this his yielding to discretion; which obliges not the victor longer, than in his own discretion he shall think fit.

And that which men do, when they demand (as it is now called) *quarter*, (which the Greeks called $Z\omega\gamma\rho\acute{\iota}\alpha$, *taking alive*,) is to evade the present fury of the victor, by submission, and to compound for their life, with ransom, or service: and therefore he that hath quarter, hath not his life given, but deferred till farther deliberation; for it is not an yielding on condition of life, but to discretion. And then only is his life in security, and his service due, when the victor hath trusted him with his corporal liberty. For slaves that work in prisons, or fetters, do it not of duty, but to avoid the cruelty of their task-masters.

The master of the servant, is master also of all he hath; and may exact the use thereof; that is to say, of his goods, of his labour, of his servants, and of his children, as often as he shall think fit. For he holdeth his life of his master, by the covenant of obedience; that is, of owning, and authorizing whatsoever the master shall do. And in case the master, if he refuse, kill him, or cast him into bonds, or otherwise punish him for his disobedience, he is himself the author of the same; and cannot accuse him of injury.

In sum, the rights and consequences of both *paternal* and *despotical* dominion, are the very same with those of a sovereign by institution; and for the same reasons: which reasons are set down in the precedent chapter. So that for a man that is monarch of divers nations, whereof he hath, in one the sovereignty by institution of the people assembled, and in another by conquest, that is by the submission of each particular, to avoid death or bonds; to demand of one nation more than of the other, from the title of conquest, as being a conquered nation, is an act of ignorance of the rights of sovereignty. For the sovereign is absolute over both alike; or else there is no sovereignty at all; and so every man may lawfully protect himself, if he can, with his own sword, which is the condition of war.

By this it appears; that a great family if it be not part of some commonwealth, is of itself, as to the rights of sovereignty, a little monarchy; whether that family consist of a man and his children; or of a man and his servants; or of a man, and his children, and servants together: wherein the father or master is the sovereign. But yet a family is not properly a commonwealth; unless it be of that power by its own number, or by other opportunities, as not to be subdued without the hazard of war. For where a number of men are manifestly too weak to defend themselves united, every one may use his own reason in time of danger, to save his own life, either by flight, or by submission to the enemy, as he shall think best; in the same manner as a very small company of soldiers, surprised by an army, may cast down their arms, and demand quarter, or run away, rather than be put to the sword. And thus much shall suffice; concerning what I find by speculation, and deduction, of sovereign rights, from the nature, need, and designs of men, in erecting of commonwealths, and putting themselves under monarchs, or assemblies, entrusted with power enough for their protection.

Let us now consider what the Scripture teacheth in the same point. To Moses, the children of *Israel* say thus: *Speak thou to us, and we will hear thee; but let not God speak to us, lest we die. (Exod. 20. 19.)* This is absolute obedience to Moses. Concerning the right of kings, God himself by the mouth of Samuel, saith, (1 *Sam.* 8. 11, 12, &c.) *This shall be the right of the king you will have to reign over you. He shall take your sons, and set them to drive his chariots, and to be his horsemen, and to run before his chariots; and gather in his harvest; and to make his engines of war, and instruments of his chariots; and shall take your daughters to make perfumes, to be his cooks, and bakers. He shall take your fields, your vine-yards, and your olive-yards, and give them to his servants. He shall take the tithe of your corn and wine, and give it to the men of his chamber, and to his other servants. He shall take your man-servants, and your maid-servants, and the choice of your youth, and employ them in his business. He shall take the tithe of your flocks; and you shall be his servants.* This is absolute power, and summed up in the last words, *you shall be his servants.* Again, when the people heard what power their king was to have, yet they consented thereto, and say thus, (*verse 19*) *we will be as all other nations, and our king shall judge our causes, and go before us, to conduct our wars.* Here is confirmed the right that sovereigns have, both to the *militia*, and to all *judicature*; in which is contained as absolute power, as one man can possibly transfer to another. Again, the prayer of king Solomon to God, was this (1 *Kings,* 3. 9): *Give to thy servant understanding, to judge thy people, and to discern between good and evil.* It belongeth therefore to the sovereign to be judge, and to prescribe the rules of *discerning good* and *evil*: which rules are laws; and therefore in him is the legislative power. Saul sought the life of *David*; yet when it was in his power to slay *Saul*, and his servants would have done it, *David* forbad them, saying, (1 *Sam.* 24. 9) *God forbid I should do such an act against my Lord, the anointed of God.* For obedience of servants St. *Paul* saith; (*Col.* 3. 20) *Servants obey your masters in all things;* and, (*Verse 22*) *children obey your par-*

ents in all things. There is simple obedience in those that are subject to paternal, or despotical dominion. Again, (*Matt.* 23. 2, 3) *The Scribes and Pharisees sit in Moses' chair, and therefore all that they shall bid you observe, that observe and do.* There again is simple obedience. And St. *Paul,* (*Titus* 3. 2) *Warn them that they subject themselves to princes, and to those that are in authority, and obey them.* This obedience is also simple. Lastly, our Saviour himself acknowledges, that men ought to pay such taxes as are by kings imposed, where he says, *Give to Caesar that which is Caesar's;* and paid such taxes himself. And that the king's word, is sufficient to take any thing from any subject, when there is need; and that the king is judge of that need: for he himself, as king of the Jews, commanded his disciples to take the ass, and ass's colt to carry him into Jerusalem, saying, (*Matth.* 21. 2, 3) *Go into the village over against you, and you shall find a she ass tied, and her colt with her, untie them, and bring them to me. And if any man ask you, what you mean by it, say the Lord hath need of them: and they will let them go.* They will not ask whether his necessity be a sufficient title; nor whether he be judge of that necessity; but acquiesce in the will of the Lord.

To these places may be added also that of *Genesis,* (*Genesis* 3. 5) *Ye shall be as gods, knowing good and evil.* And verse 11. *Who told thee that thou wast naked? hast thou eaten of the tree, of which I commanded thee thou shouldest not eat?* For the cognizance or judicature of good and evil, being forbidden by the name of the fruit of the tree of knowledge, as a trial of *Adam's* obedience; the devil to inflame the ambition of the woman, to whom that fruit already seemed beautiful, told her that by tasting it, they should be as gods, knowing *good* and *evil.* Whereupon having both eaten, they did indeed take upon them God's office, which is judicature of good and evil; but acquired no new ability to distinguish between them aright. And whereas it is said, that having eaten, they saw they were naked; no man hath so interpreted that place, as if they had been formerly blind, and saw not their own skins: the meaning is plain, that it was then they first judged their nakedness (wherein it was God's will to create them) to be uncomely; and by being ashamed, did tacitly censure God himself. And thereupon God saith, *Hast thou eaten, &c.* as if he should say, doest thou that owest me obedience, take upon thee to judge of my commandments? Whereby it is clearly, (though allegorically,) signified, that the commands of them that have the right to command, are not by their subjects to be censured, nor disputed.

So that it appeareth plainly, to my understanding, both from reason, and Scripture, that the sovereign power, whether placed in one man, as in monarchy, or in one assembly of men, as in popular, and aristocratical commonwealths, is as great, as possibly men can be imagined to make it. And though of so unlimited a power, men may fancy many evil consequences, yet the consequences of the want of it, which is perpetual war of every man against his neighbour, are much worse. The condition of man in this life shall never be without inconveniences; but there happeneth in no commonwealth any great inconvenience, but what proceeds from the subject's disobedience, and breach of those covenants, from which the commonwealth hath its being. And whosoever thinking sovereign power too great, will seek to make it less, must subject himself, to the power, that can limit it; that is to say, to a greater.

The greatest objection is, that of the practice; when men ask, where, and when, such power has by subjects been acknowledged. But one may ask them again, when or where has there been a kingdom long free from sedition and civil war. In those nations, whose commonwealths have been long-lived, and not been destroyed but by foreign war, the subjects never did dispute of the sovereign power. But howsoever, an argument from the practice of men, that have not sifted to the bottom, and with exact reason weighed the causes, and nature of commonwealths, and suffer daily those miseries, that proceed from the ignorance thereof, is invalid. For though in all places of the world, men should lay the foundation of their houses on the sand, it could not thence be inferred, that so it ought to be. The skill of making, and maintaining commonwealths, consisteth in certain rules, as doth arithmetic and geometry; not (as tennis-play) on practice only: which rules, neither poor men have the leisure, nor men that have had the leisure, have hitherto had the curiosity, or the method to find out.

CHAPTER 21

Of the Liberty of Subjects

LIBERTY, or FREEDOM, signifieth (properly) the absence of opposition; (by opposition, I mean external impediments of motion;) and may be applied no less to irrational, and inanimate creatures, than to rational. For whatsoever is so tied, or environed, as it cannot move, but within a certain space, which space is determined by the opposition of some external body, we say it hath not liberty to go further. And so of all living creatures, whilst they are imprisoned, or restrained, with walls, or chains; and of the water whilst it is kept in by banks, or vessels, that otherwise would spread itself into a larger space, we use to say, they are not at liberty, to move in such manner, as without those external impediments they would. But when the impediment of motion, is in the constitution of the thing itself, we use not to say, it wants the liberty; but the power to move; as when a stone lieth still, or a man is fastened to his bed by sickness.

And according to this proper, and generally received meaning of the word, *a* FREEMAN, *is he, that in those things, which by his strength and wit he is able to do, is not hindered to do what he has a will to.* But when the words *free*, and *liberty*, are applied to any thing but *bodies*, they are abused; for that which is not subject to motion, is not subject to impediment: and therefore, when it is said (for example) the way is free, no liberty of the way is signified, but of those that walk in it without stop. And when we say a gift is free, there is not meant any liberty of the gift, but of the giver, that was not bound by any law, or covenant to give it. So when we *speak freely*, it is not the liberty of voice, or pronunciation, but of the man, whom no law hath obliged to speak otherwise than he did. Lastly, from the use of the word *free-will*, no liberty can be inferred of the will, desire, or inclination, but the liberty of the man; which consisteth in this, that he finds no stop, in doing what he has the will, desire, or inclination to do.

Fear, and liberty are consistent; as when a man throweth his goods into the sea for *fear* the ship should sink, he doth it nevertheless very willingly, and may refuse to do it if he will: it is therefore the action of one that was *free*: so a man sometimes pays his debt, only for *fear* of imprisonment, which because nobody hindered him from detaining, was the action of a man at *liberty*. And generally all actions which men do in commonwealths, for *fear* of the law, are actions, which the doers had *liberty* to omit.

Liberty, and *necessity* are consistent: as in the water, that hath not only *liberty*, but a *necessity* of descending by the channel; so likewise in the actions which men voluntarily do: which, because they proceed from their will, proceed from *liberty*; and yet, because every act of man's will, and every desire, and inclination proceedeth from some cause, and that from another cause, in a continual chain, (whose first link is in the hand of God the first of all causes,) they proceed from *necessity*. So that to him that could see the connexion of those causes, the *necessity* of all men's voluntary actions, would appear manifest. And therefore God, that seeth, and disposeth all things, seeth also that the *liberty* of man in doing what he will, is accompanied with the *necessity* of doing that which God will, and no more, nor less.

For though men may do many things, which God does not command, nor is therefore author of them; yet they can have no passion, nor appetite to any thing, of which appetite God's will is not the cause. And did not his will assure the *necessity* of man's will, and consequently of all that on man's will dependeth, the *liberty* of men would be a contradiction, and impediment to the omnipotence and *liberty* of God. And this shall suffice, (as to the matter in hand) of that natural *liberty*, which only is properly called *liberty*.

But as men, for the attaining of peace, and conservation of themselves thereby, have made an artificial man, which we call a commonwealth; so also have they made artificial chains, called *civil laws*, which they themselves, by mutual covenants, have fastened at one end, to the lips of that man, or assembly, to whom they have given the sovereign power; and at the other end to their own ears. These bonds in their own nature but weak, may nevertheless be made to hold, by the danger, though not by the difficulty of breaking them.

In relation to these bonds only it is, that I am to speak now, of the *liberty* of *subjects*. For seeing there is no commonwealth in the world, wherein there be rules enough set down, for the regulating of all the actions, and words of men, (as being a thing impossible:) it followeth necessarily, that in all kinds of actions, by the laws praetermitted, men have the liberty, of doing what their own reasons shall suggest, for the most profitable to themselves. For if we take liberty in the proper sense, for corporal liberty; that is to say, freedom from chains, and prison, it were very absurd for men to clamour as they do, for the liberty they so manifestly enjoy. Again, if we take liberty, for an exemption from laws, it is no less absurd, for men to demand as they do, that liberty, by which all other men may be masters of their lives. And yet as absurd as it is, this is it they demand; not knowing that the laws are of no power to protect them, without a sword in the hands of a man, or men, to cause those laws to be put in execution. The liberty of a subject, lieth therefore only in those things, which in regulating their actions, the sovereign hath praetermitted: such as is the liberty to buy, and sell, and otherwise contract with one another; to choose their own abode, their own diet, their own trade of life, and institute their children as they themselves think fit; and the like.

Nevertheless we are not to understand, that by such liberty, the sovereign power of life and death, is either abolished, or limited. For it has been already shown, that nothing the sovereign representative can do to a subject, on what pretence soever, can properly be called injustice, or injury; because every subject is author of every act the sovereign doth; so that he never wanteth right to any thing, otherwise, than as he himself is the subject of God, and bound thereby to observe the laws of nature. As therefore it may, and doth often happen in commonwealths, that a subject may be put to death, by the command of the sovereign power; and yet neither do the other wrong: as when *Jephtha* caused his daughter to be sacrificed: in which, and the like cases, he that so dieth, had liberty to do the action, for which he is nevertheless, without injury put to death. And the same holdeth also in a sovereign prince, that putteth to death an innocent subject. For though the action be against the law of nature, as being contrary to equity, (as was the killing of *Uriah*, by *David*;) yet it was not an injury to *Uriah*; but to *God*. Not to *Uriah*, because the right to do what he pleased, was given him by *Uriah* himself: and yet to *God*, because *David* was *God's* subject; and prohibited all iniquity of the law of nature. Which distinction, *David* himself, when he repented the fact, evidently confirmed, saying, *To thee only have I sinned.* In the same manner, the people of *Athens*, when they banished the most potent of their commonwealth for ten years, thought they committed no injustice; and yet they never questioned what crime he had done; but what hurt he would do: nay they commanded the banishment of they know not whom; and every citizen bringing his oystershell into the market place, written with the name of him he desired should be banished, without actual accusing him, sometimes banished an *Aristides*, for his reputation of justice; and sometimes a scurrilous jester, as *Hyperbolus*, to make a jest of it. And yet a man cannot say, the sovereign people of *Athens* wanted right to banish them; or an *Athenian* the liberty to jest, or to be just.

The liberty, whereof there is so frequent and honourable mention, in the histories, and philosophy of the ancient Greeks, and Romans, and in the writings, and discourse of those that from them have received all their learning in the politics, is not the liberty of particular men; but the liberty of the commonwealth: which is the same with that, which every man then should have, if there were no civil laws, nor commonwealth at all. And the effects of it also be the same. For as amongst masterless men, there is perpetual war, of every man against his neighbour; no inheritance, to transmit to the son, nor to expect from the father; no propriety of goods, or lands; no security; but a full and absolute liberty in every particular man: so in states, and commonwealths not dependent on one another, every commonwealth, (not every man) has an absolute liberty, to do what it shall judge (that is to say, what that man, or assembly that representeth it, shall judge) most conducing to their benefit. But withal, they live in the condition of a perpetual war, and upon the confines of battle, with their frontiers armed, and cannons planted against their neighbours round about. The *Athenians*, and *Romans* were free; that is, free commonwealths: not that any particular men had the liberty to resist their own representative; but that their representative had the liberty to resist, or invade other people. There is written on the turrets of the city of *Lucca* in great characters at this day, the word *LIBERTAS*: yet no man can thence infer, that a particular man has more liberty, or immunity from the service of the commonwealth there, than in *Constantinople*. Whether a commonwealth be monarchical, or popular, the freedom is still the same.

But it is an easy thing, for men to be deceived, by the specious name of *liberty*, and for want of judgment to distinguish, mistake that for their private inheritance, and birth right, which is the right of the public only. And when the same error is confirmed by the authority of men in reputation for their writings in this subject, it is no wonder if it produce sedition, and change of government. In these western parts of the world, we are made to receive our opinions concerning the institution, and rights of commonwealths, from *Aristotle, Cicero*, and other men, Greeks and Romans, that living under popular states, derived those rights, not from the principles of nature, but transcribed them into their books, out of the practice of their own commonwealths, which were popular; as the grammarians describe the rules of language, out of the practice of the time; or the rules of poetry, out of the poems of *Homer* and *Virgil*. And because the Athenians were taught, (to keep them from desire of changing their government,) that they were freemen, and all that lived under monarchy were slaves; therefore Aristotle puts it down in his *Politics*, (*lib.* 6. *cap.* 2.) *In democracy, Liberty is to be supposed: for it is commonly held, that no man is Free in any other government.* And as Aristotle; so Cicero, and other writers have grounded their civil doctrine, on the opinions of the Romans, who were taught to hate monarchy, at first, by them that having deposed their sovereign, shared amongst them the sovereignty of *Rome*; and afterwards by their successors. And by reading of these Greek, and Latin authors, men from their childhood have gotten a habit (under a false show of liberty,) of favouring tumults, and of licentious controlling the actions of their sovereigns; and again of controlling those controllers, with the effusion of so much blood; as I think I may truly say, there was never any thing so dearly bought, as these western parts have bought the learning of the Greek and Latin tongues.

To come now to the particulars of the true liberty of a subject; that is to say, what are the things, which though commanded by the sovereign, he may nevertheless, without injustice, refuse to do; we are to consider, what rights we pass away, when we make a commonwealth; or (which is all one,) what liberty we deny ourselves, by owning all the actions (without exception) of the man, or assembly we make our sovereign. For in the act of our *submission*, consisteth both our *obligation*, and our *liberty*; which must therefore be inferred by arguments taken from thence; there being no obligation on any man, which ariseth not from some act of his own; for all men equally, are by nature free. And because such arguments, must either be drawn from the express words, *I authorise all his actions*, or from the intention of him that submitteth himself to his power, (which intention is to be understood by the end for which he so submitteth;) the obligation, and liberty of the subject, is to be derived, either from those words, (or others equivalent;) or else from the end of the institution of sovereignty, namely, the peace of the subjects within themselves, and their defence against a common enemy.

First therefore, seeing sovereignty by institution, is by covenant of every one to every one; and sovereignty by acquisition, by covenants of the vanquished to the victor, or child to the parent; it is manifest, that every subject has liberty in all those things, the right whereof cannot by covenant be transferred. I have shewn before in the 14th chapter, that covenants, not to defend a man's own body, are void. Therefore,

If the sovereign command a man (though justly condemned,) to kill, wound, or maim himself; or not to resist those that assault him; or to abstain from the use of food, air, medicine, or any other thing, without which he cannot live; yet hath that man the liberty to disobey.

If a man be interrogated by the sovereign, or his authority, concerning a crime done by himself, he is not bound (without assurance of pardon) to confess it; because no man (as I have shown in the same chapter) can be obliged by covenant to accuse himself.

Again, the consent of a subject to sovereign power, is contained in these words, *I authorize, or take upon me, all his actions;* in which there is no restriction at all, of his own former natural liberty: for by allowing him to *kill me*, I am not bound to kill myself when he commands me. It is one thing to say, *kill me, or my fellow, if you please*; another thing to say, *I will kill myself, or my fellow*. It followeth therefore, that

No man is bound by the words themselves, either to kill himself, or any other man; and consequently, that the obligation a man may sometimes have, upon the command of the sovereign to execute any dangerous, or dishonourable office, dependeth not on the words of our submission; but on the intention, which is to be understood by the end thereof. When therefore our refusal to obey, frustrates the end for which the sovereignty was ordained; then there is no liberty to refuse: otherwise there is.

Upon this ground, a man that is commanded as a soldier to fight against the enemy, though his sovereign have right enough to punish his refusal with death, may nevertheless in many cases refuse, without injustice; as when he substituteth a sufficient soldier in his place: for in this case he deserteth not the service of the commonwealth. And there is allowance to be made for natural timorousness; not only to women, (of whom no such dangerous duty is expected,) but also to men of feminine courage. When armies fight, there is on one side, or both, a running away; yet when they do it not out of treachery, but fear, they are not esteemed to do it unjustly, but dishonourably. For the same reason, to avoid battle, is not injustice, but cowardice. But he that inrolleth himself a soldier, or taketh imprest money, taketh away the excuse of a timorous nature; and is obliged, not only to go to the battle, but also not to run from it, without his captain's leave. And when the defence of the commonwealth, requireth at once the help of all that are able to bear arms, every one is obliged; because otherwise the institution of the commonwealth, which they have not the purpose, or courage to preserve, was in vain.

To resist the sword of the commonwealth, in defence of another man, guilty, or innocent, no man hath liberty; because such liberty, takes away from the sovereign, the means
of protecting us; and is therefore destructive of the very essence of government. But in
case a great many men together, have already resisted the sovereign power unjustly, or
committed some capital crime, for which every one of them expecteth death, whether
have they not the liberty then to join together, and assist, and defend one another?
Certainly they have: for they but defend their lives, which the guilty man may as well do,
as the innocent. There was indeed injustice in the first breach of their duty; their bearing
of arms subsequent to it, though it be to maintain what they have done, is no new unjust
act. And if it be only to defend their persons, it is not unjust at all. But the offer of pardon taketh from them, to whom it is offered, the plea of self-defence, and maketh their
perserverance in assisting, or defending the rest, unlawful.

As for other liberties, they depend on the silence of the law. In cases where the sovereign has prescribed no rule, there the subject hath the liberty to do, or forbear, according
to his own discretion. And therefore such liberty is in some places more, and in some less;
and in some times more, in other times less, according as they that have the sovereignty
shall think most convenient. As for example, there was a time, when in *England* a man
might enter into his own land, (and dispossess such as wrongfully possessed it,) by force.
But in aftertimes, that liberty of forcible entry, was taken away by a statute made (by the
king,) in parliament. And in some places of the world, men have the liberty of many wives:
in other places, such liberty is not allowed.

If a subject have a controversy with his sovereign, of debt, or of right of possession of
lands or goods, or concerning any service required at his hands, or concerning any penalty,
corporal, or pecuniary, grounded on a precedent law; he hath the same liberty to sue for
his right, as if it were against a subject; and before such judges, as are appointed by the
sovereign. For seeing the sovereign demandeth by force of a former law, and not by virtue
of his power; he declareth thereby, that he requireth no more, than shall appear to be due
by that law. The suit therefore is not contrary to the will of the sovereign; and consequently the subject hath the liberty to demand the hearing of his cause; and sentence,
according to that law. But if he demand, or take any thing by pretence of his power; there
lieth, in that case, no action of law: for all that is done by him in virtue of his power, is
done by the authority of every subject, and consequently, he that brings an action against
the sovereign, brings it against himself.

If a monarch, or sovereign assembly, grant a liberty to all, or any of his subjects, which
grant standing, he is disabled to provide for their safety, the grant is void; unless he
directly renounce, or transfer the sovereignty to another. For in that he might openly, (if
it had been his will,) and in plain terms, have renounced, or transferred it, and did not; it
is to be understood it was not his will; but that the grant proceeded from ignorance of the
repugnancy between such a liberty and the sovereign power: and therefore the sovereignty
is still retained; and consequently all those powers, which are necessary to the exercising
thereof; such as are the power of war, and peace, of judicature, of appointing officers, and
councillors, of levying money, and the rest named in the 18th chapter.

The obligation of subjects to the sovereign, is understood to last as long, and no longer,
than the power lasteth, by which he is able to protect them. For the right men have by nature
to protect themselves, when none else can protect them, can by no covenant be relinquished.
The sovereignty is the soul of the commonwealth; which once departed from the body, the
members do no more receive their motion from it. The end of obedience is protection; which,
wheresoever a man seeth it, either in his own, or in another's sword, nature applieth his obe-

dience to it, and his endeavour to maintain it. And though sovereignty, in the intention of them that make it, be immortal; yet is it in its own nature, not only subject to violent death, by foreign war; but also through the ignorance, and passions of men, it hath in it, from the very institution, many seeds of a natural mortality, by intestine discord.

If a subject be taken prisoner in war; or his person, or his means of life be within the guards of the enemy, and hath his life and corporal liberty given him, on condition to be subject to the victor, he hath liberty to accept the condition; and having accepted it, is the subject of him that took him; because he had no other way to preserve himself. The case is the same, if he be detained on the same terms, in a foreign country. But if a man be held in prison, or bonds, or is not trusted with the liberty of his body; he cannot be understood to be bound by covenant to subjection; and therefore may, if he can, make his escape by any means whatsoever.

If a monarch shall relinquish the sovereignty, both for himself, and his heirs; his subjects return to the absolute liberty of nature; because, though nature may declare who are his sons, and who are the nearest of his kin; yet it dependeth on his own will, (as hath been said in the precedent chapter,) who shall be his heir. If therefore he will have no heir, there is no sovereignty, nor subjection. The case is the same, if he die without known kindred, and without declaration of his heir. For then there can no heir be known, and consequently no subjection be due.

If the sovereign banish his subject; during the banishment, he is not subject. But he that is sent on a message, or hath leave to travel, is still subject; but it is, by contract between sovereigns, not by virtue of the covenant of subjection. For whosoever entereth into another's dominion, is subject to all the laws thereof; unless he have a privilege by the amity of the sovereigns, or by special licence.

If a monarch subdued by war, render himself subject to the victor; his subjects are delivered from their former obligation, and become obliged to the victor. But if he be held prisoner, or have not the liberty of his own body; he is not understood to have given away the right of sovereignty; and therefore his subjects are obliged to yield obedience to the magistrates formerly placed, governing not in their own name, but in his. For, his right remaining, the question is only of the administration; that is to say, of the magistrates and officers; which, if he have not means to name, he is supposed to approve those, which he himself had formerly appointed.

CHAPTER 24

Of the Nutrition, and Procreation of a Commonwealth

The Nutrition of a commonwealth consisteth, in the *plenty*, and *distribution* of *materials* conducing to life: in *concoction, or preparation*; and, (when concocted) in the *conveyance* of it, by convenient conduits, to the public use.

As for the plenty of matter, it is a thing limited by nature, to those commodities, which from (the two breasts of our common mother) land, and sea, God usually either freely giveth, or for labour selleth to mankind.

For the matter of this nutriment, consisting in animals, vegetals, and minerals, God hath freely laid them before us, in or near to the face of the earth; so as there needeth no more but the labour, and industry of receiving them. Insomuch as plenty dependeth (next to God's favour) merely on the labour and industry of men.

This matter, commonly called commodities, is partly *native*, and partly *foreign*: *native*, that which is to be had within the territory of the commonwealth: *foreign*, that which is imported from without. And because there is no territory under the dominion of one commonwealth, (except it be of very vast extent,) that produceth all things needful for the maintenance, and motion of the whole body; and few that produce not something more than necessary; the superfluous commodities to be had within, become no more superfluous, but supply these wants at home, by importation of that which may be had abroad, either by exchange, or by just war, or by labour: for a man's labour also, is a commodity exchangeable for benefit, as well as any other thing: and there have been commonwealths that having no more territory, than hath served them for habitation, have nevertheless, not only maintained, but also encreased their power, partly by the labour of trading from one place to another, and partly by selling the manufactures, whereof the materials were brought in from other places.

The distribution of the materials of this nourishment, is the constitution of *mine*, and *thine*, and *his*; that is to say, in one word *propriety*; and belongeth in all kinds of commonwealth to the sovereign power. For where there is no commonwealth, there is (as hath been already shown) a perpetual war of every man against his neighbour; and therefore every thing is his that getteth it, and keepeth it by force; which is neither *propriety*, nor *community*; but *uncertainty*. Which is so evident, that even *Cicero*, (a passionate defender of liberty,) in a public pleading, attributeth all propriety to the law civil. *Let the civil law,* saith he, *be once abandoned, or but negligently guarded, (not to say oppressed,) and there is nothing, that any man can be sure to receive from his ancestor, or leave to his children.* And again; *Take away the civil law, and no man knows what is his own, and what another man's.* Seeing therefore the introduction of *propriety* is an effect of commonwealth; which can do nothing but by the person that represents it, it is the act only of the sovereign; and consisteth in the laws, which none can make that have not the sovereign power. And this they well knew of old, who called that Νόμος, (that is to say, *distribution*,) which we call law; and defined justice, by *distributing* to every man *his own*.

In this distribution, the first law, is for division of the land itself: where in the sovereign assigneth to every man a portion, according as he, and not according as any subject, or any number of them, shall judge agreeable to equity, and the common good. The children of Israel, were a commonwealth in the wilderness; but wanted the commodities of the earth, till they were masters of the Land of Promise; which afterward was divided amongst them, not by their own discretion, but by the discretion of *Eleazar* the Priest, and *Joshua* their General, who, when there were twelve tribes, making them thirteen by subdivision of the tribe of *Joseph*; made nevertheless but twelve portions of the land; and ordained for the tribe of *Levi* no land; but assigned them the tenth part of the whole fruits; which division was therefore arbitrary. And though a people coming into possession of a land by war, do not always exterminate the ancient inhabitants, (as did the Jews,) but leave to many, or most, or all of them their estates; yet it is manifest they hold them afterwards, as of the victors' distribution; as the people of *England* held all theirs of *William* the *Conqueror*.

From whence we may collect, that the propriety which a subject hath in his lands, consisteth in a right to exclude all other subjects from the use of them; and not to exclude their sovereign, be it an assembly, or a monarch. For seeing the sovereign, that is to say, the commonwealth (whose person he representeth,) is understood to do nothing but in order to the common peace and security, this distribution of lands, is to be understood as done in order to the same: and consequently, whatsoever distribution he shall make in prejudice thereof, is contrary to the will of every subject, that committed his peace, and safety to his discretion, and conscience; and therefore by the will of every one of them, is to be reputed void. It is true, that a sovereign monarch, or the greater part of a sovereign assembly, may ordain the doing of many things in pursuit of their passions, contrary to their own consciences, which is a breach of trust, and of the law of nature; but this is not enough to authorize any subject, either to make war upon, or so much as to accuse of injustice, or any way to speak evil of their sovereign; because they have authorized all his actions, and in bestowing the sovereign power, made them their own. But in what cases the commands of sovereigns are contrary to equity, and the law of nature, is to be considered hereafter in another place.

In the distribution of land, the commonwealth itself, may be conceived to have a portion, and possess, and improve the same by their representative; and that such portion may be made sufficient, to sustain the whole expense to the common peace, and defence necessarily required: Which were very true, if there could be any representative conceived free from human passions, and infirmities. But the nature of men being as it is, the setting forth of public land, or of any certain revenue for the commonwealth, is in vain; and tendeth to the dissolution of government, and to the condition of mere nature, and war, as soon as ever the sovereign power falleth into the hands of a monarch, or of an assembly, that are either too negligent of money, or too hazardous in engaging the public stock, into a long or costly war. Commonwealths can endure no diet: for seeing their expense is not limited by their own appetite, but by external accidents, and the appetites of their neighbours, the public riches cannot be limited by other limits, than those which the emergent occasions shall require. And whereas in *England*, there were by the Conqueror, divers lands reserved to his own use, (besides forests, and chases, either for his recreation, or for preservation of woods,) and divers services reserved on the land he gave his subjects; yet it seems they were not reserved for his maintenance in his public, but in his natural capacity. For he, and his successors did for all that, lay arbitrary taxes on all subjects' land, when they judged it necessary. Or if those public lands, and services, were ordained as a sufficient maintenance of the commonwealth, it was contrary to the scope of the institution; being (as it appeared by those ensuing taxes) insufficient, and (as it appears by the late small revenue of the crown) subject to alienation and diminution. It is therefore in vain, to assign a portion to the commonwealth; which may sell, or give it away; and does sell and give it away when it is done by their representative.

As the distribution of lands at home; so also to assign in what places, and for what commodities, the subject shall traffic abroad, belongeth to the sovereign. For if it did belong to private persons to use their own discretion therein, some of them would be drawn for gain, both to furnish the enemy with means to hurt the commonwealth, and hurt it themselves, by importing such things, as pleasing men's appetites, be nevertheless noxious, or at least unprofitable to them. And therefore it belongeth to the commonwealth, (that is, to the sovereign only,) to approve, or disapprove both of the places, and matter of foreign traffic.

Further, seeing it is not enough to the sustentation of a commonwealth, that every man have a propriety in a portion of land, or in some few commodities, or a natural property in some useful art, and there is no art in the world, but is necessary either for the being, or well being almost of every particular man; it is necessary, that men distribute that which they can spare, and transfer their propriety therein, mutually one to another, by exchange, and mutual contract. And therefore it belongeth to the commonwealth, (that is to say, to the sovereign,) to appoint in what manner, all kinds of contract between subjects, (as buying, selling, exchanging, borrowing, lending, letting, and taking to hire,) are to be made;

and by what words and signs they shall be understood for valid. And for the matter, and distribution of the nourishment, to the several members of the commonwealth, thus much (considering the model of the whole work) is sufficient.

By concoction, I understand the reducing of all commodities, which are not presently consumed, but reserved for nourishment in time to come, to some thing of equal value, and withal so portable, as not to hinder the motion of men from place to place; to the end a man may have in what place soever, such nourishment as the place affordeth. And this is nothing else but gold, and silver, and money. For gold and silver, being (as it happens) almost in all countries of the world highly valued, is a commodious measure of the value of all things else between nations; and money (of what matter soever coined by the sovereign of a commonwealth,) is a sufficient measure of the value of all things else, between the subject of that commonwealth. By the means of which measures, all commodities, moveable, and immoveable, are made to accompany a man, to all places of his resort, within and without the place of his ordinary residence; and the same passeth from man to man, within the commonwealth; and goes round about, nourishing (as it passeth) every part thereof; in so much as this concoction, is as it were the sanguification of the commonwealth: for natural blood is in like manner made of the fruits of the earth; and circulating, nourisheth by the way, every member of the body of man.

And because silver and gold, have their value from the matter itself; they have first this privilege, that the value of them cannot be altered by the power of one, nor of a few commonwealths; as being a common measure of the commodities of all places. But base money, may easily be enhanced, or abased. Secondly, they have the privilege to make commonwealths move, and stretch out their arms, when need is, into foreign countries; and supply, not only private subjects that travel, but also whole armies with provision. But that coin, which is not considerable for the matter, but for the stamp of the place, being unable to endure change of air, hath its effect at home only; where also it is subject to the change of laws, and thereby to have the value diminished, to the prejudice many times of those that have it.

The conduits, and ways by which it is conveyed to the public use, are of two sorts; one, that conveyeth it to the public coffers; the other, that issueth the same out again for the public payments. Of the first sort, are collectors, receivers, and treasurers; of the second are the treasurers again, and the officers appointed for payment of several public or private ministers. And in this also, the artificial man maintains his resemblance with the natural; whose veins receiving the blood from the several parts of the body, carry it to the heart; where being made vital, the heart by the arteries sends it out again, to enliven, and enable for motion all the members of the same.

The procreation, or children of a commonwealth, are those we call *plantations*, or *colonies*; which are numbers of men sent out from the commonwealth, under a conductor, or governor, to inhabit a foreign country, either formerly void of inhabitants, or made void then, by war. And when a colony is settled, they are either a commonwealth of themselves, discharged of their subjection to their sovereign that sent them, (as hath been done by many commonwealths of ancient time,) in which case the commonwealth from which they went, was called their metropolis, or mother, and requires no more of them, than fathers require of the children, whom they emancipate and make free from their domestic government, which is honour, and friendship; or else they remain united to their metropolis, as were the colonies of the people of *Rome*; and then they are no commonwealths themselves, but provinces, and parts of the commonwealth that sent them. So that the right of colonies (saving honour, and league with their metropolis,) dependeth wholly on their licence, or letters, by which their sovereign authorized them to plant.

CHAPTER 26

Of Civil Laws

By CIVIL LAWS, I understand the laws, that men are therefore bound to observe, because they are members, not of this, or that commonwealth in particular, but of a commonwealth. For the knowledge of particular laws belongeth to them, that profess the study of the laws of their several countries; but the knowledge of civil law in general, to any man. The ancient law of *Rome* was called their *civil law*, from the word *civitas*, which signifies a commonwealth: and those countries, which having been under the Roman empire, and governed by that law, retain still such a part thereof as they think fit, call that part the civil law, to distinguish it from the rest of their own civil laws. But that is not it I intend to speak of here; my design being not to show what is law here, and there; but what is law; as *Plato, Aristotle, Cicero,* and divers others have done, without taking upon them the profession of the study of the law.

And first it is manifest, that law in general, is not counsel, but command; nor a command of any to any man; but only of him, whose command is addressed to one formerly obliged to obey him. And as for civil law, it addeth only the name of the person commanding, which is *persona civitatis,* the person of the commonwealth.

Which considered, I define civil law in this manner. CIVIL LAW, *is to every subject, those rules, which the commonwealth hath commanded him, by word, writing, or others sufficient sign of the will, to make use of, for the distinction of right, and wrong; that is to say, of what is contrary, and what is not contrary to the rule.*

In which definition, there is nothing that is not at first evident. For every man seeth, that some laws are addressed to all the subjects in general; some to particular provinces; some to particular vocations; and some to particular men; and are therefore laws, to every of those to whom the command is directed; and to none else. As also, that laws are the rules of just, and unjust; nothing being reputed unjust, that is not contrary to some law. Likewise that none can make laws but the commonwealth; because our subjection is to the commonwealth only: and that commands, are to be signified by sufficient signs; because a man knows not otherwise how to obey them. And therefore, whatsoever can from this definition by necessary consequence be deduced, ought to be acknowledged for truth. Now I deduce from it this that followeth.

1. The legislator in all commonwealths, is only the sovereign, be he one man, as in a monarchy, or one assembly of men, as in a democracy, or aristocracy. For the legislator is he that maketh the law. And the commonwealth only, prescribes, and commandeth the observation of those rules, which we call law: therefore the commonwealth is the legislator. But the commonwealth is no person, nor has capacity to do any thing, but by the representative, (that is, the sovereign;) and therefore the sovereign is the sole legislator. For the same reason, none can abrogate a law made, but the sovereign; because a law is not abrogated, but by another law, that forbiddeth it to be put in execution.

2. The sovereign of a commonwealth, be it an assembly, or one man, is not subject to the civil laws. For having power to make, and repeal laws, he may when he pleaseath, free himself from that subjection, by repealing those laws that trouble him, and making of new; and consequently he was free before. For he is free, that can be free when he will: nor is it possible for any person to be bound to himself; because he that can bind, can release; and therefore he that is bound to himself only, is not bound.

3. When long use obtaineth the authority of a law, it is not the length of time that maketh the authority, but the will of the sovereign signified by his silence, (for silence is sometimes an

argument of consent;) and it is no longer law, than the sovereign shall be silent therein. And therefore if the sovereign shall have a question of right grounded, not upon his present will, but upon the laws formerly made; the length of time shall bring no prejudice to his right; but the question shall be judged by equity. For many unjust actions, and unjust sentences go uncontrolled a longer time, than any man can remember. And our lawyers account no customs law, but such as are reasonable, and that evil customs are to be abolished: But the judgment of what is reasonable, and of what is to be abolished, belongeth to him that maketh the law, which is the sovereign assembly, or monarch.

4. The law of nature, and the civil law, contain each other, and are of equal extent. For the laws of nature, which consist in equity, justice, gratitude, and other moral virtues on these depending, in the condition of mere nature (as I have said before in the end of the 15th chapter,) are not properly laws, but qualities that dispose men to peace and to obedience. When a commonwealth is once settled, then are they actually laws, and not before; as being then the commands of the commonwealth; and therefore also civil laws: for it is the sovereign power that obliges men to obey them. For in the differences of private men, to declare, what is equity, what is justice, and what is moral virtue, and to make them binding, there is need of the ordinances of sovereign power, and punishments to be ordained for such as shall break them; which ordinances are therefore part of the civil law. The law of nature therefore is a part of the civil law in all commonwealths of the world. Reciprocally also, the civil law is a part of the dictates of nature. For justice, that is to say, performance of covenant, and giving to every man his own, is a dictate of the law of nature. But every subject in a commonwealth, hath covenanted to obey the civil law, (either one with another, as when they assemble to make a common representative, or with the representative it self one by one, when subdued by the sword they promise obedience, that they may receive life;) and therefore obedience to the civil law is part also of the law of nature. Civil, and natural law are not different kinds, but different parts of law; whereof one part being written, is called civil, the other unwritten, natural. But the right of nature, that is, the natural liberty of man, may be the civil law be abridged, and restrained: nay, the end of making laws, is no other, but such restraint; without the which there cannot possibly be any peace. And law was brought into the world for nothing else, but to limit the natural liberty of particular men, in such manner, as they might not hurt, but assist one another, and join together against a common enemy.

5. If the sovereign of one commonwealth, subdue a people that have lived under other written laws, and afterwards govern them by the same laws, by which they were governed before; yet those laws are the civil laws of the victor, and not of the vanquished commonwealth. For the legislator is he, not by whose authority the laws were first made, but by whose authority they now continue to be laws. And therefore where there be divers provinces, within the dominion of a commonwealth, and in those provinces diversity of laws, which commonly are called the customs of each several province, we are not to understand that such customs have their force, only from length of time; but that they were anciently laws written, or otherwise made known, for the constitutions, and statutes of their sovereigns; and are now laws, not by virtue of the prescription of time, but by the constitutions of their present sovereigns. But if an unwritten law, in all the provinces of a dominion, shall be generally observed, and no iniquity appear in the use thereof; that law can be no other but a law of nature, equally obliging all mankind.

6. Seeing then all laws, written and unwritten, have their authority, and force, from the will of the commonwealth; that is to say, from the will of the representative; which in a monarchy is the monarch, and in other commonwealths the sovereign assembly; a man may wonder from whence proceed such opinions, as are found in the books of lawyers of eminence in several commonwealths, directly, or by consequence making the legislative power depend on private men, or subordinate judges. As for example, *that the common law, hath no controller but the parliament;* which is true only where a parliament has the sovereign power, and cannot be assembled, nor dissolved, but by their own discretion. For if there be a right in any else to dissolve them, there is a right also to control them, and consequently to control their controllings.

And if there be no such right, then the controller of laws is not *parliamentum*, but *rex in parliamento*. And where a parliament is sovereign, if it should assemble never so many, or so wise men, from the countries subject to them, for whatsoever cause; yet there is no man will believe, that such an assembly hath thereby acquired to themselves a legislative power. *Item*, that the two arms of a commonwealth, are *force, and justice; the first whereof is in the king; the other deposited in the hands of the parliament.* As if a commonwealth could consist, where the force were in any hand, which justice had not the authority to command and govern.

7. That law can never be against reason, our lawyers are agreed; and that not the letter, (that is, every construction of it,) but that which is according to the intention of the legislator, is the law. And it is true: but the doubt is of whose reason it is, that shall be received for law. It is not meant of any private reason; for then there would be as much contradiction in the laws, as there is in the Schools; nor yet, (as Sir *Edward Coke* makes it,) an *artificial perfection of reason, gotten by long study, observation, and experience,* (as his was.) For it is possible long study may increase, and confirm erroneous sentences: and where men build on false grounds, the more they build, the greater is the ruin: and of those that study, and observe with equal time, and diligence, the reasons and resolutions are, and must remain discordant: and therefore it is not the *juris prudentia*, or wisdom of subordinate judges; but the reason of this our artificial man the commonwealth, and his command, that maketh law: and the commonwealth being in their representative but one person, there cannot easily arise any contradiction in the laws; and when there doth, the same reason is able, by interpretation, or alteration, to take it away. In all courts of justice, the sovereign (which is the person of the commonwealth,) is he that judgeth: the subordinate judge, ought to have regard to the reason, which moved his sovereign to make such law, that his sentence may be according thereunto; which then is his sovereign's sentence; otherwise it is his own, and an unjust one.

8. From this, that the law is a command, and a command consisteth in declaration, or manifestation of the will of him that commandeth, by voice, writing, or some other sufficient argument of the same, we may understand, that the command of the commonwealth is law only to those, that have means to take notice of it. Over natural fools, children, or madmen there is no law, no more than over brute beasts; nor are they capable of the title of just, or unjust; because they had never power to make any covenant, or to understand the consequences thereof; and consequently never took upon them to authorize the actions of any sovereign, as they must do that make to themselves a commonwealth. And as those from whom nature, or accident hath taken away the notice of all laws in general; so also every man, from whom any accident, not proceeding from his own default, hath taken away the means to take notice of any particular law, is excused, if he observe it not; and to speak properly, that law is no law to him. It is therefore necessary, to consider in this place, what arguments, and signs be sufficient for the knowledge of what is the law; that is to say, what is the will of the sovereign, as well in monarchies, as in other forms of government.

And first, if it be a law that obliges all the subjects without exception, and is not written, nor otherwise published in such places as they may take notice thereof, it is a law of nature. For whatsoever men are to take knowledge of for law, not upon other men's words, but every one from his own reason, must be such as is agreeable to the reason of all men; which no law can be, but the law of nature. The laws of nature therefore need not any publishing, nor proclamation; as being contained in this one sentence, approved by all the world, *Do not that to another, which thou thinkest unreasonable to be done by another to thyself.*

Secondly, if it be a law that obliges only some condition of men, or one particular man, and be not written, nor published by word, then also it is a law of nature; and known by the same arguments, and signs, that distinguish those in such a condition, from other subjects. For whatsoever law is not written, or some way published by him that makes it law, can be known no way, but by the reason of him that is to obey it; and is therefore also a law not only civil, but natural. For example, if the sovereign employ a public minister, without written instructions what to do; he is obliged to take for instructions the dictates of reason; as if he make a judge, the judge is to take notice, that his sentence ought to be according to the reason of his sovereign, which being always understood to be equity, he is bound to it by the law of nature: or if an ambassador, he is (in all things not contained in his written instructions) to take for instruction that which reason dictates to be most conducing to his sovereign's interest; and so of all other ministers of the sovereignty, public and private. All which instruction of natural reason may be comprehended under one name of *fidelity*; which is a branch of natural justice.

The law of nature excepted, it belongeth to the essence of all other laws, to be made known, to every man that shall be obliged to obey them, either by word, or writing, or some other act, known to proceed from the sovereign authority. For the will of another, cannot be understood, but by his own word, or act, or by conjecture taken from his scope and purpose; which in the person of the commonwealth, is to be supposed always consonant to equity and reason. And in ancient time, before letters were in common use, the laws were many times put into verse; that the rude people taking pleasure in signing, or reciting them, might the more easily retain them in memory. And for the same reason *Solomon* adviseth a man, to bind the ten commandments upon his ten fingers. And for the law which *Moses* gave to the people of Israel at the renewing of the covenant, he biddeth them to teach it their children, by discoursing of it both at home, and upon the way; at going to bed, and at rising from bed; and to write it upon the posts, and doors of their houses; and (*Deut.* 31.12) to assemble the people, man, woman, and child, to hear it read.

Nor is it enough the law be written, and published; but also that there be manifest signs, that it proceedeth from the will of the sovereign. For private men, when they have, or think they have force enough to secure their unjust designs, and convoy them safely to their ambitious ends, may publish for laws what they please, without or against the legislative authority. There is therefore requisite, not only a declaration of the law, but also sufficient signs of the author, and authority. The author, or legislator is supposed in every commonwealth to be evident, because he is the sovereign, who having been constituted by the consent of every one, is supposed by every one to be sufficiently known. And though the ignorance, and security of men be such, for the most part, as that when the memory of the first constitution of their commonwealth is worn out, they do not consider, by whose power they use to be defended against their enemies, and to have their industry protected, and to be righted when injury is done them; yet because no man that considers, can make question of it, no excuse can be derived from the ignorance of where the sovereignty is placed. And it is a dictate of natural reason, and consequently an evident law of nature, that no man ought to weaken that power, the protection whereof he hath himself demanded, or wittingly received against others. Therefore of who is sovereign, no man, but by his own fault, (whatsoever evil men suggest,) can make any doubt. The difficulty consisteth in the evidence of the authority derived from him; the removing whereof, dependeth on the knowledge of the public registers, public counsels, public ministers, and public seals; by which all laws are sufficiently verified; verified, I say, not authorized: for the verification, is but the testimony and record; not the authority of the law; which consisteth in the command of the sovereign only.

If therefore a man have a question of injury, depending on the law of nature; that is to say, on common equity; the sentence of the judge, that by commission hath authority to take cognizance of such causes, is a sufficient verification of the law of nature in that individual case. For though the advice of one that professeth the study of the law, be useful for the avoiding contention; yet it is but advice: it is the judge must tell men what is law, upon the hearing of the controversy.

But when the question is of injury, or crime, upon a written law; every man by recourse to the registers, by himself or others, may (if he will) be sufficiently informed, before he do such injury, or commit the crime, whether it be an injury, or not: nay he ought to do so: for when a man doubts whether the act he goeth about, be just, or unjust; and may inform himself, if he will; the doing is unlawful. In like manner, he that suppposeth himself injured, in a case determined by the written law, which he may by himself or others see and consider; if he complain before he consults with the law, he does unjustly, and bewrayeth a disposition rather to vex other men, than to demand his own right.

If the question be of obedience to a public officer; to have seen his commission, with the public seal, and heard it read; or to have had the means to be informed of it, if a man would, is a sufficient verification of his authority. For every man is obliged to do his best endeavour, to inform himself of all written laws, that may concern his own future actions.

The legislator known; and the laws, either by writing, or by the light of nature, sufficiently published; there wanteth yet another very material circumstance to make them obligatory. For it is not the letter, but the intendment, or meaning; that is to say, the authentic interpretation of the law (which is the sense of the legislator,) in which the nature of the law consisteth; and therefore the interpretation of the laws dependeth on the authority sovereign; and the interpreters can be none but those, which the sovereign, (to whom only the subject oweth obedience) shall appoint. For else, by the craft of an interpreter, the law may be made to bear a sense, contrary to that of the sovereign; by which means the interpreter becomes the legislator.

All laws, written, and unwritten, have need of interpretation. The unwritten law of nature, though it be easy to such, as without partiality, and passion, make use of their natural reason, and therefore leaves the violators thereof without excuse; yet considering there be very few, perhaps none, that in some cases are not blinded by self love, or some other passion; it is now become of all laws the most obscure; and has consequently the greatest need of able interpreters. The written laws, if they be short, are easily misinterpreted, from the divers significations of a word, or two: if long they be more obscure by the divers significations of many words: insomuch as no written law, delivered in few, or many words, can be well understood, without perfect understanding of the final causes, for which the law was made; the knowledge of which final causes is in the legislator. To him therefore there cannot be any knot in the law, insoluble; either by finding out the ends, to undo it by; or else by making what ends he will, (as *Alexander* did with his sword in the Gordian knot,) by the legislative power; which no other interpreter can do.

The interpretation of the laws of nature, in a commonwealth, dependeth not on the books of moral philosophy. The authority of writers, without the authority of the commonwealth, maketh not their opinions law, be they never so true. That which I have written in this treatise, concerning the moral virtues, and of their necessity, for the procuring, and maintaining peace, though it be evident truth, is not therefore presently law; but because in all commonwealths in the world, it is part of the civil law: For though it be naturally reasonable; yet it is by the sovereign power that it is law: otherwise, it were a great error, to call the laws of nature unwritten law; whereof we see so many volumes published, and in them so many contradictions of one another, and of themselves.

The interpretation of the law of nature, is the sentence of the judge constituted by the sovereign authority, to hear and determine such controversies, as depend thereon; and consisteth in the application of the law to the present case. For in the act of judicature, the judge doth no more but consider, whether the demand of the party, be consonant to natural reason, and equity; and the sentence he giveth, is therefore the interpretation of the law of nature; which interpretation is authentic; not because it is his private sentence; but because he giveth it by authority of the sovereign, whereby it becomes the sovereign's sentence; which is law for that time, to the parties pleading.

But because there is not judge subordinate, nor sovereign, but may err in a judgment of equity; if afterward in another like case he find it more consonant to equity to give a contrary sentence, he is obliged to do it. No man's error becomes his own law; nor obliges him to persist in it. Neither (for the same reason) becomes it a law to other judges, though sworn to follow it. For though a wrong sentence given by authority of the sovereign, if he know and allow it, in such laws as are mutable, be a constitution of a new law, in cases, in which every little circumstance is the same; yet in laws immutable, such as are the laws of nature, they are no laws to the same, or other judges, in the like cases for ever after. Princes succeed one another; and one judge passeth, another cometh; nay, heaven and earth shall pass; but not one title of the law of nature shall pass; for it is the eternal law of God. Therefore all the sentences of precedent judges that have ever been, cannot all together make a law contrary to natural equity: nor any examples of former judges, can warrant an unreasonable sentence, or discharge the present judge of the trouble of studying what is equity (in the case he is to judge,) from the principles of his own natural reason. For example sake, it is against the law of nature, *to punish the innocent;* and innocent is he that acquitteth himself judicially, and is acknowledged for innocent by the judge. Put the case now, that a man is accused of a capital crime, and seeing the power and malice of some enemy, and the frequent corruption and partiality of judges, runneth away for fear of the event, and afterwards is taken, and brought to a legal trial, and maketh it sufficiently appear, he was not guilty of the crime, and being thereof acquitted, is nevertheless condemned to lose his goods; this is a manifest condemnation of the innocent. I say therefore, that there is no place in the world, where this can be an interpretation of a law of nature, or be made a law by the sentences of precedent judges, that had done the same. For he that judged it first, judged unjustly; and no injustice can be a pattern of judgment to succeeding judges. A written law may forbid innocent men to fly, and they may be punished for flying: but that flying for fear of injury, should be taken for presumption of guilt, after a man is already absolved of the crime judicially, is contrary to the nature of a presumption, which hath no place after judgment given. Yet this is set down by a great lawyer for the common law of *England. If a man,* (saith he) *that is innocent, be accused of felony, and for fear flyeth for the same; albeit he judicially acquitteth himself of the felony; yet if it be found that he fled for the felony; he shall notwithstanding his innocency, forfeit all his goods, chattles, debts, and duties. For as to the forfeiture of them, the law will admit no proof against the presumption in law, grounded upon his flight.* Here you see, *an innocent man judicially acquitted, notwithstanding his innocency,* (when no written law forbad him to fly) after his acquittal, *upon a presumption in law,* condemned to lose all the goods he hath. If the law ground upon his flight a presumption of the fact, (which was capital,) the sentence ought to have been capital: if the presumption were not of the fact, for what then ought he to lose his goods? This therefore is no law of *England*; nor is the condemnation grounded upon a presumption of law, but upon the presumption of the judges. It is also against law, to say that no proof shall be admitted against a presumption of law. For all judges, sovereign and subordinate, if they refuse to hear proof, refuse to do justice: for though the sentence be just, yet the judges that condemn without hearing the proofs offered, are unjust judges; and their presumption is but prejudice; which no man ought to bring with him to the seat of justice, whatsoever precedent judgments, or examples he shall pretend to follow. There be other things of this nature, wherein men's judgments have been perverted, by trusting to precedents: but this is enough to show, that though the sentence of the judge, be a law to the party pleading, yet it is no law to any judge, that shall succeed him in that office.

In like manner, when question is of the meaning of written laws, he is not the interpreter of them, that writeth a commentary upon them. For commentaries are commonly more subject to cavil, than the text; and therefore need other commentaries; and so there will be no end of such interpretation. And therefore unless there be an interpreter authorized by the sovereign, from which the subordinate judges are not to recede, the interpreter can be no other than the ordinary judges, in the same manner, as they are in cases of the unwritten law; and their sentences are to be taken by them that plead, for laws in that particular case; but not to bind other judges, in like cases to give like judgments. For a judge may err in the interpretation even of written laws; but no error of a subordinate judge, can change the law, which is the general sentence of the sovereign.

In written laws, men use to make a difference between the letter, and the sentence of the law: and when by the letter, is meant whatsoever can be gathered from the bare words, it is well distinguished. For the significations of almost all words, are either in themselves, or in the metaphorical use of them, ambiguous; and may be drawn in argument, to make many senses; but there is only one sense of the law. But if by the letter, be meant the literal sense, then the letter, and the sentence or intention of the law, is all one. For the literal sense is that, which the legislator intended, should by the letter of the law be signified. Now the intention of the legislator is always supposed to be equity: for it were a great contumely for a judge to think otherwise of the sovereign. He ought therefore, if the word of the law do not fully authorize a reasonable sentence, to supply it with the law of nature; or if the case be difficult, to respite judgment till he have received more ample authority. For example, a written law ordaineth, that he which is thrust out of his house by force, shall be restored by force: it happens that a man by negligence leaves his house empty, and returning is kept out by force, in which case there is no special law ordained, It is evident, that this case is contained in the same law: for else there is no remedy for him at all; which is to be supposed against the intention of the legislator. Again, the word of the law, commandeth to judge according to the evidence: a man is accused falsely of a fact, which the judge saw himself done by another; and not be him that is accused. In this case neither shall the letter of the law be followed to the condemnation of the innocent, nor shall the judge give sentence against the evidence of the witnesses; because the letter of the law is to the contrary: but procure of the sovereign that another be made judge, and himself witness. So that the incommodity that follows the bare words of a written law, may lead him to the intention of the law, whereby to interpret the same the better; though no incommodity can warrant a sentence against the law. For every judge of right, and wrong, is not judge of what is commodious, or incommodious to the commonwealth.

The abilities required in a good interpreter of the law, that is to say, in a good judge, are not the same with those of an advocate; namely the study of the laws. For a judge, as he ought to take notice of the fact, from none but the witnesses; so also he ought to take notice of the law, from nothing but the statutes, and constitutions of the sovereign, alleged in the pleading, or declared to him by some that have authority from the sovereign power to declare them; and need not take care beforehand, what he shall judge; for it shall be given him what he shall say concerning the fact, by witnesses; and what he shall say in point of law, from those that shall in their pleadings show it, and by authority interpret it upon the place. the Lords of parliament in *England* were judges, and most difficult causes have been heard and determined by them; yet few of them were much versed in the study of the laws, and fewer had made profession of them: and though they consulted with lawyers, that were appointed to be present there for that purpose; yet they alone had the authority of giving sentence. In like manner, in the ordinary trials of right, twelve men of the common people, are the judges, and give sentence, not only of the fact, but of the right; and pronounce simply for the complainant, or for the defendant; that is to say, are judges not only of the fact, but also of the right: and in question of crime, not only determine whether done, or not done; but also whether it be *murder, homicide, felony, assault,* and the like, which are determinations of law: but because they are not supposed to know the law of themselves, there is one that hath authority to inform them of it, in the particular case they are to judge of. But yet if they judge not according to that he tells them, they are not subject thereby to any penalty; unless it be made appear, they did it against their consciences, or had been corrupted by reward.

The things that make a good judge, or good interpreter of the laws, are, first, *a right understanding* of that principal law of nature called *equity*; which depending not on the reading of other men's writings, but on the goodness of a man's own natural reason, and meditation, is presumed to be in those most, that have had most leisure, and had the most inclination to meditate thereon. Secondly, *contempt of unnecessary riches, and preferments.* Thirdly, *to be able in judgment to divest himself of all fear, anger, hatred, love, and compassion.* Fourthly, and lastly, *patience to hear; diligent attention in hearing; and memory to retain, digest and apply what he hath heard.*

The difference and division of the laws, has been made in divers manners, according to the different methods, of those men that have written of them. For it is a thing that dependeth not on nature, but on the scope of the writer; and is subservient to every man's proper method. In the Institutions of *Justinian,* we find seven sorts of civil laws.

1. The *edicts, constitutions,* and *epistles of the prince,* that is, of the emperor; because the whole power of the people was in him. Like these, are the proclamations of the kings of *England.*

2. *The decrees of the whole people of Rome,* (comprehending the senate,) when they were put to the question by the *senate.* These were laws, at first, by the virtue of the sovereign power residing in the people; and such of them as by the emperors were not abrogated, remained laws, by the authority imperial. For all laws that bind, are understood to be laws by his authority that has power to repeal them. Somewhat like to these laws, are the acts of parliament in England.

3. *The decrees of the common people,* (excluding the senate,) when they were put to the question by the *tribune* of the people. For such of them as were not abrogated by the emperors, remained laws by the authority imperial. Like to these, were the orders of the House of Commons in *England.*

4. *Senatus consulta,* the *order of the senate;* because when the people of *Rome* grew so numerous, as it was inconvenient to assemble them; it was thought fit by the emperor, that men should consult the senate, instead of the people: and these have some resemblance with the acts of council.

5. *The edicts of praetors,* and (in some cases) of the *aediles:* such as are the chief justices in the courts of *England.*

6. *Response prudentum;* which were the sentences, and opinions of those lawyers, to whom the emperor gave authority to interpret the law, and to give answer to such as in matter of law demanded their advice; which answers, the judges in giving judgment were obliged by the constitutions of the emperor to observe: and should be like the reports of cases judged, if other judges be by the law of *England* bound to observe them. For the judges of the common law of *England,* are not properly judges, but *juris consulti;* of whom the judges, who are either the lords, or twelve men of the country, are in point of law to ask advice.

7. Also, *unwritten customs,* (which in their own nature are an imitation of law,) by the tacit consent of the emperor, in case they be not contrary to the law of nature, are very laws.

Another division of laws, is into *natural* and *positive. Natural* are those which have been laws from all eternity; and are called not only *natural,* but also *moral* laws; consisting in the moral virtues, as justice, equity, and all habits of the mind that conduce to peace, and charity; of which I have already spoken in the fourteenth and fifteenth chapters.

Positive, are those which have not been from eternity; but have been made laws by the will of those that have had the sovereign power over others; and are either written, or made known to men, by some other argument of the will of their legislator.

Again, of positive laws, some are *human,* some *divine;* and of human positive laws, some are *distributive,* some *penal. Distributive* are those that determine the rights of the subjects, declaring to every man what it is, by which he acquireth and holdeth a propriety in lands, or goods, and a right or liberty of action: and these speak to all the subjects. *Penal* are those, which declare, what penalty shall be inflicted on those that violate the law; and speak to the ministers and officers ordained for execution. For though every one ought to be informed of the punishments ordained beforehand for their transgression; nevertheless the command is not addressed to the delinquent, (who cannot be supposed will faithfully punish himself,) but to public ministers appointed to see the penalty executed. And these penal laws are for the most part written together with the laws distributive; and are sometimes called judgments. For all laws are general judgments, or sentences of the legislator; as also every particular judgment, is a law to him, whose case is judged.

Divine positive laws (for natural laws being eternal, and universal, are all divine,) are those, which being the commandments of God, (not from all eternity, nor universally addressed to all men, but only to a certain people, or to certain persons,) are declared for such, by those whom God hath authorized to declare them. But this authority of man to declare what be these positive laws of God, how can it be known? God may command a man by a supernatural way, to deliver laws to other men. But because it is of the essence of law, that he who is to be obliged, be assured of the authority of him that declareth it, which we cannot naturally take notice to be from God, *how can a man without supernatural revelation be assured of the revelation received by the declarer?* and *how can he be bound to obey them?* For the first questions, how a man can be assured of the revelation of another, without a revelation particularly to himself, it is evidently impossible. For though a man maybe induced to believe such revelation, from the miracles they see him do, or from seeing the extraordinary sanctity of his life, or from seeing the extraordinary wisdom, or extraordinary felicity of his actions, all which are marks of God's extraordinary favour; yet they are not assured evidences of special revelation. Miracles are marvellous works: but that which is marvellous to one, may not be so to another. Sanctity may be feigned; and the visible felicities of this world, are most often the work of God by natural, and ordinary causes. And therefore no man can infallibly know by natural reason, that another has had a supernatural revelation of God's will; but only a belief; every one (as the signs thereof shall appear greater, or lesser) a firmer, or a weaker belief.

But for the second, how he can be bound to obey them; it is not so hard. For if the law declared, be not against the law of nature (which is undoubtedly God's law) and he undertake to obey it, he is bound by his own act; bound I say to obey it, but not bound to believe it: for men's belief, and interior cogitations, are not subject to the commands, but only to the operation of God, ordinary, or extraordinary. Faith of supernatural law, is not a fulfilling, but only an assenting to the same; and not a duty that we exhibit to God, but a gift which God freely giveth to whom he pleaseth; as also unbelief is not a breach of any of his laws; but a rejection of them all, except the laws natural. But this that I say, will be made yet clearer, by the examples and testimonies concerning this point in holy Scripture. The covenant God made with *Abraham* (in a supernatural manner) was thus, (*Gen.* 17. 10) *This is the covenant which thou shalt observe between me and thee and thy seed after thee. Abraham's* seed had not this revelation, nor were yet in being; yet they are a party to the covenant, and bound to obey what *Abraham* should declare to them for God's law; which they could not be, but in virtue of the obedience they owed to their parents; who (if they be subject to no other earthly power, as here in the case of *Abraham*) have sovereign power over their children and servants. Again, where God saith to *Abraham, In thee shall all nations of the earth be blessed; for I know thou wilt command thy children, and thy house after thee to keep the way of the Lord, and to observe righteousness and judgment*, it is manifest, the obedience of his family, who had no revelation, depended on their former obligation to obey their sovereign. At Mount *Sinai Moses* only went up to God; the people were forbidden to approach on pain of death; yet were they bound to obey all that Moses declared to them for God's law. Upon what ground, but on this submission of their own, *Speak thou to us, and we will hear thee; but let not God speak to us, lest we die?* By which two places it sufficiently appeareth, that in a commonwealth, a subject that has no certain and assured revelation particularly to himself concerning the will of God, is to obey for such, the command of the commonwealth: for if men were at liberty, to take for God's commandments, their own dreams, and fancies, or the dreams and fancies of private men; scarce two men would agree upon what is God's commandment; and yet in respect of them, every man would despise the commandments of the commonwealth. I conclude therefore, that in all things not contrary to the moral law, (that is to say, to the law of nature,) all subjects are bound to obey that for divine law, which is declared to be so, by the laws of the commonwealth. Which also is evident to any man's reason; for whatsoever is not against the law of nature, may be made law in the name of them that have the sovereign power; and there is no reason men should be the less obligated by it, when it is propounded in the name of God. Besides, there is no place in the world where men are permitted to pretend other commandments of God, than are declared for such by the commonwealth. Christian states punish those that revolt from Christian religion, and all other states, those that set up any religion by them forbidden. For in whatsoever is not regulated by the commonwealth, it is equity, (which is the law of nature, and therefore an eternal law of God) that every man equally enjoy his liberty.

There is also another distinction of laws, into *fundamental* and *not fundamental*, but I could never see in any author, what a fundamental law signifieth. Nevertheless one may very reasonably distinguish laws in that manner.

For a fundamental law in every commonwealth is that which being taken away, the commonwealth faileth, and is utterly dissolved; as a building whose foundation is destroyed. And therefore a fundamental law is that, by which subjects are bound to uphold whatsoever power is given to the sovereign, whether a monarch, or a sovereign assembly, without which the commonwealth cannot stand; such as is the power of war and peace, of judicature, of election of officers, and of doing whatsoever he shall think necessary for the public good. Not fundamental is that, the abrogating whereof, draweth not with it the dissolution of the commonwealth; such as are the laws concerning controversies between subject and subject. Thus much of the division of laws.

I find the words *lex civilis*, and *jus civile*, that is to say, *law* and *right civil*, promiscuously used for the same thing, even in the most learned authors; which nevertheless ought not to be so. For *right is liberty*, namely that liberty which the civil law leaves us; but *civil law* is an *obligation*; and takes from us the liberty which the law of nature gave us. Nature gave a right to every man to secure himself by his own strength, and to invade a suspected neighbour, by way of prevention: but the civil law takes away that liberty, in all cases where the protection of the law may be safely stayed for. Insomuch as *lex* and *jus*, are as different as *obligation* and *liberty*.

Likewise *laws* and *charters* are taken promiscuously for the same thing. Yet charters are donations of the sovereign; and not laws, but exemptions from law. The phrase of a law is, *jubeo, injungo, I command*, and *enjoin*: the phrase of a charter is, *dedi, concessi, I have given, I have granted*: but what is given or granted, to a man, is not forced upon him, by a law. A law may be made to bind all the subjects of a commonwealth: a liberty, or, charter is only to one man, or some one part of the people. For to say all the people of a commonwealth, have liberty in any case whatsoever; is to say, that in such case, there hath been no law made; or else having been made, is now abrogated.

CHAPTER 27

Of Crimes, Excuses, and Extenuations

A *sin*, is not only a transgression of a law, but also any contempt of the legislator. For such contempt, is a breach of all his laws at once. And therefore may consist, not only in the *commission* of a fact, or in the speaking of words by the laws forbidden or in the *omission* of what the law commandeth, but also in the *intention*, or purpose to transgress. For the purpose to break the law, is some degree of contempt of him, to whom it belongeth to see it executed. To be delighted in the imagination only, of being possessed of another man's goods, servants, or wife, without any intention to take them from him by force or fraud, is no breach of the law, that saith, *Thou shalt not covet:* nor is the pleasure a man may have in imagining, or dreaming of the death of him, from whose life he expecteth nothing but damage, and displeasure, a sin; but the resolving to put some act in execution, that tendeth thereto. For to be pleased in the fiction of that, which would please a man if it were real, is a passion so adherent to the nature both of man, and every other living creature, as to make it a sin, were to make sin of being a man. The consideration of this, has made me think them too severe, both to themselves, and others, that maintain, that the first motions of the mind, (though checked with the fear of God) be sins. But I confess it is safer to err on that hand, than on the other.

A CRIME, is a sin, consisting in the committing (by deed, or word) of that which the law forbiddeth, or the omission of what it hath commanded. So that every crime is a sin; but not every sin a crime. To intend to steal, or kill, is a sin, though it never appear in word, or fact: for God that seeth the thoughts of man, can lay it to his charge: but till it appear by something done, or said, by which the intention may be argued by a human judge, it hath not the name of crime: which distinction the Greeks observed, in the word ἁμάρτημα, and ἔγκλημα, or αἰτία; whereof the former, (which is translated *sin*,) signifieth any swerving from the law whatsoever; but the two latter, (which are translated *crime*,) signify that sin only, whereof one man may accuse another. But of intentions, which never appear by any outward act, there is no place for human accusation. In like manner the Latins by *peccatum*, which is *sin*, signify all manner of deviation from the law; but by *crimen*, (which word they derive from *cerno*, which signifies to perceive,) they mean only such sins, as may be made appear before a judge; and therefore are not mere intentions.

From this relation of sin to the law, and of crime to the civil law, may be inferred, first, that where law ceaseth, sin ceaseth. But because the law of nature is eternal, violation of covenants, ingratitude, arrogance, and all facts contrary to any moral virtue, can never cease to be sin. Secondly, that the civil law ceasing, crimes cease: for there being no other law remaining, but that of nature, there is no place for accusation; every man being his own judge, and accused only by his own conscience, and cleared by the uprightness of his own intention. When therefore his intention is right, his fact is no sin: if otherwise, his fact is sin; but not crime. Thirdly, that when the sovereign power ceaseth, crime also ceaseth: for where there is no such power, there is no protection to be had from the law; and therefore every one may protect himself by his own power: for no man in the institution of sovereign power can be supposed to give away the right of preserving his own body; for the safety whereof all sovereignty was ordained. But this is to be understood only of those, that have not themselves contributed to the taking away of the power that protected them: for that was a crime from the beginning.

The source of every crime, is some defect of the understanding; or some error in reasoning; or some sudden force of the passions. Defect in the understanding, is *ignorance;* in reasoning, *erroneous opinion.* Again, ignorance is of three sorts; of the *law,* and of the *sovereign,* and of the *penalty.* Ignorance of the law of nature excuseth no man; because every man that hath attained to the use of reason, is supposed to know, he ought not to do to another, what he would not have done to himself. Therefore into what place soever a man shall come, if he do any thing contrary to that law, it is a crime. If a man come from the *Indies* hither, and persuade men here to receive a new religion, or teach them any thing that tendeth to disobedience of the laws of this country, though he be never so well persuaded of the truth of what he teacheth, he commits a crime, and may be justly punished for the same, not only because his doctrine is false, but also because he does that which he would not approve in another, namely, that coming from hence, he should endeavour to alter the religion there. But ignorance of the civil law, shall excuse a man in a strange country, till it be declared to him; because, till then no civil law is binding.

In the like manner, if the civil law of a man's own country, be not so sufficiently declared, as he may know it if he will; nor the action against the law of nature; the ignorance is a good excuse: in other cases ignorance of the civil law, excuseth not.

Ignorance of the sovereign power, in the place of a man's ordinary residence, excuseth him not; because he ought to take notice of the power, by which he hath been protected there.

Ignorance of the penalty, where the law is declared, excuseth no man: for in breaking the law, which without a fear of penalty to follow, were not a law, but vain words, he undergoeth the penalty, though he know not what it is; because, whosoever voluntarily doth any action, accepteth all the known consequences of it; but punishment is a known consequence of the violation of the laws, in every commonwealth: which punishment, if it be determined already by the law, he is subject to that; if not, then is he subject to arbitrary punishment. For it is reason, that he which does injury, without other limitation than that of his own will, should suffer punishment without other limitation, than that of his will whose law is thereby violated.

But when a penalty, is either annexed to the crime in the law itself, or hath been usually inflicted in the like cases; there the delinquent is excused from a greater penalty. For the punishment foreknown, if not great enough to deter men from the action, is an invitement to it: because when men compare the benefit of their injustice, with the harm of their punishment, by necessity of nature they choose that which appeareth best for themselves: and therefore when they are punished more than the law had formerly determined, or more than others were punished for the same crime; it is the law that tempted, and deceiveth them.

No law, made after a fact done, can make it a crime: because if the fact be against the law of nature, the law was before the fact; and a positive law cannot be taken notice of, before it be made; and therefore cannot be obligatory. But when the law that forbiddeth a fact, is made before the fact be done; yet he that doth the fact, is liable to the penalty ordained after, in case no lesser penalty were made known before, neither by writing, nor by example, for the reason immediately before alleged.

From defect in reasoning, (that is to say, from error,) men are prone to violate the laws, three ways. First, by presumption of false principles: as when men from having observed how in all places, and in all ages, unjust actions have been authorized by the force, and victories of those who have committed them; and that potent men, breaking through the cobweb laws of their country, the weaker sort, and those that have failed in their enterprises, have been esteemed the only criminals; have thereupon taken for principles, and grounds of their reasoning, *that justice is but a vain word: that whatsoever a man can get by his own industry, and hazard, is his own: that the practice of all nations cannot be unjust: that examples of former times are good arguments of doing the like again;* and many more of that kind: which being granted, no act in itself can be a crime, but must be made so (not by the law, but) by the success of them that commit it; and the same fact be virtuous, or vicious, as fortune pleaseth; so that what *Marius* makes a crime, *Sylla* shall make meritorious, and *Caesar*, (the same laws standing) turn again into a crime, to the perpetual disturbance of the peace of the commonwealth.

Secondly, by false teachers, that either misinterpret the law of nature, making it thereby repugnant to the law civil; or by teaching for laws, such doctrines of their own, or traditions of former times, as are inconsistent with the duty of a subject.

Thirdly, by erroneous inferences from true principles; which happens commonly to men that are hasty, and precipitate in concluding, and resolving what to do; such as are they, that have both a great opinion of their own understanding, and believe that things of this nature require not time and study, but only common experience, and a good natural wit; whereof no man thinks himself unprovided: whereas the knowledge, of right and wrong, which is no less difficult, there is no man will pretend to, without great and long study. And of those defects in reasoning, there is none that can excuse (though some of them may extenuate) a crime, in any man, that pretendeth to the administration of his own private business; much less in them that undertake a public charge; because they pretend to the reason, upon the want whereof they would ground their excuse.

Of the passions that most frequently are the causes of crime, one, is vain glory, or a foolish overrating of their own worth; as if difference of worth, were an effect of their wit, or riches, or blood, or some other natural quality, not depending on the will of those that have the sovereign authority. From whence proceedeth a presumption that the punishments ordained by the laws, and extended generally to all subjects, ought not to be inflicted on them, with the same rigour they are inflicted on poor, obscure, and simple men, comprehended under the name of the *vulgar*.

Therefore it happeneth commonly, that such as value themselves by the greatness of their wealth, adventure on crimes, upon hope of escaping punishment, by corrupting public justice, or obtaining pardon by money, or other rewards.

And that such as have multitude of potent kindred; and popular men, that have gained reputation amongst the multitude, take courage to violate the laws, from a hope of oppressing the power, to whom it belongeth to put them in execution.

And that such as have a great, and false opinion of their own wisdom, take upon them to reprehend the actions, and call in question the authority of them that govern, and so to unsettle the laws with their public discourse, as that nothing shall be a crime, but what their own designs require should be so. It happeneth also to the same men, to be prone to all such crimes, as consist in craft, and in deceiving of their neighbours; because they think their designs are too subtle to be perceived. These I say are effects of a false presumption of their own wisdom. For of them that are the first movers in the disturbance of commonwealth, (which can never happen without a civil war,) very few are left alive long enough, to see their new designs established: so that the benefit of their crimes, redoundeth to posterity, and such as would least have wished it: which argues they were not so wise, as they thought they were. And those that deceive upon hope of not being observed, do commonly deceive themselves, (the darkness in which they believe they lie hidden, being nothing else but their own blindness;) and are no wiser than children, that think all hid, by hiding their own eyes.

And generally all vain-glorious men, (unless they be withal timorous,) are subject to anger; as being more prone than others to interpret for contempt, the ordinary liberty of conversation: and there are few crimes that may not be produced by anger.

As for the passions, of hate, lust, ambition, and covetousness, what crimes they are apt to produce, is so obvious to every man's experience and understanding, as there needeth nothing to be said of them, saving that they are infirmities, so annexed to the nature, both of man, and all other living creatures, as that their effects cannot be hindered, but by extraordinary use of reason, or a constant severity in punishing them. For in those things men hate, they find a continual, and unavoidable molestation; whereby either a man's patience must be everlasting, or he must be eased by removing the power of that which molesteth him. The former is difficult; the latter is many times impossible, without some violation of the law. Ambition, and covetousness are passions also that are perpetually incumbent, and pressing; whereas reason is not perpetually present, to resist them: and therefore whensoever the hope of impunity appears, their effects proceed. And for lust, what it wants in the testing, it hath in the vehemence, which sufficeth to weigh down the apprehension of all easy, or uncertain punishments.

Of all passions, that which inclineth men least to break the laws, is fear. Nay, (excepting some generous natures,) it is the only thing, (when there is appearence of profit or plea-sure by breaking the laws,) that makes men keep them. And yet in many cases a crime may be committed through fear.

For not every fear justifies the action it produceth, but the fear only of corporeal hurt, which we call *bodily fear*, and from which a man cannot see how to be delivered, but by the action. A man is assaulted, fears present death, from which he sees not how to escape, but by wounding him that assaulteth him; if he wound him to death, this is no crime; because no man is supposed at the making of a commonwealth, to have abandoned the defence of his life, or limbs, where the law cannot arrive time enough to his assistance. But to kill a man, because from his actions, or his threatenings, I may argue he will kill me when he can, (seeing I have time, and means to demand protection, from the sovereign power,) is a crime. Again, a man receives words of disgrace, or some little injuries, (for which they that made the laws, had assigned no punishment, nor thought it worthy of a man that hath the use of reason, to take notice of,) and is afraid, unless he revenge it, he shall fall into contempt, and consequently be obnoxious to the like injuries from others; and to avoid this, breaks the law, and, protects himself for the future, by the terror of his private revenge. This is a crime: for the hurt is not corporeal, but phantastical, and (though in this corner of the world, made sensible by a custom not many years since begun, amongst young and vain men,) so light, as a gallant man, and one that is assured of his own courage, cannot take notice of. Also a man may stand in fear of spirits, either through his own superstition, or through too much credit given to other men, that tell him of strange dreams and visions; and thereby be made believe they will hurt him, for doing, or omit-ting divers things, which nevertheless, to do, or omit, is contrary to the laws; and that which is so done, or omitted, is not to be excused by this fear; but is a crime. For (as I have shown before in the second chapter) dreams be naturally but the fancies remaining in sleep, after the impressions our senses had formerly received waking; and when men are by any acci-dent unassured they have slept, seem to be real visions; and therefore he that presumes to break the law upon his own, or another's dream, or pretended vision, or upon other fancy of the power of invisible spirits, than is permitted by the commonwealth, leaveth the law of nature, which is a certain offence, and followeth the imagery of his own, or another private man's brain, which he can never know whether it signifieth any thing, or nothing, nor whether he that tells his dream, say true, or lie; which if every private man should have leave to do, (as they must by the law of nature, if any one have it) there could no law be made to hold, and so all commonwealth would be dissolved.

From these different sources of crimes, it appears already, that all crimes are not (as the Stoics of old time maintained) of the same allay. There is place, not only for EXCUSE, by which that which seemed a crime, is proved to be none at all; but also for EXTENUA-TION, by which the crime, that seemed great, is made less. For though all crimes do equally deserve the name of injustice, as all deviation from a straight line is equally crookedness, which the Stoics rightly observed; yet it does not follow that all crimes are equally unjust, no more than that all crooked lines are equally crooked; which the Stoics not observing, held it as great a crime, to kill a hen, against the law, as to kill one's father.

That which totally excuseth a fact, and takes away from it the nature of a crime, can be none but that, which at the same time, taketh away the obligation of the law. For the fact committed once against the law, if he that committed it be obliged to the law, can be no other than a crime.

The want of means to know the law, totally excuseth: For the law whereof a man has no means to inform himself, is not obligatory. But the want of diligence to inquire, shall not be considered as a want of means; nor shall any man, that pretendeth to reason enough for the government of his own affairs, be supposed to want means to know the laws of nature; because they are known by the reason he pretends to: only children, and madmen are excused from offences against the law natural.

Where a man is captive, or in the power of the enemy (and he is then in the power of the enemy, when his person, or his means of living, is so,) if it be without his own fault, the obligation of the law ceaseth; because he must obey the enemy, or die; and consequently such obedience is no crime: for no man is obliged (when the protection of the law faileth,) not to protect himself, by the best means he can.

If a man, by the terror of present death, be compelled to do a fact against the law, he is totally excused; because no law can oblige a man to abandon his own preservation. And supposing such a law were obligatory; yet a man would reason thus, *If I do it not, I die presently; if I do it, I die afterwards; therefore by, doing it, there is time of life gained;* nature therefore compels him to the fact.

When a man is destitute of food, or other thing necessary for his life, and cannot preserve himself any other way, but by some fact against the law; as if in a great famine he take the food by force, or stealth, which he cannot obtain for money, nor charity; or in defence of his life, snatch away another man's sword, he is totally excused, for the reason next before alleged.

Again, facts done against the law, by the authority of another, are by that authority excused against the author; because no man ought to accuse his own fact in another, that is but his instrument: but it is not excused against a third person thereby injured; because in the violation of the law, both the author and actor are criminals. From hence it followeth that when that man, or assembly, that hath the sovereign power, commandeth a man to do that which is contrary to a former law, the doing of it is totally excused: for he ought not to condemn it himself, because he is the author; and what cannot justly be condemned by the sovereign, cannot justly be punished by any other. Besides, when the sovereign commandeth any thing to be done against his own former law, the command, as to that particular fact, is an abrogation of the law.

If that man, or assembly, that hath the sovereign power, disclaim any right essential to the sovereignty, whereby there accrueth to the subject, any liberty inconsistent with the sovereign power, that is to say, with the very being of a commonwealth, if the subject shall refuse to obey the command in any thing, contrary to the liberty granted, this is nevertheless a sin, and contrary to the duty of the subject: for he ought to take notice of what is inconsistent with the sovereignty, because it was erected by his own consent, and for his own defence; and that such liberty as is inconsistent with it, was granted through ignorance of the evil consequence thereof. But if he not only disobey, but also resist a public minister in the execution of it, then it is a crime; because he might have been righted, (without any breach of the peace,) upon complaint.

The degrees of crime are taken on divers scales, and measured, first, by the malignity of the source, or cause: secondly, by the contagion of the example: thirdly, by the mischief of the effect: and fourthly, by the concurrence of times, places, and persons.

The same fact done against the law, if it proceed from presumption of strength, riches, or friends to resist those that are to execute the law, is a greater crime than if it proceed from hope of not being discovered, or of escape by flight: for presumption of impunity by force, is a root, from whence springeth, at all times, and upon all temptations, a contempt of all laws; whereas in the latter case, the apprehension of danger, that makes a man fly, renders him more obedient for the future. A crime which we know to be so, is greater than the same crime proceeding from a false persuasion that it is lawful: for he that committeth it against his own conscience, presumeth on his force, or other power, which encourages him to commit the same again: but he that doth it by error, after the error shewn him, is conformable to the law.

He, whose error proceeds from the authority of a teacher, or an interpreter of the law publicly authorized, is not so faulty, as he whose error proceedeth from a peremptory pursuit of his own principles, and reasoning: for what is taught by one that teacheth by public authority, the commonwealth teacheth, and hath a resemblance of law, till the same authority controlleth it; and in all crimes that contain not in them a denial of the sovereign power, nor are against an evident law, excuseth totally: whereas he that groundeth his actions on his private judgment, ought according to the rectitude, or error thereof, to stand, or fall.

The same fact, if it have been constantly punished in other men, is a greater crime, than if there have been many precedent examples of impunity. For those examples are so many hopes of impunity, given by the sovereign himself: and because he which furnishes a man with such a hope, and presumption of mercy, is encourageth him to offend, hath his part in the offence; he cannot reasonably charge the offender with the whole.

A crime arising from a sudden passion, is not so great, as when the same ariseth from long meditation: for in the former case there is a place for extenuation, in the common infirmity of human nature: but he that doth it with premeditation, has used circumspection, and cast his eye, on the law, on the punishment, and on the consequence thereof to human society; all which in committing the crime, he hath contemned, and postposed to his own appetite. But there is no suddenness of passion sufficient for a total excuse: for all the time between the first knowing of the law, and the commission of the fact, shall be taken for a time of deliberation; because he ought by meditation of the law, to rectify the irregularity of his passions.

Where the law is publicly, and with assiduity, before all the people read and interpreted; a fact done against it, is a greater crime, than where men are left without such instruction, to enquire of it with difficulty, uncertainty, and interruption of their callings, and be informed by private men: for in this case, part of the fault is discharged upon common infirmity; but in the former, there is apparent negligence, which is not without some contempt of the sovereign power.

Those facts which the law expressly condemneth, but the law-maker by other manifest signs of his will tacitly approveth, are less crimes, than the same facts, condemned both by the law and lawmaker. For seeing the will of the law-maker is a law, there appear in this case two contradictory laws; which would totally excuse, if men were bound to take notice of the sovereign's approbation, by other arguments, than are expressed by his command. But because there are punishments consequent, not only to the transgression of his law, but also to the observing of it, he is in part a cause of the transgression, and therefore cannot reasonably impute the whole crime to the delinquent. For example, the law condemneth duels; the punishment is made capital: on the contrary part, he that refuseth duel, is subject to contempt and scorn, without remedy; and sometimes by the sovereign himself thought unworthy to have any charge, or preferment in war. If thereupon he accept duel; considering all men lawfully endeavour to obtain the good opinion of them that have the sovereign power, he ought not in reason to be rigorously punished; seeing part of the fault may be discharged on the punisher: which I say, not as wishing liberty of private revenges, or any other kind of disobedience; but a care in governors, not to countenance any thing obliquely, which directly they forbid. The examples of princes, to those that see them, are, and ever have been, more potent to govern their actions, than the laws themselves. And though it be our duty to do, not what they do, but what they say; yet will that duty never be performed, till it please God to give men an extraordinary, and supernatural grace to follow that precept.

Again, if we compare crimes by the mischief of their effects, first, the same fact, when it redounds to the damage of many, is greater, than when it redounds to the hurt of few. And therefore, when a fact hurteth, not only in the present, but also, (by example) in the future, it is a greater crime, than if it hurt only in the present: for the former, is a fertile crime, and multiplies to the hurt of many; the latter is barren. To maintain doctrines contrary to the religion established in the commonwealth, is a greater fault, in an authorized preacher, than in a private person: so also is it, to live profanely, incontinently, or do any irreligious act whatsoever. Likewise in a professor of the law, to maintain any point, or do any act, that tendeth to the weakening of the sovereign power, is a greater crime, than in another man: also in a man that hath such reputation for wisdom, as that his counsels are followed, or his actions imitated by many, his fact against the law, is a greater crime, than the same fact in another: for such men not only commit crime, but teach it for law to all other men. And generally all crimes are the greater, by the scandal they give; that is to say, by becoming stumbling-blocks to the weak, that look not so much upon the way they go in, as upon the light that other men carry before them.

Also facts of hostility against the present state of the commonwealth, are greater crimes, than the same acts done to private men: for the damage extends itself to all: such are the betraying of the strengths, or revealing of the secrets of the commonwealth to an enemy; also all attempts upon the representative of the commonwealth, be it a monarch, or an assembly; and all endeavours by word, or deed to diminish the authority of the same, either in the present time, or in succession; which crimes the Latins understand by *crimina laesae majestatis*, and consist in design, or act, contrary to a fundamental law.

Likewise those crimes, which render judgments of no effect, are greater crimes, than injuries done to one, or a few persons; as to receive money to give false judgment, or testimony, is a greater crime, than otherwise to deceive a man of the like, or a greater sum; because not only he has wrong, that falls by such judgments; but all judgments are rendered useless, and occasion ministered to force, and private revenges.

Also robbery, and depeculation of the public treasure, or revenues, is a greater crime, than the robbing, or defrauding of a private man; because to rob the public, is to rob many at once.

Also the counterfeit usurpation of public ministry, the counterfeiting of public seals, or public coin, than counterfeiting of a private man's person, or his seal; because the fraud thereof, extendeth to the damage of many.

Of facts against the law, done to private men, the greater crime, is that, where the damage in the common opinion of men, is most sensible. And therefore

To kill against the law, is a greater crime, than any other injury, life preserved.

And to kill with torment, greater, than simply to kill.

And mutilation of a limb, greater, than the spoiling a man of his goods.

And the spoiling a man of his goods, by terror of death, or wounds, than by clandestine surreption.

And by clandestine surreption, than by consent fraudulently obtained.

And the violation of chastity by force, greater, than by flattery.

And of a woman married, than of a woman not married.

For all these things are commonly so valued; though some men are more, and some less sensible of the same offence. But the law regardeth not the particular, but the general inclination of mankind.

And therefore the offence men take, from contumely, in words, or gesture, when they produce no other harm, than the present grief of him that is reproached, hath been neglected in the laws of the Greeks, Romans, and other both ancient, and modern commonwealths; supposing the true cause of such grief to consist, not in the contumely, (which takes no hold upon men conscious of their own virtue,) but in the pusillanimity of him that is offended by it.

Also a crime against a private man, is much aggravated by the person, time, and place. For to kill one's parent, is a greater crime, than to kill another: for the parent ought to have the honour of a sovereign, (though he have surrendered his power to the civil law,) because he had it originally by nature. And to rob a poor man, is a greater crime, than to rob a rich man; because it is to the poor a more sensible damage.

And a crime committed in the time or place appointed for devotion, is greater, than if committed at another time or place: for it proceeds from a greater contempt of the law.

Many other cases of aggravation, and extenuation might be added: but by these I have set down, it is obvious to every man, to take the altitude of any other crime proposed.

Lastly, because in almost all crimes there is an injury done, not only to some private men, but also to the commonwealth; the same crime, when the accusation is in the name of the commonwealth, is called public crime: and when in the name of a private man, a private crime; and the pleas according thereunto called public, *judicia publica,* Pleas of the Crown; or Private Pleas. As in an accusation of murder, if the accuser be a private man, the plea is a Private Plea; if the accuser be the sovereign, the plea is a Public Plea.

CHAPTER 28

Of Punishments, and Rewards

A PUNISHMENT, *is an evil inflicted by public authority, on him that hath done, or omitted that which is judged by the same authority to be a transgression of the law; to the end that the will of men may thereby the better be disposed to obedience.*

Before I infer any thing from this definition, there is a question to be answered, of much importance; which is, by what door the right, or authority of punishing in any case, came in. For by that which has been said before, no man is supposed bound by covenant, not to resist violence; and consequently it cannot be intended, that he gave any right to another to lay violent hands upon his person. In the making of a commonwealth, every man giveth away the right of defending another; but not of defending himself. Also he obligeth himself, to assist him that hath the sovereignty, in the punishing of another; but of himself not. But to covenant to assist the sovereign, in doing hurt to another, unless he that so covenanteth have a right to do it himself, is not to give him a right to punish. It is manifest therefore that the right which the commonwealth (that is, he, or they that represent it) hath to punish, is not grounded on any concession, or gift of the subjects. But I have also showed formerly, that before the institution of commonwealth, every man had a right to every thing, and to do whatsoever he thought necessary to his own preservation; subduing, hurting, or killing any man in order thereunto. And this is the foundation of that right of punishing, which is exercised in every commonwealth. For the subjects did not give the sovereign that right; but only in laying down theirs, strengthened him to use his own, as he should think fit, for the preservation of them all: so that it was not given, but left to him, and to him only; and (excepting the limits set him by natural law) as entire, as in the condition of mere nature, and of war of every one against his neighbour.

From the definition of punishment, I infer, first, that neither private revenges, nor injuries of private men, can properly be styled punishment; because they proceed not from public authority.

Secondly, that to be neglected, and unpreferred by the public favour, is not a punishment; because no new evil is thereby on any man inflicted; he is only left in the estate he was in before.

Thirdly, that the evil inflicted by public authority, without precedent public condemnation, is not to be styled by the name of punishment; but of an hostile act; because the fact for which a man is punished, ought first to be judged by public authority, to be a transgression of the law.

Fourthly, that the evil inflicted by usurped power, and judges without authority from the sovereign, is not punishment; but an act of hostility; because the acts of power usurped, have not for author, the person condemned; and therefore are not acts of public authority.

Fifthly, that all evil which is inflicted without intention, or possibility of disposing the delinquent, or (by his example) other men, to obey the laws, is not punishment; but an act of hostility; because without such an end, no hurt done is contained under that name.

Sixthly, whereas to certain actions, there be annexed by nature, divers hurtful consequences; as when a man in assaulting another, is himself slain, or wounded; or when he falleth into sickness by the doing of some unlawful act; such hurt, though in respect of God, who is the author of nature, it may be said to be inflicted, and therefore a punishment divine; yet it is not contained in the name of punishment in respect of men, because it is not inflicted by the authority of man.

Seventhly, if the harm inflicted be less than the benefit; or contentment that naturally followeth the crime committed, that harm is not within the definition; and is rather the price, or redemption, than the punishment of a crime: because it is of the nature of punishment, to have for end, the disposing of men to obey the law; which end (if it be less than the benefit of the transgression) it attaineth not, but worketh a contrary effect.

Eighthly, if a punishment be determined and prescribed in the law itself, and after the crime committed, there be a greater punishment inflicted, the excess is not punishment, but an act of hostility. For seeing the aim of punishment is not a revenge, but terror; and the terror of a great punishment unknown, is taken away by the declaration of a less, the unexpected addition is no part of the punishment. But where there is no punishment at all determined by the law, there whatsoever is inflicted, hath the nature of punishment. For he that goes about the violation of a law, wherein no penalty is determined, expecteth an indeterminate, that is to say, an arbitrary punishment.

Ninthly, harm inflicted for a fact done before there was a law that forbade it, is not punishment, but an act of hostility: for before the law, there is no transgression of the law: but punishment supposeth a fact judged, to have been a transgression of the law; therefore harm inflicted before the law made, is not punishment, but an act of hostility.

Tenthly, hurt inflicted on the representative of the commonwealth, is not punishment, but an act of hostility: because it is of the nature of punishment, to be inflicted by public authority, which is the authority only of the representative itself.

Lastly, harm inflicted upon one that is a declared enemy, falls not under the name of punishment: because seeing they were either never subject to the law, and therefore cannot transgress it; or having been subject to it, and professing to be no longer so, by consequence deny they can transgress it, all the harms that can be done them, must be taken as acts of hostility. But in declared hostility, all infliction of evil is lawful. From whence it followeth, that if a subject shall by fact, or word, wittingly, and deliberately deny the authority of the representative of the commonwealth (whatsoever penalty hath been formerly ordained for treason,) he may lawfully be made to suffer whatsoever the representative will: For in denying subjection, he denies such punishment as by the law hath been ordained; and therefore suffers as an enemy of the commonwealth; that is, according to the will of the representative. For the punishments set down in the law, are to subjects, not to enemies; such as are they, that having been by their own act subjects, deliberately revolting, deny the sovereign power.

The first, and most general distribution of punishments, is into *divine*, and *human*. Of the former I shall have occasion to speak, in a more convenient place hereafter.

Human, are those punishments that be inflicted by the commandment of man; and are either *corporal*, or *pecuniary*, or *ignominy*, or *imprisonment*, or *exile*, or mixed of these.

Corporal punishment is that, which is inflicted on the body directly, and according to the intention of him that inflicteth it: such as are stripes, or wounds, or deprivation of such pleasures of the body, as were before lawfully enjoyed.

And of these, some be *capital*, some *less* than *capital*. Capital, is the infliction of death; and that either simply, or with torment. Less than capital, are stripes, wounds, chains, and any other corporal pain, not in its own nature mortal. For if upon the infliction of a punishment death follow not in the intention of the inflictor, the punishment is not to be esteemed capital, though the harm prove mortal by an accident not to be foreseen; in which case death is not inflicted, but hastened.

Pecuniary punishment, is that which consisteth not only in the deprivation of a sum of money, but also of lands, or any other goods which are usually bought and sold for money. And in case the law, that ordaineth such a punishment, be made with design to gather money, from such as shall transgress the same, it is not properly a punishment, but the price of privilege and exemption from the law, which doth not absolutely forbid the fact, but only to those that are not able to pay the money: except where the law is natural, or part of religion; for in that case it is not an exemption from the law, but a transgression of it. As where a law exacteth a pecuniary mulct, of them that take the name of God in vain, the payment of the mulct, is not the price of a dispensation to swear, but the punishment of the transgression of a law indispensable. In like manner if the law impose a sum of money to be paid, to him that has been injured; this is but a satisfaction for the hurt done him; and extinguisheth the accusation of the party injured, not the crime of the offender.

Ignominy, is the infliction of such evil, as is made dishonourable; or the deprivation of such good, as is made honourable by the commonwealth. For there be some things honourable by nature; as the effects of courage, magnanimity, strength, wisdom, and other abilities of body and mind: others made honourable by the commonwealth; as badges, titles, offices, or any other singular mark of the sovereign's favour. The former, (though they may fail by nature, or accident,) cannot be taken away by a law; and therefore the loss of them is not punishment. But the latter, may be taken away by the public authority that made them honourable, and are properly punishments: such are degrading men condemned, of their badges, titles, and offices; or declaring them incapable of the like in time to come.

Imprisonment, is when a man is by public authority deprived of liberty; and may happen from two divers ends; whereof one is the safe custody of a man accused; the other is the inflicting of pain on a man condemned. The former is not punishment; because no man is supposed to be punished, before he be judicially heard, and declared guilty. And therefore whatsoever hurt a man is made to suffer by bonds, or restraint, before his cause be heard, over and above that which is necessary to assure his custody, is against the law of nature. But the latter is punishment, because evil, and inflicted by public authority, for somewhat that has by the same authority been judged a transgression of the law. Under this word imprisonment, I comprehend all restraint of motion, caused by an external obstacle, be it a house, which is called by the general name of a prison; or an island, as when men are said to be confined to it; or a place where men are set to work, as in old time men have been condemned to quarries, and in these times to galleys; or be it a chain, or any other such impediment.

Exile (banishment) is when a man is for a crime, condemned to depart out of the dominion of the commonwealth, or out of a certain part thereof; and during a prefixed time, or for ever, not to return into it: and seemeth not in its own nature, without other circumstances, to be a punishment; but rather an escape, or a public commandment to avoid punishment by flight. And *Cicero* says, there was never any such punishment ordained in the city of *Rome;* but calls it a refuge of men in danger. For if a man banished, be nevertheless permitted to enjoy his goods, and the revenue of his lands, the mere change of air is no punishment; nor does it tend to that benefit of the commonwealth, for which all punishments are ordained, (that is to say, to the forming of men's wills to the observation of the law;) but many times to the damage of the commonwealth. For a banished man, is a lawful enemy of the commonwealth that banished him; as being no more a member of the same. But if he be withal deprived of his lands, or goods, then the punishment lieth not in the exile, but is to be reckoned amongst punishments pecuniary.

All punishments of innocent subjects, be they great or little, are against the law of nature: For punishment is only for transgression of the law, and therefore there can be no punishment of the innocent. It is therefore a violation, first, of that law of nature, which forbiddeth all men, in their revenges, to look at any thing but some future good: For there can arrive no good to the commonwealth, by punishing the innocent. Secondly, of that, which forbiddeth ingratitude: For seeing all sovereign power, is originally given by the consent of every one of the subjects, to the end they should as long as they are obedient, be protected thereby; the punishment of the innocent, is a rendering of evil for good. And thirdly, of the law that commandeth equity; that is to say, an equal distribution of justice; which in punishing the innocent is not observed.

But the infliction of what evil soever, on an innocent man, that is not a subject, if it be for the benefit of the commonwealth, and without violation of any former covenant, is no breach of the law of nature. For all men that are not subjects, are either enemies, or else they have ceased from being so by some precedent covenants. But against enemies, whom the commonwealth judgeth capable to do them hurt, it is lawful by the original right of nature to make war; wherein the sword judgeth not, nor doth the victor make distinction of nocent, and innocent, as to the time past; nor has other respect of mercy, than as it conduceth to the good of his own people. And upon this ground it is, that also in subjects, who deliberately deny the authority of the commonwealth established, the vengeance is lawfully extended, not only to the fathers, but also to the third and fourth generation not yet in being, and consequently innocent of the fact, for which they are afflicted: because the nature of this offence, consisteth in the renouncing of subjection; which is a relapse into the condition of war, commonly called rebellion; and they that so offend, suffer not as subjects, but as enemies. For *rebellion*, is but war renewed.

Reward, is either of *gift*, or by *contract*. When by contract, it is called *salary*, and *wages*; which is benefit due for service performed, or promised. When of gift, it is benefit proceeding from the *grace* of them that bestow it, to encourage, or enable men to do them service. And therefore when the sovereign of a commonwealth appointeth a salary to any public office, he that receiveth it, is bound in justice to perform his office; otherwise, he is bound only in honour, to acknowledgment, and an endeavour of requital. For though men have no lawful remedy, when they be commanded to quit their private business, to serve the public, without reward or salary; yet they are not bound thereto, by the law of nature, nor by the institution of the commonwealth, unless the service cannot otherwise be done; because it is supposed the sovereign may make use of all their means, insomuch as the most common soldier, may demand the wages of his warfare, as a debt.

The benefits which a sovereign bestoweth on a subject, for fear of some power, and ability he hath to do hurt to the commonwealth, are not properly rewards; for they are not salaries; because there is in this case no contract supposed, every man being obliged already not to do the commonwealth disservice: nor are they graces; because they be extorted by fear, which ought not to be incident to the sovereign power: but are rather sacrifices, which the sovereign (considered in his natural person, and not in the person of the commonwealth) makes, for the appeasing the discontent of him he thinks more potent than himself; and encourage not to obedience, but on the contrary, to the continuance, and increasing of further extortion.

And whereas some salaries are certain, and proceed from the public treasure; and others uncertain, and casual, proceeding from the execution of the office for which the salary is ordained; the latter is in some cases hurtful to the commonwealth; as in the case of judicature. For where the benefit of the judges, and ministers of a court of justice, ariseth for the multitude of causes that are brought to their cognizance, there must needs follow two inconveniences: one, is the nourishing of suits; for the more suits, the greater benefit: and another that depends on that, which is contention about jurisdiction; each court drawing to itself, as many causes as it can. But in offices of execution there are not those inconveniences; because their employment cannot be increased by any endeavour of their own. And thus much shall suffice for the nature of punishment and reward; which are, as it were, the nerves and tendons, that move the limbs and joints of a commonwealth.

Hitherto I have set forth the nature of man, (whose pride and other passions have compelled him to submit himself to government;) together with the great power of his governor, whom I compared to *Leviathan*, taking that comparison out of the two last verses of the one and fortieth of *Job*; where God having set forth the great power of *Leviathan*, calleth him king of the proud. *There is nothing*, saith he, *on earth, to be compared with him. He is made so as not to be afraid. He seeth every high thing below him; and is king of all the children of pride.* But because he is mortal, and subject to decay, as all other earthly creatures are; and because there is that in heaven, (though not on earth) that he should stand in fear of, and whose laws he ought to obey; I shall in the next following chapters speak of his diseases, and the causes of his mortality; and of what laws of nature he is bound to obey.

CHAPTER 29

Of Those Things That Weaken, or Tend to the Dissolution of a Commonwealth

Though nothing can be immortal, which mortals make; yet, if men had the use of reason they pretend to, their commonwealths might be secured, at least, from perishing by internal diseases. For by the nature of their institution, they are designed to live, as long as mankind, or as the laws of nature, or as justice itself, which gives them life. Therefore when they come to be dissolved, not by external violence, but intestine disorder, the fault is not in men, as they are the *matter;* but as they are the *makers,* and orderers of them. For men, as they become at last weary of irregular jostling, and hewing one another, and desire with all their hearts, to conform themselves into one firm and lasting edifice; so for want, both of the art of making fit laws, to square their actions by, and also of humility, and patience, to suffer the rude and cumbersome points of their present greatness to be taken off, they cannot without the help of a very able architect, be compiled, into any other than a crazy building, such as hardly lasting out their own time, must assuredly fall upon the heads of their posterity.

Amongst the *infirmities* therefore of a commonwealth, I will reckon in the first place, those that arise from an imperfect institution, and resemble the diseases of a natural body, which proceed from a defectuous procreation.

Of which, this is one, *that a man to obtain a kingdom, is sometimes content with less power, than to the peace, and defence of the commonwealth is necessarily required.* From whence it cometh to pass, that when the exercise of the power laid by, is for the public safety to be resumed, it hath the resemblance of an unjust act; which disposeth great numbers of men (when occasion is presented) to rebel; in the same manner as the bodies of children, gotten by diseased parents, are subject either to untimely death, or to purge the ill quality, derived from their vicious conception, by breaking out into biles and scabs. And when kings deny themselves some such necessary power, it is not always (though sometimes), out of ignorance of what is necessary to the office they undertake; but many times out of a hope to recover the same again at their pleasure: Wherein they reason not well; because such as will hold them to their promises, shall be maintained against them by foreign commonwealths; who in order to the good of their own subjects let slip few occasions to *weaken* the estate of their neighbours. So was *Thomas Becket,* archbishop of *Canterbury,* supported against *Henry* the Second, by the Pope; the subjection of ecclesiastics to the commonwealth, having been dispensed with by *William the Conqueror* at his reception, when he took an oath, not to infringe the liberty of the church. And so were the *barons,* whose power was by *William Rufus* (to have their help in transferring the succession from his elder brother, to himself,) increased to a degree, inconsistent with the sovereign power, maintained in their rebellion against *King John,* by the French.

Nor does this happen in monarchy only. For whereas the style of the ancient Roman commonwealth, was, *the senate, and people of Rome;* neither senate, nor people pretended to the whole power; which first caused the seditions, of *Tiberius Gracchus, Caius Gracchus, Lucius Saturninus,* and others; and afterwards the wars between the senate and the people, under *Marius* and *Sylla;* and again under *Pompey* and *Caesar,* to the extinction of their democracy, and the setting up of monarchy.

The people of *Athens* bound themselves but from one only action; which was, that no man on pain of death should propound the renewing of the war for the island of *Salamis;* and yet thereby, if *Solon* had not caused to be given out he was mad, and afterwards in gesture and habit of a madman, and in verse, propounded it to the people that flocked about him, they had had an enemy perpetually in readiness, even at the gates of their city; such damage, or shifts, are all commonwealths forced to, that have their power never so little limited.

In the second place, I observe the *diseases* of a commonwealth, that proceed from the poison of seditious doctrines, whereof one is, *That every private man is judge of good and evil actions.* This is true in the condition of mere nature, where there are no civil laws; and also under civil government, in such cases as are not determined by the law. But otherwise it is manifest, that the measure of good and evil actions, is the civil law; and the judge the legislator, who is always representative of the commonwealth. From this false doctrine, men are disposed to debate with themselves, and dispute the commands of the commonwealth; and afterwards to obey, or disobey them, as in their private judgments they shall think fit. Whereby the commonwealth is distracted and *weakened*.

Another doctrine repugnant to civil society, is, that *whatsoever a man does against his conscience, is sin;* and it dependeth on the presumption of making himself judge of good and evil. For a man's conscience, and his judgment is the same thing; and as the judgment, so also the conscience may be erroneous. Therefore, though he that is subject to no civil law, sinneth in all he does against his conscience, because he has no other rule to follow but his own reason; yet it is not so with him that lives in a commonwealth; because the law is the public conscience, by which he hath already undertaken to be guided. Otherwise in such diversity, as there is of private consciences, which are but private opinions, the commonwealth must needs be distracted, and no man dare to obey the sovereign power, farther than it shall seem good in his own eyes.

It hath been also commonly taught, *that faith and sanctity, are not to be attained by study and reason, but by supernatural inspiration, or infusion,* which granted, I see not why any man should render a reason of his faith; or why every Christian should not be also a prophet; or why any man should take the law of his country, rather than his own inspiration, for the rule of his action. And thus we fall again into the fault of taking upon us to judge of good and evil; or to make judges of it, such private men as pretend to be supernaturally inspired, to the dissolution of all civil government. Faith comes by hearing, and hearing by those accidents, which guide us into the presence of them that speak to us; which accidents are all contrived by God Almighty; and yet are not supernatural, but only, for the great number of them that concur to every effect, unobservable. Faith and sanctity, are indeed not very frequent; but yet they are not miracles, but brought to pass by education, discipline, correction, and other natural ways, by which God worketh them in his elect, at such time as he thinketh fit. And these three opinions, pernicious to peace and government, have in this part of the world, proceeded chiefly from the tongues, and pens of unlearned divines; who joining the words of Holy Scripture together, otherwise than is agreeable to reason, do what they can, to make men think, that sanctity and natural reason, cannot stand together.

A fourth opinion, repugnant to the nature of a commonwealth, is this, *that he that hath the sovereign power, is subject to the civil laws.* It is true, that sovereigns are all subject to the laws of nature; because such laws be divine, and cannot by any man, or commonwealth be abrogated. But to those laws which the sovereign himself, that is, which the commonwealth maketh, he is not subject. For to be subject to laws, is to be subject to the commonwealth, that is to the sovereign representative, that is to himself; which is not subjection, but freedom from the laws. Which error, because it setteth the laws above the sovereign, setteth also a judge above him, and a power to punish him; which is to make a new sovereign; and again for the same reason a third, to punish the second; and so continually without end, to the confusion, and dissolution of the commonwealth.

A fifth doctrine, that tendeth to the dissolution of a commonwealth, is, *that every private man has an absolute propriety in his goods; such, as excludeth the right of the sovereign.* Every man has indeed a propriety that excludes the right of every other subject: and he has it only from the sovereign power; without the protection whereof, every other man should have equal right to the same. But if the right of the sovereign also be excluded, he cannot perform the office they have put him into; which is, to defend them both from foreign enemies, and from the injuries of one another; and consequently there is no longer a commonwealth.

And if the propriety of subjects, exclude not the right of the sovereign representative to their goods; much less to their offices of judicature, or execution, in which they represent the sovereign himself.

There is a sixth doctrine, plainly, and directly against the essence of a commonwealth; and it is this, *that the sovereign power may be divided.* For what is it to divide the power of a commonwealth, but to dissolve it; for powers divided mutually destroy each other. And for these doctrines, men are chiefly beholding to some of those, that making profession of the laws, endeavour to make them depend upon their own learning, and not upon the legislative power.

And as false doctrine, so also oftentimes the example of different government in a neighbouring nation, disposeth men to alteration of the form already settled. So the people of the Jews were stirred up to reject God, and to call upon the prophet *Samuel*, for a king after the manner of the nations: so also the lesser cities of *Greece,* were continually disturbed, with seditions of the aristocratical, and democratical factions; one part of almost every commonwealth, desiring to imitate the Lacedemonians; the other, the Athenians. And I doubt not, but many men, have been contented to see the late troubles in *England,* out of an imitation of the Low Countries; supposing there needed no more to grow rich, than to change, as they had done, the form of their government. For the constitution of man's nature, is of itself subject to desire novelty: When therefore they are provoked to the same, by the neighbourhood also of those that have been enriched by it, it is almost impossible for them, not to be content with those that solicit them to change; and love the first beginnings, though they be grieved with the continuance of disorder; like hot bloods, that having gotten the itch, tear themselves with their own nails, till they can endure the smart no longer.

And as to rebellion in particular against monarchy; one of the most frequent causes of it, is the reading of the books of policy, and histories of the ancient Greeks, and Romans; from which, young men, and all others that are unprovided of the antidote of solid reason, receiving a strong, and delightful impression, of the great exploits of war, achieved by the conductors of their armies, receive withal a pleasing idea, of all they have done besides; and imagine their great prosperity, not to have proceeded from the emulation of particular men, but from the virtue of their popular form of government: not considering the frequent seditions, and civil wars, produced by the imperfection of their policy. From the reading, I say, of such books, men have undertaken to kill their kings, because the Greek and Latin writers, in their books and discourses of policy, make it lawful, and laudable, for any man so to do; provided, before he do it, he call him tyrant. For they say not *regicide,* that is, killing of a king, but *tyrannicide,* that is, killing of a tyrant is lawful. From the same books, they that live under a monarch conceive an opinion, that the subjects in a popular commonwealth enjoy liberty; but that in a monarchy they are all slaves. I say, they that live under a monarchy conceive such an opinion; not they that live under a popular government: for they find no such matter. In sum, I cannot imagine, how any thing can be more prejudicial to a monarchy, than the allowing of such books to be publicly read, without present applying such correctives of discreet masters, as are fit to take away their venom: which venom I will not doubt to compare to the biting of a mad dog, which is a disease the physicians call *hydrophobia*, or *fear of water.* For as he that is so bitten, has a continual torment of thirst, and yet abhorreth water; and is in such an estate, as if the poison endeavoured to convert him into a dog: so when a monarchy is once bitten to the quick, by those democratical writers, that continually snarl at that estate; it wanteth nothing more than a strong monarch, which nevertheless out of a certain *tyrannophobia*, or fear of being strongly governed, when they have him, they abhor.

As there have been doctors, that hold there be three souls in a man; so there be also that think there may be more souls, (that is, more sovereigns,) than one, in a commonwealth; and set up a *supremacy* against the *sovereignty*; *canons* against *laws*; and a *ghostly authority* against the *civil;* working on men's minds, with words and distinctions, that of themselves signify nothing, but bewray (by their obscurity) that there walketh (as some think invisibly) another kingdom, as it were a kingdom of fairies, in the dark. Now seeing it is manifest, that the civil power, and the power of the commonwealth is the same thing; and that supremacy, and the power of making canons, and granting faculties, implieth a commonwealth; it followeth, that where one is sovereign, another supreme; where one can make laws, and another make canons; there must needs be two commonwealths, of one and the same subjects; which is a kingdom divided in itself, and cannot stand. For notwithstanding the insignificant distinction of *temporal,* and *ghostly,* they are still two kingdoms, and every subject is subject to two masters. For seeing the *ghostly* power challengeth the right to declare what is sin it challengeth by consequence to declare what is law, (sin being nothing but the transgression of the law;) and again, the civil power challenging to declare what is law, every subject must obey two masters, who both will have their commands be observed as law; which is impossible. Or, if it be but one kingdom, either the *civil*, which is the *power* of the commonwealth, must be subordinate to the *ghostly,* and then there is no sovereignty but the *ghostly;* or the *ghostly,* must be subordinate to the *temporal,* and then there is no *supremacy,* but the *temporal.* When therefore these two powers oppose one another, the commonwealth cannot but be in great danger of civil war, and dissolution. For the *civil* authority being more visible, and standing in the clearer light of natural reason, cannot choose but draw to it in all times a very considerable part of the people: and the *spiritual,* though it stand in the darkness of School distinctions, and hard words; yet because the fear of darkness, and ghosts, is greater than other fears, cannot want a party sufficient to trouble, and sometimes to destroy a commonwealth, and this is a disease which not unfitly may be compared to the epilepsy, or falling sickness (which the Jews took to be one kind of possession by spirits) in the body natural. For as in this disease, there is an unnatural spirit, or wind in the head that obstructeth the roots of the nerves, and moving them violently, taketh away the motion which naturally they should have from the power of the soul in the brain, and thereby causeth violent, and irregular motions (which men call convulsions) in the parts; insomuch as he that is seized therewith, falleth down sometimes into the water, and sometimes into the fire, as a man deprived of his senses; so also in the body politic, when the spiritual power, moveth the members of a commonwealth, by the terror of punishments, and hope of rewards (which are the nerves of it,) otherwise than by the civil power (which is the soul of the commonwealth), they ought to be moved; and by strange, and hard words suffocates their understanding, it must needs thereby distract the people, and either overwhelm the commonwealth with oppression, or cast it into the fire of a civil war.

Sometimes also in the merely civil government, there be more than one soul: as when the power of levying money, (which is the nutritive faculty,) has depended on a general assembly; the power of conduct and command, (which is the motive faculty,) on one man; and the power of making laws, (which is the rational faculty,) on the accidental consent, not only of those two, but also of a third; this endangereth the commonwealth, sometimes for want of consent to good laws; but most often for want of such nourishment, as is necessary to life, and motion. For although few perceive, that such government, is not government, but division of the commonwealth into three factions, and call it mixed monarchy; yet the truth is, that it is not one independent commonwealth, but three independent factions; nor one representative person, but three. In the kingdom of God, there may be three persons independent, without breach of unity in God that reigneth; but where men reign, that be subject to diversity of opinions, it cannot be so. And therefore if the king bear the person of the people, and the general assembly bear also the person of the people, and another assembly bear the person of a part of the people, they are not one person, nor one sovereign, but three persons, and three sovereigns.

To what disease in the natural body of man I may exactly compare this irregularity of a commonwealth, I know not. But I have seen a man, that had another man growing out of his side, with an head, arms, breast, and stomach, of his own: if he had had another man growing out of his other side, the comparison might then have been exact.

Hitherto I have named such diseases of a commonwealth, as are of the greatest, and most present danger. There be other, not so great; which nevertheless are not unfit to be observed. As first, the difficulty of raising money, for the necessary uses of the commonwealth; especially in the approach of war. This difficulty ariseth from the opinion, that every subject hath of a propriety in his lands and goods, exclusive of the sovereign's right to the use of the same. From whence it cometh to pass, that the sovereign power, which foreseeth the necessities and dangers of the commonwealth, (finding the passage of money to the public treasure obstructed, by the tenacity to the people,) whereas it ought to extend itself, to encounter, and prevent such dangers in their beginnings, contracteth itself as long as it can, and when it cannot longer, struggles with the people by stratagems of law, to obtain little sums, which not sufficing, he is fain at last violently to open the way for present supply, or perish: and being put often to these extremities, at last reduceth the people to their due temper; or else the commonwealth must perish. Insomuch as we may compare this distemper very aptly to an ague; wherein, the fleshy parts being congealed, or by venomous matter obstructed; the veins which by their natural course empty themselves into the heart, are not (as they ought to be) supplied from the arteries, whereby there succeedeth at first a cold contraction, and trembling of the limbs: and afterwards a hot, and strong endeavour of the heart, to force a passage for the blood; and before it can do that, contenteth itself with the small refreshments of such things as cool for a time, till (if nature be strong enough), it break at last the contumacy of the parts obstructed, and dissipateth the venom into sweat; or (if nature be too weak) the patient dieth.

Again, there is sometimes in a commonwealth, a disease, which resembleth the pleurisy; and that is, when the treasure of the commonwealth, flowing out of its due course, is gathered together in too much abundance in one, or a few private men, by monopolies, or by farms of the public revenues; in the same manner as the blood in a pleurisy, getting into the membrane of the breast, breedeth there an inflammation, accompanied with a fever, and painful stitches.

Also the popularity of a potent subject, (unless the commonwealth have very good caution of his fidelity,) is a dangerous disease; because the people (which should receive their motion from the authority of the sovereign,) by the flattery, and by the reputation of an ambitious man, are drawn away from their obedience to the laws, to follow a man, of whose virtues, and designs they have no knowledge. And this is commonly of more danger in a popular government, than in a monarchy; because an army is of so great force, and multitude, as it may easily be made believe, they are the people. By this means it was, that *Julius Caesar*, who was set up by the people against the senate, having won to himself the affections of his army, made himself master, both of senate and people. And this proceeding of popular, and ambitious men, is plain rebellion; and may be resembled to the effects of witchcraft.

Another infirmity of a commonwealth, is the immoderate greatness of a town, when it is able to furnish out of its own circuit, the number, and expense of a great army: as also the great number of corporations; which are as it were many lesser commonwealths in the bowels of a greater, like worms in the entrails of a natural man. To which may be added, the liberty of disputing against absolute power, by pretenders to political prudence; which though bred for the most part in the lees of the people; yet animated by false doctrines, are perpetually meddling with the fundamental laws, to the molestation of the commonwealth; like the little worms, which physicians call *ascarides*.

We may further add, the insatiable appetite, or Bulimia, of enlarging dominion; with the incurable *wounds* thereby many times received from the enemy; and the *wens*, of ununited conquests, which are many times a burthen, and with less danger lost, than kept; as also the *lethargy* of ease, and *consumption* of riot and vain expense.

Lastly, when in a war (foreign or intestine,) the enemies get a final victory; so as (the forces of the commonwealth keeping the field no longer), there is no farther protection of subjects in their loyalty; then is the commonwealth DISSOLVED, and every man at liberty to protect himself by such courses as his own discretion shall suggest unto him. For the sovereign, is the public soul, giving life and motion to the commonwealth; which expiring, the members are governed by it no more, than the carcase of a man, by his departed (though immortal) soul. For though the right of a sovereign monarch cannot be extinguished by the act of another; yet the obligation of the members may. For he that wants protection, may seek it any where; and when he hath it, is obliged (without fraudulent pretence of having submitted himself out of fear,) to protect his protection as long as he is able. But when the power of an assembly is once suppressed, the right of the same perisheth utterly; because the assembly itself is extinct; and consequently, there is no possibility for the sovereignty to re-enter.

CHAPTER 30

Of the Office of the Sovereign Representative

The office of the sovereign, (be it a monarch, or an assembly,) consisteth in the end, for which he was trusted with the sovereign power, namely the procuration of *the safety of the people;* to which he is obliged by the law of nature, and to render an account thereof to God, the author of that law, and to none but him. But by safety here, is not meant a bare preservation, but also all other contentments of life, which every man by lawful industry, without danger, or hurt to the commonwealth, shall acquire to himself.

And this is intended should be done, not by care applied to individuals, further than their protection from injuries, when they shall complain; but by a general providence, contained in public instruction, both of doctrine, and example; and in the making, and executing of good laws, to which individual persons may apply their own cases.

And because, if the essential rights of sovereignty (specified before in the eighteenth chapter) be taken away, the commonwealth is thereby dissolved, and every man returneth into the condition, and calamity of a war with every other man, (which is the greatest evil that can happen in this life;) it is the office of the sovereign, to maintain those rights entire; and consequently against his duty, first, to transfer to another, or to lay from himself any of them. For he that deserteth the means, deserteth the ends; and he deserteth the means, that being the sovereign, acknowledgeth himself subject to the civil laws; and renounceth the power of supreme judicature; or of making war, or peace by his own authority; or of judging of the necessities of the commonwealth; or of levying money, and soldiers, when, and as much as in his own conscience he shall judge necessary; or of making officers, and ministers both of war and peace; or of appointing teachers, and examining what doctrines are conformable, or contrary to the defence, peace, and good of the people. Secondly, it is against his duty, to let the people be ignorant, or misinformed of the grounds, and reasons of those his essential rights; because thereby men are easy to be seduced, and drawn to resist him, when the commonwealth shall require their use and exercise.

And the grounds of these rights, have the rather need to be diligently, and truly taught; because they cannot be maintained by any civil law, or terror of legal punishment. For a civil law, that shall forbid rebellion (and such is all resistance to the essential rights of sovereignty), is not (as a civil law) any obligation, but by virtue only of the law of nature, that forbiddeth the violation of faith; which natural obligation if men know not, they cannot know the right of any law the sovereign maketh. And for the punishment, they take it but for an act of hostility; which when they think they have strength enough, they will endeavour by acts of hostility, to avoid.

As I have heard some say, that justice is but a word, without substance: and that whatsoever a man can by force, or art, acquire to himself (not only in the condition of war, but also in a commonwealth,) is his own, which I have already showed to be false: so there be also that maintain, that there are no grounds, nor principles of reason, to sustain those essential rights, which make sovereignty absolute. For if there were, they would have been found out in some place, or other; whereas we see, there has not hitherto been any commonwealth, where those rights have been acknowledged, or challenged. Wherein they argue as ill, as if the savage people of America, should deny there were any grounds, or principles of reason, so to build a house, as to last as long as the materials, because they never yet saw any so well built. Time, and industry, produce every day new knowledge. And as the art of well building, is derived from principles of reason, observed by industrious men, that had long studied the nature of materials, and the divers effects of figure, and proportion, long after mankind began (though poorly) to build: so, long time after men have begun to constitute commonwealths, imperfect, and apt to relapse into disorder, there may principles of reason be found out, by industrious meditation, to make their constitution (excepting by external violence) everlasting. And such are those which I have in this discourse set forth: which whether they come not into the sight of those that have power to make use of them, or be neglected by them, or not, concerneth my particular interest, at this day, very little. But supposing that these of mine are not such principles of reason; yet I am sure they are principles from authority of Scripture; as I shall make it appear, when I shall come to speak of the kingdom of God, (administered by *Moses*,) over the Jews, his peculiar people by covenant.

But they say again, that though the principles be right, yet common people are not of capacity enough to be made to understand them. I should be glad, that the rich, and potent subjects of a kingdom, or those that are accounted the most learned, were no less incapable than they. But all men know, that the obstructions to this kind of doctrine, proceed not so much from the difficulty of the matter, as from the interest of them that are to learn. Potent men, digest hardly any thing that setteth up a power to bridle their affections; and learned men, any thing that discovereth their errors, and thereby lesseneth their authority: whereas the common people's minds, unless they be tainted with dependence on the potent, or scribbled over with the opinions of their doctors, are like clean paper, fit to receive whatsoever by public authority shall be imprinted in them. Shall whole nations be brought to *acquiesce* in the great mysteries of Christian religion, which are above reason; and millions of men be made believe, that the same body may be in innumerable places, at one and the same time, which is against reason; and shall not men be able, by their teaching, and preaching, protected by the law, to make that received, which is so consonant to reason, that any unprejudicated man, needs no more to learn it, than to hear it? I conclude therefore, that in the instruction of the people in the essential rights (which are the natural, and fundamental laws) of sovereignty, there is no difficulty, (whilst a sovereign has his power entire,) but what proceeds from his own fault, or the fault of those whom he trusteth in the administration of the commonwealth; and consequently, it is his duty, to cause them so to be instructed; and not only his duty, but his benefit also, and security, against the danger that may arrive to himself in his natural person, from rebellion.

And (to descend to particulars) the people are to be taught, first, that they ought not to be in love with any form of government they see in their neighbour nations, more than with their own, nor, (whatsoever present prosperity they behold in nations that are otherwise governed than they,) to desire change. For the prosperity of a people ruled by an aristocratical, or democratical assembly, cometh not from aristocracy, nor from democracy, but from the obedience, and concord of the subjects: nor do the people flourish in a monarchy, because one man has the right to rule them, but because they obey him. Take away in any kind of state, the obedience, (and consequently the concord of the people,) and they shall not only not flourish, but in short time be dissolved. And they that go about by disobedience, to do no more than reform the commonwealth, shall find they do thereby destroy it; like the foolish daughters of *Peleus*, (in the fable;) which desiring to renew the youth of their decrepid father, did by the counsel of *Medea*, cut him in pieces, and boil him, together with strange herbs, but made not of him a new man. This desire of change, is like the breach of the first of God's commandments: for there God says, *Non habebis Deos alienos;* Thou shalt not have the Gods of other nations; and in another place concerning *kings*, that they are Gods.

Secondly, they are to be taught, that they ought not to be led with admiration of the virtue of any of their fellow subjects, how high soever he stand, nor how conspicuously soever he shine in the commonwealth; nor of any assembly, (except the sovereign assembly,) so as to defer to them any obedience, or honour, appropriate to the sovereign only, whom (in their particular stations) they represent; nor to receive any influence from them, but such as is conveyed by them from the sovereign authority. For that sovereign, cannot be imagined to love his people as he ought, that is not jealous of them, but suffers them by the flattery of popular men, to be seduced from their loyalty, as they have often been, not only secretly, but openly, so as to proclaim marriage with them *in facie ecclesiciae* by preachers; and by publishing the same in the open streets: which may fitly be compared to the violation of the second of the ten commandments.

Thirdly, in consequence to this, they ought to be informed, how great a fault it is, to speak evil of the sovereign representative, (whether one man, or an assembly of men;) or to argue and dispute his power; or any way to use his name irreverently, whereby he may be brought into contempt with his people, and their obedience (in which the safety of the commonwealth consisteth) slackened. Which doctrine the third commandment by resemblance pointeth to.

Fourthly, seeing people cannot be taught this, nor when it is taught, remember it, nor after one generation past, so much as know in whom the sovereign power is placed, without setting apart from their ordinary labour, some certain times, in which they may attend those that are appointed to instruct them; it is necessary that some such times be determined, wherein they may assemble together, and (after prayers and praises given to God, the sovereign of sovereigns) hear those their duties told them, and the positive laws, such as generally concern them all, read and expounded, and be put in mind of the authority that maketh them laws. To this end had the *Jews* every seventh day, a *sabbath*, in which the law was read and expounded; and in the solemnity whereof they were put in mind, that their king was God; that having created the world in six days, he rested the seventh day; and by their resting on it from their labour, that that God was their king, which redeemed them from their servile, and painful labour in *Egypt*, and gave them a time, after they had rejoiced in God, to take joy also in themselves, by lawful recreation. So that the first table of the commandments, is spent all in setting down the sum of God's absolute power; not only as God, but as king by pact, (in peculiar) of the Jews; and may therefore give light, to those that have sovereign power conferred on them by the consent of men, to see what doctrine they ought to teach their subjects.

And because the first instruction of children, dependeth on the care of their parents; it is necessary that they should be obedient to them, whilst they are under their tuition; and not only so, but that also afterwards (as gratitude requireth,) they acknowledge the benefit of their education, by external signs of honour. To which end they are to be taught, that originally the father of every man was also his sovereign lord, with power over him of life and death; and that the fathers of families, when by instituting a commonwealth, they resigned that absolute power, yet it was never intended, they should lose the honour due unto them for their education. For to relinquish such right, was not necessary to the institution of sovereign power; nor would there be any reason, why any man should desire to have children, or take the care to nourish, and instruct them, if they were afterwards to have no other benefit from them, than from other men. And this accordeth with the fifth commandment.

Again, every sovereign ought to cause justice to be taught, which (consisting in taking from no man what is his,) is as much as to say, to cause men to be taught not to deprive their neighbours, by violence, or fraud, of any thing which by the sovereign authority is theirs. Of things held in propriety, those that are dearest to a man are his own life, and limbs; and in the next degree (in most men,) those that concern conjugal affection; and after them riches and means of living. Therefore the people are to be taught, to abstain from violence to one another's person, by private revenges; from violation of conjugal honour; and from forcible rapine, and fraudulent surreption of one another's goods. For which purpose also it is necessary they be showed the evil consequences of false judgment, by corruption either of judges or witnesses, whereby the distinction of propriety is taken away, and justice becomes of no effect: all which things are intimated in the sixth, seventh, eighth, and ninth commandments.

Lastly, they are to be taught, that not only the unjust facts, but the designs and intentions to do them, (though by accident hindered,) are injustice; which consisteth in the pravity of the will, as well as in the irregularity of the act. And this is the intention of the tenth commandment, and the sum of the second table; which is reduced all to this one commandment of mutual charity, *thou shalt love thy neighbour as thyself*: as the sum of the first table is reduced to *the love of God*; whom they had then newly received as their king.

As for the means, and conduits, by which the people may receive this instruction, we are to search, by what means so many opinions, contrary to the peace of mankind, upon weak and false principles, have nevertheless been so deeply rooted in them. I mean those, which I have in the precedent chapter specified: as that men shall judge of what is lawful and unlawful, not by the law itself, but by their own consciences; that is to say, by their own private judgments: that subjects sin in obeying the commands of the commonwealth, unless they themselves have first judged them to be lawful: that their propriety in their riches is such, as to exclude the dominion, which the commonwealth hath over the same: that it is lawful for subjects to kill such, as they call tyrants: that the sovereign power may be divided, and the like; which come to be instilled into the people by this means. They whom necessity, or covetousness keepeth attent on their trades, and labour; and they, on the other side, whom superfluity, or sloth carrieth after their sensual pleasures, (which two sorts of men take up the greatest part of mankind,) being diverted from the deep meditation, which the learning of truth, not only in the matter of natural justice, but also of all other sciences necessarily requireth, receive the notions of their duty, chiefly from divines in the pulpit, and partly from such of their neighbours, or familiar acquaintance, as having the faculty of discoursing readily, and plausibly, seem wiser and better learned in cases of law, and conscience, than themselves. And the divines, and such others as make show of learning, derive their knowledge from the universities, and from the schools of law, or from the books, which by men eminent in those schools, and universities have been published. It is therefore manifest, that the instruction of the people, dependeth wholly, on the right teaching of youth in the universities. But are not (may some man say) the universities of *England* learned enough already to do that? or is it you will undertake to teach the universities? Hard questions. Yet to the first, I doubt not to answer; that till towards the latter end of *Henry the Eighth*, the power of the Pope, was always upheld against the power of the commonwealth, principally by the universities; and that the doctrines maintained by so many preachers, against the sovereign power of the king, and by so many lawyers, and others, that had their education there, is a sufficient argument, that though the universities were not authors of those false doctrines, yet they knew not how to plant the true. For in such a contradiction of opinions, it is most certain, that they have not been sufficiently instructed; and it is no wonder, if they yet retain a relish of that subtle liquor, wherewith they were first seasoned, against the civil authority. But to the latter question, it is not fit, nor needful for me to say either aye, or no: for any man that sees what I am doing, may easily perceive what I think.

The safety of the people, requireth further, from him, or them that have the sovereign power, that justice be equally administered to all degrees of people; that is, that as well the rich and mighty, as poor and obscure persons, may be righted of the injuries done them; so as the great, may have no greater hope of impunity, when they do violence, dishonour, or any injury to the meaner sort, than when one of these, does the like to one of them: For in this consisteth equity; to which, as being a precept of the law of nature, a sovereign is as much subject, as any of the meanest of his people. All breaches of the law, are offences against the commonwealth: but there be some, that are also against private persons. Those that concern the commonwealth only, may without breach of equity be pardoned; for every man may pardon what is done against himself, according to his own discretion. But an offence against a private man, cannot in equity be pardoned, without the consent of him that is injured; or reasonable satisfaction.

The inequality of subjects, proceedeth from the acts of sovereign power; and therefore has no more place in the presence of the sovereign; that is to say, in a court of justice, than the inequality between kings, and their subjects, in the presence of the King of kings. The honour of great persons, is to be valued for their beneficence and the aids they give to men of inferior rank, or not at all. And the violences, oppressions, and injuries they do, are not extenuated, but aggravated by the greatness of their persons; because they have least need to commit them. The consequences of this partiality towards the great, proceed in this manner. Impunity maketh insolence; insolence hatred; and hatred, an endeavour to pull down all oppressing and contumelious greatness, though with the ruin of the commonwealth.

To equal justice, apperteineth also the equal imposition of taxes; the equality whereof dependeth not on the equality of riches, but on the equality of the debt, that every man oweth to the commonwealth for his defence. It is not enough, for a man to labour for the maintenance of his life; but also to fight, (if need be,) for the securing of his labour. They must either do as the Jews did after their return from captivity, in re-edifying the temple, build with one hand, and hold the sword in the other; or else they must hire others to fight for them. For the impositions, that are laid on the people by the sovereign power, are nothing else but the wages, due to them that hold the public sword, to defend private men in the exercise of several trades, and callings. Seeing then the benefit that every one receiveth thereby, is the enjoyment of life, which is equally dear to poor and rich; the debt which a poor man oweth them that defend his life, is the same which a rich man oweth for the defence of his; saving that the rich, who have the service of the poor, may be debtors not only for their own persons, but for many more. Which considered, the equality of imposition, consisteth rather in the equality of that which is consumed, than of the riches of the persons that consume the same. For what reason is there, that he which laboureth much, and sparing the fruits of his labour, consumeth little, should be more charged, than he that living idly, getteth little, and spendeth all he gets; seeing the one hath no more protection from the commonwealth, than the other? But when the impositions, are laid upon those things which men consume, every man payeth equally for what he useth: nor is the commonwealth defrauded by the luxurious waste of private men.

And whereas many men, by accident inevitable, become unable to maintain themselves by their labour; they ought not to be left to the charity of private persons; but to be provided for, (as far-forth as the necessities of nature require,) by the laws of the commonwealth. For as it is uncharitableness in any man, to neglect the impotent; so it is in the sovereign of a commonwealth, to expose them to the hazard of such uncertain charity.

But for such as have strong bodies, the case is otherwise: they are to be forced to work; and to avoid the excuse of not finding employment, there ought to be such laws, as may encourage all manner of arts; as navigation, agriculture, fishing, and all manner of manufacture that requires labour. The multitude of poor, and yet strong people still increasing, they are to be transplanted into countries not sufficiently inhabited: where nevertheless, they are not to exterminate those they find there; but constrain them to inhabit closer together, and not range a great deal of ground, to snatch what they find; but to court each little plot with art and labour, to give them their sustenance in due season. And when all the world is overcharged with inhabitants, then the last remedy of all is war; which provideth for every man, by victory, or death.

To the care of the sovereign, belongeth the making of good laws. But what is a good law? By a good law, I mean not a just law: for *no law can be unjust*. The law is made by the sovereign power, and all that is done by such power, is warranted, and owned by every one of the people; and that which every man will have so, no man can say is unjust. It is in the laws of a commonwealth, as in the laws of gaming: whatsoever the gamesters all agree on, is injustice to none of them. A good law is that, which is *needful*, for the *good of the people*, and withal *perspicuous*.

For the use of laws, (which are but rules authorized) is not to bind the people from all voluntary actions; but to direct and keep them in such a motion, as not to hurt themselves by their own impetuous desires, rashness, or indiscretion; as hedges are set, not to stop travellers, but to keep them in the way. And therefore a law that is not needful, having not the true end of a law, is not good. A law may be conceived to be good, when it is for the benefit of the sovereign; though it be not necessary for the people; but it is not so. For the good of the sovereign and people, cannot be separated. It is a weak sovereign, that has weak subjects; and a weak people, whose sovereign wanteth power to rule them at his will. Unnecessary laws are not good laws; but traps for money: which where the right of sovereign power is acknowledged, are superfluous; and where it is not acknowledged, insufficient to defend the people.

The perspicuity, consisteth not so much in the words of the law itself, as in a declaration of the causes, and motives, for which it was made. That is it, that shows us the meaning of the legislator; and the meaning of the legislator known, the law is more easily understood by few, than many words. For all words, are subject to ambiguity; and therefore multiplication of words in the body of the law, is multiplication of ambiguity: besides it seems to imply, (by too much diligence,) that whosoever can evade the words, is without the compass of the law. And this is a cause of many unnecessary processes. For when I consider how short were the laws of ancient times; and how they grew by degrees still longer; methinks I see a contention between the penners, and pleaders of the law; the former seeking to circumscribe the latter; and the latter to evade their circumscriptions; and that the pleaders have got the victory. It belongeth therefore to the office of a legislator, (such as is in all commonwealths the supreme representative, be it one man, or an assembly,) to make the reason perspicuous, why the law was made; and the body of the law itself, as short, but in as proper, and significant terms, as may be.

It belongeth also to the office of the sovereign, to make a right application of punishments, and rewards. And seeing the end of punishing is not revenge, and discharge of choler; but correction, either of the offender, or of others by his example; the severest punishments are to be inflicted for those crimes, that are of most danger to the public; such as are those which proceed from malice to the government established; those that spring from contempt of justice; those that provoke indignation in the multitude; and those, which unpunished seem authorized, as when they are committed by sons, servants, or favourites of men in authority: For indignation carrieth men, not only against the actors, and authors of injustice; but against all power that is likely to protect them; as in the case of *Tarquin;* when for the insolent act of one of his sons, he was driven out of *Rome*, and the monarchy itself dissolved. But crimes of infirmity; such as are those which proceed from great provocation, from great fear, great need, or from ignorance whether the fact be a great crime, or not, there is place many times for lenity, without prejudice to the commonwealth; and lenity when there is such place for it, is required by the law of nature. The punishment of the leaders, and teachers in a commotion; not the poor seduced people, when they are punished, can profit the commonwealth by their example. To be severe to the people, is to punish that ignorance, which may in great part be imputed to the sovereign, whose fault it was, they were no better instructed.

In like manner it belongeth to the office, and duty of the sovereign, to apply his rewards always so, as there may arise from them benefit to the commonwealth: wherein consisteth their use, and end; and is then done, when they that have well served the commonwealth, are with as little expense of the common treasure, as is possible, so well recompensed, as others thereby may be encouraged, both to serve the same as faithfully as they can, and to study the arts by which they may be enabled to do it better. To buy with money, or preferment, from a popular ambitious subject, to be quiet, and desist from making ill impressions in the minds of the people, has nothing of the nature of reward; (which is ordained not for disservice, but for service past;) nor a sign of gratitude, but of fear: nor does it tend to the benefit, but to the damage of the public. It is a contention with ambition, like that of *Hercules* with the monster *Hydra*, which having many heads, for every one that was vanquished, there grew up three. For in like manner, when the stubbornness of one popular man, is overcome with reward, there arise many more (by the example) that do the same mischief, in hope of like benefit: and as all sorts of manufacture, so also malice encreaseth by being vendible. And though sometimes a civil war, may be deferred, by such ways as that, yet the danger grows still the greater, and the public ruin more assured. It is therefore against the duty of the sovereign, to whom the public safety is committed, to reward those that aspire to greatness by disturbing the peace of their country, and not rather to oppose the beginnings of such men, with a little danger, than after a longer time with greater.

Another business of the sovereign, is to choose good counsellors; I mean such, whose advice he is to take in the government of the commonwealth. For this word counsel, *consilium*, corrupted from *considium*, is of a large signification, and comprehendeth all assemblies of men that sit together, not only to deliberate what is to be done hereafter, but also to judge of facts past, and of law for the present. I take it here in the first sense only: and in this sense, there is no choice of counsel, neither in a democracy, nor aristocracy; because the persons counselling are members of the person counselled. The choice of counsellors therefore is proper to monarchy; in which, the sovereign that endeavoureth not to make choice of those, that in every kind are the most able, dischargeth not his office as he ought to do. The most able counsellors, are they that have least hope of benefit by giving evil counsel, and most knowledge of those things that conduce to the peace, and defence of the commonwealth. It is a hard matter to know who expecteth benefit from public troubles; but the signs that guide to a just suspicion, is the soothing of the people in their unreasonable, or irremediable grievances, by men whose estates are not sufficient to discharge their accustomed expenses and may easily be observed by any one whom it concerns to know it. But to know, who has most knowledge of the public affairs, is yet harder; and they that know them, need them a great deal the less. For to know, who knows the rules almost of any art, is a great degree of the knowledge of the same art; because no man can be assured of the truth of another's rules; but he that is first taught to understand them. But the best signs of knowledge of any art, are, much conversing in it, and constant good effects of it. Good counsel comes not by lot, nor by inheritance; and therefore there is no more reason to expect good advice from the rich, or noble, in matter of state, than in delineating the dimensions of a fortress; unless we shall think there needs no method in the study of the politics, (as there does in the study of geometry,) but only to be lookers on; which is not so. For the politics is the harder study of the two. Whereas in these parts of *Europe*, it hath been taken for a right of certain persons, to have place in the highest council of state by inheritance; it is derived from the conquests of the ancient Germans; wherein many absolute lords joining together to conquer other nations, would not enter into the confederacy, without such privileges, as might be marks of difference in time following, between their posterity, and the posterity of their subjects; which privileges being inconsistent with the sovereign power, by the favour of the sovereign, they may seem to keep; but contending for them as their right, they must needs by degrees let them go, and have at last no further honour, than adhereth naturally to their abilities.

And how able soever be the counsellors in any affair, the benefit of their counsel is greater, when they give every one his advice, and the reasons of it apart, than when they do it in an assembly, by way of orations; and when they have premeditated, than when they speak on the sudden; both because they have more time, to survey the consequences of action; and are less subject to be carried away to contradiction, through envy, emulation, or other passions arising from the difference of opinion.

The best counsel, in those things that concern not other nations, but only the ease, and benefit the subjects may enjoy, by laws that look only inward, is to be taken from the general informations, and complaints of the people of each province, who are best acquainted with their own wants, and ought therefore, when they demand nothing in derogation of the essential rights of sovereignty, to be diligently taken notice of. For without those essential rights, (as I have often before said,) the commonwealth cannot at all subsist.

A commander of an army in chief, if he be not popular, shall not be beloved, nor feared as he ought to be by his army; and consequently cannot perform that office with good success. He must therefore be industrious, valiant, affable, liberal and fortunate, that he may gain an opinion both of sufficiency, and of loving his soldiers. This is popularity, and breeds in the soldiers both desire, and courage, to recommend themselves to his favour; and protects the severity of the general, in punishing (when need is) the mutinous, or negligent soldiers. But this love of soldiers, (if caution be not given of the commander's fidelity,) is a dangerous thing to sovereign power; especially when it is in the hands of an assembly not popular. It belongeth therefore to the safety of the people, both that they be good conductors, and faithful subjects, to whom the sovereign commits his armies.

But when the sovereign himself is popular; that is, reverenced and beloved of his people, there is no danger at all from the popularity of a subject. For soldiers are never so generally unjust, as to side with their captain; though they love him, against their sovereign, when they love not only his person, but also his cause. And therefore those, who by violence have at any time suppressed the power of their lawful sovereign, before they could settle themselves in his place, have been always put to the trouble of contriving their titles, to save the people from the shame of receiving them. To have a known right to sovereign power, is so popular a quality, as he that has it needs no more, for his own part, to turn the hearts of his subjects to him, but that they see him able absolutely to govern his own family: nor, on the part of his enemies, but a disbanding of their armies. For the greatest and most active part of mankind, has never hitherto been well contented with the present.

Concerning the offices of one sovereign to another, which are comprehended in that law, which is commonly called the *law of nations*, I need not say any thing in this place; because the law of nations, and the law of nature, is the same thing. And every sovereign hath the same right, in procuring the safety of his people, that any particular man can have, in procuring the safety of his own body. And the same law, that dictateth to men that have no civil government, what they ought to do, and what to avoid in regard of one another, dictateth the same to commonwealths, that is, to the consciences of sovereign princes, and sovereign assemblies; there being no court of natural justice, but in the conscience only; where not man, but God reigneth; whose laws, (such of them as oblige all mankind,) in respect of God, as he is the author of nature, are *natural;* and in respect of the same God, as he is King of kings, are *laws.* But of the kingdom of God, as King of kings, and as King also of a peculiar people, I shall speak in the rest of this discourse.

BARUCH SPINOZA

Baruch (Benedict) Spinoza (1632–1677) was born in Amsterdam, a descendent of Portuguese Marranos, that is, Jews who had fled the Inquisition for the relative safety of Holland. Virtually nothing is known of Spinoza's early life. He was educated at a traditional Jewish yeshiva where he studied Hebrew and Talmud. Spinoza was a polymath who spoke Spanish, Portuguese, and Dutch, and wrote his major philosophical works in Latin. At the age of 24, he was put under the *herem* or edict of excommunication expelling him from the synagogue. The reasons for the ban on Spinoza are not fully known, although they are almost certainly connected to the increasingly heterodox opinions on religion that he had come to espouse.

Spinoza left Amsterdam in 1660, settling first in Rijnsburg, a suburb of Leiden, and later moving to Voorsburg outside The Hague. He earned his living as a lens grinder and famously turned down an offer of a professorship at Heidelberg on the grounds that it would interfere with his independence of mind. Spinoza lived a life of uncommon detachment and isolation. He was befriended by members of some of the more liberal Protestant sects of the time, but Spinoza was not an apostate and refused to convert to Christianity. Although he lived alone and aloof, he was sought out by the leading scientists and philosophers of the day, including Leibniz and Henry Oldenburg, the secretary of the Royal Academy in London. Spinoza died of consumption in The Hague at the age of 44.

Spinoza was a writer who combined an unusual degree of boldness and secrecy. As an excommunicated Jew living on the margins of Dutch society, he knew at first hand the sting of religious persecution and the dangers of speaking one's mind openly. His signet ring bore the Latin inscription *caute*, or caution. He took pains to conceal his opinions even from those most intimate with him. With the exception of an early commentary on the philosophy of Descartes (1663), none of the other works published by Spinoza bore his name. His major work of political philosophy, the *Theologico-Political Treatise* (TPT) was published anonymously in 1670 and carried the imprimatur of a fictitious Hamburg publishing house. The work for which he is best known, the *Ethics,* was published posthumously for reasons of prudence and safety. A shorter work, *The Political Treatise*, was left unfinished at the time of his death.

At the same time that he expressed a prudent fear of the power of the multitude, Spinoza took an active stand on the major political struggles of his time. Like Machiavelli's *Prince*, which Spinoza greatly admired, the *TPT* was a passionate and partisan tract written to advance the fortunes of a political cause. This cause was the republican faction in Dutch politics championed by Jan de Witt against the monarchist faction led by the House of Orange and supported by the Calvinist clergy. Like the Collegiants and Mennonites with whom he associated, Spinoza was a republican in politics and an advocate of toleration in theology. The best state, he declared, is one where "everyone's judgment is free and unshackled" and where "each may worship God as his conscience dictates." Two years after the publication of the *TPT*, De Witt and his brother were savagely murdered by an angry mob, an action that signaled Spinoza's withdrawal from political involvement. *Ultimi barbarorum* was his final judgment on the De Witt affair.

As the title of the *TPT* implies, it is a work divided into two distinguishable, yet hardly equal, parts. The first fifteen chapters are devoted to a lengthy and painstaking critique of biblical theology. Taking up the traditional themes of prophecy, law, and miracles, Spinoza submits each in turn to withering criticism. The Bible is on his account an imaginative, but ultimately primitive, record of the mentality of an ancient culture. Its teachings were intended to instill habits of obedience and justice in superstitious and fear-driven people. The aim of the first part of the *TPT* was to liberate human reason (or philosophy) from the authority of Scripture.

Having completed the critique of theology in the first fifteen chapters of the *TPT,* Spinoza devotes the remainder of the book to the critique of politics. The *TPT* is notable as the first work of modern political philosophy to endorse democracy as the best regime (*optima Republica*). Spinoza derives the legitimacy of democratic government at least in part from premises borrowed from his most important contemporary, Thomas Hobbes. Like Hobbes, Spinoza begins with a perfectly realistic, hard-boiled picture of human nature. There is in every living being an impulse (*conatus*) toward self-preservation. It follows that in the state of nature every being has the natural right to preserve itself by whatever means are at its disposal. Like Hobbes also, Spinoza invokes the metaphor of a social contract as the means by which individuals agree with one another to reduce the state of war to a condition of peace.

Spinoza departs from Hobbes, however, in two interesting and important ways. First, because the natural right of every being is identical to its power, Spinoza draws the conclusion that the majority in any community has by definition the preponderance of right on its side. Unlike the Hobbesian contract that displays a marked preference for monarchy, for Spinoza only a democratic sovereign can ensure against the dangers of arbitrary rule stemming from the investiture of power in the hands of one person. Second, unlike Hobbes who maintained that the avoidance of war is the greatest political good, Spinoza endorses democracy for its enhancement of human freedom. Democracy is desireable because it fosters the conditions for reason and the expression of our individual faculties. To a degree developed later by Rousseau and Kant, not peace and security but freedom becomes the true end of political life. Democracy is the form of government most consistent with the modern treatment of natural right and in agreement with human liberty.

The kind of democracy advocated by Spinoza is what today would be called a *liberal democracy*. A central feature of this democracy is its incorporation of the widest possible freedom of thought and opinion. The *TPT* provides several, not necessarily consistent, justifications for toleration. In the first place, toleration is said to follow from the doctrine of natural right strictly understood. If the right of nature means the liberty to do whatever our power permits, then by nature the sovereign's power must be limited to the control of external behavior. Because "no man's mind can possibly lie wholly at the disposition of another," the sovereign must leave the contents of the mind entirely to the individual's private discretion.

The *TPT* also argues historically and pragmatically that attempts to control the content of thought have invariably backfired. Rather than produc- ing consensus and harmony, policies of intolerance and persecution have unwittingly bred conflict and opposition. The effort to criminalize opinions has led even honorable men to don the mantle of revolution. Note that unlike later defenders of toleration, Spinoza does not say that the effort to control thought violates some sacred or privileged sphere of individual privacy. Persecution is wrong, not because it is immoral, but because it is inherently self-defeating.

Most importantly, Spinoza defends freedom of speech because it fosters a certain kind of human being with certain distinctive traits of character and mind. Like John Stuart Mill in the midnineteenth century, Spinoza defends toleration, not as an end in itself but because it encourages the development of individual judgment and personal autonomy. The kind of human being envisaged by Spinoza is one who prizes individual liberty "before all things dear and precious." In the *Ethics*, Spinoza provides a particularly vivid portrait of the autonomous individual as one who strives to be independent of tradition and external sources of authority, who acts rather than being acted upon, and whose thoughts and actions stem not from envy and fear but from feelings of love and friendship. Above all, this person thinks of nothing so much as life itself and the means necessary to its enhancement. While Spinoza's idea of freedom has certain classical precedents in the works of Plato and the Stoics, it remains to a considerable degree a modern creation. To a greater extent than in the past, freedom is based on notions of individual autonomy, self-mastery, and courage.

Spinoza is one of the first thinkers to argue that the fruits of toleration are beneficial, not merely for the individual, but for society as a whole. The *TPT* draws an explicit connection between freedom of speech and the progress of the liberal arts. Like Descartes, Spinoza saw the tremendous potential locked inside the emergent sciences of nature, especially medicine, as a tool for increasing the ease and comfort of life. But Spinoza also recognized that intellectual and material progress does not take place in a vacuum. The progress of the arts and sciences is linked by him to issues of trade and commerce. Intellectual freedom is only possible in an environment that encourages commercial freedom. Spinoza's democracy is, then, necessarily a commercial republic where one finds a combination of economic, political, and religious liberty.

Spinoza's preference for the modern commercial republic is based on an emphatic rejection of the older classical republic theorized in the writings of Plato and Aristotle. For the ancients, the republic was a small, polis-like body characterized by a high degree of moral and religious homogeneity. Spinoza's defense of commercial and intellectual freedom indicates a preference for large, cosmopolitan, or "open societies" marked by a diversity of opinions and lifestyles. Furthermore, the classical republics displayed a severity and moral austerity demanding from its citizens a self-sacrificing devotion to the common good. Conversely, Spinoza's commercial republic is characterized less by virtue than by liberty in its many dimensions. Liberty is said to bring not only the progress of the arts and sciences but also the refinement and improvement of behavior. The *TPT* concludes with a ringing praise of the commercial republic of Amsterdam, where the effects of liberty are on display for all to see.

Only in the following century would Spinoza's arguments in favor of the commercial republic bear fruit in the works of Montesquieu, Hume, and Adam Smith. Everywhere the commercial republic was proposed as a more humane alternative to the theologico-political regimes that had previously dominated European thought and practice. Such a regime would favor commercial over rural interests, the city over the country, and the rule of interest and utility over the

devotion to lofty but intangible goals. The enjoyment of life rather than its mortification, a disposition to cultivate freedom rather than regret it, the celebration of the urbane pleasures of good food, companionship, the appreciation of
beauty and music—such were the goals of Spinoza's *optima Republica*.

The number of studies of Spinoza's political thought available in English
is sparse. Leo Strauss, *Spinoza's Critique of Religion,* trans. E. M. Sinclair (New
York: Schocken, 1965), puts Spinoza's political theory within the context of his
critique of theology; Yirmiyahu Yovel, *Spinoza and Other Heretics*, 2 vols.
(Princeton: Princeton University Press, 1991), examines Spinoza's excommunication against the background of the Marrano community and its influence
on his manner of writing; Lewis Feuer, *Spinoza and the Rise of Liberalism*
(Boston: Beacon, 1958), remains a useful guide to Spinoza's relation to radical
currents within Dutch politics of his time; and Steven B. Smith, "Spinoza's
Democratic Turn: Chapter 16 of the 'Theologico-Political Treatise,'" *Review of
Metaphysics,* Vol. 48, No. 2 (1994), attempts to understand Spinoza's neglected
role within the history of democratic theory.

S. B. S.

THEOLOGICO-POLITICAL TREATISE

CHAPTER XVI

Of the Foundations of a State; Of the Natural and Civil Rights of Individuals;
and Of the Rights of the Sovereign Power.

HITHERTO our care has been to separate philosophy from theology, and to show the
freedom of thought which such separation insures to both. It is now time to determine
the limits to which such freedom of thought and discussion may extend itself in the ideal
state. For the due consideration of this question we must examine the foundations of a
state, first turning our attention to the natural rights of individuals, and afterwards to
religion and the state as a whole.

By the right and ordinance of nature, I merely mean those natural laws wherewith we
conceive every individual to be conditioned by nature, so as to live and act in a given way.
For instance, fishes are naturally conditioned for swimming, and the greater for devouring
the less; therefore fishes enjoy the water, and the greater devour the less by sovereign natural right. For it is certain that nature, taken in the abstract, has sovereign right to do
anything she can; in other words, her right is co-extensive with her power. The power of
nature is the power of God, which has sovereign right over all things; and, inasmuch as
the power of nature is simply the aggregate of the powers of all her individual components, it follows that every individual has sovereign right to do all that he can; in other
words, the rights of an individual extend to the utmost limits of his power as it has been
conditioned. Now it is the sovereign law and right of nature that each individual should
endeavour to preserve itself as it is, without regard to anything but itself; therefore this

sovereign law and right belongs to every individual, namely, to exist and act according to its natural conditions. We do not here acknowledge any difference between mankind and other individual natural entities, nor between men endowed with reason and those to whom reason is unknown; nor between fools, madmen, and sane men. Whatsoever an individual does by the laws of its nature it has a sovereign right to do, inasmuch as it acts as it was conditioned by nature, and cannot act otherwise. Wherefore among men, so long as they are considered as living under the sway of nature, he who does not yet know reason, or who has not yet acquired the habit of virtue, acts solely according to the laws of his desire with as sovereign a right as he who orders his life entirely by the laws of reason.

That is, as the wise man has sovereign right to do all that reason dictates, or to live according to the Laws of reason, as also the ignorant and foolish man has sovereign right to do all that desire dictates, or to live according to the laws of desire. This is identical with the teaching of Paul, who acknowledges that previous to the law—that is, as long as men are considered of as living under the sway of nature, there is no sin.

The natural right of the individual man is thus determined, not by sound reason, but by desire and power. All are not naturally conditioned so as to act according to the laws and rules of reason; nay, on the contrary, all men are born ignorant, and before they can learn the right way of life and acquire the habit of virtue, the greater part of their life, even if they have been well brought up, has passed away. Nevertheless, they are in the meanwhile bound to live and preserve themselves as far as they can by the unaided impulses of desire. Nature has given them no other guide, and has denied them the present power of living according to sound reason; so that they are no more bound to live by the dictates of an enlightened mind, than a cat is bound to live by the laws of the nature of a lion.

Whatsoever, therefore, an individual (considered as under the sway of nature) thinks useful for himself, whether led by sound reason or impelled by the passions, that he has a sovereign right to seek and to take for himself as he best can, whether by force, cunning, entreaty, or any other means; consequently he may regard as an enemy anyone who hinders the accomplishment of his purpose.

It follows from what we have said that the right and ordinance of nature, under which all men are born, and under which they mostly live, only prohibits such things as no one desires, and no one can attain: it does not forbid strife, nor hatred, nor anger, nor deceit, nor, indeed, any of the means suggested by desire.

This we need not wonder at, for nature is not bounded by the laws of human reason, which aims only at man's true benefit and preservation; her limits are infinitely wider, and have reference to the eternal order of nature, wherein man is but a speck; it is by the necessity of this alone that all individuals are conditioned for living and acting in a particular way. If anything, therefore, in nature seems to us ridiculous, absurd, or evil, it is because we only know in part, and are almost entirely ignorant of the order and interdependence of nature as a whole, and also because we want everything to be arranged according to the dictates of our human reason; in reality that which reason considers evil, is not evil in respect to the order and laws of nature as a whole, but only in respect to the laws of our reason.

Nevertheless, no one can doubt that it is much better for us to live according to the laws and assured dictates of reason, for, as we said, they have men's true good for their object. Moreover, everyone wishes to live as far as possible securely beyond the reach of fear, and this would be quite impossible so long as everyone did everything he liked, and reason's claim was lowered to a par with those of hatred and anger; there is no one who is not ill at ease in the midst of enmity, hatred, anger, and deceit, and who does not seek to avoid them as much as he can. When we reflect that men without mutual help, or the aid of reason, must needs live most miserably, as we clearly proved in Chap. V, we shall plainly see that men must necessarily come to an agreement to live together as securely and well as possible if they are to enjoy as a whole the rights which naturally belong to them as individuals, and their life should be no more conditioned by the force and desire of individuals, but by the power and will of the whole body. This end they will be unable to attain if desire be their only guide (for by the laws of desire each man is drawn in a different direction); they must, therefore, most firmly decree and establish that they will be guided in everything by reason (which nobody will dare openly to repudiate lest he should be taken for a madman), and will restrain any desire which is injurious to a man's fellows, that they will do to all as they would be done by, and that they will defend their neighbour's rights as their own.

How such a compact as this should be entered into, how ratified and established, we will now inquire.

Now it is a universal law of human nature that no one ever neglects anything which he judges to be good, except with the hope of gaining a greater good, or from the fear of a greater evil; nor does anyone endure an evil except for the sake of avoiding a greater evil, or gaining a greater good. That is, everyone will, of two goods, choose that which he thinks the greatest; and, of two evils, that which he thinks the least. I say advisedly that which he thinks the greatest or the least, for it does not necessarily follow that he judges right. This law is so deeply implanted in the human mind that it ought to be counted among eternal truths and axioms.

As a necessary consequence of the principle just enunciated, no one can honestly promise to forego the right which he has over all things, and in general no one will abide by his promises, unless under the fear of a greater evil, or the hope of a greater good. An example will make the matter clearer. Suppose that a robber forces me to promise that I will give him my goods at his will and pleasure. It is plain (inasmuch as my natural right is, as I have shown, co-extensive with my power) that if I can free myself from this robber by stratagem, by assenting to his demands, I have the natural right to do so, and to pretend to accept his conditions. Or again, suppose I have genuinely promised someone that for the space of twenty days I will not taste food or any nourishment; and suppose I afterwards find that my promise was foolish, and cannot be kept without very great injury to myself; as I am bound by natural law and right to choose the least of two evils, I have complete right to break my compact, and act as if my promise had never been uttered. I say that I should have perfect natural right to do so, whether I was actuated by true and evident reason, or whether I was actuated by mere opinion in thinking I had promised rashly; whether my reasons were true or false, I should be in fear of a greater evil, which, by the ordinance of nature, I should strive to avoid by every means in my power.

We may, therefore, conclude that a compact is only made valid by its utility, without which it becomes null and void. It is, therefore, foolish to ask a man to keep his faith with us for ever, unless we also endeavour that the violation of the compact we enter into shall involve for the violator more harm than good. This consideration should have very great weight in forming a state. However, if all men could be easily led by reason alone, and could recognize what is best and most useful for a state, there would be no one who would not forswear deceit, for every one would keep most religiously to their compact in their desire for the chief good, namely, the preservation of the state, and would cherish good faith above all things as the shield and buckler of the commonwealth. However, it is far from being the case that all men can always be easily led by reason alone; everyone is drawn away by his pleasure, While avarice, ambition, envy, hatred, and the like so engross the mind that reason has no place therein. Hence, though men make promises with all the appearances of good faith, and agree that they will keep to their engagement, no one can absolutely rely on another man's promise unless there is something behind it. Everyone has by nature a right to act deceitfully, and to break his compacts, unless he be restrained by the hope of some greater good, or the fear of some greater evil.

However, as we have shown that the natural right of the individual is only limited by his power, it is clear that by transferring, either willingly or under compulsion, this power into the hands of another, he in so doing necessarily cedes also a part of his right; and further, that the sovereign right over all men belongs to him who has sovereign power, wherewith he can compel men by force, or restrain them by threats of the universally feared punishment of death; such sovereign right he will retain only so long as he can maintain his power of enforcing his will; otherwise he will totter on his throne, and no one who is stronger than he will be bound unwillingly to obey him.

In this manner a society can be formed without any violation of natural right, and the covenant can always be strictly kept-that is, if each individual hands over the whole of his power to the body politic, the latter will then possess sovereign natural right over all things; that is, it will have sole and unquestioned dominion, and everyone will be bound to obey, under pain of the severest punishment. A body politic of this kind is called a Democracy, which may be defined as a society which wields all its power as a whole. The sovereign power is not restrained by any laws, but everyone is bound to obey it in all things; such is the state of things implied when men either tacitly or expressly handed over to it all their power of self-defence, or in other words, all their right. For if they had wished to retain any right for themselves, they ought to have taken precautions for its defence and preservation; as they have not done so, and indeed could not have done so without dividing and consequently ruining the state, they placed themselves absolutely at the mercy of the sovereign power; and, therefore, having acted (as we have shown) as reason and necessity demanded, they are obliged to fulfil the commands of the sovereign power, however absurd these may be, else they will be public enemies, and will act against reason, which urges the preservation of the state as a primary duty. For reason bids us choose the least of two evils.

Furthermore, this danger of submitting absolutely to the dominion and will of another, is one which may be incurred with a light heart: for we have shown that sovereigns only possess this right of imposing their will, so long as they have the full power to enforce it: if such power be lost their right to command is lost also, or lapses to those who have assumed it and can keep it. Thus it is very rare for sovereigns to impose thoroughly irrational commands, for they are bound to consult their own interests, and retain their power by consulting the public good and acting according to the dictates of reason, as Seneca says, "violenta imperia nemo continuit diu." No one can long retain a tyrant's sway.

In a democracy, irrational commands are still less to be feared: for it is almost impossible that the majority of a people, especially if it be a large one, should agree in an irrational design: and, moreover, the basis and aim of a democracy is to avoid the desires as irrational, and to bring men as far as possible under the control of reason, so that they may live in peace and harmony: if this basis be removed the whole fabric falls to ruin.

Such being the ends in view for the sovereign power, the duty of subjects is, as I have said, to obey its commands, and to recognize no right save that which it sanctions.

It will, perhaps, be thought that we are turning subjects into slaves: for slaves obey commands and free men live as they like; but this idea is based on a misconception, for the true slave is he who is led away by his pleasures and can neither see what is good for him nor act accordingly: he alone is free who lives with free consent under the entire guidance of reason.

Action in obedience to orders does take away freedom in a certain sense, but it does not, therefore, make a man a slave, all depends on the object of the action. If the object of the action be the good of the state, and not the good of the agent, the latter is a slave and does himself no good. But in a state or kingdom where the weal of the whole people, and not that of the ruler, is the supreme law, obedience to the sovereign power does not make a man a slave, of no use to himself, but a subject. Therefore, that state is the freest whose laws are founded on sound reason, so that every member of it may, if he will, be free; that is, live with full consent under the entire guidance of reason.

Children, though they are bound to obey all the commands of their parents, are yet not slaves: for the commands of parents look generally to the children's benefit.

We must, therefore, acknowledge a great difference between a slave, a son, and a subject; their positions may be thus defined. A slave is one who is bound to obey his master's orders, though they are given solely in the master's interest: a son is one who obeys his father's orders, given in his own interest; a subject obeys the orders of the sovereign power, given for the common interest, wherein he is included.

I think I have now shown sufficiently clearly the basis of a democracy: I have especially desired to do so, for I believe it to be of all forms of government the most natural, and the most consonant with individual liberty. In it no one transfers his natural right so absolutely that he has no further voice in affairs, he only hands it over to the majority of a society, whereof he is a unit. Thus all men remain, as they were in the state of nature, equals.

This is the only form of government which I have treated of at length, for it is the one most akin to my purpose of showing the benefits of freedom in a state.

I may pass over the fundamental principles of other forms of government, for we may gather from what has been said whence their right arises without going into its origin. The possessor of sovereign power, whether he be one, or many, or the whole body politic, has the sovereign right of imposing any commands he pleases: and he who has either voluntarily, or under compulsion, transferred the right to defend him to another, has, in so doing, renounced his natural right and is therefore bound to obey, in all things, the commands of the sovereign power; and will be bound so to do so long as the king, or nobles, or the people preserve the sovereign power which formed the basis of the original transfer. I need add no more.

The bases and rights of dominion being thus displayed, we shall readily be able to define private civil right, wrong, justice, and injustice, with their relations to the state; and also to determine what constitutes an ally, or an enemy, or the crime of treason.

By private civil right we can only mean the liberty every man possesses to preserve his existence, a liberty limited by the edicts of the sovereign power, and preserved only by its authority: for when a man has transferred to another his right of living as he likes, which was only limited by his power, that is, has transferred his liberty and power of self-defence, he is bound to live as that other dictates, and to trust to him entirely for his defence. Wrong takes place when a citizen, or subject, is forced by another to undergo some loss or pain in contradiction to the authority of the law, or the edict of the sovereign power.

Wrong is conceivable only in an organized community: nor can it ever accrue to subjects from any act of the sovereign, who has the right to do what he likes. It can only arise, therefore, between private persons, who are bound by law and right not to injure one another. Justice consists in the habitual rendering to every man his lawful due: injustice consists in depriving a man, under the pretence of legality, of what the laws, rightly interpreted, would allow him. These last are also called equity and iniquity, because those who administer the laws are bound to show no respect of persons, but to account all men equal, and to defend every man's right equally, neither envying the rich nor despising the poor.

The men of two states become allies, when for the sake of avoiding war, or for some other advantage, they covenant to do each other no hurt, but on the contrary, to assist each other if necessity arises, each retaining his independence. Such a covenant is valid so long as its basis of danger or advantage is in force: no one enters into an engagement, or is bound to stand by his compacts unless there be a hope of some accruing good, or the fear of some evil: if this basis be removed the compact thereby becomes void: this has been abundantly shown by experience. For although different states make treaties not to harm one another, they always take every possible precaution against such treaties being broken by the stronger party, and do not rely on the compact, unless there is a sufficiently obvious object and advantage to both parties in observing it. Otherwise they would fear a breach of faith, nor would there be any wrong done thereby: for who in his proper senses, and aware of the right of the sovereign power, would trust in the promises of one who has the will and the power to do what he likes, and who aims solely at the safety and advantage of his dominion? Moreover, if we consult loyalty and religion, we shall see that no one in possession of power ought to abide by his promises to the injury of his dominion; for he cannot keep such promises without breaking the engagement he made with his subjects, by which both he and they are most solemnly bound.

An enemy is one who lives apart from the state, and does not recognize its authority either as a subject or as an ally. It is not hatred which makes a man an enemy, but the rights of the state. The rights of the state are the same in regard to him who does not recognize by any compact the state authority, as they are against him who has done the state an injury: it has the right to force him as best it can, either to submit, or to contract an alliance.

Lastly, treason can only be committed by subjects, who by compact, either tacit or expressed, have transferred all their rights to the state: a subject is said to have committed this crime when he has attempted, for whatever reason, to seize the sovereign power, or to place it in different hands. I say, *has attempted*, for if punishment were not to overtake him till he had succeeded, it would often come too late, the sovereign rights would have been acquired or transferred already.

I also say, *has attempted, for whatever reason, to seize the sovereign power*, and I recognize no difference whether such an attempt should be followed by public loss or public gain. Whatever be his reason for acting, the crime is treason, and he is rightly condemned: in war, everyone would admit the justice of his sentence. If a man does not keep to his post, but approaches the enemy without the knowledge of his commander, whatever may be his motive, so long as he acts on his own motion, even if he advances with the design of defeating the enemy, he is rightly put to death, because he has violated his oath, and infringed the rights of his commander. That all citizens are equally bound by these rights in time of peace, is not so generally recognized, but the reasons for obedience are in both cases, identical. The state must be preserved and directed by the sole authority of the sovereign, and such authority and right have been accorded by universal consent to him alone: if, therefore, anyone else attempts, without his consent, to execute any public enterprise, even though the state might (as we said) reap benefit therefrom, such person has none the less infringed the sovereign's right, and would be rightly punished for treason.

In order that every scruple may be removed, we may now answer the inquiry, whether our former assertion that everyone who has not the practice of reason, may, in the state of nature, live by sovereign natural right, according to the laws of his desires, is not in direct opposition to the law and right of God as revealed. For as all men absolutely (whether they be less endowed with reason or more) are equally bound by the Divine command to love their neighbour as themselves, it may be said that they cannot, without wrong, do injury to anyone, or live according to their desires.

This objection, so far as the state of nature is concerned, can be easily answered, for the state of nature is, both in nature and in time, prior to religion. No one knows by nature that he owes any obedience to God, nor can he attain thereto by any exercise of his reason, but solely by revelation confirmed by signs. Therefore, previous to revelation, no one is bound by a Divine law and right of which he is necessarily in ignorance. The state of nature must by no means be confounded with a state of religion, but must be conceived as without either religion or law, and consequently without sin or wrong: this is how we have described it, and we are confirmed by the authority of Paul. It is not only in respect of ignorance that we conceive the state of nature as prior to, and lacking the Divine revealed law and right; but in respect of freedom also, wherewith all men are born endowed.

If men were naturally bound by the Divine law and right, or if the Divine law and right were a natural necessity, there would have been no need for God to make a covenant with mankind, and to bind them thereto with an oath and agreement.

We must, then, fully grant that the Divine law and right originated at the time when men by express covenant agreed to obey God in all things, and ceded, as it were, their natural freedom, transferring their rights to God in the manner described in speaking of the formation of a state.

However, I will treat of these matters more at length presently.

It may be insisted that sovereigns are as much bound by the Divine law as subjects: whereas we have asserted that they retain their natural rights, and may do whatever they like.

In order to clear up the whole difficulty, which arises rather concerning the natural right than the natural state, I maintain that everyone is bound, in the state of nature, to live according to Divine law, in the same way as he is bound to fire according to the dictates of sound reason; namely, inasmuch as it is to his advantage, and necessary for his salvation; but, if he will not so live, he may do otherwise at his own risk. He is thus bound to live according to his own laws, not according to anyone else's, and to recognize no man as a judge, or as a superior in religion. Such, in my opinion, is the position of a sovereign, for he may take advice from his fellow-men, but he is not bound to recognize any as a judge, nor anyone besides himself as an arbitrator on any question of right, unless it be a prophet sent expressly by God and attesting his mission by indisputable signs. Even then he does not recognize a man, but God Himself as His judge.

If a sovereign refuses to obey God as revealed in His law, he does so at his own risk and loss, but without violating any civil or natural right. For the civil right is dependent on his own decree; and natural right is dependent on the laws of nature, which latter are not adapted to religion, whose sole aim is the good of humanity, but to the order of nature— that is, to God's eternal decree unknown to us.

This truth seems to be adumbrated in a somewhat obscurer form by those who maintain that men can sin against God's revelation, but not against the eternal decree by which He has ordained all things.

We may be asked, what should we do if the sovereign commands anything contrary to religion, and the obedience which we have expressly vowed to God? should we obey the Divine law or the human law? I shall treat of this question at length hereafter, and will therefore merely say now, that God should be obeyed before all else, when we have a certain and indisputable revelation of His will: but men are very prone to error on religious subjects, and, according to the diversity of their dispositions, are wont with considerable stir to put forward their own inventions, as experience more than sufficiently attests, so that if no one were bound to obey the state in matters which, in his own opinion concern religion, the rights of the state would be dependent on every man's judgment and passions. No one would consider himself bound to obey laws framed against his faith or superstition; and on this pretext he might assume unbounded license. In this way, the rights of the civil authorities would be utterly set at nought, so that we must conclude that the sovereign power, which alone is bound both by Divine and natural right to preserve and guard the laws of the state, should have supreme authority for making any laws about religion which it thinks fit; all are bound to obey its behests on the subject in accordance with their promise which God bids them to keep.

However, if the sovereign power be heathen, we should either enter into no engagements therewith, and yield up our lives sooner than transfer to it any of our rights; or, if the engagement be made, and our rights transferred, we should (inasmuch as we should have ourselves transferred the right of defending ourselves and our religion) be bound to obey them, and to keep our word: we might even rightly be bound so to do, except in those cases where God, by indisputable revelation, has promised His special aid against tyranny, or given us special exemption from obedience. Thus we see that, of all the Jews in Babylon, there were only three youths who were certain of the help of God, and, therefore, refused to obey Nebuchadnezzar. All the rest, with the sole exception of Daniel, who was beloved by the king, were doubtless compelled by right to obey, perhaps thinking that they had been delivered up by God into the hands of the king, and that the king had obtained and preserved his dominion by God's design. On the other hand, Eleazar, before his country had utterly fallen, wished to give a proof of his constancy to his compatriots, in order that they might follow in his footsteps, and go to any lengths, rather than allow their right and power to be transferred to the Greeks, or brave any torture rather than swear allegiance to the heathen. Instances are occurring every day in confirmation of what I here advance. The rulers of Christian kingdoms do not hesitate, with a view to strengthening their dominion, to make treaties with Turks and heathen, and to give orders to their subjects who settle among such peoples not to assume more freedom, either in things secular or religious, than is set down in the treaty, or allowed by the foreign government. We may see this exemplified in the Dutch treaty with the Japanese, which I have already mentioned.

CHAPTER XX

That in a Free State Every Man May Think What He Likes, and Say What He Thinks.

IF men's minds were as easily controlled as their tongues, every king would sit safely on his throne, and government by compulsion would cease; for every subject would shape his life according to the intentions of his rulers, and would esteem a thing true or false, good or evil, just or unjust, in obedience to their dictates. However, we have shown already (Chapter XVII) that no man's mind can possibly lie wholly at the disposition of another, for no one can willingly transfer his natural right of free reason and judgment, or be compelled so to do. For this reason government which attempts to control minds is accounted tyrannical, and it is considered an abuse of sovereignty and a usurpation of the rights of subjects, to seek to prescribe what shall be accepted as true, or rejected as false, or what opinions should actuate men in their worship of God. All these questions fall within a man's natural right, which he cannot abdicate even with his own consent.

I admit that the judgment can be biased in many ways, and to an almost incredible degree, so that while exempt from direct external control it may be so dependent on another man's words, that it may fitly be said to be ruled by him; but although this influence is carried to great lengths, it has never gone so far as to invalidate the statement, that every man's understanding is his own, and that brains are as diverse as palates.

Moses, not by fraud, but by Divine virtue, gained such a hold over the popular judgment that he was accounted superhuman, and believed to speak and act through the inspiration of the Deity; nevertheless, even he could not escape murmurs and evil interpretations. How much less then can other monarchs avoid them! Yet such unlimited power, if it exists at all, must belong to a monarch, and least of all to a democracy, where the whole or a great part of the people wield authority collectively. This is a fact which I think everyone can explain for himself.

However unlimited, therefore, the power of a sovereign may be, however implicitly it is trusted as the exponent of law and religion, it can never prevent men from forming judgments according to their intellect, or being influenced by any given emotion. It is true that it has the right to treat as enemies all men whose opinions do not, on all sub-jects, entirely coincide with its own; but we are not discussing its strict rights, but its proper course of action. I grant that it has the right to rule in the most violent manner, and to put citizens to death for very trivial causes, but no one supposes it can do this with the approval of sound judgment. Nay, inasmuch as such things cannot be done without extreme peril to itself, we may even deny that it has the absolute power to do them, or, consequently, the absolute right; for the rights of the sovereign are limited by his power.

Since, therefore, no one can abdicate his freedom of judgment and feeling; since every man is by indefeasible natural right the master of his own thoughts, it follows that men thinking in diverse and contradictory fashions, cannot, without disastrous results, be com-pelled to speak only according to the dictates of the supreme power. Not even the most experienced, to say nothing of the multitude, know how to keep silence. Men's common failing is to confide their plans to others, though there be need for secrecy, so that a gov-ernment would be most harsh which deprived the individual of his freedom of saying and teaching what he thought; and would be moderate if such freedom were granted. Still we cannot deny that authority may be as much injured by words as by actions; hence, although the freedom we are discussing cannot be entirely denied to subjects, its unlimited concession would be most baneful; we must, therefore, now inquire, how far such freedom can and ought to be conceded without danger to the peace of the state, or the power of the rulers; and this, as I said at the beginning of Chapter XVI, is my principal object.

It follows, plainly, from the explanation given above, of the foundations of a state, that the ultimate aim of government is not to rule, or restrain, by fear, nor to exact obedience, but contrariwise, to free every man from fear, that he may live in all possible security; in other words, to strengthen his natural right to exist and work without injury to himself or others.

No, the object of government is not to change men from rational beings into beasts or puppets, but to enable them to develop their minds and bodies in security, and to employ their reason unshackled; neither showing hatred, anger, or deceit, nor watched with the eyes of jealousy and injustice. In fact, the true aim of government is liberty.

Now we have seen that in forming a state the power of making laws must either be vested in the body of the citizens, or in a portion of them, or in one man. For, although men's free judgments are very diverse, each one thinking that he alone knows everything, and although complete unanimity of feeling and speech is out of the question, it is impos-sible to preserve peace, unless individuals abdicate their right of acting entirely on their own judgment. Therefore, the individual justly cedes the right of free action, though not of free reason and judgment; no one can act against the authorities without danger to the state, though his feelings and judgment may be at varience therewith; he may even speak against them, provided that he does so from rational conviction, not from fraud, anger, or hatred, and provided that he does not attempt to introduce any change on his private authority.

For instance, supposing a man shows that a law is repugnant to sound reason, and should therefore be repealed; if he submits his opinion to the judgment of the authorities (who, alone, have the right of making and repealing laws), and meanwhile acts in nowise contrary to that law, he has deserved well of the state, and has behaved as a good citizen should; but if he accuses the authorities of injustice, and stirs up the people against them, or if he seditiously strives to abrogate the law without their consent, he is a mere agitator and rebel.

Thus we see how an individual may declare and teach what he believes, without injury to the authority of his rulers, or to the public peace; namely, by leaving in their hands the entire power of legislation as it affects action, and by doing nothing against their laws, though he be compelled often to act in contradiction to what he believes, and openly feels, to be best.

Such a course can be taken without detriment to justice and dutifulness, nay, it is the one which a just and dutiful man would adopt. We have shown that justice is dependent on the laws of the authorities, so that no one who contravenes their accepted decrees can be just, while the highest regard for duty, as we have pointed out in the preceding chapter, is exercised in maintaining public peace and tranquillity; these could not be preserved if every man were to live as he pleased; therefore it is no less than undutiful for a man to act contrary to his country's laws, for if the practice became universal the ruin of states would necessarily follow.

Hence, so long as a man acts in obedience to the laws of his rulers, he in nowise contravenes his reason, for in obedience to reason he transferred the right of controlling his actions from his own hands to theirs. This doctrine we can confirm from actual custom, for in a conference of great and small powers, schemes are seldom carried unanimously, yet all unite in carrying out what is decided on, whether they voted for or against. But I return to my proposition.

From the fundamental notions of a state, we have discovered how a man may exercise free judgment without detriment to the supreme power: from the same premises we can no less easily determine what opinions would be seditious. Evidently those which by their very nature nullify the compact by which the right of free action was ceded. For instance, a man who holds that the supreme power has no rights over him, or that promises ought not to be kept, or that everyone should live as he pleases, or other doctrines of this nature in direct opposition to the above-mentioned contract, is seditious, not so much from his actual opinions and judgment, as from the deeds which they involve; for he who maintains such theories abrogates the contract which tacitly, or openly, he made with his rulers. Other opinions which do not involve acts violating the contract, such as revenge, anger, and the like, are not seditious, unless it be in some corrupt state, where superstitious and ambitious persons, unable to endure men of learning, are so popular with the multitude that their word is more valued than the law.

However, I do not deny that there are some doctrines which, while they are apparently only concerned with abstract truths and falsehoods, are yet propounded and published with unworthy motives. This question we have discussed in Chapter XV, and shown that reason should nevertheless remain unshackled. If we hold to the principle that a man's loyalty to the state should be judged, like his loyalty to God, from his actions only—namely, from his charity towards his neighbours; we cannot doubt that the best government will allow freedom of philosophical speculation no less than of religious belief. I confess that from such freedom inconveniences may sometimes arise, but what question was ever settled so wisely that no abuses could possibly spring therefrom? He who seeks to regulate everything by law, is more likely to arouse vices than to reform them. It is best to grant what cannot be abolished, even though it be in itself harmful. How many evils spring from luxury, envy, avarice, drunkenness, and the like, yet these are tolerated—vices as they are—because they cannot be prevented by legal enactments. How much more then should free thought be granted, seeing that it is in itself a virtue and that it cannot be crushed! Besides, the evil results can easily be checked, as I will show, by the secular authorities, not to mention that such freedom is absolutely necessary for progress in science and the liberal arts: for no man follows such pursuits to advantage unless his judgment be entirely free and unhampered.

But let it be granted that freedom may be crushed, and men be so bound down, that they do not dare to utter a whisper, save at the bidding of their rulers; nevertheless this can never be carried to the pitch of making them think according to authority, so that the necessary consequences would be that men would daily be thinking one thing and saying another, to the corruption of good faith, that mainstay of government, and to the fostering of hateful flattery and perfidy, whence spring stratagems, and the corruption of every good art.

It is far from possible to impose uniformity of speech, for the more rulers strive to curtail freedom of speech, the more obstinately are they resisted; not indeed by the avaricious, the flatterers, and other numskulls, who think supreme salvation consists in filling their stomachs and gloating over their money-bags, but by those whom good education, sound morality, and virtue have rendered more free. Men, as generally constituted, are most prone to resent the branding as criminal of opinions which they believe to be true, and the prescription as wicked of that which inspires them with piety towards God and man; hence they are ready to forswear the laws and conspire against the authorities, thinking it not shameful but honourable to stir up seditions and perpetuate any sort of crime with this end in view. Such being the constitution of human nature, we see that laws directed against opinions affect the generous-minded rather than the wicked, and are adapted less for coercing criminals than for irritating the upright; so that they cannot be maintained without great peril to the state.

Moreover, such laws are almost always useless, for those who hold that the opinions proscribed are sound, cannot possibly obey the law; whereas those who already reject them as false, accept the law as a kind of privilege, and make such boast of it, that authority is powerless to repeal it, even if such a course be subsequently desired.

To these considerations may be added what we said in Chapter XVIII in treating of the history of the Hebrews. And, lastly, how many schisms have arisen in the Church from the attempt of the authorities to decide by law the intricacies of theological controversy! If men were not allured by the hope of getting the law and the authorities on their side, of triumphing over their adversaries in the sight of an applauding multitude, and of acquiring honourable distinctions, they would not strive so maliciously, nor would such fury sway their minds. This is taught not only by reason but by daily examples, for laws of this kind prescribing what every man shall believe and forbidding anyone to speak or write to the contrary, have often been passed, as sops or concessions to the anger of those who cannot tolerate men of enlightenment, and who, by such harsh and crooked enactments, can easily turn the devotion of the masses into fury and direct it against whom they will.

How much better would it be to restrain popular anger and fury, instead of passing useless laws, which can only be broken by those who love virtue and the liberal arts, thus paring down the state till it is too small to harbour men of talent. What greater misfortune for a state can be conceived than that honourable men should be sent like criminals into exile, because they hold diverse opinions which they cannot disguise? What, I say, can be more hurtful than that men who have committed no crime or wickedness should, simply because they are enlightened, be treated as enemies and put to death, and that the scaffold, the terror of evil-doers, should become the arena where the highest examples of tolerance and virtue are displayed to the people with all the marks of ignominy that authority can devise?

He that knows himself to be upright does not fear the death of a criminal, and shrinks from no punishment; his mind is not wrung with remorse for any disgraceful deed: he holds that death in a good cause is no punishment, but an honour, and that death for freedom is glory.

What purpose then is served by the death of such men, what example is proclaimed? The cause for which they die is unknown to the idle and the foolish, hateful to the turbulent, loved by the upright. The only lesson we can draw from such scenes is to flatter the persecutor, or else to imitate the victim.

If formal assent is not to be esteemed above conviction, and if governments are to retain a firm hold of authority and not be compelled to yield to agitators, it is imperative that freedom of judgment should be granted, so that men may live together in harmony, however diverse, or even openly contradictory their opinions may be. We cannot doubt that such is the best system of government and open to the fewest objections, since it is the one most in harmony with human nature. In a democracy (the most natural form of government, as we have shown in Chapter XVI) everyone submits to the control of authority over his actions, but not over his judgment and reason; that is, seeing that all cannot think alike, the voice of the majority has the force of law, subject to repeal if circumstances bring about a change of opinion. In proportion as the power of free judgment is withheld we depart from the natural condition of mankind, and consequently the government becomes more tyrannical.

In order to prove that from such freedom no inconvenience arises, which cannot easily be checked by the exercise of the sovereign power, and that men's actions can easily be kept in bounds, though their opinions be at open varience, it will be well to cite an example. Such an one is not very far to seek. The city of Amsterdam reaps the fruit of this freedom in its own great prosperity and in the admiration of all other people. For in this most flourishing state, and most splendid city, men of every nation and religion live together in the greatest harmony, and ask no questions before trusting their goods to a fellow-citizen, save whether he be rich or poor, and whether he generally acts honestly, or the reverse. His religion and sect is considered of no importance: for it has no effect before the judges in gaining or losing a cause, and there is no sect so despised that its followers, provided that they harm no one, pay every man his due, and live uprightly, are deprived of the protection of the magisterial authority.

On the other hand, when the religious controversy between Remonstrants and Counter-Remonstrants began to be taken up by politicians and the States, it grew into a schism, and abundantly showed that laws dealing with religion and seeking to settle its controversies are much more calculated to irritate than to reform, and that they give rise to extreme licence: further, it was seen that schisms do not originate in a love of truth, which is a source of courtesy and gentleness, but rather in an inordinate desire for supremacy. From all these considerations it is clearer than the sun at noonday, that the true schismatics are those who condemn other men's writings, and seditiously stir up the quarrelsome masses against their authors, rather than those authors themselves, who generally write only for the learned, and appeal solely to reason. In fact, the real disturbers of the peace are those who, in a free state, seek to curtail the liberty of judgment which they are unable to tyrannize over.

I have thus shown:—I. That it is impossible to deprive men of the liberty of saying what they think. II. That such liberty can be conceded to every man without injury to the rights and authority of the sovereign power, and that every man may retain it without injury to such rights, provided that he does not presume upon it to the extent of introducing any new rights into the state, or acting in any way contrary to the existing laws. III. That every man may enjoy this liberty without detriment to the public peace, and that no inconveniences arise therefrom which cannot easily be checked. IV. That every man may enjoy it without injury to his allegiance. V. That laws dealing with speculative problems are entirely useless. VI. Lastly, that not only may such liberty be granted without prejudice to the public peace, to loyalty, and to the rights of rulers, but that it is even necessary for their preservation. For when people try to take it away, and bring to trial not only the acts which alone are capable of offending, but also the opinions of mankind, they only succeed in surrounding their victims with an appearance of martyrdom, and raise feelings of pity and revenge rather than of terror. Uprightness and good faith are thus corrupted, flatterers and traitors are encouraged, and sectarians triumph, inasmuch as concessions have been made to their animosity, and they have gained the state sanction for the doctrines of which they are the interpreters. Hence they arrogate to themselves the state authority and rights, and do not scruple to assert that they have been directly chosen by God, and that their laws are Divine, whereas the laws of the state are human, and should therefore yield obedience to the laws of God—in other words, to their own laws. Everyone must see that this is not a state of affairs conducive to public welfare. Wherefore, as we have shown in Chapter XVIII, the safest way for a state is to lay down the rule that religion is comprised solely in the exercise of charity and justice, and that the rights of rulers in sacred, no less than in secular matters, should merely have to do with actions, but that every man should think what he likes and say what he thinks.

I have thus fulfilled the task I set myself in this treatise. It remains only to call attention to the fact that I have written nothing which I do not most willingly submit to the examination and approval of my country's rulers; and that I am willing to retract anything which they shall decide to be repugnant to the laws, or prejudicial to the public good. I know that I am a man, and as a man liable to error, but against error I have taken scrupulous care, and have striven to keep in entire accordance with the laws of my country, with loyalty, and with morality.

JOHN LOCKE

John Locke (1632–1704)—philosopher, political theorist, educational theorist, political economist, scholar, statesman, and sometime physician—is one of the leading figures in the history of English letters. His friends, and enemies, included the most prominent scientists, literary figures, theologians, and politicians of his day.

Locke was born in the village of Wrington, Somerset, and was immediately surrounded by the political and religious controverises that were always to be at the center of his life. His parents were Puritans, and the parish priest who baptized him was one of the few Puritan ministers of the diocese who had survived the local bishop's attempts to drive Calvinism from the established church. It is impossible to understand Locke and the politics of seventeeth-century England without constant reference to the existence of the Church of England as the state-church. The most persistent feature of the English political landscape in the early modern period is continuing disputes about the organization of that church, its relationship to the other aspects of the life of English society, and the social and political standing of those who dissented from the Anglican establishment.

When the civil war broke out, Locke's father fought on Parliament's side in the Somerset cavalry. His reward was the admission of his son to the Westminster School in 1647. In November 1652, Locke moved to Christ Church, Oxford, the most important of the university's colleges, from which he was graduated bachelor of arts in 1655. He became master of arts three years later, and was then elected to a senior studentship (equivalent to a renewable fellowship) at Christ Church. Although he was seldom in residence after 1666, Locke retained his affiliation with Christ Church until 1683, when his presumed political activities led to his expulsion on orders from the Court. By that time, Locke, sensibly fearing for his safety, had fled to the Netherlands where he would live in exile for the next six years.

Locke met and entered the service and household of Anthony Ashley Cooper, the future Earl of Shaftesbury and one of the most powerful and important political figures of the Restoration, in 1666, the year of the famous fire that destroyed much of London. Locke became Shaftesbury's confidant, chief advisor, and assistant, as well as a friend. Over the course of the next fifteen or so years, Locke was elected to the relatively new Royal Society; traveled with, attended, and advised Shaftesbury on various personal and public matters as the latter's political fortunes rapidly rose and with equal speed plummeted, and saw to the education and marriage of Shaftesbury's son; served for a time as a member of the board of trade; invested in a new company of merchants that Shaftesbury had organized under a royal license to trade with the Bahamas; and traveled widely in France. It was also during this period that Locke wrote and revised much of the work for which he is best known by philosophers, the *Essay Concerning Human Understanding* (completed during Locke's Dutch exile and published in 1690), in which he set forth what is loosely an "empiricist" theory of knowledge.

Anti-Catholicism is a leitmotiv of English history from the Reformation until well into the nineteenth century. Since 1689, Catholics have been prohibited from holding the throne. Ten years earlier, Shaftesbury began an unsuccessful constitutional campaign to "exclude" the Roman Catholic James Duke of York from the succession. Charles II had no legitimate children, and his brother James was next in line, a prospect that Shaftesbury and his "Whig" cohorts feared. The *Two Treatises* appear to have been conceived as part of Shaftesbury's exclusion activities and were written in the early 1680s. It is likely that Shaftesbury's intention was to call the country to revolution if exclusion failed. After exclusion in fact was defeated, it was believed that Shaftesbury was masterminding a plot to overthrow the king. He left England before he could be apprehended—Locke followed a few months later—but a number of his alleged confederates was tried and executed.

Thus, Locke did not publish the *Two Treatises* until his return from exile in 1689—when it was issued anonymously—in the interim making several changes in the text and adding a preface that attempted to relate the book to the events of 1688 to 1689 and the transfer of the throne from the Catholic James II to his Protestant son-in-law and daughter, William and Mary of the Netherlands, in the "Bloodless Revolution."

The first of the *Treatises* is a detailed reply to the writings of Sir Robert Filmer, a divine-right royalist of the civil war and interregnum period, who is best known today for his *Patriarcha*. Filmer's claim that political authority is derived from God's grant of paternal (or "patriarchal") power to Adam was among the principal ingredients in the antiexclusion ideology of the 1680s. Locke's "Second Treatise" is a more consistently theoretical work than the "First," and it is there that he develops his central political and social doctrines.

We know little of the genesis of the *Letter Concerning Toleration* other than that Locke had been interested in the general subject since 1660 to 1661 and that it was completed—if not actually written—during his exile in the Netherlands, where his friends included some of the most important advocates of religious liberty. The *Letter* was composed in Latin and first published, also anonymously, in Amsterdam in 1689. It was almost immediately translated into English by the Socinian William Popple and published in London in 1690. Popple added a preface "To the Reader" that was rather more radical than the book itself appeared to be, but his translation was faithful to Locke's text. The *Letter* generated some criticism, and Locke left a final defense unfinished at his death on October 28, 1704, in the Essex home of his friends, Lord Francis and Lady Demaris Masham.

In the *Two Treatises* and the *Letter Concerning Toleration*, Locke showed himself to be an unfailing enemy of tyranny and oppression and an outspoken defender of liberty. The two works together show the centrality of religious freedom to his conception of politics and civil society. The *Two Treatises* is a bold call for revolution when the rights and liberties of the "people" have been illegitimately abridged, and *Toleration* makes it clear that the entitlement to practice the religion of one's choice without compromising the public peace and safety is paramount among those rights and liberties.

The job of government, according to Locke, is to preserve the peace and to protect and further the "natural rights" of the members of civil society and to do so in accord with natural and positive law. It is *entrusted* with this task and the power necessary to perform it by the direct grant or consent of the members of civil society in their movement from the pre- and apolitical state of nature to the world of political society. When the governors fail to rule according to law and for the "public good"—that is, when they promote some interest other than that of the public (usually their own) or when they curtail rights and liberties without warrant—they break that trust. Such behavior is the absolute and arbitrary rule defended by Filmer and other royalists as the only possible form of government and which Locke said was "no Form of Civil Government at all" (*Two Treatises*, II, Sec. 90; see also Secs. 137 and 174). When confronted by the tyranny of absolute rule, the "people" in their individual and collective capacities were permitted to reassert their natural and original powers. Ultimately, the determination of whether the trust had been abused and therefore ought to be revoked belonged, Locke said, to "any single man" (II, Sec. 168; see also II, Secs. 203, 207, and 241).

This apparently anarchic doctrine, rather like the doctrine of trust itself, is an instance of Locke's deep and realistic understanding of the nature and limits of both politics and philosophy. The right of individual resistance was hemmed in on all sides: would-be revolutionaries were obliged to consult the law of nature, to confer with their neighbors, to examine their consciences, and to be certain that the tumult they might create was not worse than the wrong they were remedying before launching what Locke called the "appeal to Heaven" (II, Secs. 20, 21, 168, 176, etc.). Even then, they were restrained by the forbearance and patience that were natural to humans and by the knowledge that in the next life they would have to answer to "a Tribunal that cannot be deceived" (II, Sec. 176).

Behind all this was Locke's theory of the state of nature, his conception of natural rights, and the doctrine of "property," for which he is probably best known today.

The state of nature was one of the established conventions of political theory by the time that Locke wrote his *Two Treatises*. It functioned as a means of accounting for the origins of government by depicting life without the benefits of organized politics and of revealing the relationship of government to human nature. Thus, the state of nature is often seen as a quasi-anthropological, reductionist hypothesis that was not asserted empirically. For Locke, it was also an important part of the polemic against Filmer's insistence that the Bible demonstrated that humans had always been subjected to government. Whether he took it seriously as anthropological reality is an open question, but the concept itself was essential to his defense of human liberty.

In the state of nature, according to Locke, there was no ownership of material possessions; everything was part of the common stock that God had provided to enable people to live. But each person did possess his or her own body and a number of natural rights, including the right to remove from this bounty of God and nature whatever was necessary to sustain life. This was done by "mixing" one's labor with what was common, thereby making it one's "property." The only limitations were that it was impermissible to appropriate more than could be used before it spoiled, and that "enough and as good" had to be left for the benefit of others (II, Secs. 31 and 33). Eventually, people became more efficient appropriators, discovered barter, and subsequently "consented" to the use of money (II, Sec. 37), which together allowed them to overcome these restrictions. All this eventually gave rise to an inegalitarian and very complex social and economic order that, Locke argued, did not violate the natural equality and liberty established by God and still was not political. For the state of nature was governed only by law of nature, "And Reason, which is that Law," could be understood by all rational adults who chose to exercise their capacities to reason (II, Sec. 6).

When it became difficult to sustain this elaborate society without formal, overarching authority, people consented to the establishment of government, the better to protect their properties and lives. They ceded to the government the power to punish wrongdoers that they had from the law of nature. Thus, the ends of government were never very far from the rights of property. When Locke talked about "property" in the state of nature—generally, before II, Section 52—he meant external goods and material possessions, which is fairly close to the most common twentieth-century meaning. But when he used the term in the context of civil society, he meant "life, liberty, and estate." This more-expansive conception introduces some puzzles into any attempt to account for the relationship of civil society to the state of nature, but it preserves the connection between the protection of property and political obligation that is one of the foundations of Locke's political theory. The Lockean formula is deceptive in its apparent simplicity: The members of civil society are those with "property"; so long as their "property" is protected by the government, people are bound to obey; the violation of their "property" by the ruler constitutes grounds for resistance. But we must not allow the words alone to beguile us into thinking—as a number of commentators have argued—that Locke's is a "bourgeois" defense of the rights of a property-owning class.

The *Letter Concerning Toleration* can be viewed in large part as a specific application of the principles of the *Two Treatises*. In the latter work, Locke advanced a conception of the magistrate as bound by the "common good," argued that the collapse of a commonwealth in which there was an attempt to impose religious uniformity would be the fault of the magistrate and not of those who resisted the imposition, and cautioned his readers by reminding them of the tribunal of God to which everyone is accountable, even though some cannot be judged by any earthly powers. What was innovative and radical about the *Letter* was the argument that religious imposition went so far beyond the legitimate competence of the magistrate as to be a ground of resistance. Locke accomplished this move by drawing a firm distinction between the secular ends of magistracy and the religious ends of churches. In doing so, he made a bolder move toward genuine religious liberty than any of his contemporaries.

Religion was a concern of civil society's—and, hence, of the magistrate's—only when particular sects preached doctrines that were "contrary to human Society, or to those moral Rules which are necessary to the preservation of Civil Society," in which case such sects were not to be tolerated. In these cases—such as Roman Catholics, whose first allegiance—was to the Pope (who claimed the power to excommunicate rulers and to discharge subjects from their duties to obey), and atheists, whose word could not be trusted—Locke claimed, toleration was denied not to religious beliefs or practices but to their deleterious consequences. Everyone else was to enjoy a full religious toleration, and Locke was confident that people with diverse religious beliefs could live at peace within one civil society.

The standard, general biography of Locke, despite many shortcomings, remains Maurice Cranston, *John Locke: A Biography* (New York: Macmillan, 1957), which should be supplemented by Ian Harris, *The Mind of John Locke:*

A study of Political Theory in Its Intellectual Setting (Cambridge: Cambridge University Press, 1994). There is no general, comprehensive work on Locke that treats his political theory along with his philosophy. However, Michael Ayers, *Locke: Epistemology and Ontology*, 2 vols. (London: Routledge, 1991), does include an extensive discussion of his ethical and natural law theories. The fullest and most reliable *historical* accounts of his political thought are John Dunn, *The Political Thought of John Locke* (Cambridge: Cambridge University Press, 1969), and John Marshall, *John Locke: Resistance, Religion, and Responsibility* (Cambridge: Cambridge University Press, 1994). Dunn has also contributed a most accessible, brief, general overview to the Past Masters Series: *Locke* (Oxford: Oxford University Press, 1984). Locke's theory of property is treated in James H. Tully, *A Discourse on Property: John Locke and His Adversaries* (Cambridge: Cambridge University Press, 1980), and Neal Wood, *John Locke and Agrarian Capitalism* (Berkeley: University of California Press, 1984). The attack on Filmer is put into a larger theoretical and historical context in Gordon Schochet, *Patriarchalism in Political Thought* (Oxford: Blackwell, 1975; 2d ed., New Brunswick, NJ: Transaction Books, 1988). Two works by A. John Simmons examine Locke's political thought and some of its implications from a nonhistorical, contemporary, philosophic perspective: *The Lockean Theory of Rights* (Princeton: Princeton University Press, 1992), and *On the Edge of Anarchy* (Princeton: Princeton University Press, 1994).

For the *Letter Concerning Toleration*, which has not attracted nearly the attention it deserves, see the essays in John Horton and Susan Mendus, eds., *John Locke: A Letter Concerning Toleration in Focus* (London: Routledge, 1991), and two articles by Gordon Schochet: "Toleration, Revolution, and Judgment in the Development of Locke's Political Thought," *Political Science*, Vol. 40 (August 1988), and "John Locke and Religious Toleration," in *The Glorious Revolution: Changing Perspectives*, Lois G. Schwoerer, ed. (Cambridge: Cambridge University Press, 1992).

G. S.

SECOND TREATISE OF GOVERNMENT

CHAPTER I

1. It having been strewn in the foregoing discourse,

1. That Adam had not, either by natural right of fatherhood, or by positive donation from God, any such authority over his children, or dominion over the world, as is pretended:

2. That if he had, his heirs, yet, had no right to it:

3. That if his heirs had, there being no law of nature, nor positive law of God, that determines, which is the right heir in all cases that may arise, the right of succession, and consequently of bearing rule, could not have been certainly determined:

4. That if even that had been determined, yet the knowledge of which is the eldest line of Adam's posterity, being so long since utterly lost, that in the races of mankind and families of the world, there remains not to one above another the least presence to be the eldest house, and to have the right of inheritance:

All these premises having, as I think, been clearly made out, it is impossible that the rulers now on earth, should make any benefit, or derive any the least shadow of authority from that, which is held to be the fountain of all power, *Adam's private dominion and paternal jurisdiction;* so that he that will not give just occasion to think that all government in the world is the product only of force and violence, and that men live together by no other rules but that of beasts, where the strongest carries it, and so lay a foundation for perpetual disorder and mischief, tumult, sedition, and rebellion (things that the followers of that hypothesis so loudly cry out against) must of necessity find out another rise of government, another original of political power, and another way of designing and knowing the persons that have it, than what Sir Robert Filmer hath taught us.

2. To this purpose, I think it may not be amiss, to set down what I take to be political power; that the power of a *magistrate* over a subject may be distinguished from that of a *father* over his children, a *master* over his servant, a *husband* over his *wife,* and a *lord* over his slave. All which distinct powers happening sometimes together in the same man, if he be considered under these different relations, it may help us to distinguish these powers one from another, and shew the difference betwixt a ruler of a commonwealth, a father of a family, and a captain of a galley.

3. *Political power,* then, I take to be a *right* of making laws and penalties of death, and consequently all less penalties for the regulating and preserving of property, and of employing the force of the community, in the execution of such laws, and in the defence of the commonwealth from foreign injury; and all this only for the public good.

CHAPTER II

Of the State of Nature

4. To understand political power, right, and derive it from its original, we must consider what state all men are naturally in, and that is, *a state of perfect freedom* to order their actions, and dispose of their possessions and persons, as they think fit, within the bounds of the law of nature; without asking leave, or depending upon the will of any other man.

A *state also of equality,* wherein all the power and jurisdiction is reciprocal, no one having more than another; there being nothing more evident, than that creatures of the same species and rank, promiscuously born to all the same advantages of nature, and the use of the same faculties, should also be equal one amongst another without subordination or subjection; unless the lord and master of them all should, by any manifest declaration of his will, set one above another, and confer on him, by an evident and clear appointment, an undoubted right to dominion and sovereignty.

5. This *equality* of men by nature, the judicious Hooker looks upon as so evident in itself, and beyond all question, that he makes it the foundation of that obligation to mutual love amongst men, on which he builds the duties we owe one another, and from whence he derives the great maxims of *justice* and *charity*. His words are, "The like natural inducement hath brought men to know, that it is no less their duty to love others than themselves; for seeing those things which are equal, must needs all have one measure; if I cannot but wish to receive good, even as much at every man's hands, as any man can wish unto his own soul, how should I look to have any part of my desire herein satisfied, unless myself be careful to satisfy the like desire, which is undoubtedly in other men, being of one and the same nature? To have any thing offered them repugnant to this desire, must

needs in all respects grieve them as much as me; so that if I do harm, I must look to suffer, there being no reason that others should shew greater measure of love to me, than they have by me shewed unto them: my desire therefore to be loved of my equals in nature, as much as possibly may be, imposeth upon me a natural duty of bearing to them-ward fully the like affection: From which relation of equality between ourselves and them that are as ourselves, what several rules and canons natural reason hath drawn, for direction of life, no man is ignorant." Eccl. Pol. L. I.

6. But though this be *a state of liberty*, yet *it is not a state of licence:* though man in that state have an uncontrollable liberty to dispose of his person or possessions, yet he has not liberty to destroy himself, or so much as any creature in his possession, but where some nobler use than its bare preservation calls for it. The *state of nature* has a law of nature to govern it, which obliges every one: And reason, which is that law, teaches all mankind, who will but consult it, that being all *equal and independent,* no one ought to harm another in his life, health, liberty, or possessions. For men being all the workmanship of one omnipotent and infinitely wise Maker; all the servants of one sovereign master, sent into the world by his order, and about his business; they are his property, whose workmanship they are, made to last during his, not another's pleasure. And being furnished with like faculties, sharing all in one community of nature, there cannot be supposed any such subordination among us, that may authorize us to destroy another, as if we were made for one another's uses, as the inferior ranks of creatures are for ours. Every one, as he is *bound to preserve himself,* and not to quit his station willfully, so by the like reason, when his own preservation comes not in competition, ought he, as much as he can, *to preserve the rest of mankind,* and may not, unless it be to do justice to an offender, take away or impair the life, or what tends to the preservation of life, the liberty, health, limb, or goods of another.

7. And that all men may be restrained from invading others rights, and from doing hurt to one another, and the law of nature be observed, which willeth the peace and *preservation of all mankind,* the *execution* of the law of nature is, in that state, put into every man's hands, whereby every one has a right to punish the transgressors of that law to such a degree as may hinder its violation. For the *law of nature* would, as all other laws that concern men in this world, be in vain, if there were no body that in the state of nature had a *power to execute* that law, and thereby preserve the innocent and restrain offenders. And if any one in the state of nature may punish another for any evil he has done, every one may do so. For in that *state of perfect equality,* where naturally there is no superiority or jurisdiction of one over another, what any may do in prosecution of that law, every one must needs have a right to do.

8. And thus, in the state of nature, *one man comes by a power over another;* but yet no absolute or arbitrary power, to use a criminal, when he has got him in his hands, according to the passionate heats, or boundless extravagancy of his own will; but only to retribute to him, so far as calm reason and conscience dictate, what is proportionate to his *transgression;* which is so much as may serve for reparation and *restraint.* For these two are the only reasons, why one man may lawfully do harm to another, which is that we call *punishment.* In transgressing the law of nature, the offender declares himself to live by another rule than that of reason and common equity, which is that measure God has set to the actions of men, for their mutual security; and so he becomes dangerous to mankind, the tye, which is to secure them from injury and violence, being slighted and broken by him. Which being a trespass against the whole species, and the peace and safety of it, provided for by the law of nature; every man upon this score, by the right he hath to preserve mankind in general, may restrain, or, where it is necessary, destroy things noxious to them, and so may bring such evil on any one, who hath transgressed that law, as may

make him repent the doing of it, and thereby deter him, and by his example others, from doing the like mischief. And in this case, and upon this ground, *every man hath a right to punish the offender, and be executioner of the law of nature.*

9. I doubt not but this will seem a very strange doctrine to some men: but before they condemn it, I desire them to resolve me, by what right any prince or state can put to death, or *punish an alien,* for any crime he commits in their country. It is certain their laws, by virtue of any sanction they receive from the promulgated will of the legislative, reach not a stranger. They speak not to him, nor, if they did, is he bound to hearken to them. The legislative authority, by which they are in force over the subjects of that common-wealth, hath no power over him. Those who have the supreme power of making laws in England, France, or Holland, are to an Indian but like the rest of the world, men without authority: And therefore, if by the law of nature every man hath not a power to punish offences against it, as he soberly judges the case to require, I see not how the magistrates of any community can *punish an alien* of another country; since in reference to him, they can have no more power, than what every man naturally may have over another.

10. Besides the crime which consists in violating the law, and varying from the right rule of reason, whereby a man so far becomes degenerate, and declares himself to quit the principles of human nature, and to be a noxious creature, there is commonly injury done to some person or other, and some other man receives damage by his transgression, in which case he who hath received any damage, has besides the right of punishment common to him with other men, a particular right to seek *reparation* from him that has done it. And any other person who finds it just, may also join with him that is injured, and assist him in recovering from the offender so much as may make satisfaction for the harm he has suffered.

11. From these *two distinct rights,* the one of *punishing* the *crime for restraint,* and pre-venting the like offence, which right of punishing is in every body; the other of taking reparation, which belongs only to the injured party; comes it to pass that the magistrate, who by being magistrate, hath the common right of punishing put into his hands, can often, where the public good demands not the execution of the law, *remit* the punishment of criminal offences by his own authority, but yet cannot *remit* the satisfaction due to any private man, for the damage he has received. That, he who has suffered the damage has a right to demand in his own name, and he alone can remit: The damnified person has this power of appropriating to himself the goods or service of the offender, *by right of self-preser-vation,* as every man has a power to punish the crime, to prevent its being committed again, *by the right he has of preserving all mankind;* and doing all reasonable things he can in order to that end: And thus it is, that every man, in the state of nature, has a power to kill a murderer, both to deter others from doing the like injury, which no reparation can com-pensate, by the example of the punishment that attends it from every body, and also *to secure* men from the attempts of a criminal, who having renounced reason, the common rule and measure, God hath given to mankind, hath by the unjust violence and slaughter he hath committed upon one, declared war against all mankind; and therefore may be destroyed as a *lion* or a *tiger,* one of those wild savage beasts, with whom men can have no society nor security: And upon this is grounded the great law of nature, "Whoso sheddeth mans blood, by man shall his blood be shed." And Cain was so fully convinced, that every one had a right to destroy such a criminal, that after the murder of his brother, he cries out, "Every one that findeth me, shall slay me;" so plain was it writ in the hearts of all mankind.

12. By the same reason may a man in the state of nature *punish the lesser breaches* of that law. It will perhaps be demanded, with death? I answer, each transgression may be *pun-ished* to that *degree,* and with so much *severity,* as will suffice to make it an ill bargain to the

offender, give him cause to repent, and terrify others from doing the like. Every offence that can be committed in the state of nature, may in the state of nature be also punished equally, and as far forth as it may, in a commonwealth: for though it would be besides my present purpose, to enter here into the particulars of the law of nature, or its *measures of punishment;* yet it is certain there is such a law, and that too, as intelligible and plain to a rational creature, and a studier of that law, as the positive laws of commonwealths, nay possibly plainer; as much as reason is easier to be understood, than the fancies and intricate contrivances of men, following contrary and hidden interests put into words; for so truly are a great part of the *municipal laws* of countries, which are only so far right, as they are founded on the law of nature, by which they are to be regulated and interpreted.

13. To this strange doctrine, viz. That *in the state of nature every one has the executive power* of the law of nature, I doubt not but it will be objected, that it is unreasonable for men to be judges in their own cases, that self-love will make men partial to themselves and their friends: And on the other side, that ill nature, passion and revenge will carry them too far in punishing others; and hence nothing but confusion and disorder will follow, and that therefore God hath certainly appointed government to restrain the partiality and violence of men. I easily grant, that civil government is the proper remedy for the inconveniencies of the state of nature, which must certainly be great, where men may be judges in their own case, since it is easy to be imagined, that he who was so unjust as to do his brother an injury, will scarce be so just as to condemn himself for it: But I shall desire those who make this objection to remember, that *absolute monarchs* are but men, and if government is to be the remedy of those evils, which necessarily follow from men's being judges in their own cases, and the state of nature is therefore not to be endured, I desire to know what kind of government that is, and how much better it is than the state of nature, where one man commanding a multitude, has the liberty to be judge in his own case, and may do to all his subjects whatever he pleases, without the least liberty to any one to question or control those who execute his pleasure? and in whatsoever he doth, whether led by reason, mistake or passion, must be submitted to? Much better it is in the state of nature, wherein men are not bound to submit to the unjust will of another: And if he that judges, judges amiss in his own, or any other case, he is answerable for it to the rest of mankind.

14. It is often asked as a mighty objection, *where are,* or ever were, there any *men in such a state of nature?* To which it may suffice as an answer at present: That since all princes and rulers of independent governments, all through the world, are in a state of nature, it is plain the world never was, nor ever will be, without numbers of men in that state. I have named all governors of independent communities, whether they are, or are not, in league with others. For it is not every compact that puts an end to the state of nature between men, but only this one of agreeing together mutually to enter into one community, and make one body politic; other promises and compacts men may make one with another, and yet still be in the state of nature. The promises and bargains for truck, &c. between the two men in the desert island, mentioned by Garcilasso de la Vega, in his history of Peru; or between a Swiss and an Indian, in the woods of America, are binding to them, though they are perfectly in a state of nature, in reference to one another. For truth and keeping of faith belongs to men as men, and not as members of society.

15. To those that say, there were never any men in the state of nature, I will not only oppose the authority of the judicious Hooker, *Eccl. Pol. lib. I. sect. 10,* where he says, "The laws which have been hitherto mentioned," i.e. the laws of nature, "do bind men absolutely, even as they are men, although they have never any settled fellowship, never any solemn agreement amongst themselves what to do or not to do, but for as much as we are not by our selves sufficient to furnish ourselves with competent store of things, need-

ful for such a life, as our nature doth desire, a life fit for the dignity of man; therefore to supply those defects and imperfections which are in us, as living singly and solely by ourselves, we are naturally induced to seek communion and fellowship with others. This was the cause of men's uniting themselves at first in politic societies." But I moreover affirm, that all men are naturally in that state, and remain so, till by their own consents they make themselves members of some politic society; and I doubt not in the sequel of this discourse to make it very clear.

CHAPTER III

Of the State of War

16. The *state of war* is a state of *enmity* and *destruction:* And therefore declaring by word or action, not a passionate and hasty, but a sedate settled design upon another man's life, *puts him in a state of war* with him against whom he has declared such an intention, and so has exposed his life to the other's power to be taken away by him, or any one that joins with him in his defence, and espouses his quarrel: it being reasonable and just I should have a right to destroy that which threatens me with destruction. For *by the fundamental law of nature, man being to be preserved* as much as possible, when all cannot be preserved, the safety of the innocent is to be preferred: And one may destroy a man who makes war upon him, or has discovered an enmity to his being, for the same reason that he may kill a *wolf* or a *lion;* because such men are not under the ties of the common law of reason, have no other rule, but that of force and violence, and so may be treated as beasts of prey, those dangerous and noxious creatures, that will be sure to destroy him whenever he falls into their power.

17. And hence it is, that he who attempts to get another man into his absolute power, does thereby *put himself into a state of war* with him; it being to be understood as a declaration of a design upon his life. For I have reason to conclude, that he who would get me into his power without my consent, would use me as he pleased when he got me there, and destroy me too when he had a fancy to it; for no body can desire to *have me in his absolute power* unless it be to compel me by force to that which is against the right of my freedom, i.e. make me a slave. To be free from such force is the only security of my preservation; and reason bids me look on him, as an enemy to my preservation, who would take away that freedom which is the fence to it; so that he who makes an *attempt to enslave* me, thereby puts himself into a state of war with me. He that, in the state of nature, *would take away the freedom* that belongs to any one in that state, must necessarily be supposed to have a design to take away every thing else, that *freedom* being the foundation of all the rest: As he that, in the state of society, would take away the freedom belonging to those of that society or commonwealth, must be supposed to design to take away from them every thing else, and so be looked on as *in a state of war*.

18. This makes it lawful for a man to *kill a thief,* who has not in the least hurt him, nor declared any design upon his life, any farther, than by the use of force, so to get him in his power, as to take away his money, or what he pleases, from him; because using force, where he has no right, to get me into his power, let his pretence be what it will, I have no reason to suppose, that he, who would *take away my liberty,* would not, when he had me in his power, take away every thing else. And therefore it is lawful for me to treat him as one

who has put *himself into a state of war* with me, i.e. kill him if I can; for to that hazard does he justly expose himself, whoever introduces a state of war, and is aggressor in it.

19. And here we have the plain *difference between the state of nature and the state of war;* which however some men have confounded, are as far distant, as a state of peace, good will, mutual assistance and preservation, and a state of enmity, malice, violence and mutual destruction, are one from another. Men living together according to reason, without a common superior on earth, with authority to judge between them, is *properly the state of nature.* But force, or a declared design of force, upon the person of another, where there is no common superior on earth to appeal to for relief, *is the state of war:* And it is the want of such an appeal gives a man the right of war even against an aggressor, though he be in society and a fellow subject. Thus a *thief,* whom I cannot harm, but by appeal to the law, for having stolen all that I am worth, I may kill, when he sets on me to rob me but of my horse or coat; because the law, which was made for my preservation, where it cannot interpose to secure my life from present force, which, if lost, is capable of no reparation, permits me my own defence, and the right of war, a liberty to kill the aggressor, because the aggressor allows not time to appeal to our common judge, nor the decision of the law, for remedy in a case where the mischief may be irreparable. *Want of a common judge with authority, puts all men in a state of nature: Force without right, upon a man's person, makes a state of war,* both where there is, and is not, a common judge.

20. But when the actual force is over, the *state of war ceases* between those that are in society, and are equally on both sides subjected to the fair determination of the law; because then there lies open the remedy of appeal for the past injury, and to prevent future harm: but where no such appeal is, as in the state of nature, for want of positive laws, and judges with authority to appeal to, *the state of war once begun, continues* with a right to the innocent party to destroy the other whenever he can, until the aggressor offers peace, and desires reconciliation on such terms as may repair any wrongs he has already done, and secure the innocent for the future: nay, where an appeal to the law, and constituted judges, lies open, but the remedy is denied by a manifest perverting of justice, and a barefaced wresting of the laws to protect or indemnify the violence or injuries of some men, or party of men, *there* it is hard to imagine any thing but *a state of war.* For wherever violence is used, and injury done, though by hands appointed to administer justice, it is still violence and injury, however coloured with the name, pretences, or forms of law, the end whereof being to protect and redress the innocent, by an unbiassed application of it, to all who are under it; wherever that is not *bona fide* done, *war is made* upon the sufferers, who having no appeal on earth to right them, they are left to the only remedy in such cases, an appeal to heaven.

21. To avoid this *state of war* (wherein there is no appeal but to heaven, and wherein every the least difference is apt to end, where there is no authority to decide between the contenders) is one *great reason of men's putting themselves into society,* and quitting the state of nature. For where there is an authority, a power on earth, from which relief can be had by *appeal,* there the continuance of the *state of war* is excluded, and the controversy is decided by that power. Had there been any such court, any superior jurisdiction on earth, to determine the right between Jephthah and the Ammonites, they had never come to *a state of war:* But we see he was forced to appeal to heaven. "The Lord the Judge," says he, "be judge this day, between the children of Israel and the children of Ammon," *Judg.* xi. 27, and then prosecuting, and relying on his appeal, he leads out his army to battle: and therefore in such controversies, where the question is put, *who shall be judge?* it cannot be meant, who shall decide the con-

troversy; every one knows what Jephthah here tells us, that "the Lord the Judge" shall judge. Where there is no judge on earth, the appeal lies to God in heaven. That question then cannot mean, who shall judge? whether another hath put himself in a *state of war* with me, and whether I may, as Jephthah did, *appeal to heaven* in it? of that I myself can only be judge in my own conscience, as I will answer it, at the great day, to the supreme judge of all men.

CHAPTER IV

Of Slavery

22. The *natural liberty* of man is to be free from any superior power on earth, and not to be under the will or legislative authority of man, but to have only the law of nature for his rule. The *liberty of man,* in society, is to be under no other legislative power; but that established, by consent, in the commonwealth; nor under the dominion of any will, or restraint of any law, but what that legislative shall enact, according to the trust put in it. Freedom then is not what Sir Robert Filmer tells us, O, A. 55. "a liberty for every one to do what he lists, to live as he pleases, and not to be tied by any laws:" But *freedom of men under government,* is, to have a standing rule to live by, common to every one of that society, and made by the legislative power erected in it; a liberty to follow my own will in all things, where the rule prescribes not; and not to be subject to the inconstant, uncertain, unknown, arbitrary will of another man: As *freedom of nature* is, to be under no other restraint but the law of nature.

23. This freedom from absolute, arbitrary power, is so necessary to, and closely joined with a man's preservation, that he cannot part with it, but by what forfeits his preservation and life together. For a man, not having the power of his own life, cannot, by compact, or his own consent, enslave himself to any one, nor put himself under the absolute, arbitrary power of another, to take away his life, when he pleases. No body can give more power than he has himself; and he that cannot take away his own life, cannot give another power over it. Indeed, having by his fault forfeited his own life, by some act that deserves death; he, to whom he has forfeited it, may (when he has him in his power) delay to take it, and make use of him to his own service, and he does him no injury by it. For, whenever he finds the hardship of his slavery outweigh the value of his life, it is in his power, by resisting the will of his master, to draw on himself the death he desires.

24. This is the perfect condition of *slavery,* which is nothing else, but *the state of war continued, between a lawful conqueror and a captive.* For, if once compact enter between them, and make an agreement for a limited power on the one side, and obedience on the other, the state of war and slavery ceases, as long as the compact endures. For, as has been said, no man can, by agreement, pass over to another that which he hath not in himself, a power over his own life.

I confess, we find among the Jews, as well as other nations, that men did sell themselves; but, it is plain, this was only to *drudgery, not to slavery.* For it is evident, the person sold was not under an absolute, arbitrary, despotical power. For the master could not have power to kill him, at any time, whom, at a certain time, he was obliged to let go free out of his service: and the master of such a servant was so far from having an arbitrary power over his life, that he could not, at pleasure, so much as maim him, but the loss of an eye, or tooth, set him free, *Exod.* xxi.

CHAPTER V

Of Property

25. Whether we consider natural *reason*, which tells us, that men, being once born, have a right to their preservation, and consequently to meat and drink, and such other things as nature affords for their subsistence: or *revelation,* which gives us an account of those grants God made of the world to Adam, and to Noah, and his sons, it is very clear, that God, as King David says, *Psal.* cxv. 16, "has given the earth to the children of men," given it to mankind in common. But this being supposed, it seems to some a very great difficulty how any one should ever come to have a *property* in any thing: I will not content myself to answer, that if it be difficult to make out *property,* upon a supposition, that God gave the world to Adam, and his posterity in common; it is impossible that any man, but one universal monarch, should have any property upon a supposition, that God gave the world to Adam, and his heirs in succession, exclusive of all the rest of his posterity. But I shall endeavour to shew, how men might come to have a *property* in several parts of that which God gave to mankind in common, and that without any express compact of all the commoners.

26. God, who hath given the world to men in common, hath also given them reason to make use of it to the best advantage of life, and convenience. The earth, and all that is therein, is given to men for the support and comfort of their being. And though all the fruits it naturally produces, and beasts it feeds, belong to mankind in common, as they are produced by the spontaneous hand of nature; and no body has originally a private dominion, exclusive of the rest of mankind, in any of them, as they are thus in their natural state: yet being given for the use of men, there must of necessity be *a means to appropriate* them some way or other, before they can be of any use, or at all beneficial to any particular man. The fruit, or venison, which nourishes the wild Indian, who knows no enclosure, and is still a tenant in common, must be his, and so his, i.e. a part of him, that another can no longer have any right to it, before it can do him any good for the support of his life.

27. Though the earth, and all inferior creatures, be common to all men, yet every man has a property in his own person: this no body has any right to but himself. The labour of his body, and the work of his hands, we may say, are properly his. Whatsoever then he removes out of the state that nature hath provided, and left it in, he hath mixed his labour with, and joined to it something that is his own, and thereby makes it his property. It being by him removed from the common state nature hath placed it in, it hath by this labour something annexed to it, that excludes the common right of other men. For this labour being the unquestionable property of the labourer, no man but he can have a right to what that is once joined to, at least where there is enough, and as good, left in common for others.

28. He that is nourished by the acorns he picked up under an oak, or the apples he gathered from the trees in the wood, has certainly appropriated them to himself. No body can deny but the nourishment is his. I ask then, when did they begin to be his? When he digested? Or when he eat? Or when he boiled? Or when he brought them home? Or when he picked them up? And it is plain, if the first gathering made them not his, nothing else could. That *labour* put a distinction between them and common: that added something to them more than nature, the common mother of all, had done; and so they became his private right. And will any one say he had no right to those acorns or apples he thus appropriated, because he had not the consent of all mankind to make them his? Was it a robbery thus to assume to himself what belonged to all in common? If such a consent as

that was necessary, man had starved, notwithstanding the plenty God had given him. We see in *commons*, which remain so by compact, that it is the taking any part of what is common, and removing it out of the state nature leaves it in, which *begins the property;* without which the common is of no use. And the taking of this or that part does not depend on the express consent of all the commoners. Thus the grass my horse has bit; the turfs my servant has cut; and the ore I have digged in any place, where I have a right to them in common with others, become my *property,* without the assignation or consent of any body. The *labour* that was mine, removing them out of that common state they were in, hath *fixed* my *property* in them.

29. By making an explicit consent of every commoner necessary to any one's appropriating to himself any part of what is given in common, children or servants could not cut the meat, which their father or master had provided for them in common, without assigning to every one his peculiar part. Though the water running in the fountain be every one's, yet who can doubt, but that in the pitcher is his only who drew it out? His *labour* hath taken it out of the hands of nature, where it was common, and belonged equally to all her children, and *hath* thereby *appropriated* it to himself.

30. Thus this law of reason makes the deer that Indian's who hath killed it; it is allowed to be his goods, who hath bestowed his labour upon it, though before it was the common right of every one. And amongst those who are counted the civilized part of mankind, who have made and multiplied positive laws to determine *property,* this original law of nature, for the *beginning of property,* in what was before common, still takes place; and by virtue thereof, what fish any one catches in the ocean, that great and still remaining common of mankind; or what ambergreise any one takes up here, is *by* the *labour* that removes it out of that common state nature left it in, *made* his *property,* who takes that pains about it. And even amongst us, the hare that any one is hunting, is thought his who pursues her during the chase. For being a beast that is still looked upon as common, and no man's private possession; whoever has employed so much *labour* about any of that kind, as to find and pursue her, has thereby removed her from the state of nature, wherein she was common, and hath *begun a property.*

31. It will perhaps be objected to this, that *if gathering the acorns, or other fruits of the earth, &c.* makes a right to them, then any one may engross as much as he will." To which I answer, Not so. The same law of nature, that does by this means give us property, does also *bound* that *property* too. "God has given us all things richly," 1 *Tim;* vi. 17, is the voice of reason confirmed by inspiration. But how far has he given it us? To *enjoy.* As much as any one can make use of to any advantage of life before it spoils, so much he may by his labour fix a property in: whatever is beyond this, is more than his share, and belongs to others. Nothing was made by God for man to spoil or destroy. And thus, considering the plenty of natural provisions there was a long time in the world, and the few spenders; and to how small a part of that provision the industry of one man could extend itself, and engross it to the prejudice of others; especially keeping within the *bounds,* set by reason, *of* what might serve for his *use;* there could be then little room for quarrels or contentions about property so established.

32. But the *chief matter of property* being now not the fruits of the earth, and the beasts that subsist on it, but the *earth it self;* as that which takes in, and carries with it all the rest: I think it is plain, that *property* in that too is acquired as the former. *As much land* as a man tills, plants, improves, cultivates, and can use the product of, so much is his *property.* He by his labour does, as it were, enclose it from the common. Nor will it invalidate his right, to say every body else has an equal title to it; and therefore he cannot appropriate, he cannot enclose, without the consent of all his fellow commoners, all mankind.

God, when he gave the world in common to all mankind, commanded man also to labour, and the penury of his condition required it of him. God and his reason commanded him to subdue the earth, i.e. improve it for the benefit of life, and therein lay out something upon it that was his own, his labour. He that, in obedience to this command of God, subdued, tilled, and sowed any part of it, thereby annexed to it something that was his *property*, which another had no title to, nor could without injury take from him.

33. Nor was this *appropriation* of any parcel of *land*, by improving it, any prejudice to any other man, since there was still enough, and as good left; and more than the yet unprovided could use. So that, in effect, there was never the less left for others because of his enclosure for himself. For he that leaves as much as another can make use of, does as good as take nothing at all. No body could think himself injured by the drinking of another man, though he took a good draught, who had a whole river of the same water left him to quench his thirst: And the case of land and water, where there is enough of both, is perfectly the same.

34. God gave the world to men in common; but since he gave it them for their benefit, and the greatest conveniences of life they were capable to draw from it, it cannot be supposed he meant it should always remain common and uncultivated. He gave it to the use of the industrious and rational, (and *labour* was to be *his title* to it) not to the fancy or covetousness of the quarrel some and contentious. He that had as good left for his improvement, as was already taken up, needed not complain, ought not to meddle with what was already improved by another's labour: If he did, it is plain he desired the benefit of another's pains, which he had no right to, and not the ground which God had given him in common with others to labour on, and whereof there was as good left, as that already possessed, and more than he knew what to do with, or his industry could reach to.

35. It is true, in *land* that is *common* in England, or any other country, where there is plenty of people under government, who have money and commerce, no one can enclose or appropriate any part, without the consent of all his fellow-commoners: Because this is left common by compact, i.e. by the law of the land, which is not to be violated. And though it be common, in respect of some men, it is not so to all mankind, but is the joint property of this country, or this parish. Besides, the remainder, after such enclosure, would not be as good to the rest of the commoners, as the whole was when they could all make use of the whole: whereas in the beginning and first peopling of the great common of the world, it was quite otherwise. The law man was under, was rather for appropriating. God commanded, and his wants forced him to *labour*. That was his *property* which could not be taken from him wherever he had fixed it. And hence subduing or cultivating the earth, and having dominion, we see are joined together. The one gave title to the other. So that God, by commanding to subdue, gave authority so far to *appropriate*: And the condition of human life, which requires labour and materials to work on, necessarily introduces private possessions.

36. The *measure of property* nature has well set by the extent of men's *labour, and the conveniences of life:* No man's labour could subdue or appropriate all; nor could his enjoyment consume more than a small part; so that it was impossible for any man, this way, to intrench upon the right of another, or acquire to himself a property, to the prejudice of his neighbour, who would still have room for as good, and as large a possession (after the other had taken out his) as before it was appropriated. This *measure* did confine every man's *possession* to a very moderate proportion, and such as he might appropriate to himself, without injury to any body, in the first ages of the world, when men were more in danger to be lost, by wandering from their company, in the then vast wilderness of the earth, than to be straitened for want of room to plant in. And the same measure may be allowed still

without prejudice to any body, as full as the world seems. For supposing a man, or family, in the state they were at first peopling of the world by the children of Adam, or Noah; let him plant in some inland, vacant places of America, we shall find that the *possessions* he could make himself, upon the *measures* we have given, would not be very large, nor, even to this day, prejudice the rest of mankind, or give them reason to complain, or think themselves injured by this man's encroachment, though the race of men have now spread themselves to all the corners of the world, and do infinitely exceed the small number was at the beginning. Nay, the extent of *ground* is of so little value, *without labour,* that I have heard it affirmed, that in Spain itself a man may be permitted to plough, sow, and reap, without being disturbed, upon land he has no other title to, but only his making use of it. But, on the contrary, the inhabitants think themselves beholden to him, who by his industry on neglected and consequently waste land, has increased the stock of corn, which they wanted. But be this as it will, which I lay no stress on; this I dare boldly affirm, that the same *rule of propriety, (viz.)* that every man should have as much as he could make use of, would hold still in the world, without straitening any body, since there is land enough in the world to suffice double the inhabitants, had not the *invention of money,* and the tacit agreement of men to put a value on it, introduced (by consent) larger possessions, and a right to them; which, how it has done, I shall by and by shew more at large.

37. This is certain, that in the beginning, before the desire of having more than man needed had altered the intrinsic value of things, which depends only on their usefulness to the life of man; or had *agreed, that a little piece of yellow metal,* which would keep without wasting or decay, should be worth a great piece of flesh, or a whole heap of corn; though men had a right to appropriate, by their labour, each one to himself as much of the things of nature as he could use: yet this could not be much, nor to the prejudice of others, where the same plenty was still left to those who would use the same industry. To which let me add, that he who appropriates land to himself by his labour, does not lessen, but increase the common stock of mankind. For the provisions serving to the support of human life, produced by one acre of enclosed and cultivated land, are (to speak much within compass) ten times more than those which are yielded by an acre of land of an equal richness lying waste in common. And therefore he that encloses land, and has a greater plenty of the conveniencies of life from ten acres, than he could have from an hundred left to nature, may truly be said to give ninety acres to mankind. For his labour now supplies him with provisions out of ten acres, which were by the product of an hundred lying in common. I have here rated the improved land very low, in making its product but as ten to one, when it is much nearer an hundred to one. For I ask, whether in the wild woods and uncultivated waste of America, left to nature, without any improvement, tillage, or husbandry, a thousand acres yield the needy and wretched inhabitants as many conveniencies of life, as ten acres equally fertile land do in Devonshire, where they are well cultivated?

Before the appropriation of land, he who gathered as much of the wild fruit, killed, caught, or tamed, as many of the beasts as he could; he that so employed his pains about any of the spontaneous products of nature, as any way to alter them from the state which nature put them in, *by* placing any of his *labour* on them, did thereby *acquire a propriety in them:* but if they perished, in his possession, without their due use; if the fruits rotted, or the venison putrified, before he could spend it, he offended against the common law of nature, and was liable to be punished; he invaded his neighbour's share, for he had *no right, farther than his use* called for any of them, and they might serve to afford him conveniencies of life.

38. The same *measures* governed the *possession of land* too: whatsoever he tilled and reaped, laid up and made use of, before it spoiled, that was his peculiar right; whatsoever

he enclosed, and could feed, and make use of, the cattle and product was also his. But if either the grass of his inclosure rotted on the ground, or the fruit of his planting perished without gathering, and laying up, this part of the earth, notwithstanding his inclosure, was still to be looked on as waste, and might be the possession of any other. Thus at the beginning, Cain might take as much ground as he could till, and make it his own land, and yet leave enough to Abel's sheep to feed on; a few acres would serve for both their possessions. But as families increased, and industry enlarged their stocks, their *possessions enlarged* with the need of them; but yet it was commonly *without any fixed property in the ground* they made use of, till they incorporated, settled themselves together, and built cities, and then, by consent, they came in time to set out the *bounds of their distinct territories,* and agree on limits between them and their neighbours; and by laws within themselves settled the *properties* of those of the same society. For we see, that in that part of the world which was first inhabited, and therefore like to be best peopled, even as low down as Abraham's time, they wandered with their flocks, and their herds, which was their substance, freely up and down; and this Abraham did, in a country where he was a stranger. Whence it is plain, that at least a great part of the *land lay in common;* that the inhabitants valued it not, nor claimed property in any more than they made use of. But when there was not room enough in the same place, for their herds to feed together, they by consent, as Abraham and Lot did, *Gen.* xiii. 5. separated and enlarged their pasture, where it best liked them. And for the same reason Esau went from his father, and his brother, and planted in Mount Seir, *Gen.* xxxvi. 6.

39. And thus, without supposing any private dominion, and property in Adam, over all the *world*, exclusive of all other men, which can no way be proved, nor any one's property be made out from it; but supposing the *world* given, as it was, to the children of men in *common,* we see how *labour* could make men distinct titles to several parcels of it, for their private uses; wherein there could be no doubt of right, no room for quarrel.

40. Nor is it so strange, as perhaps before consideration it may appear, that the *property of labour* should be able to over-balance the community of land. For it is *labour* indeed that *puts the difference of value* on every thing; and let any one consider what the difference is between an acre of land planted with tobacco or sugar, sown with wheat or barley, and an acre of the same land lying in common, without any husbandry upon it, and he will find, that the improvement of *labour makes* the far greater part of the value. I think it will be but a very modest computation to say, that of the *products* of the earth useful to the life of man, nine tenths are the *effects of labour:* nay, if we will rightly estimate things as they come to our use, and cast up the several expences about them, what in them is purely owing to *nature,* and what to *labour,* we shall find, that in most of them ninety-nine hundredths are wholly to be put on the account of *labour.*

41. There cannot be a clearer demonstration of any thing, than several nations of the Americans are of this, who are rich in land, and poor in all the comforts of life; whom nature having furnished as liberally as any other people, with the materials of plenty, i.e. a fruitful soil, apt to produce in abundance what might serve for food, raiment, and delight; yet *for want of improving it by labour,* have not one hundredth part of the conveniencies we enjoy: and a king of a large and fruitful territory there feeds, lodges, and is clad worse than a day labourer in England.

42. To make this a little clearer, let us but trace some of the ordinary provisions of life, through their several progresses, before they come to our use, and see how much they receive of their *value from human industry*. Bread, wine, and cloth, are things of daily use, and great plenty, yet notwithstanding, acorns, water, and leaves, or skins, must be our bread, drink, and cloathing, did not labour furnish us with these more useful commodi-

ties. For whatever bread is more worth than acorns, wine than water, and *cloth* or *silk,* than leaves, skins, or moss, that is *wholly owing to labour* and *industry.* The one of these being the food and raiment which unassisted nature furnishes us with; the other, provisions which our industry and pains prepare for us, which how much they exceed the other in value, when any one hath computed, he will then see how much *labour makes the far greatest part of the value* of things we enjoy in this world: and the ground which produces the materials, is scarce to be reckoned in, as any, or, at most, but a very small part of it: so little, that even amongst us, land that is left wholly to nature, that hath no improvement of pasturage, tillage, or planting, is called, as indeed it is, *waste;* and we shall find the benefit of it amount to little more than nothing.

This shews how much numbers of men are to be preferred to largeness of dominions; and that the increase of lands, and the right of employing of them, is the great art of government: and that prince, who shall be so wise and godlike, as by established laws of liberty to secure protection and encouragement to the honest industry of mankind, against the oppression of power and narrowness of party, will quickly be too hard for his neighbours; but this by the by. To return to the argument in hand.

43. An acre of land, that bears here twenty bushels of wheat, and another in America, which, with the same husbandry, would do the like, are, without doubt, of the same natural intrinsic value: but yet the benefit mankind receives from the one in a year, is worth £5, and from the other possibly not worth a penny, if all the profit an Indian received from it were to be valued, and sold here; at least, I may truly say, not one thousandth. It is *labour* then which *puts the greatest part of the value upon land,* without which it would scarcely be worth any thing: it is to that we owe the greatest part of all its useful products; for all that the straw, bran, bread, of that acre of wheat, is more worth than the product of an acre of as good land, which lies waste, is all the effect of labour. For it is not barely the ploughman's pains, the reaper's and thresher's toil, and the baker's sweat is to be counted into the *bread* we eat; the labour of those who broke the oxen, who digged and wrought the iron and stones, who felled and framed the timber employed about the plough, mill, oven, or any other utensils, which are a vast number requisite to this corn, from its being seed to be sown, to its being made bread, must all be *charged on* the account of *labour,* and received as an effect of that: nature and the earth furnished only the almost worthless materials, as in themselves. It would be a strange *catalogue of things, that industry provided and made use of, about every loaf of bread,* before it came to our use, if we could trace them; iron, wood, leather, bark, timber, stone, bricks, coals, lime, cloth, dying drugs, pitch, tar, masts, ropes, and all the materials made use of in the ship, that brought any of the commodities made use of by any of the workmen, to any part of the work, all which it would be almost impossible, at least too long, to reckon up.

44. From all which it is evident, that though the things of nature are given in common, yet man, by being master of himself, and *proprietor of his own person, and the actions or labour of it, had still in himself the great foundation of property;* and that, which made up the great part of what he applied to the support or comfort of his being, when invention and arts had improved the conveniences of life, was perfectly his own, and did not belong in common to others.

45. Thus *labour,* in the beginning, *gave a right of property,* wherever any one was pleased to employ it upon what was common, which remained a long while the far greater part, and is yet more than mankind makes use of. Men, at first, for the most part, contented themselves with what unassisted nature offered to their necessities: and though afterwards, in some parts of the world, (where the increase of people and stock, with the *use of*

money, had made land scarce, and so of some value) the several *communities* settled the bounds of their distinct territories, and by laws within themselves regulated the properties of the private men of their society, and so, by *compact* and agreement, *settled the property* which labour and industry began; and the leagues that have been made between several states and kingdoms, either expressly or tacitly disowning all claim and right to the land in the others possession, have, by common consent, given up their pretences to their natural common right, which originally they had to those countries, and so have, by *positive agreement, settled a property* amongst themselves, in distinct parts and parcels of the earth; yet there are still *great tracts of ground* to be found, which (the inhabitants thereof not having joined with the rest of mankind, in the consent of the use of their common money) *lie waste,* and are more than the people who dwell on it do, or can make use of, and so still lie in common. Though this can scarce happen amongst that part of mankind that have consented to the use of money.

46. The greatest part of *things really useful* to the life of man, and such as the necessity of subsisting made the first commoners of the world look after, as it doth the Americans now, *are* generally things of *short duration;* such as, if they are not consumed by use, will decay and perish of themselves: gold, silver, and diamonds, are things that fancy or agreement hath put the value on, more than real use, and the necessary support of life. Now of those good things which nature hath provided in common, every one had a right, (as hath been said) to as much as he could use, and property in all that he could affect with his labour; all that his industry could extend to, to alter from the state nature had put it in, was his. He that *gathered* a hundred bushels of acorns or apples, had thereby a *property* in them, they were his goods as soon as gathered. He was only to look, that he used them before they spoiled, else he took more than his share, and robbed others. And indeed it was a foolish thing, as well as dishonest, to hoard up more than he could make use of. If he gave away a part to any body else, so that it perished not uselessly in his possession, these he also made use of. And if he also bartered away plums, that would have rotted in a week, for nuts that would last good for his eating a whole year, he did no injury; he wasted not the common stock; destroyed no part of the portion of goods that belonged to others, so long as nothing perished uselessly in his hands. Again, if he would give his nuts for a piece of metal, pleased with its colour; or exchange his sheep for shells, or wool for a sparkling pebble or a diamond, and keep those by him all his life, he invaded not the right of others, he might heap up as much of these durable things as he pleased; the *exceeding of the bounds of* his *just property* not lying in the largeness of his possession, but the perishing of any thing uselessly in it.

47. And thus *came in the use of money,* some lasting thing that men might keep without spoiling, and that by mutual consent men would take in exchange for the truly useful, but perishable supports of life.

48. And as different degrees of industry were apt to give men possessions in different proportions, so this *invention of money* gave them the opportunity to continue and enlarge them. For supposing an island, separate from all possible commerce with the rest of the world, wherein there were but an hundred families, but there were sheep, horses, and cows, with other useful animals, wholesome fruits, and land enough for corn for a hundred thousand times as many, but nothing in the island, either because of its commonness, or perishableness, fit to supply the place of *money:* What reason could any one have there to enlarge his possessions beyond the use of his family and a plentiful supply to its *consumption,* either in what their own industry produced, or they could barter for like perishable, useful commodities with others? Where there is not something, both lasting and scarce, and so valuable to be hoarded up, there men will not be apt to enlarge their *possessions of*

land, were it never so rich, never so free for them to take. For I ask, what would a man value ten thousand, or an hundred thousand acres of excellent *land,* ready cultivated and well stocked too with cattle, in the middle of the inland parts of America, where he had no hopes of commerce with other parts of the world, to draw *money* to him by the sale of the product? It would not be worth the enclosing, and we should see him give up again to the wild common of nature, whatever was more than would supply the conveniences of life to be had there for him and his family.

49. Thus in the beginning all the world was America, and more so than that is now; for no such thing as *money* was any where known. Find out something that hath the *use and value of money* amongst his neighbours, you shall see the same man will begin presently to *enlarge* his possessions.

50. But since gold and silver, being little useful to the life of man in proportion to food, raiment, and carriage, has its *value* only from the consent of men, whereof *labour* yet *makes* in great part, the *measure,* it is plain, that men have agreed to a disproportionate and unequal *possession of the earth,* they having, by a tacit and voluntary consent, found out a way how a man may fairly possess more land than he himself can use the product of, by receiving in exchange for the overplus, gold and silver, which may be hoarded up without injury to any one; these metals not spoiling or decaying in the hands of the possessor. This partage of things in an inequality of private possessions, men have made practicable out of the bounds of society, and without compact, only by putting a value on gold and silver, and tacitly agreeing in the use of money. For in governments, the laws regulate the right of property, and the possession of land is determined by positive constitutions.

51. And thus, I think, it is very easy to conceive, without any difficulty *how labour could at first begin a title of property* in the common things of nature, and how the spending it upon our uses bounded it. So that there could then be no reason of quarrelling about title, nor any doubt about the largeness of possession it gave. Right and conveniency went together; for as a man had a right to all he could employ his labour upon, so he had no temptation to labour for more than he could make use of. This left no room for controversy about the title, nor for encroachment on the right of others; what portion a man carved to himself, was easily seen; and it was useless, as well as dishonest, to carve himself too much, or take more than he needed.

CHAPTER VI

Of Paternal Power

52. It may perhaps be censured as an impertinent criticism, in a discourse of this nature, to find fault with words and names, that have obtained in the world: and yet possibly it may not be amiss to offer new ones, when the old are apt to lead men into mistakes, as this of *paternal power* probably has done, which seems so to place the power of parents over their children wholly in the *father,* as if the *mother* had no share in it, whereas, if we consult reason or revelation, we shall find she hath an equal title. This may give one reason to ask, whether this might not be more properly called *parental power.* For whatever obligation nature and the right of generation lays on children, it must certainly bind them equally to both concurrent causes of it. And accordingly we see the positive law of God every where joins them together without distinction, when it commands the obedience of children: "Honour thy father and thy mother," *Exod.* xx. 12. "Whosoever curseth

his father or his mother," *Lev.* xx. 9. "Ye shall fear every man his mother and his father," *Lev.* xix. 5. "Children, obey your parents," &c. *Eph.* vi. 1, is the style of the Old and New Testament.

53. Had but this one thing been well considered, without looking any deeper into the matter, it might perhaps have kept men from running into those gross mistakes they have made, about this power of parents; which, however it might, without any great harshness, bear the name of absolute dominion, and regal authority, when under the title of *paternal power* it seemed appropriated to the father, would yet have sounded but oddly, and in the very name strewn the absurdity, if this supposed absolute power over children had been called *parental;* and thereby have discovered, that it belonged to the *mother* too. For it will but very ill serve the turn of those men, who contend so much for the absolute power and authority of the fatherhood, as they call it, that the mother should have any share in it. And it would have but ill supported the monarchy they contend for, when by the very name it appeared that that fundamental authority, from whence they would derive their government of a single person only, was not placed in one, but two persons jointly. But to let this of names pass.

54. Though I have said above, chap. ii. "That all men by nature are equal," I cannot be supposed to understand all sorts of *equality: age* or *virtue* may give men a just precedency: *excellency of parts* and *merit* may place others above the common level: *birth* may subject some, and *alliance* or *benefits* others, to pay an observance to those whom nature, gratitude, or other respects, may have made it due; and yet all this consists with the *equality,* which all men are in, in respect of jurisdiction or dominion one over another; which was the *equality* I there spoke of, as proper to the business in hand, being that *equal right,* that every man hath, *to his natural freedom,* without being subjected to the will or authority of any other man.

55. *Children,* I confess, are not born in this state of *equality,* though they are born to it. Their parents have a sort of rule and jurisdiction over them, when they come into the world, and for some time after, but it is but a temporary one. The bonds of this subjection are like the swaddling clothes they are wrapt up in, and supported by, in the weakness of their infancy: Age and reason, as they grow up, loosen them, till at length they drop quite off, and leave a man at his own free disposal.

56. Adam was created a perfect man, his body and mind in full possession of their strength and reason, and so was capable from the first instant of his being to provide for his own support and preservation; and govern his actions according to the dictates of the law of reason which God had implanted in him. From him the world is peopled with his descendants, who are all born infants, weak and helpless, without knowledge or understanding: But to supply the defects of this imperfect state, till the improvement of growth and age hath removed them, Adam and Eve, and after them all parents were, by the law of nature, *under an obligation to preserve, nourish, and educate the children,* they had begotten; not as their own workmanship, but the workmanship of their own maker, the Almighty, to whom they were to be accountable for them.

57. The law, that was to govern Adam, was the same that was to govern all his posterity, the *law of reason.* But his offspring having another way of entrance into the world, different from him, by a natural birth, that produced them ignorant and without the use of *reason,* they were not presently *under that law;* for no body can be under a law, which is not promulgated to him: and this law being promulgated or made known by *reason* only, he that is not come to the use of his *reason,* cannot be said to be *under this law;* and Adam's children, being not presently as soon as born, *under this law of reason,* were not presently free. For law, in its true notion, *is* not so much the limitation, *as the direction of a free and*

intelligent agent to his proper interest, and prescribes no farther than is for the general good of those under that law. Could they be happier without it, the law, as an useless thing, would of it self vanish: and that ill deserves the name of confinement which hedges us in only from bogs and precipices. So that, however it may be mistaken, *the end of law* is not to abolish or restrain, but *to preserve and enlarge freedom.* For in all the states of created beings capable of laws, *where there is no law, there is no freedom.* For liberty is to be free from restraint and violence from others which cannot be where there is no law: but freedom is not, as we are told, "a liberty for every man to do what he lists:" (for who could be free, when every other man's humour might domineer over him?) but a liberty to dispose, and order as he lists, his person, actions, possessions, and his whole property, within the allowance of those laws under which he is, and therein not to be subject to the arbitrary will of another, but freely follow his own.

58. The *power,* then, *that parents have* over their children, arises from that duty which is incumbent on them, to take care of their offspring during the imperfect state of childhood. To inform the mind, and govern the actions of their yet ignorant nonage, till reason shall take its place, and ease them of that trouble, is what the children want, and the parents are bound to. For God having given man an understanding to direct his actions, has allowed him a freedom of will, and liberty of acting, as properly belonging thereunto, within the bounds of that law he is under. But whilst he is in an estate, wherein he has not understanding of his own to direct his will, he is not to have any will of his own to follow: he that understands for him, must will for him too; he must prescribe to his will, and regulate his actions: but when he comes to the estate that made his *father a freeman,* the *son is a freeman* too.

59. This holds in all the laws a man is under, whether natural or civil. Is a man under the law of nature? *What made him free* of that law? What gave him a free disposing of his property according to his own will, within the compass of that law? I answer, a state of maturity, wherein he might be supposed capable to know that law, that so he might keep his actions within the bounds of it. When he has acquired that state, he is presumed to know how far that law is to be his guide, and how far he may make use of his *freedom,* and so comes to have it; till then, some body else must guide him, who is presumed to know how far the law allows a liberty. If such a state of reason, such an age of discretion *made him free,* the same shall make his son free too. Is a man under the law of England? *What made him free* of that law? That is, to have the liberty to dispose of his actions and possessions according to his own will within the permission of that law? A capacity of knowing that law. Which is supposed by that law, at the age of one and twenty years, and in some cases sooner. If this made the father free, it shall make the son free too. Till then we see the law allows the son to have no will, but he is to be guided by the will of his father or guardian, who is to understand for him. And if the father die, and fail to substitute a deputy in his trust; if he hath not provided a tutor to govern his son, during his minority, during his want of understanding; the law takes care to do it; some other must govern him, and be a will to him, till he hath *attained to a state of freedom,* and his understanding be fit to take the government of his will. But after that, the father and son are equally free as much as tutor and pupil after nonage: equally subjects of the same law together, without any dominion left in the father over the life, liberty, or estate of his son, whether they be only in the state and under the law of nature, or under the positive laws of an established government.

60. But if, through defects that may happen out of the ordinary course of nature, any one comes not to such a degree of reason, wherein he might be supposed capable of knowing the law, and so living within the rules of it; he is *never capable of being a free man,* he is

never let loose to the disposure of his own will (because he knows no bounds to it, has not understanding, its proper guide) but is continued under the tuition and government of others, all the time his own understanding is incapable of that charge. And so *lunatics* and *idiots* are never set free from the government of their parents. "Children, who are not as yet come into those years whereat they may have; and innocents which are excluded by a natural defect from ever having; thirdly, madmen, which for the present cannot possibly have the use of right reason to guide themselves; have for their guide the reason that guideth other men, which are tutors over them, to seek and procure their good for them," says Hooker, Eccl. Pol. Lib. I. Sect. 7. All which seems no more than that duty which God and nature has laid on man, as well as other creatures, to preserve their offspring, till they can be able to shift for themselves, and will scarce amount to an instance or proof of parents regal authority.

61. Thus we are *born free,* as we are born rational; not that we have actually the exercise of either: age, that brings one, brings with it the other too. And thus we see how *natural freedom and subjection to parents* may consist together, and are both founded on the same principle. A *child* is *free* by his father's title, by his father's understanding, which is to govern him till he hath it of his own. The *freedom of a man at years of discretion,* and the *subjection* of a child *to* his parents, whilst yet short of that age, are so consistent, and so distinguishable, that the most blinded contenders for monarchy, *by right of fatherhood,* cannot miss this difference; the most obstinate cannot but allow their consistency. For were their doctrine all true, were the right heir of Adam now known, and by that title settled a monarch in his throne, invested with all the absolute unlimited power, Sir Robert Filmer talks of; if he should die as soon as his heir were born, must not the child, notwithstanding he were never so free, never so much sovereign, be in subjection to his mother and nurse, to tutors and governors, till age and education brought him reason and ability to govern himself and others? The necessities of his life, the health of his body, and the information of his mind, would require him to be directed by the will of others, and not his own; and yet will any one think, that this restraint and subjection were inconsistent with, or spoiled him of, that liberty or sovereignty he had a right to, or gave away his empire to those who had the government of his nonage? This government over him only prepared him the better and sooner for it. If any body should ask me when my son is of *age to be free?* I shall answer, just when his monarch is of age to govern. "But at what time," says the judicious Hooker, Eccl. Pol. Lib. I. Sect. 6 "a man may be said to have attained so far forth the use of reason, as sufficeth to make him capable of those laws whereby he is then bound to guide his actions: this is a great deal more easy for sense to discern, than for any one by skill and learning to determine."

62. Commonwealths themselves take notice of, and allow, that there *is a time when men* are to *begin to act like free men,* and therefore till that time require not oaths of fealty, or allegiance, or other public owning of, or submission to, the government of their countries.

63. The *freedom* then of man, and liberty of acting according to his own will, is *grounded* on his having *reason,* which is able to instruct him in that law he is to govern himself by, and make him know how far he is left to the freedom of his own will. To turn him loose to an unrestrained liberty, before he has reason to guide him, is not the allowing him the privilege of his nature to be free; but to thrust him out amongst brutes, and abandon him to a state as wretched, and as much beneath that of a man, as theirs. This is that which puts the *authority* into the *parents* hands to govern the *minority* of their children. God hath made it their business to employ this care on their offspring, and hath placed in them suitable inclinations of tenderness and concern to temper this power, to apply it, as his wisdom designed it, to the children's good as long as they should need to be under it.

64. But what reason can hence advance this care of the *parents* due to their offspring into an *absolute arbitrary dominion* of the father, whose power reaches no farther than, by such a discipline as he finds most effectual, to give such strength and health to their bodies, such vigour and rectitude to their minds, as may best fit his children to be most useful to themselves and others; and, if it be necessary to his condition, to make them work, when they are able, for their own subsistence. But in this power the *mother* too has her share with the *father*.

65. Nay, *this* power so little belongs to the father by any peculiar right of nature, but only as he is guardian of his children, that when he quits his care of them, he loses his power over them, which goes along with their nourishment and education, to which it is inseparably annexed; and it belongs as much to the foster-father of an exposed child, as to the natural father of another. So little power does the bare *act of begetting* give a man over his issue; if all his care ends there, and this be all the title he hath to the name and authority of a father. And what will become of this *paternal power* in that part of the world, where one woman hath more than one husband at a time? or in those parts of America, where, when the husband and wife part, which happens frequently, the children are all left to the mother, follow her, and are wholly under her care and provision? If the father die whilst the children are young, do they not naturally every where owe the same obedience to their mother, during their minority, as to their father were he alive? And will any one say, that the mother hath a legislative power over her children? that she can make standing rules, which shall be of perpetual obligation, by which they ought to regulate all the concerns of their property, and bound their liberty all the course of their lives? or can she enforce the observation of them with capital punishments? For this is the proper *power of the magistrate,* of which the father hath not so much as the shadow. His command over his children is but temporary, and reaches not their life or property: it is but a help to the weakness and imperfection of their nonage, a discipline necessary to their education: and though a father may dispose of his own possessions as he pleases, when his children are out of danger of perishing for want, yet his power extends not to the lives or goods, which either their own industry, or another's bounty has made theirs; nor to their liberty neither, when they are once arrived to the infranchisement of the years of discretion. The *father's empire* then ceases, and can from thence forwards no more dispose of the liberty of his son, than that of any other man: and it must be far from an absolute or perpetual jurisdiction, from which a man may withdraw himself, having licence from divine authority to *leave father and mother, and cleave to his wife.*

66. But though there be a time when a child comes to be as free from subjection to the will and command of his father, as the father himself is free from subjection to the will of any body else, and they are each under no other restraint but that which is common to them both, whether it be the law of nature, or municipal law of their country; yet this freedom exempts not a son from that honour which he ought, by the law of God and nature, to pay his parents. God having made the parents instruments in his great design of continuing the race of mankind, and the occasions of life to their children; as he hath laid on them an obligation to nourish, preserve, and bring up their offspring; so he has laid on the children a perpetual obligation of *honouring their parents,* which containing in it an inward esteem and reverence to be strewn by all outward expressions, ties up the child from any thing that may ever injure or affront, disturb or endanger, the happiness or life of those from whom he received his; and engages him in all actions of defence, relief, assistance, and comfort of those, by whose means he entered into being, and has been made capable of any enjoyments of life. From this obligation no state, no freedom can absolve children. But this is very far from giving parents a power of com-

mand over their children, or an authority to make laws and dispose as they please of their lives and liberties. It is one thing to owe honour, respect, gratitude, and assistance; another to require an absolute obedience and submission. The *honour due to parents,* a monarch in his throne owes his mother, and yet this lessens not his authority, nor subjects him to her government.

67. The subjection of a minor places in the father a temporary government, which terminates with the minority of the child: and the *honour due from a child,* places in the parents a perpetual right to respect, reverence, support and compliance too, more or less, as the father's care, cost, and kindness in his education, have been more or less. This ends not with minority, but holds in all parts and conditions of a man's life. The want of distinguishing these two powers, viz. that which the father hath in the right of *tuition,* during minority, and the right of honour all his life, may perhaps have caused a great part of the mistakes about this matter. For to speak properly of them, the first of these is rather the privilege of children, and duty of parents, than any prerogative of paternal power. The nourishment and education of their children is a charge so incumbent on parents for their children's good, that nothing can absolve them from taking care of it. And though the *power of commanding and chastising* them go along with it, yet God hath woven into the principles of human nature such a tenderness for their offspring, that there is little fear that parents should use their power with too much rigour; the excess is seldom on the severe side, the strong bias of nature drawing the other way. And therefore God Almighty, when he would express his gentle dealing with the Israelites, he tells them, that though he chastened them, "he chastened them as a man chastens his son," *Deut.* viii. 5. i.e. with tenderness and affection, and kept them under no severer discipline than what was absolutely best for them, and had been less kindness to have slackened. This is that power to which children are commanded obedience, that the pains and care of their parents may not be increased, or ill rewarded.

68. On the other side, *honour* and *support,* all that which gratitude requires to return for the benefits received by and from them, is the indispensable duty of the child, and the proper privilege of the parents. This is intended for the parents advantage, as the other is for the child's; though education, the parents duty, seems to have most power, because the ignorance and infirmities of childhood stand in need of restraint and correction; which is a visible exercise of rule, and a kind of dominion. And that duty which is comprehended in the word *honour,* requires less obedience, though the obligation be stronger on grown than younger children. For who can think the command, "Children, obey your parents," requires in a man that has children of his own the same submission to his father, as it does in his yet young children to him; and that by this precept he were bound to obey all his father's commands, if, out of a conceit of authority, he should have the indiscretion to treat him still as a boy?

69. The first part then of *paternal power,* or rather duty, which is *education,* belongs so to the father, that it terminates at a certain season; when the business of education is over, it ceases of itself, and is also alienable before. For a man may put the tuition of his son in other hands; and he that has made his son an *apprentice* to another, has discharged him, during that time, of a great part of his obedience both to himself and to his mother. But all the *duty of honour,* the other part, remains nevertheless entire to them; nothing can cancel that: It is so inseparable from them both, that the father's authority cannot dispossess the mother of this right, nor can any man discharge his son from *honouring* her that bore him. But both these are very far from a power to make laws, and enforcing them with penalties that may reach estate, liberty, limbs, and life. The power of commanding ends with nonage; and though after that, *honour* and respect, support and defence, and whatsoever

gratitude can oblige a man to, for the highest benefits he is naturally capable of, be always due from a son to his parents; yet all this puts no sceptre into the father's hand, no sovereign power of commanding. He has no dominion over his son's property, or actions; nor any right that his will should prescribe to his son's in all things; however it may become his son in many things not very inconvenient to him and his family, to pay a deference to it.

70. A man may owe *honour* and respect to an ancient, or wise man; defence to his child or friend; relief and support to the distressed; and gratitude to a benefactor, to such a degree, that all he has, all he can do, cannot sufficiently pay it: but all these give no authority, no right to any one, of making laws over him from whom they are owing. And it is plain, all this is due not only to the bare title of father; not only because, as has been said, it is owing to the mother too, but because these obligations to parents, and the degrees of what is required of children, may be varied by the different care and kindness, trouble and expense, which is often employed upon one child more than another.

71. This shews the reason how it comes to pass, that *parents in societies,* where they themselves are subjects, retain a *power over their children,* and have as much right to their subjection as those who are in the state of nature. Which could not possibly be, if all political power were only paternal, and that in truth they were one and the same thing. For then, all paternal power being in the prince, the subject could naturally have none of it. But these two *powers, political* and *paternal,* are so perfectly distinct and separate, are built upon so different foundations, and given to so different ends, that every subject that is a father, has as much a paternal power over his children, as the prince has over his: and every prince, that has parents, owes them as much filial duty and obedience, as the meanest of his subjects do to theirs; and cannot therefore contain any part or degree of that kind of dominion which a prince or magistrate has over his subject.

72. Though the obligation on the parents to bring up their children, and the obligation on children to honour their parents, contain all the power on the one hand, and submission on the other, which are proper to this relation, yet there is *another power* ordinary *in the father,* whereby he has a tie on the obedience of his children; which though it be common to him with other men, yet the occasions of shewing it almost constantly happening to fathers in their private families, and the instances of it elsewhere being rare, and less taken notice of, it passes in the world for a part of paternal jurisdiction. And this is the power men generally have to *bestow their estates* on those who please them best. The possession of the father being the expectation and inheritance of the children, ordinarily in certain proportions, according to the law and custom of each country; yet it is commonly in the father's power to bestow it with a more sparing or liberal hand, according as the behaviour of this or that child hath comported with his will and humour.

73. This is no small tie on the obedience of children: and there being always annexed to the enjoyment of land a submission to the government of the country, of which that land is a part; it has been commonly supposed, that a father could *oblige his posterity to that government,* of which he himself was a subject, and that his compact held them; whereas it being only a necessary condition annexed to the land, and the inheritance of an estate which is under that government, reaches only those who will take it on that condition, and so is no natural tie or engagement, but a voluntary submission. For *every man's children* being by nature as free as himself, or any of his ancestors ever were, may, whilst they are in that freedom, choose what society they will join themselves to, what commonwealth they will put themselves under. But if they will enjoy the inheritance of their ancestors, they must take it on the same terms their ancestors had it, and submit to all the conditions annexed to such a possession. By this power indeed fathers oblige their children to obedience to themselves, even when they are past minority, and most commonly too sub-

ject them to this or that political power. But neither of these by any peculiar right of fatherhood, but by the reward they have in their hands to enforce and recompence such a compliance; and is no more power than what a Frenchman has over an Englishman, who, by the hopes of an estate he will leave him, will certainly have a strong tie on his obedience: and if, when it is left him, he will enjoy it, he must certainly take it upon the conditions annexed to the *possession of land* in that country where it lies, whether it be France or England.

74. To conclude then, though the father's power of commanding extends no farther than the minority of his children, and to a degree only fit for the discipline and government of that age; and though that honour and respect, and all that which the Latins called piety, which they indispensably owe to their parents all their lifetime, and in all estates, with all that support and defence which is due to them, gives the father no power of governing, i.e. making laws and enacting penalties on his children; though by all this he has no dominion over the property or actions of his son; yet it is obvious to conceive how easy it was, in the first ages of the world, and in places still, where the thinness of people gives families leave to separate into unpossessed quarters, and they have room to remove or plant themselves in yet vacant habitations, for the *father of the family* to become the prince[1] of it; he had been a ruler from the beginning of the infancy of his children: and since without some government it would be hard for them to live together, it was likeliest it should, by the express or tacit consent of the children when they were grown up, be in the father, where it seemed without any change barely to continue; when indeed nothing more was required to it, than the permitting the father to exercise alone, in his family, that executive power of the law of nature, which every free man naturally hath, and by that permission resigning up to him a monarchical power, whilst they remained in it. But that this was not by any *paternal right,* but only by the consent of his children, is evident from hence, that no body doubts, but if a stranger, whom chance or business had brought to his family, had there killed any of his children, or committed any other fact, he might condemn and put him to death, or otherwise punish him, as well as any of his children: which it was impossible he should do by virtue of any paternal authority over one who was not his child, but by virtue of that executive power of the law of nature, which, as a man, he had a right to: and he alone could punish him in his family, where the respect of his children had laid by the exercise of such a power, to give way to the dignity and authority they were willing should remain in him, above the rest of his family.

75. Thus it was easy, and almost natural for children, by a tacit, and scarce avoidable consent, to make way for the *father's authority and government*. They had been accustomed in their childhood to follow his direction, and to refer their little differences to him; and when they were men, who fitter to rule them? Their little properties, and less covetousness, seldom afforded greater controversies; and when any should arise, where could they have a fitter umpire than he, by whose care they had every one been sustained and brought up, and who had a tenderness for them all? It is no wonder that they made no distinction betwixt minority and full age; nor looked after one and twenty, or any other age that might make them the free disposers of themselves and fortunes, when they could have no desire to be out of their pupilage. The government they had been under during it, continued still to be more their protection than restraint: and they could no where find a greater security to their peace, liberties, and fortunes, than in the *rule of a father*.

76. Thus the natural *fathers of families* by an insensible change became the *politic monarchs* of them too: and as they chanced to live long, and leave able and worthy heirs, for several successions, or otherwise; so they laid the foundations of hereditary, or elective

kingdoms, under several constitutions and manners, according as chance, contrivance, or occasions happened to mould them. But if princes have their titles in their fathers right, and it be a sufficient proof of the natural *right of fathers* to political authority, because they commonly were those in whose hands we find, *de facto,* the exercise of government: I say, if this argument be good, it will as strongly prove, that all princes, nay princes only, ought to be priests, since it is as certain, that in the beginning, *the father of the family was priest, as that he was ruler in his own household.*

CHAPTER VII

Of Political or Civil Society

77. God having made man such a creature, that in his own judgment, it was not good for him to be alone, put him under strong obligations of necessity, convenience, and inclination, to drive him into society, as well as fitted him with understanding and language to continue and enjoy it. The first society was between man and wife, which gave beginning to that between parents and children; to which, in time, that between master and servant came to be added; and though all these might, and commonly did meet together, and make up but one family, wherein the master or mistress of it had some sort of rule proper to a family; each of these, or all together, came short of *political society,* as we shall see, if we consider the different ends, ties, and bounds of each of these.

78. *Conjugal society* is made by a voluntary compact between man and woman; and though it consist chiefly in such a communion and right in one another's bodies as is necessary to its chief end, procreation; yet it draws with it mutual support and assistance, and a communion of interests too, as necessary not only to unite their care and affection, but also necessary to their common offspring, who have a right to be nourished and maintained by them, till they are able to provide for themselves.

79. For the end of *conjunction between male and female* being not barely procreation, but the continuation of the species; this conjunction betwixt male and female ought to last, even after procreation, so long as is necessary to the nourishment and support of the young ones, who are to be sustained by those that got them, till they are able to shift and provide for themselves. This rule, which the infinite wise Maker hath set to the works of his hands, we find the inferior creatures steadily obey. In those viviparous animals which feed on grass, the *conjunction between male and female* lasts no longer than the very act of copulation; because the teat of the dam being sufficient to nourish the young, till it be able to feed on grass, the male only begets, but concerns not himself for the female or young, to whose sustenance he can contribute nothing. But in beasts of prey the conjunction lasts longer: because the dam not being able well to subsist herself, and nourish her numerous offspring by her own prey alone, a more laborious, as well as more dangerous way of living, than by feeding on grass; the assistance of the male is necessary to the maintenance of their common family, which cannot subsist till they are able to prey for themselves, but by the joint care of male and female. The same is to be observed in all birds (except some domestic ones, where plenty of food excuses the cock from feeding, and taking care of the young brood), whose young needing food in the nest, the cock and hen continue mates, till the young are able to use their wing, and provide for themselves.

80. And herein I think lies the chief, if not the only reason, *why the male and female in mankind are tied to a longer conjunction* than other creatures, viz. because the female is capa-

ble of conceiving, and *de facto* is commonly with child again, and brings forth too a new birth, long before the former is out of a dependency for support on his parents help, and able to shift for himself, and has all the assistance that is due to him from his parents: whereby the father, who is bound to take care for those he hath begot, is under an obligation to continue in conjugal society with the same woman longer than other creatures, whose young being able to subsist of themselves before the time of procreation returns again, the conjugal bond dissolves of itself, and they are at liberty, till Hymen at his usual anniversary season summons them again to choose new mates. Wherein one cannot but admire the wisdom of the great Creator, who having given to man foresight, and an ability to lay up for the future, as well as to supply the present necessity, hath made it necessary, that *society of man and wife should be more lasting,* than of male and female amongst other creatures; that so their industry might be encouraged, and their interest better united, to make provision and lay up goods for their common issue, which uncertain mixture, or easy and frequent solutions of conjugal society, would mightily disturb.

81. But though these are ties upon *mankind,* which make the *conjugal bonds* more firm and lasting in man, than the other species of animals; yet it would give one reason to inquire, why this compact, where procreation and education are secured, and inheritance taken care for, may not be made determinable, either by consent, or at a certain time, or upon certain conditions, as well as any other voluntary compacts, there being no necessity in the nature of the thing, nor to the ends of it, that it should always be for life; I mean, to such as are under no restraint of any positive law, which ordains all such contracts to be perpetual.

82. But the husband and wife, though they have but one common concern, yet having different understandings, will unavoidably sometimes have different wills too; it therefore being necessary that the last determination, i.e. the rule, should be placed somewhere; it naturally falls to the man's share, as the abler and the stronger. But this reaching but to the things of their common interest and property, leaves the wife in the full and free possession of what by contract is her peculiar right, and gives the husband no more power over her life than she has over his. The *power of the husband* being so far from that of an absolute monarch, that the *wife* has in many cases a liberty to separate from him, where natural right or their contract allows it; whether that contract be made by themselves in the state of nature, or by the customs or laws of the country they live in; and the children upon such separation fall to the father's or mother's lot, as such contract does determine.

83. For all the ends of *marriage* being to be obtained under politic government, as well as in the state of nature, the civil magistrate doth not abridge the right or power of either naturally necessary to those ends, viz. procreation and mutual support and assistance whilst they are together; but only decides any controversy that may arise between man and wife about them. If it were otherwise, and that absolute sovereignty and power of life and death naturally belonged to the husband, and were *necessary to the society between man and wife,* there could be no matrimony in any of those countries where the husband is allowed no such absolute authority. But the ends of matrimony requiring no such power in the husband, the condition of conjugal society put it not in him, it being not at all necessary to that state. Conjugal society could subsist and attain its ends without it; nay, community of goods, and the power over them, mutual assistance and maintenance, and other things belonging to conjugal society, might be varied and regulated by that contract which unites man and wife in that society, as far as may consist with procreation and the bringing up of children till they could shift for themselves; nothing being necessary to any society, that is not necessary to the ends for which it is made.

84. The *society betwixt parents and children,* and the distinct rights and powers belonging respectively to them, I have treated of so largely, in the foregoing chapter, that I shall not here need to say anything of it. And I think it is plain, that it is far different from a politic society.

85. *Master* and *servant* are names as old as history, but given to those of far different condition; for a free man makes himself a servant to another, by selling him, for a certain time, the service he undertakes to do, in exchange for wages he is to receive: and though this commonly puts him into the family of his master, and under the ordinary discipline thereof: yet it gives the master but a temporary power over him, and no greater than what is contained in the *contract* between them. But there is another sort of servants, which by a peculiar name we call *slaves,* who being captives taken in a just war, are by the right of nature subjected to the absolute dominion and arbitrary power of their masters. These men having, as I say, forfeited their lives, and with it their liberties, and lost their estates; and being in the *state of slavery,* not capable of any property, cannot in that state be considered as any part of *civil society;* the chief end whereof is the preservation of property,

86. Let us therefore consider a *master of a family* with all these subordinate relations of *wife, children, servants,* and *slaves,* united under the domestic rule of a family; which, what resemblance soever it may have in its order, offices, and number too, with a little commonwealth, yet is very far from it, both in its constitution, power, and end: or if it must be thought a monarchy, and the *paterfamilias* the absolute monarch in it, absolute monarchy will have but a very shattered and short power, when it is plain by what has been said before, that the *master of the family* has a very distinct and differently limited power, both as to time and extent, over those several persons that are in it. For excepting the slave (and the family is as much a family, and his power as *paterfamilias* as great, whether there be any slaves in his family or no) he has no legislative power of life and death over any of them, and none too but what a *mistress of a family* may have as well as he. And he certainly can have no absolute power over the whole family, who has but a very limited one over every individual in it. But how a family, or any other society of men, differ from that which is properly political society, we shall best see by considering wherein political society itself consists.

87. Man being born, as has been proved, with a title to perfect freedom, and an uncontrolled enjoyment of all the rights and privileges of the law of nature, equally with any other man, or number of men in the world, hath by nature a power, not only to preserve his property, that is, his life, liberty, and estate, against the injuries and attempts of other men; but to judge of and punish the breaches of that law in others, as he is persuaded the offence deserves, even with death itself, in crimes where the heinousness of the fact, in his opinion, requires it. But because no *political* society can be, nor subsist, without having in itself the power to preserve the property, and, in order thereunto, punish the offences of all those of that society; there and there only is *political society,* where every one of the members hath quitted his natural power, resigned it up into the hands of the community in all cases that excludes him not from appealing for protection to the law established by it. And thus all private judgment of every particular member being excluded, the community comes to be umpire by settled standing rules, indifferent, and the same to all parties; and by men having authority from the community, for the execution of those rules, decides all the differences that may happen between any members of that society concerning any matter of right; and punishes those offences which any member hath committed against the society, with such penalties as the law has established, whereby it is easy to discern, who are, and who

are not, in *political society* together. Those who are united into one body, and have a common established law and judicature to appeal to, with authority to decide controversies between them, and punish offenders, *are in civil society* one with another: but those who have no such common appeal, I mean on earth, are still in the state of nature, each being, where there is no other, judge for himself, and executioner: which is, as I have before shewed, the perfect *state of nature.*

88. And thus the commonwealth comes by a power to set down what punishment shall belong to the several transgressions which they think worthy of it, committed amongst the members of that society, (which is the *power of making laws*) as well as it has the power to punish any injury done unto any of its members, by any one that is not of it, (which is the power of war and peace,) and all this for the preservation of the property of all the members of that society, as far as is possible. But though every man who has entered into civil society, and is become a member of any commonwealth, has thereby quitted his power to punish offences against the law of nature, in prosecution of his own private judgment; yet with the judgment of offences, which he has given up to the legislative in all cases, where he can appeal to the magistrate, he has given a right to the commonwealth to employ his force, for the execution of the judgments of the commonwealth whenever he shall be called to it; which indeed are his own judgments, they being made by himself, or his representative. And herein we have the original of the legislative and executive power of civil society, which is to judge by standing laws, how far offences are to be punished, when committed within the commonwealth; and also to determine, by occasional judgments founded on the present circumstances of the fact, how far injuries from without are to be vindicated; and in both these to employ all the force of all the members, when there shall be need.

89. Whenever therefore any number of men are so united into one society, as to quit every one his executive power of the law of nature, and to resign it to the public, there and there only is a political, or civil society. And this is done, wherever any number of men, in the state of nature, enter into society to make one people, one body politic, under one supreme government; or else when any one joins himself to, and incorporates with any government already made. For hereby he authorizes the society, or, which is all one, the legislative thereof, to make laws for him, as the public good of the society shall require; to the execution whereof, his own assistance (as to his own degrees) is due. And this puts men out of a state of nature into that of a commonwealth, by setting up a judge on earth, with authority to determine all the controversies, and redress the injuries that may happen to any member of the commonwealth: which judge is the legislative, or magistrate appointed by it. And wherever there are any number of men, however associated, that have no such decisive power to appeal to, there they are still in the state of nature.

90. Hence it is evident, that absolute monarchy, which by some men is counted the only government in the world, is indeed inconsistent with civil society, and so can be no form of civil government at all; for the end of civil society being to avoid and remedy these inconveniencies of the state of nature, which necessarily follow from every man's being judge in his own case, by setting up a known authority, to which every one of that society may appeal upon any injury received, or controversy that may arise, and which every one of the[2] society ought to obey; wherever any persons are, who have not such an authority to appeal to for the decision of any difference between them, there those persons are still *in the state of nature.* And so is every *absolute prince,* in respect of those who are under his dominion.

91. For he being supposed to have all, both legislative and executive power in himself alone, there is no judge to be found, no appeal lies open to any one, who may fairly, and

indifferently, and with authority decide, and from whose decision relief and redress may be expected of any injury or inconveniency that may be suffered from the prince, or by his order: so that such a man, however intitled, *czar,* or *grand seignior,* or how you please, is as much in *the state of nature,* with all under his dominion, as he is with the rest of mankind. For wherever any two men are, who have no standing rule, and common judge to appeal to on earth, for the determination of controversies of right betwixt them, there they are still *in the state of*[3] *nature,* and under all the inconveniencies of it, with only this woful difference to the subject, or rather slave of an absolute prince; that whereas in the ordinary state of nature he has a liberty to judge of his right, and, according to the best of his power, to maintain it; now, whenever his property is invaded by the will and order of his monarch, he has not only no appeal, as those in society ought to have, but, as if he were degraded from the common state of rational creatures, is denied a liberty to judge of, or to defend his right; and so is exposed to all the misery and inconveniencies that a man can fear from one, who being in the unrestrained state of nature, is yet corrupted with flattery, and armed with power.

92. For he that thinks *absolute power purifies men's blood,* and corrects the baseness of human nature, need read but the history of this or any other age, to be convinced of the contrary. He that would have been so insolent and injurious in the woods of America, would not probably be much better in a throne; where perhaps learning and religion shall be found out to justify all that he shall do to his subjects, and the sword presently silence all those that dare question it. For what the *protection of absolute monarchy* is, what kind of fathers of their countries it makes princes to be, and to what a degree of happiness and security it carries civil society, where this sort of government is grown to perfection; he that will look into the late relation of Ceylon, may easily see.

93. *In absolute monarchies,* indeed, as well as other governments of the world, the subjects have an appeal to the law, and judges to decide any controversies, and restrain any violence that may happen betwixt the subjects themselves, one amongst another. This every one thinks necessary, and believes he deserves to be thought a declared enemy to society and mankind, who should go about to take it away. But whether this be from a true love of mankind and society, and such a charity as we all owe one to another, there is reason to doubt. For this is no more than what every man, who loves his own power, profit, or greatness, may and naturally must do, keep those animals from hurting, or destroying one another, who labour and drudge only for his pleasure and advantage; and so are taken care of, not out of any love the master has for them, but love of himself, and the profit they bring him. For if it be asked, what security, what fence is there, in such a state, *against the violence and oppression of this absolute ruler?* the very question can scarce be borne. They are ready to tell you, that it deserves death only to ask after safety. Betwixt subject and subject, they will grant, there must be measures, laws, and judges, for their mutual peace and security: but as for the ruler he ought to be *absolute,* and is above all such circumstances; because he has power to do more hurt and wrong, it is right when he does it. To ask how you may be guarded from harm, or injury, on that side where the strongest hand is to do it, is presently the voice of faction and rebellion: as if when men quitting the state of nature entered into society, they agreed that all of them but one should be under the restraint of laws, but that he should still retain all the liberty of the state of nature, increased with power, and made licentious by impunity. This is to think, that men are so foolish, that they take care to avoid what mischiefs may be done them by *pole cats,* or *foxes;* but are content, nay think it safety, to be devoured by *lions.*

94. But whatever flatterers may talk to amuse people's understandings, it hinders not men from feeling; and when they perceive, that any man, in what station soever, is out of the bounds of the civil society which they are of, and that they have no appeal on earth against any harm they may receive from him, they are apt to think themselves in the state of nature, in respect of him whom they find to be so: and to take care, as soon as they can, to have that *safety and security in civil society,* for which it was instituted, and for which only they entered into it. And therefore, though perhaps at first, (as shall be shewed more at large hereafter in the following part of this discourse) some one good and excellent man having got a pre-eminency amongst the rest, had this deference paid to his goodness and virtue, as to a kind of natural authority, that the chief rule, with arbitration of their differences, by a tacit consent devolved into his hands, without any other caution, but the assurance they had of his uprightness and wisdom; yet when time, giving authority, and (as some men would persuade us) sacredness to customs, which the negligent and unforeseen innocence of the first ages began, had brought in successors of another stamp, the people finding their properties not secure under the government, as then it was, (whereas government has no other end but the preservation of[4] property) could never be safe nor at rest, *nor think, themselves in civil society,* till the legislature was placed in collective bodies of men, call them senate, parliament, or what you please. By which means every single person became subject, equally with other the meanest men, to those laws, which he himself, as part of the legislative, had established; nor could any one, by his own authority, avoid the force of the law, when once made; nor by any presence of superiority plead exemption, thereby to license his own, or the miscarriages of any of his dependents.[5] *No man in civil society can be exempted from the laws of it.* For if any man may do what he thinks fit, and there be no appeal on earth, for redress or security against any harm he shall do; I ask, whether he be not perfectly still in the state of nature, and so can be *no part or member of that civil society:* unless any one will say, the state of nature and civil society are one and the same thing, which I have never yet found any one so great a patron of anarchy as to affirm.

CHAPTER VIII

Of the Beginning of Political Societies

95. Men being, as has been said, by nature, all free, equal, and independent, no one can be put out of this estate, and subjected to the political power of another, without his own consent. The only way, whereby any one divests himself of his natural liberty, and puts on the *bonds of civil society,* is by agreeing with other men to join and unite into a community, for their comfortable, safe, and peaceable living one amongst another, in a secure enjoyment of their properties, and a greater security against any, that are not of it. This any number of men may do, because it injures not the freedom of the rest; they are left as they were in the liberty of the state of nature. When any number of men have so *consented to make one community or government,* they are thereby presently incorporated, and make *one body politic,* wherein the *majority* have a right to act and conclude the rest.

96. For when any number of men have, by the consent of every individual, made a *community,* they have thereby made that *community* one body, with a power to act as one body, which is only by the will and determination of the majority. For that which acts any community, being only the *consent* of the individuals of it, and it being necessary to that which

greater force carries it, which is the *consent of the majority:* or else it is impossible it should act or continue one body, one community, which the consent of every individual that united into it, agreed that it should; and so every one is bound by that consent to be concluded by the majority. And therefore we see, that in assemblies, impowered to act by positive laws, where no number is set by that positive law which impowers them, the *act of the majority* passes for the act of the whole, and of course determines, as having, by the law of nature and reason, the power of the whole.

97. And thus every man, by consenting with others to make one body politic under one government, puts himself under an obligation, to every one of that society, to submit to the determination of the majority, and to be concluded by it; or else this *original compact,* whereby he with others incorporate into one society, would signify nothing, and be no compact, if he be left free, and under no other ties than he was in before in the state of nature. For what appearance would there be of any compact? What new engagement if he were no farther tied by any decrees of the society, than he himself thought fit, and did actually consent to? This would be still as great a liberty, as he himself had before his compact, or any one else in the state of nature hath, who may submit himself, and consent to any acts of it if he thinks fit.

98. For if *the consent of the majority* shall not, in reason, be received as *the act of the whole,* and conclude every individual; nothing but the consent of every individual can make any thing to be the act of the whole: But such a consent is next to impossible ever to be had, if we consider the infirmities of health, and avocations of business, which in a number, though much less than that of a commonwealth, will necessarily keep many away from the public assembly. To which if we add the variety of opinions, and contrariety of interests, which unavoidably happen in all collections of men, the coming into society upon such terms would be only like Cato's coming into the theatre, only to go out again. Such a constitution as this would make the mighty *leviathan* of a shorter duration than the feeblest creatures, and not let it outlast the day it was born in: which cannot be supposed, till we can think, that rational creatures should desire and constitute societies only to be dissolved. For where the majority cannot conclude the rest, there they cannot act as one body, and consequently will be immediately dissolved again.

99. Whosoever therefore out of a state of nature unite into a community, must be understood to give up all the power, necessary to the ends for which they unite into society, to the majority of the community, unless they expressly agreed in any number greater than the majority. And this is done by barely agreeing to *unite into one political society,* which is *all the compact* that is, or needs be, between the individuals, that enter into, or make up a commonwealth. And. thus that, which begins and actually *constitutes any political society,* is nothing, but the consent of any number of freemen capable of a majority, to unite and incorporate into such a society. And this is that, and that only, which did, or could give beginning to any lawful government in the world.

100. To this I find two objections made.

First, *That there are no instances to be found in story, of a company of men independent and equal one amongst another, that met together, and in this way began and set up a government.*

Secondly, *It is impossible of right, that men should do so, because all men being born under government, they are to submit to that, and are not at liberty to begin a new one.*

101. To the first there is this to answer, That it is not at all to be wondered, that *history* gives us but a very little account of *men, that lived together in the state of nature.* The inconveniencies of that condition and the love and want of society, no sooner brought any number of them together, but they presently united and incorporated, if they designed to

continue together. And if we may not suppose men ever to have been *in the state of nature,* because we hear not much of them in such a state, we may as well suppose the armies of Salmanasser or Xerxes were never children, because we hear little of them, till they were men, and embodied in armies. Government is every where antecedent to records, and letters seldom come in amongst a people till a long continuation of civil society has, by other more necessary arts, provided for their safety, ease, and plenty. And then they begin to look the after the history of their founders, and search into their original, when they have outlived the memory of it. For it is with commonwealths, as with particular persons, they are commonly *ignorant of their own births and infancies:* and if they know any thing of their original, they are beholden for it to the accidental records that others have kept of it. And those that we have of the beginning of any politics in the world, excepting that of the Jews, where God himself immediately interposed, and which favours not at all paternal dominion, are all either plain instances of such a beginning as I have mentioned, or at least have manifest footsteps of it.

102. He must shew a strange inclination to deny evident matter of fact, when it agrees not with his hypothesis, who will not allow, that the *beginning* of Rome and Venice were by the uniting together of several men free and independent one of another, amongst whom there was no natural superiority or subjection. And if Josephus Acosta's word may be taken, he tells us, that in many parts of America there was no government at all. "There are great and apparent conjectures," says he, "that these men, speaking of those of Peru, for a long time had neither kings nor commonwealths, but lived in troops, as they do this day in Florida, the Cheriquanas, those of Brasil, and many other nations, which have no certain kings, but as occasion is offered, in peace or war, they choose their captains as they please," 1. I. c. 25. If it be said, that every man there was born subject to his father, or the head of his family. That the subjection due from a child to a father took not away his freedom of uniting into what political society he thought fit, has been already proved. But be that as it will, these men, it is evident, were actually free; and whatever superiority some politicians now would place in any of them, they themselves claimed it not, but by consent were all equal, till by the same consent they set rulers over themselves. So that their politic societies all began from a voluntary union, and the mutual agreement of men freely acting in the choice of their governors, and forms of government.

103. And I hope those who went away from Sparta with Palantus, mentioned by Justin, 1. iii. c. 4, will be allowed to have been freemen, *independent* one of another, and to have set up a government over themselves, by their own consent. Thus I have given several examples out of history, of *people free and in the state of nature,* that being met together, incorporated and *began a commonwealth.* And if the want of such instances be an argument to prove that governments were not, nor could not be so begun, I suppose the contenders for paternal empire were better let it alone, than urge it against natural liberty. For if they can give so many instances out of history, of governments begun upon paternal right, I think (though at best an argument from what has been, to what should of right be, has no great force) one might, without any great danger, yield them the cause. But if I might advise them in the case, they would do well not to search too much into the *original of governments,* as they have begun *de facto;* lest they should find, at the foundation of most of them, something very little favourable to the design they promote, and such a power as they contend for.

104. But to conclude, reason being plain on our side, that men are naturally free, and the examples of history shewing, that the governments of the world, that were begun in peace, had their beginning laid on that foundation, and were *made by the consent of the*

people; there can be little room for doubt, either where the right is, or what has been the opinion, or practice of mankind, about the *first erecting of governments.*

105. I will not deny, that if we look back as far as history will direct us, towards the *original of commonwealths,* we shall generally find them under the government and administration of one man. And I am also apt to believe, that where a family was numerous enough to subsist by itself, and continued entire together, without mixing with others, as it often happens, where there is much land, and few people, the government commonly began *in the father.* For the father having, by the law of nature, the same power with every man else to punish, as he thought fit, any offences against that law, might thereby punish his transgressing children, even when they were men, and out of their pupilage; and they were very likely to submit to his punishment, and all join with him against the offender, in their turns, giving him thereby power to execute his sentence against any transgression, and so in effect make him the law maker, and governour over all that remained in conjunction with his family. He was fittest to be trusted; paternal affection secured their property and interest under his care; and the custom of obeying him, in their childhood, made it easier to submit to him, rather than to any other. If, therefore, they must have one to rule them, as government is hardly to be avoided amongst men that live together; who so likely to be the man as he that was their common father; unless negligence, cruelty, or any other defect of mind or body made him unfit for it? But when either the father died, and left his next heir, for want of age, wisdom, courage, or any other qualities, less fit for rule; or where several families met, and consented to continue together; there, it is not to be doubted, but they used their natural freedom to set up him whom they judged the ablest, and most likely to rule well over them. Conformable hereunto we find the people of America, who (living out of the reach of the conquering swords, and spreading domination of the two great empires of Peru and Mexico) enjoyed their own natural freedom, though, *caeteris paribus,* they commonly prefer the heir of their deceased king; yet, if they find him any way weak, or incapable, they pass him by, and set up the stoutest and bravest man for their ruler.

106. Thus, though looking back as far as records give us any account of peopling the world, and the history of nations, we commonly find the government to be in one hand; yet it destroys not that which I affirm, viz. that the *beginning of politic society* depends upon the consent of the individuals, to join into, and make one society; who, when they are thus incorporated, might set up what form of government they thought fit. But this having given occasion to men to mistake, and think, that by nature government was monarchical, and belonged to the father; it may not be amiss here to consider, why people in the beginning generally pitched upon this form; which though perhaps the father's pre-eminency might, in the first institution of some commonwealth give rise to, and place in the beginning the power in one hand; yet it is plain that the reason, that continued the form of *government in a single person,* was not any regard or respect to paternal authority; since all petty monarchies, that is, almost all monarchies, near their original, have been commonly, at least upon occasion, *elective.*

107. First then, in the beginning of things, the father's government of the childhood of those sprung from him, having accustomed them to the *rule of one man,* and taught them that where it was exercised with care and skill, with affection and love to those under it, it was sufficient to procure and preserve to men all the political happiness they sought for in society. It was no wonder that they should pitch upon, and naturally run into that form of government, which from their infancy they had been all accustomed to; and which, by experience, they had found both easy and safe. To which, if we add, that

monarchy being simple, and most obvious to men, whom neither experience had instructed in forms of government, nor the ambition or insolence of empire had taught to beware of the encroachments of prerogative, or the inconveniencies of absolute power, which monarchy in succession was apt to lay claim to, and bring upon them; it was not at all strange, that they should not much trouble themselves to think of methods of restraining any exorbitancies of those to whom they had given the authority over them, and of balancing the power of government, by placing several parts of it in different hands. They had neither felt the oppression of tyrannical dominion, nor did the fashion of the age, nor their possessions, or way of living, (which afforded little matter for covetousness or ambition) give them any reason to apprehend or provide against it; and therefore it is no wonder they put themselves into such a *frame of government,* as was not only, as I said, most obvious and simple, but also best suited to their present state and condition; which stood more in need of defence against foreign invasions and injuries, than of multiplicity of laws. The equality of a simple poor way of living, confining their desires within the narrow bounds of each man's small property, made few controversies, and so no need of many laws to decide them, or variety of officers to superintend the process, or look after the execution of justice, where there were but few trespasses, and few offenders. Since then those, who liked one another so well as to join into society, cannot but be supposed to have some acquaintance and friendship together, and some trust one in another; they could not but have greater apprehensions of others, than of one another: and therefore their first care and thought cannot but be supposed to be, how to secure themselves against foreign force. It was natural for them to put themselves under a *frame of government* which might best serve to that end, and choose the wisest and bravest man to conduct them in their wars, and lead them out against their enemies, and in this chiefly be their *ruler.*

108. Thus we see, that the *kings* of the Indians in America, which is still a pattern of the first ages in Asia and Europe, whilst the inhabitants were too few for the country, and want of people and money gave men no temptation to enlarge their possessions of land, or contest for wider extent of ground, are little more than *generals of their armies;* and though they command absolutely in war, yet at home and in time of peace they exercise very little dominion, and have but a very moderate sovereignty; the resolutions of peace and war being ordinarily either in the people, or in a council. Though the war itself, which admits not of plurality of governors, naturally devolves the command into the *king's sole authority.*

109. And thus, in Israel itself, the *chief business of their judges, and first kings,* seems to have been *to be captains in war,* and leaders of their armies; which (besides what is signified by *going out and in before the people,* which was to march forth to war, and home again at the heads of their forces) appears plainly in the story of Jephthah. The Ammonites making war upon Israel, the Gileadites in fear sent to Jephthah, a bastard of their family whom they had cast off, and article with him, if he will assist them against the Ammonites, to make him their ruler; which they do in these words, "And the people made him head and captain over them," *Judg.* xi. 11. which was, as it seems, all one as to be judge. "And he judged Israel," *Judg.* xii. 7. that is, was their captain-general, *six years.* So when Jotham upbraids the Shechemites with the obligation they had to Gideon, who had been their judge and ruler, he tells them, "He fought for you, and adventured his life far, and delivered you out of the hands of Midian," *Judg.* ix. 17. Nothing is mentioned of him, but what he did as a *general:* and indeed that is all is found in his history, or in any of the rest of the judges. And Abimelech particularly is called *king,* though at most he was but their *general.* And when, being weary of the ill conduct of Samuel's sons, the children of Israel desired a king, "like all the nations, to judge them, and to go out before them, and to

fight their battles," *1 Sam.* viii. 20. God granting their desire, says to Samuel. "I will send thee a man, and thou shalt anoint him to be captain over my people Israel, that he may save my people out of the hands of the Philistines," c. ix. 16. As if the only *business of a king* had been to lead out their armies, and fight in their defence; and accordingly at his inauguration, pouring a vial of oil upon him, declares to Saul, that "the Lord had anointed him to be captain over his inheritance," c. x. 1. And therefore those who, after Saul's being solemnly chosen and saluted *king* by the *tribes* of Mispah, were unwilling to have him their *king,* made no other objection but this, "How shall this man save us?" v. 27. as if they should have said, this man is unfit to be our king, not having skill and conduct enough in war to be able to defend us. And when God resolved to transfer the government to David, it is in these words, "But now thy kingdom shall not continue: the Lord hath sought him a man after his own heart, and the Lord hath commanded him to be captain over his people," c. xiii. 14. As if the whole kingly authority were nothing else but to be their general: and therefore the tribes who had stuck to Saul's family, and opposed David's reign, when they came to Hebron with terms of submission to him, they tell him, amongst other arguments, they had to submit to him as their king, that he was in effect their king in Saul's time, and therefore they had no reason but to receive him as their king now. "Also" (say they,) "in time past, when Saul was king over us, thou wast he that leddest out, and broughtest in Israel, and the Lord said unto thee, Thou shalt feed my people Israel, and thou shalt be a captain over Israel."

110. Thus, whether a family by degrees *grew up into a commonwealth,* and the fatherly authority being continued on to the elder son, every one in his turn growing up under it, tacitly submitted to it; and the easiness and equality of it not offending any one, every one acquiesced, till time seemed to have confirmed it, and settled a right of succession by prescription: or whether several families, or the descendants of several families, whom chance, neighbourhood, or business brought together, *uniting into society,* the need of a general, whose conduct might defend them against their enemies in war, and the great confidence the innocence and sincerity of that poor but virtuous age (such as are almost all those which begin governments, that ever come to last in the world), gave men of one another, made the first beginners of commonwealths generally put the rule into one man's hand, without any other express limitation or restraint, but what the nature of the thing and the end of government required: Whichever of those it was that at first put the rule into the hands of a single person, certain it is that no body was entrusted with it but for the public good and safety, and to those ends, in the infancies of commonwealths, those who had it, commonly used it. And unless they had done so, young societies could not have subsisted; without such nursing fathers tender and careful of the public weal, all governments would have sunk under the weakness and infirmities of their infancy, and the prince and the people had soon perished together.

111. But though the *golden age* (before vain ambition, and *amor sceleratus habendi,* evil concupiscence, had corrupted men's minds into a mistake of true power and honour) had more virtue, and consequently better governors, as well as less vicious subjects; and there was then *no stretching prerogative* on the one side, to oppress the people; nor consequently on the other, any *dispute about privilege,* to lessen or restrain the power of the magistrate; and so no contest betwixt rulers and people about governors or government: yet when ambition and luxury in future ages[6] would retain and increase the power, without doing the business for which it was given; and, aided by flattery, taught princes to have distinct and separate interests from their people; men found it necessary to examine more carefully the original and rights of government, and to find out ways to *restrain the exorbitancies,* and

prevent the abuses of that power, which they having entrusted in another's hands only for their own good, they found was made use of to hurt them.

112. Thus we may see how probable it is, that people that were naturally free, and by their own consent either submitted to the government of their father, or united together out of different families to make a government, should generally put the *rule into one man's hands,* and choose to be under the conduct of a single person, without so much as by express conditions limiting or regulating his power, which they thought safe enough in his honesty and prudence. Though they never dreamed of monarchy being *jure divino,* which we never heard of among mankind, till it was revealed to us by the divinity of this last age; nor ever allowed paternal power to have a right to dominion, or to be the foundation of all government. And thus much may suffice to shew, that, as far as we have any light from history, we have reason to conclude, that all peaceful beginnings of government have been *laid in the consent of the people.* I say peaceful, because I shall have occasion in another place to speak of conquest, which some esteem a way of beginning of governments.

The other objection I find urged against the beginning of polities, in the way I have mentioned, is this, viz.

113. *That all men being born under government, some or other, it is impossible any of them should ever be free, and at liberty to unite together, and begin a new one, or ever be able to erect a lawful government.*

If this argument be good, I ask, how came so many lawful monarchies into the world? for if any body, upon this supposition, can shew me any one man in any age of the world free to begin a lawful monarchy, I will be bound to shew him ten other *free men* at liberty at the same time to unite and begin a new government under a regal or any other form. It being demonstration, that if any one, *born under the dominion* of another, may be so free as to have a right to command others in a new and distinct empire, every one that is *born under the dominion* of another may be so free too, and may become a ruler, or subject of a distinct separate government. And so by this their own principle, either all men, however born, are free, or else there is but one lawful prince, one lawful government in the world. And then they have nothing to do, but barely to shew us which that is; which when they have done, I doubt not but all mankind will easily agree to pay obedience to him.

114. Though it be a sufficient answer to their objection, to shew that it involves them in the same difficulties that it doth those they use it against; yet I shall endeavour to discover the weakness of this argument a little farther.

"All men," say they, "are born under government, and therefore they cannot be at liberty to begin a new one. Every one is born a subject to his father, or his prince, and is therefore under the perpetual tie of subjection and allegiance." It is plain mankind never owned nor considered any such natural *subjection that they were born in,* to one or to the other, that tied them, without their own consents, to a subjection to them and their heirs.

115. For there are no examples so frequent in history, both sacred and profane, as those of men withdrawing themselves, and their obedience from the jurisdiction they were born under, and the family or community they were bred up in, and *setting up new governments* in other places, from whence sprang all that number of petty commonwealths in the beginning of ages, and which always multiplied as long as there was room enough, till the stronger, or more fortunate, swallowed the weaker; and those great ones again breaking to pieces, dissolved into lesser dominions. All which are so many testimonies against paternal sovereignty, and plainly prove, that it was not the natural right of the father descending to

his heirs, that made governments in the beginning, since it was impossible, upon that ground, there should have been so many little kingdoms; all must have been but only one universal monarchy, if men had not been *at liberty to separate themselves* from their families, and the government, be it what it will, that was set up in it, and go and make distinct commonwealths and other governments, as they thought fit.

116. This has been the practice of the world from its first beginning to this day; nor is it now any more hindrance to the freedom of mankind, that they are *born under constituted and ancient polities,* that have established laws, and set forms of government, than if they were born in the woods, amongst the unconfined inhabitants, that run loose in them. For those who would persuade us, that, *by being born under any government, we are naturally subjects to it,* and have no more any title or pretence to the freedom of the state of nature; have no other reason (bating that of paternal power, which we have already answered) to produce for it, but only, because our fathers or progenitors passed away their natural liberty, and thereby bound up themselves and their posterity to a perpetual subjection to the government which they themselves submitted to. It is true, that whatever engagements or promises any one has made for himself, he is under the obligation of them, but cannot, by any compact whatsoever, bind his children or posterity. For his son, when a man, being altogether as free as the father, any *act of the father can no more give away the liberty of the son,* than it can of any body else: he may indeed annex such conditions to the land he enjoyed as a subject of any commonwealth, as may oblige his son to be of that community, if he will enjoy those possessions which were his father's; because that estate being his father's property, he may dispose, or settle it, as he pleases.

117. And this has generally given the occasion to mistake in this matter; because commonwealths not permitting any part of their dominions to be dismembered, nor to be enjoyed by any but those of their community, the son cannot ordinarily enjoy the possessions of his father, but under the same terms his father did, by becoming a member of the society; whereby he puts himself presently under the government he finds there established, as much as any other subject of that commonwealth. And thus *the consent of freemen, born under government, which only makes them members of it,* being given separately in their turns, as each comes to be of age, and not in a multitude together; people take no notice of it, and thinking it not done at all, or not necessary, conclude they are naturally subjects as they are men.

118. But, it is plain, governments themselves understand it otherwise; they claim *no power over the son, because of that they had over the father;* nor look on children as being their subjects, by their fathers being so. If a subject of England have a child, by an English woman in France, whose subject is he? Not the king of England's; for he must have leave to be admitted to the privileges of it. Nor the king of France's: for how then has his father a liberty to bring him away, and breed him as he pleases? And who ever was judged as a traitor or deserter, if he left, or warred against a country, for being barely born in it of parents that were aliens there? It is plain then, by the practice of governments themselves, as well as by the law of right reasons, that *a child is born a subject of no country or government.* He is under his father's tuition and authority, till he comes to age of discretion; and then he is a freeman, at liberty what government he will put himself under, what body politic he will unite himself to. For if an Englishman's son, born in France, be at liberty, and may do so, it is evident there is no tie upon him by his father's being a subject of this kingdom; nor is he bound up by any compact of his ancestors. And why then hath not his son, by the same reason, the same liberty, though he be born any where else? Since the power that a father hath naturally over his children is the same, wherever they be born, and the ties of natural obligations are not bounded by the positive limits of kingdoms and commonwealths.

119. Every man being, as has been shewed, naturally free, and nothing being able to put him into subjection to any earthly power, but only his own consent; it is to be considered, what shall be understood to be a *sufficient declaration of* a man's *consent, to make him subject* to the laws of any government. There is a common distinction of an express and a tacit consent, which will concern our present case. No body doubts but an express consent, of any man entering into any society, makes him a perfect member of that society, a subject of that government. The difficulty is, what ought to be looked upon as a *tacit consent,* and how far it binds, i.e. how far any one shall be looked on to have consented, and thereby submitted to any government, where he has made no expressions of it at all. And to this I say, that every man, that hath any possessions, or enjoyment of any part of the dominions of any government, doth thereby give his *tacit consent,* and is as far forth obliged to obedience to the laws of that government, during such enjoyment, as any one under it; whether this his possession be of land, to him and his heirs for ever, or a lodging only for a week; or whether it be barely travelling freely on the highway: and, in effect, it reaches as far as the very being of any one within the territories of that government.

120. To understand this the better, it is fit to consider, that every man, when he at first incorporates himself into any commonwealth, he, by his uniting himself thereunto, annexed also, and submits to the community, those possessions which he has, or shall acquire, that do not already belong to any other government. For it would be a direct contradiction, for any one to enter into society with others for the securing and regulating of property, and yet to suppose, his land, whose property is to be regulated by the laws of the society, should be exempt from the jurisdiction of that government, to which he himself, the proprietor of the land, is a subject. By the same act therefore, whereby any one unites his person, which was before free, to any commonwealth; by the same he unites his possessions, which were before free, to it also: and they become, both of them, person and possession, subject to the government and dominion of that commonwealth, as long as it hath a being. Whoever therefore, from thenceforth, by inheritance, purchase, permission, or otherways, *enjoys any part of the land* so annexed to, and under the government *of that commonwealth, must take it with the condition* it is under; that is, *of submitting to the government of the commonwealth,* under whose jurisdiction it is, as far forth as any subject of it.

121. But since the government has a direct jurisdiction only over the land, and reaches the possessor of it, (before he has actually incorporated himself in the society) only as he dwells upon, and enjoys that; the obligation any one is under, by virtue of such enjoyment, to *submit to the government, begins and ends with the enjoyment:* so that whenever the owner, who has given nothing but such a tacit consent to the government, will, by donation, sale, or otherwise, quit the said possession, he is at liberty to go and incorporate himself into any other commonwealth; or to agree with others to begin a new one, *in vacuis locis,* in any part of the world they can find free and unpossessed: whereas he, that has once, by actual agreement, and any express declaration, given his *consent* to be of any commonwealth, is perpetually and indispensably obliged to be, and remain unalterably a subject to it, and can never be again in the liberty of the state of nature; unless, by any calamity, the government he was under comes to be dissolved, or else by some public act cuts him off from being any longer a member of it.

122. But submitting to the laws of any country, living quietly, and enjoying privileges and protection under them, *makes not a man a member of that society:* this is only a local protection and homage due to and from all those, who, not being in a state of war, come within the territories belonging to any government, to all parts whereof the force of its laws extends. But this no more *makes a man a member of that society,* a perpetual subject of

that commonwealth, than it would make a man a subject to another, in whose family he found it convenient to abide for some time, though, whilst he continued in it, he were obliged to comply with the laws, and submit to the government he found there. And thus we see, that foreigners, by living all their lives under another government, and enjoying the privileges and protection of it, though they are bound, even in conscience, to submit to its administration, as far forth as any denison; yet do not thereby come to be *subjects or members of that commonwealth*. Nothing can make any man so, but his actually entering into it by positive engagement, and express promise and compact. This is that, which I think, concerning the beginning of political societies, and that *consent which makes any one a member of any commonwealth*.

CHAPTER IX

Of the Ends of Political Society and Government

123. If man in the state of nature be so free, as has been said; if he be absolute lord of his own person and possessions, equal to the greatest, and subject to no body, why will he part with his freedom? why will he give up this empire, and subject himself to the dominion and control of any other power? To which it is obvious to answer, that though in the state of nature he hath such a right, yet the enjoyment of it is very uncertain, and constantly exposed to the invasion of others. For all being kings as much as he, every man his equal, and the greater part no strict observers of equity and justice, the enjoyment of the property he has in this state is very unsafe, very unsecure. This makes him willing to quit this condition, which, however free, is full of fears and continual dangers: and it is not without reason, that he seeks out, and is willing to join in society with others, who are already united, or have a mind to unite, for the mutual preservation of their lives, liberties, and estates, which I call by the general name, property.

124. The great and *chief end,* therefore, of men's uniting into commonwealths, and putting themselves under government, is *the preservation of their property*. To which in the state of nature there are many things wanting.

First, There wants an established, settled, known law, received and allowed by common consent to be the standard of right and wrong, and the common measure to decide all controversies between them. For though the law of nature be plain and intelligible to all rational creatures; yet men being biassed by their interest, as well as ignorant for want of studying it, are not apt to allow of it as a law binding to them in the application of it to their particular cases.

125. *Secondly,* In the state of nature there wants *a known and indifferent judge,* with authority to determine all differences according to the established law. For every one in that state being both judge and executioner of the law of nature, men being partial to themselves, passion and revenge is very apt to carry them too far, and with too much heat, in their own cases; as well as negligence, and unconcernedness, to make them too remiss in other men's.

126. *Thirdly,* In the state of nature, there often wants power to back and support the sentence when right, and to give it due execution. They who by any injustice offended, will seldom fail, where they are able, by force to make good their injustice; such resistance many times makes the punishment dangerous, and frequently destructive, to those who attempt it.

127. Thus mankind, notwithstanding all the privileges of the state of nature, being but in an ill condition, while they remain in it, are quickly driven into society. Hence it comes to pass that we seldom find any number of men live any time together in this state. The inconveniencies that they are therein exposed to, by the irregular and uncertain exercise of the power every man has of punishing the transgressions of others, make them take sanctuary under the established laws of government, and therein seek *the preservation of their property*. It is this makes them so willingly give up every one his single power of punishing, to be exercised by such alone, as shall be appointed to it amongst them; and by such rules as the community, or those authorized by them to that purpose, shall agree on. And in this we have the original *right and rise of both the legislative and executive power,* as well as of the governments and societies themselves.

128. For in the state of nature, to omit the liberty he has of innocent delights, a man has two powers.

The first is to do whatsoever he thinks fit for the preservation of himself and others within the permission of the *law of nature:* by which law, common to them all, he and all the rest of *mankind are one community*, make up one society, distinct from all other creatures. And, were it not for the corruption and viciousness of degenerate men, there would be no need of any other; no necessity that men should separate from this great and natural community, and by positive agreements combine into smaller and divided associations.

The other power a man has in the state of nature, is the *power to punish the crimes* committed against that law. Both these he gives up, when he joins in a private, if I may so call it, or particular politic society, and incorporates into any commonwealth, separate from the rest of mankind.

129. The first *power, viz. of doing whatsoever he thought fit for the preservation of himself,* and the rest of mankind, *he gives up* to be regulated by laws made by the society, so far forth as the preservation of himself and the rest of that society shall require; which laws of the society in many things confine the liberty he had by the law of nature.

130. *Secondly,* The *power of punishing he wholly gives up,* and engages his natural force, (which he might before employ in the execution of the law of nature, by his own single authority, as he thought fit) to assist the executive power of the society, as the law thereof shall require. For being now in a new state, wherein he is to enjoy many conveniencies, from the labour, assistance, and society of others in the same community, as well as protection from its whole strength; he is to part also, with as much of his natural liberty, in providing for himself, as the good, prosperity, and safety of the society shall require; which is not only necessary, but just, since the other members of the society do the like.

131. But though men, when they enter into society, give up the equality, liberty, and executive power they had in the state of nature, into the hands of the society, to be so far disposed of by the legislative, as the good of the society shall require; yet it being only with an intention in every one the better to preserve himself, his liberty and property; (for no rational creature can be supposed to change his condition with an intention to be worse) the power of the society, or legislative constituted by them, *can never be supposed to extend farther, than the common good;* but is obliged to secure every one's property, by providing against those three defects above mentioned, that made the state of nature so unsafe and uneasy. And so whoever has the legislative or supreme power of any commonwealth, is bound to govern by established standing laws, promulgated and known to the people, and not by extemporary decrees; by indifferent and upright judges, who are to decide controversies by those laws; and to employ the force of the community at home,

only in the execution of such laws; or abroad to prevent or redress foreign injuries, and secure the community from inroads and invasion. And all this to be directed to no other *end,* but the *peace, safety,* and *public good* of the people.

CHAPTER X

Of the Forms of a Commonwealth

132. The majority having, as has been shewed, upon men's first uniting into society, the whole power of the community naturally in them, may employ all that power in making laws for the community from time to time, and executing those laws by officers of their own appointing; and then the *form* of the government is a perfect *democracy:* or else may put the power of making laws into the hands of a few select men, and their heirs or successors; and then it is an *oligarchy:* or else into the hands of one man, and then it is a *monarchy:* if to him and his heirs, it is an *hereditary monarchy:* if to him only for life, but upon his death the power only of nominating a successor to return to them; an *elective monarchy.* And so accordingly of these the community may make compounded and mixed forms of government, as they think good. And if the legislative power be at first given by the majority to one or more persons only for their lives, or any limited time, and then the supreme power to revert to them again; when it is so reverted, the community may dispose of it again anew into what hands they please, and so constitute a new form of government. For the *form of government depending upon the placing* the supreme power, which is the legislative (it being impossible to conceive that an inferiour power should prescribe to a superiour, or any but the supreme make laws), according as the power of making laws is placed, such is the *form of the commonwealth.*

133. By commonwealth, I must be understood all along to mean, not a democracy, or any form of government, but *any independent community,* which the Latines signified by the word *civitas;* to which the word which best answers in our language, is *commonwealth,* and most properly expresses such a society of men, which community or city in English does not. For there may be subordinate communities in government; and city amongst us has quite a different notion from commonwealth: and therefore, to avoid ambiguity, I crave leave to use the word *commonwealth* in that sense, in which I find it used by King *James the first:* and I take it to be its genuine signification; which if any body dislike, I consent with him to change it for a better.

CHAPTER XI

Of the Extent of the Legislative Power

134. The great end of men's entering into society being the enjoyment of their properties in peace and safety, and the great instrument and means of that being the laws established in that society; *the first and fundamental positive law* of all commonwealths *is the establishing of the legislative* power; as the *first and fundamental natural law,* which is to govern even the legislative itself, *is the preservation of the society,* and (as far as will consist with the public good) of every person in it. This *legislative* is not only *the supreme power* of the common-

wealth, but sacred and unalterable in the hands where the community have once placed it; nor can any edict of any body else, in what form soever conceived, or by what power soever backed, have the force and obligation of a law, which has not its *sanction from* that *legislative* which the public has chosen and appointed; for without this the law could not have that, which is absolutely necessary to its being a *law,*[7] *the consent of the society;* over whom no body can have a power to make laws, but by their own consent, and by authority received from them; and therefore all the obedience, which by the most solemn ties any one can be obliged to pay, ultimately terminates in this supreme power, and is directed by those laws which it enacts; nor can any oaths to any foreign power whatsoever, or any domestic subordinate power, discharge any member of the society from his *obedience to the legislative,* acting pursuant to their trust; nor oblige him to any obedience contrary to the laws so enacted, or farther than they do allow; it being ridiculous to imagine one can be tied ultimately to obey any power in the society, which is not the supreme.

135. Though the legislative, whether placed in one or more, whether it be always in being, or only by intervals, though it be the supreme power in every commonwealth; yet,

First, It is *not,* nor can possibly be absolutely *arbitrary* over the lives and fortunes of the people. For it being but the joint power of every member of the society given up to that person, or assembly, which is legislator, it can be no more than those persons had in a state of nature before they entered into society, and gave up to the community. For no body can transfer to another more power than he has in himself; and no body has an absolute arbitrary power over himself, or over any other, to destroy his own life, or take away the life or property of another. A man, as has been proved, cannot subject himself to the arbitrary power of another; and having in the state of nature no arbitrary power over the life, liberty, or possession of another, but only so much as the law of nature gave him for the preservation of himself and the rest of mankind; this is all he doth, or can give up to the commonwealth, and by it to the legislative power, so that the legislative can have no more than this. Their power, in the utmost bounds of it, is *limited to the public good* of the society. It is a power, that hath no other end but preservation, and therefore can never[8] have a right to destroy, enslave, or designedly to impoverish the subjects. The obligations of the law of nature cease not in society, but only in many cases are drawn closer, and have by human laws known penalties annexed to them, to enforce their observation. Thus the law of nature stands as an eternal rule to all men, legislators as well as others. The rules that they make for other men's actions, must, as well as their own and other men's actions, be conformable to the law of nature, i.e. to the will of God, of which that is a declaration; and the *fundamental law of nature being the preservation of mankind,* no human sanction can be good or valid against it.

136. *Secondly,*[9] The legislative or supreme authority cannot assume to itself a power to rule, by extemporary, arbitrary decrees, but *is bound to dispense justice,* and decide the rights of the subject, *by promulgated, standing laws, and known authorised judges.* For the law of nature being unwritten, and so no-where to be found, but in the minds of men; they who through passion, or interest, shall miscite, or misapply it, cannot so easily be convinced of their mistake, where there is no established judge: and so it serves not, as it ought, to determine the rights, and fence the properties of those that live under it; especially where every one is judge, interpreter, and executioner of it too, and that in his own case: and he that has right on his side having ordinarily but his own single strength, hath not force enough to defend himself from injuries, or to punish delinquents. To avoid these inconveniencies, which disorder men's properties in the state of nature, men unite into societies, that they may have the united strength of the whole society to secure and defend

their properties, and may have standing rules to bound it, by which every one may know what is his. To this end it is that men give up all their natural power to the society which they enter into, and the community put the legislative power into such hands as they think fit: with this trust, that they shall be governed by *declared laws,* or else their peace, quiet, and property will still be at the same uncertainty, as it was in the state of nature.

137. Absolute arbitrary power, or governing without *settled standing laws,* can neither of them consist with the ends of society and government, which men would not quit the freedom of the state of nature for, and tie themselves up under, were it not to preserve their lives, liberties, and fortunes, and by *stated rules* of right and property to secure their peace and quiet. It cannot be supposed that they should intend, had they a power so to do, to give to any one, or more, an *absolute arbitrary power* over their persons and estates, and put a force into the magistrate's hand to execute his unlimited will arbitrarily upon them. This were to put themselves into a worse condition than the state of nature, wherein they had a liberty to defend their right against the injuries of others, and were upon equal terms of force to maintain it, whether invaded by a single man, or many in combination. Whereas by supposing they have given up themselves to the absolute arbitrary power and will of a legislator, they have disarmed themselves, and armed him, to make a prey of them when he pleases. He being in a much worse condition, who is exposed to the arbitrary power of one man, who has the command of 100,000, than he that is exposed to the arbitrary power of 100,000 single men; no body being secure, that his will, who has such a command, is better than that of other men, though his force be 100,000 times stronger. And therefore, whatever form the commonwealth is under, the ruling power ought to govern by declared and received laws, and not by extemporary dictates and undetermined resolutions. For then mankind will be in a far worse condition than in the state of nature, if they shall have armed one or a few men with the joint power of a multitude, to force them to obey at pleasure the exorbitant and unlimited decrees of their sudden thoughts, or unrestrained, and till that moment unknown wills, without having any measures set down which may guide and justify their actions; for all the power the government has, being only for the good of the society, as it ought not to be arbitrary and at pleasure, so it ought to be exercised by *established and promulgated laws;* that both the people may know their duty, and be safe and secure within the limits of the law, and the rulers too kept within their bounds, and not to be tempted, by the power they have in their hands, to employ it to such purposes, and by such measures, as they would not have known, and own not willingly.

138. *Thirdly,* The *supreme power cannot take* from any man part of his property without his own consent. For the preservation of property being the end of government, and that for which men enter into society, it necessarily supposes and requires, that the people should *have property,* without which they must be supposed to lose that, by entering into society, which was the end for which they entered into it; too gross an absurdity for any man to own. *Men* therefore *in society having property,* they have such right to the goods, which by the law of the community are theirs, that no body hath a right to take their substance or any part of it from them, without their own consent; without this they have no property at all. For I have truly no property in that, which another can by right take from me, when he pleases, against my consent. Hence it is a mistake to think, that the *supreme or legislative power* of any commonwealth can do what it will, and dispose of the estates of the subject arbitrarily, or take any part of them at pleasure. This is not much to be feared in governments where the legislative consists, wholly or in part, in assemblies which are variable, whose members, upon the dissolution of the assembly, are sub-

jects under the common laws of their country, equally with the rest. But in governments, where the legislative is in one lasting assembly always in being, or in one man, as in absolute monarchies, there is danger still, that they will think themselves to have a distinct interest from the rest of the community; and so will be apt to increase their own riches and power by taking what they think fit from the people. For a man's property is not at all secure, though there be good and equitable laws to set the bounds of it between him and his fellow subjects, if he who commands those subjects, have power to take from any private man, what part he pleases of his property, and use and dispose of it as he thinks good.

139. But government, into whatsoever hands it is put, being, as I have before shewed, intrusted with this condition, and *for this end,* that men might have and secure their properties; the prince, or senate, however it may have power to make laws, for the regulating of property between the subjects one amongst another, yet can never have a power to take to themselves the whole, or any part of the subject's property, without their own consent. For this would be in effect to leave them no property at all. And to let us see, that even absolute power where it is necessary, is not arbitrary by being absolute, but is still limited by that reason, and confined to those ends, which required it in some cases to be absolute, we need look no farther than the common practice of martial discipline. For the preservation of the army, and in it of the whole commonwealth, requires an absolute obedience to the command of every superiour officer, and it is justly death to disobey or dispute the most dangerous or unreasonable of them; but yet we see, that neither the serjeant, that could command a soldier to march up to the mouth of a cannon, or stand in a breach, where he is almost sure to perish, can command that soldier to give him one penny of his money; nor the general, that can condemn him to death for deserting his post, or for not obeying the most desperate orders, can yet, with all his absolute power of life and death, dispose of one farthing of that soldier's estate, or seize one jot of his goods; whom yet he can command any thing, and hang for the least disobedience: because such a blind obedience is necessary to that end, for which the commander has his power, viz. the preservation of the rest; but the disposing of his goods has nothing to do with it.

140. It is true, governments cannot be supported without great charge, and it is fit every one who enjoys his share of the protection, should pay out of his estate his proportion for the maintenance of it. But still it must be with his own consent, i.e. the consent of the majority, giving it either by themselves, or their representatives chosen by them. For if any one shall claim a *power to lay* and levy *taxes* on the people, by his own authority, and without such consent of the people, he thereby invades the *fundamental law of property*, and subverts the end of government. For what property have I in that, which another may by right take when he pleases, to himself?

141. *Fourthly,* The *legislative cannot transfer the power of making laws* to any other hands. For it being but a delegated power from the people, they who have it cannot pass it over to others. The people alone can appoint the form of the commonwealth, which is by constituting the legislative, and appointing in whose hands that shall be. And when the people have said, we will submit to rules, and be governed by laws made by such men, and in such forms, no body else can say other men shall make laws for them; nor can the people be bound by any laws, but such as are enacted by those whom they have chosen, and authorized to make laws for them. The power of the legislative being derived from the people by a positive voluntary grant and institution, can be no other than what that positive grant conveyed, which being only to make laws, and not to make legislators, the legislative can have no power to transfer their authority of making laws and place it in other hands.

142. These are the bounds which the trust, that is put in them by the society and the law of God and nature, have *set to the legislative* power of every commonwealth, in all forms of government.

First, They are to govern by *promulgated established laws,* not to be varied in particular cases, but to have one rule for rich and poor, for the favourite at court, and the countryman at plough.

Secondly, These laws also ought to be designed for no other end ultimately, but *the good of the people.*

Thirdly, They must *not raise taxes* on the *property of the people, without the consent of the people,* given by themselves or their deputies. And this properly concerns only such governments where the legislative is always in being, or at least where the people have not reserved any part of the legislative to deputies, to be from time to time chosen by themselves.

Fourthly, The legislative neither must *nor can transfer the power of making laws* to any body else, or place it any where, but where the people have.

CHAPTER XII

Of the Legislative, Executive, and Federative Power of the Commonwealth

143. The legislative power is that, which has a right *to direct how the force of the commonwealth* shall be employed for preserving the community and the members of it. But because those laws which are constantly to be executed, and whose force is always to continue, may be made in a little time; therefore there is no need, that the legislative should be always in being, not having always business to do. And because it may be too great a temptation to human frailty, apt to grasp at power, for the same persons, who have the power of making laws, to have also in their hands the power to execute them, whereby they may exempt themselves from obedience to the laws they make, and suit the law, both in its making and execution, to their own private advantage, and thereby come to have a distinct interest from the rest of the community, contrary to the end of society and government: therefore in well ordered commonwealths, where the good of the whole is so considered, as it ought, the legislative power is put into the hands of divers persons, who, duly assembled, have by themselves, or jointly with others, a power to make laws; which when they have done, being separated again, they are themselves subject to the laws they have made; which is a new and near tie upon them, to take care that they make them for the public good.

144. But because the laws, that are at once, and in a short time made, have a constant and lasting force, and need a *perpetual execution,* or an attendance thereunto: therefore it is necessary there should be a *power always in being,* which should see to the execution of the laws that are made, and remain in force. And thus the legislative and executive power come often to be separated.

145. There is another power in every commonwealth, which one may call *natural,* because it is that which answers to the power every man naturally had before he entered into society. For though in a commonwealth, the members of it are distinct persons still in reference to one another, and as such are governed by the laws of the society; yet in reference to the rest of mankind, they make one body, which is, as every member of it before was, still in the state of nature with the rest of mankind. Hence it is, that the controversies that happen between any man of the society with those that are out of it, are managed

by the public; and an injury done to a member of their body engages the whole in the reparation of it. So that, under this consideration, the whole community is one body in the state of nature, in respect of all other states or persons out of its community.

146. This therefore contains the power of war and peace, leagues and alliances, and all the transactions, with all persons and communities without the commonwealth; and may be called federative, if any one pleases. So the thing be understood, I am indifferent as to the name.

147. These two powers, executive and federative, though they be really distinct in themselves, yet one comprehending the execution of the municipal laws of the society within itself, upon all that are parts of it; the other the management of the *security and interest of the public without,* with all those that it may receive benefit or damage from; yet they are always almost united. And though this *federative power* in the well or ill management of it be of great moment to the commonwealth, yet it is much less capable to be directed by antecedent, standing, positive laws, than the executive; and so must necessarily be left to the prudence and wisdom of those whose hands it is in, to be managed for the public good. For the laws that concern subjects one amongst another, being to direct their actions, may well enough precede them. But what is to be done in reference to foreigners, depending much upon their actions, and the variation of designs, and interests, must be left in great part to the prudence of those who have this power committed to them, to be managed by the best of their skill, for the advantage of the commonwealth.

148. Though, as I said, the executive and federative power of every community be really distinct in themselves, yet they are hardly to be separated, and placed at the same time in the hands of distinct persons. For both of them requiring the force of the society for their exercise, it is almost impracticable to place the force of the commonwealth in distinct, and not subordinate hands; or that the executive and federative power should be placed in persons that might act separately, whereby the force of the public would be under different commands: which would be apt some time or other to cause disorder and ruin.

CHAPTER XIII

Of the Subordination of the Powers of the Commonwealth

149. Though in a constituted commonwealth, standing upon its own basis, and acting according to its own nature, that is, acting for the preservation of the community, there can be but *one supreme power,* which is the *legislative,* to which all the rest are and must be subordinate; yet the legislative being only a fiduciary power to act for certain ends, there remains still *in the people a supreme power to remove or alter the legislative,* when they find the legislative act contrary to the trust reposed in them. For all *power given with trust* for the attaining an end, being limited by that end; whenever that end is manifestly neglected or opposed, the trust must necessarily be forfeited, and the power devolve into the hands of those that gave it, who may place it anew where they shall think best for their safety and security. And thus the *community* perpetually *retains a supreme power* of saving themselves from the attempts and designs of any body, even of their legislators, whenever they shall be so foolish, or so wicked, as to lay and carry on designs against the liberties and properties of the subject. For no man, or society of men, having a power to deliver up their preservation, or consequently the means of it, to the absolute will and arbitrary

dominion of another; whenever any one shall go about to bring them into such a slavish condition, they will always have a right to preserve what they have not a power to part with; and to rid themselves of those who invade this fundamental, sacred, and unalterable law of self-preservation, for which they entered into society. And thus the community may be said in this respect to be *always the supreme power,* but not as considered under any form of government, because this power of the people can never take place till the government be dissolved.

150. In all cases, whilst the government subsists, the *legislative is the supreme power.* For what can give laws to another, must needs be superiour to him; and since the legislative is no otherwise legislative of the society, but by the right it has to make laws for all the parts, and for every member of the society, prescribing rules to their actions, and giving power of execution, where they are transgressed; the legislative must needs be the supreme, and all other powers, in any members or parts of the society, derived from and subordinate to it.

151. In some commonwealths, where the legislative is not always in being, and the executive is vested in a single person, who has also a share in the legislative; there that single person in a very tolerable sense may also be called supreme; not that he has in himself all the supreme power, which is that of law-making; but because he has in him the supreme execution, from whom all inferiour magistrates derive all their several subordinate powers, or at least the greatest part of them: having also no legislative superiour to him, there being no law to be made without his consent, which cannot be expected should ever subject him to the other part of the legislative, he is properly enough in this sense *supreme.* But yet it is to be observed, that though *oaths of allegiance* and fealty are taken to him, it is not to him as supreme legislator, but as *supreme executor* of the law, made by a joint power of him with others: allegiance being nothing but an *obedience according to law,* which when he violates, he has no right to obedience, nor can claim it otherwise, than as the public person invested with the power of the law; and so is to be considered as the image, phantom, or representative of the commonwealth, acted by the will of the society, declared in its laws; and thus he has no will, no power, but that of the law. But when he quits this representation, this public will, and acts by his own private will, he degrades himself, and is but a single private person without power, and without will, that has no right to obedience; the members owing no obedience but to the public will of the society.

152. The *executive power,* placed any where but in a person that has also a share in the legislative, is visibly subordinate and accountable to it, and may be at pleasure changed and displaced; so that it is not the *supreme executive power* that is exempt from subordination, but the *supreme executive power* vested in one, who having a share in the legislative, has no distinct superiour legislative to be subordinate and accountable to, farther than he himself shall join and consent; so that he is no more subordinate than he himself shall think fit, which one may certainly conclude will be but very little. Of other ministerial and subordinate powers in a commonwealth, we need not speak, they being so multiplied with infinite variety in the different customs and constitutions of distinct commonwealths, that it is impossible to give a particular account of them all. Only thus much, which is necessary to our present purpose, we may take notice of concerning them, that they have no manner of authority, any of them, beyond what is by positive grant and commission delegated to them, and are all of them accountable to some other power in the commonwealth.

153. It is not necessary, no, nor so much as convenient, that the *legislative* should be *always in being.* But absolutely necessary that the executive power should; because there is not always need of new laws to be made, but always need of execution of the laws that are made. When the legislative hath put the execution of the laws they make into other

hands, they have a power still to resume it out of those hands, when they find cause, and to punish for any mall-administration against the laws. The same holds also in regard of the federative power, that and the executive being both *ministerial and subordinate to the legislative,* which, as has been shewed, in a constituted commonwealth is the supreme. The legislative also in this case being supposed to consist of several persons, (for if it be a single person, it cannot but be always in being, and so will, as supreme, naturally have the supreme executive power, together with the legislative) may *assemble, and exercise their legislature,* at the times that either their original constitution, or their own adjournment, appoints, or when they please; if neither of these hath appointed any time, or there be no other way prescribed to convoke them. For the supreme power being placed in them by the people, it is always in them, and they may exercise it when they please, unless by their original constitution they are limited to certain seasons, or by an act of their supreme power they have adjourned to a certain time; and when that time comes, they have a right to assemble and act again.

154. If the legislative, or any part of it, be made up of representatives chosen for that time by the people, which afterwards return into the ordinary state of subjects, and have no share in the legislature but upon a new choice, this power of choosing must also be exercised by the people, either at certain appointed seasons, or else when they are summoned to it; and in this latter case the power of convoking the legislative is ordinarily placed in the executive, and has one of these two limitations in respect of time: that either the original constitution requires their assembling and acting at certain intervals, and then the executive power does nothing but ministerially issue directions for their electing and assembling according to due forms; or else it is left to his prudence to call them by new elections, when the occasions, or exigencies of the public require the amendment of old, or making of new laws, or the redress or prevention of any inconveniencies, that lie on, or threaten the people.

155. It may be demanded here, What if the executive power, being possessed of the force of the commonwealth, shall make use of that force to hinder the *meeting* and *acting of the legislative;* when the original constitution, or the public exigencies require it? I say, using force upon the people without authority, and contrary to the trust put in him that does so, is a state of war with the people, who have a right to *reinstate* their *legislative in the exercise* of their power. For having erected a legislative, with an intent they should exercise the power of making laws, either at certain set times, or when there is need of it; when they are hindered by any force from what is so necessary to the society, and wherein the safety and preservation of the people consists, the people have a right to remove it by force. In all states and conditions, the true remedy of force without authority, is to oppose force to it. The use of force without authority, always puts him that uses it into a *state of war,* as the aggressor; and renders him liable to be treated accordingly.

156. The *power of assembling and dismissing the legislative,* placed in the executive, gives not the executive a superiority over it, but is a fiduciary trust placed in him for the safety of the people, in a case where the uncertainty and variableness of human affairs could not bear a steady fixed rule. For it not being possible that the first framers of the government should, by any foresight, be so much masters of future events as to be able to prefix so just periods of return and duration to the *assemblies of the legislative,* in all times to come, that might exactly answer all the exigencies of the commonwealth; the best remedy could be found for this defect was to trust this to the prudence of one who was always to be present, and whose business it was to watch over the public good. Constant *frequent meetings of the legislative,* and long continuations of their assemblies, without necessary occasion, could not but be burdensome to the people, and must necessarily in time produce more

dangerous inconveniencies, and yet the quick turn of affairs might be sometimes such as to need their present help: any delay of their convening might endanger the public; and sometimes too their business might be so great, that the limited time of their sitting might be too short for their work, and rob the public of that benefit which could be had only from their mature deliberation. What then could be done in this case to prevent the community from being exposed some time or other to eminent hazard, on one side or the other, by fixed intervals and periods, set to the *meeting and acting of the legislative;* but to intrust it to the prudence of some, who being present, and acquainted with the state of public affairs, might make use of this prerogative for the public good? And where else could this be so well placed as in his hands, who was intrusted with the execution of the laws for the same end? Thus supposing the regulation of times for the *assembling and sitting of the legislative* not settled by the original constitution, it naturally fell into the hands of the executive, not as an arbitrary power depending on his good pleasure, but with this trust always to have it exercised only for the public weal, as the occurrences of times and change of affairs might require. Whether *settled periods of their convening,* or *a liberty* left to the prince for *convoking the legislative,* or perhaps a mixture of both, hath the least inconvenience attending it, it is not my business here to inquire; but only to shew, that though the executive power may have the prerogative of *convoking* and *dissolving* such *conventions of the legislative,* yet it is not thereby superiour to it.

157. Things of this world are in so constant a flux, that nothing remains long in the same state. Thus people, riches, trade, power, change their stations, flourishing mighty cities come to ruin, and prove in time neglected desolate corners, whilst other unfrequented places grow into populous countries, filled with wealth and inhabitants. But things not always changing equally, and private interest often keeping up customs and privileges, when the reasons of them are ceased; it often comes to pass, that in governments, where part of the legislative consists of representatives chosen by the people, that in tract of time this representation becomes very unequal and disproportionate to the reasons it was at first established upon. To what gross absurdities the following of custom, when reason has left it, may lead, we may be satisfied, when we see the bare name of a town, of which there remains not so much as the ruins, where scarce so much housing as a sheepcote, or more inhabitants than a shepherd is to be found, sends *as many representatives* to the grand assembly of law-makers, as a whole county numerous in people, and powerful in riches. This strangers stand amazed at, and every one must confess needs a remedy. Though most think it hard to find one; because the constitution of the legislative being the original and supreme act of the society, antecedent to all positive laws in it, and depending wholly on the people, no inferiour power can alter it. And therefore the people, when the legislative is once constituted, having, in such a government as we have been speaking of, no power to act as long as the government stands; this inconvenience is thought incapable of a remedy.

158. *Salus populi suprema lex,* is certainly so just and fundamental a rule, that he, who sincerely follows it, cannot dangerously err. If therefore the executive, who has the power of convoking the legislative, observing rather the true proportion than fashion of representation, regulates not by old custom, but true reason, the *number of members* in all places that have a right to be distinctly represented, which no part of the people, however incorporated, can pretend to, but in proportion to the assistance which it affords to the public; it cannot be judged to have set up a new legislative, but to have restored the old and true one, and to have rectified the disorders which succession of time had insensibly, as well as inevitably introduced. For it being the interest as well as intention of the people, to have a fair and equal representative; whoever brings it nearest to that, is an undoubted friend to, and establisher of the government, and cannot miss the consent and approbation of the

community. Prerogative being nothing but a power in the hands of the prince to provide
for the public good, in such cases, which depending upon unforeseen and uncertain occurrences, certain and unalterable laws could not safely direct; whatsoever shall be done manifestly for the good of the people, and the establishing the government upon its true
foundations, is, and always will be, just *prerogative*. The power of erecting new corporations, and therewith *new representatives,* carries with it a supposition that in time the *measures of representation* might vary, and those places have a just right to be represented which
before had none; and by the same reason, those cease to have a right, and be too inconsiderable for such a privilege, which before had it. It is not a change from the present state,
which perhaps corruption or decay has introduced, that makes an inroad upon the government; but the tendency of it to injure or oppress the people, and to set up one part or
party, with a distinction from, and an unequal subjection of the rest. Whatsoever cannot
but be acknowledged to be of advantage to the society, and people in general, upon just
and lasting measures, will always, when done, justify itself; and whenever the people shall
choose their *representatives upon* just and undeniably *equal measures,* suitable to the original
frame of the government, it cannot be doubted to be the will and act of the society, whoever permitted or caused them so to do.

CHAPTER XIV

Of Prerogative

159. Where the legislative and executive power are in distinct hands, (as they are in all
moderated monarchies and well-framed governments) there the good of the society
requires, that several things should be left to the discretion of him that has the executive
power. For the legislators not being able to foresee, and provide by laws, for all that may
be useful to the community, the executor of the laws having the power in his hands, has
by the common law of nature a right to make use of it for the good of the society, in many
cases, where the municipal law has given no direction, till the legislative can conveniently
be assembled to provide for it. Many things there are, which the law can by no means provide for; and those must necessarily be left to the discretion of him that has the executive
power in his hands, to be ordered by him as the public good and advantage shall require:
nay, it is fit that the laws themselves should in some cases give way to the executive power,
or rather to this fundamental law of nature and government, viz. That, as much as may
be, all the members of the society are to be preserved. For since many accidents may happen, wherein a strict and rigid observation of the laws may do harm; (as not to pull down
an innocent man's house to stop the fire, when the next to it is burning) and a man may
come sometimes within the reach of the law, which makes no distinction of persons, by an
action that may deserve reward and pardon; it is fit the ruler should have a power, in many
cases, to mitigate the severity of the law, and pardon some offenders. For the *end of government* being the *preservation of all,* as much as may be, even the guilty are to be spared,
where it can prove no prejudice to the innocent.

160. This power to act according to discretion, for the public good, without the prescription of the law, and sometimes even against it, is that which is called *prerogative*. For
since in some governments the lawmaking power is not always in being, and is usually too
numerous, and so too slow for the dispatch requisite to execution; and because also it is
impossible to foresee, and so by laws to provide for all accidents and necessities that may

concern the public, or to make such laws as will do no harm, if they are executed with an inflexible rigour on all occasions, and upon all persons that may come in their way; therefore there is a latitude left to the executive power, to do many things of choice which the laws do not prescribe.

161. This power, whilst employed for the benefit of the community, and suitably to the trust and ends of the government, *is undoubted prerogative,* and never is questioned. For the people are very seldom or never scrupulous or nice in the point; they are far from examining prerogative, whilst it is in any tolerable degree employed for the use it was meant; that is, for the good of the people, and not manifestly against it. But if there comes to be a *question* between the executive power and the people, about a thing claimed as a *prerogative,* the tendency of the exercise of such prerogative to the good or hurt of the people will easily decide that question.

162. It is easy to conceive, that in the infancy of governments, when commonwealths differed little from families in number of people, they differed from them too but little in number of laws: and the governors being as the fathers of them, watching over them, for their good, the government was almost all prerogative. A few established laws served the turn, and the discretion and care of the ruler supplied the rest. But when mistake or flattery prevailed with weak princes to make use of this power for private ends of their own, and not for the public good, the people were fain by express laws to get prerogative determined in those points wherein they found disadvantage from it: and thus declared *limitations of prerogative* were by the people found necessary in cases which they and their ancestors had left, in the utmost latitude, to the wisdom of those princes who made no other but a right use of it; that is, for the good of their people.

163. And therefore they have a very wrong notion of government, who say, that the people have *encroached upon the prerogative,* when they have got any part of it to be defined by positive laws. For in so doing they have not pulled from the prince any thing that of right belonged to him, but only declared, that that power which they indefinitely left in his or his ancestors hands, to be exercised for their good, was not a thing which they intended him when he used it otherwise. For the end of government being the good of the community, whatsoever alterations are made in it, tending to that end, cannot be an encroachment upon any body, since no body in government can have a right tending to any other end: and those only are encroachments which prejudice or hinder the public good. Those who say otherwise, speak as if the prince had a distinct and separate interest from the good of the community, and was not made for it; the root and source from which spring almost all those evils and disorders which happen in kingly governments. And indeed, if that be so, the people under his government are not a society of rational creatures, entered into a community for their mutual good; they are not such as have set rulers over themselves, to guard and promote that good; but are to be looked on as an herd of inferior creatures under the dominion of a master, who keeps them and works them for his own pleasure or profit. If men were so void of reason, and brutish, as to enter into society upon such terms, prerogative might indeed be, what some men would have it, an arbitrary power to do things hurtful to the people.

164. But since a rational creature cannot be supposed, when free, to put himself into subjection to another, for his own harm; (though, where he finds a good and wise ruler, he may not perhaps think it either necessary or useful to set precise bounds to his power in all things) prerogative can be nothing but the people's permitting their rulers to do several things, of their own free choice, where the law was silent, and sometimes too against the direct letter of the law, for the public good; and their acquiescing in it when so done. For as a good prince, who is mindful of the trust put into his hands, and careful of the

good of his people, cannot have too much prerogative, that is, power to do good; so a weak and ill prince, who would claim that power which his predecessors exercised without the direction of the law, as a prerogative belonging to him by right of his office, which he may exercise at his pleasure, to make or promote an interest distinct from that of the public, gives the people an occasion to claim their right, and limit that power, which, whilst it was exercised for their good, they were content should be tacitly allowed.

165. And therefore he that will look into the *history of England,* will find, that prerogative was always *largest* in the hands of our wisest and best princes; because the people, observing the whole tendency of their actions to be the public good, contested not what was done without law to that end: or, if any human frailty or mistake (for princes are but men, made as others) appeared in some small declinations from that end; yet it was visible, the main of their conduct tended to nothing but the care of the public. The people therefore, finding reason to be satisfied with these princes, whenever they acted without, or contrary to the letter of the law, acquiesced in what they did, and without the least complaint, let them enlarge their prerogative as they pleased; judging rightly, that they did nothing herein to the prejudice of their laws, since they acted conformably to the foundation and end of all laws, the public good.

166. Such God-like princes indeed had some title to arbitrary **power** by that argument, that would prove absolute monarchy the best government, as that which God himself governs the universe by; because such kings partook of his wisdom and goodness. Upon this is founded that saying, That the reigns of good princes have been always most dangerous to the liberties of their people. For when their successors, managing the government with different thoughts, would draw the actions of those good rulers into precedent, and make them the standard of their prerogative, as if what had been done only for the good of the people was a right in them to do, for the harm of the people, if they so pleased; it has often occasioned contest, and sometimes public disorders, before the people could recover their original right, and get that to be declared not to be prerogative, which truly was never so: since it is impossible that any body in the society should ever have a right to do the people harm; though it be very possible, and reasonable, that the people should not go about to set any bounds to the prerogative of those kings, or rulers, who themselves transgressed not the bounds of the public good. For *prerogative is nothing but the power of doing public good without a rule.*

167. The power of calling parliaments in England, as to precise time, place, and duration, is certainly a prerogative of the king, but still with this trust, that it shall be made use of for the good of the nation, as the exigencies of the times, and variety of occasions, shall require. For it being impossible to foresee which should always be the fittest place for them to assemble in, and what the best season, the choice of these was left with the executive power, as might be most subservient to the public good, and best suit the ends of parliaments.

168. The old question will be asked in this matter of prerogative, "But who shall be judge when this power is made a right use of?" I answer: between an executive power in being, with such a prerogative, and a legislative that depends upon his will for their convening, there can be no *judge on earth;* as there can be none between the legislative and the people, should either the executive or the legislative, when they have got the power in their hands, design, or go about to enslave or destroy them. The people have no other remedy in this, as in all other cases where they have no judge on earth, but to *appeal to heaven.* For the rulers, in such attempts, exercising a power the people never put into their hands, (who can never be supposed to consent that any body should rule over them for their harm) do that which they have not a right to do. And where the body of the people,

or any single man, is deprived of their right, or is under the exercise of a power without right, and have no appeal on earth, then they have a liberty to appeal to heaven, whenever they judge the cause of sufficient moment. And therefore, *though the people cannot be judge,* so as to have, by the constitution of that society, any superior power to determine and give effective sentence in the case; yet they have, by a law antecedent and paramount to all positive laws of men, reserved that ultimate determination to themselves which belongs to all mankind, where there lies no appeal on earth, viz. to judge, whether they have just cause to make their appeal to heaven. And this judgment they cannot part with, it being out of a man's power so to submit himself to another, as to give him a liberty to destroy him; God and nature never allowing a man so to abandon himself, as to neglect his own preservation: and since he cannot take away his own life, neither can he give another power to take it. Nor let any one think, this lays a perpetual foundation for disorder; for this operates not, till the inconveniency is so great, that the majority feel it, and are weary of it, and find a necessity to have it amended. But this the executive power, or wise princes, never need come in the danger of: and it is the thing, of all others, they have most need to avoid, as of all others the most perilous.

CHAPTER XV

Of Paternal, Political, and Despotical Power, Considered Together

169. Though I have had occasion to speak of these separately before, yet the great mistakes of late about government having, as I suppose, arisen from confounding these distinct powers one with another, it may not, perhaps, be amiss to consider them here together.

170. *First,* then, *Paternal or parental power* is nothing but that which parents have over their children, to govern them for the children's good, till they come to the use of reason, or a state of knowledge, wherein they may be supposed capable to understand that rule, whether it be the law of nature, or the municipal law of their country, they are to govern themselves by: capable, I say, to know it, as well as several others, who live as freemen under that law. The affection and tenderness which God hath planted in the breast of parents towards their children, makes it evident that this is not intended to be a severe arbitrary government, but only for the help, instruction, and preservation of their offspring. But happen it as it will, there is, as I have proved, no reason why it should be thought to extend to life and death, at any time, over their children, more than over any body else; neither can there be any pretence why this *parental power* should keep the child, when grown to a man, in subjection to the will of his parents, any farther than having received life and education from his parents, obliges him to respect, honour, gratitude, assistance and support, all his life, to both father and mother. And thus, it is true, the paternal is a natural government, but not at all extending itself to the ends and jurisdictions of that which is political. The *power of the father doth not reach* at all to the *property* of the child, which is only in his own disposing.

171. *Secondly, Political power* is that power which every man having in the state of nature, has given up into the hands of the society, and therein to the governors, whom the society hath set over itself, with this express or tacit trust, that it shall be employed for their good, and the preservation of their property: now this *power,* which every man has *in the state of nature,* and which he parts with to the society in all such cases where the soci-

ety can secure him, is to use such means for the preserving of his own property, as he thinks good, and nature allows him; and to punish the breach of the law of nature in others, so as (according to the best of his reason) may most conduce to the preservation of himself, and the rest of mankind. So that the *end and measure of this power,* when in every man's hands in the state of nature, being the preservation of all of his society, that is, all mankind in general; it can have no other *end or measure,* when in the hands of the magistrate, but to preserve the members of that society in their lives, liberties, and possessions; and so cannot be an absolute arbitrary power, over their lives and fortunes, which are as much as possible to be preserved; but a *power to make laws,* and annex such penalties to them, as may tend to the preservation of the whole, by cutting off those parts, and those only, which are so corrupt, that they threaten the sound and healthy, without which no severity is lawful. And this *power has its original only from compact* and agreement, and the mutual consent of those who make up the community.

172. *Thirdly,* Despotical power is an absolute, arbitrary power; one man has over another, to take away his life, whenever he pleases. This is a power, which neither nature gives, for it has made no such distinction between one man and another; nor compact can convey. For man not having such an arbitrary power over his own life, cannot give another man such a power over it; but it is *the effect only of forfeiture* which the aggressor makes of his own life, when he puts himself into the state of war with another. For having quitted reason, which God hath given to be the rule betwixt man and man, and the common bond whereby human kind is united into one fellowship and society; and having renounced the way of peace which that teaches, and made use of the force of war, to compass his unjust ends upon another, where he has no right; and so revolting from his own kind to that of beasts, by making force, which is theirs, to be his rule of right; he renders himself liable to be destroyed by the injured person, and the rest of mankind, that will join with him in the execution of justice, as any other wild beast or noxious brute, with whom mankind can have neither society nor security.[10] And thus *captives,* taken in a just and lawful war, and such only, are *subject to a despotical power;* which, as it arises not from compact, so neither is it capable of any, but is the state of war continued. For what compact can be made with a man that is not master of his own life? What condition can he perform? And if he be once allowed to be master of his own life, the *despotical arbitrary power* of his master ceases. He that is master of himself; and his own life, has a right too to the means of preserving it; so that, *as soon as compact enters, slavery ceases,* and he so far quits his absolute power, and puts an end to the state of war, who enters into conditions with his captive.

173. Nature gives the first of these, viz. *paternal power, to parents* for the benefit of their children during their minority, to supply their want of ability and understanding how to manage their property. (By property I must be understood here, as in other places, to mean that property which men have in their persons as well as goods.) *Voluntary agreement gives* the second, viz. *political power to governors* for the benefit of their subjects, to secure them in the possession and use of their properties. And *forfeiture gives* the third *despotical power to lords,* for their own benefit, over those who are stripped of all property.

174. He, that shall consider the distinct rise and extent, and the different ends of these several powers, will plainly see, that *paternal power* comes as far short of that of the *magistrate,* as *despotical* exceeds it; and that *absolute dominion,* however placed, is so far from being one kind of civil society, that it is as inconsistent with it, as slavery is with property. *Paternal power* is only where minority makes the child incapable to manage his property; *political,* where men have property in their own disposal; and *despotical,* over such as have no property at all.

CHAPTER XVI

Of Conquest

175. Though governments can originally have no other rise than that before-mentioned, nor *polities* be *founded* on any thing but *the consent of the people;* yet such have been the disorders ambition has filled the world with, that in the noise of war, which makes so great a part of the history of mankind, *this consent* is little taken notice of: and therefore many have mistaken the force of arms for the consent of the people, and reckon conquest as one of the originals of government. But conquest is as far from setting up any government, as demolishing an house is from building a new one in the place. Indeed, it often makes way for a new frame of a commonwealth, by destroying the former; but, without the consent of the people, can never erect a new one.

176. That the *aggressor,* who puts himself into the state of war with another, and *unjustly invades* another man's right, can, by such an unjust war, *never* come to *have a right over the conquered,* will be easily agreed by all men, who will not think, that robbers and pirates have a right of empire over whomsoever they have force enough to master; or that men are bound by promises, which unlawful force extorts from them. Should a robber break into my house, and with a dagger at my throat, make me seal deeds to convey my estate to him, would this give him any title? Just such a title, by his sword, has an *unjust conqueror,* who forces me into submission. The injury and the crime are equal, whether committed by the wearer of the crown, or some petty villain. The title of the offender, and the number of his followers, make no difference in the offence, unless it be to aggravate it. The only difference is, great robbers punish little ones, to keep them in their obedience; but the great ones are rewarded with laurels and triumphs; because they are too big for the weak hands of justice in this world, and have the power in their own possession, which should punish offenders. What is my remedy against a robber, that so broke into my house? Appeal to the law for justice. But perhaps justice is denied, or I am crippled and cannot stir, robbed and have not the means to do it. If God has taken away all means of seeking remedy, there is nothing left but patience. But my son, when able, may seek the relief of the law, which I am denied: he or his son may renew his appeal, till he recover his right. But the conquered, or their children, have no court, no arbitrator on earth to appeal to. Then they may appeal, as Jephthah did, to heaven, and repeat their appeal till they have recovered the native right of their ancestors, which was, to have such a legislative over them, as the majority should approve, and freely acquiesce in. If it be objected, this would cause endless trouble; I answer, no more than justice does, where she lies open to all that appeal to her. He that troubles his neighbour without a cause, is punished for it by the justice of the court he appeals to. And he that *appeals to heaven* must be sure he has right on his side; and a right too that is worth the trouble and cost of the appeal, as he will answer at a tribunal that cannot be deceived, and will be sure to retribute to every one according to the mischiefs he hath created to his fellow-subjects; that is, any part of mankind: from whence it is plain, that he that *conquers in an unjust war, can thereby have no title to the subjection and obedience of the conquered.*

177. But supposing victory favours the right side, let us consider *a conqueror in a lawful war,* and see what power he gets, and over *whom.*

First, it is plain, *he gets no power by his conquest over those that conquered with him.* They that fought on his side cannot suffer by the conquest, but must at least be as much freemen as they were before. And most commonly they serve upon terms, and on conditions to share with their leader, and enjoy a part of the spoil, and other advantages that attended the conquering sword; or at least have a part of the subdued country bestowed upon them. And *the conquering people are not, I hope, to be slaves by conquest,* and wear their laurels only to shew they are sacrifices to their leader's triumph. They that found absolute monarchy upon the title of the sword, make their heroes, who are the founders of such monarchies, arrant Drawcansirs, and forget they had any officers and soldiers that fought on their side in the battles they won, or assisted them in the subduing, or shared in possessing, the countries they mastered. We are told by some, that the English monarchy is founded in the Norman conquest, and that our princes have thereby a title to absolute dominion: which if it were true, (as by the history it appears otherwise) and that William had a right to make war on this island; yet his dominion by conquest could reach no farther than to the Saxons and Britons, that were then inhabitants of this country. The Normans that came with him, and helped to conquer, and all descended from them, are freemen, and no subjects by conquest, let that give what dominion it will. And if I, or any body else, shall claim freedom, as derived from them, it will be very hard to prove the contrary; and it is plain, the law, that has made no distinction between the one and the other, intends not there should be any difference in their freedom or privileges.

178. But supposing, which seldom happens, that the conquerors and conquered never incorporate into one people, under the same laws and freedom. Let us see next *what power a lawful conqueror has over the subdued;* and that I say is purely despotical. He has an absolute power over the lives of those who by an unjust war have forfeited them; but not over the lives or fortunes of those who engaged not in the war, nor over the possessions even of those who were actually engaged in it.

179. *Secondly,* I say then the conqueror gets no power but only over those who have actually assisted, concurred, or consented to that unjust force that is used against him. For the people having given to their governors no power to do an unjust thing, such as is to make an unjust war, (for they never had such a power in themselves) they ought not to be charged as guilty of the violence and injustice that is committed in an unjust war, any farther than they actually abet it; no more than they are to be thought guilty of any violence or oppression their governors should use upon the people themselves, or any part of their fellow-subjects, they having impowered them no more to the one than to the other. Conquerors, it is true, seldom trouble themselves to make the distinction, but they willingly permit the confusion of war to sweep all together: but yet this alters not the right; for the conqueror's power over the lives of the conquered being only because they have used force to do, or maintain an injustice, he can have that power only over those who have concurred in that force; all the rest are innocent; and he has no more title over the people of that country, who have done him no injury, and so have made no forfeiture of their lives, than he has over any other, who without any injuries or provocations, have lived upon fair terms with him.

180. *Thirdly,* The *power a conqueror gets* over those he overcomes *in a just war, is perfectly despotical:* he has an absolute power over the lives of those, who, by putting themselves in a state of war, have forfeited them; but he has not thereby a right and title to their possessions. This I doubt not but at first sight will seem a strange doctrine, it being so quite contrary to the practice of the world; there being nothing more familiar in speaking of the dominion of countries, than to say such an one conquered it. As if conquest, without any more ado, conveyed a right of possession. But when we consider, that the practice of the strong and powerful, how universal soever it may be, is seldom the rule of right, however it be one part of the subjection of the conquered, not to argue against the conditions cut out to them by the conquering sword.

181. Though in all war there be usually a complication of force and damage, and the aggressor seldom fails to harm the estate, when he uses force against the persons of those he makes war upon; yet it is the use of force only that puts a man into the state of war. For whether by force he begins the injury, or else, having quietly, and by fraud, done the injury, he refuses to make reparation, and by force maintains it, (which is the same thing, as at first to have done it by force) it is the unjust use of force that makes the war. For he that breaks open my house, and violently turns me out of doors; or, having peaceably got in, by force keeps me out; does in effect the same thing; supposing we are in such a state, that we have no common judge on earth, whom I may appeal to, and to whom we are both obliged to submit. For of such I am now speaking. It is the *unjust use of force then, that puts a man into the state of war* with another; and thereby he that is guilty of it makes a forfeiture of his life. For quitting reason, which is the rule given between man and man, and using force, the way of beasts, he becomes liable to be destroyed by him he uses force against as any savage ravenous beast, that is dangerous to his being.

182. But because the miscarriages of the father are no faults of the children, and they may be rational and peaceable, notwithstanding the brutishness and injustice of the father; the father, by his miscarriages and violence, can forfeit but his own life, but involves not his children in his guilt or destruction. His goods, which nature, that willeth the preservation of all mankind as much as is possible, hath made to belong to the children, to keep them from perishing, do still continue to belong to his children. For supposing them not to have joined in the war, either through infancy, absence, or choice, they have done nothing to forfeit them: *nor has the conqueror any right* to take them away, by the bare title of having subdued him that by force attempted his destruction; though perhaps he may have some right to them, to repair the damages he has sustained by the war, and the defence of his own right; which how far it reaches to the possessions of the conquered, we shall see by and by. So that he that *by conquest has a right over a man's person* to destroy him if he pleases, has not thereby a right *over his estate* to possess and enjoy it. For it is the brutal force the aggressor has used, that gives his adversary a right to take away his life, and destroy him if he pleases as a noxious creature; but it is damage sustained that alone gives him title to another man's goods. For, though I may kill a thief that sets on me in the highway, yet I may not (which seems less) take away his money and let him go: this would be robbery on my side. His force, and the state of war he put himself in, made him forfeit his life, but gave me no title to his goods. The *right* then *of conquest extends only to the lives* of those who joined in the war, *not to their estates*, but only in order to make reparation for the damages received, and the charges of the war; and that too with reservation of the right of the innocent wife and children.

183. Let the conqueror have as much justice on his side as could be supposed, he has no right to seize more than the vanquished could forfeit: his life is at the victor's mercy; and his service and goods he may appropriate, to make himself reparation; but he cannot take the goods of his wife and children: they too had a title to the goods he enjoyed, and their shares in the estate he possessed. For example, I in the state of nature (and all commonwealths are in the state of nature one with another) have injured another man, and refusing to give satisfaction it comes to a state of war, wherein my defending by force what I had gotten unjustly makes me the aggressor. I am conquered: my life, it is true, as forfeit, is at mercy, but not my wife's and children's. They made not the war, nor assisted in it. I could not forfeit their lives; they were not mine to forfeit. My wife had a share in my estate; that neither could I forfeit. And my children also, being born of me, had a right to be maintained out of my labour or substance. Here then is the case: the conqueror has a title to reparation for damages received, and the children have a title to their father's

estate for their subsistence. For as to the wife's share, whether her own labour, or compact, gave her a title to it, it is plain, her husband could not forfeit what was hers. What must be done in the case? I answer; the fundamental law of nature being, that all, as much as may be, should be preserved, it follows, that if there be not enough fully to satisfy both, viz. for the conqueror's losses, and children's maintenance, he that hath, and to spare, must remit something of his full satisfaction, and give way to the pressing and preferable title of those who are in danger to perish without it.

184. But supposing the *charge* and *damages of the war* are to be made up to the conqueror, to the utmost farthing; and that the children of the vanquished, spoiled of all their father's goods, are to be left to starve and perish; yet the satisfying of what shall, on this score, be due to the conqueror, will scarce give him a *title to any country he shall conquer.* For the damages of war can scarce amount to the value of any considerable tract of land, in any part of the world, where all the land is possessed, and none lies waste. And if I have not taken away the conqueror's land, which, being vanquished, it is impossible I should; scarce any other spoil I have done him can amount to the value of mine, supposing it equally cultivated, and of an extent any way coming near what I had over-run of his. The destruction of a year's product or two (for it seldom reaches four or five) is the utmost spoil that usually can be done. For as to money, and such riches and treasure taken away, these are none of nature's goods, they have but a fantastical imaginary value: nature has put no such upon them: they are of no more account by her standard, than the wampompeke of the Americans to an European prince, or the silver money of Europe would have been formerly to an American. And five years product is not worth the perpetual inheritance of land, where all is possessed, and none remains waste, to be taken up by him that is disseized: which will be easily granted, if one do but take away the imaginary value of money, the disproportion being more than between five and five hundred; though, at the same time, half a year's product is more worth than the inheritance, where there being more land than the inhabitants possess and make use of, any one has liberty to make use of the waste: but there conquerors take little care to possess themselves of the *lands of the vanquished.* No damage therefore, that men in the state of nature (as all princes and governments are in reference to one another) suffer from one another, can give a conqueror power to dispossess the posterity of the vanquished, and turn them out of that inheritance which ought to be the possession of them and their descendants to all generations. The conqueror indeed will be apt to think himself master: and it is the very condition of the subdued not to be able to dispute their right. But if that be all, it gives no other title than what bare force gives to the stronger over the weaker. And, by this reason, he that is strongest will have a right to whatever he pleases to seize on.

185. Over those then that joined with him in the war, and over those of the subdued country that opposed him not, and the posterity even of those that did, the conqueror, even in a just war, hath, by his conquest, no *right of dominion:* they are free from any subjection to him, and if their former government be dissolved, they are at liberty to begin and erect another to themselves.

186. The conqueror, it is true, usually, by the force he has over them, compels them, with a sword at their breasts, to stoop to his conditions, and submit to such a government as he pleases to afford them; but the inquiry is, what right he has to do so? If it be said, they submit by their own consent, then this allows their own *consent* to be *necessary to give the conqueror a title to rule* over them. It remains only to be considered, whether *promises extorted by force,* without right, can be thought consent, and *how far they bind.* To which I shall say, they *bind not at all;* because whatsoever another gets from me by force, I still retain the right of, and he is obliged presently to restore. He that forces my horse from me, ought presently to restore him, and I have still a right to retake him. By the same

reason, he that *forced a promise* from me, ought presently to restore it, i.e. quit me of the obligation of it: or I may resume it myself, i.e. choose whether I will perform it. For the law of nature laying an obligation on me only by the rules she prescribes, cannot oblige me by the violation of her rules: such is the extorting any thing from me by force. Nor does it at all alter the case to say, "I gave my promise," no more than it excuses the force, and passes the right, when I put my hand in my pocket and deliver my purse myself to a thief, who demands it with a pistol at my breast.

187. From all which it follows, that the *government of a conqueror*, imposed by force, on the subdued, against whom he had no right of war, or who joined not in the war against him, where he had right, *has no obligation* upon them.

188. But let us suppose that all the men of that community, being all members of the same body politic, may be taken to have joined in that unjust war, wherein they are subdued, and so their lives are at the mercy of the conqueror.

189. I say this concerns not their children who are in their minority. For since a father hath not, in himself, a power over the life or liberty of his child, no act of his can possibly forfeit it. So that the children, whatever may have happened to the fathers, are freemen, and the absolute power of the conqueror reaches no farther than the persons of the men that were subdued by him, and dies with them: and should he govern them as slaves subjected to his absolute arbitrary power, he *has* no *such right of dominion over their children.* He can have no power over them but by their own consent, whatever he may drive them to say or do; and he has no lawful authority, whilst force, and not choice, compels them to submission.

190. Every man is born with a double right: *first, a right of freedom to his person,* which no other man has a power over, but the free disposal of it lies in himself. *Secondly, a right,* before any other man, *to inherit with* his brethren his *father's goods.*

191. By the first of these, a man is *naturally free* from subjection to any government, though he be born in a place under its jurisdiction. But if he disclaim the lawful government of the country he was born in, he must also quit the right that belonged to him by the laws of it, and the possessions there descending to him from his ancestors, if it were a government made by their consent.

192. By the second, the inhabitants of any country, who are descended, and derive a title to their estates from those who are subdued, and had a government forced upon them against their free consents, *retain a right to the possession of their ancestors,* though they consent not freely to the government, whose hard conditions were by force imposed on the possessors of that country. For, the first *conqueror never having had a title to the land* of that country, the people who are the descendants of, or claim under those who were forced to submit to the yoke of a government by constraint, have always a right to shake it off, and free themselves from the usurpation or tyranny which the sword hath brought in upon them, till their rulers put them under such a frame of government as they willingly and of choice consent to. Who doubts but the Grecian christians, descendants of the ancient possessors of that country, may justly cast off the Turkish yoke, which they have so long groaned under, whenever they have an opportunity to do it? For no government can have a right to obedience from a people who have not freely consented to it; which they can never be supposed to do, till either they are put in a full state of liberty to choose their government and governors, or at least till they have such standing laws, to which they have by themselves or their representatives given their free consent; and also till they are allowed their due property, which is, so to be proprietors of what they have, that no body can take away any part of it without their own consent, without which, men under any government are not in the state of freemen, but are direct slaves under the force of war.

193. But granting that the *conqueror* in a just war has a right to the estates, as well as power over the persons of the conquered; which, it is plain, he *hath* not: nothing of absolute power will follow from hence, in the continuance of the government. Because the descendants of these being all freemen, if he grants them estates and possessions to inhabit his country (without which it would be worth nothing) whatsoever he grants them, they have, so far as it is granted, property in. The nature whereof is, that *without a man's own consent, it cannot be taken from him.*

194. Their *persons* are *free* by a native right, and their properties, be they more or less, are *their own, and at their own dispose*, and not at his; or else it is no property. Supposing the conqueror gives to one man a thousand acres, to him and his heirs for ever; to another he lets a thousand acres for his life, under the rent of £50 or £500 per annum, has not the one of these a right to his thousand acres for ever, and the other during his life, paying the said rent? and hath not the tenant for life a property in all that he gets over and above his rent, by his labour and industry during the said term, supposing it to be double the rent? Can any one say, the king, or conqueror, after his grant, may, by his power of conqueror, take away all, or part of the land from the heirs of one, or from the other during his life, he paying the rent? Or can he take away from either the goods or money they have got upon the said land, at his pleasure? If he can, then all free and voluntary contracts cease, and are void in the world; there needs nothing to dissolve them at any time but power enough: and all the grants and *promises* of *men in power* are but mockery and collusion. For can there be any thing more ridiculous than to say, I give you and yours this for ever, and that in the surest and most solemn way of conveyance can be devised; and yet it is to be understood, that I have a right, if I please, to take it away from you again to-morrow?

195. I will not dispute now, whether princes are exempt from the laws of their country; but this I am sure, they owe subjection to the laws of God and nature. No body, no power, can exempt them from the obligations of that eternal law. Those are so great, and so strong, in the case of *promises*, that omnipotency itself can be tied by them. *Grants, promises,* and *oaths,* are *bonds* that *hold the Almighty:* whatever some flatterers say to princes of the world, who all together, with all their people joined to them, are in comparison of the great God, but as a drop of the bucket, or a dust on the balance, inconsiderable, nothing!

196. The short of the *case in conquest* is this. The conqueror, if he have a just cause, has a despotical right over the persons of all that actually aided, and concurred in the war against him, and a right to make up his damage and cost out of their labour and estates, so he injure not the right of any other. Over the rest of the people, if there were any that consented not to the war, and over the children of the captives themselves, or the possessions of either, he has no power and so can have, *by virtue of conquest, no lawful title* himself *to dominion* over them, or derive it to his posterity; but is an aggressor, if he attempts upon their properties, and thereby puts himself in a state of war against them: and has no better a right of principality, he, nor any of his successors, than Hingar, or Hubba, the Danes, had here in England; or Spartacus had he conquered Italy, would have had; which is to have their yoke cast off, as soon as God shall give those under their subjection courage and opportunity to do it. Thus, notwithstanding whatever title the kings of Assyria had over Judah, by the sword, God assisted Hezekiah to throw off the dominion of that conquering empire. "And the Lord was with Hezekiah, and he prospered; wherefore he went forth, and he rebelled against the king of Assyria, and served him not," *2 Kings*, xviii. 7. Whence it is plain, that shaking off a power, which force, and not right, hath set over any one, though it hath the name of *rebellion*, yet is no offence before God, but is that which he allows and countenances, though even promises and covenants, when obtained by force, have intervened. For it is very probable, to any one that reads the story of Ahaz and

Hezekiah attentively, that the Assyrians subdued Ahaz, and deposed him, and made Hezekiah king in his father's life-time; and that Hezekiah by agreement had done him homage, and paid him tribute all this time.

CHAPTER XVII

Of Usurpation

197. As conquest may be called a foreign usurpation, so usurpation is a kind of domestic conquest; with this difference, that an usurper can never have right on his side, it being no *usurpation* but where one is got into the *possession of what another has right to*. This, so far as it is *usurpation,* is a change only of persons, but not of the forms and rules of the government; for if the usurper extend his power beyond what of right belonged to the lawful princes, or governors of the commonwealth, it is *tyranny* added to *usurpation*.

198. In all lawful governments, the designation of the persons, who are to bear rule, is as natural and necessary a part, as the form of the government itself, and is that which had its establishment originally from the people; the anarchy being much alike to have no form of government at all, or to agree, that it shall be monarchical, but to appoint no way to design the person that shall have the power, and be the monarch. Hence all commonwealths, with the form of government established, have rules also of appointing those who are to have any share in the public authority, and settled methods of conveying the right to them. For the anarchy is much alike to have no form of government at all, or to agree that it shall be monarchical, but to appoint no way to know or design the person that shall have the power and be the monarch. Whoever gets into the exercise of any part of the power, by other ways than what the laws of the community have prescribed, hath no right to be obeyed, though the form of the commonwealth be still preserved; since he is not the person the laws have appointed, and consequently not the person the people have consented to. Nor can such an *usurper*, or any deriving from him, ever have a title, till the people are both at liberty to consent, and have actually consented to allow, and confirm in him the power he hath till then usurped.

CHAPTER XVIII

Of Tyranny

199. As usurpation is the exercise of power, which another hath a right to, so *tyranny is the exercise of power beyond right,* which no body can have a right to. And this is making use of the power any one has in his hands, not for the good of those who are under it, but for his own private separate advantage.—When the governor, however intitled, makes not the law, but his will, the rule; and his commands and actions are not directed to the preservation of the properties of his people, but the satisfaction of his own ambition, revenge, covetousness, or any other irregular passion.

200. If one can doubt this to be truth, or reason, because it comes from the obscure hand of a subject, I hope the authority of a king will make it pass with him. King James the first, in his speech to the parliament, 1603, tells them thus: "I will ever prefer the

weal of the public, and of the whole commonwealth, in making of good laws and constitutions, to any particular and private ends of mine. Thinking ever the wealth and weal of
the commonwealth to be my greatest weal and worldly felicity; a point wherein a lawful
king doth directly differ from a tyrant. For I do acknowledge, that the special and greatest point of difference that is between a rightful king and an usurping tyrant, is this, that
whereas the proud and ambitious tyrant doth think his kingdom and people are only
ordained for satisfaction of his desires and unreasonable appetites, the righteous and just
king doth by the contrary acknowledge himself to be ordained for the procuring of the
wealth and property of his people." And again, in his speech to the parliament, 1609, he
hath these words: "The king binds himself by a double oath to the observation of the fundamental laws of his kingdom; tacitly, as by being a king, and so bound to protect as well
the people, as the laws of his kingdom; and expressly, by his oath at his coronation; so as
every just king, in a settled kingdom, is bound to observe that paction made to his people by his laws, in framing his government agreeable thereunto, according to that paction
which God made with Noah after the deluge: Hereafter, seed-time and harvest, and cold
and heat, and summer and winter, and day and night, shall not cease while the earth
remaineth. And therefore a king governing in a settled kingdom, leaves to be a king, and
degenerates into a tyrant, as soon as he leaves off to rule according to his laws." And a
little after, "Therefore all kings that are not tyrants, or perjured, will be glad to bound
themselves within the limits of their laws; and they that persuade them the contrary, are
vipers, and pests, both against them and the commonwealth." Thus that learned king,
who well understood the notions of things, makes the difference betwixt a *king* and a
tyrant to consist only in this, that one makes the laws the bounds of his power, and the
good of the public the end of his government; the other makes all give way to his own
will and appetite.

201. It is a mistake to think this fault is proper only to monarchies; other forms of government are liable to it, as well as that. For wherever the power, that is put in any hands for
the government of the people, and the preservation of their properties, is applied to other
ends, and made use of to impoverish, harass, or subdue them to the arbitrary and irregular commands of those that have it; there it presently becomes tyranny, whether those that
thus use it are one or many. Thus we read of the thirty tyrants at Athens, as well as one at
Syracuse; and the intolerable dominion of the decemviri at Rome was nothing better.

202. *Wherever law ends, tyranny begins*, if the law be transgressed to another's harm; and
whosoever in authority exceeds the power given him by the law, and makes use of the
force he has under his command, to compass that upon the subject, which the law allows
not, ceases in that to be a magistrate; and, acting without authority, may be opposed as
any other man, who by force invades the right of another. This is acknowledged in subordinate magistrates. He that hath authority to seize my person in the street, may be
opposed as a thief and a robber if he endeavours to break into my house to execute a writ,
notwithstanding that I know he has such a warrant, and such a legal authority, as will
impower him to arrest me abroad. And why this should not hold in the highest, as well
as in the most inferiour magistrate, I would gladly be informed. Is it reasonable that the
eldest brother, because he has the greatest part of his father's estate, should thereby have
a right to take away any of his younger brother's portions? Or, that a rich man, who
possessed a whole country, should from thence have a right to seize, when he pleased, the
cottage and garden of his poor neighbour? The being rightfully possessed of great power
and riches, exceedingly beyond the greatest part of the sons of Adam, is so far from being
an excuse, much less a reason for rapine and oppression, which the endamaging another
without authority is, that it is a great aggravation of it. For the exceeding the bounds of

authority is no more a right in a great, than in a petty officer; no more justifiable in a king than a constable; but is so much the worse in him, in that he has more trust put in him, has already a much greater share than the rest of his brethren, and is supposed, from the advantages of his education, employment, and counsellors, to be more knowing in the measures of right or wrong.

203. May the *commands* then *of a prince be opposed?* may he be resisted as often as any one shall find himself aggrieved, and but imagine he has not right done him? This will unhinge and overturn all polities, and, instead of government and order, leave nothing but anarchy and confusion.

204. To this I answer, that *force* is to be *opposed* to nothing but to unjust and unlawful *force;* whoever makes any opposition in any other case, draws on himself a just condemnation both from God and man; and so no such danger or confusion will follow, as is often suggested. For,

205. *First,* As, in some countries, the person of the prince by the law is sacred; and so, whatever he commands or does, his person is still free from all question or violence, not liable to force, or any judicial censure or condemnation. But yet opposition may be made to the illegal acts of any inferiour officer, or other commissioned by him; unless he will, by actually putting himself into a state of war with his people, dissolve the government, and leave them to that defence which belongs to every one in the state of nature. For of such things who can tell what the end will be? And a neighbour kingdom has shewed the world an odd example. In all other cases the *sacredness* of the *person exempts him from all inconveniencies,* whereby he is secure, whilst the government stands, from all violence and harm whatsoever; than which there cannot be a wiser constitution. For the harm he can do in his own person not being likely to happen often, nor to extend itself far; nor being able by his single strength to subvert the laws, nor oppress the body of the people, should any prince have so much weakness and ill-nature as to be willing to do it, the inconveniency of some particular mischiefs that may happen sometimes, when a heady prince comes to the throne, are well recompensed by the peace of the public, and security of the government, in the person of the chief magistrate, thus set out of the reach of danger: it being safer for the body that some few private men should be sometimes in danger to suffer, than that the head of the republic should be easily, and upon slight occasions, exposed.

206. *Secondly,* But this privilege belonging only to the king's person, hinders not, but they may be questioned, opposed, and resisted, who use unjust force, though they pretend a commission from him, which the law authorizes not. As is plain in the case of him that has the king's writ to arrest a man, which is a full commission from the king; and yet he that has it cannot break open a man's house to do it, nor execute this command of the king upon certain days, nor in certain places, though this commission have no such exception in it, but they are the limitations of the law, which if any one transgress, the king's commission excuses him not. For the king's authority being given him only by the law, he cannot impower any one to act against the law, or justify him, by his commission, in so doing. The *commission or command of any magistrate, where he has no authority,* being as void and insignificant, as that of any private man. The difference between the one and the other being that the magistrate has some authority so far, and to such ends, and the private man has none at all. For it is not the commission, but the authority, that gives the right of acting; and *against the laws there can be no authority.* But notwithstanding such resistance, the king's person and authority are still both secured, and so *no danger to governor or government.*

207. *Thirdly,* Supposing a government wherein the person of the chief magistrate is not thus sacred; yet this *doctrine* of the lawfulness of *resisting* all unlawful exercises of his power, *will not* upon every slight occasion endanger him, or *embroil the government.* For

where the injured party may be relieved, and his damages repaired by appeal to the law, there can be no pretence for force, which is only to be used where a man is intercepted from appealing to the law. For nothing is to be accounted hostile force, but where it leaves not the remedy of such an appeal. And it is such force alone, that puts him that uses it *into a state of war,* and makes it lawful to resist him. A man with a sword in his hand, demands my purse in the highway, when perhaps I have not twelve-pence in my pocket: this man I may lawfully kill. To another I deliver £100 to hold only whilst I alight, which he refuses to restore me, when I am got up again, but draws his sword to defend the possession of it by force, if I endeavour to retake it. The mischief this man does me is an hundred, or possibly a thousand times more than the other perhaps intended me (whom I killed before he really did me any;) and yet I might lawfully kill the one, and cannot so much as hurt the other lawfully. The reason whereof is plain; because the one using force, which threatened my life, I could not have *time to appeal* to the law to secure it: and when it was gone, it was too late to appeal. The law could not restore life to my dead carcass, the loss was irreparable: which to prevent, the law of nature gave me a right to destroy him, who had put himself into a state of war with me, and threatened my destruction. But in the other case, my life not being in danger, I may have the *benefit of appealing* to the law, and have reparation for my £100 that way.

208. *Fourthly,* But if the unlawful acts done by the magistrate be maintained (by the power he has got) and the remedy which is due by law, be by the same power obstructed: yet the *right of resisting,* even in such manifest acts of tyranny, will not suddenly, or on slight occasions, disturb the government. For if it reach no farther than some private men's cases, though they have a right to defend themselves, and to recover by force what by unlawful force is taken from them: yet the right to do so will not easily engage them in a contest, wherein they are sure to perish; it being as impossible for one, or a few oppressed men to *disturb the government,* where the body of the people do not think themselves concerned in it, as for a raving madman, or heady malecontent, to overturn a well-settled state, the people being as little apt to follow the one, as the other.

209. But if either these illegal acts have extended to the majority of the people; or if the mischief and oppression has lighted only on some few, but in such cases, as the precedent and consequences seem to threaten all; and they are persuaded in their consciences, that their laws, and with them their estates, liberties, and lives are in danger, and perhaps their religion too: how they will be hindered from resisting illegal force, used against them, I cannot tell. This is an *inconvenience,* I confess, that *attends all governments* whatsoever, when the governors have brought it to this pass, to be generally suspected of their people; the most dangerous state which they can possibly put themselves in; wherein they are the less to be pitied, because it is so easy to be avoided; it being as impossible for a governor, if he really means the good of his people, and the preservation of them, and their laws together, not to make them see and feel it, as it is for the father of a family, not to let his children see he loves and takes care of them.

210. But if all the world shall observe pretences of one kind, and actions of another; arts used to elude the law, and the trust of prerogative, (which is an arbitrary power in some things left in the prince's hand to do good, not harm, to the people) employed contrary to the end for which it was given: if the people shall find the ministers and subordinate magistrates chosen suitable to such ends, and favoured, or laid by, proportionately as they promote or oppose them: if they see several experiments made of arbitrary power, and that religion underhand favoured (though publicly proclaimed against) which is readiest to introduce it; and the operators in it supported, as much as may be; and when that cannot be done, yet approved still, and liked the better: if a *long train of actions shew the coun-*

cils all tending that way; how can a man any more hinder himself from being persuaded in his own mind, which way things are going; or from casting about how to save himself, than he could from believing the captain of the ship he was in, was carrying him, and the rest of the company, to Algiers, when he found him always steering that course, though cross winds, leaks in his ship, and want of men and provisions did often force him to turn his course another way for some time, which he steadily returned to again, as soon as the wind, weather, and other circumstances would let him?

CHAPTER XIX

Of the Dissolution of Government

211. He that will with any clearness speak of the *dissolution of government,* ought in the first place to distinguish between the *dissolution of the society* and the *dissolution of the government.* That which makes the community, and brings men out of the loose state of nature into *one politic society,* is the agreement which every one has with the rest to incorporate, and act as one body, and so be one distinct commonwealth. The usual, and almost only way whereby *this union is dissolved,* is the inroad of foreign force making a conquest upon them. For in that case, (not being able to maintain and support themselves, as *one entire* and *independent body*) the union belonging to that body which consisted therein, must necessarily cease, and so every one return to the state he was in before, with a liberty to shift for himself, and provide for his own safety, as he thinks fit, in some other society. Whenever the *society is dissolved,* it is certain the government of that society cannot remain. Thus conquerors swords often cut up governments by the roots, and mangle societies to pieces, separating the subdued or scattered multitude from the protection of, and dependence on, that society which ought to have preserved them from violence. The world is too well instructed in, and too forward to allow of, this way of dissolving of governments, to need any more to be said of it; and there wants not much argument to prove, that where the *society is dissolved,* the government cannot remain; that being as impossible, as for the frame of a house to subsist when the materials of it are scattered and dissipated by a whirlwind, or jumbled into a confused heap by an earthquake.

212. Besides this overturning from without, *governments are dissolved from within.*

First, When the *legislative is altered.* Civil society being a state of peace, amongst those who are of it, from whom the state of war is excluded by the umpirage, which they have provided in their legislative, for the ending all differences that may arise amongst any of them; it is in their legislative, that the members of a commonwealth are united, and combined together into one coherent living body. This *is the soul that gives form, life, and unity* to the commonwealth: from hence the several members have their mutual influence, sympathy, and connexion; and therefore, when the legislative is broken, or dissolved, dissolution and death follows. For, *the essence and union of the society* consisting in having one will, the legislative, when once established by the majority, has the declaring, and as it were keeping of that will. The *constitution of the legislative* is the first and fundamental act of society, whereby provision is made for the *continuation of their union,* under the direction of persons, and bonds of laws, made by persons authorized thereunto, by the consent and appointment of the people; without which no one man, or number of men, amongst them, can have authority of making laws that shall be binding to the rest. When any one, or more, shall take upon them to make laws, whom the people have not appointed so to do, they make laws without authority, which the people are not therefore bound to obey; by which means they come again to be out of subjection, and may constitute to themselves a new legislative, as they think best, being in full liberty to resist the force of those, who without authority would impose any thing upon them. Every one is at the disposure of his own will, when those who had, by the delegation of the society, the declaring of the public will, are excluded from it, and others usurp the place, who have no such authority or delegation.

213. This being usually brought about by such in the commonwealth who misuse the power they have, it is hard to consider it aright, and know at whose door to lay it, without knowing the form of government in which it happens. Let us suppose then the legislative placed in the concurrence of three distinct persons.

1. A single hereditary person, having the constant, supreme, executive power, and with it the power of convoking and dissolving the other two, within certain periods of time.
2. An assembly of hereditary nobility.
3. An assembly of representatives chosen *pro tempore*, by the people. Such a form of government supposed, it is evident.

214. *First,* That when such a single person, or prince, sets up his own arbitrary will in place of the laws, which are the will of the society, declared by the legislative, then the *legislative is changed.* For that being in effect the legislative, whose rules and laws are put in execution, and required to be obeyed; when other laws are set up, and other rules pretended, and enforced, than what the legislative, constituted by the society, have enacted, it is plain that the *legislative is changed.* Whoever introduces new laws, not being thereunto authorized, by the fundamental appointment of the society, or subverts the old, disowns and overturns the power by which they were made, and so sets up a *new legislative.*

215. *Secondly,* When the prince hinders the legislative from assembling in its due time, or from acting freely, pursuant to those ends for which it was constituted, the *legislative is altered:* for it is not a certain number of men, no, nor their meeting, unless they have also freedom of debating, and leisure of perfecting, what is for the good of the society, wherein the legislative consists: when these are taken away or altered, so as to deprive the society of the due exercise of their power, the legislative is truly altered. For it is not names that constitute governments, but the use and exercise of those powers that were intended to accompany them; so that he, who takes away the freedom, or hinders the acting of the legislative in its due seasons, in effect *takes away the legislative,* and *puts an end to the government.*

216. *Thirdly,* When, by the arbitrary power of the prince, the electors, or ways of election, are altered, without the consent, and contrary to the common interest of the people, there also the *legislative is altered.* For, if others than those whom the society hath authorized thereunto, do choose, or in another way than what the society hath prescribed, those chosen are not the legislative appointed by the people.

217. *Fourthly,* The delivery also of the people into the subjection of a foreign power, either by the prince, or by the legislative, is certainly a *change of the legislative,* and so a *dissolution of the government.* For the end why people entered into society being to be preserved one intire, free, independent society, to be governed by its own laws; this is lost, whenever they are given up into the power of another.

218. Why, in such a constitution as this, the *dissolution of the government* in these cases is to be imputed to the prince, is evident; because he, having the force, treasure, and offices of the state to employ, and often persuading himself, or being flattered by others, that as supreme magistrate, he is uncapable of control; he alone is in a condition to make great advances toward such changes, under pretence of lawful authority, and has it in his hands

to terrify or suppress opposers, as factious, seditious, and enemies to the government: whereas no other part of the legislative, or people, is capable by themselves to attempt any alteration of the legislative, without open and visible rebellion, apt enough to be taken notice of; which, when, it prevails, produces effects very little different from foreign conquest. Besides, the prince in such a form of government having the power of dissolving the other parts of the legislative, and thereby rendering them private persons, they can never in opposition to him, or without his concurrence, alter the legislative by a law, his consent being necessary to give any of their decrees that sanction. But yet, so far as the other parts of the legislative any way contribute to any attempt upon the government, and do either promote, or not, what lies in them, hinder such designs; they are guilty, and partake in this, which is certainly the greatest crime men can be guilty of one towards another.

219. There is one way more whereby such a government may be dissolved, and that is, when he who has the supreme executive power neglects and abandons that charge, so that the laws already made can no longer be put in execution. This is demonstratively to reduce all to anarchy, and so effectually to *dissolve the government*. For laws not being made for themselves, but to be, by their execution, the bonds of the society, to keep every part of the body politic in its due place and function; when that totally ceases, the *government* visibly *ceases,* and the people become a confused multitude, without order or connexion. Where there is no longer the administration of justice, for the securing of men's rights, nor any remaining power within the community to direct the force, or provide for the necessities of the public; there certainly is *no government left.* Where the laws cannot be executed, it is all one as if there were no laws; and a government without laws is, I suppose, a mystery in politics, inconceivable to human capacity, and inconsistent with human society.

220. In these and the like cases, *when the government is dissolved,* the people are at liberty to provide for themselves, by erecting a new legislative, differing from the other, by the change of persons, or form, or both, as they shall find it most for their safety and good. For the *society* can never, by the fault of another, lose the native and original right it has to preserve itself; which can only be done by a settled legislative, and a fair and impartial execution of the laws made by it. But the state of mankind is not so miserable that they are not capable of using this remedy, till it be too late to look for any. To tell *people* they *may provide for themselves,* by erecting a new legislative, when by oppression, artifice, or being delivered over to a foreign power, their old one is gone, is only to tell them, they may expect relief when it is too late, and the evil is past cure. This is in effect no more, than to bid them first be slaves, and then to take care of their liberty; and when their chains are on, tell them, they may act like freemen. This, if barely so, is rather mockery than relief; and men can never be secure from tyranny, if there be no means to escape it, till they are perfectly under it: And therefore it is, that they have not only a right to get out of it, but to prevent it.

221. There is, therefore, secondly, another way whereby *governments are dissolved,* and that is, when the legislative, or the prince either of them, act contrary to their trust.

First, The *legislative acts against the trust* reposed in them, when they endeavour to invade the property of the subject, and to make themselves, or any part of the community, masters, or arbitrary disposers of the lives, liberties, or fortunes of the people.

222. The reason why men enter into society, is the preservation of their property; and the end why they choose and authorize a legislative, is, that there may be laws made, and rules set, as guards and fences to the properties of all the members of the society: to limit the power, and moderate the dominion, of every part and member of the society. For since it can never be supposed to be the will of the society, that the legislative should have a

power to destroy that, which every one designs to secure, by entering into society, and for which the people submitted themselves to legislators of their own making, whenever the *legislators endeavour to take away and destroy the property of the people,* or to reduce them to slavery under arbitrary power, they put themselves into a state of war with the people, who are thereupon absolved from any farther obedience, and are left to the common refuge, which God hath provided for all men, against force and violence. Whensoever therefore the *legislative* shall transgress this fundamental rule of society; and either by ambition, fear, folly or corruption, *endeavour to grasp* themselves, *or put into the hands of any other an absolute power* over the lives, liberties, and estates of the people; by this breach of trust they *forfeit the power,* the people had put into their hands, for quite contrary ends, and it devolves to the people, who have a right to resume their original liberty, and, by the establishment of a new legislative, (such as they shall think fit) provide for their own safety and security, which is the end for which they are in society. What I have said here, concerning the legislative in general, holds true also concerning the supreme executor, who having a double trust put in him, both to have a part in the legislative, and the supreme execution of the law, acts against both, when he goes about to set up his own arbitrary will, as the law of the society. He *acts* also *contrary to his trust,* when he either employs the force, treasure, and offices of the society to corrupt the *representatives,* and gain them to his purposes; or openly pre-engages the *electors,* and prescribes to their choice, such, whom he has by solicitations, threats, promises, or otherwise, won to his designs: and employs them to bring in such, who have promised before-hand, what to vote, and what to enact. Thus to regulate candidates and electors, and new model the ways of election, what is it but to cut up the government by the roots, and poison the very fountain of public security? for the people having reserved to themselves the choice of their *representatives,* as the fence to their properties, could do it for no other end, but that they might always be freely chosen, and so chosen, freely act, and advise, as the necessity of the commonwealth, and the public good should, upon examination and mature debate, be judged to require. This, those who give their votes before they hear the debate, and have weighed the reasons on all sides, are not capable of doing. To prepare such an assembly as this, and endeavour to set up the declared abettors of his own will, for the true representatives of the people, and the law-makers of the society, is certainly as great a *breach of trust,* and as perfect a declaration of a design to subvert the government, as is possible to be met with. To which if one shall add rewards and punishments visibly employed to the same end, and all the arts of perverted law made use of, to take off and destroy all that stand in the way of such a design, and will not comply and consent to betray the liberties of their country, it will be past doubt what is doing. What power they ought to have in the society, who thus employ it contrary to the trust that went along with it in its first institution, is easy to determine; and one cannot but see, that he, who has once attempted any such thing as this, cannot any longer be trusted.

223. To this perhaps it will be said, that the people being ignorant, and always discontented, to lay the foundation of government in the unsteady opinion and uncertain humour of the people, is to expose it to certain ruin; and *no government will be able long to subsist,* if the people may set up a new legislative, whenever they take offence at the old one. To this I answer, quite the contrary. People are not so easily got out of their old forms as some are apt to suggest. They are hardly to be prevailed with to amend the acknowledged faults in the frame they have been accustomed to. And if there be any original defects, or adventitious ones introduced by time, or corruption: it is not an easy thing to get them changed, even when all the world sees there is an opportunity for it. This slowness and aversion in the people to quit their old constitutions, has in the many revolutions which have been seen in this kingdom, in this and former ages, still kept us

to, or, after some interval of fruitless attempts, still brought us back again to, our old legislative of king, lords, and commons: and whatever provocations have made the crown be taken from some of our princes heads, they never carried the people so far as to place it in another line.

224. But it will be said, this *hypothesis* lays a *ferment for* frequent *rebellion.* To which I *answer,*

First, No more than any other *hypothesis:* for when the people are made miserable, and find themselves *exposed to the ill usage of arbitrary power,* cry up their governors as much as you will, for *sons of Jupiter;* let them be sacred or divine, descended, or authorized from heaven; give them out for whom or what you please, the same will happen. *The people generally ill treated,* and contrary to right, will be ready upon any occasion to ease themselves of a burden that sits heavy upon them. They will wish, and seek for the opportunity, which in the change, weakness, and accidents of human affairs, seldom delays long to offer itself. He must have lived but a little while in the world, who has not seen examples of this in his time; and he must have read very little, who cannot produce examples of it in all sorts of governments in the world.

225. *Secondly,* I answer, such *revolutions happen* not upon every little mismanagement in public affairs. *Great mistakes* in the ruling part, many wrong and inconvenient laws, and all the slips of human frailty, will be *borne by the people* without mutiny or murmur. But if a long train of abuses, prevarications and artifices, all tending the same way, make the design visible to the people, and they cannot but feel what they lie under, and see whither they are going; it is not to be wondered, that they should then rouse themselves, and endeavour to put the rule into such hands which may secure to them the ends for which government was at first erected; and without which, ancient names, and specious forms, are so far from being better, that they are much worse, than the state of nature, or pure anarchy; the inconveniencies being all as great and as near, but the remedy farther off and more difficult.

226. *Thirdly,* I answer, that *this doctrine* of a power in the people of providing for their safety anew, by a new legislative, when their legislators have acted contrary to their trust, by invading their property, is the *best fence against rebellion,* and the probablest means to hinder it. For *rebellion* being an opposition, not to persons, but authority, which is founded only in the constitutions and laws of the government; those, whoever they be, who by force break through, and by force justify their violation of them, are truly and properly *rebels.* For when men, by entering into society and civil government, have excluded force, and introduced laws for the preservation of property, peace, and unity amongst themselves; those who set up force again in opposition to the laws, do *rebellare,* that is, bring back again the state of war, and are properly rebels: Which they who are in power, (by the pretence they have to authority, the temptation of force they have in their hands, and the flattery of those about them) being likeliest to do; the properest way to prevent the evil, is to shew them the danger and injustice of it, who are under the greatest temptation to run into it.

227. In both the forementioned cases, when either the legislative is changed, or the legislators act contrary to the end for which they were constituted, those who are guilty are *guilty of rebellion;* for if any one by force takes away the established legislative of any society, and the laws by them made pursuant to their trust, he thereby takes away the umpirage, which every one had consented to, for a peaceable decision of all their controversies, and a bar to the state of war amongst them. They who remove, or change the legislative, take away this decisive power, which no body can have but by the appointment and consent of the people; and so destroying the authority which the people did, and no body else can set up, and introducing a power which the people hath not authorized, they

actually *introduce a state of war,* which is that of force without authority; and thus by removing the legislative established by the society, (in whose decisions the people acquiesced and united, as to that of their own will) they untie the knot, and *expose the people anew to the state of war.* And if those, who by force take away the legislative, are *rebels,* the *legislators* themselves, as has been shewn, can be no less esteemed so; when they, who were set up for the protection and preservation of the people, their liberties and properties, shall by force invade and endeavour to take them away; and so they putting themselves into a state of war with those who made them the protectors and guardians of their peace, are properly, and with the greatest aggravation, *rebellantes,* rebels.

228. But if they, who say, "it lays a foundation for rebellion," mean that it may occasion civil wars, or intestine broils, to tell the people they are absolved from obedience when, illegal attempts are made upon their liberties or properties, and may oppose the unlawful violence of those who were their magistrates, when they invade their properties contrary to the trust put in them; and that therefore this doctrine is not to be allowed, being so destructive to the peace of the world: they may as well say, upon the same ground, that honest men may not oppose robbers or pirates, because this may occasion disorder or bloodshed. If any *mischief* come in such cases, it is not to be charged upon him who defends his own right, but *on him that invades* his neighbour's. If the innocent honest man must quietly quit all he has, for peace sake, to him who will lay violent hands upon it, I desire it may be considered, what a kind of peace there will be in the world, which consists only in violence and rapine; and which is to be maintained only for the benefit of robbers and oppressors. Who would not think it an admirable peace betwixt the mighty and the mean, when the lamb, without resistance, yielded his throat to be torn by the imperious wolf? Polyphemus's den gives us a perfect pattern of such a peace, and such a government, wherein Ulysses and his companions had nothing to do, but quietly to suffer themselves to be devoured. And no doubt Ulysses, who was a prudent man, preached up *passive obedience,* and exhorted them to a quiet submission, by representing to them of what concernment peace was to mankind; and by strewing the inconveniencies might happen, if they should offer to resist Polyphemus, who had now the power over them.

229. The end of government is the good of mankind: and which is *best for mankind,* that the people should be always exposed to the boundless will of tyranny; or that the rulers should be sometimes liable to be opposed, when they grow exorbitant in the use of their power, and employ it for the destruction, and not the preservation of the properties of their people?

230. Nor let any one say, that mischief can arise from hence, as often as it shall please a busy head, or turbulent spirit, to desire the alteration of the government. It is true, such men may stir, whenever they please; but it will be only to their own just ruin and perdition. For till the mischief be grown general, and the ill designs of the rulers become visible, or their attempts sensible to the greater part, the people, who are more disposed to suffer than right themselves by resistance, are not apt to stir. The examples of particular injustice or oppression, of here and there an unfortunate man, moves them not. But if they universally have a persuasion, grounded upon manifest evidence, that designs are carrying on against their liberties, and the general course and tendency of things cannot but give them strong suspicions of the evil intention of their governors, who is to be blamed for it? Who can help it, if they, who might avoid it, bring themselves into this suspicion? Are the people to be blamed, if they have the sense of rational creatures, and can think of things no otherwise than as they find and feel them? And is it not rather *their fault,* who put things into such a posture, that they would not have

them thought to be as they are? I grant, that the pride, ambition, and turbulency of private men, have sometimes caused great disorders in commonwealths, and factions have been fatal to states and kingdoms. But whether *the mischief* hath *oftener* begun *in the peoples wantonness,* and a desire to cast off the lawful authority of their rulers, or in *the rulers insolence,* and endeavours to get and exercise an arbitrary power over their people; whether oppression, or disobedience, gave the first rise to the disorder; I leave it to impartial history to determine. This I am sure, whoever, either ruler or subject, by force goes about to invade the rights of either prince or people, and lays the foundation for *overturning* the constitution and frame of *any just government;* is highly guilty of the greatest crime, I think, a man is capable of; being to answer for all those mischiefs of blood, rapine, and desolation, which the breaking to pieces of governments bring on a country. And he who does it, is justly to be esteemed the common enemy and pest of mankind, and is to be treated accordingly.

231. That *subjects* or *foreigners,* attempting by force on the properties of any people, may be resisted with force, is agreed on all hands. But that *magistrates,* doing the same thing, may be *resisted,* hath of late been denied: as if those who had the greatest privileges and advantages by the law, had thereby a power to break those laws, by which alone they were set in a better place than their brethren: whereas their offence is thereby the greater, both as being ungrateful for the greater share they have by the law, and breaking also that trust which is put into their hands by their brethren.

232. Whosoever uses *force without right,* as every one does in society, who does it without law, puts himself into a *state of war* with those against whom he so uses it; and in that state all former ties are cancelled, all other rights cease, and every one has a right to defend himself, and to *resist the aggressor.* This is so evident, that Barclay himself, that great assertor of the power and sacredness of kings, is forced to confess, that it is lawful for the people, in some cases, to resist their king; and that too in a chapter, wherein he pretends to shew, that the divine law shuts up the people from all manner of rebellion. Whereby it is evident, even by his own doctrine, that, since they may in some cases resist, all resisting of *princes* is not rebellion. His words are these. "Quod siquis dicat, Ergone populus tyrannicae crudelitati & furori jugulum semper praebebit? Ergone multitudo civitates suas fame, ferro, & flamma vastari, seque, conjuges, & liberos fortunae ludibrio & tyranni libidini exponi, inque omnia vitae pericula omnesque miserias & molestias a rege de luci patientur? Num illis quod omni animantium generi est a natura tributum, denegari debet, ut sc. vim vi repellant, seseq; ab injuria tueantur? Huic brevitur responsum sit, Populo universo negari defensionem, quae juris naturalis est, neque ultionem quae praeter naturam est adversus regem concedi debere. Quapropter si rex non in singulares tantum personas aliquot privatum odium exerceat, sed corpus etiam reipublicae, cujus ipse caput est, i.e. totum populum, vel insignem aliquam ejus partem immani & intoleranda saevitia seu tyrannide divexet; populo quidem hoc casu resistendi ac tuendi se ab injuria potestas competit; sed tuendi se tantum, non enim in principem invadendi: & restituendae injuriae illatae, non recedendi a debita reverentia propter acceptam injuriam. Praesentem denique impetum propulsandi non vim praeteritam ulciscendi jus habet. Horum enim alterum a natura est, ut vitam scilicet corpusque tueamur. Alterum vero contra naturam, ut inferior de superiori supplicium sumat. Quod itaque populus malum, antequam factum sit, impedire potest, ne fiat; id postquam factum est, in regem authorem sceleris vindicare non potest: populus igitur hoc amplius quam privatus quispiam habet: quod huic, vel ipsis adversariis judicibus, excepto Buchanano, nullum nisi in patientia remedium superest. Cum ille si intolerabilis tyrannus est (modicum enim ferre omnino debet) resistere cum reverentia possit." Barclay *contra Monarchom.* 1. iii. c. 8.

In English thus:

233. "But if any one should ask, Must the people then always lay themselves open to, the cruelty and rage of tyranny? Must they see their cities pillaged and laid in ashes, their wives and children exposed to the tyrant's lust and fury, and themselves and families reduced by their king to ruin, and all the miseries of want and oppression; and yet sit still? Must men alone be debarred the common privilege of opposing force with force, which nature allows so freely to all other creatures for their preservation from injury? I answer: Self-defence is a part of the law of nature; nor can it be denied the community, even against the king himself: but to revenge themselves upon him, must by no means be allowed them; it being not agreeable to that law. Wherefore if the king should shew an hatred, not only to some particular persons, but sets himself against the body of the commonwealth, whereof he is the head, and shall, with intolerable ill-usage, cruelly tyrannize over the whole, or a considerable part of the people, in this case the people have a right to resist and defend themselves from injury: but it must be with this caution, that they only defend themselves, but do not attack their prince: they may repair the damages received, but must not for any provocation exceed the bounds of due reverence and respect. They may repulse the present attempt, but must not revenge past violences. For it is natural for us to defend life and limb, but that an inferiour should punish a superiour, is against nature. The mischief which is designed them the people may prevent before it be done; but when it is done, they must not revenge it on the king, though author of the villany. This therefore is the privilege of the people in general, above what any private person hath; that particular men are allowed by our adversaries themselves (Buchanan only excepted) to have no other remedy but patience; but the body of the people may with reverence resist intolerable tyranny; for, when it is but moderate, they ought to endure it."

234. Thus far that great advocate of monarchical power allows of *resistance*.

235. It is true, he has annexed two limitations to it, to no *purpose*:

First, He says, it must be with reverence.

Secondly, It must be without retribution, or punishment; and the reason he gives is, "Because an inferiour cannot punish a superiour."

First, How to resist force without striking again, or how to *strike with* reverence, will need some skill to make intelligible. He that shall oppose an assault only with a shield to receive the blows, or in any more respectful posture, without a sword in his hand, to abate the confidence and force of the assailant, will quickly be at an end of his *resistance,* and will find such a defence serve only to draw on himself the worse usage. This is as ridiculous a way of resisting, as Juvenal thought it of fighting; "ubi to pulsas, ego vapulo tantum." And the success of the combat will be unavoidably the same he there describes it:

> *Libertas pauperis haec est:*
> *Pulsatus rogat, & pugnis concisus, adorat,*
> *Ut liceat paucis cum dentibus inde reverti.*

This will always be the event of such an imaginary *resistance*, where men may not strike again. He therefore *who may resist, must be allowed to strike.* And then let our author, or any body else, join a knock on the head, or a cut on the face, with as much *reverence* and *respect* as he thinks fit. He that can reconcile blows and reverence, may for aught I know, deserve for his pains a civil, respectful cudgelling, wherever he can meet with it.

Secondly, As to his second, "An inferiour cannot punish a superiour;" that is true, generally speaking, whilst he is his superiour. But to resist force with force, being the *state of war* that *levels the parties,* cancels all former relation of reverence, respect, and *superiority:* And then the odds that remains, is, that he, who opposes the unjust aggressor, has this *superiority* over him, that he has a right when he prevails, to punish the offender, both for the breach of the peace, and all the evils that followed upon it. Barclay therefore, in another place, more coherently to himself, denies it to be lawful to *resist* a king in any case. But he there assigns two cases, whereby a king may un-king himself. His words are,

"Quid ergo, nulline casus incidere possunt quibus populo sese erigere atque in regem impotentius dominantem arma capere & invaderejure suo suaque authoritate liceat? Nulli certe quamdiu rex manet. Semper enim ex divinis id obstat, Regem honorificato; & qui potestati resistit, Dei ordinationi resistit: non alias igitur in eum populo potestas est quam si id committat propter quod ipso jure rex esse desinat. Tunc enim se ipse principatu exuit atque in privatis constituit liber: hoc modo populus & superior efficitur, reverso ad eum sc. jure illo quod ante regem inauguratum in interregno habuit. At sunt paucorum generum commissa ejusmodi quae hunc effectum pariunt. At ego cum plurima animo perlustrem, duo tantam invenio, duos, inquam, casus quibus rex ipso facto ex rege non regem se facit & omni honore & dignitate regali atque in subditos potestate destituit; quorum etiam meminit Winzerus. Horum unus est, Si regnum disperdat, quemadmodum de Nerone fertur, quod is nempe senatum populumque Romanum, atque adeo urbem ipsam ferro flammaque vastare, ac novas sibi sedes quaerere, decrevisset. Et de Caligula, quod palam denunciarit se neque civem neque principem senatui amplius fore, inque animo habuerit interempto utriusque ordinis electissimo quoque Alexandriam commigrare, ac ut populum uno ictu interimeret, unam ei cervicem optavit. Talia cum rex aliquis meditatur & molitur serio, omnem regnandi curam & animum ilico abjicit, ac proinde imperium in subditos amittit, ut dominus servi pro derelicto habiti dominium."

236. "Alter casus est, Si rex in alicujus clientelam se contulit, ac regnum quod liberum a majoribus & populo traditum accepit, alienae ditioni mancipavit. Nam tunc quamvis forte non ea mente id agit populo plane ut incommodet: tamen quia quod praecipuum est regiae dignitatis amisit, ut summus scilicet in regno secundum Deum sit, & solo Deo inferior, atque populum etiam totum ignorantem vel invitum, cujus libertatem sartam & tectam conservare debuit in alterius gentis ditionem & potestatem dedidit, hac velut quadam regni ab alienatione efficit, ut nec quod ipse in regno imperium habuit retineat, nec in eum cui collatum voluit, juris quicquam transferat; atque ita eo facto liberum jam & suae potestatis populum relinquit, cujus rei exemplum unum annales Scotici suppeditant." Barclay *contra Monarchom.* 1. iii. c. 16.

Which in English runs thus:

237. "What then, can there no case happen wherein the people may of right, and by their own authority, help themselves, take arms, and set upon their king imperiously domineering over them? None at all, whilst he remains a king. Honour the king, and he that resists the power, resists the ordinance of God; are divine oracles that will never permit it. The people therefore can never come by a power over him, unless he does something that makes him cease to be a king. For then he divests himself of his crown and dignity, and returns to the state of a private man, and the people become free and superiour, the power which they had in the interregnum, before they crowned him king, devolving to them again. But there are but few miscarriages which bring the matter to this state. After considering it well on all sides, I can find but two. Two cases there are, I say, whereby a king, ipso facto, becomes no king, and loses all power and regal authority over his people; which are also taken notice of by Winzerus.

The first is, If he endeavour to overturn the government, that is, if he have a purpose and design to ruin the kingdom and commonwealth; as it is recorded of Nero, that he resolved to cut off the senate and people of Rome, lay the city waste with fire and sword, and then remove to some other place. And of Caligula, that he openly declared, that he would be no longer a head to the people or senate, and that he had it in his thoughts to cut off the worthiest men of both ranks, and then retire to Alexandria: and he wished that the people had but one neck, that he might dispatch them all at a blow. Such designs as these, when any king harbours in his thoughts, and seriously promotes, he immediately gives up all care and thought of the commonwealth; and consequently forfeits the power of governing his subjects, as a master does the dominion over his slaves whom he hath abandoned."

238. "The other case is, When a king makes himself the dependent of another, and subjects his kingdom which his ancestors left him, and the people put free into his hands, to the dominion of another. For however perhaps it may not be his intention to prejudice the people, yet because he has hereby lost the principal part of regal dignity, viz. to be next and immediately under God supreme in his kingdom; and also because he betrayed or forced his people, whose liberty he ought to have carefully preserved, into the power and dominion of a foreign nation. By this, as it were, alienation of his kingdom, he himself loses the power he had in it before, without transferring any the least right to those on whom he would have bestowed it; and so by this act sets the people free, and leaves them at their own disposal. One example of this is to be found in the Scotch Annals."

239. In these cases Barclay, the great champion of absolute monarchy, is forced to allow, that a king may be *resisted*, and *ceases to be a king*. That is, in short, not to multiply cases, in whatsoever he has no authority, there he is no king, and may be resisted. For wheresoever the *authority ceases, the king ceases too*, and becomes like other men who have no *authority*. And these two cases the instances differ little from those above-mentioned, to be destructive to governments, only that he has omitted the principle from which his doctrine flows; and that is, the breach of trust, in not preserving the form of government agreed on, and in not intending the end of government itself, which is the public good and preservation of property. When a king has dethroned himself, and put himself in a state of war with his people, what shall hinder them from prosecuting him who is no king, as they would any other man, who has put himself into a state of war with them; Barclay and those of his opinion would do well to tell us. This farther I desire may be taken notice of out of Barclay, that he says, "The mischief that is designed them, the people may prevent before it be done"; whereby he allows "resistance" when tyranny is but in design. "Such designs as these" (says he) "when any king harbours in his thoughts and seriously promotes, he immediately gives up all care and thought of the commonwealth;" so that, according to him, the neglect of the public good is to be taken as an evidence of such "design," or at least for a sufficient cause of "resistance." And the reason of all, he gives in these words, "Because he betrayed or forced his people, whose liberty he ought carefully to have preserved." What he adds, "into the power and dominion of a foreign nation," signifies nothing, the fault and forfeiture lying in the loss of their "liberty," which he "ought to have preserved," and not in any distinction of the persons to whose dominion they were subjected. The people's right is equally invaded, and their liberty lost, whether they are made slaves to any of their own, or a foreign nation; and in this lies the injury, and against this only have they the right of defence. And there are instances to be found in all countries, which shew, that it is not the change of nations in the persons of their governors, but the change of government, that gives the offence. Bilson, a bishop of our church, and a great stickler for the power and prerogative of princes, does, if I mistake not, in his treatise of christian subjection, acknowledge, *that princes may forfeit their power*, and their title to the obedience of their subjects; and if there needed authority in a case where reason is so plain, I could send my reader to Bractan, Fortescue, and the author of the Mirrour, and others, writers that cannot be suspected to be ignorant of our government, or enemies to it.

But I thought Hooker alone might be enough to satisfy those men, who relying on him for their ecclesiastical polity, are by a strange fate carried to deny those principles upon which he builds it. Whether they are herein made the tools of cunninger workmen, to pull down their own fabric, they were best look. This I am sure, their civil policy is so new, so dangerous, and so destructive to both rulers and people, that as former ages never could bear the broaching of it; so it may be hoped, those to come, redeemed from the impositions of these Egyptian under taskmasters, will abhor the memory of such servile flatterers, who, whilst it seemed to serve their turn, resolved all government into absolute tyranny, and would have all men born to, what their mean souls fitted them for, slavery.

240. Here, it is like, the common question will be made, *Who shall be judge,* whether the prince or legislative act contrary to their trust? This, perhaps, ill-affected and factious men may spread amongst the people, when the prince only makes use of his due prerogative. To this I reply, "The people shall be judge;" for who shall be *judge* whether his trustee or deputy acts well, and according to the trust reposed in him, but he who deputes him, and must by having deputed him, have still a power to discard him, when he fails in his trust? If this be reasonable in particular cases of private men, why should it be otherwise in that of the greatest moment, where the welfare of millions is concerned, and also where the evil, if not prevented, is greater, and the redress very difficult, dear, and dangerous?

241. But farther, this question, ("Who shall be judge?") cannot mean that there is no judge at all. For where there is no judicature on earth, to decide controversies amongst men, God in heaven is judge. He alone, it is true, is judge of the right. But *every man is judge* for himself, as in all other cases, so in this, whether another hath put himself into a state of war with him, and whether he should appeal to the supreme judge, as Jephthah did.

242. If a controversy arise betwixt a prince and some of the people, in a matter where the law is silent, or doubtful, and the thing be of great consequence, I should think the proper *umpire,* in such a case, should be the body of the *people:* for in cases where the prince hath a trust reposed in him, and is dispensed from the common ordinary rules of the law; there, if any men find themselves aggrieved, and think the prince acts contrary to, or beyond that trust, who so proper to *judge* as the body of the *people,* (who, at first, lodged that trust in him) how far they meant it should extend? But if the prince, or whoever they be in the administration, decline that way of determination, the appeal then lies no where but to heaven; force between either persons, who have no known superior on earth, or which permits no appeal to a judge on earth, being properly a state of war, wherein the appeal lies only to heaven; and in that state the *injured party must judge* for himself, when he will think fit to make use of that appeal, and put himself upon it.

243. To conclude, The *power that every individual gave the society,* when he entered into it, can never revert to the individuals gain, as long as the society lasts, but will always remain in the community; because without this there can be no community, no commonwealth, which is contrary to the original agreement: so also when the society hath placed the legislative in any assembly of men, to continue in them and their successors, with direction and authority for providing such successors, the *legislative can never revert to the people* whilst that government lasts: Because, having provided a legislative with power to continue for ever, they have given up their political power to the legislative, and cannot resume it. But if they have set limits to the duration of their legislative, and made this supreme power in any person, or assembly, only temporary; or else, when by the miscarriages of those in authority, it is forfeited; upon the forfeiture, or at the determination of the time set, *it reverts to the society,* and the people have a right to act as supreme, and continue the legislative in themselves; or erect a new form, or under the old form place it in new hands, as they think good.

Notes

1. It is no improbable opinion therefore, which the arch-philosopher was of, "That the chief person in every household was always, as it were, a king: so when numbers of households joined themselves in civil societies together, kings were the first kind of governors amongst them, which is also, as it seemeth, the reason why the name of fathers continued still in them, who, of fathers, were made rulers; as also the ancient custom of governors to do as Melchizedeck, and being kings, to exercise the office of priests, which fathers did at the first, grew perhaps by the same occasion. Howbeit, this is not the only kind of regiment that has been received in the world. The inconveniences of one kind have caused sundry others to be devised; so that in a word, all public regiment of what kind soever, seemeth evidently to have risen from the deliberate advice, consultation and composition between men, judging it convenient and behoveful; there being no impossibility in nature considered by itself, but that man might have lived without any public regiment." Hooker's Eccl. Pol. Lib. I. Sect. 10.
2. The public power of all society is above every soul contained in "the same society; and the principal use of that power is, to give laws unto all that are under it, which laws in such cases we must obey," unless there be reason shewed which may necessarily inforce, that the law of reason, or of God, doth enjoin the contrary." Hook. Eccl. Pol. Lib. I. Sect. 16.
3. "To take away all such mutual grievances, injuries and wrongs", i.e. such as attend men in the state of nature, "there was no way but only by growing into composition and agreement amongst themselves, by ordaining some kind of government public, and by yielding themselves subject thereunto, that unto whom they granted authority to rule and govern, by them the peace, tranquillity, and happy state of the rest might be procured. Men always knew that where force and injury was offered, they might be defender of themselves; they knew that however men may seek their own commodity; yet if this were done with injury unto others, it was not to be suffered, but by all men, and all good means to be withstood. Finally, they knew that no man might in reason take upon him to determine his own right, and according to his own determination proceed in maintenance thereof, in as much as every man is towards himself, and them whom he greatly affects, partial; and therefore that strifes and troubles would be endless, except they gave their common consent, all to be ordered by some, whom they should agree upon, without which consent there would be no reason that one man should take upon him to be lord or judge over another." Hooker's Eccl. Pol. Lib. I. Sect. 10.
4. "At the first, when some certain kind of regiment was once appointed, it may be that nothing was then farther thought upon for the manner of governing, but all permitted unto their wisdom and discretion, which were to rule, till by experience they found this for all parts very inconvenient, so as the thing which they had devised for a remedy, did indeed but increase the sore, which it should have cured. They saw, that to live by one man's will, became the cause of all men's misery. This constrained them to come into laws, wherein all men might see their duty beforehand, and know the penalties of trangressing them." Hooker's Eccl. Pol. Lib. I. Sect. 10.
5. "Civil law, being the act of the whole body politic, doth therefore over-rule each several part of the same body." Hooker, ibid.
6. "At first, when some certain kind of regiment was once approved, it may be nothing was then farther thought upon for the manner of governing, but all permitted unto their wisdom and discretion which were to rule, till by experience they found this for all parts very inconvenient, so as the thing which they had devised for a remedy, did indeed but increase the sore which it should have cured. They saw, that to live by one man's will, became the cause of all men's misery. This constrained them to come unto laws wherein all men might see their duty beforehand, and know the penalties of transgressing them." Hooker's Eccl. Pol. Lib. I. Sect. 10.
7. "The lawful power of making laws to command whole politic societies of men, belonging so properly unto the same entire societies, that for any prince or potentate of what kind soever upon earth, to exercise the same of himself, and not by express commission immediately and personally received from God, or else by authority derived at the first from their consent, upon whose persons they impose laws, it is no better than mere tyranny. Laws they are not therefore which public approbation hath not made so." Hooker's Eccl. Pol. Lib. I. Sect. 10. "Of this point therefore we are to note, that such men naturally have no full and perfect power to command whole politic multitudes of men, therefore utterly without our consent, we could in such sort be at no man's commandment living. And to be commanded we do consent when that society, whereof we be a part, hath at any time before consented, without revoking the same after by the like universal agreement.

Laws therefore human, of what kind so ever, are available by consent." Ibid.

8. "Two foundations there are which bear up public societies, the one a natural inclination, whereby all men desire sociable life and fellowship; the other an order, expressly or secretly agreed upon, touching the manner of their union in living together: the latter is that which we call the law of a commonweal, the very soul of a politic body, the parts whereof are by law animated, held together, and set on work in such actions as the common good requireth. Laws politic, ordained for external order and regiment amongst men, are never framed as they should be, unless presuming the will of man to be inwardly obstinate, rebellious, and averse from all obedience to the sacred laws of his nature; in a word, unless presuming man to be, in regard of his depraved mind, little better than a wild beast, they do accordingly provide notwithstanding, so to frame his outward actions, that they be no hindrance unto the common good, for which societies are instituted. Unless they do this, they are not perfect." Hooker's Eccl. Pol. Lib. I. Sect. 10.

9. "Human laws are measures in respect of men whose actions they must direct, howbeit such measures they are as have also their higher rules to be measured by, which rules are two, the law of God, and the law of nature; so that laws human must be made according to the general laws of nature, and without contradiction to any positive law of scripture, otherwise they are ill made." Hooker's Eccl. Pol. Lib. 3. Sect. 9.

"To constrain men to any thing inconvenient doth seem unreasonable." Ibid. Lib. I. Sect. 10.

10. Another copy, corrected by Mr. Locke, has it thus, "Noxious brute that is destructive to their being."

LETTER CONCERNING TOLERATION

Honored Sir,

Since you are pleased to inquire what are my thoughts about the mutual toleration of Christians in their different professions of religion, I must needs answer you freely that I esteem that toleration to be the chief characteristic mark of the true church. For whatsoever some people boast of the antiquity of places and names, or of the pomp of their outward worship; others, of the reformation of their discipline; all, of the orthodoxy of their faith—for everyone is orthodox to himself—these things, and all others of this nature, are much rather marks of men striving for power and empire over one another than of the church of Christ. Let anyone have never so true a claim to all these things, yet if he be destitute of charity, meekness, and goodwill in general toward all mankind, even to those that are not Christians, he is certainly yet short of being a true Christian himself. "The kings of the Gentiles exercise lordship over them," said our Saviour to His disciples, "but ye shall not be so" [Luke 22:25]. The business of true religion is quite another thing. It is not instituted in order to the erecting of an external pomp, nor to the obtaining of ecclesiastical dominion, nor to the exercising of compulsive force, but to the regulating of men's lives, according to the rules of virtue and piety. Whosoever will list himself under the banner of Christ must in the first place, and above all things, make war upon his own lusts and vices. It is in vain for any man to usurp the name of Christian without holiness of life, purity of manners, benignity and meekness of spirit. "Let everyone that nameth the name of Christ, depart from iniquity" [2 Tim. 2:19]. "Thou, when thou art converted, strengthen thy brethren," said our Lord to Peter [Luke 22:32]. It would, indeed, be very hard for one that appears careless about his salvation to persuade me that he were extremely concerned for mine. For it is impossible that those should sincerely and heartily apply themselves to make other people Christians who have not really embraced the Christian religion in their own hearts. If the Gospel and the apostles may be credited, no man can be a Christian without charity, and without that faith which works, not by force, but by love. Now I appeal to the consciences of those that persecute, torment, destroy, and kill other men upon pretense of religion, whether they do it out of friendship and kindness toward them or no? And I shall then indeed, and not until then, believe they do so, when I shall see those fiery zealots correcting, in the same manner, their friends and familiar acquaintance for the manifest sins they commit against the precepts of the Gospel; when I shall see them persecute with fire and sword the members of their own communion that are tainted with enormous vices, and without amendment are in danger of eternal perdition; and when I shall see them thus express their love and desire of the salvation of their souls by the infliction of torments and exercise of all manner of cruelties. For if it be out of a principle of charity, as they pretend, and love to men's souls, that they deprive them of their estates, maim them with corporal punishments, starve and torment them in noisome prisons, and in the end even take away their lives—I say, if all this be done merely to make men Christians and procure their salvation, why then do they suffer whoredom, fraud, malice, and suchlike enormities, which (according to the apostle [Rom. 1]) manifestly relish of heathenish corruption, to predominate so much and abound amongst their flocks and people? These, and suchlike things, are certainly more contrary to the glory of God, to the purity of the church, and to the salvation of souls, than any conscientious dissent from ecclesiastical decisions, or separation from public worship, whilst accompanied with innocence of life. Why then does this burning zeal for God, for the church, and for the salvation of souls—burning I say, literally, with fire and faggot—pass by those moral vices and wickednesses, without any chastisement, which are acknowledged by all men to be diametrically opposite to the profession of Christianity, and bend all its nerves either to the introducing of ceremonies, or to the establishment of opinions, which for the most part are about nice and intricate matters that exceed the capacity of ordinary understandings? Which of the parties contending about these things is in the right, which of them is guilty of schism or heresy, whether those that domineer or those that suffer, will then at last be manifest when the causes of their separation comes to be judged of. He, certainly, that follows Christ embraces His doctrine and bears His yoke, though he forsake both father and mother, separate from the public assemblies and ceremonies of his country, or whomsoever or whatsoever else he relinquishes, will not then be judged a heretic.

Now, though the divisions that are amongst sects should be allowed to be never so obstructive of the salvation of souls; yet, nevertheless, adultery, fornication, uncleanliness, lasciviousness, idolatry, and suchlike things, cannot be denied to be works of the flesh, concerning which the apostle has expressly declared [Gal. 5] that "they who do them shall not inherit the kingdom of God." Whosoever, therefore, is sincerely solicitous about the kingdom of God, and thinks it his duty to endeavor the enlargement of it amongst men, ought to apply himself with no less care and industry to the rooting out of these immoralities than to the extirpation of sects. But if anyone do otherwise, and whilst he is cruel and implacable toward those that differ from him in opinion, he be indulgent to such iniquities and immoralities as are unbecoming the name of a Christian, let such a one talk never so much of the church, he plainly demonstrates by his actions that it is another kingdom he aims at, and not the advancement of the kingdom of God.

That any man should think fit to cause another man—whose salvation he heartily desires—to expire in torments, and that even in an unconverted state, would, I confess, seem very strange to me and I think to any other also. But nobody, surely, will ever believe that such a carriage can proceed from charity, love, or goodwill. If anyone maintain that men ought to be compelled by fire and sword to profess certain doctrines, and conform to this or that exterior worship, without any regard had unto their morals; if anyone endeavor to convert those that are erroneous unto the faith, by forcing them to profess things that they do not believe and allowing them to practice things that the Gospel does not permit, it cannot be doubted indeed but such a one is desirous to have a numerous assembly joined in the same profession with himself; but that he principally intends by those means to compose a truly Christian church is altogether incredible. It is not, therefore, to be wondered at if those who do not really contend for the advancement of the true religion, and of the church of Christ, make use of arms that do not belong to the Christian warfare. If, like the Captain of our salvation, they sincerely desired the good of souls, they would tread in the steps and follow the perfect example of that Prince of Peace, who sent out His soldiers to the subduing of nations, and gathering them into His church, not armed with the sword or other instruments of force, but prepared with the Gospel of peace and with the exemplary holiness of their conversation. This was His method. Though if infidels were to be converted by force, if those that are either blind or obstinate were to be drawn off from their errors by armed soldiers, we know very well that it was much more easy for Him to do it with armies of heavenly legions than for any son of the church, how potent soever, with all his dragoons.

The toleration of those that differ from others in matters of religion is so agreeable to the Gospel of Jesus Christ, and to the genuine reason of mankind, that it seems monstrous for men to be so blind as not to perceive the necessity and advantage of it in so clear a light. I will not here tax the pride and ambition of some, the passion and uncharitable zeal of others. These are faults from which human affairs can perhaps scarce ever be perfectly freed; but yet such as nobody will bear the plain imputation of, without covering them with some specious color; and so pretend to commendation, whilst they are carried away by their own irregular passions. But, however, that some may not color their spirit of persecution and un-Christian cruelty with a pretense of care of the public weal and observation of the laws; and that others, under pretense of religion, may not seek impunity for their libertinism and licentiousness—in a word, that none may impose either upon himself or others by the pretenses of loyalty and obedience to the prince, or of tenderness and sincerity in the worship of God; I esteem it above all things necessary to distinguish exactly the business of civil government from that of religion, and to settle the just bounds that lie between the one and the other. If this be not done, there can be no end put to the controversies that will be always arising between those that have, or at least pretend to have, on the one side, a concernment for the interest of men's souls, and, on the other side, a care of the commonwealth.

The commonwealth seems to me to be a society of men constituted only for the procuring, preserving, and advancing their own civil interests.

Civil interests I call life, liberty, health, and indolency of body; and the possession of outward things, such as money, lands, houses, furniture, and the like.

It is the duty of the civil magistrate, by the impartial execution of equal laws, to secure unto all the people in general, and to every one of his subjects in particular, the just possession of these things belonging to this life. If anyone presume to violate the laws of public justice and equity, established for the preservation of those things, his presumption is to be checked by the fear of punishment consisting of the deprivation or diminution of those civil interests or goods which otherwise he might and ought to enjoy. But seeing no man does willingly suffer himself to be punished by the deprivation of any part of his goods, and much less of his liberty or life, therefore is the magistrate armed with the force and strength of all his subjects, in order to the punishment of those that violate any other man's rights.

Now that the whole jurisdiction of the magistrate reaches only to these civil concernments; and that all civil power, right and dominion is bounded and confined to the only care of promoting these things; and that it neither can nor ought in any manner to be extended to the salvation of souls, these following considerations seem unto me abundantly to demonstrate.

First, because the care of souls is not committed to the civil magistrate any more than to other men. It is not committed unto him, I say, by God; because it appears not that God has ever given any such authority to one man over another, as to compel anyone to his religion. Nor can any such power be vested in the magistrate by the consent of the people, because no man can so far abandon the care of his own salvation as blindly to leave to the choice of any other, whether prince or subject, to prescribe to him what faith or worship he shall embrace. For no man can, if he would, conform his faith to the dictates of another. All the life and power of true religion consist in the inward and full persuasion of the mind; and faith is not faith without believing. Whatever profession we make, to whatever outward worship we conform, if we are not fully satisfied in our own mind that the one is true, and the other well pleasing unto God, such profession and such practice, far from being any furtherance, are indeed great obstacles to our salvation. For in this manner, instead of expiating other sins by the exercise of religion, I say, in offering thus unto God Almighty such a worship as we esteem to be displeasing unto Him, we add unto the number of our other sins those also of hypocrisy and contempt of His Divine Majesty.

In the second place, the care of souls cannot belong to the civil magistrate because his power consists only in outward force; but true and saving religion consists in the inward persuasion of the mind, without which nothing can be acceptable to God. And such is the nature of the understanding that it cannot be compelled to the belief of anything by outward force. Confiscation of estate, imprisonment, torments, nothing of that nature can have any such efficacy as to make men change the inward judgment that they have framed of things.

It may indeed be alleged that the magistrate may make use of arguments, and thereby draw the heterodox into the way of truth and procure their salvation. I grant it; but this is common to him with other men. In teaching, instructing, and redressing the erroneous by reason, he may certainly do what becomes any good man to do. Magistracy does not oblige him to put off either humanity or Christianity; but it is one thing to persuade, another to command; one thing to press with arguments, another with penalties. This civil power alone has a right to do; to the other, goodwill is authority enough. Every man has commission to admonish, exhort, convince another of error, and, by reasoning, to draw him into truth; but to give laws, receive obedience, and compel with the sword, belongs to none but the magistrate. And upon this ground I affirm that the magistrate's power extends not to the establishing of any articles of faith or forms of worship by the force of his laws. For laws are of no force at all without penalties, and penalties in this case are absolutely impertinent, because they are not proper to convince the mind. Neither the profession of any articles of faith, nor the conformity to any outward form of worship (as has been already said), can be available to the salvation of souls unless the truth of the one, and the acceptableness of the other unto God, be thoroughly believed by those that so profess and practice. But penalties are no way capable to produce such belief. It is only light and evidence that can work a change in men's opinions; which light can in no manner proceed from corporal sufferings or any other outward penalties.

In the third place, the care of the salvation of men's souls cannot belong to the magistrate; because, though the rigor of laws and the force of penalties were capable to convince and change men's minds, yet would not that help at all to the salvation of their souls. For there being but one truth, one way to heaven, what hope is there that more men would be led into it if they had no rule but the religion of the court, and were put under the necessity to quit the light of their own reason, and oppose the dictates of their own consciences, and blindly to resign themselves up to the will of their governors and to the religion which either ignorance, ambition, or superstition had chanced to establish in the countries where they were born? In the variety and contradiction of opinions in religion, wherein the princes of the world are as much divided as in their secular interests, the narrow way would be much straitened; one country alone would be in the right, and all the rest of the world put under an obligation of following their princes in the ways that lead to destruction; and that which heightens the absurdity, and very ill suits the notion of a Deity, men would owe their eternal happiness or misery to the places of their nativity.

These considerations, to omit many others that might have been urged to the same purpose, seem unto me sufficient to conclude that all the power of civil government relates only to men's civil interests, is confined to the care of the things of this world, and hath nothing to do with the world to come.

Let us now consider what a church is. A church, then, I take to be a voluntary society of men, joining themselves together of their own accord in order to the public worshiping of God in such manner as they judge acceptable to Him, and effectual to the salvation of their souls.

I say it is a free and voluntary society. Nobody is born a member of any church; otherwise the religion of parents would descend unto children by the same right of inheritance as their temporal estates, and everyone would hold his faith by the same tenure he does his lands, than which nothing can be imagined more absurd. Thus, therefore, that matter stands. No man by nature is bound unto any particular church or sect, but everyone joins himself voluntarily to that society in which he believes he has found that profession and worship which is truly acceptable to God. The hope of salvation, as it was the only cause of his entrance into that communion, so it can be the only reason of his stay there. For if afterwards he discover anything either erroneous in the doctrine or incongruous in the worship of that society to which he has joined himself, why should it not be as free for him to go out as it was to enter? No member of a religious society can be tied with any other bonds but what proceed from the certain expectation of eternal life. A church, then, is a society of members voluntarily uniting to that end.

It follows now that we consider what is the power of this church, and unto what laws it is subject.

Forasmuch as no society, how free soever, or upon whatsoever slight occasion instituted, whether of philosophers for learning, of merchants for commerce, or of men of leisure for mutual conversation and discourse, no church or company, I say, can in the least subsist and hold together, but will presently dissolve and break in pieces, unless it be regulated by some laws, and the members all consent to observe some order. Place and time of meeting must be agreed on; rules for admitting and excluding members must be established; distinction of officers, and putting things into a regular course, and suchlike, cannot be omitted. But since the joining together of several members into this church society, as has already been demonstrated, is absolutely free and spontaneous, it necessarily follows that the right of making its laws can belong to none but the society itself; or, at least (which is the same thing), to those whom the society by common consent has authorized thereunto.

Some, perhaps, may object that no such society can be said to be a true church unless it have in it a bishop or presbyter, with ruling authority derived from the very apostles, and continued down to the present times by an uninterrupted succession.

To these I answer: In the first place, let them show me the edict by which Christ has imposed that law upon His church. And let not any man think me impertinent if in a thing of this consequence I require that the terms of that edict be very express and positive; for the promise He has made us [Matt. 18:20], that wheresoever two or three are gathered together in His name He will be in the midst of them, seems to imply the contrary. Whether such an assembly want anything necessary to a true church, pray do you consider. Certain I am that nothing can be there wanting unto the salvation of souls, which is sufficient to our purpose.

Next, pray observe how great have always been the divisions amongst even those who lay so much stress upon the divine institution and continued succession of a certain order of rulers in the church. Now their very dissension unavoidably puts us upon a necessity of deliberating and, consequently, allows a liberty of choosing that which upon consideration we prefer.

And, in the last place, I consent that these men have a ruler in their church, established by such a long series of succession as they judge necessary, provided I may have liberty at the same time to join myself to that society in which I am persuaded those things are to be found which are necessary to the salvation of my soul. In this manner ecclesiastical liberty will be preserved on all sides, and no man will have a legislator imposed upon him but whom himself has chosen.

But since men are so solicitous about the true church, I would only ask them here, by the way, if it be not more agreeable to the church of Christ to make the conditions of her communion consist in such things, and such things only, as the Holy Spirit has in the Holy Scriptures declared, in express words, to be necessary to salvation; I ask, I say, whether this be not more agreeable to the church of Christ than for men to impose their own inventions and interpretations upon others as if they were of Divine authority, and to establish by ecclesiastical laws, as absolutely necessary to the profession of Christianity, such things as the Holy Scriptures do either not mention or at least not expressly command? Whosoever requires those things in order to ecclesiastical communion, which Christ does not require in order to life eternal, he may, perhaps, indeed constitute a society accommodated to his own opinion and his own advantage; but how that can be called the church of Christ which is established upon laws that are not His, and which excludes such persons from its communion as He will one day receive into the Kingdom of Heaven, I understand not. But this being not a proper place to inquire into the marks of the true church, I will only mind those that contend so earnestly for the decrees of their own society and that cry out continually, The Church! the Church! with as much noise, and perhaps upon the same principle, as the Ephesian silversmiths did for their Diana; this, I say, I desire to mind them of, that the Gospel frequently declares that the true disciples of Christ must suffer persecution; but that the church of Christ should persecute others, and force others by fire and sword to embrace her faith and doctrine, I could never yet find in any of the books of the New Testament.

The end of a religious society (as has already been said) is the public worship of God and, by means thereof, the acquisition of eternal life. All discipline ought therefore to tend to that end, and all ecclesiastical laws to be thereunto confined. Nothing ought nor can be transacted in this society relating to the possession of civil and worldly goods. No force is here to be made use of upon any occasion whatsoever. For force belongs wholly to the civil magistrate, and the possession of all outward goods is subject to his jurisdiction.

But, it may be asked, by what means then shall ecclesiastical laws be established if they must be thus destitute of all compulsive power? I answer: They must be established by means suitable to the nature of such things, whereof the external profession and observation—if not proceeding from a thorough conviction and approbation of the mind—is altogether useless and unprofitable. The arms by which the members of this society are to be kept within their duty are exhortations, admonitions, and advices. If by these means the offenders will not be reclaimed and the erroneous convinced, there remains nothing further to be done but that such stubborn and obstinate persons who give no ground to hope for their reformation, should be cast out and separated from the society. This is the last and utmost force of ecclesiastical authority. No other punishment can thereby be inflicted than that, the relation ceasing between the body and the member which is cut off. The person so condemned ceases to be a part of that church.

These things being thus determined, let us inquire, in the next place, how far the duty of toleration extends, and what is required from everyone by it?

And, first, I hold that no church is bound, by the duty of toleration, to retain any such person in her bosom as, after admonition, continues obstinately to offend against the laws of the society. For these being the condition of communion and the bond of the society, if the breach of them were permitted without any animadversion the society would immediately be thereby dissolved. But, nevertheless, in all such cases care is to be taken that the sentence of excommunication, and the execution thereof, carry with it no rough usage of word or action whereby the ejected person may any wise be damnified in body or estate. For all force (as has often been said) belongs only to the magistrate, nor ought any private persons at any time to use force unless it be in self-defense against unjust violence. Excommunication neither does nor can, deprive the excommunicated person of any of those civil goods that he formerly possessed. All those things belong to the civil government and are under the magistrate's protection. The whole force of excommunication consists only in this: that the resolution of the society in that respect being declared, the union that was between the body and some member comes thereby to be dissolved; and that relation ceasing, the participation of some certain things which the society communicated to its members, and unto which no man has any civil right, comes also to cease. For there is no civil injury done unto the excommunicated person by the church minister's refusing him that bread and wine, in the celebration of the Lord's Supper, which was not bought with his but other men's money.

Secondly, no private person has any right in any manner to prejudice another person in his civil enjoyments because he is of another church or religion. All the rights and franchises that belong to him as a man or as a denizen are inviolably to be preserved to him. These are not the business of religion. No violence nor injury is to be offered him, whether he be Christian or pagan. Nay, we must not content ourselves with the narrow measures of bare justice; charity, bounty, and liberality must be added to it. This the Gospel enjoins, this reason directs, and this that natural fellowship we are born into requires of us. If any man err from the right way, it is his own misfortune, no injury to thee; nor therefore art thou to punish him in the things of this life because thou supposest he will be miserable in that which is to come.

What I say concerning the mutual toleration of private persons differing from one another in religion, I understand also of particular churches which stand, as it were, in the same relation to each other as private persons among themselves: nor has any one of them any manner of jurisdiction over any other; no, not even when the civil magistrate (as it sometimes happens) comes to be of this or the other communion. For the civil government can give no new right to the church, nor the church to the civil government. So that whether the magistrate join himself to any church, or separate from it, the church remains always as it was before—a free and voluntary society. It neither requires the power of the sword by the magistrate's coming to it, nor does it lose the right of instruction and excommunication by his going from it. This is the fundamental and immutable right of a spontaneous society—that it has power to remove any of its members who transgress the rules of its institution; but it cannot, by the accession of any new members, acquire any right of jurisdiction over those that are not joined with it. And therefore peace, equity, end friendship are always mutually to be observed by particular churches, in the same manner as by private persons, without any pretense of superiority or jurisdiction over one another.

That the thing may be made clearer by an example, let us suppose two churches—the one of Arminians, the other of Calvinists—residing in the city of Constantinople. Will anyone say that either of these churches has right to deprive the members of the other of their estates and liberty (as we see practiced elsewhere), because of their differing from it in some doctrines and ceremonies, whilst the Turks in the meanwhile silently stand by and laugh to see with what inhuman cruelty Christians thus rage against Christians? But if one of these churches hath this power of treating the other ill, I ask which of them it is to whom that power belongs, and by what right? It will be answered, undoubtedly, that it is the orthodox church which has the right of authority over the erroneous or heretical. This is, in great and specious words, to say just nothing at all. For every church is orthodox to itself; to others, erroneous or heretical. For whatsoever any church believes it believes to be true; and the contrary unto those things it pronounces to be error. So that the controversy between these churches about the truth of their doctrines and the purity of their worship is on both sides equal; nor is there any judge, either at Constantinople or elsewhere upon earth, by whose sentence it can be determined. The decision of that question belongs only to the Supreme Judge of all men, to whom also alone belongs the punishment of the erroneous. In the meanwhile, let those men consider how heinously they sin, who, adding injustice, if not to their error, yet certainly to their pride, do rashly and arrogantly take upon them to misuse the servants of another master, who are not at all accountable to them.

Nay, further: if it could be manifest which of these two dissenting churches were in the right, there would not accrue thereby unto the orthodox any right of destroying the other. For churches have neither any jurisdiction in worldly matters, nor are fire and sword any proper instruments wherewith to convince men's minds of error, and inform them of the truth. Let us suppose, nevertheless, that the civil magistrate inclined to favor one of them and to put his sword into their hands, that (by his consent) they might chastise the dissenters as they pleased. Will any man say that any right can be derived unto a Christian church over its brethren from a Turkish emperor? An infidel, who has himself no authority to punish Christians for the articles of their faith, cannot confer such an authority upon any society of Christians, nor give unto them a right which he has not himself. This would be the case at Constantinople; and the reason of the thing is the same in any Christian kingdom. The civil power is the same in every place. Nor can that power, in the hands of a Christian prince, confer any greater authority upon the church than in the hands of a heathen; which is to say, just none at all.

Nevertheless, it is worthy to be observed and lamented that the most violent of these defenders of the truth, the opposers of errors, the exclaimers against schism, do hardly ever let loose this their zeal for God, with which they are so warmed and inflamed, unless where they have the civil magistrate on their side. But so soon as ever court favor has given them the better end of the staff, and they begin to feel themselves the stronger, then presently peace and charity are to be laid aside. Otherwise they are religiously to be observed. Where they have not the power to carry on persecution and to become masters, there they desire to live upon fair terms and preach up toleration. When they are not strengthened with the civil power, then they can bear most patiently and unmovedly the contagion of idolatry, superstition, and heresy in their neighborhood; of which on other occasions the interest of religion makes them to be extremely apprehensive. They do not forwardly attack those errors which are in fashion at court or are countenanced by the government. Here they can be content to spare their arguments; which yet (with their leave) is the only right method of propagating truth, which has no such way of prevailing as when strong arguments and good reason are joined with the softness of civility and good usage.

Nobody, therefore, in fine, neither single persons nor churches, nay, nor even commonwealths, have any just title to invade the civil rights and worldly goods of each other upon pretense of religion. Those that are of another opinion would do well to consider with themselves how pernicious a seed of discord and war, how powerful a provocation to endless hatreds, rapines, and slaughters they thereby furnish unto mankind. No peace and security, no, not so much as common friendship, can ever be established or preserved amongst men so long as this opinion prevails that dominion is founded in grace and that religion is to be propagated by force of arms.

In the third place, let us see what the duty of toleration requires from those who are distinguished from the rest of mankind (from the laity, as they please to call us) by some ecclesiastical character and office; whether they be bishops, priests, presbyters, ministers, or however else dignified or distinguished. It is not my business to inquire here into the original of the power or dignity of the clergy. This only I say, that whencesoever their authority be sprung, since it is ecclesiastical, it ought to be confined within the bounds of the church, nor can it in any manner be extended to civil affairs, because the church itself is a thing absolutely separate and distinct from the commonwealth. The boundaries on both sides are fixed and immovable. He jumbles heaven and earth together, the things most remote and opposite, who mixes these two societies, which are in their original, end, business, and in everything perfectly distinct and infinitely different from each other. No man, therefore, with whatsoever ecclesiastical office he be dignified, can deprive another man that is not of his church and faith either of liberty or of any part of his worldly goods upon the account of that difference between them in religion. For what soever is not lawful to the whole church cannot by any ecclesiastical right become lawful to any of its members.

But this is not all. It is not enough that ecclesiastical men abstain from violence and rapine and all manner of persecution. He that pretends to be a successor of the apostles, and takes upon him the office of teaching, is obliged also to admonish his hearers of the duties of peace and goodwill toward all men, as well toward the erroneous as the orthodox; toward those that differ from them in faith and worship as well as toward those that agree with them therein. And he ought industriously to exhort all men, whether private persons or magistrates (if any such there be in his church), to charity, meekness, and toleration, and diligently endeavor to ally and temper all that heat and unreasonable averseness of mind which either any man's fiery zeal for his own sect or the craft of others has kindled against dissenters. I will not undertake to represent how happy and how great would be the fruit, both in church and state, if the pulpits everywhere sounded with this doctrine of peace and toleration, lest I should seem to reflect too severely upon those men whose dignity I desire not to detract from, nor would have it diminished either by others or themselves. But this I say, that thus it ought to be. And if anyone that professes himself to be a minister of the Word of God, a preacher of the gospel of peace, teach otherwise, he either understands not or neglects the business of his calling, and shall one day give account thereof unto the Prince of Peace. If Christians are to be admonished that they abstain from all manner of revenge, even after repeated provocations and multiplied injuries, how much more ought they who suffer nothing, who have had no harm done them, forbear violence and abstain from all manner of ill-usage toward those from whom they have received none! This caution and temper they ought certainly to use toward those who mind only their own business, and are solicitous for nothing but that (whatever men think of them) they may worship God in that manner which they are persuaded is acceptable to Him, and in which they have the strongest hopes of eternal salvation. In private domestic affairs, in the management of estates, in the conservation of bodily health, every man may consider what suits his own convenience, and follow what course he likes best. No man complains of the ill-management of his neighbor's affairs. No man is angry with another for an error committed in sowing his land or in marrying his daughter. Nobody corrects a spendthrift for consuming his substance in taverns. Let any man pull down or build or make whatsoever expenses he pleases, nobody murmurs, nobody controls him; he has his liberty. But if any man do not frequent the church, if he do not there conform his behavior exactly to the accustomed ceremonies, or if he brings not his children to be initiated in the sacred mysteries of this or the other congregation, this immediately causes an uproar. The neighborhood is filled with noise and clamor. Everyone is ready to be the avenger of so great a crime, and the zealots hardly have the patience to refrain from violence and rapine so long till the cause be heard, and the poor man be, according to form, condemned to the loss of liberty, goods, or life. Oh, that our ecclesiastical orators of every sect would apply themselves with all the strength of arguments that they are able to the confounding of men's errors! But let them spare their persons. Let them not supply their want of reasons with the instruments of force, which belong to another jurisdiction, and do ill become a churchman's hands. Let them not call in the magistrate's authority to the aid of their eloquence or learning, lest perhaps, whilst they pretend only love for the truth, this their intemperate zeal, breathing nothing but fire and sword, betray their ambition and show that what they desire is temporal dominion. For it will be very difficult to persuade men of sense that he who with dry eyes and satisfaction of mind can deliver his brother to the executioner to be burned alive does sincerely and heartily concern himself to save that brother from the flames of hell in the world to come.

In the last place, let us now consider what is the magistrate's duty in the business of toleration, which certainly is very considerable.

We have already proved that the care of souls does not belong to the magistrate. Not a magisterial care, I mean (if may so call it), which consists in prescribing by laws and compelling by punishments. But a charitable care, which consists in teaching, admonishing, and persuading, cannot be denied unto any man. The care, therefore, of every man's soul belongs unto himself, and is to be left unto himself. But what if he neglect the care of his soul? I answer: What if he neglect the care of his health or of his estate, which things are nearlier related to the government of the magistrate than the other? Will the magistrate provide by an express law that such a one shall not become poor or sick? Laws provide, as much as is possible, that the goods and health of subjects be not injured by the fraud and violence of others; they do not guard them from the negligence or ill-husbandry of the possessors themselves. No man can be forced to be rich or healthful whether he will or no. Nay, God Himself will not save men against their wills. Let us suppose, however, that some prince were desirous to force his subjects to accumulate riches or to preserve the health and strength of their bodies. Shall it be provided by law that they must consult none but Roman physicians, and shall everyone be bound to live according to their prescriptions? What, shall no potion, no broth, be taken but what is prepared either in the Vatican, suppose, or in a Geneva shop? Or, to make these subjects rich, shall they all be obliged by law to become merchants or musicians? Or shall everyone turn victualler or smith because there are some that maintain their families plentifully and grow rich in those professions? But, it may be said, there are a thousand ways to wealth, but one only way to heaven. It is well said, indeed, especially by those that plead for compelling men into this or the other way. For if there were several ways that led thither, there would not be so much as a pretense left for compulsion. But now if I be marching on with my utmost vigor in that way which, according to the sacred geography, leads straight to Jerusalem, why am I beaten and ill-used by others because, perhaps, I wear not buskins; because my hair is not of the right cut; because, perhaps, I have not been dipped in the right fashion; because I eat flesh upon the road, or some other food which agrees with my stomach; because I avoid certain by-ways, which seem unto me to lead into briars or precipices; because, amongst the several paths that are in the same road, I choose that to walk in which seems to be the straightest and cleanest; because I avoid to keep company with some travelers that are less grave, and others that are more sour than they ought to be; or, in fine, because I follow a guide that either is, or is not, clothed in white or crowned with a miter? Certainly, if we consider right, we shall find that, for the most part, they are such frivolous things as these that (without any prejudice to religion or the salvation of souls, if not accompanied with superstition or hypocrisy) might either be observed or omitted. I say they are suchlike things as these which breed implacable enmities amongst Christian brethren, who are all agreed in the substantial and truly fundamental part of religion.

But let us grant unto these zealots, who condemn all things that are not of their mode, that from these circumstances are different ends. What shall we conclude from thence? There is only one of these which is the true way to eternal happiness: but in this great variety of ways that men follow, it is still doubted which is the right one. Now, neither the care of the commonwealth nor the right enacting of laws does discover this way that leads to heaven more certainly to the magistrate than every private man's search and study discovers it unto himself I have a weak body, sunk under a languishing disease, for which (I suppose) there is one only remedy, but that unknown. Does it therefore belong unto the magistrate to prescribe me a remedy, because there is but one and because it is unknown? Because there is but one way for me to escape death, will it therefore be safe for me to do whatsoever the magistrate ordains? Those things that every man ought sincerely to inquire into himself, and by meditation, study, search, and his own endeavors attain the knowledge of, cannot be looked upon as the peculiar possession of any sort of men. Princes, indeed, are born superior unto other men in power, but in nature equal. Neither the right nor the art of ruling does necessarily carry along with it the certain knowledge of other things, and least of all of true religion. For if it were so, how could it come to pass that the lords of the earth should differ so vastly as they do in religious matters? But let us grant that it is probable the way to eternal life may be better known by a prince than by his subjects, or at least that in this incertitude of things the safest and most commodious way for private persons is to follow his dictates. You will say, what then? If he should bid you follow merchandise for your livelihood, would you decline that course for fear it should not succeed? I answer: I would turn merchant upon the prince's command, because in case I should have ill-success in trade, he is abundantly able to make up my loss some other way. If it be true, as he pretends, that he desires I should thrive and grow rich, he can set me up again when unsuccessful voyages have broken me. But this is not the case in the things that regard the life to come; if there I take a wrong course, if in that respect I am once undone, it is not in the magistrate's power to repair my loss, to ease my suffering, nor to restore me in any measure, much less entirely, to a good estate. What security can be given for the Kingdom of Heaven?

Perhaps some will say that they do not suppose this infallible judgment, that all men are bound to follow in the affairs of religion, to be in the civil magistrate, but in the church. What the church has determined, that the civil magistrate orders to be observed; and he provides by his authority that nobody shall either act or believe in the business of religion otherwise than the church teaches. So that the judgment of those things is in the church; the magistrate himself yields obedience thereunto, and requires the like obedience from others. I answer: Who sees not how frequently the name of the church, which was venerable in time of the apostles, has been made use of to throw dust in the people's eyes, in the following ages? But, however, in the present case it helps us not. The one only narrow way which leads to heaven is not better known to the magistrate than to private persons, and therefore I cannot safely take him for my guide who may probably be as ignorant of the way as myself, and who certainly is less concerned for my salvation than I myself am. Amongst so many kings of the Jews, how many of them were there whom any Israelite, thus blindly following, had not fallen into idolatry, and thereby into destruction? Yet nevertheless, you bid me be of good courage, and tell me that all is now safe and secure, because the magistrate does not now enjoin the observance of his own decrees in matters of religion, but only the decrees of the church. Of what church? I beseech you. Of that, certainly, which likes him best. As if he that compels me by laws and penalties to enter into this or the other church did not interpose his own judgment in the matter. What difference is there whether he lead me himself or deliver me over to be led by others? I depend both ways upon his will, and it is he that determines both ways of my eternal state. Would an Israelite that had worshiped Baal upon the command of his king have been in any better condition because somebody had told him that the king ordered nothing in religion upon his own head, nor commanded anything to be done by his subjects in divine worship but what was approved by the counsel of priests and declared to be of divine right by the doctors of their church? If the religion of any church become therefore true and saving because the head of that sect, the prelates and priests, and those of that tribe, do all of them, with all their might, extol and praise it, what religion can ever be accounted erroneous, false, and destructive? I am doubtful concerning the doctrine of the Socinians, I am suspicious of the way of worship practiced by the Papists or Lutherans; will it be ever a jot safer for me to join either unto the one or the other of those churches, upon the magistrate's command, because he commands nothing in religion but by the authority and counsel of the doctors of that church?

But, to speak the truth, we must acknowledge that the church (if a convention of clergymen, making canons, must be called by that name) is for the most part more apt to be influenced by the court than the court by the church. How the church was under the vicissitude of orthodox and Arian emperors is very well known. Or if those things be too remote, our modern English history affords us fresh examples in the reigns of Henry VIII, Edward VI, Mary, and Elizabeth, how easily and smoothly the clergy changed their decrees, their articles of faith, their form of worship, everything according to the inclination of those kings and queens. Yet were those kings and queens of such different minds in point of religion, and enjoined thereupon such different things, that no man in his wits (I had almost said none but an atheist) will presume to say that any sincere and upright worshiper of God could, with a safe conscience, obey their several decrees. To conclude, it is the same thing whether a king, that prescribes laws to another man's religion pretend to do it by his own judgment or by the ecclesiastical authority and advice of others. The decisions of churchmen, whose differences and disputes are sufficiently known, cannot be any sounder or safer than his; nor can all their suffrages joined together add a new strength to the civil power. Though this also must be taken notice of—that princes seldom have any regard to the suffrages of ecclesiastics that are not favorers of their own faith and way of worship.

But, after all, the principal consideration and which absolutely determines this controversy is this: Although the magistrate's opinion in religion be sound, and the way that he appoints be truly evangelical, yet, if I be not thoroughly persuaded thereof in my own mind, there will be no safety for me in following it. No way whatsoever that I shall walk in against the dictates of my conscience will ever bring me to the mansions of the blessed. I may grow rich by an art that I take not delight in, I may be cured of some disease by remedies that I have not faith in; but I cannot be saved by a religion that I distrust and by a worship that I abhor. It is in vain for an unbeliever to take up the outward show of another man's profession. Faith only and inward sincerity are the things that procure acceptance with God. The most likely and most approved remedy can have no effect upon the patient if his stomach reject it as soon as taken; and you will in vain cram a medicine down a sick man's throat which his particular constitution will be sure to turn into poison. In a word, whatsoever may be doubtful in religion, yet this at least is certain, that no religion which I believe not to be true can be either true or profitable unto me. In vain, therefore, do princes compel their subjects to come into their church communion, under pretense of saving their souls. If they believe, they will come of their own accord; if they believe not, their coming will nothing avail them. How great soever, in fine, may be the pretense of goodwill and charity, and concern for the salvation of men's souls, men cannot be forced to be saved whether they will or no. And therefore, when all is done, they must be left to their own consciences.

Having thus at length freed men from all dominion over one another in matters of religion, let us now consider what they are to do. All men know and acknowledge that God ought to be publicly worshiped; why otherwise do they compel one another unto the public assemblies? Men, therefore, constituted in this liberty, are to enter into some religious society, that they meet together, not only for mutual edification, but to own to the world that they worship God, and offer unto His Divine Majesty such service as they themselves are not ashamed of, and such as they think not unworthy of Him, nor unacceptable to Him; and finally, that by the purity of doctrine, holiness of life, and decent form of worship, they may draw others unto the love of the true religion, and perform such other things in religion as cannot be done by each private man apart.

These religious societies I call churches; and these, I say, the magistrate ought to tolerate, for the business of these assemblies of the people is nothing but what is lawful for every man in particular to take care of—I mean the salvation of their souls; not in this case is there any difference between the national church and other separated congregations.

But as in every church there are two things especially to be considered—the outward form and rites of worship, and the doctrines and articles of faith—these things must be handled each distinctly that so the whole matter of toleration may the more clearly be understood.

Concerning outward worship, I say, in the first place, that the magistrate has no power to enforce by law, either in his own church or much less in another, the use of any rites or ceremonies whatsoever in the worship of God. And this, not only because these churches are free societies, but because whatsoever is practiced in the worship of God is only so far justifiable as it is believed by those that practice it to be acceptable unto Him. Whatsoever is not done with that assurance of faith is neither well in itself, nor can it be acceptable to God. To impose such things, therefore, upon any people, contrary to their own judgment, is in effect to command them to offend God, which, considering that the end of all religion is to please Him, and that liberty is essentially necessary to that end, appears to be absurd beyond expression.

But perhaps it may be concluded from hence that I deny unto the magistrate all manner of power about indifferent things, which, if it be not granted, the whole subject matter of lawmaking is taken away. No, I readily grant that indifferent things, and perhaps none but such, are subjected to the legislative power. But it does not therefore follow that the magistrate may ordain whatsoever he pleases concerning anything that is indifferent. The public good is the rule and measure of all lawmaking. If a thing be not useful to the commonwealth, though it be never so indifferent, it may not presently be established by law.

And further, things never so indifferent in their own nature, when they are brought into the church and worship of God, are removed out of the reach of the magistrate's jurisdiction, because in that use they have no connection at all with civil affairs. The only business of the church is the salvation of souls, and it no way concerns the commonwealth, or any member of it, that this or the other ceremony be there made use of. Neither the use nor the omission of any ceremonies in those religious assemblies does either advantage or prejudice the life, liberty, or estate of any man. For example, let it be granted that the washing of an infant with water is in itself an indifferent thing; let it be granted also that the magistrate understand such washing to be profitable to the curing or preventing of any disease the children are subject unto, and esteem the matter weighty enough to be taken care of by a law. In that case he may order it to be done. But will anyone therefore say that a magistrate has the same right to ordain by law that all children shall be baptized by priests in the sacred font in order to the purification of their souls? The extreme difference of these two cases is visible to everyone at first sight. Or let us apply the last case to the child of a Jew, and the thing speaks itself. For what hinders but a Christian magistrate may have subjects that are Jews? Now, if we acknowledge that such an injury may not be done unto a Jew as to compel him, against his own opinion, to practice in his religion a thing that is in its nature indifferent, how can we maintain that anything of this kind may be done to a Christian?

Again, things in their own nature indifferent cannot, by any human authority, be made any part of the worship of God—for this very reason: because they are indifferent. For, since indifferent things are not capable, by any virtue of their own, to propitiate the Deity, no human power or authority can confer on them so much dignity and excellence as to enable them to do it. In the common affairs of life that use of indifferent things which God has not forbidden is free and lawful, and therefore in those things human authority has place. But it is not so in matters of religion. Things indifferent are not otherwise lawful in the worship of God than as they are instituted by God Himself, and as He, by some positive command, has ordained them to be made a part of that worship which He will vouchsafe to accept at the hands of poor sinful men. Nor, when an incensed Deity shall ask us, "Who has required these or suchlike things at your hands?" will it be enough to answer Him that the magistrate commanded them. If civil jurisdiction extend thus far, what might not lawfully be introduced into religion? What hodgepodge of ceremonies, what superstition inventions, built upon the magistrate's authority, might not (against conscience) be imposed upon the worshipers of God? For the greatest part of these ceremonies and superstitions consists in the religious use of such things as are in their own nature indifferent; nor are they sinful upon any other account than because God is not the author of them. The sprinkling of water, and the use of bread and wine, are both in their own nature and in the ordinary occasions of life altogether indifferent. Will any man therefore say that these things could have been introduced into religion, and made a part of divine worship, if not by divine institution? If any human authority or civil power could have done this, why might it not also enjoin the eating of fish and drinking of ale in the holy banquet as a part of divine worship? Why not the sprinkling of the blood of beasts in churches, and expiations by water or fire, and abundance more of this kind? But these things, how indifferent soever they be in common uses, when they come to be annexed unto divine worship, without divine authority, they are as abominable to God as the sacrifice of a dog. And why is a dog so abominable? What difference is there between a dog and a goat, in respect of the divine nature, equally and infinitely distant from all affinity with matter, unless it be that God required the use of one in His worship, and not of the other? We see, therefore, that indifferent things, how much soever they be under the power of the civil magistrate, yet cannot, upon that pretense, be introduced into religion and imposed upon religious assemblies because, in the worship of God, they wholly cease to be indifferent. He that worships God does it with design to please Him and procure His favor. But that cannot be done by him who, upon the command of another, offers unto God that which he knows will be displeasing to Him, because not commanded by Himself. This is not to please God, or appease His wrath, but willingly and knowingly to provoke Him by a manifest contempt, which is a thing absolutely repugnant to the nature and end of worship.

But it will be here asked: "If nothing belonging to divine worship be left to human discretion, how is it then that churches themselves have the power of ordering anything about the time and place of worship, and the like?" To this I answer that in religious worship we must distinguish between what is part of the worship itself and what is but a circumstance. That is a part of the worship which is believed to be appointed by God and to be well-pleasing to Him, and therefore that is necessary. Circumstances are such things which, though in general they cannot be separated from worship, yet the particular instances or modifications of them are not determined, and therefore they are indifferent. Of this sort are the time and place of worship, habit, and posture of him that worships. These are circumstances, and perfectly indifferent, where God has not given any express command about them. For example: amongst the Jews the time and place of their worship, and the habits of those that officiated in it, were not mere circumstances, but a part of the worship itself, in which, if anything were defective or different from the institution, they could not hope that it would be accepted by God. But these, to Christians under the liberty of the Gospel, are mere circumstances of worship, which the prudence of every church may bring into such use as shall be judged most subservient to the end of order, decency, and edification. But, even under the Gospel, those who believe the first or the seventh day to be set apart by God, and consecrated still to His worship, to them that portion of time is not a simple circumstance, but a real part of Divine worship, which can neither be changed nor neglected.

In the next place: As the magistrate has no power to impose by his laws the use of any rites and ceremonies in any church, so neither has he any power to forbid the use of such rites and ceremonies as are already received, approved, and practiced by any church; because, if he did so, he would destroy the church itself, the end of whose institution is only to worship God with freedom after its own manner.

You will say, by this rule, if some congregations should have a mind to sacrifice infants, or (as the primitive Christians were falsely accused) lustfully pollute themselves in promiscuous uncleanliness, or practice any other such heinous enormities, is the magistrate obliged to tolerate them because they are committed in a religious assembly? I answer, No. These things are not lawful in the ordinary course of life, nor in any private house; and therefore neither are they so in the worship of God, or in any religious meeting. But, indeed, if any people congregated upon account of religion should be desirous to sacrifice a calf, I deny that that ought to be prohibited by a law. Meliboeus, whose calf it is, may lawfully kill his calf at home, and burn any part of it that he thinks fit. For no injury is thereby done to anyone, no prejudice to another man's goods. And for the same reason he may kill his calf also in a religious meeting. Whether the doing so be well-pleasing to God or no, it is their part to consider that do it. The part of the magistrate is only to take care that the commonwealth receive no prejudice, and that there be no injury done to any man, either in life or estate. And thus what may be spent on a feast may be spent on a sacrifice. But if peradventure such were the state of things that the interest of the commonwealth required all slaughter of beasts should be forborne for some while, in order to the increasing of the stock of cattle that had been destroyed by some extraordinary murrain, who sees not that the magistrate, in such a case, may forbid all his subjects to kill any calves for any use whatsoever? Only it is to be observed that, in this case, the law is not made about a religious but a political matter; nor is the sacrifice, but the slaughter of calves, thereby prohibited.

By this we see what difference there is between the church and the commonwealth. Whatsoever is lawful in the commonwealth cannot be prohibited by the magistrate in the church. Whatsoever is permitted unto any of his subjects for their ordinary use neither can nor ought to be forbidden by him to any sect of people for their religious uses. If any man may lawfully take bread or wine, either sitting or kneeling in his own house, the law ought not to abridge him of the same liberty in his religious worship; though in the church the use of bread and wine be very different, and be there applied to the mysteries of faith and rites of divine worship. But those things that are prejudicial to the common-weal of a people in their ordinary use, and are therefore forbidden by laws, those things ought not to be permitted to churches in their sacred rites. Only the magistrate ought always to be very careful that he do not misuse his authority to the oppression of any church, under pretense of public good.

It may be said, what if a church be idolatrous, is that also to be tolerated by the magistrate? I answer, what power can be given to the magistrate for the suppression of an idolatrous church which may not in time and place be made use of to the ruin of an orthodox one? For it must be remembered that the civil power is the same everywhere, and the religion of every prince is orthodox to himself. If, therefore, such a power be granted unto the civil magistrate in spirituals, as that at Geneva, for example, he may extirpate, by violence and blood, the religion which is there reputed idolatrous; by the same rule another magistrate, in some neighboring country, may oppress the reformed religion, and, in India, the Christian. The civil power can either change everything in religion, according to the prince's pleasure, or it can change nothing. If it be once permitted to introduce anything into religion, by the means of laws and penalties, there can be no bounds put to it; but it will in the same manner be lawful to alter everything, according to that rule of truth which the magistrate has framed unto himself. No man whatsoever ought therefore to be deprived of his terrestrial enjoyments upon account of his religion. Not even Americans, subjected unto a Christian prince, are to be punished either in body or goods for not embracing our faith and worship. If they are persuaded that they please God in observing the rites of their own country, and that they shall obtain happiness by that means, they are to be left unto God and themselves. Let us trace this matter to the bottom. Thus it is: an inconsiderable and weak number of Christians, destitute of everything, arrive in a pagan country; these foreigners beseech the inhabitants, by the bowels of humanity, that they would succor them with the necessaries of life; those necessaries are given them, habitations are granted, and they all join together and grow up into one body of people. The Christian religion by this means takes root in that country and spreads itself, but does not suddenly grow the strongest. While things are in this condition, peace, friendship, faith, and equal justice are preserved amongst them. At length the magistrate becomes a Christian, and by that means their party becomes the most powerful. Then immediately all compacts are to be broken, all civil rights to be violated, that idolatry may be extirpated; and unless these innocent pagans, strict observers of the rules of equity and the law of nature, and no ways offending against the laws of the society, I say, unless they will forsake their ancient religion and embrace a new and strange one, they are to be turned out of the lands and possessions of their forefathers, and perhaps deprived of life itself. Then, at last, it appears what zeal for the church, joined with the desire of dominion, is capable to produce, and how easily the pretense of religion and of the care of souls serves for a cloak to covetousness, rapine, and ambition.

Now whosoever maintains that idolatry is to be rooted out of any place by laws, punishments, fire, and sword, may apply this story to himself. For the reason of the thing is equal, both in America and Europe. And neither pagans there nor any dissenting Christians here can, with any right, be deprived of their worldly goods by the predominating faction of a courtchurch; nor are any civil rights to be either changed or violated upon account of religion in one place more than another.

But idolatry, say some, is a sin and therefore not to be tolerated. If they said it were therefore to be avoided, the inference were good. But it does not follow that because it is a sin it ought therefore to be punished by the magistrate. For it does not belong unto the magistrate to make use of his sword in punishing everything, indifferently, that he takes to be a sin against God. Covetousness, uncharitableness, idleness, and many other things are sins, by the consent of men, which yet no man ever said were to be punished by the magistrate. The reason is because they are not prejudicial to other men's rights, nor do they break the public peace of societies. Nay, even the sins of lying and perjury are nowhere punishable by laws, unless in certain cases in which the real turpitude of the thing and the offense against God are not considered, but only the injury done unto men's neighbors and to the commonwealth. And what if in another country, to a Mahometan or a pagan prince, the Christian religion seem false and offensive to God; may not the Christians for the same reason, and after the same manner, be extirpated there?

But it may be urged further that, by the law of Moses, idolaters were to be rooted out. True, indeed, by the law of Moses; but that is not obligatory to us Christians. Nobody pretends that everything generally enjoined by the law of Moses ought to be practiced by Christians; but there is nothing more frivolous than that common distinction of moral, judicial, and ceremonial law which men ordinarily make use of. For no positive law whatsoever can oblige any people but those to whom it is given. "Hear, O Israel," sufficiently restrains the obligations of the law of Moses only to that people. And this consideration alone is answer enough unto those that urge the authority of the law of Moses for the inflicting of capital punishment upon idolaters. But, however, I will examine this argument a little more particularly.

The case of idolaters, in respect of the Jewish commonwealth, falls under a double consideration. The first is of those who, being initiated in the Mosaical rites and made citizens of that commonwealth, did afterwards apostatize from the worship of the God of Israel. These were proceeded against as traitors and rebels, guilty of no less than high treason. For the commonwealth of the Jews, different in that from all others, was an absolute theocracy; nor was there, or could there be, any difference between that commonwealth and the church. The laws established there concerning the worship of One Invisible Deity were the civil laws of that people and a part of their political government, in which God Himself was the legislator. Now, if anyone can show me where there is a commonwealth at this time, constituted upon that foundation, I will acknowledge that the ecclesiastical laws do there unavoidably become a part of the civil, and that the subjects of that government both may and ought to be kept in strict conformity with that church by the civil power. But there is absolutely no such thing under the Gospel as a Christian commonwealth. There are, indeed, many cities and kingdoms that have embraced the faith of Christ, but they have retained their ancient form of government, with which the law of Christ hath not at all meddled. He, indeed, hath taught men how, by faith and good works, they may obtain eternal life; but He instituted no commonwealth. He prescribed unto His followers no new and peculiar form of government, nor put He the sword into any magistrate's hand, with commission to make use of it in forcing men to forsake their former religion and receive His.

Secondly, foreigners and such as were strangers to the commonwealth of Israel were not compelled by force to observe the rites of the Mosaical law; but, on the contrary, in the very same place where it is ordered that an Israelite that was an idolater should be put to death [Exod. 22:20, 21], there it is provided that strangers should not be vexed nor oppressed. I confess that the seven nations that possessed the land which was promised to the Israelites were utterly to be cut off, but this was not singly because they were idolaters. For if that had been the reason, why were the Moabites and other nations to be spared? No, the reason is this: God being in a peculiar manner the King of the Jews, He could not suffer the adoration of any other deity (which was properly an act of high treason against Himself) in the land of Canaan, which was His kingdom. For such a manifest revolt could no ways consist with His dominion, which was perfectly political in that country. All idolatry was therefore to be rooted out of the bounds of His kingdom, because it was an acknowledgment of another god, that is to say, another king, against the laws of empire. The inhabitants were also to be driven out, that the entire possession of the land might be given to the Israelites. And for the like reason the Emims and the Horims were driven out of their countries by the children of Esau and Lot, and their lands, upon the same grounds, given by God to the invaders [Deut. 2]. But, though all idolatry was thus rooted out of the land of Canaan, yet every idolater was not brought to execution. The whole family of Rahab, the whole nation of the Gibeonites, articled with Joshua and were allowed by treaty; and there were many captives amongst the Jews who were idolaters. David and Solomon subdued many countries without the confines of the Land of Promise, and carried their conquests as far as Euphrates. Amongst so many captives taken, so many nations reduced under their obedience, we find not one man forced into the Jewish religion and the worship of the true God, and punished for idolatry, though all of them were certainly guilty of it. If anyone indeed, becoming a proselyte, desired to be made a denizen of their commonwealth, he was obliged to submit to their laws, that is, to embrace their religion. But this he did willingly, on his own accord, not by constraint. He did not unwillingly submit, to show his obedience, but he sought and solicited for it as a privilege. And, as soon as he was admitted, he became subject to the laws of the commonwealth by which all idolatry was forbidden within the borders of the land of Canaan. But that law (as I have said) did not reach to any of those regions, however subjected unto the Jews, that were situated without those bounds.

Thus far concerning outward worship. Let us now consider articles of faith.

The articles of religion are some of them practical and some speculative. Now, though both sorts consist in the knowledge of truth, yet these terminate simply in the understanding, those influence the will and manners. Speculative opinions, therefore, and articles of faith (as they are called) which are required only to be believed, cannot be imposed on any church by the law of the land. For it is absurd that things should be enjoined by laws which are not in men's power to perform. And to believe this or that to be true does not depend upon our will. But of this enough has been said already. But (will some say) let men at least profess that they believe. A sweet religion, indeed, that obliges men to dissemble and tell lies, both to God and man, for the salvation of their souls! If the magistrate thinks to save men thus, he seems to understand little of the way of salvation. And if he does it not in order to save them, why is he so solicitous about the articles of faith as to enact them by a law?

Further, the magistrate ought not to forbid the preaching or professing of any speculative opinions in any church, because they have no manner of relation to the civil rights of the subjects. If a Roman Catholic believe that to be really the body of Christ which another man calls bread, he does no injury thereby to his neighbor. If a Jew do not believe the New Testament to be the Word of God, he does not thereby alter anything in men's civil rights. If a heathen doubt of both Testaments, he is not therefore to be punished as a pernicious citizen. The power of the magistrate and the estates of the people may be equally secure whether any man believe these things or no. I readily grant that these opinions are false and absurd. But the business of laws is not to provide for the truth of opinions, but for the safety and security of the commonwealth, and of every particular man's goods and person. And so it ought to be. For the truth certainly would do well enough if she were once left to shift for herself. She seldom has received, and I fear never will receive, much assistance from the power of great men, to whom she is but rarely known and more rarely welcome. She is not taught by laws, nor has she any need of force to procure her entrance into the minds of men. Errors indeed prevail by the assistance of foreign and borrowed succors. But if truth makes not her way into the understanding by her own light, she will be but the weaker for any borrowed force violence can add to her. Thus much for speculative opinions. Let us now proceed to practical ones.

A good life, in which consists not the least part of religion and true piety, concerns also the civil government; and in it lies the safety both of men's souls and of the commonwealth. Moral actions belong therefore to the jurisdiction both of the outward and inward court, both of the civil and domestic governor; I mean both of the magistrate and conscience. Here, therefore, is great danger, lest one of these jurisdictions entrench upon the other and discord arise between the keeper of the public peace and the overseers of souls. But if what has been already said concerning the limits of both these governments be rightly considered, it will easily remove all difficulty in this matter.

Every man has an immortal soul, capable of eternal happiness or misery, whose happiness depending upon his believing and doing those things in this life which are necessary to the obtaining of God's favor, and are prescribed by God to that end. It follows from thence, first, that the observance of these things is the highest obligation that lies upon mankind, and that our utmost care, application, and diligence ought to be exercised in the search and performance of them; because there is nothing in this world that is of any consideration in comparison with eternity. Secondly, that seeing one man does not violate the right of another by his erroneous opinions and undue manner of worship, nor is his perdition any prejudice to another man's affairs, therefore, the care of each man's salvation belongs only to himself. But I would not have this understood as if I meant hereby to condemn all charitable admonitions and affectionate endeavors to reduce men from errors, which are indeed the greatest duty of a Christian. Anyone may employ as many exhortations and arguments as he pleases, toward the promoting of another man's salvation. But all force and compulsion are to be forborne. Nothing is to be done imperiously. Nobody is obliged in that manner to yield obedience unto the admonitions or injunctions of another, further than he himself is persuaded. Every man in that has the supreme and absolute authority of judging for himself. And the reason is because nobody else is concerned in it, nor can receive any prejudice from his conduct therein.

But besides their souls, which are immortal, men have also their temporal lives here upon earth; the state whereof being frail and fleeting, and the duration uncertain, they have need of several outward conveniences to the support thereof, which are to be procured or preserved by pains and industry. For those things that are necessary to the comfortable support of our lives are not the spontaneous products of nature, nor do offer themselves fit and prepared for our use. This part therefore draws on another care, and necessarily gives another employment. But the pravity of mankind being such that they had rather injuriously prey upon the fruits of other men's labors than take pains to provide for themselves, the necessity of preserving men in the possession of what honest industry has already acquired, and also of preserving their liberty and strength, whereby they may acquire what they further want, obliges men to enter into society with one another, that by mutual assistance and joint force they may secure unto each other their properties, in the things—that contribute to the comfort and happiness of this life, leaving in the meanwhile to every man the care of his own eternal happiness, the attainment whereof can neither be facilitated by another man's industry, nor can the loss of it turn to another man's prejudice, nor the hope of it be forced from him by any external violence. But, forasmuch as men thus entering into societies, grounded upon their mutual compacts of assistance for the defense of their temporal goods, may, nevertheless, be deprived of them, either by the rapine and fraud of their fellow citizens or by the hostile violence of foreigners, the remedy of this evil consists in arms, riches, and multitude of citizens; the remedy of the other in laws; and the care of all things relating both to one and the other is committed by the society to the civil magistrate. This is the original, this is the use, and these are the bounds of the legislative (which is the supreme) power in every commonwealth. I mean that provision may be made for the security of each man's private possessions, for the peace, riches, and public commodities of the whole people, and, as much as possible, for the increase of their inward strength against foreign invasions.

These things being thus explained, it is easy to understand to what end the legislative power ought to be directed, and by what measures regulated; and that is the temporal good and outward prosperity of the society, which is the sole reason of men's entering into society, and the only thing they seek and aim at in it. And it is also evident what liberty remains to men in reference to their eternal salvation, and that is, that everyone should do what he in his conscience is persuaded to be acceptable to the Almighty, on whose good pleasure and acceptance depends their eternal happiness. For obedience is due, in the first place, to God, and afterwards to the laws.

But some may ask, What if the magistrate should enjoin anything by his authority that appears unlawful to the conscience of a private person? I answer that if government be faithfully administered and the counsels of the magistrates be indeed directed to the public good, this will seldom happen. But if, perhaps, it do so fall out, I say that such a private person is to abstain from the action that he judges unlawful, and he is to undergo the punishment which it is not unlawful for him to bear. For the private judgment of any person concerning a law enacted in political matters, for the public good, does not take away the obligation of that law, nor deserve a dispensation. But if the law indeed be concerning things that lie not within the verge of the magistrate's authority (as, for example, that the people, or any party amongst them, should be compelled to embrace a strange religion and join in the worship and ceremonies of another church), men are not in these cases obliged by that law, against their consciences. For the political society is instituted for no other end, but only to secure every man's possession of the things of this life. The care of each man's soul, and of the things of heaven, which neither does belong to the commonwealth nor can be subjected to it, is left entirely to every man's self. Thus the safeguard of men's lives and of the things that belong unto this life is the business of the commonwealth; and the preserving of those things unto their owners is the duty of the magistrate. And therefore the magistrate cannot take away these worldly things from this man or party and give them to that, nor change propriety amongst fellow subjects (no, not even by a law), for a cause that has no relation to the end of civil government, I mean for their religion, which whether it be true or false does no prejudice to the worldly concerns of their fellow subjects, which are the things that only belong unto the care of the commonwealth.

But what if the magistrate believe such a law as this to be for the public good? I answer: as the private judgment of any particular person, if erroneous, does not exempt him from the obligation of law, so the private judgment (as I may call it) of the magistrate does not give him any new right of imposing laws upon his subjects which neither was in the constitution of the government granted him nor ever was in the power of the people to grant, much less if he make it his business to enrich and advance his followers and fellow sectaries with the spoils of others. But what if the magistrate believe that he has a right to make such laws, and that they are for the public good, and his subjects believe the contrary? Who shall be judge between them? I answer, God alone. For there is no judge upon earth between the supreme magistrate and the people. God, I say, is the only Judge in this case, who will retribute unto everyone at the last day according to his deserts, that is, according to his sincerity and uprightness in endeavoring to promote piety and the public weal and peace of mankind. But what shall be done in the meanwhile? I answer: The principal and chief care of everyone ought to be of his own soul first, and, in the next place, of the public peace; though yet there are very few will think it is peace there where they see all laid waste.

There are two sorts of contests amongst men, the one managed by law, the other by force; and these are of that nature that where the one ends, the other always begins. But it is not my business to inquire into the power of the magistrate in the different constitutions of nations. I only know what usually happens where controversies arise without a judge to determine them. You will say, then, the magistrate being the stronger will have his will, and carry his point. Without doubt; but the question is not here concerning the doubtfulness of the event, but the rule of right.

But to come to particulars. I say, first, no opinions contrary to human society, or to those moral rules which are necessary to the preservation of civil society, are to be tolerated by the magistrate. But of these, indeed, examples in any church are rare. For no sect can easily arrive to such a degree of madness as that it should think fit to teach, for doctrines or religion, such things as manifestly undermine the foundations of society, and are, therefore, condemned by the judgment of all mankind; because their own interest, peace, reputation, everything would be thereby endangered.

Another more secret evil, but more dangerous to the commonwealth, is when men arrogate to themselves and to those of their own sect some peculiar prerogative covered over with a specious show of deceitful words, but in effect opposite to the civil right of the community. For example: we cannot find any sect that teaches, expressly and openly, that men are not obliged to keep their promise; that princes may be dethroned by those that differ from them in religion; or that the dominion of all things belongs only to themselves. For these things, proposed thus nakedly and plainly, would soon draw on them the eye and hand of the magistrate, and awaken all the care of the commonwealth to a watchfulness against the spreading of so dangerous an evil. But, nevertheless, we find those that say the same things in other words. What else do they mean who teach that faith is not to be kept with heretics? Their meaning, forsooth, is that the privilege of breaking faith belongs unto themselves; for they declare all that are not of their communion to be heretics, or at least may declare them so whensoever they think fit. What can be the meaning of their asserting that kings excommunicated forfeit their crowns and king-doms? It is evident that they thereby arrogate unto themselves the power of deposing kings, because they challenge the power of excommunication as the peculiar right of their hierarchy. That dominion is founded in grace is also an assertion by which those that maintain it do plainly lay claim to the possession of all things. For they are not so want-ing to themselves as not to believe, or at least as not to profess, themselves to be the truly pious and faithful. These, therefore, and the like, who attribute unto the faithful, reli-gious, and orthodox, that is, in plain terms, unto themselves, any peculiar privilege or power above other mortals, in civil concernments; or who upon pretense of religion do challenge any manner of authority over such as are not associated with them in their eccle-siastical communion, I say these have no right to be tolerated by the magistrate, as nei-ther those that will not own and teach the duty of tolerating all men in matters of mere religion. For what do all these and the like doctrines signify but that they may and are ready upon any occasion to seize the government and possess themselves of the estates and fortunes of their fellow subjects; and that they only ask leave to be tolerated by the magistrate so long until they find themselves strong enough to effect it?

Again: That church can have no right to be tolerated by the magistrate which is con-stituted upon such a bottom that all those who enter into it do thereby *ipso facto* deliver themselves up to the protection and service of another prince. For by this means the magistrate would give way to the settling of a foreign jurisdiction in his own country, and suffer his own people to be listed, as it were, for soldiers against his own government. Nor does the frivolous and fallacious distinction between the court and the church afford any remedy to this inconvenience; especially when both the one and the other are equally sub-ject to the absolute authority of the same person who has not only power to persuade the members of his church to whatsoever he lists, either as purely religion or in order there-unto, but can also enjoin it them on pain of eternal fire. It is ridiculous for anyone to profess himself to be a Mahometan only in his religion, but in everything else a faithful subject to a Christian magistrate, whilst at the same time he acknowledges himself bound to yield blind obedience to the Mufti of Constantinople, who himself is entirely obedient to the Ottoman Emperor and frames the feigned oracles of that religion according to his pleasure. But this Mahometan living amongst Christians would yet more apparently renounce their government if he acknowledged the same person to be head of his church who is the supreme magistrate in the state.

Lastly, those are not at all to be tolerated who deny the being of a God. Promises, covenants, and oaths, which are the bonds of human society, can have no hold upon an atheist. The taking away of God, though but even in thought, dissolves all; besides also, those that by their atheism undermine and destroy all religion can have no pretense of religion whereupon to challenge the privilege of a toleration. As for other practical opin-ions, though not absolutely free from all error, if they do not tend to establish domination over others, or civil impunity to the church in which they are taught, there can be no rea-son why they should not be tolerated.

It remains that I say something concerning those assemblies which being vulgarly called, and perhaps having sometimes been conventicles and nurseries of factions and seditions, are thought to afford the strongest matter of objection against this doctrine of toleration. But this has not happened by anything peculiar unto the genius of such assem-blies, but by the unhappy circumstances of an oppressed or ill-settled liberty. These accusations would soon cease if the law of toleration were once so settled that all churches were obliged to lay down toleration as the foundation of their own liberty, and teach that liberty of conscience is every man's natural right, equally belonging to dissenters as to themselves; and that nobody ought to be compelled in matters of religion either by law or force. The establishment of this one thing would take away all ground of complaints and tumults upon account of conscience; and these causes of discontents and animosities being once removed, there would remain nothing in these assemblies that were not more peaceable and less apt to produce disturbance of state than in any other meetings whatsoever. But let us examine particularly the heads of these accusations.

You will say that assemblies and meetings endanger the public peace and threaten the commonwealth. I answer, if this be so, why are there daily such numerous meetings in markets and courts of judicature? Why are crowds upon the Exchange and a concourse of people in cities suffered? You will reply, those are civil assemblies, but these we object against are ecclesiastical. I answer, it is a likely thing indeed that such assemblies as are altogether remote from civil affairs should be most apt to embroil them. Oh, but civil assemblies are composed of men that differ from one another in matters of religion, but these ecclesiastical meetings are of persons that are all of one opinion. As if an agreement in matters of religion were in effect a conspiracy against the commonwealth; or as if men would not be so much the more warmly unanimous in religion the less liberty they had of assembling. But it will be urged still that civil assemblies are open and free for anyone to enter into, whereas religious conventicles are more private, and thereby give opportunity to clandestine machinations. I answer that this is not strictly true, for many civil assemblies are not open to everyone. And if some religious meetings be private, who are they (I beseech you) that are to be blamed for it, those that desire or those that forbid their being public? Again, you will say that religious communion does exceedingly unite men's minds and affections to one another, and is therefore the more dangerous. But if this be so, why is not the magistrate afraid of his own church, and why does he not forbid their assemblies as things dangerous to his government? You will say because he himself is a part and even the head of them. As if he were not also a part of the commonwealth and the head of the whole people!

Let us therefore deal plainly. The magistrate is afraid of other churches, but not of his own, because he is kind and favorable to the one, but severe and cruel to the other. These he treats like children and indulges them even to wantonness. Those he uses as slaves, and how blamelessly soever they demean themselves, recompenses them no otherwise than by galleys, prisons, confiscations, and death. These he cherishes and defends; those he continually scourges and oppresses. Let him turn the tables. Or let those dissenters enjoy but the same privileges in civils as his other subjects, and he will quickly find that these religious meetings will be no longer dangerous. For if men enter into seditious conspiracies, it is not religion inspires them to it in their meetings, but their sufferings and oppressions that make them willing to ease themselves. Just and moderate governments are everywhere quiet, everywhere safe; but oppression raises ferments and makes men struggle to cast off an uneasy and tyrannical yoke. I know that seditions are very frequently raised upon pretense of religion, but it is as true that for religion subjects are frequently ill treated and live miserably. Believe me, the stirs that are made proceed not from any peculiar temper of this or that church or religious society, but from the common disposition of all mankind, who when they groan under any heavy burden endeavor naturally to shake off the yoke that galls their necks. Suppose this business of religion were let alone, and that there were some other distinction made between men and men upon account of their different complexions, shapes, and features, so that those who have black hair (for example) or gray eyes should not enjoy the same privileges as other citizens; that they should not be permitted either to buy or sell, or live by their callings; that parents should not have the government and education of their own children; that all should either be excluded from the benefit of the laws or meet with partial judges—can it be doubted but these persons, thus distinguished from others by the color of their hair and eyes, and united together by one common persecution, would be as dangerous to the magistrate as any others that had associated themselves merely upon the account of religion? Some enter into company for trade and profit, others for want of business have their clubs for claret. Neighborhood joins some, and religion others. But there is only one thing which gathers people into seditious commotions, and that is oppression.

You will say, What, will you have people to meet at divine service against the magistrate's will? I answer, Why, I pray, against his will? Is it not both lawful and necessary that they should meet? Against his will, do you say? That is what I complain of; that is the very root of all the mischief. Why are assemblies less sufferable in a church than in a theater or market? Those that meet there are not either more vicious or more turbulent than those that meet elsewhere. The business in that is that they are ill used, and therefore they are not to be suffered. Take away the partiality that is used toward them in matters of common right, change the laws, take away the penalties unto which they are subjected, and all things will immediately become safe and peaceable; nay, those that are averse to the religion of the magistrate will think themselves so much the more bound to maintain the peace of the commonwealth as their condition is better in that place than elsewhere; and all the several separate congregations, like so many guardians of the public peace, will watch one another, that nothing may be innovated or changed in the form of the government, because they can hope for nothing better than what they already enjoy—that is, an equal condition with their fellow subjects under a just and moderate government. Now if that church which agrees in religion with the prince be esteemed the chief support of any civil government, and that for no other reason (as has already been shown) than because the prince is kind and the laws are favorable to it, how much greater will be the security of government where all good subjects, of whatsoever church they be, without any distinction upon account of religion, enjoying the same favor of the prince and the same benefit of the laws, shall become the common support and guard of it, and where none will have any occasion to fear the severity of the laws but those that do injuries to their neighbors and offend against the civil peace?

That we may draw toward a conclusion. The sum of all we drive at is that every man may enjoy the same rights that are granted to others. Is it permitted to worship God in the Roman manner? Let it be permitted to do it in the Geneva form also. Is it permitted to speak Latin in the market place? Let those that have a mind to it be permitted to do it also in the church. Is it lawful for any man in his own house to kneel, stand, sit, or use any other posture, and to clothe himself in white or black, in short or in long garments? Let it not be made unlawful to eat bread, drink wine, or wash with water in the church. In a word, whatsoever things are left free by law in the common occasions of life, let them remain free unto every church in divine worship. Let no man's life or body or house or estate suffer any manner of prejudice upon these accounts. Can you allow of the Presbyterian discipline? Why should not the Episcopal also have what they like? Ecclesiastical authority, whether it be administered by the hands of a single person or many, is everywhere the same; and neither has any jurisdiction in things civil, nor any manner of power of compulsion, nor anything at all to do with riches and revenues.

Ecclesiastical assemblies and sermons are justified by daily experience and public allowance. These are allowed to people of some one persuasion, why not to all? If anything pass in a religious meeting seditiously and contrary to the public peace, it is to be punished in the same manner, and no otherwise than as if it had happened in a fair or market. These meetings ought not to be sanctuaries for factious and flagitious fellows. Nor ought it to be less lawful for men to meet in churches than in halls; nor are one part of the subjects to be esteemed more blamable for their meeting together than others. Everyone is to be accountable for his own actions, and no man is to be laid under a suspicion or odium for the fault of another. Those that are seditious, murderers, thieves, robbers, adulterers, slanderers, etc, of whatsoever church, whether national or not, ought to be punished and suppressed. But those whose doctrine is peaceable, and whose manners are pure and blameless, ought to be upon equal terms with their fellow subjects. Thus if solemn assemblies, observations of festivals, public worship be permitted to any one sort of professors, all these things ought to be permitted to the Presbyterians, Independents, Anabaptists, Arminians, Quakers, and others, with the same liberty. Nay, if we may openly speak the truth, and as becomes one man to another, neither pagan nor Mahometan nor Jew ought to be excluded from the civil rights of the commonwealth because of his religion. The Gospel commands no such thing. The church which "judgeth not those that are without" [1 Cor. 5:12, 13] wants it not. And the commonwealth, which embraces indifferently all men that are honest, peaceable, and industrious, requires it not. Shall we suffer a pagan to deal and trade with us, and shall we not suffer him to pray unto and worship God? If we allow the Jews to have private houses and dwellings amongst us, why should we not allow them to have synagogues? Is their doctrine more false, their worship more abominable, or is the civil peace more endangered by their meeting in public than in their private houses? But if these things may be granted to Jews and pagans, surely the condition of any Christians ought not to be worse than theirs in a Christian commonwealth.

You will say, perhaps, Yes, it ought to be; because they are more inclinable to factions, tumults, and civil wars. I answer, Is this the fault of the Christian religion? If it be so, truly the Christian religion is the worst of all religions, and ought neither to be embraced by any particular person nor tolerated by any commonwealth. For if this be the genius, this the nature of the Christian religion, to be turbulent and destructive to the civil peace, that church itself which the magistrate indulges will not always be innocent. But far be it from us to say any such thing of that religion which carries the greatest opposition to covetousness, ambition, discord, contention, and all manner of inordinate desires; and is the most modest and peaceable religion that ever was. We must therefore seek another cause of those evils that are charged upon religion. And if we consider right, we shall find it to consist wholly in the subject that I am treating of. It is not the diversity of opinions (which cannot be avoided), but the refusal of toleration to those that are of different opinions (which might have been granted), that has produced all the bustles and wars that have been in the Christian world upon account of religion. The heads and leaders of the church, moved by avarice and insatiable desire of dominion, making use of the immoderate ambition of magistrates and the credulous superstition of the giddy multitude, have incensed and animated them against those that dissent from themselves, by preaching unto them, contrary to the laws of the Gospel and to the precepts of charity, that schismatics and heretics are to be outed of their possessions and destroyed. And thus have they mixed together and confounded two things that are in themselves most different, the church and the commonwealth. Now as it is very difficult for men patiently to suffer themselves to be stripped of the goods which they have got by their honest industry and, contrary to all the laws of equity, both human and divine, to be delivered up for a prey to other men's violence and rapine, especially when they are otherwise altogether blameless;

and that the occasion for which they are thus treated does not at all belong to the jurisdiction of the magistrate, but entirely to the conscience of every particular man, for the
conduct of which he is accountable to God only; what else can be expected but that these
men, growing weary of the evils under which they labor, should in the end think it lawful for them to resist force with force, and to defend their natural rights (which are not
forfeitable upon account of religion) with arms as well as they can? That this has been
hitherto the ordinary course of things is abundantly evident in history, and that it will
continue to be so hereafter is but too apparent in reason. It cannot, indeed, be otherwise
so long as the principle of persecution for religion shall prevail, as it has done hitherto,
with magistrate and people, and so long as those that ought to be the preachers of peace
and concord shall continue with all their art and strength to excite men to arms and sound
the trumpet of war. But that magistrates should thus suffer these incendiaries and disturbers of the public peace might justly be wondered at if it did not appear that they have
been invited by them unto a participation of the spoil, and have therefore thought fit to
make use of their covetousness and pride as means whereby to increase their own power.
For who does not see that these good men are indeed more ministers of the government
than ministers of the Gospel, and that by flattering the ambition and favoring the dominion of princes and men in authority, they endeavor with all their might to promote that
tyranny in the commonwealth which otherwise they should not be able to establish in the
church? This is the unhappy agreement that we see between the church and state.
Whereas if each of them would contain itself within its own bounds—the one attending
to the worldly welfare of the commonwealth, the other to the salvation of souls—it is
impossible that any discord should ever have happened between them. *Sed pudet haec oppro-
bria, etc.* God Almighty grant, I beseech Him, that the gospel of peace may at length be
preached, and that civil magistrates, growing more careful to conform their own consciences to the law of God and less solicitous about the binding of other men's consciences
by human laws, may, like fathers of their country, direct all their counsels and endeavors
to promote universally the civil welfare of all their children, except only of such as are
arrogant, ungovernable, and injurious to their brethren; and that all ecclesiastical men,
who boast themselves to be the successors of the apostles, walking peaceably and modestly
in the apostles' steps, without intermeddling with state affairs, may apply themselves
wholly to promote the salvation of souls.

FAREWELL

Perhaps it may not be amiss to add a few things concerning heresy and schism. A Turk
is not, nor can be, either heretic or schismatic to a Christian; and if any man fall off from
the Christian faith to Mahometism, he does not thereby become a heretic or schismatic,
but an apostate and an infidel. This nobody doubts of; and by this it appears that men of
different religions cannot be heretics or schismatics to one another.

We are to inquire, therefore, what men are of the same religion. Concerning which it
is manifest that those who have one and the same rule of faith and worship are of the same
religion; and those who have not the same rule of faith and worship are of different religions. For since all things that belong unto that religion are contained in that rule, it
follows necessarily that those who agree in one rule are of one and the same religion, and
vice versa. Thus Turks and Christians are of different religions, because these take the
Holy Scriptures to be the rule of their religion, and those the Alcoran. And for the same
reason there may be different religions also even amongst Christians. The Papists and
Lutherans, though both of them profess faith in Christ, and are therefore called Christians,
yet are not both of the same religion, because these acknowledge nothing but the Holy

Scriptures to be the rule and foundation of their religion, those take in also traditions and the decrees of Popes, and of these together make the rule of their religion; and thus the Christians of St. John (as they are called) and the Christians of Geneva are of different religions, because these also take only the Scriptures, and those I know not what traditions, for the rule of their religion.

This being settled, it follows, first, that heresy is a separation made in ecclesiastical communion between men of the same religion for some opinions no way contained in the rule itself; and, secondly, that amongst those who acknowledge nothing but the Holy Scriptures to be their rule of faith, heresy is a separation made in their Christian communion for opinions not contained in the express words of Scripture. Now this separation may be made in a twofold manner:

1. When the greater part, or by the magistrate's patronage the stronger part, of the church separates itself from others by excluding them out of her communion because they will not profess their belief of certain opinions which are not the express words of the Scripture. For it is not the paucity of those that are separated, nor the authority of the magistrate, that can make any man guilty of heresy, but he only is a heretic who divides the church into parts, introduces names and marks of distinction, and voluntarily makes a separation because of such opinions.

2. When anyone separates himself from the communion of a church because that church does not publicly profess some certain opinions which the Holy Scriptures do not expressly teach.

Both these are heretics because they err in fundamentals, and they err obstinately against knowledge; for when they have determined the Holy Scriptures to be the only foundation of faith, they nevertheless lay down certain propositions as fundamental which are not in the Scripture, and because others will not acknowledge these additional opinions of theirs, nor build upon them as if they were necessary and fundamental, they therefore make a separation in the church, either by withdrawing themselves from others or expelling the others from them. Nor does it signify anything for them to say that their confessions and symbols are agreeable to Scripture and to the analogy of faith; for if they be conceived in the express words of Scripture, there can be no question about them because those things are acknowledged by all Christians to be of divine inspiration, and therefore fundamental. But if they say that the articles which they require to be professed are consequences deduced from the Scripture, it is undoubtedly well done of them who believe and profess such things as seem unto them so agreeable to the rule of faith. But it would be very ill done to obtrude those things upon others unto whom they do not seem to be the indubitable doctrines of the Scripture; and to make a separation for such things as these, which neither are nor can be fundamental, is to become heretics; for I do not think there is any man arrived to that degree of madness as that he dare give out his consequences and interpretations of Scripture as divine inspirations, and compare the articles of faith that he has framed according to his own fancy with the authority of Scripture. I know there are some propositions so evidently agreeable to Scripture that nobody can deny them to be drawn from thence, but about those, therefore, there can be no difference. This only I say—that however clearly we may think this or the other doctrine to be deduced from Scripture, we ought not therefore to impose it upon others as a necessary article of faith because we believe it to be agreeable to the rule of faith, unless we would be content also that other doctrines should be imposed upon us in the same manner, and that we should be compelled to receive and profess all the different and contradictory opinions of Lutherans, Calvinists, Remonstrants, Anabaptists, and other sects which the contrivers of symbols, systems, and confessions are accustomed to deliver to their followers as genuine and necessary deductions from the Holy Scripture. I cannot but wonder at the extravagant arrogance of those men who think that they themselves can explain things necessary to salvation more clearly than the Holy Ghost, the eternal and infinite wisdom of God.

Thus much concerning heresy, which word in common use is applied only to the doctrinal part of religion. Let us now consider schism, which is a crime near akin to it; for both these words seem unto me to signify an ill-grounded separation in ecclesiastical communion made about things not necessary. But since use, which is the supreme law in matter of language, has determined that heresy relates to errors in faith, and schism to those in worship or discipline, we must consider them under that distinction.

Schism, then, for the same reasons that have already been alleged, is nothing else but a separation made in the communion of the church upon account of something in divine worship or ecclesiastical discipline that is not any necessary part of it. Now, nothing in worship or discipline can be necessary to Christian communion but what Christ our legislator, or the apostles by inspiration of the Holy Spirit, have commanded in express words.

In a word, he that denies not anything that the Holy Scriptures teach in express words, nor makes a separation upon occasion of anything that is not manifestly contained in the sacred text—however he may be nicknamed by any sect of Christians and declared by some or all of them to be utterly void of true Christianity—yet in deed and in truth this man cannot be either a heretic or schismatic.

These things might have been explained more largely and more advantageously, but it is enough to have hinted at them thus briefly to a person of your parts.

MONTESQUIEU

Charles-Louis de Secondat, Baron de Montesquieu, was born on January 19, 1689, at the château of La Brède, located near the city of Bordeaux in southwestern France. While in Paris during 1755, he contracted a fever on January 29 and died on February 10 amidst the usual eighteenth-century tug of war between priests eager to announce a deathbed profession of orthodoxy and the equally vehement denials of the avant-garde thinkers, the *philosophes*, that he had wavered at the final moment in his commitment to the cause of the Enlightenment.

Whatever the circumstances of his death, the undeniable truth of Montesquieu's life is that he was a great and pioneering figure of the French Enlightenment, and that his sphere of intellectual influence spanned many foreign lands, reaching as far west as the American colonies and as far east as the Russia of Catherine the Great. All the *philosophes*—Diderot, d'Alembert, Helvétius, among others—accepted and built on certain of his themes. His efforts to reform the cruel laws that treated crimes as sins became theirs, and the same holds for his plea on behalf of religious tolerance of Protestants and Jews, his corresponding outcry against the Revocation of the Edict of Nantes and the Spanish Inquisition, and his denunciation of the bloody conquests of the Spaniards in the Americas.

Although Paris was the center of French culture, there was no need for Montesquieu to travel to the capital to gain his initial intellectual inspiration when in his own Gasçon backyard he could learn so much from the great Montaigne (1533–1592), author of the *Essays*. Nauseated by the brutality of the wars of religion, disgusted by the murderous actions of the Spaniards searching for gold in the New World, Montaigne found more humanity among cannibals than in the ranks of the European conquerors. Cannibals kill humans only when hungry; Europeans kill sometimes for aristocratic sport, at other times to accumulate pieces of a shiny metal, or to plant their flag and crucifix on foreign soil. Who, then, is the savage? Montesquieu seconded Montaigne's opinion and added that the slave trade in his century proved Europeans were far from enlightened during the age of the Enlightenment.

Montesquieu also shared with Montaigne a philosophical skepticism, a denial that absolute truth is accessible to the human mind. How intolerable is intolerance when certainty is beyond our grasp, all knowledge deriving from the senses and hence relative to our persons. In his notebook, Montesquieu commented that the mistake of most philosophers had been to ignore that the terms *beautiful, good, noble, grand,* and *perfect* are "relative to the beings who use them." One and only one absolute existed for Montesquieu, the absolute evil of despotism. To ward off the worst possibilities was in consequence his primary concern, and to that end he, unlike Montaigne, gave a great deal of thought to political institutions—and to the social, economic, and cultural prerequisites of limited rule. In general, he discovered that Protestant, commercial, and constitutionalist Holland and England represented the best Europe had to offer, just as Catholic, economically retarded, and politically absolutist

Spain and Portugal represented the worst. Above all, Montesquieu believed, France must avoid following in the historical footsteps of reactionary and regressive Spain.

Although the *philosophes* reiterated his specific findings, Montesquieu remained a unique figure among his kind in his method of reasoning. In contrast to his Parisian compatriots who espoused philosophies of natural rights and utilitarianism, he conducted his studies through the comparative method. The "more than/less than" judgments of comparative analysis suited his skeptical outlook and assisted him in anchoring his aspirations, not in the utopian speculation for which he had no use, but in concrete historical possibilities. Bored though he was with his legal duties at the *parlement* of Bordeaux, Montesquieu made effective use of his training in the law while writing his masterpiece, *The Spirit of the Laws* (1748), a path-breaking adventure in what is now known as the *sociology of law*.

As early as 1721, Montesquieu established his reputation as a writer with the publication of his *Persian Letters*. Then, as now, the first of his major writings was received by his readers as a witty, sly, satirical work, poking fun at the pretence of Europeans, the French in particular. His audience was titillated, it is true, by the sometimes sexually frank letters passed back and forth between the traveler, Usbek, and his wives sequestered in the Persian harem. No one, however, paid much attention to the underlying significance of Montesquieu's portrait of the battle of the sexes in Persia. Hence, a year before his death, Montesquieu found it necessary to write a new preface to the *Persian Letters*, in which he pointed out that the book was a novel, not a series of disjointed letters. In effect, Montesquieu implied that the story of the eventual rebellion of Roxane against her despotic husband was the chief meaning of the work. Usbek is an enlightened man, a kind of Persian *philosophe,* but he is also a good Persian male and as such has been inured from birth to regard women as property. Persia is a despotic country, and the family, in consequence, is a miniature despotism.

It was always Montesquieu's position that despotic power benefits no one, not even the despot. And so it is that Usbek acknowledges how completely jealousy consumes him. We can well imagine his devastation on learning that Roxane has taken her life rather than lie again in his arms.

Montesquieu's first major publication presents a depiction of what he will call "Oriental despotism" in the *Spirit of the Laws.* His second book, the *Considerations on the Greatness of the Romans and the Cause of Their Decline* (1734), concerns the model of the ancient civic republic, which likewise reappears in his magnum opus. Athenians, Spartans, and Romans were as politically free as Persians were enslaved, yet Montesquieu's monograph on the Roman republic reprises the theme of despotism in its account of war and aggrandizement. Having accepted Machiavelli's claim that the Romans were the most ruthless and conniving power-politicians of all times, Montesquieu adds that the despotism they perpetrated abroad caused the decline of their civic virtue at home. Expansion of the Roman city-state steadily undermined the civic ethos, in that it fostered a yearning for privacy and personal wealth; the time had arrived when the Romans would conclude that the life of citizenship takes up too many evenings.

In the *Spirit of the Laws,* Montesquieu posited that each type of political regime was reinforced by a characteristic social ethos, despotism by "fear," the ancient republic by (civic) "virtue," and he added a newly conceptualized model of a monarchical regime, complemented by the social principle of "honor." By *monarchy*, Montesquieu understood the social and political structure that had evolved from the chaos of feudalism to the divine-right absolutism of the Old Regime. What prevented this government from doing its worst were the "intermediary bodies," the First and Second Estates, and the massive and tangled world of privileges and exemptions that were to be struck down during the French Revolution. If the society of the Old Regime revolved around a code of aristocratic honor, that was because the prerevolutionary bourgeoisie wanted to join rather than displace the nobility. Moliere's *Bourgeois Gentleman* is the classic statement of middle-class aspirations to buy a noble title and put on aristocratic airs.

The key term in Montesquieu's use of the comparative method is *feudalism*. When comparing the Western world to the Eastern, he held that it was the presence of royal absolutism on both sides of the globe that made regimes comparable; it was the presence of feudal social structures in countries such as France and their absence in Persia or China that differentiated Oriental despotism from Western kingship. Take away the structure of feudal privileges and inequalities, keep the absolute monarch, and France will become a despotic state. No sooner did Voltaire read the chapters devoted to the study of "intermediary bodies," their prominence in Europe and nonexistence elsewhere, than he concluded that Montesquieu had written the *Spirit of the Laws* to apologize for the vested interests of the nobility to which he was born.

Had Voltaire read *The Spirit of the Laws* more carefully, he would have noted that, to Montesquieu, the feudal factor did more than differentiate West from East. It also permitted him to compare one Western country with another, because each of the various European societies had evolved from a common feudal embryo. Poland and Hungary, with their weak monarchs, unruly nobility, downtrodden peasantry, and anemic urban centers were in the eighteenth century as France had been during the Middle Ages. Montesquieu's depiction of the Middle Ages as a time when a multitude of local despots dominated the countryside proves how little love he had for the First and Second Estates when they did not serve as "intermediary bodies" blocking the arbitrary will of an absolute monarch.

How reluctant Montesquieu was to count on intermediary bodies under any circumstances is evident in his frequent remarks on Spain. Supposedly an absolute monarchy modified by clergy and nobles, the Spanish regime was in truth, and with disastrous consequences, the captive of the intermediary powers. As it turns out, a divine-right monarch all too frequently is dictated to by the Church, which in Spain led to the Inquisition and in France led to the Revocation of the Edict of Nantes, a measure depriving the French monarch of his most economically productive subjects, the Protestant Huguenots. Not reasons of state but hatreds of the clergy are what motivates public policy in Europe, which hardly needs to import Oriental despotism by abolishing the intermediary bodies when the retention of the feudal social structure so effectively produces a homegrown variety of despotic government. What damage the Church does not do, the nobility inflicts upon the Spanish nation: Aristocratic "honor," envied even by the middle class, disdains commerce, such that all nobles and would-be nobles prefer a life of leisure and conspicuous consumption to one of entrepreneurship. A work ethic has no chance to take root in Spain where both the clergy and the nobility remove the lands from productivity. Once the leading power of Europe, Spain (like Portugal) has become the village idiot of the Western world.

If the retention of intermediary bodies (Spain) was no guarantee against despotism, neither did their demise automatically entail the advent of a despotic regime. "Abolish the privileges of the lords, the clergy, and cities in a monarchy," wrote Montesquieu, "and you will soon have a popular state, or else a despotic government." Across the Channel, he spied a "popular state." "The English, to favor their liberty, have abolished all the intermediate powers of which their monarchy was composed." Having consumed its Old Regime during the upheavals of the seventeenth century, England had emerged as a postfeudal society, and was freer than ever before because it held fast to its constitutional politics at the same time that it discarded its social past.

England was the freest country on the face of the earth, Holland the second freest. Both nations were commercial republics, Holland explicitly so, whereas England is a "republic hiding under the form of a monarchy." Although he admired civic virtue, Montesquieu feared the suppression of private life in the ancient republics. His was a modern notion of freedom that would be safeguarded by the checks and balances, the separation of powers, he spelled out in the famous Book XI, Chapter 6, of *The Spirit of the Laws*.

Montesquieu was, in short, a champion of what today is known as liberalism. All his writings were devoted to combating prejudice, inhumanity, and arbitrary government. His message was one of tolerance, acceptance of diversity, and moderation. "Political liberty is found only in moderate governments. . . . Who dares say it? Virtue itself has need of limits." Mutual forebearance, not religious or ideological righteousness, is what makes for a socio-political order in which common human decency is indeed common.

Robert Shackleton's *Montesquieu* (Oxford: Oxford University Press, 1961) is the standard biography. Jean Starobinski, *Montesquieu par lui-même* (Paris: Seuil, 1953), offers autobiographical jottings and commentary. Judith Shklar, *Montesquieu* (Oxford: Oxford University Press, 1987), is the best brief study. Mark Hulliung, *Montesquieu and the Old Regime* (Berkeley: University of California Press, 1976), provides a comprehensive interpretation.

M. H.

THE SPIRIT OF THE LAWS[1]

PREFACE

If amidst the infinite number of subjects contained in this book, there is any thing, which, contrary to my expectation, may possibly offend, I can at least assure the public, that it was not inserted with an ill intention: For I am not naturally of a captious temper. Plato thanked the Gods, that he was born in the same age with Socrates: and for my part, I give thanks to the Almighty, that I was born a subject of that government under which I live; and that it is his pleasure I should obey those, whom he has made me love.

[1]Translated by Thomas Nugent, spelling updated, footnotes omitted.

I beg one favor of my readers, which I fear will not be granted me; this is, that they will not judge by a few hours of reading, of the labour of twenty years; that they will approve or condemn the book entire, and not a few particular phrases. If they would serve into the design of the author, they can do it no other way so completely, as by searching into the design of the work.

I have first of all considered mankind; and the result of my thoughts has been, that amidst such an infinite diversity of laws and manners, they were not solely conducted by the caprice of fancy.

I have laid down the first principles, and have found that the particular cases follow naturally from them; that the histories of all nations are only consequences of them; and that every particular law is connected with another law, or depends on some other of a more general extent.

When I have been obliged to look back into antiquity, I have endeavoured to assume the spirit of the ancients, lest I should consider those things as alike, which are really different; and lest I should miss the difference of those which appear to be alike.

I have not drawn my principles from my prejudices, but from the nature of things.

Here a great many truths will not appear, till we have seen the chain which connects them with others. The more we enter into particulars, the more we shall perceive the certainty of the principles on which they are founded. I have not even given all these particulars, for who could mention them all without a most insupportable fatigue?

The reader will not here meet with any of those bold flights, which seem to characterize the works of the present age. When things are examined with ever so small a degree of extent, the sallies of imagination must vanish; these generally arise from the mind's collecting all its powers to view only one side of the subject, while it leaves the other unobserved.

I write not to censure any thing established in any country whatsoever. Every nation will here find the reasons on which its maxims are founded; and this will be the natural inference, that to propose alterations, belongs only to those who are so happy as to be born with a genius capable of penetrating into the entire constitution of a state.

It is not a matter of indifference, that the minds of the people be enlightened. The prejudices of the magistrate have arisen from national prejudice. In a time of ignorance they have committed even the greatest evils without the least scruple; but in an enlightened age they even tremble, while conferring the greatest blessings. They perceive the ancient abuses; they see how they must be reformed; but they are sensible also of the abuses of the reformation. They let the evil continue if they fear a worse; they are content with a lesser good, if they doubt of a greater. They examine into the parts, to judge of them in connection; they examine all the causes to discover their different effects.

Could I but succeed so as to afford new reasons to every man to love his prince, his country, his laws; new reasons to render him more sensible in every nation and government of the blessings he enjoys, I should think myself the most happy of mortals.

Could I but succeed so as to persuade those who command, to increase their knowledge in what they ought to prescribe; and those who obey, to find a new pleasure resulting from their obedience, I should think myself the most happy of mortals.

The most happy of mortals should I think myself, could I contribute to make mankind recover from their prejudices. By prejudices, I here mean, not that which renders men ignorant of some particular things, but whatever renders them ignorant of themselves.

It is in endeavouring to instruct mankind, that we are best able to practice that general virtue, which comprehends the love of all. Man, that flexible being, conforming in society to the thoughts and impressions of others, is equally capable of knowing his own nature, whenever it is laid open to his view; and of losing the very sense of it, when this idea is banished from his mind.

Often have I begun, and as often have I laid aside this undertaking. I have a thousand times given the leaves I have written to the winds: I every day felt my paternal hands fall. I have followed my object without any fixed plan: I have known neither rules nor exceptions; I have found the truth, only to lose it again. But when I had once discovered my first principles, every thing I sought for appeared; and in the course of twenty years, I have seen my work begun, grow up, advanced, and finished.

If this work meets with success, I shall owe it chiefly to the grandeur and majesty of the subject. However I do not think that I have been totally deficient in point of genius. When I have seen what so many great men both in France, England and Germany have said before me, I have been lost in admiration: but I have not lost my courage: I have said with Corregio, And I also am a painter.

BOOK I

Of Laws in General

CHAPTER 1

Of the Relation of Laws to Different Beings

Laws in their most general signification, are the necessary relations derived from the nature of things. In this sense all beings have their laws, the Deity has his laws, the material world its laws, the intelligences superior to man have their laws, the beasts their laws, man his laws.

Those who assert that *a blind fatality produced the various effects we behold in this world,* are guilty of a very great absurdity; for can any thing be more absurd than to pretend that a blind fatality could be productive of intelligent beings?

There is then a primitive reason; and laws are the relations which subsist between it and different beings, and the relations of these beings among themselves.

God is related to the universe as creator and preserver; the laws by which he has created all things, are those by which he preserves them. He acts according to these rules because he knows them; he knows them because he has made them; and he made them because they are relative to his wisdom and power.

As we see that the world, though formed by the motion of matter, and void of understanding, subsists notwithstanding through so long a succession of ages, its motion must certainly be directed by invariable laws: and could we imagine another world, it must also have constant rules, or must inevitably perish.

Thus the creation which seems an arbitrary act, supposes laws as invariable as those of the fatality of the Atheists. It would be absurd to say, that the Creator might govern the world without those rules, since without them it could not subsist.

These rules are a fixt and invariable relation. In bodies moved the motion is received, increased, diminished, lost, according to the relations of the quantity of matter and velocity; each diversity is *uniformity,* each change is *constancy.*

Particular intelligent beings may have laws of their own making, but they have some likewise which they never made. Before there were intelligent beings, they were possible; they had therefore possible relations, and consequently possible laws. Before laws were made, there were relations of possible justice. To say that there is nothing just or unjust but what is commanded or forbidden by positive laws, is the same thing as saying that before the describing of a circle all the radii were not equal.

We must therefore acknowledge relations of justice antecedent to the positive law by which they are established: as for instance, that if human societies existed, it would be right to conform to their laws; if there were intelligent beings that had received a benefit of another being, they ought to be grateful; if one intelligent being had created another intelligent being, the latter ought to continue in its original state of dependance; if one intelligent being injures another, it deserves a retaliation of the injury, and so on.

But the intelligent world is far from being so well governed as the physical. For though the former has also its laws which of their own nature are invariable, yet it does not conform to them so exactly as the physical world. This is because on the one hand particular intelligent beings are of a finite nature and consequently liable to error; and on the other, their nature requires them to be free agents. Hence they do not steadily conform to their primitive laws; and even those of their own instituting they frequently infringe.

Whether brutes be governed by the general laws of motion, or by a particular movement, is what we cannot determine. Be that as it will, they have not a more intimate relation to God than the rest of the material world; and sensation is of no other use to them, than in the relation they have either with other particular beings, or with themselves.

By the allurement of pleasure they preserve the being of the individual, and by the same allurement they preserve their species. They have natural laws, because they are united by sensations; positive laws they have none, because they are not connected by knowledge. And yet they do not conform invariably to their natural laws; these are better observed by vegetables, that have neither intellectual nor sensitive faculties.

Brutes are deprived of the high advantages which we have; but they have some which we have not. They have not our hopes, but they are without our fears; they are subject like us to death, but without knowing it; even most of them are more attentive than we to self-preservation, and do not make so bad a use of their passions.

Man, as a physical being, is, like other bodies, governed by invariable laws. As an intelligent being, he incessantly transgresses the laws established by God, and changes those which he himself has established. He is left to his own direction, though he is a limited being, subject like all finite intelligences, to ignorance and error; even the imperfect knowledge he has, he loses as a sensible creature, and is hurried away by a thousand impetuous passions. Such a being might every instant forget his Creator; God has therefore reminded him of his duty by the laws of religion. Such a being is liable every moment to forget himself; philosophy has provided against this by the laws of morality. Formed to live in society, he might forget his fellow creatures; legislators have therefore by political and civil laws confined him to his duty.

CHAPTER 2

Of the Laws of Nature

Antecedent to all these laws are those of nature, so called because they derive their force entirely from our frame and being. In order to have a perfect knowledge of these laws, we must consider man before the establishment of society: the laws received in such a state would be those of nature.

The law which imprinting in our minds the idea of a Creator inclines us to him, is the first in importance, though not in order, of natural laws. Man in a state of nature would have the faculty of knowing, before he had any acquired knowledge. Plain it is that his first ideas would be far from being of a speculative nature; he would think of the preservation of his being, before he would investigate its origin. Such a man would feel nothing in himself at first but impotency and weakness; his fears and apprehensions would be excessive; as appears from instances (were there any necessity of proving it) of savages found in forests, trembling at the motion of a leaf, and flying from every shadow.

In this state every man would fancy himself inferior, instead of being sensible of his equality. No danger would there be therefore of their attacking one another; peace would be the first law of nature.

The natural impulse or desire which Hobbes attributes to mankind of subduing one another, is far from being well founded. The idea of empire and dominion is so complex, and depends on so many other notions, that it could never be the first that would occur to human understandings.

Hobbes inquires, *For what reason do men go armed, and have locks and keys to fasten their doors, if they be not naturally in a state of war?* But is it not obvious that he attributes to man before the establishment of society, what cannot happen but in consequence of this establishment, which furnishes them with motives for hostile attacks and self-defence.

Next to a sense of his weakness man would soon find himself sensible of his wants. Hence another law of nature would prompt him to seek for nourishment.

Fear, I have observed, would incline men to shun one another; but the marks of this fear being reciprocal would soon induce them to associate. Besides, this association would quickly follow from the very pleasure one animal feels at the approach of another of the same species. Again, the attraction arising from the difference of sexes would enhance this pleasure, and the natural inclination they have for each other, would form a third law.

Beside the sense or instinct which man has in common with brutes, he has the advantage of attaining to acquired knowledge; and thereby has a second tie which brutes have not. Mankind have therefore a new motive of uniting, and a fourth law of nature arises from the desire of living in society.

CHAPTER 3

Of Positive Laws

As soon as mankind enter into a state of society, they lose the sense of their weakness, the equality ceases, and then commences the state of war.

Each particular society begins to feel its strength, whence arises a state of war betwixt different nations. The individuals likewise of each society become sensible of their strength; hence the principal advantages of this society they endeavour to convert to their own emolument, which constitutes between them a state of war.

These two different kinds of military states give rise to human laws. Considered as inhabitants of so great a planet which necessarily implies a variety of nations, they have laws relative to their mutual intercourse, which is what we call the *law of nations*. Considered as members of a society that must be properly supported, they have laws relative to the governors and the governed; and this we call *politic law*. They have also another sort of laws relating to the mutual communication of citizens among themselves; by which is understood the *civil law*.

The law of nations is naturally founded on this principle, that different nations ought in time of peace to do one another all the good they can, and in time of war as little harm as possible, without prejudicing their real interests.

The object of war is victory; victory aims at conquest; conquest at preservation. From this and the preceding principle all those laws are derived which constitute the *law of nations*.

All countries have a law of nations, not excepting the Iroquois themselves, though they devour their prisoners: for they send and receive ambassadors, and understand the rights of war and peace. The mischief is that this law of nations is not founded on true principles.

Besides the law of nations relating to all societies, there is a *politic law* for each particularly considered. No society can subsist without a form of government. *The conjunction of the particular forces of individuals,* as Gravina well observes, *constitutes what we call a political state.*

The general force may be in the hands of a single person, or of many. Some have thought that nature having established paternal authority, the government of a single person was most conformable to nature. But the example of paternal authority proves nothing. For if the power of a father is relative to a single government, that of brothers after the death of a father, or that of cousin-germans after the decease of brothers, are relative to a government of many. The political power necessarily comprehends the union of several families.

Better is it to say that the government most conformable to nature, is that whose particular disposition best agrees with the humour and disposition of the people in whose favour it is established.

The particular force of individuals cannot be united without a conjunction of all their wills. *The conjunction of those wills,* as Gravina again very justly observes, *is what we call the CIVIL STATE.*

Law in general is human reason, inasmuch as it governs all the inhabitants of the earth; the political and civil laws of each nation ought to be only the particular cases in which this human reason is applied.

They should be adapted in such a manner to the people for whom they are made, as to render it very unlikely for those of one nation to be proper for another.

They should be relative to the nature and principle of the actual, or intended government; whether they form this principle, as in the case of political laws, or whether they support it, as may be said of civil institutions.

They should be relative to the climate, whether hot or cold, of each country, to the quality of the soil, to its situation and bigness, to the manner of living of the natives, whether husbandmen, huntsmen, or shepherds; they should have a relation to the degree of liberty which the constitution will bear; to the religion of the inhabitants, to their inclinations, riches, number, commerce, manners, and customs. In fine they have relations amongst themselves, as also with their origin, with the object of the legislator, and with the order of things on which they are established, in all which different lights they ought to be considered.

This is what I have undertaken to perform in the following work. These relations I shall examine, which form all together what we call the *Spirit of Laws*.

I have not separated the political from the civil laws; for as I do not pretend to treat of laws, but of their spirit, and as this spirit consists in the various relations which the laws may have with different things, it is not so much my business to follow the natural order of laws, as that of these relations and things.

I shall first examine the relation which laws have with the nature and principle of each government; and as this principle has a strong influence on laws, I shall make it my business to understand it thoroughly; and if I can but once establish it, the laws will soon appear to flow from thence as from their source. I shall proceed afterwards to other more particular relations.

BOOK II

CHAPTER 1

Of the Nature of the Three Different Governments

There are three species of government; *republic, monarchical,* and *despotic.* In order to discover their nature, it is sufficient to recollect the common notion, which supposes three definitions or rather three facts, that the *republican government is that in which the body or only a part of the people is possessed of the supreme power: monarchy that in which a single person governs but by fixed established laws: a despotic government, that in which a single person directs every thing by his own will and caprice.*

This is what I call the nature of each government; we must examine now which are those laws that follow this nature directly, and consequently are the first fundamental laws.

CHAPTER 2

Of the Republican Government, and the Laws Relative to Democracy

When the body of the people in a republic are possessed of the supreme power, this is called a *democracy.*

In a democracy the people are in some respects the sovereign, and in others the subject.

There can be no sovereign but by suffrage, which are their own will; and the sovereign's will is the sovereign himself. The laws therefore which establish the right of suffrage, are fundamental to this government. In fact, it is as important to regulate in a republic, in what manner, by whom, to whom, and concerning what, suffrages are to be given, as it is in a monarchy to know who is the prince and after what manner he ought to govern. . . .

It is an essential point to fix the number of citizens that are to form the public assemblies; otherwise it might be uncertain whether the whole body or only a part of the people have voted. At Sparta the number was fixed to ten thousand. But at Rome, that had sometimes all its inhabitants without its walls, and sometimes all Italy and a great part of the world within them; at Rome, I say, this number was never fixed, which was one of the principal causes of its ruin.

The people in whom the supreme power resides, ought to do of themselves whatever conveniently they can; and what they cannot well do, they must commit to the management of ministers.

The ministers are not properly theirs, unless they have the nomination of them; it is therefore a fundamental maxim in this government, that the people should choose their ministers, that is, their magistrates.

They have occasion as well as monarchs, and even more than they, to be directed by a council or senate. But to have a proper confidence in them, they should have the choosing of the members; whether the election be made by themselves, as at Athens; or by some magistrate deputed for the purpose, as was customary at Rome on certain occasions.

The people are extremely well qualified for choosing those whom they are to entrust with part of their authority. They can tell when a person has been often in battle, and has had particular success; they are therefore very capable of electing a general. They can tell when a judge is assiduous in his office, when he gives general satisfaction, and has never been charged with bribery. These are all facts of which they can have better information in a public forum, than a monarch in his palace. But are they able to manage an affair, to find out and make a proper use of places, occasions, moments? No, this is beyond their capacity. . . .

The public business must however be carried on, with a certain motion neither too quick nor too slow. But the action of the common people is always either too remiss or too violent. Sometimes with a hundred thousand arms they overturn all before them; and sometimes with a hundred thousand feet they creep like insects.

In a popular state the inhabitants are divided into certain classes. It is in the manner of making this division that great legislators have signalized themselves; and it is on this the duration and prosperity of democracy have always depended.

Servius Tullius followed the spirit of aristocracy in the distribution of his classes. We find in Livy and in Dionysius Halicarnassus, in what manner he lodged the right of suffrage in the hands of the principal citizens. He had divided the people of Rome into a hundred and ninety three centuries, which formed six classes; and ranking the rich, who were in smaller numbers, in the first centuries; and those in middling circumstances, who were more numerous, in the following centuries; he flung the indigent multitude into the last; and as each century had but one vote, it was property rather than numbers that decided the elections.

Solon divided the people of Athens into four classes. In this he was directed by the spirit of democracy, his intention not being to fix those who were to choose, but those who were capable of being chosen; wherefore leaving to each citizen the right of election, he made the judges eligible from each of those four classes; but the magistrates he ordered to be chosen only out of the first three, which consisted of citizens of easy fortunes.

As the division of those who have a right of suffrage is a fundamental law in a republic, so the manner also of giving this suffrage is another fundamental law.

The suffrage by *lot* is natural to democracy; as that by *choice* is to aristocracy.

The suffrage by *lot* is a method of electing that offends no one; it lets each citizen entertain reasonable hopes of serving his country.

But as this method is naturally defective, it has been the glorious endeavour of the most eminent legislators to regulate and amend it.

Solon made a law at Athens that military employments should be conferred by choice, but that senators and judges should be elected by lot.

The same legislator ordained, that civil magistracies, attended with great expense, should be given by choice; and the others by lot.

But in order to amend the suffrage by lot, he made a rule that none but those who presented themselves should be elected; that the person elected should be examined by judges, and that every one should have a right to accuse him if he were unworthy of the office: this participated at the same time of the suffrage by lot, and of that by choice. When the time of their magistracy was expired, they were obliged to submit to another judgment in regard to the manner they had behaved. People who were utterly unqualified, must by this means have been extremely backward in giving in their names to be drawn by lot.

The law which determines the manner of giving the suffrages is likewise fundamental in a democracy. It is a question of some importance, whether the suffrages ought to be public or secret. Cicero observes, that the laws which rendered them secret towards the close of the republic, were the cause of its decline. But as this is differently practiced in different republics, I shall offer here my thoughts concerning this subject.

The people's suffrages ought doubtless to be public; and this should be considered as a fundamental law of democracy. The lower sort of people ought to be directed by those of higher rank, and restrained within bounds by the gravity of certain personages. Hence by rendering the suffrages secret in the Roman republic all was lost; it was no longer possible to direct a populace that sought its own destruction.

Intriguing in a senate is dangerous; dangerous it is also in a body of nobles; but not so in the people whose nature it is to act through passion. In countries where they have no share in the government, we often see them as much inflamed on the account of an actor, as they could possibly have been for state affairs. The misfortune of a republic is, when there are no more intrigues; and this happens when the people are corrupted by dint of money: in which case they grow indifferent to public concerns, and passionately desirous of lucre. Careless of the government, and of every thing belonging to it, they quietly wait for their salary.

It is likewise a fundamental law in democracies, that the people should have the sole power to enact laws. And yet there are a thousand occasions on which it is necessary the senate should have a power of decreeing; nay it is frequently proper to make some trial of a law before it is established. The constitutions of Rome and Athens were extremely wise. The decrees of the senate had the force of laws for the space of a year, and did not become perpetual till they were ratified by the consent of the people.

CHAPTER 4

Of the Relation of Laws to the Nature of Monarchial Government

The intermediate, subordinate and dependent powers, constitute the nature of monarchical government, that is, of that in which a single person governs by fundamental laws. I said, *intermediate, subordinate* and *dependent powers*. In fact, in monarchies the prince is the source of all power political and civil. These fundamental laws necessarily suppose the intermediate channels through which the power flows: for if there be only the momentary and capricious will of a single person to govern the state, nothing can be fixed, and, of course there can be no fundamental law.

The most natural, intermediate and subordinate power is that of the nobility. This in some measure seems to be essential to a monarchy, whose fundamental maxim is, *no monarch, no nobility; no nobility, no monarch;* but there may be a despotic prince.

There are men who have endeavoured in some countries in Europe to abolish all the jurisdiction of the nobility; not perceiving that they were driving at the very thing that was done by the parliament of *England.* Abolish the privileges of the lords, of the clergy, and of the cities in a monarchy, and you will soon have a popular state, or else an arbitrary government.

The courts of a considerable kingdom in Europe have been striking for many ages at the patrimonial jurisdiction of the lords and clergy. We do not pretend to censure these sage magistrates; but we leave it to the public to judge, how far this may alter the constitution.

Far am I from being prejudiced in favour of the privileges of the clergy; however, I should be glad their jurisdiction were once fixed. The question is not whether their jurisdiction was justly established; but whether it be really established; whether it constitutes a part of the laws of the country, and is in every respect relative to those laws; whether between two powers acknowledged independent, the conditions ought not to be reciprocal; and whether it be not the same thing with respect to a good subject, to defend the prerogative of the prince, or the limits which from time immemorial he has prescribed to his authority.

Though the ecclesiastic power is so dangerous in a republic, yet it is extremely proper in a monarchy, especially of the absolute kind. What would become of *Spain* and *Portugal* since the subversion of their laws, were it not for this only barrier against the torrent of arbitrary power? A barrier that is always useful when there is no other: for as a despotic government is productive of the most frightful calamities to human nature, the very evil that restrains it, is beneficial to the subject.

As the ocean which seems to threaten to overflow the whole earth, is stopped by weeds and by little pebbles that lie scattered along the shore; so monarchs whose power seems unbounded, are restrained by the smallest obstacles, and suffer their natural pride to be subdued by supplication and prayer. . . .

It is not enough to have intermediate powers in a monarchy; there must be also a depositary of the laws. This depositary can be only the political bodies, who promulge the new laws, and revive the obsolete. The natural ignorance of the nobility, their indolence, and contempt of civil government, require there should be a body invested with a power of reviving and executing the laws which would be otherwise buried in oblivion. The prince's council are not a proper depositary. They are naturally the depositaries of the momentary will of the prince, and not of the fundamental laws. Besides the prince's council continually changes; it is neither permanent, nor numerous; neither has it a sufficient share of the confidence of the people; consequently it is incapable to set them right in difficult conjunctures, or to reduce them to proper obedience.

Despotic governments, where there are no fundamental laws, have no such kind of depositary. Hence it is that religion has generally so much influence in those countries, because it forms a kind of permanent depositary; and if this cannot be said of religion, it may of the customs that are respected instead of laws.

CHAPTER 5

Of the Laws Relative to the Nature of a Despotic Government

From the nature of a despotic power it follows that the single person invested with this power, commits the execution of it also to a single person. A man who his senses continually inform, that he himself is every thing, and his subjects nothing, is naturally lazy, voluptuous, and ignorant. In consequence of this, he neglects the management of public affairs. But were he to commit the administration to many, there would be continual disputes between them; they would form intrigues to be his first slave; and the prince would be obliged to take the reins into his own hands. It is therefore more natural for him to resign it to a vizier, and to invest him with the same power as himself. The creation of a vizier is a fundamental law of this government.

It is related of a pope, that he had raised an infinite number of difficulties to prevent his election, from a thorough conviction of his incapacity. At length he was prevailed on to accept of the pontificate; and resigned the administration entirely to his nephew. He was soon struck with surprise, and said, *I should never have thought that these things were so easy.* The same may be said of the princes of the East. When from the prison, where eunuchs have enervated both their hearts and understanding, and where they frequently conceal from them their very condition, they are drawn forth in order to be raised to the throne; they are at first amazed: but as soon as they have got a vizier, and have abandoned themselves in their seraglio to the most brutal passions, pursuing, in the middle of a prostituted court, the most capricious extravagancies, they could never have dreamt to find matters so easy.

The greater the extent of an empire, the greater is the seraglio; and consequently so much the more is the prince intoxicted with pleasure. Hence the more nations such a prince has to govern, the less he attends to the government; the greater his affairs, the less he makes them the subject of his deliberations.

BOOK III

CHAPTER 1

Difference Between the Nature and Principle of Government

After having examined the laws relative to the nature of each government, we must investigate those that relate to its principle.

There is this difference between the nature and principle of government, that its nature is that by which it is constituted, and its principle that by which it is made to act. One is its particular structure, and the other the human passions which set it in motion.

Now laws ought to be no less relative to the principle than to the nature of each government. We must therefore inquire into this principle, which shall be the subject of this third book.

CHAPTER 2

Of the Principle of Different Governments

I have already observed that it is the nature of a republican government, that either the collective body of the people, or particular families should be possessed of the sovereign power: of a monarchy, that the prince should have this sovereign power, but in the execution of it should be directed by established laws: of a despotic government, that a single person should rule according to his own will and caprice. No more do I want to enable me to discover their three principles; these are from thence most naturally derived. I shall begin with a republican government, and in particular with that of democracy.

CHAPTER 3

Of the Principle of Democracy

There is no great share of probity necessary to support a monarchical or despotic government. The force of laws in one, and the prince's arm in the other, are sufficient to direct and maintain the whole. But in a popular state, one spring more is necessary, namely *virtue*.

What I have here advanced, is confirmed by the unanimous testimony of historians, and is extremely agreeable to the nature of things. For it is clear that in a monarchy, where he who commands the execution of the laws generally thinks himself above them, there is less need of virtue than in a popular government, where the person entrusted with the execution of the laws, is sensible of his being subject to their direction, and that he must submit to their authority.

Clear it is also that a monarch, who through bad council or indolence ceases to enforce the execution of the laws, may easily repair the evil; he has only to change his council; or to shake off this indolence. But when in a popular government, there is a suspension of the laws, as this can proceed only from the corruption of the republic, the state is certainly undone.

A very droll spectacle it was in the last century to behold the impotent efforts the English made for the establishment of democracy. As those who had a share in the direction of public affairs were void of all virtue, as their ambition was inflamed by the success of the most daring of their members, as the spirit of a faction was suppressed only by that of a succeeding faction, the government was continually changing; the people amazed at so many revolutions fought everywhere for a democracy without being able to find it. At length after a series of tumultuary motions and violent shocks, they were obliged to have recourse to the very government they had so odiously proscribed. . . .

When virtue is banished, ambition invades the hearts of those who are capable of receiving it, and avarice possesses the whole community. Desires then change their objects; what they were fond of before, becomes now indifferent; they were free with laws, and they want to be free without them; every citizen is like a slave who has escaped from his master's house; what was maxim is called rigor; to rule they give the name of constraint; and of fear to attention. Frugality then, and not the thirst of gain, passes for avarice.

Athens was possessed of the same number of forces, when she triumphed with so much glory, and when with so much infamy she was enslaved. When Philip attempted to reign in Greece, and appeared at the gates of Athens, she had even then lost nothing but time. We may see in Demosthenes how difficult it was to awake her; she dreaded Philip not as an enemy of her liberty, but of her pleasures.

CHAPTER 5

That Virtue is Not the Principle
of Monarchical Government

In monarchies, policy makes people do great things with as little virtue as she can. Thus in the finest machines, art has contrived as few movements, springs, and wheels as possible.

The state subsists independent of the love of our country, of the thirst of true glory, of self-denial, of the sacrifice of our dearest interests, and of all those heroic virtues which we admire in the ancients, and which to us are known only by story.

The laws supply here the place of those virtues; they are by no means wanted, and the state dispenses with them: an action performed here in secret is in some measure of no consequence.

Though all crimes be of their own nature public, yet there is a distinction between crimes that are really public, and those that are private, which are so called, because they are more injurious to individuals than to the whole society.

Now in republics private crimes are more public, that is, they attack the constitution more than they do individuals; and in monarchies public crimes are more private, that is, they are more prejudicial to private people than to the constitution.

I beg that no one will take what I have said amiss; my observations are founded on the unanimous testimony of historians. I am not ignorant that virtuous princes are no such very rare sight; but I venture to affirm that in a monarchy it is extremely difficult for the people to be virtuous.

Let us compare what the historians of all ages have said concerning the courts of monarchs; let us recollect the conversations and sentiments of people of all countries in respect to the abandoned character of courtiers; and we shall find, that these are not mere airy speculations, but things confirmed by a sad and melancholy experience.

Ambition with idleness, baseness with pride, the thirst of riches without labour, aversion to truth; flattery, treason, perfidy, violation of engagements, contempt of civil duties, fear of the prince's virtue, hope from his weakness, but above all, the perpetual ridicule of virtue; are, I think, the characteristic by which the courtiers of all ages and countries have been constantly distinguished. Now it is exceeding difficult for the leading men of the nation to be knaves and for the inferior sort of people to be honest; for the former to be cheats, and for the latter to consent to be duped.

But if there should chance to be some unlucky honest man among the people, Cardinal Richelieu in his political testament seems to hint that a prince should take care not to employ him. So true is it that virtue is not the spring of this government!

CHAPTER 6

In What Manner Virtue is Supplied in a Monarchical Government

But it is high time for me to have done with this subject, lest I should be suspected of writing a satire against monarchical government. Far be it from me; if monarchy wants one spring, it is provided with another. Honor, that is, the prepossessions of every person and every rank, supplies the place of virtue, and is everywhere her representative: here it is capable of inspiring the most glorious actions; and joined with the force of laws it may lead us to the end of government as well as virtue itself.

Hence in well policied monarchies, they are almost all good subjects, and very few honest men; for to be an honest man, an honest intention is necessary.

CHAPTER 7

Of the Principle of Monarchy

A monarchical government supposes, as we have already observed, preeminences, ranks, and likewise a noble descent. Now as it is the nature of honor to aspire to preferments and distinguishing titles, it is therefore properly placed in this government.

Ambition is pernicious in a republic. But in a monarchy it has some good effects; it gives life to the government, and is attended with this advantage, that it is no way dangerous, because it may be continually checked.

It is with this kind of government as with the system of the universe, in which there is a power that constantly repels all bodies from the center, and a power of gravitation that attracts them to it. Honor sets all the parts of the body politic in motion; by its very action it connects them, and thus each individual advances the public good, while he only thinks of promoting his own particular interest.

True it is, that, philosophically speaking, it is a false honor which moves all the parts of the government; but even this false honor is as useful to the public, as true honor could possibly prove to private people.

Is it not a very great point, to oblige men to perform the most difficult actions, such as require a great degree of fortitude and spirit, without any other recompense, than the fame and reputation arising from the actions themselves?

CHAPTER 8

That Honor is Not the Principle of Despotic Governments

Honor is far from being the principle of despotic governments; men being here all upon a level, no one can prefer himself to another; men being here all slaves, they can give themselves no preference at all.

Besides, as honor has its laws and rules, as it knows not how to submit, as it depends in great measure on a man's own caprice, and not on that of another person; it can be found only in countries in which the constitution is fixed, and where they are governed by settled laws.

How can a despotic prince bear with any such thing as honor? Honor glories in contempt of life, and here the prince's whole strength consists in the power of taking it away. How can honor ever bear with a despotic prince? It has its fixed rules, and constant caprices; but a despotic prince is directed by no rule, and his own caprices destroy all others.

Honor therefore, a thing unknown in despotic governments, where very often they have not so much as a fit word to express it, is the prevailing principle in monarchies; here it gives life to the whole body politic, to the laws, and even to the virtues themselves.

CHAPTER 9

Of the Principle of Despotic Government

As virtue is necessary in a republic, and in a monarchy honor, so fear is necessary in a despotic government: with regard to virtue, there is no occasion for it at all, and honor would be extremely dangerous.

Here the immense power of the prince is devolved entirely upon those to whom he is pleased to entrust it. Persons capable of setting a value upon themselves would be likely to create revolutions. Fear must therefore depress all their spirits, and extinguish even the least sense of ambition.

A moderate government may, whenever it pleases, and without any danger, relax its springs. It supports itself by its laws, and by its own force. But when a despotic prince ceases one single moment to lift up his arm, when he cannot instantly demolish those whom he has entrusted with the first posts and employments, all is over; for as fear, the spring of this government, no longer subsists, the people are left without a protector.

CHAPTER 10

Difference on Obedience in Moderate and Despotic Governments

In despotic states that nature of the government requires the most passive obedience; and when once the prince's will is made known, it ought infallibly to produce its effect.

Here they have no limitations or restrictions, no mediums, terms, equivalents, parleys, or remonstrances; nothing equal or better to propose; man is a creature that submits to the absolute will of a creature like himself.

In a country like this they are no more allowed to represent their fears in respect to a future event, than to excuse their bad success by the capriciousness of fortune. Man's portion here, like that of beasts, is instinct, compliance and punishment.

Little does it then avail to plead the sentiments of nature, respect for a father, tenderness for a wife and children, the laws of honor, or an ill state of health; the orders are given, and that is sufficient.

In Persia when the king has condemned a person, it is no longer lawful to mention his name, or to intercede in his favor. Though he were drunk and beside himself, yet the decree must be executed; otherwise he would contradict himself, and the law admits of no contradiction. This has been the way of thinking in this country in all ages.

There is one thing however that may be opposed to the prince's will; namely religion. They will abandon a parent, nay they will kill him, if the prince so commands; but he cannot oblige them to drink wine. The laws of religion are of a superior nature, because they bind the prince as well as the subject. But, with respect to the law of nature it is otherwise; the prince is no longer supposed to be a man.

CHAPTER 11

Reflections on the Foregoing

Such are the principles of the three sorts of government: which does not imply that in a particular republic they actually are, but that they ought to be, virtuous: nor does it prove, that in a particular monarchy they are actuated by honor, or in a particular despotic government by fear; but that they ought to be directed by these principles, otherwise the government is imperfect.

BOOK IV

CHAPTER 1

Of the Laws of Education

The laws of education are the first impressions we receive; and as they prepare us for civil life, each particular family ought to be governed pursuant to the plan of the great family which comprehends them all.

If the people in general have a principle, their constituent parts, that is, the several families, will have one also. The laws of education will be therefore different in each species of government; in monarchies they will have honor for their object, in republics virtue, in despotic governments fear.

CHAPTER 2

Of Education in Monarchies

It is not from colleges or academies that the principal branch of education in monarchies is derived; it is when we set out in the world that our education in some measure commences. This is the school of what we call honor, that universal preceptor which ought everywhere to be our guide.

There it is that we constantly see and hear three things, *that we should have a certain nobleness in our virtues, a kind of frankness in our morals, and a particular politeness in our behaviour.*

The virtues we are there taught, are less what we owe to others, than to ourselves; they are not so much what assimilates us to, as what distinguishes us from, our fellow citizens.

There the actions of men are not judged as good, but as beautiful; not as just, but as great; not as reasonable, but as extraordinary. . . .

In fine, the education of monarchies requires a certain politeness of behaviour. Men born for society, are born to please one another; and a person that would break through the rules of decorum, by shocking those he conversed with, would so far lose the public esteem as to become incapable of doing any good.

But politeness, generally speaking, does not derive its original from so pure a source. It arises from a desire of distinguishing our selves. It is pride that renders us polite: we feel a pleasing vanity in being remarked for a behaviour that shows in some measure we are not meanly born, and that we have not been bred up with those who in all ages have been considered as the scum of the people. . . .

There is nothing so strongly inculcated in monarchies, by the laws, by religion, and honor, as submission to the prince's will; but this very honor tells us that the prince ought never to command a dishonourable action, because this would render us incapable to serve him. . . .

There is nothing that honor more strongly recommends to the nobility, than to serve their prince in a military capacity. In fact this is their favourite profession, because its dangers, its success, and even its miscarriages are the road to grandeur. . . .

Honor therefore has its supreme laws, to which education is obliged to conform. The chief of these are, that we are allowed to set a value upon our fortune, but it is absolutely forbidden to set any value upon our lives.

The second is, that when we are raised to a post or rank, we should never do or permit any thing which may seem to imply that we look upon ourselves as inferior to the rank we hold.

The third is, that those things which honor forbids are more rigorously forbidden, when the laws do not concur in the prohibition; and those it commands are more strongly insisted upon, when they happen not to be commanded by law.

CHAPTER 3

Of Education in a Despotic Government

As education in monarchies tends only to raise and ennoble the mind, so in despotic governments its only aim is to debase it.

Excessive obedience supposes ignorance in the person that obeys, the same it supposes in him that commands; for he has no occasion to deliberate, to doubt, to reason; he has only to will.

In despotic states each house is a separate government. As education therefore consists chiefly in social converse, it must be here very much limited; all it does is to strike the heart with fear, and to imprint in the understanding a very simple notion of a few principles of religion. Learning here proves dangerous, emulation fatal; and as to virtue, Aristotle cannot think there is any one virtue belonging to slaves; if so, education in despotic countries is confined within a very narrow compass.

Here therefore education is in some measure needless; to give something one must take away every thing; and begin with making a bad subject in order to make a good slave.

For why should education take pains in forming a good citizen, only to make him share in the public misery? If he loved his country, he would strive to relax the springs of government; if he miscarried, he would be undone; if he succeeded, he would expose himself, the prince, and his country to ruin.

CHAPTER 5

Of Education in a Republican Government

It is in a republican government that the whole power of education is required. The fear of despotic governments rises naturally of itself amidst threats and punishments; the honor of monarchies is favoured by the passions, and favours them in its turn: but virtue is a self-renunciation which is always arduous and painful.

This virtue may be defined, as the love of the laws and of our country. As this love requires a constant preference of public to private interest, it is the source of all the particular virtues; for they are nothing more than this very preference itself.

This love is peculiar to democracies. In these alone the government is entrusted to private citizens. Now government is like every thing else: to preserve it, we must love it.

Has it ever been heard that kings were not fond of monarchy, or that despotic princes hated arbitrary power?

Every thing therefore depends on establishing this love in a republic, and to inspire it ought to be the principal business of education: but the surest way of instilling it into children, is for parents to set them an example.

People have it generally in their power to communicate their knowledge to their children; but they are still better able to transfuse their passions.

If this happens not to be the case, it is because the impressions made at home are effaced by those they have received abroad.

It is not the young people that degenerate: they are not spoilt till those of maturer age are already sunk in corruption.

BOOK VIII

CHAPTER 1

General Idea of this Book

The corruption of each government generally begins with that of the principles.

CHAPTER 2

Of the Corruption of the Principle of Democracy

The principle of democracy is corrupted, not only when the spirit of equality is extinct, but likewise when they fall into a spirit of extreme equality, and when every citizen wants to be upon a level with those he has chosen to command him. Then the people, incapable of bearing the very power they have entrusted, want to do every thing of themselves, to debate for the senate, to execute for the magistrates, and to strip the judges.

When this is the case, virtue can no longer subsist in the republic. The people want to exercise the functions of the magistrates; who cease to be revered. The deliberations of the senate are slighted; all respect is then laid aside for the senators, and consequently for old age. If respect ceases for old age, it will cease also for parents; deference to husbands will be likewise thrown off, and submission to masters. This licentiousness will soon captivate the mind; and the restraint of command be as fatiguing as that of obedience. Wives, children, slaves, will shake off all subjection. No longer will there be any such thing as manners, order, or virtue. . . .

Democracy hath therefore two excesses to avoid, the spirit of inequality which leads to aristocracy or monarchy; and the spirit of extreme equality, which leads to despotic power, as the latter is completed by conquest.

CHAPTER 3

Of the Spirit of Extreme Equality

As distant as heaven is from earth, so is the true spirit of equality from that of extreme equality. The former does not consist in managing so that every body should command, or that no one should be commanded; but in obeying and commanding our equals. It endeavours not to be without a master, but that its masters should be none but its equals.

In the state of nature indeed, all men are born equal; but they cannot continue in this equality. Society makes them lose it, and they recover it only by means of the laws.

Such is the difference between a well and an ill policied democracy, that in the former men are equal only as citizens, but in the latter they are equal also as magistrates, senators, judges, fathers, husbands, masters.

The natural place of virtue is near to liberty; but it is not nearer to extreme liberty than to servitude.

CHAPTER 4

Particular Cause of the Corruption of the People

Great success, especially when chiefly owing to the people, swells them so high with pride, that it is impossible to manage them. Jealous of their magistrates they soon become jealous likewise of the magistracy; enemies to those that govern, enemies they soon prove to the constitution. Thus it was the victory of Salamine over the Persians that corrupted the republic of Athens; and thus the defeat of the Athenians ruined the republic of Syracuse.

CHAPTER 6

Of the Corruption of the Principle of Monarchy

As democracies are destroyed when the people despoil the senate, magistrates and judges of their functions; so monarchies are corrupted when the prince insensibly deprives societies of their prerogatives, or cities of their privileges. In the first case the multitude usurp a despotic power; in the second it is usurped by a single person. . . .

Monarchy is destroyed, when a prince thinks he shows a greater exertion of power in changing than in conforming to the order of things; when he deprives some of his subjects of their hereditary employments to bestow them arbitrarily upon others, and when he is fonder of being guided by his fancy than by his judgment.

Monarchy is destroyed when the prince directing every thing entirely to himself, calls that state to his capital, the capital to his court, and the court to his own person.

Monarchy is destroyed in fine, when the prince mistakes his authority, his situation, and the love of his people; and when he is not fully persuaded that a monarch ought to think himself secure, as a despotic prince ought to think himself in danger.

CHAPTER 7

The Same Subject Continued

The principle of monarchy is corrupted, when the first dignities are marks of the first servitude, when the great men are stripped of popular respect, and rendered the low tools of arbitrary power.

It is still more corrupted, when honor is set up in contradiction to honors, and when men are capable of being loaded at the very same time with infamy and dignities.

It is corrupted when the prince changes his justice into severity; when he puts like the Roman emperors a Medusa's head on his breast; and when he assumes that menacing and terrible air which Commodus ordered to be given to his statues.

Again it is corrupted, when mean and abject souls grow vain of the pomp attending their servitude; and imagine that the motive which induces them to be entirely devoted to their prince, exempts them from all duty to their country.

But if it be true, (and indeed the experience of all ages has shown it) that in proportion as the power of the monarch becomes boundless and immense, his security diminishes; is the corrupting this power, is the altering its very nature, a less crime than that of high treason against the prince?

CHAPTER 8

Danger of the Corruption of the Principle of Monarchical Government

The danger is not when the state passes from one moderate to another moderate government, as from a republic to a monarchy, or from a monarchy to a republic; but when it precipitates from a moderate to a despotic government.

Most of the European nations are still governed by principles of morality. But if through a long abuse of power, or through hurry of conquest, despotic sway should prevail to a certain degree; neither morals nor climate would be able to withstand its baleful influence: and then human nature would be exposed, for some time at least, even in this beautiful part of the world, to the insults with which she has been abused in the other three.

CHAPTER 10

Of the Corruption of the Principles of Despotic Government

The principle of despotic government is subject to a continual corruption, because it is in its very nature corrupt. Other governments are destroyed by particular accidents which do violence to the principles of each constitution; this is ruined by its own intrinsic imperfection, when no accidental causes impede or corrupt the principles on which it is founded. It maintains itself therefore only when circumstances drawn from the climate, religion, situation, or genius of the people, oblige it to follow some order, and to admit of some rule. By these things its nature is forced without being changed; its ferocity remains; and it is made tame and tractable only for a time.

CHAPTER 11

Natural Effects of the Goodness and Corruption of the Principles

When once the principles of government are corrupted, the very best laws become bad and turn against the state; when the principles are sound, even bad laws have the same effect as good; the force of the principle draws everything to it.

CHAPTER 12

The Same Subject Continued

. . . When once a republic is corrupted, there is no possibility of remedying any of the rising evils but by removing the corruption and restoring its lost principles: every other correction is either useless or a new evil.

CHAPTER 15

Sure Methods of Preserving the Three Principles

I shall not be able to make myself rightly understood, till the reader has perused the four following chapters.

CHAPTER 16

Distinctive Properties of a Republic

It is natural to a republic to have only a small territory; otherwise it cannot long subsist. In a large republic there are men of large fortunes, and consequently of less moderation; there are too great deposits to entrust into the hands of a single subject; interests are divided; an ambitious person soon becomes sensible that he may be happy, great, and glorious, by oppressing his fellow citizens; and that he might raise himself to grandeur on the ruins of his country.

In a large republic the public good is sacrificed to a thousand views; it is subordinate to exceptions; and depends on accidents. In a small one, the interest of the public is easier perceived, better understood, and more within the reach of every citizen; abuses have a lesser extent, and of course are less protected.

The long duration of the republic of Sparta was owing to its having always continued with the same extent of territory after all its wars. The sole aim of Sparta was liberty; and the sole advantage of its liberty, glory.

It was the spirit of the Greek republics to be as contented with their territories, as with their laws. Athens was first fired with ambition and gave it to Lacedemon; but it was an ambition rather of commanding a free people, than of governing slaves; rather of directing than of breaking the union. All was lost upon the starting up of monarchy, a government whose spirit is more turned to increase and advancement.

Excepting particular circumstances, it is difficult for any other than a republican government to subsist long in a single town. A prince of so petty a state would naturally endeavour to oppress, because his power would be great while the means of enjoying it or of causing it to be respected, would be very inconsiderable. The consequence of this would be that he would trample upon his people. On the other hand, such a prince might be easily crushed by a foreign or even by a domestic force; the people might every instant unite and rise up against him. Now as soon as a prince of a single town is expelled, the quarrel is over; but if he has many towns, it only begins.

CHAPTER 17

Distinctive Properties of a Monarchy

A monarchical state ought to be of a moderate bigness. Were it small, it would form itself into a republic: were it very large, the nobility, possessed of great estates, far from the inspection of the prince, with a private court of their own, and secure moreover from sudden executions by the laws and manners of the country, such a nobility, I say, might throw off their allegiance, having nothing to fear from too slow and too distant a punishment.

Thus Charlemain had scarce founded his empire when he was obliged to divide it; whether the governors of the provinces refused to obey; or whether in order to keep them more under subjection there was a necessity of parcelling the empire into several kingdoms.

After the decease of Alexander his empire was divided. How was it possible for those Greek and Macedonian chiefs, who were each of them free and independent, or commanders at least of the victorious bands dispersed throughout that vast conquest, how was it possible, I say, for them to obey?

Attila's empire was dissolved soon after his death; such a number of kings, who were no longer under restraint, could not resume their fetters.

The sudden establishment of unlimited power is a remedy which in those cases may prevent a dissolution: but how dreadful the remedy, that after the enlargement of dominion, opens a new scene of misery!

The rivers hasten to mingle their waters with the sea; and monarchies lose themselves in despotic power.

CHAPTER 19

Distinctive Properties of a Despotic Government

A large empire supposes a despotic authority in the person that governs. It is necessary that the quickness of the prince's resolutions should supply the distance of the places they are sent to; that fear should prevent the carelessness of the remote governor or magistrate; that the law should be derived from a single person, and should change continually according to the accidents which incessantly multiply in a state in proportion to its bigness.

CHAPTER 20

Consequence of the Preceding Chapters

If it be therefore the natural property of small states to be governed as a republic, of middling ones to be subject to a monarch, and of large empires to be swayed by a despotic prince; the consequence is, that in order to preserve the principles of the established government, the state must be supported in the extent it has acquired, and that the spirit of this state will change in proportion as it contracts or extends its limits.

CHAPTER 21

Of the Empire of China

. . . Our missionaries take notice of the vast empire of China, as of an admirable government, that has a proper mixture of fear, honor, and virtue. Consequently I must have given an idle distinction, in establishing the principles of the three governments.

But I cannot conceive what this so much boasted honor can be among people that will not do the least thing without blows.

Again, our mercantile people are far from giving us any idea of that virtue so much talked of by the missionaries; we need only consult them in relation to the robberies and extortions of the mandarins.

Besides, Father *Parennin's* letters concerning the emperor's proceedings against some new-converted princes of the blood who had incurred his displeasure, plainly show us a continued plan of tyranny, and inhuman injuries committed by rule, that is in cool blood.

We have likewise Monsieur *de Marian's,* and the same Father *Parennin's* letters on the government of China. After some pertinent questions and answers, the whole wonder vanishes.

BOOK XI

CHAPTER 1

General Idea

I make a distinction between the laws that form political liberty with regard to the constitution, and those by which it is formed in respect to the citizen. The former shall be the subject of this book; the latter I shall examine in the next.

CHAPTER 2

Different Significations Given to the Word Liberty

There is no word whatsoever that has admitted of more various significations, and has made more different impressions on human minds, than that of Liberty. Some have taken it for a facility of deposing a person on whom they had conferred a tyrannical authority; others for the power of choosing a person whom they are obliged to obey; others for the right of bearing arms, and of being thereby enabled to use violence; others in fine for the privilege of being governed by a native of their own country or by their own laws. A certain nation, for a long time thought liberty consisted in the privilege of wearing a long beard. Some have annexed this name to one form of government, in exclusion of others: Those who had a republican taste, applied it to this government; those who liked a monarchical state, gave it to monarchies. Thus they all have applied the name of liberty to the government most conformable to their own customs and inclinations: and as in a republic people have not so constant and so present a view of the instruments of the evils they complain of, and likewise as the laws seem there to speak more, and the executors of the laws less, it is generally attributed to republics, and excluded from monarchies. In fine as in democracies the people seem to do very near whatever they please, liberty has been placed in this sort of government, and the power of the people has been confounded with their liberty.

CHAPTER 3

In What Liberty Consists

It is true that in democracies the people seem to do what they please; but political liberty does not consist in an unrestrained freedom. In governments, that is, in societies directed by laws, liberty can consist only in the power of doing what we ought to will, and in not being constrained to do what we ought not to will.

We must have continually present to our minds the difference between independence and liberty. Liberty is a right of doing whatever the laws permit; and if a citizen could do what they forbid, he would no longer be possessed of liberty, because all his fellow citizens would have the same power.

CHAPTER 4

The Same Subject Continued

Democratic and aristocratic states are not necessarily free. Political liberty is to be met with only in moderate governments: yet even in these it is not always met with. It is there only when there is no abuse of power: but constant experience shows us, that every man invested with power is apt to abuse it; he pushes on till he comes to the utmost limit. Is it not strange, though true, to say, that virtue itself has need of limits?

To prevent the abuse of power, it is necessary that by the very disposition of things power should be a check to power. A government may be so constituted, as no man shall be compelled to do things to which the law does not oblige him, nor forced to abstain from things which the law permits.

CHAPTER 5

Of the End or View of Different Governments

Though all governments have the same general end, which is that of preservation, yet each has another particular view. Increase of dominion was the view of Rome; war, of Sparta; religion, of the Jewish laws; commerce, that of Marseilles; public tranquillity, that of the laws of China; navigation, of the laws of Rhodes; natural liberty, that of the policy of the Savages; in general the pleasures of the prince, that of despotic states; that of monarchies, the prince's and the kingdom's glory; the independence of individuals is the end aimed at by the laws of Poland, and from thence results the oppression of the whole.

One nation there is also in the world, that has for the direct end of its constitution political liberty. We shall examine presently the principles on which this liberty is founded: if they are found, liberty will appear as in a mirror.

To discover political liberty in a constitution, no great labour is requisite. If we are capable of seeing it where it exists, why should we go any further in search of it?

CHAPTER 6

Of the Constitution of England

In every government there are three sorts of power: the legislative; the executive in respect to things dependent on the law of nations; and the executive, in regard to things that depend on the civil laws.

By virtue of the first, the prince or magistrate enacts temporary or perpetual laws, and amends or abrogates those that have been already enacted. By the second, he makes peace or war, sends or receives embassies, establishes the public security, and provides against invasions. By the third, he punishes crimes, or determines the disputes that arise between individuals. The latter we shall call the judiciary power, and the other simply the executive power of the state.

The political liberty of the subject is a tranquillity of mind, arising from the opinion each person has of his safety. In order to have this liberty, it is requisite the government be so constituted as one man need not be afraid of another.

When the legislative and executive powers are united in the same person, or in the same body of magistracy, there can be then no liberty; because apprehensions may arise, lest the same monarch or senate should enact tyrannical laws, to execute them in a tyrannical manner.

Again, there is no liberty, if the power of judging be not separated from the legislative and executive powers. Were it joined with the legislative, the life and liberty of the subject would be exposed to arbitrary control; for the judge would be then the legislator. Were it joined to the executive power, the judge might behave with all the violence of an oppressor.

Miserable indeed would be the case, were the same man, or the same body whether of the nobles or of the people, to exercise those three powers, that of enacting laws, that of executing the public resolutions, and that of judging the crimes or differences of individuals.

Most kingdoms of Europe enjoy a moderate government, because the prince who is invested with the two first powers, leaves the third to his subjects. In Turkey, where these three powers are united in the Sultan's person, the subjects groan under the weight of tyranny and oppression. . . .

The judiciary power ought not to be given to a standing senate; it should be exercised by persons taken from the body of the people, at certain times of the year, and pursuant to a form and manner prescribed by law, in order to erect a tribunal that should last only as long as necessity requires.

By this means the power of judging, a power so terrible to mankind, not being annexed to any particular state or profession, becomes, as it were, invisible. People have not then the judges continually present to their view; they fear the office, but not the magistrate.

In accusations of a deep or criminal nature, it is proper the person accused should have the privilege of choosing in some measure his judges in concurrence with the law; or at least he should have a right to except against so great a number, that the remaining part may be deemed his own choice.

The other two powers may be given rather to magistrates or permanent bodies, because they are not exercised on any private subject; one being no more than the general will of the state, and the other the execution of that general will.

But though the tribunals ought not to be fixed, yet the judgments ought, and to such a degree, as to be always conformable to the exact letter of the law. Were they to be the private opinion of the judge, people would then live in society without knowing exactly the obligations it lays them under.

The judges ought likewise to be in the same station as the accused, or in other words, his peers, to the end that he may not imagine he is fallen into the hands of persons inclined to treat him with rigor.

If the legislature leaves the executive power in possession of a right to imprison those subjects who can give security for their good behaviour, there is an end of liberty; unless they are taken up, in order to answer without delay to a capital crime. In this case they are really free, being subject only to the power of the law.

But should the legislature think itself in danger by some secret conspiracy against the state, or by a correspondence with a foreign enemy, it might authorise the executive power, for a short and limited time, to imprison suspected persons, who in that case would lose their liberty only for a while, to preserve it for ever. . . .

As in a free state, every man who is supposed a free agent, ought to be his own governor; so the legislative power should reside in the whole body of the people. But since this is impossible in large states, and in small ones is subject to many inconveniences; it is fit that the people should act by their representatives, what they cannot act by themselves.

The inhabitants of a particular town are much better acquainted with its wants and interests, than with those of other places; and are better judges of the capacity of their neighbours, than of that of the rest of their countrymen. The members therefore of the legislature should not be chosen from the general body of the nation; but it is proper that in every considerable place, a representative should be elected by the inhabitants.

The great advantage of representatives is their being capable of discussing affairs. For this the people collectively are extremely unfit, which is one of the greatest inconveniences of a democracy.

It is not at all necessary that the representatives who have received a general instruction from their electors, should wait to be particularly instructed on every affair, as is practised in the diets of Germany. True it is that by this way of proceeding, the speeches of the deputies might with greater propriety be called the voice of the nation: but on the other hand this would throw them into infinite delays, would give each deputy a power of controlling the assembly; and on the most urgent and pressing occasions the springs of the nation might be stopped by a single caprice.

When the deputies, as Mr. Sidney well observes, represent a body of people as in Holland, they ought to be accountable to their constituents: but it is a different thing in England, where they are deputed by boroughs.

All the inhabitants of the several districts ought to have a right of voting at the election of a representative, except such as are in so mean a situation, as to be deemed to have no will of their own.

One great fault there was in most of the ancient republics; that the people had a right to active resolutions, such as require some execution, a thing of which they are absolutely incapable. They ought to have no hand in the government but for the choosing of representatives, which is within their reach. For though few can tell the exact degree of men's capacities, yet there are none but are capable of knowing in general whether the person they choose is better qualified than most of his neighbours.

Neither ought the representative body to be chosen for active resolutions, for which it is not so fit; but for the enacting of laws, or to see whether the laws already enacted be duly executed, a thing they are very capable of, and which none indeed but themselves can properly perform.

In a state there are always persons distinguished by their birth, riches, or honors: but were they to be confounded with the common people, and to have only the weight of a single vote like the rest, the common liberty would be their slavery, and they would have no interest in supporting it, as most of the popular resolutions would be against them. The share they have therefore in the legislature ought to be proportioned to the other advantages they have in the state; which happens only when they form a body that has a right to put a stop to the enterprises of the people, as the people have a right to oppose any encroachment of theirs.

The legislative power is therefore committed to the body of the nobles, and to the body chosen to represent the people, which have each their assemblies and deliberations apart, each their separate view and interests.

Of the three powers above-mentioned the judiciary is in some measure next to nothing. There remain therefore only two; and as these have need of a regulating power to temper them, the part of the legislative body composed of the nobility, is extremely proper for this very purpose.

The body of the nobility ought to be hereditary. In the first place it is so in its own nature; and in the next there must be a considerable interest to preserve its prerogatives; prerogatives that in themselves are obnoxious to popular envy, and of course in a free state are always in danger.

But as an hereditary power might be tempted to pursue its own particular interests, and forget those of the people; it is proper that where they may reap a singular advantage from being corrupted, as in the laws relating to the supplies, they should have no other share in the legislation, than the power of refusing, and not that of enacting.

By *the power of enacting*, I mean the right of ordaining by their own authority, or of amending what has been ordained by others. By the *power of refusing*, I would be understood to mean the right of annulling a resolution taken by another; which was the power of the tribunes at Rome. And though the person possessed of the privilege of refusing may likewise have the right of approving, yet this approbation passes for no more than a declaration, that he intends to make no use of his privilege of refusing, and is derived from that very privilege.

The executive power ought to be in the hands of a monarch; because this branch of government, which has always need of expedition, is better administered by one than by many: whereas, whatever depends on the legislative power, is oftentimes better regulated by many than by a single person.

But if there was no monarch, and the executive power was committed to a certain number of persons selected from the legislative body, there would be an end then of liberty; by reason the two powers would be united, as the same persons would actually sometimes have, and would moreover be always able to have, a share in both.

Were the legislative body to be a considerable time without meeting, this would likewise put an end to liberty. For of two things one would naturally follow; either that there would be no longer any legislative resolutions, and then the state would fall into anarchy; or that these resolutions would be taken by the executive power which would render it absolute.

It would be needless for the legislative body to continue always assembled. This would be troublesome to the representatives, and moreover would cut out too much work for the executive power, so as to take off its attention from executing, and oblige it to think only of defending its own prerogatives and the right it has to execute.

Again, were the legislative body to be always assembled, it might happen to be kept up only by filling the vacant places of the deceased members with new representatives; and in that case, if the legislative body was once corrupted, the evil would be past all remedy. When different legislative bodies succeed one another, the people who have a bad opinion of that which is actually sitting, may reasonably entertain some hopes of the next: but were it to be always the same body, the people upon seeing it once corrupted, would no longer expect any good from its laws; and of course they would either become desperate or fall into a state of indolence.

The legislative body should not assemble of itself. For a body is supposed to have no will but when it is assembled; and besides were it not to assemble unanimously, it would be impossible to determine which was really the legislative body, the part assembled, or the other. And if it had a right to prorogue itself, it might happen never to be prorogued; which would be extremely dangerous in case it should ever attempt to encroach on the executive power. Besides there are seasons, some more proper than others, for assembling the legislative body: it is fit therefore that the executive power should regulate the time of convening as well as the duration of those assemblies, according to the circumstances and exigencies of state known to itself.

Were the executive power not to have a right of putting a stop to the encroachments of the legislative body, the latter would become despotic; for as it might arrogate to itself what authority it pleased, it would soon destroy all the other powers.

But it is not proper on the other hand that the legislative power should have a right to stop the executive. For as the execution has its natural limits, it is useless to confine it; besides the executive power is generally employed in momentary operations. The power therefore of the Roman tribunes was faulty, as it put a stop not only to the legislation, but likewise to the execution itself; which was attended with infinite mischiefs.

But if the legislative power in a free government has no right to stay the executive, it has a right and ought to have the means of examining in what manner its laws have been executed.

But whatever may be the issue of that examination, the legislative body ought not to have a power of judging the person, nor of course the conduct of him who is entrusted with the executive power. His person should be sacred, because as it is necessary for the good of the state to prevent the legislative body from rendering themselves arbitrary, the moment he is accused or tried, there is an end of liberty.

In this case the state would be no longer a monarchy, but a kind of republican, though not a free, government. But as the person entrusted with the executive power cannot abuse it without bad counsellors, and such as hate the laws as ministers, though the laws favour them as subjects; these men may be examined and punished.

Though in general the judiciary power ought not to be united with any part of the legislative, yet this is liable to three exceptions founded on the particular interest of the party accused.

The great are always obnoxious to popular envy; and were they to be judged by the people, they might be in danger from their judges, and would moreover be deprived of the privilege which the meanest subject is possessed of in a free state, of being tried by their peers. The nobility for this reason ought not to be cited before the ordinary courts of judicature, but before that part of the legislature which is composed of their own body.

It is possible that the law, which is clear-sighted in one sense, and blind in another, might in some cases be too severe. But as we have already observed, the national judges are no more, than the mouth that pronounces the words of the law, mere passive beings incapable of moderating either its force or rigor. That part therefore of the legislative body, which we have just now observed to be a necessary tribunal on another occasion, is also a necessary tribunal in this; it belongs to its supreme authority to moderate the law in favour of the law itself, by mitigating the sentence.

It might also happen that a subject entrusted with the administration of public affairs, may infringe the rights of the people, and be guilty of crimes which the ordinary magistrates either could not, or would not punish. But in general the legislative power cannot judge; and much less can it be a judge in this particular case, where it represents the party concerned, which is the people. It can only therefore impeach. But before what court shall it bring its impeachment? Must it go and demean itself before the ordinary tribunals, which are its inferiors, and being composed moreover of men who are chosen from the people as well as itself, will naturally be swayed by the authority of so powerful an accuser? No: in order to preserve the dignity of the people, and the security of the subject, the legislative part which represents the people, must bring in its charge before the legislative part which represents the nobility, who have neither the same interests nor the same passions.

Here is an advantage which this government has over most of the ancient republics, where there was this abuse, that the people were at the same time both judge and accuser.

The executive power, pursuant to what has been already said, ought to have a share in the legislature by the power of refusing, otherwise it would soon be stripped of its prerogatives. But should the legislative power usurp a share of the executive, the latter would be equally undone.

If the prince were to have a share in the legislature by the power of enacting, liberty would be lost. But as it is necessary he should have a share in the legislature for the support of his own prerogative, this share must consist in the power of refusing.

The change of government at Rome was owing to this, that neither the senate who had one part of the executive power, nor the magistrates who were entrusted with the other, had the right of refusing, which was entirely lodged in the people.

Here then is the fundamental constitution of the government we are treating of. The legislative body being composed of two parts, one checks the other, by the mutual privilege of refusing. They are both checked by the executive power, as the executive is by the legislative.

These three powers should naturally form a state of repose or inaction. But as there is a necessity for movement in the course of human affairs, they are forced to move, but still to move in concert.

As the executive power has no other part in the legislative than the privilege of refusing, it can have no share in the public debates. It is not even necessary that it should propose, because as it may always disapprove of the resolutions that shall be taken, it may likewise reject the decisions on those proposals which were made against its will.

In some ancient commonwealths, where public debates were carried on by the people in a body, it was natural for the executive power to propose and debate with the people, otherwise their resolutions must have been attended with a strange confusion.

Were the executive power to determine the raising of public money, otherwise than by giving its consent, liberty would cease; because it would become legislative in the most important point of legislation.

If the legislative power was to settle the subsidies, not from year to year, but for ever, it would run the risk of losing its liberty, because the executive power would no longer be dependent; and when once it was possessed of such a perpetual right, it would be a matter of indifference, whether it held it of itself, or of another. The same may be said, if it should come to a resolution of entrusting, not an annual, but a perpetual command of the sea and land forces to the executive power.

To prevent the executive power from being capable of oppressing, it is requisite that the armies, with which it is entrusted, should consist of the people, and have the same spirit as the people, as was the case at Rome till the time of *Marius*. To obtain this end, there are only two ways, either that the persons employed in the army, should have sufficient property to answer for their conduct to their fellow subjects, and be enlisted only for a year, as was customary at Rome: or if there should be a standing army, composed chiefly of the most despicable part of the nation, the legislative power should have a right to disband them as soon as it pleased; the soldiers should live in common with the rest of the people; and no separate camp, barracks, or fortress, should be suffered.

When once an army is established, it ought not to depend immediately on the legislative, but on the executive power; and this from the very nature of the thing; its business consisting more in action than in deliberation.

From a manner of thinking that prevails amongst mankind, they set a higher value upon courage than timorousness, on activity than prudence, on strength than counsel. Hence the army will ever despise a senate, and respect their own officers. They will naturally slight the orders sent them by a body of men, whom they look upon as cowards, and therefore unworthy to command them. So that as soon as the army depends on the legislative body, the government becomes a military one; and if the contrary has ever happened, it has been owing to some extraordinary circumstances. It is because the army was always kept divided; it is because it was composed of several bodies, that depended each on their particular province; it is because the capital towns were strong places, defended by their natural situation, and not garrisoned with regular troops.

Holland for instance, is still safer than Venice; she might drown, or starve the revolted troops; for as they are not quartered in towns that are capable to furnish them with necessary subsistence; this subsistence is of course precarious.

Whoever shall read the admirable treatise of Tacitus on the manners of the Germans, will find that it is from them the English have borrowed the idea of their political government. This beautiful system was invented first in the woods.

As all human things have an end, the state we are speaking of will lose its liberty, will perish. Have not Rome, Sparta, and Carthage perished? It will perish when the legislative power shall be more corrupt than the executive.

It is not my business to examine whether the English actually enjoy this liberty, or not. Sufficient it is for my purpose to observe, that it is established by their laws; and I inquire no further.

Neither do I pretend by this to undervalue other governments, nor to say that this extreme political liberty ought to give uneasiness to those who have only a moderate share of it. How should I have any such design, I who think that even the excess of reason is not always desirable, and that mankind generally find their account better in mediums than in extremes?

Harrington in his *Oceana* has also inquired into the highest point of liberty to which the constitution of a state may be carried. But of him indeed it may be said, that for want of knowing the nature of real liberty, he busied himself in pursuit of an imaginary one, and that he built a Chalcedon though had a Byzantium before his eyes.

CHAPTER 7

Of the Monarchies We Are Acquainted With

The monarchies we are acquainted with have not, like that we have been speaking of, liberty for their direct view: their only aim is the subject's, the state's, and the prince's glory. But from this glory there results a spirit of liberty, which in those governments may perform as great things, and may contribute as much perhaps to happiness, as liberty itself.

Here the three powers are not distributed and founded on the model of the constitution above-mentioned; they have each a particular distribution, according to which they border more or less on political liberty; and if they did not border upon it, monarchy would degenerate into despotic government.

BOOK XV

In What manner the Laws of Civil Slavery Relate to the Nature of the Climate

CHAPTER 1

Of Civil Slavery

Slavery, properly so called, is the establishment of a right which gives to one man such a power over another as renders him absolute master of his life and fortune. The state of slavery is in its own nature bad. It is neither useful to the master nor to the slave; not to the slave, because he can do nothing through a motive of virtue; nor to the master, because by having an unlimited authority over his slaves he insensibly accustoms himself to the want of all moral virtues, and thence becomes fierce, hasty, severe, choleric, voluptuous, and cruel.

In despotic countries, where they are already in a state of political servitude, civil slavery is more tolerable than in other governments. Every one ought to be satisfied in those countries with necessaries and life. Hence the condition of a slave is hardly more burdensome than that of a subject.

But in a monarchical government, where it is of the utmost importance that human nature should not be debased or dispirited, there ought to be no slavery. In democracies, where they are all upon equality; and in aristocracies, where the laws ought to use their utmost endeavors to procure as great an equality as the nature of the government will permit, slavery is contrary to the spirit of the constitution: it only contributes to give a power and luxury to the citizens which they ought not to have.

CHAPTER 2

Origin of the Right of Slavery Among the Roman Civilians

One would never have imagined that slavery should owe its birth to pity, and that this should have been excited in three different ways.

The law of nations to prevent prisoners from being put to death has allowed them to be made slaves. The civil law of the Romans empowered debtors, who were subject to be ill used by their creditors, to sell themselves. And the law of nature requires that children whom a father in a state of servitude is no longer able to maintain should be reduced to the same state as the father.

These reasons of the civilians are all false. It is false that killing in war is lawful, unless in a case of absolute necessity: but when a man has made another his slave, he cannot be said to have been under a necessity of taking away his life, since he actually did not take it away. War gives no other right over prisoners than to disable them from doing any further harm by securing their persons. All nations concur in detesting the murdering of prisoners in cold blood.

Neither is it true that a freeman can sell himself. Sale implies a price; now when a person sells himself, his whole substance immediately devolves to his master; the master, therefore, in this case, gives nothing, and the slave receives nothing. You will say he has a *peculium*. But this *peculium* goes along with the person. If it is not lawful for a man to kill himself because he robs his country of his person, for the same reason he is not allowed to barter his freedom. The freedom of every citizen constitutes a part of the public liberty, and in a democratic state is even a part of the sovereignty. To sell one's freedom is so repugnant to all reason as can scarcely be supposed in any man. If liberty may be rated with respect to the buyer, it is beyond all price to the seller. The civil law, which authorizes a division of goods among men, cannot be thought to rank among such goods a part of the men who were to make this division. The same law annuls all iniquitous contracts; surely then it affords redress in a contract where the grievance is most enormous.

The third way is birth, which falls with the two former; for if a man could not sell himself, much less could he sell an unborn infant. If a prisoner of war is not to be reduced to slavery, much less are his children.

The lawfulness of putting a malefactor to death arises from this circumstance: the law by which he is punished was made for his security. A murderer, for instance, has enjoyed the benefit of the very law which condemns him; it has been a continual protection to him; he cannot, therefore, object to it. But it is not so with the slave. The law of slavery can never be beneficial to him; it is in all cases against him, without ever being for his advantage; and therefore this law is contrary to the fundamental principle of all societies.

If it be pretended that it has been beneficial to him, as his master has provided for his subsistence, slavery, at this rate, should be limited to those who are incapable of earning their livelihood. But who will take up with such slaves? As to infants, nature, who has supplied their mothers with milk, had provided for their sustenance; and the remainder of their childhood approaches so near the age in which they are most capable of being of service that he who supports them cannot be said to give them an equivalent which can entitle him to be their master.

Nor is slavery less opposed to the civil law than to that of nature. What civil law can restrain a slave from running away, since he is not a member of society, and consequently has no interest in any civil institutions? He can be retained only by a family law, that is, by the master's authority.

CHAPTER 3

Another Origin of the Right of Slavery

I would as soon say that the right of slavery proceeds from the contempt of one nation for another, founded on a difference in customs.

Lopez de Gama relates "that the Spaniards found near St. Martha several basketfuls of crabs, snails, grasshoppers, and locusts, which proved to be the ordinary provision of the natives. This the conquerors turned to a heavy charge against the conquered." The author owns that this, with their smoking and trimming their beards in a different manner, gave rise to the law by which the Americans became slaves to the Spaniards.

Knowledge humanizes mankind, and reason inclines to mildness; but prejudices eradicate every tender disposition.

CHAPTER 4

Another Origin of the Right of Slavery

I would say that religion gives its professors a right to enslave those who dissent from it, in order to render its propagation more easy.

This was the notion that encouraged the ravagers of America in their iniquity. Under the influence of this idea they founded their right of enslaving so many nations; for these robbers, who would absolutely be both robbers and Christians, were superlatively devout.

Louis XIII was extremely uneasy at a law by which all the Negroes of his colonies were to be made slaves; but it being strongly urged to him as the readiest means for their conversion, he acquiesced without further scruple.

CHAPTER 5

Of the Slavery of the Negroes

Were I to vindicate our right to make slaves of the Negroes, these should be my arguments:—

The Europeans, having extirpated the Americans, were obliged to make slaves of the Africans, for clearing such vast tracts of land.

Sugar would be too dear if the plants which produce it were cultivated by any other than slaves.

These creatures are all over black, and with such a flat nose that they can scarcely be pitied.

It is hardly to be believed that God, who is a wise Being, should place a soul, especially a good soul, in such a black ugly body.

It is so natural to look upon color as the criterion of human nature, that the Asiatics, among whom eunuchs are employed, always deprive the blacks of their resemblance to us by a more opprobrious distinction.

The color of the skin may be determined by that of the hair, which, among the Egyptians, the best philosophers in the world, was of such importance that they put to death all the red-haired men who fell into their hands.

The Negroes prefer a glass necklace to that gold which polite nations so highly value. Can there be a greater proof of their wanting common sense ?

It is impossible for us to suppose these creatures to be men, because, allowing them to be men, a suspicion would follow that we ourselves are not Christians.

Weak minds exaggerate too much the wrong done to the Africans. For were the case as they state it, would the European powers, who make so many needless conventions among themselves, have failed to enter into a general one, in behalf of humanity and compassion?

CHAPTER 7

Another Origin of the Right of Slavery

There is another origin of the right of slavery, and even of the most cruel slavery which is to be seen among men.

There are countries where the excess of heat enervates the body, and renders men so slothful and dispirited that nothing but the fear of chastisement can oblige them to perform any laborious duty: slavery is there more reconcilable to reason; and the master being as lazy with respect to his sovereign as his slave is with regard to him, this adds a political to a civil slavery.

Aristotle endeavors to prove that there are natural slaves; but what he says is far from proving it. If there be any such, I believe they are those of whom I have been speaking.

But as all men are born equal, slavery must be accounted unnatural, though in some countries it be founded on natural reason; and a wide difference ought to be made between such countries, and those in which even natural reason rejects it, as in Europe, where it has been so happily abolished.

Plutarch, in the " Life of Numa," says that in Saturn's time there was neither slave nor master. Christianity has restored that age in our climates.

CHAPTER 8

Inutility of Slavery Among Us

Natural slavery, then, is to be limited to some particular parts of the world. In all other countries, even the most servile drudgeries may be performed by freemen.

Experience verifies my assertion. Before Christianity had abolished civil slavery in Europe, working in the mines was judged too toilsome for any but slaves or malefactors: at present there are men employed in them who are known to live comfortably. The magistrates have, by some small privileges, encouraged this profession: to an increase of labor they have joined an increase of gain; and have gone so far as to make those people better pleased with their condition than with any other which they could have embraced.

No labor is so heavy but it may be brought to a level with the workman's strength, when regulated by equity, and not by avarice. The violent fatigues which slaves are made to undergo in other parts may be supplied by a skilful use of ingenious machines. The Turkish mines in the Bannat of Temeswaer, though richer than those of Hungary, did not yield so much; because the working of them depended entirely on the strength of their slaves.

I know not whether this article be dictated by my understanding or by my heart. Possibly there is not that climate upon earth where the most laborious services might not with proper encouragement be performed by freemen. Bad laws having made lazy men, they have been reduced to slavery because of their laziness.

BOOK XIX

CHAPTER 27

How the Laws Contribute to Form the Manner, Customs, and Character of a Nation

The customs of an enslaved people are a part of their servitude, those of a free people are a part of their liberty.

I have spoken in the eleventh book of a free people, and have given the principles of their constitution: let us now see the effects which follow from this liberty, the character it is capable of forming, and the customs which naturally result from it.

I do not deny that the climate may have produced a great part of the laws, manners, and customs of this nation; but I maintain that its manners and customs have a close connection with its laws.

As there are in this state two visible powers—the legislative and executive—and as every citizen has a will of his own, and may at pleasure assert his independence, most men have a greater fondness for one of these powers than for the other, and the multitude have commonly neither equity nor sense enough to show an equal affection to both.

And as the executive power, by disposing of all employments, may give great hopes, and no fears, every man who obtains any favor from it is ready to espouse its cause; while it is liable to be attacked by those who have nothing to hope from it.

All the passions being unrestrained, hatred, envy, jealousy, and an ambitious desire of riches and honors, appear in their extent; were it otherwise, the state would be in the condition of a man weakened by sickness, who is without passions because he is without strength.

The hatred which arises between the two parties will always subsist, because it will always be impotent.

These parties being composed of freemen, if the one becomes too powerful for the other, as a consequence of liberty this other is depressed; while the citizens take the weaker side, with the same readiness as the hands lend their assistance to remove the infirmities and disorders of the body.

Every individual is independent, and being commonly led by caprice and humor, frequently changes parties; he abandons one where he left all his friends, to unite himself to another in which he finds all his enemies: so that in this nation it frequently happens that the people forget the laws of friendship, as well as those of hatred.

The sovereign is here in the same case with a private person; and against the ordinary maxims of prudence is frequently obliged to give his confidence to those who have most offended him, and to disgrace the men who have best served him: he does that by necessity which other princes do by choice.

As we are afraid of being deprived of the blessing we already enjoy, and which may be disguised and misrepresented to us; and as fear always enlarges objects, the people are uneasy under such a situation, and believe themselves in danger, even in those moments when they are most secure.

As those who with the greatest warmth oppose the executive power dare not avow the self-interested motives of their opposition, so much the more do they increase the terrors of the people, who can never be certain whether they are in danger or not. But even this contributes to make them avoid the real dangers, to which they may, in the end, be exposed.

But the legislative body having the confidence of the people, and being more enlightened than they, may calm their uneasiness, and make them recover from the bad impressions they have entertained.

This is the great advantage which this government has over the ancient democracies, in which the people had an immediate power; for when they were moved and agitated by the orators, these agitations always produced their effect.

But when an impression of terror has no certain object, it produces only clamor and abuse; it has, however, this good effect, that it puts all the springs of government into motion, and fixes the attention of every citizen. But if it arises from a violation of the fundamental laws, it is sullen, cruel, and produces the most dreadful catastrophes.

Soon we should see a frightful calm, during which everyone would unite against that power which had violated the laws.

If, when the uneasiness proceeds from no certain object, some foreign power should threaten the state, or put its prosperity or its glory in danger, the little interests of party would then yield to the more strong and binding, and there would be a perfect coalition in favor of the executive power.

But if the disputes were occasioned by a violation of the fundamental laws, and a foreign power should appear, there would be a revolution that would neither alter the constitution nor the form of government. For a revolution formed by liberty becomes a confirmation of liberty.

A free nation may have a deliverer: a nation enslaved can have only another oppressor.

For whoever is able to dethrone an absolute prince has a power sufficient to become absolute himself.

As the enjoyment of liberty, and even its support and preservation consist in every man's being allowed to speak his thoughts, and to lay open his sentiments, a citizen in this state will say or write whatever the laws do not expressly forbid to be said or written.

A people like this, being always in a ferment, are more easily conducted by their passions than by reason, which never produces any great effect in the mind of man; it is therefore easy for those who govern to make them undertake enterprises contrary to their true interest.

This nation is passionately fond of liberty, because this liberty is real; and it is possible for it, in its defence, to sacrifice its wealth, its ease, its interest, and to support the burden of the heaviest taxes, even such as a despotic prince durst not lay upon his subjects.

But as the people have a certain knowledge of the necessity of submitting to those taxes, they pay them from the well-founded hope of their discontinuance; their burdens are heavy, but they do not feel their weight: while in other states the uneasiness is infinitely greater than the evil.

This nation must therefore have a fixed and certain credit, because it borrows of itself and pays itself. It is possible for it to undertake things above its natural strength, and employ against its enemies immense sums of fictitious riches, which the credit and nature of the government may render real.

To preserve its liberty, it borrows of its subjects: and the subjects, seeing that its credit would be lost if ever it were conquered, have a new motive to make fresh efforts in defence of its liberty.

This nation, inhabiting an island, is not fond of conquering, because it would be weakened by distant conquests—especially as the soil of the island is good, for it has then no need of enriching itself by war: and as no citizen is subject to another, each sets a greater value on his own liberty than on the glory of one or any number of citizens.

Military men are there regarded as belonging to a profession which may be useful but is often dangerous, and as men whose very services are burdensome to the nation: civil qualifications are therefore more esteemed than the military.

This nation, which liberty and the laws render easy, on being freed from pernicious prejudices, has become a trading people; and as it has some of those primitive materials of trade out of which are manufactured such things as from the artist's hand receive a considerable value, it has made settlements proper to procure the enjoyment of this gift of heaven in its fullest extent.

As this nation is situated towards the north, and has many superfluous commodities, it must want also a great number of merchandise which its climate will not produce: it has therefore entered into a great and necessary intercourse with the southern nations; and making choice of those states whom it is willing to favor with an advantageous commerce, it enters into such treaties with the nation it has chosen as are reciprocally useful to both.

In a state where, on the one hand, the opulence is extreme, and on the other the taxes are excessive, they are hardly able to live on a small fortune without industry. Many, therefore, under a pretence of travelling, or of health, retire from amongst them, and go in search of plenty, even to the countries of slavery.

A trading nation has a prodigious number of little particular interests; it may then injure or be injured in an infinite number of ways. Thus it becomes immoderately jealous, and is more afflicted at the prosperity of others than it rejoices at its own.

And its laws, otherwise mild and easy, may be so rigid with respect to the trade and navigation carried on with it, that it may seem to trade only with enemies.

If this nation sends colonies abroad, it must rather be to extend its commerce than its dominion.

As men are fond of introducing into other places what they have established amongst themselves, they have given the people of the colonies their own form of government; and this government carrying prosperity along with it, they have raised great nations in the forests they were sent to inhabit.

Having formerly subdued a neighboring nation, which by its situation, the goodness of its ports, and the nature of its products, inspires it with jealousy, though it has given this nation its own laws, yet it holds it in great dependence: the subjects there are free and the state itself in slavery.

The conquered state has an excellent civil government, but is oppressed by the law of nations. Laws are imposed by one country on the other, and these are such as render its prosperity precarious, and dependent on the will of a master.

The ruling nation inhabiting a large island, and being in possession of a great trade, has with extraordinary ease grown powerful at sea; and as the preservation of its liberties requires that it should have neither strongholds nor fortresses nor land forces, it has occasion for a formidable navy to defend it against invasions; a navy which must be superior to that of all other powers, who, employing their treasures in wars on land, have not sufficient for those at sea.

The empire of the sea has always given those who have enjoyed it a natural pride; because, thinking themselves capable of extending their insults wherever they please, they imagine that their power is as boundless as the ocean.

This nation has a great influence in the affairs of its neighbors; for as its power is not employed in conquests, its friendship is more courted, and its resentment more dreaded, than could naturally be expected from the inconstancy of its government, and its domestic divisions.

Thus it is the fate of the executive power to be almost always disturbed at home and respected abroad.

Should this nation on some occasions become the centre of the negotiations of Europe, probity and good faith would be carried to a greater height than in other places; because the ministers being frequently obliged to justify their conduct before a popular council, their negotiations could not be secret; and they would be forced to be, in this respect, a little more honest.

Besides, as they would in some sort be answerable for the events which an irregular conduct might produce, the surest, the safest way for them would be to take the straightest path.

If the nobles were formerly possessed of an immoderate power, and the monarch had found the means of abasing them by raising the people, the point of extreme servitude must have been that between humbling the nobility and that in which the people began to feel their power.

Thus this nation, having been formerly subject to an arbitrary power, on many occasions preserves the style of it, in such a manner as to let us frequently see upon the foundation of a free government the form of an absolute monarchy.

With regard to religion, as in this state every subject has a free will, and must consequently be either conducted by the light of his own mind or by the caprice of fancy, it necessarily follows that everyone must either look upon all religion with indifference, by which means they are led to embrace the established religion, or they must be zealous for religion in general, by which means the number of sects is increased.

It is not impossible but that in this nation there may be men of no religion, who would not, however, bear to be obliged to change that which they would choose, if they cared to choose any; for they would immediately perceive that their lives and fortunes are not more peculiarly theirs than their manner of thinking, and that whoever would deprive them of the one might even with better reason take away the other.

If, amongst the different religions, there is one that has been attempted to be established by methods of slavery, it must there be odious; because as we judge of things by the appendages we join with them, it could never present itself to the mind in conjunction with the idea of liberty.

The laws against those who profess this religion could not, however, be of the sanguinary kind; for liberty can never inflict such punishments; but they may be so rigorous as to do all the mischief that can be done in cold blood.

It is possible that a thousand circumstances might concur to give the clergy so little credit, that other citizens may have more. Therefore, instead of a separation, they have chosen rather to support the same burdens as the laity, and in this respect to make only one body with them; but as they always seek to conciliate the respect of the people, they distinguish themselves by a more retired life, a conduct more reserved, and a greater purity of manners.

The clergy not being able to protect religion, nor to be protected by it, only seek to persuade; their pens therefore furnish us with excellent works in proof of a revelation and of the providence of the Supreme Being.

Yet the state prevents the sitting of their assemblies, and does not suffer them to correct their own abuses; it chooses thus, through a caprice of liberty, rather to leave their reformation imperfect than to suffer the clergy to be the reformers.

Those dignities which make a fundamental part of the constitution are more fixed than elsewhere; but, on the other hand, the great in this country of liberty are nearer upon a level with the people; their ranks are more separated, and their persons more confounded.

As those who govern have a power which, in some measure, has need of fresh vigor every day, they have a greater regard for such as are useful to them than for those who only contribute to their amusement: we see, therefore, fewer courtiers, flatterers, and parasites; in short, fewer of all those who make their own advantage of the folly of the great.

Men are less esteemed for frivolous talents and attainments than for essential qualities; and of this kind there are but two, riches and personal merit.

They enjoy a solid luxury, founded, not on the refinements of vanity, but on that of real wants; they ask nothing of nature but what nature can bestow.

The rich enjoy a great superfluity of fortune, and yet have no relish for frivolous amusements; thus, many having more wealth than opportunities of expense, employ it in a fantastic manner: in this nation they have more judgment than taste.

As they are always employed about their own interest, they have not that politeness which is founded on indolence; and they really have not leisure to attain it.

The era of Roman politeness is the same as that of the establishment of arbitrary power. An absolute government produces indolence, and this gives birth to politeness.

The more people there are in a nation who require circumspect behavior, and care not to displease, the more there is of politeness. But it is rather the politeness of morals than that of manners which ought to distinguish us from barbarous nations.

In a country where every man has, in some sort, a share in the administration of the government, the women ought scarcely to live with the men. They are therefore modest, that is, timid; and this timidity constitutes their virtue: whilst the men without a taste for gallantry plunge themselves into a debauchery, which leaves them at leisure, and in the enjoyment of their full liberty.

Their laws not being made for one individual more than another, each considers himself a monarch; and, indeed, the men of this nation are rather confederates than fellow-subjects.

As the climate has given many persons a restless spirit and extended views, in a country where the constitution gives every man a share in its government and political interests, conversation generally turns upon politics: and we see men spend their lives in the calculation of events which, considering the nature of things and caprices of fortune, or rather of men, can scarcely be thought subject to the rules of calculation.

In a free nation it is very often a matter of indifference whether individuals reason well or ill; it is sufficient that they do reason: hence springs that liberty which is a security from the effects of these reasonings.

But in a despotic government, it is equally pernicious whether they reason well or ill; their reasoning is alone sufficient to shock the principle of that government.

Many people who have no desire of pleasing abandon themselves to their own particular humor; and most of those who have wit and ingenuity are ingenious in tormenting themselves: filled with contempt or disgust for all things, they are unhappy amidst all the blessings that can possibly contribute to promote their felicity.

As no subject fears another, the whole nation is proud: for the pride of kings is founded only on their independence.

Free nations are haughty; others may more properly be called vain.

But as these men who are naturally so proud live much by themselves, they are commonly bashful when they appear among strangers; and we frequently see them behave for a considerable time with an odd mixture of pride and ill-placed shame.

The character of the nation is more particularly discovered in their literary performances, in which we find the men of thought and deep meditation.

As society gives us a sense of the ridicule of mankind, retirement renders us more fit to reflect on the folly of vice. Their satirical writings are sharp and severe, and we find amongst them many Juvenals, without discovering one Horace.

In monarchies extremely absolute, historians betray the truth, because they are not at liberty to speak it; in states remarkably free, they betray the truth, because of their liberty itself; which always produces divisions, everyone becoming as great a slave to the prejudices of his faction as he could be in a despotic state.

Their poets have more frequently an original rudeness of invention than that particular kind of delicacy which springs from taste; we there find something which approaches nearer to the bold strength of a Michaelangelo than to the softer graces of a Raphael.

BOOK XXV

Of Laws in Relation to the Establishment of Religion and Its External Polity

CHAPTER 9

Of Toleration in Point of Religion

We are here politicians, and not divines: but the divines themselves must allow that there is a great difference between tolerating and approving a religion.

When the legislator has believed it a duty to permit the exercise of many religions, it is necessary that it should enforce also a toleration amongst these religions themselves. It is a principle that every religion which is persecuted, becomes itself persecuting: for as soon as by some accidental turn it arises from persecution, it attacks the religion which persecuted it; not as a religion, but as a tyranny.

It is necessary then that the laws require from the several religions, not only that they shall not embroil the state, but that they shall not raise disturbances amongst themselves. A citizen does not fulfil the laws, by not disturbing the government; it is requisite, that he should not trouble any citizen whomsoever.

CHAPTER 11

Of Changing a Religion

A prince who undertakes to destroy or to change the established religion of his kingdom, must greatly expose himself. If his government is despotic, he runs the risk of seeing a revolution, which from some kind of tyranny or other is never a new thing in such states. The cause of this revolution is, that a state cannot change its religion, manners, and customs in an instant, and with the same rapidity as the prince publishes the ordinance which establishes a new religion.

Besides, the ancient religion is connected with the constitution of the kingdom, and the new one is not: the former agrees with the climate, and very often the new one is opposite to it. Moreover, the citizens, disgusted with their laws, look upon the government already established with contempt; they conceive a jealousy against the two religions, instead of a firm belief in one; and in a word, these revolutions give the state, at least for some time, both bad citizens, and bad believers.

CHAPTER 12

Of Penal Laws

Penal laws ought to be avoided, in respect to religion; they imprint fear, it is true; but as religion has also penal laws which inspire fear, the one is effaced by the other: and between these two different kinds of fear, the mind becomes hardened.

The threatenings of religion are so terrible, and its promises so great, that when they actuate the mind, whatever efforts the magistrates may use to oblige us to renounce it, they seem to leave us nothing when they deprive us of the exercise of our religion; and to bereave us of nothing, when we are freely allowed to profess it.

It is not therefore in filling the soul with this great object, in hastening its approach to that important moment in which it ought to be of the highest importance, that they can succeed in detaching the soul from it. A more certain way is to attack religion by favours, by the conveniences of life, by hopes of fortune; not by that which revives, but by that which extinguishes, the sense of its duty; not by that which shocks it, but by that which throws it into indifference, at the time when other passions actuate our minds, and those which religion inspires are hushed into silence. A general rule in changing a religion; the invitations should be much stronger than the penalties.

The temper of the human mind has appeared even in the nature of the punishments they have employed. If we take a survey of the persecutions in Japan, we shall find that they were more shocked at cruel torments than at long sufferings, which rather weary than affright; which are the more difficult to surmount from their appearing less difficult.

In a word, history sufficiently informs us, that penal laws have never had any other effect but to destroy.

CHAPTER 13

A Most Humble Remonstrance to the Inquisitors of Spain and Portugal

A Jewess of ten years of age, who was burnt at Lisbon at the last *Auto-da-fe*, gave occasion to the following little piece; the most idle, I believe, that ever was wrote. When we attempt to prove things so evident, we are sure never to convince.

The author declares, that though a Jew, he has a respect for the Christian religion; and that he should be glad to take away from the princes who are not Christians, a plausible presence for persecuting this religion.

"You complain," says he to the inquisitors, "that the emperor of Japan caused all the Christians in his dominions to be burnt by a slow fire. But he will answer, we treat you who do not believe like us, as you yourselves treat those who do not believe like you: you can only complain of your weakness, which has hindered you from exterminating us, and which has enabled us to exterminate you.

"But it must be confessed, that you are much more cruel than this emperor. You put us to death, who believe only what you believe, because we do not believe *all* that you believe. We follow a religion, which you yourselves know to have been formerly dear to God. We think that God loves it still, and you think that he loves it no more: and because you judge thus, you make those suffer by sword and fire, who hold an error so pardonable as to believe that God still loves what he once loved.

"If you are cruel to us, you are much more so to our children; you cause them to be burnt, because they follow the inspirations given them by those whom the law of nature, and the laws of all nations teach them to regard as gods.

"You deprive yourselves of the advantage you have over the Mahometans, with respect to the manner in which their religion was established. When they boast of the number of their believers, you tell them that they have obtained them by violence, and that they have extended their religion by the sword: why then do you establish yours by fire?

"When you would bring us over to you, we object a source from which you glory to descend. You reply to us, that though your religion is new, it is divine; and you prove it from its growing amidst the persecution of Pagans, and when watered by the blood of your martyrs: but at present you play the part of the Dioclesians, and make us take yours.

We conjure you, not by the mighty God whom both you and we serve, but by that Christ who, you tell us, took upon him a human form, to propose himself for an example for you to follow; we conjure you to behave to us, as he himself would behave was he upon earth. You would have us be Christians, and you will not be so yourselves.

"But if you will not be Christians, be at least men: treat us as you would, if having only the weak light of justice which nature bestows, you had not a religion to conduct, and a revelation to enlighten you.

"If heaven has had so great a love for you, as to make you see the truth, you have received a great favour: but is it for children who have received the inheritance of their father, to hate those who have not?

If you have this truth, hide it not from us by the manner in which you propose it. The characteristic of truth is its triumph over hearts and minds, and not that impotency which you confess, when you would force us to receive it by your tortures.

"If you were wise, you would not put us to death for no other reason, but because we are unwilling to deceive you. If your Christ is the son of God, we hope he will reward us for being so unwilling to profane his mysteries; and we believe, that the God whom both you and we serve, will not punish us for having suffered death for a religion which he formerly gave us, only because we believe that he still continues to give it.

"You live in an age in which the light of nature shines more bright than it has ever done; in which philosophy has enlightened human understandings; in which the morality of your gospel has been more known; in which the respective rights of mankind, with regard to each other, and the empire which one conscience has over another, are best understood. If you do not therefore shake off your ancient prejudices, which whilst unregarded, mingle with your passions, it must be confessed, that you are incorrigible, incapable of any degree of light, or instruction; and a nation must be very unhappy that gives authority to such men.

"Would you have us frankly tell you our thoughts? You consider us rather as your enemies, than as the enemies of your religion: for if you loved your religion, you would not suffer it to be corrupted by such gross ignorance.

"It is necessary that we should advertise you of one thing, that is, if any one in times to come shall dare to assert, that in the age in which we live the people of Europe were civilized, you will be cited to prove that they were barbarians; and the idea they will have of you, will be such as will dishonour your age, and spread hatred over all your contemporaries."

JEAN-JACQUES ROUSSEAU

Jean-Jacques Rousseau (1712–1778) was born in Geneva. His mother died two days later, and his father—a watchmaker—fled when Rousseau was 10. Raised by his uncle, Rousseau left Geneva at 16 and eventually settled in Paris in the early 1740s. Despite the geographic separation, Rousseau maintained a strong public identification with Geneva throughout much of his life. He came to intellectual maturity in absolutist France, in debate with the leading thinkers of the French Enlightenment, but the image of Geneva as a small, self-governing republic, in which the people are sovereign and all citizens are subject to law, continued to provide political bearings.

Whereas Rousseau's early experience in Geneva inspired his political thought, his theory of human nature came to him later, and in a flash, as he walked from Paris to Vincennes in 1749 (he was on his way to visit Diderot, then imprisoned in the château of Vincennes). Reflecting on a question set by the Academy of Dijon—"Has the restoration of the sciences and the arts contributed to the purification of morals?"—Rousseau was overtaken, he says, by a flood of ideas, "a thousand lights." Lying at the heart of this "sudden inspiration" was the thought that dominated his subsequent writing: "that man is naturally good, and that it is solely by [our] institutions that men become wicked." This conception of natural goodness—an alternative to the Augustinian doctrine of original sin and the Hobbesian theory of human nature—is, as Rousseau explained to Archbishop Beaumont of Paris, the "fundamental principle of all morals," and the basis of "all my writings."

Unified by this fundamental idea, Rousseau's principal writings on human nature and politics fall into three groups. In his early, "critical" essays— the *Discourse on the Arts and Sciences* (1750), *Discourse on the Origins of Inequality* (1755), and *Letter to M. d'Alembert on the Theater* (1758)—he challenges the Enlightenment view that the advance of science and understanding has improved the human condition, making human life freer, happier, and more virtuous. Rousseau rejects this complacent view, and reveals a darker side to intellectual progress. Connecting enlightenment with the evolution of constraint, unhappiness, and vice, he explains how human beings, though naturally good, have been corrupted. His more positive writings—*Of the Social Contract, Emile,* the best-selling novel *New Heloise* (1761), *Letters from the Mountain* (1764), and constitutional proposals for Corsica (1765) and Poland (1772)—present a scheme of political institutions and a program of education that would cure our corrupt condition, restoring freedom through virtue and providing us with a life suited to our nature. In his autobiographical, confessional writings—including his *Confessions, Reveries of the Solitary Walker,* and *Rousseau, Judge of Jean-Jacques,* all published after Rousseau's death— Rousseau testifies to his own authenticity, insisting that he has not been caught up in the web of deception, hypocrisy, and manipulation that defines conventional society. These writings, though intensely personal and self-revealing, also present a universal message: Rousseau's own uncorrupted sincerity is evidence of humanity's natural goodness, and illustrates the possibility of extricating ourselves from self-imposed misery and vice.

Rousseau's political philosophy describes the terms of that extrication. The fundamental political problem, he says, is "to find a form of association that defends and protects the person and goods of each associate with all the common force, and by means of which each one uniting with all, nevertheless obeys only himself and remains as free as before." The importance of this problem reflects the central role in our nature of self-love and freedom. Because we love ourselves, we cannot be indifferent to the security of our person and goods. But not just any form of protection will do. We are "born free," with a capacity to choose and to regulate our own conduct. This capacity is the source of humanity's special worth, of our standing as moral agents who can make claims on others and take responsibility for our conduct. Freedom is so fundamental that "renouncing one's liberty is renouncing one's dignity as a man, the rights of humanity and even its duties." So we must find a form of security that does not demand such renunciation.

Of The Social Contract presents Rousseau's solution: a political society that achieves a "harmony of obedience and freedom." In this society, obedience to authority does not require a subordination of will that denies our freedom and corrupts our sensibilities. The proposed harmony is puzzling. How *could* each person accept political authority, thus uniting with all for common security, while obeying only himself or herself, achieving the "moral freedom" that consists in giving the law to oneself, and so remaining "as free as before?"

Rousseau's explanation has two components, corresponding to two kinds of doubt about the possibility of such a political society—doubts about *content* and *motivation*.

The problem of content arises because accepting authority, which is required for security, appears to involve letting oneself be ruled by the decisions of others (perhaps the majority). To show that self-government can be reconciled with the chains of social connection and bonds of political authority, we need some way to dispel this appearance—to show that the idea of such reconciliation is even coherent.

Rousseau's conception of a society guided by a *general will* addresses this problem. In such a society, the political obligations of citizens are fixed by laws; those laws reflect a shared understanding of the common good; and that understanding expresses an equal concern for the good of each citizen. Because the content of the conception of the common good reflects an equal concern with the well-being of each citizen, the society provides security for the person and goods of each. Because citizens share the conception, and it is embodied in law, each citizen remains free in fulfilling legal obligations. Those obligations are acceptable to citizens as free agents because each can regard the obligations to the common good as self-imposed.

Rousseau's solution to the fundamental problem requires, then, that the parties to the social compact treat each other as equals, both in the institution of equal citizenship and in regulating conduct by reference to reasons of the common good. To institutionalize and sustain the supremacy of the general will, Rousseau proposes a system of nonrepresentative, direct democracy. Citizens themselves are to assemble regularly to reaffirm their social bonds, evaluate the performance of the executive, and choose the fundamental laws that will best advance their common good.

Even if we grant, however, that the society of the general will solves the content problem, we may still wonder whether such an ideal society is a human possibility. It requires, after all, a shared conception of, and allegiance to, the common good. But widespread vice—selfishness, pride, jealousy, envy-naturally prompts the thought that this ideal is inconsistent with human motivations.

Hobbes would certainly have rejected Rousseau's view for this reason. Surveying what he called the "known natural inclinations of mankind," Hobbes found desires for individual preservation and happiness; he noted the strength of human fears about violent death; he observed (in at least some people) passions of pride, jealousy, and envy rooted in a sense of natural differences of worth and a concern that relative social standing mirror those presumptively natural differences. And he found that people are often blinded by passion into acting for near-term advantages and against their own longer-term interests. Departing from these observations, he concluded that we need a sovereign with unconditional authority, whose power is sufficient to overawe subjects, tame their pride with fear, and ensure the social peace required to protect human life and happiness.

Hobbes's defense of political submission is driven, in short, by his general pessimism about human capacities for self-regulation. More particularly, he was skeptical about the motivational power of reason of the common good because he did not see human beings as moved by a concern to treat others as equals. Concerned with preservation and happiness, we have at most an instrumental concern with equality; and insofar as we are prone to pride, we will reject equality as inconsistent with our naturally superior worth and an insult to our dignity.

Rousseau's case for the motivational possibility of a general will and the political autonomy it makes possible would have been simpler had he rejected Hobbes's psychological observations. But Rousseau found little basis for disagreeing with Hobbes's dismal description: "Men are wicked," he says in the *Discourse on the Origins of Inequality*, adding that "a sad and constant experience makes proof unnecessary." We observe widespread vice, and underlying that vice can discern a "frenzy to distinguish ourselves," an "ardent desire to raise one's relative fortune less out of genuine need than in order to place oneself above others." This frenzy and desire, in turn, have roots in an inflated, false sense of self-worth; struck by differences of social station, we fail to see that "man is the same in all stations."

This description naturally prompts the pessimistic thought that the society of the general will is incompatible with human motivations, that human nature has no place for the commitment to equality and the common good required for political autonomy. And if we could directly infer intrinsic properties of human nature from observed motivations—if, for example, the "ardent desire" for advantage over others were an original predisposition, or the inflated sense of self-worth an original sentiment—that pessimistic thought would be true, and we would be compelled to reject the possibility of a political society in which citizens give the law to themselves. But we are not required to accept that direct inference, and therefore not required to draw the pessimistic implications. That is the point of Rousseau's *Second Discourse*. It presents, as Rousseau describes it, a "genealogy of vice." The point of that genealogy is to turn back an argument that begins with the "sad and constant experience" of human vice, that attributes such vice to a natural desire for advantage, or a naturally exaggerated sense of our own worth, and that ends by rejecting as unrealistic an ideal of free association among equals. Rousseau's strategy is to explain all human vice in terms of social circumstance, without postulating any original predisposition to it: Although human beings are *naturally good,* the experience of social inequality encourages the desire for advantage and inflamed sense of self-worth that produce constraint, vice, and misery.

Rousseau's explanation, then, constitutes a defense of human nature. And that defense permits us to hope, with reason, for a society whose members respect one another as equals, and in so doing respond to the demands of self-love and freedom.

On the unity of Rousseau's writings, see Ernst Cassirer, *The Question of Jean-Jacques Rousseau,* translated and edited by Peter Gay (Bloomington: University of Indiana Press, 1963). Jean Starobinski provides a psychological interpretation of Rousseau's work, underscoring Rousseau's concern for transparency in human relations, in *Jean-Jacques Rousseau: Transparency and Obstruction,* trans. Arthur Goldhammer (Chicago: University of Chicago Press, 1988). On the theory of natural goodness, see Arthur Melzer, *The Natural Goodness of Man: The System of Rousseau's Thought* (Chicago: University of Chicago Press, 1990), and Joshua Cohen, "The Natural Goodness of Humanity," in *Reclaiming the History of Ethics: Essays for John Rawls,* Barbara Herman, Christine Korsgaard, and Andrews Reath, eds. (Cambridge: Cambridge University Press, 1996). For a discussion of Rousseau's political thought against the background of early modern political theory, see Robert Derathe, *Jean-Jacques Rousseau et la Science Politique de son Temps* (Paris: Presses Universitaire de France, 1950). For a discussion of Rousseau's views in connection with Genevan culture and politics, see John Stephenson Spink, *Jean-Jacques Rousseau et Gèneve: essai sur les idées politiques et religieuses de Rousseau dans leur relation avec la penseé genevoise au XVIIIe* (Paris: Boívín, 1934). On Rousseau's conception of democracy, in relation to traditional debate about democracy and political conflict in eighteenth-century Geneva, see James Miller, *Rousseau: Dreamer of Democracy* (New Haven: Yale University Press, 1984). On Rousseau's critique of representative government, see Richard Fralin, *Rousseau and Representation* (New York: Columbia University Press, 1978). The best discussion of Rousseau's psychological views is N. J. Dent's *Rousseau* (Oxford: Blackwell, 1988). For Rousseau's views on women, see Susan Moller Okin, *Women and Political Thought* (Princeton: Princeton University Press, 1979), Part 3; and Joel Schwartz, *The Sexual Politics of Jean-Jacques Rousseau* (Chicago: University of Chicago Press, 1984). Patrick Riley provides an illuminating account of the theological background to Rosseau's conception of the general will in *The General Will Before Rousseau: The Transformation of the Divine into the Civic* (Princeton: Princeton University Press, 1986).

J. C.

A DISCOURSE ON A SUBJECT PROPOSED BY THE ACADEMY OF DIJON: WHAT IS THE ORIGIN OF INEQUALITY AMONG MEN, AND IS IT AUTHORIZED BY NATURAL LAW?

Non in depravatis, sed in his quae bene secundum naturam se habent considerandum est quid sit naturale.
Aristotle, *Politics*, Book i, Chapter 2.

[We should consider what is natural not in things which are depraved but in those which are rightly ordered according to nature.]

DEDICATION TO THE REPUBLIC OF GENEVA

Most honourable, magnificent and sovereign lords, convinced that only a virtuous citizen can confer on his country honours which it can accept, I have been for thirty years past working to make myself worthy to offer you some public homage; and, this fortunate opportunity supplementing in some degree the insufficiency of my efforts, I have thought myself entitled to follow in embracing it the dictates of the zeal which inspires me, rather than the right which should have been my authorization. Having had the happiness to be born among you, how could I reflect on the equality which nature has ordained between men, and the inequality which they have introduced, without reflecting on the profound wisdom by which both are in this State happily combined and made to coincide, in the manner that is most in conformity with natural law, and most favourable to society, to the maintenance of public order and to the happiness of individuals? In my researches after the best rules common sense can lay down for the constitution of a government, I have been so struck at finding them all in actuality in your own, that even had I not been born within your walls I should have thought it indispensable for me to offer this picture of human society to that people, which of all others seems to be possessed of its greatest advantages, and to have best guarded against its abuses.

If I had had to make choice of the place of my birth, I should have preferred a society which had an extent proportionate to the limits of the human faculties; that is, to the possibility of being well governed: in which every person being equal to his occupation, no one should be obliged to commit to others the functions with which he was entrusted: a State, in which all the individuals being well known to one another, neither the secret machinations of vice, nor the modesty of virtue should be able to escape the notice and judgment of the public; and in which the pleasant custom of seeing and knowing one another should make the love of country rather a love of the citizens than of its soil.

Translated by G. D. H. Cole, revised by J. H. Brumfitt and John C. Hall, updated by P. D. Jimack. Everyman's Library, David Campbell Publishers Ltd. Reprinted by permission of the publisher.

I should have wished to be born in a country in which the interest of the Sovereign and that of the people must be single and identical; to the end that all the movements of the machine might tend always to the general happiness. And as this could not be the case, unless the Sovereign and the people were one and the same person, it follows that I should have wished to be born under a democratic government, wisely tempered.

I should have wished to live and die free: that is, so far subject to the laws that neither I, nor anybody else, should be able to cast off their honourable yoke: the easy and salutary yoke which the haughtiest necks bear with the greater docility, as they are made to bear no other.

I should have wished then that no one within the State should be able to say he was above the law; and that no one without should be able to dictate so that the State should be obliged to recognize his authority. For, be the constitution of a government what it may, if there be within its jurisdiction a single man who is not subject to the law, all the rest are necessarily at his discretion. And if there be a national ruler within, and a foreign ruler without, however they may divide their authority, it is impossible that both should be duly obeyed, or that the State should be well governed.

I should not have chosen to live in a republic of recent institution, however excellent its laws; for fear the government, being perhaps otherwise framed than the circumstances of the moment might require, might disagree with the new citizens, or they with it, and the State run the risk of overthrow and destruction almost as soon as it came into being. For it is with liberty as it is with those solid and succulent foods, or with those generous wines which are well adapted to nourish and fortify robust constitutions that are used to them, but ruin and intoxicate weak and delicate constitutions to which they are not suited. Peoples once accustomed to masters are not in a condition to do without them. If they attempt to shake off the yoke they still more estrange themselves from freedom, as, by mistaking for it an unbridled licence to which it is diametrically opposed, they nearly always manage, by their revolutions, to hand themselves over to seducers, who only make their chains heavier than before. The Roman people itself, a model for all free peoples, was wholly incapable of governing itself when it escaped from the oppression of the Tarquins. Debased by slavery, and the ignominious tasks which had been imposed upon it, it was at first no better than a stupid mob, which it was necessary to control and govern with the greatest wisdom; in order that, being accustomed by degrees to breathe the health-giving air of liberty, minds which had been enervated or rather brutalized under tyranny, might gradually acquire that severity of morals and spirit of fortitude which made it at length the people of all most worthy of respect. I should, then, have sought out for my country some peaceful and happy Republic, of an antiquity that lost itself, as it were, in the night of time: which had experienced only such shocks as served to manifest and strengthen the courage and patriotism of its subjects; and whose citizens, long accustomed to a wise independence, were not only free, but worthy to be so.

I should have wished to choose myself a country, diverted, by a fortunate impotence, from the brutal love of conquest, and secured, by a still more fortunate situation, from the fear of becoming itself the conquest of other States: a free city situated between several nations, none of which should have any interest in attacking it, while each had an interest in preventing it from being attacked by the others; in short, a Republic which should have nothing to tempt the ambition of its neighbours, but might reasonably depend on their assistance in case of need. It follows that a republican State so happily situated could have nothing to fear but from itself; and that, if its members trained themselves to the use of arms, it would be rather to keep alive that military ardour and courageous spirit which are so proper among freemen, and tend to keep up their taste for liberty, than from the necessity of providing for their defence.

I should have sought a country, in which the right of legislation was vested in all the citizens; for who can judge better than they of the conditions under which they had best dwell together in the same society? Not that I should have approved of *plebiscita*, like those among the Romans; in which the rulers in the State, and those most interested in its preservation, were excluded from the deliberations on which in many cases its security depended; and in which, by the most absurd inconsistency, the magistrates were deprived of rights which the meanest citizens enjoyed.

On the contrary, I should have desired that, in order to prevent self-interested and ill-conceived projects, and all such dangerous innovations as finally ruined the Athenians, each man should not be at liberty to propose new laws at pleasure; but that this right should belong exclusively to the magistrates; and that even they should use it with so much caution, the people, on its side, be so reserved in giving its consent to such laws, and the promulgation of them be attended with so much solemnity, that before the constitution could be upset by them, there might be time enough for all to be convinced, that it is above all the great antiquity of the laws which makes them sacred and venerable, that men soon learn to despise laws which they see daily altered, and that States, by accustoming themselves to neglect their ancient customs under the pretext of improvement, often introduce greater evils than those they endeavour to remove.

I should have particularly avoided, as necessarily ill-governed, a Republic in which the people, imagining themselves in a position to do without magistrates, or at least to leave them with only a precarious authority, should imprudently have kept for themselves the administration of civil affairs and the execution of their own laws. Such must have been the rude constitution of primitive governments, directly emerging from a state of nature; and this was another of the vices that contributed to the downfall of the Republic of Athens.

But I should have chosen a community in which the individuals, content with sanctioning their laws, and deciding the most important public affairs in general assembly and on the motion of the rulers, had established honoured tribunals, carefully distinguished the several departments, and elected year by year some of the most capable and upright of their fellow-citizens to administer justice and govern the State; a community, in short, in which the virtue of the magistrates thus bearing witness to the wisdom of the people, each class reciprocally did the other honour. If in such a case any fatal misunderstandings arose to disturb the public peace, even these intervals of blindness and error would bear the marks of moderation, mutual esteem, and a common respect for the laws; which are sure signs and pledges of a reconciliation as lasting as sincere. Such are the advantages, most honourable, magnificent, and sovereign lords, which I should have sought in the country in which I should have chosen to be born. And if providence had added to all these a delightful situation, a temperate climate, a fertile soil, and the most beautiful countryside under Heaven, I should have desired only, to complete my felicity, the peaceful enjoyment of all these blessings, in the bosom of this happy country; to live at peace in the sweet society of my fellow-citizens, and practising towards them, from their own example, the duties of friendship, humanity, and every other virtue, to leave behind me the honourable memory of a good man, and an upright and virtuous patriot.

But if, less fortunate or too late grown wise, I had seen myself reduced to end an infirm and languishing life in other climates, vainly regretting that peaceful repose which I had forfeited in the imprudence of youth, I should at least have entertained the same feelings in my heart, though denied the opportunity of making use of them in my native country. Filled with a tender and disinterested love for my distant fellow-citizens, I should have addressed them from my heart, much in the following terms.

'My dear fellow-citizens, or rather my brothers, since the ties of blood, as well as the laws, unite almost all of us, it gives me pleasure that I cannot think of you, without thinking at the same time of all the blessings you enjoy, and of which none of you, perhaps, more deeply feels the value than I who have lost them. The more I reflect on your civil and political condition, the less can I conceive that the nature of human affairs could admit of a better. In all other governments, when there is a question of ensuring the greatest good of the State, nothing gets beyond projects and ideas, or at best bare possibilities. But as for you, your happiness is complete, and you have nothing to do but enjoy it; you require nothing more to be made perfectly happy than to know how to be satisfied with being so. Your sovereignty, acquired or recovered by the sword, and maintained for two centuries past by your valour and wisdom, is at length fully and universally acknowledged. Your boundaries are fixed, your rights confirmed, and your repose secured by honourable treaties. Your constitution is excellent, being not only dictated by the profoundest wisdom, but guaranteed by great and friendly powers. Your State enjoys perfect tranquillity; you have neither wars nor conquerors to fear; you have no other master than the wise laws you have yourselves made; and these are administered by upright magistrates of your own choosing. You are neither so wealthy as to be enervated by effeminacy, and thence to lose, in the pursuit of frivolous pleasures, the taste for real happiness and solid virtue; nor poor enough to require more assistance from abroad than your own industry is sufficient to procure you. In the meantime the precious privilege of liberty, which in great nations is maintained only by submission to the most exorbitant impositions, costs you hardly anything for its preservation.

May a Republic, so wisely and happily constituted, last for ever, for an example to other nations, and for the felicity of its own citizens! This is the only prayer you have left to make, the only precaution that remains to be taken. It depends, for the future, on yourselves alone (not to make you happy, for your ancestors have saved you that trouble), but to render that happiness lasting, by your wisdom in its enjoyment. It is on your constant union, your obedience to the laws, and your respect for their ministers, that your preservation depends. If there remains among you the smallest trace of bitterness or distrust, hasten to destroy it, as an accursed leaven which sooner or later must bring misfortune and ruin on the State. I conjure you all to look into your hearts, and to hearken to the secret voice of conscience. Is there any among you who can find, throughout the universe, a more upright, more enlightened, and more honourable body than your magistracy? Do not all its members set you an example of moderation, of simplicity of manners, of respect for the laws, and of the most sincere harmony? Place, therefore, without reserve, in such wise superiors, that salutary confidence which reason ever owes to virtue. Consider that they are your own choice, that they justify that choice, and that the honours due to those whom you have dignified are necessarily yours by reflection. Not one of you is so ignorant as not to know that, when the laws lose their force and those who defend them their authority, security and liberty are universally impossible. Why, therefore, should you hesitate to do that cheerfully and with just confidence which you would all along have been bound to do by your true interest, your duty, and reason itself?

Let not a culpable and pernicious indifference to the maintenance of the constitution ever induce you to neglect, in case of need, the prudent advice of the most enlightened and zealous of your fellow-citizens; but let equity, moderation, and firmness of resolution continue to regulate all your proceedings, and to exhibit you to the whole universe as the example of a valiant and modest people, jealous equally of their honour and of their liberty. Beware particularly, as the last piece of advice I shall give you, of sinister constructions and venomous rumours, the secret motives of which are often more dangerous than the actions at which they are levelled. A whole house will be awake and take the first alarm given by a good and trusty watch-dog, who barks only at the approach of thieves; but we hate the importunity of those noisy curs, which are perpetually disturbing the public repose, and whose continual ill-timed warnings prevent our attending to them, when they may perhaps be necessary.

And you, most honourable and magnificent lords, the worthy and revered magistrates of a free people, permit me to offer you in particular my duty and homage. If there is in the world a station capable of conferring honour on those who fill it, it is undoubtedly that which virtue and talents combine to bestow, that of which you have made yourselves worthy, and to which you have been promoted by your fellow-citizens. Their worth adds a new lustre to your own; while, as you have been chosen, by men capable of governing others, to govern themselves, I cannot but hold you as much superior to all other magistrates, as a free people, and particularly that over which you have the honour to preside, is by its wisdom and its reason superior to the populace of other States.

Be it permitted me to cite an example of which there ought to have existed better records, and one which will be ever near to my heart. I cannot recall to mind, without the sweetest emotions, the memory of that virtuous citizen, to whom I owe my being and by whom I was often instructed, in my infancy, in the respect which is due to you. I see him still, living by the work of his hands, and feeding his soul on the sublimest truths. I see the works of Tacitus, Plutarch, and Grotius, lying before him in the midst of the tools of his trade. At his side stands his dear son, receiving, alas with too little profit, the tender instructions of the best of fathers. But, if the follies of youth made me for a while forget his wise lessons, I have at length the happiness to be conscious that, whatever propensity one may have to vice, it is not easy for an education, with which love has mingled, to be entirely thrown away.

Such, my most honourable and magnificent lords, are the citizens, and even the common inhabitants of the State which you govern; such are those intelligent and sensible men, of whom, under the name of workmen and the people, it is usual, in other nations, to have a low and false opinion. My father, I own with pleasure, was in no way distinguished among his fellow-citizens. He was only such as they all are; and yet, such as he was, there is no country in which his acquaintance would not have been coveted and cultivated even with advantage by men of the highest character. It would not become me, nor is it, thank Heaven, at all necessary for me to remind you of the regard which such men have a right to expect of their magistrates, to whom they are equal both by education and by the rights of nature and birth, and inferior only, by their own will, by that preference which they owe to your merit, and, for giving you, can claim some sort of acknowledgment on your side. It is with a lively satisfaction I understand that the greatest candour and condescension attend, in all your behaviour towards them, on that gravity which becomes the ministers of the law; and that you so well repay them, by your esteem and attention, the respect and obedience which they owe to you. This conduct is not only just but prudent; as it happily tends to obliterate the memory of many unhappy events which ought to be buried in eternal oblivion. It is also so much the more judicious, as it tends to make this generous and equitable people find a pleasure in their duty; to make them naturally love to do you honour, and to cause those who are the most zealous in the maintenance of their own rights to be at the same time the most disposed to respect yours.

It ought not to be thought surprising that the rulers of a civil society should have the welfare and glory of their communities at heart: but it is uncommonly fortunate for the peace of men, when those persons who look upon themselves as the magistrates, or rather the masters, of a more holy and sublime country, show some love for the earthly country which maintains them. I am happy in having it in my power to make so singular an exception in our favour, and to be able to rank, among its best citizens, those zealous depositaries of the sacred articles of faith established by the laws, those venerable shepherds of souls whose powerful and captivating eloquence is so much the better calculated to bear to men's hearts the maxims of the gospel, as they are themselves the first to put them into practice. All the world knows of the great success with which the art of the pulpit is cultivated at Geneva; but men are so used to hearing divines preach one thing and practise another, that few have a chance of knowing how far the spirit of Christianity, holiness of manners, severity towards themselves, and indulgence towards their neighbours, prevail throughout the whole body of our ministers. It is, perhaps, given to the city of Geneva alone to produce the edifying example of so perfect a union between its clergy and men of letters. It is in great measure on their wisdom, their known moderation, and their zeal for the prosperity of the State that I build my hopes of its perpetual tranquillity. At the same time, I notice, with a pleasure mingled with surprise and veneration, how much they detest the frightful maxims of those accursed and barbarous men, of whom history furnishes us with more than one example; who, in order to support the pretended rights of God, that is to say their own interests, have been so much the less sparing of human blood, as they were more hopeful their own in particular would be always respected.

I must not forget that precious half of the Republic which makes the happiness of the other; and whose sweetness and prudence preserve its tranquillity and virtue. Amiable and virtuous daughters of Geneva, it will be always the lot of your sex to govern ours. Happy are we, so long as your chaste influence, solely exercised within the limits of conjugal union, is exerted only for the glory of the State and the happiness of the public. It was thus the female sex commanded at Sparta; and thus you deserve to command at Geneva. What man can be such a barbarian as to resist the voice of honour and reason, coming from the lips of an affectionate wife? Who would not despise the vanities of luxury, on beholding the simple and modest attire which, from the lustre it derives from you, seems the most favourable to beauty? It is your task to perpetuate, by your insinuating influence and your innocent and amiable rule, a respect for the laws of the State, and harmony among the citizens. It is yours to reunite divided families by happy marriages; and, above all things, to correct, by the persuasive sweetness of your lessons and the modest graces of your conversation, those extravagances which our young people pick up in other countries, whence, instead of many useful things by which they might profit, they bring home hardly anything, besides a puerile air and a ridiculous manner, acquired among loose women, but an admiration for I know not what so-called grandeur, and paltry recompenses for being slaves, which can never come near the real greatness of liberty. Continue, therefore, always to be what you are, the chaste guardians of our morals, and the sweet security for our peace, exerting on every occasion the privileges of the heart and of nature, in the interests of duty and virtue.

I flatter myself that I shall never be proved to have been mistaken in building on such a foundation my hopes of the general happiness of the citizens and the glory of the Republic. It must be confessed, however, that with all these advantages, it will not shine with that lustre, by which the eyes of most men are dazzled; a puerile and fatal taste for which is the most mortal enemy of happiness and liberty.

Let our dissolute youth seek elsewhere light pleasures and long repentances. Let our pretenders to taste admire elsewhere the grandeur of palaces, the beauty of equipages, sumptuous furniture, the pomp of public entertainments, and all the refinements of luxury and effeminacy. Geneva boasts nothing but men; such a sight has nevertheless a value of its own, and those who have a taste for it are well worth the admirers of all the rest.

Deign, most honourable, magnificent, and sovereign lords, to receive, and with equal goodness, this respectful testimony of the interest I take in your common prosperity. And, if I have been so unhappy as to be guilty of any indiscreet transport in this glowing effusion of my heart, I beseech you to pardon me, and to attribute it to the tender affection of a true patriot, and to the ardent and legitimate zeal of a man, who can imagine for himself no greater felicity than to see you happy.

Most honourable, magnificent, and sovereign lords, I am, with the most profound respect,

Your most humble and obedient servant and fellow-citizen.

Chambéry,   J. J. Rousseau
June 12, 1754

PREFACE

Of all human sciences the most useful and most imperfect appears to me to be that of mankind: and I will venture to say, the single inscription on the Temple of Delphi contained a precept more difficult and more important than is to be found in all the huge volumes that moralists have ever written. I consider the subject of the following discourse as one of the most interesting questions philosophy can propose, and unhappily for us, one of the most thorny that philosophers can have to solve. For how shall we know the source of inequality between men, if we do not begin by knowing mankind? And how shall man hope to see himself as nature made him, across all the changes which the succession of place and time must have produced in his original constitution? How can he distinguish what is fundamental in his nature from the changes and additions which his circumstances and the advances he has made have introduced to modify his primitive condition? Like the statue of Glaucus, which was so disfigured by time, seas, and tempests, that it looked more like a wild beast than a god, the human soul, altered in society by a thousand causes perpetually recurring, by the acquisition of a multitude of truths and errors, by the changes happening to the constitution of the body, and by the continual jarring of the passions, has, so to speak, changed in appearance, so as to be hardly recognizable. Instead of a being acting constantly from fixed and invariable principles, instead of that celestial and majestic simplicity, impressed on it by its divine Author, we find it only the frightful contrast of passion mistaking itself for reason, and of understanding grown delirious.

It is still more cruel that, as every advance made by the human species removes it still farther from its primitive state, the more discoveries we make, the more we deprive ourselves of the means of making the most important of all. Thus it is, in one sense, by our very study of man, that the knowledge of him is put out of our power.

It is easy to perceive that it is in these successive changes in the constitution of man that we must look for the origin of those differences which now distinguish men, who, it is allowed, are as naturally equal among themselves as were the animals of every kind, before physical causes had introduced those varieties now observable among some of them.

It is, in fact, not to be conceived that these primary changes, however they may have arisen, could have altered, all at once and in the same manner, every individual of the species. It is natural to think that, while the condition of some of them grew better or worse, and they were acquiring various good or bad qualities not inherent in their nature, there were others who continued a longer time in their original condition. Such was doubtless the first source of the inequality of mankind, which it is much easier to point out thus in general terms, than to assign with precision to its actual causes.

Let not my readers therefore imagine that I flatter myself with having seen what it appears to me so difficult to discover. I have here entered upon certain arguments, and risked some conjectures, less in the hope of solving the difficulty, than with a view to throwing some light upon it, and reducing the question to its proper form. Others may easily proceed farther on the same road, and yet no one find it very easy to get to the end. For it is by no means a light undertaking to distinguish properly between what is original and what is artificial in the actual nature of man, or to form a true idea of a state which no longer exists, perhaps never did exist, and probably never will exist; and of which it is, nevertheless, necessary to have true ideas, in order to form a proper judgment of our present state. It requires, indeed, more philosophy than can be imagined to enable any one to determine exactly what precautions he ought to take, in order to make solid observations on this subject; and it appears to me that a good solution of the following problem would be not unworthy of the Aristotles and Plinys of the present age. *What experiments would have to be made, to discover the natural man? And how are those experiments to be made in a state of society?*

So far am I from undertaking to solve this problem, that I think I have sufficiently considered the subject, to venture to declare beforehand that our greatest philosophers would not be too good to direct such experiments, and our most powerful sovereigns to make them. Such a combination we have very little reason to expect, especially attended with the perseverance, or rather succession of intelligence and goodwill necessary on both sides to success.

These investigations, which are so difficult to make, and have been hitherto so little thought of, are, nevertheless, the only means that remain of obviating a multitude of difficulties which deprive us of the knowledge of the real foundations of human society. It is this ignorance of the nature of men which casts so much uncertainty and obscurity on the true definition of natural right: for, the idea of right, says Burlamaqui, and more particularly that of natural right, are ideas manifestly relative to the nature of man. It is then from this very nature itself, he goes on, from the constitution and state of man, that we must deduce the first principles of this science.

We cannot see without surprise and disgust how little agreement there is between the different authors who have treated this great subject. Among the more important writers there are scarcely two of the same mind about it. Not to speak of the ancient philosophers, who seem to have done their best purposely to contradict one another on the most fundamental principles, the Roman jurists subjected man and the other animals indiscriminately to the same natural law, because they considered, under that name, rather the law which nature imposes on herself than that which she prescribes to others; or rather because of the particular acceptation of the term 'law' among those jurists; who seem on this occasion to have understood nothing more by it than the general relations established by nature between all animated beings, for their common preservation. The moderns, understanding by the term 'law' merely a rule prescribed to a moral being, that is to say intelligent, free, and considered in his relations to other beings, consequently confine the jurisdiction of natural law to man, as the only animal endowed with reason. But, defining this law, each after his own fashion, they have established it on such metaphysical principles, that there are very few persons among us capable of comprehending them, much less of discovering them for themselves. So that the definitions of these learned men, all differing in everything else, agree only in this, that it is impossible to comprehend the law of nature, and consequently to obey it, without being a very subtle casuist and a profound metaphysician. All which is as much as to say that mankind must have employed, in the establishment of society, a capacity which is acquired only with great difficulty, and by very few persons, even in a state of society.

Knowing so little of nature, and agreeing so ill about the meaning of the word 'law', it would be difficult for us to fix on a good definition of natural law. Thus all the definitions we meet with in books, setting aside their defect in point of uniformity, have yet another fault, in that they are derived from many kinds of knowledge, which men do not possess naturally, and from advantages of which they can have no idea until they have already departed from that state. Modern writers begin by inquiring what rules it would be expedient for me to agree on for their common interest, and then give the name of natural law to a collection of these rules, without any other proof than the good that would result from their being universally practised. This is undoubtedly a simple way of making definitions, and of explaining the nature of things by almost arbitrary conveniences.

But as long as we are ignorant of the natural man, it is in vain for us to attempt to determine either the law originally prescribed to him, or that which is best adapted to his constitution. All we can know with any certainty respecting this law is that, if it is to be a law, not only the wills of those it obliges must be sensible of their submission to it; but also, to be natural, it must come directly from the voice of nature.

Throwing aside, therefore, all those scientific books, which teach us only to see men such as they have made themselves, and contemplating the first and most simple operations of the human soul, I think I can perceive in it two principles prior to reason, one of them deeply interesting us in our own welfare and preservation, and the other exciting a natural repugnance at seeing any other sensible being, and particularly any of our own species, suffer pain or death. It is from the agreement and combination which the understanding is in a position to establish between these two principles, without its being necessary to introduce that of sociability, that all the rules of natural right appear to me to be derived—rules which our reason is afterwards obliged to establish on other foundations, when by its successive developments it has been led to suppress nature itself.

In proceeding thus, we shall not be obliged to make man a philosopher before he is a man. His duties toward others are not dictated to him only by the later lessons of wisdom; and, so long as he does not resist the internal impulse of compassion, he will never hurt any other man, nor even any sentient being, except on those lawful occasions on which his own preservation is concerned and he is obliged to give himself the preference. By this method also we put an end to the time-honoured disputes concerning the participation of animals in natural law: for it is clear that, being destitute of intelligence and liberty, they cannot recognize that law; as they partake, however, in some measure of our nature, in consequence of the sensibility with which they are endowed, they ought to partake of natural right; so that mankind is subjected to a kind of obligation even toward the brutes. It appears, in fact, that if I am bound to do no injury to my fellow-creatures, this is less because they are rational than because they are sentient beings: and this quality, being common both to men and beasts, ought to entitle the latter at least to the privilege of not being wantonly ill-treated by the former.

The very study of the original man, of his real wants, and the fundamental principles of his duty, is besides the only proper method we can adopt to obviate all the difficulties which the origin of moral inequality presents, on the true foundations of the body politic, on the reciprocal rights of its members, and on many other similar topics equally important and obscure.

If we look at human society with a calm and disinterested eye, it seems, at first, to show us only the violence of the powerful and the oppression of the weak. The mind is shocked at the cruelty of the one, or is induced to lament the blindness of the other; and as nothing is less permanent in life than those external relations, which are more frequently produced by accident than wisdom, and which are called weakness or power, riches or poverty, all human institutions seem at first glance to be founded merely on banks of shifting sand. It is only by taking a closer look, and removing the dust and sand that surround the edifice, that we perceive the immovable basis on which it is raised, and learn to respect its foundations. Now, without a serious study of man, his natural faculties and their successive development, we shall never be able to make these necessary distinctions, or to separate, in the actual constitution of things, that which is the effect of the divine will, from the innovations attempted by human art. The political and moral investigations, therefore, to which the important question before us leads, are in every respect useful; while the hypothetical history of government affords a lesson equally instructive to mankind.

In considering what we should have become, had we been left to ourselves, we should learn to bless Him, whose gracious hand, correcting our institutions, and giving them an immovable basis, has prevented those disorders which would otherwise have arisen from them, and caused our happiness to come from those very sources which seemed likely to involve us in misery.

> *Quem te deus esse*
> *Jussit, et humana quà parte locatus es in re,*
> *Disce.*

Persius, Satires, iii. 71

[Learn what God ordered you to be and your place in the human condition.]

A DISSERTATION
ON THE ORIGIN AND FOUNDATION
OF THE INEQUALITY OF MANKIND

It is of man that I have to speak; and the question I am investigating shows me that it is to men that I must address myself: for questions of this sort are not asked by those who are afraid to honour truth. I shall then confidently uphold the cause of humanity before the wise men who invite me to do so, and shall not be dissatisfied if I acquit myself in a manner worthy of my subject and of my judges.

I conceive that there are two kinds of inequality among the human species; one, which I call natural or physical, because it is established by nature, and consists in a difference of age, health, bodily strength, and the qualities of the mind or of the soul: and another, which may be called moral or political inequality, because it depends on a kind of convention, and is established, or at least authorized, by the consent of men. This latter consists of the different privileges which some men enjoy to the prejudice of others; such as that of being more rich, more honoured, more powerful, or even in a position to exact obedience.

It is useless to ask what is the source of natural inequality, because that question is answered by the simple definition of the word. Again, it is still more useless to inquire whether there is any essential connection between the two inequalities; for this would be only asking, in other words, whether those who command are necessarily better than those who obey, and if strength of body or of mind, wisdom, or virtue are always found in particular individuals, in proportion to their power or wealth: a question fit perhaps to be discussed by slaves in the hearing of their masters, but highly unbecoming to reasonable and free men in search of the truth.

The subject of the present discourse, therefore, is more precisely this. To mark, in the progress of things, the moment at which right took the place of violence and nature became subject to law, and to explain by what sequence of miracles the strong came to submit to serve the weak, and the people to purchase imaginary repose at the expense of real felicity.

The philosophers, who have inquired into the foundations of society, have all felt the necessity of going back to a state of nature; but not one of them has got there. Some of them have not hesitated to ascribe to man, in such a state, the idea of just and unjust, without troubling themselves to show that he must be possessed of such an idea, or that it could be of any use to him. Others have spoken of the natural right of every man to keep what belongs to him, without explaining what they meant by 'belongs'. Others again, beginning by giving the strong authority over the weak, proceeded directly to the birth of government, without regard to the time that must have elapsed before the meaning of the words 'authority' and 'government' could have existed among men. Every one of them, in short, constantly dwelling on wants, avidity, oppression, desires, and pride, has transferred to the state of nature ideas which were acquired in society; so that, in speaking of the savage, they described the social man. It has not even entered into the heads of most of our writers to doubt whether the state of nature ever existed; but it is clear from the Holy Scriptures that the first man, having received his understanding and commandments immediately from God, was not himself in such a state; and that, if we give such credit to the writings of Moses as every Christian philosopher ought to give, we must deny that, even before the deluge, men were ever in the pure state of nature; unless, indeed, they fell back into it from some very extraordinary circumstance; a paradox which it would be very embarrassing to defend, and quite impossible to prove.

Let us begin then by laying all facts aside, as they do not affect the question. The investigations we may enter into, in treating this subject, must not be considered as historical truths, but only as mere conditional and hypothetical reasonings, rather calculated to explain the nature of things, than to ascertain their actual origin; just like the hypotheses which our physicists daily form respecting the formation of the world. Religion commands us to believe that God Himself having taken men out of a state of nature immediately after the creation, they are unequal only because it is His will they should be so: but it does not forbid us to form conjectures based solely on the nature of man, and the beings around him, concerning what might have become of the human race, if it had been left to itself. This then is the question asked me, and that which I propose to discuss in the following discourse. As my subject interests mankind in general, I shall endeavour to make use of a style adapted to all nations, or rather, forgetting time and place, to attend only to men to whom I am speaking. I shall suppose myself in the Lyceum of Athens, repeating the lessons of my masters, with Plato and Xenocrates for judges, and the whole human race for audience.

O man, of whatever country you are, and whatever your opinions may be, behold your history, such as I have thought to read it, not in books written by your fellow-creatures, who are liars, but in nature, which never lies. All that comes from her will be true; nor will you meet with anything false, unless I have involuntarily put in something of my own. The times of which I am going to speak are very remote: how much are you changed from what you once were! It is, so to speak, the life of your species which I am going to write, after the qualities which you have received, which your education and habits may have depraved, but cannot have entirely destroyed. There is, I feel, an age at which the individual man would wish to stop: you are about to inquire about the age at which you would have liked your whole species to stand still. Discontented with your present state, for reasons which threaten your unfortunate descendants with still greater discontent, you will perhaps wish it were in your power to go back; and this feeling should be a panegyric on your first ancestors, a criticism of your contemporaries, and a terror to the unfortunates who will come after you.

The First Part

Important as it may be, in order to judge rightly of the natural state of man, to consider him from his origin, and to examine him, as it were, in the embryo of his species, I shall not follow his organization through its successive developments, nor shall I stay to inquire what his animal system must have been at the beginning, in order to become at length what it actually is. I shall not ask whether his long nails were at first, as Aristotle supposes, only crooked talons; whether his whole body, like that of a bear, was not covered with hair; or whether the fact that he walked upon all fours, with his looks directed toward the earth, confined to a horizon of a few paces, did not at once point out the nature and limits of his ideas. On this subject I could form none but vague and almost imaginary conjectures. Comparative anatomy has as yet made too little progress, and the observations of naturalists are too uncertain, to afford an adequate basis for any solid reasoning. So that, without having recourse to the supernatural information given us on this head, or paying any regard to the changes which must have taken place in the internal, as well as the external, conformation of man, as he applied his limbs to new uses, and fed himself on new kinds of food, I shall suppose his conformation to have been at all times what it appears to us at this day; that he always walked on two legs, made use of his hands as we do, directed his looks over all nature, and measured with his eyes the vast expanse of the heavens.

If we strip this being, thus constituted, of all the supernatural gifts he may have received, and all the artificial faculties he can have acquired only by a long process; if we consider him, in a word, just as he must have come from the hands of nature, we behold in him an animal weaker than some, and less agile than others; but, taking him all round, the most advantageously organized of any. I see him satisfying his hunger at the first oak, and slaking his thirst at the first brook: finding his bed at the foot of the tree which afforded him a repast; and, with that, all his wants supplied.

While the earth was left to its natural fertility and covered with immense forests, whose trees were never mutilated by the axe, it would present on every side both sustenance and shelter for every species of animal. Men, dispersed up and down among the rest, would observe and imitate their industry, and thus attain even to the instinct of the beasts, with the advantage that, whereas every species of brutes was confined to one particular instinct, man, who perhaps has not any one peculiar to himself, would appropriate them all, and live upon most of those different foods, which other animals shared among themselves; and thus would find his subsistence much more easily than any of the rest.

Accustomed from their infancy to the inclemencies of the weather and the rigour of the seasons, inured to fatigue, and forced, naked and unarmed, to defend themselves and their prey from other ferocious animals, or to escape them by flight, men would acquire a robust and almost unalterable constitution. The children, bringing with them into the world the excellent constitution of their parents, and fortifying it by the very exercises which first produced it, would thus acquire all the vigour of which the human frame is capable. Nature in this case treats them exactly as Sparta treated the children of her citizens: those who come well formed into the world she renders strong and robust, and all the rest she destroys; differing in this respect from our modern communities, in which the State, by making children a burden to their parents, kills them indiscriminately before they are born.

The body of a savage man being the only instrument he understands, he uses it for various purposes, of which ours, for want of practice, are incapable: for our industry deprives us of that force and agility which necessity obliges him to acquire. If he had had an axe, would he have been able with his naked arm to break so large a branch from a tree? If he had had a sling, would he have been able to throw a stone with so great velocity? If he had had a ladder, would he have been so nimble in climbing a tree? If he had had a horse, would he have been himself so swift of foot? Give civilized man time to gather all his machines about him, and he will no doubt easily beat the savage; but if you would see a still more unequal contest, set them together naked and unarmed, and you will soon see the advantage of having all our forces constantly at our disposal, of being always prepared for every event, and of carrying one's self, as it were, perpetually whole and entire about one.

Hobbes contends that man is naturally intrepid, and is intent only upon attacking and fighting. Another illustrious philosopher holds the opposite, and Cumberland and Pufendorf also affirm that nothing is more timid and fearful than man in the state of nature; that he is always in a tremble, and ready to fly at the least noise or the slightest movement. This may be true of things he does not know; and I do not doubt his being terrified by every novelty that presents itself, when he neither knows the physical good or evil he may expect from it, nor can make a comparison between his own strength and the dangers he is about to encounter. Such circumstances, however, rarely occur in a state of nature, in which all things proceed in a uniform manner, and the face of the earth is not subject to those sudden and continual changes which arise from the passions and caprices of bodies of men living together. But savage man, living dispersed among other animals, and finding himself betimes in a situation to measure his strength with theirs, soon comes to compare himself with them; and, perceiving that he surpasses them more in adroitness than they surpass him in strength, learns to be no longer afraid of them. Set a bear, or a wolf, against a robust, agile, and resolute savage, as they all are, armed with stones and a good cudgel, and you will see that the danger will be at least on both sides, and that, after a few trials of this kind, wild beasts, which are not fond of attacking each other, will not be at all ready to attack man, whom they will have found to be as wild and ferocious as themselves. With regard to such animals as have really more strength than man has adroitness, he is in the same situation as all weaker animals, which notwithstanding are still able to subsist; except indeed that he has the advantage that, being equally swift of foot, and finding an almost certain place of refuge in every tree, he is at liberty to take or leave it at every encounter, and thus to fight or fly, as he chooses. Add to this that it does not appear that any animal naturally makes war on man, except in case of self-defence or excessive hunger, or betrays any of those violent antipathies, which seem to indicate that one species is intended by nature for the food of another.

This is doubtless why negroes and savages are so little afraid of the wild beasts they may meet in the woods. The Caribs of Venezuela among others live in this respect in absolute security and without the smallest inconvenience. Though they are almost naked, Francis Corréal tells us, they expose themselves freely in the woods, armed only with bows and arrows; but no one has ever heard of one of them being devoured by wild beasts.

But man has other enemies more formidable, against which he is not provided with such means of defence: these are the natural infirmities of infancy, old age, and illness of every kind, melancholy proofs of our weakness, of which the two first are common to all animals, and the last belongs chiefly to man in a state of society. With regard to infancy, it is observable that the mother, carrying her child always with her, can nurse it with much greater ease than the females of many other animals, which are forced to be perpetually going and coming, with great fatigue, one way to find subsistence, and another to suckle or feed their young. It is true that if the woman happens to perish, the infant is in great danger of perishing with her; but this risk is common to so many other species of animals, whose young take a long time before they are able to provide for themselves. And if our infancy is longer than theirs, our lives are longer in proportion; so that all things are in this respect fairly equal; though there are other rules to be considered regarding the duration of the first period of life, and the number of young, which do not affect the present subject. In old age, when men are less active and perspire little, the need for food diminishes with the ability to provide it. As the savage state also protects them from gout and rheumatism, and old age is, of all ills, that which human aid can least alleviate, they cease to be, without others perceiving that they are no more, and almost without perceiving it themselves.

With respect to sickness, I shall not repeat the vain and false declamations which most healthy people pronounce against medicine; but I shall ask if any solid observations have been made from which it may be justly concluded that, in the countries where the art of medicine is most neglected, the mean duration of man's life is less than in those where it is most cultivated. How indeed can this be the case, if we bring on ourselves more diseases than medicine can furnish remedies? The great inequality in manner of living, the extreme idleness of some, and the excessive labour of others, the easiness of exciting and gratifying our sensual appetites, the too exquisite foods of the wealthy which over-heat and fill them with indigestion, and, on the other hand, the unwholesome food of the poor, often, bad as it is, insufficient for their needs, which induces them, when opportunity offers, to eat voraciously and overcharge their stomachs; all these, together with sitting up late, and excesses of every kind, immoderate transports of every passion, fatigue, mental exhaustion, the innumerable pains and anxieties inseparable from every condition of life, by which the mind of man is incessantly tormented; these are too fatal proofs that the greater part of our ills are of our own making, and that we might have avoided them nearly all by adhering to that simple, uniform, and solitary manner of life which nature prescribed. If she destined man to be healthy, I venture to say that a state of reflection is one contrary to nature and that the man who meditates is a depraved animal. When we think of the good constitution of the savages, at least of those whom we have not ruined with our spirituous liquors, and reflect that they are troubled with hardly any disorders, save wounds and old age, we are tempted to believe that, in following the history of civil society, we shall be telling also that of human sickness. Such, at least, was the opinion of Plato, who inferred from certain remedies prescribed, or approved, by Podalirius and Machaon at the siege of Troy, that several sicknesses which these remedies gave rise to in his time, were not then known to mankind; and Celsus tells us that diet, which is now so necessary, was first invented by Hippocrates.

Being subject therefore to so few causes of sickness, man, in the state of nature, can have no need of remedies, and still less of physicians: nor is the human race in this respect worse off than other animals, and it is easy to learn from hunters whether they meet with many infirm animals in the course of the chase. It is certain they frequently meet with such as carry the marks of having been considerably wounded, with many that have had bones or even limbs broken, yet have been healed without any other surgical assistance than that of time, or any other regimen than that of their ordinary life. At the same time their cures seem not to have been less perfect, for their not having been tortured by incisions, poisoned with drugs, or wasted by fasting. In short, however useful medicine, properly administered, may be among us, it is certain that, if the savage, when he is sick and left to himself, has nothing to hope but from nature, he has, on the other hand, nothing to fear but from his disease; which renders his situation often preferable to our own.

We should beware, therefore, of confounding the savage man with the men we have daily before our eyes. Nature treats all the animals left to her care with a predilection that seems to show how jealous she is of that right. The horse, the cat, the bull, and even the ass are generally of greater stature, and always more robust, and have more vigour, strength, and courage, when they run wild in the forests than when bred in the stall. By becoming domesticated, they lose half these advantages; and it seems as if all our care to feed and treat them well serves only to deprave them. It is thus with man also: as he becomes sociable and a slave, he grows weak, timid, and servile; his effeminate way of life totally enervates his strength and courage. To this it may be added that there is still a greater difference between savage and civilized man than between wild and tame beasts; for men and brutes having been treated alike by nature, the several conveniences in which men indulge themselves still more than they do their beasts, are so many additional causes of their deeper degeneracy.

It is not therefore so great a misfortunate to these primitive men, nor so great an obstacle to their preservation, that they go naked, have no dwellings, and lack all the superfluities which we think so necessary. If their skins are not covered with hair, they have no need of such covering in warm climates; and, in cold countries, they soon learn to appropriate the skins of the beasts they have overcome. If they have but two legs to run with, they have two arms to defend themselves with, and provide for their wants. Their children are slowly and with difficulty taught to walk; but their mothers are able to carry them with ease; an advantage which other animals lack, as the mother, if pursued, is forced either to abandon her young, or to regulate her pace by theirs. Unless, in short, we suppose a singular and fortuitous concurrence of circumstances of which I shall speak later, and which could well never come about, it is plain in every state of the case, that the man who first made himself clothes or a dwelling was furnishing himself with things not at all necessary; for he had till then done without them, and there is no reason why he should not have been able to put up in manhood with the same kind of life as had been his in infancy.

Solitary, indolent, and perpetually accompanied by danger, the savage cannot be fond of sleep; his sleep too must be light, like that of the animals, which think but little and may be said to slumber all the time they do not think. Self-preservation being his chief and almost sole concern, he must exercise most those faculties which are most concerned with attack or defence, either for overcoming his prey, or for preventing him from becoming the prey of other animals. On the other hand, those organs which are perfected only by softness and sensuality will remain in a gross and imperfect state, incompatible with any sort of delicacy; so that, his senses being divided on this head, his touch and taste will be extremely coarse, his sight, hearing, and smell exceedingly fine and subtle. Such in general is the animal condition, and such, according to the narratives of travellers, is that of most savage nations. It is therefore no matter for surprise that the Hottentots of the Cape of Good Hope distinguish ships at sea, with the naked eye, at as great a distance as the Dutch can do with their telescopes; or that the savages of America should trace the Spaniards, by their smell, as well as the best dogs could have done; or that these barbarous peoples feel no pain in going naked, or that they use large quantities of pimento with their food, and drink the strongest European liquors like water.

Hitherto I have considered merely the physical man; let us now take a view of him on his metaphysical and moral side.

I see nothing in any animal but an ingenious machine, to which nature hath given senses to wind itself up, and to guard itself, to a certain degree, against anything that might tend to disorder or destroy it. I perceive exactly the same things in the human machine, with this difference, that in the operations of the brute, nature is the sole agent, whereas man has some share in his own operations, in his character as a free agent. The one chooses and refuses by instinct, the other from an act of free will: hence the brute cannot deviate from the rule prescribed to it, even when it would be advantageous for it to do so; and, on the contrary, man frequently deviates from such rules to his own prejudice. Thus a pigeon would be starved to death by the side of a dish of the choicest meats, and a cat on a heap of fruit or grain; though it is certain that either might find nourishment in the foods which it thus rejects with disdain, did it think of trying them. Hence it is that dissolute men run into excesses which bring on fevers and death; because the mind depraves the senses, and the will continues to speak when nature is silent.

Every animal has ideas, since it has senses; it even combines those ideas in a certain degree; and it is only in degree that man differs, in this respect, from the brute. Some philosophers have even maintained that there is a greater difference between one man and another than between some men and some beasts. It is not, therefore, so much the understanding that constitutes the specific difference between the man and the brute, as the human quality of free agency. Nature lays her commands on every animal, and the brute obeys her voice. Man receives the same impulsion, but at the same time knows himself at liberty to acquiesce or resist: and it is particularly in his consciousness of this liberty that the spirituality of his soul is displayed. For physics may explain, in some measure, the mechanism of the senses and the formation of ideas; but in the power of willing or rather of choosing, and in the feeling of this power, nothing is to be found but acts which are purely spiritual and wholly inexplicable by the laws of mechanism.

Yet, if the difficulties attending all these questions should still leave room for dispute about this difference between men and brutes, there is another very specific quality which distinguishes them, and which will admit of no dispute. This is the faculty of self-improvement, which, by the help of circumstances, gradually develops all the rest of our faculties, and is inherent in the species as in the individual: whereas a brute is, at the end of a few months, all he will ever be during his whole life, and his species, at the end of a thousand years, exactly what it was the first year of that thousand. Why is man alone liable to grow into a dotard? Is it not because he returns, in this, to his primitive state; and that, while the brute, which has acquired nothing and has therefore nothing to lose, still retains the force of instinct, man, who loses, by age or accident, all that his *perfectibility* had enabled him to gain, falls by this means lower than the brutes themselves? It would be melancholy, were we forced to admit that this distinctive and almost unlimited faculty is the source of all human misfortunes; that it is this which, in time, draws man out of his original state, in which he would have spent his days insensibly in peace and innocence; that it is this faculty, which, successively producing in different ages his discoveries and his errors, his vices and his virtues, makes him at length a tyrant both over himself and over nature.[1] It would be shocking to be obliged to regard as a benefactor the man who first suggested to the Oroonoko Indians the use of the boards they apply to the temples of their children, which secure to them some part at least of their imbecility and original happiness.

Savage man, left by nature solely to the direction of instinct, or rather indemnified for what he may lack by faculties capable at first of supplying its place, and afterwards of raising him much above it, must accordingly begin with purely animal functions: thus seeing and feeling must be his first condition, which would be common to him and all other animals. To will, and not to will, to desire and to fear, must be the first, and almost the only operations of his soul, till new circumstances occasion new developments of his faculties.

Whatever moralists may hold, the human understanding is greatly indebted to the passions, which, it is universally allowed, are also much indebted to the understanding. It is by the activity of the passions that our reason is improved; for we desire knowledge only because we wish to enjoy; and it is impossible to conceive any reason why a person who has neither fears nor desires should give himself the trouble of reasoning. The passions, again, originate in our wants, and their progress depends on that of our knowledge; for we cannot desire or fear anything, except from the idea we have of it, or from the simple impulse of nature. Now savage man, being destitute of every species of enlightenment, can have no passions save those of the latter kind: his desires never go beyond his physical wants. The only goods he recognizes in the universe are food, a female, and sleep: the only evils he fears are pain and hunger. I say pain, and not death: for no animal can know what it is to die; the knowledge of death and its terrors being one of the first acquisitions made by man in departing from an animal state.

It would be easy, were it necessary, to support this opinion by facts, and to show that, in all the nations of the world, the progress of the understanding has been exactly proportionate to the wants which the peoples had received from nature, or been subjected to by circumstances, and in consequence to the passions that induced them to provide for those necessities. I might instance the arts, rising up in Egypt and expanding with the inundation of the Nile. I might follow their progress into Greece, where they took root afresh, grew up and towered to the skies, among the rocks and sands of Attica, without being able to germinate on the fertile banks of the Eurotas: I might observe that in general, the people of the North are more industrious than those of the South, because they cannot get on so well without being so: as if nature wanted to equalize matters by giving their understandings the fertility she had refused to their soil.

But who does not see, without recurring to the uncertain testimony of history, that everything seems to remove from savage man both the temptation and the means of changing his condition? His imagination paints no pictures; his heart makes no demands on him. His few wants are so readily supplied, and he is so far from having the knowledge which is needful to make him want more, that he can have neither foresight nor curiosity. The face of nature becomes indifferent to him as it grows familiar. He sees in it always the same order, the same successions: he has not understanding enough to wonder at the greatest miracles; nor is it in his mind that we can expect to find that philosophy man needs, if he is to know how to notice for once what he sees every day. His soul, which nothing disturbs, is wholly wrapped up in the feeling of its present existence, without any idea of the future, however near at hand; while his projects, as limited as his views, hardly extend to the close of day. Such, even at present, is the extent of the native Caribbean's foresight: he will improvidently sell you his cottonbed in the morning, and come crying in the evening to buy it again, not having foreseen he would want it again the next night.

The more we reflect on this subject, the greater appears the distance between pure sensation and the most simple knowledge: it is impossible indeed to conceive how a man, by his own powers alone, without the aid of communication and the spur of necessity, could have bridged so great a gap. How many ages may have elapsed before mankind were in a position to behold any other fire than that of the heavens! What a multiplicity of chances must have happened to teach them the commonest uses of that element! How often must they have let it out before they acquired the art of reproducing it! and how often may not such a secret have died with him who had discovered it! What shall we say of agriculture, an art which requires so much labour and foresight, which is so dependent on others that it is plain it could only be practiced in a society which had at least begun, and which does not serve so much to draw the means of subsistence from the earth—for these it would produce of itself—but to compel it to produce what is most to our taste? But let us suppose that men had so multiplied that the natural produce of the earth was no longer sufficient for their support; a supposition, by the way, which would prove such a life to be very advantageous for the human race; let us suppose that, without forges or workshops, the instruments of husbandry had dropped from the sky into the hands of savages; that they had overcome their natural aversion to continual labour; that they had learnt so much foresight for their needs; that they had divined how to cultivate the earth, to sow grain and plant trees; that they had discovered the arts of grinding corn, and of setting the grape to ferment—all being things that must have been taught them by the gods, since it is not to be conceived how they could discover them for themselves—yet after all this, what man among them would be so absurd as to take the trouble of cultivating a field, which might be stripped of its crop by the first comer, man or beast, that might take a liking to it; and how should each of them resolve to pass his life in wearisome labour, when, the more necessary to him the reward of his labour might be, the surer he would be of not getting it? In a word, how could such a situation induce men to cultivate the earth, till it was regularly parcelled out among them; that is to say, till the state of nature had been abolished?

Were we to suppose savage man as trained in the art of thinking as philosophers make him; were we, like them, to suppose him a very philosopher capable of investigating the sublimest truths, and of forming, by highly abstract chains of reasoning, maxims of reason and justice, deduced from the love of order in general, or the known will of his Creator; in a word, were we to suppose him as intelligent and enlightened, as he must have been, and is in fact found to have been, dull and stupid, what advantage would accrue to the species, from all such metaphysics, which could not be communicated by one to another, but must end with him who made them? What progress could be made by mankind, while dispersed in the woods among other animals? and how far could men improve or mutually enlighten one another, when, having no fixed habitation, and no need of one another's assistance, the same persons hardly met twice in their lives, and perhaps then, without knowing one another or speaking together?

Let it be considered how many ideas we owe to the use of speech; how far grammar exercises the understanding and facilitates its operations. Let us reflect on the inconceivable pains and the infinite space of time that the first invention of languages must have cost. To these reflections add what preceded, and then judge how many thousand ages must have elapsed in the successive development in the human mind of those operations of which it is capable.

I shall here take the liberty for a moment, of considering the difficulties of the origin of languages, on which subject I might content myself with a simple repetition of the Abbé Condillac's investigations, as they fully confirm my system, and perhaps even first suggested it. But it is plain, from the manner in which this philosopher solves the difficulties he himself raises, concerning the origin of arbitrary signs, that he assumes what I question, viz. that a kind of society must already have existed among the first inventors of language. While I refer, therefore, to his observations on this head, I think it right to give my own, in order to exhibit the same difficulties in a light adapted to my subject. The first which presents itself is to conceive how language can have become necessary; for as there was no communication among men and no need for any, we can neither conceive the necessity of this invention, nor the possibility of it, if it was not somehow indispensable. I might affirm, with many others, that languages arose in the domestic intercourse between parents and their children. But this expedient would not obviate the difficulty, and would besides involve the blunder made by those who, in reasoning on the state of nature, always import into it ideas gathered in a state of society. Thus they constantly consider families as living together under one roof, and the individuals of each as observing among themselves a union as intimate and permanent as that which exists among us, where so many common interests unite them: whereas, in this primitive state, men had neither houses, nor huts, nor any kind of property whatever; every one lived where he could, seldom for more than a single night; the sexes united without design, as accident, opportunity, or inclination brought them together, nor had they any great needs of words to communicate their designs to each other; and they parted with the same indifference. The mother gave suck to her children at first for her own sake; and afterwards, when habit had made them dear, for theirs: but as soon as they were strong enough to go in search of their own food, they forsook her of their own accord; and, as they had hardly any other method of not losing one another than that of remaining continually within sight, they soon became quite incapable of recognizing one another when they happened to meet again. It is further to be observed that the child, having all his wants to explain, and of course more to say to his mother than the mother could have to say to him, must have borne the brunt of the task of invention, and the language he used would be of his own device, so that the number of languages would be equal to that of the individuals speaking them, and the variety would be increased by the vagabond and roving life they led, which would not give time for any idiom to become constant. For to say that the mother dictated to her child the words he was to use in asking her for one thing or another, is an explanation of how languages already formed are taught, but by no means explains how languages were originally formed.

We will suppose, however, that this first difficulty is obviated. Let us for a moment then take ourselves as being on this side of the vast space which must lie between a pure state of nature and that in which languages had become necessary, and, admitting their necessity, let us inquire how they could first be established. Here we have a new and worse difficulty to grapple with; for if men need speech to learn to think, they must have stood in much greater need of the art of thinking, to be able to invent that of speaking. And though we might conceive how the articulate sounds of the voice came to be taken as the conventional interpreters of our ideas, it would still remain for us to inquire what could have been the interpreters of this convention for those ideas, which, answering to no sensible objects, could not be indicated either by gesture or voice; so that we can hardly form any tolerable conjectures about the origin of this art of communicating our thoughts and establishing a correspondence between minds: an art so sublime, that far distant as it is from its origin, philosophers still behold it at such an immeasurable distance from perfection, that there is none rash enough to affirm it will ever reach it, even though the revolutions time necessarily produces were suspended in its favour, though prejudice should be banished from our academies or condemned to silence, and those learned societies should devote themselves uninterruptedly for whole ages to this thorny question.

The first language of mankind, the most universal and vivid, in a word the only language man needed, before he had occasion to exert his eloquence to persuade assembled multitudes, was the simple cry of nature. But as this was excited only by a sort of instinct on urgent occasions, to implore assistance in case of danger, or relief in case of suffering, it could be of little use in the ordinary course of life, in which more moderate feelings prevail. When the ideas of men began to expand and multiply, and closer communication took place among them, they strove to invent more numerous signs and a more copious language. They multiplied the inflexions of the voice, and added gestures, which are in their own nature more expressive, and depend less for their meaning on a prior determination. Visible and movable objects were therefore expressed by gestures, and audible ones by imitative sounds: but, as hardly anything can be indicated by gestures, except objects actually present or easily described, and visible actions; as they are not universally useful—for darkness or the interposition of a material object destroys their efficacy—and as besides they rather request than secure our attention; men at length bethought themselves of substituting for them the articulate sounds of the voice, which, without bearing the same relation to any particular ideas, are better calculated to express them all, as conventional signs. Such an institution could only be made by common consent, and must have been effected in a manner not very easy for men whose gross organs had not been accustomed to any such exercise. It is also in itself still more difficult to conceive, since such a common agreement must have had motives, and it seems that speech must needs have existed before its use could be established.

It is reasonable to suppose that the first words which men used had for them a much wider meaning than the ones we use in languages which have already developed, and that, ignorant as they were of the division of discourse into its constituent parts, they at first gave every single word the sense of a whole proposition. When they began to distinguish subject and attribute, and noun and verb, which was itself no common effort of genius, substantives were at first only so many proper names; the present infinitive was the only tense of verbs; and the very idea of adjectives must have been developed with great difficulty; for every adjective is an abstract idea, and abstractions are painful and unnatural operations.

Every object at first received a particular name without regard to genus or species, which these primitive originators were not in a position to distinguish; every individual presented itself to their minds in isolation, as they are in the picture of nature. If one oak was called A, another was called B; for the primitive idea of two things is that they are not the same, and it often takes a long time for what they have in common to be seen: so that, the narrower the limits of their knowledge of things, the more copious their dictionary must have been. The difficulty of using such a vocabulary could not be easily removed; for, to arrange beings under common and generic denominations, it became necessary to know their distinguishing properties: the need arose for observation and definition, that is to say, for natural history and metaphysics of a far more developed kind than men can at that time have possessed.

Add to this, that general ideas cannot be introduced into the mind without the assistance of words, nor can the understanding seize them except by means of propositions. This is one of the reasons why animals cannot form such ideas, or ever acquire that capacity for self-improvement which depends on them. When a monkey goes from one nut to another, are we to conceive that he entertains any general idea of that kind of fruit, and compares its archetype with the two individual nuts? Assuredly he does not; but the sight of one of these nuts recalls to his memory the sensations which he received from the other, and his eyes, being modified after a certain manner, give information to the palate of the modification it is about to receive. Every general idea is purely intellectual; if the imagination meddles with it ever so little, the idea immediately becomes particular. If you endeavour to trace in your mind the image of a tree in general, you never attain to your end. In spite of all you can do, you will have to see it as great or little, bare or leafy, light or dark, and were you capable of seeing nothing in it but what is common to all trees, it would no longer be like a tree at all. Purely abstract beings are perceivable in the same manner, or are only conceivable by the help of language. The definition of a triangle alone gives you a true idea of it: the moment you imagine a triangle in your mind, it is some particular triangle and not another, and you cannot avoid giving it sensible lines on a coloured area. We must then make use of propositions and of language in order to form general ideas. For no sooner does the imagination cease to operate than the understanding proceeds only by the help of words. If then the first inventors of speech could give names only to ideas they already had, it follows that the first substantives could be nothing more than proper names.

But when our new grammarians, by means of which I have no conception, began to extend their ideas and generalize their terms, the ignorance of the inventors must have confined this method within very narrow limits; and, as they had at first gone too far in multiplying the names of individuals, from ignorance of their genus and species, they made afterwards too few of these, from not having considered beings in all their specific differences. It would indeed have needed more knowledge and experience than they could have, and more pains and inquiry than they would have bestowed, to carry these destinations to their proper length. If, even today, we are continually discovering new species, which have hitherto escaped observation, let us reflect how many of them must have escaped men who judged things merely from their first appearance! It is superfluous to add that the primitive classes and the most general notions must necessarily have escaped their notice also. How, for instance, could they have understood or thought of the words matter, spirit, substance, mode, figure, motion, when even our philosophers, who have so long been making use of them, have themselves the greatest difficulty in understanding them; and when, the ideas attached to them being purely metaphysical, there are no models of them to be found in nature?

But I stop at this point, and ask my judges to suspend their reading a while, to consider, after the invention of physical substantives, which is the easiest part of language to invent, that there is still a great way to go, before the thoughts of men will have found perfect expression and constant form, such as would answer the purposes of public speaking, and produce their effect on society. I beg of them to consider how much time must have been spent, and how much knowledge needed, to find out numbers, abstract terms, aorists, and all the tenses of verbs, particles, syntax, the method of connecting propositions, the forms of reasoning, and all the logic of speech. For myself, I am so aghast at the increasing difficulties which present themselves, and so well convinced of the almost demonstrable impossibility that languages should owe their original institution to merely human means, that I leave, to any one who will undertake it, the discussion of the difficult problem: which was the more necessary, the existence of society to the invention of language, or the invention of language to the establishment of society. But be the origins of language and society what they may, it may be at least inferred, from the little care which nature has taken to unite mankind by mutual wants, and to facilitate the use of speech, that she has contributed little to make them sociable, and has put little of her own into all they have done to create such bonds of union. It is in fact impossible to conceive why, in a state of nature, one man should stand more in need of the assistance of another, than a monkey or a wolf of the assistance of another of its kind: or, granting that he did, what motives could induce that other to assist him; or, even then, by what means they could agree about the conditions. I know it is incessantly repeated that man would in such a state have been the most miserable of creatures; and indeed, if it be true, as I think I have proved, that he must have lived many ages, before he could have either desire or an opportunity of emerging from it, this would only be an accusation against nature, and not against the being which she had thus unhappily constituted. But as I understand the word 'miserable', it either has no meaning at all, or else signifies only a painful privation of something, or a state of suffering either in body or soul. I should be glad to have explained to me, what kind of misery a free being, whose heart is at ease and whose body is in health, can possibly suffer. I would like to know which is the more likely to become insupportable to those who take part in it: the life of society or the life of nature. We hardly see anyone around us except people who are complaining of their existence; many even deprive themselves of it if they can and all divine and human laws put together can hardly put a stop to this disorder. I would like to know if anyone has heard of a savage who took it into his head, when he was free, to complain of life and to kill himself. Let us be less arrogant, then, when we judge on which side real misery is found. Nothing, on the other hand, could be more miserable than a savage exposed to the dazzling light of our 'civilization', tormented by our passions and reasoning about a state different from his own. It appears that providence most wisely determined that the faculties, which he potentially possessed, should develop themselves only as occasion offered to exercise them, in order that they might not be superfluous or perplexing to him, by appearing before their time, nor slow and useless when the need for them arose. In instinct alone, he had all he required for living in the state of nature; and with a developed understanding he has only just enough to support life in society.

It appears, at first view, that men in a state of nature, having no moral relations or determinate obligations one with another, could not be either good or bad, virtuous or vicious; unless we take these terms in a physical sense, and call, in an individual, those qualities vices which may be injurious to his preservation, and those virtues which contribute to it; in which case, he would have to be accounted most virtuous, who put least check on the pure impulses of nature. But without deviating from the ordinary sense of the words, it will be proper to suspend the judgment we might be led to form on such a state, and be on our guard against our prejudices, till we have weighed the matter in the scales of impartiality, and seen whether virtues or vices preponderate among civilized men: and whether their virtues do them more good than their vices do harm; till we have discovered whether the progress of the sciences sufficiently indemnifies them for the mischiefs they do one another, in proportion as they are better informed of the good they ought to do; or whether they would not be, on the whole, in a much happier condition if they had nothing to fear or to hope from any one, than as they are, subjected to universal dependence, and obliged to take everything from those who engage to give them nothing in return.

Above all, let us not conclude, with Hobbes, that because man has no idea of goodness, he must be naturally wicked; that he is vicious because he does not know virtue; that he always refuses to do his fellow-creatures services which he does not think they have a right to demand; or that by virtue of the right he justly claims to all he needs, he foolishly imagines himself the sole proprietor of the whole universe. Hobbes had seen clearly the defects of all the modern definitions of natural right: but the consequences which he deduces from his own show that he understands it in an equally false sense. In reasoning on the principles he lays down, he ought to have said that the state of nature, being that in which the care for our own preservation is the least prejudicial to that of others, was consequently the best calculated to promote peace, and the most suitable for mankind. He does say the exact opposite, in consequence of having improperly admitted, as a part of savage man's care for self-preservation, the gratification of a multitude of passions which are the work of society, and have made laws necessary. A bad man, he says, is a robust child. But it remains to be proved whether man in a state of nature is this robust child:

and, should we grant that he is, what would he infer? Why truly, that if this man, when robust and strong, were dependent on others as he is when feeble, there is no extravagance he would not be guilty of; that he would beat his mother when she was too slow in giving him her breast; that he would strangle one of his younger brothers, if he should be troublesome to him, or bite the leg of another, if he put him to any inconvenience. But that man in the state of nature is both strong and dependent involves two contrary suppositions. Man is weak when he is dependent, and is his own master before he comes to be strong. Hobbes did not reflect that the same cause, which prevents a savage from making use of his reason, as our jurists hold, prevents him also from abusing his faculties, as Hobbes himself allows: so that it may be justly said that savages are not bad merely because they do not know what it is to be good: for it is neither the development of the understanding nor the restraint of law that hinders them from doing ill; but the peacefulness of their passions, and their ignorance of vice: *tanto plus in illis proficit vitiorum ignoratio, quam in his cognitio virtutis.*[2] There is another principle which has escaped Hobbes; which, having been bestowed on mankind, to moderate, on certain occasions, the impetuosity of *amour-propre,* or, before its birth, the desire of self-preservation, tempers the ardour with which he pursues his own welfare, by an innate repugnance at seeing a fellow-creature suffer.[3] I think I need not fear contradiction in holding man to be possessed of the only natural virtue, which could not be denied him by the most violent detractor of human virtue. I am speaking of compassion, which is a disposition suitable to creatures so weak and subject to so many evils as we certainly are: by so much the more universal and useful to mankind, as it comes before any kind of reflection; and at the same time so natural, that the very brutes themselves sometimes give evident proofs of it. Not to mention the tenderness of mothers for their offspring and the perils they encounter to save them from danger, it is well known that horses show a reluctance to trample on living bodies. One animal never passes by the dead body of another of its species without disquiet: some even give their fellows a sort of burial; while the mournful lowings of the cattle when they enter the slaughter-house show the impressions made on them by the horrible spectacle which meets them. We find, with pleasure, the author of *The Fable of the Bees* obliged to own that man is a compassionate and sensible being, and laying aside his cold subtlety of style, in the example he gives, to present us with the pathetic description of a man who, from a place of confinement, is compelled to behold a wild beast tear a child from the arms of its mother, grinding its tender limbs with its murderous teeth, and tearing its palpitating entrails with its claws. What horrid agitation must not the eye-witness of such a scene experience, although he would not be personally concerned! What anguish would he not suffer at not being able to give any assistance to the fainting mother and the dying infant!

Such is the pure emotion of nature, prior to all kinds of reflection! Such is the force of natural compassion, which the greatest depravity of morals has as yet hardly been able to destroy! for we daily find at our theatres men affected, nay, shedding tears at the sufferings of a wretch who, were he in the tyrant's place, would probably even add to the torments of his enemies; like the bloodthirsty Sulla, who was so sensitive to ills he had not caused, or that Alexander of Pheros who did not dare to go and see any tragedy acted, for fear of being seen weeping with Andromache and Priam, though he could listen without emotion to the cries of all the citizens who were daily strangled at his command.

Mollisima corda
Humano generi dare se natura fatetur
Quae lacrimas dedit.

Juvenal, *Satires,* XV. 131[4]

Mandeville well knew that, in spite of all their morality, men would have never been better than monsters, had not nature bestowed on them a sense of compassion, to aid their reason: but he did not see that from this quality alone flow all those social virtues, of which he denied man the possession. But what is generosity, clemency, or humanity but compassion applied to the weak, to the guilty, or to mankind in general? Even benevolence and friendship are, if we judge rightly, only the effects of compassion, constantly set upon a particular object: for how is it different to wish that another person may not suffer pain and uneasiness and to wish him happy? Were it even true that pity is no more than a feeling which puts us in the place of the sufferer, a feeling obscure yet lively in a savage, developed yet feeble in civilized man; this truth would have no other consequence than to confirm my argument. Compassion must, in fact, be the stronger, the more the animal beholding any kind of distress identifies himself with the animal that suffers. Now, it is plain that such identification must have been much more perfect in a state of nature than it is in a state of reason. It is reason that engenders *amour-propre*, and reflection that confirms it: it is reason which turns man's mind back upon itself, and divides him from everything that could disturb or afflict him. It is philosophy that isolates him, and bids him say, at sight of the misfortunes of others: 'Perish if you will, I am secure.' Nothing but such general evils as threaten the whole community can disturb the tranquil sleep of the philosopher, or tear him from his bed. A murder may with impunity be committed under his window; he has only to put his hands to his ears and argue a little with himself, to prevent nature, which is shocked within him, from identifying itself with the unfortunate sufferer. Uncivilized man has not this admirable talent; and for want of reason and wisdom, is always foolishly ready to obey the first promptings of humanity. It is the populace that flocks together at riots and street brawls, while the wise man prudently makes off. It is the mob and the market-women, who part the combatants, and stop decent people from cutting one another's throats.

It is then certain that compassion is a natural feeling, which, by moderating the activity of love of self in each individual, contributes to the preservation of the whole species. It is this compassion that hurries us without reflection to the relief of those who are in distress: it is this which in a state of nature supplies the place of laws, morals, and virtues, with the advantage that none are tempted to disobey its gentle voice: it is this which will always prevent a sturdy savage from robbing a weak child or a feeble old man of the sustenance they may have with pain and difficulty acquired, if he sees a possibility of providing for himself by other means: it is this which, instead of inculcating that sublime maxim of rational justice, *Do to others as you would have them do unto you,* inspires all men with that other maxim of natural goodness, much less perfect indeed, but perhaps more useful; *Do good to yourself with as little evil as possible to others.* In a word, it is rather in this natural feeling than in any subtle arguments that we must look for the cause of that repugnance, which every man would experience in doing evil, even independently of the maxims of education. Although it might belong to Socrates and other minds of the like craft to acquire virtue by reason, the human race would long since have ceased to be, had its preservation depended only on the reasonings of the individuals composing it.

With passions so little active, and so good a curb, men, being rather wild than wicked, and more intent to guard themselves against the mischief that might be done them, than to do mischief to others, were by no means subject to very perilous dissensions. They maintained no kind of intercourse with one another, and were consequently strangers to vanity, deference, esteem, and contempt; they had not the least idea of 'mine' and 'thine', and no true conception of justice; they looked upon every violence to which they were subjected, rather as an injury that might easily be repaired than as a crime that ought to be punished; and they never thought of taking revenge, unless perhaps mechanically and on the spot, as a dog will sometimes bite the stone which is thrown at him. Their quarrels therefore would seldom have very bloody consequences; for the subject of them would be merely the question of subsistence. But I am aware of one greater danger, which remains to be noticed.

Of the passions that stir the heart of man, there is one which makes the sexes necessary to each other, and is extremely ardent and impetuous; a terrible passion that braves danger, surmounts all obstacles, and in its transports seems calculated to bring destruction on the human race which it is really destined to preserve. What must become of men who are left to this brutal and boundless rage, without modesty, without shame, and daily upholding their amours at the price of their blood?

It must, in the first place, be allowed that, the more violent the passions are, the more are laws necessary to keep them under restraint. But, setting aside the inadequacy of laws to effect this purpose, which is evident from the crimes and disorders to which these passions daily give rise among us, we should do well to inquire if these evils did not spring up with the laws themselves; for in this case, even if the laws were capable of repressing such evils, it is the least that could be expected from them, that they should check a mischief which would not have arisen without them.

Let us begin by distinguishing between the physical and moral ingredients in the feeling of love. The physical part of love is that general desire which urges the sexes to union with each other. The moral part is that which determines and fixes this desire exclusively upon one particular object; or at least gives it a greater degree of energy toward the object thus preferred. It is easy to see that the moral part of love is a factitious feeling, born of social usage, and enhanced by the women with much care and cleverness, to establish their empire, and put in power the sex which ought to obey. This feeling, being founded on certain ideas of beauty and merit which a savage is not in a position to acquire, and on comparisons which he is incapable of making, must be for him almost non-existent; for, as his mind cannot form abstract ideas of proportion and regularity, so his heart is not susceptible to the feelings of love and admiration, which are even insensibly produced by the application of these ideas. He follows solely the character nature has implanted in him, and not tastes which he could never have acquired; so that every woman equally answers his purpose.

Men in a state of nature being confined merely to what is physical in love, and fortunate enough to be ignorant of those excellences, which whet the appetite while they increase the difficulty of gratifying it, must be subject to fewer and less violent fits of passion, and consequently fall into fewer and less violent disputes. The imagination, which causes such ravages among us, never speaks to the heart of savages, who quietly await the impulses of nature, yield to them involuntarily, with more pleasure than ardour, and, their wants once satisfied, lose the desire. It is therefore incontestable that love, as well as all other passions, must have acquired in society that glowing impetuosity, which makes it so often fatal to mankind. And it is the more absurd to represent savages as continually cutting one another's throats to indulge their brutality, because this opinion is directly contrary to experience; the Caribbeans, who have as yet least of all deviated from the state of nature, being in fact the most peaceable of people in their amours, and the least subject to jealousy, though they live in a hot climate which seems always to inflame the passions.

With regard to the inferences that might be drawn, in the case of several species of animals, the males of which fill our poultry yards with blood and slaughter, or in spring make the forests resound with their quarrels over their females; we must begin by excluding all those species, in which nature has plainly established, in the comparative power of the sexes, relations different from those which exist among us: thus we can base no conclusion about men on the habits of fighting cocks. In those species where the proportion is better observed, these battles must be entirely due to the scarcity of females in comparison with males; or, what amounts to the same thing, to the intervals during which the female constantly refuses the advances of the male: for if each female admits the male but during two months in the year, it is the same as if the number of females were five-sixths less. Now, neither of these two cases is applicable to the human species, in which the number of females usually exceeds that of males, and among whom it has never been observed, even among savages, that the females have, like those of other animals, their stated times of passion and indifference. Moreover, in several of these species, the individuals all take fire at once, and there comes a fearful moment of universal passion, tumult, and disorder among them; a scene which is never beheld in the human species, whose love is not thus seasonal. We must not then conclude from the combats of such animals for the enjoyment of the females, that the case would be the same with mankind in a state of nature: and, even if we drew such a conclusion, we see that such contests do not exterminate other kinds of animals, and we have no reason to think they would be more fatal to ours. It is indeed clear that they would do still less mischief than is the case in a state of society; especially in those countries in which, morals being still held in some repute, the jealousy of lovers and the vengeance of husbands are the daily cause of duels, murders, and even worse crimes; where the obligation of eternal fidelity only occasions adultery, and the very laws of honour and continence necessarily increase debauchery and lead to the multiplication of abortions.

Let us conclude then that man in a state of nature, wandering up and down the forests, without industry, without speech, and without home, an equal stranger to war and to all ties, neither standing in need of his fellow-creatures nor having any desire to hurt them, and perhaps even not distinguishing them one from another; let us conclude that, being self-sufficient and subject to so few passions, he could have no feelings or knowledge but such as befitted his situation; that he felt only his actual necessities, and disregarded everything he did not think himself immediately concerned to notice, and that his understanding made no greater progress than his vanity. If by accident he made any discovery, he was the less able to communicate it to others, as he did not know even his own children. Every art would necessarily perish with its inventor, where there was no kind of education among men, and generations succeeded generations without the least advance; when, all setting out from the same point, centuries must have elapsed in the barbarism of the first ages; when the race was already old, and man remained a child.

If I have expatiated at such length on this supposed primitive state, it is because I had so many ancient errors and inveterate prejudices to eradicate, and therefore thought it incumbent on me to dig down to their very root, and show, by means of a true picture of the state of nature, how far even the natural inequalities of mankind are from having that reality and influence which modern writers suppose.

It is in fact easy to see that many of the differences between men which are ascribed to nature stem rather from habit and the diverse modes of life of men in society. Thus a robust or delicate constitution, and the strength or weakness attaching to it, are more frequently the effects of a hardy or effeminate method of education than of the original endowment of the body. It is the same with the powers of the mind; for education not only makes a difference between such as are cultured and such as are not, but even increases the differences which exist among the former, in proportion to their respective degrees of culture: as the distance between a giant and a dwarf on the same road increases with every step they take. If we compare the prodigious diversity, which obtains in the education and manner of life of the various orders of men in the state of society, with the uniformity and simplicity of animal and savage life, in which every one lives on the same kind of food and in exactly the same manner, and does exactly the same things, it is easy to conceive how much less the difference between man and man must be in a state of nature than in a state of society, and how greatly the natural inequality of mankind must be increased by the inequalities of social institutions.

But even if nature really affected, in the distribution of her gifts, that partiality which is imputed to her, what advantage would the greatest of her favourites derive from it, to the detriment of others, in a state that admits of hardly any kind of relation between them? Where there is no love, of what advantage is beauty? Of what use is wit to those who do not converse, or cunning to those who have no business with others? I hear it constantly repeated that, in such a state, the strong would oppress the weak; but what is here meant by oppression? Some, it is said, would violently domineer over others, who would groan under a servile submission to their caprices. This indeed is exactly what I observe to be the case among us; but I do not see how it can be inferred of men in a state of nature, who could not easily be brought to conceive what we mean by dominion and servitude. One man, it is true, might seize the fruits which another had gathered, the game he had killed, or the cave he had chosen for shelter; but how would he ever be able to exact obedience, and what ties of dependence could there be among men without possessions? If, for instance, I am driven from one tree, I can go to the next; if I am disturbed in one place, what hinders me from going to another? Again, should I happen to meet with a man so much stronger than myself, and at the same time so depraved, so indolent, and so bar-barous, as to compel me to provide for his sustenance while he himself remains idle; he must take care not to have his eyes off me for a single moment; he must bind me fast before he goes to sleep, or I shall certainly either knock him on the head or make my escape. That is to say, he must in such a case voluntarily expose himself to much greater trouble than he seeks to avoid, or can give me. After all this, let him be off his guard ever so little; let him but turn his head aside at any sudden noise, and I shall be instantly twenty paces off, lost in the forest, and, my fetters burst asunder, he would never see me again.

Without my expatiating thus uselessly on these details, every one must see that as the bonds of servitude are formed merely by the mutual dependence of men on one another and the reciprocal needs that unite them, it is impossible to make any man a slave, unless he be first reduced to a situation in which he cannot do without the help of others: and, since such a situation does not exist in a state of nature, every one is there his own mas-ter, and the law of the strongest is of no effect.

Having proved that the inequality of mankind is hardly felt, and that its influence is next to nothing in a state of nature, I must next show its origin and trace its progress in the successive developments of the human mind. Having shown that human *perfectibility,* the social virtues, and the other faculties which natural man potentially possessed, could never develop of themselves, but must require the fortuitous concurrence of many foreign causes that might never arise, and without which he would have remained for ever in his primitive conditions, I must now collect and consider the different accidents which may have improved the human understanding while depraving the species, and made man wicked while making him sociable; so as to bring him and the world from that distant period to the point at which we now behold them.

I confess that, as the events I am going to describe might have happened in various ways, I have nothing to determine my choice but conjectures: but such conjectures become reasons when they are the most probable that can be drawn from the nature of things, and the only means of discovering the truth. The consequences, however, which I mean to deduce will not be barely conjectural; as, on the principles just laid down, it would be impossible to form any other theory that would not furnish the same results, and from which I could not draw the same conclusions.

This will be a sufficient apology for my not dwelling on the manner in which the lapse of time compensates for the little probability in the events; on the surprising power of trivial causes, when their action is constant; on the impossibility, on the one hand, of destroying certain hypotheses, though on the other we cannot give them the certainty of known matters of fact, on its being within the province of history, when two facts are given as real, and have to be connected by a series of intermediate facts, which are unknown or supposed to be so, to supply such facts as may connect them; and on its being in the province of philosophy when history is silent, to determine similar facts to serve the same end; and lastly, on the influence of similarity, which, in the case of events, reduces the facts to a much smaller number of different classes than is commonly imagined. It is enough for me to offer these hints to the consideration of my judges, and to have so arranged that the general reader has no need to consider them at all.

The Second Part

The first man who, having enclosed a piece of ground, bethought himself of saying 'this is mine', and found people simple enough to believe him, was the real founder of civil society. From how many crimes, wars, and murders, from how many horrors and misfortunes might not any one have saved mankind, by pulling up the stakes, or filling up the ditch, and crying to his fellows: 'Beware of listening to this impostor; you are undone if you once forget that the fruits of the earth belong to us all, and the earth itself to nobody.' But there is great probability that things had then already come to such a pitch, that they could no longer continue as they were; for the idea of property depends on many prior ideas, which could only be acquired successively, and cannot have been formed all at once in the human mind. Mankind must have made very considerable progress, and acquired considerable knowledge and industry which they must also have transmitted and increased from age to age, before they arrived at this last point of the state of nature. Let us then go farther back, and endeavour to unify under a single point of view that slow succession of events and discoveries in the most natural order.

Man's first feeling was that of his own existence, and his first care that of self-preservation. The produce of the earth furnished him with all he needed, and instinct told him how to use it. Hunger and other appetites made him at various times experience various modes of existence; and among these was one which urged him to propagate his species—a blind propensity that, having nothing to do with the heart, produced a merely animal act. The want once gratified, the two sexes knew each other no more; and even the offspring was nothing to its mother, as soon as it could do without her.

Such was the condition of infant man; the life of an animal limited at first to mere sensations, and hardly profiting by the gifts nature bestowed on him, much less capable of entertaining a thought of forcing anything from her. But difficulties soon presented themselves, and it became necessary to learn how to surmount them: the height of the trees, which prevented him from gathering their fruits, the competition of other animals desirous of the same fruits, and the ferocity of those who sought to deprive man himself of life, all obliged him to apply himself to bodily exercises. He had to be active, swift of foot, and vigorous in fight. Natural weapons, stones, and sticks, were easily found: he learnt to surmount the obstacles of nature, to contend in case of necessity with other

animals, and to dispute for the means of subsistence even with other men, or to indemnify himself for what he was forced to give up to a stronger.

In proportion as the human race grew more numerous, men's cares increased. The difference of soils, climates, and seasons, must have introduced some differences into their
manner of living. Barren years, long and sharp winters, scorching summers which parched
the fruits of the earth, must have demanded a new industry. On the seashore and the banks
of rivers, they invented the hook and line, and became fishermen and eaters of fish. In the
forests they made bows and arrows, and became huntsmen and warriors. In cold countries
they clothed themselves with the skins of the beasts they had slain. The lightning, a volcano, or some lucky chance acquainted them with fire, a new resource against the rigours
of winter: they next learned how to preserve this element, then how to reproduce it, and
finally how to prepare with it the flesh of animals which before they had eaten raw.

The way these different beings and phenomena impinged on him and on each other
must naturally have engendered in man's mind the awareness of certain relationships.
Thus the relationships which we denote by the terms great, small, strong, weak, swift,
slow, fearful, bold, and the like, almost insensibly compared at need, must have at length
produced in him a kind of reflection, or rather a mechanical prudence, which would indicate to him the precautions most necessary to his security.

The new intelligence which resulted from this development increased his superiority
over other animals, by making him sensible of it. He would now endeavour, therefore, to
ensnare them, would play them a thousand tricks, and though many of them might surpass him in swiftness or in strength, would in time become the master of some and the
scourge of others. Thus, the first time he looked into himself, he felt the first emotion of
pride; and, at a time when he scarce knew how to distinguish the different orders of
beings, by looking upon his species as of the highest order, he prepared the way for
assuming pre-eminence as an individual.

Other men, it is true, were not then to him what they now are to us, and he had no
greater intercourse with them than with other animals; yet they were not neglected in his
observations. The conformities, which he would in time discover between them, and
between himself and his female, led him to judge of others which were not then perceptible; and finding that they all behaved as he himself would have done in like circumstances, he naturally inferred that their manner of thinking and acting was altogether in
conformity with his own. This important truth, once deeply impressed on his mind, must
have induced him, from an intuitive feeling more certain and much more rapid than any
kind of reasoning, to pursue the rules of conduct, which he had best observe towards
them, for his own security and advantage.

Taught by experience that the love of well-being is the sole motive of human actions,
he found himself in a position to distinguish the few cases, in which mutual interest
might justify him in relying upon the assistance of his fellows; and also the still fewer
cases in which a conflict of interests might give cause to suspect them. In the former case,
he joined in the same herd with them, or at most in some kind of loose association, that
laid no restraint on its members, and lasted no longer than the transitory occasion that
formed it. In the latter case, every one sought his own private advantage, either by open
force, if he thought himself strong enough, or by address and cunning, if he felt himself
the weaker.

In this manner, men may have insensibly acquired some gross ideas of mutual undertakings, and of the advantages of fulfilling them: that is, just so far as their present and
apparent interest was concerned; for they were perfect strangers to foresight, and were so
far from troubling themselves about the distant future, that they hardly thought of the

morrow. If a deer was to be taken, every one saw that, in order to succeed, he must abide faithfully by his post: but if a hare happened to come within the reach of any one of them, it is not to be doubted that he pursued it without scruple, and, having seized his prey, cared very little, if by so doing he caused his companions to miss theirs.

It is easy to understand that such intercourse would not require a language much more refined than that of rooks or monkeys, who associate together for much the same purpose. Inarticulate cries, plenty of gestures, and some imitative sounds, must have been for a long time the universal language; and by the addition, in every country, of some conventional articulate sounds (of which, as I have already intimated, the first institution is not too easy to explain) particular languages were produced; but these were rude and imperfect, and nearly such as are now to be found among some savage nations.

Hurried on by the rapidity of time, by the abundance of things I have to say, and by the almost insensible progress of things in their beginnings, I pass over in an instant a multitude of ages; for the slower the events were in their succession, the more rapidly may they be described.

These first advances enabled men to make others with greater rapidity. In proportion as they grew enlightened, they grew industrious. They ceased to fall asleep under the first tree, or in the first cave that afforded them shelter; they invented several kinds of implements of hard and sharp stones, which they used to dig up the earth, and to cut wood; then they made huts out of branches, and afterwards learnt to plaster them over with mud and clay. This was the epoch of a first revolution, which established and distinguished families, and introduced a kind of property, in itself the source of a thousand quarrels and conflicts. As, however, the strongest were probably the first to build themselves huts which they felt themselves able to defend, it may be concluded that the weak found it much easier and safer to imitate, than to attempt to dislodge them: and of those who were once provided with huts, none could have any inducement to appropriate that of his neighbour; not indeed so much because it did not belong to him, as because it could be of no use, and he could not make himself master of it without exposing himself to a desperate battle with the family which occupied it.

The first expansions of the human heart were the effects of a novel situation, which united husbands and wives, fathers and children, under one roof. The habit of living together soon gave rise to the finest feelings known to humanity, conjugal love and paternal affection. Every family became a little society, the more united because liberty and reciprocal attachment were the only bonds of its union. The sexes, whose manner of life had been hitherto the same, began now to adopt different ways of living. The women became more sedentary, and accustomed themselves to mind the hut and their children, while the men went abroad in search of their common subsistence. From living a softer life, both sexes also began to lose something of their strength and ferocity: but, if individuals became to some extent less able to encounter wild beasts separately, they found it, on the other hand, easier to assemble and resist in common.

The simplicity and solitude of man's life in this new condition, the paucity of his wants, and the implements he had invented to satisfy them, left him a great deal of leisure, which he employed to furnish himself with many conveniences unknown to his fathers: and this was the first yoke he inadvertently imposed on himself, and the first source of the evils he prepared for his descendants. For, besides continuing thus to enervate both body and mind, these conveniences lost with use almost all their power to please, and even degenerated into real needs, till the want of them became far more disagreeable than the possession of them had been pleasant. Men would have been unhappy at the loss of them, though the possession did not make them happy.

We can here see a little better how the use of speech became established, and insensibly improved in each family, and we may form a conjecture also concerning the manner in which various causes may have extended and accelerated the progress of language, by making it more and more necessary. Floods or earthquakes surrounded inhabited districts with precipices or waters: revolutions of the globe tore off portions from the continent, and made them islands. It is readily seen that among men thus collected and compelled to live together, a common idiom must have arisen much more easily than among those who still wandered through the forests of the continent. Thus it is very possible that after their first essays in navigation the islanders brought over the use of speech to the continent: and it is at least very probable that communities and languages were first established in islands, and even came to perfection there before they were known on the mainland.

Everything now begins to change its aspect. Men, who have up to now been roving in the woods, by taking to a more settled manner of life, come gradually together, form separate bodies, and at length in every country arises a distinct nation, united in character and manners, not by regulations or laws, but by uniformity of life and food, and the common influence of climate. Permanent neighbourhood could not fail to produce, in time, some connection between different families. Young people of opposite sexes lived in neighbouring huts and the casual unions between them which resulted from the call of nature soon led, as they came to know each other better, to another kind which was no less pleasant and more permanent. They became accustomed to looking more closely at the different objects of their desires and to making comparisons; imperceptibly they acquired ideas of beauty and merit which led to feelings of preference. In consequence of seeing each other often, they could not do without seeing each other constantly. A tender and pleasant feeling insinuated itself into their souls, and the least opposition turned it into an impetuous fury: with love arose jealousy; discord triumphed, and human blood was sacrificed to the gentlest of all passions.

As ideas and feelings succeeded one another, and heart and head were brought into play, men continued to lay aside their original wildness; their private connections became every day more intimate as their limits extended. They accustomed themselves to assemble before their huts round a large tree; singing and dancing, the true offspring of love and leisure, became the amusement, or rather the occupation, of men and women thus assembled together with nothing else to do. Each one began to consider the rest, and to wish to be considered in turn; and thus a value came to be attached to public esteem. Whoever sang or danced best, whoever was the handsomest, the strongest, the most dexterous, or the most eloquent, came to be of most consideration; and this was the first step towards inequality, and at the same time towards vice. From these first distinctions arose on the one side vanity and contempt and on the other shame and envy: and the fermentation caused by these new leavens ended by producing combinations fatal to innocence and happiness.

As soon as men began to value one another, and the idea of consideration had got a footing in the mind, every one put in his claim to it, and it became impossible to refuse it to any with impunity. Hence arose the first obligations of civility even among savages; and every intended injury became an affront; because, besides the hurt which might result from it, the party injured was certain to find in it a contempt for his person, which was often more insupportable than the hurt itself.

Thus, as every man punished the contempt shown him by others, in proportion to his opinion of himself, revenge became terrible, and men bloody and cruel. This is precisely the state reached by most of the savage nations known to us: and it is for want of having made a proper distinction in our ideas, and seen how very far they already are from the state of nature, that so many writers have hastily concluded that man is naturally cruel, and requires civil institutions to make him more mild; whereas nothing is more gentle than man in his primitive state, as he is placed by nature at an equal distance from the stupidity of brutes, and the fatal ingenuity of civilized man. Equally confined by instinct and reason to the sole care of guarding himself against the mischiefs which threaten him, he is restrained by natural compassion from doing any injury to others, and is not led to do such a thing even in return for injuries received. For, according to the axiom of the wise Locke, 'There can be no injury, where there is no property.'

But it must be remarked that the society thus formed, and the relations thus established among men, required of them qualities different from those which they possessed from their primitive constitution. Morality began to appear in human actions, and every one, before the institution of law, was the only judge and avenger of the injuries done him, so that the goodness which was suitable in the pure state of nature was no longer proper in the new-born state of society. Punishments had to be made more severe, as opportunities of offending became more frequent, and the dread of vengeance had to take the place of the rigour of the law. Thus, though men had become less patient, and their natural compassion had already suffered some diminution, this period of expansion of the human faculties, keeping a just mean between the indolence of the primitive state and the petulant activity of our *amour-propre,* must have been the happiest and most stable of epochs. The more we reflect on it, the more we shall find that this state was the least subject to revolutions, and altogether the very best man could experience; so that he can have departed from it only through some fatal accident, which, for the public good, should never have happened. The example of savages, most of whom have been found in this state, seems to prove that men were meant to remain in it, that it is the real youth of the world, and that all subsequent advances have been apparently so many steps towards the perfection of the individual, but in reality towards the decrepitude of the species.

So long as men remained content with their rustic huts, so long as they were satisfied with clothes made of the skins of animals and sewn together with thorns and fish-bones, adorned themselves only with feathers and shells, and continued to paint their bodies different colours, to improve and beautify their bows and arrows, and to make with sharp-edged stones fishing boats or clumsy musical instruments; in a word, so long as they undertook only what a single person could accomplish, and confined themselves to such arts as did not require the joint labour of several hands, they lived free, healthy, honest, and happy lives, in so far as their nature allowed, and they continued to enjoy the pleasures of mutual and independent intercourse. But from the moment one man began to stand in need of the help of another; from the moment it appeared advantageous to any one man to have enough provisions for two, equality disappeared, property was introduced, work became indispensable, and vast forests became smiling fields, which man had to water with the sweat of his brow, and where slavery and misery were soon seen to germinate and grow up with the crops.

Metallurgy and agriculture were the two arts which produced this great revolution. The poets tell us it was gold and silver, but, for the philosophers, it was iron and corn, which first civilized men, and ruined humanity. Thus both were unknown to the savages of America, who for that reason are still savage: the other nations also seem to have continued in a state of barbarism while they praised only one of these arts. One of the best reasons, perhaps, why Europe has been, if not longer, at least more constantly and highly civilized than the rest of the world, is that it is at once the most abundant in iron and the most fertile in corn.

It is difficult to conjecture how men first came to know and use iron; for it is impossible to suppose they would of themselves think of digging the ore out of the mine, and preparing it for smelting, before they knew what would be the result. On the other hand, we have the less reason to suppose this discovery the effect of any accidental fire, as mines are only formed in barren places, bare of trees and plants; so that it looks as if nature had taken pains to keep the fatal secret from us. There remains, therefore, only the extraordinary accident of some volcano which, by ejecting metallic substances already in fusion, suggested to the spectators the idea of imitating the natural operation. And we must further conceive them as possessed of uncommon courage and foresight, to undertake so laborious a work, with so distant a prospect of drawing advantage from it; yet these qualities are united only in minds more advanced than we can suppose those of these first discoverers to have been.

With regard to agriculture, the principles of it were known long before they were put in practice; and it is indeed hardly possible that men, constantly employed in drawing their subsistence from plants and trees, should not readily acquire a knowledge of the means made use of by nature for the propagation of plant life. It was in all probability very long, however, before their industry took that turn, either because trees, which together with hunting and fishing afforded them food, did not require their attention; or because they were ignorant of the use of corn, or without instruments to cultivate it; or because they lacked foresight to future needs; or lastly, because they were without means of preventing others from robbing them of the fruit of their labour.

When they grew more industrious, it is natural to believe that they began, with the help of sharp stones and pointed sticks, to cultivate a few vegetables or roots around their huts; though it was long before they knew how to prepare corn, or were provided with the implements necessary for raising it in any large quantity; not to mention how essential it is, for husbandry, to consent to immediate loss, in order to reap a future gain—a precaution very foreign to the turn of a savage's mind; for, as I have said, he hardly foresees in the morning what he will need at night.

The invention of the other arts must therefore have been necessary to compel mankind to apply themselves to agriculture. No sooner were artificers wanted to smelt and forge iron, than others were required to maintain them; the more hands that were employed in manufactures, the fewer were left to provide for the common subsistence, though the number of mouths to be furnished with food remained the same: and as some required commodities in exchange for their iron, the rest at length discovered the method of making iron serve for the multiplication of commodities. By this means the arts of husbandry and agriculture were established on the one hand, and the art of working metals and multiplying their uses on the other.

The cultivation of the earth necessarily brought about its distribution; and property, once recognized, gave rise to the first rules of justice; for, to secure each man his own, it had to be possible for each to have something. Besides, as men began to look forward to the future, and all had something to lose, every one had reason to apprehend that reprisals would follow any injury he might do to another. This origin is so much the more natural, as it is impossible to conceive how property can come from anything but manual labour: for what else can a man add to things which he does not originally create, so as to make them his own property? It is the husbandman's labour alone that, giving him a title to the produce of the ground he has tilled, gives him a claim also to the land itself, at least till harvest; and so, from year to year, a constant possession which is easily transformed into property. When the ancients, says Grotius, gave to Ceres the title of Legislatrix, and to a festival celebrated in her honour the name of Thesmophoria, they meant by that that the distribution of lands had produced a new kind of right: that is to say, the right of property, which is different from the right deducible from the law of nature.

In this state of affairs, equality might have been sustained, had the talents of individuals been equal, and had, for example, the use of iron and the consumption of commodities always exactly balanced each other; but, as there was nothing to preserve this balance, it was soon distributed; the strongest did most work; the most skilful turned his labour to best account; the most ingenious devised methods of diminishing his labour: the husbandman wanted more iron, or the smith more corn, and, while both laboured equally, the one gained a great deal by his work, while the other could hardly support himself. Thus natural inequality unfolds itself insensibly with that of combination, and the difference between men, developed by their different circumstances, becomes more sensible and permanent in its effects, and begins to have an influence, in the same proportion, over the lot of individuals.

Matters once at this pitch, it is easy to imagine the rest. I shall not detain the reader with a description of the successive invention of other arts, the development of language, the trial and utilization of talents, the inequality of fortunes, the use and abuse of riches, and all the details connected with them which the reader can easily supply for himself. I shall confine myself to a glance at mankind in this new situation.

Behold then all human faculties developed, memory and imagination in full play, *amour-propre* interested, reason active, and the mind almost at the highest point of its perfection. Behold all the natural qualities in action, the rank and condition of every man assigned him; not merely his share of property and his power to serve or injure others, but also his wit, beauty, strength or skill, merit or talents: and these being the only qualities capable of commanding respect, it soon became necessary to possess or to affect them.

It now became the interest of men to appear what they really were not. To be and to seem became two totally different things; and from this distinction sprang insolent pomp and cheating trickery, with all the numerous vices that go in their train. On the other hand, free and independent as men were before, they were now, in consequence of a multiplicity of new wants, brought into subjection, as it were, to all nature, and particularly to one another; and each became in some degree a slave even in becoming the master of other men: if rich, they stood in need of the services of others; if poor, of their assistance; and even a middle condition did not enable them to do without one another. Man must now, therefore, have been perpetually employed in getting others to interest themselves in his lot, and in making them, apparently at least, if not really, find their advantage in promoting his own. Thus he must have been sly and artful in his behaviour to some, and imperious and cruel to others; being under a kind of necessity to ill-use all the persons of whom he stood in need, when he could not frighten them into compliance, and did not judge it his interest to be useful to them. Insatiable ambition, the thirst of raising their respective fortunes, not so much from real want as from the desire to surpass others, inspired all men with a vile propensity to injure one another, and with a secret jealousy, which is the more dangerous, as it puts on the mask of benevolence, to carry its point with greater security. In a word, there arose rivalry and competition on the one hand, and conflicting interests on the other, together with a secret desire on both of profiting at the expense of others. All these evils were the first effects of property, and the inseparable attendants of growing inequality.

Before the invention of signs to represent riches, wealth could hardly consist in anything but lands and cattle, the only real possessions men can have. But, when inheritances so increased in number and extent as to occupy the whole of the land, and to border on one another, one man could aggrandize himself only at the expense of another; at the same time the supernumeraries, who had been too weak or too indolent to make such acquisitions, and had grown poor without sustaining any loss, because, while they saw everything change around them, they remained still the same, were obliged to receive their subsistence, or steal it, from the rich; and this soon bred, according to their different characters, dominion and slavery, or violence and rapine. The wealthy, on their part, had no sooner begun to taste the pleasure of command, than they disdained all others, and, using their old slaves to acquire new, thought of nothing but subduing and enslaving their neighbours; like ravenous wolves, which, having once tasted human flesh, despise every other food and thenceforth seek only men to devour.

Thus, as the most powerful or the most miserable considered their might or misery as a kind of right to the possessions of others, equivalent, in their opinion, to that of property, the destruction of equality was attended by the most terrible disorders. Usurpations by the rich, robbery by the poor, and the unbridled passions of both, suppressed the cries of natural compassion and the still feeble voice of justice, and filled men with avarice, ambition, and vice. Between the tide of the strongest and that of the first occupier, there arose perpetual conflicts, which never ended but in battles and bloodshed. The new-born state of society thus gave rise to a horrible state of war; men thus harassed and depraved were no longer capable of retracing their steps or renouncing the fatal acquisitions they had made, but, labouring by the abuse of the faculties which do them honour, merely to their own confusion, brought themselves to the brink of ruin.

> Attonitus novitate mali, divesque miserque,
> Effugere optat opes; et quae modo voverat odit.[5]

It is impossible that men should not at length have reflected on so wretched a situation, and on the calamities that overwhelmed them. The rich, in particular, must have felt how much they suffered by a constant state of war, of which they bore all the expense; and in which, though all risked their lives, they alone risked their property. Besides, however speciously they might disguise their usurpations, they knew that they were founded on precarious and false titles; so that, if others took from them by force what they themselves had gained by force, they would have no reason to complain. Even those who had been enriched by their own industry, could hardly base their proprietorship on better claims. It was in vain to repeat: 'I built this well; I gained this spot by my industry.' Who gave you your standing, it might be answered, and what right have you to demand payment of us for doing what we never asked you to do? Do you not know that numbers of your fellow-creatures are starving, for want of what you have too much of? You ought to have had the express and universal consent of mankind, before appropriating more of the common subsistence than you needed for your own maintenance. Destitute of valid reasons to justify and sufficient strength to defend himself, able to crush individuals with ease, but easily crushed himself by a troop of bandits, one against all, and incapable, on account of mutual jealousy, of joining with his equals against numerous enemies united by the common hope of plunder, the rich man, thus urged by necessity, conceived at length the profoundest plan that ever entered the mind of man: this was to employ in his favour the forces of those who attacked him, to make allies of his adversaries, to inspire them with different maxims, and to give them other institutions as favourable to himself as the law of nature was unfavourable.

With this view, after having represented to his neighbours the horror of a situation which armed every man against the rest, and made their possessions as burdensome to them as their wants, and in which no safety could be expected either in riches or in poverty, he readily devised plausible arguments to make them close with his design. 'Let us join,' said he, 'to guard the weak from oppression, to restrain the ambitious, and secure to every man the possession of what belongs to him: let us institute rules of justice and peace, to which all without exception may be obliged to conform; rules that may in some measure make amends for the caprices of fortune, by subjecting equally the powerful and the weak to the observance of reciprocal obligations. Let us, in a word, instead of turning our forces against ourselves, collect them in a supreme power which may govern us by wise laws, protect and defend all the members of the association, repulse their common enemies, and maintain eternal harmony among us.'

Far fewer words to this purpose would have been enough to impose on men so bar-barous and easily seduced; especially as they had too many disputes among themselves to do without arbitrators, and too much ambition and avarice to go long without masters. All ran headlong to their chains, in hopes of securing their liberty; for they had just wit enough to perceive the advantages of political institutions, without experience enough to enable them to foresee the dangers. The most capable of foreseeing the dangers were the very persons who expected to benefit by them; and even the most prudent judged it not inexpedient to sacrifice one part of their freedom to ensure the rest; as a wounded man has his arm cut off to save the rest of his body.

Such was, or may well have been, the origin of society and law, which bound new fet-ters on the poor, and gave new powers to the rich; which irretrievably destroyed natural liberty, eternally fixed the law of property and inequality, converted clever usurpation into unalterable right, and, for the advantage of a few ambitious individuals, subjected all mankind to perpetual labour, slavery, and wretchedness. It is easy to see how the estab-lishment of one community made that of all the rest necessary, and how, in order to make head against united forces, the rest of mankind had to unite in turn. Societies soon mul-tiplied and spread over the face of the earth, till hardly a corner of the world was left in which a man could escape the yoke, and withdraw his head from beneath the sword which he saw perpetually hanging over him by a thread. Civil right having thus become the common rule among the members of each community, the law of nature maintained its place only between different communities, where, under the name of the right of nations, it was qualified by certain tacit conventions, in order to make commerce practicable, and serve as a substitute for natural compassion, which lost, when applied to societies, almost all the influence it had over individuals, and survived no longer except in some great cosmopolitan spirits, who, breaking down the imaginary barriers that separate different peoples, follow the example of our Sovereign Creator, and include the whole human race in their benevolence.

But bodies politic, remaining thus in a state of nature among themselves, presently experienced the inconveniences which had obliged individuals to forsake it; for this state became still more fatal to these great bodies than it had been to the individuals of whom they were composed. Hence arose national wars, battles, murders, and reprisals, which shock nature and outrage reason; together with all those horrible prejudices which class among the virtues the honour of shedding human blood. The most distinguished men hence learned to consider cutting each other's throats a duty; at length men massacred their fellow-creatures by thousands without so much as knowing why, and committed more murders in a single day's fighting, and more violent outrages in the sack of a single town, than were committed in the state of nature during whole ages over the whole earth. Such were the first effects which we can see to have followed the division of mankind into different communities. But let us return to their institution.

I know that some writers have given other explanations of the origin of political soci-eties, such as the conquest of the powerful, or the association of the weak. It is, indeed, indifferent to my argument which of these causes we choose. That which I have just laid down, however, appears to me the most natural for the following reasons. First: because, in the first case, the right of conquest, being no right in itself, could not serve as a foundation on which to build any other; the victor and the vanquished people still remained with respect to each other in the state of war, unless the vanquished, restored to the full possession of their liberty, voluntarily made choice of the victor for their chief. For till then, whatever capitulation may have been made being founded on violence, and therefore *ipso facto* void, there could not have been on this hypothesis either a real society or body politic, or any law other than that of the strongest. Secondly: because the words 'strong' and 'weak' are, in the second case, ambiguous; for during the interval between the establishment of a right of property, or prior occupancy, and that of political government, the meaning of these words is better expressed by the terms 'rich' and 'poor'; because, in fact, before the institution of laws, men had no other way of reducing their equals to submission, than by attacking their goods, or making some of their own over to them. Thirdly: because, as the poor had nothing but their freedom to lose, it would have been in the highest degree absurd for them to resign voluntarily the only good they still enjoyed, without getting anything in exchange: whereas the rich having feelings, if I may so express myself, in every part of their possessions, it was much easier to harm them, and therefore more necessary for them to take precautions against it; and, in short, because it is more reasonable to suppose a thing to have been invented by those to whom it would be of service, than by those whom it must have harmed.

Government had, in its infancy, no regular and constant form. The want of experience and philosophy prevented men from seeing any but present inconveniences, and they thought of providing against others only as they presented themselves. In spite of the endeavours of the wisest legislators, the political state remained imperfect, because it was little more than the work of chance; and, as it had begun ill, though time revealed its defects and suggested remedies, the original faults were never repaired. It was continually being patched up, when the first task should have been to get the site cleared and all the old materials removed, as was done by Lycurgus at Sparta, if a stable and fasting edifice was to be erected. Society consisted at first merely of a few general conventions, which every member bound himself to observe; and for the performance of covenants by the whole body went security to each individual. Experience only could show the weakness of such a constitution, and how easily it might be infringed with impunity, from the difficulty of convicting men of faults, where the public alone was to be witness and judge: the laws could not but be eluded in many ways; disorders and inconveniences could not but multiply continually, till it became necessary to commit the dangerous trust of public authority to private persons, and the care of enforcing obedience to the deliberations of the people to the magistrate. For to say that chiefs were chosen before the confederacy was formed, and that the administrators of the laws were there before the laws themselves, is too absurd a supposition to consider seriously.

It would be as unreasonable to suppose that men at first threw themselves irretrievably and unconditionally into the arms of an absolute master, and that the first expedient which proud and unsubdued men hit upon for their common security was to run headlong into slavery. For what reason, in fact, did they take to themselves superiors, if it was not in order that they might be defended from oppression, and have protection for their lives, liberties, and properties, which are, so to speak, the constituent elements of their being? Now, in the relations between man and man, the worst that can happen is for one to find himself at the mercy of another, and it would have been inconsistent with common sense to begin by bestowing on a chief the only things they wanted his help to preserve. What equivalent could he offer them for so great a right? And if he had presumed to exact it under pretext of defending them, would he not have received the answer recorded in the fable: 'What more can the enemy do to us?' It is therefore beyond dispute, and indeed the fundamental maxim of all political right, that people have set up chiefs to protect their liberty, and not to enslave them. 'If we have a prince,' said Pliny to Trajan, 'it is to save ourselves from having a master.'

Politicians indulge in the same sophistry about the love of liberty as philosophers about the state of nature. They judge, by what they see, of very different things, which they have not seen; they attribute to man a natural propensity to servitude, because the slaves within their observation are seen to bear the yoke with patience; they fail to reflect that it is with liberty as with innocence and virtue; the value is known only to those who possess them, and the taste for them is forfeited when they are forfeited themselves. 'I know the charms of your country,' said Brasidas to a Satrap, who was comparing the life at Sparta with that at Persepolis, 'but you cannot know the pleasures of mine.'

An unbroken horse erects his mane, paws the ground and starts back impetuously at the sight of the bridle; while one which is properly trained suffers patiently even whip and spur: so savage man will not bend his neck to the yoke to which civilized man submits without a murmur, but prefers the most turbulent state of liberty to the most peaceful slavery. We cannot therefore, from the servility of nations already enslaved, judge of the natural disposition of mankind for or against slavery; we should go by the prodigious efforts of every free people to save itself from oppression. I know that the former are for ever holding forth in praise of the tranquillity they enjoy in their chains, and that they call a state of wretched servitude a state of peace: *miserrimam servitutem pacem appellant*.[6] But when I observe the latter sacrificing pleasure, peace, wealth, power, and life itself to the preservation of that one treasure, which is so disdained by those who have lost it; when I see free-born animals dash their brains out against the bars of their cage, from an innate impatience of captivity; when I behold numbers of naked savages, that despise European pleasures, braving hunger, fire, the sword, and death, to preserve nothing but their independence, I feel that it is not for slaves to argue about liberty.

With regard to paternal authority, from which some writers have derived absolute government and all society, it is enough, without going back to the contrary arguments of Locke and Sidney, to remark that nothing on earth can be farther from the ferocious spirit of despotism than the mildness of that authority which looks more to the advantage of him who obeys than to that of him who commands; that, by the law of nature, the father is the child's master no longer than his help is necessary; that from that time they are both equal, the son being perfectly independent of the father, and owing him only respect, and not obedience. For gratitude is a duty which ought to be paid, but not a right to be exacted: instead of saying that civil society is derived from paternal authority, we ought to say rather that the latter derives its principal force from the former. No individual was ever acknowledged as the father of many, till his sons and daughters remained settled around him. The goods of the father, of which he is really the master, are the ties which keep his children in dependence, and he may bestow on them, if he pleases, no share of his property, unless they merit it by constant deference to his will. But the subjects of an arbitrary despot are so far from having the like favour to expect from their chief, that they themselves and everything they possess are his property, or at least are considered by him as such; so that they are forced to receive, as a favour, the little of their own he is pleased to leave them. When he despoils them, he does but justice, and mercy in that he permits them to live.

By proceeding thus to test fact by right, we should discover as little reason as truth in the voluntary establishment of tyranny. It would also be no easy matter to prove the validity of a contract binding on only one of the parties, where all the risk is on one side, and none on the other; so that no one could suffer but he who bound himself. This hateful system is indeed, even in modern times, very far from being that of wise and good monarchs, and especially of the kings of France; as may be seen from several passages in their edicts; particularly from the following passage in a celebrated edict published in 1667 in the name and by order of Louis XIV.

'Let it not, therefore, be said that the Sovereign is not subject to the laws of his State; since the contrary is a true proposition of the right of nations, which flattery has sometimes attacked but good princes have always defended as the tutelary divinity of their dominions. How much more legitimate is it to say with the wise Plato, that the perfect felicity of a kingdom consists in the obedience of subjects to their prince, and of the prince to the laws, and in the laws being just and constantly directed to the public good!'[7]

I shall not stay here to inquire whether, as liberty is the noblest faculty of man, it is not degrading our very nature, reducing ourselves to the level of the brutes, which are mere slaves of instinct, and even an affront to the Author of our being, to renounce without reserve the most precious of all His gifts, and to bow to the necessity of committing all the crimes He has forbidden, merely to gratify a mad or a cruel master; or if this sublime craftsman ought not to be less angered at seeing His workmanship entirely destroyed than thus dishonoured. I will waive (if my opponents please) the authority of Barbeyrac, who, following Locke, roundly declares that no man can so far sell his liberty as to submit to an arbitrary power which may use him as it likes. *For,* he adds, *this would be to sell his own life, of which he is not master.* I shall ask only what right those who were not afraid thus to debase themselves could have to subject their posterity to the same ignominy, and to renounce for them those blessings which they do not owe to the liberality of their progenitors, and without which life itself must be a burden to all who are worthy of it.

Pufendorf says that we may divest ourselves of our liberty in favour of other men, just as we transfer our property from one to another by contracts and agreements. But this seems a very weak argument. For in the first place, the property I alienate becomes quite foreign to me, nor can I suffer from the abuse of it; but it very nearly concerns me that my liberty should not be abused, and I cannot without incurring the guilt of the crimes I may be compelled to commit, expose myself to become an instrument of crime. Besides, the right of property being only a convention of human institution, men may dispose of what they possess as they please: but this is not the case with the essential gifts of nature, such as life and liberty, which every man is permitted to enjoy, and of which it is at least doubtful whether any have a right to divest themselves. By giving up the one, we degrade our being; by giving up the other, we do our best to annul it; and, as no temporal good can indemnify us for the loss of either, it would be an offence against both reason and nature to renounce them at any price whatsoever. But, even if we could transfer our liberty, as we do our property, there would be a great difference with regard to the children, who enjoy the father's substance only by the transmission of his right; whereas, liberty being a gift which they hold from nature as being men, their parents have no right whatever to deprive them of it. As then, to establish slavery, it was necessary to do violence to nature, so, in order to perpetuate such a right, nature would have to be changed. Jurists who have gravely determined that the child of a slave comes into the world a slave, have decided, in other words, that a man shall come into the world not a man.

I regard it then as certain, that government did not begin with arbitrary power, but that this is the depravation, the extreme term, of government, and brings it back, finally, to just the law of the strongest, which it was originally designed to remedy. Supposing, however, it had begun in this manner, such power, being in itself illegitimate, could not have served as a basis for the laws of society, nor, consequently, for the inequality they instituted.

Without entering at present upon the investigations which still remain to be made into the nature of the fundamental compact underlying all government, I content myself with adopting the common opinion concerning it, and regard the establishment of the political body as a real contract between the people and the chiefs chosen by them: a contract by which both parties bind themselves to observe the laws therein expressed, which form the ties of their union. The people having in respect of their social relations concentrated all their wills in one, the several articles, concerning which this will is explained, become so many fundamental laws, obligatory on all the members of the State without exception, and one of these articles regulates the choice and power of the magistrates appointed to watch over the execution of the rest. This power extends to everything which may maintain the constitution, without going so far as to alter it. It is accompanied by honours, in order to bring the laws and their administrators into respect. The ministers are also distinguished by personal prerogatives, in order to recompense them for the cares and labour which good administration involves. The magistrate, on his side, binds himself to use the power he is entrusted with only in conformity with the intention of his constituents, to maintain them all in the peaceable possession of what belongs to them, and to prefer on every occasion the public interest to his own.

Before experience had shown, or knowledge of the human heart enabled men to foresee, the unavoidable abuses of such a constitution, it must have appeared so much the more excellent, as those who were charged with the care of its preservation had themselves most interest in it; for magistracy and the rights attaching to it being based solely on the fundamental laws, the magistrates would cease to be legitimate as soon as these ceased to exist; the people would no longer owe them obedience; and as not the magistrates, but the laws, are essential to the being of a State, the members of it would regain the right to their natural liberty.

If we reflect with ever so little attention on this subject, we shall find new arguments to confirm this truth, and be convinced from the very nature of the contract that it cannot be irrevocable; for, if there were no superior power capable of ensuring the fidelity of the contracting parties, or compelling them to perform their reciprocal engagements, the parties would be sole judges in their own cause, and each would always have a right to renounce the contract, as soon as he found that the other had violated its terms, or that they no longer suited his convenience. It is upon this principle that the right of abdication may possibly be founded. Now, if, as here, we consider only what is human in this institution, it is certain that, if the magistrate, who has all the power in his own hands, and appropriates to himself all the advantages of the contract, has none the less a right to renounce his authority, the people, who suffer for all the faults of their chief, must have a much better right to renounce their dependence. But the terrible and innumerable quarrels and disorders that would necessarily arise from so dangerous a privilege, show, more than anything else, how much human governments stood in need of a more solid basis than mere reason, and how expedient it was for the public tranquillity that the divine will should interpose to invest the sovereign authority with a sacred and inviolable character, which might deprive subjects of the fatal right of disposing of it. If the world had received no other advantages from religion, this would be enough to impose on men the duty of adopting and cultivating it, abuses and all, since it has been the means of saving more blood than fanaticism has ever spilt. But let us follow the thread of our hypothesis.

The different forms of government owe their origin to the differing degrees of inequality which existed between individuals at the time of their institution. If there happened to be any one man among them pre-eminent in power, virtue, riches, or personal influence, he became sole magistrate, and the State assumed the form of monarchy. If several, nearly equal in point of eminence, stood above the rest, they were elected jointly, and formed an aristocracy. Again, among a people who had deviated less from a state of nature, and between whose fortune or talents there was less disproportion, the supreme administration was retained in common, and a democracy was formed. It was discovered in process of time which of these forms suited men the best. Some peoples continued to be ruled solely by their laws; others soon came to obey masters. Citizens wished to preserve their liberty; subjects, however, irritated at seeing others enjoying a blessing they had lost, thought only of making slaves of their neighbours. In a word, on the one side arose riches and conquests, and on the other happiness and virtue.

In these different governments, all the offices were at first elective; and when the influence of wealth did not carry the day, the preference was given to merit, which gives a natural ascendancy, and to age, which is experienced in business and deliberate in council. The Elders of the Hebrews, the Gerontes at Sparta, the Senate at Rome, and the very etymology of our word Seigneur, show how old age was once held in veneration. But the more often the choice fell upon old men, the more often elections had to be repeated, and the more they became a nuisance; intrigues set in, factions were formed, party feeling grew bitter, civil wars broke out; the lives of individuals were sacrificed to the pretended happiness of the State; and at length men were on the point of relapsing into their primitive anarchy. Ambitious chiefs profited by these circumstances to perpetuate their offices in their own families: at the same time the people, already used to dependence, ease, and the conveniences of life, and already incapable of breaking its fetters, agreed to an increase of its slavery, in order to secure its tranquillity. Thus magistrates, having become hereditary, contracted the habit of considering their offices as a family estate, and themselves as proprietors of the communities of which they were at first only the officers, of regarding their fellow-citizens as their slaves, and numbering them, like cattle, among their belongings, and of calling themselves the equals of the gods and kings of kings.

If we follow the progress of inequality in these various revolutions, we shall find that the establishment of laws and of the right of property was its first term, the institution of magistracy the second, and the conversion of legitimate into arbitrary power the third and last; so that the condition of rich and poor was authorized by the first period; that of powerful and weak by the second; and only by the third that of master and slave, which is the last degree of inequality, and the term at which all the rest remain, when they have got so far, till the government is either entirely dissolved by new revolutions, or brought back again to legitimacy.

To understand this progress as necessary we must consider not so much the motives for the establishment of the body politic, as the forms it assumes in actuality, and the faults that necessarily attend it: for the flaws which make social institutions necessary are the same as make the abuse of them unavoidable. If we except Sparta, where the laws were mainly concerned with the education of children, and where Lycurgus established such morality as practically made laws needless—for laws as a rule, being weaker than the passions, restrain men without altering them—it would not be difficult to prove that every government, which scrupulously complied with the ends for which it was instituted, and guarded carefully against change and corruption, was set up unnecessarily. For a country in which no one evaded the laws and no one made a bad use of the powers of a magistrate would require neither laws nor magistrates.

Political distinctions necessarily produce civil distinctions. The growing inequality between the people and its leaders is soon felt by individuals and among them it takes a

thousand different forms according to their passions, their talents and their circumstances. The magistrate could not usurp illegitimate power without the help of creatures
to whom he is forced to give a share of that power. Besides, individuals only allow themselves to be oppressed so far as they are hurried on by blind ambition, and, looking rather
below than above them, come to love authority more than independence, and submit to
slavery, that they may in turn enslave others. It is no easy matter to reduce to obedience a
man who has no ambition to command; nor would the most adroit politician find it possible to enslave a people whose only desire was to be independent. But inequality easily
makes its way among cowardly and ambitious minds, which are ever ready to run the risks
of fortune, and almost indifferent whether they command or obey, as it is favourable or
adverse. Thus, there must have been a time, when the eyes of the people were so fascinated, that their rulers had only to say to the least of men, 'Be great, you and all your posterity,' to make him immediately appear great in the eyes of every one as well as in his
own. His descendants took still more upon them, in proportion to their distance from
him; the more obscure and uncertain the cause, the greater the effect: the greater the
number of idlers one could count in a family, the more illustrious it was held to be.

If this were the place to go into details, I could readily explain how, even without the
intervention of government, inequality of credit and authority became unavoidable
among private persons, as soon as their union in a single society made them compare
themselves one with another, and take into account the differences which they found out
from the continual intercourse every man had to have with his neighbours.[8] These differences are of several kinds; but riches, nobility or rank, power and personal merit being the
principal distinctions by which men form an estimate of each other in society, I could
prove that the harmony or conflict of these different forces is the surest indication of the
good or bad constitution of a State. I could show that among these four kinds of inequality, personal qualities being the origin of all the others, wealth is the one to which they
are all reduced in the end; for, as riches tend most immediately to the prosperity of individuals, and are easiest to communicate, they are used to purchase every other distinction.
By this observation we are enabled to judge pretty exactly how far a people has departed
from its primitive constitution, and of its progress towards the extreme term of corruption. I could explain how much this universal desire for reputation, honours, and advancement, which inflames us all, exercises and holds up to comparison our faculties and
powers; how it excites and multiplies our passions, and, by creating universal competition
and rivalry, or rather enmity, among men, occasions numberless failures, successes, and
disturbances of all kinds by making so many aspirants run the same course. I could show
that it is to this desire of being talked about, and this unremitting rage of distinguishing
ourselves, that we owe the best and the worst things we possess, both our virtues and our
vices, our science and our errors, our conquerors and our philosophers; that is to say, a
great many bad things, and a very few good ones. In a word, I could prove that, if we have
a few rich and powerful men on the pinnacle of fortune and grandeur, while the crowd
grovels in want and obscurity, it is because the former prize what they enjoy only in so far
as others are destitute of it; and because, without changing their condition, they would
cease to be happy the moment the people ceased to be wretched.

These details alone, however, would furnish matter for a considerable work, in which
the advantages and disadvantages of every kind of government might be weighed, as they
are related to man in the state of nature, and at the same time all the different aspects,
under which inequality has up to the present appeared, or may appear in ages yet to come,
according to the nature of the several governments, and the alterations which time must
unavoidably occasion in them, might be demonstrated. We should then see the multitude

oppressed from within, in consequence of the very precautions it had taken to guard against foreign tyranny. We should see oppression continually gain ground without its being possible for the oppressed to know where it would stop, or what legitimate means was left them of checking its progress. We should see the rights of citizens and the freedom of nations slowly extinguished, and the complaints, protests, and appeals of the weak treated as seditious murmurings. We should see the honour of defending the common cause confined by statecraft to a mercenary part of the people. We should see taxes made necessary by such means, and the disheartened husbandman deserting his fields even in the midst of peace, and leaving the plough to gird on the sword. We should see fatal and capricious codes of honour established; and the champions of their country sooner or later becoming its enemies, and for ever holding their daggers to the breasts of their fellow-citizens. The time would come when they would be heard saying to the oppressor of their country:

> *Pectore si fratris gladium juguloque parentis*
> *Condere me jubeas, gravidaeque in viscera partu*
> *Conjugis, invita peragam tamen omnia dextra.*
>
> Lucan, i. 376[9]

From great inequality of fortunes and conditions, from the vast variety of passions and of talents, of useless and pernicious arts, of vain sciences, would arise a multitude of prejudices equally contrary to reason, happiness, and virtue. We should see the magistrates fomenting everything that might weaken men united in society, by promoting dissension among them; everything that might sow in it the seeds of actual division, while it gave society the air of harmony; everything that might inspire the different ranks of people with mutual hatred and distrust, by setting the rights and interests of one against those of another, and so strengthen the power which comprehended them all.

It is from the midst of this disorder and these revolutions, that despotism, gradually raising up its hideous head and devouring everything that remained sound and untainted in any part of the State, would at length trample on both the laws and the people, and establish itself on the ruins of the republic. The times which immediately preceded this last change would be times of trouble and calamity; but at length the monster would swallow up everything, and the people would no longer have either chiefs or laws, but only tyrants. From this moment there would be no question of virtue or morality; for despotism (*cui ex honesto nulla est spes*), wherever it prevails, admits no other master; it no sooner speaks than probity and duty lose their weight and blind obedience is the only virtue which slaves can still practise.

This is the last term of inequality, the extreme point that closes the circle, and meets that from which we set out. Here all private persons return to their first equality, because they are nothing; and, subjects having no law but the will of their master, and their master no restraint but his passions, all notions of good and all principles of equity again vanish. There is here a complete return to the law of the strongest, and so to a new state of nature, differing from that we set out from; for the one was a state of nature in its first purity, while this is the consequence of excessive corruption. There is so little difference between the two states in other respects, and the contract of government is so completely dissolved by despotism, that the despot is master only so long as he remains the strongest; as soon as he can be expelled, he has no right to complain of violence. The popular insurrection that ends in the death or deposition of a Sultan is as lawful an act as those by which he disposed, the day before, of the lives and fortunes of his subjects. As he was maintained by force alone, it is force alone that overthrows him. Thus everything takes place according to the natural order; and, whatever may be the result of such frequent and precipitate revolutions, no one man has reason to complain of the injustice of another, but only of his own ill fortune or indiscretion.

If the reader thus discovers and retraces the lost and forgotten road, by which man must have passed from the state of nature to the state of society; if he carefully restores, along with the intermediate situations which I have just described, those which want of time has compelled me to suppress, or my imagination has failed to suggest, he cannot fail to be struck by the vast distance which separates the two states. It is in tracing this slow succession that he will find the solution of a number of problems of politics and morals, which philosophers cannot settle. He will feel that, men being different in different ages, the reason why Diogenes could not find a man was that he sought among his contemporaries a man of an earlier period. He will see that Cato died with Rome and liberty, because he did not fit the age in which he lived; the greatest of men served only to astonish a world which he would certainly have ruled, had he lived five hundred years sooner. In a word, he will explain how the soul and the passions of men insensibly change their very nature; why our wants and pleasures in the end seek new objects; and why, the original man having vanished by degrees, society offers to us only an assembly of artificial men and factitious passions, which are the work of all these new relations, and without any real foundation in nature. We are taught nothing on this subject, by reflection, that is not entirely confirmed by observation. The savage and the civilized man differ so much in the bottom of their hearts and in their inclinations, that what constitutes the supreme happiness of one would reduce the other to despair. The former breathes only peace and liberty; he desires only to live and be free from labour; even the *ataraxia* of the Stoic falls far short of his profound indifference to every other object. Civilized man, on the other hand, is always moving, sweating, toiling, and racking his brains to find still more laborious occupations: he goes on in drudgery to his last moment, and even seeks death to put himself in a position to live, or renounces life to acquire immortality. He pays his court to men in power, whom he hates, and to the wealthy, whom he despises; he stops at nothing to have the honour of serving them; he is not ashamed to value himself on his own meanness and their protection; and, proud of his slavery, he speaks with disdain of those, who have not the honour of sharing it. What a sight would the perplexing and envied labours of a European minister of State present to the eyes of a Caribbean! How many cruel deaths would not this indolent savage prefer to the horrors of such a life, which is seldom even sweetened by the pleasure of doing good! But, for him to see into the motives of all this solicitude the words 'power, and 'reputation' would have to bear some meaning in his mind; he would have to know that there are men who set a value on the opinion of the rest of the world; who can be made happy and satisfied with themselves rather on the testimony of other people than on their own. In reality, the source of all these differences is, that the savage lives within himself, while social man lives constantly outside himself, and only knows how to live in the opinion of others, so that he seems to receive the consciousness of his own existence merely from the judgment of others concerning him. It is not to my present purpose to insist on the indifference to good and evil which arises from this disposition, in spite of our many fine works on morality, or to show how, everything being reduced to appearances, there is but art and mummery in even honour, friendship, virtue, and often vice itself, of which we at length learn the secret of boasting; to show, in short, how, always asking others what we are, and never daring to ask ourselves, in the midst of so much philosophy, humanity, and civilization, and of such sublime codes of morality, we have nothing to show for ourselves but a frivolous and deceitful appearance, honour without virtue, reason without wisdom, and pleasure without happiness. It is sufficient that I have proved that this is not by any means the original state of man, but that it is merely the spirit of society, and the inequality which society produces, that thus transform and alter all our natural inclinations.

I have endeavoured to trace the origin and progress of inequality, and the institution and abuse of political societies, as far as these are capable of being deduced from the nature of man merely by the light of reason, and independency of those sacred dogmas which give the sanction of divine right to sovereign authority. It follows from this survey that, as there is hardly any inequality in the state of nature, all the inequality which now prevails owes its strength and growth to the development of our faculties and the advance of the human mind, and becomes at last permanent and legitimate by the establishment of property and laws. Secondly, it follows that moral inequality, authorized by positive right alone, clashes with natural right, whenever it is not proportionate to physical inequality—a distinction which sufficiently determines what we ought to think of that species of inequality which prevails in all civilized countries; since it is plainly contrary to the law of nature, however defined, that children should command old men, fools wise men, and that the privileged few should gorge themselves with superfluities, while the starving multitude are in want of the bare necessities of life.

Appendix

A famous author, reckoning up the good and evil of human life, and comparing the aggregates, finds that our pains greatly exceed our pleasures: so that, all things considered, human life is not at all a valuable gift. This conclusion does not surprise me; for the writer drew all his arguments from man in civilization. Had he gone back to the state of nature, his inquiries would clearly have had a different result, and man would have been seen to be subject to very few evils not of his own creation. It has indeed cost us not a little trouble to make ourselves as wretched as we are. When we consider, on the one hand, the immense labours of mankind, the many sciences brought to perfection, the arts invented, the powers employed, the deeps filled up, the mountains levelled, the rocks shattered, the rivers made navigable, the tracts of land cleared, the lakes emptied, the marshes drained, the enormous structures erected on land, and the teeming vessels that cover the sea; and, on the other hand, estimate with ever so little thought, the real advantages that have accrued from all these works to mankind, we cannot help being amazed at the vast disproportion there is between these things, and deploring the infatuation of man, which, to gratify his silly pride and vain self-admiration, induces him eagerly to pursue all the miseries he is capable of feeling, though beneficent nature had kindly placed them out of his way.

That men are actually wicked, a sad and continual experience of them proves beyond doubt: but, all the same I think I have shown that man is naturally good. What then can have depraved him to such an extent, except the changes that have happened in his constitution, the advances he has made, and the knowledge he has acquired? We may admire human society as much as we please; it will be none the less true that it necessarily leads men to hate each other in proportion as their interests clash, and to do one another apparent services, while they are really doing every imaginable mischief. What can be thought of a relation, in which the interest of every individual dictates rules directly opposite to those the public reason dictates to the community in general—in which every man finds his profit in the misfortunes of his neighbour? There is not perhaps any man in a comfortable position who has not greedy heirs, and perhaps even children, secretly wishing for his death; not a ship at sea, of which the loss would not be good news to some merchant or other; not a house, in which some debtor of bad faith would not be glad to see reduced to ashes with all the papers it contains; not a nation which does not rejoice at the disasters that befall its neighbours. Thus it is that we find our advantage in the misfortunes of our fellow-creatures, and that the loss of one man almost always constitutes the prosperity of another. But it is still more pernicious that public calamities are the objects of the hopes and expectations of innumerable individuals. Some desire sickness, some mortality, some war, and some famine. I have seen men wicked enough to weep for sorrow at the prospect of a plentiful season; and the great and fatal fire of London, which cost so many unhappy persons their lives or their fortunes, made the fortunes of perhaps ten thousand others. I know that Montaigne censures Demades the Athenian for having caused to be punished a workman who, by selling his coffins very dear, was a great gainer by the deaths of his fellow-citizens; but, the reason alleged by Montaigne being that everybody ought to be punished, my point is clearly confirmed by it. Let us penetrate, therefore, the superficial appearances of benevolence, and survey what passes in the inmost recesses of the heart. Let us reflect what must be the state of things, when men are forced to caress and destroy one another at the same time; when they are born enemies by duty, and knaves by interest. It will perhaps be said that society is so formed that every man gains by serving the rest. That would be all very well, if he did not gain still more by injuring them. There is no legitimate profit so great, that it cannot be greatly exceeded by what may be made illegitimately; we always gain more by hurting our neighbours than by doing them good. Nothing is required but to know how to act with impunity; and to this end the powerful employ all their strength, and the weak all their cunning.

Savage man, when he has dined, is at peace with all nature, and the friend of all his fellow-creatures. If a dispute arises about a meal, he rarely comes to blows, without having first compared the difficulty of conquering his antagonist with the trouble of finding subsistence elsewhere: and, as pride does not come in, it all ends in a few blows; the victor eats, and the vanquished seeks provision somewhere else, and all is at peace. The case is quite different with man in the state of society, for whom first necessaries have to be provided, and then superfluities; delicacies follow next, then immense wealth, then subjects, and then slaves. He enjoys not a moment's relaxation; and what is yet stranger, the less natural and pressing his wants, the more headstrong are his passions, and, still worse, the more he has it in his power to gratify them; so that after a long course of prosperity, after having swallowed up treasures and ruined multitudes, the hero ends up by cutting every throat till he finds himself, at last, sole master of the world. Such is in miniature the moral picture, if not of human life, at least of the secret pretensions of the heart of civilized man.

Compare without partiality the state of the citizen with that of the savage, and trace out, if you can, how many inlets the former has opened to pain and death, besides those of his vices, his wants, and his misfortunes. If you reflect on the mental afflictions that prey on us, the violent passions that waste and exhaust us, the excessive labour with which the poor are burdened, the still more dangerous indolence to which the wealthy give themselves up, so that the poor perish of want, and the rich of surfeit; if you reflect but a moment on the heterogeneous mixtures and pernicious seasonings of foods; the corrupt state in which they are frequently eaten; on the adulteration of medicines, the wiles of those who sell them, the mistakes of those who administer them, and the poisonous vessels in which they are prepared; on the epidemics bred by foul air in consequence of great numbers of men being crowded together, or those which are caused by our delicate way of living, by our passing from our houses into the open air and back again, by the putting on or throwing off our clothes with too little care, and by all the precautions which sensuality has converted into necessary habits, and the neglect of which sometimes costs us our life or health; if you take into account the conflagrations and earthquakes, which, devouring or overwhelming whole cities, destroy the inhabitants by thousands, in a world, if you add together all the dangers with which these causes are always threatening us, you will see how dearly nature makes us pay for the contempt with which we have treated her lessons.

I shall not here repeat, what I have elsewhere said of the calamities of war; but wish that those, who have sufficient knowledge, were willing or bold enough to make public the details of the villainies committed in armies by the contractors for commissariat and hospitals: we should see plainly that their monstrous frauds, already none too well concealed, which cripple the finest armies in less than no time, occasion greater destruction among the soldiers than the swords of the enemy.

The number of people who perish annually at sea, by famine, the scurvy, pirates, fire, and shipwrecks, affords matter for another shocking calculation. We must also place to the credit of the establishment of property, and consequently so the institution of society, assassinations, poisonings, highway robberies, and even the punishments inflicted on the wretches guilty of these crimes; which, though expedient to prevent greater evils, yet by making the murder of one man cost the lives of two or more, double the loss to the human race.

What shameful methods are sometimes practised to prevent the birth of men, and cheat nature; wither by brutal and depraved appetites which insult her most beautiful work—appetites unknown to savages or mere animals, which can spring only from the corrupt imagination of mankind in civilized countries; or by secret abortions, the fitting effects of debauchery and vitiated notions of honour; or by the exposure or murder of multitudes of infants, who fall victims to the poverty of their parents, or the cruel shame of their mothers; or, finally, by the mutilation of unhappy wretches, part of whose life, with their hope of posterity, is given up to vain singing, or, still worse, the brutal jealousy of other men: a mutilation which, in the last case, becomes a double outrage against nature from the treatment of those who suffer it, and from the use to which they are destined. But is it not a thousand times more common and more dangerous for paternal rights openly to offend against humanity? How many talents have not been thrown away, and inclinations forced, by the unwise constraint of fathers? How many men, who would have distinguished themselves in a fitting estate, have died dishonoured and wretched in another for which they had no taste! How many happy, but unequal, marriages have been broken or disturbed, and how many chaste wives have been dishonoured, by an order of things continually in contradiction with that of nature! How many good and virtuous husbands and wives are reciprocally punished for having been ill-assorted! How many young and unhappy victims of their parents' avarice plunge into vice, or pass their melancholy days in tears, groaning in the indissoluble bonds which their hearts repudiate and gold alone has formed! Fortunate sometimes are those whose courage and virtue remove them from life before inhuman violence makes them spend it in crime or in despair. Forgive me, fathers and mothers, who are ever to be pitied: I regret having to increase your pain; I only hope it may serve as an eternal and terrible example to anyone who dares, in the very name of nature, to violate the most sacred of natural rights.

If I have spoken only of those ill-starred unions which are the result of our system, is it to be thought that those over which love and sympathy preside are free from disadvantages? What if I should undertake to show humanity attacked in its very source, and even in the most sacred of all ties, in which fortune is consulted before nature, and, the disorders of society confounding all virtue and vice, continence becomes a criminal precaution, and a refusal to give life to a fellow-creature, an act of humanity? But, without drawing aside the veil which hides all these horrors, let us content ourselves with pointing out the evil which others will have to remedy.

To all this add the multiplicity of unhealthy trades, which shorten men's lives or destroy their bodies, such as working in the mines, and the preparing of metals and minerals, particularly lead, copper, mercury, cobalt, and arsenic: add those other dangerous trades which are daily fatal to many tilers, carpenters, masons, and miners; put all these together and we can see in the establishment and perfection of societies, the reasons for that diminution of our species, which has been noticed by many philosophers.

Luxury, which cannot be avoided among men greedy for their own comfort and for the respect of others, soon completes the evil which society had begun and, under the pretence of giving bread to the poor whom it should never have made such, impoverishes all the rest, and sooner or later depopulates the state. Luxury is a remedy much worse than the disease it sets up to cure; or rather it is in itself the greatest of all evils, for every State, great or small: for, in order to maintain all the servants and vagabonds it creates, it brings oppression and ruin on the citizen and the labourer; it is like those scorching winds, which, covering the trees and plants with devouring insects, deprive useful animals of their subsistence and spread famine and death wherever they blow.

From society and the luxury to which it gives birth arise the liberal and mechanical arts, commerce, letters, and all those superfluities which make industry flourish, and enrich and ruin nations. The reason for such destruction is plain. It is easy to see, from the very nature of agriculture, that it must be the least lucrative of all the arts; for, its produce being the most universally necessary, the price must be proportionate to the abilities of the very poorest of mankind.

From the same principle may be deduced this rule, that the arts in general are more lucrative in proportion as they are less useful; and that, in the end, the most useful becomes the most neglected. From this we may learn what to think of the real advantages of industry and the actual effects of its progress.

Such are the sensible causes of all the miseries, into which opulence at length plunges the most celebrated nations. In proportion as arts and industry flourish, the despised husbandman, burdened with the taxes necessary for the support of luxury, and condemned to pass his days between labour and hunger, forsakes his native field, to seek in towns the bread he ought to carry thither. The more our capital cities strike the vulgar eye with admiration, the greater reason is there to lament the sight of the abandoned countryside, the large tracts of land that lie uncultivated, the roads crowded with unfortunate citizens turned beggars or highwaymen, and doomed to end their wretched lives either on a dunghill or on the gallows. Thus the State grows rich on the one hand, and feeble and depopulated on the other; the mightiest monarchies, after having taken immense pains to enrich and depopulate themselves, fall at last a prey to some poor nation, which has yielded to the fatal temptation of invading them, and then, growing opulent and weak in its turn, is itself invaded and ruined by some other.

Would someone be so kind as to explain to us what produced the hordes of barbarians who overran Europe, Asia and Africa for so many centuries? Was their prodigious increase due to their industry and arts, to the wisdom of their laws, or to the excellence of their political system? Let the learned tell us why, instead of multiplying to such a degree, these fierce and brutal men, without sense or science, without education, and without restraint, did not destroy each other hourly in quarrelling over the productions of their fields and woods. Let them tell us how these wretches could have the presumption to oppose such clever people as we were, so well trained in military discipline, and possessed of such excellent laws and institutions: and why, since society has been brought to perfection in northern countries, and so much pains taken to instruct their inhabitants in their social duties and in the art of living happily and peaceably together, we see them no longer produce such numberless hosts as they used once to send forth to be the plague and terror of other nations. I fear someone may at last answer me by saying, that all these fine things, arts, sciences, and laws, were wisely invented by men, as a salutary plague, to prevent the too great multiplication of mankind, lest the world, which was given us for a habitation, should in time be too small for its inhabitants.

What, then, is to be done? Must we destroy society, abolish *mine* and *yours* and go back to living in the forests with the bears? This is the sort of conclusion my adversaries would come to and I would sooner forestall it than leave to them the shame of drawing it. O you, who have never heard the voice of heaven, who think man destined only to live this little life and die in peace; you, who can resign in the midst of populous cities your fatal acquisitions, your restless spirits, your corrupt hearts and endless desires; resume, since it depends entirely on yourselves, your ancient and primitive innocence: retire to the woods, there to lose the sight and remembrance of the crimes of your contemporaries; and be not apprehensive of degrading your species, by renouncing its advances in order to renounce its vices. As for men like me, whose passions have destroyed their original simplicity, who can no longer subsist on plants or acorns, or live without laws and magistrates; those who were honoured in their first father with supernatural instructions; those who discover, in the design of giving human actions at the start a morality which they must otherwise have been so long in acquiring, the reason for a precept in itself indifferent and inexplicable on every other system; those, in short, who are persuaded that the Divine Being has called all mankind to be partakers in the happiness and perfection of celestial intelligences, all these will endeavour to merit the eternal prize they are to expect from the practice of those virtues, which they make themselves follow in learning to know them. They will respect the sacred bonds of their respective communities; they will love their fellow-citizens, and serve them with all their might: they will scrupulously obey the laws, and all those who make or administer them; they will particularly honour those wise and good princes, who find means of preventing, curing, or even palliating all these evils and abuses, by which we are constantly threatened; they will animate the zeal of their deserving rulers, by showing them, without flattery or fear, the importance of their office and the severity of their duty. But they will not therefore have less contempt for a constitution that cannot support itself without the aid of so many splendid characters, much oftener wished for than found; and from which, notwithstanding all their pains and solicitude, there always arise more real calamities than even apparent advantages.

Notes

1. See Appendix, p. 414.
2. [Justin, *Hist.* ii, 2. So much more does the ignorance of vice profit the one sort than the knowledge of virtue the other.]
3. *Amour-propre* must not be confused with love of self: for they differ both in themselves and in their effects. Love of self is a natural feeling which leads every animal to look to its own preservation, and which, guided in man by reason and modified by compassion, creates humanity and virtue. *Amour-propre* is a purely relative and factitious feeling, which arises in the state of society, leads each individual to make more of himself than of any other, causes all the mutual damage men inflict one on another, and is the real source of the 'sense of honour'. This being understood, I maintain that, in our primitive condition, in the true state of nature, *amour-propre* did not exist; for as each man regarded himself as the only observer of his actions, the only being in the universe who took any interest in him, and the sole judge of his deserts, no feeling arising from comparisons he could not

be led to make could take root in his soul; and for the same reason, he could know neither hatred nor the desire for revenge, since these passions can spring only from a sense of injury: and as it is the contempt or the intention to hurt, and not the harm done, which constitutes the injury, men who neither valued nor compared themselves could do one another much violence, when it suited them, without feeling any sense of injury. In a word, each man, regarding his fellows almost as he regarded animals of different species, might seize the prey of a weaker or yield up his own to a stronger, and yet consider these acts of violence as mere natural occurrences, without the slightest emotion of insolence or despite, or nay other feeling than the joy or grief of success or failure.

4. [Nature avows she gave the human race the softest hearts, who gave them tears.]

5. [Ovid, *Metamorphoses*, xi. 127.

Both rich and poor, shocked at their new found ills,

Would fly from wealth, and lose what they had sought.]

6. [Tacitus, *Hist.* iv. 17. The most wretched slavery they call peace.]

7. *Of the Rights of the Most Christian Queen over various States of the Monarchy of Spain,* 1667.

8. Distributive justice would oppose this rigorous equality of the state of nature, even were it practicable in civil society; as all the members of the State owe it their services in proportion to their talents and abilities, they ought, on their side, to be distinguished and favoured in proportion to the services they have actually rendered. It is in this sense we must understand that passage of Isocrates, in which he extols the primitive Athenians, for having determined which of the two kinds of equality was the most useful, viz. that which consists in dividing the same advantages indiscriminately among all the citizens, or that which consists in distributing them to each according to his deserts. These able politicians, adds the orator, banishing that unjust inequality which makes no distinction between good and bad men, adhered inviolably to that which rewards and punishes every man according to his deserts.

But in the first place, there never existed a society, however corrupt some may have become, where no difference was made between the good and the bad; and with regard to morality, where no measures can be prescribed by law exact enough to serve as a practical rule for a magistrate, it is with great prudence that, in order not to leave the fortune or quality of the citizens to his discretion, it prohibits him from passing judgment on persons and confines his judgment to actions. Only morals such as those of the ancient Romans can bear censors, and such a tribunal among us would throw everything into confusion. The difference between good and bad men is determined by public esteem; the magistrate being strictly a judge of right alone; whereas the public is the truest judge of morals, and is of such integrity and penetration on this head, that although it may be sometimes deceived, it can never be corrupted. The rank of citizens ought, therefore, to be regulated, not according to their personal merit—for this would put it in the power of the magistrate to apply the law almost arbitrarily—but according to the actual services done to the State, which are capable of being more exactly estimated.

9. [If you order me to thrust my sword in my brother's breast or my father's throat or the bowels of my pregnant wife, I will do all this though with an unwilling right arm.]

OF THE SOCIAL CONTRACT
OR
PRINCIPLES OF POLITICAL RIGHT

PREFATORY NOTE

This little treatise is extracted from a more extensive work undertaken at an earlier time without consideration of my capacity, and long since abandoned. Of the various fragments that might be selected from what was accomplished, the following is the most considerable, and appears to me the least unworthy of being offered to the public. The rest no longer exists.

Book One

I want to inquire whether, taking men as they are and laws as they can be, it is possible to have some legitimate and certain rule of administration in civil affairs. In this investigation I shall always strive to ally what right permits with what interest prescribes, so that justice and utility may not be divided.

I enter upon this inquiry without proving the importance of my subject. I shall be asked whether I am a prince or a legislator that I write on Politics. I reply that I am not, and that it is for this reason that I write on Politics. If I were a prince or a legislator, I should not waste my time in saying what ought to be done; I should do it or remain silent.

Having been born a citizen of a free State, and a member of the sovereign, however feeble an influence my voice may have in public affairs, the right to vote upon them is sufficient to impose on me the duty of informing myself about them. I feel happy, whenever I meditate on governments, always to find in my researches new reasons for loving that of my own country!

I. *Subject of This First Book*

Man is born free, and everywhere he is in chains. One believes himself the master of others, and yet he is a greater slave than they. How has this change come about? I do not know. What can render it legitimate? I believe that I can settle this question.

If I considered only force and the results that proceed from it, I should say that so long as a People is compelled to obey and does obey, it does well; but that, so soon as it can shake off the yoke and does shake it off, it does better; for, recovering its liberty by the same right by which it was taken away, either it is justified in resuming it, or there was no justification for depriving them of it. But the social order is a sacred right which serves as a basis for all others. Yet this right does not come from nature; it is therefore based on conventions. The question is to know what these conventions are. Before coming to that, I must establish what I have just laid down.

Translated by Charles M. Sheroverj; reprinted with his permission.

II. Of the First Societies

The most ancient of all societies, and the only natural one, is the family. Nevertheless children remain bound to their father only as long as they have need of him for their own preservation. As soon as this need ceases, the natural bond is dissolved. The children freed from the obedience which they owe to their father, and the father from the cares which he owes to his children, become equally independent. If they remain united, it is no longer naturally but voluntarily, and the family itself is kept together only by convention.

This common liberty is a consequence of man's nature. His first law is to attend to his own preservation, his first cares are those which he owes to himself, and as soon as he comes to years of discretion, being sole judge of the means adapted for his own preservation, he becomes thereby his own master.

The family is, then, if you will, the primitive model of political societies; the chief is the image of the father, while the people are the image of the children; and all, being born free and equal, only alienate their liberty for their own advantage. The whole difference is that, in the family, the father's love for his children repays him for the care that he bestows upon them; while, in the State, the pleasure of commanding makes up for the chief's lack of love for his people.

Grotius denies that all human authority is established for the benefit of the governed! He cites slavery as an example. His most invariable mode of reasoning is to establish right by fact.[1] A more rational method could be employed, but none more favorable to Tyrants.

It is then doubtful, according to Grotius, whether the human race belongs to a hundred men, or whether these hundred men belong to the human race; and he appears throughout his book to incline to the former opinion, which is also that of Hobbes. In this way we have mankind divided like herds of cattle, each of which has a master, who looks after it in order to devour it.

Just as a herdsman is of a superior nature to his herd, so chiefs, who are the herdsmen of man are also of a superior nature to their people. Thus, according to Philo's account, the Emperor Caligula reasoned, inferring well enough from this analogy that kings are gods, or that men are brutes.

The reasoning of Caligula is tantamount to that of Hobbes and Grotius. Aristotle, before them all, had likewise said that men are not naturally equal, but that some are born for slavery and others for domination.

Aristotle was right, but he mistook the effect for the cause. Every man born in slavery is born for slavery; nothing is more certain. Slaves lose everything in their chains, even the desire to escape from them; they love their servitude as the companions of Ulysses loved their brutishness.[2] If, then, there are slaves by nature, it is because there have been slaves contrary to nature. Force made the first slaves; their cowardice perpetuated them.

I have said nothing about King Adam nor about Emperor Noah, the father of three great Monarchs who shared the universe, like the children of Saturn with whom they are supposed to be identical. I hope that my moderation will give satisfaction; for, as I am a direct descendant of one of these Princes, and perhaps of the eldest branch, how do I know whether, by examination of titles, I might not find myself the legitimate king of the human race? Be that as it may, one cannot deny that Adam was Sovereign of the world, as Robinson was of his island, so long as he was its sole inhabitant; and it was a convenient feature of that empire that the monarch, secure on his throne, had nothing to fear from rebellions, or wars, or conspirators.

III. Of the Right of the Strongest

The strongest man is never strong enough to be always master, unless he transforms his force into right, and obedience into duty. Hence the right of the strongest—a right assumed ironically in appearance, and really established in principle. But will this word never be explained to us? Force is a physical power; I do not see what morality can result from its effects. To yield to force is an act of necessity, not of will; it is at most an act of prudence. In what sense could it be a duty?

Let us suppose for a moment this pretended right. I say that nothing results from it but an inexplicable muddle. For as soon as force constitutes right, the effect changes with the cause; every force which overcomes the first succeeds to its right (privilege). As soon as one can disobey with impunity, he may do so legitimately; and since the strongest is always in the right, it remains merely to act in such a way that one may be the strongest. But what sort of a right perishes when force ceases? If it is necessary to obey by compulsion, there is no need to obey by duty; and if men are no longer forced to obey, obligation is at an end. Obviously, then, this word "right" adds nothing to force; it means nothing here at all.

Obey the powers that be. If that means yield to force, the precept is good but superfluous; I warrant that it will never be violated. All power comes from God, I admit; but every disease does also. Does it follow that we are prohibited from calling in a physician? If a brigand should surprise me in the recesses of a wood: not only am I bound to give up my purse when forced, but am I also in conscience bound to do so when I might conceal it? For after all, the pistol which he holds is also a power.

Let us agree, then, that might does not make right, and that we are obligated to obey only legitimate powers. Thus my original questions ever recurs.

IV. Of Slavery

Since no man has a natural authority over his fellow men, and since force is not the source of right, conventions remain as the basis of all legitimate authority among men.

If an individual, says Grotius, can alienate his liberty and become the slave of a master, why should a whole people not be able to alienate theirs, and subject themselves to a king? In this there are a good many equivocal words that require explanation; but let us confine ourselves to the word *alienate*. To alienate is to give or sell. Now a man who becomes another's slave does not give himself; he sells himself at the very least for his subsistence; but why does a people sell itself? Far from a king supplying to his subjects their subsistence, he draws his from them; and according to Rabelais, a king does not live on little. Do subjects, then, give up their persons on condition that their goods also shall be taken? I do not see what is left for them to keep.

It will be said that the despot secures to his subjects civil peace. Just so; but what do they gain by that, if the wars which his ambition brings upon them, together with his insatiable greed and the vexations of his administration, dishearten them more than their own dissensions would? What do they gain if this peace itself is one of their miseries? One lives peacefully also in dungeons; is this enough to find them good? The Greeks confined in the cave of the Cyclops lived peacefully until their turn came to be devoured.

To say that a man gives himself for nothing is to say something absurd and inconceivable; such an act is illegitimate and worthless, for the simple reason that he who performs it is not in his right mind. To say the same thing of a whole people is to suppose a people of madmen; and madness does not make right.

Even if each person could alienate himself, he could not alienate his children; they are born men and free; their liberty belongs to them, and no one has a right to dispose of it except themselves. Before they have come to an age of discretion, the father can, in their name, stipulate conditions for their preservation and welfare, but not surrender them irrevocably and unconditionally; for such a bequest is contrary to the ends of nature, and exceeds the rights of paternity. It would be necessary, therefore, to ensure that an arbitrary government might be legitimate, that with each generation the people have the option of accepting it or rejecting it; but in that case this government would no longer be arbitrary.

To renounce one's liberty is to renounce one's quality as a man, the rights of humanity and even its duties. For whoever renounces everything there is no possible compensation. Such renunciation is incompatible with man's nature; and to deprive his actions of all morality is tantamount to depriving his will of all freedom. Finally, a convention which stipulates absolute authority on the one side and unlimited obedience on the other is vain and contradictory. Is it not clear that one is under no obligations whatsoever toward a man from whom one has a right to demand everything? And does not this single condition, without equivalent, without exchange, entail the nullity of the act? For what right would my slave have against me, since all that he has belongs to me? His right being mine, this right of me against myself is a meaningless phrase.

Grotius and others derive from war another origin for the pretended right of slavery. The victor having, according to them, the right of slaying the vanquished, the latter may purchase his life at the cost of his freedom; a convention so much the more legitimate that it turns to the profit of both.

But it is clear that this pretended right of slaying the vanquished in no way results from the state of war. Men are not naturally enemies, if only for the reason that, living in their primitive independence, they have no mutual relations sufficiently durable to constitute a state of peace or a sense of war. It is the relation of things and not of men which constitutes war; and the state of war cannot arise from simple personal relations, but only from real relations; private war—war between man and man—cannot exist either in the state of nature, where there is no settled ownership, or in the social state, where everything is under the authority of the laws.

Private combats, duels, and encounters are acts which do not at all constitute a state; and with respect to the private wars authorized by the Establishments of Louis IX, king of France, and suspended by the Peace of God, they were abuses of the feudal government, an absurd system if ever there was one, contrary both to the principles of natural right and to all good polity.

War, then, is not a relation between man and man, but a relation between State and State, in which individuals are enemies only by accident, not as men, nor even as citizens,[3] but as soldiers; not as members of the fatherland, but as its defenders. In short, each State can have as enemies only other States and not individual men, inasmuch as it is impossible to fix any true relation between things of different natures.

This principle is also comfortable to the established maxims of all ages and to the constant practice of all civilized peoples. Declarations of war are not so much warnings to the powers as to their subjects. The foreigner, whether king, or private person, or people, who robs, slays, or detains subjects without declaring war against the prince, is not an enemy, but a brigand. Even in open war, a just prince, while he rightly takes possession of all that belongs to the public in an enemy country, respects the person and property of individuals; he respects the rights on which his own are founded. The aim of war being the destruction of the enemy State, we have a right to slay its defenders so long as they bear arms; but as soon as they lay them down and surrender, ceasing to be enemies or instruments of the enemy, they become again simply men, and one has no further right over their lives. Sometimes it is possible to destroy the State without killing a single one of its members. But war confers no right except what is necessary to its end. These principles are not those of Grotius; they are not based on the authority of poets, but are derived from the nature of things, and are founded on reason.

With regard to the right of conquest, it has no other foundation than the law of the strongest. If war does not confer on the victor the right of slaying vanquished peoples, this right, which he does not possess, cannot be the foundation of a right to enslave them. One has a right to slay an enemy only when it is impossible to enslave him; the right to enslave him is not derived from the right to kill him. It is, therefore, an iniquitous exchange to make him purchase his life, over which the victor has no right, at the cost of his liberty. In establishing the right of life and death upon the right of slavery, and the right of slavery upon the right of life and death—is it not clear that one falls into a vicious circle?

Even if we suppose this terrible right of killing everybody, I say that a slave made in war, or a conquered people, is under no obligation at all to a master, except to obey him so far as compelled. In taking an equivalent for his life the victor has conferred no favor on him: instead of killing him unprofitably, the victor has destroyed him for his own advantage. Far, then, from having acquired over him any authority linked to that of force, the state of war subsists between them as before, their relation even is the effect of it; and the exercise of the right of war does not presuppose any treaty of peace. They have made a convention. Be it so; but this convention, far from terminating the state of war, presupposes its continuance.

Thus, in whatever way we view things, the right of slavery is null, not only because it is illegitimate, but because it is absurd and meaningless. These words, *slavery* and *right,* are contradictory; they are mutually exclusive. Whether addressed by a man to a man, or by a man to a people, such a speech as this will always be equally foolish: *I make a convention with you wholly at your expense and wholly for my profit, which I shall observe as long as I please and which you also shall observe as long as I please.*

V. That It Is Always Necessary to Go Back to a First Convention

Even if I were in accord with all that I have so far refuted, those who favor despotism would be no farther advanced. There will always be a great difference between subduing a multitude and ruling a society. If scattered men, however numerous they may be, are subjected successively to a single person, this seems to me only a case of master and slaves, not of a people and its chief: they form, if you will, an aggregation, but not an association, for they have neither public property nor a body politic. Such a man, had he enslaved half the world, is always only one individual; his interest, separated from that of the rest, is always only a private interest. If he dies, his empire after him is left scattered and disunited, as an oak dissolves and becomes a heap of ashes after the fire has consumed it.

A people, says Grotius, can give itself to a king. According to Grotius, a people, then, is a people before it gives itself to a king. This gift itself is a civil act, and presupposes a public deliberation. Hence, before examining the act by which a people elects a king, it would be good to examine the act by which a people is a people. For this act being necessarily anterior to the other, is the real foundation of the society.

In fact, if there were no anterior convention, where, unless the election were unanimous, would be the obligation upon the minority to submit to the decision of the majority? And whence do the hundred who desire a master derive the right to vote on behalf of

ten who do not desire one? The law of the plurality of votes is itself established by convention, and presupposes unanimity at least once.

VI. Of The Social Pact

I suppose that men have reached a point at which the obstacles that endanger their preservation in the state of nature prevail by their resistance over the forces which each individual can exert in order to maintain himself in that state. Then this primitive condition can
no longer subsist, and the human race would perish unless it changed its manner of being.

Now as men cannot create any new forces, but only unite and direct those that exist,
they have no other means of self-preservation than to form by aggregation a sum of forces
which may overcome the resistance, to put them in action by a single motive power, and
to make them work in concert.

This sum of forces can be produced only by the combination of many; but the strength
and freedom of each man being the primary instruments of his preservation, how can he
pledge them without injuring himself, and without neglecting the care which he owes to
himself? This difficulty, applied to my subject, may be stated in these terms:

"To find a form of association which defends and protects with the whole force of the
community the person and goods of every associate, and by means of which each, uniting
with all, nevertheless obeys only himself, and remains as free as before." Such is the fundamental problem to which the social contract gives the solution.

The clauses of this contract are so determined by the nature of the act that the slightest modification would render them vain and ineffectual; so that, although perhaps they
have never been formally enunciated, they are everywhere the same, everywhere tacitly
admitted and recognized; until, the social pact being violated, each man regains his initial rights and recovers his natural liberty, while losing the conventional liberty for which
he renounced it.

These clauses, rightly understood, are all reducible to one only, namely the total alienation of each associate, with all of his rights, to the whole community: For, in the first
place, as each gives himself up entirely, the condition is equal for all, and, the condition
being equal for all, no one has any interest in making it burdensome to others.

Further, the alienation being made without reserve, the union is as perfect as it can
be, and no associate has anything more to claim. For if some rights were left to individuals, since there would be no common superior who could judge between them and
the public, each, being on some point his own judge, would soon claim to be so on all; the
state of nature would still subsist, and the association would necessarily become tyrannical or useless.

Finally, each, in giving himself to all, gives himself to nobody; and as there is not one
associate over whom we do not acquire the same rights which we concede to him over ourselves, we gain the equivalent of all that we lose, and more power to preserve what we have.

If, then, everything which is not of the essence of the social pact is set aside, one finds
that it reduces itself to the following terms: *Each of us puts in common his person and his whole
power under the supreme direction of the general will; and in return we receive in a body every member as an indivisible part of the whole.*

Forthwith, instead of the particular person of each contracting part, this act of association produces a moral and collective body, which is composed of as many members as the
assembly has voices, and which receives from this same act its unity, its common *self* [*moi*],
its life, and its will. This public person, which is thus formed by the union of all the

individual members, formerly took the name of *City*[4] and now takes that of *Republic* or *body politic*, which is called by its members *State* when it is passive, *Sovereign* when it is active, *Power* when it is compared to similar bodies. With regard to the associates, they take collectively the name of *people*, and are called individually *Citizens*, as participating in the sovereign authority, and *Subjects*, as subjected to the laws of the State. But these terms are often confused and are mistaken one for another; it is sufficient to know how to distinguish them when they are used with complete precision.

VII. Of the Sovereign

One sees by this formula that the act of association includes a reciprocal engagement between the public and the individual, and that each individual, contracting so to speak with himself, is engaged in a double relation: namely, as a member of the Sovereign toward individuals, and as a member of the State toward the Sovereign. But we cannot apply here the maxim of civil right that no one is bound by engagements made with himself; for there is a great difference between being obligated to oneself and to a whole of which one forms a part.

It is necessary to note further that the public deliberation which can obligate all subjects to the Sovereign in consequence of the two different relations under which each of them is regarded cannot, for a contrary reason, bind the Sovereign to itself; and that accordingly it is contrary to the nature of the body politic for the Sovereign to impose on itself a law which it cannot transgress. As it can only be considered under one and the same relation, it is in the position of an individual contracting with himself; thus we see that there is not, nor can there be, any kind of fundamental law obligatory for the body of the people, not even the social contract. This does not imply that such a body cannot perfectly well enter into engagements with others in what does not derogate from this contract; for, with regard to foreigners, it becomes a simple being, an individual.

But the body politic or Sovereign, deriving its existence only from the sanctity of the contract, can never bind itself, even to others, in anything that derogates from the original act, such as to alienate some portion of itself, or submission to another Sovereign. To violate the act by which it exists would be to annihilate itself; and what is nothing produces nothing.

As soon as this multitude is thus united into one body, it is impossible to injure one of the members without attacking the body; still less to injure the body without the members feeling the effects. Thus duty and interest equally obligate the two contracting parties to give mutual assistance; and the same men should seek to combine in this twofold relationship all the advantages which are attendant on it.

Now the Sovereign, being formed only of the individuals who compose it, neither has nor can have any interest contrary to theirs; consequently the Sovereign power needs no guarantee toward its subjects, because it is impossible that the body should wish to injure all its members; and we shall see hereafter that it can injure no one in particular. The Sovereign, for the simple reason that it is, is always everything that it ought to be.

But this is not the case with respect to the relation of subjects to the Sovereign, which, notwithstanding the common interest, would have no security for the performance of their engagements, unless it found means to ensure their fidelity.

Indeed, each individual may, as a man, have a particular will contrary to, or divergent from, the general will which he has as a Citizen. His private interest may speak to him quite differently from the common interest; his absolute and naturally independent existence may make him regard what he owes to the common cause as a gratuitous contribution, the loss of which will be less harmful to others than will the payment of it be onerous to him; and viewing the moral person that constitutes the State as a being of reason because it is not a man, he would be willing to enjoy the rights of a citizen without being willing to fulfill the duties of a subject: an injustice, the progress of which would bring about the ruin of the body politic.

In order, then, that the social pact may not be a vain formula, it tacitly includes this engagement, which can alone give force to the others—that whoever refuses to obey the general will shall be constrained to do so by the whole body; which means nothing else than that he shall be forced to be free; for such is the condition which, giving each Citizen to his Fatherland, guarantees him from all personal dependence, a condition that makes up the spark and interplay of the political mechanism, and alone renders legitimate civil engagements, which, without it, would be absurd and tyrannical, and subject to the most enormous abuse.

VIII. *Of the Civil State*

This passage from the state of nature to the civil state produces in man a very remarkable change, by substituting in his conduct injustice for instinct, and by giving his actions the morality that they previously lacked. It is only when the voice of duty succeeds physical impulsion, and right succeeds appetite, that man, who till then had only looked after himself, sees that he is forced to act on other principles, and to consult his reason before listening to his inclinations. Although, in this state, he is deprived of many advantages he holds from nature, he gains such great ones in return, that his faculties are exercised and developed; his ideas are expanded; his feelings are ennobled; his whole soul is exalted to such a degree that, if the abuses of this new condition did not often degrade him below that from which he has emerged, he should ceaselessly bless the happy moment that removed him from it forever, and transformed him from a stupid and ignorant animal into an intelligent being and a man.

Let us reduce this whole balance to terms easy to compare. What man loses by the social contract is his natural liberty and an unlimited right to anything which tempts him and which he is able to attain; what he gains is civil liberty and the ownership of all that he possesses. In order not to be mistaken about these compensations, we must clearly distinguish natural liberty, which is limited only by the force of the individual, from civil liberty, which is limited by the general will; and possession, which is only the result of force or the right of the first occupant, from ownership, which can only be based on a positive title.

Besides the preceding, one can add to the acquisitions of the civil state the moral freedom which alone renders man truly master of himself; for the impulsion of mere appetite is slavery, and obedience to the law one prescribes to oneself is freedom. But I have already said too much on this subject, and the philosophical meaning of the term *liberty* does not belong to my subject here.

IX. *Of Real Property*

Each member of the community gives himself up to it at the moment of its formation, just as he actually is, himself and all his force, of which the goods he possesses form a part.

It is not that by this act possession changes its nature in changing hands and becomes property in those of the Sovereign; but, as the powers of the City are incomparably greater than those of an individual, public possession is also, in fact, more secure and more irrevocable, without being more legitimate, at least for foreigners. For the State, with regard to its members, is master of all their property by the social contract, which in the State serves as the basis of all rights; but with regard to other powers it is master only by right of first occupant which it holds from private individuals.

The right of first occupant, although more real than that of the strongest, becomes a true right only after the establishment of property [ownership]. Every man has by nature a right to all that is necessary to him; but the positive act which makes him owner of certain goods excludes him from the rest. His portion having been allotted, he ought to confine himself to it, and he has no further right against the community. That is why the right of first occupant, so weak in the state of nature, is respected by every member of a civil society. In this right one respects not so much what belongs to others as what does not belong to oneself.

Generally, in order to authorize the right of first occupant over any land whatsoever, the following conditions are needed. First, the land must not yet be inhabited by anyone; second, a man must occupy only the area required for his subsistence; third, he must take possession of it not by an empty ceremony but by labor and cultivation, the only mark of ownership which, in the absence of legal title, ought to be respected by others.

Indeed, to grant the right of first occupant according to necessity and labor, is it not to extend this right as far as it can go? Can one assign limits to this right? Will the mere setting foot on common ground be sufficient to presume an immediate claim to the ownership of it? Will the power of driving away other men from it for a moment suffice to deprive them of the right of ever returning to it? How can a man or a people take possession of an immense territory and rob the whole human race of it except by a punishable usurpation, since henceforth other men are deprived of the place of residence and sustenance which nature gives to them in common? When Núñez de Balboa on the seashore took possession of the Pacific Ocean and of the whole of South America in the name of the crown of Castile, was this sufficient to dispossess all the inhabitants, and exclude from it all the Princes in the world? On this stand, such ceremonies might have been multiplied vainly enough; and the Catholic King in his cabinet might, by a single stroke, have taken possession of the whole universe; only cutting off afterward from his empire what was previously occupied by other Princes.

It can be understood how the lands of individuals, united and contiguous, become public territory, and how the right of sovereignty, extending itself from the subjects to the land which they occupy, becomes at once real and personal; this places the possessors in greater dependence, and makes their own powers a guarantee for their fidelity. An advantage which ancient monarchs do not appear to have clearly sensed, for, calling themselves only Kings of the Persians or Scythians or Macedonians, they seem to have viewed themselves as chiefs of men rather than as owners of countries. Those of today call themselves more cleverly Kings of France, Spain, England, etc. In thus holding the land they are quite sure of holding its inhabitants.

What is remarkable about this alienation is that the community, in receiving the property of individuals, far from robbing them of it, only assures them lawful possession, and changes usurpation into true right, enjoyment into ownership. Then the possessors, being considered as depositaries of the public property, and their rights being respected by all members of the State, and maintained with all its power against the foreign intruder, have, as it were, by a transfer advantageous to the public and still more to themselves, acquired all that they have given up. This is a paradox which is easily explained by distinguishing between the rights which the Sovereign and the owner have over the same property, as shall be seen later.

It may also happen that men begin to unite before they possess anything, and that afterward taking over territory sufficient for all, they enjoy it in common, or share it among themselves, either equally or in proportions fixed by the Sovereign. In whatever manner this acquisition is made, the right which every individual has over his own property is always subordinate to the right which the community has over all; otherwise there would be neither solidity in the social union, nor real force in the exercise of Sovereignty.

I shall close this chapter and this book with a remark which ought to serve as a basis for the whole social system; it is that instead of destroying natural equality, the fundamental pact, on the contrary, substitutes a moral and legitimate equality for the physical inequality which nature imposed upon men, so that, although unequal in strength or talent, they all become equal by convention and legal right.[5]

Book Two

I. That Sovereignty Is Inalienable

The first and most important consequence of the principles established above is that the general will can only direct the forces of the State in keeping with the end for which it was instituted, which is the common good; for if the opposition of private interests has made the establishment of societies necessary, the harmony of these same interests has made it possible. That which is common to these different interests forms the social bond; and if there were not some point in which all interests agree, no society could exist. Now it is only on this common interest that the society should be governed.

I say, then, that sovereignty, being only the exercise of the general will, can never be alienated, and that the Sovereign, which is only a collective being, can be represented only by itself; power can well be transmitted, but will cannot.

In fact, if it is not impossible that a private will agree on some point with the general will, it is at least impossible that this agreement should be lasting and constant, for the private will naturally tends to preferences, and the general will to equality. It is still more impossible to have a guarantee for this agreement; even though it should always exist, it would be an effect not of art but of chance. The Sovereign may indeed say: I now will what a certain man wills, or at least what he says that he wills; but it cannot say: what that man wills tomorrow, I shall also will; since it is absurd that the will should bind itself for the future and since it is not incumbent on any will to consent to anything contrary to the good of the being that wills. If, then, the people promises simply to obey, it dissolves itself by that act, it loses its quality as a people; at the instant that there is a master, there is no longer a Sovereign, and forthwith the body politic is destroyed.

This is not to say that the orders of the chiefs cannot pass for expressions of the general will, so long as the Sovereign, free to oppose them, does not do so. In such case, from the universal silence one should presume the consent of the people. This will be explained at greater length.

II. That Sovereignty Is Indivisible

For the same reason that sovereignty is inalienable, it is indivisible. For either the will is general[6] or it is not; it is the will either of the body of the people, or only of a part. In the first case, this declared will is an act of sovereignty and constitutes law. In the second case, it is only a private will, or an act of magistracy; it is at most a decree.

But our political men, not being able to divide sovereignty in its principles, divide it in its object: they divide it into force and will, into legislative power and executive power; into rights of taxation, of justice, and of war; into internal administration and power of treating with foreigners: sometimes they confound all these parts and sometimes separate them. They make the Sovereign to be a fantastic being formed of borrowed pieces; it is as if they composed a man from several bodies, one having eyes, another having arms, another having feet, and nothing more. Charlatans of Japan, it is said, cut up a child before the eyes of the spectators; then, throwing all its limbs, one after another, into the air, they make the child come back down alive and whole. Such almost are the juggler's tricks of our politicians; after dismembering the social body by a deception worthy of a carnival, they recombine the parts, one knows not how.

This error comes from not having formed exact notions of sovereign authority, and from having taken as parts of this authority what are only emanations from it. Thus, for example, the act of declaring war and that of making peace have been looked at as acts of sovereignty; but this is not the case, since each of these acts is not a law, but only an application of the law, a particular act which determines the case of the law, as will be clearly seen when the idea attached to the word *law* will be fixed.

In following out the other divisions in the same way, one would find that whenever sovereignty appears divided, a mistake has been made; that the rights which are taken as parts of that sovereignty are all subordinate to it, and always suppose supreme wills of which these rights are merely the execution.

One could not say to what extent this lack of exactitude has made obscure the conclusions of authors in matters of political right, when they wished to judge the respective rights of kings and peoples along the principles they had established. Anyone can see, in Chapters III and IV of the first book of Grotius, how this learned man and his translator, Barbeyrac, became entangled and embarrassed in their sophisms, fearful of saying too much or not saying enough according to their views, and of offending the interests they needed to conciliate. Grotius, having taken refuge in France through discontent with his own fatherland, and wishing to pay court to Louis XIII, to whom his book is dedicated, spares nothing to despoil the people of all their rights and, in the most artful manner, to bestow them on kings. This also would clearly have been the wish of Barbeyrac, who dedicated his translation to the king of England, George I. But unfortunately, the expulsion of James II, which he calls abdication, forced him to be guarded, to equivocate, to evade, in order not to make William appear a usurper. If these two writers had adopted true principles, all their difficulties would have been lifted, and they would have always been coherent; but they would have regretfully spoken the truth and would have paid court only to the people. For truth hardly leads to fortune, and the people confer no ambassadorships, university chairs, or pensions.

III. Whether the General Will Can Err

It follows from what precedes that the general will is always upright and always tends toward the public utility; but it does not follow that the deliberations of the people always have the same rectitude. One wishes always his own good, but does not always discern it. The people is never corrupted, though often deceived, and then only does it seem to will that which is bad.

There is often a great difference between the will of all and the general will; the latter regards only the common interest, the other regards private interests and is only the sum of particular wills: but remove from these wills the pluses and minuses which cancel each other out[7] and the general will remains as the sum of the differences.

If, when an adequately informed people deliberates, the Citizens having no communication among themselves, from the large number of small differences the general will would always result, and the deliberation would always be good. But when factions are formed, partial associations at the expense of the whole, the will of each of these associations becomes general with regard to its members, and particular with regard to the State: one is then able to say that there are no longer as many voters as there are men, but only as many as there are associations. The differences become less numerous and yield a less general result. Finally, when one of these associations is so large that it overcomes the rest, you no longer have a sum of small differences as the result, but a unique difference; then there no longer is a general will, and the opinion which dominates is only a private opinion.

It matters, then, in order to have the general will expressed well, that there be no partial societies in the State, and that each Citizen speak only his own opinions.[8] Such was the unique and sublime institution of the great Lycurgus. But if there are partial associations, it is necessary to multiply their number and so prevent inequality, as was done by Solon, Numa, and Servius. These precautions are the only valid ones, in order that the general will always be enlightened and that the people are not deceived.

IV. Of the Limits of the Sovereign Power

If the State or the City is only a moral person whose life consists in the union of its members, and if the most important of its cares is that of its own conservation, it needs a universal and compulsive force to move and dispose every part in the manner most appropriate for the whole. As nature gives each man an absolute power over all his limbs, the social pact gives the body politic an absolute power over all its members, and it is the same power which, directed by the general will, bears, as I have said, the name of sovereignty.

But beyond the public person, we have to consider the private persons who compose it, and whose life and liberty are naturally independent of it. It is then necessary to distinguish clearly the respective rights of the Citizens and of the Sovereign[9] as well as between the duties which the former have to fulfill as subjects and the natural right which they ought to enjoy in their quality as men.

Granted that whatever part of his power, his goods, and his liberty each alienates by the social pact is only that part whose use is important to the community; we must also agree that the Sovereign alone is judge of that importance.

All the services that a citizen can render to the State, he owes to it as soon as the Sovereign demands them; but the Sovereign, on its side, cannot impose any burden on its subjects that is useless to the community; it cannot even wish to do so; because under the law of reason nothing happens without cause, just as under the law of nature.

The engagements which bind us to the social body are obligatory only because they are mutual, and their nature is such that in fulfilling them one cannot work for others without also working for oneself. Why is the general will always upright, and why do all constantly desire the well-being of each, if not because no one appropriates this word *each* to himself without thinking of himself as voting on behalf of all? This proves that equality of right and the notion of justice it produces derive from the preference which each gives to himself, and consequently from the nature of man; that the general will, to be truly such, must be just in its object as in its essence; that it ought to proceed from all in order to be applicable to all; and that it loses its natural rectitude when it is directed to some individual and determinate object, because in that case, judging from what is foreign to us, we have no true principle of equity to guide us.

In effect, so soon as a matter of fact or particular right is in question on a point which has not been regulated by a previous general convention, the affair becomes contentious. It is a lawsuit in which the interested individuals are one of the parties and the public the other, but in which I perceive neither the law which must be followed, nor the judge who should decide. It would be ridiculous to wish to refer the matter for an express decision of the general will, which can only be the decision of one of the parties, and which, consequently, is for the other party only a will that is foreign, partial, and inclined on such an occasion to injustice as well as it is subject to error. Thus, just as a particular will cannot represent the general will, the general will in turn changes its nature when it has a particular object and cannot, as general, decide about either a man or a fact. When the people of Athens, for example, named or deposed their chiefs, decreed honor to one, imposed penalties on another, and by multitudes of particular decrees exercised indiscriminately all the functions of government, the people no longer had any general will properly so called; it no longer acted as Sovereign but as Magistrate. This will appear contrary to common ideas, but I must be allowed time to set forth my own.

What generalizes the will, one must see from this, is not so much the number of voices as the common interest that unites them; for, in this institution, each necessarily submits to the conditions that he imposes on others: an admirable accord of interest and justice which gives to common deliberations a spirit of equity that seems to disappear in the discussion of any particular affair, for want of a common interest to unite and identify the ruling principle of the judge with that of the party.

By whatever path we return to our principle, we always arrive at the same conclusion: the social pact establishes among citizens such an equality that they all engage themselves under the same conditions and ought to enjoy the same rights. Thus, by the nature of the pact, every act of sovereignty, that is to say every authentic act of the general will, obligates or favors all the citizens equally; so that the Sovereign knows only the body of the nation, and distinguishes none of those who compose it. What then is properly an act of sovereignty? It is not a convention of the superior with an inferior, but a convention of the body with each of its members. A legitimate convention, because it has the social contract for its base; equitable, because it is common to all; useful, because it can have no object other than the general welfare; and firm, because it has for its guarantee the public force and supreme power. So long as the subjects submit only to such conventions, they obey no one, but only their own will; and to ask how far the respective rights of the Sovereign and the Citizens extend is to ask up to which point the latter can engage themselves, each toward all and all toward each.

One sees thereby that the Sovereign power, wholly absolute, wholly sacred, wholly inviolable as it is, neither passes nor can pass the limits of general conventions, and that every man can fully dispose of what is left to him of his goods and his liberty by these conventions; so that the Sovereign never has a right to burden one subject more than another, because then the matter becomes individual, and its power is no longer competent.

These distinctions once admitted, it is so false that in the social contract there is, on the part of individuals, any real renunciation, that their situation, as a result of this contract, is in reality preferable to what it was before: instead of an alienation they have only made an advantageous exchange of an uncertain and precarious mode of existence for a better and more assured one, of natural independence for liberty, of the power to injure others for their own safety, and of their strength, which others might overcome, for a right which the social union renders invincible. Their life itself, which they have dedicated to the State, is continually protected by it; and when they expose their lives for its defense, what do they do but restore what they have received from it? What do they do but what they would do more frequently and with more risk in the state of nature, when, engaging in inevitable struggles, they would defend at the peril of their lives their means of preserving it? All have to fight, if need be, for the fatherland, it is true; but then no one ever has to fight for himself. Do we not gain, still, to run this risk for that which assures our safety, a part of the risks we would have to run for ourselves as soon as our security was taken away?

V. Of the Right of Life and Death

One asks how individuals having no right to dispose of their own lives can transmit to the Sovereign this right which they do not possess? This question appears difficult to resolve only because it is poorly posed. Every man has a right to risk his own life in order to preserve it. Has it ever been said that one who throws himself out of a window to escape from a fire is guilty of suicide? Has this crime, indeed, ever been imputed to a man who perishes in a storm although, on embarking, he was not ignorant of the danger?

The social treaty has as its end the conservation of the contracting parties. He who desires the end desires also the means, and these means are inseparable from some risks, even from some losses. He who desires to preserve his life at the expense of others ought also to give it up for them when necessary. Still, the Citizen is no longer judge of the peril to which the law requires that he expose himself; and when the Prince has said to him: "It is expedient for the State that you die," he should die; because it is only on this condition that he has lived in security until then, and his life is no longer only a benefit of nature, but a conditional gift of the State.

The penalty of death inflicted on criminals can be seen almost from the same viewpoint: it is in order not to be the victim of a murderer that a person consents to die if he becomes one. In this treaty, far from disposing of his own life, one only thinks of guaranteeing it, and it is not to be presumed that any of the contracting members plans at that time to be hanged.

Besides, every malefactor, attacking the social right, becomes by his crimes a rebel and traitor to his fatherland; he ceases to be a member of it by violating its laws, and even makes war against it. The conservation of the State then is incompatible with his own, so one of the two must perish, and when the guilty one is executed, it is less as a Citizen than as an enemy. The proceedings, the judgment, are the proofs and declaration that he has broken the social treaty, and consequently is no longer a member of the State. Yet as he is acknowledged to be such, at least by his residence, he ought to be removed from it by exile as a violator of the pact, or by death as a public enemy; for one such enemy is not a moral person, but a man, and it is then that the right of war is to slay the vanquished.

But, one will say, the condemnation of a Criminal is a particular act. Agreed: likewise, this condemnation does not concern the Sovereign; it is a right which it can confer though it is itself unable to exercise. All my ideas hold together, but I do not know how to explain them all at once.

Besides, the frequency of physical punishment is always a sign of weakness or indolence in the Government. There is no one so wicked who could not be made good for something. One has a right to execute, even as an example, only someone who cannot be preserved with danger.

As regards the right to pardon or to exempt a guilty person from the penalty imposed by the law and pronounced by the judge, it belongs only to that which is above both the judge and the law, that is to say to the Sovereign; still, its right in this is not very distinct, and the cases of using it are very rare. In a well-governed State there are few punishments, not because many pardons are given, but because there are few criminals; the multitude of crimes assures their impunity when the State declines. Under the Roman Republic neither the senate nor the consuls attempted to grant pardons; the people themselves did not grant any, although they sometimes revoked their own judgments. Frequent pardons announce that crimes will soon need them no longer, and each sees to where that leads. But I feel my heart murmur and hold back my pen; let us leave these questions for discussion to the just man who has never done wrong and who never has had need of pardon himself.

VI. Of the Law

By the social pact we have given existence and life to the body politic; it is now a matter of giving it movement and will through legislation. For the original act by which this body is formed and united still determines nothing with respect to what it should do to preserve itself.

What is good and conforming to order is such by the nature of things and independent of human conventions. All justice comes from God, he alone is the source; but if we knew how to receive it from so high, we would need neither government nor laws. Without doubt there is a universal justice emanating from reason alone; but this justice, in order to be admitted among us, must be reciprocal. Considering things from a human viewpoint, the laws of justice, lacking a natural sanction, are ineffectual among men; they only bring good to the wicked and evil to the just man when he observes them with everyone else and no one observes them with him. Conventions and laws are then needed in order to unite rights with duties and to bring justice to its object. In the state of nature, where everything is common, I owe nothing to those to whom I have promised nothing, and I recognize as belonging to others only what is useless to me. It is not so in the civil state, where all the rights are fixed by the law.

But what then is a law? As long as one continues to attach to this word only metaphysical ideas, one will continue to reason without understanding, and when one will have said what a law of nature is, one will not have a better idea of what is a law of the State.

I have already said that there is no general will concerning a particular object. In effect, this particular object is either in the State or outside the State. If it is outside the State, a will that is foreign to it is not general in relation to it; and if within the State, that object is part of it; then there is formed between the whole and its part a relation which makes the whole two separate entities, of which the part is one, and the whole less this same part is the other. But the whole less one part is not the whole, and so long as the relation subsists, there is no longer any whole but two unequal parts: from which it follows that the will of one of them is no longer general in relation to the other.

But when the whole people decrees for the whole people, it considers only itself; and if a relation is then formed, it is between the entire object from one point of view and the whole object from another point of view, without any division of the whole. It is this act that I call a law.

When I say that the object of the laws is always general, I mean that the law considers the subjects in a body and the actions as abstract, never a man as an individual nor a particular action. Thus the law can very well decree that there will be privileges, but it cannot confer them on anyone by name; the law can create several Classes of Citizens, even assign the characteristics that confer a right to membership in these Classes, but it cannot name specific persons to be admitted to them; it can establish a royal Government and a hereditary succession, but it cannot elect a king or appoint a royal family; in a word, no function that relates to an individual object belongs to the legislative power.

On this idea one sees instantly that it is no longer necessary to ask who is responsible for making the laws, since they are acts of the general will; nor whether the Prince is above the laws, since he is a member of the State; nor if the law can be unjust, since no one is unjust to himself; nor how one is free and subject to the laws, since they are only registers of our wills.

One sees further that the law uniting the universality of the will with that of the object, what any man, whoever he may be, orders on his own, is not a law; what is ordered even by the Sovereign regarding a particular object is not a law, but a decree, not an act of sovereignty, but of magistracy.

I therefore call every State ruled by laws a Republic, under whatever form of administration it could have; for then only the public interest governs and the public entity [Latin: *res publica*] is real. Every legitimate Government is republican;[10] I will explain later what Government is.

Laws are properly only the conditions of the civil association. The People, submitting to the laws, ought to be their author; it concerns only those who are associating together to regulate the conditions of the society. But how will they regulate them? Will it be in a common accord by sudden inspiration? Does the body politic have an organ to announce its will? Who will give it the foresight necessary to frame its acts and publish them in advance, or how will it pronounce them at the moment of need? How will a blind multitude, which often does not know what it wants because it rarely knows what is good for it, carry out an enterprise so great and also difficult as a system of legislation? By itself the people always wants the good, but by itself does not always discern it. The general will is always upright, but the judgment which guides it is not always enlightened. It is necessary to make it see objects as they are, sometimes as they ought to appear, to point out the good road it seeks, to guard it from the seduction of private wills, to bring before its eyes considerations of places and times, to balance the attraction of present and tangible advantages against the danger of distant and hidden evils. Private individuals see the good they reject; the public wants the good it does not see. All have equal need of guides. It is necessary to obligate the former to conform their wishes to their reason; it is necessary to teach the latter to know what it wants. Then from public enlightenment results the union of the understanding and the will in the social body, hence the precise concourse of the parts, and finally the maximum force of the whole. From this arises the necessity of a Legislator.

VII. Of the Legislator

In order to discover the best rules of society which are suitable to nations, there would be needed a superior intelligence who saw all the passions of men and who had not experienced any of them; who would have no relation to our nature and yet knew it thoroughly; whose happiness would not depend on us and who would be quite willing to occupy himself with ours; finally, one who, preparing for himself a distant glory in the progress of time, could work in one age and find satisfaction in another.[11] Gods would be needed to give laws to men.

The same reasoning that Caligula used as to fact, Plato used with regard to right in order to define the civil or royal person whom he seeks in his book on ruling [i.e., the *Statesman*]. But if it is true that a great Prince is a rare man, what will a great Legislator be? The first has only to follow the model which the other has to propose. The latter is the engineer who invents the machine, the former is only the workman who puts it in readiness and makes it work. In the birth of societies, says Montesquieu, it is the chiefs of republics who make the institutions, and afterward it is the institutions which form the chiefs of republics.

He who dares to undertake the instituting of a people ought to feel himself capable, as it were, of changing human nature; of transforming each individual, who in himself is a perfect and solitary whole, into part of a greater whole from which this individual receives in some way his life and his being; of altering the constitution of man so as to reinforce it; of substituting a partial and moral existence for the physical and independent existence we have all received from nature. It is necessary, in a word, to remove man's own forces in order to give him some that are strange and which he is not able to use without the help of others. The more these natural forces are dead and annihilated, the greater and more durable are those acquired, the more too is the institution solid and perfect: so that if each Citizen is nothing, and can be nothing, except in combination with all others, and if the force acquired by the whole be equal or superior to the sum of the natural forces of all individuals, one can say that legislation has attained the highest possible point of perfection.

The Legislator is in all respects an extraordinary man in the State. If he ought to be so by his genius, he is not less so by his function. It is not magistracy, it is not sovereignty. This office, which constitutes the republic, does not enter into its constitution; it is a particular and superior function which has nothing in common with human dominion; for if he who controls men should not have control over the laws, he who has control over the laws should not control men; otherwise, the laws, as ministers of his passions, would often serve only to perpetuate his acts of injustice; he would never be able to prevent his private views from corrupting the sacredness of his work.

When Lycurgus gave laws to his fatherland, he began by abdicating the throne. It was the custom of most Greek towns to entrust the establishment of their laws to foreigners. The modern republics of Italy have often imitated this practice; the republic of Geneva also found it worked well.[12] Rome, in its finest age, saw all the crimes of Tyranny reborn in its bosom, and itself on the verge of peril, because of having united legislative authority and sovereign power in the same hands.

Yet the Decemvirs themselves never arrogated the right to pass any law on their sole authority. "Nothing that we propose to you," they said to the people, "can pass into law without your consent. Romans, be yourselves the authors of the laws that ought to secure your happiness."

He who drafts the laws, then, does not have or should not have any legislative right, and even the people cannot, if it wishes, divest itself of this incommunicable right, because according to the fundamental pact, only the general will obligates individuals and one cannot be assured that a particular will has conformed to the general will until after it has been submitted to the free votes of the people; I have already said that, but it is not useless to repeat it.

Thus one finds at the same time in the work of legislation two things which seem incompatible: an enterprise above human force, and to execute it an authority that is nothing.

Another difficulty merits attention. Wise men who wish to speak their own language to the people instead of using the common speech will not be understood. Besides, there are a thousand kinds of ideas that it is impossible to translate into the language of the people. Very general views and very remote objects are equally beyond their grasp: each individual, appreciating no other plan of government than that which relates to his private interest, appreciates with difficulty the advantages he should receive from the continual privations which good laws impose. For a newly formed people to be able to appreciate the sane maxims of politics and to follow the fundamental rules of statecraft, it would be necessary that the effect could become the cause; that the social spirit, which ought to be the accomplishment of the institution, would preside over the institution itself; and that men be already, prior to the laws, that which they should become by means of them. Since the Legislator is able to employ neither force nor reasoning, he must have recourse to an authority of a different order, which can win without violence and persuade with convincing.

This is what in all times has forced the fathers of nations to have recourse to the intervention of heaven, and to give the Gods credit for their own wisdom, to the end that the peoples, brought under the laws of the State as to those of nature, and recognizing the same power in the formation of man and in that of the city, obey with liberty and bear with docility the yoke of public felicity.

This sublime reason which rises above the reach of common men the Legislator places in the mouth of the immortals in order to win over by divine authority those unable to be moved by human prudence.[13] But not every man can make the Gods speak or be believed when he announces himself as their interpreter. The great soul of the Legislator is the true miracle which should prove his mission. Any man can engrave stone tablets, or buy an oracle, or feign a secret relationship with some divinity, or train a bird to speak in his ear, or find some other crude means of imposing on the people. He who knows only this could even assemble by chance a crowd of madmen, but he will never found an empire and his extravagant work will soon perish with him. Vain delusions form a transient bond; only wisdom renders it durable. The Judaic law which still subsists, and that of the child of Ishmael, which has ruled half the world for ten centuries, still proclaim today the great men who enunciated them; and while proud philosophy or blind party spirit sees in them only lucky impostors, the true student of politics admires in their institutions this great and powerful genius who presides over durable institutions.

It is not necessary to conclude from this with Warburton that politics and religions have among us a common object, but rather that in the origin of nations, one serves as instrument of the other.

VIII. Of the People

Just as an architect, before raising a large building, observes and tests the soil in order to see if it is able to sustain the weight, the wise instructor does not begin by drawing up laws that are good in themselves, but first examines whether the people for whom he intends them are fitted to support them. This is why Plato refused to provide laws to the Arcadians and Cyrenians, knowing that these two peoples were rich and could not tolerate equality; it is for this reason that one witnessed good laws and wicked men in Crete, because Minos had only disciplined a people steeped in vice.

A thousand nations have flourished on earth which never could have borne good laws; and even those which could have done so, for as long as they lasted, had only a short time to do so. Most Peoples, as most men, are docile only in their youth; they become incorrigible as they age. Once customs are established and prejudices have taken root, it is a dangerous and vain enterprise to want to reform them; the people are not able to tolerate their evils being touched even in order to destroy them, like those stupid and cowardly patients who quiver at the sight of a doctor.

To be sure, just as some diseases unhinge men's minds and remove the memory of the past, it is sometimes found during the lifetime of States violent epochs in which revolutions do to the people what certain crises do to individuals, in which the horror of the past takes the place of forgetfulness, and in which the State, inflamed by civil wars, is reborn, so to speak, from its ashes and regains the vigor of youth in springing from the arms of death. Such was Sparta at the time of Lycurgus, such as Rome after the Tarquins, and such among us were Holland and Switzerland after the expulsion of the Tyrants.

But these events are rare; they are exceptions, the reason for which is always found in the particular constitution of the excepted State. They could not even happen twice with the same people, for it can make itself free when it is still barbarous, but it cannot do so when the civil strength is exhausted. Then troubles can destroy it without revolutions being able to reestablish it, and as soon as its chains are broken, it falls apart and ceases to exist. It then needs a master, not a liberator. Free Peoples, remember this maxim: "One can acquire liberty, but one can never recover it."

Youth is not infancy. For Nations as for men there is a time of youth, or, if one prefers, of maturity, that must elapse before subjecting them to laws; but the maturity of a people is not always easy to discern, and if it is anticipated, the work is ruined. One people is capable of discipline on its birth, another is not after ten centuries. The Russians will never be truly civilized, because they were too early. Peter had an imitative genius; he did not have the true genius which creates and makes everything out of nothing. A few of the things he did were good, the majority were ill-timed. He saw that his people was barbarous, he did not see that it was not ready for a lawful order; he wished to civilize it when it was only needed to discipline it. He wished at first to make Germans, Englishmen, when he should have begun by making Russians: he prevented his subjects from ever becoming what they might have been, by persuading them that they were what they were not. It is in this way that a French Tutor trains his pupil to shine for a moment in childhood, and then never to be anything. The Russian Empire will want to subjugate Europe and will itself be subjugated. The Tartars, its subjects or its neighbors, will become its masters and ours. This revolution seems to me inevitable. All the Kings of Europe are working in concert to accelerate it.

IX. (Continued)

As nature has set limits to the stature of a well-formed man, beyond which there are only Giants and Dwarfs, so too, with regard to the best constitution of a State, there are limits to the possible extent it may have so that it should be neither too large to be well governed, nor too small to maintain itself. There is in every body politic a *maximum* of force that should not be exceeded, and which is often distended as it grows larger. The more the social bond is extended, the more it is loosened; and generally a small State is proportionally stronger than a large one.

A thousand reasons demonstrate this maxim. In the first place, administration becomes more difficult at great distances, as a weight becomes heavier at the end of a longer lever. It also becomes more burdensome in proportion as its levels are multiplied: for each town has first its own administration, for which the people pay, each district its own, still paid for by the people, then each province, then the large governments, the Satrapies, the Viceroyalties, which need always to be funded more lavishly as one goes higher, and always at the expense of the unfortunate people; finally comes the supreme administration which overwhelms everyone. So many surcharges continually exhaust the subjects: far from being well governed by all these different orders, they are less well governed than if they had only one above them. Meanwhile, hardly any resources remain for emergencies; and when it is necessary to have recourse to them, the State is always on the brink of ruin.

This is not all; not only does the Government have less vigor and speed to enforce observation of the laws, prevent harassments, correct abuses, prevent seditious enterprises which are undertaken in remote places; but the people have less affection for their chiefs, who are never seen, for the fatherland, which to their eyes is like the world, and for their fellow citizens, most of whom are strangers.

The same laws cannot be suitable for so many diverse provinces which have different customs, who live under contrasting climates, and cannot tolerate the same form of government. Different laws only engender trouble and confusion among peoples who, living under the same chiefs and in continual communication, mingle or intermarry in different areas, and submitting to different customs, never know if their patrimony is really theirs. Talents are hidden, virtues ignored, vices unpunished, in that multitude of men, unknown to each other, whom the seat of the supreme administration brings together in one place. The Chiefs, overwhelmed with work, see nothing for themselves; clerks govern the State. Finally, the measures necessary to maintain the general authority, which so many distant Officers wish to evade or impose, absorb all public attention; there remains none for the welfare of the people, and barely any for its defense if needed; and thus a body too large for its constitution collapses and perishes under its own weight.

On the other side, the State ought to provide itself a certain base for its solidity, to resist the shocks it will not fail to experience and the efforts which it will be constrained to make in order to sustain itself: for all peoples have a kind of centrifugal force, by which they continually act against one another, tending to aggrandize themselves at the expense of their neighbors, like the vortices of Descartes. Thus weak men risk being quickly swallowed up and none can preserve himself except by placing himself in a kind of equilibrium with all, which renders the pressure almost equal.

One sees that there are reasons for expansion and reasons for contraction, and it is not the least talent of the student of politics to find between the two the most advantageous proportion to the conservation of the State. One can say in general that the former, being only external and relative, ought to be subordinated to the others, which are internal and absolute; a strong and wholesome constitution is the first thing to be sought, and one should count more on the vigor born out of a good government than on the resources provided by a large territory.

Besides, one has seen States so constituted that the necessity of conquest entered into their constitution itself, and that, in order to maintain themselves, they were forced to expand ceaselessly. Perhaps they prided themselves greatly on this happy necessity, which nevertheless showed them, with the limit of their greatness, the inevitable moment of their fall.

X. (Continued)

One can measure a body politic in two ways: namely, by the extent of its territory and by the number of its people; and there is between them a suitable ratio according to which the State can be given its true dimension. Men make the State and it is the terrain that nourishes the men: the relation is then that the land should suffice for the maintenance of its inhabitants, and that there be as many inhabitants as the land can nourish. It is in this proportion that is found the *maximum* power of a given number of people; for if the terrain is too large, guarding it is onerous, its cultivation insufficient, its products superfluous; this is the proximate cause of defensive wars. If there is not enough land, the State finds it necessary to supplement its produce at the discretion of its neighbors; this is the proximate cause of offensive wars. Every people which has by its position no alternative between commerce or war is inherently weak; it depends on its environment, it depends on its neighbors, it depends on events; it has nothing but an uncertain and brief existence. It subjugates and changes situations or it is subjugated and is nothing. It is able to conserve itself as free only through being petty or grand.

One is not able to provide an arithmetically fixed ratio between the extent of land and the number of men, a relation that is reciprocally sufficient because of the differences which are found in the qualities of terrain, in degrees of fertility, in the nature of produce, in the influence of climate, as much as in the temperaments of the men who inhabit it, some of whom consume little in a fertile country, others much from a barren soil. It is also necessary to have regard to the greater or lesser fecundity of the women, to what the country is able to have that is more or less favorable to the population, to the number of men the legislator is able to bring together by his institutions; so the legislator ought to found his judgment not on what he does see but on what he can foresee, not focus his vision on the actual condition of the population but on what it should naturally become. Finally, there are a thousand occasions where the particular contingencies of place require or permit that more territory be embraced than seems necessary. Thus men will spread out in a mountainous country, where the natural products, the woods, the pastures, require less labor, where experience teaches that women are more fecund than in the plains, and where a great amount of sloping land can provide only a small horizontal base, the only one that can be counted on for vegetation. Or, on the other hand, people can restrict themselves to the seashore, even among nearly sterile rocks and sand; because fishing there can supplement in large part the products of the earth, because men ought to be more concentrated in order to repel pirates, and besides, it is much easier to relieve the country, by colonies, of too many inhabitants.

To these conditions for the institution of a people it is necessary to add one which cannot replace the others, but without which they are all useless: it is that they enjoy abundance and peace; for the time in which the State is organized, as that when a battalion is formed, is the instant when the body is least capable of resistance and most easily destroyed. One would resist better in absolute disorder than in a moment of ferment, when each is occupied with his own status and not the common danger. Should a war, a famine, a sedition arise in this time of crisis, the State is inevitably overturned.

Many governments have indeed been established during such storms; but then it is those governments themselves that destroy the State. Usurpers always bring about or choose disjointed times, in order to pass, under the cover of public terror, destructive laws which the people would never adopt when calm. The choice of the moment of instituting a government is one of the surest signs by which one can distinguish the work of the Legislator from that of the Tyrant.

What people is then suitable for legislation? That which finds itself already bound by some union of origin, interest, or convention, but still has never carried the true yoke of the laws; that which has neither customs nor superstitions deeply rooted; that which does not fear being set upon by a sudden invasion, which, without entering into the quarrels of its neighbors, can alone resist each of them, or is able to use the aid of one to repulse the other; that whose every member can be known by all, and where no man is charged with a greater burden than he can bear; that which is able to get along without other peoples and which all other peoples are able to get along without;[14] that which is neither rich nor poor, and can be self-sufficient; finally, that which unites the steadfastness of an ancient people with the docility of a new one. What renders the work of legislation arduous is less what it must establish than that which it must destroy; and that which renders success so rare is the impossibility of finding the simplicity of nature joined to the needs of society. All these conditions, it is true, are difficult to bring together. Thus one sees few well-constituted States.

There is still in Europe one country capable of legislation; it is the Isle of Corsica. The valor and constancy with which this brave people have known how to recover and defend their liberty well deserves that some wise man should teach them how to save it. I have a feeling that one day this small Isle will astound Europe.

XI. Of the Diverse Systems of Legislation

If one seeks to find precisely what constitutes the greatest good of all, which ought to be the goal of every system of legislation, one will find that it reduces itself to two principal objects, *liberty* and *equality*. Liberty, because all self-dependence is so much force taken away from the body of the State; equality because liberty cannot subsist without it.

I have already said what civil liberty is; with regard to equality, it is necessary not to understand by this word that every degree of power and of wealth should be absolutely the same, but that, as to power, it should be above all violence and never exercised except in virtue of position and the laws; and as to wealth, no citizen should be so opulent as to be able to buy another, and none so poor as to be constrained to sell himself.[15] This presumes on the side of the mighty moderation, of goods and influence, and on the side of the lowly, moderation of avarice and of covetousness.

This equality is said to be a chimerical fantasy which cannot exist in practice. But if abuse is inevitable, does it follow that abuse should not be at least regulated? It is precisely because the force of things always tends to destroy equality that the force of legislation should always tend to maintain it.

But these general objects of every good institution ought to be modified in each country by the relations that arise, as much from the local situation as from the character of the inhabitants, and it is upon these relations that arise, as much from the local situation as from the character of the inhabitants, and it is upon these relations that it is necessary to assign to each people a particular institutional system, which should be the best, not perhaps in itself, but for the State for which it is designed. For example, is the soil barren and sterile; or the country too densely populated? Turn your care to industry and the arts, whose products you will exchange for the provisions you lack. On the other hand, do you occupy rich plains and fertile hillsides? On a good terrain, do you lack inhabitants? Give your care to agriculture, which multiplies the population, and drive away the arts, which only further depopulate the country by gathering the few inhabitants in a few places.[16] Do you occupy extended and convenient shores? Cover the sea with vessels, cultivate commerce and navigation; you will have a brief and brilliant existence. Does the sea bathe nearly inaccessible rocks on your beaches? Remain barbarians and fish-eaters; you will live more tranquilly, perhaps better, and surely more happily. In a word, beyond the maxims common to all, each People contains within itself some cause which orders them in a particular manner and renders its legislation appropriate to itself alone. Thus, in ancient times the Hebrews and recently the Arabs had made religion their principal object, the Athenians letters, Carthage and Tyre commerce, Rhodes navigation, Sparta war, and Rome virtue. The author of *The Spirit of the Laws* has shown us many examples of the art by which the legislator directs the institution toward each of these objects.

What renders the constitution of a State truly solid and durable is when the proper means are so observed that natural relations and the laws always fall into concert on the same points, and that the latter, so to speak, only assure, accompany, and rectify the former. But if the Legislator, mistaking his object, takes a principle different from that which arises from the nature of things, the one tending to servitude and the other to liberty, the one to wealth and the other to increasing population, the one to peace and the other to conquest, one will see the imperceptible enfeeblement of the laws, the impairment of the constitution, and the State will not cease to be agitated until destroyed or changed, and invincible nature will have retaken her empire.

XII. Division of the Laws

To organize the whole, to give the best possible form to the public entity, there are diverse relations to consider. First of all, the action of the entire body operating on itself, that is, the relation of all to all, or of the Sovereign to the State, this relation being composed, as we shall see later, of the relations of the intermediate terms.

The laws which govern this relationship carry the name of political laws, and are also called fundamental laws, not without some reason if these laws are wise. For if there is in each State only one good way of ordering it, the people who have found it ought to adhere to it: but if the established order is bad, why should one take as fundamental laws which prevent it from being good? Besides, in every situation, a people is always the master of changing its laws, even the best; for if it pleases a people to do itself harm, who has the right to prevent it?

The second relation is that of the members among themselves or with the entire body, and this relation ought to be in the first case as little as in the second case it is as great as possible: so that each Citizen should be in a perfect independence of all the others, and in an excessive dependence on the City; which is always achieved by the same means; because only the force of the State secures the liberty of its members. It is from this second relation that the civil laws arise.

One can consider a third kind of relation between man and the law, namely that of punishable disobedience, and it is this which gives rise to the establishment of the criminal laws, which are basically less a particular species of law than the sanction of all the others.

To these three types of law is joined a fourth, the most important of all; it is engraved neither in marble nor in bronze, but in the hearts of the citizens; it is the true constitution of the State; every day it takes on new force; when the other laws age or wither away, it revives or supplements them, and conserves a people in the spirit of its institution, imperceptibly substituting the force of habit for that of authority. I speak of habitual conduct, of customs, and especially of opinion; a part of the laws unknown to our political thinkers, but on which the success of everything else depends; something with which the great Legislator secretly occupies himself while he seems to concern himself with particular regulations that are only the frame of the vault, of which moral customs, slower to arise, finally form the immovable Keystone.

Among these diverse Classes, the political laws, which constitute the form of Government, are alone relevant to my subject.

Book Three

Before speaking of the diverse forms of Government, let us try to fix the precise meaning of that word, which has not yet been very well explained.

I. Of Government in General

I warn the reader that this chapter should be read with care, and that I do not know the art of being clear to those who do not wish to be attentive.

Every free action has two causes which concur to produce it, the one moral, namely the will that determines the act; the other physical, namely the power that executes it. When I walk toward an object, it is first necessary that I want to go there; in the second place, that my feet carry me there. Should a paralytic wish to run, should an agile man not wish to do so, both will remain where they are. The body politic has the same motive power: in it one likewise distinguishes force and will. The latter is under the name of *legislative power*, the former under the name of *executive power*. Nothing is or should be done there [in the body politic] without their concurrence.

We have seen that the legislative power belongs to the people, and can belong to it alone. It is easy to see, on the contrary, by the principles already established, that the executive power cannot belong to the general public as Legislative or Sovereign; because this power consists only in particular acts which are not the province of the law, nor consequently of the Sovereign, all of whose acts can only be laws.

It is then necessary for the public force to have an appropriate agent that unifies it and puts it to work according to the directions of the general will, which serves as the means of communication between the State and the Sovereign, which in some way accomplishes in the public person what the union of soul and body does in man. This is in the State the reason for Government, improperly confused with the Sovereign, of which it is only the Minister.

What then is the Government? An intermediate body established between the subjects and the Sovereign for their mutual correspondence, charged with the execution of the laws, and to the maintenance of liberty, both civil and political.

The members of this body are called Magistrates or *Kings,* that is to say *Governors;* and the body as a whole bears the name of *Prince.*[17] Thus those who claim that the act by which a people submits to its chiefs is not a contract are quite correct. It is absolutely only a commission, an employment in which simple officers of the Sovereign exercise in its name the power which it has entrusted to them, and which it can limit, modify, and take back when it pleases to do so, since the alienation of such a right is incompatible with the nature of the social body, and contrary to the goal of the association.

I then call *Government* or supreme administration the legitimate exercise of the executive power, and Prince or Magistrate, the man or the body charged with that administration.

In the Government are found the intermediary forces, whose relationship composes the relation of the whole to the whole or of the Sovereign to the State. One can represent this last relation by that of the extremes of a continuous proportion, of which the proportional mean is the Government. The Government receives from the Sovereign the orders it gives to the people, and so that the State may be in good equilibrium it is necessary, all things considered that there be equality between the product or power of the Government taken in itself and the product or power of the citizens, who are sovereigns on one side and subjects on the other.

Further, one could not alter any of these three terms without instantly destroying the proportion. If the Sovereign wishes to govern, or if the Magistrate wishes to provide laws, or if the subjects refuse to obey, disorder takes the place of regularity, force and will no longer act in concert, and the State falls into despotism or anarchy. Finally, as there is only one proportional mean in each relationship, only one good government is possible in a State. But, as a thousand events can change the relationships of a people, different Governments are able to be good not only for diverse peoples, but for the same people at different times.

To try to give an idea of the diverse relations which reign between the two extremes, I will take as an example the number of people, as an easy relationship to express.

Suppose the State is composed of ten thousand citizens. The Sovereign can only be considered collectively and as a body. But each private person in his quality as subject is considered as an individual. Thus the Sovereign is to the subject as ten thousand to one; this is to say that each member of the State is only one ten thousandth of the sovereign authority, even he is entirely subjected to it. Should the people be composed of one hundred thousand men, the condition of the subjects does not change, and each bears equally the entire dominion of the laws, while his vote, reduced to one hundred thousandth, has ten times less influence in their forming. The subject, then, always remains one, the ratio of the Sovereign to the subject always increases in proportion to the number of Citizens. Whence it follows that the larger the State grows, the more liberty diminishes.

When I say that the ratio increases, I understand that it is farther removed from equality. Thus the larger the ratio in the geometric sense, the lesser the relation in the everyday sense; in the first, the relation is considered according to the quantity measured by the quotient, and in the latter, considered according to identity, estimated by similarity.

Now the less the individual wills relate to the general will, that is to say customary conduct to the laws, the more repressive force has to be increased. The Government, then, in order to be good, should be relatively stronger as the people becomes more numerous.

On the other hand, the growth of the State giving the trustees of public authority more temptations and means to abuse their power, the more the Government has to have force to contain the people, the more force the Sovereign should have in turn in order to contain the Government. I speak here not of an absolute force, but of the relative force of the diverse parts of the State.

It follows from this double ratio that the continued proportion between the Sovereign, the Prince, and the people is hardly an arbitrary idea, but a necessary consequence of the nature of the political body. It follows further that one of the extremes, namely the people as subject, being fixed and represented by unity, whenever the double ratio increases or diminishes, the single ratio increases or diminishes similarly, and consequently the middle term is changed. This serves to show that there is no one constitution of Government unique and absolute, but that it is possible to have as many Governments of different natures as there are States of different sizes.

If, in reducing this system to ridicule, one would say that in order to find this proportional mean, and form the body of Government, it is only necessary, according to me, to take the square root of the number of the people, I would respond that I take that number here only as an example, that the relations of which I speak are measured not solely by the number of men, but in general by the amount of action, which results from combining a multitude of causes; that, moreover, if to express myself in fewer words I borrow geometric terms for a moment, I am aware of the fact that geometric precision has no place in moral quantities.

The Government is on a small scale what the body politic which contains it is on the large scale. It is a moral person endowed with certain faculties, active as the Sovereign, passive as the State, and one can break it down into other, similar relations, from which consequently arise a new proportion, and still another within this, similar to the order of tribunals, until one arrives at an indivisible middle term, that is to say one sole chief or supreme magistrate, who is able to be represented, in the middle of this progression, much as the unifying element between the series of fractions and that of whole numbers.

Without embarrassing ourselves with this multiplication of terms, let us be content to consider the Government as a new body within the State, distinct from the people and the Sovereign, and intermediate between the two.

The essential difference between these two bodies is that the State exists by itself, and the Government exists only through the Sovereign. Thus only the dominant will of the Prince is or ought to be the general will or the law; its force is only the public force concentrated in itself: as soon as it wishes to derive from itself some absolute and independent act, the bond tying the whole together begins to loosen. Finally, if it should happen that the Prince have a particular will more active than that of the Sovereign, and if, in order to obey this private will, he use some of the public force which is in its hands, so that there would be, so to speak, two Sovereigns, one of right and the other of fact: at that instant the social union would vanish and the body politic be dissolved.

However, for the body of the Government to have an existence, a real life that distinguishes it from the body of the State, for all its members to be able to act in concert and fulfill the purpose for which it has been instituted, it needs a particular *self*, a sensibility common to its members, a force, a will of its own that tends toward its own conservation. This particular existence presumes assemblies, councils, a power to deliberate, to resolve, rights, titles, privileges which belong exclusively to the Prince, and which render the condition of the magistrate more honorable, in proportion to which it is more arduous. The difficulties lie in the method of disposing, within the whole, this subordinate whole, in such a way that it may not weaken the general constitution while strengthening its own; that it always distinguish its particular force directed to its own conservation from the public force directed to the conservation of the State, and that, in a word, it always be ready to sacrifice the Government to the people and not the people to the Government.

Besides, although the artificial body of the Government is the product of another artificial body, and has in some respects only a borrowed and subordinate life, that does not prevent it from being able to act with more or less vigor or speed, to enjoy, so to speak, more or less robust health. Finally, without directly departing from the goal for which it was instituted, it can deviate more or less from it according to the manner in which it is constituted.

From all these differences arise the diverse relations that the Government ought to have with the body of the State, according to the accidental and particular relationships by which that same State is modified. For often the Government that is best in itself will become the most vicious, if its relations are not altered according to the defects of the body politic to which it belongs.

II. Of the Principle Which Constitutes the Diverse Forms of Government

In order to expose the general cause of these differences, it is necessary to distinguish here the Prince and the Government, as I have already distinguished the State from the Sovereign.

The body of the magistracy can be composed of a greater or lesser number of members. We have said that the relation of the Sovereign to the subjects was greater as the number of people was greater, and by an evident analogy we can say the same of the Government with regard to the Magistrates.

Now the total force of the Government, being always that of the State, does not vary: from which it follows that the more of that force it uses on its own members, the less remains for it to act on the whole people.

Thus the more numerous are the Magistrates, the weaker the Government. As that maxim is fundamental, let us apply it to clarify it better.

We can distinguish in the person of the magistrate three essentially different wills. First, the individual's own will, which tends only to his private advantage; second, the common will of the magistrates, which relates itself uniquely to the advantage of the Prince, and which can be called the corporate will, being general in relation to the Government, and particular in relation to the State, of which the Government is a part; third, the will of the people, or the sovereign will, which is general as much in relation to the State considered as the whole, as in relation to the Government considered as part of the whole.

In a perfect system of legislation, the particular or individual will ought to be null, the corporate will proper to the Government very subordinate, and consequently the general or sovereign will always dominant and the sole rule of all the others.

According to the natural order, on the contrary, these different wills become more active as they become more concentrated. Thus the general will is always the weakest, the corporate will has the second rank, and the private will is first of all; so that in the Government each member is first himself, then Magistrate, and then citizen, a gradation directly opposed to what the social order requires.

Granting this, suppose that the whole Government is in the hands of one man. The particular will and the corporate will are then perfectly united, and consequently the latter is in the highest possible degree of intensity. Further, as it is the degree of will on which the use of force depends, and the absolute force of the Government does not vary, it follows that the most active of Governments is that of one man.

On the contrary, suppose we unite the Government with the legislative authority; let us make the Sovereign into the Prince and all of the Citizens into as many Magistrates. Then the corporate will, confounded with the general will, will be no more active than it and will leave to the particular will its full force. Thus the Government, always with the same absolute force, will have attained its *minimum* relative force or activity.

These relations are incontestable, and other considerations also serve to confirm them. One sees, for example, that each magistrate is more active in his group than each citizen is in his, and consequently the particular will has much more influence in the acts of the Government than in those of the Sovereign; for each magistrate is nearly always charged with some function of Government, while each citizen, taken separately, exercises no function of sovereignty. Besides, the more a State is extended, the more its real force is increased even though not by reason of its size: but if the State remains the same, the magistrates may well be multiplied without the Government acquiring any more real force, because that force is the force of the State, whose measure remains unchanged. Thus the relative force or activity of the Government diminishes, without its absolute or real force being able to increase.

It is also certain that public matters are expedited more slowly as more people are charged with them, that in giving too much importance to prudence one does not give enough to fortune, that one lets opportunity escape, and that owing to excessive deliberation the fruits of deliberation are often lost.

I have just proved that the Government is weakened as the magistrates are multiplied, and I have already proved that the larger the population, the more the repressive force should be increased. From this it follows that the ratio of the magistrates to the Government ought to be the inverse ratio of subjects to Sovereign; this is to say that the more the State grows, the more the Government should shrink; so that the number of chiefs diminishes as the number of people is increased.

But I speak here only of the relative force of Government, not of its rectitude: for, on the contrary, the more numerous the magistracy, the more the corporate will approaches the general will; whereas under a single magistrate, this same corporate will is, I have said, only a particular will. Thus one loses on one side what one gains on the other, and the art of the Legislator is to know how to fix the point where the force and the will of the Government are always combined in the reciprocal proportion most advantageous to the State.

III. Division of Governments

We have seen in the preceding chapter why one distinguishes the diverse species or forms of Governments by the number of members who compose them; it remains to see here how this division is made.

The Sovereign can, in the first place, commit the charge of Government to all the people or the majority of the people, in such a way that more citizens are magistrates than simply individual citizens. One gives to this form of government the name of *Democracy*.

Or it can confine the Government to the hands of a small number, so that there are more simple Citizens than magistrates; this form bears the name of *Aristocracy*.

Finally, it can concentrate the whole Government in the hands of one sole magistrate from whom all the others derive their power. This third form is the most common and is called *Monarchy* or royal Government.

One should note that all these forms or at least the first two are more or less variable and may indeed have a considerable range; for Democracy can embrace all the people or be restricted to half. Aristocracy, in its turn, can confine itself to half the number down to the smallest, indeterminately. Royalty itself is susceptible to some division. Sparta always had two Kings by its constitution; and one has seen in the Roman Empire as many as eight Emperors at one time without being able to say that the Empire was divided. Thus there is a point where each form of Government blends with the next, and one sees that, under three sole types, Government can really be divided into as many diverse forms as the State has Citizens.

There is more: this same Government being in some respects able to subdivide itself into other parts, one part administered in one manner and the other part in another, from these three combined forms there can emerge a multitude of mixed forms, each of which is multipliable by all the simple forms.

In all times, there has been much dispute about the best form of Government, without considering that each of them is the best in certain cases, and the worst in others.

If in different States the number of supreme magistrates should be in an inverse ratio to that of the Citizens, it follows that generally Democratic Government suits small states, Aristocratic medium-sized, and Monarchical large ones. This rule is immediately derived from the principle, but how count the multitude of circumstances which can furnish exceptions?

IV. Of Democracy

He who makes the law knows better than anyone how it ought to be executed and interpreted. It seems then that there could be no better constitution than the one in which the executive power is joined to the legislative. But it is just that which renders this Government insufficient in certain regards, because things that ought to be distinguished are not, and the prince and the Sovereign, being the same person, only form as it were a Government without a Government.

It is not good that he who makes the laws execute them, nor that the body of the people turn their attention away from general considerations in order to give it to particular objects. Nothing is more dangerous than the influence of private interests in public affairs, and the abuse of laws by the Government is a lesser evil than the corruption of the Legislator, the inevitable result of private considerations. Then, the State having been corrupted in its substance, all reform becomes impossible. A people who would never abuse the Government would not abuse independence either; a people who would always govern well would have no need of being governed.

To take the term in a rigorous sense, there has never existed a true Democracy, and it will never exist. It is contrary to the natural order that the greater number should govern and that the lesser number should be governed. One cannot imagine the people remaining constantly assembled in order to attend to public affairs, and one readily sees that it would not know how to establish commissions for this purpose without the form of the administration changing.

In fact, I think it possible to lay down as a principle that when the functions of the government are divided among several tribunals, sooner or later those with the fewest members acquire the greatest authority, if only because of the facility in expediting the public business which naturally brings this about.

Besides, how many things difficult to unite does this Government presume! First, a very small State where the people are easily assembled and where each citizen can easily know all the others; second, a great simplicity of moral customs, which prevents a multitude of public matters and thorny discussions; next, a great equality of rank and fortune, without which equality in rights and authority would not long subsist; finally, little or no luxury because luxury either is the result of wealth or renders it necessary; it corrupts both the rich and the poor, the one by possession, the other by covetousness; it sells the fatherland to indolence and vanity; it deprives the State of all its citizens in order to enslave some to others, and all to opinion.

That is why a celebrated author has named virtue as the principle of the Republic, for all these conditions could not subsist without virtue; but failing to make the necessary distinctions, this great genius often lacked accuracy and sometimes clarity, and did not see that the Sovereign authority being everywhere the same, the same principle ought to function in every well-constituted State, more or less, it is true, according to the form of Government.

Let us add that there is no Government so subject to civil wars and internal agitations as the Democratic or popular, because there is none which tends so strongly and continually to change its form, nor demands more vigilance and courage in order to be maintained in its own form. It is especially in this constitution that the Citizen ought to arm himself with force and steadfastness and to say each day of his life from his heart what a virtuous Palatine[18] said in the Diet of Poland: "Malo periculosam libertatem quam quietum servitium." [I prefer liberty with danger to peace with slavery.]

If there were a people of Gods, it would govern itself democratically. A Government so perfect is not suited to men.

V. Of Aristocracy

We have here two very distinct moral persons, namely the Government and the Sovereign, and consequently two general wills, the one in relation to all the citizens, the other solely for the members of the administration. Thus, although the Government is able to regulate its internal policy as it pleases, it is never able to speak to the people in the name of the Sovereign, that is to say in the name of the people itself; this must never be forgotten.

The first societies governed themselves aristocratically. The family heads deliberated among themselves about public affairs. The young people deferred without distress to the authority of experience. Hence the names of *Priests, Ancients, Senate, Elders*. The savages of North America still govern themselves this way in our day, and are very well governed.

But, as the inequality due to institutions prevailed over natural inequality, wealth or power[19] was preferred to age, and Aristocracy became elective. Finally, the power transmitted with the father's goods to the children created patrician families, rendering the Government hereditary, and one witnessed Senators twenty years of age.

There are then three kinds of Aristocracy: natural, elective, hereditary. The first is suited only for simple peoples; the third is the worst of all governments. The second is the best: it is Aristocracy properly named.

Beyond the advantage of the distinction between the two powers, aristocracy has that of the choice of its members; for in popular Government all the Citizens are born magistrates; but this one limits them to a small number, and they only become so by election:[20] a means by which probity, insight, experience, and all the other reasons for public preference and esteem are so many new guarantees of being wisely governed.

Additionally, assemblies are more conveniently held, public affairs are better discussed, expedited with more order and diligence, the repute of the State is better sustained abroad by venerable Senators than by an unknown or scorned multitude.

In a word, it is the best and most natural order that the wisest should govern the multitude, when it is certain that they will govern it for its profit and not for their own; there being no need to uselessly multiply devices, nor to do with twenty thousand men what one hundred well-chosen men can do still better. But it need be remarked that the corporate interest begins here to direct the public force less under the rule of the general will, and that another inevitable propensity removes from the laws a part of the executive power.

With regard to particular proprieties, a State should not be so small, nor a people so simple and righteous, that the execution of the laws immediately ensues from the public will, as in a good Democracy. Nor again must a nation be so large that the chiefs, dispersed in order to govern, are able to determine the Sovereign each in his own department, and begin by making themselves independent in order to finally become the masters.

But if Aristocracy requires some fewer virtues than popular Government, it requires others which are properly its own; as moderation among the wealthy and contentment among the poor; for it seems that a rigorous equality would be out of place there; it was not even observed in Sparta.

Further, if this form permits a certain inequality of fortune, it is indeed so that generally the administration of public affairs should be entrusted to those who are better able to give their time to it, but not, as Aristotle claims, so that the wealthy always be preferred. On the contrary, it is important that an opposite choice should sometimes inform the people that there are more important reasons for preference in the merits of men than in their wealth.

VI. Of Monarchy

Up to this point we have considered the Prince as a moral and collective person, united by the force of the laws, and entrusted with the executive power in the State. We now have to consider this power united in the hands of one natural person, a real man, who alone has the right to dispose of it according to the laws. He is what one calls a Monarch or a King.

Completely contrary to other administrations where a collective entity represents an individual, in this one an individual represents a collective entity; so that the moral unity which constitutes the Prince is at the same time a physical unity, in which all the faculties which the law combines in the other with such effort are found naturally combined.

Thus the will of the people, and the will of the Prince, and the public force of the State, and the private force of the Government, all respond to the same motive, all the mechanisms of the machine are in the same hand, everything works to the same end; there are no opposing movements that cancel each other, and one can imagine no kind of constitution in which a lesser effort produces more notable an action. Archimedes tranquilly seated on the shore and effortlessly pulling along a large Vessel represents to me a skillful monarch governing his vast States from his private study, and making everything move while appearing to be motionless.

But if there is no Government that has more vigor, there is none where the private will has greater sway and more easily dominates others; everything works to the same end, it is true, but this end is not the goal of public happiness, and the very force of the Administration ceaselessly operates to the detriment of the State.

Kings want to be absolute, and from afar one calls out to them that the best means for being so is to make themselves loved by their peoples. This maxim is very fine and even very true in some respects. Unfortunately, it will always be jeered at in the Courts. Power which comes from the love of the peoples is without doubt the greater; but it is precarious and conditional, and never will satisfy Princes. The best Kings wish to be able to be wicked if it pleases them, without ceasing to be the masters. A political sermonizer will tell them in vain that the power of the people being their own, their greatest interest is that the people should be flourishing, numerous, formidable. They know very well that is not true. Their personal interest is first that the People be weak, miserable, and never able to resist them. I admit that, supposing the subjects always perfectly submissive, the interest of the Prince should then be that the people are powerful, to the end that this power, being his own, would make him formidable to his neighbors; but this interest is only secondary and subordinate, and as the two suppositions are incompatible, it is natural that Princes always give preference to the maxim which is most immediately useful to them. It is this that Samuel strongly represented to the Hebrews; it is this that Machiavelli made evident. While feigning to give lessons to the Kings he has given great ones to the peoples. *The Prince* of Machiavelli is the book of republicans.[21]

We have found, by general relationships, that monarchy is suitable only to large States, and we find this again by examining it itself. The more numerous the public administration, the more the ratio of the Prince to the subjects diminishes and approaches equality, so that this relation is one of equality even as in Democracy. This same ratio increases as the Government shrinks, and it is at its *maximum* when the Government is in the hands of a single man. Then there is found too great a distance between the Prince and the People, and the State lacks cohesiveness. In order to create this, intermediary orders are needed. Princes, Grandees, and the nobility are necessary to fill them. Now none of this is suited to a small State, which is ruined by all these distinctions.

But if it is difficult that a large State be well governed, it is much more difficult that it be well governed by one man alone, and everyone knows what happens when the King appoints deputies.

An essential and inevitable defect which will always place monarchical government beneath the republican is that in the latter the public voice hardly ever raises to the highest positions any but enlightened and capable men, who fill them with honor; whereas those who attain rank in monarchies are most often merely petty bunglers, petty rascals, petty intriguers, whose petty talents, which enable them to attain high posts in the Courts, only serve to show the public their ineptitude as soon as they have attained these posts. The people is mistaken in its choice much less than the Prince, and a man of true merit is almost as rare in the ministry as a fool at the head of a republican government. Also, when by some lucky chance one of those men born to govern takes control of public business in a monarchy almost wrecked by this crowd of fine managers, one is totally surprised by the resources that he finds, and it is an epoch-making event in a country.

For a monarchical State to be well governed, it would be necessary that its size or extent be proportionate to the capabilities of he who governs. It is easier to conquer than to rule. With a sufficient lever, the world can be moved by a finger, but to sustain it requires the shoulders of Hercules. Should the State be the least bit large, the Prince is nearly always too small for it. When on the contrary it happens that the State is too small for its chief, which is very rare, it is still badly governed, because the chief, always following the grandeur of his views, forgets the people's interest, and makes them no less discontent by the abuse of his overabundant talents than does a chief limited by those which he lacks. It would require, so to speak, that a kingdom enlarge or contract itself in every reign according to the capacity of the Prince; rather, as the talents of a Senate are more stable, the State is able to have permanent boundaries and the administration would not go on any less well.

The most perceptible inconvenience of the Government of a single person is the lack of that continual succession which forms in the other two an uninterrupted bond. One King dies, another is needed; elections leave dangerous intervals, they are stormy, and unless the Citizens have a disinterestedness and integrity which this Government hardly manages to permit, intrigue and corruption intermingle throughout. It is difficult for one to whom the State has been sold not to sell it in turn, and recoup for himself from the helpless the money that the powerful have extorted from him. Sooner or later everything becomes venal under such an administration, and the peace which is enjoyed under kings is worse than the disorder of these interregnums.

What has been done to prevent these ills? Crowns have been made hereditary in certain families, and an order of succession has been established which prevents any dispute at the death of Kings. That is to say, substituting the inconvenience of regencies for that of elections, an apparent tranquillity has been preferred to a wise administration, and it is preferred to risk having infants, monsters, or imbeciles for chiefs than having to argue over the choice of good Kings; it has not been considered that in thus exposing oneself to the risk of this alternative, one sets nearly all the odds against himself. It was a very sensible reply that Dionysius the Younger gave to his father, who, reproaching him for a dishonorable action, said: "Have I given you such an example?" "Ah," replied the son, "your father was not king."

Everything conspires to deprive a man elevated to command others of justice and reason. Much trouble is taken, it is said, to teach young Princes the art of ruling: it does not seem that this education profits them. One would do better to begin by teaching them the art of obeying. The greatest kings celebrated by history were not brought up to rule; it is a science that one has never mastered less than after having studied it too much, and that one acquires better by obeying than by commanding. *Nam ultissimus idem ac brevissimus bonarum malarumque rerum delectus, cogitare quid aut nolueris sub alio principe, aut volueris.* [Because the best and shortest way to discover what is good and what is bad is to ask what you would have wished to happen or not to happen, if another than you had been king.][22]

One consequence of this lack of coherence is the instability of royal government, which, being regulated alternatively on one level and then on another, according to the character of the ruling Prince or of the people ruling for him, cannot long maintain a fixed aim or a consistent course of conduct: this variation, which always makes the state drift from maxim to maxim, from project to project, does not take place in other Governments, where the prince is always the same. Thus one sees that in general if there is more cunning in a Court, there is more wisdom in a Senate, and that Republics go to their goals by more constant and better-followed policies; whereas each revolution in the [royal] Ministry produces one in the State; the maxim common to all Ministers, and nearly all Kings, being to take up the reverse of their predecessors in everything.

From this same incoherence is found the solution of a sophism very familiar to all defenders of royalty; not only is civil Government compared to the Government of the household and the prince to the father of the family, an error already refuted, but all the virtues of which he will have need are liberally ascribed to this magistrate, while always supposing that the Prince is what he ought to be; with the aid of this supposition royal Government is evidently preferable to any other, because it is incontestably the strongest, and in order to also be the best, it lacks only a corporate will more conformable to the general will.

But if, according to Plato[23] the king by nature is such a rare person, how many times will nature and fortune converge to crown him? And if royal education necessarily corrupts those who receive it, what should one hope from a succession of men trained to rule? It is surely deliberate self-deception to confound royal Government with that of a good King. To see what this Government is in itself, it is necessary to consider it under stupid or wicked Princes; for they will come to the Throne as such, or the Throne will make them such.

These difficulties have not escaped our Authors, but they are not embarrassed by them. The remedy is, they say, to obey without a murmur. God gives bad Kings in his anger, and one must endure them as chastisements from Heaven. This discourse is edifying, without doubt; but I do not know if it is not more appropriate to the pulpit than in a book about politics. What is to be said of a doctor who promises miracles and whose entire art is to exhort his sick charge to have patience? One knows well that it is necessary to suffer a bad Government when one has one: the question should be how to find a good one.

VII. Of Mixed Governments

Properly speaking, there is no simple Government. A single Chief must have subordinate magistrates; a popular Government must have a Chief. Thus, in the partition of the executive power, there is always a gradation from the greater number to the less, with this difference, that sometimes the greater number depends on the lesser number, and sometimes the lesser number on the greater number.

Sometimes there is an equal division, either when the constituent parts are in mutual dependence, as in the Government of England; or when the authority of each part is independent but imperfect, as in Poland. This latter form is bad, because there is no unity in the government, and the State lacks cohesion.

Which is better, a simple Government or a mixed Government? This question is much debated among political thinkers, and it requires the same response I have already given concerning every form of Government.

Simple Government is best in itself, solely because it is simple. But when the executive power does not depend enough on the legislative, that is to say when there is a greater ratio between the Prince and the Sovereign than between the people and the Prince, this defect of proportion must be remedied by dividing the Government; for then all its parts have no less authority over the subjects, and their division renders all of them together less strong against the Sovereign.

The same disadvantage is also prevented by establishing intermediate magistrates who, leaving the Government in its entirety, only serve to balance the two powers and to maintain their respective rights. Then the Government is not mixed, it is tempered.

One can remedy the opposite disadvantage by similar means, and when the Government is too loose, Tribunals can be established to concentrate it: this is practiced in all Democracies. In the first case one divides the Government to weaken it, and in the second, in order to reinforce it; for the *maximum* force and weakness are found equally in simple Governments, whereas the mixed forms provide a medium force.

VIII. *That Every Form of Government Is Not Appropriate for Every Country*

Liberty, not being a fruit of all climates, is not within the reach of all peoples. The more one contemplates this principle established by Montesquieu, the more one senses its truth. The more one contests it, the more one is given occasion to establish it by new proofs.

In all the Governments of the world the public person consumes, yet produces nothing. From where, then, comes the substance it consumes? From the labor of its members. It is the surplus of private individuals that produces what is needed by the public. Hence it follows that the civil State can subsist only as long as the labor of men produces more than their own needs.

Now this excess is not the same in all countries of the world. In several it is considerable, in other it is moderate, in others null, in others negative. This ratio depends on the fertility of the climate, the kind of labor which the soil requires, the nature of its products, the physical strength of its inhabitants, the greater or lesser consumption necessary for them, and on several other similar ratios of which it is composed.

On the other hand, all Governments are not of the same nature; some are more or less ravenous, and the differences are based on this other principle, that the further public contributions are removed from their source, the more burdensome they are. This burden is not to be measured by the amount of taxes but by the path they must take in order to return to the hands from which they came; when this circulation is prompted and well established, it is unimportant whether little or much is paid; the people is always rich and finances always thrive. On the contrary, however little the People gives, when this small sum does not revert to it, by always giving it soon exhausts itself; the State is never wealthy, and the people is always destitute.

It follows that the greater the distance from the people to the Governments increases, the more burdensome do the tributes become: thus in a Democracy the people is least encumbered, in Aristocracy more so, and in Monarchy, it carries the greatest weight. Monarchy then is suited only to wealthy nations; Aristocracy, to States of moderate wealth and size; Democracy, to small and poor States.

In effect, the more one reflects on it, the more one finds in this the difference between free States and monarchies: in the first, everything is used for the common utility; in the others, the public and private forces are reciprocal, and the former are augmented by the weakening of the latter. Finally, in place of governing the subjects in order to render them happy, despotism makes them miserable in order to govern them.

There are then in each climate natural causes by which we can assign the form of Government toward which the force of the climate leads it, and we can even say what kind of inhabitants it should have. Unproductive and sterile places where the produce does not repay the labor ought to remain uncultivated and deserted, or should only be inhabited by Savage Peoples. The places where human labor yields only bare necessities should be inhabited by barbarous peoples, all polity being an impossibility there; places where the excess of the produce over the labor is moderate are suitable for free peoples; those where abundant and fertile soil yields much produce for little labor want to be governed monarchically, so that the excess of the subjects' surplus may be consumed by the luxury of the Prince; for it is better that this excess should be absorbed by the government than dissipated by private individuals. There are exceptions, I know: but these exceptions themselves confirm the rule, in that sooner or later they produce revolutions which restore things to the order of nature.

Let us always distinguish general laws from the particular causes which can modify their effect. Even if the whole south were covered with Republics and the entire north with despotic States, it would not be less true that, through the effect of climate, despotism is suited to warm countries, barbarism to cold countries, and a good polity to the intermediate regions. I see, however, that one can agree with the principle and still be able to dispute its application; one could say that there are very fertile cold countries and some very unproductive southern ones. But this difficulty is only one for those who do not examine the thing in all its relationships. It is necessary, as I have already said, to consider those of work, labor, consumption, etc.

Let us suppose that of two pieces of land equal in size, one produces five units and the other ten. If the inhabitants of the former consume four and those of the latter nine, the excess of the first product will be 1/5 and that of the second 1/10. The ratio between these two surpluses being then the inverse of the produce of each, the piece of land which yields only five will produce a surplus double that of the piece of land which produces ten.

But it is not a question of a doubled product, and I do not believe that any person dares in general to claim the fertility of the cold countries to be even equal to that of the warm countries. At any rate, let us suppose this equality; let us, if one wishes, put England in balance with Sicily, and Poland with Egypt. More to the south we will have Africa and the Indies; farther north we will have nothing more. For this equality of produce, what difference is there in cultivation? In Sicily it is only necessary to scratch the soil; in England what effort is demanded to work it! Now where more hands are needed to obtain the same product, the surplus should necessarily be less.

Consider, beyond this, that the same quantity of men consume much less in the warm countries. The climate requires only that people should be sober in order to be in good health: Europeans who want to live as at home all perish from dysentery and indigestion. "We are," says Chardin, "carnivorous beasts, wolves, in comparison with Asians. Some attribute the sobriety of the Persians to the fact that their country is scantily cultivated, but I believe on the contrary that their country is less abundant in food because the inhabitants need less. If their frugality," he continues, "resulted from the scarcity of the country, it would only be the poor who ate little, whereas it is so of the people generally; and one would eat more or less in each province according to the fertility of the country, whereas the same sobriety is found everywhere in the kingdom. They pride themselves greatly on their manner of living, saying that one need only look at their complexion to see that it is much better than those of the Christians. Indeed, the complexion of the Persians is smooth; while that of their subjects, the Armenians, who live in European fashion, is coarse and blotchy, and their bodies are fat and heavy."

The more one approached the equator, the less do people live on. They eat nearly no meat; rice, maize, couscous, millet, cassava are their ordinary foods. There are in the Indies millions of men whose nutrition costs less than a penny a day. We see in Europe itself noticeable differences in appetite between northern and southern peoples. A Spaniard will live eight days on a German's dinner. In the countries where men are most voracious, luxury itself is directed toward matters of consumption. In England it is displayed on a table loaded with meats; in Italy you are regaled with sugar and flowers.

Luxury in clothing again offers similar differences. In climates where seasonal changes are sudden and violent, one has clothes that are better and simpler; in those where one dresses only for ornament, splendor is more sought than utility, for clothes themselves are a luxury. In Naples you will see men every day promenade along the Posillipo with gold-embroidered coats but no stockings. It is the same with regard to buildings: one gives everything for magnificence when one fears no damage from the weather. In Paris, in London, one wishes to be warmly and comfortably housed. In Madrid one has superb salons, but no windows that shut, and one sleeps in a mere rat hole.

The foods are much more substantial and succulent in warm countries; this is a third difference which cannot fail to influence the second. Why does one eat so many vegetables in Italy? Because they are good, nourishing, of excellent flavor. In France, where they are grown only with water, they are not nourishing and scarcely count for anything on the tables. They do not, however, take up less ground and cost at least as much effort to cultivate. Experience shows that the wheat of Barbary, inferior in other respects to that of France, yields much more flour, and that French wheat in turn yields more than the wheat of the north. From this one can infer that a similar gradation is generally observable in the same direction from the equator to the pole. Now is it not a clear disadvantage to have an equal quantity of product with a lesser quantity of nourishment?

To all these different considerations I can add one which springs from and strengthens them: warm countries have less need of inhabitants than cold countries, and would be able to nourish a greater number; hence a double surplus is produced, always to the advantage of despotism. The greater the area inhabited by the same number of inhabitants, the more difficult rebellions become; because concerted action cannot be taken promptly and secretly, and because it is always easy for the Government to discover projects and to cut communications; but the closer together a numerous people is packed, the less is the Government able to usurp from the Sovereign: the chiefs deliberate as safely in their rooms as the Prince in his council, and the crowd is assembled as quickly in the squares as the troops in their quarters. The advantage of a tyrannical Government in this regard is then to act over great distances. With the aid of the points of support which it establishes, its power increases with distance like that of levers.[24] The power of the people, on the contrary, acts only when concentrated; it evaporates and disappears when spread out, like the effect of gunpowder scattered on the ground, which only takes fire grain by grain. The least populous countries are thus the best adapted for tyranny: ferocious beasts reign only in deserts.

IX. Of the Signs of a Good Government

When one then asks what is absolutely the best Government, one poses a question as insoluble as indeterminate; or, if you wish, it has as many correct solutions as there are possible combinations in the absolute and relative positions of peoples.

But if one asked by what sign one can know that a given people is well or badly governed, this would be another thing, and the question of fact could be resolved.

However, it is not resolved, because each wants to do so in his own way. The subjects extol public tranquillity, the Citizens the liberty of private individuals; the one prefers the security of possessions, the other that of persons; one holds that the best Government is the most severe, the other maintains that it is the mildest; one believes that crimes should be punished, and the other that they should be prevented; one finds it good to be feared by neighbors, the other prefers to be ignored by them; one is satisfied when money circulates, the other demands that the people have bread. Even though agreement should be had on these and similar points, would we have advanced? Moral quantities lacking any precise measure, if there were agreement on the sign, how could there be about its evaluation?

For my part, I am always astounded that such a simple sign is overlooked, or that one has the bad faith not to admit it. What is the end of political association? It is the preservation and the prosperity of its members. And what is the surest sign that they are preserved and prospering? It is their number and population. Do not go then to look elsewhere for this much-disputed sign. All other things being equal, the Government under which, without external aids, without naturalizations, without colonies, the Citizens become populous and multiply most is infallibly the best; that under which a people diminish and wither away is the worst. Calculators, it is now your concern; count, measure, compare.[25]

X. Of the Abuse of the Government, and of Its Tendency to Degenerate

As the private will incessantly acts against the general will, so the Government makes a continual effort against the Sovereignty. The more this effort increases, the more the constitution deteriorates, and as there is here no other corporate will which, by resisting that of the Prince, would balance it, sooner or later there must come a time when the Prince finally oppresses the Sovereign and breaks the social treaty. It is this inherent and inevitable vice that, from the birth of the body politic, tends without respite to destroy it, just as old age and death finally destroy the body of a man.

There are two general ways by which a Government degenerates: namely, when it shrinks, or when the State dissolves.

The government shrinks when it passes from a large to a small number, that is from Democracy to Aristocracy, and from Aristocracy to Royalty. That is its natural inclination.[26] If it were to go backward from a small number to a large one, it could be said that it slackens, but this inverse progress is impossible.

In effect, the government only changes its form when its exhausted mainspring leaves it too weakened to be able to preserve itself. Now if it would slacken more as it extends itself, its force would become completely null, and it would subsist still less. It is then necessary to wind and adjust the spring as it unravels; otherwise the State which it sustains will fall into ruin.

The dissolution of the State can occur in two ways.

First, when the Prince no longer administers the State in accordance with laws and usurps the sovereign power. Then a remarkable change occurs; it is not the Government but the State that shrinks: I mean to say that the large State dissolves and another is formed within it, composed solely of the members of the Government, and it is for the rest of the People only its master and tyrant. So that at the instant that the Government usurps sovereignty, the social pact is broken; and all ordinary Citizens, returning by right to their natural liberty, are forced but no longer obligated to obey.

The same situation also occurs when the members of the Government separately usurp the power which they only ought to exercise as a body; this is no less a violation of the laws, and produces a still greater disorder. Then one has, so to say, as many Princes as Magistrates; and the State, no less divided than the Government, perishes or changes its form.

When the State dissolves, the abuse of Government, whatever it might be, takes the common name of *anarchy*. To distinguish, Democracy degenerates into *Ochlocracy*, Aristocracy into *Oligarchy*; I should add that Royalty degenerates into *Tyranny*, but this last word is equivocal and requires explanation.

In the ordinary sense, a Tyrant is a King who governs with violence and without regard to justice and to the laws. In the precise sense, a Tyrant is a private individual who arrogates royal authority to himself without having a right to it. It is thus that the Greeks understood this word Tyrant: they gave it indifferently to good and bad Princes whose authority was not legitimate. Hence *Tyrant* and *usurper* are two perfectly synonymous words.[27]

To give different names to different things, I call the usurper of royal authority a *Tyrant*, and the usurper of the Sovereign power a *Despot*. The Tyrant is he who intrudes himself contrary to the laws in order to govern according to the law; the Despot is he who places himself above the laws themselves. Thus the Tyrant may not be a Despot but the Despot is always a Tyrant.

XI. Of the Death of the Body Politic

Such is the natural and inevitable inclination of the best-constituted Governments. If Sparta and Rome have perished, what State can hope to last forever? If we wish to form a durable establishment, let us then not seek to make it eternal. In order to succeed, one should neither attempt the impossible, nor flatter oneself with giving to the work of men a solidity that human things do not admit of.

The body politic, just as the human body, begins to die at its moment of birth and carries within itself the causes of its destruction. But each can have a constitution more or less robust and suited to preserve it for a longer or shorter time. The constitution of man is the work of nature; that of the State is the work of art. It does not rest with men to prolong their lives; it is the responsibility of men to prolong that of the State as far as possible, by giving it the best constitution that it can have. The best-constituted will come to an end, but later than another, if no unforeseen accident brings about its premature destruction.

The principle of political life is in the Sovereign authority. The legislative power is the heart of the Sovereign authority. The legislative power is the heart of the State, the executive power is its brain, which gives movement to all the parts. The brain can fall into paralysis and the individual still lives. A man remains an imbecile and lives, but as soon as the heart has ceased its functions, the animal is dead.

It is not by the laws that the State subsists, but by the legislative power. The law of yesterday does not obligate today, but tacit consent is presumed from silence, and the sovereign is deemed to confirm continually the laws which it does not abrogate while being able to do so. Whatever it has once declared it wills it wills always, until the declaration is revoked.

Why then is so much respect paid to ancient laws? It is for that very reason. One must believe that it is only the excellence of ancient wills which has enabled them to be so long preserved: if the Sovereign had not constantly recognized them as salutary, it would have revoked them a thousand times. That is why, far from being weakened, the laws unceasingly acquire new strength in every well-constituted State; the prejudice in favor of antiquity renders them more venerable each day; in contrast, wherever the laws weaken as they grow older, it is proof that there is no longer legislative power, and that the State no longer lives.

XII. How the Sovereign Authority Is Maintained

The Sovereign, having no other force than the legislative power, acts only by the laws; and the laws being only authentic acts of the general will, the Sovereign can only act when the people is assembled. The people assembled, it will be said, what a chimera! It is a chimera today, but it was not two thousand years ago. Have men changed their nature?

The limits of the possible in moral things are less narrow than we think. It is our weaknesses, our vices, our prejudices which shrink them. Sordid souls do not believe in great men: vile slaves smile with a mocking air at the word *liberty*.

From what has been done let us consider what can be done. I will not speak of the ancient republics of Greece; but the Roman Republic was, it seems to me, a large State, and the town of Rome a large town. The last census in Rome showed four hundred thousand citizens bearing arms, and the last enumeration of the Empire more than four million Citizens without counting subjects, foreigners, women, infants, slaves.

What unimaginable difficulty in assembling frequently the immense population of this capital and its environs! However, few weeks passed without the Roman people being assembled, even several times. And it exercised not only the rights of sovereignty, but part of those of Government. It handled certain matters, it judged certain causes, and in the public assembly the whole people were also often magistrate as Citizen.

By going back to the earliest times of Nations, one would find that most of the ancient governments, even monarchies such as those of the Macedonians and the Franks, had similar Councils. Be it as it may, this single incontestable fact answers all difficulties. To argue from the existent to the possible produces a consequence that seems good to me.

XIII. (Continued)

It is not sufficient that the assembled people should have once fixed the constitution of the State giving sanction to a body of laws; it is not sufficient that it should have established a perpetual Government, or that it should have once and for all provided for the election of magistrates. Beyond the extraordinary assemblies which unforeseen events can require, there is need for fixed and periodical ones which nothing can abolish or postpone, so that on the appointed day the people be legitimately convoked by the law, without need for any other formal convocation.

But excepting these assemblies lawful solely by their date, every assembly of the People that has not been convoked by the magistrates charged with the purpose and according to prescribed forms ought to be regarded as illegitimate, and all that is done in it as null; because the order to be assembled itself should emanate from the law.

As for the more or less frequent resumption of legitimate assemblies, they depend on so many considerations that one could not know how to give them precise rules. Still, one can say in general that the more force the Government has, the more frequently should the Sovereign show itself.

This, I will be told, may be good for a single town; but what is to be done when the State comprises several towns? Will the Sovereign authority be divided? or should it be concentrated in a single town and subjugate all the rest?

I reply that one should do neither one nor the other. First, the sovereign authority is simple and one, and cannot be divided without being destroyed. In the second place, a town, no more than a Nation, can be legitimately subject to another, because the essence of the body politic is first the harmony of the obedience and liberty, and these words *subject* and *sovereign* are identical correlatives whose idea is united under the single word Citizen.

I reply again that it is always an evil to combine several towns into a single city, and that, wishing to create this union, one should not flatter oneself in expecting that the natural drawbacks can be avoided. One cannot object that the abuse of large States cannot be brought against someone who only wants small ones; but how give to small States enough force to resist the large ones? Just as each of the Greek towns resisted the great King, and as more recently Holland and Switzerland resisted the house of Austria.

In any case, if one cannot reduce the State to just boundaries, there is one expedient: it is to not allow a capital, to make the Government sit alternatively in each town, and to assemble in it, each in turn the Estates of the country.

Populate the territory equally, extend the same rights everywhere, carry abundance and life everywhere; thus the State will become at once the strongest and best governed possible. Remember that the walls of the towns are formed only from the debris of rural houses. For each Palace I see rising in the capital, I believe I see an entire rural country laid in ruins.

XIV. (Continued)

The moment the People is legitimately assembled in Sovereign body, all jurisdiction of the Government ceases; the executive power is suspended, and the person of the humblest Citizen is as sacred and inviolable as that of the first Magistrate, because where the Represented part is found, there is no longer a Representative. Most of the tumults that arose in Rome in the *comitia* came from having ignored or neglected this rule. The Consuls then were only the Presidents of the People, the Tribunes simple Speakers,[28] the Senate was nothing at all.

These intervals of suspension, when the Prince recognizes or ought to recognize an actual superior, have always been fearful for him; and these assemblies of the people who are the shield of the body politic and the curb of the Government, have been in all times the horror of the chiefs: hence such men never lack concerns, objections, obstacles, promises, in order to discourage citizens from assemblies. When the latter are avaricious, cowardly, fainthearted, and more loving of repose than of liberty, they do not long hold out against the redoubled efforts of the Government: it is thus that, as the resisting force is ceaselessly augmented, the Sovereign authority evaporates at the end, and most cities fall and perish before their time.

But between Sovereign authority and arbitrary Government there is sometimes introduced an intermediate power of which one must speak.

XV. Of Deputies or Representatives

As soon as public service ceases to be the principal concern of the Citizens, and they prefer to serve with their purses instead of their persons, the State is already nearly in ruin. Is it necessary to march to combat? they pay for troops and remain at home; is it necessary to go to the Council? they name deputies and remain at home. By dint of laziness and money, they finally have soldiers to enslave the fatherland and representatives to sell it.

It is the worry over commerce and the arts, the greedy pursuit of gain, indolence, and the love of comforts, which exchange personal services for money. One gives part of his profit in order to augment it at his convenience. Give money and soon enough you will have chains. This word *finance* is a slave's word; it is unknown in the City. In a truly free State the citizens do everything with their arms and nothing with money. Far from paying to exempt themselves from their duties, they will pay to perform them Themselves. I am certainly far from commonly held ideas; I believe that forced labor is less contrary to liberty than taxes.

The better the State is constituted, the more do public affairs outweigh private ones in the minds of the Citizens. There is even a much smaller number of private affairs, because as the sum of general well-being provides considerably more to that of each individual, less remains to be sought by individual exertions. In a well-conducted city each hastens to the assemblies; under a bad Government nobody wants to take a step to attend them, because no one takes an interest in what is done there, as it is foreseen that the general will does not prevail; and so in the end domestic concerns absorb everything. Good laws lead to better laws; bad laws bring on worse ones. As soon as someone says of the affairs of the State *Why is it important to me?* one should count the State as lost.

The cooling of the love of the fatherland, the activity of private interest, the immensity of States, conquests, the abuse of Government, have suggested the procedure of using Deputies or Representatives of the people in the assemblies of the Nation. This is what in certain countries one dares to call the Third Estate. Thus the particular interest of two orders is placed at first and second rank; the public interest is only at the third.

Sovereignty cannot be represented for the same reason that it cannot be alienated; it consists essentially in the general will, and the will cannot be represented: it is itself, or it is something other; there is no middle ground. The deputies of the people then are not and cannot be its representatives, they are only its commissioners; they can conclude nothing definitively. Every law that the People in person has not ratified is null; it is not a law. The English people thinks itself free, but is greatly mistaken; it is only free during the election of the members of Parliament: as soon as they are elected, it is enslaved, it is nothing. In the short moments of its liberty, the use made of it well merits its loss.

The idea of Representatives is modern: it comes to us from feudal Government, from that iniquitous and absurd Government in which the human species is degraded, and where the name of man is dishonored. In the ancient Republics and even in the Monarchies, the people never had representatives; they did not know this word. It is yet noteworthy that in Rome, where the Tribunes were so sacred, one could not even imagine that they might usurp the functions of the people, and in the midst of such a large multitude, they never tried to pass a single Plebiscite on their own authority. One can, however, imagine the embarrassment sometimes caused by the crowd by what occurred in the times of the Gracchi, when a part of the Citizens gave their vote from the rooftops.

Where right and liberty are everything, inconveniences are nothing. Among this wise people, everything was estimated in its just measure; it allowed the Lictors to do what the Tribunes would not have dared to do; it did not fear that the Lictors would wish to represent it.

To explain, however, how the Tribunes sometimes represented it, it suffices to understand how the Government represents the Sovereign. The Law being only the declaration of the general will, it is clear that, in the legislative power, the people cannot be represented; but it can and ought to be in the executive power, which is only force applied to the Law. This shows on close examination that very few Nations have laws. Be that as it may, it is certain that the Tribunes, not having any part of the executive power, were never able to represent the Roman people by right of their office, but only by usurping those of the Senate.

Among the Greeks, everything the people had to do it did by itself: it was unceasingly assembled in the public square. It lived in a mild climate; it was not avaricious; slaves did its work; its prime business was its liberty. Not having the same advantages, how conserve the same rights? Your more rigorous climate gives you more needs,[29] six months of the year the public square is not usable, your indistinct tongues cannot be understood in the open air; you give more for your own gain than for your liberty, and you fear slavery far less than misery.

What! is liberty only maintained with the support of servitude? Perhaps. The two extremes meet. Everything not in nature has its inconveniences, and civil society more than all the rest. There are such unfortunate circumstances where one can save his liberty only at the expense of another, and where the citizen can only be perfectly free when the slave is completely enslaved. Such was the position of Sparta. As for you modern peoples, you have no slaves, but you are slaves; you pay for their liberty with your own. You boast of your preference in vain; I find in it more of cowardice than of humanity.

I do mean by all this neither that slaves are necessary nor that the right of slavery is legitimate, since I have proved the contrary: I only state the reasons why modern peoples who believe themselves free have Representatives, and why ancient peoples did not. Be that as it may, the instant that a People gives itself Representatives, it is no longer free; it is no more.

All things considered, I do not see that it should henceforth be possible for the Sovereign to preserve among us the exercise of its rights unless the City is very small. But if it is very small, will it be subjugated? No. I will show later[30] how the external power of a great People can be united with the convenient polity and good order of a small State.

XVI. *That the Institution of the Government Is Not a Contract*

The Legislative power once well established, it is a matter of establishing the executive power as well; for this latter, only operating by particular acts, not being of the essence of the other, is naturally separate from it. If it were possible for the Sovereign, considered as such, to have executive power, right and fact would be so confounded that one would no longer know what is law and what is not, and the body politic thus denatured would soon fall prey to the violence against which it was instituted.

The Citizens being all equal by the social contract, all can prescribe what all ought to do, whereas no one has a right to make another do what he does not do himself. Now it is properly this right, that the Sovereign gives to the Prince in instituting the Government.

Several have held that the act of this establishment was a contract between the People and the chiefs it gives itself; a contract by which is stipulated between the two parties the conditions under which the latter obligates itself to command and the former to obey. One will agree, I am sure, that this is a strange manner of contracting. But let us see if this opinion is tenable.

First, the supreme authority can no more be modified than alienated; to limit it is to destroy it. It is absurd and contradictory that the Sovereign give itself a superior; to obligate oneself to obey a master is to go back to one's full liberty.

Further, it is evident that this contract of the people with such or such persons would be a particular act. Whence it follows that this contract would be neither a law nor an act of sovereignty, and consequently it would be illegitimate.

One sees also that the contracting parties would be under the law of nature alone and without any guarantee of their reciprocal engagements, which is repugnant in every way to the civil state. He who has force in hand being always the master of its use, we might as well give the name of contract to the act of a man who would say to another: "I give you all my goods, on the condition that you will return to me whatever pleases you."

There is only one contract in the State; it is that of association, and that alone excludes all others. No public Contract can be imagined which would not be a violation of the first.

XVII. Of the Institution of the Government

Under what idea, then, must we conceive the act by which the Government is instituted? I will first note that this act is complex or composed of two others: namely, the establishment of the law and the execution of the law.

By the first the Sovereign resolves that there will be a body of Government established under such form; and it is clear that this act is a law.

By the second, the People name the chiefs who will be entrusted with the established Government. Now this naming, being a particular act, is not a second law, but only a consequence of the first and a function of Government.

The difficulty is to understand how one can have an act of Government before the Government exists, and how the People, who is only Sovereign or subject, can become Prince or Magistrate in certain circumstances.

It is here that is uncovered one of those astounding properties of the body politic, by which it reconciles seemingly contradictory operations. For here occurs a sudden conversion of Sovereignty into Democracy; so that, without any perceivable change, and solely by a new relation of all to all, the Citizens having become Magistrates pass from general acts to particular acts, and from the law to its execution.

This changing of relation is not a subtlety of speculation without example in practice: it occurs every day in the Parliament of England, where the lower Chamber on certain occasions turns itself into a Committee of the Whole, in order to better discuss its business, and thus becomes a simple commission, from the Sovereign Court that it was the preceding moment; as such it then reports to itself, as the House of Commons, what it decided in the Committee of the Whole, and deliberates again under one title about what it has already resolved under another.

Such is the advantage proper to Democratic Government, that it can be established in fact by a simple act of the general will. After this, that provisional Government remains in office, if such form is adopted, or establishes in the name of the Sovereign the Government prescribed by the law, and thus all is according to rule. It is not possible to institute the Government in any other legitimate manner without renouncing the principles heretofore established.

XVIII. *Means of Preventing Usurpation of the Government*

From these clarifications it follows, in confirmation of Chapter XVI [p. 461–462], that the act which institutes the Government is not a contract but a Law, that those entrusted with the executive power are not the masters of the people but its officers, whom it can establish and depose when it pleases, that there is no question for them of contracting but of obeying, and that in undertaking the functions which the State imposes on them, they are only fulfilling their duty as Citizens, without having any sort of right to dispute about the conditions.

When it happens that the People institutes a hereditary Government, be it monarchical in one family, or aristocratic in an order of Citizens, it is not an engagement that it undertakes: it is a provisional form which it gives to the administration, until it pleases it to put in order another.

It is true that these changes are always dangerous, and that the established Government must only be touched if it becomes incompatible with the public good; but this circumspection is a maxim of politics and not a rule of right, and the State is no more bound to leave civil authority to its chiefs than military authority to its Generals.

It is also true that in such a case one should observe with greatest care all the requisite formalities in order to distinguish a regular and legitimate act from a seditious tumult, and the will of a whole people from the clamors of a faction. Especially in this odious case one should only concede in full rigor of what is right what cannot be refused, and it is also from this obligation that the Prince draws a great advantage in preserving its power despite the people, without anyone being able to say that it has usurped the power. For in seeming to exercise only its rights, it could very easily extend them, and under the pretext of maintaining the public peace obstruct the assemblies destined to reestablish good order; so that it takes advantage of a silence it prevents from being broken, or of irregularities it has had committed, in order to suppose in its favor the consent of those whom fear silences and to punish those who dare to speak. It is thus that the Decemvirs, having first been elected for one year, then continued for another, tried to retain their power perpetually by not permitting the *comitia* to assemble; and it is by this easy means that all governments in the world, when once invested with public force, sooner or later usurp the Sovereign authority.

The periodical assemblies of which I have already spoken are suited to prevent or defer this evil, especially when they have no need of formal convocation; for then the Prince would not be able to prevent them without openly declaring himself violator of the laws and enemy of the State.

The opening of these assemblies, which have for their only object the maintenance of the social treaty, should always be done with two propositions that cannot be suppressed, and which pass separately by vote.

The first: "Whether it pleases the Sovereign to preserve the present form of Government."

The second: "Whether it please the People to leave the administration to those presently charged with it."

I presume here what I believe I have demonstrated: namely, that there is in the State no fundamental law which cannot be revoked, not even the social pact; for if all the Citizens assemble in order to break this pact by common accord, one cannot doubt that it would be very legitimately broken. Grotius even thinks that each person can renounce the State of which he is a member, and regain his natural liberty and his goods on leaving the country.[31] Now it would be absurd that all the Citizens together cannot do what each of them can do separately.

Book Four

I. That the General Will Is Indestructible

As long as several men together consider themselves as a single body, they have only one will which relates to the common preservation and to the general well-being. Then all the activities of the State are vigorous and simple, its maxims are clear and luminous, it has no entangled and conflicting interests, the common good is clearly apparent everywhere and only good sense is needed to perceive it. Peace, union, equality, are enemies of political subtleties. Upright and simple men are hard to deceive because of their simplicity; snares and refined pretexts do not impose upon them; they are not even clever enough to be duped. When one sees among the happiest people in the world groups of peasants regulating the affairs of State under an oak tree and always conducting themselves wisely, can one keep from scorning the refinement of other nations, who render themselves illustrious and miserable with so much art and mystery?

A State thus governed has need of very few Laws, and to the extent that it becomes necessary to promulgate new ones, this necessity is universally seen. The first man who proposes them does no more than say what all have already felt, and there is no question of intrigues or eloquence in order to pass into law what each has already resolved to do, as soon as he is sure that the others will do likewise.

What deceives those who reason is that seeing only States badly constituted from their origin, they are impressed by the impossibility of maintaining a similar polity in such States. They laugh on imagining all the follies to which a cunning knave, an insinuating speaker, could persuade the people of Paris or London. They do not know that Cromwell would have been put to hard labor by the people of Berne, and the Duke of Beaufort imprisoned by the Genevans.

But when the social bond begins to loosen and the State to weaken; when private interests being to make themselves felt and the small societies to influence the great one, the common interest degenerates and finds opponents: unanimity reigns no more in the votes, the general will is no longer the will of all, contradictions, debates arise, and the best advice does not pass without disputes.

Finally, when the State, near its ruin, subsists only as a vain and illusory form, when the social bond is broken in all hearts, when the vilest interest impudently takes on the sacred name of the public good, then the general will becomes mute; all, guided by secret motives, no longer express their opinions as Citizens, as if the State had never existed; and they falsely pass under the name of Laws iniquitous decrees which have only private interest as their goal.

Does it follow from this that the general will is annihilated or corrupted? No, it is always constant, unalterable, and pure; but it is subordinated to others that prevail over it. Each, detaching his own interest from the common interest, sees clearly that he cannot completely separate himself from it, but his part in the public evil does not seem anything to him compared with the exclusive good he intends to appropriate. This private good excepted, he wishes the general good for his own interest as strongly as anyone else. Even in selling his vote for money he does not extinguish the general will in himself; he eludes it. The fault he commits is to change the status of the question and to answer another than what he has been asked; so that instead of saying by his vote, "It is advantageous to the State," he says, "It is advantageous to a certain man or a certain party that such or such a motion passes." Thus the law of public order in the assemblies is not so much to maintain the general will as to make sure that it always is questioned and that it always responds.

I could here present many reflections on the simple right of voting in every act of sovereignty; a right which nothing is able to take away from the Citizens; and on the right to state opinions, to propose, divide, to discuss, that the Government has always great care to leave only to its members; but this important matter would require a separate treatise, and I cannot say everything in this one.

II. Of Voting

From the preceding chapter one sees that the manner in which general affairs are managed gives a sufficiently accurate indication of the actual state of the habitual conduct, and the health of the body politic. The more harmony reigns in the assemblies, that is to say the closer opinions approach unanimity, the more dominant is the general will; but long debates, dissensions, tumult, indicate the ascendancy of private interests and the decline of the State.

This seems less evident when two or more orders enter into its constitution, as in Rome the Patricians and the Plebeians, whose quarrels often troubled the *comitia*, even in the finest times of the republic; but this exception is more apparent than real, for then, by the vice inherent in the body politic, there are, so to speak, two States in one: what is not true of the two together is true of each separately. And in fact, even in the stormiest times the plebiscites of the people, when the Senate did not interfere with them, always passed tranquillity and by a large majority of votes: the Citizens having only one interest, the people only one will.

At the other extremity of the circle unanimity returns. It is when the citizens, having fallen into slavery, no longer have either liberty or will. Then fright and flattery change votes into acclamations; one no longer deliberates, but adores or curses. Such was the vile manner of expressing opinions in the Senate under the Emperors. Sometimes it was done with ridiculous precautions. Tacitus observed that under Otho, the Senators, in overwhelming Vitellius with execrations, arranged to make a frightening noise at the same time so that if, by chance, he became the master, he would not know what each of them had said.

From these diverse considerations arise the maxims by which one ought to regulate the manner of counting the votes and comparing opinions, according to whether the general will is more or less easy to know, and the State more or less declining.

There is only one single law which by its nature requires unanimous consent. It is the social pact: for civil association is the most voluntary act in the world; every man being born free and master of himself, no one can, under any pretext whatever, subjugate him without his assent. To decide that the son of a slave is born a slave is to decide that he is not born a man.

If, then, at the time of the social pact, there are found some opponents of it, their opposition does not invalidate the contract, it only prevents them from being included in it: they are foreigners among citizens. When the State is instituted, consent is in residence; to live in a territory is to submit oneself to sovereignty.[32]

Outside of this basic contract, the voice of the greater number always obliges all the others; it is a consequence of the contract itself. But one asks how a man can be free and forced to conform to wills that are not his own. How are opponents free and yet subject to laws to which they have not consented?

I respond that the question is poorly posed. The citizen consents to all the laws, even those which are passed despite him, and even to those that punish him when he dares to violate any of them. The constant will of all the members of the State is the general will: by it they are citizens and free.[33] When a law is proposed in the assembly of the People, what is asked of them is not precisely whether they approve the proposition or reject it, but whether or not it conforms to the general will which is their own: each in giving his vote states his opinion on that question, and from the counting of the votes is taken the declaration of the general will. When the opinion contrary to mine prevails, that only proves that I was mistaken, and that what I had considered to be the general will was not. If my private opinion had prevailed, I would have done something other than I had wanted to do, and then I would not have been free.

This supposes, it is true, that all the characteristics of the general will are still in the majority; when they cease to be there, whichever side one takes, there is no longer any liberty.

In showing earlier how private wills have been substituted for the general will in public deliberations, I have sufficiently indicated the practicable means for preventing this abuse; I will speak of it again later on. With regard to the proportional number of the votes required to declare this will, I have also stated the principles by which one can determine it. The difference of a single vote breaks a tie, only one opposed breaks unanimity; but between unanimity and a tie vote there are many unequal divisions, at each of which one can fix this number according to the condition and needs of the body politic.

Two general maxims can serve to regulate these ratios: the one, that the more important and serious the deliberations, the closer the prevailing opinion should approach unanimity; the other, that the more the matter requires speed of decision, the more one can reduce the prescribed difference in the division of opinions: in deliberations that must be resolved immediately, a majority by one vote should suffice. The first of these maxims seems more suitable to laws, and the second to business matters. Be that as it may, it is by their combination that the best ratios are established by which a majority can decide.

III. Of Elections

With regard to the elections of the Prince and the Magistrates, which are, as I have said, complex acts, there are two routes by which to proceed: namely, by choice and by lot. Both have been employed in diverse Republics, and a very complicated mixture of the two is still seen in the election of the Doge of Venice.

"Voting by lot," Says Montesquieu, "is of the nature of democracy." I agree, but how is that? "Drawing lots," he continues, "is a mode of election that afflicts no one: it leaves to each citizen a reasonable hope of serving the fatherland." These are not the reasons.

If we note that the election of the chiefs is a function of Government and not of Sovereignty, one will see why the way of drawing lots is in the nature of Democracy, where the administration is so much better as its acts are less multiplied.

In every true Democracy, the magistracy is not an advantage, but an onerous responsibility which cannot be justly imposed on one individual rather than on another. The law alone can impose this responsibility on the one whose lot is drawn. For then, the condition being equal for all, and the choice dependent on no human will, there is no private application that alters the universality of the law.

In an Aristocracy, the Prince chooses the Prince, the Government is preserved by itself, and it is there that voting is appropriate.

The example of the election of the Doge of Venice far from destroying this distinction confirms it; this combined form is suitable to a mixed government. For it is an error to take the Government of Venice as a true Aristocracy. If the People there have no part in the Government, the nobility there is the people itself. A multitude of poor poverty-stricken noblemen never approach any magistracy, and have for their nobility only the empty title of Excellency and the right to attend the grand Council. This grand Council being as numerous as our general council in Geneva, its illustrious members have no more privileges than our simple Citizens. It is certain that, setting aside the extreme disparity of the two Republics, the burghers of Geneva exactly correspond to the Venetian patricians; our natives and inhabitants correspond to the Townsmen and people of Venice; our peasants correspond to the subjects on the mainland: finally, in whatever manner we consider this Republic, apart from its size, its Government is no more aristocratic than ours. The whole difference is that, not having any chief for life, we do not have the same need to draw lots.

Elections by lot would have few disadvantages in a true Democracy, where, all being equal in moral conduct and talents as in maxims and fortune, the choice would become almost indifferent. But I have already said that there is no true Democracy.

When choice and lot are combined, the first should be used in positions that require special talents, such as military offices; the other is suitable for those in which good sense, justice, and integrity suffice, such as judicial responsibilities; because in a well-constituted State these qualities are common to all citizens.

Neither lot nor voting has any place in a monarchical Government. The Monarch being by right the sole Prince and the one Magistrate, the choice of his lieutenants belongs only to him. When the Abbé de Saint-Pierre proposed to multiply the Councils of the king of France, and to elect the members by ballot, he did not see that he was proposing to change the form of the Government.

It would remain for me to speak of the manner of casting and collecting the votes in the assembly of the people; but perhaps the account of the Roman practice in that respect will explain more clearly all the maxims which I might be able to establish. It is not unworthy of a judicious reader to see in some detail how public and private affairs were treated in a Council of two hundred thousand men.

IV. Of the Roman Comitia

We have no trustworthy records of the early times of Rome; there is even a great probability that most things which have been reported are fables,[34] and in general the most instructive part of the annals of peoples, which is the history of their founding, is the most defective. Experience teaches us every day of the causes giving rise to the revolutions of empires: but as peoples are no longer being formed, we hardly have anything but conjectures to explain how they were formed.

The practices one finds established at least testify that these practices had an origin. Of the traditions that reach back to these origins, those which the greatest authorities support and which the strongest reasons confirm ought to be accepted as most certain. These are the maxims that I have tried to follow in inquiring how the freest and most powerful people on earth exercised its supreme power.

After the foundation of Rome, the nascent Republic, that is to say the army of the founder, composed of Albans, Sabines, and foreigners, was divided into three classes, which took from this division the names of *Tribes*. Each of these Tribes was subdivided into ten *Curiae* [sections], and each *Curia* into *Decuriae* [ten subsections], at the head of which were placed chiefs called *Curiones* and *Decuriones*.

Beyond this, a body of one hundred Horsemen or Knights, called *Centuria*, was drawn from each Tribe, by which one sees that these divisions, not very necessary in a market town, were at first only military. But it seems that an instinct for greatness induced the little town of Rome from the first to organize itself in a manner suitable to the capital of the world.

From this first division, one disadvantage soon resulted. The tribe of the Albans[35] and that of the Sabines[36] remained always in the same condition, while that of the foreigners[37] increased continually through perpetual influx of new members and soon surpassed the other two. The remedy Servius found for this dangerous abuse was to change the division, and in place of the one based on races, which he abolished, he substituted another, drawn from the districts of the city occupied by each Tribe. In place of the three Tribes he made four, each of which occupied one of the hills of Rome and bore its name. Thus, by remedying the current inequality, he also prevented it for the future; and in order that this might be a division not only of places but of men, he forbade the inhabitants of one quarter to move to another; which prevented the races from blending together.

He also doubled the three old centuries of Cavalry, and added twelve others to them, but always under the old names; a simple and judicious means by which he effected a distinction between the body of Knights and that of the People, without making the latter murmur.

To these four urban Tribes Servius added fifteen others, called rustic Tribes, because they were formed of inhabitants of the countryside, divided into the same number of cantons. Subsequently the same number of new ones was formed, and the Roman People finally found itself divided into thirty-five Tribes, a number which remained fixed until the end of the Republic.

From this distinction between the urban Tribes and the rural Tribes resulted an effect worthy of note, because there is no other instance of it, and because Rome owed to it both the preservation of her moral customs and the growth of her empire. It might be supposed that the urban Tribes soon arrogated to themselves the power and the honors, and were ready to debase the rustic Tribes: it was quite the reverse. One knows the taste of the early Romans for life in the countryside. This taste derived from their wise founder, who united to liberty rustic and military labor, and relegated so to speak to the town the arts, crafts, intrigue, fortune, and slavery.

Thus, as all the illustrious men of Rome lived in the country and cultivated their land, it was customary to seek only there the supporters of the Republic. This condition, being that of the worthiest Patricians, was honored by everyone; the simple and laborious life of

the Villagers was preferred to the idle and slack life of the Burghers of Rome, and someone who would have been only an unhappy proletarian in the town, by working in the
fields, became a respected Citizen. It is not without reason, said Varro, that our magnanimous ancestors established in the Village the nurseries of those robust and valiant men
who defended them in times of war and nourished them in times of peace. Pliny says positively that the Tribes of the fields were honored because of the men who composed them;
whereas the cowards whom one wanted to disgrace were transferred as a mark of ignominy
into the urban Tribes. The Sabine Appius Claudius, having come to settle in Rome, was
overwhelmed there with honors and enrolled in a rustic Tribe which took the name of his
family. Finally, freedmen all entered the urban Tribes, never the rural; and during the
whole of the Republic there is not a single example of any of these freedmen attaining any
seat in the magistracy even though he had become a citizen.

This maxim was excellent; but it was pushed so far that finally a change and certainly
an abuse of policy resulted from it.

First, the Censors, after having long arrogated the right of arbitrarily transferring citizens from one Tribe to another, permitted most of them to be enrolled in whichever
pleased them; this permission, which surely served no use, removed one of the great
strengths of the censorship. Additionally, as the Great and the powerful all enrolled themselves in the Tribes of the countryside, and the freedmen became citizens remaining with
the population in the urban ones, the Tribes in general no longer had any particular place
or territory; but all found themselves so intermingled that it was impossible to distinguish the members of each except by the registers, so that the idea of the word *Tribe* thus
passed from the real to the personal, or rather became nearly chimerical.

It also happened that the urban Tribes, being nearer at hand, were often found to be
the strongest in the *comitia*, and sold the State to those who deigned to buy the votes of
the rabble which composed them.

With regard to the *Curiae*, the founder having formed ten in each tribe, the entire
Roman people then enclosed in the walls of the town consisted of thirty *Curiae*, each of
which had its temples, its gods, its officers, its priests, and its festivals, called *compitalia*,
resembling the *paganalia* which the rural tribes later had.

In Servius's new apportionment, the number thirty being incapable of equal distribution into four Tribes, he was unwilling to touch them; and the *Curiae*, independent of the
tribes, became another division of the inhabitants of Rome. But there was no question of
Curiae either in the rural tribes or in the people who composed them, because the Tribes
having become a purely civil establishment, and another policy to levy troops having been
introduced, the military divisions of Romulus were found superfluous. Thus, although
every Citizen was enrolled in a Tribe, there were many who were not enrolled in a *Curia*.

Servius made yet a third division, which had no relation to the two preceding ones, but
became by its effects the most important of all. He distributed the whole Roman people
into six classes, which he distinguished neither by residence nor by individual attributes,
but by property. So the first classes were filled by the rich, the last by the poor, and the
middle by those who enjoyed a moderate fortune. These six classes were subdivided into
one hundred and ninety-three other bodies, called centuries; and these bodies were so distributed that the first class alone comprised more than half, and the last counted for only
one subdivision, even though it alone contained more than half of the inhabitants of Rome.

In order that the people would not so clearly discern the consequences of this last form,
Servious pretended to give it a military aspect; he introduced into the second class two
centuries of armorers, and two centuries of war instruments into the fourth. In each class,
except the last, he distinguished the young and the old, that is to say those who were

obligated to bear arms and those whose age exempted them by law; this distinction, more than that of property, produced the necessity of frequently redoing the census or enumeration. Finally, he wished the assembly to be held in the Campus Martius, and that all who were of age to serve gather there with their arms.

The reason he did not follow in the last class this same division of young and old is that the populace of which it was composed was not accorded the honor of bearing Arms for the fatherland: it was necessary to have hearths in order to obtain the right of defending them; and out of those innumerable troops of beggars with which the armies of Kings today glitter, there is no one perhaps who would not have been chased with disdain from a Roman cohort, when soldiers were the defenders of liberty.

One further distinguished, however, in the last class, the *proletarians* from those one called the *capite censi*. The first, not completely destitute, at least sometimes gave Citizens to the State, sometimes even soldiers when the need was pressing. As for those who had nothing at all, and could only be tallied by a head count, they were regarded as wholly worthless, and Marius was the first who deigned to enroll them.

Without deciding here if this third enumeration was good or bad in itself, I think I can affirm that it was made practicable only by the simple habits of the early Romans, their disinterestedness, their taste for agriculture, their dislike of commerce and the ardent pursuit of gain. Where is the modern people among whom rapacious greed, restlessness of spirit, intrigue, continual changes of residence, and perpetual revolutions of fortunes would have let such an institution endure for twenty years without overturning the whole State? It is even well to note that customary conduct and the censorship were stronger than this institution in correcting the vices in Rome, and that many a rich man was relegated to the class of the poor for having made too great a display of his wealth.

From all this one can easily understand why mention is scarcely ever made of more than five classes, although there were really six. The sixth, providing neither soldiers to the army nor voters to the *Campus Martius*,[38] and being of almost no use to the Republic, rarely counted for anything.

Such were the different divisions of the Roman people. Let us now see the effect they produced in the assemblies. These assemblies, when legitimately convoked were called *Comitia*: ordinarily they were held in the Roman Forum or in the *Campus Martius*, and were distinguished as *comitia* by *Curiae*, by Centuries, and by Tribes, according to which of these three forms they were organized: the *comitia* by *Curiae* was instituted by Romulus; those by Centuries by Servius; those by tribes by the Tribunes of the people. No law received sanction, no magistrate was elected, except in the *comitia*; and as no Citizen was not enrolled in a *Curia*, in a Century, or in a Tribe, it follows that no citizen was excluded from the right of voting, and that the Roman people was truly Sovereign by right and in fact.

In order that the *Comitia* be legitimately assembled and that what was done there have the force of law, three conditions were necessary: the first that the body or the Magistrate who convoked them be invested with the necessary authority; the second that the assembly be held on one of the days permitted by the law; the third that the auguries be favorable.

The reason for the first regulation need not be explained. The second is a matter of policy: thus it was not permitted to hold the *Comitia* on feast and market days, when country people coming to Rome on business did not have time to spend the day in the Forum. By the third, the Senate bridled a proud and restless people, and appropriately tempered the ardor of seditious Tribunes; but these found more than one way to elude this hindrance.

Laws and the election of chiefs were not the only points submitted to the judgment of the *Comitia*; the Roman people having usurped the most important functions of Government, it can be said that the destiny of Europe was settled in its assemblies. This variety of objects gave rise to the various forms these assemblies took according to the matters which had to be decided.

In order to judge these diverse forms, it suffices to compare them. Romulus, in instituting the *Curiae*, sought to contain the Senate by means of the people and the people by means of the Senate, while dominating both equally. He thus gave the people by this form all the authority of numbers in order to balance that of power and of riches left to the patricians. But, according to the spirit of Monarchy, he left more advantage to the patricians through the influence of their Clients upon the majority of votes. This admirable institution of Patrons and Clients was a masterpiece of politics and humanity without which the Patriciate, so contrary to the spirit of the Republic, would not have been able to subsist. Rome alone has had the honor of giving to the world such a fine example from which no abuse ever resulted and which nevertheless has never been followed.

This same form of *Curiae* having subsisted under the Kings down to Servius, and the region of the last Tarquin not having been considered legitimate, the royal laws came to be generally designated by the name of *leges curiatae*.

Under the Republic the *Curiae*, always limited to the four urban tribes, and containing only the populace of Rome, could suit neither the Senate, which was at the head of the Patricians, nor the Tribunes, who, although plebeians, were at the head of the comfortably situated citizens. They fell then into disrepute, and their degradation was such that their thirty assembled Lictors did what the *comitiae* by *Curiae* should have done.

The division by Centuries was so favourable to the Aristocracy that one does see at first how the Senate did not always prevail in the *Comitia* of that name, and by which the consuls, Censors, and other curial Magistrates were elected. In effect, of the one hundred and ninety-three centuries which formed the six classes of the whole Roman people, the first Class comprising ninety-eight, and the votes being counted only by Centuries, this first class alone outnumbered all the others in votes. When all these Centuries were in accord, one did not even continue to count the votes; what the smallest number had decided passed for a decision of the multitude; and one can say that in the *comitia* by centuries, business was more regulated by the majority of money than by votes.

But this extreme authority was moderated by two means: first, the Tribunes usually, and a great number of Plebeians always, being in the class of the rich, balanced the influence of the Patricians in this first class.

The second means consisted in this, that instead of making the Centuries begin to vote according to their order, which would have always begun with the first, one century was drawn by lot and that once[39] proceeded alone to the election; after that all the Centuries, called another day according to their rank, repeated the same election and ordinarily confirmed it. One thus took the authority of example away from rank to give it to lot, according to the principle of Democracy.

From this practice another advantage resulted; the Citizens from the countryside had the time between the two elections to inform themselves of the merit of the candidate provisionally named, so that they could vote knowledgeably. But, under the pretext of haste, this practice came to be abolished, and the two elections took place on the same day.

The *Comitia* by Tribe, were properly the Council of the Roman people. They were only convoked by the Tribunes; in them the Tribunes were elected and passed their plebiscites. Not only did the Senate have no rank in them, it did not have even the right to attend; and, forced to obey laws on which they were not able to vote, the Senators, in this regard, were less free than the lowest Citizens. This injustice was altogether mistaken, and alone sufficed to invalidate the decrees of a body to which all members were not admitted.

Should all the patricians have attended these *comitia* according to the right they had as Citizens, becoming then simple private individuals, they would hardly have had influence in a formal vote that relied on a head count, and in which the least proletarian had as much power as the Prince of the Senate.

One sees then that besides the order which resulted from these diverse divisions for the counting of the votes of such a great People, the divisions were not reduced to forms indifferent in themselves, but each had effects relative to the purposes for which it was preferred.

Without entering into this in greater detail, it follows from the preceding explanations that the *comitia* by Tribes was more favorable to popular Government, and the *comitia* by Centuries to Aristocracy. With regard to the *comitia* by *Curiae*, where only the populace of Rome formed the majority, as they were only good for favoring tyranny and evil design, they deserved to fall into discredit, the seditious themselves abstaining from a means which only too plainly would reveal their projects. It is certain that the entire majesty of the Roman People was found only in the *Comitia* by Centuries, which were alone complete; seeing that the rural tribes were absent from the *Comitia* by *Curiae* and the Senate and the Patricians from the *Comitia* by Tribes.

As to the manner of collecting the votes, it was among the early Romans as simple as their customary conduct, although still less simple than in Sparta. Each gave his vote with a loud voice, and a registrar wrote them down accordingly; a majority of votes in each tribe determined the vote of the tribe, a majority of votes among the tribes determined the vote of the people, and so with the *Curiae* and Centuries. This usage was good as long as honesty reigned among the Citizens, and each was ashamed to vote publicly for an unjust opinion or on an unworthy subject; but when the people became corrupted and votes were bought, it was preferred that votes to be given in secret in order to contain purchasers by distrust, and to furnish scoundrels the means of not being traitors.

I know that Cicero blames this change and attributes to it in part the ruin of the republic. But although I feel the weight that one should have for Cicero's authority here, I cannot share his opinion. I think, on the contrary, that because not enough similar changes were made, the fall of the State was accelerated. As the diet of healthy persons is unfit for the sick, so we should not wish to govern a corrupt people by the same Laws appropriate to a good people. Nothing proves this maxim better than the duration of the republic of Venice, the semblance of which still exists uniquely because its laws are only suited for wicked men.

To each Citizen, then, tablets were distributed for each to vote without others knowing his opinion. New formalities were also established for the collection of the tablets, the counting of the votes, the comparison of the numbers, etc. This did not prevent the Officers in charge of these functions[40] from being suspect. Finally, in order to prevent intrigue and traffic in votes, edicts were passed, the multitude of which demonstrates their uselessness.

Toward the closing years it was often found necessary to resort to extraordinary expedients in order to compensate for the insufficiency of the laws. Sometimes miracles were alleged; but this means, which could deceive the people, could not deceive those who governed them: sometimes one suddenly convoked an assembly before the Candidates had had the time to conduct their intrigues; sometimes one used a whole meeting for speaking when the people were seen ready to take the bad side. But at last ambition eluded everything; and it is incredible that in the midst of such abuses, this immense people, by favor of its ancient regulations, did not fail to elect Magistrates, to pass laws, to judge cases, to expedite its public and private business, with almost as much facility as the Senate itself could have done.

V. Of the Tribunate

When an exact proportion between the constitutive parts of the State cannot be established, or when indestructible causes incessantly alter their relations, then a special magistracy is instituted, which is not incorporated into the others, but which places each term back into its true relation with the others, and serves as a liaison or a middle term, either between the Prince and the People, or between the Prince and the Sovereign, or if necessary between the two sides at the same time.

This body, which I will call the *Tribunate*, is the preserver of the laws and of the legislative power. Sometimes it serves to protect the Sovereign against the Government, as the Tribunes of the people did in Rome; sometimes to sustain the government against the people, as the Council of Ten now does in Venice; and sometimes to maintain the balance on either side, as the Ephors did in Sparta.

The Tribunate is not a constitutive part of the City, and should have no share of the legislative or executive power, but it is in this that its power is greater: for, able to do nothing, it can prevent everything. It is more sacred and revered, as defender of the laws, than the Prince who executes them and the Sovereign who gives them. This was very clearly seen in Rome when the proud patricians, who always despised the entire people, were forced to flinch before a simple officer of the people, who had neither auspices nor jurisdiction.

The Tribunate wisely tempered is the strongest buttress of a good constitution; but if it has even a little too much force it dislocates everything: weakness is not in its nature; and provided that it is something, it is never less than it should be.

It degenerates into tyranny when it usurps the executive power of which it is only the moderator, and when it wishes to dispense laws which it should only protect. The enormous power of the Ephors, which was without danger as long as Sparta preserved its moral customs, accelerated the corruption once it had begun. The blood of Agis, slain by these tyrants, was avenged by his successor; the crime and the punishment of the Ephors equally hastened the fall of the Republic; and after Cleomenes, Sparta was no longer anything. Again, Rome perished in the same way and the excessive power of the tribunes, usurped by degree, finally served, with the aid of laws made for liberty, as a safeguard of the emperors who destroyed it. As for the Council of Ten in Venice, it is a Tribunal of blood, equally horrible to the Patricians and to the People, and far from resolutely defending the laws, it only serves, after their degradation, to strike secret blows which no one dares to notice.

The Tribunate is weakened, like the Government, by multiplication of its members. When the Tribunes of the Roman people, originally two in number, later five, wanted to double this number, the Senate let them do so, being quite sure of controlling some by the others; this did not fail to happen.

The best means of preventing the usurpations of such a formidable body, a means which until now no Government has deemed expedient, would be not to render this body permanent, but to set intervals during which it would remain suppressed. These intervals, which should not be long enough to let abuses have time to become established, can be fixed by law, in such a manner that they can easily be abridged in case of need by extraordinary commissions.

This means seems to me without inconvenience, because, as I have said, the Tribunate, forming no part of the constitution, can be removed without the constitution suffering; and it seems to be efficacious, because a newly established magistrate begins not with the power his predecessor had but only with that which the law gives him.

VI. Of the Dictatorship

The inflexibility of laws, which prevents them from adapting to events, can in certain cases render them pernicious and cause the ruin of the State in a crisis. The order and slowness of formalities demand a space of time which circumstances sometimes refuse. A thousand cases can present themselves for which the legislator has not provided, and it is a very necessary foresight to sense that everything cannot be foreseen.

It is then not necessary to want to strengthen political institutions so much that the power to suspend their effect is removed. Even Sparta let her laws lie dormant.

But only the greatest dangers can outweigh the danger of altering the public order, and the sacred power of the laws should never be arrested unless it is a matter of the safety of the fatherland. In these rare and obvious cases, public security is provided for by a special act which entrusts its responsibility to the most worthy. This commission can be conferred in two ways, according to the kind of danger.

If, in order to remedy it, it suffices to augment the activity of the government, one may concentrate this activity in one or two of its members. Thus it is not the authority of the laws that is changed but only the form of their administration. But if the danger is such that the formal process of the law is an obstacle to guaranteeing them, then a supreme chief is named who silences all the laws and suspends for a moment the Sovereign authority; in such case, the general is not doubted, and it is evident that the first intention of the people is that the State should not perish. In this way the suspension of the legislative authority does not abolish it: the magistrate who silences it cannot make it speak; he dominates it without power to represent it; he can do everything except make laws.

The first means was employed by the Roman Senate when it charged the Consuls by a consecrated formula to provide for the safety of the republic. The second was employed when one of the two consuls named a Dictator,[41] a usage of which Alba had given the example to Rome.

In the early days of the Republic, recourse had often been had to the Dictatorship, because the State still was not firmly enough set to be able to maintain itself solely by the force of its constitution.

Moral customs rendering superfluous at that time many precautions which would have been necessary in another time, one did not fear either that a Dictator would abuse his authority or that he would try to retain it beyond his term. On the contrary, it seemed that such great power was a burden to him in whom it was vested, so that he hastened to divest himself of it; as if it were too painful and perilous a position to take the place of the laws!

Thus it is not the danger of abuse, but that of degradation, that makes me blame the indiscreet use of this supreme magistracy in early times. For as long as it was wasted on elections, dedications, and pure formalities, it was feared that it would become less formidable when needed, and that one would accustom oneself to regard it as an empty title which was employed only in empty ceremonies.

Toward the end of the Republic, the Romans, having become more circumspect, were as unreasonably sparing in the use of the Dictatorship as they had formerly been unreasonably wasteful of it. It was easy to see that their fear was ill-founded, that the very weakness of the capital then formed its security against the magistrates in its own core, that a Dictator would be able in certain cases to defend public liberty without being able to assail it, and that the chains of Rome would not be forged in Rome itself, but in its armies: the slight resistance of Marius against Sulla, of Pompey against Caesar, plainly demonstrated what could be expected from the authority within against the force from without.

This error made them commit great mistakes. Such, for example, was not naming a Dictator in the Catiline affair: as for it was only a question of the interior of the town and, at most, some province of Italy, a Dictator, with the unlimited authority that the laws gave him, would have easily dissipated the conspiracy, which was stifled only by a combination of happy accidents which human prudence would never have anticipated.

Instead of that, the senate contented itself to hand all its power over to the Consuls; whence it happened that Cicero in order to act efficaciously was constrained to exceed this power on an important point, and although the first transports of joy gave approval to his conduct, later he was justly called to account for the blood of Citizens shed contrary to the laws; a reproach which one could not have made against a Dictator. But the eloquence of the Consul carried all; and he himself, although a Roman, preferring his glory more than his fatherland, sought not so much the most legitimate and the surest means of saving the State, but to have all the honor from this affair.[42] Thus he was justly honored as liberator of Rome, and justly punished as violator of the laws. However, brilliant his recall, it is certain that it was a pardon.

Additionally, in whatever manner this important commission may be conferred, it is important to fix its duration to a very short term which can never be prolonged. In the crises that call for its being established, the State is soon destroyed or saved, and after the current need is passed, the Dictatorship becomes tyrannical or useless. In Rome the Dictators held office for only six months, the majority abdicated before this term. If the term had been longer, perhaps they would have been tempted to prolong it still further, as the Decemvirs did theirs of one year. The Dictator had only the time to deal with the need which had led to his election; he did not have time to come up with other projects.

VII. Of the Censorship

Just as the declaration of the general will is done by the law, the declaration of public judgment is done by the censorship; public opinion is the kind of law of which the Censor is the Minister, and which he applies only to particular cases, as does the Prince.

Far from being the arbiter of the opinion of the people, then, the censorial tribunal only declares it, and as soon as it deviates from that opinion, its decisions are vain and ineffectual.

It is useless to distinguish the moral customs of a nation from the objects of its esteem; for all these things come from the same principle and are necessarily confounded. Among all the peoples of the world, it is not nature but general opinion that decides the choice of their pleasures. Reform the opinions of men and their customs and manners will themselves be purified. One always likes what is good or what one finds to be so, but it is on this judgment that one deceives oneself: it is therefore this judgment which needs adjusting. He who judges customs judges honor, and he who judges honor takes his law from opinion.

The opinions of a people arise from its constitution; although the law does not regulate customs, it is legislation that gives them birth: when legislation is impaired customs degenerate, but then the judgment of the Censors will not do what the force of the laws has not done.

It follows from this that the Censorship can be useful to conserve customs, but never to reestablish them. Establish Censors while the laws are vigorous; as soon as they have lost vigor, everything is desperate; nothing that is legitimate has any force when the laws no longer have any.

The Censorship maintains moral customs by preventing opinions from being corrupted, by conserving their rectitude through wise applications, sometimes even in fixing them when they are still uncertain. The use of seconds in duels, carried to madness in the kingdom of France, was abolished there by these few words in an edict of the king: "As for those who have the cowardice to name seconds." This judgment, anticipating that of the public, decided it immediately. But when the same edicts wished to proclaim that it was also cowardice to fight duels, which is very true, but contrary to the common opinion, the public mocked this decision, on which its judgment was already formed.

I have already said elsewhere[43] that public opinion not being subject to constraint, there should be no vestige of this in the tribunal established to represent it. One cannot admire too much that art which this resource, wholly lost along moderns, was put to work among the Romans and better still among the Lacedaemonians [Spartans].

A man of bad moral conduct having proposed a good recommendation in the council of Sparta, the Ephors, without taking notice, arranged for a virtuous citizen to offer the same advice. What honor for the one, what shame for the other, without having to give either praise or blame to either of the two! Certain drunkards of Samos[44] defiled the tribunal of the Ephors; the next day by public Edict the Samians were permitted to be filthy. A true punishment would have been less severe than such impunity. When Sparta declared what was or was not decent, Greece did not appeal from its judgments.

VIII. Of Civil Religion

Men has at first no other Kings than the Gods, no other Government than the Theocratic. They reasoned like Caligula; and at that time they reasoned aptly. It requires a long change of sentiments and ideas in order for one to resolve to take one's peer for a master, and to flatter oneself that this would be good.

From the sole fact that one placed God at the head of each political society, it followed that there were as many Gods as peoples. Two peoples foreign to each other, and nearly always enemies, could not recognize the same master for very long. Two armies engaged in battle with each other could not obey the same chief. Thus from national divisions polytheism resulted, and from this came theological and civil intolerance, which are naturally the same, as will be stated later.

The fantasy the Greeks had of rediscovering their Gods among barbarous peoples came from that other notion they had of regarding themselves as the natural Sovereigns of those peoples. But it is a ridiculous erudition of our own day that revolves around the notion that the Gods of diverse nations are identical: as if Moloch, Saturn, and Chronos could be the same God; as if the Baal of the Phoenicians, the Zeus of the Greeks, and the Jupiter of the Latins could be the same; as if something could remain common among different chimerical Beings bearing different names!

Should one ask how under paganism, when each State had its own cult and its Gods, there were no wars of religion? I respond that it was for the very reason that each State, having its own cult as well as its own Government, did not distinguish between its Gods and its laws. Political war was also Theological; the districts of the Gods were so to speak fixed by the borders of the Nations. The God of one people had no right over other peoples. The Gods of the pagans were not jealous Gods; they partitioned among themselves the empire of the world: Moses himself and the Hebrew people sometimes countenanced this idea by speaking of the God of Israel. It is true they regarded the Gods of the Canaanites, a proscribed people devoted to destruction and whose place they were to occupy, as nothing; but see how they spoke of the divinities of neighboring peoples whom they were forbidden to attack: "The possession of that which belongs to Chamos, your god," said Jephthah to the Ammonites, "is it not legitimately yours? We possess by the same title the lands that our victorious God has acquired."[45] In that, it seems to me, there was a well-recognized parity between the rights of Chamos and those of the God of Israel.

But when the Jews, subjected to the Kings of Babylon and later to the Kings of Syria, wished to persist in not recognizing any other God than their own, this refusal, regarded as a rebellion against the victor, brought on them the persecutions we read of in their history, and of which no other example is seen before Christianity.[46]

Each Religion having then been uniquely attached to the laws of the Sate which prescribed it, there was no other manner of converting a people than to subjugate it, no other missionaries than conquerors, and as the obligation to change cults became the law of the conquered, it was necessary to conquer before speaking of it. Far from men combating for the Gods, it was, as in Homer, the Gods who combated for men; each asked his own god for victory, and paid for it with new altars. The Romans, before taking a place, summoned its Gods to abandon it, and when they left to the Tarrantines their angered Gods, they then regarded those Gods as subject to their own and forced to pay them homage. To the vanquished they left their own Gods just as they left them their own laws. A crown for Jupiter in the Capitol was often the only tribute they imposed.

Finally, the Romans having extended with their empire their cult and their Gods, and having often themselves adopted those of the conquered by granting to them the right of the City, the peoples of this vast empire imperceptibly found themselves having multitudes of Gods and cults, nearly everywhere the same: and that is how paganism was finally known in the world as only one and the same Religion.

It was in these circumstances that Jesus came to establish upon the earth a Spiritual kingdom; this, separating the theological from the political system, ended the unity of the State, and caused the internal divisions which have never ceased to agitate Christian peoples. For as this new idea of a kingdom in another world was unable to enter into the heads of pagans, they always regarded the Christians as true rebels who, under a hypocritical submission, only sought the moment to render themselves independent and masters, and to adroitly usurp the authority they pretended to respect in their weakness. Such was the cause of the persecutions.

What the pagans feared has happened; then everything changed its appearance, the humble Christians changed their language, and soon one saw this pretended kingdom of the other world become under a visible chief the most violent despotism in this world.

However, as there has always been a Prince and civil laws, there resulted from this double power a perpetual conflict of jurisdiction which has rendered all good polity impossible in Christian States; and one has never been able to come to know whether one was obligated to obey the master or the priest.

Many peoples, however, even in Europe or its vicinity, have wished to conserve or reestablish the ancient system, but without success; the spirit of Christianity has wholly won. The sacred cult has always remained or again become independent of the Sovereign, and without a necessary bond with the body of the State. Mohammed had very sound views, he tied his political system together well, and as long as the form of this government subsisted under his successors the Caliphs, this Government was exactly unified, and in that regard good. But the Arabs, having become flourishing, lettered, polished, soft, and cowardly, were subjugated by barbarians: then the division between the two powers began again; although it may be less apparent among the Mohammedans than among the Christians. It is there nonetheless, especially in the sect of Ali, and there are States, such as Persia, where it is unceasingly felt.

Among us, the kings of England have established themselves chiefs of the Church, as have the Czars: but, by this title, they have rendered themselves less its masters than its Ministers; they have acquired less the right to change it than the power to maintain it; they are not its legislators, they are only its Princes. Wherever the clergy forms a body,[47] it is master and legislator in its fatherland. There are then two powers, two Sovereigns, in England and in Russia, as everywhere else.

Of all the Christian authors, the philosopher Hobbes is the only one who has clearly seen the evil and the remedy, who has dared to propose uniting the two heads of the eagle, and bring everything back to political unity, without which no State or Government will ever be well constituted. But he should have seen that the dominating spirit of Christianity was incompatible with his system, and that the interest of the priest would always be stronger than that of the State. It is not so much what is horrible and false in his political theory as what it has that is just and true that has rendered it odious.[48]

I believe that in developing the historical facts under this viewpoint, one would easily refute the opposed sentiments of Bayle and Warburton, one of whom claims that no Religion is useful to the body politic, and the other that to the contrary, Christianity is its strongest support. To the first, one could prove that no State was ever founded without Religion serving as its base, and to the second, that Christian law is more injurious than useful to a firm constitution of the State. In order to make myself understood, it is only needed to give a little more precision to the overly vague ideas of Religion relative to my subject.

Religion considered by its relation to the society, which is either general or particular, can also be divided into two kinds: namely, the Religion of man and that of the Citizen. The first, without temples, without altars, without rites, limited to the purely internal worship of the Supreme God and to the eternal duties of morality, is the pure and simple Religion of the Gospel, the true Theism, and what one can call the divine natural right. The other, inscribed in a single country, gives it its Gods, its proper and tutelary patrons; its has its dogmas, its rites, it external worship prescribed by the laws: outside of the single Nation that follows it, all is for it infidel, foreign, barbarous; it extends the duties and rights of man only as far as its altars. Such were all the Religions of the early peoples, to which one can give the name of divine, civil, or positive right.

There is a third, more bizarre kind of Religion which, giving to men two legislations, two chiefs, two fatherlands, subjects them to contradictory duties and prevents them from being able to be at one time devout and Citizens. Such is the religion of the Lamas, such is that of the Japanese, such is Roman Christianity. One can call this the religion of the Priest. There results from it a kind of mixed unsociable right which has no name.

Considered politically, these three kinds of religions all have their defects. The third is so evidently bad that it is a waste of time to amuse oneself demonstrating it. Whatever destroys social unity is worthless. All institutions which place man in contradiction with himself are worthless.

The second is good insofar as it unites divine worship with the love of the laws, and by making the fatherland the object of the adoration of the Citizens it teaches them that to serve the State is to serve the tutelary God. It is one kind of theocracy, in which there should be no other pontiff but the Prince, nor other priests than the magistrates. Then to die for one's country is to go to martyrdom, to violate the laws is to be impious, and to subject a guilty man to public execration is to deliver him to the anger of the gods: *sacer esto*.

But it is bad in that being founded on error and on falsehood it deceives men, renders them credulous, superstitious, and drowns the true worship of the Divinity in a vain ceremonial. It is again bad when, becoming exclusive and tyrannical, it renders a people sanguinary and intolerant, so that it breathes only murder and massacre, and believes it is performing a holy action by killing whoever does not admit its gods. This places such a people in a natural state of war with all others, very detrimental to its own security.

There remains then the Religion of man or Christianity, not that of today, but that of the Gospel, which is altogether different. By this holy, sublime, and true Religion, men, children of the same God, all recognize themselves as brothers, and the society which unites them is not even dissolved at death.

But this Religion, having no particular relation with the body politic, leaves to the laws only the force that they derive from themselves without adding any other to them, and thus one of the great bonds of a particular society remains ineffective. What is more, far from attaching the hearts of the Citizens to the State, it detaches them as from all things of the earth; I know nothing more contrary to the social spirit.

We are told that a people of true Christians would form the most perfect society that one can imagine. I see only one great difficulty in this supposition; it is that a society of true Christians would no longer be a society of men.

I even say that this supposed society with all its perfection would be neither the strongest nor the most durable. By dint of being perfect, it would lack cohesion; its destructive vice would be in its very perfection.

Each would fulfill his duty; the people would be subject to the laws, the chiefs would be just and moderate, the magistrates honest and incorruptible; the soldiers would despise death; there would be neither vanity nor luxury: all this is very good, but let us look further.

Christianity is an entirely spiritual religion, only occupied by things of Heaven; the fatherland of the Christian is not of this world. He does his duty, it is true, but he does it with a profound indifference to the good or bad outcome of his cares. Provided he has nothing for which to reproach himself, it is of little import to him whether all fares well or poorly here below. If the State is flourishing, he hardly dares to enjoy the public felicity, for he fears to take selfish pride in the glory of his country; if the State declines, he blesses the hand of God that weighs down heavily on his people.

In order that the society be peaceable and harmony be maintained, all Citizens without exception would have to be equally good Christians. But if unfortunately there is found in it a single ambitious man, a single hypocrite, a Catiline, for example, a Cromwell, such a man very certainly would have an advantage over his pious compatriots. The Christian charity does not easily permit one to think ill of one's neighbor. As soon as he will have found by some ruse the art of imposing on them and securing to himself a part of the public authority, behold a man invested with dignity. God wills that he should be respected; soon he is a power; God wills that one obeys him; does the depositary of this power abuse it? He is the rod with which God punishes his children. It would violate conscience to chase out the usurper: it would be necessary to trouble the public peace, to use violence, to shed blood; all this is not accordant with the meekness of the Christian; and after all, does it matter whether one is free or serf in this vale of misery? The essential thing is to go to paradise, and resignation is only one more means toward that.

Does some foreign war occur? The Citizens march to combat without distress; none among them thinks of flight; they do their duty, but without passion for victory; they know better how to die than how to conquer. Whether they are victors or vanquished, does it matter? Doesn't Providence know better than they what they need? Imagine what advantage a proud, impetuous, passionate enemy can wrest from their stoicism. Place them against those courageous people consumed with an ardent love of glory and the fatherland; suppose your Christian Republic facing Sparta or Rome: the pious Christians will be beaten, crushed, destroyed, before they have had time to know where they are, or they will owe their safety only to the scorn their enemies have for them. To my mind it was a fine oath that the soldiers of Fabius took; they did not swear to die or conquer, they swore to return as conquerors, and kept their oath. Never would Christians have done such a thing; they would have believed they were tempting God.

But I am mistaken in speaking of a Christian Republic; each of these two words excludes the other. Christianity only preaches servitude and dependence. Its spirit is too favorable to tyranny for it not to always profit by it. True Christians are made to be slaves; they know it and are hardly moved by it; this short life has too little value in their eyes.

We are told Christian troops are excellent. I deny it. Let me be shown such. As for me, I do not know of any Christian Troops. I am told of the Crusades. Without disputing the valor of the Crusaders, I will note that, far from being Christians, they were soldiers of the priest, they were Citizens of the Church: they battled for its Spiritual country, which the Church had rendered temporal, one knows not how. Properly regarded, this returns us to paganism: as the Gospel does not establish a national Religion, any holy war is impossible among Christians.

Under the pagan emperors Christian soldiers were brave; all the Christian authors affirm this, and I believe it: there was a competition for honor against the pagan Troops. As soon as the Emperors became Christians this competition no longer subsisted; and when the cross had driven out the eagle, all Roman valor disappeared.

But setting aside political considerations, let us return to right, and settle the principles on this important point. The right which the social pact gives to the Sovereign over the subjects does not pass, as I have said, the limits of public utility.[49] The subjects then owe no account of their opinions to the Sovereign except as these opinions are important to the community. Now it matters greatly to the State that each Citizen have a Religion which makes him love his duties; but the dogmas of this Religion concern neither the State nor its members except as these dogmas relate to morality and to the duties that anyone who professes it is bound to fulfill toward others. Each may have in addition whatever opinions please him, without it being the Sovereign's business to know what they are. For as the Sovereign has no competence in the other world, whatever may be the destiny of the subjects in the life to come is not its affair, provided that they are good citizens in this life.

There is then a purely civil profession of faith, the articles of which it is the business of the Sovereign to settle, not precisely as dogmas of religion, but as sentiments of sociability, without which it is impossible to be a good Citizen or faithful subject.[50] Without being able to obligate anyone to believe them, it can banish from the State anyone who does not believe them; it can banish him, not as impious, but as unsociable, as incapable of sincerely loving the laws, and justice, and of sacrificing at need his life to his duty. If anyone, after publicly acknowledging these dogmas, behaves as though he does not believe them, he should be punished by death; he has committed the greatest of crimes, he has lied before the laws.

The dogmas of this civil religion ought to be simple, few in number, stated with precision, without explanations or commentaries. The existence of the Deity, powerful, intelligent, beneficent, prescient, and provident; the life to come, the happiness of the just, the punishment of the wicked, the sanctity of the social Contract and the Laws: these are the positive dogmas. As for the negative dogmas, I limit them to only one, intolerance: it belongs in the creeds we have excluded.

Those who distinguish civil intolerance from theological intolerance are, in my opinion, mistaken. These two kinds of intolerance are inseparable. It is impossible to live in peace with people whom one believes to be damned; to love them would be to hate God who punishes them: it is absolutely necessary that they be reclaimed or tormented. Wherever theological intolerance is admitted, it is impossible that it not have some civil effect,[51] and as soon as it has any, the Sovereign is no longer Sovereign, even in temporal matters; from then on the Priests are the true masters; the Kings are only their officers.

Now that there is no longer and can never be an exclusive national Religion, one should tolerate all those which tolerate the others, so far as their dogmas have nothing contrary to the duties of the Citizen. But whoever dares to say: *outside of the Church there is no salvation,* ought to be chased from the State, unless the State be the Church, and the Prince be the Pontiff. Such a dogma is good only in a Theocratic Government; in any other it is pernicious. The reason for which Henry IV embraced the Roman Religion ought to make any honest man, and especially any Prince who would know how to reason, leave it.

IX. Conclusion

After having set forth the true principles of political right and attempted to found the State on its base, it would remain to support it by its external relations; this would comprise the law of the peoples, commerce, the right of war and conquest, the public right, alliances, negotiations, treaties, etc. But all that forms a new object which is too vast for my limited scope; I should always have confined myself to what is nearer to me.

Notes

1. "Learned researches in public law are often nothing but the history of ancient abuses; and to devote much labor to studying them is misguided pertinacity" (*Treatise on the Interests of France in Relation to Her Neighbors,* by M. L. M. d'A.). That is exactly what Grotius did.
2. See a small treatise by Plutarch, entitled *That Brutes Employ Reason.*
3. The Romans, who understood and respected the rights of war better than any nation in the world, carried their scruples so far in this respect that no citizen was allowed to serve as a volunteer without enlisting expressly against the enemy, and by name against a specific enemy. A legion in which Cato the Younger made his first campaign under Popilius having been reformed, Cato the Elder wrote to Popilius that, if he consented to his son's continuing to serve under him, it was necessary that he take a new military oath, because, the first being annulled, he could no longer bear arms against the enemy. And Cato also wrote to his son to abstain from appearing in battle until he had taken this new oath. I know that it will be possible to urge against me the siege of Clusium and other particular cases; but I cite laws and customs. No nation has transgressed its laws less frequently than the Romans, and no nation has had laws so admirable.
4. The real meaning of this word has almost completely disappeared among the moderns; the majority take a town for a city, and a burgher for a citizen. They do not know that houses make the town, and that citizens make the city. This very mistake once cost the Carthaginians dear. I have never read of the title *Cives* being given to the subjects of a prince, not even in ancient times to the Macedonians, nor, in our days, to the English, although nearer liberty than all the rest. The French alone employ familiarly this name *citizen,* because they have no true idea of it, as we can see from their dictionaries; but for this fact, they would, by assuming it, commit the crime of contempt. The name, among them, expresses a virtue, not a right. When Bodin wanted to give an account of our citizens and burghers he made a gross blunder, mistaking the one for the other. M. d'Alembert has not erred in this, and, in his article *Geneva,* has clearly distinguished the four orders of men (even five, counting mere foreigners) which exist in our town, and of which only two compose the republic. No other French author I know of has understood the real meaning of the word *citizen.*
5. Under bad governments, this equality is only apparent and illusory; it serves only to keep the poor man in his misery and the rich in his usurpations. In fact, laws are always useful to those who possess

and injurious to those who have nothing; whence it follows that the social state is advantageous to men only so far as they all have something, and none of them has too much.

6. For a will to be general, it is not always necessary that it be unanimous, but it is necessary for all the voices to be counted; any formal exclusion destroys the generality.

7. "Every interest," says M. d'A. "has different principles. The accord of two private interests is formed by opposition to that of a third." He might have added that the accord of all interests is formed by opposition of it to each. Unless there were different interests, the common interest would scarcely be felt and would never meet with any obstacles; everything would go of itself, and politics would cease to be an art.

8. "It is true," says Machiavelli, "that some divisions harm the republic while others are beneficial to it; those that are injurious are accompanied by cabals and factions; those that assist it are maintained without cabals and factions. No founder of a republic can provide against enmities within it, and so he therefore ought to provide at least that there shall be cabals" (*History of Florence*, Book VII).

9. Attentive readers, I beg you, do not hasten to accuse me here of contradiction. I have not been able to avoid it in these terms, owing to the poverty of the language; but wait.

10. I do not understand by this word only an Aristocracy or a Democracy, but in general any government directed by the general will, which is the law. In order to be legitimate, the Government must not confound itself with the Sovereign, but should be its minister; then monarchy itself is a republic. This will be clarified in the next book.

11. A people only become famous when its legislation begins to decline. One does not know for how many centuries the institutions of Lycurgus conferred happiness on the Spartans before they came to be known by the rest of Greece.

12. Those who consider Calvin only as a theologian poorly understand the extent of his genius. The drafting of our wise Edicts, in which he played a large part, does him as much honor as his *Institutes*. Whatever revolution time may bring about in our cult, so long as the love of fatherland and of liberty will not be extinguished among us, the memory of that great man will not cease to be blessed.

13. "And truly," says Machiavelli, "there never was any lawgiver among any people who did not have recourse to God, for otherwise his laws would not have been accepted, for many benefits are known to a prudent man who does not have reasons evident enough to enable him to persuade others" (*Discourses on Titus Livy*, I, 11).

14. If, of two neighboring peoples, one is not able to get along without the other, this would be a very difficult situation for the first, and very dangerous for the second. Every wise nation, in such case, would be forced to quickly deliver the other from this dependence. The Republic of Thlascala, an enclave in the Mexican Empire, preferred to deny itself salt rather than buy it from Mexicans or even accept it gratuitously. The wise Thlascalans saw the trap hidden under that liberality. They kept themselves free; and this small State, enclosed within that great Empire, finally was the instrument of its ruin.

15. Do you wish, then, to give stability to the State? Bring the two extremes together as much as possible: allow neither excess opulence nor beggars. These two conditions, naturally inseparable, are equally fatal to the common good; from one springs the fomenters of tyranny, from the other the tyrants: it is always between them that the trading of public liberty transpires: one buys it, the other sells it.

16. Any branch of foreign commerce, says M. d'Argenson, diffuses a deceptive utility through the kingdom generally; it can only enrich a few individuals, even some towns, but the nation as a whole gains nothing, and the people are none the better for it.

17. It is for this reason that in Venice the name of *most Serene Prince* is given to the college, even when the Doge does not attend it.

18. The Palatine of Posen, father of the king of Poland, duke of Lorraine.

19. It is clear that the word *optimates*, among the ancients, meant not the best, but the most powerful.

20. It is very important to regulate by laws the form of the election of the magistrates, because leaving it to the will of the prince, one could not escape falling into hereditary Aristocracy, as happened in the Republics of *Venice* and *Berne*. Also, the first has long been a dissolved State; but the second maintains itself by the extreme wisdom of its Senate: it is a very honorable and very dangerous exception.

21. Machiavelli was an honest man and a good citizen; but, attached to the house of Medici, he was forced, during the oppression of his fatherland, to disguise his love for liberty. The mere choice of his execrable hero sufficiently manifests his secret intention; and the opposition of the maxims of his book *The Prince* and those of his *Discourses on Titus Livy* and his *History of Florence* shows that this profound political thinker has had until now only superficial or corrupt readers. The court of Rome has sternly prohibited his book; I certainly believe it: it is that court which he most clearly depicts.

22. Tacitus, *Histories* [I, 16].

23. The *Statesman*.

24. This does not contradict what I said before (Book Two, IX) on the inconveniences of large States; for if it were there a matter of the authority of the government over its members, it is here that of its power against the subjects. Its scattered members serve as points of support to it for acting upon the people at a distance, but it has no point of support for acting on its members themselves. Thus, in one case, the length of the lever in fact is weakness, and in the other case it is power.

25. One should judge on the same principle the centuries which merit preference regarding the prosperity of the human race. Those in which literature and art were seen to flourish have been too much admired, without the secret object of their cultivation being penetrated, without their fatal consequences being considered. *"Idque apud imperitos humanitas vocabatur, quum pars servitutis esset"* (Tacitus, *Agricola*, XXI). [Fools bestowed the word *humanity* on what was already the beginning of slavery.] Shall we never detect in the maxims of books the gross self-interest which makes the Authors speak? No, whatever they may say, when, despite its brilliancy, a country is being depopulated, it is untrue that all goes well, and it is not enough that a poet should have an income of one hundred thousand livres for his epoch to be the best of all. The apparent repose and tranquillity of the chiefs must be regarded less than the welfare of entire nations and especially of the most populous states. Hail lays waste a few cantons, but it rarely causes scarcity. Riots and civil wars greatly startle the chiefs, but they do not produce the real misfortunes of peoples, who may even relax while it is being disputed who shall tyrannize over them. It is from their permanent condition that their real prosperity or calamities arise; when all remains crushed under the yoke, it is then that everything withers; it is then that the chiefs destroy them at their leisure: *"ubi solitudinem faciunt, pacem appellant"* (Tacitus, *Agricola*, XXXI). ["where they create solitude (when they have made the country into desert), they say that peace regins"]. When the quarrels of the great agitated the kingdom of France, and the coadjutor of Paris carried a dagger in his pocket to the *Parlement*, that did not prevent the French people from living happily and in large numbers in free and honorable ease. Ancient Greece flourished in the midst of the most cruel wars; blood flowed there in streams, and the whole country was covered with men. It seemed, said Machiavelli, that amid murders, proscriptions, and civil wars our republic became more powerful; the virtue of its citizens, their customary conduct, their independence, were more effective in strengthening it than all its dissensions had been in weakening it. A little agitation give strength to men's souls, and what truly makes the species prosper is not so much peace as liberty.

26. The slow formation and the progress of the republic of Venice in its lagoons offers a notable example of this succession; and it is indeed astounding that, after more than twelve hundred years, the Venetians seem to be still in only the second stage, which began with the *Serrar di Consiglio* [Closing of the Council] in 1198. As for the ancient Dukes, for whom they are reproached, whatever the *Squittinio della libertà veneta* may say, it is proved that they were not their sovereigns.

One will not fail to cite as an objection the Roman Republic as having pursued a completely opposite development, passing from Monarchy to Aristocracy, and from Aristocracy to Democracy. I am far from thinking about it in this way.

The first establishment of Romulus was a mixed Government, which promptly degenerated into Despotism. For some particular reason, the State perished before its time, as we see a newly born baby die before reaching manhood. The expulsion of the Tarquins was the true epoch of the birth of the Republic. But it did not assume a stable form at first, because it only completed half of the work by not abolishing the patriciate. For in this manner, the hereditary Aristocracy, which is the worst of the legitimate administrations, remaining in conflict with the Democracy, always an uncertain and fluctuating form of government, was not settled until the establishment of the Tribunes, as Machiavelli has proved; only then was there a true Government and a true Democracy. In fact, the people were at the time not only Sovereign, but also magistrate and judge; the Senate was only a subordinate tribunal to temper or concentrate the Government; and the consuls themselves, although patricians as well as first magistrates and absolute generals in war, were in Rome only the presidents of the people.

From that time on, the Government was also seen to follow its natural propensity and tend strongly to Aristocracy. The Patriciate abolishing itself, as it were, the Aristocracy was no longer in the body of Patricians as it was in Venice and Genoa, but in the body of the Senate, composed of patricians and plebeians, and also in the body of the Tribunes when they began to usurp active power; for words make no difference to things, and when the people has chiefs who govern for it, it is always an Aristocracy.

From the abuses of the Aristocracy were born the civil wars and the triumvirate. Sulla, Julius Caesar, Augustus, became in fact true Monarchs; and finally, under the despotism of Tiberius, the State was dissolved. Roman history does not then refute my principle: it confirms it.

27. *"Omnes enim et habentur et dicuntur tyranni, qui potestate utuntur perpetua in ea civitate quae libertate usa est"* (Cornelius Nepos, *Life of Militades,* VIII). [All are considered and called tyrants, who hold perpetual power in a State that has had liberty.] It is true that Aristotle (*Nicomachean Ethics*, VIII, 10) distinguishes the tyrant from the king, in that the first governs for his own benefit and the latter solely for the benefit of his subjects; but beyond the fact that generally all the Greek authors have taken the word *Tyrant* in another sense, as appears most clearly in Xenophon's *Hiero*, it would seem to follow from Aristotle's distinction that since the beginning of the world not a single King has yet existed.

28. Nearly in the sense that one gives this name in the Parliament of England. The resemblance of these offices would have placed the Consuls and the Tribunes in conflict, even if all jurisdiction had been suspended.

29. To adopt in cold countries the luxury and indolence of the Orientals is to wish to be given their chains; it is to submit to them more necessarily than they do.

30. It is this which I intended to do in a sequel to this work, when in considering foreign relations I would come to confederations. This is a wholly new matter and one where the principles have still to be established.

31. It being well understood that one does not leave in order to evade his duty and avoid serving the fatherland at the moment it has need of us. Flight then would be criminal and punishable; it would no longer be withdrawal, but desertion.

32. This should always be understood for a free State; for otherwise family, goods, need for asylum, necessity, or violence can detain an inhabitant in the country despite himself; and then his residence alone no longer supposes his consent to the contract or to the violations of the contract.

33. In Genoa, one reads in front of the prisons and on the chains of those condemned to the galleys the word *Libertas*. This application of the motto is fine and just. It is only the malefactors in all states who prevent the Citizen from being free. In a country where all such people would be in the Galleys, one would enjoy the most perfect liberty.

34. The name *Rome*, which presumably comes from *Romulus*, is Greek and means *force*; the name *Numa* is also Greek, and means *law*. What is the likelihood that the first two kings of that town bore in advance names so well related to what they did?

35. Ramnenses.

36. Tatienses.

37. Luceres.

38. I say to the *Campus Martius* because it was there that the *comitia* were assembled by *centuriae:* in the two other forms, the people were assembled in the *Forum* or elsewhere; and then the *capite censi* had as much influence and authority as the first Citizens.

39. This *Centuria,* thus chosen by lot, was called *proerogativa,* because its suffrage was demanded first; hence came the word *prerogative.*

40. *Custodes, distributores, regatores suffragiorum.* [Inspectors, canvassers, clerks of the voting.]

41. This nomination was made at night and in secret, as if it were shameful to place a man above the laws.

42. He could not satisfy himself in this by proposing a dictator, not being able to name himself and not being sure that his colleague would nominate him.

43. I only indicate in this chapter that which I have treated in much greater length in the *Letter to M. d'Alembert.*

44. They were from another island, but the delicacy of our language prohibits naming it on this occasion.

45. *"Nonne ea quae possidet Chamos deus tuus, tibi jure debentur?"* Such is the text of the Vulgate. Father de Carrierés has translated it: "Do you not believe you have a right to possess what belongs to Chamos your God?" I am ignorant of the force of the Hebrew text; but I see that, in the Vulgate, Jephthah positively recognized the right of the god Chamos, and that the French translator weakens this acknowledgment by an "according to you" which is not in the Latin.

46. There is strongest evidence that the war of the Phoenicians, called a sacred war, was not a war of religion. Its object was to punish sacrileges, not to subdue nonbelievers.

47. It is well to note that it is not so much formal assemblies, as those in France, which tie the clergy into a body, but the communion of the Churches. Communion and excommunication are the social pact of the clergy, a pact by which they will always be the master of peoples and of kings. All the priests who communicate together are fellow citizens, be they from the two ends of the world. This invention is a masterpiece of politics. There is nothing similar among pagan priests, thus they have never constituted a body of clergy.

48. Note, among others, in a letter from Grotius to his brother on April 11, 1643, what this learned man approved and what he blamed in the book *De Cive*. It is true that, inclined to indulgence, he seems to pardon the author for his good points for the sake of the bad ones: but everyone is not so lenient.

49. "In the republic," says M. d'A., "each is perfectly free in that which does not injure others." That is the invariable limit; it cannot be more exactly stated. I have not been able to refuse myself the pleasure of sometimes citing this manuscript, although it is not known to the public, in order to render honor to the memory of an illustrious and respectable man, who had preserved even in the ministry the heart of a true citizen, and upright and sound views on the government of his country.

50. Caesar, pleading for Catiline, tried to establish the dogma of the mortality of the soul; Cato and Cicero, in order to refute him, did not amuse themselves philosophizing: they contented themselves with showing that Caesar spoke as a bad citizen and advanced a doctrine pernicious to the state. Indeed, it was that which the Roman Senate had to judge, and not a question of theology.

51. Marriage, for example, being a civil contract has civil effects, without which it is impossible that society subsist. Let us suppose then that a clergy ascribe to itself alone the right of performing this act, a right it must necessarily usurp in every intolerant religion; then is it not clear that in asserting the authority of the Church it renders empty that of the prince, who will have no other subjects than those the clergy is willing to give him? Master of which people can or cannot marry, according to whether they hold or do not hold such or such doctrine, according to whether they admit or reject such or such a formula, according to whether they are more or less devoted to it, is it not clear that by behaving prudently and keeping firm, the Church alone will dispose of inheritances, offices, citizens, and the State itself, which cannot subsist when composed only of bastards? But, it will be said, men will appeal against such abuses; they will adjourn, decree, seize temporal holdings. What a pity! The clergy, however little it may have, I do not say of courage but of good sense, will let this be done and go its way; it will quietly permit appealing, adjourning, decreeing, seizing, and will end by being the master. It is not, it seems to me, a great sacrifice to abandon a part when one is sure of taking possession of the whole.

DAVID HUME

The most far-ranging of early modern British philosophers, David Hume (1711–1776) was born in Edinburgh, Scotland, to a modestly prosperous, small landholding family. When David was two years old, his father died. By the age of 12, Hume was studying at Edinburgh University. Between 1734 and 1737, he drafted what was to become his first, and now widely regarded as his greatest, work: *A Treatise of Human Nature*. Two volumes ("Of the Understanding" and "Of the Passions") appeared in 1739 when Hume was 28, and the final volume ("Of Morals") in 1740. But Hume was greatly disappointed in the lack of attention to the work, later claiming it "fell deadborn from the press." His *Essays, Moral, Political, and Literary*, including "Of Parties in General," were published in 1741 to 1742. Over the years, Hume revised these essays and added others such as "Of the Original Contract" (1748).

Eventually, Hume reworked the ideas he had first propounded in the *Treatise* in the form of shorter, and he believed, better-written, pieces, including *An Enquiry Concerning the Principles of Morals* (1751), which by Hume's estimation was his "incomparably" finest work. Hume published his six-volume *The History of England* between 1754 and 1762, and it became the standard reference for nearly a century. The autobiographical *My Own Life*, and other essays, including "Of the Origin of Government," were published posthumously in 1777. The controversial *Dialogues Concerning Natural Religion* finally appeared in 1779.

Between 1763 and 1766, Hume lived in Paris, where he became a celebrated intellectual companion to famous French Enlightenment figures. In 1766, he brought Rousseau back with him to England. Having tried to help the emotionally unstable Rousseau flee from persecution in Switzerland, Hume was stunned when Rousseau accused him of treachery.

For the last two years of his life, Hume endured illness. In late summer of 1776, he received a visit from Adam Smith, one of his closest friends. Encouraged to see Hume in good spirits, Smith "could not help entertaining some faint hopes" of a recovery. "Your hopes are groundless," the older philosopher replied. Hume "then diverted himself" by depicting an imaginary dialogue with the mythological boatman who conveys people to the netherworld. Asking for more time to correct his works and to see how the public would then receive them, Hume envisioned himself bluntly rebuffed: "There will be no end to such excuses. . . . Get into the boat this instant, you lazy, loitering rogue." Hume died soon thereafter.

For Hume, it would be a myth to suppose that people were originally "savage" loners, devoid of trust, in desperate need of government to save them from ceaseless strife. Human beings are naturally motivated, not only by self-concern but by various benevolent inclinations as well: self-sacrificing devotion to their children, pity for the unfortunate, and a measure of genuine kindness towards friends and immediate neighbors. Indeed, the basic unit of human life is the family, and individuals "are trained up by their parents to some rule of conduct and behavior" (*Enquiry Concerning the Principles of*

Morals [EPM], III, I). Moreover, families can live in society with one another even without government, so long as they are few in number and have comparatively modest material aspirations. Society enables people to combine their powers, benefit from division of labor and specialization of tasks, and reduce one another's exposure to "fortune and accidents" (*Treatise, III, II, II*).

But as naturally sociable as people are, society is not immune to serious destabilizing influences. In Hume's view, conflict over "external" goods is especially threatening to the peace and stability of society. This is because of their "easy and loose transition." To secure social peace, Hume urges that there be "stability of possessions" and transference only by "consent" (rather than by force and fraud). But these lofty ideas need to be filled in by more specific guidelines. Such norms—regulating the allocation and use of external goods (property) and fixing the conditions under which people can regard one another as obligated (contract)—are the rules of what Hume calls "justice."

If people were wholly and unlimitedly benevolent, *or* if resources were infinitely abundant, there would be no need for justice. But benevolence, though real, is limited. Moreover, material resources, though generally sufficient for everyone's survival, are not so abundant as to permit everyone to take as much as might seem desirable. So in the circumstances that normally prevail, a scheme of justice is socially necessary.

But which rules of justice can best serve the purpose of securing social peace? Hume had earlier rejected the proposal that each particular good be assigned to whichever individual would make the best personal, or public, use of it. In the *Enquiry*, he considers, and rejects for much the same reasons, a different proposal: Distribute material goods in proportion to each person's moral merit. Because different people can so easily interpret such rules in such different (and typically self-serving) ways, their adoption is more likely to exacerbate than to resolve conflict. The rule "to each equally" seems more promising but suffers from at least two fatal defects: (1) Without differential rewards, society will become far less productive; so strict equality causes more poverty than it alleviates. (2) In the face of inevitable differences in talent, industry, and care, people will wind up with unequal possessions, no matter how equal the initial distribution. To identify and correct such departures from equality, there will have to be frequent interference in people's lives; authority so extensive "must soon degenerate into tyranny."

How then *should* "stability of possession" be achieved? For Hume, appropriate rules of property must be clear and relatively easy to apply. Familiar property rules (e.g., title belongs to the current possessor, or the first possessor, or the longest possessor) are useful, if somewhat conventional, stipulations. In the *Enquiry*, Hume suggests that some considerations are less arbitrarily connected to the support of society. "Who cannot see," he asks, that "whatever is produced or improved by a man's art or industry ought, for ever, to be secured to him"? This rule is evidently not a mere product of the "finer turns of the imagination"; but in contrast with Locke, neither is it grounded in some natural right to the products of one's own labor. The point is simply to encourage productive work.

In the *Treatise*, Hume had described schemes of justice as a "remedy" that "is not deriv'd from nature, but from artifice." That justice is an "artificial" virtue might mislead someone into thinking that it is not really a virtue at all, or not to be taken as seriously as other virtues. In an appendix to the *Enquiry*, Hume clarified himself with the aid of a brilliant metaphor: Acts of benevolence may be compared to stones placed one by one on a wall—*each* stone makes a positive difference. While acts of justice are like stones in a vaulted arch—there must be an overall scheme or design to which *most* of the stones conform if the structure is to stand at all.

Granted the social need for rules of justice, is it also necessary to have government enforce the rules? If human beings were perfectly just, government might be unnecessary. But people are typically led astray by the tendency to prefer what is "near" to what is "remote." Thus, self-love typically favors present satisfaction over long-term well-being; and benevolent concern is liable to confine itself to a small circle of friends and neighbors without regard to the larger public interest. Hume argues that although we cannot change our natures, we can "change our circumstances" by setting up appropriate forms of government. Under a wisely arranged political system, the protection of the public interest is made to be in the *personal* interest of those individuals who hold positions of public authority.

From the discussion thus far one might suppose that government's role is limited to keeping the peace, upholding property rights, and enforcing contracts. But in the *Treatise*, Hume clearly associates government with more ambitious public policies as well. As society grows bigger, Hume sees government playing an essential role in coordinating large-scale cooperative endeavors and punishing individuals who try to free-ride on the efforts of others. "Thus bridges are built; harbours open'd; ramparts rais'd; canals form'd; fleets equip'd; and armies disciplin'd; every where by the care of government, which tho' compos'd of men subject to all human infirmities, becomes, by one of the finest and most subtle inventions imaginable . . . in some measure, exempte from all these infirmities" (*Treatise*, III, II, VII).

Hume's initial enthusiasm about this "finest" invention would be tempered in his later writings as he came to recognize more fully the sources of conflict among citizens, and the potential for negligence and corruption in public officials. Thus in "Of Parties in General," Hume laments the ways in which division along theological, ideological, and even racial lines can be at least as destabilizing as conflicts of economic interest. And in such essays as "Of the Origin of Government," Hume grapples with the objection that even "the magistrate himself may often be negligent, or partial, or unjust in his administration." He then indicates two ways of modifying the design of political institutions that could help keep public officials in the service of public, not merely private, interests. Echoing Montesquieu and anticipating Madison, he suggests that there must be "a partition of powers among several members." In addition, those who have a share of the power, thus divided, "must act by general and equal laws, that are previously known." Thus the "invention" of government is actually "finest" when power is so distributed as to create checks and balances against abuse and corruption, and when it is exercised not in an arbitrary or highly discretionary way but according to the principles of rule by law.

Even if we grant that government is a good idea, when is a particular claim to governmental authority legitimate? And when, if ever, is resistance to putative authority justifiable? Hume argues against the claim that a government is legitimate *only* if originally formed by an agreement between itself and the people. For one thing, if we try to ground the duty of allegiance to government in the duty to do what we have given our word to do, there is still the problem of explaining how and why we are bound to keep our word. And it would be circular to respond "because we have given our word to do so." In the end, we can only justify the duty of keeping our word by appealing to what is necessary to the support of society. But this same consideration will *directly* ground our duty of allegiance to government as well. So appealing to contract is an inadequately roundabout way of getting to the ultimate source of political legitimacy and dutiful allegiance.

In opposition to the doctrine of absolute monarchy, Hume recognizes that legitimate authority is not unconditional. To be sure, the "total dissolution" of government is one of the most "terrible" things that can happen. Yet there have been rulers whose tyranny was so contrary to fundamental human interests that it would be a "perversion of common sense" to condemn those who took up arms against them. Hence, "Where a civil law is so perverse as to cross all the interests of society, it loses all its authority, and men judge by the ideas of natural justice, which are conformable to those interests" (*EPM*, III, II, n. 3). Hume obviously believes that such circumstances are rare, but hardly impossible; and that while violent revolution is not to be contemplated lightly, it is sometimes the only viable remaining course. The philosophical point is that disobedience is not to be based on an appeal either to natural rights or to some fictitious original contract, whose terms one alleges to have been violated. Rather, if the justification for having and obeying government is the "general interests and necessities of society," then disobedience can be justified on the same ground. But is there some precise way to know when it is right to resist authority? No. For "'tis certainly impossible for the laws, or even for philosophy, to establish any *particular* rules, by which we may know when resistance is lawful; and decide all controversies which may arise on that subject" (*Treatise*, III, II, X).

Such reluctance to produce an exact formula for political life is characteristic of Hume's approach. In his last political essay, "Of the Origin of Government," for example, we are told that in the contest "between Authority and Liberty. . . neither of them can absolutely prevail," but we are not told very much more about the exact scope of either. When doing political theory, why paint with so broad a brush? For Hume there is a deeper reason, reflecting his own empiricist temperament: "I am apt . . . to entertain a suspicion, that the world is still too young to fix many general truths in politics" ("Of Civil Liberty"). Though we must try to find a sensible middle ground between unacceptable extremes, there is a limit to the precision we can sensibly expect to achieve without greater historical experience and deeper understanding of human nature.

For excellent general studies of Hume's thought, see Norman Kemp Smith's *The Philosophy of David Hume* (London: Macmillan, 1964); Barry Stroud's *Hume* (London: Routledge & Kegan Paul, 1977); and Annette C. Baier's *A Progress of Sentiments: Reflections on Hume's Treatise* (Cambridge: Harvard University Press, 1991).

A lucid introduction to Hume's ethical thought, helpfully placing it in the context of the British moral tradition from which it evolved, is *Hume's Moral Theory* (London: Routledge & Kegan Paul, 1980) by J. L. Mackie. Hume's ideas about value, virtue, and justice are carefully examined in light of their psychological underpinnings by Pall S. Ardal in *Passion and Value in Hume's Treatise* (Edinburgh: Edinburgh University Press, 1989).

Looking at Hume from the perspective of contemporary political philosophy, Brian Barry provides a searching analysis in *Theories of Justice* (Berkeley:

University of California Press, 1989, Vol. 1, Chap. 4). In *Hume's Philosophy of Common Life* (Chicago: University of Chicago Press, 1984), Donald W. Livingston interprets Hume as a political conservative. The opposite case for regarding Hume as a would-be reformer of established political practices is ably argued by John B. Stewart in *Opinion and Reform in Hume's Political Philosophy* (Princeton: Princeton University Press, 1992). Frederick G. Whelan's *Order and Artifice in Hume's Political Philosophy* (Princeton: Princeton University Press, 1985) shows how Hume treats history and experience as sources of political value.

A. K.

AN ENQUIRY CONCERNING THE PRINCIPLES OF MORALS

Section III

PART I

Of Justice

That Justice is useful to society, and consequently that *part* of its merit, at least, must arise from that consideration, it would be a superfluous undertaking to prove. That public utility is the *sole* origin of justice, and that reflections on the beneficial consequences of this virtue are the *sole* foundation of its merit; this proposition, being more curious and important, will better deserve our examination and enquiry.

Let us suppose, that nature has bestowed on the human race such profuse *abundance* of all *external* conveniences, that, without any uncertainty in the event, without any care or industry on our part, every individual finds himself fully provided with whatever his most voracious appetites can want, or luxurious imagination wish or desire. His natural beauty, we shall suppose, surpasses all acquired ornaments: The perpetual clemency of the seasons renders useless all cloaths or covering: The raw herbage affords him the most delicious fare; the clear fountain, the richest beverage. No laborious occupation required: No tillage: No navigation. Music, poetry, and contemplation, form his sole business: Conversation, mirth, and friendship his sole amusement.

It seems evident, that, in such a happy state, every other social virtue would flourish, and receive tenfold encrease; but the cautious, jealous virtue of justice would never once have been dreamed of. For what purpose make a partition of goods, where every one has already more than enough? Why give rise to property, where there cannot possibly be any injury? Why call this object *mine*, when, upon the seizing of it by another, I need but stretch out my hand to possess myself of what is equally valuable? Justice, in that case, being totally USELESS, would be an idle ceremonial, and could never possibly have place in the catalogue of virtues.

We see, even in the present necessitous condition of mankind, that, wherever any benefit is bestowed by nature in an unlimited abundance, we leave it always in common among the whole human race, and make no subdivisions of right and property. Water and air, though the most necessary of all objects, are not challenged as the property of individuals; nor can any man commit injustice by the most lavish use and enjoyment of these blessings. In fertile extensive countries, with few inhabitants, land is regarded on the same footing. And no topic is so much insisted on by those, who defend the liberty of the seas, as the unexhausted use of them in navigation. Were the advantages, procured by navigation, as inexhaustible, these reasoners had never had any adversaries to refute; nor had any claims ever been advanced of a separate, exclusive dominion over the ocean.

It may happen, in some countries, at some periods, that there be established a property in water, none in land; [1] If the latter be in greater abundance than can be used by the inhabitants, and the former be found, with difficulty, and in very small quantities.

Again; suppose, that, though the necessities of human race continue the same as at present, yet the mind is so enlarged, and so replete with friendship and generosity, that every man has the utmost tenderness for every man, and feels no more concern for his own interest than for that of his fellows: It seems evident, that the USE of justice would, in this case, be suspended by such an extensive benevolence; nor would the divisions and barriers of property and obligation have ever been thought of. Why should I bind another, by a deed or promise, to do me any good office, when I know that he is already prompted, by the strongest inclination, to seek my happiness, and would, of himself, perform the desired service; except the hurt, he thereby receives, be greater than the benefit accruing to me? in which case, he knows, that, from my innate humanity and friendship, I should be the first to oppose myself to his imprudent generosity. Why raise land-marks between my neighbour's field and mine, when my heart has made no division between our interests; but shares all his joys and sorrows with the same force and vivacity as if originally my own? Every man, upon this supposition, being a second self to another, would trust all his interests to the discretion of every man; without jealousy, without partition, without distinction. And the whole human race would form only one family; where all would lie in common, and be used freely, without regard to property; but cautiously too, with as entire regard to the necessities of each individual, as if our own interests were most intimately concerned.

In the present disposition of the human heart, it would, perhaps, be difficult to find compleat instances of such enlarged affections; but still we may observe, that the case of families approaches towards it; and the stronger the mutual benevolence is among the individuals, the nearer it approaches; till all distinction of property be, in a great measure, lost and confounded among them. Between married persons, the cement of friendship is by the laws supposed so strong as to abolish all division of possessions: and has often, in reality, the force ascribed to it. And it is observable, that, during the ardour of new enthusiasms, when every principle is inflamed into extravagance, the community of goods has frequently been attempted: and nothing but experience of its inconveniencies, from the returning or disguised selfishness of men, could make the imprudent fanatics adopt anew the ideas of justice and of separate property. So true is it, that this virtue derives its existence entirely from its necessary *use* to the intercourse and social state of mankind.

To make this truth more evident, let us reverse the foregoing suppositions; and carrying every thing to the opposite extreme, consider what would be the effect of these new situations. Suppose a society to fall into such want of all common necessaries, that the utmost frugality and industry cannot preserve the greater number from perishing, and the whole from extreme misery: It will readily, I believe, be admitted, that the strict laws of justice are suspended, in such a pressing emergence, and give place to the stronger motives of necessity and self-preservation. Is it any crime, after a shipwreck, to seize whatever means or instrument of safety one can lay hold of, without regard to former limitations of property? Or if a city besieged were perishing with hunger; can we imagine, that men will see any means of preservation before them, and lose their lives, from a scrupulous regard to what, in other situations, would be the rules of equity and justice? The USE and TENDENCY of that virtue is to procure happiness and security, by preserving order in society: But where the society is ready to perish from extreme necessity, no greater evil can be dreaded from violence and injustice; and every man may now provide for himself by all the means, which prudence can dictate, or humanity permit. The public, even in less urgent necessities, opens granaries, without the consent of proprietors; as justly supposing, that the authority of magistracy may, consistent with equity, extend so far: But were any number of men to assemble, without the tye of laws or civil jurisdiction; would an equal partition of bread in a famine, though effected by power and even violence, be regarded as criminal or injurious?

Suppose likewise, that it should be a virtuous man's fate to fall into the society of ruffians, remote from the protection of laws and government; what conduct must he embrace in that melancholy situation? He sees such a desperate rapaciousness prevail; such a disregard to equity, such contempt of order, such stupid blindness to future consequences, as must immediately have the most tragical conclusion, and must terminate in destruction to the greater number, and in a total dissolution of society to the rest. He, mean while, can have no other expedient than to arm himself, to whomever the sword he seizes, or the buckler, may belong: To make provision of all means of defence and security: And his particular regard to justice being no longer of USE to his own safety or that of others, he must consult the dictates of self preservation alone, without concern for those who no longer merit his care and attention.

When any man, even in political society, renders himself, by his crimes, obnoxious to the public, he is punished by the laws in his goods and person; that is, the ordinary rules of justice are, with regard to him, suspended for a moment, and it becomes equitable to inflict on him, for the *benefit* of society, what, otherwise, he could not suffer without wrong or injury.

The rage and violence of public war; what is it but a suspension of justice among the warring parties, who perceive, that this virtue is now no longer of any *use* or advantage to them? The laws of war, which then succeed to those of equity and justice, are rules calculated for the *advantage* and *utility* of that particular state, in which men are now placed. And were a civilized nation engaged with barbarians, who observed no rules even of war; the former must also suspend their observance of them, where they no longer serve to any purpose; and must render every action or rencounter as bloody and pernicious as possible to the first aggressors.

Thus, the rules of equity or justice depend entirely on the particular state and condition, in which men are placed, and owe their origin and existence to that UTILITY, which results to the public from their strict and regular observance. Reverse, in any considerable circumstance, the condition of men: Produce extreme abundance or extreme necessity: Implant in the human breast perfect moderation and humanity, or perfect rapaciousness and malice: By rendering justice totally *useless,* you thereby totally destroy its essence, and suspend its obligation upon mankind.

The common situation of society is a medium amidst all these extremes. We are naturally partial to ourselves, and to our friends; but are capable of learning the advantage resulting from a more equitable conduct. Few enjoyments are given us from the open and liberal hand of nature; but by art, labour, and industry, we can extract them in great abundance. Hence the ideas of property become necessary in all civil society: Hence justice derives its usefulness to the public: And hence alone arises its merit and moral obligation.

These conclusions are so natural and obvious, that they have not escaped even the poets, in their descriptions of the felicity, attending the golden age or the reign of SATURN. The seasons, in that first period of nature, were so temperate, if we credit these agreeable fictions, that there was no necessity for men to provide themselves with cloaths and houses, as a security against the violence of heat and cold: The rivers flowed with wine and milk: The oaks yielded honey; and nature spontaneously produced her greatest delicacies. Nor were these the chief advantages of that happy age. Tempests were not alone removed from nature; but those more furious tempests were unknown to human breasts, which now cause such uproar, and engender such confusion. Avarice, ambition, cruelty, selfishness, were never heard of: Cordial affection, compassion, sympathy, were the only movements with which the mind was yet acquainted. Even the punctilious distinction of *mine* and *thine* was banished from among that happy race of mortals, and carried with it the very notion of property and obligation, justice and injustice.

This *poetical* fiction of the *golden age* is, in some respects, of a piece with the *philosophical* fiction of the *state of nature*; only that the former is represented as the most charming and most peaceable condition, which can possibly be imagined; whereas the latter is painted out as a state of mutual war and violence, attended with the most extreme necessity. On the first origin of mankind, we are told, their ignorance and savage nature were so prevalent, that they could give no mutual trust, but must each depend upon himself, and his own force or cunning for protection and security. No law was heard of: No rule of justice known: No distinction of property regarded: Power was the only measure of right; and a perpetual war of all against all was the result of men's untamed selfishness and barbarity.[2]

Whether such a condition of human nature could ever exist, or if it did, could continue so long as to merit the appellation of a *state*, may justly be doubted. Men are necessarily born in a family-society, at least; and are trained up by their parents to some rule of conduct and behaviour. But this must be admitted, that, if such a state of mutual war and violence was ever real, the suspension of all laws of justice, from their absolute inutility, is a necessary and infallible consequence.

The more we vary our views of human life, and the newer and more unusual the lights are, in which we survey it, the more shall we be convinced, that the origin here assigned for the virtue of justice is real and satisfactory.

Were there a species of creatures, intermingled with men, which, though rational, were possessed of such inferior strength, both of body and mind, that they were incapable of all resistance, and could never, upon the highest provocation, make us feel the effects of their resentment; the necessary consequence, I think, is, that we should be bound, by the laws of humanity, to give gentle usage to these creatures, but should not, properly speaking, lie under any restraint of justice with regard to them, nor could they possess any right or property, exclusive of such arbitrary lords. Our intercourse with them could not be called society, which supposes a degree of equality; but absolute command on the one side, and servile obedience on the other. Whatever we covet, they must instantly resign: Our permission is the only tenure, by which they hold their possessions: Our compassion and kindness the only check, by which they curb our lawless will: And as no inconvenience ever results from the exercise of a power, so firmly established in nature, the restraints of justice and property, being totally *useless*, would never have place in so unequal a confederacy.

This is plainly the situation of men, with regard to animals; and how far these may be said to possess reason, leave it to others to determine. The great superiority of civilized

EUROPEANS above barbarous INDIANS, tempted us to imagine ourselves on the same footing with regard to them, and made us throw off all restraints of justice, and even of
humanity, in our treatment of them. In many nations, the female sex are reduced to like
slavery, and are rendered incapable of all property, in opposition to their lordly masters.
But though the males, when united, have, in all countries, bodily force sufficient to maintain this severe tyranny; yet such are the insinuation, address, and charms of their fair
companions, that women are commonly able to break the confederacy, and share with the
other sex in all the rights and privileges of society.

Were the human species so framed by nature as that each individual possessed within
himself every faculty, requisite both for his own preservation and for the propagation of
his kind: Were all society and intercourse cut off between man and man, by the primary
intention of the supreme Creator: It seems evident, that so solitary a being would be as
much incapable of justice, as of social discourse and conversation. Where mutual regards
and forbearance serve to no manner of purpose, they would never direct the conduct of any
reasonable man. The headlong course of the passions would be checked by no reflection on
future consequences. And as each man is here supposed to love himself alone, and to
depend only on himself and his own activity for safety and happiness, he would, on every
occasion to the utmost of his power, challenge the preference above every other being, to
none of which he is bound by any ties, either of nature or of interest.

But suppose the conjunction of the sexes to be established in nature, a family immediately arises; and particular rules being found requisite for its subsistence, these are immediately embraced; though without comprehending the rest of mankind within their
prescriptions. Suppose, that several families unite together into one society, which is
totally disjoined from all others, the rules, which preserve peace and order, enlarge themselves to the utmost extent of that society; but becoming then entirely useless, lose their
force when carried one step farther. But again suppose, that several distinct societies
maintain a kind of intercourse for mutual convenience and advantage, the boundaries
of justice still grow larger, in proportion to the largeness of men's views, and the force of
their mutual connexions. History, experience, reason sufficiently instruct us in this natural
progress of human sentiments, and in the gradual enlargement of our regards to justice,
in proportion as we become acquainted with the extensive utility of that virtue.

PART II

If we examine the *particular* laws, by which justice is directed, and property determined;
we shall still be presented with the same conclusion. The good of mankind is the only
object of all these laws and regulations. Not only it is requisite, for the peace and interest
of society, that men's possessions should be separated; but the rules, which we follow,
in making the separation, are such as can best be contrived to serve farther the interests
of society.

We shall suppose, that a creature, possessed of reason, but unacquainted with human
nature, deliberates with himself what RULES of justice or property would best promote
public interest, and establish peace and security among mankind: His most obvious
thought would be, to assign the largest possessions to the most extensive virtue, and give
every one the power of doing good, proportioned to his inclination. In a perfect theocracy,
where a being, infinitely intelligent, governs by particular volitions, this rule would certainly have place, and might serve to the wisest purposes: But were mankind to execute
such a law; so great is the uncertainty of merit, both from its natural obscurity, and from

the self-conceit of each individual, that no determinate rule of conduct would ever result from it; and the total dissolution of society must be the immediate consequence. Fanatics may suppose, *that dominion is founded on grace*, and *that saints alone inherit the earth*; but the civil magistrate very justly puts these sublime theorists on the same footing with common robbers, and teaches them by the severest discipline, that a rule, which, in speculation, may seem the most advantageous to society, may yet be found, in practice, totally pernicious and destructive.

That there were *religious* fanatics of this kind in ENGLAND, during the civil wars, we learn from history; though it is probable, that the obvious *tendency* of these principles excited such horror in mankind, as soon obliged the dangerous enthusiasts to renounce, or at least conceal their tenets. Perhaps, the *levellers*, who claimed an equal distribution of property, were a kind of *political* fanatics, which arose from the religious species, and more openly avowed their pretensions; as carrying a more plausible appearance, of being practicable in themselves, as well as useful to human society.

It must, indeed, be confessed, that nature is so liberal to mankind, that, were all her presents equally divided among the species, and improved by art and industry, every individual would enjoy all the necessaries, and even most of the comforts of life; nor would ever be liable to any ills, but such as might accidentally arise from the sickly frame and constitution of his body. It must also be confessed, that, wherever we depart from this equality, we rob the poor of more satisfaction than we add to the rich, and that the slight gratification of a frivolous vanity, in one individual, frequently costs more than bread to many families, and even provinces. It may appear withal, that the rule of equality, as it would be highly *useful*, is not altogether *impracticable*; but has taken place, at least in an imperfect degree, in some republics; particularly that of SPARTA; where it was attended, it is said, with the most beneficial consequences. Not to mention, that the AGRARIAN laws, so frequently claimed in ROME, and carried into execution in many GREEK cities, proceeded, all of them, from a general idea of the utility of this principle.

But historians, and even common sense, may inform us, that, however specious these ideas of *perfect* equality may seem, they are really, at bottom, *impracticable*; and were they not so, would be extremely *pernicious* to human society. Render possessions ever so equal, men's different degrees of art, care, and industry will immediately break that equality. Or if you check these virtues, you reduce society to the most extreme indigence; and instead of preventing want and beggary in a few, render it unavoidable to the whole community. The most rigorous inquisition too is requisite to watch every inequality on its first appearance; and the most severe jurisdiction, to punish and redress it. But besides, that so much authority must soon degenerate into tyranny, and be exerted with great partialities; who can possibly be possessed of it, in such a situation as is here supposed? Perfect equality of possessions, destroying all subordination, weakens extremely the authority of magistracy, and must reduce all power nearly to a level, as well as property.

We may conclude, therefore, that, in order to establish laws for the regulation of property, we must be acquainted with the nature and situation of man; must reject appearances, which may be false, though specious; and must search for those rules, which are, on the whole, most *useful* and *beneficial*. Vulgar sense and slight experience are sufficient for this purpose; where men give not way to too selfish avidity, or too extensive enthusiasm.

Who sees not, for instance, that whatever is produced or improved by a man's art or industry ought, for ever, to be secured to him, in order to give encouragement to such *useful* habits and accomplishments? That the property ought also to descend to children and relations, for the same *useful* purpose? That it may be alienated by consent, in order to beget that commerce and intercourse, which is so *beneficial* to human society? And that all contracts and promises ought carefully to be fulfilled, in order to secure mutual trust and confidence, by which the general *interest* of mankind is so much promoted?

Examine the writers on the laws of nature; and you will always find, that, whatever principles they set out with, they are sure to terminate here at last, and to assign, as the ultimate reason for every rule which they establish, the convenience and necessities of mankind. A concession thus extorted, in opposition to systems, has more authority, than if it had been made in prosecution of them.

What other reason, indeed, could writers ever give, why this must be *mine* and that *yours*; since uninstructed nature, surely, never made any such distinction? The objects, which receive those appellations, are, of themselves, foreign to us; they are totally disjoined and separated from us; and nothing but the general interests of society can form the connexion.

Sometimes, the interests of society may require a rule of justice in a particular case; but may not determine any particular rule, among several, which are all equally beneficial. In that case, the slightest *analogies* are laid hold of, in order to prevent that indifference and ambiguity, which would be the source of perpetual dissention. Thus possession alone, and first possession, is supposed to convey prosperity, where no body else has any preceding claim and pretension. Many of the reasonings of lawyers are of this analogical nature, and depend on very slight connexions of the imagination.

Does any one scruple, in extraordinary cases, to violate all regard to the private property of individuals, and sacrifice to public interest a distinction, which had been established for the sake of that interest? The safety of the people is the supreme law: All other particular laws are subordinate to it, and dependent on it: And if, in the *common* course of things, they be followed and regarded; it is only because the public safety and interest *commonly* demand so equal and impartial an administration.

Sometimes both *utility* and *analogy* fail, and leave the laws of justice in total uncertainty. Thus, it is highly requisite, that prescription or long possession should convey property; but what number of days or months or years should be sufficient for that purpose, it is impossible for reason alone to determine. *Civil laws* here supply the place of the natural *code*, and assign different terms for prescription, according to the different *utilities*, proposed by the legislator. Bills of exchange and promissory notes, by the laws of most countries, prescribe sooner than bonds, and mortgages, and contracts of a more formal nature.

In general, we may observe, that all questions of property are subordinate to authority of civil laws, which extend, restrain, modify, and alter the rules of natural justice, according to the particular *convenience* of each community. The laws have, or ought to have, a constant reference to the constitution of government, the manners, the climate, the religion, the commerce, the situation of each society. A late author of genius, as well as learning, has prosecuted this subject at large, and has established, from these principles, a system of political knowledge, which abounds in ingenious and brilliant thoughts, and is not wanting in solidity.[3]

What is a man's property? Any thing, which it is lawful for him, and for him alone, to use. *But what rule have we, by which we can distinguish these objects?* Here we must have recourse to statutes, customs, precedents, analogies, and a hundred other circumstances; some of which are constant and inflexible, some variable and arbitrary. But the ultimate point, in which they all professedly terminate, is, the interest and happiness of human society. Where this enters not into consideration, nothing can appear more whimsical, unnatural, and even superstitious, than all or most of the laws of justice and of property.

Those, who ridicule vulgar superstitions, and expose the folly of particular regards to meats, days, places, postures, apparel, have an easy task; while they consider all the qualities and relations of the objects, and discover no adequate cause for that affection or antipathy, veneration or horror, which have so mighty an influence over a considerable part of mankind. A SYRIAN would have starved rather than taste pigeon; an EGYPTIAN would not have approached bacon: But if these species of food be examined by the senses of sight, smell, or taste, or scrutinized by the sciences of chymistry, medicine, or physics; no difference is ever found between them and any other species, nor can that precise circumstance be pitched on, which may afford a just foundation for the religious passion. A fowl on Thursday is lawful food; on Friday abominable: Eggs, in this house, and in this diocese, are permitted during Lent; a hundred paces farther, to eat them is a damnable sin. This earth or building, yesterday was profane; to-day, by the muttering of certain words, it has become holy and sacred. Such reflections as these, in the mouth of a philosopher, one may safely say, are too obvious to have any influence; because they must always, to every man, occur at first sight; and where they prevail not, of themselves, they are surely obstructed by education, prejudice, and passion, not by ignorance or mistake.

It may appear to a careless view, or rather a too abstracted reflection, that there enters a like superstition into all the sentiments of justice; and that, if a man expose its object, or what we call property, to the same scrutiny of sense and science, he will not, by the most accurate enquiry, find any foundation for the difference made by moral sentiment. I may lawfully nourish myself from this tree; but the fruit of another of the same species, ten paces off, it is criminal for me to touch. Had I worne this apparel an hour ago, I had merited the severest punishment; but a man, by pronouncing a few magical syllables, has now rendered it fit for my use and service. Were this house placed in the neighbouring territory, it had been immoral for me to dwell in it; but being built on this side of the river, it is subject to a different municipal law, and, by its becoming mine, I incur no blame or censure. The same species of reasoning, it may be thought, which so successfully exposes superstition, is also applicable to justice; nor is it possible, in the one case more than in the other, to point out, in the object, that precise quality or circumstance, which is the foundation of the sentiment.

But there is this material difference between *superstition* and *justice,* that the former is frivolous, useless, and burdensome; the latter is absolutely requisite to the well-being of mankind and existence of society. When we abstract from this circumstance (for it is too apparent ever to be overlooked) it must be confessed, that all regards to right and property, seem entirely without foundation, as much as the grossest and most vulgar superstition. Were the interests of society nowise concerned, it is as unintelligible, why another's articulating certain sounds implying consent, should change the nature of my actions with regard to a particular object, as why the reciting of a liturgy by a priest, in a certain habit and posture, should dedicate a heap of brick and timber, and render it, thenceforth and for ever, sacred.[4]

These reflections are far from weakening the obligations of justice, or diminishing any thing from the most sacred attention to property. On the contrary, such sentiments must acquire new force from the present reasoning. For what stronger foundation can be desired or conceived for any duty, than to observe, that human society, or even human nature could not subsist, without the establishment of it; and will still arrive at greater degrees of happiness and perfection, the more inviolable the regard is, which is paid to that duty?

The dilemma seems obvious: As justice evidently tends to promote public utility and to support civil society, the sentiment of justice is either derived from our reflecting on that tendency, or like hunger, thirst, and other appetites, resentment, love of life, attachment to offspring, and other passions, arises from a simple original instinct in the human breast, which nature has implanted for like salutary purposes. If the latter be the case, it follows, that property, which is the object of justice, is also distinguished by a simple, original instinct, and is not ascertained by any argument or reflection. But who is there that ever heard of such an instinct? Or is this a subject, in which new discoveries can be made? We may as well attempt to discover, in the body, new senses, which had before escaped the observation of all mankind.

But farther, though it seems a very simple proposition to say, that nature, by an instinctive sentiment, distinguishes property, yet in reality we shall find, that there are required for that purpose ten thousand different instincts, and these employed about objects of the greatest intricacy and nicest discernment. For when a definition of *property* is required, that relation is found to resolve itself into any possession acquired by occupation, by industry, by prescription, by inheritance, by contract, &c. Can we think, that nature, by an original instinct, instructs us in all these methods of acquisition?

These words too, inheritance and contract, stand for ideas infinitely complicated; and to define them exactly, a hundred volumes of laws, and a thousand volumes of commentators, have not been found sufficient. Does nature, whose instincts in men are simple, embrace such complicated and artificial objects, and create a rational creature, without trusting any thing to the operation of his reason?

But even though all this were admitted, it would not be satisfactory. Positive laws can certainly transfer property. Is it by another original instinct, that we recognize the authority of kings and senates, and mark all the boundaries of their jurisdiction? Judges too, even though their sentence be erroneous and illegal, must be allowed, for the sake of peace and order, to have decisive authority, and ultimately to determine property. Have we original, innate ideas of praetors and chancellors and juries? Who sees not, that all these institutions arise merely from the necessities of human society?

All birds of the same species, in every age and country, build their nests alike: In this we see the force of instinct. Men, in different times and places, frame their houses differently: Here we perceive the influence of reason and custom. A like inference may be drawn from comparing the instinct of generation and the institution of property.

How great soever the variety of municipal laws, it must be confessed, that their chief out-lines pretty regularly concur; because the purposes, to which they tend, are every where exactly similar. In like manner, all houses have a roof and walls, windows and chimneys; though diversified in their shape, figure, and materials. The purposes of the latter, directed to the conveniences of human life, discover not more plainly their origin from reason and reflection, than do those of the former, which point all to a like end.

I need not mention the variations, which all the rules of property receive from the finer turns and connexions of the imagination, and from the subtilties and abstractions of law-topics and reasonings. There is no possibility of reconciling this observation to the notion of original instincts.

What alone will beget a doubt concerning the theory, on which I insist, is the influence of education and acquired habits, by which we are so accustomed to blame injustice, that we are not, in every instance, conscious of any immediate reflection on the pernicious consequences of it. The views the most familiar to us are apt, for that very reason, to escape us; and what we have very frequently performed from certain motives, we are apt likewise to continue mechanically, without recalling, on every occasion, the reflections, which first determined us. The convenience, or rather necessity, which leads to justice, is so universal, and every where points so much to the same rules, that the habit takes place in all societies: and it is not without some scrutiny, that we are able to ascertain its true origin. The matter, however, is not so obscure, but that, even in common life, we have, every moment, recourse to the principle of public utility, and ask, *What must become of the world, if such practices prevail? How could society subsist under such disorders?* Were the distinction or separation of possessions entirely useless, can any one conceive, that it ever should have obtained in society?

Thus we seem, upon the whole, to have attained a knowledge of the force of that principle here insisted on, and can determine what degree of esteem or moral approbation may result from reflections on public interest and utility. The necessity of justice to the support of society is the SOLE foundation of that virtue; and since no moral excellence is more highly esteemed, we may conclude, that this circumstance of usefulness has, in general, the strongest energy, and most entire command over our sentiments. It must, therefore, be the source of a considerable part of the merit ascribed to humanity, benevolence, friendship, public spirit, and other social virtues of that stamp; as it is the SOLE source of the moral approbation paid to fidelity, justice, veracity, integrity, and those other estimable and useful qualities and principles. It is entirely agreeable to the rules of philosophy, and even of common reason; where any principle has been found to have a great force and energy in one instance, to ascribe to it a like energy in all similar instances. This indeed is NEWTON's chief rule of philosophizing.[5]

Notes

1. GENESIS, Chapter xiii. and xxi.

2. This fiction of a state of nature, as a state of war, was not first started by Mr. Hobbes, as is commonly imagined. Plato endeavours to refute an hypothesis very like it in the second, third, and fourth books *de republica*. Cicero, on the contrary, supposes it certain and universally acknowledged in the following passage. "*Quis enim vestrûm, judices, ignorat, ita naturam rerum tulisse, ut quodam tempore homines, nondum neque naturali, neque civili jure descripto, fusi per agros, ac dispersi vagarentur tantumque haberent quantum manu ac viribus, per caedem ac vulnera, aut eripere, aut retinere potuissent? Qui igitur primi virtute et consilio praestanti extiterunt, ii perspecto genere humanae docilitatis atque ingenii, dissipatos, unum in locum congregarunt, eosque ex feritate illa ad justitiam ac mansuetudinem transduxerunt. Tum res ad communem utilitatem, quas publicas appellamus, tum conventicula hominum, quae postea civitates nominatae sunt, tum domicilia conjuncta, quas urbes dicamus, invento et divino et humano jure, moenibus sepserunt. Atque inter hanc vitam, perpolitam humanitate, et illam immanem, nihil tam interest quam Jus atque Vis. Horum utro uti nolimus, altero est utendum. Vim volumus extingui? Jus valeat necesse est, id est, judicia, quibus omne jus continetur. Judicia displicent, aut nulla sunt? Vis dominetur necesse est. Haec vident omnes.*" Pro Sext. 1. 42. [Can there be anyone among you, jurors, who does not know that nature had brought things about so that, at one time, before natural or civil law was discerned, scattered and landless men roamed the countryside, men who had just as much as they had been able to snatch by force and defend by bloodshed and violence? Then those men who first stood out for their exceptional virtue and judgment, having recognized men's natural talent for training and ingenuity, brought the nomads together and led them from savagery into justice and mildness. And after human and divine law were discovered, then matters were arranged for the general good, which we call public affairs, then common meeting places, which were later called communities, and eventually homes were brought within walls, which we call cities. And so there is no more difference between this orderly civilized life, and that former savagery, than there is between Law and Violence. If we prefer not to use one of these, we must use the other. Do we want violence eradicated? Then law must prevail, i.e., the verdicts in which all law is contained. Are the verdicts disliked or ignored? Then violence must prevail. Everyone understands this.]

3. The author of *L'Esprit des Loix.* This illustrious writer, however, sets out with a different theory, and supposes all right to be founded on certain *rapports* or relations; which is a system, that in my opinion, never will be with true philosophy. Father Malebranche, as far as I can learn, was the first that started this abstract theory of morals, which was afterwards adopted by Cudworth, Clarke, and others; and as it excludes all sentiment, and pretends to found every thing on reason, it has not wanted followers in this philosophic age. See Section I. and Appendix I. With regard to justice, the virtue

here treated of, the inference against this theory seems short and conclusive. Property is allowed to be dependent on civil laws; civil laws are allowed to have no other object, but the interest of society: This therefore must be allowed to be the sole foundation of property and justice. Not to mention, that our obligation itself to obey the magistrate and his laws is founded on nothing but the interests of society.

If the ideas of justice, sometimes, do not follow the dispositions of civil law: we shall find, that these cases, instead of objections, are confirmations of the theory delivered above. Where a civil law is so perverse as to cross all the interests of society, it loses all its authority, and men judge by the ideas of natural justice, which are conformable to those interests. Sometimes also civil laws, for useful purposes, require a ceremony or form to any deed; and where that is wanting, their decrees run contrary to the usual tenour of justice; but one who takes advantage of such chicanes, is not commonly regarded as an honest man. Thus, the interests of society require, that contracts be fulfilled; and there is not a more material article either of natural or civil justice: But the omission of a trifling circumstance will often, by law, invalidate a contract, *in foro humano*, but not *in foro conscientiae*, as divines express themselves. In these cases, the magistrate is supposed only to withdraw his power of enforcing the right, not to have altered the right. Where his intention extends to the right, and is conformable to the interests of society; it never fails to alter the right; a clear proof of the origin of justice and of property, as assigned above.

4. It is evident, that the will or consent alone never transfers property, nor causes the obligation of a promise (for the same reasoning extends to both) but the will must be expressed by words or signs, in order to impose a tye upon any man. The expression being once brought in as subservient to the will, soon becomes the principal part of the promise; nor will a man be less bound by his word, though he secretly give a different direction to his intention, and withhold the assent of his mind. But though the expression makes, on most occasions, the whole of the promise, yet it does not always so; and one who should make use of any expression, of which he knows not the meaning, and which he uses without any sense of the consequences, would not certainly be bound by it. Nay, though he know its meaning, yet if he use it in jest only, and with such signs as evidently show, that he has no serious intention of binding himself, he would not lie under any obligation of performance; but it is necessary, that the words be a perfect expression of the will, without any contrary signs. Nay, even this we must not carry so far as to imagine, that one, whom, by our quickness of understanding, we conjecture, from certain signs, to have an intention of deceiving us, is not bound by his expression or verbal promise, if we accept of it; but must limit this conclusion to those cases where the signs are of a different nature from those of deceit. All these contradictions are easily accounted for, if justice arise entirely from its usefulness to society; but will never be explained on any other hypothesis.

It is remarkable, that the moral decisions of the *Jesuits* and other relaxed casuists, were commonly formed in prosecution of some such subtilties of reasoning as are here pointed out, and proceed as much from the habit of scholastic refinement as from any corruption of the heart, if we may follow the authority of Mons. Bayle. See his Dictionary, article Loyola. And why has the indignation of mankind risen so high against these casuists, but because every one perceived, that human society could not subsist were such practices authorized, and that morals must always be handled with a view to public interest, more than philosophical regularity? If the secret direction of the intention, said every man of sense, could invalidate a contract; where is our security? And yet a metaphysical schoolman might think, that where an intention was supposed to be requisite, if that intention really had not place, no consequence ought to follow, and no obligation be imposed. The casuistical subtilties may not be greater than the subtilties of lawyers, hinted at above, but as the former are pernicious, and the latter *innocent* and even *necessary*, this is the reason of the very different reception they meet with from the world.

It is a doctrine of the church of Rome, that the priest, by a secret direction of his intention, can invalidate any sacrament. This position is derived from a strict and regular prosecution of the obvious truth, that empty words alone, without any meaning or intention in the speaker, can never be attended with any effect. If the same conclusion be not admitted in reasonings concerning civil contracts, where the affair is allowed to be of so much less consequence than the eternal salvation of thousands, it proceeds entirely from men's sense of the danger and inconvenience of the doctrine in the former case: And we may thence observe, that however positive, arrogant, and dogmatical any superstition may appear, it never can convey any thorough persuasion of the reality of its objects, or put them, in any degree, on a balance with the common incidents of life, which we learn from daily observation and experimental reasoning.

5. Principia, lib. iii.

OF PARTIES IN GENERAL

Of all men, that distinguish themselves by memorable *atchievements*, the first place of honour seems due to Legislators and founders of states, who transmit a system of laws and institutions to secure the peace, happiness, and liberty of future generations. The influence of useful inventions in the arts and sciences may, perhaps, extend farther than that of wise laws, whose effects are limited both in time and place; but the benefit arising from the former, is not so sensible as that which results from the latter. Speculative sciences do, indeed, improve the mind; but this advantage reaches only to a few persons, who have leisure to apply themselves to them. And as to practical arts, which encrease the commodities and enjoyments of life, it is well known, that men's happiness consists not so much in an abundance of these, as in the peace and security with which they possess them; and those blessings can only be derived from good government. Not to mention, that general virtue and good morals in a state, which are so requisite to happiness, can never arise from the most refined precepts of philosophy, or even the severest injunctions of religion; but must proceed entirely from the virtuous education of youth, the effect of wise laws and institutions. I must, therefore, presume to differ from Lord Bacon in this particular, and must regard antiquity as somewhat unjust in its distribution of honours, when it made gods of all the inventors of useful arts, such as Ceres Bacchus Aesculapius; and dignify legislators, such as Romulus and Theseus, only with the appellation of demigods and heroes.

As much as legislators and founders of states ought to be honoured and respected among men, as much ought the founders of sects and factions to be detested and hated; because the influence of faction is directly contrary to that of laws. Factions subvert government, render laws impotent, and beget the fiercest animosities among men of the same nation, who ought to give mutual assistance and protection to each other. And what should render the founders of parties more odious is, the difficulty of extirpating these weeds, when once they have taken root in any state. They naturally propagate themselves for many centuries, and seldom end but by the total dissolution of that government, in which they are sown. They are, besides, plants which grow most plentifully in the richest soil; and though absolute governments be not wholly free from them, it must be confessed, that they rise more easily, and propagate themselves faster in free governments, where they always infect the legislature itself, which alone could be able, by the steady application of rewards and punishments, to eradicate them.

Factions may be divided into Personal and Real that is, into factions, founded on personal friendship or animosity among such as compose the contending parties, and into those founded on some real difference of sentiment or interest. The reason of this distinction is obvious; though I must acknowledge, that parties are seldom found pure and unmixed, either of the one kind or the other. It is not often seen, that a government divides into factions, where there is no difference in the views of the constituent members, either real or apparent, trivial or material: And in those factions, which are founded on the most real and most material difference, there is always observed a great deal of personal animosity or affection. But notwithstanding this mixture, a party may be denominated either personal or real, according to that principle which is predominant, and is found to have the greatest influence.

Personal factions arise most easily in small republics. Every domestic quarrel, there, becomes an affair of state. Love, vanity, emulation, any passion, as well as ambition and resentment, begets public division. The Neri and Bianchi of Florence the Fregosi and Adorni of Genoa, the Colonesi and Orsini of modern Rome, were parties of this kind.

Men have such a propensity to divide into personal factions, that the smallest appearance of real difference will produce them. What can be imagined more trivial than the difference between one colour of livery and another in horse races? Yet this difference begat two most inveterate factions in the Greek empire, the Prasini and Veneti who never suspended their animosities, till they ruined that unhappy government.

We find in the Roman history a remarkable dissension between two tribes, the Pollia and Papiria, which continued for the space of near three hundred years, and discovered itself in their suffrages at every election of magistrates.[1]

This faction was the more remarkable, as it could continue for so long a tract of time; even though it did not spread itself, nor draw any of the other tribes into a share of the quarrel. If mankind had not a strong propensity to such divisions, the indifference of the rest of the community must have suppressed this foolish animosity, that had not any aliment of new benefits and injuries, of general sympathy and antipathy, which never fail to take place, when the whole state is rent into two equal factions.

Nothing is more usual than to see parties, which have begun upon a real difference, continue even after that difference is lost. When men are once inlisted on opposite sides, they contract an affection to the persons with whom they are united, and an animosity against their antagonists: And these passions they often transmit to their posterity. The real difference between Guelf and Ghibbelline was long lost in Italy, before these factions were extinguished. The Guelfs adhered to the pope, the Ghibbellines to the emperor; yet the family of Sforza, who were in alliance with the emperor, though they were Guelfs, being expelled from Milan by the king of France assisted by Jacomo Trivulzio and the Ghibbellines, the pope concurred with the latter, and they formed leagues with the pope against the emperor.[2]

The civil wars which arose some few years ago in Morocco, between the *blacks* and *whites*, merely on account of their complexion, are founded on a pleasant difference. We laugh at them; but I believe, were things rightly examined, we afford much more occasion of ridicule to the Moors. For, what are all the wars of religion, which have prevailed in this polite and knowing part of the world? They are certainly more absurd than the Moorish civil wars. The difference of complexion is a sensible and a real difference: But the controversy about an article of faith, which is utterly absurd and unintelligible, is not a difference in sentiment, but in a few phrases and expressions, which one party accepts of, without understanding them; and the other refuses in the same manner.

Real factions may be divided into those from *interest*, from *principle* and from *affection*. Of all factions, the first are the most reasonable, and the most excusable. Where two orders of men, such as the nobles and people, have a distinct authority in a government, not very accurately balanced and modelled, they naturally follow a distinct interest; nor can we reasonably expect a different conduct, considering that degree of selfishness implanted in human nature. It requires great skill in a legislator to prevent such parties; and many philosophers are of opinion, that this secret, like the *grand elixir*, or *perpetual motion*, may amuse men in theory, but can never possibly be reduced to practice. In despotic governments, indeed, factions often do not appear; but they are not the less real; or rather, they are more real and more pernicious, upon that very account. The distinct orders of men, nobles and people, soldiers and merchants, have all a distinct interest; but the more powerful oppresses the weaker with impunity, and without resistance; which begets a seeming tranquillity in such governments.

There has been an attempt in England to divide the *landed* and *trading* part of the nation; but without success. The interests of these two bodies are not really distinct, and never[3] will be so, till our public debts encrease to such a degree, as to become altogether oppressive and intolerable.

Parties from *principle*, especially abstract speculative principle, are known only to modern times, and are, perhaps, the most extraordinary and unaccountable *phoenomenon*, that has yet appeared in human affairs. Where different principles beget a contrariety of conduct, which is the case with all different political principles, the matter may be more easily explained. A man, who esteems the true right of government to lie in one man, or one family, cannot easily agree with his fellow-citizen, who thinks that another man or family is possessed of this right. Each naturally wishes that right may take place, according to his own notions of it. But where the difference of principle is attended with no contrariety of action, but every one may follow his own way, without interfering with his neighbour, as happens in all religious controversies; what madness, what fury can beget such unhappy and such fatal divisions?

Two men travelling on the highway, the one east, the other west, can easily pass each other, if the way be broad enough: But two men, reasoning upon opposite principles of religion, cannot so easily pass, without shocking; though one should think, that the way were also, in that case, sufficiently broad, and that each might proceed, without interruption, in his own course. But such is the nature of the human mind, that it always lays hold on every mind that approaches it; and as it is wonderfully fortified by an unanimity of sentiments, so is it shocked and disturbed by any contrariety. Hence the eagerness, which most people discover in a dispute; and hence their impatience of opposition, even in the most speculative and indifferent opinions.

This principle, however frivolous it may appear, seems to have been the origin of all religious wars and divisions. But as this principle is universal in human nature, its effects would not have been confined to one age, and to one sect of religion, did it not there concur with other more accidental causes, which raise it to such a height, as to produce the greatest misery and devastation. Most religions of the ancient world arose in the unknown ages of government, when men were as yet barbarous and uninstructed, and the prince, as well as peasant, was disposed to receive, with implicit faith, every pious tale or fiction, which was offered him. The magistrate embraced the religion of the people, and entering cordially into the care of sacred matters, naturally acquired an authority in them, and united the ecclesiastical with the civil power. But the *Christian* religion arising, while principles directly opposite to it were firmly established in the polite part of the world, who despised the nation that first broached this novelty; no wonder, that, in such circumstances, it was but little countenanced by the civil magistrate, and that the priesthood was allowed to engross all the authority in the new sect. So bad a use did they make of this power, even in those early times, that the primitive persecutions may, perhaps, *in part*,[3] be ascribed to the violence instilled by them into their followers. And the same principles of priestly government continuing, after Christianity became the established religion, they have engendered a spirit of persecution, which has ever since been the poison of human society, and the source of the most inveterate factions in every government. Such divisions, therefore, on the part of the people, may justly be esteemed factions of *principle;* but, on the part of the priests, who are the prime movers, they are really factions of *interest.*

There is another cause (beside the authority of the priests, and the separation of the ecclesiastical and civil powers) which has contributed to render Christendom the scene of religious wars and divisions. Religions, that arise in ages totally ignorant and barbarous, consist mostly of traditional tales and fictions, which may be different in every sect, without being contrary to each other; and even when they are contrary, every one adheres to the tradition of his own sect, without much reasoning or disputation. But as philosophy was widely spread over the world, at the time when Christianity arose, the teachers of the new sect were obliged to form a system of speculative opinions; to divide, with some accuracy, their articles of faith; and to explain, comment, confute, and defend with all the subtilty of argument and science. Hence naturally arose keenness in dispute, when the Christian religion came to be split into new divisions and heresies: And this keenness assisted the priests in their policy, of begetting a mutual hatred and antipathy among their deluded followers. Sects of philosophy, in the ancient world, were more zealous than parties of religion; but in modern times, parties of religion are more furious and enraged than the most cruel factions that ever arose from interest and ambition.

I have mentioned parties from *affection* as a kind of *real* parties, beside those from *interest* and *principle.* By parties from affection, I understand those which are founded on the different attachments of men towards particular families and persons, whom they desire to rule over them. These factions are often very violent; though, I must own, it may seem unaccountable, that men should attach themselves so strongly to persons, with whom they are no wise acquainted, whom perhaps they never saw, and from whom they never received, nor can ever hope for any favour. Yet this we often find to be the case, and even with men, who, on other occasions, discover no great generosity of spirit, nor are found to be easily transported by friendship beyond their own interest. We are apt to think the relation between us and our sovereign very close and intimate. The splendour of majesty and power bestows an importance on the fortunes even of a single person. And when a man's good-nature does not give him this imaginary interest, his ill-nature will, from spite and opposition to persons whose sentiments are different from his own.

Notes

1. As this fact has not been much observed by antiquaries or politicians, I shall deliver it in the words of the Roman historian. *Populus* Tusculanus *cum conjugibus ac liberis* Romam *venit: Ea multitudo, veste mutata, & specie reorum tribus circuit, genibus se omnium advolvens. Plus itaque misericordia ad paenoeveniam impetrandam, quam causa ad crimen purgandum valuit. Tribus omnes praeter* Polliam, *antiquarunt legem. Polliae sententia fuit, puberes verberatos necari, liberos conjugesque sub corona lege belli venire: Memoriamque ejus irae* Tusculanis *in paenoe tam atrocis auctores mansisse ad patris aetatem constat; nec quemquam fere ex* Pollia *tribu candidatum* Papiram *ferre solitam,* T. LIVII, lib. 8. 37. The Castelani and Nicolloti are two mobbish factions in Venice, who frequently box together, and then lay aside their quarrels presently. [*The History of Rome,* trans. by D. Spillan *et al.,* 4 vols. (London: G. Bell & Sons, Ltd., 1911), Vol. I, p. 555 (8.37): "The Tusculans, with their wives and children, came to Rome. The whole party in mourning habits, like persons under accusation, went round the tribes, throwing themselves at the feet of the citizens. The compassion thus excited operated more effectually toward procuring them pardon, than all their arguments did towards clearing them of guilt. Every one of the tribes, except the Pollian, negatived the proposition. The sentence of the Pollian tribe, was that the grown-up males should be beaten and put to death, and their wives and children sold by auction, according to the rules of war. It appears that the resentment which rose against the advisers of so rigorous a measure, was retained in memory by the Tusculans down to the age of our fathers; and that hardly any candidate of the Pollian tribe could, ever since, gain the votes of the Papirian."]

2. Lewis XII.

3. I say, *in part*; For it is a vulgar error to imagine, that the ancients were as great friends to toleration as the English or Dutch are at present. The laws against external superstition, amongst the Romans, were as ancient as the time of the twelve tables; and the Jews as well as Christians were sometimes punished by them; though, in general, these laws were not rigorously executed. Immediately after the conquest of Gaul, they forbad all but the natives to be initiated into the religion of the Druids; and this was a kind of persecution. In about a century after this conquest, the emperor, Claudius, quite abolished that superstition by penal laws; which would have been a very grievous persecution, if the imitation of the Roman manners had not, before-hand, weaned the Gauls from their ancient prejudices. Suetonius *in vita* Claudii. Pliny ascribes the abolition of the Druidical superstitions to Tiberius, probably because that emperor had taken some steps towards restraining them (lib. xxx. cap. i.). This is an instance of the usual caution and moderation of the Romans in such cases; and very different from their violent and sanguinary method of treating the *Christians.* Hence we may entertain a suspicion, that those furious persecutions of *Christianity* were in some measure owing to the imprudent zeal and bigotry of the first propagators of that sect; and Ecclesiastical history affords us many reasons to confirm this suspicion.

OF THE ORIGINAL CONTRACT

As no party, in the present age, can well support itself, without a philosophical or speculative system of principles, annexed to its political or practical one; we accordingly find, that each of the factions, into which this nation is divided, has reared up a fabric of the former kind, in order to protect and cover that scheme of actions, which it pursues.

The people being commonly very rude builders, especially in this speculative way, and more especially still, when actuated by party-zeal; it is natural to imagine, that their workmanship must be a little unshapely, and discover evident marks of that violence and hurry, in which it was raised. The one party, by tracing up government to the Deity, endeavour to render it so sacred and inviolate, that it must be little less than sacrilege, however tyrannical it may become, to touch or invade it, in the smallest article. The other party, by founding government altogether on the consent of the People, suppose that there is a kind of *original contract,* by which the subjects have tacitly reserved the power of resisting their sovereign, whenever they find themselves aggrieved by that authority, with which they have, for certain purposes, voluntarily entrusted him. These are the speculative principles of the two parties; and these too are the practical consequences deduced from them.

I shall venture to affirm, *That both these* systems *of speculative principles are just; though not in the sense, intended by the parties*: And, *That both the* schemes *of practical consequences are prudent; though not in the extremes, to which each party, in opposition to the other, has commonly endeavoured to carry them.*

That the Deity is the ultimate author of all government will never be denied by any, who admit a general providence, and allow, that all events in the universe are conducted by an uniform plan, and directed to wise purposes. As it is impossible for the human race to subsist, at least in any comfortable or secure state, without the protection of government; this institution must certainly have been intended by that beneficent Being, who means the good of all his creatures: And as it has universally, in fact, taken place, in all countries, and all ages; we may conclude, with still greater certainty, that it was intended by that omniscient Being, who can never be deceived by any event or operation. But since he gave rise to it, not by any particular or miraculous interposition, but by his concealed and universal efficacy; a sovereign cannot, properly speaking, be called his vice-gerent, in any other sense than every power or force, being derived from him, may be said to act by his commission. Whatever actually happens is comprehended in the general plan or intention of providence; nor has the greatest and most lawful prince any more reason, upon that account, to plead a peculiar sacredness or inviolable authority, than an inferior magistrate, or even an usurper, or even a robber and a pyrate. The same divine superintendant, who, for wise purposes, invested a Titus or a Trajan with authority, did also, for purposes, no doubt, equally wise, though unknown, bestow power on a Borgia or an Angria. The same causes, which gave rise to the sovereign power in every state, established likewise every petty jurisdiction in it, and every limited authority. A constable, therefore, no less than a king, acts by a divine commission, and possesses an indefeasible right.

When we consider how nearly equal all men are in their bodily force, and even in their mental powers and faculties, till cultivated by education; we must necessarily allow, that nothing but their own consent could, at first, associate them together, and subject them to any authority. The people, if we trace government to its first origin in the woods and deserts, are the source of all power and jurisdiction, and voluntarily, for the sake of peace and order, abandoned their native liberty, and received laws from their equal and companion. The conditions, upon which they were willing to submit, were either expressed, or were so clear and obvious, that it might well be esteemed superfluous to express them. If this, then, be meant by the *original contract,* it cannot be denied, that all government is, at first, founded on a contract, and that the most ancient rude combinations of mankind were formed chiefly by that principle. In vain, are we asked in what records this charter of our liberties is registered. It was not written on parchment, nor yet on leaves or barks of trees. It preceded the use of writing and all the other civilized arts of life. But we trace it plainly in the nature of man, and in the equality, or something approaching equality, which we find in all the individuals of that species. The force, which now prevails, and which is founded on fleets and armies, is plainly political, and derived from authority, the effect of established government. A man's natural force consists only in the vigour of his limbs, and the firmness of his courage; which could never subject multitudes to the command of one. Nothing but their own consent, and their sense of the advantages resulting from peace and order, could have had that influence.

Yet even this consent was long very imperfect, and could not be the basis of a regular administration. The chieftain, who had probably acquired his influence during the continuance of war, ruled more by persuasion than command; and till he could employ force to reduce the refractory and disobedient, the society could scarcely be said to have attained a state of civil government. No compact or agreement, it is evident, was expressly formed for general submission; an idea far beyond the comprehension of savages: Each exertion of authority in the chieftain must have been particular, and called forth by the present exigencies of the case: The sensible utility, resulting from his interposition, made these exertions become daily more frequent; and their frequency gradually produced an habitual, and, if you please to call it so, a voluntary, and therefore precarious, acquiescence in the people.

But philosophers, who have embraced a party (if that be not a contradiction in terms) are not contented with these concessions. They assert, not only that government in its earliest infancy arose from consent or rather the voluntary acquiescence of the people; but also, that, even at present, when it has attained full maturity, it rests on no other foundation. They affirm, that all men are still born equal, and owe allegiance to no prince or government, unless bound by the obligation and sanction of a *promise*. And as no man, without some equivalent, would forego the advantages of his native liberty, and subject himself to the will of another; this promise is always understood to be conditional, and imposes on him no obligation, unless he meet with justice and protection from his sovereign. These advantages the sovereign promises him in return; and if he fail in the execution, he has broken, on his part, the articles of engagement, and has thereby freed his subject from all obligations to allegiance. Such, according to these philosophers, is the foundation of authority in every government; and such the right of resistance, possessed by every subject.

But would these reasoners look abroad into the world, they would meet with nothing that, in the least, corresponds to their ideas, or can warrant so refined and philosophical a system. On the contrary, we find, every where, princes, who claim their subjects as their property, and assert their independent right of sovereignty, from conquest or succession. We find also, every where, subjects, who acknowledge this right in their prince, and suppose themselves born under obligations of obedience to a certain sovereign, as much as under the ties of reverence and duty to certain parents. These connexions are always conceived to be equally independent of our consent, in Persia and China; in France and Spain; and even in Holland and England, wherever the doctrines above-mentioned have not been carefully inculcated. Obedience or subjection becomes so familiar, that most men never make any enquiry about its origin or cause, more than about the principle of gravity, resistance, or the most universal laws of nature. Or if curiosity ever move them; as soon as they learn, that they themselves and their ancestors have, for several ages, or from time immemorial, been subject to such a form of government or such a family; they immediately acquiesce, and acknowledge their obligation to allegiance. Were you to preach, in most parts of the world, that political connexions are founded altogether on voluntary consent or a mutual promise, the magistrate would soon imprison you, as seditious, for loosening the ties of obedience; if your friends did not before shut you up as delirious, for advancing such absurdities. It is strange, that an act of the mind, which every individual is supposed to have formed, and after he came to the use of reason too, otherwise it could have no authority; that this act, I say, should be so much unknown to all of them, that, over the face of the whole earth, there scarcely remain any traces or memory of it.

But the contract, on which government is founded, is said to be the *original contract*; and consequently may be supposed too old to fall under the knowledge of the present generation. If the agreement, by which savage men first associated and conjoined their force, be here meant, this is acknowledged to be real; but being so ancient, and being obliterated by a thousand changes of government and princes, it cannot now be supposed to retain any authority. If we would say any thing to the purpose, we must assert, that every particular government, which is lawful, and which imposes any duty of allegiance on the subject, was, at first, founded on consent and a voluntary compact. But besides that this supposes the consent of the fathers to bind the children, even to the most remote generations, (which republican writers will never allow) besides this, I say, it is not justified by history or experience, in any age or country of the world.

Almost all the governments, which exist at present, or of which there remains any record in story, have been founded originally, either on usurpation or conquest, or both, without any presence of a fair consent, or voluntary subjection of the people. When an artful and bold man is placed at the head of an army or faction, it is often easy for him, by employing, sometimes violence, sometimes false pretences, to establish his dominion over a people a hundred times more numerous than his partizans. He allows no such open communication, that his enemies can know, with certainty, their number or force. He gives them no leisure to assemble together in a body to oppose him. Even all those, who are the instruments of his usurpation, may wish his fall; but their ignorance of each other's intention keeps them in awe, and is the sole cause of his security. By such arts as these, many governments have been established; and this is all the *original contract*, which they have to boast of.

The face of the earth is continually changing, by the encrease of small kingdoms into great empires, by the dissolution of great empires into smaller kingdoms, by the planting of colonies, by the migration of tribes. Is there any thing discoverable in all these events, but force and violence? Where is the mutual agreement or voluntary association so much talked of?

Even the smoothest way, by which a nation may receive a foreign master, by marriage or a will, is not extremely honourable for the people; but supposes them to be disposed of, like a dowry or a legacy, according to the pleasure or interest of their rulers.

But where no force interposes, and election takes place; what is this election so highly vaunted? It is either the combination of a few great men, who decide for the whole, and will allow of no opposition: Or it is the fury of a multitude, that follow a seditious ringleader, who is not known, perhaps, to a dozen among them, and who owes his advancement merely to his own impudence, or to the momentary caprice of his fellows.

Are these disorderly elections, which are rare too, of such mighty authority, as to be the only lawful foundation of all government and allegiance?

In reality, there is not a more terrible event, than a total dissolution of government, which gives liberty to the multitude, and makes the determination or choice of a new establishment depend upon a number, which nearly approaches to that of the body of the people: For it never comes entirely to the whole body of them. Every wise man, then, wishes to see, at the head of a powerful and obedient army, a general, who may speedily seize the prize, and give to the people a master, which they are so unfit to chuse for themselves. So little correspondent is fact and reality to those philosophical notions.

Let not the establishment at the *Revolution* deceive us, or make us so much in love with a philosophical origin to government, as to imagine all others monstrous and irregular. Even that event was far from corresponding to these refined ideas. It was only the succession, and that only in the regal part of the government, which was then changed: And it was only the majority of seven hundred, who determined that change for near ten millions. I doubt not, indeed, but the bulk of those ten millions acquiesced willingly in the determination: But was the matter left, in the least, to their choice? Was it not justly supposed to be, from that moment, decided, and every man punished, who refused to submit to the new sovereign? How otherwise could the matter have ever been brought to any issue or conclusion?

The republic of Athens was, I believe, the most extensive democracy, that we read of in history: Yet if we make the requisite allowances for the women, the slaves, and the strangers, we shall find, that that establishment was not, at first, made, not any law ever voted, by a tenth part of those who were bound to pay obedience to it: Not to mention the islands and foreign dominions, which the Athenians claimed as theirs by right of conquest. And as it is well known, that popular assemblies in that city were always full of licence and disorder, notwithstanding the institutions and laws by which they were checked: How much more disorderly must they prove, where they form not the established constitution, but meet tumultuously on the dissolution of the ancient government, in order to give rise to a new one? How chimerical must it be to talk of a choice in such circumstances?

The Acheans enjoyed the freest and most perfect democracy of all antiquity; yet they employed force to oblige some cities to enter into their league, as we learn from Polybius.

Harry the IVth and Harry the VIIth of England, had really no title to the throne but a parliamentary election; yet they never would acknowledge it, lest they should thereby weaken their authority. Strange, if the only real foundation of all authority be consent and promise!

It is in vain to say, that all governments are or should be, at first, founded on popular consent, as much as the necessity of human affairs will admit. This favours entirely my pretension. I maintain, that human affairs will never admit of this consent; seldom of the appearance of it. But that conquest or usurpation, that is, in plain terms, force, by dissolving the ancient governments, is the origin of almost all the new ones, which were ever established in the world. And that in the few cases, where consent may seem to have taken place, it was commonly so irregular, so confined, or so much intermixed either with fraud or violence, that it cannot have any great authority.

My intention here is not to exclude the consent of the people from being one just foundation of government where it has place. It is surely the best and most sacred of any. I only pretend, that it has very seldom had place in any degree, and never almost in its full extent. And that therefore some other foundation of government must also be admitted.

Were all men possessed of so inflexible a regard to justice, that, of themselves, they would totally abstain from the properties of others; they had for ever remained in a state of absolute liberty, without subjection to any magistrate or political society: But this is a state of perfection, of which human nature is justly deemed incapable. Again; were all men possessed of so perfect an understanding, as always to know their own interests, no form of government had ever been submitted to, but what was established on consent, and was fully canvassed by every member of the society: But this state of perfection is likewise much superior to human nature. Reason, history, and experience shew us, that all political societies have had an origin much less accurate and regular; and were one to choose a period of time, when the people's consent was the least regarded in public transactions, it would be precisely on the establishment of a new government. In a settled constitution, their inclinations are often consulted; but during the fury of revolutions, conquests, and public convulsions, military force or political craft usually decides the controversy.

When a new government is established, by whatever means, the people are commonly dissatisfied with it, and pay obedience more from fear and necessity, than from any idea of allegiance or of moral obligation. The prince is watchful and jealous, and must carefully guard against every beginning or appearance of insurrection. Time, by degrees, removes all these difficulties, and accustoms the nation to regard, as their lawful or native princes, that family, which, at first, they considered as usurpers or foreign conquerors. In order to found this opinion, they have no recourse to any notion of voluntary consent or promise, which, they know, never was, in this case, either expected or demanded. The original establishment was formed by violence, and submitted to from necessity. The subsequent administration is also supported by power, and acquiesced in by the people, not as a matter of choice, but of obligation. They imagine not, that their consent gives their prince a title: But they willingly consent, because they think, that, from long possession, he has acquired a title, independent of their choice or inclination.

Should it be said, that, by living under the dominion of a prince, which one might leave, every individual has given a *tacit* consent to his authority, and promised him obedience; it may be answered, that such an implied consent can only have place, where a man imagines, that the matter depends on his choice. But where he thinks (as all mankind do who are born under established governments) that by his birth he owes allegiance to a certain prince or certain form of government; it would be absurd to infer a consent or choice, which he expressly, in this case, renounces and disclaims.

Can we seriously say, that a poor peasant or artizan has a free choice to leave his country, when he knows no foreign language or manners, and lives from day to day, by the small wages which he acquires? We may as well assert, that a man, by remaining in a vessel, freely consents to the dominion of the master; though he was carried on board while asleep, and must leap into the ocean, and perish, the moment he leaves her.

What if the prince forbid his subjects to quit his dominions; as in Tiberius's time, it was regarded as a crime in a Roman knight that he had attempted to fly to the Parthians, in order to escape the tyranny of that emperor?[2] Or as the ancient Muscovites prohibited all travelling under pain of death? And did a prince observe, that many of his subjects were seized with the frenzy of migrating to foreign countries, he would doubtless, with great reason and justice, restrain them, in order to prevent the depopulation of his own kingdom. Would he forfeit the allegiance of all his subjects, by so wise and reasonable a law? Yet the freedom of their choice is surely, in that case, ravished from them.

A company of men, who should leave their native country, in order to people some uninhabited region, might dream of recovering their native freedom; but they would soon find, that their prince still laid claim to them, and called them his subjects, even in their new settlement. And in this he would but act conformably to the common ideas of mankind.

The truest *tacit* consent of this kind, that is ever observed, is when a foreigner settles in any country, and is beforehand acquainted with the prince, and government, and laws, to which he must submit: Yet is his allegiance, though more voluntary, much less expected or depended on, than that of a natural born subject. On the contrary, his native prince still asserts a claim to him. And if he punish not the renegade, when he seizes him in war with his new prince's commission; this clemency is not founded on the municipal law, which in all countries condemns the prisoner; but on the consent of princes, who have agreed to this indulgence, in order to prevent reprisals.

Did one generation of men go off the stage at once, and another succeed, as is the case with silk-worms and butterflies, the new race, if they had sense enough to choose their government, which surely is never the case with men, might voluntarily, and by general consent, establish their own form of civil polity, without any regard to the laws or precedents, which prevailed among their ancestors. But as human society is in perpetual flux, one man every hour going out of the world, another coming into it, it is necessary, in order to preserve stability in government, that the new brood should conform themselves to the established constitution, and nearly follow the path which their fathers, treading in the footsteps of theirs, had marked out to them. Some innovations must necessarily have place in every human institution, and it is happy where the enlightened genius of the age give these a direction to the side of reason, liberty, and justice: but violent innovations no individual is entitled to make: they are even dangerous to be attempted by the legislature: more ill than good is ever to be expected from them: and if history affords examples to the contrary, they are not to be drawn into precedent, and are only to be regarded as proofs, that the science of politics affords few rules, which will not admit of some exception, and which may not sometimes be controuled by fortune and accident. The violent innovations in the reign of Henry VIII proceeded from an imperious monarch, seconded by the appearance of legislative authority: Those in the reign of Charles I were derived from faction and fanaticism; and both of them have proved happy in the issue: But even the former were long the source of many disorders, and still more dangers; and if the measures of allegiance were to be taken from the latter, a total anarchy must have place in human society, and a final period at once be put to every government.

Suppose, that an usurper, after having banished his lawful prince and royal family, should establish his dominion for ten or a dozen years in any country, and should preserve so exact a discipline in his troops, and so regular a disposition in his garrisons, that no insurrection had ever been raised, or even murmur heard, against his administration: Can it be asserted, that the people, who in their hearts abhor his treason, have tacitly consented to his authority, and promised him allegiance, merely because, from necessity, they live under his dominion? Suppose again their native prince restored, by means of an army, which he levies in foreign countries: They receive him with joy and exultation, and shew plainly with what reluctance they had submitted to any other yoke. I may now ask, upon what foundation the prince's title stands? Not on popular consent surely: For though the people willingly acquiesce in his authority, they never imagine, that their consent made him sovereign. They consent; because they apprehend him to be already, by birth, their lawful sovereign. And as to that tacit consent, which may now be inferred from their living under his dominion, this is no more than what they formerly gave to the tyrant and usurper.

When we assert, that all lawful government arises from the consent of the people, we certainly do them a great deal more honour than they deserve, or even expect and desire from us. After the Roman dominions became too unwieldly for the republic to govern them, the people, over the whole known world, were extremely grateful to Augustus for that authority, which, by violence, he had established over them; and they shewed an equal disposition to submit to the successor, whom he left them, by his last will and testament. It was afterwards their misfortune, that there never was, in one family, any long regular succession; but that their line of princes was continually broken, either by private assassinations or public rebellions. The *praetorian* bands, on the failure of every family, set up one emperor; the legions in the East a second; those in Germany, perhaps, a third: And the sword alone could decide the controversy. The condition of the people, in that mighty monarchy, was to be lamented, not because the choice of the emperor was never left to them; for that was impracticable: But because they never fell under any succession of masters, who might regularly follow each other. As to the violence and wars and bloodshed, occasioned by every new settlement; these were not blameable, because they were inevitable.

The house of Lancaster ruled in this island about sixty years; yet the partizans of the white rose seemed daily to multiply in England. The present establishment has taken place during a still longer period. Have all views of right in another family been utterly extinguished; even though scarce any man now alive had arrived at years of discretion, when it was expelled, or could have consented to its dominion, or have promised it allegiance? A sufficient indication surely of the general sentiment of mankind on this head. For we blame not the partizans of the abdicated family, merely on account of the long time, during which they have preserved their imaginary loyalty. We blame them for adhering to a family, which, we affirm, has been justly expelled, and which, from the moment the new settlement took place, had forfeited all title to authority.

But would we have a more regular, at least a more philosophical, refutation of this principle of an original contract or popular consent; perhaps, the following observations may suffice.

All *moral* duties may be divided into two kinds. The *first* are those, to which men are impelled by a natural instinct or immediate propensity, which operates on them, independent of all ideas of obligation, and of all views, either to public or private utility. Of this nature are, love of children, gratitude to benefactors, pity to the unfortunate. When we reflect on the advantage, which results to society from such humane instincts, we pay them the just tribute of moral approbation and esteem: But the person, actuated by them, feels their power and influence, antecedent to any such reflection.

The *second* kind of moral duties are such as are not supported by any original instinct of nature, but are performed entirely from a sense of obligation, when we consider the necessities of human society, and the impossibility of supporting it, if these duties were neglected. It is thus *justice* or a regard to the property of others, *fidelity* or the observance of promises, become obligatory, and acquire an authority over mankind. For as it is evident, that every man loves himself better than any other person, he is naturally impelled to extend his acquisitions as much as possible; and nothing can restrain him in this propensity, but reflection and experience, by which he learns the pernicious effects of that licence, and the total dissolution of society which must ensue from it. His original inclination, therefore, or instinct, is here checked and restrained by a subsequent judgment or observation.

The case is precisely the same with the political or civil duty of *allegiance* as with the natural duties of justice and fidelity. Our primary instincts lead us, either to indulge ourselves in unlimited freedom, or to seek dominion over others: And it is reflection only which engages us to sacrifice such strong passions to the interests of peace and public order. A small degree of experience and observation suffices to teach us, that society cannot possibly be maintained without the authority of magistrates, and that this authority must soon fall into contempt, where exact obedience is not payed to it. The observation of these general and obvious interests is the source of all allegiance, and of that moral obligation, which we attribute to it.

What necessity, therefore, is there to found the duty of *allegiance* or obedience to magistrates on that of *fidelity* or a regard to promises, and to suppose, that it is the consent of each individual, which subjects him to government; when it appears, that both allegiance and fidelity stand precisely on the same foundation, and are both submitted to by mankind, on account of the apparent interests and necessities of human society? We are bound to obey our sovereign, it is said; because we have given a tacit promise to that purpose. But why are we bound to observe our promise? It must here be asserted, that the commerce and intercourse of mankind, which are of such mighty advantage, can have no security where men pay no regard to their engagements. In like manner, may it be said, that men could not live at all in society, at least in a civilized society, without laws and magistrates and judges, to prevent the encroachments of the strong upon the weak, of the violent upon the just and equitable. The obligation to allegiance being of like force and authority with the obligation to fidelity, we gain nothing by resolving the one into the other. The general interests or necessities of society are sufficient to establish both.

If the reason be asked of that obedience, which we are bound to pay to government, I readily answer, *because society could not otherwise subsist*: And this answer is clear and intelligible to all mankind. Your answer is, *because we should keep our word*. But besides, that no body, till trained in a philosophical system, can either comprehend or relish this answer: Besides this, I say, you find yourself embarrassed, when it is asked, *why we are bound to keep our word?* Nor can you give any answer, but what would, immediately, without any circuit, have accounted for our obligation to allegiance.

But *to whom is allegiance due? And who is our lawful sovereign?* This question is often the most difficult of any, and liable to infinite discussions. When people are so happy, that they can answer, *Our present sovereign, who inherits, in a direct line, from ancestors, that have governed us for many ages;* this answer admits of no reply; even though historians, in tracing up to the remotest antiquity, the origin of that royal family, may find, as commonly happens, that its first authority was derived from usurpation and violence. It is confessed, that private justice, or the abstinence from the properties of others, is a most cardinal virtue: Yet reason tells us, that there is no property in durable objects, such as lands or houses, when carefully examined in passing from hand to hand, but must, in some period, have been founded on fraud and injustice. The necessities of human society, neither in private nor public life, will allow of such an accurate enquiry: And there is no virtue or moral duty, but what may, with facility, be refined away, if we indulge a false philosophy, in sifting and scrutinizing it, by every captious rule of logic, in every light or position, in which it may be placed.

The questions with regard to private property have filled infinite volumes of law and philosophy, if in both we add the commentators to the original text; and in the end, we may safely pronounce, that many of the rules, there established, are uncertain, ambiguous, and arbitrary. The like opinion may be formed with regard to the succession and rights of princes and forms of government. Several cases, no doubt, occur, especially in the infancy of any constitution, which admit of no determination from the laws of justice and equity: And our historian Rapin pretends, that the controversy between Edward the Third and Philip de Valois was of this nature, and could be decided only by an appeal to heaven, that is, by war and violence.

Who shall tell me, whether Germanicus or Drusus ought to have succeeded to Tiberius, had he died, while they were both alive, without naming any of them for his successor? Ought the right of adoption to be received as equivalent to that of blood, in a nation, where it had the same effect in private families, and had already, in two instances, taken place in the public? Ought Germanicus to be esteemed the elder son because he was born before Drusus; or the younger, because he was adopted after the birth of his brother? Ought the right of the elder to be regarded in a nation, where he had no advantage in the succession of private families? Ought the Roman empire at that time to be deemed hereditary, because of two examples; or ought it, even so early, to be regarded as belonging to the stronger or to the present possessor, as being founded on so recent an usurpation?

Commodus mounted the throne after a pretty long succession of excellent emperors, who had acquired their title, not by birth, or public election, but by the fictitious rite of adoption. That bloody debauchee being murdered by a conspiracy suddenly formed between his wench and her gallant, who happened at that time to be *Proetorian Proefect;* these immediately deliberated about choosing a master to human kind, to speak in the style of those ages; and they cast their eyes on Pertinax. Before the tyrant's death was known, the *Proefect* went secretly to that senator, who, on the appearance of the soldiers, imagined that his execution had been ordered by Commodus. He was immediately saluted emperor by the officer and his attendants; cheerfully proclaimed by the populace; unwillingly submitted to by the guards; formally recognized by the senate; and passively received by the provinces and armies of the empire.

The discontent of the *Proetorian* bands broke out in a sudden sedition, which occasioned the murder of that excellent prince: And the world being now without a master and without government, the guards thought proper to set the empire formally to sale. Julian, the purchaser, was proclaimed by the soldiers, recognized by the senate, and submitted to by the people; and must also have been submitted to by the provinces, had not the envy of the legions begotten opposition and resistance. Pescennius Niger in Syria elected himself emperor, gained the tumultuary consent of his army, and was attended with the secret good-will of the senate and people of Rome. Albinus in Britain found an equal right to set up his claim; but Severus, who governed Pannonia, prevailed in the end above both of them. That able politician and warrior, finding his own birth and dignity too much inferior to the imperial crown, professed, at first, an intention only of revenging the death of Pertinax. He marched as general into Italy; defeated Julian; and without our being able to fix any precise commencement even of the soldiers' consent, he was from necessity acknowledged emperor by the senate and people; and fully established in his violent authority by subduing Niger and Albinus.[3]

Inter haec Gordianus Caesar (says Capitolinus, speaking of another period) *sublatus a militibus.* Imperator *est appellatus, quia non erat alius in proesenti.* It is to be remarked, that Gordian was a boy of fourteen years of age.

Frequent instances of a like nature occur in the history of the emperors; in that of Alexander's successors; and of many other countries: Nor can any thing be more unhappy than a despotic government of this kind; where the succession is disjointed and irregular, and must be determined, on every vacancy, by force or election. In a free government, the matter is often unavoidable, and is also much less dangerous. The interests of liberty may there frequently lead the people, in their own defence, to alter the succession of the crown. And the constitution, being compounded of parts, may still maintain a sufficient stability, by resting on the aristocratical or democratical members, though the monarchical be altered, from time to time, in order to accommodate it to the former.

In an absolute government, when there is no legal prince, who has a title to the throne, it may safely be determined to belong to the first occupant. Instances of this kind are but too frequent, especially in the eastern monarchies. When any race of princes expires, the will or destination of the last sovereign will be regarded as a title. Thus the edict of Lewis the XIVth, who called the bastard princes to the succession in case of the failure of all the legitimate princes, would, in such an event, have some authority.[4] Thus the will of Charles the Second disposed of the whole Spanish monarchy. The cession of the ancient proprietor, especially when joined to conquest, is likewise deemed a good title. The general obligation, which binds us to government, is the interest and necessities of society; and this obligation is very strong. The determination of it to this or that particular prince or form of government is frequently more uncertain and dubious. Present possession has considerable authority in these cases, and greater than in private property; because of the disorders which attend all revolutions and changes of government.

We shall only observe, before we conclude, that, though an appeal to general opinion may justly, in the speculative sciences of metaphysics, natural philosophy, or astronomy, be deemed unfair and inconclusive, yet in all questions with regard to morals, as well as criticism, there is really no other standard, by which any controversy can ever be decided. And nothing is a clearer proof, that a theory of this kind is erroneous, than to find, that it leads to paradoxes, repugnant to the common sentiments of mankind, and to the practice and opinion of all nations and all ages. The doctrine, which founds all lawful government on an *original contract*, or consent of the people, is plainly of this kind; nor has the most noted of its partizans, in prosecution of it, scrupled to affirm, *that absolute monarchy is inconsistent with civil society, and so can be no form of civil government at all;*[5] *and that the supreme power in a state cannot take from any man, by taxes and impositions, any part of his property, without his own consent or that of his representatives.*[6] What authority any moral reasoning can have, which leads into opinions so wide of the general practice of mankind, in every place but this single kingdom, it is easy to determine.

The only passage I meet with in antiquity, where the obligation of obedience to government is ascribed to a promise, is in Plato's *Crito*: where Socrates refuses to escape from prison, because he had tacitly promised to obey the laws. Thus he builds a *tory* consequence of passive obedience, on a *whig* foundation of the original contract.

New discoveries are not to be expected in these matters. If scarce any man, till very lately, ever imagined that government was founded on compact, it is certain, that it cannot, in general, have any such foundation.

The crime of rebellion among the ancients was commonly expressed by the terms νεωτερίζειν, *novas res moliri*.

Notes

1. Lib. ii. cap. 38.
2. Tacit. Ann. vi. cap. 14.
3. Herodian, lib. ii.
4. It is remarkable, that, in the remonstrance of the duke of Bourbon and the legitimate princes, against this destination of Louis the XIVth, the doctrine of the *original contract* is insisted on, even in that absolute government. The French nation, say they, chusing Hugh Capet and his posterity to rule over them and their posterity, where the former line fails, there is a tacit right reserved to choose a new royal family; and this right is invaded by calling the bastard princes to the throne, without the consent of the nation. But the Comte de Boulainvilliers, who wrote in defence of the bastard princes, ridicules this notion of an original contract, especially when applied to Hugh Capet; who mounted the throne, says he, by the same arts, which have ever been employed by all conquerors and usurpers. He got his title, indeed, recognized by the states after he had put himself in possession: But is this a choice or contract? The Comte de Boulainvilliers, we may observe, was a noted republican; but being a man of learning, and very conversant in history, he knew that the people were never almost consulted in these revolutions and new establishment, and that time alone bestowed right and authority on what was commonly at first founded on force and violence. See *Etat de la France*, Vol. III.
5. See Locke on Government, Chapter vii. Section 90.
6. Id. Chapter xi. Section 138, 139, 140.

OF THE ORIGIN OF GOVERNMENT

Man, born in a family, is compelled to maintain society, from necessity, from natural inclination, and from habit. The same creature, in his farther progress, is engaged to establish political society, in order to administer justice; without which there can be no peace among them, nor safety, nor mutual intercourse. We are, therefore, to look upon all the vast apparatus of our government, as having ultimately no other object or purpose but the distribution of justice, or, in other words, the support of the twelve judges. Kings and parliaments, fleets and armies, officers of the court and revenue, ambassadors, ministers, and privy-counsellors, are all subordinate in their end to this part of administration. Even the clergy, as their duty leads them to inculcate morality, may justly be thought, so far as regards this world, to have no other useful object of their institution.

All men are sensible of the necessity of justice to maintain peace and order; and all men are sensible of the necessity of peace and order for the maintenance of society. Yet, notwithstanding this strong and obvious necessity, such is the frailty or perverseness of our nature! it is impossible to keep men, faithfully and unerringly, in the paths of justice. Some extraordinary circumstances may happen, in which a man finds his interests to be more promoted by fraud or rapine, than hurt by the breach which his injustice makes in the social union. But much more frequently, he is seduced from his great and important, but distant interests, by the allurement of present, though often very frivolous temptations. This great weakness is incurable in human nature.

Men must, therefore, endeavour to palliate what they cannot cure. They must institute some persons, under the appellation of magistrates, whose peculiar office it is, to point out the decrees of equity, to punish transgressors, to correct fraud and violence, and to oblige men, however reluctant, to consult their own real and permanent interests. In a word, Obedience is a new duty which must be invented to support that of Justice; and the tyes of equity must be corroborated by those of allegiance.

But still, viewing matters in an abstract light, it may be thought, that nothing is gained by this alliance, and that the factitious duty of obedience, from its very nature, lays as feeble a hold of the human mind, as the primitive and natural duty of justice. Peculiar interests and present temptations may overcome the one as well as the other. They are equally exposed to the same inconvenience. And the man, who is inclined to be a bad neighbour, must be led by the same motives, well or ill understood, to be a bad citizen and subject. Not to mention, that the magistrate himself may often be negligent, or partial, or unjust in his administration.

Experience, however, proves, that there is a great difference between the cases. Order in society, we find, is much better maintained by means of government; and our duty to the magistrate is more strictly guarded by the principles of human nature, than our duty to our fellow-citizens. The love of dominion is so strong in the breast of man, that many, not only submit to, but court all the dangers, and fatigues, and cares of government; and men, once raised to that station, though often led astray by private passions, find, in ordinary cases, a visible interest in the impartial administration of justice. The persons, who first attain this distinction by the consent, tacit or express, of the people, must be endowed with superior personal qualities of valour, force, integrity, or prudence, which command respect and confidence: and after government is established, a regard to birth, rank, and station has a mighty influence over men, and enforces the decrees of the magistrate. The prince or leader exclaims against every disorder, which disturbs his society. He summons all his partizans and all men of probity to aid him in correcting and redressing it: and he is readily followed by all indifferent persons in the execution of his office. He soon acquires the power of rewarding these services; and in the progress of society, he establishes subordinate ministers and often a military force, who find an immediate and a visible interest, in supporting his authority. Habit soon consolidates what other principles of human nature had imperfectly founded; and men, once accustomed to obedience, never think of departing from that path, in which they and their ancestors have constantly trod, and to which they are confined by so many urgent and visible motives.

But though this progress of human affairs may appear certain and inevitable, and though the support which allegiance brings to justice, be founded on obvious principles of human nature, it cannot be expected that men should beforehand be able to discover them, or foresee their operation. Government commences more casually and more imperfectly. It is probable, that the first ascendant of one man over multitudes begun during a state of war; where the superiority of courage and of genius discovers itself most visibly, where unanimity and concert are most requisite, and where the pernicious effects of disorder are most sensibly felt. The long continuance of that state, an incident common among savage tribes, enured the people to submission; and if the chieftain possessed as much equity as prudence and valour, he became, even during peace, the arbiter of all differences, and could gradually, by a mixture of force and consent, establish his authority. The benefit sensibly felt from his influence, made it be cherished by the people, at least by the peaceable and well disposed among them; and if his son enjoyed the same good qualities, government advanced the sooner to maturity and perfection; but was still in a feeble state, till the farther progress of improvement procured the magistrate a revenue, and enabled him to bestow rewards on the several instruments of his administration, and to inflict punishments on the refractory and disobedient. Before that period, each exertion of his influence must have been particular, and founded on the peculiar circumstances of the case. After it, submission was no longer a matter of choice in the bulk of the community, but was rigorously exacted by the authority of the supreme magistrate.

In all governments, there is a perpetual intestine struggle, open or secret, between Authority and Liberty; and neither of them can ever absolutely prevail in the contest. A great sacrifice of liberty must necessarily be made in every government; yet even the authority, which confines liberty, can never, and perhaps ought never, in any constitution, to become quite entire and uncontroulable. The sultan is master of the life and fortune of any individual; but will not be permitted to impose new taxes on his subjects: a French monarch can impose taxes at pleasure; but would find it dangerous to attempt the lives and fortunes of individuals. Religion also, in most countries, is commonly found to be a very intractable principle; and other principles or prejudices frequently resist all the authority of the civil magistrate; whose power, being founded on opinion, can never subvert other opinions, equally rooted with that of his title to dominion. The government, which, in common appellation, receives the appellation of free, is that which admits of a partition of power among several members, whose united authority is no less, or is commonly greater than that of any monarch; but who, in the usual course of administration, must act by general and equal laws, that are previously known to all the members and to all their subjects. In this sense, it must be owned, that liberty is the perfection of civil society; but still authority must be acknowledged essential to its very existence: and in those contests, which so often take place between the one and the other, the latter may, on that account, challenge the preference. Unless perhaps one may say (and it may be said with some reason) that a circumstance, which is essential to the existence of civil society, must always support itself, and needs be guarded with less jealousy, than one that contributes only to its perfection, which the indolence of men is so apt to neglect, or their ignorance to overlook.

ADAM SMITH

Adam Smith (1723–1790) was a luminary in what is now called "the Scottish Enlightenment." Relatively little is known about his private life; he did not write an autobiography, and in spite of his fame as well as his friendship with leading figures of the day (such as Hume and Voltaire), his correspondence reveals surprisingly little about him as a man. He was clearly of stern character, strict discipline, sceptical disposition (and thus much opposed to extravagant religious or political claims), and complete trustworthiness. In many ways he appears to have been the perfect Stoic, needing little, independent, self-directed, and with emotions under watchful supervision. He did not live a monastic life, however; he had a wide circle of friends from many walks of life and regularly participated in meetings of literary, scientific, and business circles.

Smith attended Glasgow University, where he studied with Francis Hutcheson, and then Oxford, on the educational quality of which he subsequently commented caustically in the *Wealth of Nations*. Between 1748 and 1751, Smith lectured at Edinburgh under the patronage of Lord Kames; his topics were rhetoric, belles lettres, and jurisprudence. Student notes of Smith's lectures have survived, and while imperfect as such notes must be, the notes show that Smith possessed an impressive knowledge of the history of rhetoric and literature, backed up by a command of the relevant languages, ancient and modern. From the start, Smith also evinced a deep interest in the uses and development of language (as is shown by his first publications) and put his command of rhetoric to work in his own writings.

In 1751, Smith was named professor of logic at Glasgow University; he taught logic (which he rapidly transformed into a course on rhetoric), jurisprudence, and political theory. The next year, he became professor of moral philosophy at Glasgow, and his subject expanded to include ethics. After rising to the position of vice-rector of the university, Smith resigned his chair in 1764 in order to serve as traveling tutor to the third Duke of Buccleuch. Smith spent the next several years in France, where he met many of the leading *philosophes*, as well as French political economists. By 1767, he had returned to his native Kirkcaldy, where he lived with his mother (Smith never married) and worked on further revision of his books, as well as on drafts of others. In 1778, he was named commissioner of customs for Scotland and of Salt Duties, and relocated to Edinburgh. A decade later, he also served as rector of Glasgow University. As appropriate to his international reputation and position, Smith was consulted about various issues of the day, including about relations with the American colonies.

Smith published just two books, *The Theory of Moral Sentiments* (first edition 1759) and *An Inquiry into the Nature and Causes of the Wealth of Nations* (first edition 1776), each in a series of emended and expanded editions. From the first editions on, these two books were remarkably successful, and with impressive speed elevated Smith to the stature of an international celebrity. His work was rapidly translated into several languages and taken seriously by thinkers of the order of Burke, Hume, Bentham, Kant, and Hegel. Smith conceived of these books as parts of a much more extended corpus that was to have included a "Philosophical History of the Liberal and Elegant Arts"; a treatment of "natural jurisprudence" (an analysis of the "natural rules of justice" or "general principles of law and government"); and a detailed account of the evolution of these rules of natural justice. Unfortunately, Smith instructed that almost all of his unpublished manuscripts were to be destroyed on his death. Two sets of student notes of his lectures on jurisprudence were discovered long after, and they help us understand what part of the missing system might have looked like. A number of posthumously published essays (now available in a volume entitled *Essays on Philosophical Subjects*), along with the student notes of his lectures on rhetoric, give us a reasonable picture of his "philosophical history" of rhetoric, the imitative arts, and both philosophy and science. These essays demonstrate Smith's vast and imaginative grasp of those areas and outline a philosophy of science that seeks to account for theory acceptance in broadly "aesthetic" terms. The "psychology" of inquiry, and the connection between knowledge, rhetoric, and aesthetics, clearly fascinated Smith, as is evident in the *Theory of Moral Sentiments* as well.

In the *Theory of Moral Sentiments*, he sought to answer two questions. The first is "wherein does virtue consist? Or what is the tone of temper and tenour of conduct, which constitutes the excellent and praise-worthy character, the character which is the natural object of esteem, honour, and approbation?" The second treats of what we might call the "psychology of ethics" or "moral psychology." As Smith put it, "by what power or faculty in the mind is it, that this [excellent and praise-worthy] character, whatever it be, is recommended to us?" His answer to the first question—viz., that virtue is to be understood as the "mean" or the appropriate pitch of a passion or emotion in the given case—revives parts of the Aristotelian view of virtue. His answer to the second question built on Hume's theory of *sympathy*, a term denoting our ability to put ourselves imaginatively in the situation of another, as well as on the notion of the "impartial spectator." Sympathy is possible thanks to the imagination; for Smith the moral imagination is the glue that holds society together. As we judge others, so they judge us; we learn early on to view ourselves through the eyes of others, to imagine what they are imagining about us. For Smith, society is a spectatorial, theatrical affair. As we naturally seek the approval of others and they of us—thanks to *sympathy*—we feel bound to each other's praise and blame. Smith's view of the "self" is thoroughly social, and is ultimately at odds with perfectionist doctrines such as those of Plato, Aristotle, and Aquinas. However, we are also capable of viewing ourselves through the eyes of an imagined, impartial spectator; the judgments of a given society are not necessarily final.

Smith throughout exhibits scepticism about metaphysical and theological views of virtue and of the psychology of morals. The self-understanding of reasonable moral actors ought to serve as the moral philosopher's guide. Smith's discussion in the *Theory of Moral Sentiments* ranges from the motivation for wealth getting to the psychological causes of dangerous religious and political fanaticism. The threat of fanaticism concerned Smith deeply, as it did so many other thinkers of the period (including Thomas Jefferson and James Madison): "Of all the corrupters of moral sentiments . . . faction and fanaticism have always been by far the greatest." Smith's criticisms of wealth getting are as merciless as those of many traditional moralists; yet he also reconciles us to our desire to "better our own condition" by observing the ways in which it is both natural and productive. Here as elsewhere, Smith shows himself capable of both critical detachment from the phenomena he analyzes and moderation in his hopes for amelioration.

The *Wealth of Nations* attempts to explain why free economic, political, and religious markets are not only more efficient (when properly regulated) in increasing the wealth of nations but also more in keeping with nature, more likely to win the approval of an impartial spectator than would monopolistic alternatives, and of course praiseworthy because supportive of liberty. The book thus makes a broad-gauged case for a modern commercial society. Taken together, Smith's two books attempt to show how virtue, liberty, and material welfare can complement each other. He shows full awareness of the potentially dehumanizing force of what was later called *capitalism*, and sought remedies for it in schemes for liberal education and properly organized religion. He harshly criticized colonialism, slavery, and racism. Book V of the *Wealth of Nations* offers an ingeneous "free market" solution to the problem of religious faction, one which depends on the assumptions in the *Theory of Moral Sentiments* about the psychology of moderation and fanaticism, a solution that strikingly foreshadows James Madison's famous proposals in the tenth of fifty-first *Federalist* for controlling civil strife. Smith hopes that the result of fair competition among religions will be to "reduce the doctrine of the greater part of them to that pure and rational religion, free from every mixture of absurdity, imposture, or fanaticism, such as wise men have in all ages of the world wished to see established." Unlike Marx, Smith did not take religion to be the opium of the people; nor did he think that the religious impulse can, or should, be extirpated. He thought that it can have a constructive role, but under conditions of liberty of religious belief. The argument in the *Wealth of Nations* in favor of liberty is not only based on its utility in the service of wealth but also on its connection with justice and the flourishing of virtues such as moderation and prudence. The relationship between liberal institutional arrangements (such as the separation between church and state) and virtue is a circular one for Smith. The wrong arrangements elicit fanaticism and corruption, which in turn further illiberal institutions.

In the "obvious and simple system of natural liberty," Smith writes, "every man, as long as he does not violate the laws of justice, is left perfectly free to pursue his own interest his own way, and to bring both his industry and capital into competition with those of any other man, or order of men." The government is left with the duties of promoting public works, protecting society from invasion, and protecting its citizens from one other. These are areas in which the efforts of individuals are insufficient. In Smith's hands, these supply a wide entrance for government intervention in society, and he is never dogmatic in defining precisely what government may or may not do. Smith does not advocate mere laissez-faire, and he sees a role for the state in regulating, or encouraging, or even supporting the arts, education, commerce, and many other areas.

In complex ways, Smith's work self-consciously synthesizes ancient and modern thought; it is both of the Enlightenment and the counter-Enlightenment, as is clear in Smith's subtle discussions of the relationship between commerce and virtue. Smith provides a fascinating window on the old "quarrel between ancients and moderns." He does so with marked self-consciousness about its approach, showing a sophisticated awareness of his own methodology and rhetoric.

The combination of the incompleteness of Smith's corpus, his decision in the two published books not to comment on the unity of the moral philosophy and political economy, the dialectical quality of his writing, the intrinsic difficulty of the issues, and the eclecticism of his thinking, have made it a challenge to articulate the unity of his project. The problem of the unity of Smith's books became a *cause célèbre* in nineteenth-century German scholarship, where it gained the impressive technical designation of "das Adam-Smith Problem." The alleged problem consisted in part in the unity of the doctrine of *sympathy* and benevolence of the one work, with that of selfishness and acquisitiveness of the other. While stated thus, the problem is based on a misunderstanding of the terms *sympathy* and *self-interest*. At a deeper level, the questions of the relationship between self-interest and duty towards others, between socially derived morals and independent moral norms, remains. But these are general philosophical problems, and to Smith's credit he thought them through with integrity and an open mind. His general argument in favor of a modern commercial republic is nuanced and qualified as appropriate, and is all the more powerful for it.

The secondary literature on Smith is vast. A small sample of the widely divergent but fine work on Smith would include V. Brown's *Adam Smith's Discourse: Canonicity, Commerce and Conscience* (London: Routledge, 1994), a book that deploys recent literary theory in a novel interpretation of Smith; J. Cropsey's classic *Polity and Economy: An Interpretation of the Principles of Adam Smith* (Westport, CT: Greenwood Press, 1977), in which Smith is placed in the decisively "modern" tradition of political philosophy stemming from Machiavelli and Hobbes; and K. Haakonssen's *The Science of a Legislator: The Natural Jurisprudence of David Hume & Adam Smith* (Cambridge: Cambridge University Press, 1981), a work exploring Smith's theory of justice and arguing for the centrality of "natural jurisprudence" to Smith's philosophy. *Wealth and Virtue* (Cambridge: Cambridge University Press, 1983), edited by I. Hont & M. Ignatieff, contains useful essays about Smith's seemingly paradoxical arguments on this classical theme. D. D. Raphael's *Adam Smith* (Oxford: Oxford University Press, 1985) supplies a useful and precise overview of Smith and his thought. A. S. Skinner's *A System of Social Science: Paper Relating to Adam Smith* (Oxford: Clarendon Press, 1979) brings together a number of his seminal papers on Smith, while D. Winch's *Adam Smith's Politics: An Essay in Historiographic Revision* (Cambridge: Cambridge University Press, 1978) counters the view that Smith assimilated "politics" to "economics," and with attention to the historical context reconstructs the substance of Smith's political theory. For an overview of the secondary literature, see M. B. Lightwood's *A Selected Bibliography of Significant Works About Adam Smith* (Philadelphia: University of Pennsylvania Press, 1984), and F. Cordasco's & B. Franklin's *Adam Smith: A Bibliographical Checklist* (New York: B. Franklin, 1950).

C. L. G.

THE THEORY OF MORAL SENTIMENTS

PART IV

Of the Effect of Utility upon the Sentiment of Approbation

CHAPTER 1

Of the beauty which the appearance of Utility bestows upon all the productions of art,
and of the extensive influence of this species of Beauty

That utility is one of the principal sources of beauty has been observed by every body, who
has considered with any attention what constitutes the nature of beauty. The conveniency
of a house gives pleasure to the spectator as well as its regularity, and he is as much hurt
when he observes the contrary defect, as when he sees the correspondent windows of different forms, or the door not placed exactly in the middle of the building. That the fitness
of any system or machine to produce the end for which it was intended, bestows a certain
propriety and beauty upon the whole, and renders the very thought and contemplation of
it agreeable, is so very obvious that nobody has overlooked it.

The cause too, why utility pleases, has of late been assigned by an ingenious and agreeable philosopher, who joins the greatest depth of thought to the greatest elegance of
expression, and possesses the singular and happy talent of treating the abstrusest subjects
not only with the most perfect perspicuity, but with the most lively eloquence. The utility of any object, according to him, pleases the master by perpetually suggesting to him
the pleasure or conveniency which it is fitted to promote. Every time he looks at it, he is
put in mind of this pleasure; and the object in this manner becomes a source of perpetual
satisfaction and enjoyment. The spectator enters by sympathy into the sentiments of the
master, and necessarily views the object under the same agreeable aspect. When we visit
the palaces of the great, we cannot help conceiving the satisfaction we should enjoy if we
ourselves were the masters, and were possessed of so much artful and ingeniously contrived accommodation. A similar account is given why the appearance of inconveniency
should render any object disagreeable both to the owner and to the spectator.

But that this fitness, this happy contrivance of any production of art, should often be
more valued, than the very end for which it was intended; and that the exact adjustment
of the means for attaining any conveniency or pleasure, should frequently be more
regarded, than that very conveniency or pleasure, in the attainment of which their whole
merit would seem to consist, has not, so far as I know, been yet taken notice of by any
body. That this however is very frequently the case, may be observed in a thousand
instances, both in the most frivolous and in the most important concerns of human life.

When a person comes into his chamber, and finds the chairs all standing in the middle
of the room, he is angry with his servant, and rather than see them continue in that disorder, perhaps takes the trouble himself to set them all in their places with their backs to
the wall. The whole propriety of this new situation arises from its superior conveniency in
leaving the floor free and disengaged. To attain this conveniency he voluntarily puts himself to more trouble than all he could have suffered from the want of it; since nothing was
more easy, than to have set himself down upon one of them, which is probably what he

does when his labour is over. What he wanted therefore, it seems, was not so much this conveniency, as that arrangement of things which promotes it. Yet it is this conveniency which ultimately recommends that arrangement, and bestows upon it the whole of its propriety and beauty.

A watch, in the same manner, that falls behind above two minutes in a day, is despised by one curious in watches. He sells it perhaps for a couple of guineas, and purchases another at fifty, which will not lose above a minute in a fortnight. The sole use of watches however, is to tell us what o'clock it is, and to hinder us from breaking any engagement, or suffering any other inconveniency by our ignorance in that particular point. But the person so nice with regard to this machine, will not always be found either more scrupulously punctual than other men, or more anxiously concerned upon any other account, to know precisely what time of day it is. What interests him is not so much the attainment of this piece of knowledge, as the perfection of the machine which serves to attain it.

How many people ruin themselves by laying out money on trinkets of frivolous utility? What pleases these lovers of toys is not so much the utility, as the aptness of the machines which are fitted to promote it. All their pockets are stuffed with little conveniencies. They contrive new pockets, unknown in the clothes of other people, in order to carry a greater number. They walk about loaded with a multitude of baubles, in weight and sometimes in value not inferior to an ordinary Jew's-box, some of which may sometimes be of some little use, but all of which might at all times be very well spared, and of which the whole utility is certainly not worth the fatigue of bearing the burden.

Nor is it only with regard to such frivolous objects that our conduct is influenced by this principle; it is often the secret motive of the most serious and important pursuits of both private and public life.

The poor man's son, whom heaven in its anger has visited with ambition, when he begins to look around him, admires the condition of the rich. He finds the cottage of his father too small for his accommodation, and fancies he should be lodged more at his ease in a palace. He is displeased with being obliged to walk a-foot, or to endure the fatigue of riding on horseback. He sees his superiors carried about in machines, and imagines that in one of these he could travel with less inconveniency. He feels himself naturally indolent, and willing to serve himself with his own hands as little as possible; and judges, that a numerous retinue of servants would save him from a great deal of trouble. He thinks if he had attained all these, he would sit still contentedly, and be quiet, enjoying himself in the thought of the happiness and tranquillity of his situation. He is enchanted with the distant idea of this felicity. It appears in his fancy like the life of some superior rank of beings, and, in order to arrive at it, he devotes himself for ever to the pursuit of wealth and greatness. To obtain the conveniencies which these afford, he submits in the first year, nay in the first month of his application, to more fatigue of body and more uneasiness of mind than he could have suffered through the whole of his life from the want of them. He studies to distinguish himself in some laborious profession. With the most unrelenting industry he labours night and day to acquire talents superior to all his competitors. He endeavours next to bring those talents into public view, and with equal assiduity solicits every opportunity of employment. For this purpose he makes his court to all mankind; he serves those whom he hates, and is obsequious to those whom he despises. Through the whole of his life he pursues the idea of a certain artificial and elegant repose which he may never arrive at, for which he sacrifices a real tranquillity that is at all times in his power, and which, if in the extremity of old age he should at last attain to it, he will find to be in no respect preferable to that humble security and contentment which he had abandoned for it. It is then, in the in last dregs of life, his body wasted with toil and diseases, his mind galled and ruffled by the memory of a thousand injuries and disappointments which he imagines he has met with from the injustice of his enemies, or from the perfidy and ingratitude of his friends, that he begins at last to find that wealth and greatness are mere trinkets of frivolous utility, no more adapted for procuring ease of body or tranquillity of mind than the tweezer-cases of the lover of toys; and like them too, more troublesome to the person who carries them about with him than all the advantages they can afford him are commodious. There is no other real difference between them, except that the conveniencies of the one are somewhat more observable than those of the other. The palaces, the gardens, the equipage, the retinue of the great, are objects of which the obvious conveniency strikes every body. They do not require that their masters should point out to us wherein consists their utility. Of our own accord we readily enter into it, and by sympathy enjoy and thereby applaud the satisfaction which they are fitted to afford him. But the curiosity of a tooth-pick, of an ear-picker, of a machine for cutting the nails, or of any other trinket of the same kind, is not so obvious. Their conveniency may perhaps be equally great, but it is not so striking, and we do not so readily enter into the satisfaction of the man who possesses them. They are therefore less reasonable subjects of vanity than the magnificence of wealth and greatness; and in this consists the sole advantage of these last. They more effectually gratify that love of distinction so natural to man. To one who was to live alone in a desolate island it might be a matter of doubt, perhaps, whether a palace, or a collection of such small conveniencies as are commonly contained in a tweezer-case, would contribute most to his happiness and enjoyment. If he is to live in society, indeed, there can be no comparison, because in this, as in all other cases, we constantly pay more regard to the sentiments of the spectator, than to those of the person principally concerned, and consider rather how his situation will appear to other people, than how it will appear to himself. If we examine, however, why the spectator distinguishes with such admiration the condition of the rich and the great, we shall find that it is not so much upon account of the superior ease or pleasure which they are supposed to enjoy, as of the numberless artificial and elegant contrivances for promoting this ease or pleasure. He does not even imagine that they are really happier than other people: but he imagines that they possess more means of happiness. And it is the ingenious and artful adjustment of those means to the end for which they were intended, that is the principal source of his admiration. But in the languor of disease and the weariness of old age, the pleasures of the vain and empty distinctions of greatness disappear. To one, in this situation, they are no longer capable of recommending those toilsome pursuits in which they had formerly engaged him. In his heart he curses ambition, and vainly regrets the ease and the indolence of youth, pleasures which are fled for ever, and which he has foolishly sacrificed for what, when he has got it, can afford him no real satisfaction. In this miserable aspect does greatness appear to every man when reduced either by spleen or disease to observe with attention his own situation, and to consider what it is that is really wanting to his happiness. Power and riches appear then to be, what they are, enormous and operose machines contrived to produce a few trifling conveniencies to the body, consisting of springs the most nice and delicate, which must be kept in order with the most anxious attention, and which in spite of all our care are ready every moment to burst into pieces, and to crush in their ruins their unfortunate possessor. They are immense fabrics, which it requires the labour of a life to raise, which threaten every moment to overwhelm the person that dwells in them, and which while they stand, though they may save him from some smaller inconveniencies, can protect him from none of the severer inclemencies of the season. They keep off the summer shower, not the winter storm, but leave him always as much, and sometimes more exposed than before, to anxiety, to fear, and to sorrow; to diseases, to danger, and to death.

But though this splenetic philosophy, which in time of sickness or low spirits is familiar to every man, thus entirely depreciates those great objects of human desire, when in
better health and in better humour, we never fail to regard them under a more agreeable
aspect. Our imagination, which in pain and sorrow seems to be confined and cooped up
within our own persons, in times of ease and prosperity expands itself to every thing
around us. We are then charmed with the beauty of that accommodation which reigns in
the palaces and oeconomy of the great; and admire how every thing is adapted to promote
their ease, to prevent their wants, to gratify their wishes, and to amuse and entertain their
most frivolous desires. If we consider the real satisfaction which all these things are capable of affording, by itself and separated from the beauty of that arrangement which is fitted
to promote it, it will always appear in the highest degree contemptible and trifling. But
we rarely view it in this abstract and philosophical light. We naturally confound it in our
imagination with the order, the regular and harmonious movement of the system, the
machine or economy by means of which it is produced. The pleasures of wealth and greatness, when considered in this complex view, strike the imagination as something grand
and beautiful and noble, of which the attainment is well worth all the toil and anxiety
which we are so apt to bestow upon it.

And it is well that nature imposes upon us in this manner. It is this deception which
rouses and keeps in continual motion the industry of mankind. It is this which first
prompted them to cultivate the ground, to build houses, to found cities and commonwealths, and to invent and improve all the sciences and arts, which ennoble and embell-
ish human life; which have entirely changed the whole face of the globe, have turned the
rude forests of nature into agreeable and fertile plains, and made the track less and barren
ocean a new fund of subsistence, and the great high road of communication to the different nations of the earth. The earth by these labours of mankind has been obliged to re-
double her natural fertility, and to maintain a greater multitude of inhabitants. It is to no
purpose, that the proud and unfeeling landlord views his extensive fields, and without a
thought for the wants of his brethren, in imagination consumes himself the whole harvest
that grows upon them. The homely and vulgar proverb, that the eye is larger than the
belly, never was more fully verified than with regard to him. The capacity of his stomach
bears no proportion to the immensity of his desires, and will receive no more than that
of the meanest peasant. The rest he is obliged to distribute among those, who prepare, in
the nicest manner, that little which he himself makes use of, among those who fit up the
palace in which this little is to be consumed, among those who provide and keep in order
all the different baubles and trinkets, which are employed in the oeconomy of greatness;
all of whom thus derive from his luxury and caprice, that share of the necessaries of life,
which they would in vain have expected from his humanity or his justice. The produce of
the soil maintains at all times nearly that number of inhabitants which it is capable of
maintaining. The rich only select from the heap what is most precious and agreeable.
They consume little more than the poor, and in spite of their natural selfishness and rapacity, though they mean only their own conveniency, though the sole end which they propose from the labours of all the thousands whom they employ, be the gratification of their
own vain and insatiable desires, they divide with the poor the produce of all their
improvements. They are led by an invisible hand to make nearly the same distribution of
the necessaries of life, which would have been made, had the earth been divided into equal
portions among all its inhabitants, and thus without intending it, without knowing it,
advance the interest of the society, and afford means to the multiplication of the species.
When Providence divided the earth among a few lordly masters, it neither forgot nor
abandoned those who seemed to have been left out in the partition. These last too enjoy

their share of all that it produces. In what constitutes the real happiness of human life, they are in no respect inferior to those who would seem so much above them. In ease of body and peace of mind, all the different ranks of life are nearly upon a level, and the beggar, who suns himself by the side of the highway, possesses that security which kings are fighting for.

The same principle, the same love of system, the same regard to the beauty of order, of art and contrivance, frequently serves to recommend those institutions which tend to promote the public welfare. When a patriot exerts himself for the improvement of any part of the public police, his conduct does not always arise from pure sympathy with the happiness of those who are to reap the benefit of it. It is not commonly from a fellow-feeling with carriers and waggoners that a public-spirited man encourages the mending of high roads. When the legislature establishes premiums and other encouragements to advance the linen or woollen manufactures, its conduct seldom proceeds from pure sympathy with the wearer of cheap or fine cloth, and much less from that with the manufacturer or merchant. The perfection of police, the extension of trade and manufactures, are noble and magnificent objects. The contemplation of them pleases us, and we are interested in whatever can tend to advance them. They make part of the great system of government, and the wheels of the political machine seem to move with more harmony and ease by means of them. We take pleasure in beholding the perfection of so beautiful and grand a system, and we are uneasy till we remove any obstruction that can in the least disturb or encumber the regularity of its motions. All constitutions of government, however, are valued only in proportion as they tend to promote the happiness of those who live under them. This is their sole use and end. From a certain spirit of system, however, from a certain love of art and contrivance, we sometimes seem to value the means more than the end, and to be eager to promote the happiness of our fellow-creatures, rather from a view to perfect and improve a certain beautiful and orderly system, than from any immediate sense or feeling of what they either suffer or enjoy. There have been men of the greatest public spirit, who have shown themselves in other respects not very sensible to the feelings of humanity. And on the contrary, there have been men of the greatest humanity, who seem to have been entirely devoid of public spirit. Every man may find in the circle of his acquaintance instances both of the one kind and the other. Who had ever less humanity, or more public spirit, than the celebrated legislator of Muscovy? The social and well-natured James the First of Great Britain seems, on the contrary, to have had scarce any passion, either for the glory or the interest of his country. Would you awaken the industry of the man who seems almost dead to ambition, it will often be to no purpose to describe to him the happiness of the rich and the great; to tell him that they are generally sheltered from the sun and the rain, that they are seldom hungry, that they are seldom cold, and that they are rarely exposed to weariness, or to want of any kind. The most eloquent exhortation of this kind will have little effect upon him. If you would hope to succeed, you must describe to him the conveniency and arrangement of the different apartments in their palaces; you must explain to him the propriety of their equipages, and point out to him the number, the order, and the different offices of all their attendants. If any thing is capable of making impression upon him, this will. Yet all these things tend only to keep off the sun and the rain, to save them from hunger and cold, from want and weariness. In the same manner, if you would implant public virtue in the breast of him who seems heedless of the interest of his country, it will often be to no purpose to tell him, what superior advantages the subjects of a well-governed state enjoy; that they are better lodged, that they are better clothed, that they are better fed. These considerations will commonly make no great impression. You will be more likely to persuade, if you describe

the great system of public police which procures these advantages, if you explain the connexions and dependencies of its several parts, their mutual subordination to one another,
and their general subserviency to the happiness of the society; if you show how this system might be introduced into his own country, what it is that hinders it from taking
place there at present, how those obstructions might be removed, and all the several
wheels of the machine of government be made to move with more harmony and smooth-
ness, without grating upon one another, or mutually retarding one another's motions. It
is scarce possible that a man should listen to a discourse of this kind, and not feel himself
animated to some degree of public spirit. He will, at least for the moment, feel some
desire to remove those obstructions, and to put into motion so beautiful and so orderly a
machine. Nothing tends so much to promote public spirit as the study of politics, of the
several systems of civil government, their advantages and disadvantages, of the constitution of our own country, its situation, and interest with regard to foreign nations, its commerce, its defence, the disadvantages it labours under, the dangers to which it may be
exposed, how to remove the one, and how to guard against the other. Upon this account
political disquisitions, if just, and reasonable, and practicable, are of all the works of speculation the most useful. Even the weakest and the worst of them are not altogether without their utility. They serve at least to animate the public passions of men, and rouse them
to seek out the means of promoting the happiness of the society.

CHAPTER II

Of the beauty which the appearance of Utility bestows upon the characters and actions of men; and how far the perception of this beauty may be regarded as one of the original principles of approbation

The characters of men, as well as the contrivances of art, or the institutions of civil government, may be fitted either to promote or to disturb the happiness both of the individual and of the society. The prudent, the equitable, the active, resolute, and sober character
promises prosperity and satisfaction, both to the person himself and to every one connected with him. The rash, the insolent, the slothful, effeminate, and voluptuous, on the
contrary, forebodes ruin to the individual, and misfortune to all who have any thing to do
with him. The first turn of mind has at least all the beauty which can belong to the most
perfect machine that was ever invented for promoting the most agreeable purpose: and the
second, all the deformity of the most awkward and clumsy contrivance. What institution
of government could tend so much to promote the happiness of mankind as the general
prevalence of wisdom and virtue? All government is but an imperfect remedy for the deficiency of these. Whatever beauty, therefore, can belong to civil government upon account
of its utility, must in a far superior degree belong to these. On the contrary, what civil policy can be so ruinous and destructive as the vices of men? The fatal effects of bad government arise from nothing, but that it does not sufficiently guard against the mischiefs
which human wickedness gives occasion to.

   This beauty and deformity which characters appear to derive from their usefulness or
inconveniency, are apt to strike, in a peculiar manner, those who consider, in an abstract
and philosophical light, the actions and conduct of mankind. When a philosopher goes to
examine why humanity is approved of, or cruelty condemned, he does not always form
to himself, in a very clear and distinct manner, the conception of any one particular action

either of cruelty or of humanity, but is commonly contented with the vague and indeterminate idea which the general names of those qualities suggest to him. But it is in particular instances only that the propriety or impropriety, the merit or demerit of actions is very obvious and discernible. It is only when particular examples are given that we perceive distinctly either the concord or disagreement between our own affections and those of the agent, or feel a social gratitude arise towards him in the one case, or a sympathetic resentment in the other. When we consider virtue and vice in an abstract and general manner, the qualities by which they excite these several sentiments seem in a great measure to disappear, and the sentiments themselves become less obvious and discernible. On the contrary, the happy effects of the one and the fatal consequences of the other seem then to rise up to the view, and as it were to stand out and distinguish themselves from all the other qualities of either.

The same ingenious and agreeable author who first explained why utility pleases, has been so struck with this view of things, as to resolve our whole approbation of virtue into a perception of this species of beauty which results from the appearance of utility. No qualities of the mind, he observes, are approved of as virtuous, but such as are useful or agreeable either to the person himself or to others; and no qualities are disapproved of as vicious but such as have a contrary tendency. And Nature, indeed, seems to have so happily adjusted our sentiments of approbation and disapprobation, to the conveniency both of the individual and of the society, that after the strictest examination it will be found, I believe, that this is universally the case. But still I affirm, that it is not the view of this utility or hurtfulness which is either the first or principal source of our approbation and disapprobation. These sentiments are no doubt enhanced and enlivened by the perception of the beauty or deformity which results from this utility or hurtfulness. But still, I say, they are originally and essentially different from this perception.

For first of all, it seems impossible that the approbation of virtue should be a sentiment of the same kind with that by which we approve of a convenient and well-contrived building; or that we should have no other reason for praising a man than that for which we commend a chest of drawers.

And secondly, it will be found, upon examination, that the usefulness of any disposition of mind is seldom the first ground of our approbation; and that the sentiment of approbation always involves in it a sense of propriety quite distinct from the perception of utility. We may observe this with regard to all the qualities which are approved of as virtuous, both those which, according to this system, are originally valued as useful to ourselves, as well as those which are esteemed on account of their usefulness to others.

The qualities most useful to ourselves are, first of all, superior reason and understanding, by which we are capable of discerning the remote consequences of all our actions, and of foreseeing the advantage or detriment which is likely to result from them: and secondly, self-command, by which we are enabled to abstain from present pleasure or to endure present pain, in order to obtain a greater pleasure or to avoid a greater pain in some future time. In the union of those two qualities consists the virtue of prudence, of all the virtues that which is most useful to the individual.

With regard to the first of those qualities, it has been observed on a former occasion, that superior reason and understanding are originally approved of as just and right and accurate, and not merely as useful or advantageous. It is in the abstruser sciences, particularly in the higher parts of mathematics, that the greatest and most admired exertions of human reason have been displayed. But the utility of those sciences, either to the individual or to the public, is not very obvious, and to prove it, requires a discussion which is not always very easily comprehended. It was not, therefore, their utility which first recommended them to the public admiration. This quality was but little insisted upon, till it became necessary to make some reply to the reproaches of those, who, having themselves no taste for such sublime discoveries, endeavoured to depreciate them as useless.

That self-command, in the same manner, by which we restrain our present appetites, in order to gratify them more fully upon another occasion, is approved of, as much under the aspect of propriety, as under that of utility. When we act in this manner, the sentiments which influence our conduct seem exactly to coincide with those of the spectator. The spectator does not feel the solicitations of our present appetites. To him the pleasure which we are to enjoy a week hence, or a year hence, is just as interesting as that which we are to enjoy this moment. When for the sake of the present, therefore, we sacrifice the future, our conduct appears to him absurd and extravagant in the highest degree, and he cannot enter into the principles which influence it. On the contrary, when we abstain from present pleasure, in order to secure greater pleasure to come, when we act as if the remote object interested us as much as that which immediately presses upon the senses, as our affections exactly correspond with his own, he cannot fail to approve of our behaviour: and as he knows from experience, how few are capable of this self-command, he looks upon our conduct with a considerable degree of wonder and admiration. Hence arises that eminent esteem with which all men naturally regard a steady perseverance in the practice of frugality, industry, and application, though directed to no other purpose than the acquisition of fortune. The resolute firmness of the person who acts in this manner, and in order to obtain a great though remote advantage, not only gives up all present pleasures, but endures the greatest labour both of mind and body, necessarily commands our approbation. That view of his interest and happiness which appears to regulate his conduct, exactly tallies with the idea which we naturally form of it. There is the most perfect correspondence between his sentiments and our own, and at the same time, from our experience of the common weakness of human nature, it is a correspondence which we could not reasonably have expected. We not only approve, therefore, but in some measure admire his conduct, and think it worthy of a considerable degree of applause. It is the consciousness of this merited approbation and esteem which is alone capable of supporting the agent in this tenour of conduct. The pleasure which we are to enjoy ten years hence interests us so little in comparison with that which we may enjoy to-day, the passion which the first excites, is naturally so weak in comparison with that violent emotion which the second is apt to give occasion to, that the one could never be any balance to the other, unless it was supported by the sense of propriety, by the consciousness that we merited the esteem and approbation of every body, by acting in the one way, and that we became the proper objects of their contempt and derision by behaving in the other.

Humanity, justice, generosity, and public spirit, are the qualities most useful to others. Wherein consists the propriety of humanity and justice has been explained upon a former occasion, where it was shewn how much our esteem and approbation of those qualities depended upon the concord between the affections of the agent and those of the spectators.

The propriety of generosity and public spirit is founded upon the same principle with that of justice. Generosity is different from humanity. Those two qualities, which at first sight seem so nearly allied, do not always belong to the same person. Humanity is the virtue of a woman, generosity of a man. The fair-sex, who have commonly much more tenderness than ours, have seldom so much generosity. That women rarely make considerable donations, is an observation of the civil law. Humanity consists merely in the exquisite fellow-feeling which the spectator entertains with the sentiments of the persons principally concerned, so as to grieve for their sufferings, to resent their injuries, and to rejoice at their good fortune. The most humane actions require no self-denial, no self-command, no great exertion of the sense of propriety. They consist only in doing what this exquisite sympathy would of its own accord prompt us to do. But it is otherwise with generosity. We never are generous except when in some respect we prefer some other person to ourselves, and sacrifice some great and important interest of our own to an equal interest of a friend or of a superior. The man who gives up his pretensions to an office that was the great object of his ambition, because he imagines that the services of another are better entitled to it; the man who exposes his life to defend that of his friend, which he judges to be of more importance; neither of them act from humanity, or because they feel more exquisitely what concerns that other person than what concerns themselves. They both consider those opposite interests, not in the light in which they naturally appear to themselves, but in that in which they appear to others. To every bystander, the success or preservation of this other person may justly be more interesting than their own; but it cannot be so to themselves. When to the interest of this other person, therefore, they sacrifice their own, they accommodate themselves to the sentiments of the spectator, and by an effort of magnanimity act according to those views of things which, they feel, must naturally occur to any third person. The soldier who throws away his life in order to defend that of his officer, would perhaps be but little affected by the death of that officer, if it should happen without any fault of his own; and a very small disaster which had befallen himself might excite a much more lively sorrow. But when he endeavours to act so as to deserve applause, and to make the impartial spectator enter into the principles of his conduct, he feels, that to every body but himself, his own life is a trifle compared with that of his officer, and that when he sacrifices the one to the other, he acts quite properly and agreeably to what would be the natural apprehensions of every impartial bystander.

It is the same case with the greater exertions of public spirit. When a young officer exposes his life to acquire some inconsiderable addition to the dominions of his sovereign, it is not because the acquisition of the new territory is, to himself, an object more desireable than the preservation of his own life. To him his own life is of infinitely more value than the conquest of a whole kingdom for the state which he serves. But when he compares those two objects with one another, he does not view them in the light in which they naturally appear to himself, but in that in which they appear to the nation he fights for. To them the success of the war is of the highest importance; the life of a private person of scare any consequence. When he puts himself in their situation, he immediately feels that he cannot be too prodigal of his blood, if, by shedding it, he can promote so valuable a purpose. In thus thwarting, from a sense of duty and propriety, the strongest of all natural propensities, consists the heroism of his conduct. There is many an honest Englishman, who, in his private station, would be more seriously disturbed by the loss of a guinea, than by the national loss of Minorca, who yet, had it been in his power to defend that fortress, would have sacrificed his life a thousand times rather than, through his fault, have let it fall into the hands of the enemy. When the first Brutus led forth his own sons to a capital punishment, because they had conspired against the rising liberty of Rome, he sacrificed what, if he had consulted his own breast only, would appear to be the stronger to the weaker affection. Brutus ought naturally to have felt much more for the death of his own sons, than for all that probably Rome could have suffered from the want of so great an example. But he viewed them, not with the eyes of a father, but with those of a Roman citizen. He entered so thoroughly into the sentiments of this last character, that he paid no regard to that tie, by which he himself was connected with them; and to a Roman citizen, the sons even of Brutus seemed contemptible, when put into the balance with the smallest interest of Rome. In these and in all other cases of this kind, our admiration is not so much founded upon the utility, as upon the unexpected, and on that account the great, the noble, and exalted propriety of such actions. This utility, when we come to view it, bestows upon them, undoubtedly, a new beauty, and upon that account still further recommends them to our approbation. This beauty, however, is chiefly perceived by men of reflection and speculation, and is by no means the quality which first recommends such actions to the natural sentiments of the bulk of mankind.

It is to be observed, that so far as the sentiment of approbation arises from the perception of this beauty of utility, it has no reference of any kind to the sentiments of others. If it was possible, therefore, that a person should grow up to manhood without any communication with society, his own actions might, notwithstanding, be agreeable or disagreeable to him on account of their tendency to his happiness or disadvantage. He might perceive a beauty of this kind in prudence, temperance, and good conduct, and a deformity in the opposite behaviour: he might view his own temper and character with that sort of satisfaction with which we consider a well-contrived machine, in the one case; or with that sort of distaste and dissatisfaction with which we regard a very awkward and clumsy contrivance, in the other. As these perceptions, however, are merely a matter of taste, and have all the feebleness and delicacy of that species of perceptions, upon the justness of which what is properly called taste is founded, they probably would not be much attended to by one in this solitary and miserable condition. Even though they should occur to him, they would by no means have the same effect upon him, antecedent to his connexion with society, which they would have in consequence of that connexion. He would not be cast down with inward shame at the thought of this deformity; nor would he be elevated with secret triumph of mind from the consciousness of the contrary beauty. He would not exult from the notion of deserving reward in the one case, nor tremble from the suspicion of meriting punishment in the other. All such sentiments suppose the idea of some other being, who is the natural judge of the person that feels them; and it is only by sympathy with the decisions of this arbiter of his conduct, that he can conceive, either the triumph of self-applause, or the shame of self-condemnation.

THE WEALTH OF NATIONS

INTRODUCTION AND PLAN OF THE WORK

The annual labour of every nation is the fund which originally supplies it with all the necessaries and conveniences of life which it annually consumes, and which consist always, either in the immediate produce of that labour, or in what is purchased with that produce from other nations.

According therefore, as this produce, or what is purchased with it, bears a greater or smaller proportion to the number of those who are to consume it, the nation will be better or worse supplied with all the necessaries and conveniences for which it has occasion.

But this proportion must in every nation be regulated by two different circumstances; first, by the skill, dexterity, and judgment with which its labour is generally applied; and, secondly, by the proportion between the number of those who are employed in useful labour, and that of those who are not so employed. Whatever be the soil, climate, or

extent of territory of any particular nation, the abundance or scantiness of its annual supply must, in that particular situation, depend upon those two circumstances.

The abundance or scantiness of this supply too seems to depend more upon the former
of those two circumstances than upon the latter. Among the savage nations of hunters and
fishers, every individual who is able to work, is more or less employed in useful labour,
and endeavours to provide, as well as he can, the necessaries and conveniencies of life, for
himself, or such of his family or tribe as are either too old, or too young, or too infirm to
go a hunting and fishing. Such nations, however, are so miserably poor, that, from mere
want, they are frequently reduced, or, at least, think themselves reduced, to the necessity
sometimes of directly destroying, and sometimes of abandoning their infants, their old
people, and those afflicted with lingering diseases, to perish with hunger, or to be
devoured by wild beasts. Among civilized and thriving nations, on the contrary, though a
great number of people do not labour at all, many of whom consume the produce of ten
times, frequently of a hundred times more labour than the greater part of those who work;
yet the produce of the whole labour of the society is so great, that all are often abundantly
supplied, and a workman, even of the lowest and poorest order, if he is frugal and industrious, may enjoy a greater share of the necessaries and conveniences of life than it is possible for any savage to acquire.

The causes of this improvement, in the productive powers of labour, and the order,
according to which its produce is naturally distributed among the different ranks and
conditions of men in the society, make the subject of the First Book of this Inquiry.

Whatever be the actual state of the skill, dexterity, and judgment with which labour
is applied in any nation, the abundance or scantiness of its annual supply must depend,
during the continuance of that state, upon the proportion between the number of those
who are annually employed in useful labour, and that of those who are not so employed.
The number of useful and productive labourers, it will hereafter appear, is every where in
proportion to the quantity of capital stock which is employed in setting them to work,
and to the particular way in which it is so employed. The Second Book, therefore, treats
of the nature of capital stock, of the manner in which it is gradually accumulated, and of
the different quantities of labour which it puts into motion, according to the different
ways in which it is employed.

Nations tolerably well advanced as to skill, dexterity, and judgment, in the application
of labour, have followed very different plans in the general conduct or direction of it; and
those plans have not all been equally favourable to the greatness of its produce. The policy of some nations has given extraordinary encouragement to the industry of the country;
that of others to the industry of towns. Scarce any nation has dealt equally and impartially
with every sort of industry. Since the downfall of the Roman empire, the policy of Europe
has been more favourable to arts, manufactures, and commerce, the industry of towns;
than to agriculture, the industry of the country. The circumstances which seem to have
introduced and established this policy are explained in the Third Book.

Though those different plans were, perhaps, first introduced by the private interests
and prejudices of particular orders of men, without any regard to, or foresight of, their
consequences upon the general welfare of the society; yet they have given occasion to very
different theories of political economy; of which some magnify the importance of that
industry which is carried on in towns, others of that which is carried on in the country.
Those theories have had a considerable influence, not only upon the opinions of men of
learning, but upon the public conduct of princes and sovereign states. I have endeavoured,
in the Fourth Book, to explain, as fully and distinctly as I can, those different theories,
and the principal effects which they have produced in different ages and nations.

To explain in what has consisted the revenue of the great body of the people, or what has been the nature of those funds which, in different ages and nations, have supplied their annual consumption, is the object of these Four first Books. The Fifth and last Book treats of the revenue of the sovereign, or commonwealth. In this Book I have endeavoured to show; first, what are the necessary expences of the sovereign, or commonwealth; which of those expences ought to be defrayed by the general contribution of the whole society; and which of them, by that of some particular part only, or of some particular members of it; secondly, what are the different methods in which the whole society may be made to contribute towards defraying the expences incumbent on the whole society, and what are the principal advantages and inconveniencies of each of those methods: and, thirdly and lastly, what are the reasons and causes which have induced almost all modern governments to mortgage some part of this revenue, or to contract debts, and what have been the effects of those debts upon the real wealth, the annual produce of the land and labour of the society.

BOOK I

Of the Causes of Improvement in the productive Powers of Labour, and of the Order according to which its Produce is naturally distributed among the different Ranks of the People

CHAPTER I

Of the Division of Labour

The greatest improvement in the productive powers of labour, and the greater part of the skill, dexterity, and judgment with which it is any where directed, or applied, seem to have been the effects of the division of labour.

The effects of the division of labour, in the general business of society, will be more easily understood, by considering in what manner it operates in some particular manufactures. It is commonly supposed to be carried further in some very trifling ones; not perhaps that it really is carried further in them than in others of more importance: but in those trifling manufactures which are destined to supply the small wants of but a small number of people, the whole number of workmen must necessarily be small; and those employed in every different branch of the work can often be collected into the same workhouse, and placed at once under the view of the spectator. In those great manufactures, on the contrary, which are destined to supply the great wants of the great body of the people, every different branch of the work employs so great a number of workmen, that it is impossible to collect them all into the same workhouse. We can seldom see more, at one time, than those employed in one single branch. Though in such manufactures, therefore, the work may really be divided into a much greater number of parts, than in those of a more trifling nature, the division is not near so obvious, and has accordingly been much less observed.

To take an example, therefore, from a very trifling manufacture; but one in which the division of labour has been very often taken notice of, the trade of the pin-maker; a workman not educated to this business (which the division of labour has rendered a distinct trade), nor acquainted with the use of the machinery employed in it (to the invention of which the same division of labour has probably given occasion), could scarce, perhaps, with his utmost industry, make one pin in a day, and certainly could not make twenty. But in the way in which this business is now carried on, not only the whole work is a peculiar trade, but it is divided into a number of branches, of which the greater part are likewise peculiar trades. One man draws out the wire, another straights it, a third cuts it, a fourth points it, a fifth grinds it at the top for receiving the head; to make the head requires two or three distinct operations; to put it on, is a peculiar business, to whiten the pins is another; it is even a trade by itself to put them into the paper; and the important business of making a pin is, in this manner, divided into about eighteen distinct operations, which, in some manufactories, are all performed by distinct hands, though in others the same man will sometimes perform two or three of them. I have seen a small manufactory of this kind where ten men only were employed, and where some of them consequently performed two or three distinct operations. But though they were very poor, and therefore but indifferently accommodated with the necessary machinery, they could, when they exerted themselves, make among them about twelve pounds of pins in a day. There are in a pound upwards of four thousand pins of a middling size. Those ten persons, therefore, could make among them upwards of forty-eight thousand pins in a day. Each person, therefore, making a tenth part of forty-eight thousand pins, might be considered as making four thousand eight hundred pins in a day. But if they had all wrought separately and independently, and without any of them having been educated to this peculiar business, they certainly could not each of them have made twenty, perhaps not one pin in a day; that is, certainly, not the two hundred and fortieth, perhaps not the four thousand eight hundredth part of what they are at present capable of performing, in consequence of a proper division and combination of their different operations. . . .

This great increase of the quantity of work, which, in consequence of the division of labour, the same number of people are capable of performing, is owing to three different circumstances; first, to the increase of dexterity in every particular workman; secondly, to the saving of the time which is commonly lost in passing from one species of work to another; and lastly, to the invention of a great number of machines which facilitate and abridge labour, and enable one man to do the work of many.

First, the improvement of the dexterity of the workman necessarily increases the quantity of the work he can perform, and the division of labour, by reducing every man's business to some one simple operation, and by making this operation the sole employment of his life, necessarily increases very much the dexterity of the workman. A common smith, who, though accustomed to handle the hammer, has never been used to make nails, if upon some particular occasion he is obliged to attempt it, will scarce, I am assured, be able to make above two or three hundred nails in a day, and those too very bad ones. A smith who has been accustomed to make nails, but whose sole or principal business has not been that of a nailer, can seldom with his utmost diligence make more than eight hundred or a thousand nails in a day. I have seen several boys under twenty years of age who had never exercised any other trade but that of making nails, and who, when they exerted themselves, could make, each of them, upwards of two thousand three hundred nails in a day. The making of a nail, however, is by no means one of the simplest operations. The same person blows the bellows, stirs or mends the fire as there is occasion, heats the iron, and forges every part of the nail: In forging the head too he is obliged to change his tools. The different operations into which the making of a pin, or of a metal button, is subdivided, are all of them much more simple, and the dexterity of the person, of whose life it has been the sole business to perform them, is usually much greater. The rapidity with which some of the operations of those manufactures are performed, exceeds what the human hand could, by those who had never seen them, be supposed capable of acquiring.

Secondly, the advantage which is gained by saving the time commonly lost in passing from one sort of work to another, is much greater than we should at first view be apt to imagine it. It is impossible to pass very quickly from one kind of work to another, that is carried on in a different place, and with quite different tools. A country weaver, who cultivates a small farm, must lose a good deal of time in passing from his loom to the field, and from the field to his loom. When the two trades can be carried on in the same workhouse, the loss of time is no doubt much less. It is even in this case, however, very considerable. A man commonly saunters a little in turning his hand from one sort of employment to another. When he first begins the new work he is seldom very keen and hearty; his mind, as they say, does not go to it, and for some time he rather trifles than applies to good purpose. The habit of sauntering and of indolent careless application, which is naturally, or rather necessarily acquired by every country workman who is obliged to change his work and his tools every half hour, and to apply his hand in twenty different ways almost every day of his life; renders him almost always slothful and lazy, and incapable of any vigorous application even on the most pressing occasions. Independent, therefore, of his deficiency in point of dexterity, this cause alone must always reduce considerably the quantity of work which he is capable of performing.

Thirdly, and lastly, every body must be sensible how much labour is facilitated and abridged by the application of proper machinery. It is unnecessary to give any example. I shall only observe, therefore, that the invention of all those machines by which labour is so much facilitated and abridged, seems to have been originally owing to the division of labour. Men are much more likely to discover easier and readier methods of attaining any object, when the whole attention of their minds is directed towards that single object, than when it is dissipated among a great variety of things. But in consequence of the division of labour, the whole of every man's attention comes naturally to be directed towards some one very simple object. It is naturally to be expected, therefore, that some one or other of those who are employed in each particular branch of labour should soon find out easier and readier methods of performing their own particular work, wherever the nature of it admits of such improvement. A great part of the machines made use of in those manufactures in which labour is most subdivided, were originally the inventions of common workmen, who, being each of them employed in some very simple operation, naturally turned their thoughts towards finding out easier and readier methods of performing it. Whoever has been much accustomed to visit such manufactures, must frequently have been shewn very pretty machines, which were the inventions of such workmen, in order to facilitate and quicken their own particular part of the work. In the first fire-engines, a boy was constantly employed to open and shut alternately the communication between the boiler and the cylinder, according as the piston either ascended or descended. One of those boys, who loved to play with his companions, observed that, by tying a string from the handle of the valve, which opened this communication, to another part of the machine, the valve would open and shut without his assistance, and leave him at liberty to divert himself with his play-fellows. One of the greatest improvements that has been made upon this machine, since it was first invented, was in this manner the discovery of a boy who wanted to save his own labour.

All the improvements in machinery, however, have by no means been the inventions of those who had occasion to use the machines. Many improvements have been made by the ingenuity of the makers of the machines, when to make them became the business of a peculiar trade; and some by that of those who are called philosophers or men of speculation, whose trade it is, not to do any thing, but to observe every thing; and who, upon that account, are often capable of combining together the powers of the most distant and dissimilar objects. In the progress of society, philosophy or speculation becomes, like every other employment, the principal or sole trade and occupation of a particular class of citizens. Like every other employment too, it is subdivided into a great number of different branches, each of which affords occupation to a peculiar tribe or class of philosophers; and this subdivision of employment in philosophy, as well as in every other business, improves dexterity, and saves time. Each individual becomes more expert in his own peculiar branch, more work is done upon the whole, and the quantity of science is considerably increased by it.

It is the great multiplication of the productions of all the different arts, in consequence of the division of labour, which occasions, in a well-governed society, that universal opulence which extends itself to the lowest ranks of the people. Every workman has a great quantity of his own work to dispose of beyond what he himself has occasion for; and every other workman being exactly in the same situation, he is enabled to exchange a great quantity of his own goods for a great quantity, or, what comes to the same thing, for the price of a great quantity of theirs. He supplies them abundantly with what they have occasion for, and they accommodate him as amply with what he has occasion for, and a general plenty diffuses itself through all the different ranks of the society.

Observe the accommodation of the most common artificer or day-labourer in a civilized and thriving country, and you will perceive that the number of people of whose industry a part, though but a small part, has been employed in procuring him this accommodation, exceeds all computation. The woollen coat, for example, which covers the day-labourer, as coarse and rough as it may appear, is the produce of the joint labour of a great multitude of workmen. The shepherd, the sorter of the wool, the wool-comber or carder, the dyer, the scribbler, the spinner, the weaver, the fuller, the dresser, with many others, must all join their different arts in order to complete even this homely production. How many merchants and carriers, besides, must have been employed in transporting the materials from some of those workmen to others who often live in a very distant part of the country! How much commerce and navigation in particular, how many ship-builders, sailors, sail-makers, rope-makers, must have been employed in order to bring together the different drugs made use of by the dyer, which often come from the remotest corners of the world! What a variety of labour too is necessary in order to produce the tools of the meanest of those workmen! To say nothing of such complicated machines as the ship of the sailor, the mill of the fuller, or even the loom of the weaver, let us consider only what a variety of labour is requisite in order to form that very simple machine, the shears with which the shepherd clips the wool. The miner, the builder of the furnace for smelting the ore, the feller of the timber, the burner of the charcoal to be made use of in the smelting-house, the brick-maker, the bricklayer, the workmen who attend the furnace, the mill-wright, the forger, the smith, must all of them join their different arts in order to produce them. Were we to examine, in the same manner, all the different parts of his dress and household furniture, the coarse linen shirt which he wears next his skin, the shoes which cover his feet, the bed which he lies on, and all the different parts which compose it, the kitchen-grate at which he prepares his victuals, the coals which he makes use of for that purpose, dug from the bowels of the earth, and brought to him perhaps by a long sea and a long land carriage, all the other utensils of his kitchen, all the furniture of his table, the knives and forks, the earthen or pewter plates upon which he serves up and divides his victuals, the different hands employed in preparing his bread and his beer, the glass window which lets in the heat and the light, and keeps out the wind and the rain, with all the knowledge and art requisite for preparing that beautiful and happy invention, without which these northern parts of the world could scarce have afforded a very comfortable habitation, together with the tools of all the different workmen employed in producing those different conveniencies; if we examine, I say, all these things, and consider what a variety of labour is employed about each of them, we shall be sensible that without the assistance and co-operation of many thousands, the very meanest person in a civilized country could not be provided, even according to, what we very falsely imagine, the easy and simple manner in which he is commonly accommodated. Compared, indeed, with the more extravagant luxury of the great, his accommodation must no doubt appear extremely simple and easy; and yet it may be true, perhaps, that the accommodation of an European prince does not always so much exceed that of an industrious and frugal peasant, as the accommodation of the latter exceeds that of many an African king, the absolute master of the lives and liberties of ten thousand naked savages.

CHAPTER II

Of the Principle which gives occasion to the Division of Labour

This division of labour, from which so many advantages are derived, is not originally the effect of any human wisdom, which foresees and intends that general opulence to which it gives occasion. It is the necessary, though very slow and gradual consequence of a certain propensity in human nature which has in view no such extensive utility; the propensity to truck, barter, and exchange one thing for another.

Whether this propensity be one of those original principles in human nature, of which no further account can be given; or whether, as seems more probable, it be the necessary consequence of the faculties of reason and speech, it belongs not to our present subject to enquire. It is common to all men, and to be found in no other race of animals, which seem to know neither this nor any other species of contracts. Two greyhounds, in running down the same hare, have sometimes the appearance of acting in some sort of concert. Each turns her towards his companion, or endeavours to intercept her when his companion turns her towards himself. This, however, is not the effect of any contract, but of the accidental concurrence of their passions in the same object at that particular time. Nobody ever saw a dog make a fair and deliberate exchange of one bone for another with another dog. Nobody ever saw one animal by its gestures, and natural cries signify to another, this is mine, that yours; I am willing to give this for that. When an animal wants to obtain something either of a man or of another animal, it has no other means of persuasion but to gain the favour of those whose service it requires. A puppy fawns upon its dam, and a spaniel endeavours by a thousand attractions to engage the attention of its master who is at dinner, when it wants to be fed by him. Man sometimes uses the same arts with his brethren, and when he has no other means of engaging them to act according to his inclinations, endeavours by every servile and fawning attention to obtain their good will. He has not time, however, to do this upon every occasion. In civilized society he stands at all times in need of the co-operation and assistance of great multitudes, while his whole life is scarce sufficient to gain the friendship of a few persons. In almost every other race of animals each individual, when it is grown up to maturity, is intirely independent, and in its natural state has occasion for the assistance of no other living creature. But man has almost constant occasion for the help of his brethren, and it is in vain for him to expect it from their benevolence only. He will be more likely to prevail if he can interest their self-love in his favour, and shew them that it is for their own advantage to do for him what he requires of them. Whoever offers to another a bargain of any kind, proposes to do this. Give me that which I want, and you shall have this which you want, is the meaning of every such offer; and it is in this manner that we obtain from one another the far greater part of those good offices which we stand in need of. It is not from the benevolence of the butcher, the brewer, or the baker, that we expect our dinner, but from their regard to their own interest. We address ourselves, not to their humanity but to their self-love, and never talk to them of our own necessities but of their advantages. Nobody but a beggar chuses to depend chiefly upon the benevolence of his fellow-citizens. Even a beggar does not depend upon it entirely. The charity of well-disposed people, indeed, supplies him with the whole fund of his subsistence. But though this principle ultimately provides him with all the necessaries of life which he has occasion for, it neither does nor can provide him with them as he has occasion for them. The greater part of his occasional wants are supplied in the same manner as those of other people, by treaty, by barter, and by purchase. With the money which one man gives him he purchases food. The old cloaths which another bestows upon him he exchanges for other old cloaths which suit him better, or for lodging, or for food, or for money, with which he can buy either food, cloaths, or lodging, as he has occasion.

As it is by treaty, by barter, and by purchase, that we obtain from one another the greater part of those mutual good offices which we stand in need of, so it is this same trucking disposition which originally gives occasion to the division of labour. In a tribe of hunters or shepherds a particular person makes bows and arrows, for example, with more readiness and dexterity than any other. He frequently exchanges them for cattle or for venison with his companions; and he finds at last that he can in this manner get more cattle and venison, than if he himself went to the field to catch them. From a regard to his own interest, therefore, the making of bows and arrows grows to be his chief business, and he becomes a sort of armourer. Another excels in making the frames and covers of their little huts or moveable houses. He is accustomed to be of use in this way to his neighbours, who reward him in the same manner with cattle and with venison, till at last he finds it his interest to dedicate himself entirely to this employment, and to become a sort of house-carpenter. In the same manner a third becomes a smith or a brazier, a fourth a tanner or dresser of hides or skins, the principal part of the clothing of savages. And thus the certainty of being able to exchange all that surplus part of the produce of his own labour, which is over and above his own consumption, for such parts of the produce of other men's labour as he may have occasion for, encourages every man to apply himself to a particular occupation, and to cultivate and bring to perfection whatever talent or genius he may possess for that particular species of business.

The difference of natural talents in different men is, in reality, much less than we are aware of; and the very different genius which appears to distinguish men of different professions, when grown up to maturity, is not upon many occasions so much the cause, as the effect of the division of labour. The difference between the most dissimilar characters, between a philosopher and a common street porter, for example, seems to arise not so much from nature, as from habit, custom, and education. When they came into the world, and for the first six or eight years of their existence, they were, perhaps, very much alike, and neither their parents nor play-fellows could perceive any remarkable difference. About that age, or soon after, they come to be employed in very different occupations. The difference of talents comes then to be taken notice of, and widens by degrees, till at last the vanity of the philosopher is willing to acknowledge scarce any resemblance. But without the disposition to truck, barter, and exchange, every man must have procured to himself every necessary and conveniency of life which he wanted. All must have had the same duties to perform, and the same work to do, and there could have been no such difference of employment as could alone give occasion to any great difference of talents.

As it is this disposition which forms that difference of talents, so remarkable among men of different professions, so it is this same disposition which renders that difference useful. Many tribes of animals acknowledged to be all of the same species, derive from nature a much more remarkable distinction of genius, than what, antecedent to custom and education, appears to take place among men. By nature a philosopher is not in genius and disposition half so different from a street porter, as a mastiff is from a greyhound, or a greyhound from a spaniel, or this last from a shepherd's dog. Those different tribes of animals, however, though all of the same species, are of scarce any use to one another. The strength of the mastiff is not, in the least, supported either by the swiftness of the greyhound, or by the sagacity of the spaniel, or by the docility of the shepherd's dog. The effects of those different geniuses and talents, for want of the power or disposition to barter and exchange, cannot be brought into a common stock, and do not in the least contribute to the better accommodation and conveniency of the species. Each animal is still obliged to support and defend itself, separately and independently, and derives no sort of advantage from that variety of talents with which nature has distinguished its fellows. Among men, on the contrary, the most dissimilar geniuses are of use to one another; the different produces of their respective talents, by the general disposition to truck, barter, and exchange, being brought, as it were, into common stock, where every man may purchase whatever part of the produce of other men's talents he has occasion for.

CHAPTER IV

Of the Origin and Use of Money

When the division of labour has been once thoroughly established, it is but a very small part of a man's wants which the produce of his own labour can supply. He supplies the far greater part of them by exchanging that surplus part of the produce of his own labour, which is over and above his own consumption, for such parts of the produce of other men's labour as he has occasion for. Every man thus lives by exchanging, or becomes in some measure a merchant, and the society itself grows to be what is properly a commercial society.

But when the division of labour first began to take place, this power of exchanging must frequently have been very much clogged and embarrassed in its operations. One man, we shall suppose, has more of a certain commodity than he himself has occasion for, while another has less. The former consequently would be glad to dispose of, and the latter to purchase, a part of this superfluity. But if this latter should chance to have nothing that the former stands in need of, no exchange can be made between them. The butcher has more meat in his shop than he himself can consume, and the brewer and the baker would each of them be willing to purchase a part of it. But they have nothing to offer in exchange, except the different productions of their respective trades, and the butcher is already provided with all the bread and beer which he has immediate occasion for. No exchange can, in this case, be made between them. He cannot be their merchant, nor they his customers; and they are all of them thus mutually less serviceable to one another. In order to avoid the inconveniency of such situations, every prudent man in every period of society, after the first establishment of the division of labour, must naturally have endeavoured to manage his affairs in such a manner, as to have at all times by him, besides the peculiar produce of his own industry, a certain quantity of some one commodity or other, such as he imagined few people would be likely to refuse in exchange for the produce of their industry.

Many different commodities, it is probable, were successively both thought of and employed for this purpose. In the rude ages of society, cattle are said to have been the common instrument of commerce; and, though they must have been a most inconvenient one, yet in old times we find things were frequently valued according to the number of cattle which had been given in exchange for them. The armour of Diomede, says Homer, cost only nine oxen; but that of Glaucus cost an hundred oxen. Salt is said to be the common instrument of commerce and exchanges in Abyssinia; a species of shells in some parts of the coast of India; dried cod at Newfoundland; tobacco in Virginia; sugar in some of our West India colonies; hides or dressed leather in some other countries; and there is at this day a village in Scotland where it is not uncommon, I am told, for a workman to carry nails instead of money to the baker's shop or the ale-house.

In all countries, however, men seem at last to have been determined by irresistible reasons to give the preference, for this employment, to metals above every other commodity. Metals can not only be kept with as little loss as any other commodity, scarce any thing being less perishable than they are, but they can likewise, without any loss, be divided into any number of parts, as by fusion those parts can easily be re-united again; a quality which no other equally durable commodities possess, and which more than any other quality renders them fit to be the instruments of commerce and circulation. The man who wanted to buy salt, for example, and had nothing but cattle to give in exchange for it, must have been obliged to buy salt to the value of a whole ox, or a whole sheep at a time. He could seldom buy less than this, because what he was to give for it could seldom be divided without loss; and if he had a mind to buy more, he must, for the same reasons, have been obliged to buy double or triple the quantity, the value, to wit, of two or three oxen, or of two or three sheep. If, on the contrary, instead of sheep or oxen, he had metals to give in exchange for it, he could easily proportion the quantity of the metal to the precise quantity of the commodity which he had immediate occasion for. . . .

It is in this manner that money has become in all civilized nations the universal instrument of commerce, by the intervention of which goods of all kinds are bought and sold, or exchanged for one another.

What are the rules which men naturally observe in exchanging them either for money or for one another, I shall now proceed to examine. These rules determine what may be called the relative or exchangeable value of goods.

The word Value, it is to be observed, has two different meanings, and sometimes expresses the utility of some particular object, and sometimes the power of purchasing other goods which the possession of that object conveys. The one may be called 'value in use;' the other, 'value in exchange.' The things which have the greatest value in use have frequently little or no value in exchange; and, on the contrary, those which have the greatest value in exchange have frequently little or no value in use. Nothing is more useful than water: but it will purchase scarce any thing; scarce any thing can be had in exchange for it. A diamond, on the contrary, has scarce any value in use; but a very great quantity of other goods may frequently be had in exchange for it.

In order to investigate the principles which regulate the exchangeable value of commodities, I shall endeavour to shew,

First, what is the real measure of this exchangeable value; or, wherein consists the real price of all commodities,

Secondly, what are the different parts of which this real price is composed or made up.

And, lastly, what are the different circumstances which sometimes raise some or all of these different parts of price above, and sometimes sink them below their natural or ordinary rate; or, what are the causes which sometimes hinder the market price, that is, the actual price of commodities, from coinciding exactly with what may be called their natural price.

I shall endeavour to explain, as fully and distinctly as I can, those three subjects in the three following chapters, for which I must very earnestly entreat both the patience and attention of the reader: his patience in order to examine a detail which may perhaps in some places appear unnecessarily tedious; and his attention in order to understand what may, perhaps, after the fullest explication which I am capable of giving of it, appear still in some degree obscure. I am always willing to run some hazard of being tedious in order to be sure that I am perspicuous; and after taking the utmost pains that I can to be perspicuous, some obscurity may still appear to remain upon a subject in its own nature extremely abstracted.

CHAPTER V

Of the real and nominal Price of Commodities, or of their Price in Labour, and their Price in Money

Every man is rich or poor according to the degree in which he can afford to enjoy the necessaries, conveniencies, and amusements of human life. But after the division of labour has once thoroughly taken place, it is but a very small part of these with which a man's own labour can supply him. The far greater part of them he must derive from the labour of other people, and he must be rich or poor according to the quantity of that labour which he can command, or which he can afford to purchase. The value of any commodity, therefore, to the person who possesses it, and who means not to use or consume it himself, but to exchange it for other commodities, is equal to the quantity of labour which it enables him to purchase or command. Labour, therefore, is the real measure of the exchangeable value of all commodities.

The real price of every thing, what every thing really costs to the man who wants to acquire it, is the toil and trouble of acquiring it. What every thing is really worth to the man who has acquired it, and who wants to dispose of it or exchange it for something else, is the toil and trouble which it can save to himself, and which it can impose upon other people. What is bought with money or with goods is purchased by labour as much as what we acquire by the toil of our own body. That money or those goods indeed save us this toil. They contain the value of a certain quantity of labour which we exchange for what is supposed at the time to contain the value of an equal quantity. Labour was the first price, the original purchase money that was paid for all things. It was not by gold or by silver, but by labour, that all the wealth of the world was originally purchased; and its value, to those who possess it and who want to exchange it for some new productions, is precisely equal to the quantity of labour which it can enable them to purchase or command.

Wealth, as Mr. Hobbes says, is power. But the person who either acquires, or succeeds to a great fortune, does not necessarily acquire or succeed to any political power, either civil or military. His fortune may, perhaps, afford him the means of acquiring both, but the mere possession of that fortune does not necessarily convey to him either. The power which that possession immediately and directly conveys to him, is the power of purchasing; a certain command over all the labour, or over all the produce of labour which is then in the market. His fortune is greater or less, precisely in proportion to the extent of this power; or to the quantity either of other men's labour, or, what is the same thing, of the produce of other men's labour, which it enables him to purchase or command. The exchangeable value of every thing must always be precisely equal to the extent of this power which it conveys to its owner.

But though labour be the real measure of the exchangeable value of all commodities, it is not that by which their value is commonly estimated. It is often difficult to ascertain the proportion between two different quantities of labour. The time spent in two different sorts of work will not always alone determine this proportion. The different degrees of hardship endured, and of ingenuity exercised, must likewise be taken into account. There may be more labour in an hour's hard work than in two hours easy business; or in an hour's application to a trade which it cost ten years labour to learn, than in a month's industry at an ordinary and obvious employment. But it is not easy to find any accurate measure either of hardship or ingenuity. In exchanging indeed the different productions of different sorts of labour for one another, some allowance is commonly made for both. It is adjusted, however, not by any accurate measure, but by the higgling and bargaining of the market, according to that sort of rough equality which, though not exact, is sufficient for carrying on the business of common life.

Every commodity besides, is more frequently exchanged for, and thereby compared with, other commodities than with labour. It is more natural, therefore, to estimate its exchangeable value by the quantity of some other commodity than by that of the labour which it can purchase. The greater part of people too understand better what is meant by a quantity of a particular commodity, than by a quantity of labour. The one is a plain palpable object; the other an abstract notion, which, though it can be made sufficiently intelligible, is not altogether so natural and obvious.

But when barter ceases, and money has become the common instrument of commerce, every particular commodity is more frequently exchanged for money than for any other commodity. The butcher seldom carries his beef or his mutton to the baker, or the brewer, in order to exchange them for bread or for beer, but he carries them to the market, where he exchanges them for money, and afterwards exchanges that money for bread and for beer. The quantity of money which he gets for them regulates too the quantity of bread and beer which he can afterwards purchase. It is more natural and obvious to him, therefore, to estimate their value by the quantity of money, the commodity for which he immediately exchanges them, than by that of bread and beer, the commodities for which he can exchange them only by the intervention of another commodity; and rather to say that his butcher's meat is worth threepence or fourpence a pound, than that it is worth three or four pounds of bread, or three or four quarts of small beer. Hence it comes to pass, that the exchangeable value of every commodity is more frequently estimated by the quantity of money, than by the quantity either of labour or of any other commodity which can be had in exchange for it.

Gold and silver, however, like every other commodity, vary in their value, are sometimes cheaper and sometimes dearer, sometimes of easier and sometimes of more difficult purchase. The quantity of labour which any particular quantity of them can purchase or command, or the quantity of other goods which it will exchange for, depends always upon the fertility or barrenness of the mines which happen to be known about the time when such exchanges are made. The discovery of the abundant mines of America reduced, in the sixteenth century, the value of gold and silver in Europe to about a third of what it had been before. As it cost less labour to bring those metals from the mine to the market, so when they were brought thither they could purchase or command less labour; and this revolution in their value, though perhaps the greatest, is by no means the only one of which history gives some account. But as a measure of quantity, such as the natural foot, fathom, or handful, which is continually varying in its own quantity, can never be an accurate measure of the quantity of other things; so a commodity which is itself continually varying in its own value, can never be an accurate measure of the value of other commodities. Equal quantities of labour, at all times and places, may be said to be of equal value to the labourer. In his ordinary state of health, strength and spirits; in the ordinary degree of his skill and dexterity, he must always lay down the same portion of his ease, his liberty, and his happiness. The price which he pays must always be the same, whatever may be the quantity of goods which he receives in return for it. Of these, indeed, it may sometimes purchase a greater and sometimes a smaller quantity; but it is their value which varies, not that of the labour which purchases them. At all times and places that is dear which it is difficult to come at, or which it costs much labour to acquire; and that cheap which is to be had easily, or with very little labour. Labour alone, therefore, never varying in its own value, is alone the ultimate arid real standard by which the value of all commodities can at all times and places be estimated and compared. It is their real price; money is their nominal price only.

But though equal quantities of labour are always of equal value to the labourer, yet to the person who employs him they appear sometimes to be of greater and sometimes of smaller value. He purchases them sometimes with a greater and sometimes with a smaller quantity of goods, and to him the price of labour seems to vary like that of all other things. It appears to him dear in the one case, and cheap in the other. In reality, however, it is the goods which are cheap in the one case, and dear in the other.

In this popular sense, therefore, labour, like commodities, may be said to have a real and a nominal price. Its real price may be said to consist in the quantity of the necessaries and conveniencies of life which are given for it; its nominal price, in the quantity of money. The labourer is rich or poor, is well or ill rewarded, in proportion to the real, not to the nominal price of his labour. . . .

CHAPTER VI

Of the component Parts of the Price of Commodities

In that early and rude state of society which precedes both the accumulation of stock and the appropriation of land, the proportion between the quantities of labour necessary for acquiring different objects seems to be the only circumstance which can afford any rule for exchanging them for one another. If among a nation of hunters, for example, it usually costs twice the labour to kill a beaver which it does to kill a deer, one beaver should naturally exchange for or be worth two deer. It is natural that what is usually the produce of two days or two hours labour, should be worth double of what is usually the produce of one day's or one hour's labour.

If the one species of labour should be more severe than the other, some allowance will naturally be made for this superior hardship; and the produce of one hour's labour in the one way may frequently exchange for that of two hours labour in the other.

Or if the one species of labour requires an uncommon degree of dexterity and ingenuity, the esteem which men have for such talents, will naturally give a value to their produce, superior to what would be due to the time employed about it. Such talents can seldom be acquired but in consequence of long application, and the superior value of their produce may frequently be no more than a reasonable compensation for the time and labour which must be spent in acquiring them. In the advanced state of society, allowances of this kind, for superior hardship and superior still, are commonly made in the wages of labour; and something of the same kind must probably have taken place in its earliest and rudest period.

In this state of things, the whole produce of labour belongs to the labourer; and the quantity of labour commonly employed in acquiring or producing any commodity, is the only circumstance which can regulate the quantity of labour which it ought commonly to purchase, command, or exchange for.

As soon as stock has accumulated in the hands of particular persons, some of them will naturally employ it in setting to work industrious people, whom they will supply with materials and subsistence, in order to make a profit by the sale of their work, or by what their labour adds to the value of the materials. In exchanging the complete manufacture either for money, for labour, or for other goods, over and above what may be sufficient to pay the price of the materials, and the wages of the workmen, something must be given for the profits of the undertaker of the work who hazards his stock in this adventure. The value which the workmen add to the materials, therefore, resolves itself in this case into two parts, of which the one pays their wages, the other the profits of their employer upon the whole stock of materials and wages which he advanced. He could have no interest to employ them, unless he expected from the sale of their work something more than what was sufficient to replace his stock to him; and he could have no interest to employ a great stock rather than a small one, unless his profits were to bear some proportion to the extent of his stock.

The profits of stock, it may perhaps be thought, are only a different name for the wages of a particular sort of labour, the labour of inspection and direction. They are, however, altogether different, are regulated by quite different principles, and bear no proportion to the quantity, the hardship, or the ingenuity of this supposed labour of inspection and direction. They are regulated altogether by the value of the stock employed, and are greater or smaller in proportion to the extent of this stock. Let us suppose, for example, that in some particular place, where the common annual profits of manufacturing stock are ten per cent, there are two different manufactures, in each of which twenty workmen are employed at the rate of fifteen pounds a year each, or at the expence of three hundred a year in each manufactory. Let us suppose too, that the coarse materials annually wrought up in the one cost only seven hundred pounds, while the finer materials in the other cost seven thousand. The capital annually employed in the one will in this case amount only to one thousand pounds; whereas that employed in the other will amount to seven thousand three hundred pounds. At the rate of ten per cent, therefore, the undertaker of the one will expect an yearly profit of about one hundred pounds only; while that of the other will expect about seven hundred and thirty pounds. But though their profits are so very different, their labour of inspection and direction may be either altogether or very nearly the same. In many great works, almost the whole labour of this kind is committed to some principal clerk. His wages properly express the value of this labour of inspection and direction. Though in settling them some regard is had commonly, not only to his labour and skill, but to the trust which is reposed in him, yet they never bear any regular proportion to the capital of which he oversees the management; and the owner of this capital, though he is thus discharged of almost all labour, still expects that his profits should bear a regular proportion to his capital. In the price of commodities, therefore, the profits of stock constitute a component part altogether different from the wages of labour, and regulated by quite different principles.

In this state of things, the whole produce of labour does not always belong to the labourer. He must in most cases share it with the owner of the stock which employs him.

Neither is the quantity of labour commonly employed in acquiring or producing any commodity, the only circumstance which can regulate the quantity which it ought commonly to purchase, command, or exchange for. An additional quantity, it is evident, must be due for the profits of the stock which advanced the wages and furnished the materials of that labour.

As soon as the land of any country has all become private property, the landlords, like all other men, love to reap where they never sowed, and demand a rent even for its natural produce. The wood of the forest, the grass of the field, and all the natural fruits of the earth, which, when land was in common, cost the labourer only the trouble of gathering them, come, even to him, to have an additional price fixed upon them. He must then pay for the licence to gather them; and must give up to the landlord a portion of what his labour either collects or produces. This portion, or, what comes to the same thing, the price of this portion, constitutes the rent of land, and in the price of the greater part of commodities makes a third component part.

The real value of all the different component parts of price, it must be observed, is measured by the quantity of labour which they can, each of them, purchase or command. Labour measures the value not only of that part of price which resolves itself into labour, but of that which resolves itself into rent, and of that which resolves itself into profit. . . .

BOOK IV

Of Systems of Political Economy

INTRODUCTION

Political economy, considered as a branch of the science of a statesman or legislator, proposes two distinct objects; first, to provide a plentiful revenue or subsistence for the people, or more properly to enable them to provide such a revenue or subsistence for themselves; and secondly, to supply the state or commonwealth with a revenue sufficient for the publick services. It proposes to enrich both the people and the sovereign.

The different progress of opulence in different ages and nations, has given occasion to two different systems of political economy, with regard to enriching the people. The one may be called the system of commerce, the other that of agriculture. I shall endeavour to explain both as fully and distinctly as I can, and shall begin with the system of commerce. It is the modern system, and is best understood in our own country and in our own times.

CHAPTER II

Of Restraints upon the Importation from Foreign Countries of Such Goods as Can Be Produced at Home

. . . Every individual is continually exerting himself to find out the most advantageous employment for whatever capital he can command. It is his own advantage, indeed, and not that of the society, which he has in view. But the study of his own advantage naturally, or rather necessarily leads him to prefer that employment which is most advantageous to the society.

First, every individual endeavours to employ his capital as near home as he can, and consequently as much as he can in the support of domestick industry; provided always that he can thereby obtain the ordinary, or not a great deal less than the ordinary profits of stock.

Thus upon equal or nearly equal profits, every wholesale merchant naturally prefers the home-trade to the foreign trade of consumption, and the foreign trade of consumption to the carrying trade. In the home-trade his capital is never so long out of his sight as it frequently is in the foreign trade of consumption. He can know better the character and situation of the persons whom he trusts, and if he should happen to be deceived, he knows better the laws of the country from which he must seek redress. In the carrying trade, the capital of the merchant is, as it were, divided between two foreign countries, and no part of it is ever necessarily brought home, or placed under his own immediate view and command. The capital which an Amsterdam merchant employs in carrying corn from Konnigsberg to Lisbon, and fruit and wine from Lisbon to Konnigsberg, must generally be the one-half of it at Konnigsberg and the other half at Lisbon. No part of it need ever come to Amsterdam. The natural residence of such a merchant should either be at Konnigsberg or Lisbon, and it can only be some very particular circumstances which can make him prefer the residence of Amsterdam. The uneasiness, however, which he feels at being separated so far from his capital, generally determines him to bring part both of the Konnigsberg goods which he destines for the market of Lisbon, and of the Lisbon goods which he destines for that of Konnigsberg, to Amsterdam: and though this necessarily subjects him to a double charge of loading and unloading, as well as to the payment of some duties and customs, yet for the sale of having some part of his capital always under his own view and command, he willingly submits to this extraordinary charge; and it is in this manner that every country which has any considerable share of the carrying trade, becomes always the emporium, or general market, for the goods of all the different countries whose trade it carries on. The merchant, in order to save a second loading and unloading, endeavours always to sell in the home-market as much of the goods of all those different countries as he can, and thus, so far as he can, to convert his carrying trade into a foreign trade of consumption. A merchant, in the same manner, who is engaged in the foreign trade of consumption, when he collects goods for foreign markets, will always be glad, upon equal or nearly equal profits, to sell as great a part of them at home as he can. He saves himself the risk and trouble of exportation, when, so far as he can, he thus converts his foreign trade of consumption into a home-trade. Home is in this manner the center, if I may say so, round which the capitals of the inhabitants of every country are continually circulating, and towards which they are always tending, though by particular causes they may sometimes be driven off and repelled from it towards more distant employments. But a capital employed in the home-trade, it has already been shown, necessarily puts into motion a greater quantity of domestic industry, and gives revenue and employment to a greater number of the inhabitants of the country, than an equal capital employed in the foreign trade of consumption: and one employed in the foreign trade of consumption has the same advantage over an equal capital employed in the carrying trade. Upon equal, or only nearly equal profits, therefore, every individual naturally inclines to employ his capital in the manner in which it is likely to afford the greatest support to domestick industry, and to give revenue and employment to the greatest number of people of his own country.

Secondly, every individual who employs his capital in the support of domestick industry, necessarily endeavours so to direct that industry, that its produce may be of the greatest possible value.

The produce of industry is what it adds to the subject or materials upon which it is employed. In proportion as the value of this produce is great or small, so will likewise be the profits of the employer. But it is only for the sake of profit that any man employs a capital in the support of industry; and he will always, therefore, endeavour to employ it in the support of that industry of which the produce is likely to be of the greatest value or to exchange for the greatest quantity either of money or of other goods.

But the annual revenue of every society is always precisely equal to the exchangeable value of the whole annual produce of its industry, or rather is precisely the same thing with that exchangeable value. As every individual, therefore, endeavours as much as he can both to employ his capital in the support of domestick industry, and so to direct that industry that its produce may be of the greatest value; every individual necessarily labours to render the annual revenue of the society as great as he can. He generally, indeed, neither intends to promote the publick interest, nor knows how much he is promoting it. By preferring the support of domestick to that of foreign industry, he intends only his own security; and by directing that industry in such a manner as its produce may be of the greatest value, he intends only his own gain, and he is in this, as in many other cases, led by an invisible hand to promote an end which was no part of his intention. Nor is it always the worse for the society that it was no part of it. By pursuing his own interest he frequently promotes that of the society more effectually than when he really intends to promote it. I have never known much good done by those who affected to trade for the publick good. It is an affectation, indeed, not very common among merchants, and very few words need be employed in dissuading them from it.

What is the species of domestick industry which his capital can employ, and of which the produce is likely to be of the greatest value, every individual, it is evident, can, in his local situation, judge much better than any statesman or lawgiver can do for him. The stateman, who should attempt to direct private people in what manner they ought to employ their capitals, would not only load himself with a most unnecessary attention, but assume an authority which could safely be trusted, not only to no single person, but to no council or senate whatever, and which would nowhere be so dangerous as in the hands of a man who had folly and presumption enough to fancy himself fit to exercise it. . . .

CHAPTER IX

Of the Agricultural Systems . . .

. . . All systems either of preference or of restraint, therefore, being thus completely taken away, the obvious and simple system of natural liberty establishes itself of its own accord. Every man, as long as he does not violate the laws of justice, is left perfectly free to pursue his own interest his own way, and to bring both his industry and capital into competition with those of any other man, or order of men. The sovereign is completely discharged from a duty, in the attempting to perform which he must always be exposed to innumerable delusions, and for the proper performance of which no human wisdom or knowledge could ever be sufficient; the duty of superintending the industry of private people, and of directing it towards the employments most suitable to the interest of the society. According to the system of natural liberty, the sovereign has only three duties to attend to; three duties of great importance, indeed, but plain and intelligible to common understandings: first, the duty of protecting the society from the violence and invasion of other independent societies; secondly, the duty of protecting, as far as possible, every member of the society from the injustice or oppression of every other member of it, or the duty of establishing an exact administration of justice; and, thirdly, the duty of erecting and maintaining certain pub-lick works and certain publick institutions, which it can never be for the interest of any individual, or small number of individuals, to erect and maintain; because the profit could never repay the expence to any individual or small number of individuals, though it may frequently do much more than repay it to a great society. . . .

The proper performance of those several duties of the sovereign necessarily supposes a certain expence; and this expence again necessarily requires a certain revenue to support it. In the following book, therefore, I shall endeavour to explain; first, what are the neces-sary expences of the sovereign or commonwealth; and which of those expences ought to be defrayed by the general contribution of the whole society; and which of them, by that of some particular part only, or of some particular members of the society: secondly, what are the different methods in which the whole society may be made to contribute towards defraying the expences incumbent on the whole society, and what are the principal advan-tages and inconveniencies of each of those methods: and, thirdly, what are the reasons and causes which have induced almost all modern governments to mortgage some part of this revenue, or to contract debts, and what have been the effects of those debts upon the real wealth, the annual produce of the land and labour of the society. The following book, therefore, will naturally be divided into three chapters.

BOOK V

Of the Revenue of the Sovereign or Commonwealth

CHAPTER I

Of the Expences of the Sovereign or Commonwealth

. . . The expence of defending the society, and that of supporting the dignity of the chief magistrate, are both laid out for the general benefit of the whole society. It is reasonable, therefore, that they should be defrayed by the general contribution of the whole society, all the different members contributing, as nearly as possible, in proportion to their respec-tive abilities.

The expence of the administration of justice too, may, no doubt, be considered as laid out for the benefit of the whole society. There is no impropriety, therefore, in its being defrayed by the general contribution of the whole society. The persons, however, who give occasion to this expence are those who, by their injustice in one way or another, make it necessary to seek redress or protection from the courts of justice. The persons again most immediately benefited by this expence, are those whom the courts of justice either restore to their rights, or maintain in their rights. The expence of the administration of justice, therefore, may very properly be defrayed by the particular contribution of one or other, or both of those two different sets of persons, according as different occasions may require, that is, by the fees of court. It cannot be necessary to have recourse to the general contri-bution of the whole society, except for the conviction of those criminals who have not themselves any estate or fund sufficient for paying those fees.

Those local or provincial expences of which the benefit is local or provincial (what is laid out, for example, upon the police of a particular town or district) ought to be defrayed by a local or provincial revenue, and ought to be no burden upon the general revenue of the society. It is unjust that the whole society should contribute towards an expence of which the benefit is confined to a part of the society.

The expence of maintaining good roads and communications is, no doubt, beneficial to the whole society, and may, therefore, without any injustice, be defrayed by the general contribution of the whole society. This expence, however, is most immediately and directly beneficial to those who travel or carry goods from one place to another, and to those who consume such goods. . . .

The expence of the institutions for education and religious instruction, is likewise, no doubt, beneficial to the whole society, and may, therefore, without injustice, be defrayed by the general contribution of the whole society. This expence, however, might perhaps with equal propriety, and even with some advantage, be defrayed altogether by those who receive the immediate benefit of such education and instruction, or by the voluntary contribution of those who think they have occasion for either the one or the other.

When the institutions or publick works which are beneficial to the whole society, either cannot be maintained altogether, or are not maintained altogether by the contribution of such particular members of the society as are most immediately benefited by them, the deficiency must in most cases be made up by the general contribution of the whole society. The general revenue of the society, over and above defraying the expence of defending the society, and of supporting the dignity of the chief magistrate, must make up for the deficiency of many particular branches of revenue. The sources of this general or publick revenue, I shall endeavour to explain in the following chapter.

CHAPTER II

Of the Sources of the general or publick Revenue of the Society

The revenue which must defray, not only the expence of defending the society and of supporting the dignity of the chief magistrate, but all the other necessary expences of government, for which the constitution of the state has not provided any particular revenue, may be drawn, either, first, from some fund which peculiarly belongs to the sovereign or commonwealth, and which is independent of the revenue of the people; or, secondly, from the revenue of the people.

PART II

Of Taxes

. . . Before I enter upon the examination of particular taxes, it is necessary to premise the four following maxims with regard to taxes in general.

I. The subjects of every state ought to contribute towards the support of the government, as nearly as possible, in proportion to their respective abilities; that is, in proportion to the revenue which they respectively enjoy under the protection of the state. The expence of government to the individuals of a great nation, is like the expence of management to the joint tenants of a great estate who are all obliged to contribute in proportion to their respective interests in the estate. In the observation or neglect of this maxim consists, what is called the equality or inequality of taxation. Every tax, it must be observed once for all, which falls finally upon one only of the three sorts of revenue above-mentioned, is necessarily unequal, in so far as it does not affect the other two. In the following examination of different taxes I shall seldom take much further notice of this sort of inequality, but shall, in most cases, confine my observations to that inequality which is occasioned by a particular tax falling unequally even upon that particular sort of private revenue which is affected by it.

II. The tax which each individual is bound to pay ought to be certain, and not arbitrary. The time of payment, the manner of payment, the quantity to be paid, ought all to be clear and plain to the contributor, and to every other person. Where it is otherwise, every person subject to the tax is put more or less in the power of the tax-gatherer, who can either aggravate the tax upon any obnoxious contributor, or extort, by the terror of such aggravation, some present or perquisite to himself. The uncertainty of taxation encourages the insolence and favours the corruption of an order of men who are naturally unpopular, even where they are neither insolent nor corrupt. The certainty of what each individual ought to pay is, in taxation, a matter of so great importance, that a very considerable degree of inequality, it appears, I believe, from the experience of all nations, is not near so great an evil as a very small degree of uncertainty.

III. Every tax ought to be levied at the time, or in the manner in which it is most likely to be convenient for the contributor to pay it. A tax upon the rent of land or of houses, payable at the same term at which such rents are usually paid, is levied at the time when it is most likely to be convenient for the contributor to pay; or, when he is most likely to have wherewithal to pay. Taxes upon such consumable goods as are articles of luxury, are all finally paid by the consumer, and generally in a manner that is very convenient for him. He pays them by, little and little, as he has occasion to buy the goods. As he is at liberty too, either to buy, or not to buy as he pleases, it must be his own fault if he ever suffers any considerable inconveniency from such taxes.

IV. Every tax ought to be so contrived as both to take out and to keep out of the pockets of the people as little as possible, over and above what it brings into the publick treasury of the state. A tax may either take out or keep out of the pockets of the people a great deal more than it brings into the publick treasury, in the four following ways. First, the levying of it may require a great number of officers, whose salaries may eat up the greater part of the produce of the tax, and whose perquisites may impose another additional tax upon the people. Secondly, it may obstruct the industry of the people, and discourage them from applying to certain branches of business which might give maintenance and employment to great multitudes. While it obliges the people to pay, it may thus diminish, or perhaps destroy some of the funds, which might enable them more easily to do so. Thirdly, by the forfeitures and other penalties which those unfortunate individuals incur who attempt unsuccessfully to evade the tax, it may frequently ruin them, and thereby put an end to the benefit which the community might have received from the employment of their capitals. An injudicious tax offers a great temptation to smuggling. But the penalties of smuggling must rise in proportion to the temptation. The law, contrary to all the ordinary principles of justice, first creates the temptation, and then punishes those who yield to it; and it commonly enhances the punishment too in proportion to the very circumstance which ought certainly to alleviate it, the temptation to commit the crime. Fourthly, by subjecting the people to the frequent visits, and the odious examination of the tax-gatherers, it may expose them to much unnecessary trouble, vexation, and oppression; and though vexation is not, strictly speaking, expence, it is certainly equivalent to the expence at which every man would be willing to redeem himself from it. It is in some one or other of these four different ways that taxes are frequently so much more burdensome to the people than they are beneficial to the sovereign.

CHAPTER III

Of Publick Debts

. . . A country abounding with merchants and manufacturers, necessarily abounds with a set of people through whose hands not only their own capitals, but the capitals of all those who either lend them money, or trust them with goods, pass as frequently, or more frequently, than the revenue of a private man, who, without trade or business, lives upon his income, passes through his hands. The revenue of such a man can regularly pass through his hands only once in a year. But the whole amount of the capital and credit of a merchant, who deals in a trade of which the returns are very quick, may sometimes pass through his hands two, three, or four times in a year. A country abounding with merchants and manufacturers, therefore, necessarily abounds with a set of people who have it at all times in their power to advance, if they chuse to do so, a very large sum of money to government. Hence the ability in the subjects of a commercial state to lend.

Commerce and manufactures can seldom flourish long in any state which does not enjoy a regular administration of justice, in which the people do not feel themselves secure in the possession of their property, in which the faith of contracts is not supported by law, and in which the authority of the state is not supposed to be regularly employed in enforcing the payment of debts from all those who are able to pay. Commerce and manufactures, in short, can seldom flourish in any state in which there is not a certain degree of confidence in the justice of government. The same confidence which disposes great merchants and manufacturers, upon ordinary occasions, to trust their property to the protection of a particular government; disposes them, upon extraordinary occasions, to trust that government with the use of their property. By lending money to government, they do not even for a moment diminish their ability to carry on their trade and manufactures. On the contrary, they commonly augment it. The necessities of the state render government upon most occasions willing to borrow upon terms extremely advantageous to the lender. The security which it grants to the original creditor, is made transferable to any other creditor, and, from the universal confidence in the justice of the state, generally sells in the market for more than was originally paid for it. The merchant or monied man makes money by lending money to government, and instead of diminishing, increases his trading capital. He generally considers it as a favor, therefore, when the administration admits him to share in the first subscription for a new loan. Hence the inclination or willingness in the subjects of a commercial state to lend.

The government of such a state is very apt to repose itself upon this ability and willingness of its subjects to lend it their money on extraordinary occasions. It foresees the facility of borrowing, and therefore dispenses itself from the duty of saving.

In a rude state of society there are no great mercantile or manufacturing capitals. The individuals who hoard whatever money they can save, and who conceal their hoard, do so from a distrust of the justice of government, from a fear that if it was known that they had a hoard, and where that hoard was to be found, they would quickly be plundered. In such a state of things few people would be able, and nobody would be willing, to lend their money to government on extraordinary exigencies. The sovereign feels that he must provide for such exigencies by saving, because he foresees the absolute impossibility of borrowing. This foresight increases still further his natural disposition to save.

The progress of the enormous debts which at present oppress, and will in the long-run probably ruin, all the great nations of Europe, has been pretty uniform. Nations, like private men, have generally begun to borrow upon what may be called personal credit, without assigning or mortgaging any particular fund for the payment of the debt; and when this resource has failed them, they have gone on to borrow upon assignments or mortgages of particular funds. . . .

It is not contrary to justice that . . . America should contribute towards the discharge of the publick debt of Great Britain.

The expence of the peace establishment of the colonies was, before the commencement of the present disturbances, very considerable, and is an expence which may, and if no revenue can be drawn from them, ought certainly to be saved altogether. This constant expence in time of peace, though very great, is insignificant in comparison with what the defence of the colonies has cost us in time of war. The last war, which was undertaken altogether on account of the colonies, cost Great Britain, it has already been observed, upwards of ninety millions. The Spanish war of 1739 was principally undertaken on their account; in which, and in the French war that was the consequence of it, Great Britain spent upwards of forty millions, a great part of which ought justly to be charged to the colonies. In those two wars the colonies cost Great Britain much more than double the sum which the national debt amounted to before the commencement of the first of them. Had it not been for those wars that debt might, and probably would by this time, have been completely paid; and had it not been for the colonies, the former of those wars might not, and the latter certainly would not have been undertaken. It was because the colonies were supposed to be provinces of the British empire, that this expence was laid out upon them. But countries which contribute neither revenue nor military force towards the support of the empire, cannot be considered as provinces. They may perhaps be considered as appendages, as a sort of splendid and showy equipage; of the empire. But if the empire can no longer support the expence of keeping up this equipage, it ought certainly to lay it down; and if it cannot raise its revenue in proportion to its expence, it ought, at least, to accommodate its expence to its revenue. If the colonies, notwithstanding their refusal to submit to British taxes, are still to be considered as provinces of the British empire, their defence in some future war may cost Great Britain as great an expence as it ever has done in any former war. The rulers of Great Britain have, for more than a century past, amused the people with the imagination that they possessed a great empire on the west side of the Atlantic. This empire, however, has hitherto existed in imagination only. It has hitherto been, not an empire, but the project of an empire; not a gold mine, but the project of a gold mine; a project which has cost, which continues to cost, and which, if pursued in the same way as it has been hitherto, is likely to cost immense expence, without being likely to bring any profit; for the effects of the monopoly of the colony trade, it has been shewn; are, to the great body of the people, mere loss instead of profit. It is surely now time that our rulers should either realize this golden dream, in which they have been indulging themselves, perhaps, as well as the people; or, that they should awake from it themselves, and endeavour to awaken the people. If the project cannot be compleated, it ought to be given up. If any of the provinces of the British empire cannot be made to contribute towards the support of the whole empire, it is surely time that Great Britain should free herself from the expence of defending those provinces in time of war, and of supporting any part of their civil or military establishments in time of peace, and endeavour to accommodate her future views and designs to the real mediocrity of her circumstances.

IMMANUEL KANT

Kant (1724–1804) was born in Königsberg (Kaliningrad), the fourth of nine children of poor and uneducated parents. His father was a harness maker; his fervently pietistic mother died in 1737. With financial help from the family pastor, Kant attended (1732–1740) the Collegium Fredericianum, a pietistic school that aroused in him a lifelong disgust with religious authorities and rituals. The next six years were spent studying quite broadly at Königsberg's Albertina University, where Kant contributed to his upkeep through private lessons and billiard winnings. He was nevertheless obliged to quit when his father died in 1746, and he spent the subsequent nine years as a private tutor with wealthy families in East Prussia. He returned to Königsberg in 1755, defended a master's thesis about fire, and took up an unsalaried teaching post at the university. Living off small lecture fees, Kant taught up to thirty-four hours a week on many subjects (including theology, natural law, astronomy, logic, physics—even fireworks, meteorology, and fortress construction), until he was finally appointed (salaried) professor for logic and metaphysics in 1770. While teaching at Albertina (1755–1796), Kant enjoyed great popularity and respect among his students and colleagues. He was dean of his faculty several times and twice president of the university. Especially during the earlier years, Kant also had an active social life, regularly entertaining at home and visiting the homes and salons of the leading citizens. The image of him as an egghead and sourpuss owes more to Heinrich Heine's imagination than to the facts, though it is true, of course, that Kant never married, never traveled, and worked quite hard throughout his life.

Between 1749 and 1770, Kant published essays in logic, theology, philosophy, aesthetics, and, especially, in the sciences. His theory of how matter concentrated to form our solar system and galaxies (1755), ignored at the time, blossomed in the next century as the Kant-Laplace hypothesis, and his essay on incongruent counterparts (1768) undercut Leibniz's relational account of space. In his Latin inaugural dissertation of 1770, Kant presented a radical account of space and time as subjective forms of our human sensibility, which therefore presents us with mere appearances of things. Trying to complete this account, Kant found he could not sustain his view that through our understanding, at least, we can know things as they really are. Despite much lighter teaching duties, he published nothing during his next "silent" decade. The result of his struggles is the *Critique of Pure Reason* (1781), which, after initial consternation and dismissal by the academic establishment, came to be widely accepted as the greatest philosophical work of all time.

After the immense labors of the first *Critique,* Kant—a tiny, now frail and sickly man of 57—burst into print, publishing in rapid succession dozens of highly original and consequential works on many topics. The most important among these are: *Prolegomena to Any Future Metaphysics* in 1783; "Idea for a University History" and "What Is Enlightenment?" in 1784; *Groundwork of the Metaphysics of Morals* in 1785; "What Does It Mean to Orient Oneself in

Thought?" and *Metaphysical Foundations of Natural Science* in 1786; a substantially reworked second edition of the *Critique of Pure Reason* in 1787; *Critique of Practical Reason* in 1788; *Critique of Judgment* in 1790; "On the Saying: That May Be True in Theory, But Does Not Hold Good in Practice" and *Religion Within the Limits of Reason Alone* in 1793; *Perpetual Peace* in 1795; *Metaphysics of Morals* in 1797; and *The Contest of the Faculties* and *Anthropology Considered From a Pragmatic Viewpoint* in 1798. Kant gave his final lecture in July 1796 and began work on another monumental work, now known as the *Opus Postumum,* which his deteriorating faculties did not allow him to complete. He died in Königsberg with his genius fully recognized all over Germany as well as abroad: As of 1804, publications about him and his work stood at a staggering 2,800. In the presence of thousands, Kant's emaciated body was laid to rest in the professors' tomb of the cathedral, under a plaque with a famous quote from his second *Critique*:

> Two things fill the mind with ever new and increasing admiration and awe, the oftener and more steadily we reflect on them: the starry heavens above me and the moral law within me (Vol. V, p. 161).

(Kant's works are standardly cited by volume and page numbers of the Prussian Academy Edition.)

Kant expressed what animated his practical (moral and political) philosophy in a later personal note:

> I am a scholar by inclination. I feel the whole thirst for knowledge and the greedy urge to make progress therein and also the satisfaction with every acquisition. There was a time when I thought this alone could constitute the honor of humanity and I despised the ignorant crowd. Rousseau has set me straight. That delusive superiority disappears, I learn to honor human beings, and I would regard myself as more useless than the common laborer if I did not believe that this reflection can give a worth to all others, [namely] to realize the rights of humankind" (Vol. XX, p. 44).

What are these rights? The central idea of Kant's practical philosophy is that of freedom, comprising inner freedom as independence from inclinations and external freedom as a domain of action safe from invasion by others. Each person has a right to the largest domain of external freedom that is consistent with a like domain for everyone else; and each therefore has a duty to restrict his own external freedom so that it is consistent with a like freedom for all. Such self-restraint is required by our own reason, which issues only this one categorical command: to recognize and to treat every person endowed with reason as having the same ultimate moral value and claims as oneself. In subordinating one's inclinations to this imperative, one respects the external freedom of others and attains inner freedom, or autonomy, for oneself.

Kant may have thought until the late 1780s that government and hence political philosophy are necessary only as accommodations to the galling fact that most human beings are not willing to practice the required self-restraint. But in the later texts here reproduced, Kant came to a better understanding: There are several schemes for defining mutually consistent, equal, and maximal domains of external freedom; and, if persons restrain themselves according to different such schemes, then mutual consistency is not achieved. Even persons of wholly good will would therefore need a legislative authority to coordinate upon one eligible scheme, and—since laws cannot settle their own interpretation—also a judicial authority. Persons whose will is less than wholly good need enforcement, too, because no one is morally required to honor the rights of others so long as he lacks assurances that he will not, in doing so, endanger his own (Vol. VIII, p. 349n.; Vol. VI, p. 307). Without a government fulfilling these three functions the rights of humankind cannot be realized "since each will have his own right to do *what seems right and good to him*" (Vol. VI, p. 312).

Persons ought then to coexist in a juridical condition, the specifics of which Kant presents as the object of a social contract. This is little more than a metaphor: In contrast to Locke and Rousseau, there is no suggestion that this contract did or must actually take place. And, in contrast to Hobbes and Rawls, he also does not engage in prudential reasoning in behalf of persons who might coexist in various possible alternative social conditions. Kant's social contract has then no independent moral force: The right form of human coexistence requires no justification through prudence or agreement. Grounded in reason, it is fully justified; it overrules prudence and demands agreement: It is our unconditional moral duty to consent to, and to uphold, just institutions.

Just institutions involve a consistent distribution of external freedoms supported by a common political authority. Ideally, legislation should impose that scheme of consistent, equal, and maximal domains of external freedom that optimally promotes human enlightenment and culture. And ideally, political authority should exemplify a republican constitution, in which ultimate political authority (sovereignty) is exercised by the people, who legislate through representatives, and in which the sovereign delegates executive and judicial authority to magistrates and judges. In patent contradiction to these abstract ideals, Kant also contends that women should not be equal under the law and that they, and all economic dependents, should be disenfranchised.

Because a juridical condition is crucial for securing external freedom, and for facilitating inner freedom, it becomes Kant's supreme concern: Where it is absent, persons "who can mutually influence one another" ought to create it and may compel one another to do so (Vol. VIII, p. 349n.). Where it is present, persons ought to obey the laws even if they are flawed and even if the two conditions of a republican constitution are not met; "Any *law-governed* constitution, even if it is only in small measure just, is better than none at all" (Vol. VIII, p. 373n.). Here Kant comes very close to Hobbes: A juridical condition requires one sovereign as the ultimate court of appeal in all conflicts. If sovereignty were divided or limited in any way, then conflicts over the precise location of the division or the limits would be left without a legal path of authoritative resolution. There can then be no genuine division of powers, only delegation of authority: "The sovereign may divest the ruler [executive] of his power, depose him, or reform his administration" (Vol. VI, p. 317). Nor can there be a right to resistance or rebellion—an existing juridical condition may be reformed only from the top.

In "On the Saying . . . ," Kant nevertheless insists that his view differs importantly from Hobbes's: Each human being has inalienable rights that, though he must not enforce them against the sovereign, the latter is duty-bound to respect and to realize. But Kant here exaggerates the contrast, as even Hobbes is not an unqualified proponent of might-makes-right. In Chapter XXX of his *Leviathan,* he contends that, while all laws promulgated by the sovereign are ipso facto just and hence ought to be obeyed by the subjects, the sovereign ought to promulgate only laws that are good, i.e., "*needfull,* for the *good of the people,* and withall *perspicuous.*" (cp. also the introduction to the *Leviathan,* where Hobbes complains about "the barbarous state of men in power, towards their inferiors"). Hobbes and Kant agree, then, that there are duties of the sovereign, and differ only about their status and content.

How does Kant's account apply to our world, where persons within various territories coexist in a juridical condition while relations across their boundaries are still in a state of nature? Kant's Second Definitive Article in *Perpetual Peace* demands the creation of a free association of sovereign states, which became the model for the League of Nations. He hoped that, within such an association, international disputes would be resolved through negotiations, especially if the member states have republican constitutions under which the people, as sovereign, decide about war or peace. Yet Kant's discussion of this article nonetheless ends with a ringing endorsement of a world republic: It is only because existing states "absolutely do not wish to . . . give up their savage (lawless) freedom, adjust themselves to public coercive laws, and thus establish a continuously growing international state" that we must, "if all is not to be lost," replace "the positive idea of a world republic [with] the negative surrogate of an alliance" (Vol. VIII, p. 357). I conjecture that, seeing the road to a world republic blocked for the foreseeable future, Kant thought it important to concentrate on the morally inferior but far more attainable ideal of the best-possible semijuridical condition. What he did not and, given his Hobbesian commitments, could not see are the intermediate possibilities involving a juridical condition without one ultimate court of appeal: a genuine vertical division of political authority as exemplified today by the United States and the European Union.

Good general works on Kant's life and work are Ernst Cassirer, *Kant's Life and Thought* (New Haven: Yale University Press, 1971 [1918]); Otfried Höffe, *Immanuel Kant* (Albany: SUNY Press, 1995 [1983]); and Paul Guyer, ed., *The Cambridge Companion to Kant* (Cambridge: Cambridge University Press, 1992). On the political issues raised in the following selections, see especially Patrick Riley, *Kant's Political Philosophy* (Totowa: Rowman & Littlefield, 1983); Howard Williams, *Kant's Political Philosophy* (New York: St. Martin's Press, 1983); and Allen Rosen, *Kant's Theory of Justice* (Ithaca, NY: Cornell University Press, 1993). On Kant's political thought more generally, see Jeffrie Murphy, *Kant: The Philosophy of Right* (London: Macmillan, 1979); Susan Meld Shell, *The Rights of Reason* (Toronto: Toronto University Press, 1980); Yirmiahu Yovel, *Kant and the Philosophy of History* (Princeton: Princeton University Press, 1980); Harry Van der Linden, *Kantian Ethics and Socialism* (Indianapolis: Hackett, 1988); and Leslie A. Mulholland, *Kant's System of Rights* (New York: Columbia University Press, 1990).

T. W. P.

ON THE OLD SAW: THAT MAY BE RIGHT IN THEORY BUT IT WON'T WORK IN PRACTICE

II. ON THE RELATION OF THEORY TO PRACTICE IN CONSTITUTIONAL LAW

(*contra* Hobbes)

Among the contracts that enable groups of people to unite in a society (*pactum sociale*), the one to be found a civil constitution between them (*pactum unionis civilis*) is a special kind. As far as *execution* is concerned, it has much in common with any other contract aimed at the joint promotion of some purpose; it is essentially different from the rest, however, in the principle of what it founds (*constitutionis civilis*). The union of many people for some common end which they all *have* is found in all social contracts. But their union as an end in itself—as the end that everyone *ought to have,* and thus as the first and unconditioned duty in each external relationship of human beings who cannot avoid influencing one another—does not occur in a society unless it has attained to the civil state, i.e., unless it constitutes a community. The end, now, which in such an external relation is in itself a duty, and itself the supreme formal condition of all other external duties (*conditio sine qua non*), is the legal order (the right) of people *under public coercive laws*, by which each can be assigned his own, and each protected against the incursions of all others.

Yet the concept of external law as such derives completely from the concept of *freedom* in the external relations of men to one another. It has nothing whatever to do with the pursuit of happiness, the end which all men have by nature, or with the prescription of means to that end. There simply must not be any mingling of that law as such with the end of happiness posing as its determining ground. *Law* is the limitation of each man's freedom to the condition of its consistency with everyone's freedom to the extent possible in accordance with a universal law. And *public law* is the totality of the *external laws* that serve to make such thoroughgoing consistency possible. Since every limitation of freedom by another's arbitrary will is termed coercion, it follows that a civil constitution is a relationship of *free* men who are nonetheless subject to coercive laws, their overall freedom in relation to others notwithstanding. They are subject to those laws because reason itself wills it so, pure reason which legislates a priori and irrespective of the empirical ends that have been summed up under the general name happiness. For human ideas regarding those ends differ greatly, and each man seeks them in a different place, so that their will cannot be brought under a common principle nor, consequently, under an external law consistent with everyone's freedom.

The civil state, viewed purely as a legal state, is thus based a priori upon the following principles:

1. The *freedom* of each member of society as a *human being;*
2. The *equality* of each member with every other member as a *subject of the state;*
3. The *independence* of each member of the community as a *citizen.*

Translated by E. B. Ashton. Reprinted by permission of the University of Pennsylvania Press.

These principles are not laws given by a state already established, but they are the only laws that make it possible to found a state in accordance with pure rational principles of external human law as such. Therefore:

1. Human *freedom* as a principle for the constitution of a community I express in this formula: No man can compel me to be happy after his fashion, according to his conception of the wellbeing of someone else. Instead, everybody may pursue his happiness in the manner that seems best to him, provided he does not infringe on other people's freedom to pursue similar ends, i.e., on another's right to do whatever can coexist with every man's freedom under a possible universal law.

If a government were founded on the principle of benevolence toward the people, as a *father's* toward his children—in other words, if it were a *paternalistic government (imperium paternale)* with the subjects, as minors, unable to tell what is truly beneficial or detrimental to them, obliged to wait for the head of state to judge what should constitute their happiness and be kind enough to desire it also—such a government would be the worst conceivable *despotism.* It would be a constitution that cancels every freedom of the subjects, who retain no rights at all. A *patriotic* rather than *paternalistic* government *(imperium, non paternale, sed patrioticum)* is the only one conceivable for people capable of having rights, and also the only one conceivable for a benevolent ruler. For the *patriotic* way of thinking is that which makes everyone in the state, including the ruler, look upon the community as his mother's womb, or on the country as his father's land where he himself came into being, and which he must leave behind as a cherished pledge, in order to protect the rights of the community by laws issuing from the common will, not deeming himself entitled to subject it to the uses of his unconditional discretion.

This right to freedom belongs to every member of the community as a human being, provided he is a being capable of having rights at all.

2. The *equality* of subjects may be phrased as follows: Each member of the community has rights that entitle him to coerce every other member. Only the community's head is excepted from that coercion. Not being a member of the community but its creator or preserver, he also is authorized to coerce without being subject to legal coercion himself. Whoever is *subject* to laws in a state is a subject; that is to say, coercion by laws applies to him as to all other members of the community, with the sole exception of one single (physical or moral) person, the head of state, who is the only one capable of exerting all legal coercion. For if he too could be coerced he would not be the head of the state, and the sequence of subordination would continue upwards ad infinitum. And if there were two persons free from coercion, neither of them would be subject to coercive laws and neither one could wrong the other—which is impossible.

But this thorough equality of persons as the subjects of a state is quite consistent with the greatest inequality in the quantity and degree of their possessions, whether these be physical or mental superiority, external gifts of fortune, or simply rights (of which there can be many) with respects to others. One man's welfare, therefore, is greatly dependent on another's will, as the poor man's on the will of the rich; one must obey, as a child its parents or a wife her husband, when the other commands; or, one will serve as a day-laborer while the other pays wages, and so forth. And yet, as subjects all of them are equal *before the law* which, as the expression of the general will, can only be singular, and concerns the form of the right, not the matter or the object to which I have a right. For it is only by means of the public law and its executor, the head of state, that a man can coerce anyone else, but by the same means everyone else will resist him in like measure; and no one can lose this capacity to coerce—i.e., to have rights against others—except in consequence of his own crime. Nor can a man give it up of his own accord; there is no contract, no legal act, by which he can put himself in the position of having no rights any more, only duties. For if he were to do so, he would be depriving himself of the right to make a contract, and so the contract would cancel itself.

This idea of the human equality of men as subjects in a community results in the following formula: Each member of the community must be permitted to rise in it to any status or class (appropriate to a subject) to which his talent, industry, and luck may take him. And his fellow subjects may not block his way by any *hereditary* prerogative, as members of some specific privileged class, to keep him and his heirs beneath that class forever.

For right consists merely in limiting everybody else's freedom to the point where it can coexist with my freedom according to a universal law, and the public law in a community is no more than a state of actual legislation in accordance with this principle and combined with power. Due to his legislation, consequently, all members of a people live as subjects in a state of law *(status iuridicus)*, namely, in a state of equilibrium between the effect and counter-effect of wills that limit each other in accordance with the universal law of freedom. This is what we call the civil state; and in that state the *innate right* of everyone is the *same* (i.e., until he takes an action affecting that right), entitling him to compel all others to observe the bounds within which their use of their freedom is compatible with mine. Since a man's birth is not an *action* of his and thus does not bring upon him unequal legal status, nor subject him to any coercive laws other than those which he, as a subject of the sole supreme lawmaking power, shares with all the rest, there can be no one member of the community, no fellow subject, who is innately privileged over another. No man can leave to his descendants any prerogative of the *status* he holds in the community; nor can he forcibly keep them, who are qualified by birth to be masters, so to speak, from rising by their own merits to higher levels in the order of ranks—where one is superior, another inferior, though neither is *imperans* while the other is *subjectus*. A man may leave his heirs everything else; and in a sequence of descendants, considerable inequality of financial circumstances may result between the members of a community, between wage earners, tenants, landowners and the laborers who till the land, and so on. Only one thing he cannot prevent: the right of the less favored to rise to the same favored circumstances if enabled to do so by their talent, industry, and luck. For otherwise the testator would be allowed to coerce without being coercible in turn by the reaction of others, and would exceed the level of a fellow subject.

Nor can a man living in the legal framework of a community be stripped of this quality by anything save his own crime. He can never lose it, neither by contract nor by acts of war *(occupatio bellica)*, for no legal act, neither his own nor another's, can terminate his proprietary rights in himself. No such act can put him into the class of domestic animals which we use at will for any kind of service and keep in that state without their consent for as long as we please, albeit with the restriction—sometimes religiously sanctioned, as among the Hindus—that they not be maimed or killed. No matter what his circumstances, a man may be deemed happy as long as he knows that the law does not discriminate in favor of his fellow subjects, that if he fails to rise to their level it is not due to the irresistible will of others but solely to himself, to his own faculties or resolve, or to circumstances for which he can hold no one else responsible.[1]

3. *Independence (sibisufficientia)* of a member of a community as a *citizen,* that is to say, a co-legislator. With regard to legislation all men are free and equal *under* public law as already enacted, though they are not equal with respect to the right to *enact* that law. Those who are not able to have this right are still, as members of the community, required to obey its law, and share in its protection, though not as *citizens* but only as *partakers* in the law's protection.

For all rights depend upon laws. But a public law that determines what all men are to be legally permitted or forbidden is the act of a public will from which all rights issue, and which must therefore be incapable of wronging anyone. There is but one will for which this is possible: the will of the people as a whole (when all decide about all, and each, accordingly, decides about himself)—because the one man to whom each person can do no legal wrong is himself. If it is otherwise, any decision made for all by a will other than the will of all might be an injustice, and a further law would still be required to limit such a will's enactments. Thus no particular will can serve as lawmaker for a community. (In fact, the very concept of a community is made up of the coinciding concepts of the external freedom, the equality, and the *unity* of the will of *all* and, since the combination of the first two requires voting, independence is the premise of the last.) This basic law, which can emerge only from the general, united popular will, is called the *original contract.*

Every man who has the right to vote on this legislation is termed a *citizen (citoyen,* i.e., a *citizen* of the *state,* not of a city or borough, a *bourgeois).* The only necessary qualification, aside from the *natural* one of not being a child or a woman, is that he be *his own master (sui iuris):* that he own some sort of property—among which may be counted any skill, craft, fine art, or science that supports him. This is to say that whenever he needs to acquire things from others in order to live, he will acquire them only by *disposing* of what is *his own,*[2] not by allowing others to use his services, so that he will not, in the proper sense of the word, be anyone's servant but the community's. Here, then, craftsmen and large (or small) landowners are all equal, each entitled to cast one vote only. We may disregard the question how one man can rightly come to own more land than his own hands can put to use (for acquisition by armed conquest is not original acquisition), and how so many who otherwise would have been capable of acquiring permanent property happen to be reduced to serving that landowner for their livelihood. In any event it would conflict with the previous principle, equality, if the large landowning class were so privileged by law that either its descendants would always remain large landowners (of the feudal type, whose estates could not be divided by sale or inheritance so as to benefit more of the people), or that in case of such division none but members of a certain, arbitrarily chosen class could acquire any part of the estates. The large landed proprietor eliminates the votes of as many smaller proprietors as could occupy his place; thus he is not voting in their name and, consequently, has only one vote.

It is necessary, then, to rely exclusively on the ability, industry, and luck of each community member, that these will enable each of them in time to acquire a part of the community, and enable all to acquire the whole. But these differences cannot be taken into account in the making of the general laws. The number of eligible voters on legislation must be set one per capital of property owners, and not according to the size of their possessions.

Yet *all* of those who have this right to vote must agree that the public law is just. Otherwise there would be a legal conflict between those who agree and those who disagree, and the resolution of that conflict would require an additional, higher principle of law. Since we cannot expect unanimity of a whole people, however, the only attainable outcome to be foreseen is a majority of votes—and not a majority of direct voters, in a large nation, but only a majority of those delegated as representatives of the people. The acceptance by general consent, hence by *contract,* of the principle that this majority suffices must be the supreme ground on which to establish a civil constitution.

Conclusions

Here we have an original contract on which alone a civil and thus consistently legal constitution among men can be based and a community established.

Yet this contract, which we call *contractus originarius* or *pactum sociale,* as the coalition of every particular and private will within a people into a common public will for purposes of purely legal legislation, need by no means to be presupposed as a fact. It is not necessary first to demonstrate historically, so to speak, that a people, whose rights and duties we have inherited, must really have performed such an act *at some time* and must have left us, by word of mouth or in writing, some reliable news or instrument of it, before we are to consider ourselves bound by an existing civil constitution. It is rather a *mere idea* of reason, albeit one with indubitable practical reality, obligating every lawmaker to frame his laws so that they *might* have come from the united will of an entire people, and to regard any subject who would be a citizen as if he had joined in voting for such a will. For this is the touchstone of the legitimacy of all public law. If a law is so framed that all the people *could not possibly* give it their consent—as, for example, a law granting the hereditary *privilege* of *master status* to a certain class of *subjects*—the law is unjust; but if it is *at all possible* that a people might agree on it, then the people's duty is to look upon the law as just, even assuming that their present situation or the tenor of their present way of thinking were such that, if consulted, they would probably refuse to agree.[3]

But this restriction obviously applies to the lawmaker's judgment only, not to the subject's. If a people were to judge that a certain actual legislation will with the utmost probability deprive them of their happiness—what can such a people do? Should they not resist? The answer can be only: they can do nothing but obey. For the question is not what happiness the subject may expect from the establishment of a community or from its administration. Rather, the issue is first of all the legal order which is thereby to be secured for all. This is the supreme principle from which all maxims concerning a community must start, and which is not limited by any other principle. Regarding happiness no universally valid principle of legislation can be given. For both the circumstances of the time and the high contradictory and constantly changing delusions in which each man seeks his happiness (and no one can prescribe for him where he should seek it) render all fixed principles impossible and unfit by themselves to serve as principles of legislation. The proposition *salus publica suprema civitatis lex est*—the public welfare is the community's highest law—remains undiminished in validity and public esteem; but the common weal to be considered *first of all* is precisely that legal constitution which secures the freedom of everyone by means of laws, leaving him to pursue his happiness by whichever way seems best to him as long as he does not infringe upon that universal freedom under the law and thus upon the rights of other fellow subjects.

When the supreme power makes laws that are initially aimed at happiness—at the prosperity of citizens, at population, and the like—this is not done for the purpose of establishing a civil constitution. It is done simply as a means to *secure the state of law,* chiefly against the people's foreign enemies. The head of state must have the authority to judge by himself alone whether such laws are needed for the community to flourish as it must in order to safeguard its strength and stability, internally as well as against foreign foes. But the purpose is not to make the people happy, against their will as it were; the only purpose is to make them exist as a community.[4] The lawmaker may err in judging whether or not those measures are *prudently* taken; but there can be no error of judgment when he asks himself whether or not the law is in accord with the legal principle. For here he possesses that infallible yardstick (and a priori at that)—the idea of the original contract. (He need not wait for experience, as he must in following the principle of happiness, to instruct him first about the suitability of his means.) Just as long as it is not self-contradictory to assume that all the people consent to such a law, however distasteful they may find it, the law is in accord with justice. But if a public law is in accord with justice, if it is unimpeachable, irreprehensible from the point of view of the right, it carries with it the authority to coerce and, conversely, a ban on any active resistance to the lawmaker's will. In other words, the power in the state that lends effect to the law is irresistible, and there is no legally existing community that does not have such power to crush all inner resistance, since this resistance would be following a maxim whose general application would destroy all civil constitutions in which alone men can have rights.

It follows that any resistance to the supreme lawmaking power, any incitement of dissatisfied subjects to action, any uprising that bursts into rebellion—that all this is the worst, most punishable crime in a community. For it shatters the community's foundations. And this ban is *absolute,* so unconditional that even though that supreme power or its agent, the head of state, may have broken the original contract, even though in the subject's eyes he may have forfeited the right to legislate by empowering the government to rule tyrannically by sheer violence, even then the subject is allowed no resistance, no violent counteraction. The reason is that once a civil constitution exists, a people no longer have the right to judge how that constitution ought to be administered. For suppose they had such a right and their judgment ran counter to that of the actual head of state: who is to decide which side is right? Neither one can act as a judge in his own case. To decide between the head and the people there would have to be a head above the head—which is self-contradictory.

Nor, by the way, can a sort of *right of necessity (ius in casu necessitatis)*—which supposed *right* to do *wrong* in extreme (physical) need is an absurdity anyway[5]—arise here to provide a way in which the barrier blocking the people's own power could be lifted. For the head of state is just as apt to justify his harsh treatment of the subjects by their recalcitrance as they are to justify their rebellion with complaints of their undue suffering at his hands. And who is to decide? The one who is in control of the supreme administration of public justice, and this is precisely the head of state—he alone can decide. And no one in the community can thus have a right to contest that control of his.

And yet there are estimable men who maintain that in certain circumstances the subject does have the right to oppose his superior with force. Among them I will here mention only Achenwall who, in presenting his doctrines of natural law,[6] exhibits great caution, precision, and modesty. He says: "If the danger from enduring further the injustice of its head poses a greater threat to the community than may be feared from taking up arms against him, then the people may resist him; on the strength of this right they may set aside their contract of submission and depose him as a tyrant." And he concludes: "In this fashion (respective to their former overlord) the people return to a state of nature."

I can well believe that in an actual case neither Achenwall nor any of the good men who have aired their minds in agreement with him on this point would ever have lent their counsel or consent to such dangerous undertakings. And as for the uprisings in which the Swiss, the Dutch, or even the British won their much vaunted constitutions, there can be hardly a doubt that if those revolts had miscarried, readers of their history would view the execution of their now so exalted initiators as nothing more than the well-earned punishment of high political criminals. For the outcome usually colors our judgment of the legal grounds, though it was uncertain while the latter are certain. As far as these legal grounds are concerned—granting even that such a rebellion might do no wrong to a prince (who may have violated, say, a *joyeuse entrée,* or an actual underlying contract with his people)—it is clear that the people by pursuing their rights in this manner have done the greatest wrong. For this manner, if adopted as a maxim, would render every legal constitution insecure and introduce a state of utter lawlessness *(status naturalis)* in which all rights would lose at least their effectiveness.

Since so many right-thinking authors have this tendency to argue the people's case (to the people's own ruin), I will note only that this is due, at times, to a common fallacy whereby, while talking of the principle of right, they shift the ground of their judgment to the principle of happiness. At other times, no document can be produced of a contract actually submitted to the community, accepted by its head, and sanctioned by both. Having assumed the idea of an original contract—an idea that always provides the rational basis—to be something that must have happened in *actual fact,* they believe the people to have always retained the right to depart from the contract whenever, in the people's own judgment, there is a gross violation of it.[7]

It is plain to see here what mischief the principle of happiness (and happiness is really incapable of any determinate principle) causes in constitutional law, just as it does in morality, despite the best intentions of those who teach it. The sovereign wants to make the people happy according to his own notions and becomes a despot; the people will not be deprived of the universal human claim to their own happiness and become rebels. If one had asked, to begin with, what is right—and the principles of this are a priori certain and cannot be bungled by any empiricist—the idea of the social contract would retain its unimpeachable prestige. It would not do so as a fact, as Danton would have it when he declares that without such a fact all property and all rights contained in the actually existing constitution are null and void. But the idea would retain its prestige solely as the rational principle for judging any public lawful constitution as such. And one would see that until a general will exists, the people possess no right at all to coerce their ruler, since it is only through him that they can legally coerce. Yet, once that general will exists, there can be no popular coercion of the rule, because then the people themselves would be the supreme ruler. Consequently, the people never have any right of coercion (any right to be refractory in word or deed) against the head of state.

This theory is also amply confirmed in practice. In Great Britain, whose people boast of their constitution as if it were the model for all the world, we nonetheless find the constitution completely silent on what the people have a right to do in case the monarch should transgress the contract of 1688. In other words: if he wanted to violate it, the constitution, in the absence of any specific law, secretly reserves the right to rebel. That the constitution should contain a law for such a case—a law to justify the overthrow of the existing constitution which is the source of all particular laws (even assuming a breach of contract)—is a clear contradiction, because then it would have to contain a publicly constituted[8] opposing power, a second head of state to protect the people's right against the first. And there would have to be a third, then, to decide which of the two sides is right.

Worried, moreover, about such charges in the event their enterprise should fail, those popular guides (or guardians, if you will) who frightened the monarch away preferred to impute to him a voluntary surrender of the reins of government rather than to arrogate to themselves a right to depose him—a claim that would have brought the constitution into a flagrant contradiction with itself.

Surely I will not be accused of flattering the monarch too much with this kind of inviolability; and so I hope also to be spared the charge of favoring the people too much when

I say that they, too, have inalienable rights against the head of state, even though these rights cannot be coercive.

Hobbes is of the opposite opinion. According to him (*de Cive,* Chapter 7, section 14) the head of state is bound by no contractual obligation toward the people. He cannot wrong the citizens, he may dispose of them as he wishes. This thesis would be quite true if "wrong" were understood to give the injured a coercive right against the man who inflicted the wrong; but stated in such general terms the proposition is terrifying.

The nonrecalcitrant subject must be able to assume that his sovereign does not *want* to wrong him. On this assumption, since every man has inalienable rights which he cannot give up even if he would, and concerning which he is himself entitled to judge, the wrong that a citizen believes himself to have suffered can be due only to an error, or to the ignorance of certain consequences that follow from laws made by the supreme power. Accordingly the citizen must be free to inform the public of his views on whatever in the sovereign decrees appears to him as a wrong against the community, and he must have this freedom with the sovereign's own approval. For to assume that the head might never be in error, never in ignorance of anything, would be to imagine him graced with divine intuitions and exalted above all men. *Freedom of the pen*—within the bounds of respect and affection for the constitution one lives under, kept within those bounds by the subjects' liberal way of thinking which the constitution itself instills in them (and to which the pens automatically restrict one another, lest they lose their freedom)—this is the sole shield of popular rights. For to deny the people this freedom would not merely deprive them of every claim to justice in regard to the supreme commander (according to Hobbes); it would also deprive the supreme commander, whose will commands the subjects as citizens only by representing the general will of the people, of any knowledge of matters which he himself would change if only he knew them. Hence, to limit this freedom would bring him into contradiction with himself. But to make the head apprehensive that public unrest might be incited if men were to think for themselves and to think out loud amounts to arousing in him distrust of his own power or even hatred of his own people.

There is a universal principle by which a people must judge its rights *negatively*—i.e., must judge what the supreme legislature, in all good faith, might be deemed *not to have ordained.* This principle is contained in the proposition: *Whatever resolution the people cannot make about themselves, the lawmaker cannot make about the people.*

Suppose, for example, a law were to command the permanent establishment of a previously decreed state religion. Could this be viewed as expressing the lawmaker's real will and intent? One should first ask himself whether a people *may* enact a law to the effect that certain tenets of faith and outward religious forms, once adopted, should remain forever; that is, may a people prevent itself (in its future generations) from progressing in religious insight or from correcting what may be old errors? It will be clear then that an original contract in which the people made such a law would be null and void in itself, because it runs counter to the destiny and to the ends of mankind. A law so made is thus not to be regarded as the monarch's true will, and remonstrances may be made to him.

But in each case in which something of the kind has nevertheless been decreed by supreme legislation, general and public judgments on it may be offered, but resistance in word or deed must never be mobilized.

What must prevail in every community is *obedience,* bowing to coercive laws that suffer no exception within the mechanism of the state constitution. But at the same time a *spirit of freedom* must prevail, since in matters of universal human duty everyone wants to be rationally convinced of the justice of this coercion, lest he come into contradiction with himself. Obedience without the spirit of freedom is the effective cause of all *secret societies.* For it is a natural calling of mankind to communicate with one another, especially about what concerns man in general; with the cultivation of this freedom those societies would disappear.

And how else could a government obtain the knowledge that promotes its own essential intent than by allowing the spirit of freedom, a spirit so worthy of respect both in its origin and its effects, to express itself?

Nowhere will a practice that avoids all pure rational principles disparage theory more arrogantly than in the question of what a good state constitution requires. This is because a long-standing legal constitution gradually causes the people to make it their rule to judge both their happiness and their rights by the state of affairs in which everything so far has functioned peacefully—but not, conversely, to evaluate the state of affairs by concepts of both their rights and happiness with which reason supplies them. The rule is, rather, always to prefer that passive state to the perilous position of seeking a better one, a position to which Hippocrates' advice to physicians applies: *iudicium anceps, experimentum periculosum*—decision is difficult, experiment perilous. All constitutions of sufficiently long standing, whatever their flaws and for all their differences, yield the same result: one is content with the constitution one lives under. Hence, from the viewpoint of *the people's welfare,* no theory properly applies to all; instead, everything rests on a practice submissive to experience.

But if there is something in reason which the term "constitutional law" can express, and if men who face each other in the antagonism of their freedom find in this concept a unifying force—if it shows them an objective, practical reality (and here no reference must be made to whatever well-being or ill-being it may cause them, for that can be learned only by experience)—it is based on a priori principles, because experience cannot teach us what is right. And then, there is a *theory* of constitutional law with which all practice, to be valid, must agree.

The only argument to be advanced against this thesis is that while men have in their heads the idea of rights that are their due, their hard hearts make them incapable and unworthy of being treated accordingly, so that they may and must be kept in order by a supreme power acting solely on rules of prudence. Yet this desperate leap (*salto mortale*) is such that, once we are talking not of right but of power only, the people may try their own power and jeopardize every legal constitution. Unless there is something which rationally compels immediate respect, such as human rights, all influences upon human choice will be incapable of curbing human freedom. But when the right, joined by benevolence, makes its voice heard, human nature shows itself not too depraved to listen diferentially. (*Tum pietate gravem meritisque si forte virum quem/Conspexere silent arrectisque auribus adstant:* Once they behold a man weighty with merits and righteousness, they stand in silence, pricking up their ears. Virgil.)

III. ON THE RELATION OF THEORY TO PRACTICE IN INTERNATIONAL LAW— A GENERAL-PHILANTHROPIC, I.E., COSMOPOLITAN VIEW[9]

(*contra* Mendelssohn)

Are we to love the human race as a whole, or is it an object to be viewed with displeasure, an object that has our best wishes (lest we become misanthropic) but never our best expectations, and from which, therefore, we would rather avert our eyes?

The answer to this question depends on our answer to another question. Are there tendencies in human nature which allow us to infer that the species will always progress toward the better, and that the evil of present and past times will be lost in the good of the future? If so, we could love the species at least for its constant approach to the good; if not, we would have to loathe or despise it, no matter what the affectations of a universal love of mankind—which would then be, at most, a well-meaning love, not a love well pleased—may say to the contrary. What is and remains evil, notably the evil and deliberate mutual violation of the most sacred human rights, this we cannot avoid loathing, even when we try our hardest to love it. We hate it—not that we would harm people, but that we would have as little to do with them as possible.

Moses Mendelssohn was of the latter opinion (*Jerusalem,* Section Two, pp. 44–47), opposing it to his friend Lessing's hypothesis of mankind undergoing a divine education. To him it is chimera "that the whole of mankind down here should be moving ever forward, perfecting itself in the sequence of times."

We see, he says, the human race as a whole "performing slight oscillations, and it has never taken a few forward steps without relapsing soon after, twice as fast, into its former condition." (This is exactly the boulder of Sisyphus; in this way one assumes, with the Hindus, that the earth is a place of penance for old sins now beyond recall.) "Men progress but mankind constantly wavers within the same fixed limits; viewed as a whole it maintains at all periods of time about the same level of morality, the same measure of religion and irreligion, virtue and vice, happiness(?) and misery."

He introduces this assertion (p. 46) by saying, "You want to guess what Providence intends for mankind? Forge no hypotheses" (earlier he had called them "theory"); "just look around at what is really happening, and if you can, survey the history of all ages and look at what has happened from the beginning. This is the fact; this must have been part of the intention; this must have been approved or at least included in the plans of wisdom."

I take a different view.

If it is a sight fit for a god to see a virtuous man wrestle with tribulations and temptations and yet stand firm, it is a sight most unfit, I will not say for a god, but for the commonest man of good will to see the human race from period to period take upward steps toward virtue, only to see it soon after relapsing just as deeply into vice and misery. To watch this tragedy for a while may perhaps be touching and instructive, but eventually the curtain has to fall. For in the long run the tragedy becomes a farce, and though the actors, fools that they are, do not tire of it, the spectator will. After one or two acts he has had enough of it; he can correctly assume that the never-ending play is forever the same. If it is only a play, the punishment at the end may make up for his unpleasant sensations.

But in real life to pile vice upon countless vice (though interrupted by virtues), just so that some day there will be plenty to punish, would be repugnant, at least by our conception, even to the morality of a wise creator and governor of the world.

I may be allowed to assume, therefore, that our species, progressing steadily in civilization as is its natural end, is also making strides for the better in regard to the moral end of its existence, and that this progress will be *interrupted* now and then, but never *broken off.* I do not have to prove this assumption; the burden of proof is on its opponent. I rest my case on this: I have the innate duty (though in respect of moral character required I am not so good as I should and hence could be) so to affect posterity through each member in the sequence of generations in which I live, simply as a human being, that future generations will become continually better (which also must be assumed to be possible), and that this duty may thus rightfully be passed on from one generation to the next. Let any number of doubts be drawn from history to dispute my hopes, doubts which, if conclusive, might move me to abandon a seemingly futile labor; but as long as the futility cannot be made wholly certain, I cannot exchange my duty (as the *liquidum*) for the rule of prudence not to attempt the unfeasible (as the *illiquidum,* because it is a mere hypothesis). I may always be and remain unsure whether an improvement in the human race can be hoped for; but this can invalidate neither the maxim nor its necessary presupposition that in a practical respect it be feasible.

Without this hope for better times the human heart would never have been warmed by a serious desire to do something useful for the common good; this hope has always influenced the labors of right-thinking men. Even the excellent Mendelssohn must have reckoned with it when he so zealously strove for the enlightenment and welfare of the nation to which he belonged. For he could not reasonably hope to accomplish them by himself, all alone, unless others after him continued advancing on the same path. Despite the depressing sight, not so much of ills that oppress mankind from natural causes as of those men inflict upon each other, the mind is cheered by the prospect that things may be better in future—a quite unselfish benevolence, since we shall long be in our graves and shall not reap the fruits which we have helped to sow. Empirical arguments against the success of these resolves, which rest on hope, are insufficient here. The argument that what has not succeeded so far will therefore never succeed, does not even justify the abandonment of a pragmatic or technological intention (as that of air travel by aerostatic balloons, for instance), much less than abandonment of a moral intention that becomes a duty unless its accomplishment is demonstrably impossible. Besides, there is a good deal of evidence to show that in our age, compared with all earlier ones, mankind has by and large really made considerable moral progress for the better. (Short-time arrests can prove nothing to the contrary.) And it can also be shown that the screaming about an irresistibly growing depravation of mankind comes from the very fact that, upon reaching a higher level of morality, we can see farther ahead, and that the severity of our judgments about what we are compared with what we ought to be—in other words, our self-criticism—increases the higher we have climbed on the moral ladder in all of what we have come to know of the world's course.

If we ask, then, by what means we might maintain and possibly accelerate this perpetual progress for the better, we soon see that this immeasurable success will depend not so much on what *we* do (on what education we give to the young, for instance), or on the method *we* ought to use to accomplish it. Instead, it will depend upon what human *nature* will do in and with us to *force* us into a track to which we would not easily accommodate ourselves on our own. For we can look only to nature, or rather, because the attainment of this end requires supreme wisdom, the *Providence* for a success that will affect the whole and thence the parts, while on the contrary, the *designs* of men start with the parts, if indeed they do not stop there. The whole as such is too large for men; they can extend their ideas to it, but not their influence, chiefly since the design of one man will repel another, so that they would hardly reach agreement on a design of their own free intention.

Just as universal violence and the resulting distress were finally bound to make a people decide that they should submit to the coercion of public laws, which reason itself prescribes for them as remedy, and found a state under a *civil constitution,* even so the distress of ceaseless warfare, in which states in turn seek to reduce or subjugate each other, must eventually bring the states under a *cosmopolitan* constitution even against their will. Such general peace may pose an even greater threat to freedom from another quarter by leading to the most terrible despotism, as has repeatedly happened in the case of oversized states. Yet the distress of ceaseless warfare must compel them to adopt a condition which, although not a cosmopolitan community under one head, is still lawful—a *federation* under jointly agreed *international law.*

For the advancing civilization of the states, accompanied by a growing inclination to expand by cunning or by force at the other's expense, means the multiplication of wars. To maintain standing armies, to add to them constantly more men at the same pay, to keep them in training and equip them with ever more numerous tools of war, all this is bound to produce higher and higher costs. The price of all necessities keeps rising, without any hope of a corresponding increase in the supply of the metals of which they are made. And no peace lasts long enough for the peacetime savings to match the cost of the next war, a complaint for which the invention of national debts is an ingenious but ultimately self-destructive nostrum. As a result, impotence must finally accomplish what good will ought to have done but did not: the organization of every state's internal affairs so that the decisive voice on whether or not to wage war is not that of the head of state—for whom the war costs actually nothing—but that of the people, who pay for it. (This necessarily presupposes, of course, the realization of that idea of the original contract.) For the people are hardly likely to plunge themselves into penury—which never touches the head of state—out of sheer lust of expansion or because of supposed purely verbal insults. And so their descendants will not be burdened with debts they have not brought on themselves; they too—due not to any love for them, but only to the self-love of each era— will be able to progress toward an ever better condition, even in a moral sense; because any community unable to harm others by force must rely on justice alone, and may have grounds to hope for help from other communities of the same constitution.

This, however, is just an opinion and mere hypothesis, as uncertain as all judgments claiming to state the sole adequate natural cause for an intended effect that is not wholly in our power. And, as has been shown above, even as such an hypothesis it contains no principle for its enforcement by the subjects of an existing state; rather, it contains an enforcement for uncoercible heads of state. In the usual order of things it is not in human nature to relinquish power voluntarily; yet, in pressing circumstances, it is not impossible. So we may consider it a not inadequate expression of the moral hopes and wishes of men (conscious of their weakness) to look to *Providence* for the circumstances required. They may hope that since it is the *purpose* of *mankind,* of the entire species, to achieve its final destiny by the free use of its powers as far as they go, Providence will bring about an outcome to which the purposes of *men,* considered separately, run directly counter. For this very counteraction of inclinations, the fonts of evil, gives reason free play to subjugate them all and to inaugurate a reign of the good that is self-sustaining, once it exists, in place of the reign of self-destructive evil.

Nowhere does human nature appear less lovable than in the relations of whole nations to each other. No state's independence or possessions are even for a moment safe from the others. The will to subjugate another, or encroach upon what belongs to him, is always present; and warlike preparations for defense, which often make peace more burdensome and more destructive of domestic welfare than war itself, may never be relaxed. For this the only possible remedy is international law based on public statutes backed by power, statutes to which every state would have to submit in analogy to civil or constitutional law for individuals. For an enduring universal peace by means of the so-called *balance of power in Europe* is a mere chimera, rather like Swift's house whose architect had built it in such perfect accordance with all the laws of equilibrium that a sparrow lighting on the roof made it promptly collapse.

"But states," it will be said, "will never submit to such coercive laws; and the proposal of a universal international state, whose authority all individual states should voluntarily accept and whose laws they should obey, may sound ever so nice in the theory of an Abbé de Saint-Pierre or a Rousseau, but it will not work in practice. Has it not always been ridiculed by great statesmen, and more yet by heads of state, as a pedantically childish academic idea?"

I for my part put my trust in the theory that proceeds from the principle of justice, concerning how relations between individuals and states *ought to be*. The theory commends to the earthly demigods the maxim to proceed so that each of their quarrels become the introduction to such a universal international state and, thus, to assume as a practical possibility that it *can be*.

At the same time, however, I trust *(in subsidium)* in the nature of things, which compels one to go where he would rather not *(fata volentem ducunt, nolentem trahunt*—fate guides the willing and drags the unwilling). In this I also take human nature into account. Since respect for right and duty is still alive in human nature, I cannot, or will not, consider it so steeped in evil that in the end, after many unsuccessful attempts, moral-practical reason should not triumph and show human nature also to be lovable. So, even from a cosmopolitan viewpoint my assertion stands: what is valid in theory, on rational grounds, is valid also in practice.

Notes

1. If we want to link the word "gracious" with a determinate concept differentiating it from "kind," "benevolent," "protective," and the like, we can use it only for a person who is not subject to legal coercion. In other words, since it is the head of the *state government* who effects and grants every benefit possible under public law (for the *sovereign* who gives those laws is invisible, as it were; he is the law personified, not its agent), that head alone, as the only one not subject to legal coercion, can rightly be titled "gracious lord." Even in an aristocracy, as in Venice for example, the *Senate* is the only "gracious lord." All the nobles who constitute it are subjects (not even the *Doge* excepted, for the Grand Council alone is the sovereign) and, as far as the execution of the laws is concerned, the equals of everyone else. Every subject has the right to coerce any one of them.

   Princes—i.e., those who have a hereditary right to the rule—are styled "gracious lords" by courtesy, court fashion, on account of their prospects and claims; but in their proprietary status they are fellow subjects nonetheless, and their humblest servant must have the right to coerce them legally through the head of state.

   As for the gracious (more properly, noble) ladies, it might be considered that it is their *status* together with their *sex* which gives them a claim to this title (a claim, consequently, only upon the male sex), and this owing to the refinement of manners (called gallantry), whereby the male believes to do himself greater honor in proportion as he concedes greater prerogatives to the fair sex.

2. The producer of an *opus* can convey it to another by transfer, just as if it were his property; but

praestatio operae is not such a transfer. The domestic servant, the shop clerk, the laborer, even the hairdresser—these are mere *operarii,* not *artifices* in the broader sense, and they are not members of the state, hence not entitled to be citizens. Although my relations to the man I give my firewood to cut, and to the tailor to whom I give my cloth with which to make me a garment, seem altogether similar, yet the first differs from the second as the hairdresser differs from the wigmaker (even if I have given him the hair for my wig) or the day-laborer from the artist or craftsman who fashions a work that belongs to him until he has been paid. The latter, acting as a tradesman, will exchange his property *(opus)* with others; the former will permit others to use his services *(operam).*

It is, I confess, somewhat difficult to determine just what it takes to be able to claim the status of being one's own master.

3. If, for example, a proportional war tax were levied on all subjects, the fact that it is onerous would not permit them to call it unjust on the grounds that the war, in their view, was unnecessary. This they have no right to judge, because there is always *the possibility* that the war is unavoidable and the tax indispensable, and hence must be considered lawful in the judgment of the subjects. But if in such a war the property of certain owners is onerously commandeered while others, equally situated, are spared this burden, it is easy to see that all the people cannot consent to such a law, and because they cannot consider such an unequal distribution of burdens as just, they are entitled at least to remonstrate against it.

4. This includes certain import restrictions in order to promote the use of purchasing power for the subjects' own good rather than to benefit foreigners and to stimulate foreign industry; because the state, without a prosperous people, would not be strong enough to resist foreign enemies or to maintain itself as a community.

5. There is only one *casus necessitatis*—the case in which an *absolute duty* conflicts with one that, though perhaps major, is still only a *conditional duty.* For example, to save the state from calamity it may be necessary to betray one's relative, perhaps a father or son. To save the state from calamity is an unconditional duty, but it is only a conditional duty to avert the relative's unhappiness (as long as he has not become guilty of a crime against the state). Reporting a relative's plans to the authorities may be performed with extreme reluctance, but is compelled by necessity, to wit, moral necessity.

But when a shipwrecked man pushes another off his raft to save his own life, then to say that he had a right to do so because of his (physical) need is totally false. For I have a duty to save my life only on condition that I can do so without committing a crime. But I have an unconditional duty not to take the life of someone else who is not injuring me nor even causing the danger threatening mine. Even so, the professors of law are quite consistent in making legal allowance for such emergency acts. For the authorities cannot attach any *punishment* to this injunction, because that punishment would have to be death. And it would be an absurd law that threatened death to one who refuses to die voluntarily in a dangerous situation.

6. *Ius Naturae. Editio 5ta. Paris posterior,* Sections 203 to 206.

7. No matter how the people's real contract with their sovereign may be violated, they cannot immediately react *as a community,* but only as a mob. For the former constitution has been torn up by the people, while their organization as a new *community* is still to occur. This is when the state of anarchy arises with all its at least potential horrors. And the wrong in that situation is whatever each of the people's parties inflicts on the other. This also emerges from an example cited, where the rebellious subjects of that state finally sought to force on each other a constitution that would have become far more oppressive than the one discarded—namely, the prospect of being devoured by clerics and aristocrats instead of being able to look to an all-governing head for a more equitable distribution of the state's burdens.

8. No right in the state can be insidiously concealed, as it were, by way of a secret reservation, least of all the right which the people presume to be a part of the constitution. For all constitutional laws must be conceived as deriving from a public will. If the constitution were to permit rebellion, it would have to state publicly the right to rebel and the way to exercise it.

9. It is not immediately apparent how a general *philanthropic* presupposition relates to a *cosmopolitan* constitution, and how the latter relates to the foundation of international law as the only condition in which those human tendencies that make our species lovable can be properly developed. The conclusion of this part will make that connection plain.

PERPETUAL PEACE

We need not try to decide whether this satirical inscription, (once found on a Dutch innkeeper's signboard above the picture of a churchyard) is aimed at mankind in general, or at the rulers of states in particular, unwearying in their love of war, or perhaps only at the philosophers who cherish the sweet dream of perpetual peace. The author of the present sketch would make one stipulation, however. The practical politician stands upon a definite footing with the theorist: with great self-complacency he looks down upon him as a mere pedant whose empty ideas can threaten no danger to the state (starting as it does from principles derived from experience), and who may always be permitted to knock down his eleven skittles at once without a worldly-wise statesman needing to disturb himself. Hence, in the event of a quarrel arising between the two, the practical statesman must always act consistently, and not scent danger to the state behind opinions ventured by the theoretical politician at random and publicly expressed. With which saving clause *(clausula salvatoria)* the author will herewith consider himself duly and expressly protected against all malicious misinterpretation.

FIRST SECTION

Containing the Preliminary Articles of Perpetual Peace Between States

1. "No treaty of peace shall be regarded as valid, if made with the secret reservation of material for a future war."

For then it would be a mere truce, a mere suspension of hostilities, not peace. A peace signifies the end of all hostilities and to attach to it the epithet "eternal" is not only a verbal pleonasm, but matter of suspicion. The causes of a future war existing, although perhaps not yet known to the high contracting parties themselves, are entirely annihilated by the conclusion of peace, however acutely they may be ferreted out of documents in the public archives. There may be a mental reservation of old claims to be thought out at a future time, which are, none of them, mentioned at this stage, because both parties are too much exhausted to continue the war, while the evil intention remains of using the first favourable opportunity for further hostilities. Diplomacy of this kind only Jesuitical casuistry can justify: it is beneath the dignity of a ruler, just as acquiescence in such processes of reasoning is beneath the dignity of his minister, if one judges the facts as they really are.

If, however, according to present enlightened ideas of political wisdom, the true glory of a state lies in the uninterrupted development of its power by every possible means, this judgment must certainly strike one as scholastic and pedantic.

2. "No state having an independent existence—whether it be great or small—shall be acquired by another through inheritance, exchange, purchase or donation."

For a state is not a property *(patrimonium)*, as may be the ground on which its people are settled. It is a society of human beings over whom no one but itself has the right to rule and to dispose. Like the trunk of a tree, it has its own roots, and to graft it on to

Translated by M. Campbell Smith.

another state is to do away with its existence as a moral person, and to make of it a thing. Hence it is in contradiction to the idea of the original contract without which no right over a people is thinkable.[1] Everyone knows to what danger the bias in favour of these modes of acquisition has brought Europe (in other parts of the world it has never been known). The custom of marriage between states, as if they were individuals, has survived even up to the most recent times and is regarded partly as a new kind of industry by which ascendency may be acquired through family alliances, without any expenditure of strength; partly as a device for territorial expansion. Moreover, the hiring out of the troops of one state to another to fight against an enemy not at war with their native country is to be reckoned in this connection; for the subjects are in this way used and abused at will as personal property.

3. "Standing armies *(miles perpetuus)* shall be abolished in course of time."

For they are always threatening other states with war by appearing to be in constant readiness to fight. They incite the various states to outrival one another in the number of their soldiers, and to this number no limit can be set. Now, since owing to the sums devoted to this purpose, peace at last becomes even more oppressive than a short war, these standing armies are themselves the cause of wars of aggression, undertaken in order to get rid of this burden. To which we must add that the practice of hiring men to kill or to be killed seems to imply a use of them as mere machines and instruments in the hand of another (namely, the state) which cannot easily be reconciled with the right of humanity in our own person. The matter stands quite differently in the case of voluntary periodical military exercise on the part of citizens of the state, who thereby seek to secure themselves and their country against attack from without.

The accumulation of treasure in a state would in the same way be regarded by other states as a menace of war, and might compel them to anticipate this by striking the first blow. For of the three forces, the power of arms, the power of alliance and the power of money, the last might well become the most reliable instrument of war, did not the difficulty of ascertaining the amount stand in the way.

4. "No national debts shall be contracted in connection with the external affairs of the state."

This source of help is above suspicion, where assistance is sought outside or within the state, on behalf of the economic administration of the country (for instance, the improvement of the roads, the settlement and support of new colonies, the establishment of granaries to provide against seasons of scarcity, and so on). But, as a common weapon used by the Powers against one another, a credit system under which debts go on indefinitely increasing and are yet always assured against immediate claims (because all the creditors do not put in their claim at once) is a dangerous money power. This ingenious invention of a commercial people in the present century is, in other words, a treasure for the carrying on of war which may exceed the treasures of all the other states taken together, and can only be exhausted by a threatening deficiency in the taxes—an event, however, which will long be kept off by the very briskness of commerce resulting from the reaction of this system on industry and trade. The ease, then, with which war may be waged, coupled with the inclination of rulers towards it—an inclination which seems to be implanted in human nature—is a great obstacle in the way of perpetual peace. The prohibition of this system must be laid down as a preliminary article of perpetual peace, all the more necessarily because the final inevitable bankruptcy of the state in question must involve in the loss many who are innocent; and this would be a public injury to these states. Therefore other nations are at least justified in uniting themselves against such an one and its pretensions.

5. "No state shall violently interfere with the constitution and administration of another."

For what can justify it in so doing? The scandal which is here presented to the subjects of another state? The erring state can much more serve as a warning by exemplifying the great evils which a nation draws down on itself through its own lawlessness. Moreover, the bad example which one free person gives another, (as *scandalum acceptum*) does no injury to the latter. In this connection, it is true, we cannot count the case of a state which has become split up through internal corruption into two parts, each of them representing by itself an individual state which lays claim to the whole. Here the yielding of assistance to one faction could not be reckoned as interference on the part of a foreign state with the consitution of another, for here anarchy prevails. So long, however, as the inner strife has not yet reached this state the interference of other powers would be a violation of the rights of an independent nation which is only struggling with internal disease. It would therefore itself cause a scandal, and make the autonomy of all states insecure.

6. "No state at war with another shall countenance such modes of hostility as would make mutual confidence impossible in a subsequent state of peace: such are the employment of assassins *(percussores)* or of poisoners *(venefici)*, breaches of capitulation, the instigating and making use of treachery *(perduellio)* in the hostile state."

These are dishonourable strategems. For some kind of confidance in the disposition of the enemy must exist even in the midst of war, as otherwise peace could not be concluded, and the hostilities would pass into a war of extermination *(bellum internecinum)*. War, however, is only our wretched expedient of asserting a right by force, an expedient adopted in the state of nature, where no court of justice exists which could settle the matter in dispute. In circumstances like these, neither of the two parties can be called an unjust enemy, because this form of speech presupposes a legal decision: the issue of the conflict—just as in the case of the so-called judgments of God—decides on which side right is. Between states, however, no punitive war *(bellum punitivum)* is thinkable, because between them a relation of superior and inferior does not exist. Whence it follows that a war of extermination, where the process of annihilation would strike both parties at once and all right as well, would bring about perpetual peace only in the great graveyard of the human race. Such a war then, and therefore also the use of all means which lead to it, must be absolutely forbidden. That the methods just mentioned do inevitably lead to this result is obvious from the fact that these infernal arts, already vile in themselves, on coming into use, are not long confined to the sphere of war. Take, for example, the use of spies *(uti exploratoribus)*. Here only the dishonesty of others is made use of; but vices such as these, when once encouraged, cannot in the nature of things be stamped out and would be carried over into the state of peace, where their presence would be utterly destructive to the purpose of that state.

Although the laws stated are, objectively regarded, (*i.e.* in so far as they affect the action of rulers) purely prohibitive laws *(leges prohibitivæ)*, some of them *(leges strictæ)* are strictly valid without regard to circumstances and urgently require to be enforced. Such are Nos. I, 5, 6. Others, again, (like Nos. 2, 3, 4) although not indeed exceptions to the maxims of law, yet in respect of the practical application of these maxims allow subjectively of a certain latitude to suit particular circumstances. The enforcement of these *leges latæ* may be legitimately put off, so long as we do not lose sight of the ends at which they aim. This purpose of reform does not permit of the deferment of an act of restitution (as, for example, the restoration to certain states of freedom of which they have been deprived in the manner described in article 2) to an infinitely distant date—as Augustus used to say, to the "Greek Kalends", a day that will never come. This would be to sanction non-restitution. Delay is permitted only with the intention that restitution should not be made too precipitately and so defeat the purpose we have in view. For the prohibition refers here only to the *mode of acquisition* which is to be no longer valid, and not to the *fact of possession* which, although indeed it has not the necessary title of right, yet at the time of so-called acquisition was held legal by all states, in accordance with the public opinion of the time.[2]

SECOND SECTION

Containing the Definitive Articles of a Perpetual Peace Between States

A state of peace among men who live side by side is not the natural state (*status naturalis*), which is rather to be described as a state of war: that is to say, although there is not perhaps always actual open hostility, yet there is a constant threatening that an outbreak may occur. Thus the state of peace must be *established*. For the mere cessation of hostilities is no guarantee of continued peaceful relations, and unless this guarantee is given by every individual to his neighbour—which can only be done in a state of society regulated by law—one man is at liberty to challenge another and treat him as an enemy.[3]

First Definitive Article of Perpetual Peace

I. "The civil constitution of each state shall be republican."

The only constitution which has its origin in the idea of the original contract, upon which the lawful legislation of every nation must be based, is the republican.[4] It is a constitution, in the first place, founded in accordance with the principle of the freedom of the members of society, as human beings: secondly, in accordance with the principle of the dependence of all, as subjects, on a common legislation: and, thirdly, in accordance with the law of the equality of the members as citizens. It is then, looking at the question of right, the only constitution whose fundamental principles lie at the basis of every form of civil constitution. And the only question for us now is, whether it is also the one constitution which can lead to perpetual peace.

Now the republican constitution apart from the soundness of its origin, since it arose from the pure source of the concept of right, has also the prospect of attaining the desired result, namely, perpetual peace. And the reason is this. If, as must be so under this constitution, the consent of the subjects is required to determine whether there shall be war or not, nothing is more natural than that they should weigh the matter well, before undertaking such a bad business. For in decreeing war, they would of necessity be resolving to bring down the miseries of war upon their country. This implies: they must fight themselves; they must hand over the costs of the war out of their own property; they must do their poor best to make good the devastation which it leaves behind; and finally, as a crowning ill, they have to accept a burden of debt which will embitter even peace itself, and which they can never pay off on account of the new wars which are always impending. On the other hand, in a government where the subject is not a citizen holding a vote, (i.e. in a constitution which is not republican), the plunging into war is the least serious thing in the world. For the ruler is not a citizen, but the owner of the state, and does not lose a whit by the war, while he goes on enjoying the delights of his table or sport, or of his pleasure palaces and gala days. He can therefore decide on war for the most trifling reasons, as if it were a kind of pleasure party. Any justification of it that is necessary for the sake of decency he can leave without concern to the diplomatic corps who are always only too ready with their services.

The following remarks must be made in order that we may not fall into the common error of confusing the republican with the democratic constitution. The forms of the state (*civitas*) may be classified according to either of two principles of division:—the difference of the persons who hold the supreme authority in the state, and the manner in which the people are governed by their ruler whoever he may be. The first is properly called the form of sovereignty (*forma imperii*), and there can be only three constitutions differing in this respect: where, namely, the supreme authority belongs to only one, to several individuals working together, or to the whole people constituting the civil society. Thus we have autocracy or the sovereignty of a monarch, aristocracy or the sovereignty of the nobility, and democracy or the sovereignty of the people. The second principle of division is the form of government (*forma regiminis*), and refers to the way in which the state makes use of its supreme power: for the manner of government is based on the constitution, itself the act of that universal will which transforms a multitude into a nation. In this respect the form of government is either republican or despotic. Republicanism is the political principle of severing the executive power of the government from the legislature. Despotism is that principle in pursuance of which the state arbitrarily puts into effect laws which it has itself made: consequently it is the administration of the public will, but this is identical with the private will of the ruler. Of these three forms of a state, democracy, in the proper sense of the word, is of necessity despotism, because it establishes an executive power, since all decree regarding—and, if need be, against—any individual who dissents from them. Therefore the "whole people", so-called, who carry their measure are really not all, but only a majority: so that here the universal will is in contradiction with itself and with the principle of freedom.

Every form of government in fact which is not representative is really no true constitution at all, because a law-giver may no more be, in one and the same person, the administrator of his own will, than the universal major premise of a syllogism may be, at the same time, the subsumption under itself of the particulars contained in the minor premise. And, although the other two constitutions, autocracy and aristocracy, are always defective in so far as they leave the way open for such a form of government, yet there is at least always a possibility in these cases, that they may take the form of a government in accordance with the spirit of a representative system. Thus Frederick the Great used at least to say that he was "merely the highest servant of the state."[5] The democratic constitution, on the other hand, makes this impossible, because under such a government every one wishes to be master. We may therefore say that the smaller the staff of the executive—that is to say, the number of rulers—and the more real, on the other hand, their representation of the people, so much the more is the government of the state in accordance with a possible republicanism; and it may hope by gradual reforms to raise itself to that standard. For this reason, it is more difficult under an aristocracy than under a monarchy—while under a democracy it is impossible except by a violent revolution—to attain to this, the one perfectly, lawful constitution. The kind of government,[6] however, is of infinitely more importance to the people than the kind of constitution, although the greater or less aptitude of a people for this ideal greatly depends upon such external form. The form of government, however, if it is to be in accordance with the idea of right, must embody the representative system in which alone a republican form of administration is possible and without which it is despotic and violent, be the constitution what it may. None of the ancient so-called republics were aware of this, and they necessarily slipped into absolute despotism which, of all despotisms, is most endurable under the sovereignty of one individual.

Second Definitive Article of Perpetual Peace

II. "The law of nations shall be founded on a federation of free states."

Nations, as states, may be judged like individuals who, living in the natural state of society—that is to say, uncontrolled by external law—injure one another through their very proximity. Every state, for the sake of its own security, may—and ought to—demand that its neighbour should submit itself to conditions, similar to those of the civil society where the right of every individual is guaranteed. This would give rise to a federation of nations which, however, would not have to be a State of nations. That would involve a contradiction. For the term "state" implies the relation of one who rules to those who obey—that is to say, of lawgiver to the subject people: and many nations in one state would constitute only one nation, which contradicts our hypothesis, since here we have to consider the right of one nation against another, in so far as they are so many separate states and are not to be fused into one.

The attachment of savages to their lawless liberty, the fact that they would rather be at hopeless variance with one another than submit themselves to a legal authority consti-tuted by themselves, that they therefore prefer their senseless freedom to a reason—gov-erned liberty, is regarded by us with profound contempt as barbarism and uncivilisation and the brutal degradation of humanity. So one would think that civilised races, each formed into a state by itself, must come out of such an abandoned condition as soon as they possibly can. On the contrary, however, every state thinks rather that its majesty (the "majesty" of a people is an absurd expression) lies just in the very fact that it is subject to no external legal authority; and the glory of the ruler consists in this, that, without his requiring to expose himself to danger, thousands stand at his command ready to let them-selves be sacrificed for a matter of no concern to them.[7] The difference between the sav-ages of Europe and those of America lies chiefly in this, that, while many tribes of the latter have been entirely devoured by their enemies, Europeans know a better way of using the vanquished than by eating them; and they prefer to increase through them the num-ber of their subjects, and so the number of instruments at their command for still more widely spread war.

The depravity of human nature shows itself without disguise in the unrestrained rela-tions of nations to each other, while in the law-governed civil state much of this is hidden by the check of government. This being so, it is astonishing that the word "right" has not yet been entirely banished from the policies of war as pedantic, and that no state has yet ventured to publicly advocate this point of view. For Hugo Grotius, Puffendorf, Vattel and others—Job's comforters, all of them—are always quoted in good faith to justify an attack, although their codes, whether couched in philosophical or diplomatic terms, have not—

nor can have—the slightest legal force, because states, as such, are under no common external authority; and there is no instance of a state having ever been moved by argument to desist from its purpose, even when this was backed up by the testimony of such great men. This homage which every state renders—in words at least—to the idea of right, proves that, although it may be slumbering, there is, notwithstanding, to be found in man a still higher natural moral capacity by the aid of which he will in time gain the mastery over the evil principle in his nature, the existence of which he is unable to deny. And he hopes the same of others; for otherwise the word "right" would never be uttered by states who wish to wage war, unless to deride it like the Gallic Prince who declared:—"The privilege which nature gives the strong is that the weak must obey them."[8]

The method by which states prosecute their rights can never be by process of law—as it is where there is an external tribunal—but only by war. Through this means, however, and its favourable issue, victory, the question of right is never decided. A treaty of peace makes, it may be, an end to the war of the moment, but not to the conditions of war which at any time may afford a new pretext for opening hostilities; and this we cannot exactly condemn as unjust, because under these conditions everyone is his own judge. Notwithstanding, not quite the same rule applies to states according to the law of nations as holds good of individuals in a lawless condition according to the law of nature, namely, "that they ought to advance out of this condition." This is so, because, as states, they have already within themselves a legal constitution, and have therefore advanced beyond the stage at which others, in accordance with their ideas of right, can force them to come under a wider legal constitution. Meanwhile, however, reason, from her throne of the supreme law-giving moral power, absolutely condemns war as a morally lawful proceeding, and makes a state of peace, on the other hand, an immediate duty. Without a compact between the nations, however, this state of peace cannot be established or assured. Hence there must be an alliance of a particular kind which we may call a covenant of peace (*foedus pacificum*), which would differ from a treaty of peace (*pactum pacis*) in this respect, that the latter merely puts an end to one war, while the former would seek to put an end to war for ever. This alliance does not aim at the gain of any power whatsoever of the state, but merely at the preservation and security of the freedom of the state for itself and of other allied states at the same time. The latter do not, however, require, for this reason, to submit themselves like individuals in the state of nature to public laws and coercion. The practicability or objective reality of this idea of federation which is to extend gradually over all states and so lead to perpetual peace can be shewn. For, if Fortune ordains that a powerful and enlightened people should form a republic,—which by its very nature is inclined to perpetual peace—this would serve as a centre of federal union for other states wishing to join, and thus secure conditions of freedom among the states in accordance with the idea of the law of nations. Gradually, through different unions of this kind, the federation would extend further and further.

It is quite comprehensible that a people should say:—"There shall be no war among us, for we shall form ourselves into a state, that is to say, constitute for ourselves a supreme legislative, administrative, and judicial power which will settle our disputes peaceably." But if this state says:—"There shall be no war between me and other states, although I recognise no supreme law-giving power which will secure me my rights and whose rights I will guarantee;" then it is not at all clear upon what grounds I could base my confidence in my right, unless it were the substitute for that compact on which civil society is based—namely, free federation which reason must necessarily connect with the idea of the law of nations, if indeed any meaning is to be left in that concept at all.

There is no intelligible meaning in the idea of the law of nations as giving a right to make war; for that must be a right to decide what is just, not in accordance with universal, external laws limiting the freedom of each individual, but by means of one-sided maxims applied by force. We must then understand by this that men of such ways of thinking are quite justly served, when they destroy one another, and thus find perpetual peace in the wide grave which covers all the abominations of acts of violence as well as the authors of such deeds. For states, in their relation to one another, there can be, according to reason, no other way of advancing from that lawless condition which unceasing war implies, than by giving up their savage lawless freedom, just as individual men have done, and yielding to the coercion of public laws. Thus they can form a State of nations (*civitas gentium*), one, too, which will be ever increasing and would finally embrace all the peoples of the earth. States, however, in accordance with their understanding of the law of nations, by no means desire this, and therefore reject *in hypothesi* what is correct *in thesi*. Hence, instead of the positive idea of a world-republic, if all is not to be lost, only the negative substitute for it, a federation averting war, maintaining its ground and ever extending over the world may stop the current of this tendency to war and shrinking from the control of law. But even then there will be a constant danger that this propensity may break out.[9]

"*Furor impius intus—fremit horridus ore cruento.*" (Virgil.)

Third Definitive Article of Perpetual Peace

III. "The rights of men, as citizens of the world, shall be limited to the conditions of universal hospitality."

We are speaking here, as in the previous articles, not of philanthropy, but of right; and in this sphere hospitality signifies the claim of a stranger entering foreign territory to be treated by its owner without hostility. The latter may send him away again, if this can be done without causing his death; but, so long as he conducts himself peaceably, he must not be treated as an enemy. It is not a right to be treated as a guest to which the stranger can lay claim—a special friendly compact on his behalf would be required to make him for a given time an actual inmate—but he has a right of visitation. This right to present themselves to society belongs to all mankind in virtue of our common right of possession on the surface of the earth on which, as it is a globe, we cannot be infinitely scattered, and must in the end reconcile ourselves to existence side by side: at the same time, originally no one individual had more right than another to live in any one particular spot. Uninhabitable portions of the surface, ocean and desert, split up the human community, but in such a way that ships and camels—"the ship of the desert"—make it possible for men to come into touch with one another across these unappropriated regions and to take advantage of our common claim to the face of the earth with a view to a possible intercommunication. The inhospitality of the inhabitants of certain sea coasts—as, for example, the coast of Barbary—in plundering ships in neighbouring seas or making slaves of shipwrecked mariners; or the behaviour of the Arab Bedouins in the deserts, who think that proximity to nomadic tribes constitutes a right to rob, is thus contrary to the law of nature. This right to hospitality, however—that is to say, the privilege of strangers arriving on foreign soil—does not amount to more than what is implied in a permission to make an attempt at intercourse with the original inhabitants. In this way far distant territories may enter into peaceful relations with one another. These relations may at last come under the public control of law, and thus the human race may be brought nearer the realisation of a cosmopolitan constitution.

Let us look now, for the sake of comparison, at the inhospitable behaviour of the civilised nations, especially the commercial states of our continent. The injustice which they exhibit on visiting foreign lands and races—this being equivalent in their eyes to conquest—is such as to fill us with horror. America, the negro countries, the Spice Islands, the Cape etc. were, on being discovered, looked upon as countries which belonged to nobody; for the native inhabitants were reckoned as nothing. In Hindustan, under the pretext of intending to establish merely commercial depots, the Europeans introduced foreign troops; and, as a result, the different states of Hindustan were stirred up to far-spreading wars. Oppression of the natives followed, famine, insurrection, perfidy and all the rest of the litany of evils which can afflict mankind.

China[10] and Japan (Nipon) which had made an attempt at receiving guests of this kind, have now taken a prudent step. Only to a single European people, the Dutch, has China given the right of access to her shores (but not of entrance into the country), while Japan has granted both these concessions; but at the same time they exclude the Dutch who enter, as if they were prisoners, from social intercourse with the inhabitants. The worst, or from the standpoint of ethical judgment the best, of all this is that no satisfaction is derived from all this violence, that all these trading companies stand on the verge of ruin, that the Sugar Islands, that seat of the most horrible and deliberate slavery, yield no real profit, but only have their use indirectly and for no very praiseworthy object—namely, that of furnishing men to be trained as sailors for the men-of-war and thereby contributing to the carrying on of war in Europe. And this has been done by nations who make a great ado about their piety, and who, while they are quite ready to commit injustice, would like, in their orthodoxy, to be considered among the elect.

The intercourse, more or less close, which has been everywhere steadily increasing between the nations of the earth, has now extended so enormously that a violation of right in one part of the world is felt all over it. Hence the idea of a cosmopolitan right is no fantastical, high-flown notion of right, but a complement of the unwritten code of law—constitutional as well as international law—necessary for the public rights of mankind in general and thus for the realisation of perpetual peace. For only by endeavouring to fulfil the conditions laid down by this cosmopolitan law can we flatter ourselves that we are gradually approaching that ideal.

FIRST SUPPLEMENT

Concerning the Guarantee of Perpetual Peace

This guarantee is given by no less a power than the great artist nature (*natura dædala rerum*) in whose mechanical course is clearly exhibited a predetermined design to make harmony spring from human discord, even against the will of man. Now this design, although called Fate when looked upon as the compelling force of a cause, the laws of whose operation are unknown to us, is, when considered as the purpose manifested in the course of nature, called Providence,[11] the deep lying wisdom of a Higher Cause, directing itself towards the ultimate practical end of the human race and predetermining the course of things with a view to its realisation. This Providence we do not, it is true, perceive in the cunning contrivances [*Kunstanstalten*] of nature; nor can we even conclude from the fact of their existence that it is there; but, as in every relation between the form of things and their final cause, we can, and must, supply the thought of a Higher Wisdom, in order that we may be able to form an idea of the possible existence of these products after the analogy of human works of art. [*Kunsthand*]. The representation to ourselves of the relation and agreement of these formations of nature to the moral purpose for which they were made and which reason directly prescribes to us, is an Idea, it is true, which is in theory superfluous; but in practice it is dogmatic, and its objective reality is well established. Thus we see, for example, with regard to the ideal of perpetual peace, that it is our duty to make use of the mechanism of nature for the realisation of that end. Moreover, in a case like this where we are interested merely in the theory and not in the religious question, the use of the word "nature" is more appropriate than that of "providence", in view of the limitations of human reason, which, in considering the relation of effects to their causes, must keep within the limits of possible experience. And the term "nature" is also less presumptuous than the other. To speak of a Providence knowable by us would be boldly to put on the wings of Icarus in order to draw near to the mystery of its unfathomable purpose.

Before we determine the surety given by nature more exactly, we must first look at what ultimately makes this guarantee of peace necessary—the circumstances in which nature has carefully placed the actors in her great theatre. In the next place, we shall proceed to consider the manner in which she gives this surety.

The provisions she has made are as follows: (1) she has taken care that men *can* live in all parts of the world; (2) she has scattered them by means of war in all directions, even into the most inhospitable regions, so that these too might be populated; (3) by this very means she has forced them to enter into relations more or less controlled by law. It is surely wonderful that, on the cold wastes round the Arctic Ocean, there is always to be found moss for the reindeer to scrape out from under the snow, the reindeer itself either serving as food or to draw the sledge of the Ostiak or Samoyedes. And salt deserts which would otherwise be left unutilised have the camel, which seems as if created for travelling in such lands. This evidence of design in things, however, is still more clear when we come to know that, besides the fur-clad animals of the shores of the Arctic Ocean, there are seals, walruses and whales whose flesh furnishes food and whose oil fire for the dwellers in these regions. But the providential care of nature excites our wonder above all, when we hear of the driftwood which is carried—whence no one knows—to these treeless shores: for without the aid of this material the natives could neither construct their craft, nor weapons, nor huts for shelter. Here too they have so much to do, making war against wild animals, that they live at peace with one another. But what drove them originally into these regions was probably nothing but war.

Of animals, used by us as instruments of war, the horse was the first which man learned to tame and domesticate during the period of the peopling of the earth; the elephant belongs to the late period of the luxury of states already established. In the same way, the art of cultivating certain grasses called cereals—no longer known to us in their original form—and also the multiplication and improvement, by transplanting and grafting, of the original kinds of fruit—in Europe, probably only two species, the crab-apple and wild pear—could only originate under the conditions accompanying established states where the rights of property are assured. That is to say it would be after man, hitherto existing in lawless liberty, had advanced beyond the occupations of a hunter,[12] a fisherman or a shepherd to the life of a tiller of the soil, when salt and iron were discovered,—to become, perhaps, the first articles of commerce between different peoples,—and were sought far and near. In this way the peoples would be at first brought into peaceful relation with one another, and so come to an understanding and the enjoyment of friendly intercourse, even with their most distant neighbours.

Now while nature provided that men could live on all parts of the earth, she also at the same time despotically willed that they *should* live everywhere on it, although against

their own inclination and even although this imperative did not presuppose an idea of
duty which would compel obedience to nature with the force of a moral law. But, to attain
this end, she has chosen war. So we see certain peoples, widely separated, whose common
descent is made evident by affinity in their languages. Thus, for instance, we find the
Samoyedes on the Arctic Ocean, and again a people speaking a similar language on the
Altai Mts., 200 miles [*Meilen*] off, between whom has pressed in a mounted tribe, warlike in character and of Mongolian origin, which has driven one branch of the race far
from the other, into the most inhospitable regions where their own inclination would certainly not have carried them.[13] In the same way, through the intrusion of the Gothic and
Sarmatian tribes, the Finns in the most northerly regions of Europe, whom we call
Laplanders, have been separated by as great a distance from the Hungarians, with whose
language their own is allied. And what but war can have brought the Esquimos to the
north of America, a race quite distinct from those of that country and probably European
adventurers of prehistoric times? And war too, nature's method of populating the earth,
must have driven the Pescherais, in South America as far as Patagonia. War itself, however, is in need of no special stimulating cause, but seems engrafted in human nature, and
is even regarded, as something noble in itself to which man is inspired by the love of glory
apart from motives of self-interest. Hence, among the savages of America as well as those
of Europe in the age of chivalry, martial courage is I looked upon as of great value in itself,
not merely when a war is going on, as is reasonable enough, but in order that there should
be war: and thus war is often entered upon merely to exhibit this quality. So that an
intrinsic dignity is held to attach to war in itself, and even philosophers eulogise it as an
ennobling, refining influence on humanity, unmindful of the Greek proverb, "War is evil,
in so far as it makes more bad people than it takes away."

So much, then, of what nature does for her own ends with regard to the human race as
members of the animal world. Now comes the question which touches the essential points
in this design of a perpetual peace:—"What does nature do in this respect with reference
to the end which man's own reason sets before him as a duty? and consequently what does
she do to further the realisation of his moral purpose? How does she guarantee that what
man, by the laws of freedom, ought to do and yet fails to do, he will do, without any infringement of his freedom by the compulsion of nature and that, moreover, this shall be
done in accordance with the three forms of public right—constitutional or political law,
international law and cosmopolitan law?" When I say of nature that she *wills* that this or
that should take place, I do not mean that she imposes upon us the duty to do it—for only
the free, unrestrained, practical reason can do that—but that she does it herself, whether
we will or not. *"Fata volentem ducunt, nolentem trahunt."*

I. Even if a people were not compelled through internal discord to submit to the
restraint of public laws, war would bring this about, working from without. For, according to the contrivance of nature which we have mentioned, every people finds another
tribe in its neighbourhood, pressing upon it in such a manner that it is compelled to form
itself internally into a state to be able to defend itself as a power should. Now the republican constitution is the only one which is perfectly adapted to the rights of man, but it
is also the most difficult to establish and still more to maintain. So generally is this recognised that people often say the members of a republican state would require to be angels,
because men, with their self-seeking propensities, are not fit for a constitution of so sublime a form. But now nature comes to the aid of the universal, reason-derived will which,
much as we honour it, is in practice powerless. And this she does, by means of these very
self-seeking propensities, so that it only depends—and so much lies within the power of
man—on a good organisation of the state for their forces to be so pitted against one

another, that the one may check the destructive activity of the other or neutralise its effect. And hence, from the standpoint of reason, the result will be the same as if both forces did not exist, and each individual is compelled to be, if not a morally good man, yet at least a good citizen. The problem of the formation of the state, hard as it may sound, is not insoluble, even for a race of devils, granted that they have intelligence. It may be put thus:—"Given a multitude of rational beings who, in a body, require general laws for their own preservation, but each of whom, as an individual, is secretly inclined to exempt himself from this restraint: how are we to order their affairs and how establish for them a constitution such that, although their private dispositions may be really antagonistic, they may yet so act as a check upon one another, that, in their public relations, the effect is the same as if they had no such evil sentiments." Such a problem must be capable of solution. For it deals, not with the moral reformation of mankind, but only with the mechanism of nature; and the problem is to learn how this mechanism of nature can be applied to men, in order so to regulate the antagonism of conflicting interests in a people that they may even compel one another to submit to compulsory laws and thus necessarily bring about the state of peace in which laws have force. We can see, in states actually existing, although very imperfectly organised, that, in externals, they already approximate very nearly to what the Idea of right prescribes, although the principle of morality is certainly not the cause. A good political constitution, however, is not to be expected as a result of progress in morality; but rather, conversely, the good moral condition of a nation is to be looked for, as one of the first fruits of such a constitution. Hence the mechanism of nature, working through the self-seeking propensities of man (which of course counteract one another in their external effects), may be used by reason as a means of making way for the realisation of her own purpose, the empire of right, and, as far as is in the power of the state, to promote and secure in this way internal as well as external peace. We may say, then, that it is the irresistible will of nature that right shall at last get the supremacy. What one here fails to do will be accomplished in the long run, although perhaps with much inconvenience to us. As Bouterwek says, "If you bend the reed too much it breaks: he who would do too much does nothing."

2. The idea of international law presupposes the separate existence of a number of neighbouring and independent states; and, although such a condition of things is in itself already a state of war, (if a federative union of these nations does not prevent the outbreak of hostilities) yet, according to the Idea of reason, this is better than that all the states should be merged into one under a power which has gained the ascendancy over its neighbours and gradually become a universal monarchy. For the wider the sphere of their jurisdiction, the more laws lose in force; and soulless despotism, when it has choked the seeds of good, at last sinks into anarchy. Nevertheless it is the desire of every state, or of its ruler, to attain to a permanent condition of peace in this very way; that is to say, by subjecting the whole world as far as possible to its sway. But nature wills it otherwise. She employs two means to separate nations, and prevent them from intermixing: namely, the differences of language and of religion.[14] These differences bring with them a tendency to mutual hatred, and furnish pretexts for waging war. But, none the less, with the growth of culture and the gradual advance of men to greater unanimity of principle, they lead to concord in a state of peace which, unlike the despotism we have spoken of, (the churchyard of freedom) does not arise from the weakening of all forces, but is brought into being and secured through the equilibrium of these forces in their most active rivalry.

3. As nature wisely separates nations which the will of each state, sanctioned even by the principles of international law, would gladly unite under its own sway by stratagem or force; in the same way, on the other hand, she united nations whom the principle of a

cosmopolitan right would not have secured against violence and war. And this union she brings about through an appeal to their mutual interests. The commercial spirit cannot co-exist with war, and sooner or later it takes possession of every nation. For, of all the forces which lie at the command of a state, the power of money is probably the most reliable. Hence states find themselves compelled—not, it is true, exactly from motives of morality—to further the noble end of peace and to avert war, by means of mediation, wherever it threatens to break out, just as if they had made a permanent league for this purpose. For great alliances with a view to war can, from the nature of things, only very rarely occur, and still more seldom succeed.

In this way nature guarantees the coming of perpetual peace, through the natural course of human propensities: not indeed with sufficient certainty to enable us to prophesy the future of this ideal theoretically, but yet clearly enough for practical purposes. And thus this guarantee of nature makes it a duty that we should labour for this end, an end which is no mere chimera.

SECOND SUPPLEMENT

A Secret Article for Perpetual Peace

A secret article in negotiations concerning public rights is, when looked at objectively or with regard to the meaning of the term, a contradiction. When we view it, however, from the subjective standpoint, with regard to the character and condition of the person who dictates it, we see that it might quite well involve some private consideration, so that he would regard it as hazardous to his dignity to acknowledge such an article as originating from him.

The only article of this kind is contained in the following proposition:—"The opinions of philosophers, with regard to the conditions of the possibility of a public peace, shall be taken into consideration by states armed for war."

It seems, however, to be derogatory to the dignity of the legislative authority of a state—to which we must of course attribute all wisdom—to ask advise from subjects (among whom stand philosophers) about the rules of its behaviour to other states. At the same time, it is very advisable that this should be done. Hence the state will silently invite suggestion for this purpose, while at the same time keeping the fact secret. This amounts to saying that the state will allow philosophers to discuss freely and publicly the universal principles governing the conduct of war and establishment of peace; for they will do this of their own accord, if no prohibition is laid upon them. The arrangement between states, on this point, does not require that a special agreement should be made, merely for this purpose; for it is already involved in the obligation imposed by the universal reason of man which gives the moral law. We would not be understood to say that the state must give a preference to the principles of the philosopher, rather than to the opinions of the jurist, the representative of state authority; but only that he should be heard. The latter, who has chosen for a symbol the scales of right and the sword of justice, generally uses that sword not merely to keep off all outside influences from the scales; for, when one pan of the balance will not go down, he throws his sword into it; and then *Væ victis!* The jurist, not being a moral philosopher, is under the greatest temptation to do this, because it is his business only to apply existing laws and not to investigate whether these are not themselves in need of improvement; and this actually lower function of his profession he looks upon as the nobler, because it is linked to power (as is the case also in both the other faculties, theology and medicine). Philosophy occupies a very low position compared with this combined power. So that it is said, for example, that she is the handmaid of theology; and the same has been said of her position with regard to law and medicine. It is not quite clear, however, "whether she bears the torch before these gracious ladies, or carries the train."

That kings should philosophise, or philosophers become kings, is not to be expected. But neither is it to be desired; for the possession of power is inevitably fatal to the free exercise of reason. But it is absolutely indispensable, for their enlightenment as to the full significance of their vocations, that both kings and sovereign nations, which rule themselves in accordance with laws of equality, should not allow the class of philosophers to disappear, nor forbid the expression of their opinions, but should allow them to speak openly. And since this class of men, by their very nature, are incapable of instigating rebellion or forming unions for purposes of political agitation, they should not be suspected of propagandism.

APPENDIX I

On the Disagreement Between Morals and Politics with Reference to Perpetual Peace

In an objective sense, morals is a practical science, as the sum of laws exacting unconditional obedience, in accordance with which we *ought* to act. Now, once we have admitted the authority of this idea of duty, it is evidently inconsistent that we should think of saying that we *cannot* act thus. For, in this case, the idea of duty falls to the ground of itself; "*ultra posse nemo obligatur.*" Hence there can be no quarrel between politics, as the practical science of right, and morals, which is also a science of right, but theoretical. That is, theory cannot come into conflict with practice. For, in that case, we would need to understand under the term "ethics" or "morals" a universal doctrine of expediency, or, in other words, a theory of precepts which may guide us in choosing the best means for attaining ends calculated for our advantage. This is to deny that a science of morals exists.

Politics says, "Be wise as serpents"; morals adds the limiting condition, "and guileless as doves." If these precepts cannot stand together in one command, then there is a real quarrel between politics and morals. But if they can be completely brought into accord, then the idea of any antagonism between them is absurd, and the question of how best to make a compromise between the two points of view ceases to be even raised. Although the saying, "Honesty is the best policy," expresses a theory which, alas, is often contradicted in practice, yet the likewise theoretical maxim, "Honesty is better than any policy," is exalted high above every possible objection, is indeed the necessary condition of all politics.

The Terminus of morals does not yield to Jupiter, the Terminus of force; for the latter remains beneath the sway of Fate. In other words, reason is not sufficiently enlightened to survey the series of predetermining causes which would make it possible for us to predict with certainty the good or bad results of human action, as they follow from the mechanical laws of nature; although we may hope that things will turn out as we should desire. But what we have to do, in order to remain in the path of duty guided by the rules of wisdom, reason makes everywhere perfectly clear, and does this for the purpose of furthering her ultimate ends.

The practical man, however, for whom morals is mere theory, even while admitting that what ought to be can be, bases his dreary verdict against our well-meant hopes really on this: he pretends that he can foresee from his observation of human nature, that men will never be willing to do what is required in order to bring about the wished-for results leading to perpetual peace. It is true, that the will of all individual men to live under a legal constitution according to the principles of liberty—that is to say, the distributive unity of the wills of all—is not sufficient to attain this end. We must have the collective unity of their united will: all as a body must determine these new conditions. The solution of this difficult problem is required in order that civil society should be a whole. To all this diversity of individual wills there must come a uniting cause, in order to produce a common will which no distributive will is able to give. Hence, in the practical realisation of that idea, no other beginning of a law-governed society can be counted upon than one that is brought about by force: upon this force, too, public law afterwards rests. This state of things certainly prepares us to meet considerable deviation in actual experience from the theoretical idea of perpetual peace, since we cannot take into account the moral character and disposition of a law-giver in this connection, or expect that, after he has united a wild multitude into one people, he will leave it to them to bring about a legal constitution by their common will.

It amounts to this. Any ruler who has once got the power in his hands will not let the people dictate laws for him. A state which enjoys an independence of the control of external law will not submit to the judgment of the tribunals of other states, when it has to consider how to obtain its rights against them. And even a continent, when it feels its superiority to another, whether this be in its way or not, will not fail to take advantage of an opportunity offered of strengthening its power by the spoliation or even conquest of this territory. Hence all theoretical schemes, connected with constitutional, international or cosmopolitan law, crumble away into empty impracticable ideals. While, on the other hand, a practical science, based on the empirical principles of human nature, which does not disdain to model its maxims on an observation of actual life, can alone hope to find a sure foundation on which to build up a system of national policy.

Now certainly, if there is neither freedom nor a moral law founded upon it, and every actual or possible event happens in the mere mechanical course of nature, then politics, as the art of making use of this physical necessity in things for the government of men, is the whole of practical wisdom and the idea of right is an empty concept. If, on the other hand, we find that this idea of right is necessarily to be conjoined with politics and even to be raised to the position of a limiting condition of that science, then the possibility of reconciling them must be admitted. I can thus imagine a moral politician, that is to say, one who understands the principles of statesmanship to be such as do not conflict with morals; but I cannot conceive of a political moralist who fashions for himself such a system of ethics as may serve the interest of statesmen.

The moral politician will always act upon the following principle:—"If certain defects which could not have been avoided are found in the political constitution or foreign relations of a state, it is a duty for all, especially for the rulers of the state, to apply their whole energy to correcting them as soon as possible, and to bringing the constitution and political relations on these points into conformity with the Law of Nature, as it is held up as a model before us in the idea of reason; and this they should do even at a sacrifice of their own interest." Now it is contrary to all politics—which is, in this particular, in agreement with morals—to dissever any of the links binding citizens together in the state or nations in cosmopolitan union, before a better constitution is there to take the place of what has been thus destroyed. And hence it would be absurd indeed to demand that every imperfection in political matters must be violently altered on the spot. But, at the same time, it may be required of a ruler at least that he should earnestly keep the maxim in mind which points to the necessity of such a change; so that he may go on constantly approaching the end to be realised, namely, the best possible constitution according to the laws of right. Even although it is still under despotic rule, in accordance with its constitution as then existing, a state may govern itself on republican lines, until the people gradually become capable of being influenced by the mere idea of the authority of law, just as if it had physical power. And they become accordingly capable of self-legislation, their faculty for which is founded on original right. But if, through the violence of revolution, the product of a bad government, a constitution more in accord with the spirit of law were attained even by unlawful means, it should no longer be held justifiable to bring the people back to the old constitution, although, while the revolution was going on, every one who took part in it by use of force or stratagem, may have been justly punished as a rebel. As regards the external relations of nations, a state cannot be asked to give up its constitution, even although that be a despotism (which is, at the same time, the strongest constitution where foreign enemies are concerned), so long as it runs the risk of being immediately swallowed up by other states. Hence, when such a proposal is made, the state whose constitution is in question must at least be allowed to defer acting upon it until a more convenient time.[15]

It is always possible that moralists who rule despotically, and are at a loss in practical matters, will come into collision with the rules of political wisdom in many ways, by adopting measures without sufficient deliberation which show themselves afterwards to have been overestimated. When they thus offend against nature, experience must gradually lead them into a better track. But, instead of this being the case, politicians who are fond of moralising do all they can to make moral improvement impossible and to perpetuate violations of law, by extenuating political principles which are antagonistic to the idea of right, on the pretext that human nature is not capable of good, in the sense of the ideal which reason prescribes.

These politicians, instead of adopting an open, straightforward way of doing things (as they boast), mix themselves up in intrigue. They get at the authorities in power and say what will please them; their sole bent is to sacrifice the nation, or even, if they can, the whole world, with the one end in view that their own private interest may be forwarded. This is the manner of regular jurists (I mean the journeyman lawyer not the legislator), when they aspire to politics. For, as it is not their business to reason too nicely over legislation, but only to enforce the laws of the country, every legal constitution in its existing form and, when this is changed by the proper authorities, the one which takes its place, will always seem to them the best possible. And the consequence is that everything is purely mechanical. But this adroitness in suiting themselves to any circumstances may lead them to the delusion that they are also capable of giving an opinion about the principles of political constitutions in general, in so far as they conform to ideas of right, and are therefore not empirical, but *a priori*. And they may therefore brag about their knowledge of men,—which indeed one expects to find, since they have to deal with so many— without really knowing the nature of man and what can be made of it, to gain which knowledge a higher standpoint of anthropological observation than theirs is required. Filled with ideas of this kind, if they trespass outside their own sphere on the boundaries of political and international law, looked upon as ideals which reason holds before us, they can do so only in the spirit of chicanery. For they will follow their usual method of making everything conform mechanically to compulsory laws despotically made and enforced, even here, where the ideas of reason recognise the validity of a legal compulsory force, only when it is in accordance with the principles of freedom through which a permanently valid constitution becomes first of all possible. The would-be practical man, leaving out of account this idea of reason, thinks that he can solve this problem empirically by looking to the way in which those constitutions which have best survived the test of time were established, even although the spirit of these may have been generally contrary to the idea of right. The principles which he makes use of here, although indeed he does not make them public, amount pretty much to the following sophistical maxims.

1. *Fac et excusa.* Seize the most favourable opportunity for arbitrary usurpation—either of the authority of the state over its own people or over a neighbouring people; the justification of the act and extenuation of the use of force will come much more easily and gracefully, when the deed is done, than if one has to think out convincing reasons for taking this step and first hear through all the objections which can be made against it. This is especially true in the first case mentioned, where the supreme power in the state also controls the legislature which we must obey without any reasoning about it. Besides, this show of audacity in a statesman even lends him a certain semblance of inward conviction of the justice of his action; and once he has got so far the god of success (*bonus eventus*) is his best advocate.

2. *Si fecisti, nega.* As for any crime you have committed, such as has, for instance, brought your people to despair and thence to insurrection, deny that it has happened owing to any fault of yours. Say rather that it is all caused by the insubordination of your subjects, or, in the case of your having usurped a neighbouring state, that human nature is to blame; for, if a man is not ready to use force and steal a march upon his neighbour, he may certainly count on the latter forestalling him and taking him prisoner.

3. *Divide et impera.* That is to say, if there are certain privileged persons, holding authority among the people, who have merely chosen you for their sovereign as *primus inter pares,* bring about a quarrel among them, and make mischief between them and the people. Now back up the people with a dazzling promise of greater freedom; everything will now depend unconditionally on your will. Or again, if there is a difficulty with foreign states, then to stir up dissension among them is a pretty sure means of subjecting first one and then the other to your sway, under the pretext of aiding the weaker.

It is true that nowadays no body is taken in by these political maxims, for they are all familiar to everyone. Moreover, there is no need of being ashamed of them, as if their injustice were too patent. For the great Powers never feel shame before the judgment of the common herd, but only before one another; so that as far as this matter goes, it is not the revelation of these guiding principles of policy that can make rulers ashamed, but only the unsuccessful use of them. For as to the morality of these maxims, politicians are all agreed. Hence there is always left political prestige on which they can safely count; and this means the glory of increasing their power by any means that offer.[16]

In all these twistings and turnings of an immoral doctrine of expediency which aims at substituting a state of peace for the warlike conditions in which men are placed by nature, so much at least is clear;—that men cannot get away from the idea of right in their private any more than in their public relations; and that they do not dare (this is indeed most strikingly seen in the concept of an international law) to base politics merely on the manipulations of expediency and therefore to refuse all obedience to the idea of a public right. On the contrary, they pay all fitting honour to the idea of right in itself, even although they should, at the same time, devise a hundred subterfuges and excuses to avoid it in practice, and should regard force, backed up by cunning, as having the authority which comes from being the source and unifying principle of all right. It will be well to put an end to this sophistry, if not to the injustice it extenuates, and to bring the false advocates of the mighty of the earth to confess that it is not right but might in whose interest they speak, and that it is the worship of might from which they take their cue, as if in this matter they had a right to command. In order to do this, we must first expose the delusion by which they deceive themselves and others; then discover the ultimate principle from which their plans for a perpetual peace proceed; and thence show that all the evil which stands in the way of the realisation of that ideal springs from the fact that the political moralist begins where the moral politician rightly ends and that, by subordinating principles to an end or putting the cart before the horse, he defeats his intention of bringing politics into harmony with morals.

In order to make practical philosophy consistent with itself, we must first decide the following question:—In dealing with the problems of practical reason must we begin from its material principle—the end as the object of free choice—or from its formal principle which is based merely on freedom in its external relation?—from which comes the following law:—"Act so that thou canst will that thy maxim should be a universal law, be the end of thy action what it will."

Without doubt, the latter determining principle of action must stand first; for, as a principle of right, it carries unconditional necessity with it, whereas the former is obligatory only if we assume the empirical conditions of the end set before us,—that is to say, that it is an end capable of being practically realised. And if this end—as, for example, the end of perpetual peace—should be also a duty, this same duty must necessarily have been deduced from the formal principle governing the maxims which guide external action. Now the first principle is the principle of the political moralist; the problems of constitutional, international and cosmopolitan law are mere technical problems (*problema technicum*). The second or formal principle, on the other hand, as the principle of the moral politician who regards it as a moral problem (*problema morale*), differs widely from the other principle in its methods of bringing about perpetual peace, which we desire not only as a material good, but also as a state of things resulting from our recognition of the precepts of duty.

To solve the first problem—that, namely, of political expediency—much knowledge of nature is required, that her mechanical laws may be employed for the end in view. And yet the result of all knowledge of this kind is uncertain, as far as perpetual peace is concerned. This we find to be so, whichever of the three departments of public law we take. It is uncertain whether a people could be better kept in obedience and at the same time prosperity by severity or by baits held out to their vanity; whether they would be better governed under the sovereignty of a single individual or by the authority of several acting together; whether the combined authority might be better secured merely, say, by an official nobility or by the power of the people within the state; and, finally, whether such conditions could be long maintained. There are examples to the contrary in history in the case of all forms of government, with the exception of the only true republican constitution, the idea of which can occur only to a moral politician. Still more uncertain is a law of nations, ostensibly established upon statutes devised by ministers; for this amounts in fact to mere empty words, and rests on treaties which, in the very act of ratification, contain a secret reservation of the right to violate them. On the other hand, the solution of the second problem—the problem of political wisdom—forces itself, we may say, upon us; it is quite obvious to every one, and puts all crooked dealings to shame; it leads, too, straight to the desired end, while at the same time, discretion warns us not to drag in the conditions of perpetual peace by force, but to take time and approach this ideal gradually as favourable circumstances permit.

This may be expressed in the following maxim:—"Seek ye first the kingdom of pure practical reason and its righteousness, and the object of your endeavour, the blessing of perpetual peace, will be added unto you." For the science of morals generally has this peculiarity,—and it has it also with regard to the moral principles of public law, and therefore with regard to a science of politics knowable *a priori*,—that the less it makes a man's conduct depend on the end he has set before him, his purposed material or moral gain, so much the more, nevertheless, does it conform in general to this end. The reason for this is that it is just the universal will, given *a priori*, which exists in a people or in the relation of different peoples to one another, that alone determines what is lawful among men. This union of individual wills, however, if we proceed consistently in practice, in observance of the mechanical laws of nature, may be at the same time the cause of bringing about the result intended and practically realizing the idea of right. Hence it is, for example, a principle of moral politics that a people should unite into a state according to the only valid concepts of right, the ideas of freedom and equality; and this principle is not based on expediency, but upon duty. Political moralists, however, do not deserve a hearing, much and sophistically as they may reason about the existence, in a multitude of men forming a society, of certain natural tendencies which would weaken those principles and defeat their intention. They may endeavour to prove their assertion by giving instances of badly organised constitutions, chosen both from ancient and modern times, (as, for example, democracies without a representative system); but such arguments are to be treated with contempt, all the more, because a pernicious theory of this kind may perhaps even bring about the evil which it prophesies. For, in accordance with such reasoning, man is thrown into a class with all other living machines which only require the consciousness that they are not free creatures to make them in their own judgment the most miserable of all beings.

Fiat justitia, pereát mundus. This saying has become proverbial, and although it savours a little of boastfulness, is also true. We may translate it thus:—"Let justice rule on earth, although all the rogues in the world should go to the bottom." It is a good, honest principle of right cutting off all the crooked ways made by knavery or violence. It must not, however, be misunderstood as allowing anyone to exercise his own rights with the utmost severity, a course in contradiction to our moral duty; but we must take it to signify an obligation, binding upon rulers, to refrain from refusing to yield anyone his rights or from curtailing them, out of personal feeling or sympathy for others. For this end, in particular, we require, firstly, that a state should have an internal political constitution, established according to the pure principles of right; secondly, that a union should be formed between this state and neighbouring or distant nations for a legal settlement of their differences, after the analogy of the universal state. This proposition means nothing more than this:—Political maxims must not start from the idea of a prosperity and happiness which are to be expected from observance of such precepts in every state; that is, not from the end which each nation makes the object of its will as the highest empirical principle of political wisdom; but they must set out from the pure concept of the duty of right, from the "*ought*" whose principle is given *a priori* through pure reason. This is the law, whatever the material consequences may be. The world will certainly not perish, by any means, because the number of the wicked people in it is becoming fewer. The morally bad has one peculiarity, inseparable from its nature;—in its purposes, especially in relation to other evil influences, it is in contradiction with itself, and counteracts its own natural effect, and thus makes room for the moral principle of good, although advance in this direction may be slow.

Hence objectively, in theory, there is no quarrel between morals and politics. But subjectively, in the self-seeking tendencies of men (which we cannot actually call their morality, as we would a course of action based on maxims of reason,) this disagreement in principle exists and may always survive; for it serves as a whetstone to virtue. According to the principle, *Tu ne cede malis, sed contra audentior ito,* the true courage of virtue in the present case lies not so much in facing the evils and self-sacrifices which must be met here as in firmly confronting the evil principle in our own nature and conquering its wiles. For this is a principle far more dangerous, false, treacherous and sophistical which puts forward the weakness in human nature as a justification for every transgression.

In fact the political moralist may say that a ruler and people, or nation and nation do *one another* no wrong, when they enter on a war with violence or cunning, although they do wrong, generally speaking, in refusing to respect the idea of right which alone could establish peace for all time. For, as both are equally wrongly disposed to one another, each transgressing the duty he owes to his neighbour, they are both quite rightly served, when they are thus destroyed in war. This mutual destruction stops short at the point of extermination, so that there are always enough of the race left to keep this game going on through all the ages, and a far-off posterity may take warning by them. The Providence that orders the course of the world is hereby justified. For the moral principle in mankind never becomes extinguished, and human reason, fitted for the practical realisation of ideas of right according to that principle, grows continually in fitness for that purpose with the ever advancing march of culture; while at the same time, it must be said, the guilt of transgression increases as well. But it seems that, by no theodicy or vindication of the justice of God, can we justify Creation in putting such a race of corrupt creatures into the world at all, if, that is, we assume that the human race neither will nor can ever be in a happier condition than it is now. This standpoint, however, is too high a one for us to judge from, or to theorise, with the limited concepts we have at our command, about the wisdom of that supreme Power which is unknowable by us. We are inevitably driven to such despairing conclusions as these, if we do not admit that the pure principles of right have objective reality—that is to say, are capable of being practically realised—and consequently that action must be taken on the part of the people of a state and, further, by states in relation to one another, whatever arguments empirical politics may bring forward against this course. Politics in the real sense cannot take a step forward without first paying homage to the principles of morals. And, although politics, *per se,* is a difficult art, in its union with morals no art is required; for in the case of a conflict arising between the two sciences, the moralist can cut asunder the knot which politics is unable to untie. Right must be held sacred by man, however great the cost and sacrifice to the ruling power. Here is no half-and-half course. We cannot devise a happy medium between right and expediency, a right pragmatically conditioned. But all politics must bend the knee to the principle of right, and may, in that way, hope to reach, although slowly perhaps, a level whence it may shine upon men for all time.

APPENDIX II

Concerning the Harmony of Politics with Morals According to
the Transcendental Idea of Public Right.

If I look at public right from the point of view of most professors of law, and abstract from its *matter* or its empirical elements, varying according to the circumstances given in our experience of individuals in a state or of states among themselves, then there remains the *form* of publicity. The possibility of this publicity, every legal title implies. For without it there could be no justice, which can only be thought as before the eyes of men; and, without justice, there would be no right, for, from justice only, right can come.

This characteristic of publicity must belong to every legal title. Hence, as, in any particular case that occurs, there is no difficulty in deciding whether this essential attribute is present or not, (whether, that is, it is reconcilable with the principles of the agent or not), it furnishes an easily applied criterion which is to be found *a priori* in the reason, so that in the particular case we can at once recognise the falsity or illegality of a proposed claim (*praetensio juris*), as it were by an experiment of pure reason.

Having thus, as it were, abstracted from all the empirical elements contained in the concept of a political and international law, such as, for instance, the evil tendency in human nature which makes compulsion necessary, we may give the following proposition as the *transcendental formula* of public right:—"All actions relating to the rights of other men are wrong, if the maxims from which they follow are inconsistent with publicity."

This principle must be regarded not merely as ethical, as belonging to the doctrine of virtue, but also as juridical, referring to the rights of men. For there is something wrong in a maxim of conduct which I cannot divulge without at once defeating my purpose, a maxim which must therefore be kept secret, if it is to succeed, and which I could not publicly acknowledge without infallibly stirring up the opposition of everyone. This necessary and universal resistance with which everyone meets me, a resistance therefore evident *a priori,* can be due to no other cause than the injustice with which such a maxim threatens everyone. Further, this testing principle is merely negative; that is, it serves only as a means by which we may know when an action is unjust to others. Like axioms, it has a certainty incapable of demonstration; it is besides easy of application as appears from the following examples of public right.

1. Constitutional law. Let us take in the first place the public law of the state (*jus civitatis*), particularly in its application to matters within the state. Here a question arises which many think difficult to answer, but which the transcendental principle of publicity solves quite readily:—"Is revolution a legitimate means for a people to adopt, for the purpose of throwing off the oppressive yoke of a so-called tyrant (*non titulo, sed exercitio talis*)?" The rights of a nation are violated in a government of this kind, and no wrong is done to the tyrant in dethroning him. Of this there is no doubt. None the less, it is in the highest degree wrong of the subjects to prosecute their rights in this way; and they would be just as little justified in complaining, if they happened to be defeated in their attempt and had to endure the severest punishment in consequence.

A great many reasons for and against both sides of this question may be given, if we seek to settle it by a dogmatic deduction of the principles of right. But the transcendental principle of the publicity of public right can spare itself this diffuse argumentation. For, according to that principle, the people would ask themselves, before the civil contract was made, whether they could venture to publish maxims, proposing insurrection when a favourable opportunity should present itself. It is quite clear that if, when a constitution is established, it were made a condition that force may be exercised against the sovereign under certain circumstances, the people would be obliged to claim a lawful authority higher than his. But in that case, the so-called sovereign would be no longer sovereign: or, if both powers, that of the sovereign and that of the people, were made a condition of the constitution of the state, then its establishment (which was the aim of the people) would be impossible. The wrongfulness of revolution is quite obvious from the fact that openly to acknowledge maxims which justify this step would make attainment of the end at which they aim impossible. We are obliged to keep them secret. But this secrecy would not be necessary on the part of the head of the state. He may say quite plainly that the ringleaders of every rebellion will be punished by death, even although they may hold that it was he who first transgressed the fundamental law. For, if a ruler is conscious of possessing irresistible sovereign power (and this must be assumed in every civil constitution, because a sovereign who has not power to protect any individual member of the nation against his neighbour has also not the right to exercise authority over him), then he need have no fear that making known the maxims which guide him will cause the defeat of his plans. And it is quite consistent with this view to hold that, if the people are successful in their insurrection, the sovereign must return to the rank of a subject, and refrain from inciting rebellion with a view to regaining his lost sovereignty. At the same time he need have no fear of being called to account for his former administration.

2. International law. There can be no question of an international law, except on the assumption of some kind of a law-governed state of things, the external condition under which any right can belong to man. For the very idea of international law, as public right, implies the publication of a universal will determining the rights and property of each individual nation; and this *status juridicus* must spring out of a contract of some sort which may not, like the contract to which the state owes its origin, be founded upon compulsory laws, but may be, at the most, the agreement of a permanent free association such as the federation of the different states, to which we have alluded above. For, without the control of law to some extent, to serve as an active bond of union among different merely natural or moral individuals,—that is to say, in a state of nature,—there can only be private law. And here we find a disagreement between morals, regarded as the science of right, and politics. The criterion, obtained by observing the effect of publicity on maxims, is just as easily applied, but only when we understand that this agreement binds the contracting states solely with the object that peace may be preserved among them, and between them and other states; in no sense with a view to the acquisition of new territory or power. The following instances of antinomy occur between politics and morals, which are given here with the solution in each case.

a. "When either of these states has promised something to another, (as, for instance, assistance, or a relinquishment of certain territory, or subsidies and such like), the question may arise whether, in a case where the safety of the state thus bound depends on its evading the fulfillment of this promise, it can do so by maintaining a right to be regarded as a double person:—firstly, as sovereign and accountable to no one in the state of which that sovereign power is head; and, secondly, merely as the highest official in the service of that state, who is obliged to answer to the state for every action. And the result of this is that the state is acquitted in its second capacity of any obligation to which it has committed itself in the first." But, if a nation or its sovereign proclaimed these maxims, the natural consequence would be that every other would flee from it, or unite with other states to oppose such pretensions. And this is a proof that politics, with all its cunning, defeats its own ends, if the test of making principles of action public, which we have indicated, be applied. Hence the maxim we have quoted must be wrong.

b. "If a state which has increased its power to a formidable extent (*potentia tremenda*) excites anxiety in its neighbours, is it right to assume that, since it has the means, it will also have the will to oppress others; and does that give less powerful states a right to unite and attack the greater nation without any definite cause of offence ?" A state which would here answer openly in the affirmative would only bring the evil about more surely and speedily. For the greater power would forestall those smaller nations, and their union would be but a weak reed of defence against a state which knew how to apply the maxim, *divide et impera.* This maxim of political expediency then, when openly acknowledged, necessarily defeats the end at which it aims, and is therefore wrong.

c. "If a smaller state by its geographical position breaks up the territory of a greater, so as to prevent a unity necessary to the preservation of that state, is the latter not justified in subjugating its less powerful neighbour and uniting the territory in question with its own?" We can easily see that the greater state dare not publish such a maxim beforehand; for either all smaller states would without loss of time unite against it, or other powers would contend for this booty. Hence the impracticability of such a maxim becomes evident under the light of publicity. And this is a sign that it is wrong, and that in a very great degree; for, although the victim of an act of injustice may be of small account, that does not prevent the injustice done from being very great.

3. Cosmopolitan law. We may pass over this department of right in silence, for, owing to its analogy with international law, its maxims are easily specified and estimated.

In this principle of the incompatibility of the maxims of international law with their publicity, we have a good indication of the non-agreement between politics and morals regarded as a science of right. Now we require to know under what conditions these maxims do agree with the law of nations. For we cannot conclude that the converse holds, and that all maxims which can bear publicity are therefore just. For anyone who has a decided supremacy has no need to make any secret about his maxims. The condition of a law of nations being possible at all is that, in the first place, there should be a law-governed state of things. If this is not so, there can be no public right, and all right which we can think of outside the law-governed state,—that is to say, in the state of nature,—is mere private right. Now we have seen above that something of the nature of a federation between nations, for the sole purpose of doing away with war, is the only rightful condition of things reconcilable with their individual freedom. Hence the agreement of politics and morals is only possible in a federative union, a union which is necessarily given *a priori,* according to the principles of right. And the lawful basis of all politics can only be the establishment of this union in its widest possible extent. Apart from this end, all political sophistry is folly and veiled injustice. Now this sham politics has a casuistry, not to be excelled in the best Jesuit school. It has its mental reservation (*reservatio mentalis*): as in the drawing up of a public treaty in such terms as we can, if we will, interpret when occasion serves to our advantage; for example, the distinction between the *status quo* in fact (*de fait*) and in right (*de droit*). Secondly, it has its probabilism; when it pretends to discover evil intentions in another, or makes the probability of their possible future ascendency a lawful reason for bringing about the destruction of other peaceful states. Finally, it has its philosophical sin (*peccatum philosophicum, peccatillum, baggatelle*) which is that of holding it a trifle easily pardoned that a smaller state should be swallowed up, if this be to the gain of a nation much more powerful; for such an increase in power is supposed to tend to the greater prosperity of the whole world.[17]

Duplicity gives politics the advantage of using one branch or the other of morals, just as suits its own ends. The love of our fellowmen is a duty: so too is respect for their rights. But the former is only conditional: the latter, on the other hand, an unconditional, absolute imperative duty; and anyone who would give himself up to the sweet consciousness of well-doing must be first perfectly assured that he has not transgressed its commands. Politics has no difficulty in agreeing with morals in the first sense of the term, as ethics, to secure that men should give to superiors their rights. But when it comes to morals, in its second aspect, as the science of right before which politics must bow the knee, the politician finds it prudent to have nothing to do with compacts and rather to deny all reality to morals in this sense, and reduce all duty to mere benevolence. Philosophy could easily frustrate the artifices of a politics like this, which shuns the light of criticism, by publishing its maxims, if only statesmen would have the courage to grant philosophers the right to ventilate their opinions.

With this end in view, I propose another principle of public right, which is at once transcendental and affirmative. Its formula would be as follows:—"All maxims which require publicity, in order that they may not fail to attain their end, are in agreement both with right and politics."

For, if these maxims can only attain the end at which they aim by being published, they must be in harmony with the universal end of mankind, which is happiness; and to be in sympathy with this (to make the people contented with their lot) is the real business of politics. Now, if this end should be attainable only by publicity, or in other words, through the removal of all distrust of the maxims of politics, these must be in harmony with the right of the people; for a union of the ends of all is only possible in a harmony with this right.

I must postpone the further development and discussion of this principle till another opportunity. That it is a transcendental formula is quite evident from the fact that all the empirical conditions of a doctrine of happiness, or the *matter* of law, are absent, and that it has regard only to the *form* of universal conformity to law.

If it is our duty to realise a state of public right, if at the same time there are good grounds for hope that this ideal may be realised, although only by an approximation advancing *ad infinitum,* then perpetual peace, following hitherto falsely so-called conclusions of peace, which have been in reality mere cessations of hostilities, is no mere empty idea. But rather we have here a problem which gradually works out its own solution and, as the periods in which a given advance takes place towards the realisation of the ideal of perpetual peace will, we hope, become with the passing of time shorter and shorter, we must approach ever nearer to this goal.

Notes

1. An hereditary kingdom is not a state which can be inherited by another state, but one whose sovereign power can be inherited by another physical person. The state then acquires a ruler, not the

ruler as such (that is, as one already possessing another realm) the state.

2. It has been hitherto doubted, not without reason, whether there can be laws of permission (*leges permissivae*) of pure reason as well as commands (*leges praeceptivae*) and prohibitions (*leges prohibitivae*). For law in general has a basis of objective practical necessity: permission, on the other hand, is based upon the contingency of certain actions in practice. It follows that a law of permission would enforce what cannot be enforced; and this would envolve a contradiction, if the object of the law should be the same in both cases. Here, however, in the present case of a law of permission, the presupposed prohibition is aimed merely at the future manner of acquisition of a right—for example, acquisition through inheritance: the exemption from this prohibition (i.e. the permission) refers to the present state of possession. In the transition from a state of nature to the civil state, this holding of property can continue as a *bona fide*, if usurpatory, ownership, under the new social conditions, in accordance with a permission of the Law of Nature. Ownership of this kind, as soon as its true nature becomes known, is seen to be mere nominal possession (*possessio putativa*) sanctioned by opinion and customs in a natural state of society. After the transition stage is passed, such modes of acquisition are likewise forbidden in the subsequently evolved civil state: and this power to remain in possession would not be admitted if the supposed acquisition had taken place in the civilized community. It would be bound to come to an end as an injury to the right of others, the moment its illegality became patent.

I have wished here only by the way to draw the attention of teachers of the Law of Nature to the idea of a *lex permissiva* which presents itself spontaneously in any system of rational classification. I do so chiefly because use is often made of this concept in civil law with reference to statutes; with this difference, that the law of prohibition stands alone by itself, while permission is not, as it ought to be, introduced into that law as a limiting clause, but is thrown among the exceptions. Thus "this or that is forbidden",—say, Nos. 1, 2, 3, and so on in an infinite progression,—while permissions are only added to the law incidentally: they are not reached by the application of some principle, but only by groping about among cases which have actually occurred. Were this not so, qualifications would have had to be brought into the formula of laws of prohibition which would have immediately transformed them into laws of permission. Count von Windischgrätz, a man whose wisdom was equal to his discrimination, urged this very point in the form of a question propounded by him for a prize essay. One must therefore regret that this ingenious problem has been so soon neglected and left unsolved. For the possibility of a formula similar to those of mathematics is the sole real test of a legislation that would be consistent. Without this, the so-called *jus certum* will remain forever a mere pious wish: we can have only general laws valid on the whole; no general laws possessing the universal validity which the concept law seems to demand.

3. It is usually accepted that a man may not take hostile steps against any one, unless the latter has already injured him by act. This is quite accurate, if both are citizens of a law-governed state. For, in becoming a member of this community, each gives the other the security he demands against injury, by means of the supreme authority exercising control over them both. The individual, however, (or nation) who remains in a mere state of nature deprives me of this security and does me injury, by mere proximity. There is perhaps no active (*facto*) molestation, but there is a state of lawlessness (*status injustus*) which, by its very existence, offers a continual menace to me. I can therefore compel him, either to enter into relations with me under which we are both subject to law, or to withdraw from my neighbourhood. So that the postulate upon which the following articles are based is:—"All men who have the power to exert a mutual influence upon one another must be under a civil government of some kind."

A legal constitution is, according to the nature of the individuals who compose the state:—

(1) A constitution formed in accordance with the right of citizenship of the individuals who constitute a nation (*jus civitatis*).

(2) A constitution whose principle is international law which determines the relations of states (*jus gentium*).

(3) A constitution formed in accordance with cosmopolitan law, in as far as individuals and states, standing in an external relation of mutual reaction, may be regarded as citizens of one world-state (*jus cosmopoliticum*).

This classification is not an arbitrary one, but is necessary with reference to the idea of perpetual peace. For, if even one of these units of society were in a position physically to influence another, while yet remaining a member of a primitive order of society, then a state of war would be joined with these primitive conditions; and from this it is our present purpose to free ourselves.

4. Lawful, that is to say, external freedom cannot be defined, as it so often is, as the right "to do whatever one likes, so long as this does not wrong anyone else." For what is this right? It is the possibility of actions which do not lead to the injury of others. So the explanation of a "right" would be something like this:—"Freedom is the possibility of actions which do not injure anyone. A man does not wrong another—whatever his action—if he does not wrong another": which is empty tautology. My external (lawful) freedom is rather to be explained in this way: it is the right through which I could have given my consent. In exactly the same way, external (legal) equality in a state is that relation of the subjects in consequence of which no individual can legally bind or oblige another to anything, without at the same time submitting himself to the law which ensures that he can, in his turn, be bound and obliged in like manner by this other.

The principle of lawful independence requires no explanation, as it is involved in the general concept of a constitution. The validity of this hereditary and inalienable right, which belongs of necessity to mankind, is affirmed and ennobled by the principle of a lawful relation between man himself and higher beings, if indeed he believes in such beings. This is so, because he thinks of himself, in accordance with these very principles, as a citizen of a transcendental world as well as of the world of sense. For, as far as my freedom goes, I am bound by no obligation even with regard to Divine Laws—which are apprehended by me only through my reason—except in so far as I could have given my assent to them; for it is through the law of freedom of my own reason that I first form for myself a concept of a Divine Will. As for the principle of equality, in so far as it applies to the most sublime being in the universe next to God—a being I might perhaps figure to myself as a mighty emanation of the Divine spirit,—there is no reason why, if I perform my duty in the sphere in which I am placed, as that aeon does in his, the duty of obedience alone should fall to my share, the right to command to him. That this principle of equality, (unlike the principle of freedom), does not apply to our relation to God is due to the fact that, to this being alone, the idea of duty does not belong.

As for the right to equality which belongs to all citizens as subject, the solution of the problem of the admissibility of an hereditary nobility hinges on the following question:—"Does social rank—acknowledged by the state to be higher in the case of one subject than another—stand above desert, or does merit take precedence of social standing?" Now it is obvious that, if high position is combined with good family, it is quite uncertain whether merit, that is to say, skill and fidelity in office, will follow as well. This amounts to granting the favoured individual a commanding position without any question of desert; and to that, the universal will of the people—expressed in an original contract which is the fundamental principle of all right—would never consent. For it does not follow that a nobleman is a man of noble character. In the case of the official nobility, as one might term the rank of higher magistracy—which one must acquire by merit—the social position is not attached like property to the person but to his office, and equality is not thereby disturbed; for, if a man gives up office, he lays down with it his official rank and falls back into the rank of his fellows.

5. The lofty appellations which are often given to a ruler—such as the Lord's Anointed, the Administrator of the Divine Will upon earth and Vicar of God—have been many times censured as flattery gross enough to make one giddy. But it seems to me without cause. Far from making a prince arrogant, names like these must rather make him humble at heart, if he has any intelligence—which we take for granted he has—and reflects that he has undertaken an office which is too great for any human being. For, indeed, it is the holiest which God has on earth—namely, the right of ruling mankind: and he must ever live in fear of injuring this treasure of God in some respect or other.

6. Mallet du Pan boasts in his seemingly brilliant but shallow and superficial language that, after many years experience, he has come at last to be convinced of the truth of the well known saying of Pope:—

> "For Forms of Government let fools contest;
> Whate'er is best administered is best."

If this means that the best administered government is best administered, then, in Swift's phrase, he has cracked a nut to find a worm in it. If it means, however, that the best conducted government is also the best kind of government,—that is, the best form of political constitution,—then it is utterly false: for examples of wise administration are no proof of the kind of government. Whoever ruled better than Titus and Marcus Aurelius, and yet the one left Domitian, the other Commodus, as his successor? This could not have happened where the constitution was a good one, for their absolute unfitness for the position was early enough known, and the power of the emperor was sufficiently great to exclude them.

7. A Greek emperor, who magnanimously volunteered to settle by a duel his quarrel with a Bulgarian prince, got the following answer: "A smith who has tongs will not pluck the glowing iron from the fire with his hands."

8. On the conclusion of peace at the end of a war, it might not be unseemly for a nation to appoint a day of humiliation, after the festival of thanksgiving, on which to invoke the mercy of Heaven for the terrible sin which the human race are guilty of, in their continued unwillingness to submit (in their relations with other states) to a law-governed constitution, preferring rather in the pride of their independence to use the barbarous method of war, which after all does not really settle what is wanted, namely, the right of each state in a quarrel. The feasts of thanksgiving during a war for a victorious battle, the hymns which are sung—to use the Jewish expression—"to the Lord of Hosts" are not in less strong contrast to the ethical idea of a father of mankind; for, apart from the indifference these customs show to the way in which nations seek to establish their rights—sad enough as it is—these rejoicings bring in an element of exultation that a great number of lives, or at least the happiness of many, has been destroyed.

9. On the conclusion of peace at the end of a war, it might not be unseemly for a nation to appoint a day of humiliation, after the festival of thanksgiving, on which to invoke the mercy of Heaven for the terrible sin which the human race are guilty of, in their continued unwillingness to submit (in their relations with other states) to a law-governed constitution, preferring rather in the pride of their independence to use the barbarous method of war, which after all does not really settle what is wanted, namely, the right of each state in a quarrel. The feasts of thanksgiving during a war for a victorious battle, the hymns which are sung—to use the Jewish expression—"to the Lord of Hosts" are not in less strong contrast to the ethical idea of a father of mankind; for, apart from the indifference these customs show to the way in which nations seek to establish their rights—sad enough as it is—these rejoicings bring in an element of exultation that a great number of lives, or at least the happiness of many, has been destroyed.

10. In order to call this great empire by the name which it gives itself—namely, China, not Sina or a word of similar sound—we have only to look at Georgii: *Alphab. Tibet.,* pp. 651 to 654, particularly *note* b., below. According to the observation of Professor Fischer of St. Petersburg, there is really no particular name which it always goes by: the most usual is the word *Kin,* i.e. gold, which the inhabitants of Tibet call *Ser.* Hence the emperor is called the king of gold, i.e. the king of the most splendid country in the world. This word *Kin* may probably be *chin* in the empire itself, but be pronounced *Kin* by the Italian missionaries on account of the gutturals. Thus we see that the country of the Seres, so often mentioned by the Romans, was China: the silk, however, was despatched to Europe across Greater Tibet, probably through Smaller Tibet and Bucharia, through Persia and then on. This leads to many reflections as to the antiquity of this wonderful state, as compared with Hindustan, at the time of its union with Tibet and thence with Japan. On the other hand, the name Sina or Tschina which is said to be given to this land by neighbouring peoples leads to nothing.

Perhaps we can explain the ancient intercourse of Europe with Tibet—a fact at no time widely known—by looking at what Hesychius has preserved on the matter. I refer to the shout, Κονξ Ομπαξ (*Konx Ompax*), the cry of the Hierophants in the Eleusinian mysteries (cf. *Travels of Anacharsis the Younger,* Part V., p. 447, seq.). For, according to Georgii *Alph. Tibet.,* the word *Concioa* which bears a striking resemblance to *Konx* means God. *Pah-cio* (*ib.* p. 520) which might easily be pronounced by the Greeks like *pax* means *promulgator legis,* the divine principle permeating nature (called also, on p. 177, *Cencresi*). *Om,* however, which La Croze translated by *benedictus,* i.e. blessed, can when applied to the Deity mean nothing but beatified (p. 507). Now P. Franz, Horatius, when he asked the Lhamas of Tibet, as he often did, what they understood by God (*Concioa*) always got the answer:—"It is the assembly of all the saints," *i.e.* the assembly of those blessed ones who have been born again according to the faith of the Lama and, after many wanderings in changing forms, have at last returned to God, to Burchane: that is to say, they are beings to be worshipped, souls which have undergone transmigration (p. 223). So the mysterious expression *Konx Ompax* ought probably to mean the holy (*Konx*), blessed, (*Om*) and wise (*Pax*) supreme Being pervading the universe, the personification of nature. Its use in the Greek mysteries probably signified monotheism for the Epoptes, in distinction from the polytheism of the people, although elsewhere P. Horatius scented atheism here. How that mysterious word came by way of Tibet to the Greeks may be explained as above; and, on the other hand, in this way is made probable an early intercourse of Europe with China across Tibet, earlier perhaps than the communication with Hindustan.

11. In the mechanical system of nature to which man belongs as a sentient being, there appears, as the underlying ground of its existence, a certain *form* which we cannot make intelligible to ourselves except by thinking into the physical world the idea of an end preconceived by the Author of the universe: this predetermination of nature on the part of God we generally call Divine Providence. In so far as this providence appears in the origin of the universe, we speak of Providence as founder of this world (*providentia conditrix; semel jussit, semper parent.* Augustine). As it maintains the course of nature, however, according to universal laws of adaptation to preconceived ends, we call it a ruling providence (*providentia gubernatrix*). Further, we name it the guiding providence (*providentia directrix*), as it appears in the world for special ends, which we could not foresee, but suspect only from the result. Finally, regarding particular events as divine purposes, we speak no longer of providence, but of dispensation (*directio extraordinaria*). As this term, however, really suggests the idea of miracles, although the events are not spoken of by this name, the desire to fathom dispensation, as such, is a foolish presumption in men. For, from one single occurrence, to jump at the conclusion that there is a particular principle of efficient causes and that this event is an end and not merely the natural sequence of a design quite unknown to us is absurd and presumptuous, in however pious and humble a spirit we may speak to it. In the same way to distinguish between a universal and a particular providence when regarding it *materialiter*, in its relation to actual objects in the world (to say, for instance, that there may be, indeed, a providence for the preservation of the different species of creation, but that individuals are left to chance) is false and contradictory. For providence is called universal for the very reason that no single thing may be thought of as shut out from its care. Probably the distinction of two kinds of providence, *formaliter* or subjectively considered, had reference to the manner in which its purposes are fulfilled. So that we have ordinary providence (e.g. the yearly decay and awakening to new life in nature with change of season) and what we may call unusual or special providence (e.g. the bringing of timber by ocean currents to Arctic shores where it does not grow, and where without this aid the inhabitants could not live). Here, although we can quite well explain the physico-mechanical cause of these phenomena—in this case, for example, the banks of the rivers in temperate countries are over-grown with trees, some of which fall into the water and are carried along, probably by the Gulf Stream—we must not overlook the teleological cause which points to the providential care of a ruling wisdom above nature. But the concept, commonly used in the schools of philosophy, of a co-operation on the part of the Deity or a concurrence (*concursus*) in the operations going on in the world of sense, must be dropped. For it is, firstly, self-contradictory to couple the like and the unlike together (*gryphes jungere equis*) and to let Him who is Himself the entire cause of the changes in the universe make good any shortcomings in His own predetermining providence (which to require this must be defective) during the course of the world; for example, to say that the physician has restored the sick with the help of God—that is to say that He has been present as a support. For *causa solitariae non juvat*. God created the physician as well as his means of healing; and we must ascribe the result wholly to Him, if we will go back to the supreme First Cause which, theoretically, is beyond our comprehension. Or we can ascribe the result entirely to the physician, in so far as we follow up this event, as explicable in the chain of physical causes, according to the order of nature. Secondly, moreover, such a way of looking at this question destroys all the fixed principles by which we judge an effect. But, from the ethico-practical point of view which looks entirely to the transcendental side of things, the idea of a divine concurrence is quite proper and even necessary: for example, in the faith that God will make good the imperfection of our human justice, if only our feelings and intentions are sincere; and that He will do this by means beyond our comprehension, and therefore we should not slacken our efforts after what is good. Whence it follows, as a matter of course, that no one must attempt to explain a good action as a mere event in time by this *concursus;* for that would be

to pretend a theoretical knowledge of the supersensible and hence be absurd,

12. Of all modes of livelihood the life of the hunter is undoubtedly most incompatible with a civilised condition of society. Because, to live by hunting, families must isolate themselves from their neighbours, soon becoming estranged and spread over widely scattered forests, to be before long on terms of hostility, since each requires a great deal of space to obtain food and raiment. God's command to Noah not to shed blood (I. *Genesis*, IX. 4–6) is frequently quoted, and was afterwards—in another connection it is true—made by the baptised Jews a condition to which Christians, newly converted from heathendom, had to conform. Cf. *Acts* XV, 20; XXI. 25. This command seems originally to have been nothing else than a prohibition of the life of the hunter; for here the possibility of eating raw flesh must often occur, and, in forbidding the one custom, we condemn the other.

13. The question might be put:—"If it is nature's will that these Arctic shores should not remain unpopulated, what will become of their inhabitants, if, as is to be expected, at some time or other no more driftwood should be brought to them? For we may believe that, with the advance of civilisation, the inhabitants of temperate zones will utilise better the wood which grows on the banks of their rivers, and not let it fall into the stream and so be swept away." I answer: the inhabitants of the shores of the River Obi, the Yenisei, the Lena will supply them with it through trade, and take in exchange the animal produce in which the seas of Arctic shores are so rich—that is if nature has first of all brought about peace among them.

14. Difference of religion! A strange expression, as if one were to speak of different kinds of morality. There may indeed be different historical forms of belief,—that is to say, the various means which have been used in the course of time to promote religion,—but they are mere subjects of learned investigation, and do not really lie within the sphere of religion. In the same way there are many religious works—the *Zendavesta, Veda, Koran,* etc.—but there is only one religion, binding for all men and for all times. These books are each no more than the accidental mouthpiece of religion, and may be different according to differences in time and place.

15. These are *permissive* laws of reason which allow us to leave a system of public law, when it is tainted by injustice, to remain just as it is, until everything is entirely revolutionised through an internal development, either spontaneous, or fostered and matured by peaceful influences. For any legal constitution whatsoever, even although it conforms only slightly with the spirit of law is better than none at all—that is to say, anarchy, which is the fate of a precipitate reform. Hence, as things now are, the wise politician will look upon it as his duty to make reforms on the lines marked out by the ideal of public law. He will not use revolutions, when these have been brought about by natural causes, to extenuate still greater oppression than caused them, but will regard them as the voice of nature, calling upon him to make such thorough reforms as will bring about the only lasting constitution, a lawful constitution based on the principles of freedom.

16. It is still sometimes denied that we find, in members of a civilised community, a certain depravity rooted in the nature of man; and it might, indeed, be alleged with some show of truth that not an innate corruptness in human nature, but the barbarism of men, the defect of a not yet sufficiently developed culture, is the cause of the evident antipathy to law which their attitude indicates. In the external relations of states, however, human wickedness shows itself incontestably, without any attempt at concealment. Within the state, it is covered over by the compelling authority of civil laws. For, working against the tendency every citizen has to commit acts of violence against his neighbour, there is the much stronger force of the government which not only gives an appearance of morality to the whole state (*causae non causae*), but, by checking the outbreak of lawless propensities, actually aids the moral qualities of men considerably, in their development of a direct respect for the law. For every individual thinks that he himself would hold the idea of right sacred and follow faithfully what it prescribes, if only he could expect that everyone else would do the same. This guarantee is in part given to him by the government; and a great advance is made by this step which is not deliberately moral, towards the ideal of fidelity to the concept of duty for its own sake without thought of return. As, however, every man's good opinion of himself presupposes an evil disposition in everyone else, we have an expression of their mutual judgment of one another, namely, that when it comes to hard facts, none of them are worth much; but whence this judgment comes remains unexplained, as we cannot lay the blame on the nature of man, since he is a being in the possession of freedom. The respect for the idea of right, of which it is absolutely impossible for

man to divest himself, sanctions in the most solemn manner the theory of our power to conform to its dictates. And hence every man sees himself obliged to act in accordance with what the idea of right prescribes, whether his neighbours fulfil their obligation or not.

17. We can find the voucher for maxims such as these in Herr Hofrichter Garve's essay, *On the Connection of Morals with Politics,* 1788. This worthy scholar confesses at the very beginning that he is unable to give a satisfactory answer to this question. But his sanction of such maxims, even when coupled with the admission that he cannot altogether clear away the arguments raised against them, seems to be a greater concession in favour of those who shew considerable inclination to abuse them, than it might perhaps be wise to admit.

THE DECLARATION OF INDEPENDENCE

In Congress, July 4th, 1776
The Unanimous Declaration Of The Thirteen States of America

When in the Course of human events, it becomes necessary for one people to dissolve the political bands which have connected them with another, and to assume among the Powers of the earth, the separate and equal station to which the Laws of Nature and of Nature's God entitle them, a decent respect to the opinions of mankind requires that they should declare the causes which impel them to the separation.

We hold these truths to be self-evident, that all men are created equal, that they are endowed by their Creator with certain unalienable Rights, that among these are Life, Liberty and the pursuit of Happiness. That to secure these rights, Governments are instituted among Men, deriving their just powers from the consent of the governed, That whenever any Form of Government becomes destructive of these ends, it is the Right of the People to alter or to abolish it, and to institute new Government, laying its foundation on such principles and organizing its powers in such form, as to them shall seem most likely to effect their Safety and Happiness. Prudence, indeed, will dictate that Governments long established should not be changed for light and transient causes; and accordingly all experience hath shown, that mankind are more disposed to suffer, while evils are sufferable, than to right themselves by abolishing the forms to which they are accustomed. But when a long train of abuses and usurpations, pursuing invariably the same Object evinces a design to reduce them under absolute Despotism, it is their right, it is their duty, to throw off such Government, and to provide new Guards for their future security.—Such has been the patient sufferance of these Colonies; and such is now the necessity which constrains them to alter their former Systems of Government. The history of the present King of Great Britain is a history of repeated injuries and usurpations, all having in direct object the establishment of an absolute Tyranny over these States. To prove this, let Facts be submitted to a candid world.

He has refused his Assent to Laws, the most wholesome and necessary for the public good.

He has forbidden his Governors to pass Laws of immediate and pressing importance, unless suspended in their operation till his Assent should be obtained; and when so suspended, he has utterly neglected to attend to them.

He has refused to pass other Laws for the accommodation of large districts of people, unless those people would relinquish the right of Representation in the Legislature, a right inestimable to them and formidable to tyrants only.

He has called together legislative bodies at places unusual, uncomfortable, and distant from the depository of their Public Records, for the sole purpose of fatiguing them into compliance with his measures.

He has dissolved Representative Houses repeatedly, for opposing with manly firmness his invasions on the rights of the people.

He has refused for a long time, after such dissolutions, to cause others to be elected; whereby the Legislative Powers, incapable of Annihilation, have returned to the People at large for their exercise; the State remaining in the mean time exposed to all the dangers of invasion from without, and convulsions within.

He has endeavoured to prevent the population of these States; for that purpose obstructing the Laws of Naturalization of Foreigners; refusing to pass others to encourage their migration hither, and raising the conditions of new Appropriations of Lands.

He has obstructed the Administration of Justice, by refusing his Assent to Laws for establishing Judiciary Powers.

He has made Judges dependent on his Will alone, for the tenure of their offices, and the amount and payment of their salaries.

He has erected a multitude of New Offices, and sent hither swarms of Officers to harass our People, and eat out their substance.

He has kept among us, in times of peace, Standing Armies without the Consent of our legislature.

He has affected to render the Military independent of and superior to the Civil Power.

He has combined with others to subject us to a jurisdiction foreign to our constitution, and unacknowledged by our laws; giving his Assent to their acts of pretended legislation:

For quartering large bodies of armed troops among us:

For protecting them, by a mock Trial, from Punishment for any Murders which they should commit on the Inhabitants of these States:

For cutting off our Trade with all parts of the world:

For imposing taxes on us without our Consent:

For depriving us in many cases, of the benefits of Trial by Jury:

For transporting us beyond Seas to be tried for pretended offences:

For abolishing the free System of English Laws in a neighbouring Province, establishing therein an Arbitrary government, and enlarging its Boundaries so as to render it at once an example and fit instrument for introducing the same absolute rule into these Colonies:

For taking away our Charters, abolishing our most valuable Laws, and altering fundamentally the Forms of our Governments:

For suspending our own Legislature, and declaring themselves invested with Power to legislate for us in all cases whatsoever.

He has abdicated Government here, by declaring us out of his Protection and waging War against us.

He has plundered our seas, ravaged our Coasts, burnt our towns, and destroyed the lives of our people.

He is at this time transporting large armies of foreign mercenaries to compleat the works of death, desolation and tyranny, already begun with circumstances of Cruelty & perfidy scarcely paralleled in the most barbarous ages, and totally unworthy the Head of a civilized nation.

He has constrained our fellow Citizens taken Captive on the high Seas to bear Arms against their Country, to become the executioners of their friends and Brethren, or to fall themselves by their Hands.

He has excited domestic insurrections amongst us, and has endeavoured to bring on the inhabitants of our frontiers, the merciless Indian Savages, whose known rule of warfare, is an undistinguished destruction of all ages, sexes and conditions.

In every stage of these Oppressions We have Petitioned for Redress in the most humble terms: Our repeated Petitions have been answered only by repeated injury. A Prince, whose character is thus marked by every act which may define a Tyrant, is unfit to be the ruler of a free People.

Nor have We been wanting in attention to our British brethren. We have warned them from time to time of attempts by their legislature to extend an unwarrantable jurisdiction over us. We have reminded them of the circumstances of our emigration and settlement here. We have appealed to their native justice and magnanimity, and we have conjured them by the ties of our common kindred to disavow these usurpations, which, would inevitably interrupt our connections and correspondence. They too have been deaf to the voice of justice and of consanguinity. We must, therefore, acquiesce in the necessity, which denounces our Separation, and hold them, as we hold the rest of mankind, Enemies in War, in Peace Friends.

We, therefore, the Representatives of the united States of America, in General Congress, Assembled, appealing to the Supreme Judge of the world for the rectitude of our intentions, do, in the Name, and by Authority of the good People of these Colonies, solemnly publish and declare, That these United Colonies are, and of Right ought to be Free and Independent States; that they are Absolved from all Allegiance to the British Crown, and that all political connection between them and the State of Great Britain, is and ought to be totally dissolved; and that as Free and Independent States, they have full Power to levy War, conclude Peace, contract Alliances, establish Commerce, and to do all other Acts and Things which Independent States may of right do. And for the support of this Declaration, with a firm reliance on the Protection of Divine Providence, we mutually pledge to each other our Lives, our Fortunes and our sacred Honor.

THE CONSTITUTION OF THE UNITED STATES

We the people of the United States, in Order to form a more perfect Union, establish justice, insure domestic Tranquillity, provide for the common defence, promote the general Welfare, and secure the Blessings of Liberty to ourselves and our Posterity, do ordain and establish this Constitution of the United States of America.

Article I

Sec. 1. All legislative Powers herein granted shall be vested in a Congress of the United States, which shall consist of a Senate and House of Representatives.

Sec. 2. The House of Representatives shall be composed of Members chosen every second Year by the People of the several States, and the Electors in each State shall have the Qualifications requisite for Electors of the most numerous Branch of the State Legislature.

No Person shall be a Representative who shall not have attained to the Age of twenty five Years, and been seven Years a Citizen of the United States, and who shall not, when elected, be an Inhabitant of that State in which he shall be chosen.

Representatives and direct Taxes shall be apportioned among the several States which may be included within this Union, according to their respective Numbers, which shall be determined by adding to the whole Number of free Persons, including those bound to Service for a Term of Years, and excluding Indians not taxed, three fifths of all other Persons. The actual Enumeration shall be made within three Years after the first Meeting of the Congress of the United States, and within every subsequent Term of ten Years, in such Manner as they shall by Law direct. The Number of Representatives shall not exceed one for every thirty Thousand, but each State shall have at Least one Representative; and until such enumeration shall be made, the State of New Hampshire shall be entitled to chuse three, Massachusetts eight, Rhode-Island and Providence Plantations one, Connecticut five, New-York six, New Jersey four, Pennsylvania eight, Delaware one, Maryland six, Virginia ten, North Carolina five, South Carolina five, and Georgia three.

When vacancies happen in the Representation from any State, the Executive Authority thereof shall issue Writs of Election to fill such Vacancies.

The House of Representatives shall chuse their Speaker and other Officers; and shall have the sole Power of Impeachment.

Sec. 3. The Senate of the United States shall be composed of two Senators from each State, chosen by the Legislature thereof, for six Years; and each Senator shall have one Vote.

Immediately after they shall be assembled in Consequence of the first Election, they shall be divided as equally as may be into three Classes. The Seats of the Senators of the first Class shall be vacated at the Expiration of the second Year, of the second Class at the Expiration of the fourth Year, and of the third Class at the Expiration of the sixth Year, so that one third may be chosen every second Year; and if Vacancies happen by Resignation, or otherwise, during the Recess of the Legislature of any State, the Executive thereof may make temporary Appointments until the next Meeting of the Legislature, which shall then fill such Vacancies.

No Person shall be a Senator who shall not have attained to the Age of thirty Years, and been nine Years a Citizen of the United States, and who shall not, when elected, be an Inhabitant of that State for which he shall be chosen.

The Vice President of the Untied States shall be President of the Senate, but shall have no Vote, unless they be equally divided.

The Senate shall chuse their other, Officers, and also a President pro tempore, in the Absence of the Vice President, or when he shall exercise the Office of President of the United States.

The Senate shall have the sole Power to try all Impeachments. When sitting for that Purpose, they shall be on Oath or Affirmation. When the President of the United States is tried, the Chief justice shall preside: And no Person shall be convicted without the Concurrence of two thirds of the Members present.

Judgment in Cases of Impeachment shall not extend further than to removal from Office, and disqualification to hold and enjoy any Office of honor, Trust or Profit under the United States: but the Party convicted shall nevertheless be liable and subject to Indictment, Trial, Judgment and Punishment, according to Law.

Sec. 4. The Times, Places and Manner of holding elections for Senators and Representatives, shall be prescribed in each State by the Legislature thereof; but the Congress may at any time by Law make or alter such Regulations, except as to the Places of Chusing Senators.

The Congress shall assemble at least once in every Year, and such Meeting shall be on the first Monday in December, unless they shall by Law appoint a different Day.

Sec. 5. Each House shall be the Judge of the Elections, Returns and Qualifications of its own Members, and a Majority of each shall constitute a Quorum to do business; but a smaller Number may adjourn from day to day, and may be authorized to compel the Attendance of absent Members, in such Manner, and under such Penalties as each House may provide.

Each House may determine the Rules of its Proceedings, punish its Members for disorderly Behaviour, and with the Concurrence of two thirds, expel a Member.

Each House shall keep a Journal of its Proceedings, and from time to time publish the same, excepting such Parts as may in their judgment require Secrecy; and the Yeas and Nays of the Members of either House on any question shall, at the Desire of one fifth of those Present, be entered on the Journal.

Neither House, during the Session of Congress, shall, without the Consent of the other, adjourn for more than three days, nor to any other Place than that in which the two Houses shall be sitting.

Sec. 6. The Senators and Representatives shall receive a Compensation for their Services, to be ascertained by Law, and paid out of the Treasury of the United States. They shall in all Cases, except Treason, Felony and Breach of the Peace, be privileged from Arrest during their Attendance at the Session of their respective Houses, and in going to and returning from the same; and for any Speech or Debate in either House, they shall not be questioned in any other Place.

No Senator or Representative shall, during the Time for which he was elected, be appointed to any civil Office under the Authority of the United States which shall have been created, or the Emoluments whereof shall have been encreased during such time; and no Person holding any Office under the United States, shall be a Member of either House during his Continuance in Office.

Sec. 7. All Bills for raising Revenue shall originate in the House of Representatives; but the Senate may propose or concur with Amendments as on other Bills.

Every Bill which shall have passed the House of Representatives and the Senate, shall, before it become a Law, be presented to the President of the United States; If he approve he shall sign it, but if not he shall return it, with his Objections to the House in which it shall have originated, who shall enter the Objections at large on their Journal, and proceed to reconsider it. If after such Reconsideration two thirds of that House shall agree to pass the Bill, it shall be sent, together with the Objections, to the other House, by which it shall likewise be reconsidered, and if approved by two thirds of that House, it shall become a Law. But in all such Cases the Votes of both Houses shall be determined by Yeas and Nays, and the Names of the Persons voting for and against the Bill shall be entered on the journal of each House respectively. If any Bill shall not be returned by the President within ten Days (Sundays excepted) after it shall have been presented to him, the Same shall be a Law, in like Manner as if he had signed it, unless the Congress by their Adjournment prevent its Return, in which Case it shall not be a Law.

Every Order, Resolution, or Vote to which the Concurrence of the Senate and House of Representatives may be necessary (except on a question of Adjournment) shall be presented to the President of the Untied States; and before the Same shall take Effect, shall be approved by him, or being disapproved by him, shall be repassed by two thirds of the Senate and House of Representatives, according to the Rules and Limitations prescribed in the Case of a Bill.

Sec. 8. The Congress shall have Power to lay and collect Taxes, Duties, Imposts and Excises, to pay the Debts and provide for the common Defence and general Welfare of the United States; but all Duties, Imposts and Excises shall be uniform throughout the United States;

To borrow Money on the credit of the United States;

To regulate Commerce with foreign Nations, and among the several States, and with the Indian Tribes;

To establish an uniform Rule of Naturalization, and uniform Laws on the Subject of Bankruptcies throughout the United States;

To coin Money, regulate the Value Thereof, and of foreign Coin, and fix the standard of Weights and Measures;

To provide for the Punishment of counterfeiting the Securities and current Coin of the United States;

To establish Post Offices and post Roads;

To promote the Progress of Science and useful Arts, by securing for limited Times to Authors and Inventors the exclusive Right to their respective Writings and Discoveries;

To constitute Tribunals inferior to the supreme Court;

To define and punish Piracies and Felonies committed on the high Seas, and Offences against the Law of Nations;

To declare War, grant Letters of Marque and Reprisal, and make Rules concerning Captures on Land and Water;

To raise and support Armies, but no Appropriation of Money to that Use shall be for a longer Term than two Years;

To provide and maintain a Navy;

To make Rules for the Government and Regulation of the land and naval Forces;

To provide for calling forth the Militia to execute the Laws of the Union, suppress Insurrections and repel Invasions;

To provide for organizing, arming, and disciplining the Militia, and for governing such Part of them as may be employed in the Service of the United States, reserving to the States respectively, the Appointment of the Officers, and the Authority of training the Militia according to the discipline prescribed by Congress;

To exercise exclusive Legislation in all Cases whatsoever, over such District (not exceeding ten Miles square) as may, by Cession of particular States, and the Acceptance of Congress, become the Seat of the Government of the United States, and to exercise like Authority over all Places purchased by the Consent of the Legislature of the State in which the Same shall be, for the Erection of Forts, Magazines, Arsenals, dock-Yards, and other needful Buildings;—And

To make all Laws which shall be necessary and proper for carrying into Execution the foregoing Powers, and all other Powers vested by this Constitution in the Government of the United States, or in any Department or Officer thereof.

Sec. 9. The Migration or Importation of such Persons as any of the States now existing shall think proper to admit, shall not be prohibited by the Congress prior to the Year one thousand eight hundred and eight, but a Tax or duty may be imposed on such Importation, not exceeding ten dollars for each Person.

The Privilege of the Writ of Habeas Corpus shall not be suspended, unless when in Cases of Rebellion or Invasion the public Safety may require it.

No Bill of Attainder or ex post facto Law shall be passed.

No Capitation, or other direct, Tax shall be laid, unless in Proportion to the Census or Enumeration herein before directed to be taken.

No Tax or Duty shall be laid on Articles exported from any State.

No Preference shall be given by any Regulation of Commerce or Revenue to the Ports of one State over those of another: nor shall Vessels bound to, or from, one State, be obliged to enter, clear, or pay Duties in another.

No Money shall be drawn from the Treasury, but in Consequence of Appropriations made by Law; and a regular Statement and Account of the Receipts and Expenditures of all public Money shall be published from time to time.

No Title of Nobility shall be granted by the United States: And no Person holding any Office of Profit or Trust under them, shall, without the Consent of the Congress, accept of any present, Emolument, Office, or Title, of any kind whatever, from any King, Prince or Foreign State.

Sec. 10. No State shall enter into any Treaty, Alliance, or Confederation; grant Letters of Marque and Reprisal; coin Money; emit Bills of Credit; make any Thing but gold and silver Coin a Tender in Payment of Debts; pass any Bill of Attainder, ex post facto Law, or Law impairing the Obligation of Contracts, or grant any Title of Nobility.

No State shall, without the Consent of the Congress, lay any Imposts or Duties on Imports or Exports, except what may be absolutely necessary for executing its inspection Laws: and the net Produce of all Duties and Imposts, laid by any State on Imports or Exports, shall be for the Use of the Treasury of the United States, and all such Laws shall be subject to the Revision and Controul of the Congress.

No State shall, without the Consent of Congress, lay any Duty of Tonnage, keep Troops, or Ships of War in time of Peace, enter in any Agreement or Compact with another State, or with a foreign Power, or engage in War, unless actually invaded, or in such imminent Danger as will not admit of delay.

Article II

Sec. 1. The executive Power shall be vested in a President of the United States of America. He shall hold his Office during the Term of four Years, and, together with the Vice President, chosen for the same Term, be elected, as follows.

Each State shall appoint, in such Manner as the Legislature thereof may direct, a Number of Electors, equal to the whole Number of Senators and Representatives to which the State may be entitled in the Congress: but no Senator or Representative, or Person holding an Office of Trust or Profit under the United States, shall be appointed an Elector.

The Electors shall meet in their respective States, and vote by Ballot for two Persons, of whom one at least shall not be an Inhabitant of the same State with themselves. And they shall make a List of all the Persons voted for, and of the Number of Votes for each; which List they shall sign and certify, and transmit sealed to the Seat of the Government of the United States, directed to the President of the Senate. The President of the Senate shall, in the Presence of the Senate and House of Representatives, open all the Certificates, and the Votes shall then be counted. The Person having the greatest Number of Votes shall be the President, if such Number be a Majority of the whole Number of Electors appointed; and if there be more than one who have such Majority, and have an equal Number of Votes, then the House of Representatives shall immediately chuse by Ballot one of them for President; and if no person have a Majority, then from the five highest on the List the said House shall in like Manner chuse the President. But in chusing the President, the Votes shall be taken by States, the Representation from each State having one Vote; A quorum for this Purpose shall consist of a Member or Members from two thirds of the States, and a majority of all the States shall be necessary to a Choice. In every Case, after the Choice of the President, the Person having the greatest Number of Votes of the Electors shall be the Vice President. But if there should remain two or more who have equal Votes, the Senate shall chuse from them by Ballot the Vice President.

The Congress may determine the Time of chusing the Electors, and the Day on which they shall give their Votes; which Day shall be the same throughout the United States.

No Person except a natural born Citizen, or a Citizen of the United States, at the time of the Adoption of this Constitution, shall be eligible to the Office of President; neither shall any Person be eligible to that Office who shall not have attained to the Age of thirty five Years, and been fourteen Years a Resident within the United States.

In Case of the Removal of the President from Office, or of his Death, Resignation, or Inability to discharge the Powers and Duties of the said Office, the Same shall devolve on the Vice President, and the Congress may by law provide for the Case of Removal, Death, Resignation or Inability, both of the President and Vice President, declaring what Officer shall then act as President, and such Office shall act accordingly, until the Disability be removed, or a President shall be elected.

The President shall, at stated Times, receive for his Services, a Compensation, which shall neither be encreased nor diminished during the Period for which he shall have been elected, and he shall not receive within that Period any other Emolument from the United States, or any of them.

Before he enter on the Execution of his Office, he shall take the following Oath or Affirmation:—"I do solemnly swear (or affirm) that I will faithfully execute the Office of President of the United States, and will to the best of my Ability, preserve, protect and defend the Constitution of the United States."

Sec. 2. The President shall be commander in Chief of the Army and Navy of the United States, and of the Militia of the several States, when called into the actual Service of the United States; he may require the Opinion, in writing, of the principal Officer in each of the executive Departments, upon any Subject relating to the Duties of their respective Officers, and he shall have Power to grant Reprieves and Pardons for Offenses against the United States, except in Cases of Impeachment.

He shall have Power, by and with the Advice and Consent of the Senate, to make Treaties, provided two thirds of the Senators present concur; and he shall nominate, and by and with the Advice and Consent of the Senate, shall appoint Ambassadors, other public Ministers and Consuls, Judges of the supreme Court, and all other Officers of the United States, whose Appointments are not herein otherwise provided for, and which shall be established by Law: but the Congress may by Law vest the Appointment of such inferior Officers, as they think proper, in the President alone, in the Courts of Law, or in the Heads of Departments.

The President shall have Power to fill up all Vacancies that may happen during the Recess of the Senate, by granting Commissions which shall expire at the End of their next Session.

Sec. 3. He shall from time to time give to the Congress Information of the State of the Union, and recommend to their consideration such Measures as he shall judge necessary and expedient; he may, on extraordinary Occasion, convene both Houses, or either of them, and in Case of Disagreement between them, with Respect to the Time of Adjournment, he may adjourn them to such Time as he shall think proper; he shall receive Ambassadors and other public Ministers; he shall take Care that the Laws be faithfully executed, and shall Commission all the Officers of the United States.

Sec. 4. The President, Vice President and all civil Officers of the United States, shall be removed from Office on Impeachment for, and Conviction of, Treason, Bribery, or other high Crimes and Misdemeanors.

Article III

Sec. 1. The judicial Power of the United States, shall be vested in one supreme Court, and in such inferior Courts as the Congress may from time to time ordain and establish. The judges, both of the supreme and inferior Courts, shall hold their Offices during good Behaviour, and shall, at stated Times, receive for their Services, a Compensation, which shall not be diminished during their Continuance in Office.

Sec. 2. The judicial Power shall extend to all Cases, in Law and Equity, arising under this Constitution, the Laws of the United States, and Treaties made, or which shall be made, under their Authority;—to all Cases Affecting Ambassadors, other public Ministers and Consuls;—to all Cases of admiralty and maritime jurisdiction;—to

Controversies to which the United States shall be a Party;—to Controversies between two or more States;—between a State and Citizens of another State;—between Citizens of different States;—between Citizens of the same State claiming Lands under Grants of different States, and between a State, or the citizens thereof, and foreign States, Citizens or Subjects.

In all Cases affecting Ambassadors, other public Ministers and Consuls, and those in which a State shall be Party, the supreme Court shall have original jurisdiction. In all the other cases before mentioned, the supreme Court shall have appellate jurisdiction, both as to Law and Fact, with such Exceptions, and under such Regulations as the Congress shall make.

The Trial of all Crimes, except in Cases of Impeachment, shall be by jury; and such Trial shall be held in the State where the said Crimes shall have been committed; but when not committed within any State, the Trial shall be at such Place or Places as the Congress may by Law have directed.

Sec. 3. Treason against the United States, shall consist only in levying War against them, or in adhering to their Enemies, giving them Aid and Comfort. No Person shall be convicted of Treason unless on the Testimony of two Witnesses to the same overt Act, or on Confession in open Court.

The Congress shall have Power to declare the Punishment of Treason, but no Attainder of Treason shall work Corruption of Blood, or Forfeiture except during the Life of the Person attainted.

Article IV

Sec. 1. Full Faith and Credit shall be given in each State to the Public Acts, Records, and judicial Proceedings of every other State. And the Congress may by general Laws prescribe the Manner in which such Acts, Records and Proceedings shall be proved, and the Effect thereof.

Sec. 2. The Citizens of each State shall be entitled to all Privileges and Immunities of Citizens in the Several States.

A Person charged in any State with Treason, Felony, or other Crime, who shall flee from justice, and be found in another State, shall on Demand of the executive Authority of the State from which he fled, be delivered up, to be removed to the State having jurisdiction of the Crime.

No Person held to Service or Labour in one State, under the Laws thereof, escaping into another, shall, in Consequence of any Law or Regulation therein, be discharged from such Service or Labour, but shall be delivered up on Claim of the Party to whom such Service or Labour may be due.

Sec. 3. New States may be admitted by the Congress into this Union; but no new States shall be formed or erected within the jurisdiction of any other State; nor any State be formed by the junction of two or more States, or Parts of States, without Consent of the Legislatures of the States concerned as well as of the Congress.

The Congress shall have Power to dispose of and make all needful Rules and Regulations respecting the Territory or other Property belonging to the United States; and nothing in this Constitution shall be so construed as to Prejudice any Claims of the United States, or of any particular State.

Sec. 4. The United States shall guarantee to every State in this Union a Republican Form of Government, and shall protect each of them against Invasion; and on Application of the Legislature, or of the Executive (when the Legislature cannot be convened) against domestic Violence.

Article V

The Congress, whenever two thirds of both Houses shall deem it necessary, shall propose Amendments to this Constitution, or, on the Application of the Legislatures of two thirds of the several States, shall call a Convention for proposing Amendments, which, in either Case, shall be valid to all Intents and Purposes, as Part of this Constitution, when ratified by the Legislatures of three fourths of the several States, or by Conventions in three fourths thereof, as the one or the other Mode of Ratification may be proposed by the Congress; Provided that no Amendment which may be made prior to the Year One thousand eight hundred and eight shall in any Manner affect the first and fourth Clauses in the Ninth Section of the first Article; and that no State, without its Consent, shall be deprived of its equal Suffrage in the Senate.

Article VI

All Debts contracted and Engagements entered into, before the Adoption of this Constitution, shall be as valid against the United States under this Constitution, as under the Confederation.

This Constitution, and the Laws of the United States which shall be made in Pursuance thereof; and all Treaties made, or which shall be made, under the Authority of the United States, shall be the supreme Law of the Land; and the judges in every State shall be bound thereby, any Thing in the Constitution or Laws of any State to the Contrary notwithstanding.

The Senators and Representatives before mentioned, and the Members of the several State Legislatures, and all executive and judicial Officers, both of the United States and of the several States, shall be bound by Oath or Affirmation, to support this Constitution; but no religious Test shall ever be required as a Qualification to any Office or public Trust under the United States.

Article VII

The Ratification of the Conventions of nine States, shall be sufficient for the Establishment of this Constitution between the States so ratifying the Same.

Done in Convention by the Unanimous Consent of the States present the Seventeenth Day of September in the Year of our Lord one thousand seven hundred and Eighty seven and of the Independence of the United States of America the Twelfth. In witness whereof We have hereunto subscribed our Names,

Attest William Jackson Secretary

Geo: Washington—Presidt.
and deputy from Virginia

Delaware
Geo: Read
Gunning Bedford junr
John Dickinson
Richard Bassett
Jaco: Broom

Maryland
James McHenry
Dan of St Thos. Jenifer
Danl Carroll

Virginia
John Blair—
James Madison Jr.

North Carolina
Wm. Blount
Richd. Dobbs Spaight.
Hu Williamson

South Carolina
J. Rutledge
Charles Cotesworth Pinckney
Charles Pinckney
Pierce Butler

Georgia
William Few
Abr Baldwin

New Hampshire
John Langdon
Nicholas Gilman

Massachusetts
Nathaniel Gorham
Rufus King

Connecticut
Wm: Saml. Johnson
Roger Sherman

New York
Alexander Hamilton

New Jersey
Wil: Livingston
David Brearley
Wm. Paterson.
Jona: Dayton

Pennsylvania
B Franklin
Thomas Mifflin
Robt Morris
Geo. Clymer
Thos. FitzSimons
Jared Ingersoll
James Wilson
Gouv. Morris

Articles in Addition to, and Amendment of, the Constitution of the United States of America, proposed by Congress, and ratified by the Legislatures of the several States, pursuant to the fifth Article of the original Constitution.

Article I

Congress shall make no law respecting an establishment of religion, or prohibiting the free exercise thereof; or abridging the freedom of speech, or of the press; or the right of the people peaceably to assemble, and to petition the government for a redress of grievances.

Article II

A well regulated Militia, being necessary to the Security of a free State, the right of the people to keep and bear Arms, shall not be infringed.

Article III

No Soldier shall, in time of peace be quartered in any house, without the consent of the Owner, nor in time of war, but in a manner to be prescribed by law.

Article IV

The right of the people to be secure in their persons, houses, papers, and effects, against unreasonable searches and seizures, shall not be violated, and no Warrants shall issue, but upon probable cause, supported by Oath or affirmation, and particularly describing the place to be searched, and the persons or things to be seized.

Article V

No person shall be held to answer for a capital, or otherwise infamous crime, unless on a presentment or indictment of a Grand Jury, except in cases arising in the land or naval forces, or in the Militia, when in actual service in time of War or public danger; nor shall any person be subject for the same offence to be twice put in jeopardy of life or limb; nor shall be compelled in any criminal case to be a witness against himself, nor be deprived of life, liberty, or property, without due process of law; nor shall private property be taken for public use, without just compensation.

Article VI

In all criminal prosecutions, the accused shall enjoy the right to a speedy and public trial, by an impartial jury of the State and district wherein the crime shall have been committed, which district shall have been previously ascertained by law, and to be informed of the nature and cause of the accusation; to be confronted with the witnesses against him; to have compulsory process for obtaining witnesses in his favor, and to have the Assistance of Counsel for his defence.

Article VII

In Suits at common law, where the value in controversy shall exceed twenty dollars, the right of trial by jury shall be preserved, and no fact tried by a jury, shall be otherwise reexamined in any Court of the United States, than according to the rules of the common law.

Article VIII

Excessive bail shall not be required, nor excessive fines imposed, nor cruel and unusual punishments inflicted.

Article IX

The enumeration in the Constitution, of certain rights, shall not be construed to deny or disparage others retained by the people.

Article X

The powers not delegated to the United States by the Constitution, nor prohibited by it to the States, are preserved to the States respectively, or to the people.

Article XI

The Judicial power of the United States shall not be construed to extend to any suit in law or equity, commenced or prosecuted against one of the United States by Citizens of another State, or by Citizens or Subjects of any Foreign State.

Article XII

The Electors shall meet in their respective states, and vote by ballot for President and Vice-President, one of whom, at least, shall not be an inhabitant of the same state with themselves; they shall name in their ballots the person voted for as President, and in distinct ballots the person voted for as Vice-President, and they shall make distinct lists of all persons voted for as President, and of all persons voted for as Vice-President, and of the number of votes for each, which lists they shall sign and certify, and transmit sealed to the seat of the government of the United States, directed to the President of the Senate;—The President of the Senate shall, in the presence of the Senate and House of Representatives, open all the certificates and the votes shall then be counted;—The person having the greatest number of votes for President, shall be the President, if such number be a majority of the whole number of Electors appointed; and if no person have such majority, then from the persons having the highest numbers not exceeding three on the list of those voted for as President, the House of Representatives shall choose immediately, by ballot, the President. But in choosing the President the votes shall be taken by states, the representation from each state having one vote; a quorum for this purpose shall consist of a member or members from two-thirds of the states, and a majority of all the states shall be necessary to a choice. And if the House of Representatives shall not choose a President whenever the right of choice shall devolve upon them, before the fourth day of March next following, then the Vice-President shall act as President, as in the case of the death or other constitutional disability of the President.—The person having the greatest number of votes as Vice-President shall be the Vice-President, if such number be a majority of the whole number of Electors appointed, and if no person have a majority, then from the two highest numbers on the list the Senate shall choose the Vice-President; a quorum for the purpose shall consist of two-thirds of the whole number of Senators, and a majority of the whole number shall be necessary to a choice. But no person constitutionally ineligible to the office of President shall be eligible to that of Vice-President of the United States.

Article XIII

Sec. 1. Neither slavery nor involuntary servitude, except as a punishment for crime whereof the party shall have been duly convicted, shall exist within the United States, or any place subject to their jurisdiction.

Sec. 2. Congress shall have power to enforce this article by appropriate legislation.

Article XIV

Sec. 1. All persons born or naturalized in the United States, and subject to the jurisdiction thereof, are citizens of the United States and of the State wherein they reside. No State shall make or enforce any law which shall abridge the privileges or immunities of citizens of the United States; nor shall any State deprive any person of life, liberty, or property, without due process of law; nor deny to any person within its jurisdiction the equal protection of the laws.

Sec. 2. Representatives shall be apportioned among the several States according to their respective numbers, counting the whole number of persons in each State, excluding Indians not taxed. But when the right to vote at any election for the choice of electors for President and Vice President of the United States, Representatives in Congress, the Executive and Judicial officers of a State, or the members of the Legislature thereof, is denied to any of the male inhabitants of such State, being twenty-one years of age, and citizens of the United States, or in any way abridged, except for participation in rebellion, or other crime, the basis of representation therein shall be reduced in the proportion which the number of such male citizens shall bear to the whole number of male citizens twenty-one years of age in such State.

Sec. 3. No person shall be a Senator or Representative in Congress, or elector of President and Vice President, or hold any office, civil or military, under the United States, or under any State, who, having previously taken an oath, as a member of Congress, or as an officer of the United States, or as a member of any State legislature, or as an executive or judicial officer of any State, to support the Constitution of the United States, shall have engaged in insurrection or rebellion against the same, or given aid or comfort to the enemies thereof. But Congress may by a vote of two-thirds of each House, remove such disability.

Sec. 4. The validity of the public debt of the United States, authorized by law, including debts incurred for payment of pensions and bounties for services in suppressing insurrection or rebellion, shall not be questioned. But neither the United States nor any State shall assume or pay any debt or obligation incurred in aid of insurrection or rebellion against the United States, or any claim for the loss or emancipation of any slave; but all such debts, obligations and claims shall be held illegal and void.

Sec. 5. The Congress shall have power to enforce, by appropriate the legislation, the provisions of this article.

Article XV

Sec. 1. The right of citizens of the United States to vote shall not be denied or abridged by the United States or by any State on account of race, color, or previous condition of servitude.

Sec. 2. The Congress shall have power to enforce this article by appropriate legislation.

Article XVI

The Congress shall have power to lay and collect taxes on incomes, from whatever source derived, without apportionment among the several States, and without regard to any census or enumeration.

Article XVII

The Senate of the United States shall be composed of two Senators from each State, elected by the people thereof, for six years; and each Senator shall have one vote. The electors in each State shall have the qualifications requisite for electors of the most numerous branch of the State legislatures.

When vacancies happen in the representation of any State in the Senate, the executive authority of such State shall issue writs of election to fill such vacancies: *Provided,* That the legislature of any State may empower the executive thereof to make temporary appointments until the people fill the vacancies by election as the legislature may direct.

This amendment shall not be so construed as to affect the election or term of any Senator chosen before it becomes valid as part of the Constitution.

Article XVIII

Sec. 1. After one year from the ratification of this article the manufacture, sale, or transportation of intoxicating liquors within, the importation thereof into, or the exportation thereof from the United States and all territory subject to the jurisdiction thereof for beverage purposes is hereby prohibited.

Sec. 2. The Congress and the several States shall have concurrent power to enforce this article by appropriate legislation.

Sec. 3. This article shall be inoperative unless it shall have been ratified as an amendment to the Constitution by the legislatures of the several States, as provided in the Constitution, within seven years from the date of the submission hereof to the States by the Congress.

Article XIX

The right of citizens of the United States to vote shall not be denied or abridged by the United States or by any State on account of sex.

Congress shall have power to enforce this article by appropriate legislation.

Article XX

Sec. 1. The terms of the President and Vice President shall end at noon on the 20th day of January, and the terms of Senators and Representatives at noon on the 3d day of January, of the years in which such terms would have ended if this article had not been ratified; and the terms of their successors shall then begin.

Sec. 2. The Congress shall assemble at least once in every year, and such meeting shall begin at noon on the 3d day of January, unless they shall by law appoint a different day.

Sec. 3. If, at the time fixed for the beginning of the term of the President, the President elect shall have died, the Vice President elect shall become President. If a President shall not have been chosen before the time fixed for the beginning of his term, or if the President elect shall have failed to qualify, then the Vice President elect shall act as President until a President shall have qualified; and the Congress may by law provide for the case wherein neither a President elect nor a Vice President elect shall have qualified, declaring who shall then act as President, or the manner in which one who is to act shall be selected, and such person shall act accordingly until a President or Vice President shall have qualified.

Sec. 4. The Congress may by law provide for the case of the death of any of the persons from whom the House of Representatives may choose a President whenever the right of choice shall have devolved upon them, and for the case of the death of any of the persons from whom the Senate may choose a Vice President whenever the right of choice shall have devolved upon them.

Sec. 5. Sections 1 and 2 shall take effect on the 15th day of October following the ratification of this article.

Sec. 6. This article shall be inoperative unless it shall have been ratified as an amendment to the Constitution by the legislatures of three-fourths of the several States within seven years from the date of its submission.

Article XXI

Sec. 1. The eighteenth article of amendment to the Constitution of the United States is hereby repealed.

Sec. 2. The transportation or importation into any State, Territory, or possession of the United States for delivery or use therein of intoxicating liquors, in violation of the laws thereof, is hereby prohibited.

Sec. 3. This article shall be inoperative unless it shall have been ratified as an amendment to the Constitution by conventions in the several States, as provided in the Constitution, within seven years from the date of the submission hereof to the States by the Congress.

Article XXII

Sec. 1. No person shall be elected to the office of the President more than twice, and no person who has held the office of President, or acted as President, for more than two years of a term to which some other person was elected President shall be elected to the office of the President more than once. But this Article shall not apply to any person holding the office of President when this Article was proposed by the Congress, and shall not prevent any person who may be holding the office of President, or acting as President during the term within which this Article becomes operative from holding the office of President or acting as President during the remainder of such term.

Sec. 2. This article shall be inoperative unless it shall have been ratified as an amendment to the Constitution by the legislatures of three-fourths of the several States within seven years from the date of its submission to the States by the Congress.

Article XXIII

Sec. 1. The District constituting the seat of Government of the United States shall appoint in such manner as the Congress may direct:

A number of electors of President and Vice President equal to the whole number of Senators and Representatives in Congress to which the District would be entitled if it were a State, but in no event more than the least populous State; they shall be in addition to those appointed by the States, but they shall be considered, for the purposes of the election of President and Vice President, to be electors appointed by a State; and they shall meet in the District and perform such duties as provided by the twelfth article of amendment.

Sec. 2. The Congress shall have power to enforce this article by appropriate legislation.

Article XXIV

The right of citizens of the United States to vote in any primary or other election for President or Vice President, for electors for President or Vice President, or for Senator or Representative in Congress, shall not be denied or abridged by the United States or any State by reason of failure to pay any poll tax or other tax.

Sec. 2. The Congress shall have power to enforce this article by appropriate legislation.

Article XXV

Sec. 1. In case of the removal of the President from office or of his death or resignation, the Vice President shall become President.

Sec. 2. Whenever there is a vacancy in the office of the Vice President, the President shall nominate a Vice President who shall take office upon confirmation by a majority vote of both Houses of Congress.

Sec. 3. Whenever the President transmits to the President pro tempore of the Senate and the Speaker of the House of Representatives his written declaration that he is unable to discharge the powers and duties of his office, and until he transmits to them a written declaration to the contrary, such powers and duties shall be discharged by the Vice President as Acting President.

Sec. 4. Whenever the Vice President and a majority of either the principal officers of the executive departments or of such other body as Congress may by law provide, transmit to the President pro tempore of the Senate and the Speaker of the House of Representatives their written declaration that the President is unable to discharge the powers and duties of his office, the Vice President shall immediately assume the powers and duties of the office as Acting President.

Thereafter, when the President transmits to the President pro tempore of the Senate and the Speaker of the House of Representatives his written declaration that no inability exists, he shall resume the powers and duties of his office unless the Vice President and a majority of either the principal officers of the executive department or of such other body as Congress may by law provide, transmit within four days to the President pro tempore of the Senate and the Speaker of the House of Representatives their written declaration that the President is unable to discharge the powers and duties of his office. Thereupon Congress shall decide the issue, assembling within forty-eight hours for that purpose if not in session. If the Congress, within twenty-one days after receipt of the latter written declaration, or, if Congress is not in session, within twenty-one days after Congress is required to assemble, determines by two-thirds vote of both Houses that the President is unable to discharge the powers and duties of his office, the Vice President shall continue to discharge the same as Acting President; otherwise, the President shall resume the powers and duties of his office.

Article XXVI

Sec. 1. The right of citizens of the United States, who are eighteen years of age or older, to vote shall not be denied or abridged by the United States or by any State on account of age.

Sec. 2. The Congress shall have power to enforce this article by appropriate legislation.

Article XXVII

No law, varying the compensation for the services of the Senators and Representatives, shall take effect, until an election of Representatives shall have intervened.

THE FEDERALIST PAPERS

The Federalist Papers, also referred to as *The Federalist*, were written by Alexander Hamilton, James Madison, and John Jay (under the pseudonym Publius, or the Public Man) in order to persuade the citizens of New York State to vote in favor of ratification of the proposed Constitution. The papers appeared in various New York journals from October 1787 through May 1788. They were an answer to attacks by opponents of the Constitution, particularly a series of articles under the signature of Cato (assumed at the time to be the governor, George Clinton, but he may have been an associate). The Antifederalists or opponents of the new Constitution won the election by a two-to-one margin. Through skillful maneuvering in the ratification convention, the Federalists were able to secure a vote in favor of ratification by the narrow margin of 31 to 29.

The authors of *The Federalist Papers* kept their anonymity for several years. It is now generally agreed that Hamilton wrote fifty-one numbers, Madison twenty-six, Jay five, and Hamilton and Madison together three. The papers were published immediately as a book, then republished in 1799 and 1802, and continually since then. They won immediate acclaim as an authoritative expression of the theory behind the Constitution. Charles A. Beard called *The Federalist Papers* the greatest work of political theory ever written by Americans, and the greatest work of political science in any language.

The main organizer of the enterprise, Alexander Hamilton (1755–1804) was born in the West Indies island of Nevis, the illegitimate son of a Scottish merchant and an Englishwoman, herself a native of the West Indies. Abandoned by his father, Alexander worked as a clerk in an import-export firm in Saint-Croix. With the help of his employer, and also of a clergyman who recognized his intellectual ability, he arrived in New York in 1772. He met and became friendly with John Jay, entering King's College (later Columbia) the following year. Winning a commission as an artillery officer, he participated in several battles, and was chosen by George Washington as an aide-de-camp. In 1780 Hamilton married Elizabeth Schuyler, the daughter of a wealthy landowner, which assured him social position. After the war he became one of New York's leading lawyers, participated actively in politics, and was a delegate to Congress. Under the new government, Hamilton served as secretary of the treasury (1789–1795), then returned to the practice of law, continuing to play an active role in politics. He was killed in a duel with Aaron Burr.

James Madison (1751–1836) was descended from early English immigrants to Virginia. His family maintained a large plantation and estate in Orange County, not far from Jefferson's Monticello. Madison attended the College of New Jersey (later Princeton), a stronghold of revolutionary sentiment, graduating in 1771. He entered politics in 1774, first in his native Orange County, then as a member of the Virginia Convention. He and Thomas Jefferson became close friends and political associates. He was chosen to be a member of the Virginia Council of State, which advised and shared responsibility with the governor. In this capacity he served with governors Patrick

Henry and Thomas Jefferson. Both Madison and Jefferson condemned the lack of an independent executive in wartime Virginia. Madison was chosen as a delegate to the Continental Congress in 1780; he played a major role in the Philadelphia Convention in 1787. After adoption of the new Constitution, Madison was elected to the House of Representatives, and worked closely with Jefferson in opposing the emerging Federalist party. He left Congress in 1797, served a term in the Virginia legislature, and became secretary of state (1801–1809) under President Jefferson. He succeeded Jefferson as president (1809–1817).

John Jay (1745–1829) was the oldest and at the time best known of the authors. Jay was descended from French Huguenot merchants of La Rochelle who fled to America after the revocation of the Edict of Nantes. He married Sarah Livingston, gaining entry into one of the wealthiest Whig families of New Jersey. After attending King's College, he became a successful lawyer, and was elected a delegate to the Continental Congress in 1774. An active political career began: He drafted a constitution for the state of New York, served as chief justice of the New York Supreme Court, was elected president of the Continental Congress in 1778, then was named ambassador to Spain, later joining Benjamin Franklin in Paris to negotiate peace with Britain. On his return to New York in 1784, Jay was named secretary for foreign affairs under the Articles of Confederation, in which post he was still serving when he contributed to the *Federalist Papers*. Subsequently he became the first chief justice of the United States (1789). As special envoy he negotiated a treaty with Britain (1794), then resigned as chief justice to serve as governor of New York (1795–1801).

The very first of the Federalist papers, written by Hamilton (according to legend, overnight in the cabin of the sloop taking him back to New York from legal business in Albany) posed the question: "whether societies of men are really capable or not of establishing good government from reflection and choice, or whether they are forever destined to depend for their political constitutions on accident and force." The immediate and most obvious meaning was whether the citizens of New York, after hearing arguments on both sides, would vote in favor of ratification of the new Constitution. A "wrong" choice, said Hamilton, should be considered the "general misfortune of mankind." Hamilton also sought to highlight the significance of the ratification process itself. The Americans thought they were in the forefront of the struggle against feudalism, a system they condemned as degrading to humanity, based on accident of birth and force of tradition. But in an age of enlightenment, people were active agents of their own destiny. The first Federalist paper was the opening salvo of a global democratic revolution.

Hamilton and Jay then analyzed the defects of the government under the Articles of Confederation. Most obvious was its inability to defend the nation in dealing with foreign powers, to resolve conflicts among the states (who were creating barriers to the flow of commerce and laying rival claims to the western territories), and to levy taxes directly instead of depending on the states for contributions. In addition, Madison stressed the tendency to disregard minority rights by local majorities in the states. He challenged Montesquieu's advocacy of small republics linked together by compact, which was popular among Antifederalists.

For Publius, the defects of the Confederation would be remedied by a strong general government, levying its own taxes, able to deal on terms of equality with foreign powers, capable of defending a larger public interest and of avoiding internecine strife, and protecting rights of individuals and minorities. It would have the power to enforce its decisions directly on individuals, through courts.

For Madison, popular government did not mean direct participation by the people in government (called, in Number 10, *pure democracy*). Direct popular rule was not feasible in governing a large territory; it was not desirable even when feasible. The very form of government itself is defective in that skilled orators could sway the populace by appealing to their passions. In a republic, the people elect representatives who can "refine and enlarge upon the public views." Representation also makes it possible to create checks and balances in order to avoid abuse of power and allow time for reflection and reconsideration.

The major cause of instability in popular government, argued Madison in Number 10, is "faction" and the spirit of party. So long as men have different "faculties," and the liberty to develop them, they will have different opinions and hold different types of property, which is the most durable source of faction. Madison's conception of property makes a break with the feudal emphasis on land ownership; he rather grants equal validity to commercial and manufacturing interests, describing an interaction characteristic of modern economies. One role of government is to protect the faculties of men; but Madison and Hamilton believed that government should regulate property and reduce the disparity between wealth and poverty. The new Constitution helps control the effects of faction principally by extending the Republic in order to take in a greater variety of interests, thus making it difficult for any one faction to dominate. But this was only a tendency. An extended republic might also be paralyzed by the conflict among factions and parties. Hence, the need for an "energetic government" with a "proper structure."

Government must be able to defend a public good over and beyond the clash of factions. The public good is characterized by a long-term view, as opposed to immediate interests. In Rhode Island, cited several times by Publius, a majority in the state legislature, representing debtors, authorized the issuance of paper money that rapidly became worthless. To secure a short-term advantage, the dominant majority thus sacrificed its own long-term interest in commercial exchange based on mutual confidence and economic growth. Government protects the "permanent and aggregate interests of the community" by creating the infrastructure of an expanding economy ("new improvements" like roads and canals, observed Madison in Number 14, along with a sound currency, a system of justice, schools).

Interests must be represented in government, but not be able to dominate. Government must be capable of action, but with provision for deliberation. Separation of the branches of government permits each branch to specialize in different functions, thereby becoming more effective in their totality. An executive was to embody the principle of "energy," Hamilton explained in Number 70, while the legislature was best suited to perform the indispensable functions of representation and conciliation of interests, reflection, and judgment. The role of the judicial power was to uphold clearly stated limits set down in the fundamental law; it was not anticipated that the judicial branch would be able to interpret the "spirit" of the Constitution. Hamilton's argument in Numbers 78 to 84 remains a source of inspiration for both defenders and opponents of judicial activism. Each branch would be given sufficient power to defend itself, noted Madison in Numbers 47 and 51, thus maintaining the system of specialized functions. It is particularly important in a republic, he emphasized in Number 48, to prevent the legislature from encroaching upon the executive, for that would lead to instability, chaos, and ultimately a call for a dictator. The alternative to Union, warned Hamilton in Number 85, was anarchy, civil war, and "perhaps the military despotism of a victorious demagogue."

The reputation of *The Federalist* has reflected the evolution of the Constitution it explained and justified. The victory of the North in the Civil War seemed to vindicate the supremacy of the general government over the states, and its role in promoting the growth of a modern society. But the social and economic tensions of industrialization led some progressives and socialists to view the Constitution as a mechanism, and *The Federalist* as a theory serving the interests of a dominant capitalist class by making property rights inviolable and preventing the formation of a popular and anticapitalist majority. The rise of fascism and communism, and the growing crisis of communism after World War II, led to a new appreciation of *The Federalist* and of the success of the American revolutionaries in establishing a stable republic that averted dictatorship, preserved individual liberties, and promoted the growth of an increasingly prosperous society. There is renewed interest in *The Federalist* today by Europeans seeking to create unity out of diversity through the European Union, and by the peoples of former Communist systems striving to establish viable representative institutions.

Hamilton has been the subject of many biographies. Forrest McDonald, *Alexander Hamilton, A Biography* (New York: W. W. Norton, 1979), is good on intellectual influences; John C. Miller, *Alexander Hamilton and the Growth of the New Nation* (New York: Harper and Row, 1959), emphasizes political factors; Clinton Rossiter, *Alexander Hamilton and the Constitution* (New York: Harcourt, Brace & World, 1964), is valuable for Hamilton's political and constitutional thought; Jacob Cooke, *Alexander Hamilton* (New York: Scribner, 1982), draws upon Freudian theory in appraising his personality. On Madison: Irving Brant, *The Fourth President: A Life of James Madison* (Indianapolis: Bobbs-Merrill, 1970), is a one-volume abridgment of the author's monumental six-volume biography; Ralph Ketcham, *James Madison* (New York: Macmillan, 1971), pays special attention to politics; Drew R. McCoy, *The Last of the Fathers: James Madison and the Republican Legacy* (New York: Cambridge University Press, 1989), deals with the evolution of Madison's views on the crises of the early years of the Republic, notably nullification and slavery. For a lively account of the role played by the three Publii in the making of the Constitution and the ratification debate, see Richard B. Morris, *Witnesses at the Creation: Hamilton, Madison, Jay, and the Constitution* (New York: Henry Holt, 1985).

Among the critical works: Douglas Adair, *Fame and the Founding Fathers* (New York: W. W. Norton, 1974), argues that David Hume was a major source; and Garry Wills, *Explaining America: The Federalist* (New York: Doubleday & Co., 1981), explicates the text of *The Federalist*, and follows Adair in attributing decisive influence to Hume and the Scottish Enlightenment. More diverse influences are identified by contributors to Allan Bloom, ed., *Confronting the Constitution* (Washington, DC: American Enterprise Institute, 1990). Analytic themes (separation of powers, justice, rule of law, constitutionalism) are treated by contributors to Charles R. Kesler, ed., *Saving the Revolution: The Federalist Papers and the American Founding* (New York: Free Press, 1987).

Scholarly and balanced treatments include: David F. Epstein, *The Political Theory of The Federalist* (Chicago: University of Chicago Press, 1984); and George W. Carey, *The Federalist: Design for a Constitutional Republic* (Urbana: University of Illinois Press, 1989). Samuel H. Beer, *To Make a Nation: The Rediscovery of American Federalism* (Cambridge: Harvard University Press, 1993), deals with the theory of federalism expounded in *The Federalist,* and assesses the evolution of the system. On *The Federalist* as a model of political science, see the essay by Harvey C. Mansfield, Jr., in Allan Bloom, ed., *Confronting the Constitution,* cited above.

B. E. B.

THE FEDERALIST PAPERS

NUMBER 1

After an unequivocal experience of the inefficiency of the subsisting federal government, you are called upon to deliberate on a new Constitution for the United States of America. The subject speaks its own importance; comprehending in its consequences nothing less than the existence of the Union, the safety and welfare of the parts of which it is composed, the fate of an empire in many respects the most interesting in the world. It has been frequently remarked that it seems to have been reserved to the people of this country, by their conduct and example, to decide the important question, whether societies of men are really capable or not of establishing good government from reflection and choice, or whether they are forever destined to depend for their political constitutions on accident and force. If there be any truth in the remark, the crisis at which we are arrived may with propriety be regarded as the era in which that decision is to be made; and a wrong election of the part we shall act may, in this view, deserve to be considered as the general misfortune of mankind.

This idea will add the inducements of philanthropy to those of patriotism, to heighten the solicitude which all considerate and good men must feel for the event. Happy will it be if our choice should be directed by a judicious estimate of our true interests, unperplexed and unbiased by considerations not connected with the public good. But this is a thing more ardently to be wished than seriously to be expected. The plan offered to our deliberations affects too many particular interests, innovates upon too many local institutions, not to involve in its discussion a variety of objects foreign to its merits, and of views, passions and prejudices little favorable to the discovery of truth.

Among the most formidable of the obstacles which the new Constitution will have to encounter may readily be distinguished the obvious interest of a certain class of men in every State to resist all changes which may hazard a diminution of the power, emolument, and consequence of the offices they hold under the State establishments; and the perverted ambition of another class of men, who will either hope to aggrandize themselves by the confusions of their country, or will flatter themselves with fairer prospects of elevation from the subdivision of the empire into several partial confederacies than from its union under one government.

It is not, however, my design to dwell upon observations of this nature. I am well aware that it would be disingenuous to resolve indiscriminately the opposition of any set of men (merely because their situations might subject them to suspicion) into interested or ambitious views. Candor will oblige us to admit that even such men may be actuated by upright intentions; and it cannot be doubted that much of the opposition which has made its appearance, or may hereafter make its appearance, will spring from sources, blameless at least, if not respectable—the honest errors of minds led astray by preconceived jealousies and fears. So numerous indeed and so powerful are the causes which serve to give a false bias to the judgment, that we, upon many occasions, see wise and good men on the wrong as well as on the right side of questions of the first magnitude to society. This circumstance, if duly attended to, would furnish a lesson of moderation to those who are ever so much persuaded of their being in the right in any controversy. And a further reason for caution, in this respect, might be drawn from the reflection that we are not always sure that those who advocate the truth are influenced by purer principles than their antagonists. Ambition, avarice, personal animosity, party opposition, and many other motives not more laudable than these, are apt to operate as well upon those who support as those who oppose the right side of a question. Were there not even inducements to moderation, nothing could be more ill-judged than that intolerant spirit which has, at all times, characterized political parties. For in politics, as in religion, it is equally absurd to aim at making proselytes by fire and sword. Heresies in either can rarely be cured by persecution.

And yet, however just these sentiments will be allowed to be, we have already sufficient indications that it will happen in this as in all former cases of great national discussion. A torrent of angry and malignant passions will be let loose. To judge from the conduct of the opposite parties, we shall be led to conclude that they will mutually hope to evince the justness of their opinions, and to increase the number of their converts by the loudness of their declamations and the bitterness of their invectives. An enlightened zeal for the energy and efficiency of government will be stigmatized as the offspring of a temper fond of despotic power and hostile to the principles of liberty. An over-scrupulous jealousy of danger to the rights of the people, which is more commonly the fault of the head than of the heart, will be represented as mere presence and artifice, the stale bait for popularity at the expense of the public good. It will be forgotten, on the one hand, that jealousy is the usual concomitant of love, and that the noble enthusiasm of liberty is apt to be infected with a spirit of narrow and illiberal distrust. On the other hand, it will be equally forgotten that the vigor of government is essential to the security of liberty; that, in the contemplation of a sound and well-informed judgment, their interest can never be separated; and that a dangerous ambition more often lurks behind the specious mask of zeal for the rights of the people than under the forbidding appearance of zeal for the firmness and efficiency of government. History will teach us that the former has been found a much more certain road to the introduction of despotism than the latter, and that of those men who have overturned the liberties of republics, the greatest number have begun their career by paying an obsequious court to the people; commencing demagogues, and ending tyrants.

In the course of the preceding observations, I have had an eye, my fellow-citizens, to putting you upon your guard against all attempts, from whatever quarter, to influence your decision in a matter of the utmost moment to your welfare, by any impressions other than those which may result from the evidence of truth. You will, no doubt, at the same time, have collected from the general scope of them, that they proceed from a source not unfriendly to the new Constitution. Yes, my countrymen, I own to you that, after having given it an attentive consideration, I am clearly of opinion it is your interest to adopt it. I am convinced that this is the safest course for your liberty, your dignity, and your happiness. I affect not reserves which I do not feel. I will not amuse you with an appearance of deliberation when I have decided. I frankly acknowledge to you my convictions, and I will freely lay before you the reasons on which they are founded. The consciousness of good intentions disdains ambiguity. I shall not, however, multiply professions on this head. My motives must remain in the depository of my own breast. My arguments will be open to all, and may be judged of by all. They shall at least be offered in a spirit which will not disgrace the cause of truth.

I propose, in a series of papers, to discuss the following interesting particulars:—*The utility of the Union to your political prosperity—The insufficiency of the present Confederation to preserve that Union—The necessity of a government at least equally energetic with the one proposed, to the attainment of this object—The conformity of the proposed Constitution to the true principles of republican government—Its analogy to your own State constitution—*and lastly, *The additional security which its adoption will afford to the preservation of that species of government, to liberty, and to property.*

In the progress of this discussion I shall endeavor to give a satisfactory answer to all the objections which shall have made their appearance, that may seem to have any claim to your attention.

It may perhaps be thought superfluous to offer arguments to prove the utility of the Union, a point, no doubt, deeply engraved on the hearts of the great body of the people in every State, and one, which it may be imagined, has no adversaries. But the fact is, that we already hear it whispered in the private circles of those who oppose the new Constitution, that the thirteen States are of too great extent for any general system, and that we must of necessity resort to separate confederacies of distinct portions of the whole.[1] This doctrine will, in all probability, be gradually propagated, till it has votaries enough to countenance an open avowal of it. For nothing can be more evident, to those who are able to take an enlarged view of the subject, than the alternative of an adoption of the new Constitution or a dismemberment of the Union. It will therefore be of use to begin by examining the advantages of that Union, the certain evils, and the probable dangers, to which every State will be exposed from its dissolution. This shall accordingly constitute the subject of my next address.   Publius [Hamilton]

NUMBER 10

Among the numerous advantages promised by a well-constructed Union, none deserves to be more accurately developed than its tendency to break and control the violence of faction. The friend of popular governments never finds himself so much alarmed for their character and fate, as when he contemplates their propensity to this dangerous vice. He will not fail, therefore, to set a due value on any plan which, without violating the principles to which he is attached, provides a proper cure for it. The instability, injustice, and confusion introduced into the public councils, have, in truth, been the mortal diseases under which popular governments have everywhere perished; as they continue to be the favorite and fruitful topics from which the adversaries to liberty derive their most specious declamations. The valuable improvements made by the American constitutions on the popular models, both ancient and modern, cannot certainly be too much admired; but it would be an unwarrantable partiality, to contend that they have as effectually obviated the danger on this side, as was wished and expected. Complaints are everywhere heard from our most considerate and virtuous citizens, equally the friends of public and private faith, and of public and personal liberty, that our governments are too unstable, that the public good is disregarded in the conflicts of rival parties, and that measures are too often decided, not according to the rules of justice and the rights of the minor party, but by the superior force of an interested and overbearing majority. However anxiously we may wish that these complaints had no foundation, the evidence of known facts will not permit us to deny that they are in some degree true. It will be found, indeed, on a candid review of our situation, that some of the distresses under which we labor have been erroneously charged on the operation of our governments; but it will be found, at the same time, that other causes will not alone account for many of our heaviest misfortunes; and, particularly, for that prevailing and increasing distrust of public engagements, and alarm for private rights, which are echoed from one end of the continent to the other. These must be chiefly, if not wholly, effects of the unsteadiness and injustice with which a factious spirit has tainted our public administrations.

By a faction, I understand a number of citizens, whether amounting to a majority or minority of the whole, who are united and actuated by some common impulse of passion, or of interest, adverse to the rights of other citizens, or to the permanent and aggregate interests of the community.

There are two methods of curing the mischiefs of faction: the one, by removing its causes; the other, by controlling its effects.

There are again two methods of removing the causes of faction: the one, by destroying the liberty which is essential to its existence; the other, by giving to every citizen the same opinions, the same passions, and the same interests.

It could never be more truly said than of the first remedy, that it was worse than the disease. Liberty is to faction what air is to fire, an aliment without which it instantly expires. But it could not be less folly to abolish liberty, which is essential to political life, because it nourishes faction, than it would be to wish the annihilation of air, which is essential to animal life, because it imparts to fire its destructive agency.

The second expedient is as impracticable as the first would be unwise. As long as the reason of man continues fallible, and he is at liberty to exercise it, different opinions will be formed. As long as the connection subsists between his reason and his self-love, his opinions and his passions will have a reciprocal influence on each other; and the former will be objects to which the latter will attach themselves. The diversity in the faculties of men, from which the rights of property originate, is not less an insuperable obstacle to a uniformity of interests. The protection of these faculties is the first object of government. From the protection of different and unequal faculties of acquiring property, the possession of different degrees and kinds of property immediately results; and from the influence of these on the sentiments and views of the respective proprietors, ensues a division of the society into different interests and parties.

The latent causes of faction are thus sown in the nature of man; and we see them everywhere brought into different degrees of activity, according to the different circumstances of civil society. A zeal for different opinions concerning religion, concerning government, and many other points, as well of speculation as of practice; an attachment to different leaders ambitiously contending for pre-eminence and power; or to persons of other descriptions whose fortunes have been interesting to the human passions, have, in turn, divided mankind into parties, inflamed them with mutual animosity, and rendered them much more disposed to vex and oppress each other than to co-operate for their common good. So strong is this propensity of mankind to fall into mutual animosities, that where no substantial occasion presents itself, the most frivolous and fanciful distinctions have been sufficient to kindle their unfriendly passions and excite their most violent conflicts. But the most common and durable source of factions has been the various and unequal distribution of property. Those who hold and those who are without property have ever formed distinct interests in society. Those who are creditors, and those who are debtors, fall under a like discrimination. A landed interest, a manufacturing interest, a mercantile interest, a moneyed interest, with many lesser interests, grow up of necessity in civilized nations, and divide them into different classes, actuated by different sentiments and views. The regulation of these various and interfering interests forms the principal task of modern legislation, and involves the spirit of party and faction in the necessary and ordinary operations of the government.

No man is allowed to be a judge in his own cause, because his interest would certainly bias his judgment, and, not improbably, corrupt his integrity. With equal, nay with greater reason, a body of men are unfit to be both judges and parties at the same time; yet what are many of the most important acts of legislation, but so many judicial determinations, not indeed concerning the rights of single persons, but concerning the rights of large bodies of citizens? And what are the different classes of legislators but advocates and parties to the causes which they determine? Is a law proposed concerning private debts? It is a question to which the creditors are parties on one side and the debtors on the other. Justice ought to hold the balance between them. Yet the parties are, and must be, themselves the judges; and the most numerous party, or, in other words, the most powerful faction must be expected to prevail. Shall domestic manufactures be encouraged, and in what degree, by restrictions on foreign manufactures? are questions which would be differently decided by the landed and the manufacturing classes, and probably by neither with a sole regard to justice and the public good. The apportionment of taxes on the various descriptions of property is an act which seems to require the most exact impartiality; yet there is, perhaps, no legislative act in which greater opportunity and temptation are given to a predominant party to trample on the rules of justice. Every shilling with which they overburden the inferior number, is a shilling saved to their own pockets.

It is in vain to say that enlightened statesmen will be able to adjust these clashing interests, and render them all subservient to the public good. Enlightened statesmen will not always be at the helm. Nor, in many cases, can such an adjustment be made at all without taking into view indirect and remote considerations, which will rarely prevail over the immediate interest which one party may find in disregarding the rights of another or the good of the whole.

The inference to which we are brought is, that the *causes* of faction cannot be removed, and that relief is only to be sought in the means of controlling its *effects*.

If a faction consists of less than a majority, relief is supplied by the republican principle, which enables the majority to defeat its sinister views by regular vote. It may clog the administration, it may convulse the society; but it will be unable to execute and mask its violence under the forms of the Constitution. When a majority is included in a faction, the form of popular government, on the other hand, enables it to sacrifice to its ruling passion or interest both the public good and the rights of other citizens. To secure the public good and private rights against the danger of such a faction, and at the same time to preserve the spirit and the form of popular government, is then the great object to which our inquiries are directed. Let me add that it is the great desideratum by which this form of government can be rescued from the opprobrium under which it has so long labored, and be recommended to the esteem and adoption of mankind.

By what means is this object attainable? Evidently by one of two only. Either the existence of the same passion or interest in a majority at the same time must be prevented, or the majority, having such coexistent passion or interest, must be rendered, by their number and local situation, unable to concert and carry into effect schemes of oppression. If the impulse and the opportunity be suffered to coincide, we well know that neither moral nor religious motives can be relied on as an adequate control. They are not found to be such on the injustice and violence of individuals, and lose their efficacy in proportion to the number combined together, that is, in proportion as their efficacy becomes needful.

From this view of the subject it may be concluded that a pure democracy, by which I mean a society consisting of a small number of citizens, who assemble and administer the government in person, can admit of no cure for the mischiefs of faction. A common passion or interest will, in almost every case, be felt by a majority of the whole: a communication and concert result from the form of government itself; and there is nothing to check the inducements to sacrifice the weaker party or an obnoxious individual. Hence it is that such democracies have ever been spectacles of turbulence and contention; have ever been found incompatible with personal security or the rights of property; and have in general been as short in their lives as they have been violent in their deaths. Theoretic politicians, who have patronized this species of government, have erroneously supposed that by reducing mankind to a perfect equality in their political rights, they would, at the same time, be perfectly equalized and assimilated in their possessions, their opinions, and their passions.

A republic, by which I mean a government in which the scheme of representation takes place, opens a different prospect, and promises the cure for which we are seeking. Let us examine the points in which it varies from pure democracy, and we shall comprehend both the nature of the cure and the efficacy which it must derive from the Union.

The two great points of difference between a democracy and a republic are: first, the delegation of the government, in the latter, to a small number of citizens elected by the rest; secondly, the greater number of citizens, and greater sphere of country, over which the latter may be extended.

The effect of the first difference is, on the one hand, to refine and enlarge the public views, by passing them through the medium of a chosen body of citizens, whose wisdom may best discern the true interest of their country, and whose patriotism and love of justice will be least likely to sacrifice it to temporary or partial considerations. Under such a regulation, it may well happen that the public voice, pronounced by the representatives of the people, will be more consonant to the public good than if pronounced by the people themselves, convened for the purpose. On the other hand, the effect may be inverted. Men of factious tempers, of local prejudices, or of sinister designs, may, by intrigue, by corruption, or by other means, first obtain the suffrages, and then betray the interests, of the people. The question resulting is, whether small or extensive republics are more favorable to the election of proper guardians of the public weal; and it is clearly decided in favor of the latter by two obvious considerations:

In the first place, it is to be remarked that, however small the republic may be, the representatives must be raised to a certain number, in order to guard against the cabals of a few; and that, however large it may be, they must be limited to a certain number, in order to guard against the confusion of a multitude. Hence, the number of representatives in the two cases not being in proportion to that of the two constituents, and being proportionally greater in the small republic, it follows that, if the proportion of fit characters be not less in the large than in the small republic, the former will present a greater option, and consequently a greater probability of a fit choice.

In the next place, as each representative will be chosen by a greater number of citizens in the large than in the small republic, it will be more difficult for unworthy candidates to practice with success the vicious arts by which elections are too often carried; and the suffrages of the people being more free, will be more likely to centre in men who possess the most attractive merit and the most diffusive and established characters.

It must be confessed that in this, as in most other cases, there is a mean, on both sides of which inconveniences will be found to lie. By enlarging too much the number of electors, you render the representative too little acquainted with all their local circumstances and lesser interests; as by reducing it too much, you render him unduly attached to these, and too little fit to comprehend and pursue great and national objects. The federal Constitution forms a happy combination in this respect; the great and aggregate interests being referred to the national, the local and particular to the State legislatures.

The other point of difference is, the greater number of citizens and extent of territory which may be brought within the compass of republican than of democratic government; and it is this circumstance principally which renders factious combinations less to be dreaded in the former than in the latter. The smaller the society, the fewer probably will be the distinct parties and interests composing it; the fewer the distinct parties and interests, the more frequently will a majority be found of the same party; and the smaller the number of individuals composing a majority, and the smaller the compass within which they are placed, the more easily will they concert and execute their plans of oppression. Extend the sphere and you take in a greater variety of parties and interests; you make it less probable that a majority of the whole will have a common motive to invade the rights of other citizens; or if such a common motive exists, it will be more difficult for all who feel it to discover their own strength, and to act in unison with each other. Besides other impediments, it may be remarked that, where there is a consciousness of unjust or dishonorable purposes, communication is always checked by distrust in proportion to the number whose concurrence is necessary.

Hence, it clearly appears, that the same advantage which a republic has over a democracy, in controlling the effects of faction, is enjoyed by a large over a small republic,—is enjoyed by the Union over the States composing it. Does the advantage consist in the substitution of representatives whose enlightened views and virtuous sentiments render them superior to local prejudices and to schemes of injustice? It will not be denied that the representation of the Union will be most likely to possess these requisite endowments. Does it consist in the greater security afforded by a greater variety of parties, against the event of any one party being able to outnumber and oppress the rest? In an equal degree does the increased variety of parties comprised within the Union, increase this security. Does it, in fine, consist in the greater obstacles opposed to the concert and accomplishment of the secret wishes of an unjust and interested majority? Here, again, the extent of the Union gives it the most palpable advantage.

The influence of factious leaders may kindle a flame within their particular States, but will be unable to spread a general conflagration through the other States. A religious sect may degenerate into a political faction in a part of the Confederacy; but the variety of sects dispersed over the entire face of it must secure the national councils against any danger from that source. A rage for paper money, for an abolition of debts, for an equal division of property, or for any other improper or wicked project, will be less apt to pervade the whole body of the Union than a particular member of it; in the same proportion as such a malady is more likely to taint a particular county or district, than an entire State.

In the extent and proper structure of the Union, therefore, we behold a republican remedy for the diseases most incident to republican government. And according to the degree of pleasure and pride we feel in being republicans, ought to be our zeal in cherishing the spirit and supporting the character of Federalists.   Publius [Madison]

NUMBER 15

To the People of the State of New York:

In the course of the preceding papers, I have endeavored, my fellow-citizens, to place before you, in a clear and convincing light, the importance of Union to your political safety and happiness. I have unfolded to you a complication of dangers to which you would be exposed, should you permit that sacred knot which binds the people of America together to be severed or dissolved by ambition or by avarice, by jealousy or by misrepresentation. In the sequel of the inquiry through which I propose to accompany you, the truths intended to be inculcated will receive further confirmation from facts and arguments hitherto unnoticed. If the road over which you will still have to pass should in some places appear to you tedious or irksome, you will recollect that you are in quest of information on a subject the most momentous which can engage the attention of a free people, that the field through which you have to travel is in itself spacious, and that the difficulties of the journey have been unnecessarily increased by the mazes with which sophistry has beset the way. It will be my aim to remove the obstacles from your progress in as compendious a manner as it can be done, without sacrificing utility to despatch.

In pursuance of the plan which I have laid down for the discussion of the subject, the point next in order to be examined is the "insufficiency of the present Confederation to the preservation of the Union." It may perhaps be asked what need there is of reasoning or proof to illustrate a position which is not either controverted or doubted, to which the understandings and feelings of all classes of men assent, and which in substance is admitted by the opponents as well as by the friends of the new Constitution. It must in truth be acknowledged that, however these may differ in other respects, they in general appear to harmonize in this sentiment, at least, that there are material imperfections in our national system, and that something is necessary to be done to rescue us from impending anarchy. The facts that support this opinion are no longer objects of speculation. They have forced themselves upon the sensibility of the people at large, and have at length extorted from those, whose mistaken policy has had the principal share in precipitating the extremity at which we are arrived, a reluctant confession of the reality of those defects in the scheme of our federal government, which have been long pointed out and regretted by the intelligent friends of the Union.

We may indeed with propriety be said to have reached almost the last stage of national humiliation. There is scarcely any thing that can wound the pride or degrade the character of an independent nation which we do not experience. Are there engagements to the performance of which we are held by every tie respectable among men? These are the subjects of constant and unblushing violation. Do we owe debts to foreigners and to our own citizens contracted in a time of imminent peril for the preservation of our political existence? These remain without any proper or satisfactory provision for their discharge. Have we valuable territories and important posts in the possession of a foreign power which, by express stipulations, ought long since to have been surrendered? These are still retained, to the prejudice of our interests, not less than of our rights. Are we in a condition to resent or to repel the aggression? We have neither troops, nor treasury, nor government.[2] Are we even in a condition to remonstrate with dignity? The just imputations on our own faith, in respect to the same treaty, ought first to be removed. Are we entitled by nature and compact to a free participation in the navigation of the Mississippi? Spain excludes us from it. Is public credit an indispensable resource in time of public danger? We seem to have abandoned its cause as desperate and irretrievable. Is commerce of importance to national wealth? Ours is at the lowest point of declension. Is respectability in the eyes of foreign powers a safeguard against foreign encroachments? The imbecility of our government even forbids them to treat with us. Our ambassadors abroad are the mere pageants of mimic sovereignty. Is a violent and unnatural decrease in the value of land a symptom of national distress? The price of improved land in most parts of the country is much lower than can be accounted for by the quantity of waste land at market, and can only be fully explained by that want of private and public confidence, which are so alarmingly prevalent among all ranks, and which have a direct tendency to depreciate property of every kind. Is private credit the friend and patron of industry? That most useful kind which relates to borrowing and lending is reduced within the narrowest limits, and this still more from an opinion of insecurity than from the scarcity of money. To shorten an enumeration of particulars which can afford neither pleasure nor instruction, it may in general be demanded, what indication is there of national disorder, poverty, and insignificance that could befall a community so peculiarly blessed with natural advantages as we are, which does not form a part of the dark catalogue of our public misfortunes.

This is the melancholy situation to which we have been brought by those very maxims and councils which would now deter us from adopting the proposed Constitution; and which, not content with having conducted us to the brink of a precipice, seem resolved to plunge us into the abyss that awaits us below. Here, my countrymen, impelled by every motive that ought to influence an enlightened people, let us make a firm stand for our safety, our tranquillity, our dignity, our reputation. Let us at last break the fatal charm which has too long seduced us from the paths of felicity and prosperity.

It is true, as has been before observed, that facts, too stubborn to be resisted, have produced a species of general assent to the abstract proposition that there exist material defects in our national system; but the usefulness of the concession, on the part of the old adversaries of federal measures, is destroyed by a strenuous opposition to a remedy, upon the only principles that can give it a chance of success. While they admit that the government of the United States is destitute of energy, they contend against conferring upon it those powers which are requisite to supply that energy. They seem still to aim at things repugnant and irreconcilable; at an augmentation of federal authority, without a diminution of State authority; at sovereignty in the Union, and complete independence in the members. They still, in fine, seem to cherish with blind devotion the political monster of an *imperium in imperio*. This renders a full display of the principal defects of the Confederation necessary, in order to show that the evils we experience do not proceed from minute or partial imperfections, but from fundamental errors in the structure of the building, which cannot be amended otherwise than by an alteration in the first principles and main pillars of the fabric.

The great and radical vice in the construction of the existing Confederation is in *the principle* of Legislation for States or Governments, in their Corporate or Collective Capacities, and as contradistinguished from the Individuals of which they consist. Though this principle does not run through all the powers delegated to the Union, yet it pervades and governs those on which the efficacy of the rest depends. Except as to the rule of apportionment, the United States has an indefinite discretion to make requisitions for men and money; but they have no authority to raise either, by regulations extending to the individual citizens of America. The consequence of this is, that though in theory their resolutions concerning those objects are laws, constitutionally binding on the members of the Union, yet in practice they are mere recommendations which the States observe or disregard at their option.

It is a singular instance of the capriciousness of the human mind, that after all the admonitions we have had from experience on this head, there should still be found men who object to the new Constitution, for deviating from a principle which has been found the bane of the old, and which is in itself evidently incompatible with the idea of Government; a principle, in short, which, if it is to be executed at all, must substitute the violent and sanguinary agency of the sword to the mild influence of the magistracy.

There is nothing absurd or impracticable in the idea of a league or alliance between independent nations for certain defined purposes precisely stated in a treaty regulating all the details of time, place, circumstance, and quantity; leaving nothing to future discretion; and depending for its execution on the good faith of the parties. Compacts of this kind exist among all civilized nations, subject to the usual vicissitudes of peace and war, of observance and non-observance, as the interests or passions of the contracting powers dictate. In the early part of the present century there was an epidemical rage in Europe for this species of compacts, from which the politicians of the times fondly hoped for benefits which were never realized. With a view to establishing the equilibrium of power and the peace of that part of the world, all the resources of negotiations were exhausted, and triple and quadruple alliances were formed; but they were scarcely formed before they were broken, giving an instructive but afflicting lesson to mankind, how little dependence is to be placed on treaties which have no other sanction than the obligations of good faith, and which oppose general considerations of peace and justice to the impulse of any immediate interest or passion.

If the particular States in this country are disposed to stand in a similar relation to each other, and to drop the project of a general Discretionary Superintendence, the scheme would indeed be pernicious, and would entail upon us all the mischiefs which have been enumerated under the first head; but it would have the merit of being, at least, consistent and practicable. Abandoning all views towards a confederate government, this would bring us to a simple alliance offensive and defensive; and would place us in a situation to be alternate friends and enemies of each other, as our mutual jealousies and rivalships, nourished by the intrigues of foreign nations, should prescribe to us.

But if we are unwilling to be placed in this perilous situation; if we still will adhere to the design of a national government, or, which is the same thing, of a superintending power, under the direction of a common council, we must resolve to incorporate into our plan those ingredients which may be considered as forming the characteristic difference between a league and a government; we must extend the authority of the Union to the persons of the citizens,—the only proper objects of government.

Government implies the power of making laws. It is essential to the idea of a law, that it be attended with a sanction; or, in other words, a penalty or punishment for disobedience. If there be no penalty annexed to disobedience, the resolutions or commands which pretend to be laws will, in fact, amount to nothing more than advice or recommendation. This penalty, whatever it may be, can only be inflicted in two ways: by the agency of the courts and ministers of justice, or by military force; by the Coercion of the magistracy, or by the Coercion of arms. The first kind can evidently apply only to men; the last kind must of necessity, be employed against bodies politic, or communities, or States. It is evident that there is no process of a court by which the observance of the laws can, in the last resort, be enforced. Sentences may be denounced against them for violations of their duty;

but these sentences can only be carried into execution by the sword. In an association where the general authority is confined to the collective bodies of the communities that compose it, every breach of the laws must involve a state of war; and military execution must become the only instrument of civil obedience. Such a state of things can certainly not deserve the name of government, nor would any prudent man choose to commit his happiness to it.

There was a time when we were told that breaches, by the States, of the regulations of the federal authority were not to be expected; that a sense of common interest would preside over the conduct of the respective members, and would beget a full compliance with all the constitutional requisitions of the Union. This language, at the present day, would appear as wild as a great part of what we now hear from the same quarter will be thought, when we shall have received further lessons from that best oracle of wisdom, experience. It at all times betrayed an ignorance of the true springs by which human conduct is actuated, and belied the original inducements to the establishment of civil power. Why has government been instituted at all? Because the passions of men will not conform to the dictates of reason and justice, without constraint. Has it been found that bodies of men act with more rectitude or greater disinterestedness than individuals? The contrary of this has been inferred by all accurate observers of the conduct of mankind; and the inference is founded upon obvious reasons. Regard to reputation has a less active influence, when the infamy of a bad action is to be divided among a number, than when it is to fall singly upon one. A spirit of faction, which is apt to mingle its poison in the deliberations of all bodies of men, will often hurry the persons of whom they are composed into improprieties and excesses, for which they would blush in a private capacity.

In addition to all this, there is, in the nature of sovereign power, an impatience of control, that disposes those who are invested with the exercise of it, to look with an evil eye upon all external attempts to restrain or direct its operations. From this spirit it happens, that in every political association which is formed upon the principle of uniting in a common interest a number of lesser sovereignties, there will be found a kind of eccentric tendency in the subordinate or inferior orbs, by the operation of which there will be a perpetual effort in each to fly off from the common centre. This tendency is not difficult to be accounted for. It has its origin in the love of power. Power controlled or abridged is almost always the rival and enemy of that power by which it is controlled or abridged. This simple proposition will teach us, how little reason there is to expect, that the persons intrusted with the administration of the affairs of the particular members of a confederacy will at all times be ready, with perfect good-humor, and an unbiased regard to the public weal, to execute the resolutions or decrees of the general authority. The reverse of this results from the constitution of human nature.

If, therefore, the measures of the Confederacy cannot be executed without the intervention of the particular administrations, there will be little prospect of their being executed at all. The rulers of the respective members, whether they have a constitutional right to do it or not, will undertake to judge of the propriety of the measures themselves. They will consider the conformity of the thing proposed or required to their immediate interests or aims; the momentary conveniences or inconveniences that would attend its adoption. All this will be done; and in a spirit of interested and suspicious scrutiny, without that knowledge of national circumstances and reasons of state, which is essential to a right judgment, and with that strong predilection in favor of local objects, which can hardly fail to mislead the decision. The same process must be repeated in every member of which the body is constituted; and the execution of the plans, framed by the councils of the whole, will always fluctuate on the discretion of the ill-informed and prejudiced opinion of every part. Those who have been conversant in the proceedings of popular assemblies; who have seen how difficult it often is, where there is no exterior pressure of circumstances, to bring them to harmonious resolutions on important points, will readily conceive how impossible it must be to induce a number of such assemblies, deliberating at a distance from each other, at different times, and under different impressions, long to cooperate in the same views and pursuits.

In our case, the concurrence of thirteen distinct sovereign wills is requisite, under the Confederation, to the complete execution of every important measure that proceeds from the Union. It has happened as was to have been foreseen. The measures of the Union have not been executed; the delinquencies of the States have, step by step, matured themselves to an extreme, which has, at length, arrested all the wheels of the national government, and brought them to an awful stand. Congress at this time scarcely possess the means of keeping up the forms of administration, till the States can have time to agree upon a more substantial substitute for the present shadow of a federal government. Things did not come to this desperate extremity at once. The causes which have been specified produced at first only unequal and disproportionate degrees of compliance with the requisitions of the Union. The greater deficiencies of some States furnished the pretext of example and the temptation of interest to the complying, or to the least delinquent States. Why should we do more in proportion than those who are embarked with us in the same political voyage? Why should we consent to bear more than our proper share of the common burden? These were suggestions which human selfishness could not withstand, and which even speculative men, who looked forward to remote consequences, could not, without hesitation, combat. Each State, yielding to the persuasive voice of immediate interest or convenience, has successively withdrawn its support, till the frail and tottering edifice seems ready to fall upon our heads, and to crush us beneath its ruins.   Publius [Hamilton]

NUMBER 39

The last paper having concluded the observations which were meant to introduce a candid survey of the plan of government reported by the convention, we now proceed to the execution of that part of our undertaking.

The first question that offers itself is, whether the general form and aspect of the government be strictly republican. It is evident that no other form would be reconcilable with the genius of the people of America; with the fundamental principles of the Revolution; or with that honorable determination which animates every votary of freedom, to rest all our political experiments on the capacity of mankind for self-government. If the plan of the convention, therefore, be found to depart from the republican character, its advocates must abandon it as no longer defensible.

What, then, are the distinctive characters of the republican form? Were an answer to this question to be sought, not by recurring to principles, but in the application of the term by political writers, to the constitutions of different States, no satisfactory one would ever be found. Holland, in which no particle of the supreme authority is derived from the people, has passed almost universally under the denomination of a republic. The same title has been bestowed on Venice, where absolute power over the great body of the people is exercised, in the most absolute manner, by a small body of hereditary nobles. Poland, which is a mixture of aristocracy and of monarchy in their worst forms, has been dignified with the same appellation. The government of England, which has one republican branch only, combined with an hereditary aristocracy and monarchy, has, with equal impropriety, been frequently placed on the list of republics. These examples, which are nearly as dissimilar to each other as to a genuine republic, show the extreme inaccuracy with which the term has been used in political disquisitions.

If we resort for a criterion to the different principles on which different forms of government are established, we may define a republic to be, or at least may bestow that name on, a government which derives all its powers directly or indirectly from the great body of the people, and is administered by persons holding their offices during pleasure, for a limited period, or during good behavior. It is *essential* to such a government that it be derived from the great body of the society, not from an inconsiderable proportion, or a favored class of it; otherwise a handful of tyrannical nobles, exercising their oppressions by a delegation of their powers, might aspire to the rank of republicans, and claim for their government the honorable title of republic. It is *sufficient* for such a government that the persons administering it be appointed, either directly or indirectly, by the people; and that they hold their appointments by either of the tenures just specified; otherwise every government in the United States, as well as every other popular government that has been or can be well organized or well executed, would be degraded from the republican character. According to the constitution of every State in the Union, some or other of the officers of government are appointed indirectly only by the people. According to most of them, the chief magistrate himself is so appointed. And according to one, this mode of appointment is extended to one of the coordinate branches of the legislature. According to all the constitutions, also, the tenure of the highest offices is extended to a definite period, and in many instances, both within the legislative and executive departments, to a period of years. According to the provisions of most of the constitutions, again, as well as according to the most respectable and received opinions on the subject, the members of the judiciary department are to retain their offices by the firm tenure of good behavior.

On comparing the Constitution planned by the convention with the standard here fixed, we perceive at once that it is, in the most rigid sense, conformable to it. The House of Representatives, like that of one branch at least of all the State legislatures, is elected immediately by the great body of the people. The Senate, like the present Congress, and the Senate of Maryland, derives its appointment indirectly from the people. The President is indirectly derived from the choice of the people, according to the example in most of the States. Even the judges with all other officers of the Union, will, as in the several States, be the choice, though a remote choice, of the people themselves. The duration of the appointments is equally conformable to the republican standard, and to the model of State constitutions. The House of Representatives is periodically elective, as in all the States; and for the period of two years, as in the State of South Carolina. The Senate is elective, for the period of six years; which is but one year more than the period of the Senate of Maryland, and but two more than that of the Senates of New York and Virginia. The President is to continue in office for the period of four years; as in New York and Delaware the chief magistrate is elected for three years, and in South Carolina for two years. In the other States the election is annual. In several of the States, however, no constitutional provision is made for the impeachment of the chief magistrate. And in Delaware and Virginia he is not impeachable till out of office. The President of the United States is impeachable at any time during his continuance in office. The tenure by which the judges are to hold their places, is, as it unquestionably ought to be, that of good behavior. The tenure of the ministerial offices generally, will be a subject of legal regulation, conformably to the reason of the case and the example of the State constitutions.

Could any further proof be required of the republican complexion of this system, the most decisive one might be found in its absolute prohibition of titles of nobility, both under the federal and the State governments; and in its express guaranty of the republican form to each of the latter.

"But it was not sufficient," say the adversaries of the proposed Constitution, "for the convention to adhere to the republican form. They ought, with equal care, to have preserved the *federal* form, which regards the Union as a *Confederacy* of sovereign states; instead of which, they have framed a *national* government, which regards the Union as a *consolidation* of the States." And it is asked by what authority this bold and radical innovation was undertaken? The handle which has been made of this objection requires that it should be examined with some precision.

Without inquiring into the accuracy of the distinction on which the objection is founded, it will be necessary to a just estimate of its force, first, to ascertain the real character of the government in question; secondly, to inquire how far the convention were authorized to propose such a government; and thirdly, how far the duty they owed to their country could supply any defect of regular authority.

First.—In order to ascertain the real character of the government, it may be considered in relation to the foundation on which it is to be established; to the sources from which its ordinary powers are to be drawn; to the operation of those powers; to the extent of them; and to the authority by which future changes in the government are to be introduced.

On examining the first relation, it appears, on one hand, that the Constitution is to be founded on the assent and ratification of the people of America, given by deputies elected for the special purpose; but, on the other, that this assent and ratification is to be given by the people, not as individuals composing one entire nation, but as composing the distinct and independent States to which they respectively belong. It is to be the assent and ratification of the several States, derived from the supreme authority in each State,—the authority of the people themselves. The act, therefore, establishing the Constitution, will not be a *national*, but a *federal* act.

That it will be a federal and not a national act, as these terms are understood by the objectors; the act of the people, as forming so many independent States, not as forming one aggregate nation, is obvious from this single consideration, that it is to result neither from the decision of a *majority* of the people of the Union, nor from that of a *majority* of the States. It must result from the *unanimous* assent of the several States that are parties to it, differing no otherwise from their ordinary assent than in its being expressed, not by the legislative authority, but by that of the people themselves. Were the people regarded in this transaction as forming one nation, the will of the majority of the whole people of the United States would bind the minority, in the same manner as the majority in each State must bind the minority; and the will of the majority must be determined either by a comparison of the individual votes, or by considering the will of the majority of the States as evidence of the will of a majority of the people of the United States. Neither of these rules has been adopted. Each State, in ratifying the Constitution, is considered as a sovereign body, independent of all others, and only to be bound by its own voluntary act. In this relation, then, the new Constitution will, if established, be a *federal*, and not a *national* constitution.

The next relation is, to the sources from which the ordinary powers of government are to be derived. The House of Representatives will derive its powers from the people of America; and the people will be represented in the same proportion, and on the same principle, as they are in the legislature of a particular State. So far the government is *national*, not *federal*. The Senate, on the other hand, will derive its powers from the States, as political and coequal societies; and these will be represented on the principle of equality in the Senate, as they now are in the existing Congress. So far the government is *federal,* not *national.* The executive power will be derived from a very compound source. The immediate election of the President is to be made by the States in their political characters. The votes allotted to them are in a compound ratio, which considers them partly as distinct and coequal societies, partly as unequal members of the same society. The eventual election, again, is to be made by that branch of the legislature which consists of the national representatives; but in this particular act they are to be thrown into the form of individual delegations, from so many distinct and coequal bodies politic. From this aspect of the government, it appears to be of a mixed character, presenting at least as many *federal* as *national* features.

The difference between a federal and national government, as it relates to the *operation of the government,* is supposed to consist in this, that in the former the powers operate on the political bodies composing the Confederacy, in their political capacities; in the latter, on the individual citizens composing the nation, in their individual capacities. On trying the Constitution by this criterion, it falls under the *national,* not the *federal* character; though perhaps not so completely as has been understood. In several cases, and particularly in the trial of controversies to which States may be parties, they must be viewed and proceeded against in their collective and political capacities only. So far the national countenance of the government on this side seems to be disfigured by a few federal features. But this blemish is perhaps unavoidable in any plan; and the operation of the government on the people, in their individual capacities, in its ordinary and most essential proceedings, may, on the whole, designate it, in this relation, a *national* government.

But if the government be national with regard to the *operation* of its powers, it changes its aspect again when we contemplate it in relation to the extent of its powers. The idea of a national government involves in it, not only an authority over the individual citizens, but an indefinite supremacy over all persons and things, so far as they are objects of lawful government. Among a people consolidated into one nation, this supremacy is completely vested in the national legislature. Among communities united for particular purposes, it is vested partly in the general and partly in the municipal legislatures. In the former case, all local authorities are subordinate to the supreme; and may be controlled, directed, or abolished by it at pleasure. In the latter, the local or municipal authorities form distinct and independent portions of the supremacy, no more subject, within their respective spheres, to the general authority, than the general authority is subject to them, within its own sphere. In this relation, then, the proposed government cannot be deemed a *national* one; since its jurisdiction extends to certain enumerated objects only, and leaves to the several States a residuary and inviolable sovereignty over all other objects. It is true that in controversies relating to the boundary between the two jurisdictions, the tribunal which is ultimately to decide, is to be established under the general government. But this does not change the principle of the case. The decision is to be impartially made, according to the rules of the Constitution; and all the usual and most effectual precautions are taken to secure this impartiality. Some such tribunal is clearly essential to prevent an appeal to the sword and a dissolution of the compact; and that it ought to be established under the general rather than under the local governments, or, to speak more properly, that it could be safely established under the first alone, is a position not likely to be combated.

If we try the Constitution by its last relation to the authority by which amendments are to be made, we find it neither wholly *national* nor wholly *federal.* Were it wholly national, the supreme and ultimate authority would reside in the *majority* of the people of the Union; and this authority would be competent at all times, like that of a majority of every national society, to alter or abolish its established government. Were it wholly federal, on the other hand, the concurrence of each State in the Union would be essential to every alteration that would be binding on all. The mode provided by the plan of the convention is not founded on either of these principles. In requiring more than a majority, and particularly in computing the proportion by *States*, not by citizens, it departs from the *national* and advances towards the *federal* character; in rendering the concurrence of less than the whole number of States sufficient, it loses again the *federal* and partakes of the *national* character

The proposed Constitution, therefore, is, in strictness, neither a national nor a federal Constitution, but a composition of both. In its foundation it is federal, not national; in the sources from which the ordinary powers of the government are drawn, it is partly federal and partly national; in the operation of these powers, it is national, not federal; in the extent of them, again, it is federal, not national; and, finally, in the authoritative mode of introducing amendments, it is neither wholly federal nor wholly national.

Publius [Madison]

NUMBER 47

Having reviewed the general form of the proposed government and the general mass of power allotted to it, I proceed to examine the particular structure of this government, and the distribution of this mass of power among its constituent parts.

One of the principal objections inculcated by the more respectable adversaries to the Constitution, is its supposed violation of the political maxim, that the legislative, executive, and judiciary departments ought to be separate and distinct. In the structure of the federal government, no regard, it is said, seems to have been paid to this essential precaution in favor of liberty. The several departments of power are distributed and blended in such a manner as at once to destroy all symmetry and beauty of form, and to expose some of the essential parts of the edifice to the danger of being crushed by the disproportionate weight of other parts.

No political truth is certainly of greater intrinsic value, or is stamped with the authority of more enlightened patrons of liberty, than that on which the objection is founded. The accumulation of all powers, legislative, executive, and judiciary, in the same hands, whether of one, a few, or many, and whether hereditary, self-appointed, or elective, may justly be pronounced the very definition of tyranny. Were the federal Constitution, therefore, really chargeable with the accumulation of power, or with a mixture of powers, having a dangerous tendency to such an accumulation, no further arguments would be necessary to inspire a universal reprobation of the system. I persuade myself, however, that it will be made apparent to every one, that the charge cannot be supported, and that the maxim on which it relies has been totally misconceived and misapplied. In order to form correct ideas on this important subject, it will be proper to investigate the sense in which the preservation of liberty requires that the three great departments of power should be separate and distinct.

The oracle who is always consulted and cited on this subject is the celebrated Montesquieu. If he be not the author of this invaluable precept in the science of politics, he has the merit at least of displaying and recommending it most effectually to the attention of mankind. Let us endeavor, in the first place, to ascertain his meaning on this point.

The British Constitution was to Montesquieu what Homer has been to the didactic writers on epic poetry. As the latter have considered the work of the immortal bard as the perfect model from which the principles and rules of the epic art were to be drawn, and by which all similar works were to be judged, so this great political critic appears to have viewed the Constitution of England as the standard, or to use his own expression, as the mirror of political liberty; and to have delivered, in the form of elementary truths, the several characteristic principles of that particular system. That we may be sure, then, not to mistake his meaning in this case, let us recur to the source from which the maxim was drawn.

On the slightest view of the British Constitution, we must perceive that the legislative, executive, and judiciary departments are by no means totally separate and distinct from each other. The executive magistrate forms an integral part of the legislative authority. He alone has the prerogative of making treaties with foreign sovereigns, which, when made, have, under certain limitations, the force of legislative acts. All the members of the judiciary department are appointed by him, can be removed by him on the address of the two Houses of Parliament, and form, when he pleases to consult them, one of his constitutional councils. One branch of the legislative department forms also a great constitutional council to the executive chief, as, on another hand, it is the sole depositary of judicial power in cases of impeachment, and is invested with the supreme appellate jurisdiction in all other cases. The judges, again, are so far connected with the legislative department as often to attend and participate in its deliberations, though not admitted to a legislative vote.

From these facts, by which Montesquieu was guided, it may clearly be inferred that, in saying "There can be no liberty where the legislative and executive powers are united in the same person, or body of magistrates," or, "if the power of judging be not separated from the legislative and executive powers," he did not mean that these departments ought to have no *partial agency* in, or no *control* over, the acts of each other. His meaning, as his own words import, and still more conclusively as illustrated by the example in his eye, can amount to no more than this, that where the *whole* power of one department is exercised by the same hands which possess the *whole* power of another department, the fundamental principles of a free constitution are subverted. This would have been the case in the constitution examined by him, if the king, who is the sole executive magistrate, had possessed also the complete legislative power, or the supreme administration of justice; or if the entire legislative body had possessed the supreme judiciary, or the supreme executive authority. This, however is not among the vices of that constitution. The magistrate in whom the whole executive power resides cannot of himself make a law, though he can put a negative on every law; nor administer justice in person, though he has the appointment of those who do administer it. The judges can exercise no executive prerogative, though they are shoots from the executive stock; nor any legislative function, though they may be advised with by the legislative councils. The entire legislature can perform no judiciary act, though by the joint act of two of its branches the judges may be removed from their offices, and though one of its branches is possessed of the judicial power in the last resort. The entire legislature, again, can exercise no executive prerogative, though one of its branches constitutes the supreme executive magistracy, and another, on the impeachment of a third, can try and condemn all the subordinate officers in the executive department.

The reasons on which Montesquieu grounds his maxim are a further demonstration of his meaning. "When the legislative and executive powers are united in the same person or body," says he, "there can be no liberty, because apprehensions may arise lest *the same* monarch or senate should *enact* tyrannical laws to *execute* them in a tyrannical manner." Again: "Were the power of judging joined with the legislative, the life and liberty of the subject would be exposed to arbitrary control, for *the judge* would then be *the legislator*.

Were it joined to the executive power, *the judge* might behave with all the violence of *an oppressor*." Some of these reasons are more fully explained in other passages; but briefly stated as they are here, they sufficiently establish the meaning which we have put on this celebrated maxim of this celebrated author.

If we look into the constitutions of the several States, we find that, notwithstanding the emphatical and, in some instances, the unqualified terms in which this axiom has been laid down, there is not a single instance in which the several departments of power have been kept absolutely separate and distinct. New Hampshire, whose constitution was the last formed, seems to have been fully aware of the impossibility and inexpediency of avoiding any mixture whatever of these departments, and has qualified the doctrine by declaring "that the legislative, executive, and judiciary powers ought to be kept as separate from, and independent of, each other *as the nature of a free government will admit; or as is consistent with that chain of connection that binds the whole fabric of the constitution in one indissoluble bond of unity and amity.*" Her constitution accordingly mixes these departments in several respects. The Senate, which is a branch of the legislative department, is also a judicial tribunal for the trial of impeachments. The President, who is the head of the executive department, is the presiding member also of the Senate; and, besides an equal vote in all cases, has a casting vote in case of a tie. The executive head is himself eventually elective every year by the legislative department, and his council is every year chosen by and from the members of the same department. Several of the officers of state are also appointed by the legislature. And the members of the judiciary department are appointed by the executive department.

The constitution of Massachusetts has observed a sufficient though less pointed caution, in expressing this fundamental article of liberty. It declares "that the legislative departments shall never exercise the executive and judicial powers, or either of them; the executive shall never exercise the legislative and judicial powers, or either of them; the judicial shall never exercise the legislative and executive powers, or either of them." This declaration corresponds precisely with the doctrine of Montesquieu, as it has been explained, and is not in a single point violated by the plan of the convention. It goes no farther than to prohibit any one of the entire departments from exercising the powers of another department. In the very constitution to which it is prefixed, a partial mixture of powers has been admitted. The executive magistrate has a qualified negative on the legislative body, and the Senate, which is a part of the legislature, is a court of impeachment for members both of the executive and judiciary departments. The members of the judiciary department, again, are appointable by the executive department, and removable by the same authority on the address of the two legislative branches. Lastly, a number of the officers of government are annually appointed by the legislative department. As the appointment to offices, particularly executive offices, is in its nature an executive function, the compilers of the constitution have, in this last point at least, violated the rule established by themselves.

I pass over the constitutions of Rhode Island and Connecticut, because they were formed prior to the Revolution, and even before the principle under examination had become an object of political attention.

The constitution of New York contains no declaration on this subject; but appears very clearly to have been framed with an eye to the danger of improperly blending the different departments. It gives, nevertheless, to the executive magistrate, a partial control over the legislative department; and, what is more, gives a like control to the judiciary department; and even blends the executive and judiciary departments in the exercise of this control. In its council of appointment members of the legislature are associated with the executive authority, in the appointment of officers, both executive and judiciary. And its court for the trial of impeachments and correction of errors is to consist of one branch of the legislature and the principal members of the judiciary department.

The constitution of New Jersey has blended the different powers of government more than any of the preceding. The governor, who is the executive magistrate, is appointed by the legislature; is chancellor and ordinary, or surrogate of the State; is a member of the Supreme Court of Appeals, and president, with a casting vote, of one of the legislative branches. The same legislative branch acts again as executive council of the governor, and with him constitutes the Court of Appeals. The members of the judiciary department are appointed by the legislative department, and removable by one branch of it, on the impeachment of the other.

According to the constitution of Pennsylvania, the president, who is the head of the executive department, is annually elected by a vote in which the legislative department predominates. In conjunction with an executive council, he appoints the members of the judiciary department, and forms a court of impeachment for trial of all officers, judiciary as well as executive. The judges of the Supreme Court and justices of the peace seem also to be removable by the legislature; and the executive power of pardoning in certain cases, to be referred to the same department. The members of the executive council are made *ex-officio* justices of peace throughout the State.

In Delaware, the chief executive magistrate is annually elected by the legislative department. The speakers of the two legislative branches are vice-presidents in the executive department. The executive chief, with six others, appointed, three by each of the legislative branches, constitutes the Supreme Court of Appeals; he is joined with the legislative department in the appointment of the other judges. Throughout the States, it appears that the members of the legislature may at the same time be justices of the peace; in this State, the members of one branch of it are *ex-officio* justices of the peace; as are also the members of the executive council. The principal officers of the executive department are appointed by the legislative; and one branch of the latter forms a court of impeachments. All officers may be removed on address of the legislature.

Maryland has adopted the maxim in the most unqualified terms; declaring that the legislative, executive, and judicial powers of government ought to be forever separate and distinct from each other. Her constitution, notwithstanding, makes the executive magistrate appointable by the legislative department; and the members of the judiciary by the executive department.

The language of Virginia is still more pointed on this subject. Her constitution declares, "that the legislative, executive, and judiciary departments shall be separate and distinct; so that neither exercise the powers properly belonging to the other; nor shall any person exercise the powers of more than one of them at the same time, except that the justices of county courts shall be eligible to either House of Assembly." Yet we find not only this express exception, with respect to the members of the inferior courts, but that the chief magistrate, with his executive council, are appointable by the legislature; that two members of the latter are triennially displaced at the pleasure of the legislature; and that all the principal offices, both executive and judiciary, are filled by the same department. The executive prerogative of pardon, also, is in one case vested in the legislative department.

The constitution of North Carolina, which declares "that the legislative, executive, and supreme judicial powers of government ought to be forever separate and distinct from each other," refers, at the same time, to the legislative department, the appointment not only of the executive chief, but all the principal officers within both that and the judiciary department.

In South Carolina, the constitution makes the executive magistracy eligible by the legislative department. It gives to the latter, also, the appointment of the members of the judiciary department, including even justices of the peace and sheriffs; and the appointment of officers in the in the executive department, down to captains in the army and navy of the State.

In the constitution of Georgia, where it is declared "that the legislative, executive, and judiciary departments shall be separate and distinct, so that neither exercise the powers properly belonging to the other," we find that the executive department is to be filled by appointments of the legislature; and the executive prerogative of pardon to be finally exercised by the same authority. Even justices of the peace are to be appointed by the legislature.

In citing these cases, in which the legislative, executive, and judiciary departments have not been kept totally separate and distinct, I wish not to be regarded as an advocate for the particular organizations of the several State governments. I am fully aware that among the many excellent principles which they exemplify, they carry strong marks of the haste, and still stronger of the inexperience, under which they were framed. It is but too obvious that in some instances the fundamental principle under consideration has been violated by too great a mixture, and even an actual consolidation, of the different powers; and that in no instance has a competent provision been made for maintaining in practice the separation delineated on paper. What I have wished to evince is, that the charge brought against the proposed Constitution, of violating the sacred maxim of free government, is warranted neither by the real meaning annexed to that maxim by its author, nor by the sense in which it has hitherto been understood in America. This interesting subject will be resumed in the ensuing paper.   Publius [Madison]

NUMBER 48

It was shown in the last paper that the political apothegm there examined does not require that the legislative, executive, and judiciary departments should be wholly unconnected with each other. I shall undertake, in the next place, to show that unless these departments be so far connected and blended as to give to each a constitutional control over the others, the degree of separation which the maxim requires, as essential to a free government, can never in practice be duly maintained.

It is agreed on all sides, that the powers properly belonging to one of the departments ought not to be directly and completely administered by either of the other departments. It is equally evident, that none of them ought to possess, directly or indirectly, an overruling influence over the others, in the administration of their respective powers. It will not be denied, that power is of an encroaching nature, and that it ought to be effectually restrained from passing the limits assigned to it. After discriminating, therefore, in theory, the several classes of power, as they may in their nature be legislative, executive, or judiciary, the next and most difficult task is to provide some practical security for each, against the invasion of the others. What this security ought to be, is the great problem to be solved.

Will it be sufficient to mark, with precision, the boundaries of these departments, in the constitution of the government, and to trust to these parchment barriers against the encroaching spirit of power? This is the security which appears to have been principally relied on by the compilers of most of the American constitutions. But experience assures us, that the efficacy of the provision has been greatly overrated; and that some more adequate defence is indispensably necessary for the more feeble, against the more powerful, members of the government. The legislative department is everywhere extending the sphere of its activity, and drawing all power into its impetuous vortex.

The founders of our republics have so much merit for the wisdom which they have displayed, that no task can be less pleasing than that of pointing out the errors into which they have fallen. A respect for truth, however, obliges us to remark, that they seem never for a moment to have turned their eyes from the danger to liberty from the overgrown and all-grasping prerogative of an hereditary magistrate, supported and fortified by an hereditary branch of the legislative authority. They seem never to have recollected the danger from legislative usurpations, which, by assembling all power in the same hands, must lead to the same tyranny as is threatened by executive usurpations.

In a government where numerous and extensive prerogatives are placed in the hands of an hereditary monarch, the executive department is very justly regarded as the source of danger, and watched with all the jealousy which a zeal for liberty ought to inspire. In a democracy, where a multitude of people exercise in person the legislative functions, and are continually exposed, by their incapacity for regular deliberation and concerted measures, to the ambitious intrigues of their executive magistrates, tyranny may well be apprehended, on some favorable emergency, to start up in the same quarter. But in a representative republic, where the executive magistracy is carefully limited, both in the extent and the duration of its power; and where the legislative power is exercised by an assembly, which is inspired, by a supposed influence over the people, with an intrepid confidence in its own strength; which is sufficiently numerous to feel all the passions which actuate a multitude, yet not so numerous as to be incapable of pursuing the objects of its passions, by means which reason prescribes; it is against the enterprising ambition of this department that the people ought to indulge all their jealousy and exhaust all their precautions.

The legislative department derives a superiority in our governments from other circumstances. Its constitutional powers being at once more extensive, and less susceptible of precise limits, it can, with the greater facility, mask, under complicated and indirect measures, the encroachments which it makes on the coordinate departments. It is not unfrequently a question of real nicety in legislative bodies, whether the operation of a particular measure will, or will not, extend beyond the legislative sphere. On the other side, the executive power being restrained within a narrower compass, and being more simple in its nature, and the judiciary being described by landmarks still less uncertain, projects of usurpation by either of these departments would immediately betray and defeat themselves. Nor is this all: as the legislative department alone has access to the pockets of the people, and has in some constitutions full discretion, and in all a prevailing influence, over the pecuniary rewards of those who fill the other departments, a dependence is thus created in the latter, which gives still greater facility to encroachments of the former.

I have appealed to our own experience for the truth of what I advance on this subject. Were it necessary to verify this experience by particular proofs, they might be multiplied without end. I might find a witness in every citizen who has shared in, or been attentive to, the course of public administrations. I might collect vouchers in abundance from the records and archives of every State in the Union. But as a more concise, and at the same time equally satisfactory, evidence, I will refer to the example of two States, attested by two unexceptionable authorities.

The first example is that of Virginia, a State which, as we have seen, has expressly declared in its constitution, that the three great departments ought not to be intermixed. The authority in support of it is Mr. Jefferson, who, besides his other advantages for remarking the operation of the government, was himself the chief magistrate of it. In order to convey fully the ideas with which his experience had impressed him on this subject, it will be necessary to quote a passage of some length from his very interesting "Notes on the State of Virginia," p. 195. "All the powers of government, legislative, executive, and judiciary, result to the legislative body. The concentrating these in the same hands, is precisely the definition of despotic government. It will be no alleviation, that these powers will be exercised by a plurality of hands, and not by a single one. One hundred and seventy-three despots would surely be as oppressive as one. Let those who doubt it, turn their eyes on the republic of Venice. As little will it avail us, that they are chosen by ourselves. An *elective despotism* was not the government we fought for; but one which should not only be founded on free principles, but in which the powers of government should be so divided and balanced among several bodies of magistracy, as that no one could transcend their legal limits, without being effectually checked and restrained by the others. For this reason, that convention which passed the ordinance of government, laid its foundation on this basis, that the legislative, executive, and judiciary departments should be separate and distinct, so that no person should exercise the powers of more than one of them at the same time. *But no barrier was provided between these several powers.* The judiciary and the executive members were left dependent on the legislative for their subsistence in office, and some of them for their continuance in it. If, therefore, the legislature assumes executive and judiciary powers, no opposition is likely to be made; nor, if made, can be effectual; because in that case they may put their proceedings into the form of acts of Assembly, which will render them obligatory on the other branches. They have accordingly, *in many* instances, *decided rights* which should have been left to *judiciary controversy, and the direction of the executive, during the whole time of their session, is becoming habitual and familiar.*"

The other State which I shall take for an example is Pennsylvania; and the other authority, the Council of Censors, which assembled in the years 1783 and 1784. A part of the duty of this body, as marked out by the constitution, was "to inquire whether the constitution had been preserved inviolate in every part; and whether the legislative and executive branches of government had performed their duty as guardians of the people, or assumed to themselves, or exercised, other or greater powers than they are entitled to by the constitution." In the execution of this trust, the council were necessarily led to a comparison of both the legislative and executive proceedings, with the constitutional powers of these departments; and from the facts enumerated, and to the truth of most of which both sides in the council subscribed, it appears that the constitution had been flagrantly violated by the legislature in a variety of important instances.

A great number of laws had been passed, violating, without any apparent necessity, the rule requiring that all bills of a public nature shall be previously printed for the consideration of the people; although this is one of the precautions chiefly relied on by the constitution against improper acts of the legislature.

The constitutional trial by jury had been violated, and powers assumed which had not been delegated by the constitution.

Executive powers had been usurped.

The salaries of the judges, which the constitution expressly requires to be fixed, had been occasionally varied; and cases belonging to the judiciary department frequently drawn within legislative cognizance and determination.

Those who wish to see the several particulars falling under each of these heads, may consult the journals of the council, which are in print. Some of them, it will be found, may be imputable to peculiar circumstances connected with the war; but the greater part of them may be considered as the spontaneous shoots of an ill-constituted government.

It appears, also, that the executive department had not been innocent of frequent breaches of the constitution. There are three observations, however, which ought to be made on this head: *first,* a great proportion of the instances were either immediately produced by the necessities of the war, or recommended by Congress or the commander-in-chief; *secondly,* in most of the other instances, they conformed either to the declared or the known sentiments of the legislative department; *thirdly,* the executive department of Pennsylvania is distinguished from that of the other States by the number of members composing it. In this respect, it has as much affinity to a legislative assembly as to an executive council. And being at once exempt from the restraint of an individual responsibility for the acts of the body, and deriving confidence from mutual example and joint influence, unauthorized measures would, of course, be more freely hazarded, than where the executive department is administered by a single hand, or by a few hands.

The conclusion which I am warranted in drawing from these observations is, that a mere demarcation on parchment of the constitutional limits of the several departments, is not a sufficient guard against those encroachments which lead to a tyrannical concentration of all the powers of government in the same hands.   Publius [Madison]

NUMBER 51

To what expedient, then, shall we finally resort, for maintaining in practice the necessary partition of power among the several departments, as laid down in the Constitution? The only answer that can be given is, that as all these exterior provisions are found to be inadequate the defect must be supplied, by so contriving the interior structure of the government as that its several constituent parts may, by their mutual relations, be the means of keeping each other in their proper places. Without presuming to undertake a full development of this important idea, I will hazard a few general observations, which may perhaps place it in a clearer light, and enable us to form a more correct judgment of the principles and structure of the government planned by the convention.

In order to lay a due foundation for that separate and distinct exercise of the different powers of government, which to a certain extent is admitted on all hands to be essential to the preservation of liberty, it is evident that each department should have a will of its own; and consequently should be so constituted that the members of each should have as little agency as possible in the appointment of the members of the others. Were this principle rigorously adhered to, it would require that all the appointments for the supreme executive, legislative, and judiciary magistracies should be drawn from the same fountain of authority, the people, through channels having no communication whatever with one another. Perhaps such a plan of constructing the several departments would be less difficult in practice than it may in contemplation appear. Some difficulties, however, and some additional expense would attend the execution of it. Some deviations, therefore, from the principle must be admitted. In the constitution of the judiciary department in particular, it might be inexpedient to insist rigorously on the principle: first, because peculiar qualifications being essential in the members, the primary consideration ought to be to select that mode of choice which best secures these qualifications; secondly, because the permanent tenure by which the appointments are held in that department, must soon destroy all sense of dependence on the authority conferring them.

It is equally evident, that the members of each department should be as little dependent as possible on those of the others, for the emoluments annexed to their offices. Were the executive magistrate, or the judges, not independent of the legislature in this particular, their independence in every other would be merely nominal.

But the great security against a gradual concentration of the several powers in the same department, consists in giving to those who administer each department the necessary constitutional means and personal motives to resist encroachments of the others. The provision for defence must in this, as in all other cases, be made commensurate to the danger of attack. Ambition must be made to counteract ambition. The interest of the man must be connected with the constitutional rights of the place. It may be a reflection on human nature, that such devices should be necessary to control the abuses of government. But what is government itself, but the greatest of all reflections on human nature? If men were angels, no government would be necessary. If angels were to govern men, neither external nor internal controls on government would be necessary. In framing a government which is to be administered by men over men, the great difficulty lies in this: you must first enable the government to control the governed; and in the next place oblige it to control itself. A dependence on the people is, no doubt, the primary control on the government; but experience has taught mankind the necessity of auxiliary precautions.

This policy of supplying, by opposite and rival interests, the defect of better motives, might be traced through the whole system of human affairs, private as well as public. We see it particularly displayed in all the subordinate distributions of power, where the constant aim is to divide and arrange the several offices in such a manner as that each may be a check on the other—that the private interest of every individual may be a sentinel over the public rights. These inventions of prudence cannot be less requisite in the distribution of the supreme powers of the State.

But it is not possible to give to each department an equal power of self-defence. In republican government, the legislative authority necessarily predominates. The remedy for this inconveniency is to divide the legislature into different branches; and to render them, by different modes of election and different principles of action, as little connected with each other as the nature of their common functions and their common dependence on the society will admit. It may even be necessary to guard against dangerous encroachments by still further precautions. As the weight of the legislative authority requires that it should be thus divided, the weakness of the executive may require, on the other hand, that it should be fortified. An absolute negative on the legislature appears, at first view, to be the natural defence with which the executive magistrate should be armed. But perhaps it would be neither altogether safe nor alone sufficient. On ordinary occasions it might not be exerted with the requisite firmness, and on extraordinary occasions it might be perfidiously abused. May not this defect of an absolute negative be supplied by some qualified connection between this weaker department and the weaker branch of the stronger department, by which the latter may be led to support the constitutional rights of the former, without being too much detached from the rights of its own department?

If the principles on which these observations are founded be just, as I persuade myself they are, and they be applied as a criterion to the several State constitutions, and to the federal Constitution, it will be found that if the latter does not perfectly correspond with them, the former are infinitely less able to bear such a test.

There are, moreover, two considerations particularly applicable to the federal system of America, which place that system in a very interesting point of view.

First. In a single republic, all the power surrendered by the people is submitted to the administration of a single government; and the usurpations are guarded against by a division of the government into distinct and separate departments. In the compound republic of America, the power surrendered by the people is first divided between two distinct governments, and then the portion allotted to each subdivided among distinct and separate departments. Hence a double security arises to the rights of the people. The different governments will control each other, at the same time that each will be controlled by itself.

Second. It is of great importance in a republic not only to guard the society against the oppression of its rulers, but to guard one part of the society against the injustice of the other part. Different interests necessarily exist in different classes of citizens. If a majority be united by a common interest, the rights of the minority will be insecure. There are but two methods of providing against this evil: the one by creating a will in the community independent of the majority—that is, of the society itself; the other, by comprehending in the society so many separate descriptions of citizens as will render an unjust combination of a majority of the whole very improbable, if not impracticable. The first method prevails in all governments possessing an hereditary or self-appointed authority. This, at best, is but a precarious security; because a power independent of the society may as well espouse the unjust views of the major, as the rightful interests of the minor party, and may possibly be turned against both parties. The second method will be exemplified in the federal republic of the United States. Whilst all authority in it will be derived from and dependent on the society, the society itself will be broken into so many parts, interests and classes of citizens, that the rights of individuals, or of the minority, will be in little danger from interested combinations of the majority. In a free government the security for civil rights must be the same as that for religious rights. It consists in the one case in the multiplicity of interests, and in the other in the multiplicity of sects. The degree of security in both cases will depend on the number of interests and sects; and this may be presumed to depend on the extent of country and number of people comprehended under the same government. This view of the subject must particularly recommend a proper federal system to all the sincere and considerate friends of republican government, since it shows that in exact proportion as the territory of the Union may be formed into more circumscribed Confederacies, or States, oppressive combinations of a majority will be facilitated; the best security, under the republican forms, for the rights of every class of citizens, will be diminished; and consequently the stability and independence of some member of the government, the only other security, must be proportionally increased. Justice is the end of government. It is the end of civil society. It ever has been and ever will be pursued until it be obtained, or until liberty be lost in the pursuit. In a society under the forms of which the stronger faction can readily unite and oppress the weaker, anarchy may as truly be said to reign as in a state of nature, where the weaker individual is not secured against the violence of the stronger; and as, in the latter state, even the stronger individuals are prompted, by the uncertainty of their condition, to submit to a government which may protect the weak as well as themselves; so, in the former state, will the more powerful factions or parties be gradually induced, by a like motive, to wish for a government which will protect all parties, the weaker as well as the more powerful. It can be little doubted that if the State of Rhode Island was separated from the Confederacy and left to itself, the insecurity of rights under the popular form of government within such narrow limits would be displayed by such reiterated oppressions of factious majorities that some power altogether independent of the people would soon be called for by the voice of the very factions whose misrule had proved the necessity of it. In the extended republic of the United States, and among the great variety of interests, parties, and sects which it embraces, a coalition of a majority of the whole society could seldom take place on any other principles than those of justice and the general good; whilst there being thus less danger to a minor from the will of a major party, there must be less pretext, also, to provide for the security of the former, by introducing into the government a will not dependent on the latter, or, in other words, a will independent of the society itself. It is no less certain than it is important, notwithstanding the contrary opinions which have been entertained, that the larger the society, provided it lie within a practical sphere, the more duly capable it will be of self-government. And happily for the *republican cause,* the practicable sphere may be carried to a very great extent, by a judicious modification and mixture of the *federal principle.*   Publius [Madison]

NUMBER 63

A *fifth* desideratum, illustrating the utility of a senate, is the want of a due sense of national character. Without a select and stable member of the government, the esteem of foreign powers will not only be forfeited by an unenlightened and variable policy, proceeding from the causes already mentioned, but the national councils will not possess that sensibility to the opinion of the world, which is perhaps not less necessary in order to merit, than it is to obtain, its respect and confidence.

An attention to the judgment of other nations is important to every government for two reasons: the one is, that, independently of the merits of any particular plan or measure, it is desirable, on various accounts, that it should appear to other nations as the offspring of a wise and honorable policy; the second is, that in doubtful cases, particularly where the national councils may be warped by some strong passion or momentary interest, the presumed or known opinion of the impartial world may be the best guide that can be followed. What has not America lost by her want of character with foreign nations; and how many errors and follies would she not have avoided, if the justice and propriety of her measures had, in every instance, been previously tried by the light in which they would probably appear to the unbiased part of mankind?

Yet however requisite a sense of national character may be, it is evident that it can never be sufficiently possessed by a numerous and changeable body. It can only be found in a number so small that a sensible degree of the praise and blame of public measures may be the portion of each individual; or in an assembly so durably invested with public trust, that the pride and consequence of its members may be sensibly incorporated with the reputation and prosperity of the community. The half-yearly representatives of Rhode Island would probably have been little affected in their deliberations on the iniquitous measures of that State, by arguments drawn from that light in which such measures would be viewed by foreign nations, or even by the sister States; whilst it can scarcely be doubted that if the concurrence of a select and stable body had been necessary, a regard to national character alone would have prevented the calamities under which that misguided people is now laboring.

I add, as a *sixth* defect, the want, in some important cases, of a due responsibility in the government to the people, arising from that frequency of elections which in other cases produces this responsibility. This remark will, perhaps, appear not only new, but paradoxical. It must nevertheless be acknowledged, when explained, to be as undeniable as it is important.

Responsibility, in order to be reasonable, must be limited to objects within the power of the responsible party, and in order to be effectual, must relate to operations of that power, of which a ready and proper judgment can be formed by the constituents. The objects of government may be divided into two general classes: the one depending on measures which have singly an immediate and sensible operation; the other depending on a succession of well-chosen and well-connected measures, which have a gradual and perhaps unobserved operation. The importance of the latter description to the collective and permanent welfare of every country, needs no explanation. And yet it is evident that an assembly elected for so short a term as to be unable to provide more than one or two links in a chain of measures, on which the general welfare may essentially depend, ought not to be answerable for the final result, any more than a steward or tenant, engaged for one year, could be justly made to answer for places or improvements which could not be accomplished in less than half a dozen years. Nor is it possible for the people to estimate the *share* of influence which their annual assemblies may respectively have on events resulting from the mixed transactions of several years. It is sufficiently difficult to preserve a personal responsibility in the members of a *numerous* body, for such acts of the body as have an immediate, detached, and palpable operation on its constituents.

The proper remedy for this defect must be an additional body in the legislative department, which, having sufficient permanency to provide for such objects as require a continued attention, and a train of measures, may be justly and effectually answerable for the attainment of those objects.

Thus far I have considered the circumstances which point out the necessity of a well-constructed Senate only as they relate to the representatives of the people. To a people as little blinded by prejudice or corrupted by flattery as those whom I address, I shall not scruple to add, that such an institution may be sometimes necessary as a defence to the people against their own temporary errors and delusions. As the cool and deliberate sense of the community ought, in all governments, and actually will, in all free governments, ultimately prevail over the views of its rulers; so there are particular moments in public affairs when the people, stimulated by some irregular passion, or some illicit advantage, or misled by the artful misrepresentations of interested men, may call for measures which they themselves will afterwards be the most ready to lament and condemn. In these critical moments, how salutary will be the interference of some temperate and respectable body of citizens, in order to check the misguided career, and to suspend the blow meditated by the people against themselves, until reason, justice, and truth can regain their authority over the public mind? What bitter anguish would not the people of Athens have often escaped if their government had contained so provident a safeguard against the tyranny of their own passions? Popular liberty might then have escaped the indelible reproach of decreeing to the same citizens the hemlock on one day and statues on the next.

It may be suggested, that a people spread over an extensive region cannot, like the crowded inhabitants of a small district, be subject to the infection of violent passions, or to the danger of combining in pursuit of unjust measures. I am far from denying that this is a distinction of peculiar importance. I have, on the contrary, endeavored in a former paper to show, that it is one of the principal recommendations of a confederated republic. At the same time, this advantage ought not to be considered as superseding the use of auxiliary precautions. It may even be remarked, that the same extended situation, which will exempt the people of America from some of the dangers incident to lesser republics, will expose them to the inconveniency of remaining for a longer time under the influence of those misrepresentations which the combined industry of interested men may succeed in distributing among them.

It adds no small weight to all these considerations, to recollect that history informs us of no long-lived republic which had not a senate. Sparta, Rome, and Carthage are, in fact, the only states to whom that character can be applied. In each of the two first there was a senate for life. The constitution of the senate in the last is less known. Circumstantial evidence makes it probable that it was not different in this particular from the two others. It is at least certain, that it had some quality or other which rendered it an anchor against popular fluctuations; and that a smaller council, drawn out of the senate, was appointed not only for life, but filled up vacancies itself. These examples, though as unfit for the imitation, as they are repugnant to the genius, of America, are, notwithstanding, when compared with the fugitive and turbulent existence of other ancient republics, very instructive proofs of the necessity of some institution that will blend stability with liberty. I am not unaware of the circumstances which distinguish the American from other popular governments, as well ancient as modern; and which render extreme circumspection necessary, in reasoning from one case to the other. But after allowing due weight to this consideration, it may still be maintained, that there are many points of similitude which render these examples not unworthy of our attention. Many of the defects, as we have seen, which can only be supplied by a senatorial institution, are common to a numerous assembly frequently elected by the people, and to the people themselves. There are others peculiar to the former, which require the control of such an institution. The people can never wilfully betray their own interests; but they may possibly be betrayed by the representatives of the people; and the danger will be evidently greater where the whole legislative trust is lodged in the hands of one body of men, than where the concurrence of separate and dissimilar bodies is required in every public act.

The difference most relied on, between the American and other republics, consists in the principle of representation; which is the pivot on which the former move, and which is supposed to have been unknown to the latter, or at least to the ancient part of them. The use which has been made of this difference, in reasonings contained in former papers, will have shown that I am disposed neither to deny its existence nor to undervalue its importance. I feel the less restraint, therefore, in observing, that the position concerning the ignorance of the ancient governments on the subject of representation, is by no means precisely true in the latitude commonly given to it. Without entering into a disquisition which here would be misplaced, I will refer to a few known facts, in support of what I advance.

In the most pure democracies of Greece, many of the executive functions were performed, not by the people themselves, but by officers elected by the people, and *representing* the people in their *executive* capacity.

Prior to the reform of Solon, Athens was governed by nine Archons, annually *elected by the people at large.* The degree of power delegated to them seems to be left in great obscurity. Subsequent to that period, we find an assembly, first of four, and afterwards of six hundred members, annually *elected by the people;* and *partially* representing them in their *legislative* capacity, since they were not only associated with the people in the function of making laws, but had the exclusive right of originating legislative propositions to the people. The senate of Carthage, also, whatever might be its power, or the duration of its appointment, appears to have been elective by the suffrages of the people. Similar instances might be traced in most, if not all the popular governments of antiquity.

Lastly, in Sparta we meet with the Ephori, and in Rome with the Tribunes; two bodies, small indeed in numbers, but annually *elected by the whole body of the people,* and considered as the *representatives* of the people, almost in their *plenipotentiary* capacity. The Cosmi of Crete were also annually *elected by the people,* and have been considered by some authors as an institution analogous to those of Sparta and Rome, with this difference only, that in the election of that representative body the right of suffrage was communicated to a part only of the people.

From these facts, to which many others might be added, it is clear that the principle of representation was neither unknown to the ancients nor wholly overlooked in their political constitutions. The true distinction between these and the American governments, lies in *the total exclusion of the people, in their collective capacity,* from any share in the *latter,* and not in the *total exclusion of the representatives of the people* from the administration of the *former.* The distinction, however, thus qualified, must be admitted to leave a most advantageous superiority in favor of the United States. But to insure to this advantage its full effect, we must be careful not to separate it from the other advantage, of an extensive territory. For it cannot be believed, that any form of representative government could have succeeded within the narrow limits occupied by the democracies of Greece.

In answer to all these arguments, suggested by reason, illustrated by examples, and enforced by our own experience, the jealous adversary of the Constitution will probably content himself with repeating, that a senate appointed not immediately by the people, and for the term of six years, must gradually acquire a dangerous preeminence in the government, and finally transform it into a tyrannical aristocracy.

To this general answer, the general reply ought to be sufficient, that liberty may be endangered by the abuses of liberty as well as by the abuses of power; that there are numerous instances of the former as well as of the latter; and that the former, rather than the latter, are apparently most to be apprehended by the United States. But a more particular reply may be given.

Before such a revolution can be effected, the Senate, it is to be observed, must in the first place corrupt itself; must next corrupt the State legislatures; must then corrupt the House of Representatives; and must finally corrupt the people at large. It is evident that the Senate must be first corrupted before it can attempt an establishment of tyranny. Without corrupting the State legislatures, it cannot prosecute the attempt, because the periodical change of members would otherwise regenerate the whole body. Without exerting the means of corruption with equal success on the House of Representatives, the opposition of that co-equal branch of the government would inevitably defeat the attempt; and without corrupting the people themselves, a succession of new representatives would speedily restore all things to their pristine order. Is there any man who can seriously persuade himself that the proposed Senate can, by any possible means within the compass of human address, arrive at the object of a lawless ambition, through all these obstructions?

If reason condemns the suspicion, the same sentence is pronounced by experience. The constitution of Maryland furnishes the most apposite example. The Senate of that State is elected, as the federal Senate will be, indirectly by the people, and for a term less by one year only than the federal Senate. It is distinguished, also, by the remarkable prerogative of filling up its own vacancies within the term of its appointment, and, at the same time, is not under the control of any such rotation as is provided for the federal Senate. There are some other lesser distinctions, which would expose the former to colorable objections, that do not lie against the latter. If the federal Senate, therefore, really contained the danger which has been so loudly proclaimed, some symptoms at least of a like danger ought by this time to have been betrayed by the Senate of Maryland, but no such symptoms have appeared. On the contrary, the jealousies at first entertained by men of the same description with those who view with terror the correspondent part of the federal Constitution, have been gradually extinguished by the progress of the experiment; and the Maryland constitution is daily deriving, from the salutary operation of this part of it, a reputation in which it will probably not be rivaled by that of any State in the Union.

But if any thing could silence the jealousies on this subject, it ought to be the British example. The Senate there, instead of being elected for a term of six years, and of being unconfined to particular families or fortunes, is an hereditary assembly of opulent nobles. The House of Representatives, instead of being elected for two years, and by the whole body of the people, is elected for seven years, and, in very great proportion, by a very small proportion of the people. Here, unquestionably, ought to be seen in full display the aristocratic usurpations and tyranny which are at some future period to be exemplified in the United States. Unfortunately, however, for the anti-federal argument, the British history informs us that this hereditary assembly has not been able to defend itself against the continual encroachments of the House of Representatives; and that it no sooner lost the support of the monarch, than it was actually crushed by the weight of the popular branch.

As far as antiquity can instruct us on this subject, its examples support the reasoning which we have employed. In Sparta, the Ephori, the annual representatives of the people, were found an overmatch for the senate for life, continually gained on its authority and finally drew all power into their own hands. The Tribunes of Rome, who were the representatives of the people, prevailed, it is well known, in almost every contest with the senate for life, and in the end gained the most complete triumph over it. The fact is the more remarkable, as unanimity was required in every act of the Tribunes, even after their number was augmented to ten. It proves the irresistible force possessed by that branch of a free government, which has the people on its side. To these examples might be added that of Carthage, whose senate, according to the testimony of Polybius, instead of drawing all power into its vortex, had, at the commencement of the second Punic War, lost almost the whole of its original portion.

Besides the conclusive evidence resulting from this assemblage of facts, that the federal Senate will never be able to transform itself, by gradual usurpations, into an independent and aristocratic body, we are warranted in believing, that if such a revolution should ever happen from causes which the foresight of man cannot guard against, the House of Representatives, with the people on their side, will at all times be able to bring back the Constitution to its primitive form and principles. Against the force of the immediate representatives of the people, nothing will be able to maintain even the constitutional authority of the Senate, but such a display of enlightened policy, and attachment to the public good, as will divide with that branch of the legislature the affections and support of the entire body of the people themselves.   Publius [Madison]

NUMBER 70

There is an idea, which is not without its advocates, that a vigorous Executive is inconsistent with the genius of republican government. The enlightened well-wishers to this species of government must at least hope that the supposition is destitute of foundation; since they can never admit its truth, without at the same time admitting the condemnation of their own principles. Energy in the Executive is a leading character in the definition of good government. It is essential to the protection of the community against foreign attacks; it is not less essential to the steady administration of the laws; to the protection of property against those irregular and high-handed combinations which sometimes interrupt the ordinary course of justice; to the security of liberty against the enterprises and assault of ambition, of faction, and of anarchy. Every man the least conversant in Roman story, knows how often that republic was obliged to take refuge in the absolute power of a single man, under the formidable title of Dictator, as well against the intrigues of ambitious individuals who aspired to the tyranny, and the seditions, of whole classes of the community whose conduct threatened the existence of all government, as against the invasions of external enemies who menaced the conquest and destruction of Rome.

There can be no need, however, to multiply arguments or examples on this head. A feeble Executive implies a feeble execution of the government. A feeble execution is but another phrase for a bad execution; and a government ill executed, whatever it may be in theory, must be, in practice, a bad government.

Taking it for granted, therefore, that all men of sense will agree in the necessity of an energetic Executive, it will only remain to inquire, what are the ingredients which constitute this energy? How far can they be combined with those other ingredients which constitute safety in the republican sense? And how far does this combination characterize the plan which has been reported by the convention?

The ingredients which constitute energy in the Executive are, first, unity; secondly, duration; thirdly, an adequate provision for its support; fourthly, competent powers.

The ingredients which constitute safety in the republican sense are, first, a due dependence on the people; secondly, a due responsibility.

Those politicians and statesmen who have been the most celebrated for the soundness of their principles and for the justice of their views, have declared in favor of a single Executive and a numerous legislature. They have, with great propriety, considered energy as the most necessary qualification of the former, and have regarded this as most applicable to power in a single hand; while they have, with equal propriety, considered the latter as best adapted to deliberation and wisdom, and best calculated to conciliate the confidence of the people and to secure their privileges and interests.

That unity is conducive to energy will not be disputed. Decision, activity, secrecy, and despatch will generally characterize the proceedings of one man in a much more eminent degree than the proceedings of any greater number; and in proportion as the number is increased, these qualities will be diminished.

This unity may be destroyed in two ways: either by vesting the power in two or more magistrates of equal dignity and authority; or by vesting it ostensibly in one man, subject, in whole or in part, to the control and co-operation of others, in the capacity of counsellors to him. Of the first, the two Consuls of Rome may serve as an example; of the last, we shall find examples in the constitutions of several of the States. New York and New Jersey if I recollect right, are the only States which have intrusted the executive authority wholly to single men.[3] Both these methods of destroying the unity of the Executive have their partisans; but the votaries of an executive council are the most numerous. They are both liable, if not to equal, to similar objections, and may in most lights be examined in conjunction.

The experience of other nations will afford little instruction on this head. As far, however, as it teaches anything, it teaches us not to be enamoured of plurality in the Executive. We have seen that the Achaeans, on an experiment of two Praetors, were induced to abolish one. The Roman history records many instances of mischiefs to the republic from the dissensions between the Consuls, and between the military Tribunes, who were at times substituted for the Consuls. But it gives us no specimens of any peculiar advantages derived to the state from the circumstance of the plurality of those magistrates. That the dissensions between them were not more frequent or more fatal, is matter of astonishment, until we advert to the singular position in which the republic was almost continually placed, and to the prudent policy pointed out by the circumstances of the state, and pursued by the Consuls, of making a division of the government between them. The patricians engaged in a perpetual struggle with the plebeians for the preservation of their ancient authorities and dignities; the Consuls, who were generally chosen out of the former body, were commonly united by the personal interest they had in the defence of the privileges of their order. In addition to this motive of union, after the arms of the republic had considerably expanded the bounds of its empire, it became an established custom with the Consuls to divide the administration between themselves by lot— one of them remaining at Rome to govern the city and its environs, the other taking command in the more distant provinces. This expedient must, no doubt, have had great influence in preventing those collisions and rivalships which might otherwise have embroiled the peace of the republic.

But quitting the dim light of historical research, attaching ourselves purely to the dictates of reason and good sense, we shall discover much greater cause to reject than to approve the idea of plurality in the Executive, under any modification whatever.

Wherever two or more persons are engaged in any common enterprise or pursuit, there is always danger of difference of opinion. If it be a public trust or office, in which they are clothed with equal dignity and authority, there is peculiar danger of personal emulation and even animosity. From either, and especially from all these causes, the most bitter dissensions are apt to spring. Whenever these happen, they lessen the respectability, weaken the authority, and distract the plans and operations of those whom they divide. If they should unfortunately assail the supreme executive magistracy of a country, consisting of a plurality of persons, they might impede or frustrate the most important measures of the government, in the most critical emergencies of the state. And what is still worse, they might split the community into the most violent and irreconcilable factions, adhering differently to the different individuals who composed the magistracy.

Men often oppose a thing, merely because they have had no agency in planning it, or because it may have been planned by those whom they dislike. But if they have been consulted, and have happened to disapprove, opposition then becomes, in their estimation, an indispensable duty of self-love. They seem to think themselves bound in honor, and by all the motives of personal infallibility, to defeat the success of what has been resolved upon contrary to their sentiments. Men of upright, benevolent tempers have too many opportunities of remarking, with horror, to what desperate lengths this disposition is sometimes carried, and how often the great interests of society are sacrificed to the vanity, to the conceit, and to the obstinacy of individuals, who have credit enough to make their passions and their caprices interesting to mankind. Perhaps the question now before the public may, in its consequences, afford melancholy proofs of the effects of this despicable frailty, or rather detestable vice, in the human character.

Upon the principles of a free government, inconveniences from the source just mentioned must necessarily be submitted to in the formation of the legislature; but it is unnecessary, and therefore unwise, to introduce them into the constitution of the Executive. It is here too that they may be most pernicious. In the legislature, promptitude of decision is oftener an evil than a benefit. The differences of opinion, and the jarrings of parties in that department of the government, though they may sometimes obstruct salutary plans, yet often promote deliberation and circumspection, and serve to check excesses in the majority. When a resolution too is once taken, the opposition must be at an end. That resolution is a law, and resistance to it punishable. But no favorable circumstances palliate or atone for the disadvantages of dissension in the executive department. Here, they are pure and unmixed. There is no point at which they cease to operate. They serve to embarrass and weaken the execution of the plan or measure to which they relate, from the first step to the final conclusion of it. They constantly counteract those qualities in the Executive which are the most necessary ingredients in its composition,—vigor and expedition, and this without any counterbalancing good. In the conduct of war, in which the energy of the Executive is the bulwark of the national security, every thing would be to be apprehended from its plurality.

It must be confessed that these observations apply with principal weight to the first case supposed—that is, to a plurality of magistrates of equal dignity and authority, a scheme, the advocates for which are not likely to form a numerous sect; but they apply, though not with equal, yet with considerable weight to the project of a council, whose concurrence is made constitutionally necessary to the operations of the ostensible Executive. An artful cabal in that council would be able to distract and to enervate the whole system of administration. If no such cabal should exist, the mere diversity of views and opinions would alone be sufficient to tincture the exercise of the executive authority with a spirit of habitual feebleness and dilatoriness.

But one of the weightiest objections to a plurality in the Executive, and which lies as much against the last as the first plan, is, that it tends to conceal faults and destroy responsibility. Responsibility is of two kinds—to censure and to punishment. The first is the more important of the two, especially in an elective office. Man, in public trust, will much oftener act in such a manner as to render him unworthy of being any longer trusted, than in such a manner as to make him obnoxious to legal punishment. But the multiplication of the Executive adds to the difficulty of detection in either case. It often becomes impossible, amidst mutual accusations, to determine on whom the blame or the punishment of a pernicious measure, or series of pernicious measures, ought really to fall. It is shifted from one to another with so much dexterity, and under such plausible appearances, that the public opinion is left in suspense about the real author. The circumstances which may have led to any national miscarriage of misfortune are sometimes so complicated that, where there are a number of actors who may have had different degrees and kinds of agency, though we may clearly see upon the whole that there has been mismanagement, yet it may be impracticable to pronounce to whose account the evil which may have been incurred is truly chargeable.

"I was overruled by my council. The council were so divided in their opinions that it was impossible to obtain any better resolution on the point." These and similar pretexts are constantly at hand, whether true or false. And who is there that will either take the trouble or incur the odium of a strict scrutiny into the secret springs of the transaction? Should there be found a citizen zealous enough to undertake the unpromising task, if there happen to be collusion between the parties concerned, how easy it is to clothe the circumstances with so much ambiguity, as to render it uncertain what was the precise conduct of any of those parties.

In the single instance in which the governor of this State is coupled with a council— that is, in the appointment to offices, we have seen the mischiefs of it in the view now under consideration. Scandalous appointments to important offices have been made. Some cases, indeed, have been so flagrant that ALL PARTIES have agreed in the impropriety of the thing. When inquiry has been made, the blame has been laid by the governor on the members of the council, who, on their part, have charged it upon his nomination; while the people remain altogether at a loss to determine, by whose influence their interests have been committed to hands so unqualified and so manifestly improper. In tenderness to individuals, I forbear to descend to particulars.

It is evident from these considerations, that the plurality of the Executive tends to deprive the people of the two greatest securities they can have for the faithful exercise of any delegated power, *first,* the restraints of public opinion, which lose their efficacy, as well on account of the division of the censure attendant on bad measures among a number, as on account of the uncertainty on whom it ought to fall; and, *secondly,* the opportunity of discovering with facility and clearness the misconduct of the persons they trust, in order either to their removal from office, or to their actual punishment in cases which admit of it.

In England, the king is a perpetual magistrate; and it is a maxim which has obtained for the sake of the public peace, that he is unaccountable for his administration, and his person sacred. Nothing, therefore, can be wiser in that kingdom, than to annex to the king a constitutional council, who may be responsible to the nation for the advice they give. Without this, there would be no responsibility whatever in the executive department—an idea inadmissible in a free government. But even there the king is not bound by the resolutions of his council, though they are answerable for the advice they give. He is the absolute master of his own conduct in the exercise of his office, and may observe or disregard the counsel given to him at his sole discretion.

But in a republic, where every magistrate ought to be personally responsible for his behavior in office, the reason which in the British Constitution dictates the propriety of a council, not only ceases to apply, but turns against the institution. In the monarchy of Great Britain, it furnishes a substitute for the prohibited responsibility of the chief magistrate, which serves in some degree as a hostage to the national justice for his good behavior. In the American republic, it would serve to destroy, or would greatly diminish, the intended and necessary responsibility of the Chief Magistrate himself.

The idea of a council to the Executive, which has so generally obtained in the State constitutions, has been derived from that maxim of republican jealousy which considers power as safer in the hands of a number of men than of a single man. If the maxim should be admitted to be applicable to the case, I should contend that the advantage on that side would not counterbalance the numerous disadvantages on the opposite side. But I do not think the rule at all applicable to the executive power. I clearly concur in opinion, in this particular, with a writer whom the celebrated Junius pronounces to be "deep, solid, and ingenious," that "the executive power is more easily confined when it is ONE";[4] that it is far more safe there should be a single object for the jealousy and watchfulness of the people; and, in a word that all multiplication of the Executive is rather dangerous than friendly to liberty.

A little consideration will satisfy us, that the species of security sought for in the multiplication of the Executive, is unattainable. Numbers must be so great as to render combination difficult, or they are rather a source of danger than of security. The united credit and influence of several individuals must be more formidable to liberty, than the credit and influence of either of them separately. When power, therefore, is placed in the hands of so small a number of men, as to admit of their interests and views being easily combined in a common enterprise, by an artful leader, it becomes more liable to abuse, and more dangerous when abused, than if it be lodged in the hands of one man; who, from the very circumstance of his being alone, will be more narrowly watched and more readily suspected, and who cannot unite so great a mass of influence as when he is associated with others. The Decemvirs of Rome, whose name denotes their number,[5] were more to be dreaded in their usurpation than any ONE of them would have been. No person would think of proposing an Executive much more numerous than that body; from six to a dozen have been suggested for the number of the council. The extreme of these numbers, is not too great for an easy combination; and from such a combination America would have more to fear, than from the ambition of any single individual. A council to a magistrate who is himself responsible for what he does, are generally nothing better than a clog upon his good intentions, are often the instruments and accomplices of his bad, and are almost always a cloak to his faults.

I forbear to dwell upon the subject of expense; though it be evident that if the council should be numerous enough to answer the principal end aimed at by the institution, the salaries of the members, who must be drawn from their homes to reside at the seat of government, would form an item in the catalogue of public expenditures too serious to be incurred for an object of equivocal utility. I will only add that, prior to the appearance of the Constitution, I rarely met with an intelligent man from any of the States, who did not admit, as the result of experience, that the UNITY of the executive of this State was one of the best of the distinguishing features of our constitution.   Publius [Hamilton]

NUMBER 78

We proceed now to an examination of the judiciary department of the proposed government.

In unfolding the defects of the existing Confederation, the utility and necessity of a federal judicature have been clearly pointed out. It is the less necessary to recapitulate the considerations there urged, as the propriety of the institution in the abstract is not disputed; the only questions which have been raised being relative to the manner of constituting it, and to its extent. To these points, therefore, our observations shall be confined.

The manner of constituting it seems to embrace these several objects: 1st. The mode of appointing the judges. 2d. The tenure by which they are to hold their places. 3d. The partition of the judiciary authority between different courts, and their relations to each other.

First. As to the mode of appointing the judges; this is the same with that of appointing the officers of the Union in general, and has been so fully discussed in the two last numbers, that nothing can be said here which would not be useless repetition.

Second. As to the tenure by which the judges are to hold their places: this chiefly concerns their duration in office; the provisions for their support; the precautions for their responsibility.

According to the plan of the convention, all judges who may be appointed by the United States are to hold their offices *during good behavior;* which is comfortable to the most approved of the State constitutions, and among the rest, to that of this State. Its propriety having been drawn into question by the adversaries of that plan, is no light symptom of the rage for objection, which disorders their imaginations and judgments. The standard of good behavior for the continuance in office of the judicial magistracy, is certainly one of the most valuable of the modern improvements in the practice of government. In a monarchy it is an excellent barrier to the despotism of the prince; in a republic it is a no less excellent barrier to the encroachments and oppressions of the representative body. And it is the best expedient which can be devised in any government, to secure a steady, upright, and impartial administration of the laws.

Whoever attentively considers the different departments of power must perceive, that, in a government in which they are separated from each other, the judiciary, from the nature of its functions, will always be the least dangerous to the political rights of the Constitution; because it will be least in a capacity to annoy or injure them. The Executive not only dispenses the honors, but holds the sword of the community. The legislature not only commands the purse, but prescribes the rules by which the duties and rights of every citizen are to be regulated. The judiciary, on the contrary, has no influence over either the sword or the purse; no direction either of the strength or of the wealth of the society; and can take no active resolution whatever. It may truly be said to have neither FORCE nor WILL but merely judgment; and must ultimately depend upon the aid of the executive arm even for the efficacy of its judgments.

This simple view of the matter suggests several important consequences. It proves incontestably, that the judiciary is beyond comparison the weakest of the three departments of power[6]; that it can never attack with success either of the other two; and that all possible care is requisite to enable it to defend itself against their attacks. It equally proves, that though individual oppression may now and then proceed from the courts of justice, the general liberty of the people can never be endangered from that quarter; I mean so long as the judiciary remains truly distinct from both the legislature and the Executive. For I agree, that "there is no liberty, if the power of judging be not separated from the legislative and executive powers."[7] And it proves, in the last place, that as liberty can have nothing to fear from the judiciary alone, but would have every thing to fear from its union with either of the other departments; that as all the effects of such a union must ensue from a dependence of the former on the latter, notwithstanding a nominal and apparent separation; that as, from the natural feebleness of the judiciary, it is in continual jeopardy of being overpowered, awed, or influenced by its coordinate branches; and that as nothing can contribute so much to its firmness and independence as permanency in office, this quality may therefore be justly regarded as an indispensable ingredient in its constitution, and, in a great measure, as the citadel of the public justice and the public security.

The complete independence of the courts of justice is peculiarly essential in a limited Constitution. By a limited Constitution, I understand one which contains certain specified exceptions to the legislative authority; such, for instance, as that it shall pass no bills of attainder, no *ex-post-facto* laws, and the like. Limitations of this kind can be preserved in practice no other way than through the medium of courts of justice, whose duty it must be to declare all acts contrary to the manifest tenor of the Constitution void. Without this, all the reservations of particular rights or privileges would amount to nothing.

Some perplexity respecting the rights of the courts to pronounce legislative acts void, because contrary to the Constitution, has arisen from an imagination that the doctrine would imply a superiority of the judiciary to the legislative power. It is urged that the authority which can declare the acts of another void, must necessarily be superior to the one whose acts may be declared void. As this doctrine is of great importance in all the American constitutions, a brief discussion of the ground on which it rests cannot be unacceptable.

There is no position which depends on clearer principles, than that every act of a delegated authority, contrary to the tenor of the commission under which it is exercised, is void. No legislative act, therefore, contrary to the Constitution, can be valid. To deny this, would be to affirm, that the deputy is greater than his principal; that the servant is above his master; that the representatives of the people are superior to the people themselves; that men acting by virtue of powers, may do not only what their powers do not authorize, but what they forbid.

If it be said that the legislative body are themselves the constitutional judges of their own powers, and that the construction they put upon them is conclusive upon the other department, it may be answered, that this cannot be the natural presumption, where it is not to be collected from any particular provisions in the Constitution. It is not otherwise to be supposed, that the Constitution could intend to enable the representatives of the people to substitute their *will* to that of their constituents. It is far more rational to suppose, that the courts were designed to be an intermediate body between the people and the legislature, in order, among other things, to keep the latter within the limits assigned to their authority. The interpretation of the laws is the proper and peculiar province of the courts. A constitution is, in fact, and must be regarded by the judges, as a fundamental law. It therefore belongs to them to ascertain its meaning, as well as the meaning of any particular act proceeding from the legislative body. If there should happen to be an irreconcilable variance between the two, that which has the superior obligation and validity ought, of course, to be preferred; or, in other words, the Constitution ought to be preferred to the statute, the intention of the people to the intention of their agents.

Nor does this conclusion by any means suppose a superiority of the judicial to the legislative power. It only supposes that the power of the people is superior to both; and that where the will of the legislature, declared in its statutes, stands in opposition to that of the people, declared in the Constitution, the judges ought to be governed by the latter rather than the former. They ought to regulate their decisions by the fundamental laws, rather then by those which are not fundamental.

This exercise of judicial discretion, in determining between two contradictory laws, is exemplified in a familiar instance. It not uncommonly happens, that there are two statutes existing at one time, clashing in whole or in part with each other, and neither of them containing any repealing clause or expression. In such a case, it is the province of the courts to liquidate and fix their meaning and operation. So far as they can, by any fair construction, be reconciled to each other, reason and law conspire to dictate that this should be done; where this is impracticable, it becomes a matter of necessity to give effect to one, in exclusion of the other. The rule which has obtained in the courts for determining their relative validity is, that the last in order of time shall be preferred to the first. But this is a mere rule of construction, not derived from any positive law, but from the nature and reason of the thing. It is a rule not enjoined upon the courts by legislative provision, but adopted by themselves, as consonant to truth and propriety, for the direction of their conduct as interpreters of the law. They thought it reasonable, that between the interfering acts of an *equal* authority, that which was the last indication of its will should have the preference.

But in regard to the interfering acts of a superior and subordinate authority, of an original and derivative power, the nature and reason of the thing indicate the converse of that rule as proper to be followed. They teach us that the prior act of a superior ought to be preferred to the subsequent act of an inferior and subordinate authority; and that accordingly, whenever a particular statute contravenes the Constitution, it will be the duty of the judicial tribunals to adhere to the latter and disregard the former.

It can be of no weight to say that the courts, on the pretence of a repugnancy, may substitute their own pleasure to the constitutional intentions of the legislature. This might as well happen in the case of two contradictory statutes; or it might as well happen in every adjudication upon any single statute. The courts must declare the sense of the law; and if they should be disposed to exercise WILL instead of JUDGMENT, the consequence would equally be the substitution of their pleasure to that of the legislative body. The observation, if it prove any thing, would prove that there ought to be no judges distinct from that body.

If, then, the courts of justice are to be considered as the bulwarks of a limited Constitution against legislative encroachments, this consideration will afford a strong argument for the permanent tenure of judicial offices, since nothing will contribute so much as this to that independent spirit in the judges which must be essential to the faithful performance of so arduous a duty.

This independence of the judges is equally requisite to guard the Constitution and the rights of individuals from the effects of those ill humors, which the arts of designing men, or the influence of particular conjunctures, sometimes disseminate among the people themselves, and which, though they speedily give place to better information, and more deliberate reflection, have a tendency, in the meantime, to occasion dangerous innovations in the government, and serious oppressions of the minor party in the community. Though I trust the friends of the proposed Constitution will never concur with its enemies,[8] in questioning that fundamental principle of republican government, which admits the right of the people to alter or abolish the established Constitution, whenever they find it inconsistent with their happiness, yet it is not to be inferred from this principle, that the representatives of the people, whenever a momentary inclination happens to lay hold of a majority of their constituents, incompatible with the provisions in the existing Constitution, would, on that account, be justifiable in a violation of those provisions; or that the courts would be under a greater obligation to connive at infractions in this shape, than when they had proceeded wholly from the cabals of the representative body. Until the people have, by some solemn and authoritative act, annulled or changed the established form, it is binding upon themselves collectively, as well as individually; and no presumption, or even knowledge, of their sentiments, can warrant their representatives in a departure from it, prior to such an act. But it is easy to see, that it would require an uncommon portion of fortitude in the judges to do their duty as faithful guardians of the Constitution, where legislative invasions of it had been instigated by the major voice of the community.

But it is not with a view to infractions of the Constitution only, that the independence of the judges may be an essential safeguard against the effects of occasional ill humors in the society. These sometimes extend no farther than to the injury of the private rights of particular classes of citizens, by unjust and partial laws. Here also the firmness of the judicial magistracy is of vast importance in mitigating the severity and confining the operation of such laws. It not only serves to moderate the immediate mischiefs of those which may have been passed, but it operates as a check upon the legislative body in passing them; who, perceiving that obstacles to the success of iniquitous intention are to be expected from the scruples of the courts, are in a manner compelled, by the very motives of the injustice they meditate, to qualify their attempts. This is a circumstance calculated to have more influence upon the character of our governments, than but few may be aware of. The benefits of the integrity and moderation of the judiciary have already been felt in more States than one; and though they may have displeased those whose sinister expectations they may have disappointed, they must have commanded the esteem and applause of all the virtuous and disinterested. Considerate men, of every description, ought to prize whatever will tend to beget or fortify that temper in the courts; as no man can be sure that he may not be to-morrow the victim of a spirit of injustice, by which he may be a gainer today. And every man must now feel, that the inevitable tendency of such a spirit is to sap the foundations of public and private confidence, and to introduce in its stead universal distrust and distress.

That inflexible and uniform adherence to the rights of the Constitution, and of individuals, which we perceive to be indispensable in the courts of justice, can certainly not be expected from judges who hold their offices by a temporary commission. Periodical appointments, however regulated, or by whomsoever made, would, in some way or other, be fatal to their necessary independence. If the power of making them was committed either to the Executive or legislature, there would be danger of an improper complaisance to the branch which possessed it; if to both, there would be an unwillingness to hazard the displeasure of either; if to the people, or to persons chosen by them for the special purpose, there would be too great a disposition to consult popularity, to justify a reliance that nothing would be consulted but the Constitution and the laws.

There is yet a further and a weightier reason for the permanency of the judicial offices, which is deducible from the nature of the qualifications they require. It has been frequently remarked, with great propriety, that a voluminous code of laws is one of the inconveniences necessarily connected with the advantages of a free government. To avoid an arbitrary discretion in the courts, it is indispensable that they should be bound down by strict rules and precedents, which serve to define and point out their duty in every particular case that comes before them; and it will readily be conceived from the variety of controversies which grow out of the folly and wickedness of mankind, that the records of those precedents must unavoidably swell to a very considerable bulk, and must demand long and laborious study to acquire a competent knowledge of them. Hence it is, that there can be but few men in the society who will have sufficient skill in the laws to qualify them for the stations of judges. And making the proper deductions for the ordinary depravity of human nature, the number must be still smaller of those who unite the requisite integrity with the requisite knowledge. These considerations apprise us, that the government can have no great option between fit character; and that a temporary duration in office, which would naturally discourage such characters from quitting a lucrative line of practice to accept a seat on the bench, would have a tendency to throw the administration of justice into hands less able, and less well qualified, to conduct it with utility and dignity. In the present circumstances of this country, and in those in which it is likely to be for a long time to come, the disadvantages on this score would be greater than they may at first sight appear; but it must be confessed, that they are far inferior to those which present themselves under the other aspects of the subject.

Upon the whole, there can be no room to doubt that the convention acted wisely in copying from the models of those constitutions which have established *good behavior* as the tenure of their judicial offices, in point of duration; and that so far from being blamable on this account, their plan would have been inexcusably defective, if it had wanted this important feature of good government. The experience of Great Britain affords an illustrious comment on the excellence of the institution.   Publius [Hamilton]

Notes

1. The same idea, tracing the arguments to their consequences is held out in several of the late publications against the new Constitution.—Publius
2. "I mean for the Union."—Publius
3. New York has no council except for the single purpose of appointing to offices; New Jersey has a council whom the governor may consult. But I think, from the terms of the constitution, their resolutions do not bind him.—Publius
4. De Lolme.—Publius
5. Ten.—Publius
6. The celebrated Montesquieu, speaking of them, says: "Of the three powers above mentioned, the judiciary is next to nothing."—"Spirit of Laws," Vol. I, p. 186.—Publius
7. *Idem*, p. 181.—Publius
8. *Vide* "Protest of the Minority of the Convention of Pennsylvania," Martin's Speech, etc.—Publius

THE DECLARATION OF THE RIGHTS OF MAN AND OF THE CITIZEN

The Declaration was adopted August 26, 1789, by the French Constituent Assembly and served as a preamble to the French constitution of 1791.

The representatives of the people of France, formed into a National Assembly, considering that ignorance, neglect, or contempt of human rights, are the sole causes of public misfortunes and corruptions of Government, have resolved to set forth in a solemn declaration, these natural, imprescriptible, and inalienable rights: that this declaration being constantly present to the minds of the members of the body social, they may be for ever kept attentive to their rights and their duties; that the acts of the legislative and executive powers of government, being capable of being every moment compared with the end of political institutions, may be respected; and also, that the future claims of the citizens, being directed by simple and incontestable principles, may tend to the maintenance of the Constitution, and the general happiness.

For these reasons, the National Assembly doth recognize and declare, in the presence of the Supreme Being, and with the hope of his blessing and favour, the following *sacred* rights of men and of citizens:

I. Men are born, and always continue, free and equal in respect of their rights. Civil distinctions, therefore, can be founded only on public utility.

II. The end of all political associations, is the preservation of the natural and imprescriptible rights of man; and these rights are liberty, property, security, and resistance of oppression.

III. The nation is essentially the source of all sovereignty; nor can any individual, or any body of men, be entitled to any authority which is not expressly derived from it.

IV. Political liberty consists in the power of doing whatever does not injure another. The exercise of the natural rights of every man, has no other limits than those which are necessary to secure to every *other* man the free exercise of the same rights; and these limits are determinable only by the law.

V. The law ought to prohibit only actions hurtful to society. What is not prohibited by the law, should not be hindered; nor should any one be compelled to that which the law does not require.

Translated by Thomas Paine.

VI. The law is an expression of the will of the community. All citizens have a right to concur, either personally, or by their representatives, in its formation. It should be the same to all, whether it protects or punishes; and all being equal in its sight, are equally eligible to all honours, places, and employments, according to their different abilities, without any other distinction than that created by their virtues and talents.

VII. No man should be accused, arrested, or held in confinement, except in cases determined by the law, and according to the forms which it has prescribed. All who promote, solicit, execute, or cause to be executed, arbitrary orders, ought to be punished, and every citizen called upon, or apprehended by virtue of the law, ought immediately to obey, and renders himself culpable by resistance.

VIII. The law ought to impose no other penalties but such as are absolutely and evidently necessary; and no one ought to be punished, but in virtue of a law promulgated before the offence, and legally applied.

IX. Every man being presumed innocent till he has been convicted, whenever his detention becomes indispensable, all rigour to him, more than is necessary to secure his person, ought to be provided against by the law.

X. No man ought to be molested on account of his opinions, not even on account of his *religious* opinions, provided his avowal of them does not disturb the public order established by law.

XI. The unrestrained communication of thoughts and opinions being one of the most precious rights of man, every citizen may speak, write, and publish freely, provided he is responsible for the abuse of this liberty, in cases determined by law.

XII. A public force being necessary to give security to the rights of men and of citizens, that force is instituted for the benefit of the community and not for the particular benefit of the persons to whom it is intrusted.

XIII. A common contribution being necessary for the support of the public force, and for defraying the other expenses of government, it ought to be divided equally among the members of the community, according to their abilities.

XIV. Every citizen has a right, either by himself or his representative, to a free voice in determining the necessity of public contributions, the appropriation of them, and their account, mode of assessment, and duration.

XV. Every community has had a right to demand of all its agents an account of their conduct.

XVI. Every community in which a separation of powers and a security of rights is not provided for, wants a constitution.

XVII. The right to property being inviolable and sacred, no one ought to be deprived of it, except in cases of evident public necessity, legally ascertained, and on condition of a previous just indemnity.

EDMUND BURKE

Edmund Burke (1729–1797), was born in Dublin, Ireland, the son of a solici-
tor. He attended Trinity College in Dublin, and graduated in 1748. He began
the study of law at the Middle Temple in London in 1750, but he did not complete his studies. He embarked instead on a literary career and formed friendships with a number of prominent literary figures, including Dr. Samuel
Johnson. In 1757 he became secretary to Lord Rockingham, which was the
beginning of a long, distinguished, and controversial political career. Burke
represented the city of Bristol in Parliament, but following a defeat for reelec-
tion, he was given a seat from a safe "pocket borough" by Lord Rockingham.
Burke was a leader of the Rockingham element of the Whig Party, and he was
active on behalf of his native Ireland, in the prolonged impeachment proceedings against Warren Hastings, and as a critic of the French Revolution and its
English admirers.

Burke's most famous works are a satire of Lord Bolingbrooke, *A Vindication of Natural Society* (1756), and *A Philosophical Inquiry into the Origins
of Our Ideas of the Sublime and Beautiful* (1757), which influenced Kant's aesthetics, and the classic *Reflections on the Revolution in France* (1790).

Critics of conservatism often complain of being unable to isolate a distinctive body of conservative doctrine, but perhaps it is possible to discover a
cohesive set of attitudes or beliefs shared by most if not all conservatives. Here
it may be useful to regard Edmund Burke as the quintessential conservative.
One conservative attitude Burke exemplifies is the tendency not so much to
ignore principle as to place as narrow a construction on principle as possible.
With his training in law and his parliamentary experience, Burke preferred to
speak in terms of constitutional principles. Burke was a champion of the
American colonists in their dispute with the British government, but unlike
Jefferson who linked the dispute to the inalienable rights of man, Burke was
content to insist that the Americans were simply defending their rights as
Englishmen. Also, although Burke was an heir to the English Revolution of 1688
to 1689, he chose to interpret it as involving "a small and temporary deviation"
from the strict order of regular hereditary succession. Another conservative attitude Burke illustrates lies in his belief that "metaphysical" speculation, or the
dogmatic assertion of "abstract" rights, is often pernicious whether in the British
government's insistence on its rights of taxation over the American colonies or
in the French Third Estate's insistence on its rights against the monarchy and
the aristocracy. Nowhere was the harmful effect more evident to Burke than in the
French Declaration of the Rights of Man. Burke's condemnation of the Rights of
Man was so harsh and sweeping that some scholars have concluded Burke
believed only in historical rights resulting from orderly, constitutional change,
but this is not the case. Like Locke, Burke believed that men have natural rights
to life, liberty, and property, but he affirmed that the "real" rights of man lie in
the advantages that civil society makes possible. He cautioned that the effective
exercise of these rights depends very much on a proper understanding of the
historical context and on a sense of prudence. Burke strongly opposed contem-

porary English proposals for universal manhood suffrage and for greater freedom for the Dissenters on the ground that political and religious liberties were
adequately provided for under existing laws. In situations where no one could
reasonably view governmental misconduct as simply an interruption or denial
of historical constitutional rights, Burke appealed to the principles of natural
law, as he did eloquently and repeatedly in the (unsuccessful) impeachment
proceedings against Warren Hastings of the East India Company. Here Burke
defended India against what he regarded as despotism and misrule by
Englishmen, and, since no one could plausibly maintain that the people of
India were being denied their rights as Englishmen, Burke rested his case
squarely on the principles of natural law. Since Burke's commitment to the natural law has been questioned, it is important to note that Burke had read every
defender of the natural law, with the possible exception of Aquinas, and as a
devout Anglican Burke would have found it difficult to ignore the natural law
tradition of the Anglican Church. Religious faith is another attitude that Burke
shares with most but not all conservatives. Burke saw the natural moral law as
that portion of the divine law that is accessible to human reason and is applicable to all men. However, he believed that the ways in which it is applicable
depend greatly on the historical circumstances of a people. Arrangements that
promote the peace, prosperity, and liberty of a people depend on many variables, including, he thought, the participation of Divine Providence. Another
conservative attitude we find in Burke lies in his belief that a country consists of
complementary and not opposed social classes or groups. Burke saw the legislator not as a spokesman for the particular interests of a given constituency but
as a representative of the long-term interests of the nation as a whole. He saw
no opposition between land and commerce, which helps explain the difficulty
Marxists have experienced over whether to classify Burke as a champion of a
dying feudal order or of an emerging commercial class. What Burke did believe
in was the free market ideas of Adam Smith, but he also stressed the importance
of charity. Although he sometimes condemned factions, Burke, unlike James
Madison, did not regard society as being typically subject to the pressures of
opposed factions, and we find in Burke nothing like the American idea of a system of checks and balances in a federal system as a means of offsetting the divi-
siveness of faction. Burke's belief in the essential harmony of classes and groups
in society was subject to one important caveat. He distrusted intellectuals as
a group, especially when they were no longer moored (as he had been) to an
aristocratic patron or to the Church. In all matters of practical reason, Burke
believed it important to remember (as one of our contemporary political
philosophers has put it) that the view we adopt is always a view from somewhere, a fact that he believed his enemies, such as the French *philosophes*,
failed to comprehend. Burke himself can be regarded as attempting to explain
and justify the practices of what he believed to be on the whole a just constitutional regime. Although he was reluctant to appeal to first principles, this was
due in large part to his belief that these principles had found satisfactory expression in the English constitutional monarchy. This may, of course, strike us as premature self-congratulation, but what is enduring perhaps is Burke's insight that,
given the frailties of human nature and the vagaries of circumstance, we may
never enjoy a point of view from which we can correctly say that a given society
is entirely just. Although Burke believed the natural rights of man are "sacred,"
he rejected the view that the individuals who possess these rights are isolated
and atomic. For Burke, an individual person is far more than the "rights bearer"

that has been the focus of modern liberal thought. He is a member of a society with a common culture and set of traditions, and he has duties arising from his position in society.

A recent conservative critic has complained that when a tradition becomes Burkian it is already dead or dying, but this is because of the exaggerated importance he has attached to Burke's contrasts between tradition and reason and between the stability of tradition and conflict. For Burke, tradition, in a viable constitutional regime, is the product of successful conflict resolutions over many generations, and neither death nor stagnation need occur so long as we have change and piecemeal reform in which practical reason does not neglect the historical circumstances of a people. Burke's cherished ideas of prejudice, prescription, and presumption have the function of ensuring that conflict does not override the stability that tradition provides. Prejudice on Burke's view is the latent wisdom found in many but not all the opinions of a people; prescription is the recognition that rights may be established by the long exercise of their corresponding powers; and presumption is a lawyerly way of saying that rights based on prescription should prevail unless there is overwhelming evidence that they should be altered. This is Burke's (and Hume's) way of ensuring that change will not be at the expense of ordered liberty.

The definitive political biography of Burke is Carl B. Cone's two-volume *Burke and the Nature of Politics* (Lexington: University of Kentucky Press, 1957 and 1964). Two natural law interpretations of Burke that differ on important points are Peter J. Stanlis, *Edmund Burke and the Natural Law* (Ann Arbor: University of Michigan Press, 1958), and Burleigh Taylor Wilkins, *The Problem of Burke's Political Philosophy* (Oxford: Oxford University Press, 1967). For a Marxist critique of Burke, see C. B. MacPherson, *Edmund Burke* (Oxford: Oxford University Press, 1980). See also J. G. A. Pocock's *Introduction to Edmund Burke: Reflections on the Revolution in France* (Indianapolis: Hackett Publishing Company, 1987), and Alasdair MacIntyre, *After Virtue* (Notre Dame, IN: Notre Dame University Press, 1984).

B. T. W.

REFLECTIONS ON THE REVOLUTION IN FRANCE

It appears to me as if I were in a great crisis, not of the affairs of France alone, but of all Europe, perhaps of more than Europe. All circumstances taken together, the French Revolution is the most astonishing that has hitherto happened in the world. The most wonderful things are brought about in many instances by means the most absurd and ridiculous; in the most ridiculous modes; and, apparently, by the most contemptible instruments. Everything seems out of nature in this strange chaos of levity and ferocity, and of all sorts of crimes jumbled together with all sorts of follies. In viewing this monstrous tragic-comic scene, the most opposite passions necessarily succeed, and sometimes mix with each other in the mind; alternate contempt and indignation; alternate laughter and tears; alternate scorn and horror.

It cannot, however, be denied, that to some this strange scene appeared in quite another point of view. Into them it inspired no other sentiments than those of exultation and rapture. They saw nothing in what has been done in France, but a firm and temperate exertion of freedom: so consistent, on the whole, with morals and with piety as to make it deserving not only of the secular applause of dashing Machiavellian politicians, but to render it a fit theme for all the devout effusions of sacred eloquence.

On the forenoon of the 4th of November last, Doctor Richard Price, a nonconforming minister of eminence, preached at the dissenting meeting-house of the Old Jewry, to his club or society, a very extraordinary miscellaneous sermon, in which there are some good moral and religious sentiments, and not ill expressed, mixed up in a sort of porridge of various political opinions and reflections; but the Revolution in France is the grand ingredient in the cauldron. . . . His doctrines affect our constitution in its vital parts. He tells the Revolution Society in this political sermon, that his Majesty "is almost the *only* lawful king in the world, because the *only* one who owes his crown to the *choice of his people.*". . .

This doctrine, as applied to the prince now on the British throne, either is nonsense, and therefore neither true or false, or it affirms a most unfounded, dangerous, illegal, and unconstitutional position. According to this spiritual doctor of politics, if his Majesty does not owe his crown to the choice of his people, he is no *lawful king.* Now nothing can be more untrue than that the crown of this kingdom is so held by his Majesty. Therefore if you follow their rule, the king of Great Britain, who most certainly does not owe his high office to any form of popular election, is in no respect better than the rest of the gang of usurpers, who reign, or rather rob, all over the face of this miserable world, without any sort of right or title to the allegiance of their people. . . . If you admit this interpretation, how does their idea of election differ from our idea of inheritance? And how does the settlement of the crown in the Brunswick line derived from James the First come to legalize our monarchy, rather than that of any of the neighboring countries? At some time or other, to be sure, all the beginners of dynasties were chosen by those who called them to govern. There is ground enough for the opinion that all the kingdoms of Europe were, at a remote period, elective, with more or fewer limitations in the objects of choice. But whatever kings might have been here, or elsewhere, a thousand years ago, or in whatever manner the ruling dynasties of England or France may have begun, the king of Great Britain, is, at this day, king by a fixed rule of succession, according to the laws of his country; and whilst the legal conditions of the compact of sovereignty are performed by him (as they are performed), he holds his crown in contempt of the choice of the Revolution Society, who have not a single vote for a king amongst them, either individually or collectively; though I make no doubt they would soon erect themselves into an electoral college, if things were ripe to give effect to their claim. His Majesty's heirs and successors, each in his time and order, will come to the crown with the same contempt of their choice with which his Majesty has succeeded to that he wears.

Whatever may be the success of evasion in explaining away the gross error of *fact,* which supposes that his Majesty (though he holds it in concurrence with the wishes) owes his crown to the choice of his people; yet nothing can evade their full explicit declaration, concerning the principle of a right in the people to choose; which right is directly maintained, and tenaciously adhered to. All the oblique insinuations concerning election bottom in this proposition, and are referable to it. Lest the foundation of the king's exclusive legal title should pass for a mere rant of adulatory freedom, the political divine proceeds dogmatically to assert, that, by the principles of the Revolution, the people of England have acquired three fundamental rights, all which, with him, compose one system, and lie together in one short sentence; namely, that we have acquired a right,

1. "To choose our own governors."
2. "To cashier them for misconduct."
3. "To frame a government for ourselves."

This new, and hitherto unheard-of, bill of rights, though made in the name of the whole people, belongs to those gentlemen and their faction only. The body of the people of England have no share in it. They utterly disclaim it. They will resist the practical assertion of it with their lives and fortunes. They are bound to do so by the laws of their country, made at the time of that very Revolution which is appealed to in favor of the fictitious rights claimed by the society which abuses its name.

These gentlemen of the Old Jewry, in all their reasonings on the Revolution of 1688, have a Revolution which happened in England about forty years before, and the late French Revolution, so much before their eyes, and in their hearts, that they are constantly confounding all the three together. It is necessary that we should separate what they confound. We must recall their erring fancies to the acts of the Revolution which we revere, for the discovery of its true *principles*. If the *principles* of the Revolution of 1688 are anywhere to be found, it is in the statute called the Declaration of Right. In that most wise, sober, and considerate declaration, drawn up by great lawyers and great statesmen, and not by warm and inexperienced enthusiasts, not one word is said, nor one suggestion made, of a general right "to choose our own *governers; to cashier them for misconduct; and to *form* a government for *ourselves.*" . . .

You will observe, that from Magna Charta to the Declaration of Right, it has been the uniform policy of our constitution to claim and assert our liberties, as an *entailed inheritance* derived to us from our forefathers, and to be transmitted to our posterity; as an estate specially belonging to the people of this kingdom, without any reference whatever to any other more general or prior right. By this means our constitution preserves a unity in so great a diversity of its parts. We have an inheritable crown; an inheritable peerage; and a House of Commons and a people inheriting privileges, franchises, and liberties, from a long line of ancestors.

This policy appears to me to be the result of profound reflection; or rather the happy effect of following nature, which is wisdom without reflection, and above it. A spirit of innovation is generally the result of a selfish temper and confined views. People will not look forward to posterity, who never look backward to their ancestors. Besides, the people of England well know, that the idea of inheritance furnishes a sure principle of conservation and a sure principle of transmission; without at all excluding a principle of improvement. It leaves acquisition free; but it secures what it acquires. Whatever advantages are obtained by a state proceeding on these maxims, are locked fast as in a sort of family settlement; grasped as in a kind of mortmain for ever. By a constitutional policy, working after the pattern of nature, we receive, we hold, we transmit our government and our privileges, in the same manner in which we enjoy and transmit our property and our lives. The institutions of policy, the goods of fortune, the gifts of providence, are handed down to us, and from us, in the same course and order. Our political system is placed in a just correspondence and symmetry with the order of the world, and with the mode of extensive decreed to a permanent body composed of transitory parts; wherein, by the disposition of a stupendous wisdom, moulding together the great mysterious incorporation of the human race, the whole, at one time, is never old, or middle-aged, or young, but, in a condition of unchangeable constancy, moves on through the varied tenor of perpetual decay, fall, renovation, and progression. Thus, by preserving the method of nature in the conduct of the state, in what we improve, we are never wholly new; in what we retain, we are never wholly obsolete. By adhering in this manner and on those principles to our fore-fathers, we are guided not by the superstition of antiquarians, but by the spirit of philo-sophic analogy. In this choice of inheritance we have given to our frame of polity the image of a relation in blood; binding up the constitution of our country with our dearest domestic ties; adopting our fundamental laws into the bosom of our family affections; keeping inseparable, and cherishing with the warmth of all their combined and mutually reflected charities, our state, our hearths, our sepulchres, and our altars.

Through the same plan of a conformity to nature in our artificial institutions, and by calling in the aid of her unerring and powerful instincts, to fortify the fallible and feeble contrivances of our reason, we have derived several other, and those no small benefits, from considering our liberties in the light of an inheritance. Always acting as if in the presence of canonized forefathers, the spirit of freedom, leading in itself to misrule and excess, is tempered with an awful gravity. This idea of a liberal descent inspires us with a sense of habitual native dignity which prevents that upstart insolence almost inevitably adhering to and disgracing those who are the first acquirers of any distinction. By this means our liberty becomes a noble freedom. It carries an imposing and majestic aspect. It has a pedi-gree and illustrious ancestors. It has its bearings, and its ensigns armorial. It has its gallery of portraits; its monumental inscriptions; its records, evidences, and titles. We procure reverence to our civil institutions on the principle upon which nature teaches us to revere individual men; on account of their age, and on account of those from whom they are descended. All you sophisters cannot produce anything better adapted to preserve a rational and manly freedom than the course that we have pursued, who have chosen our nature rather than our speculations, our breasts rather than our inventions, for the great conservatories and magazines of our rights and privileges.

You might, if you pleased, have profited of our example, and have given to your recov-ered freedom a correspondent dignity. Your privileges, though discontinued, were not lost to memory. Your constitution, it is true, whilst you were out of possession, suffered waste and dilapidation; but you possessed in some parts the walls, and, in all, the foundations, of a noble and venerable castle. You might have repaired those walls; you might have built on those old foundations. Your constitution was suspended before it was perfected; but you had the elements of a constitution very nearly as good as could be wished. In your old states you possessed that variety of parts corresponding with the various descriptions of which your community was happily composed; you had all the combination, and all that opposition of interests, you had that action and counteraction, which, in the natural and in the political world, from the reciprocal struggle of discordant powers, draws out the harmony of the universe. These opposed and conflicting interests, which you considered as so great a blemish in your old and in our present constitution, interpose a salutary check to all precipitate resolutions. They render deliberation a matter not of choice, but of necessity; they make all change a subject of *compromise,* which naturally begets modera-tion; they produce *temperaments* preventing the sore evil of harsh, crude, unqualified refor-mations; and rendering all the headlong exertions of arbitrary power, in the few or in the many, for ever impracticable. Though the diversity of members and interests, general lib-erty had as many securities as there were separate views in the several orders; whilst by pressing down the whole by the weight of a real monarchy, the separate parts would have been prevented from warping, and starting from their allotted places.

You had all these advantages in your ancient states; but you chose to act as if you had never been moulded into civil society, and had everything to begin anew. You began ill, because you began by despising everything that belonged to you. You set up your trade without a capital. If the last generations of your country appeared without much lustre in your eyes, you might have passed them by, and derived your claims from a more early race of ancestors. Under a pious predilection for those ancestors, your imaginations would have realized in them a standard of virtue and wisdom, beyond the vulgar practice of the hour: and you would have risen with the example to whose imitation you aspired. Respecting your forefathers, you would have been taught to respect yourselves. You would not have chosen to consider the French as a people of yesterday, as a nation of low-born servile wretches until the emancipating year of 1789. . . .

Compute your gains: see what is got by those extravagant and presumptuous speculations which have taught your leaders to despise all their predecessors, and all their contemporaries, and even to despise themselves, until the moment in which they became truly despicable. By following those false lights, France has bought undisguised calamities at a higher price than any nation has purchased the most unequivocal blessings! France has bought poverty by crime! France has not sacrificed her virtue to her interest, but she has abandoned her interest, that she might prostitute her virtue. All other nations have begun the fabric of a new government, or the reformation of an old, by establishing originally, or by enforcing with greater exactness, some rites or other of religion. All other people have laid the foundations of civil freedom in severer manners, and a system of a more austere and masculine morality. France, when she let loose the reins of regal authority, doubled the license of a ferocious dissoluteness in manners, and of an insolent irreligion in opinions and practices; and has extended through all ranks of life, as if she were communicating some privilege, or laying open some secluded benefit, all the unhappy corruptions that usually were the disease of wealth and power. This is one of the new principles of equality in France. . . .

Believe me, Sir, those who attempt to level, never equalise. In all societies, consisting of various descriptions of citizens, some description must be uppermost. The levellers therefore only change and pervert the natural order of things; they load the edifice of society, by setting up in the air what the solidity of the structure requires to be on the ground. The associations of tailors and carpenters, of which the republic (of Paris, for instance) is composed, cannot be equal to the situation, into which, by the worst of usurpations, an usurpation on the prerogatives of nature, you attempt to force them.

The Chancellor of France at the opening of the States, said, in a tone of oratorical flourish, that all occupations were honourable. If he meant only, that no honest employment was disgraceful, he would not have gone beyond the truth. But in asserting that anything is honourable, we imply some distinction in its favor. The occupation of a hair-dresser, or of a working tallow-chandler, cannot be a matter of honor to any person—to say nothing of a number of other more servile employments. Such descriptions of men ought not to suffer oppression from the state; but the state suffers oppression, if such as they, either individually or collectively, are permitted to rule. In this you think you are combating prejudice, but you are at war with nature.

I do not, my dear Sir, conceive you to be of that sophistical, captious spirit, or of that uncandid dulness, as to require, for every general observation or sentiment, an explicit detail of the correctives and exceptions, which reason will presume to be included in all the general propositions which come from reasonable men. You do not imagine, that I wish to confine power, authority, and distinction to blood, and names, and titles. No, Sir. There is no qualification for government but virtue and wisdom, actual or presumptive. Wherever they are actually found, they have, in whatever state, condition, profession or trade, the passport of Heaven to human place and honor. Woe to the country which would madly and impiously reject the service of the talents and virtues, civil, military, or religious, that are given to grace and serve it; and would condemn to obscurity everything formed to diffuse lustre and glory around a state! Woe to that country too, that, passing into the opposite extreme, considers a low education, a mean contracted view of things, a sordid, mercenary occupation, as a preferable title to command! Everything ought to be open; but not indifferently to every man. No rotation; no appointment by lot; no mode of election operating in the spirit of sortition, or rotation, can be generally good in a government conversant in extensive objects. Because they have no tendency, direct or indirect, to select the man with a view to the duty, or to accommodate the one to the other. I do not hesitate to say, that the road to eminence and power from obscure condition, ought not to be made too easy, nor a thing too much of course. If rare merit be the rarest of all rare things, it ought to pass through some sort of probation. The temple of honor ought to be seated on an eminence. If it be opened through virtue, let it be remembered too, that virtue is never tried but by some difficulty and some struggle.

Nothing is a due and adequate representation of a state, that does not represent its ability, as well as its property. But as ability is a vigorous and active principle, and as property is sluggish, inert, and timid, it never can be safe from the invasions of ability, unless it be, out of all proportion, predominant in the representation. It must be represented too in great masses of accumulation, or it is not rightly protected. The characteristic essence of property, formed out of the combined principles of its acquisition and conservation, is to be *unequal*. The great masses therefore which excite envy, and tempt rapacity, must be put out of the possibility of danger. Then they form a natural rampart about the lesser properties in all their gradations. The same quantity of property, which is by the natural course of things divided among many, has not the same operation. Its defensive power is weakened as it is diffused. In this diffusion each man's portion is less than what, in the eagerness of his desires, he may flatter himself to obtain by dissipating the accumulations of others. The plunder of the few would indeed give but a share inconceivably small in the distribution to the many. But the many are not capable of making this calculation; and those who lead them to rapine never intend this distribution. . . .

It is said, that twenty-four millions ought to prevail over two hundred thousand. True; if the constitution of a kingdom be a problem of arithmetic. This sort of discourse does well enough with the lamp-post for its second: to men who *may* reason calmly, it is ridiculous. The will of the many and their interest must very often differ; and great will be the difference when they make an evil choice. A government of five hundred country attorneys and obscure curates is not good for twenty-four millions of men, though it were chosen by eight-and-forty millions; nor is it the better for being guided by a dozen of persons of quality, who have betrayed their trust in order to obtain that power. At present, you seem in everything to have strayed out of the high road of nature. The property of France does not govern it. Of course property is destroyed, and rational liberty has no existence. All you have got for the present is a paper circulation and a stock-jobbing constitution: and as to the future, do you seriously think that the territory of France, upon the republican system of eighty-three independent municipalities (to say nothing of the parts that compose them), can ever be governed as one body, or can ever be set in motion by the impulse of one mind? When the National Assembly has completed its work, it will have accomplished its ruin. These commonwealths will not long bear a state of subjection to the republic of Paris. They will not bear that this one body should monopolize the captivity of the king, and the dominion over the Assembly calling itself national. Each will keep its own portion of the spoil of the church to itself; and it will not suffer either that spoil, or the more just fruits of their industry, or the natural produce of their soil, to be sent to swell the insolence, or pamper the luxury, of the mechanics of Paris. In this they will see none of the equality, under the pretence of which they have been tempted to throw off their allegiance to their sovereign, as well as the ancient constitution of their country. There can be no capital city in such a constitution as they have lately made. They have forgot, that when they framed democratic governments, they had virtually dismembered their country. The person, whom they persevere in calling king, has not power left to him by the hundredth part sufficient to hold together this collection of republics. The republic of Paris will endeavor indeed to complete the debauchery of the army, and illegally to perpetuate the Assembly, without resort to its constituents, as the means of continuing its despotism. It will make efforts, by becoming the heart of a boundless paper circulation, to draw everything to itself; but in vain. All this policy in the end will appear as feeble as it is now violent. . . .

Far am I from denying in theory, full as far is my heart from withholding in practice (if I were of power to give or to withhold), the *real* rights of men. In denying their false claims of right, I do not mean to injure those which are real, and are such as their pretended rights would totally destroy. If civil society be made for the advantage of man, all the advantages for which it is made become his right. It is an institution of beneficence; and law itself is only beneficence acting by a rule. Men have a right to live by that rule; they have a right to do justice, as between fellows, whether their fellows are in public function or in ordinary occupation. They have a right to the fruits of their industry; and to the means of making their industry fruitful. They have a right to the acquisitions of their parents; to the nourishment and improvement of their offspring; to instruction in life, and to consolation in death. Whatever each man can separately do, without trespassing upon others, he has a right to do for himself; and he has a right to a fair portion of all which society, with all its combinations of skill and force, can do in his favor. In this partnership all men have equal rights; but not to equal things. He that has but five shillings in the partnership, has as good a right to it, as he that has five hundred pounds has to his larger proportion. But he has not a right to an equal dividend in the product of the joint stock; and as to the share of power, authority, and direction which each individual ought to have in the management of the state, that I must deny to be amongst the direct original rights of man in civil society; for I have in my contemplation the civil social man, and no other. It is a thing to be settled by convention.

If civil society be the offspring of convention, that convention must be its law. That convention must limit and modify all the descriptions of constitution which are formed under it. Every sort of legislative, judicial, or executory power are its creatures. They can have no being in any other state of things; and how can any man claim under the conventions of civil society, rights which do not so much as suppose its existence? rights which are absolutely repugnant to it? One of the first motives to civil society, and which becomes one of its fundamental rules, is, *that no man should be judge in his own case.* By this each person has at once divested himself of the first fundamental right of uncovenanted man, that is, to judge for himself, and to assert his own cause. He abdicates all right to be his own governor. He inclusively, in a great measure, abandons the right of self-defence, the first law of nature. Men can not enjoy the rights of an uncivil and of a civil state together. That he may obtain justice, he gives up his right of determining what it is in points the most essential to him. That he may secure some liberty, he makes a surrender in trust of the whole of it.

Government is not made in virtue of natural rights, which may and do exist in total independence of it; and exist in much greater clearness, and in a much greater degree of abstract perfection: but their abstract perfection is their practical defect. By having a right to everything they want everything. Government is a contrivance of human wisdom to provide for human *wants*. Men have a right that these wants should be provided for by this wisdom. Among these wants is to be reckoned the want, out of civil society, of a sufficient restraint upon their passions. Society requires not only that the passions of individuals should be subjected, but that even in the mass and body, as well as in the individuals, the inclinations of men should frequently be thwarted, their will controlled, and their passions brought into subjection. This can only be done *by a power out of themselves;* and not, in the exercise of its function, subject to that will and to those passions which it is its office to bridle and subdue. In this sense the restraints on men, as well as their liberties, are to be reckoned among their rights. But as the liberties and the restrictions vary with times and circumstances, and admit of infinite modifications, they cannot be settled upon any abstract rule; and nothing is so foolish as to discuss them upon that principle.

The moment you abate anything from the full rights of men, each to govern himself, and suffer any artificial, positive limitation upon those rights, from that moment the whole organization of government becomes a consideration of convenience. This it is which makes the constitution of a state, and the due distribution of its powers, a matter of the most delicate and complicated skill. It requires a deep knowledge of human nature and human necessities, and of the things which facilitate or obstruct the various ends, which are to be pursued by the mechanism of civil institutions. The state is to have recruits to its strength, and remedies to its distempers. What is the use of discussing a man's abstract right to food or medicine? The question is upon the method of procuring and administering them. In that deliberation I shall always advise to call in the aid of the farmer and the physician, rather than the professor of metaphysics.

The science of constructing a commonwealth, or renovating it, or reforming it, is, like every other experimental science, not to be taught *à priori.* Nor is it a short experience that can instruct us in that practical science; because the real effects of moral causes are not always immediate; but that which in the first instance is prejudicial may be excellent in its remoter operation; and its excellence may arise even from the ill effects it produces in the beginning. The reverse also happens: and very plausible schemes, with very pleasing commencements, have often shameful and lamentable conclusions. In states there are often some obscure and almost latent causes, things which appear at first view of little moment, on which a very great part of its prosperity or adversity may most essentially depend. The science of government being therefore so practical in itself, and intended for such practical purposes, a matter which requires experience, and even more experience than any person can gain in his whole life, however sagacious and observing he may be, it is with infinite caution that any man ought to venture upon pulling down an edifice, which has answered in any tolerable degree for ages the common purposes of society, or on building it up again, without having models and patterns of approved utility before his eyes.

These metaphysic rights entering into common life, like rays of light which pierce into a dense medium, are, by the laws of nature, refracted from their straight line. Indeed in the gross and complicated mass of human passions and concerns, the primitive rights of men undergo such a variety of refractions and reflections, that it becomes absurd to talk of them as if they continued in the simplicity of their original direction. The nature of man is intricate; the objects of society are of the greatest possible complexity: and therefore no simple disposition or direction or power can be suitable either to man's nature, or to the quality of his affairs. When I hear the simplicity of contrivance aimed at and boasted of in any new political constitutions, I am at no loss to decide that the artificers are grossly ignorant of their trade, or totally negligent of their duty. The simple governments are fundamentally defective, to say no worse of them. If you were to contemplate society in but one point of view, all these simple modes of polity are infinitely captivating. In effect each would answer its single end much more perfectly than the more complex is able to attain in its complex purposes. But it is better that the whole should be imperfectly and anomalously answered, than that, while some parts are provided for with great exactness, others might be totally neglected, or perhaps materially injured, by the overcare of a favorite member.

The pretended rights of these theorists are all extremes: and in proportion as they are metaphysically true, they are morally and politically false. The rights of men are in a sort of *middle,* incapable of definition, but not impossible to be discerned. The rights of men in governments are their advantages; and these are often in balances between differences of good; in compromises sometimes between good and evil, and sometimes between evil and evil. Political reason is a computing principle; adding, subtracting, multiplying, and dividing, morally and not metaphysically, or mathematically, true moral denominations.

By these theorists the right of the people is almost always sophistically confounded with their power. The body of the community, whenever it can come to act, can meet with no effectual resistance; but till power and right are the same, the whole body of them has no right inconsistent with virtue, and the first of all virtues, prudence. Men have no right to what is not reasonable, and to what is not for their benefit. . . .

History will record, that on the morning of the 6th of October, 1789, the king and queen of France, after a day of confusion, alarm, dismay, and slaughter, lay down, under the pledged security of public faith, to indulge nature in a few hours of respite, and troubled, melancholy repose. From this sleep the queen was first startled by the voice of the sentinel at her door, who cried out to her to save herself by flight—that this was the last proof of fidelity he could give—that they were upon him, and he was dead. Instantly he was cut down. A band of cruel ruffians and assassins, reeking with his blood, rushed into the chamber of the queen, and pierced with a hundred strokes of bayonets and poniards the bed, from whence this persecuted woman had but just time to fly almost naked, and, through ways unknown to the murderers, had escaped to seek refuge at the feet of a king and husband, not secure of his own life for a moment.

This king, to say no more of him, and this queen, and their infant children (who once would have been the pride and hope of a great and generous people), were then forced to abandon the sanctuary of the most splendid palace in the world, which they left swimming in blood, polluted by massacre, and strewed with scattered limbs and mutilated carcasses. Thence they were conducted into the capital of their kingdom. Two had been selected from the unprovoked, unresisted, promiscuous slaughter, which was made of the gentlemen of birth and family who composed the king's body guard. These two gentlemen, with all the parade of an execution of justice, were cruelly and publicly dragged to the block, and beheaded in the great court of the palace. Their heads were stuck upon spears, and led the procession; whilst the royal captives who followed in train were slowly moved along, amidst the horrid yells, and shrilling screams, and frantic dances, and infamous contumelies, and all the unutterable abominations of the furies of hell, in the abused shape of the vilest of women. After they had been made to taste, drop by drop, more than the bitterness of death, in the slow torture of a journey of twelve miles, protracted to six hours, they were, under a guard, composed of those very soldiers who had thus conducted them through this famous triumph, lodged in one of the old palaces of Paris, now converted into a bastille for kings. . . .

It is now sixteen or seventeen years since I saw the queen of France, then the dauphiness, at Versailles; and surely never lighted on this orb, which she hardly seemed to touch, a more delightful vision. I saw her just above the horizon, decorating and cheering the elevated sphere she just began to move in,—glittering like the morning-star, full of life, and splendor, and joy. Oh! what a revolution! and what a heart must I have to contemplate without emotion that elevation and that fall! Little did I dream when she added titles of veneration to those of enthusiastic, distant, respectful love, that she should ever be obliged to carry the sharp antidote against disgrace concealed in that bosom; little did I dream that I should have lived to see such disasters fallen upon her in a nation of gallant men, in a nation of men of honor, and of cavaliers. I thought ten thousand swords must have leaped from their scabbards to avenge even a look that threatened her with insult. But the age of chivalry is gone. That of sophisters, economists, and calculators, has succeeded; and the glory of Europe is extinguished for ever. Never, never more shall we behold that generous loyalty to rank and sex, that proud submission, that dignified obedience, that subordination of the heart, which kept alive, even in servitude itself, the spirit of an exalted freedom. The unbought grace of life, the cheap defence of nations, the nurse of manly sentiment and heroic enterprise, is gone! It is gone, that sensibility of principle, that chastity of honor, which felt a stain like a wound, which inspired courage whilst it mitigated ferocity, which ennobled whatever it touched, and under which vice itself lost half its evil, by losing all its grossness.

This mixed system of opinion and sentiment had its origin in the ancient chivalry; and the principle, though varied in its appearance by the varying state of human affairs, subsisted and influenced through a long succession of generations, even to the time we live in. If it should ever be totally extinguished, the loss I fear will be great. It is this which has given its character to modern Europe. It is this which has distinguished it under all its forms of government, and distinguished it to its advantage, from the states of Asia, and possibly from those states which flourished in the most brilliant periods of the antique world. It was this, which, without confounding ranks, had produced a noble equality, and handed it down through all the gradations of social life. It was this opinion which mitigated kings into companions, and raised private men to be fellows with kings. Without force or opposition, it subdued the fierceness of pride and power; it obliged sovereigns to submit to the soft collar of social esteem, compelled stern authority to submit to elegance, and gave a dominating vanquisher of laws to be subdued by manners.

But now all is to be changed. All the pleasing illusions, which made power gentle and obedience liberal, which harmonized the different shades of life, and which, by a bland assimilation, incorporated into politics the sentiments which beautify and soften private society, are to be dissolved by this new conquering empire of light and reason. All the decent drapery of life is to be rudely torn off. All the superadded ideas, furnished from the wardrobe of a moral imagination, which the heart owns, and the understanding ratifies, as necessary to cover the defects of our naked, shivering nature, and to raise it to dignity in our own estimation, are to be exploded as a ridiculous, absurd, and antiquated fashion.

On this scheme of things, a king is but a man, a queen is but a woman; a woman is but an animal, and an animal not of the highest order. All homage paid to the sex in general as such, and without distinct views, is to be regarded as romance and folly. Regicide, and parricide, and sacrilege, are but fictions of superstition, corrupting jurisprudence by destroying its simplicity. The murder of a king, or a queen, or a bishop, or a father, are only common homicide; and if the people are by any chance, or in any way, gainers by it, a sort of homicide much the most pardonable, and into which we ought not to make too severe a scrutiny.

On the scheme of this barbarous philosophy, which is the offspring of cold hearts and muddy understandings, and which is as void of solid wisdom as it is destitute of all taste and elegance, laws are to be supported only by their own terrors, and by the concern which each individual may find in them from his own private speculations, or can spare to them from his own private interests. In the groves of *their* academy, at the end of every vista, you see nothing but the gallows. Nothing is left which engages the affections on the part of the commonwealth. On the principles of this mechanic philosophy, our institutions can never be embodied, if I may use the expression, in persons; so as to create in us love, veneration, admiration, or attachment. But that sort of reason which banishes the affections is incapable of filling their place. These public affections, combined with manners, are required sometimes as supplements, sometimes as correctives, always as aids to law. . . . When the old feudal and chivalrous spirit of *fealty,* which, by freeing kings from fear, freed both kings and subjects from the precautions of tyranny, shall be extinct in the minds of men, plots and assassinations will be anticipated by preventive murder and preventive confiscation, and that long roll of grim and bloody maxims, which form the political code of all power, not standing on its own honor, and the honor of those who are to obey it. Kings will be tyrants from policy, when subjects are rebels from principle.

When ancient opinions and rules of life are taken away, the loss cannot possibly be estimated. From that moment we have no compass to govern us; nor can we know distinctly to what port we steer. Europe, undoubtedly, taken in a mass, was in a flourishing condition the day on which your revolution was completed. How much of that prosperous state was owing to the spirit of our old manners and opinions is not easy to say; but as such causes cannot be indifferent in their operation, we must presume, that, on the whole, their operation was beneficial.

We are but too apt to consider things in the state in which we find them, without sufficiently adverting to the causes by which they have been produced, and possibly may be upheld. Nothing is more certain than that our manners, our civilization, and all the good things which are connected with manners and with civilization, have, in this European world of ours, depended for ages upon two principles; and were indeed the result of both combined; I mean the spirit of a gentleman, and the spirit of religion. The nobility and the clergy, the one by profession, the other by patronage, kept learning in existence, even in the midst of arms and confusions, and whilst governments were rather in their causes, than formed. Learning paid back what it received to nobility and to priesthood; and paid it usury, by enlarging their ideas, and by furnishing their minds. Happy if they had all continued to know their indissoluble union, and their proper place! Happy if learning, not debauched by ambition, had been satisfied to continue the instructor, and not aspired to be the master! Along with its natural protectors and guardians, learning will be cast into the mire, and trodden down under the hoofs of a swinish multitude . . . .

I hear it is sometimes given out in France, that what is doing among you is after the example of England. I beg leave to affirm, that scarcely anything done with you has originated from the practice or the prevalent opinions of this people, either in the act or in the spirit of the proceeding. Let me add, that we are as unwilling to learn these lessons from France, as we are sure that we never taught them to that nation. The cabals here, who take a sort of share in your transactions, as yet consist of but a handful of people. . . .

As such cabals have not existed in England, so neither has the spirit of them had any influence in establishing the original frame of our constitution, or in any one of the several reparations and improvements it has undergone. The whole has been done under the auspices, and is confirmed by the sanctions of religion and piety. The whole has emanated from the simplicity of our national character, and from a sort of native plainness and directness of understanding, which for a long time characterized those men who have successively obtained authority amongst us. This disposition still remains, at least in the great body of the people.

We know, and what is better, we feel inwardly, that religion is the basis of civil society, and the source of all good and of all comfort. In England we are so convinced of this, that there is no rust of superstition, with which the accumulated absurdity of the human mind might have crusted it over in the course of ages, that ninety-nine in a hundred of the people of England would not prefer to impiety. We shall never be such fools as to call in an enemy to the substance of any system to remove its corruptions, to supply its defects, or to perfect its construction. If our religious tenets should ever want a further elucidation, we shall not call on atheism to explain them. We shall not light up our temple from that unhallowed fire. It will be illuminated with other lights. It will be perfumed with other incense, than the infectious stuff which is imported by the smugglers of adulterated metaphysics. If our ecclesiastical establishment should want a revision, it is not avarice or rapacity, public or private, that we shall employ for the audit, or receipt, or application of its consecrated revenue. Violently condemning neither the Greek nor the Armenian, nor, since heats are subsided, the Roman system of religion, we prefer the Protestant; not because we think it has less of the Christian religion in it, but because, in our judgment, it has more. We are Protestants, not from indifference, but from zeal.

We know, and it is our pride to know, that man is by his constitution a religious animal; that atheism is against, not only our reason, but our instincts; and that it cannot prevail long. But if, in the moment of riot, and in a drunken delirium from the hot spirit drawn out of the alembic of hell, which in France is now so furiously boiling, we should uncover our nakedness by throwing off that Christian religion which has hitherto been our boast and comfort, and one great source of civilization amongst us, and amongst many other nations, we are apprehensive (being well aware that the mind will not endure a void) that some uncouth, pernicious, and degrading superstition might take place of it.

For that reason, before we take from our establishment the natural, human means of estimation, and give it up to contempt, as you have done, and in doing it have incurred the penalties you well deserve to suffer, we desire that some other may be presented to us in the place of it. We shall then form our judgment.

On these ideas, instead of quarrelling with establishments, as some do, who have made a philosophy and a religion of their hostility to such institutions, we cleave closely to them. We are resolved to keep an established church, an established monarchy, an established aristocracy, and an established democracy, each in the degree it exists, and in no greater. . . .

Society is indeed a contract. Subordinate contracts for objects of mere occasional interest may be dissolved at pleasure—but the state ought not to be considered as nothing better than a partnership agreement in a trade of pepper and coffee, calico or tobacco, or some other such low concern, to be taken up for a little temporary interest, and to be dissolved by the fancy of the parties. It is to be looked on with other reverence; because it is not a partnership in things subservient only to the gross animal existence of a temporary and perishable nature. It is a partnership in all science; a partnership in all art; a partnership in every virtue, and in all perfection. As the ends of such a partnership cannot be obtained in many generations, it becomes a partnership not only between those who are living, but between those who are living, those who are dead, and those who are to be born. Each contract of each particular state is but a clause in the great primæval contract of eternal society, linking the lower with the higher natures, connecting the visible and invisible world, according to a fixed compact sanctioned by the inviolable oath which holds all physical and all moral natures, each in their appointed place. This law is not subject to the will of those, who by an obligation above them, and infinitely superior, are bound to submit their will to that law. The municipal corporations of that universal kingdom are not morally at liberty at their pleasure, and on their speculations of a contingent improvement, wholly to separate and tear asunder the bands of their subordinate community, and to dissolve it into an unsocial, uncivil, unconnected chaos of elementary principles. It is the first and supreme necessity only, a necessity that is not chosen, but chooses, a necessity paramount to deliberation, that admits no discussion, and demands no evidence, which alone can justify a resort to anarchy. This necessity is no exception to the rule; because this necessity itself is a part too of that moral and physical disposition of things, to which man must be obedient by consent or force; but if that which is only submission to necessity should be made the object of choice, the law is broken, nature is disobeyed, and the rebellious are outlawed, cast forth, and exiled, from this world of reason, and order, and peace, and virtue, and fruitful penitence, into the antagonist world of madness, discord, vice, confusion, and unavailing sorrow. . . .

When all the frauds, impostures, violences, rapines, burnings, murders, confiscations, compulsory paper currencies, and every description of tyranny and cruelty employed to bring about and to uphold this Revolution, have their natural effect, that is, to shock the moral sentiments of all virtuous and sober minds, the abettors of this philosophic system immediately strain their throats in a declaration against the old monarchial government of France. . . . Have these gentlemen never heard, in the whole circle of the worlds of theory and practice, of anything between the despotism of the monarch and the despotism of the multitude? Have they never heard of a monarchy directed by laws, controlled and balanced by the great hereditary wealth and hereditary dignity of a nation; and both again controlled by a judicious check from the reason and feeling of the people at large, acting by a suitable and permanent organ? Is it then impossible that a man may be found, who, without criminal ill intention, or pitiable absurdity, shall prefer such a mixed and tempered government to either of the extremes; and who may repute that nation to be destitute of all wisdom and of all virtue, which, having in its choice to obtain such a government with ease, *or rather to confirm it when actually possessed,* thought proper to commit a thousand crimes, and to subject their country to a thousand evils, in order to avoid it? Is it then a truth so universally acknowledged, that a pure democracy is the only tolerable form into which human society can be thrown, that a man is not permitted to hesitate about its merits, without the suspicion of being a friend to tyranny, that is, of being a foe to mankind?

I do not know under what description to class the present ruling authority in France. It affects to be a pure democracy, though I think it in a direct train of becoming shortly a mischievous and ignoble oligarchy. But for the present I admit it to be a contrivance of the nature and effect of what it pretends to. I reprobate no form of government merely upon abstract principles. There may be situations in which the purely democratic form will become necessary. There may be some (very few, and very particularly circumstanced) where it would be clearly desirable. This I do not take to be the case of France, or of any other great country. Until now, we have seen no examples of considerable democracies. The ancients were better acquainted with them. Not being wholly unread in the authors, who had seen the most of those constitutions, and who best understood them, I cannot help concurring with their opinion, that an absolute democracy, no more than absolute monarchy, is to be reckoned among the legitimate forms of government. They think it rather the corruption and degeneracy, than the sound constitution of a republic. If I recollect rightly, Aristotle observes, that democracy has many striking points of resemblance with a tyranny. Of this I am certain, that in a democracy, the majority of the citizens is capable of exercising the most cruel oppressions upon the minority, whenever strong divisions prevail in that kind of polity, as they often must; and that oppression of the minority will extend to far greater numbers, and will be carried on with much greater fury, than can almost ever be apprehended from the dominion of a single sceptre. In such a popular persecution, individual sufferers are in a much more deplorable condition than in any other. Under a cruel prince they have the balmy compassion of mankind to assuage the smart of their wounds; they have the plaudits of the people to animate their generous constancy under their sufferings: but those who are subjected to wrong under multitudes, are deprived of all external consolation. They seem deserted by mankind, overpowered by a conspiracy of their whole species. . . .

Corporate bodies are immortal for the good of the members, but not for their punishment. Nations themselves are such corporations. As well might we in England think of waging inexpiable war upon all Frenchmen for the evils which they have brought upon us in the several periods of our mutual hostilities. You might, on your part, think yourselves justified in falling upon all Englishmen on account of the unparalleled calamities brought on the people of France by the unjust invasions of our Henrys and our Edwards. Indeed we should be mutually justified in this exterminatory war upon each other, full as much as you are in the unprovoked persecution of your present countrymen, on account of the conduct of men of the same name in other times.

We do not draw the moral lessons we might from history. On the contrary, without care it may be used to vitiate our minds and to destroy our happiness. In history a great volume is unrolled for our instruction, drawing the materials of future wisdom from the past errors and infirmities of mankind. It may, in the perversion, serve for a magazine, furnishing offensive and defensive weapons for parties in church and state, and supplying the means of keeping alive, or reviving, dissensions and animosities, and adding fuel to civil fury. History consists, for the greater part, of the miseries brought upon the world by pride, ambition, avarice, revenge, lust, sedition, hypocrisy, ungoverned zeal, and all the train of disorderly appetites, which shake the public with the same

> *troublous storms that toss*
> *The private state, and render life unsweet. . . .*

Your citizens of Paris formerly had lent themselves as the ready instruments to slaughter the followers of Calvin, at the infamous massacre of St. Bartholomew. What should we say to those who could think of retaliating on the Parisians of this day the abominations and horrors of that time? They are indeed brought to abhor *that* massacre. Ferocious as they are, it is not difficult to make them dislike it; because the politicians and fashionable teachers have no interest in giving their passions exactly the same direction. Still, however, they find it their interest to keep the same savage dispositions alive. It was but the other day that they caused this very massacre to be acted on the stage for the diversion of the descendants of those who committed it. In this tragic farce they produced the cardinal of Lorraine in his robes of function, ordering general slaughter. Was this spectacle intended to make the Parisians abhor persecution, and loathe the effusion of blood?—No; it was to teach them to persecute their own pastors; it was to excite them, by raising a disgust and horror of their clergy, to an alacrity in hunting down to destruction an order, which, if it ought to exist at all, ought to exist not only in safety, but in reverence. It was to stimulate their cannibal appetites (which one would think had been gorged sufficiently) by variety and seasoning; and to quicken them to an alertness in new murders and massacres, if it should suit the purpose of the Guises of the day. An Assembly, in which sat a multitude of priests and prelates, was obliged to suffer this indignity at its door. The author was not sent to the galleys, nor the players to the house of correction. Not long after this exhibition, those players came forward to the Assembly to claim the rites of that very religion which they had dared to expose, and to show their prostituted faces in the senate, whilst the archbishop of Paris, whose function was known to his people only by his prayers and benedictions, and his wealth only by his alms, is forced to abandon his house, and to fly from his flock (as from ravenous wolves), because, truly, in the sixteenth century, the cardinal of Lorraine was a rebel and a murderer.

Such is the effect of the perversion of history, by those, who, for the same nefarious purposes, have perverted every other part of learning. But those who will stand upon that elevation of reason, which places centuries under our eye, and brings things to the true point of comparison, which obscures little names, and effaces the colors of little parties, and to which nothing can ascend but the spirit and moral quality of human actions, will say to the teachers of the Palais Royal,—The cardinal of Lorraine was the murderer of the sixteenth century, you have the glory of being the murderers in the eighteenth; and this is the only difference between you. But history in the nineteenth century, better understood, and better employed, will, I trust, teach a civilized posterity to abhor the misdeeds of both these barbarous ages. It will teach future priests and magistrates not to retaliate upon the speculative and inactive atheists of future times, the enormities committed by the present practical zealots and furious fanatics of that wretched error, which, in its quiescent state, is more than punished, whenever it is embraced. It will teach posterity not to make war upon either religion or philosophy, for the abuse which the hypocrites of both have made of the two most valuable blessings conferred upon us by the bounty of the universal Patron, who in all things eminently favors and protects the race of man.

JEREMY BENTHAM

Jeremy Bentham is the best known of the English utilitarians, a group of philosophical radicals working at the end of the eighteenth and beginning of the nineteenth centuries to formulate and apply utilitarian principles as criteria for the detailed criticism and reform of law, politics, and social institutions.

Bentham was born in 1748; he was educated at Westminster School and Queen's College, Oxford. He was admitted to the English bar in 1769, but soon forswore the practice of law as it is, for the more solitary, less remunerative, but temperamentally more congenial study of the law as it ought to be. In his earliest writings—*A Fragment on Government*, published in 1776, and *A Comment upon the Commentaries* (unpublished until 1928)—Bentham attacked the characterization of the common law and the English Constitution in William Blackstone's *Commentaries on the Laws of England* (1767), an attack that continues in the later chapters of the extract presented here.

Throughout his life, Bentham insisted that law could be understood only in terms of the determinate commands of an identifiable sovereign backed up by sanctions of some sort. He was a legal positivist, not in the sense that he thought law was or should be morally neutral or value-free, but in the sense that he rejected the idea of natural law, regarding laws instead as social facts, though of course *mutable* social facts that the community was entitled to take charge of and change and improve for the sake of the general welfare. Since law sprang from the human will, law making was to be evaluated in the same way as all other conduct concerning other people—by its tendency to promote the happiness of those affected. On this account, the student of law and politics had a twofold function: first to find out what the existing state of the law was and the effects of its operation on society, and second, to work out what the greatest-happiness principle demanded in the particular circumstances of a given society, to propose rules and institutions for putting those demands into effect, and to persuade powerful sovereigns to include those proposals in the content of their sanctioned commands.

This utilitarian approach to law, politics, and ethics was a product of the intellectual optimism that dominated continental philosophy in the eighteenth century. Under the influence of Enlightenment figures like Cesare Beccaria and Claude Helvetius, Bentham developed a precisely formulated version of utilitarianism, which he set out in perhaps his best-known work, *An Introduction to the Principles of Morals and Legislation* (1789). (The extract that follows is from an adaptation of the *Introduction* published originally in French by Bentham's disciple Etienne Dumont.)

Bentham's utilitarianism is at once a psychological theory and a normative principle: "Nature has placed mankind under the governance of two sovereign masters, *pain* and *pleasure*. It is for them alone to determine what we ought to do, as well as to determine what we shall do." The "ought" side of this equation is pretty clear. The utilitarian principle approves or disapproves of actions, including legislative actions, by their effects on the happiness of the members of the community ("the greatest happiness of the greatest number"), and Bentham provided an elaborate account of the various dimensions on which pleasure and pain would have to be measured in the "moral arithmetic" that legislative calculations ought ideally to involve.

What is less clear is how this comports with the "is" side of his theory, the view about psychological motivation. If sovereigns are motivated in fact by pleasure and pain, they are likely to pass laws that promote their own interests rather than those of their subjects. Bentham never really came to terms with this difficulty in his earlier work, but by the beginning of the nineteenth century he had become convinced that the promotion of the greatest happiness of the greatest number could be secured only by giving the greatest number some degree of influence over the careers (and thus the happiness) of their legislators, making the latter effectively accountable to them. In this way the tension between the normative and the psychological sides of Benthamism generated a pretty powerful argument for democracy.

The paradigm of utilitarian moral calculation—adding costs and benefits to members of the community, multiplying each one by its intensity and discounting it by its uncertainty—dominated Bentham's thought throughout his life. He did not believe it could be applied meticulously "to every moral judgment or to every legislative operation." And he did believe it should be supplemented by what he called "axioms of mental pathology," i.e., empirical generalizations "expressive of the connexion between such occurrences as are continually taking place, or liable to take place, and the pleasures and pains representing the result of them." (The law of the diminishing marginal utility of money is a good example.) But the calculus of utility was "always to be kept in view," if only as a way of discrediting other less consequentialist—and on Bentham's account less rational—approaches to politics, such as appeals to tradition, religion, or natural law.

In particular, it is Bentham's consequentialism that explains his antipathy to that other great reforming creed of his day, the doctrine of natural rights expounded by the American and French revolutionaries. Though he supported both revolutions, he regarded the invocation of rights as a dangerous argument stopper in politics: "When I hear of natural rights . . . I always see in the background a cluster of daggers and pikes introduced into the National Assembly." The problem with rights was conceptual as well as political. Bentham's polemic *Anarchical Fallacies* (written in the 1790s as a response to the French Declaration of the Rights of Man and the Citizen) is famous for the quip, "Natural rights is simple nonsense: natural and imprescriptible rights, rhetorical nonsense—nonsense upon stilts," and the word *nonsense* here is not just a term of abuse but the mark of another Bentham's convictions: the need for analytical clarity and linguistic precision. This concern is apt to seem pedantic to us, or even cranky in the context of Bentham's obsession with elaborate taxonomies and coining of new terms such as *demosio-tameutic* to settle problems of definition. We forget, though, how riddled with confusion political and legal discourse was in Bentham's day and how often verbal equivocation was put to the service of reaction. Macaulay was not exaggerating when he described Bentham as "the man who found jurisprudence a gibberish and left it a science."

Much the same can be said about Bentham's more practical schemes for legal and social reform. In his later years, Bentham sent out a steady stream of legislative and constitutional proposals touching almost every aspect of public affairs, from the codification of civil law to the detailed design of prisons. The recipients included not only the government of his own country but also those of Russia, France, Spain, and particularly the new republics of North and South America. During this period, the previously solitary Bentham accumulated a number of acolytes who took on the task of making his often illegible and chaotic manuscripts available in orderly form to the general public. (This process continues, with no end in sight, to this day.) He died in 1832, surrounded by these acolytes and by well over 70,000 pages of manuscript material.

That few of Bentham's proposals were ever taken up directly by those who received them might lead us to regard this body of work as the cranky production of a utilitarian Mad Hatter, closeted in his study and beguiled by the intricacies of his own crabbed system. In fact, his lasting legacy was the spirit of rational reform that came to dominate English politics through the work of those whose intelligence and political instincts were molded by Bentham's example. We tend to underestimate this legacy now, because we take for granted many of the reforms that were animated by the rational, radical, and calculating spirit of Benthamism. It is easy to forget how savage and chaotic the English criminal law was until the utilitarians set about campaigning for its reform and rationalization in the nineteenth century. It was not just the criminal law. One commentator offered this list in the London *Times*, a century after Bentham's death:

> The reform of the representative system in Parliament; the removal of defects in the jury system, the abolition of imprisonment for debt, the sweeping away of usury laws, reform of the law of evidence, reform of the Poor Law, the establishment of a national system of education, an extension of the idea of savings banks, cheap postage, a complete and uniform Register of Births, Deaths and Marriages, a Code for Merchant Shipping, protection of inventors, uniform and scientific methods of drafting Acts of Parliament, the passing of public health legislation. . . .

To us, the commentator remarked, the list makes quite dull reading. But in 1800 it was an heroic adventure, "for when Bentham set forth his polity all these things were impossible, absurd, ridiculous. Great intellects waved them away. . . ."

Thus we should read the extract that follows not just as a practical manifesto, but as an earnest, if rather labored, attempt to found a new political culture, not forgetting how hard it was at the beginning of the nineteenth century to sustain thinking in these or any similar terms in public life, against the baying of prejudice, terror, superstition, equivocation, and humbug that for time immemorial had greeted any attempt to rehabilitate the fabric of English society and its law.

There are excellent discussions of Bentham's political philosophy in Ross Harrison, *Bentham* (London: Routledge, 1983); in "The Arguments of the Philosophers" series, in Douglas Long, *Bentham on Liberty* (Toronto: University of Toronto Press, 1977); and in Nancy Rosenblum, *Bentham's Theory of the State* (Cambridge: Harvard University Press, 1978). For his legal theory, see Gerald Postema, *Bentham and the Common Law Tradition* (Oxford: Clarendon Press, 1986), and *Essays on Bentham* (Oxford: Clarendon Press, 1983) by one of this century's most distinguished Bentham editors, H. L. A. Hart.

J. W.

PRINCIPLES OF LEGISLATION

CHAPTER I

The Principle of Utility

The Public Good ought to be the object of the legislator; General Utility ought to be the foundation of his reasonings. To know the true good of the community is what constitutes the science of legislation; the art consists in finding the means to realize that good.

The principle of *utility,* vaguely announced, is seldom contradicted; it is even looked upon as a sort of commonplace in politics and morals. But this almost universal assent is only apparent. The same ideas are not attached to this principle; the same value is not given to it; no uniform and logical manner of reasoning results from it.

To give it all the efficacy which it ought to have, that is, to make it the foundation of a system of reasonings, three conditions are necessary.

First,—To attach clear and precise ideas to the word *utility,* exactly the same with all who employ it.

Second,—To establish the unity and the sovereignty of this principle, by rigorously excluding every other. It is nothing to subscribe to it in general; it must be admitted without any exception.

Third,—To find the processes of a moral arithmetic by which uniform results may be arrived at.

The causes of dissent from the doctrine of utility may all be referred to two false principles, which exercise an influence, sometimes open and sometimes secret, upon the judgments of men. If these can be pointed out and excluded, the true principle will remain in purity and strength.

These three principles are like three roads which often cross each other, but of which only one leads to the wished-for destination. The traveller turns often from one into another, and loses in these wanderings more than half his time and strength. The true route is however the easiest; it has mile-stones which cannot be shifted, it has inscriptions, in a universal language, which cannot be effaced; while the two false routes have only contradictory direction in enigmatical characters. But without abusing the language of allegory, let us seek to give a clear idea of the true principle, and of its two adversaries.

Nature has placed man under the empire of *pleasure* and of *pain.* We owe to them all our ideas; we refer to them all our judgments and all the determinations of our life. He who pretends to withdraw himself from this subjection knows not what he says. His only object is to seek pleasure and to shun pain, even at the very instant that he rejects the greatest pleasures or embraces pains the most acute. These eternal and irresistible sentiments ought to be the great study of the moralist and the legislator. The *principle of utility* subjects everything to these two motives.

Utility is an abstract term. It expresses the property or tendency of a thing to prevent some evil or to procure some good. *Evil* is pain, or the cause of pain. *Good* is pleasure, or the cause of pleasure. That which is comfortable to the utility, or the interest of an individual, is what tends to augment the total sum of his happiness. That which is conformable to the utility, or the interest of a community, is what tends to augment the total sum of happiness of the individuals that compose it.

Translated by Richard Hildreth.

A *principle* is a first idea, which is made the beginning or basis of a system of reasonings. To illustrate it by a sensible image, it is a fixed point to which the first link of a chain is attached. Such a principle must be clearly evident—to illustrate and to explain it must secure its acknowledgment. Such are the axioms of mathematics; they are not proved directly; it is enough to show that they cannot be rejected without falling into absurdity.

The *logic of utility* consists in setting out, in all the operations of the judgment, from the calculation or comparison of pains and pleasures, and in not allowing the interference of any other idea.

I am a partisan of the *principle of utility* when I measure my approbation or disapprobation of a public or private act by its tendency to produce pleasure or pain; when I employ the words *just, unjust, moral, immoral, good, bad,* simply as collective terms including the ideas of certain pains or pleasures; it always being understood that I use the words *pain* and *pleasure* in their ordinary signification, without inventing any arbitrary definition for the sake of excluding certain pleasures or denying the existence of certain pains. In this matter we want no refinement, no metaphysics. It is not necessary to consult Plato, nor Aristotle. *Pain* and *pleasure* are what everybody feels to be such—the peasant and the prince, the unlearned as well as the philosopher.

He who adopts the *principle of utility,* esteems virtue to be a good only on account of the pleasures which result from it; he regards vice as an evil only because of the pains which it produces. Moral good is *good* only by its tendency to produce physical good. Moral evil is *evil* only by its tendency to produce physical evil; but when I say *physical,* I mean the pains and pleasures of the soul as well as the pains and pleasures of sense. I have in view man, such as he is, in his actual constitution.

Programs for Reform

If the partisan of the *principle of utility* finds in the common list of virtues an action from which there results more pain than pleasure, he does not hesitate to regard that pretended virtue as a vice; he will not suffer himself to be imposed upon by the general error; he will not lightly believe in the policy of employing false virtues to maintain the true.

If he finds in the common list of offenses some indifferent action, some innocent pleasure, he will not hesitate to transport this pretended offence into the class of lawful actions; he will pity the pretended criminals, and will reserve his indignation for their persecutors.

CHAPTER II

The Ascetic Principle[1]

This principle is exactly the rival, the antagonist of that which we have just been examining. Those who follow it have a horror of pleasures. Everything which gratifies the senses, in their view, is odious and criminal. They found morality upon privations, and virtue upon the renouncement of one's self. In one word, the reverse of the partisans of utility, they approve everything which tends to diminish enjoyment, they blame everything, which tends to augment it.

This principle has been more or less followed by two classes of men, who in other respects have scarce any resemblance, and who even affect a mutual contempt. The one class are philosophers, the other, devotees. The ascetic philosophers, animated by the hope of applause, have flattered themselves with the idea of seeming to rise above humanity, by despising vulgar pleasures. They expect to be paid in reputation and in glory, for all the sacrifices which they seem to make to the severity of their maxims. The ascetic devotees are foolish people, tormented by vain terrors. Man, in their eyes, is but a degenerate being, who ought to punish himself without ceasing for the crime of being born, and never to turn off his thoughts from that gulf of eternal misery which is ready to open beneath his feet. Still, the martyrs to these absurd opinions have, like all others, a fund of hope. Independent of the worldly pleasures attached to the reputation of sanctity, these atrabilious pietists flatter themselves that every instant of voluntary pain here below will procure them an age of happiness in another life. Thus, even the ascetic principle reposes upon some false idea of utility. It acquired its ascendancy only through mistake.[2]

The devotees have carried the ascetic principle much further than the philosophers. The philosophical party has confined itself to censuring pleasures; the religious sects have turned the infliction of pain into a duty. The stoics said that pain was not an evil; the Jansenists maintained that it was actually a good. The philosophical party never reproved pleasures in the mass, but only those which it called gross and sensual, while it exalted the pleasures of sentiment and understanding. It was rather a preference for the one class, than a total exclusion of the other. Always despised, or disparaged under its true name, pleasure was received and applauded when it took the titles of *honour, glory, reputation, decorum,* or *self-esteem.*

Not to be accused of exaggerating the absurdity of the ascetics, I shall mention the least unreasonable origin which can be assigned to their system.

It was early perceived that the attraction of pleasure might seduce into pernicious acts; that is, acts of which the good was not equivalent to the evil. To forbid these pleasures, in consideration of their bad effects, is the object of sound morals and good laws. But the ascetics have made a mistake, for they have attacked pleasure itself; they have condemned it in general; they have made it the object of a universal prohibition, the sign of a reprobate nature; and it is only out of regard for human weakness that they have had the indulgence to grant some particular exemptions.

CHAPTER III

The Arbitrary Principle; or the Principle of Sympathy and Antipathy

This principle consists in approving or blaming by sentiment, without giving any other reason for the decision except the decision itself. *I love; I hate;* such is the pivot on which this principle turns. An action is judged to be good or bad, not because it is conformable, or on the contrary, to the interest of those whom it affects, but because it pleases or displeases him who judges. He pronounces sovereignly; he admits no appeal; he does not think himself obliged to justify his opinion by any consideration relative to the good of society. "It is my interior persuasion; it is my intimate conviction; I feel it; sentiment consults nobody; the worse for him who does not agree with me—he is not a man, he is a monster in human shape." Such is the despotic tone of these decisions.

But, it may be asked, are there men so unreasonable as to dictate their particular sentiments as laws, and to arrogate to themselves the privilege of infallibility? What you call the *principle of sympathy and antipathy* is not a principle of reasoning; it is rather the negation, the annihilation of all principle. A true anarchy of ideas results from it; since every man having an equal right to give *his* sentiments as a universal rule, there will no longer be any common measure, no ultimate tribunal to which we can appeal.

Without doubt the absurdity of this principle is sufficiently manifest. No man, therefore, is bold enough to say openly, "I wish you to think as I do, without giving me the trouble to reason with you." Every one would revolt against a pretension so absurd. Therefore, recourse is had to diverse inventions of disguise. Despotism is veiled under some ingenious phrase. Of this the greater part of philosophical systems are a proof.

One man tells you that he has in himself something which has been given him to teach what is good and what is evil; and this he calls either his *conscience* or his *moral sense.* Then, working at his case, he decides such a thing to be good, such another to be bad. Why? Because my moral sense tells me so; because my conscience approves or disapproves it.

Another comes and the phrase changes. It is no longer the moral sense,—it is *common sense* which tells him what is good and what is bad. This common sense is a sense, he says, which belongs to everybody; but then he takes good care in speaking of everybody to make no account of those who do not think as he does.

Another tells you that this moral sense and this common sense are but dreams; that the *understanding* determines what is good and what is bad. His understanding tells him so and so; all good and wise men have just such an understanding as he has. As to those who do not think in the same way, it is a clear proof that their understandings are defective or corrupt.

Another tells you that he has an *eternal and immutable rule of right,* which rule commands this and forbids that; then he details to you his own particular sentiments, which you are obliged to receive as so many branches of the eternal rule of right.

You hear a multitude of professors, of jurists, of magistrates, of philosophers, who make the *law of nature* echo in your ears. They all dispute, it is true, upon every point of their system; but no matter—each one proceeds with the same confident intrepidity, and utters his opinions as so many chapters of the *law of nature.* The phrase is sometimes modified, and we find in its place, *natural right, natural equity, the rights of man,* etc.

One philosopher undertakes to build a moral system upon what he calls *truth;* according to him, the only evil in the world is lying. If you kill your father, you commit a crime, because it is a particular fashion of saying that he is not your father. Everything which this philosopher does not like, he disapproves under the pretext that it is a sort of falsehood—since it amounts to asserting that we ought to do what ought not to be done. . . .

To sum up—the *ascetic principle* attacks utility in front. The *principle of sympathy* neither rejects it nor admits it; it pays no attention to it; it floats at hazard between good and evil. The ascetic principle is so unreasonable, that its most senseless followers have never attempted to carry it out. The principle of sympathy and antipathy does not prevent its partisans from having recourse to the principle of utility. This last alone neither asks nor admits any exceptions. *Qui non sub me contra me;* that which is not under me is against me; such is its motto. According to this principle, to legislate is an affair of observation and calculation; according to the ascetics, it is an affair of fanaticism; according to the principle of sympathy and antipathy, it is a matter of humour, of imagination, of taste. The first method is adapted to philosophers; the second to monks; the third is the favourite of wits, of ordinary moralists, of men of the world, of the multitude.

CHAPTER IV

Operation of These Principles Upon Legislation

. . . The principle which has exercised the greatest influence upon governments, is that of sympathy and antipathy. In fact, we must refer to that principle all those specious objects which governments pursue, without having the general good for a single and independent aim; such as good morals, equality, liberty, justice, power, commerce, religion; objects respectable in themselves, and which ought to enter into the views of the legislator; but which too often lead him astray, because he regards them as ends, not as means. He substitutes them for public happiness, instead of making them subordinate to it.

Thus, a government, entirely occupied with wealth and commerce, looks upon society as a workshop, regards men only as productive machines, and cares little how much it torments them, provided it makes them rich. The customs, the exchanges, the stocks, absorb all its thoughts. It looks with indifference upon a multitude of evils which it might easily cure. It wishes only for a great production of the means of enjoyment, while it is constantly putting new obstacles in the way of enjoying.

Other governments esteem power and glory as the sole means of public good. Full of disdain for those states which are able to be happy in a peaceful security, they must have intrigues, negotiations, wars and conquests. They do not consider of what misfortunes this glory is composed, and how many victims these bloody triumphs require. The *éclat* of victory, the acquisition of a province, conceal from them the desolation of their country, and make them mistake the true end of government.

Many persons do not inquire if a state be well administered; if the laws protect property and persons; if the people are happy. What they require, without giving attention to anything else, is political liberty—that is, the most equal distribution which can be imagined of political power. Wherever they do not see the form of government to which they are attached, they see nothing but slaves; and if these pretended slaves are well satisfied with their condition, if they do not desire to change it, they despise and insult them. In their fanaticism they are always ready to stake all the happiness of a nation upon a civil war, for the sake of transporting power into the hands of those whom an invincible ignorance will not permit to use it, except for their own destruction. . . .

CHAPTER VII

Pains and Pleasures Considered as Sanctions

The will cannot be influenced except by motives; but when we speak of *motives* we speak of *pleasures* or *pain*. A being whom we could not effect either by painful or pleasurable emotions would be completely independent of us.

The pain or pleasure which is attached to a law form what is called its sanction. The laws of one state are not laws in another because they have no sanction there, no obligatory force.

Pleasures and pains may be distinguished into four classes:

1st. Physical.

2nd. Moral.

3rd. Political.

4th. Religious.

Consequently, when we come to consider pains and pleasures under the character of punishments and rewards, attached to certain rules of conduct, we may distinguish four sanctions.

1st. Those pleasures and pains which may be expected from the ordinary course of nature, acting by itself, without human intervention, compose the *natural* or *physical sanction.*

2nd. The pleasures or pains which may be expected from the action of our fellow-men, in virtue of their friendship or hatred, of their esteem or their contempt—in one word, of their spontaneous disposition towards us, compose the *moral sanction;* or it may be called the *popular sanction, sanction of public opinion, sanction of honour, sanction of the pains and pleasures of sympathy.*

3rd. The pleasures or pains which may be expected from the action of the magistrate, in virtue of the laws, compose the *political sanction;* it may also be called the *legal sanction.*

4th. The pleasures or pains which may be expected in virtue of the threats or promises of religion, compose the *religious sanction.*

A man's house is destroyed by fire. Is it in consequence of his imprudence?—It is a pain of the natural sanction. Is it by the sentence of a judge?—It is a pain of the political sanction. Is it by the malice of his neighbours?—It is a pain of the popular sanction. Is it supposed to be the immediate act of an offended Divinity?—In such a case it would be a pain of the religious sanction, or vulgarly speaking, a judgement of God.

It is evident from this example that the same sort of pains belong to all the sanctions. The only difference is in the circumstances which produce them.

This classification will be very useful in the course of this work. It is an easy and uniform nomenclature, absolutely necessary to distinguish and describe the different kinds of moral powers, those intellectual levers which constitute the machinery of the human heart.

These four sanctions do not act upon all men in the same manner, nor with the same degree of force. They are sometimes rivals, sometimes allies, and sometimes enemies. When they agree, they operate with an irresistible power; when they are in opposition, they mutually enfeeble each other; when they are rivals, they produce uncertainties and contradictions in the conduct of men.

Four bodies of laws may be imagined, corresponding to these four sanctions. The highest point of perfection would be reached if these four codes constituted but one. This perfection, however, is as yet far distant, though it may not be impossible to attain it. But the legislator ought always to recollect that he can operate directly only by means of the political sanction. The three others must necessarily be its rivals or its allies, its antagonists or its ministers. If he neglects them in his calculations, he will be deceived in his results; but if he makes them subservient to his views, he will gain an immense power. There is no chance of uniting them, except under the standard of utility.

The natural sanction is the only one which always acts; the only one which works of itself; the only one which is unchangeable in its principal characteristics. It insensibly draws all the others to it, corrects their deviations, and produces whatever uniformity there is in the sentiments and the judgments of men.

The popular sanction and the religious sanction are more variable, more dependant upon human caprices. Of the two, the popular sanction is more equal, more steady, and more constantly in accordance with the principle of utility. The force of the religious sanction is more unequal, more apt to change with times and individuals, more subject to dangerous deviations. It grows weak by repose, but revives by opposition.

In some respects the political sanction has the advantage of both. It acts upon all men with a more equal force; it is clearer and more precise in is precepts; it is surer and more exemplary in its operations; finally, it is more susceptible of being carried to perfection. Its progress has an immediate influence upon the progress of the other two; but it embraces only actions of a certain kind; it has not a sufficient hold upon the private conduct of individuals; it cannot proceed except upon proofs which it is often impossible to obtain; and secrecy, force, or stratagem are able to escape it. It thus appears, from considering what each of these sanctions can effect, and what they cannot, that neither ought to be rejected, but that all should be employed and directed towards the same end. They are like magnets, of which the virtue is destroyed when they are presented to each other by their contrary poles, while their power is doubled when they are united by the poles which correspond.

It may be observed, in passing, that the systems which have most divided men have been founded upon an exclusive preference given to one or the other of these sanctions. Each has had its partisans, who have wished to exalt it above the others. Each has had its enemies, who have sought to degrade it by showing its weak side, exposing its errors, and developing all the evils which have resulted from it, without making any mention of its good effects. Such is the true theory of all those paradoxes which elevate nature against society, politics against religion, religion against nature and government, and so on.

Each of these sanctions is susceptible of error, that is to say, of some applications contrary to the principle of utility. But by applying the nomenclature above explained, it is easy to indicate by a single word the seat of the evil. Thus, for example, the reproach which after the punishment of a criminal falls upon an innocent family is an error of the popular sanction. The offence of usury, that is, of receiving interest above the legal interest, is an error of the political sanction. Heresy and magic are errors of the religious sanction. Certain sympathies and antipathies are errors of the natural sanction. The first germ of mistake exists in some single sanction, whence it commonly spreads into the others. It is necessary, in all these cases, to discover the origin of the evil before we can select or apply the remedy.

CHAPTER VIII

The Measure of Pleasures and Pains

The sole object of the legislator is to increase pleasures and to prevent pains; and for this purpose he ought to be well acquainted with their respective values. As pleasures and pains are the only instruments which he employs, he ought carefully to study their power.

If we examine the *value* of a pleasure, considered in itself, and in relation to a single individual, we shall find that it depends upon four circumstances,—

1st. *Its intensity.*
2nd. *Its duration.*
3rd. *Its certainty.*
4th. *Its proximity.*

The value of a pain depends upon the same circumstances.

But it is not enough to examine the value of pleasures and pains as if they were isolated and independent. Pains and pleasures may have other pains and pleasures as their consequences. Therefore, if we wish to calculate the *tendency* of an act from which there results an immediate pain or pleasure, we must take two additional circumstances into the account, viz.—

5th. *Its productiveness.*

6th. *Its purity.*

A *productive pleasure* is one which is likely to be followed by other pleasures of the same kind.

A *productive pain* is one which is likely to be followed by other pains of the same kind.

A *pure pleasure* is one which is not likely to produce pains.

A *pure pain* is one which is not likely to produce pleasures.

When the calculation is to be made in relation to a collection of individuals, yet another element is necessary,—

7th. *Its extent.*

That is, the number of persons who are likely to find themselves affected by this pain or pleasure.

When we wish to value an action, we must follow in detail all the operations above indicated. These are the elements of moral calculation; and legislation thus becomes a matter of arithmetic. The *evil* produced is the outgo, the *good* which results is the income. The rules of this calculation are like those of any other. This is a slow method, but a sure one; while what is called sentiment is a prompt estimate, but apt to be deceptive. It is not necessary to recommence this calculation upon every occasion. When one has become familiar with the process; when he has acquired the justness of estimate which results from it; he can compare the sum of good and evil with so much promptitude as scarcely to be conscious of the steps of the calculation. It is thus that we perform many arithmetical calculations, almost without knowing it. The analytical method, in all its details, becomes essential, only when some new or complicated matter arises; when it is necessary to clear up some disputed point, or to demonstrate a truth to those who are yet unacquainted with it.

This theory of moral calculation, though never clearly explained, has always been followed in practice; at least, in every case where men have had clear ideas of their interest. What is it, for example, that makes up the value of a landed estate? Is it not the amount of pleasure to be derived from it? and does not this value vary according to the length of time for which the estate is to be enjoyed; according to the nearness or the distance of the moment when the possession is to begin; according to the certainty or uncertainty of its being retained?

Errors, whether in legislation or the moral conduct of men, may be always accounted for by a mistake, a forgetfulness, or a false estimate of some one of these elements, in the calculation of good and evil.

CHAPTER IX

Circumstances Which Affect Sensibility

All causes of pleasure do not give the same pleasure to all; all causes of pain do not always produce the same pain. It is in this that *difference of sensibility* consists. This difference is in degree, or in kind: in degree, when the impression of a given cause upon many individuals is uniform, but unequal; in kind, when the same cause produces opposite sensations in different individuals.

This difference of sensibility depends upon certain circumstances which influence the physical or moral condition of individuals, and which, being changed, produce a corresponding change in their feelings. This is an experimental fact. Things do not affect us in the same manner in sickness and ill health, in plenty and in poverty, in infancy and old age. But a view so general is not sufficient; it is necessary to go deeper into the human heart. Lyonet wrote a quarto volume upon the anatomy of the caterpillar; morals are in need of an investigator as patient and philosophical. I have not courage to imitate Lyonet. I shall think it sufficient if I open a new point of view—if I suggest a surer method to those who wish to pursue this subject.

The foundation of the whole is *temperament,* or the original constitution. By this word I understand that radical and primitive disposition which attends us from our birth, and which depends upon physical organization, and the nature of the soul.

But although this radical constitution is the basis of all the rest, this basis lies so concealed that it is very difficult to get at it, so as to distinguish those varieties of sensibility which it produces from those which belong to other causes.

It is the business of the physiologist to distinguish these temperaments; to follow out their mixtures; and to trace their effects. But these grounds are as yet too little known to justify the moralist or legislator in founding anything upon them. . . .

CHAPTER X

Analysis of Political Good and Evil.—How They are Diffused Through Society

It is with government as with medicine; its only business is the choice of evils. Every law is an evil, for every law is an infraction of liberty. Government, I repeat it, has but the choice of evils. In making that choice, what ought to be the object of the legislator? He ought to be certain of two things: 1st, that in every case, the acts which he undertakes to prevent are really evils; and, 2nd, that these evils are greater than those which he employs to prevent them.

He has then two things to note—the evil of the offence, and the evil of the law; the evil of the malady, and the evil of the remedy.

An evil seldom comes alone. A portion of evil can hardly fall upon an individual, without spreading on every side, as from a centre. As it spreads, it takes different forms. We see an evil of one kind coming out of an evil of another kind; We even see evil coming out of good, and good out of evil. . . .

The propagation of good is less rapid and less sensible than that of evil. The seed of good is not so productive in hopes as the seed of evil is fruitful in alarms. But this difference is abundantly made up, for good is a necessary result of natural causes which operate always; while evil is produced only by accident, and at intervals.

Society is so constituted that, in labouring for our particular good, we labour also for the good of the whole. We cannot augment our own means of enjoyment without augmenting also the means of others. Two nations, like two individuals, grow rich by a mutual commerce; and all exchange is founded upon reciprocal advantages.

It is fortunate also that the effects of evil are not always evil. They often assume the contrary quality. Thus, juridical punishments applied to offenses, although they produce an evil of the first order, are not generally regarded as evils, because they produce a good of the second order. They produce alarm and danger,—but for whom? Only for a class of evil-doers, who are voluntary sufferers. Let them obey the laws, and they will be exposed neither to danger nor alarm.

We should never be able to subjugate, however imperfectly, the vast empire of evil, had we not learned the method of combatting one evil by another. It has been necessary to enlist auxiliaries among pains, to oppose other pains which attack us on every side. So, in the art of curing pains of another sort, poisons well applied have proved to be remedies.

CHAPTER XII

The Limits Which Separate Morals from Legislation

Morality in general is the art of directing the actions of men in such a way as to produce the greatest possible sum of good.

Legislation ought to have precisely the same object.

But although these two arts, or rather sciences, have the same end they differ greatly in extent. All actions, whether public or private, fall under the jurisdiction of morals. It is a guide which leads the individual, as it were, by the hand through all the details of his life, all his relations with his fellows. Legislation cannot do this; and, if it could, it ought not to exercise a continual interference and dictation over the conduct of men.

Morality commands each individual to do all that is advantageous to the community, his own personal advantages included. But there are many acts useful to the community which legislation ought not to command. There are also many injurious actions which it ought not to forbid, although morality does so. In a word, legislation has the same centre with morals, but it has not the same circumference.

There are two reasons for this difference: 1st. Legislation can have no direct influence upon the conduct of men, except by punishments. Now these punishments are so many evils, which are not justifiable, except so far as there results from them a greater sum of good. But, in many cases in which we might desire to strengthen a moral precept by a punishment, the evil of the punishment would be greater than the evil of the offence. The means necessary to carry the law into execution would be of a nature to spread through society a degree of alarm more injurious than the evil intended to be prevented.

2nd. Legislation is often arrested by the danger of overwhelming the innocent in seeking to punish the guilty. Whence comes this danger? From the difficulty of defining an offence, and giving a clear and precise idea of it. For example, hardheartedness, ingratitude, perfidy, and other vices which the popular sanction punishes, cannot come under the power of the laws, unless they are defined as exactly as theft, homicide, or perjury.

But, the better to distinguish the true limits of morals and legislation, it will be well to refer to the common classification of moral duties.

Private morality regulates the actions of men, either in that part of their conduct in which they alone are interested, or in that which may affect the interests of others. The actions which affect a man's individual interest compose a class called, perhaps improperly, *duties to ourselves;* and the quality or disposition manifested in the accomplishment of those duties receives the name of *prudence.* That part of conduct which relates to others composes a class of actions called *duties to others.* Now there are two ways of consulting the happiness of others: the one negative, abstaining from diminishing it; the other positive, labouring to augment it. The first constitutes *probity;* the second is *beneficence.*

Morality upon these three points needs the aid of the law; but not in the same degree, nor in the same manner.

I. The rules of prudence are almost always sufficient of themselves. If a man fails in what regards his particular private interest, it is not his will which is in fault, it is his understanding. If he does wrong, it can only be through mistake. The fear of hurting himself is a motive of repression sufficiently strong; it would be useless to add to it the fear of an artificial pain.

Does any one object, that facts show the contrary? That excesses of play, those of intemperance, the illicit intercourse between the sexes, attended so often by the greatest dangers, are enough to prove that individuals have not always sufficient prudence to abstain from what hurts them?

Confining myself to a general reply, I answer, in the first place, that, in the greater part of these cases, punishment would be so easily eluded, that it would be inefficacious; secondly, that the evil produced by the penal law would be much beyond the evil of the offence.

Suppose, for example, that a legislator should feel himself authorized to undertake the extirpation of drunkenness and fornication by direct laws. He would have to begin by a multitude of regulations. The first inconvenience would therefore be a complexity of laws. The easier it is to conceal these vices, the more necessary it would be to resort to severity of punishment, in order to destroy by the terror of examples the constantly recurring hope of impunity. This excessive rigour of laws forms a second inconvenience not less grave than the first. The difficulty of procuring proofs would be such that it would be necessary to encourage informers, and to entertain an army of spies. This necessity forms a third inconvenience, greater than either of the others. Let us compare the results of good and evil. Offenses of this nature, if that name can be properly given to imprudences, produce no alarm; but the pretended remedy would spread a universal terror; innocent or guilty, every one would fear for himself or his connexions; suspicions and accusations would render society dangerous; we should fly from it; we should involve ourselves in mystery and concealment; we should shun all the disclosures of confidence. Instead of suppressing one vice, the laws would produce other vices, new and more dangerous.

It is true that example may render certain excesses contagious; and that an evil which would be almost imperceptible, if it acted only upon a small number of individuals, may become important by its extent. All that the legislator can do in reference to offenses of this kind is, to submit them to some slight punishment in cases of scandalous notoriety. This will be sufficient to give them a taint of illegality, which will excite the popular sanction against them.

It is in cases of this kind that legislators have governed too much. Instead of trusting to the prudence of individuals, they have treated them like children, or slaves. They have suffered themselves to be carried away by the same passion which has influenced the founders of religious orders, who, to signalize their authority, and through a littleness of spirit, have held their subjects in the most abject dependence, and have traced for them, day by day, and moment by moment, their occupations, their food, their rising up, their lying down, and all the petty details of their life. There are celebrated codes, in which are found a multitude of clogs of this sort; there are useless restraints upon marriage; punishments decreed against celibacy; sumptuary laws regulating the fashion of dress, the expense of festivals, the furniture of houses, and the ornaments of women; there are numberless details about ailments, permitted or forbidden; about ablutions of such or such a kind; about the purifications which health or cleanliness require; and a thousand similar puerilities, which add, to all the inconveniences of useless restraint, that of besotting the people, by covering these absurdities with a veil of mystery, to disguise their folly.

Yet more unhappy are the States in which it is attempted to maintain by penal laws a uniformity of religious opinions. The choice of their religion ought to be referred entirely to the prudence of individuals. If they are persuaded that their eternal happiness depends upon a certain form of worship or a certain belief, what can a legislator oppose to an interest so great? It is not necessary to insist upon this truth—it is generally acknowledged; but, in tracing the boundaries of legislation, I cannot forget those which it is the most important not to overstep.

As a general rule, the greatest possible latitude should be left to individuals, in all cases in which they can injure none but themselves, for they are the best judges of their own interests. If they deceive themselves, it is to be supposed that the moment they discover their error they will alter their conduct. The power of the law need interfere only to prevent them from injuring each other. It is there that restraint is necessary; it is there that the application of punishments is truly useful, because the rigour exercised upon an individual becomes in such a case the security of all.

II. It is true that there is a natural connection between prudence and probity; for our own interest, well understood, will never leave us without motives to abstain from injuring our fellows. . . .

A man enlightened as to his own interest will not indulge himself in a secret offence through fear of contracting a shameful habit, which sooner or later will betray him; and because the having secrets to conceal from the prying curiosity of mankind leaves in the heart a sediment of disquiet, which corrupts every pleasure. All he can acquire at the expense of security cannot make up for the loss of that; and, if he desires a good reputation, the best guarantee he can have for it is his own esteem.

But, in order that an individual should perceive this connection between the interests of others and his own, he needs an enlightened spirit and a heart free from seductive passions. The greater part of men have neither sufficient light, sufficient strength of mind, nor sufficient moral sensibility to place their honesty above the aid of the laws. The legislator must supply the feebleness of this natural interest by adding to it an artificial interest, more steady and more easily perceived.

More yet. In many cases morality derives its existence from the law; that is, to decide whether the action is morally good or bad, it is necessary to know whether the laws permit or forbid it. It is so of what concerns property. A manner of selling or acquiring, esteemed dishonest in one country, would be irreproachable in another. It is the same with offenses against the state. The state exists only by law, and it is impossible to say what conduct in this behalf morality requires of us before knowing what the legislator has decreed. There are countries where it is an offence to enlist into the service of a foreign power, and others in which such a service is lawful and honourable.[3]

III. As to beneficence some distinctions are necessary. The law may be extended to general objects, such as the care of the poor; but, for details, it is necessary to depend upon private morality. Beneficence has its mysteries, and loves best to employ itself upon evils so unforeseen or so secret that the law cannot reach them. Besides, it is to individual free will that benevolence owes its energy. If the same acts were commanded, they would no longer be benefits, they would lose their attractions and their essence. It is morality and especially religion, which here form the necessary complement to legislation, and the sweetest tie of humanity.

However, instead of having done too much in this respect, legislators have not done enough. They ought to erect into an offence the refusal or the omission of a service to humanity when it would be easy to render it, and when some distinct ill clearly results from the refusal; such, for example, as abandoning a wounded man in a solitary road without seeking any assistance for him; not giving information to a man who is ignorantly meddling with poisons; not reaching out the hand to one who has fallen into a ditch from which he cannot extricate himself; in these, and other similar cases, could any fault be found with a punishment, exposing the delinquent to a certain degree of shame, or subjecting him to a pecuniary responsibility for the evil which he might have prevented?

I will add, that legislation might be extended further than it is in relation to the interests of the inferior animals. I do not approve the laws of the Hindus on this subject. There are good reasons why animals should serve for the nourishment of man, and for destroying those which incommode us. We are the better for it, and they are not the worse; for they have not, as we have, long and cruel anticipations of the future; and the death which they receive at our hands may always be rendered less painful than that which awaits them in the inevitable course of nature. But what can be said to justify the useless torments they are made to suffer; the cruel caprices which are exercised upon them? Among the many reasons which might be given for making criminal such gratuitous cruelties, I confine myself to that which relates to my subject. It is a means of cultivating a general sentiment of benevolence, and of rendering men more mild; or at least of preventing that brutal depravity, which, after fleshing itself upon animals, presently demands human suffering to satiate its appetite.[4]

CHAPTER XIII

False Methods of Reasoning on the Subject of Legislation

It has been the object of this introduction to give a clear idea of the principle of utility, and of the method of reasoning conformable to that principle. There results from it a legislative logic, which can be summed up in a few words. What is it to offer a *good reason* with respect to a law? It is to allege the good or evil which the law tends to produce: so much good, so many arguments in its favour; so much evil, so many arguments against it; remembering all the time that good and evil are nothing else than pleasure and pain.

What is it to offer a *false reason?* It is the alleging for or against a law something else than its good or evil effects.

Nothing can be more simple, yet nothing is more new. It is not the principle of utility which is new; on the contrary, that principle is necessarily as old as the human race. All the truth there is in morality, all the good there is in the laws, emanate from it; but utility has often been followed by instinct, while it has been combatted by argument. If in books of legislation it throws out some sparks here and there, they are quickly extinguished in the surrounding smoke. BECCARIA is the only writer who deserves to be noted as an exception; yet even in his work there is some reasoning drawn from false sources.

It is upwards of two thousand years since Aristotle undertook to form, under the title of *Sophisms,* a complete catalogue of the different kinds of false reasoning. This catalogue, improved by the information which so long an interval might furnish, would here have its place and its uses. But such an undertaking would carry me too far. I shall be content with presenting some heads of error on the subject of legislation. By means of such a contrast, the principle of utility will be put into a clearer light.

I. Antiquity Is Not a Reason. The antiquity of a law may create a prejudice in its favour; but in itself, it is not a reason. If the law in question has contributed to the public good, the older it is, the easier it will be to enumerate its good effects, and to prove its utility by a direct process.

2. The Authority of Religion is Not a Reason. Of late, this method of reasoning has gone much out of fashion, but till recently its use was very extensive. The work of Algernon Sidney is full of citation from the *Old Testament*, and he finds there the foundation of a system of Democracy, as Bossuet had found the principle of absolute power. Sidney wished to combat the partisans of divine right and passive obedience with their own weapons.

If we suppose that a law emanates from the Deity, we suppose that it emanates from supreme wisdom, and supreme bounty. Such a law, then, can only have for its object the most eminent utility; and this utility, put into a clear light, will always be an ample justification of the law.

3. Reproach of Innovation Is Not a Reason. To reject innovation is to reject progress; in what condition should we be, if that principle had been always followed? All which exists had had a beginning; all which is established has been innovation. Those very persons who approve a law to-day because it is ancient, would have opposed it as new when it was first introduced.

4. An Arbitrary Definition is Not a Reason. Nothing is more common, among jurists and political writers, than to base their reasonings, and even to write long works, upon a foundation of purely arbitrary definitions. This artifice consists in taking a work in a particular sense, foreign from its common usage; in employing that word as no one ever employed it before; and in puzzling the reader by an appearance of profoundness and of mystery.

Montesquieu himself has fallen into this fault in the very beginning of his work. Wishing to give a definition of law, he proceeds from metaphor to metaphor; he brings together the most discordant objects—the Divinity, the material world, superior intelligence, beasts and men. We learn, at last, that *laws are relations; and eternal relations.* Thus the definition is more obscure than the thing to be defined. The word *law*, in its proper sense, excites in every mind a tolerably clear idea, the word *relation* excites no idea at all. The word *law*, in its figurative sense, produces nothing, but equivocations; and Montesquieu, who ought to have dissipated the darkness has only increased it.

It is the character of a false definition, that it can only be employed in a particular way. That author, a little further on (ch. iii.), gives another definition. *Law in general,* he says, *is human reason, in so far as it governs all the people of the earth.* These terms are more familiar; but no clear idea results from them. Is it the fact, that so many laws, contradictory, ferocious, or absurd, and in a perpetual state of change, are always *human reason*? It would seem that reason, so far from being the law, is often in opposition to it.

This first chapter of Montesquieu has given occasion to an abundance of nonsense. The brain has been racked in search of metaphysical mysteries, where none in fact exist. Even Beccaria has suffered himself to be carried away by this obscure notion of *relations.* To interrogate a man in order to know whether he is innocent or guilty, is to force him, he tells us, to accuse himself. To this procedure he objects; and why? because, as he says, it is to *confound all relations.*[5] But what does that mean? To enjoy, to suffer, to cause enjoyment, to cause suffering: those are expressions which I understand; but to follow relations and to confound relations, is what I do not understand at all. These abstract terms do not excite any idea in my mind; they do not awaken any sentiment. I am absolutely indifferent about *relations:—pleasures* and *pains* are what interest me.

Rousseau has not been satisfied with the definition of Montesquieu. He has given his own, which he announces as a great discovery. *Law,* he says, *is the expression of the general will.* There are, then, no laws except where the people have spoken in a body. There is no law except in an absolute democracy. Rousseau has suppressed, by this supreme decree, all existing laws; and at the same time he has deprived of the possibility of existence all those which are likely to be made hereafter,—the legislation of the republic of San Marino alone excepted.

5. Metaphors Are Not Reasons. I mean either metaphor properly so called, or allegory, used at first for illustration or ornament, but afterwards made the basis of an argument.

Blackstone, so great an enemy of all reform, that he has gone so far as to find fault with the introduction of the English language into the reports of cases decided by the courts, has rejected no means of inspiring his readers with the same prejudice. He represents the law as a castle, as a fortress, which cannot be altered without being weakened. I allow that he does not advance this metaphor as an argument; but why does he employ it? To gain possession of the imagination; to prejudice his readers against every idea of reform; to excite in them an artificial fear of all innovation in the laws. There remains in the mind a false image, which produces the same effect with false reasoning. He ought to have recollected that this allegory might be employed against himself. When they see the law turned into a castle, is it not natural for ruined suitors to represent it as a castle inhabited by robbers?

A man's house, say the English, is his castle. This poetical expression is certainly no reason; for if a man's house be his castle by night, why not by day? If it is an inviolable asylum for the owner, why is it not so for every person whom he chooses to receive there? The course of justice is sometimes interrupted in England by this puerile notion of liberty. Criminals seem to be looked upon like foxes; they are suffered to have their burrows, in order to increase the sports of the chase.

A church in Catholic countries is the *House of God.* This metaphor has served to establish asylums for criminals. It would be a mark of disrespect for the Divinity to seize by force those who had taken refuge in his house.

The *balance of trade* has produced a multitude of reasonings founded upon metaphor. It has been imagined that in the course of mutual commerce nations rose and sank like the scales of a balance loaded with unequal weights; people have been terribly alarmed at what appeared to them a want of equilibrium; for it has been supposed that what one nation gained the other must lose, as if a weight had been transferred from one scale to another.

The word *mother-country* has produced a great number of prejudices and false reasonings in all questions concerning colonies and the parent state. Duties have been imposed upon colonies, and they have been accused of offenses, founded solely upon the metaphor of their filial dependence.

6. A Fiction is Not a Reason. I understand by fiction an assumed fact notoriously false, upon which one reasons as if it were true. . . .

Blackstone, in the seventh chapter of his first book, in speaking of the royal authority, has given himself up to all the puerility of fiction. The king, he tells us, is everywhere present; he can do no wrong; he is immortal.

These ridiculous paradoxes, the fruits of servility, so far from furnishing just ideas of the prerogatives of royalty, only serve to dazzle, to mislead, and to give to reality itself an air of fable and of prodigy. But these fictions are not mere sparkles of imagination. He makes them the foundation of many reasonings. He employs them to explain certain royal prerogatives, which might be justified by very good arguments, without perceiving how much the best cause is injured by attempting to prop it up by falsehoods. *The judges,* he tells us, *are mirrors, in which the image of the king is reflected.* What puerility! Is it not exposing to ridicule the very objects which he designs to render the most respectable?

But there are fictions more bold and more important, which have played a great part in politics, and which have produced celebrated works; these are *contracts*.

The *Leviathan* of Hobbes, a work now-a-days but little known, and detested through prejudice and at second-hand as a defence of despotism, is an attempt to base all political society upon a pretended contract between the people and the sovereign. The people by this contract have renounced their natural liberty, which produced nothing but evil; and have deposited all power in the hands of the prince. All opposing wills have been united in his, or rather annihilated by it. That which he wills is taken to be the will of all his subjects. When David brought about the destruction of Uriah, he acted in that matter with Uriah's consent, for Uriah had consented to all that David might command. The prince, according to this system, might sin against God, but he could not sin against man, because all his actions proceeded from the general consent. It was impossible to entertain the idea of resisting him, because such an idea implied the contradiction of resisting one's self.

Locke, whose name is as dear to the friends of liberty as that of Hobbes is odious, has also fixed the basis of government upon a contract. He agrees that there is a contract between the prince and the people; but according to him the prince takes an engagement to govern according to the laws, and for the public good; while the people, on their side, take an engagement of obedience so long, as the prince remains faithful to the conditions in virtue of which he receives the crown.

Rousseau rejects with indignation the idea of this bilateral contract between the prince and the people. He has imagined a *social contract,* by which all are bound to all, and which is the only legitimate basis of government. Society exists only by virtue of this free convention of associates.

These three systems—so directly opposed—agree, however, in beginning the theory of politics with a fiction, for these three contracts are equally fictitious. They exist only in the imagination of their authors. Not only we find no trace of them in history, but everywhere we discover proofs to the contrary. . . .

It is not necessary to make the happiness of the human race dependent on a fiction. It is not necessary to erect the social pyramid upon a foundation of sand, or upon a clay which slips from beneath it. Let us leave such trifling to children; men ought to speak the language of truth and reason.

The true political tie is the immense interest which men have in maintaining a government. Without a government there can be no security, no domestic enjoyments, no property, no industry. It is in this fact that we ought to seek the basis and the reason of all governments, whatever may be their origin and their form; it is by comparing them with their object that we can reason with solidity upon their rights and their obligations, without having recourse to pretended contracts which can only serve to produce interminable disputes.

7. Fancy is Not a Reason. Nothing is more common than to say, *reason decides, eternal reason orders,* etc. But what is this reason? If it is not a distinct view of good or evil, it is mere fancy; it is a despotism, which announces nothing but the interior persuasion of him who speaks. Let us see upon what foundation a distinguished jurist has sought to establish the paternal authority. A man of ordinary good sense would not see much difficulty in that question; but your learned men find a mystery everywhere.

"The right of a father over his children," says Cocceiji, "is founded in reason;—for, 1st, Children are born in a house, of which the father is the master; 2nd, They are born in a family of which he is the chief; 3rd, They are of his seed, and a part of his body." These are the reasons from which he concludes, among other things, that a man of forty ought not to marry without the consent of a father, who in the course of nature must by that time be in his dotage. What there is common to these three reasons is, that none of them has any relation to the interests of the parties. The author consults neither the welfare of father nor that of the children.

The right of a father is an improper phrase. The question is not of an unlimited, nor of an indivisible right. There are many kinds of rights which may be granted or refused to a father, each for particular reasons. . . .

And here we may remark an essential difference between false principles and the true one. The principle of utility, applying itself only to the interests of the parties, bends to circumstances, and accommodates itself to every case. False principles, being founded upon things which have nothing to do with individual interests, would be inflexible if they were consistent. Such is the character of this pretended right founded upon birth. The son naturally belongs to the father, because the matter of which the son is formed once circulated in the father's veins. No matter how unhappy he renders his son;—it is impossible to annihilate his right, because we cannot make his son cease to be his son. The corn of which your body is made formerly grew in my field; how is it that you are not my slave?

8. Antipathy and Sympathy Are Not Reasons. Reasoning by antipathy is most common upon subjects connected with penal law; for we have antipathies against actions reputed to be crimes; antipathies against individuals reputed to be criminals; antipathies against the ministers of justice; antipathies against such and such punishments. This false principle has reigned like a tyrant throughout this vast province of law. Beccaria first dared openly to attack it. His arms were of celestial temper; but if he did much towards destroying the usurper, he did very little towards the establishment of a new and more equitable rule.

It is the principle of antipathy which leads us to speak of offenses as *deserving* punishment. It is the corresponding principle of sympathy which leads us to speak of certain action as *meriting* reward. This word *merit* can only lead to passion and to error. It is *effects,* good or bad, which we ought alone to consider.

But when I say that *antipathies and sympathies are no reason,* I mean those of legislator; for the antipathies and sympathies of the people may be reasons, and very powerful ones. However odd or pernicious a religion, a law, a custom may be, it is of no consequence, so long as the people are attached to it. To take away an enjoyment or a hope, chimerical though it may be, is to do the same injury as if we took away a real hope, a real enjoyment. In such a case the pain of a single individual becomes, by sympathy, the pain of all. Thence results a crowd of evils; antipathy against a law which wounds the general prejudice; antipathy against the whole code of that law is a part; antipathy against the government which carries the laws into execution; a disposition not to aid in their execution; a disposition secretly to oppose it; a disposition to oppose it openly and by force; a disposition to destroy a government which sets itself in opposition to the popular will—all the evils produced by those offences, which, in a collective shape, form that sad compound called *rebellion* or *civil war*—all the evils produced by the punishments which are resorted to as a means of putting a stop to those offences. Such is the succession of fatal consequences which are always ready to arise from fancies and prejudices violently opposed. The legislator ought to yield to the violence of a current which carries away everything that obstructs it. But let us observe, that in such a case, the fancies themselves are not the reason that determines the legislator; his reason is the evils which threaten to grow out of an opposition to those fancies.

But ought the legislator to be a slave to the fancies of those whom he governs? No. Between an imprudent opposition and a servile compliance there is a middle path, honourable and safe. It is to combat these fancies with the only arms that can conquer them—

example and instruction. He must enlighten the people, he must address himself to the public reason; he must give time for error to be unmasked. Sound reasons, clearly set forth, are of necessity stronger than false ones. But the legislator ought not to show himself too openly in these instructions, for fear of compromising himself with the public ignorance. Indirect means will better answer his end.

It is to be observed, however, that too much deference for prejudices is a more common fault than the contrary excess. The best projects of laws are for ever stumbling against this common objection—"Prejudice is opposed to it; the people will be offended!" But how is that known? How has public opinion been consulted? What is its organ? Have the whole people but one uniform notion on this subject? Have all the individuals of the community the same sentiment, including perhaps nine out of ten, who never heard the subject spoken of? Besides, if the people are in error, are they compelled always to remain so? Will not an influx of light dissipate the darkness which produces error? Can we expect the people to possess sound knowledge, while it is yet unattained by their legislators, by those who are regarded as the wise men of the land? Have there not been examples of other nations who have come out of similar ignorance, and where triumphs have been achieved over the same obstacles?

After all, popular prejudice serves oftener as a pretext than as a motive. It is a convenient cover for the weakness of statesmen. The ignorance of the people is the favourite argument of pusillanimity and of indolence; while the real motives are prejudices from which the legislators themselves have not been able to get free. The name of the people is falsely used to justify their leaders.

9. Begging the Question is Not a Reason. The *petito principii*, or begging the question, is one of the sophisms which is noted by Aristotle; but it is a Proteus which conceals itself artfully, and is reproduced under a thousand forms.

Begging the question, or rather assuming the question, consists in making use of the very proposition in dispute, as though it were already proved.

This false procedure insinuates itself into morals and legislation, under the disguise of *sentimental* or *impassioned* terms; that is, terms which, beside their principle sense, carry with them an accessory idea of praise or blame. Neuter terms are those which simply express the thing in question, without any attending presumption of good or evil; without introducing any foreign idea of blame or approbation.

Now it is to be observed that an impassioned term envelops a proposition not expressed, but understood, which always accompanies its employment, though in general unperceived by those who employ it. This concealed proposition implies either blame or praise; but the implication is always vague and undetermined.

Do I desire to connect an idea of utility with a term which commonly conveys an accessory idea of blame? I shall seem to advance a paradox, and to contradict myself. For example, should I say that such a piece of luxury is a good thing? The proposition astonishes those who are accustomed to attach to this word luxury a sentiment of disapprobation.

How shall I be able to examine this particular point without awakening a dangerous association? I must have recourse to a neuter word; I must say, for example, *such a manner of spending one's revenue* is good. This turn of expression runs counter to no prejudice, and permits an impartial examination of the object in question. When Helvetius advanced the idea that all actions have interest for their motive, the public cried out against his doctrine without stopping to understand it. Why? Because the word *interest* has an odious sense; a common acceptation, in which it seems to exclude every motive of pure attachment and of benevolence.

How many reasonings upon political subjects are founded upon nothing but impassioned terms! People suppose they are giving a reason for a law, when they say that it is conformable to the principles of monarchy or of democracy. But that meant nothing. If there are persons in whose minds these words are associated with an idea of approbation, there are others who attach contrary ideas to them. Let these two parties begin to quarrel, the dispute will never come to an end, except through the weariness of the combatants. For, before beginning a true examination, we must renounce these impassioned terms, and calculate the effects of the proposed law in good and evil.

Blackstone admires in the British constitution the combination of the three forms of government; and he hence concludes that it must possess the collected good qualities of monarchy, aristocracy, and democracy. How happened it that he did not perceive, that without changing his premises, a conclusion might be drawn from them, diametrically opposite, yet equally just; to wit, that the British constitution must unite all the particular *faults* of democracy, aristocracy, and monarchy?

To the word *independence,* there are attached certain accessory ideas of dignity and virtue; to the word *dependence,* accessory ideas of inferiority and corruption. Hence it is that the panegyrists of the British constitution admire the *independence* of the three powers of which the legislature is composed. This, in their eyes, is the masterpiece of politics; the happiest trait in that whole scheme of government. On the other side, those who would detract from the merits of that constitution, are always insisting upon the actual *dependence* of one or the other of its branches. Neither the praise nor the censure contain any reasons.

As to the fact, the pretended independence does not exist. The king and the greater part of the lords have a direct influence upon the election of the House of Commons. The king has the power of dissolving that House at any moment; a power of no little efficacy. The king exercises a direct influence by honourable and lucrative employments, which he gives or takes away at pleasure. On the other side, the king is dependent upon the two Houses, and particularly upon the Commons, since he cannot maintain himself without money and troops,—two principal and essential matters which are wholly under the control of the representatives of the people. What pretence has the House of Lords to be called independent, while the king can augment its number at pleasure, and change the vote in his favour by the creation of new lords; exercising too, as he does, an additional influence on the temporal peers, by the prospect of advancement in the ranks of the peerage; and on the bishops, by the bait of ecclesiastical promotion?

Instead of reasoning upon a deceptive word, let us consider effects. It is the reciprocal dependence of these three powers which produces their agreement; which subjects them to fixed rules, which gives them a steady and systematic operation. Hence the necessity of mutual respect, attention, concession, and moderation. If they were absolutely independent, there would be continual shocks between them. It would often be necessary to appeal to force; and the result would be a state of anarchy.

I cannot refrain from giving two other examples of this error of reasoning, founded upon the misuse of terms.

If we attempt a theory upon the subject of *national presentation,* in following out all that appears to be a natural consequence of that abstract idea, we come at last to the conclusion that *universal suffrage* out to be established; and to the additional conclusion that the representatives out to be re-chosen as frequently as possible, in order that the national representation may deserve to be esteemed such.

In deciding these same questions according to the principle of utility, it will not do to reason upon words; we must look only at effects. In the election of a legislative assembly, the right of suffrage should not be allowed except to those who are esteemed by the nation fit to exercise it; for a choice made by men who do not possess the national confidence will weaken the confidence of the nation in the assembly so chosen.

Men who would be thought fit to be electors, are those who cannot be presumed to possess political integrity, and a sufficient degree of knowledge. Now we cannot presume upon the political integrity of those whom want exposes to the temptation of selling themselves; nor of those who have no fixed abode; nor of those who have been found guilty in the courts of justice of certain offenses forbidden by the law. We cannot presume a sufficient degree of knowledge in women, whom their domestic condition withdraws from the conduct of public affairs; in children and adults beneath a certain age; in those who are deprived by their proverty of the first elements of education, etc. etc.

It is according to these principles, and others like them, that we ought to fix the conditions necessary for becoming an elector; and it is in like manner, upon the advantages and disadvantages of frequent elections, without paying any attention to arguments drawn from abstract terms, that we ought to reason in establishing the duration of a legislative assembly.

The last example I shall give will be taken from *contracts:* I mean those political fictions to which this name has been applied by their authors.

When Locke and Rousseau reason upon this pretended contracts; when they affirm that the social or political contract includes such and such a clause, can they prove it otherwise than by the general utility which is supposed to result from it? Grant that this contract which has never been reduced to writing is, however, in full existence. On what depends all its force? It is not upon its utility? Why ought we to fulfil our engagements? Because the faith of promises is the basis of society. It is for the advantage of all that the promises of every indiviual should be faithfully observed. There would no longer be any security among men, no commerce, no confidence;—it would be necessary to go back to the woods, if engagements did not possess an obligatory force. It is the same with these political contracts. It is their utility which makes them binding. When they become injurious, they lose their force. If a king had taken an oath to render his subjects unhappy, would such an engagement be valid? If the people were sworn to obey him at all events, would they be bound to suffer themselves to be exterminated by a Nero or a Caligula, rather than violate their promise? If there resulted from the contract effects universally injurious, could there be any sufficient reason for maintaining it? It cannot be denied, then, that the validity of a contract is at bottom only a question of utility—a little wrapped up, a little disguised, and, in consequence, more susceptible of false interpretations.

10. An Imaginary Law is Not a Reason. Natural law, natural rights are two kinds of fictions or metaphors, which play so great a part in books of legislation that they deserve to be examined by themselves.

The primitive sense of the word *law,* and the ordinary meaning of the word, is—the will or command of a legislator. The *law of nature* is a figurative expression, in which nature is represented as a being; and such and such a disposition is attributed to her, which is figuratively called a law. In this sense, all the general inclinations of men, all those which appear to exist independently of human societies, and from which must proceed the establishment of political and civil law, are called *laws of nature.* This is the true sense of the phrase.

But this is not the way in which it is understood. Authors have taken it in a direct sense; as if there had been a real code of natural laws. They appeal to these laws; they cite them, and they oppose them, clause by clause, to the enactments of legislators. They do not see that these natural laws are laws of their own invention; that they are all at odds among themselves as to the contents of this pretended code; that they affirm without proof; that systems are as numerous as authors; and that, in reasoning in this manner, it is necessary to be always beginning anew, because every one can advance what he pleases touching laws which are only imaginary, and so keep on disputing for ever.

What is natural to man is sentiments of pleasure or pain, what are called inclinations. But to call these sentiments and these inclinations laws, is to introduce a false and dangerous idea. It is to set language in opposition to itself; for it is necessary to make *laws* precisely for the purpose of restraining these inclinations. Instead of regarding them as laws, they must be submitted to laws. It is against the strongest natural inclinations that it is necessary to have laws the most repressive. If there were a law of nature which directed all men towards their common good, laws would be useless; it would be employing a creeper to uphold an oak; it would be kindling a torch to add light to the sun.

Blackstone, in speaking of the obligation of parents to provide for the support of their children, says, "that it is a principle of natural law, a duty imposed by nature itself, and by the proper act of the parents in bringing the children into the world. Montesquieu, he adds, "observes with reason, that the natural obligation of the father to support his children, is what has caused the establishment of marriage, which points out the person who ought to fulfill this obligation" (Book i, Chap. 16).

Parents *are inclined* to support their children; parents *ought* to support their children; these are two distinct propositions. The first does not suppose the second; the second does not suppose the first. There are, without doubt, the strongest reasons for imposing upon parents the obligation to bring up their children. Why have not Blackstone and Montesquieu mentioned those reasons? Why do they refer us to what they call the law of nature? What is this law of nature, which needs to be propped up by a secondary law from another legislator? If this natural obligation exists, as Montesquieu says it does, far from serving as the foundation of marriage, it proves its inutility,—at least for the end which he assigns. One of the objects of marriage is, precisely to supply the insufficiency of natural affection. It is designed to convert into obligation that inclination of parents, which would not always be sufficiently strong to surmount the pains and embarrassments of education.

Men are very well disposed to provide for their own support. It has not been necessary to make laws to oblige them to that. If the disposition of parents to provide for the support of their children had been constantly and universally as strong, legislators never would have thought of turning it into an obligation.

The exposure of infants, so common in ancient Greece, is still practised in China, and to a greater extent. To abolish this practice, would it not be necessary to allege other reasons besides this pretended law of nature, which here is evidently at fault?

The word *rights,* the same as the word *law,* has two senses; the one a proper sense, the other a metaphorical sense. *Rights,* properly so called, are the creatures of *law* properly so called, real laws give birth to real rights. *Natural rights* are the creatures of natural law; they are a metaphor which derives its origin from another metaphor.

What there is natural in men is means,—faculties. But to call these means, these faculties, *natural rights,* is again to put language in opposition to itself. For *rights* are established to insure the exercise of means and faculties. The right is the *guarantee;* the faculty is the thing guaranteed. How can we understand each other with a language which confounds under the same term things so different? Where would be the nomenclature of the arts, if we gave to the *mechanic* who makes an article the same name as to the article itself?

Real rights are always spoken of in a legal sense; natural rights are often spoken of in a sense that may be called anti-legal. When it is said, for example, that *law cannot avail against natural rights,* the word *rights* is employed in a sense above the law; for, in this use of it, we acknowledge rights which attack the law; which overturn it, which annul it. In this anti-legal sense, the word *right* is the greatest enemy of reason, and the most terrible destroyer of governments.

There is no reasoning with fanatics, armed with *natural rights,* which each one understands as he pleases, and applies as he sees fit; of which nothing can be yielded, nor retrenched; which are inflexible, at the same time that they are unintelligible; which are consecrated as dogmas, from which it is a crime to vary. Instead of examining laws by their effects, instead of judging them as good or bad, they consider them in relation to these pretended natural rights; that is to say, they substitute for the reasoning of experience the chimeras of their own imaginations.

This is not a harmless error; it passes from speculation into practice. "Those laws must be obeyed, which are accordant with nature; the others are null in fact; and instead of obeying them, they ought to be resisted. The moment natural rights are attacked, every good citizen ought to rouse up in their defence. These rights, evidence in themselves, do not need to be proved; it is sufficient to declare them. How prove what is evident already? To doubt implies a want of sense, or a fault of intellect," &c.

But not to be accused of gratuitously ascribing such seditious maxims to these inspired politicians of nature, I shall cite a passage from Blackstone, directly to the point; and I choose Blackstone, because he is, of all writers, the one who has shown the most profound respect for the authority of governments. In speaking of these pretended laws of nature, and of the laws of revelation, he says: "Human laws must not be permitted to contradict these; if a human law commands a thing forbidden by the natural or divine law, we are bound to transgress that human law," &c. (1 Comm. p. 43).

Is not this arming every fanatic against all governments? In the immense variety of ideas respecting natural and Divine law, cannot some reason be found for resisting all human laws? Is there a single state which can maintain itself a day, if each individual holds himself bound in conscience to resist the laws, whenever they are not conformed to his particular ideas of natural or Divine law? What a cut-throat scene of it we should have between all the interpreters of the code of nature, and all the interpreters of the law of God!

"The pursuit of happiness is a natural right." The pursuit of happiness is certainly a natural inclination; but can it be declared to be a right?——That depends on the way in which it is pursued. The assassin pursues his happiness, or what he esteems such, by committing an assassination. Has he a right to do so? If not, why declare that he has? What tendency is there in such a declaration to render men more happy or more wise?

Turgot was a great man; but he had adopted the general opinion without examining it. Inalienable and natural rights were the despotism or the dogmatism which he wished to exercise, without himself perceiving it. If he saw no reason to doubt a proposition; if he judged it evidently true; he referred it, without going further, to natural right, to eternal justice. Henceforward he made use of it as an article of faith, which he was no longer permitted to examine.

Utility having been often badly applied, understood in a narrow sense, and having lent its name to crimes, has appeared contrary to eternal justice. It thus became degraded, and acquired a mercenary reputation. It needs courage to restore it to honour, and to re-establish reasoning upon its true basis.

I propose a treaty of conciliation with the partisans of natural rights. If *nature* has made such or such a law, those who cite it with so much confidence, those who have modestly taken upon themselves to be its interpreters, must suppose that nature had some reasons for her law. Would it not be surer, shorter and more persuasive, to give us those reasons directly, instead of urging upon us the will of this unknown legislator, as itself an authority?

All these false methods of reasoning can always be reduced to one or the other of the two false principles. This fundamental distinction is very useful in getting rid of words, and rendering ideas more clear. To refer such or such an argument to one or another of the false principles, is like tying weeds into bundles, to be thrown into the fire.

I conclude with a general observation. The language of error is always obscure and indefinite. An abundance of words serves to cover a paucity and a falsity of ideas. The oftener terms are changed, the easier it is to delude the reader. The language of truth is uniform and simple. The same ideas are always expressed by the same terms. Everything is referred to pleasures or to pains. Every expression is avoided which tends to disguise or intercept the familiar idea, that from such and such actions result such and such pleasures and pains. Trust not to me, but to experience, and especially your own. Of two opposite methods of action, do you desire to know which should have the preference? Calculate their effects in good and evil, and prefer that which promises the greater sum of good.

Notes

1. *Ascetic,* by its etymology, signifies *one who exercises.* It was applied to the monks, to indicate their favorite practices of devotion and penitence.
2. This mistake consists in representing the Deity in words, as a being of infinite benevolence, yet ascribing to him prohibitions and threats which are the attributes of an implacable being, who uses his power only to satisfy his malevolence.

    We might ask these ascetic theologians what life is good for, if not for the pleasures it procures us?—and what pledge we have for the goodness of God in another life, if he has forbidden the enjoyment of this?
3. Here we touch upon one of the most difficult of questions. If the law is not what it ought to be; if it openly combats the principle of utility; ought we to obey it? Ought we to violate it? Ought we to remain neuter between the law which commands an evil, and morality which forbids it? The solution of this question involves considerations both of prudence and benevolence. We ought to examine if it is more dangerous to violate the law than to obey it; we ought to consider whether the probable evils of disobedience are less or greater than the probable evils of disobedience.
4. See *Barrow's Voyage to the Cape of Good Hope,* for the cruelties of the Dutch settlers toward their cattle and their slaves.
5. Beccaria. Chap. xii
6. I say "have to." For only when the means of production and distribution have *actually* outgrown the form of management by joint-stock companies and when, therefore, the taking them over by the state has become *economically* inevitable, only then—even if it is the state of today that effects this— is there an economic advance, the attainment of another step preliminary to the taking over of all productive forces by society itself. But of late, since Bismarck went in for state ownership of industrial establishments, a kind of spurious socialism has arisen, degenerating, now and again, into something of flunkyism, that without more ado declares *all* state ownership, even of the Bismarckian sort, to be socialistic. Certainly if the taking over by the state of the tobacco industry is socialistic, then Napoleon and Metternich must be numbered among the founders of socialism. If the Belgian state, for quite ordinary political and financial reasons, itself constructed its chief railway lines; if Bismarck, not under any economic compulsion, took over for the state the chief Prussian lines, simply to be the better able to have them in hand in case of war, to bring up the railway employees as voting cattle for the government, and especially to create for himself a new source of income independent of parliamentary votes—this was in no sense a socialistic measure, directly or indirectly, consciously or unconsciously. Otherwise the Royal Maritime Company, the Royal porcelain manufacture, and even the regimental tailor of the army would also be socialistic institutions, or even, as was seriously proposed by a sly dog in Frederick William III's reign, the taking over by the state of the brothels.

7. A few figures may serve to give an approximate idea of the enormous expansive force of the modern means of production, even under the capitalist pressure. According to Mr. Giffen, the total wealth of Great Britain and Ireland amounted, in round numbers, in

1814 to £2,200,000,000
1865 to £6,100,000,000
1875 to £8,500,000,000

As an instance of the squandering of means of production and of products during a crisis the total loss in the German iron industry alone, in the crisis 1873–78, was given at the Second German Industrial Congress (Berlin, February 21, 1878) as £22,750,000.

ALEXIS DE TOCQUEVILLE

Alexis (Charles-Henri Maurice Clérel) de Tocqueville (1805–1859) was born in Paris into an aristocratic family with strong ties to the monarchy. His father, Hervé, was in sympathy with the Revolution in 1789 at first, hoping that a constitutional monarchy might emerge. He remained faithful to the king when the Revolution took a radical turn. In 1793, Hervé married the granddaughter of Malesherbes, the liberal aristocrat who helped conduct the defense of Louis XVI before the Convention. In 1794 Malesherbes was arrested and executed. Hervé and his wife also were arrested and imprisoned under the Terror, but were released after Robespierre's fall. The experience of the Tocqueville family during the Revolution had a powerful effect subsequently on Alexis, who continued a tradition of loyalty to the Bourbons, sympathy with the progressive aspects of the Revolution, and horror over the Terror.

Alexis was tutored at home as a child, then entered school in Metz, where his father held the powerful post of prefect. He took up the study of law in Paris, from 1823 to 1826, preparing himself to become a magistrate. As a student he was influenced by the lectures of François Guizot, whose liberal views he found congenial. In 1827, Alexis was appointed an unpaid apprentice judge in Versailles, where he became friendly with a young deputy prosecutor, Gustave de Beaumont. Alexis was twenty-five years old when the July Revolution led to the overthrow and exile of Charles X, who was replaced by the more liberal Louis-Philippe of Orléans. Alexis did not regret the fall of Charles X, but he would have preferred to see the king's grandson succeed under a regency, thus preserving the continuity of the Bourbon line. He reluctantly decided to swear the loyalty oath required of civil servants, but felt vulnerable because of his family's well-known links to the Bourbons. To remove himself from a difficult and distasteful political situation, he decided to visit North America. He and Beaumont sought and received permission from the ministry of the interior to study prison reform (an issue being hotly debated in France) in America. Both young friends were eager to use this mission, which was unpaid, to study at first hand the operation of political institutions in a more egalitarian society than France.

Tocqueville and Beaumont arrived in New York on May 9, 1831, returning to France from New York on February 20 of the following year. Their nine-month sojourn took place at the end of Andrew Jackson's first term in office. The two friends traveled widely, spoke to many leading figures (including President Jackson), and read deeply. Upon their return, they met their immediate obligation to produce a report, which appeared as a joint book in 1833, *On the Penitentiary System in the United States and Its Application in France*. It won a literary prize and acclaim for the authors. In 1832, Beaumont had been dismissed as a deputy public prosecutor because he refused to take on a politically charged case. Tocqueville resigned his post in protest, though he probably would have abandoned his career in any case. In 1835, Beaumont published a novel on the racial problem in America, *Marie, or Slavery in the United States*.

After a visit to England, Tocqueville settled down in Paris, and in one year of intensive work wrote the first part of *Democracy in America,* published in January 1835. For Tocqueville, America was in all likelihood the future of France. He believed it inevitable that social position would be based on merit, not birth. But he feared that increasing equality of conditions might destroy the institutions that traditionally safeguarded individual liberties. Following the lead of *The Federalist Papers,* Tocqueville argued that tyranny of the majority was the greatest danger in a popular government, but it could be prevented. The people must be persuaded, in their own interest, to accept limits on their power and leadership by the more educated. A proper separation of powers, including an executive "that has strength of its own," could avert abuses of power while providing effective government. Yet those best able to govern were being driven out of politics because they could not bring themselves to flatter the people. This young aristocrat believed that a constitutional monarchy (hardly a serious prospect in America) would offer greater protection for liberties and call forth more virtuous leaders. The book was an instant success, bringing its author fame and considerable income. A year later, Alexis married Mary Mottely, an Englishwoman of middle-class background residing in France. The marriage remained childless.

In the next five years, he worked on the second part of *Democracy in America,* which appeared in 1840. The tone was more somber, as he shifted attention from America (which he never again saw) to more abstract considerations on equality and liberty. America became an illustration of his general reflections rather than the principal subject. Developments in France made him more pessimistic about the prospect of preserving liberty and avoiding the rise of an interventionist, authoritarian state. In the period between 1835 and 1840, he also wrote three essays on subjects of continuing interest to him: a memoir on poverty, published in Cherbourg in 1835; an article in the *London and Westminister Review* in 1836, "The Social and Political State of France Before and After 1789"; and commentary on Algeria in a local newspaper.

Tocqueville thought it a duty of the wellborn and educated to assume political responsibilities. He first presented himself as a candidate for election to the Chamber of Deputies in 1837, in the district of Valognes, near his château in the Manche, but lost. He succeeded in the election of 1839 and was handily reelected thereafter. He also was elected president of the departmental council, a tribute to his ability to cultivate local constituencies. In the Chamber, Tocqueville was independent, but close to the dynastic left (faithful to legitimist principles, yet favoring liberal reforms). He took a special interest in policy toward Algeria (where he traveled extensively), prison reform, and defense of religious schools from state control.

In the Revolution of February 1848, which he had predicted in a speech to the Chamber a few weeks beforehand, he opposed the demands of the Paris workers and denounced socialism as a threat to liberty. But he accepted the Republic and was elected under the newly instituted universal suffrage by an overwhelming majority to the Constituent Assembly in April 1848. Tocqueville was chosen as one of the eighteen members of the committee charged with drafting a new constitution. He took a strong position on three issues: opposing inclusion of a right to work, because it would lead to socialism and extinction of liberty; defending bicameralism (but was outvoted); and favoring the principle of popular election of the president, provided his power was effectively checked. The committee accorded vast powers to a popularly elected president. Tocqueville's prediction came true: In a country with a strong monarchical tradition, such a president could not be anything but "a pretender to the Crown." During the June riots, he supported General Cavaignac's repressive measures. Tocqueville campaigned half-heartedly for Cavaignac in the presidential election in December, which Louis-Napoleon Bonaparte won by a 3-to-1 margin. Elected to the new Legislative Assembly in May 1849, Tocqueville agreed the following month to serve as minister for foreign affairs. His tenure lasted four months, coming to an end in a clash between the President and the Assembly. He opposed Louis-Napoleon's coup d'état of December 2, 1851. After an overnight imprisonment, he was ousted from all political offices.

In forced retirement, Tocqueville wrote a lively account of the Revolution of 1848 and the subsequent seizure of power by Louis-Napoleon. These *Souvenirs* (Recollections) were published posthumously in 1893. Tocqueville then decided to devote himself to writing, returning to his lifelong concern with the French Revolution. At first he planned to begin with the seizure of power by Napoleon Bonaparte (the 18th Brumaire), working backward to see how the Revolution had prepared the way for a new empire rather than restoration of the Old Regime. But to answer this historical riddle, he found it necessary to start with the structure of power in the Old Regime. Publication of *The Old Regime and the Revolution* in 1856 reestablished his literary reputation. Tocqueville traced the roots of Bonapartism to the despotism and class consciousness of the Old Regime. The failure of the French nobility to absorb the rising middle class left a void that was filled by a centralizing monarchy. The French love of liberty reawakened in the 1780s in a society with no other aristocracy than a single all-powerful administration. "Liberty's head," he observed, was placed on "the body of a slave." Yet the mass of the people had made important gains under the Revolution, in material well-being and above all in their dignity, so that they resisted the appeals of legitimists who wished to revive the Old Regime. Tocqueville died before he could write the second part of the book on Bonapartism.

Tocqueville's reputation grew in the first few decades after his death, but went into virtual eclipse by the end of the century. His attachment to Bourbon legitimism and aristocratic values appeared increasingly irrelevant as French opinion solidified around the Third Republic. The emergence of social democracy as a powerful movement throughout Europe and then the Bolshevik Revolution in Russia made his opposition to working-class demands and socialism seem outdated. His reputation was kept alive in the United States, where *Democracy in America* remained a classic, and where the liberal tradition he incarnated was strong. After World War II, Tocqueville came back into vogue. The reaction to the excesses of Stalinism revived interest in his analysis of the origins of dictatorship in the very structure of a progressive revolution. Widespread concern over the suppression of liberty by majorities (as evidenced by popular support for fascism in Germany and the Vichy government in France), tendencies toward conformity in mass societies, bureaucratic authoritarianism, and welfare dependency also made Tocqueville newly relevant.

The best biography is André Jardin, *Alexis de Tocqueville* (New York: Farrar, Strauss & Giroux, 1988). George W. Pierson, *Tocqueville and Beaumont in America* (New York: Oxford University Press, 1938), is indispensable on the adventures of the two young aristocrats in Jacksonian America. James T. Schleifer, *The Making of Tocqueville's Democracy in America* (Chapel Hill: University of

North Carolina Press, 1980), is a detailed treatment of the evolution of Tocqueville's thought as he wrote the two volumes, calling attention also to the importance of *The Federalist* as a source. Jean-Claude Lamberti, *Tocqueville and the Two Democracies* (Cambridge: Harvard University Press, 1989), follows the development of Tocqueville's constant comparison between the United States and France. Seymour Drescher, *Tocqueville and England* (Cambrige: Harvard University Press, 1964), links Tocqueville's views on English history and society to his public career and the French historical situation.

Works dealing with analytic themes (modernization, democracy, liberty, equality, centralization, and revolution) include: Seymour Drescher, *Dilemmas of Democracy: Tocqueville and Modernization* (Pittsburgh: University of Pittsburgh Press, 1968); the symposium volume edited by Abraham Eisenstadt, *Reconsidering Tocqueville's Democracy in America* (New Brunswick: Rutgers University Press, 1988); Jack Lively, *The Social and Political Thought of Alexis de Tocqueville* (Oxford: Clarendon Press, 1962); Irving M. Zeitlin, *Liberty, Equality, and Revolution in Alexis de Tocqueville* (Boston: Little, Brown, 1971); and Marvin Zetterbaum, *Tocqueville and the Problem of Democracy* (Stanford: Stanford University Press, 1967). The sympathetic treatment of Tocqueville in Raymond Aron, *Main Currents in Sociological Thought* (New York: Basic Books, 1965), and François Furet, *Interpreting the French Revolution* (New York: Cambridge University Press, 1981), contributed to the revival of interest in his thought in France.

B. E. B.

DEMOCRACY IN AMERICA

PART II

CHAPTER 6

The Real Advantages Derived by American Society from Democratic Government

Before beginning this chapter I must remind the reader of something already mentioned several times in the course of this book.

The political constitution of the United States seems to me to be one of the forms that democracy can give to its government, but I do not think that American institutions are the only ones, or the best, that a democratic nation might adopt.

So in pointing out the blessings which the Americans derive from democratic government, I am far from claiming or from thinking that such advantages can only be obtained by the same laws.

The general tendency of laws under the sway of American democracy
and the instincts of those who apply them

The vices of democracy are immediately apparent. Its advantages only become clear in the long run. American democracy is often clumsy, but the general tendency of its laws is advantageous. Under American democracy public officials have no permanent interests differing from those of the majority. The results of this.

The vices and weaknesses of democratic government are easy to see; they can be proved by obvious facts, whereas its salutary influence is exercised in an imperceptible and almost secret way. Its defects strike one at first glance, but its good qualities are revealed only in the long run.

The laws of American democracy are often defective or incomplete; they sometimes violate acquired rights or sanction dangerous ones; even If they were good, their frequent changes would be a great evil. All this is seen at first glance.

How, then, do the American republics maintain themselves and prosper?

In laws one should make a careful distinction between the aim sought and the way in which they progress toward that aim, and between their absolute and their relative excellence.

Suppose that the lawgiver's aim is to favor the interests of the few at the expense of the many; his measures are so combined as to accomplish the proposed aim in the shortest time and with least possible effort. The law will be well contrived, but its object bad; its very efficiency will make it the more dangerous.

In general the laws of a democracy tend toward the good of the greatest number, for they spring from the majority of all the citizens, which may be mistaken but which cannot have an interest contrary to its own.

But those of an aristocracy do tend to monopolize power and wealth in the hands of a few, because in the nature of things an aristocracy is a minority.

One can therefore say in general terms that democracy's aim in its legislation is more beneficial to humanity than that of aristocracy in its lawmaking.

But there its advantages end.

An aristocracy is infinitely more skillful in the science of legislation than democracy can ever be. Being master of itself, it is not subject to transitory impulses; it has far-sighted plans and knows how to let them mature until the favorable opportunity offers. An aristocracy moves forward intelligently; it knows how to make the collective force of all its laws converge on one point at one time.

A democracy is not like that; its laws are almost always defective or untimely.

Therefore the measures of democracy are more imperfect than those of an aristocracy; it often unintentionally works against itself; but its aim is more beneficial.

Suppose a society so organized by nature or by its constitution that it can tolerate the passing effect of bad laws and can without disaster await the result of the *general tendency* of its laws, and in such a case you will appreciate that democratic government, for all its faults, is yet the best suited of all to make society prosper.

That is just what does happen in the United States; I here repeat what I have described elsewhere: the great privilege of the Americans is to be able to make retrievable mistakes.

I would say something similar about the public officials.

It is easy to see that American democracy often makes mistakes in the choice of men to whom it entrusts power, but it is not so easy to say why the state prospers in their hands.

Notice first that in a democratic state, though the rulers be less honest or less capable, the governed are more enlightened and more alert.

In democracies the people, constantly occupied as they are with their affairs and jealous of their rights, prevent their representative from deviating from a general line indicated by their interests.

Note also that although a democratic magistrate may use his power worse than another, he generally holds it for a shorter time.

But there is a more general and satisfactory reason than any of these.

No doubt it is important for nations that their rulers should possess virtues and talents, but perhaps it is even more important for them that the rulers should not have interests contrary to those of the mass of the governed, for in that case their virtues might become almost useless and their talents disastrous.

I have said that it was important for the rulers not to have interests contrary or different from those of the mass of the ruled. I do not say that they should have interests similar to those of *all* the governed, for I don't suppose that such a thing has ever happened.

No one has yet found a political structure that equally favors the growth and prosperity of all the classes composing society. These classes have formed something like distinct nations within the same nation, and experience has proved it almost as dangerous completely to entrust the fate of all to one of these as it is to make one nation arbiter of the destiny of another. When the rich alone rule, the interests of the poor are always in danger; and when the poor make the law, the interests of the rich run great risks. What, then, is the advantage of democracy? The real advantage of democracy is not, as some have said, to favor the prosperity of all, but only to serve the well-being of the greatest number.

In the United States those who are entrusted with the direction of public affairs are often inferior both in capacity and in morality to those whom an aristocracy might bring to power; but their interest is mingled and identified with that of the majority of their fellow citizens. Hence they may often prove untrustworthy and make great mistakes, but they will never systematically follow a tendency hostile to the majority; they will never turn the government into something exclusive and dangerous.

The bad administration of one magistrate under a democracy is, moreover, an isolated fact that has an influence only during the short period of his tenure of office. Corruption and incapacity are not common interests capable of linking men in any permanent fashion.

A corrupt or incapable magistrate will not combine his efforts with another magistrate's simply because the latter is corrupt or incapable too, and these two men will never work in concert so that corruption or incapacity may flourish among their posterity. Quite the contrary, the ambition and intrigues of the one will help to unmask the other. Generally speaking, in a democracy the vices of a magistrate are altogether personal.

But under aristocratic rule public men have a class interest which, though it sometimes agrees with that of the majority, is more often distinct therefrom. That interest forms a lasting common link between them; it invites them to unite and combine their endeavors toward an aim which is not always the happiness of the greatest number. It not only forms a link between the actual rulers but also unites them with a considerable section of the ruled, for many of the citizens, without having any office, form part of the aristocracy.

The aristocratic magistrate therefore finds constant support within society, as well as from the government.

This common objective which in aristocracies unites the magistrates with the interests of one portion of their contemporaries identifies them also, so to say, with that of future generations. They work for the future as well as for the present. Hence the aristocratic magistrate is impelled at the same time and in the same direction by the passions of the ruled, by his own, and, I might almost say, by the passions of those who come after him.

How can we be surprised if he puts up no resistance? So in aristocracies one often sees class spirit carrying away even those who are not corrupted by it and finds that they are unconsciously shaping society gradually to their convenience and that of their descendants.

I do not know if there has ever been another aristocracy as liberal as that of England or one that has uninterruptedly furnished the government with men so worthy and so enlightened.

Nevertheless, it is easy to see that in English legislation the poor man's welfare has in the end often been sacrificed to that of the rich, and the rights of the greatest number have been sacrificed to the privileges of the few; and so England now contains within herself every extreme of human fate, and one there finds wretchedness almost as great as the greatness of her power and glory.

In the United States, where public officials have no class interest to promote, the general and continuous course of the government is beneficial, although the rulers are often inept and sometimes contemptible.

There is therefore at the bottom of democratic institutions some hidden tendency which often makes men promote the general prosperity, in spite of their vices and their mistakes, whereas in aristocratic institutions there is sometimes a secret bias which, in spite of talents and virtues, leads men to contribute to the afflictions of their fellows. In this way it may come about that under aristocratic governments public men do evil without intending it, and in democracies they bring about good results of which they have never thought.

Public spirit in the United States

Instinctive patriotism. Well-considered patriotism. Their different characteristics. Why nations must strive with all their strength toward the second when the first has disappeared. The efforts of the Americans to achieve this. Individual interest intimately linked to that of the country.

There is a patriotism which mainly springs from the disinterested, undefinable, and unpondered feeling that ties a man's heart to the place where he was born. This instinctive love is mingled with a taste for old habits, respect for ancestors, and memories of the past;

those who feel it love their country as one loves one's father's house. They love the peace they enjoy there; they are attached to the quiet habits they have formed; they are attached to the memories it recalls; and they even find a certain attraction in living there in obedience. This same patriotism is often also exalted by religious zeal, and then it works wonders. It is itself a sort of religion; it does not reason, but believes, feels, and acts. Some nations have in a sense personified their country and see the monarch as standing for it. Hence they have transferred some of the feelings of patriotism to him, and they boast of his triumphs and are proud of his power. There was a time under the old monarchy when the French experienced a sort of joy in surrendering themselves irrevocably to the arbitrary will of their monarch and said with pride: "We live under the most powerful king in the world."

Like all unpondered passions, this patriotism impels men to great ephemeral efforts, but not to continuous endeavor. Having saved the state in time of crisis, it often lets it decay in time of peace

When peoples are still simple in their mores and firm in their belief, when society gently rests on an ancient order of things whose legitimacy is not contested, then that instinctive patriotism prevails.

There is also another sort of patriotism more rational than that; less generous, perhaps less ardent, but more creative and more lasting, it is engendered by enlightenment, grows by the aid of laws and the exercise of rights, and in the end becomes, in a sense, mingled with personal interest. A man understands the influence which his country's well-being has on his own; he knows the law allows him to contribute to the production of this well-being, and he takes an interest in his country's prosperity, first as a thing useful to him and then as something he has created.

But sometimes there comes a time in the life of nations when old customs are changed, mores destroyed, beliefs shaken, and the prestige of memories has vanished, but when nonetheless enlightenment has remained incomplete and political rights are ill-assured or restricted. Then men see their country only by a weak and doubtful light; their patriotism is not centered on the soil, which in their eyes is just inanimate earth, nor on the customs of their ancestors, which they have been taught to regard as a yoke, nor on religion, which they doubt, nor on the laws, which they do not make, nor on the lawgiver, whom they fear ant scorn. So they find their country nowhere, recognizing neither its own nor any borrowed features, and they retreat into a narrow and unenlightened egoism. Such men escape from prejudices without recognizing the rule of reason; they have neither the instinctive patriotism of a monarchy nor the reflective patriotism of a republic, but have come to a halt between the two amid confusion and misery.

What can be done in such a condition? Retreat. But nations do not return to the feelings of their youth any more than men return to the innocent tastes of their infancy; they may regret them, but they cannot bring them back to life. Therefore it is essential to march forward and hasten to make the people see that individual interest is linked to that of the country, for disinterested patriotism has fled beyond recall.

Certainly I am far from claiming that in order to reach this result the exercise of political rights must immediately be granted to every man; but I do say that the most powerful way, and perhaps the only remaining way, in which to interest men in their country's fate is to make them take a share in its government. In our day it seems to me that civic spirit is inseparable from the exercise of political rights, and I think that henceforward in Europe the numbers of the citizens will be found to increase or diminish in proportion to the extension of those rights.

How is it that in the United States, where the inhabitants arrived but yesterday in the land they occupy, whither they brought with them neither customs nor memories, where they meet for the first time without knowing each other, where, to say it in one word, the instinct of country can hardly exist—how does it come about that each man is as interested in the affairs of his township, of his canton, and of the whole state as he is in his own affairs? It is because each man in his sphere takes an active part in the government of society.

The common man in the United States has understood the influence of the general prosperity on his own happiness, an idea so simple but nevertheless so little understood by the people. Moreover, he is accustomed to regard that prosperity as his own work. So he sees the public fortune as his own, and he works for the good of the state, not only from duty or from pride, but, I dare almost say, from greed.

There is no need to study the institutions or the history of the Americans to recognize the truth of what has just been said, for their mores are sufficient evidence of it. The American, taking part in everything that is done in his country, feels a duty to defend anything criticized there, for it is not only his country that is being attacked, but himself; hence one finds that his national pride has recourse to every artifice and descends to every childishness of personal vanity.

Nothing is more annoying in the ordinary intercourse of life than this irritable patriotism of the Americans. A foreigner will gladly agree to praise much in their country, but he would like to be allowed to criticize something, and that he is absolutely refused.

So America is the land of freedom where, in order not to offend anybody, the foreigner may speak freely neither about individuals nor about the state, neither about the ruled nor about the rulers, neither about public undertakings nor about private ones—indeed, about nothing that one comes across, except perhaps the climate and the soil, but yet one meets Americans ready to defend both of these, as if they had a share in forming them.

In our day we must make up our minds and dare to choose between the patriotism of all and the government of the few, for one cannot combine at the same time the social strength and activity given by the first with the guarantees of tranquillity sometimes provided by the second.

The idea of rights in the United States

No great people is without an idea of rights. How such a conception can be imparted to a nation. Respect for rights in the United States. Source of that respect.

Next to virtue as a general idea, nothing, I think is so beautiful as that of rights, and indeed the two ideas are mingled. The idea of rights is nothing but the conception of virtue applied to the world of politics.

By means of the idea of rights men have defined the nature of license and of tyranny. Guided by its light, we can each of us be independent without arrogance and obedient without servility. When a man submits to force, that surrender debases him; but when he accepts the recognized right of a fellow mortal to give him orders, there is a sense in which he rises above the giver of the commands. No man can be great without virtue, nor any nation great without respect for rights; one might almost say that without it there can be so society, for what is a combination of rational and intelligent beings held together by force alone?

I keep asking myself how, in our day, this conception may be taught to mankind and made, so to say, palpable to their senses; and I find one only, namely, to give them all the peaceful use of certain rights. One can see how this works among children, who are men except in strength and in experience; when a baby first begins to move among things outside himself, instinct leads him to make use of anything his hands can grasp; he has no idea of other people's property, no even that it exists; but as he is instructed in the value of things and discovers that he too may be despoiled, he becomes more circumspect, and in the end is led to respect for others that which he wishes to be respected for himself.

As for a child with his toys, so is it later for a man with all his belongings. Why is it that in America, the land par excellence of democracy, no one makes that outcry against property in general that often echoes through Europe? Is there any need to explain? It is because there are no proletarians in America. Everyone, having some possession to defend, recognizes the right to property in principle.

It is the same in the world of politics. The American man of the people has conceived a high idea of political rights because he has some; he does not attack those of others, in order that his own may not be violated. Whereas the corresponding man in Europe would be prejudiced against all authority, even the highest, the American uncomplaining obeys the lowest of his officials.

This truth is illustrated even in the smallest details of a nation's life. In France there are few pleasures exclusively reserved for the higher classes of society; the poor man is admitted almost everywhere where the rich can go, so one finds him behaving decently and with proper consideration for pleasures in which he shares. In England, where enjoyment is the privilege of the rich, who also monopolize power, people complain that when a poor man does furtively steal into the exclusive haunts of the rich he has a taste for causing pointless damage there. Why be surprised at that? Trouble has been taken to see that he has nothing to lose.

Democratic government makes the idea of political rights penetrate right down to the least of citizens, just as the division of property puts the general idea of property rights within reach of all. That, in my view, is one of its greatest merits.

I am not asserting it to be an easy matter to teach all men to make use of political rights; I only say that when that can happen, the results are important.

And I would add that if ever there was a century in which such an attempt should be made, that century is ours.

Do you not see that religions are growing weak and that the conception of the sanctity of rights is vanishing? Do you not see that mores are changing and that the moral conception of rights is being obliterated with them?

Do you notice how on all sides beliefs are giving way to arguments, and feelings to calculations? If amid this universal collapse you do not succeed in linking the idea of rights to personal interest, which provides the only stable point in the human heart, what other means will be left to you to govern the world, if not fear?

So, then, when I am told that laws are feeble and the governed turbulent, that passions are lively and virtue powerless, and that in this situation one must not dream of increasing the rights of democracy, I answer that it is for these very reasons that one must consider doing so, and in truth, I think the governments have an even greater interest in doing this than has society, for governments perish but society cannot die. However, I do not wish to press the example of America too far.

In America the people were invested with political rights at a time when it was difficult for them to make ill use of them because the citizens were few and their mores simple. As they have grown more powerful, the Americans have not appreciably increased the powers of democracy; rather they have extended its domain.

There can be no doubt that the moment when political rights are granted to a people who have till then been deprived of them is a time of crisis, a crisis which is often necessary but always dangerous.

A child may kill when he does not understand the value of life; he carries off other people's property before he knows that his own may be snatched from him. The man of the people, at the moment when political rights are granted to him, is much in the same position with respect to those rights as is a child faced by the whole of nature, and it is then that famous phrase applies: *homo puer robustus.*

This truth can be tested even in America. Those states in which the citizens have longest enjoyed their rights are those in which they still best know how to use them.

It cannot be repeated too often: nothing is more fertile in marvels than the art of being free, but nothing is harder than freedom's apprenticeship. The same is not true of despotism. Despotism often presents itself as the repairer of all the ills suffered, the support of just rights, defender of the oppressed, and founder of order. Peoples are lulled to sleep by the temporary prosperity it engenders, and when they do wake up, they are wretched. But liberty is generally born in stormy weather, growing with difficulty amid civil discords, and only when it is already old does one see the blessings it has brought.

Respect for law in the United States

American respect for law. Paternal affection they feel for it. Personal interest of everybody in increasing the law's strength.

It is not always feasible to call on the whole people, either directly or indirectly, to take its part in lawmaking, but no one can deny that when that can be done the law derives great authority therefrom. This popular origin, though often damaging to the wisdom and quality of legislation, gives it peculiar strength.

There is prodigious force in the expression of the wills of a whole people. When it stands out in broad daylight, even the imagination of those who would like to contest it is somehow smothered.

Parties are well aware of this truth.

For that reason, whenever possible they cast doubts on the majority's validity. Having failed to gain a majority from those who voted, they claim it among those who abstained from voting, and if that fails them, they claim a majority among those who have no right to vote.

In the United States, except for slaves, servants, and paupers fed by the township, no one is without a vote and, hence, an indirect share in lawmaking. Therefore those who would like to attack the laws are forced to adopt ostensibly one of two courses: they must either change the nation's opinion or trample its wishes under foot.

There is a second reason, too, more direct and powerful in its effect, namely, that every American feels a sort of personal interest in obeying the laws, for a man who is not today one of the majority party may be so tomorrow, and so he may soon be demanding for laws of his choosing that respect which he now professes for the lawgiver's will. Therefore, however annoying a law may be, the American will submit to it, not only as the work of the majority but also as his own doing; he regards it as a contract to which he is one of the parties.

So in the United States there is no numerous and perpetually turbulent crowd regarding the law as a natural enemy to fear and to suspect. On the contrary, one is bound to notice that all classes, show great confidence in their country's legislation, feeling a sort of paternal love for it.

I am wrong in saying all classes. As in America, the European ladder of power has been turned upside down; the wealthy find themselves in a position analogous to that of the poor in Europe: it is they who often mistrust the law. As I have said elsewhere, the real advantage of democratic government is not that it guarantees the interests of all, as is sometimes claimed, but just that it does protect those of the greatest number. In the United States, where the poor man rules, the rich have always some fear that he may abuse his power against them.

This state of mind among the wealthy may produce a silent discontent, but it creates no violent trouble for society, for the same reason which prevents the rich man from trusting the lawgiver also prevents him from defying his commands. Because he is rich he does not make the law, and because of his wealth he does not dare to break it. Among civilized nations it is generally only those with nothing to lose who revolt. Hence, though democratic laws may not always deserve respect, they are almost always respected, for those who usually break the laws cannot fail to obey those they have made and from which they profit, and those citizens who might have an interest in infringing them are impelled both by character and by circumstance to submit to the lawgiver's will, whatever it may be. Moreover, in America the people obey the law not only because it is their work but also because they can change it if by any chance it does injure them; they submit to it primarily as self-imposed evil, and secondly as a passing one.

Activity prevailing in all parts of the political body in the United States; the influence thereby exerted on society.

The political activity prevailing in the United States is harder to conceive than the freedom and equality found there. The continual feverish activity of the legislatures is only an episode and an extension of a movement that is universal. How difficult an American finds it to be occupied with his own business only. Political agitation spills over into civil society. The industrial activity of the Americans is in part due to this. Indirect advantages derived by society from democratic government.

When one passes from a free country into another which is not so, the contrast is very striking: there, all is activity and bustle; here all seems calm and immobile. In the former, betterment and progress are the questions of the day; in the latter, one might suppose that society, having acquired every blessing, longs for nothing but repose in which to enjoy them. Nevertheless, the country which is in such a rush to attain happiness is generally richer and more prosperous than the one that seems contented with its lot. And considering them one by one, it is hard to understand how this one daily discovers so many new needs, while the other seems conscious of so few.

While this remark applies to free countries that have preserved the forms of monarchy and to those dominated by an aristocracy, it is even more true of democratic republics. In them it is not only one section of the people that undertakes to better the state of society, for the whole nation is concerned therewith. It is not just the necessities and comforts of one class that must be provided for, but those of all classes at once.

It is not impossible to conceive the immense freedom enjoyed by the Americans, and one can also form an idea of their extreme equality, but the political activity prevailing in the United States is something one could never understand unless one had seen it.

No sooner do you set foot on American soil than you find yourself in a sort of tumult; a confused clamor rises on every side, and a thousand voices are heard at once, each expressing some social requirements. All around you everything is on the move: here the people of a district are assembled to discuss the possibility of building a church; there they are busy choosing a representative; further on, the delegates of a district are hurrying to town to consult about some local improvements; elsewhere it's the village farmers who have left their furrows to discuss the plan for a road or a school. One group of citizens assembles for the sole object of announcing that they disapprove of the government's course, while others unite to proclaim that the men in office are the fathers of their country. And here is yet another gathering which regards drunkenness as the main source of ills in the state and has come to enter into a solemn undertaking to give an example of temperance.[1]

The great political movement which keeps American legislatures in a state of continual agitation, and which alone is noticed from outside, is only an episode and a sort of extension of the universal movement, which begins in the lowest ranks of the people and thence spreads successively through all classes of citizens. No one could work harder to be happy.

It is hard to explain the place filled by political concerns in the life of an American. To take a hand in the government of society and to talk about it is his most important business and, so to say, the only pleasure he knows. That is obvious even in the most trivial habits of his life; even the women often go to public meetings and forget household cares while they listen to political speeches. For them clubs to some extent take the place of theaters. An American does not know how to converse, but he argues; he does not talk, but expatiates. He always speaks to you as if addressing a meeting, and if he happens to get excited, he will say "Gentlemen" when addressing an audience of one.

The inhabitant in some countries shows a sort of repugnance in accepting the political rights granted to him by the law; it strikes him as a waste of time to spend it on communal interests, and he likes to shut himself up in a narrow egoism, of which four ditches with hedges on top define the precise limits.

But if an American should be reduced to occupying himself with his own affairs, at that moment half his existence would be snatched from him; he would feel it as a vast void in his life and would become incredibly unhappy.[2]

I am convinced that if despotism ever came to be established in the United States it would find it even more difficult to overcome the habits that have sprung from freedom than to conquer the love of, freedom itself.

That constantly renewed agitation introduced by democratic government into political life passes, then, into civil society. Perhaps, taking everything into consideration, that is the greatest advantage of democratic government, and I praise it much more on account of what it causes to be done than for what it does.

It is incontestible that the people often manage public affairs very badly, but their concern therewith is bound to extend their mental horizon and shake them out of the rut of ordinary routine. A man of the people, when asked to share the task of governing society, acquires a certain self-esteem. Since he then has power, the brains of very enlightened people are put at his disposal. Constant efforts are made to enlist his support, and he learns from a thousand different efforts to deceive him. In politics he takes a part in undertakings he has not thought of, and they give him a general taste for enterprise. Daily new improvements to communal property are suggested to him, and that starts him wishing to improve his own. He may not be more virtuous or happier than his forebears, but he is more enlightened and active. I have no doubt that democratic institutions, combined with the physical nature of the land, are the indirect reason, and not, as is often claimed, the direct one, for the prodigious industrial expansion seen in the United States. It is not the laws' creation, but the people have learned to achieve it by making the laws.

When the enemies of democracy claim that a single man does his appointed task better than the government of all, I think they are right. There is more consistency in one man's rule than in that of a multitude, assuming equal enlightenment on either side; one man is more persevering, has more idea of the whole problem, attends more closely to details, and is a better judge of men. Anyone who denies that either has never seen a democratic republic or bases his view on too few examples. Democracy, even when local circumstances and the character of the people allow it to maintain itself, does not display a regular or methodical form of government. That is true. Democratic freedom does not carry its undertakings through as perfectly as an intelligent despotism would; it often abandons them before it has reaped the profit, or embarks on perilous ones; but in the long run it produces more; each thing is less well done, but more things are done. Under its sway it is not especially the things accomplished by the public administration that are great, but rather those things done without its help and beyond its sphere. Democracy does not provide a people with the most skillful of governments, but it does that which the most skillful government often cannot do: it spreads throughout the body social a restless activity, superabundant force, and energy never found elsewhere, which, however little favored by circumstance, can do wonders. Those are its true advantages.

In this century, when the destinies of the Christian world seem in suspense, some hasten to assail democracy as a hostile power while it is still growing; others already worship this new deity emerging from chaos. But both parties have an imperfect knowledge of the object of their hate or their desire; they fight in the dark and strike at random.

What do you expect from society and its government? We must be clear about that.

Do you wish to raise mankind to an elevated and generous view of the things of this world? Do you want to inspire men with a certain scorn of material goods? Do you hope to engender deep convictions and prepare the way for acts of profound devotion?

Are you concerned with refining mores, elevating manners, and causing the arts to blossom? Do you desire poetry, renown, and glory?

Do you set out to organize a nation so that it will have a powerful influence over all others? Do you expect it to attempt great enterprises and, whatever be the result of its efforts, to leave a great mark on history?

If in your view that should be the main object of men in society, do not support democratic government; it surely will not lead you to that goal.

But if you think it profitable to turn man's intellectual and moral activity toward the necessities of physical life and use them to produce well-being, if you think that reason is more use to men than genius, if your object is not to create heroic virtues but rather tranquil habits, if you would rather contemplate vices than crimes and prefer fewer transgressions at the cost of fewer splendid deeds, if in place of a brilliant society you are content to live in one that is prosperous, and finally, if in your view the main object of government is not to achieve the greatest strength or glory for the nation as a whole but to provide for every individual therein the utmost well-being, protecting him as far as possible from all afflictions, then it is good to make conditions equal and to establish a democratic government.

But if there is no time left to make a choice, and if a force beyond human control is already carrying you along regardless of your desires toward one of these types of government, then at least seek to derive from it all the good that it can do; understanding its good instincts as well as its evil inclinations, try to restrain the latter and promote the former.

CHAPTER 7

The Omnipotence of the Majority in the United States and its Effects

The natural strength of the majority in democracies. Most of the American constitutions have artificially increased this natural strength. How? Pledged delegates. Moral power of the majority. View of its infallibility. Respects for its rights. What increases it in the United States.

The absolute sovereignty of the will of the majority is the essence of democratic government, for in democracies there is nothing outside the majority capable of resisting it.

Most American constitutions have sought further artificially to increase this natural strength of the majority.[3]

Of all political powers, the legislature is the one most ready to obey the wishes of the majority. The Americans wanted the members of the legislatures to be appointed *directly* by the people and for a *very short* term of office so that they should be obliged to submit not only to the general views but also to the passing passions of their constituents.

The members of both houses have been chosen from the same class and appointed in the same way, so that the activity of the legislative body is almost as quick and just as irresistible as that of a single assembly.

Having constituted the legislature in this way, almost all the powers of government were concentrated in its hands.

At the same time as the law increased the strength of naturally powerful authorities, it increasingly weakened those that were by nature feeble. It gave the representatives of the executive neither stability nor independence, and by subjecting them completely to the caprices of the legislature, deprived them of what little influence the nature of democratic government might have allowed them to enjoy.

In several states the majority elected the judges, and in all they depended in a way on the legislature, whose members had the right annually to fix their salaries.

Custom has gone even beyond the laws.

A custom is spreading more and more in the United States which will end by making the guarantees of representative government vain; it frequently happens that the electors, when they nominate a deputy, lay down a plan of conduct for him and impose some positive obligations on him which he cannot avoid. It is as if, with tumult threatening, the majority were deliberating in the marketplace.

In America several particular circumstances also tend to make the power of the majority not only predominant but irresistible.

The moral authority of the majority is partly based on the notion that there is more enlightenment and wisdom in a numerous assembly than in a single man, and the number of the legislators is more important than how they are chosen. It is the theory of equality applied to brains. This doctrine attacks the last asylum of human pride; for that reason the minority is reluctant in admitting it and takes a long time to get used to it. Like all powers, and perhaps more than any other of them, the power of the majority needs to have proved lasting to appear legitimate. When it is beginning to establish itself, it enforces obedience by constraint; it is only when men have long lived under its laws that they begin to respect it.

The idea that the majority has a right based on enlightenment to govern society was brought to the United States by its first inhabitants; and this idea, which would of itself be enough to create a free nation, has by now passed into mores and affects even the smallest habits of life.

Under the old monarchy the French took it as a maxim that the king could do no wrong, and when he did do wrong, they thought the fault lay with his advisers. This made obedience wonderfully much easier. One could grumble against the law without ceasing to love and respect the lawgiver. The Americans take the same view of the majority.

The moral authority of the majority is also founded on the principle that the interest of the greatest number should be preferred to that of those who are fewer. Now, it is easy to understand that the respect professed for this right of the greatest number naturally grows or shrinks according to the state of the parties. When a nation is divided between several great irreconcilable interests, the privilege of the majority is often disregarded, for it would be too unpleasant to submit to it.

If there existed in America one class of citizens whom the legislators were trying to deprive of certain exclusive privileges possessed for centuries and wanted to force them down from a high station to join the ranks of the crowd, it is probable that minority would not easily submit to its laws.

But as men equal among themselves came to people the United States, there is as yet no natural or permanent antagonism between the interests of the various inhabitants.

There are states of society in which those who are in the minority cannot hope to win the majority over, for to do so would involve abandoning the very aim of the struggle in which they are engaged abandoning the very aim of the struggle in which they are engaged against it. An aristocracy, for instance, could not become a majority without giving up its exclusive privileges, and if it did let them go, it would no longer be an aristocracy.

In the United States, political questions cannot arise in such general and absolute fashion, and all the parties are ready to recognize the rights of the majority because they all hope one day to profit themselves by them.

Hence the majority in the United States has immense actual power and a power of opinion which is almost as great. When once its mind is made up on any question, there are, so to say, no obstacles which can retard, much less halt, its progress and give it time to hear the wails of those it crushes as it passes.

The consequences of this state of affairs are fate-laden and dangerous for the future.

How in America the omnipotence of the majority increases the legislative and administrative instability natural to democracies

How the Americans increase the legislative instability natural to democracies by changing their legislators every year and by giving them almost limitless power. The same effect on the administration. In America the drive toward social improvements is infinitely greater but less continuous than in Europe.

I have spoken before of the vices natural to democratic government, and every single one of them increases with the growing power of the majority.

To begin with the most obvious of all:

Legislative instability is an ill inherent in democratic government because it is the nature of democracies to bring new men to power. But this ill is greater or less according to the power and means of action accorded to the legislator.

In America the lawmaking authority has been given sovereign power. This authority can carry out anything it desires quickly and irresistibly, and its representatives change annually. That it is to say, just that combination has been chosen which most encourages democratic instability and allows the changing wishes of democracy to be applied to the most important matters.

Thus American laws have a shorter duration than those of any other country in the world today. Almost all American constitutions have been amended within the last thirty years, and so there is no American state which has not modified the basis of its laws within that period.

As of the laws themselves, it is enough to glance at the archives of the various states of the Union to realize that in America the legislator's activity never slows down. Not that American democracy is by nature more unstable than any other, but it has been given the means to carry the natural instability of its inclinations into the making of laws.[4]

The omnipotence of the majority and the rapid as well as absolute manner in which its decisions are executed in the United States not only make the law unstable but have a like effect on the execution of the law and on public administrative activity.

As the majority is the only power whom it is important to please, all its projects are taken up with great ardour; but as soon as its attention is turned elsewhere, all these efforts cease; whereas in free European states, where the administrative authority has an independent existence and an assured position, the legislator's wishes continue to be executed even when he is occupied by other matters.

Much more zeal and energy are brought to bear in America on certain improvements than anywhere else.

In Europe an infinitely smaller social force is employed, but more continuously.

A few years ago some pious people undertook to make the state of the prisons better. The public was roused by their exhortations, and the reform of criminals became a popular cause.

New prisons were then built. For the first time the idea of reforming offenders as well as punishing them penetrated into the prisons. But that happy revolution in which the public cooperated with such eagerness and which the simultaneous efforts of the citizens rendered irresistible could not be accomplished in a moment.

Alongside the new penitentiaries, built quickly in response to the public's desire, the old prisons remained and housed a great number of the guilty. These seemed to become more unhealthy and more corrupting at the same rate as the new ones became healthy and devoted to reform. This double effect is easily understood: the majority, preoccupied with the idea of founding a new establishment, had forgotten the already existing ones. Everybody's attention was turned away from the matter that no longer held their master's and supervision ceased. The salutary bonds of discipline were first stretched and then soon broken. And beside some prison that stood as a durable monument to the gentleness and enlightenment of our age, there was a dungeon recalling the barbarities of the Middle Ages.

Tyranny of the majority

How the principle of the sovereignty of the people should be understood. Impossibility of conceiving a mixed government. Sovereign power must be placed somewhere. Precautions which one should take to moderate its action. These precautions have not been taken in the United States. Result thereof.

I regard it as an impious and detestable maxim that in matters of government the majority of a people has the right to do everything, and nevertheless I place the origin of all powers in the will of the majority. Am I in contradiction with myself?

There is one law which has been made, or at least adopted, not by the majority of this or that people, but by the majority of all men. That law is justice.

Justice therefore forms the boundary to each people's right.

A nation is like a jury entrusted to represent universal society and to apply the justice which is its law. Should the jury representing society have greater power than that very society whose laws it applies?

Consequently, when I refuse to obey an unjust law, by no means deny the majority's right to give orders; I only appeal from the sovereignty of the people to the sovereignty of the human race.

There are those not afraid to say that in matters which only concern itself a nation cannot go completely beyond the bounds of justice and reason and that there is therefore no need to fear giving total power to the majority representing it. But that is the language of a slave.

What is a majority, in its collective capacity, if not an individual with opinions, and usually with interests, contrary to those of another individual, called the minority? Now, if you admit that a man vested with omnipotence can abuse it against his adversaries, why not admit the same concerning a majority? Have men, by joining together, changed their character? By becoming stronger, have they become more patient of obstacles?[5] For my part, I cannot believe that, and I will never grant to several that power to do everything which I refuse to a single man.

It is not that I think that in order to preserve liberty one can mix several principles within the same government in such a way that they will be really opposed to one another.

I have always considered what is called a mixed government to be a chimera. There is in truth no such thing as a mixed government (in the sense usually given to the words), since in any society one finds in the end some principle of action that dominates all the others.

Eighteenth-century England, which has been especially cited as an example of this type of government, was an essentially aristocratic state, although it contained within itself great elements of democracy, for laws and mores were so designed that the aristocracy could always prevail in the long run and manage public affairs as it wished.

The mistake is due to those who, constantly seeing the interests of the great in conflict with those of the people, have thought only about the struggle and have not paid attention to the result thereof, which was more important. When a society really does have a mixed government, that is to say, one equally shared between contrary principles, either a revolution breaks out or that society breaks up.

I therefore think it always necessary to place somewhere one social power superior to all others, but I believe that freedom is in danger when that power finds no obstacle that can restrain its course and give it time to moderate itself.

Omnipotence in itself seems a bad and dangerous thing. I think that its exercise is beyond man's strength, whoever he be, and that only God can be omnipotent without danger because His wisdom and justice are always equal to His power. So there is no power on earth in itself so worthy of respect or vested with such a sacred right that I would wish to let it act without control and dominate without obstacles. So when I see the right and capacity to do all given to any authority whatsoever, whether it be called people or king, democracy or aristocracy, and whether the scene of action is a monarchy or a republic, I say: the germ of tyranny is there, and I will go look for other laws under which to live.

My greatest complaint against democratic government as organized in the United States is not, as many Europeans make out, its weakness, but rather its irresistible strength. What I find most repulsive in America is not the extreme freedom reigning there but the shortage of guarantees against tyranny.

When a man or a party suffers an injustice in the United States, to whom can he turn? To public opinion? That is what forms the majority. To the legislative body? It represents the majority and obeys it blindly. To the executive power? It is appointed by the majority and serves as its passive instrument. To the police? They are nothing but the majority under arms. A jury? The jury is the majority vested with the right to pronounce judgment; even the judges in certain states are elected by the majority. So, however iniquitous or unreasonable the measure which hurts you, you must submit.[6]

But suppose you were to have a legislative body so composed that it represented the majority without being necessarily the slave of its passions, an executive power having a strength of its own, and a judicial power independent of the other two authorities; then you would still have a democratic government, but there would be hardly any remaining risk of tyranny.

I am not asserting that at the present time in America there are frequent acts of tyranny. I do say that one can find no guarantee against it there and that the reasons for the government's gentleness must be sought in circumstances and in mores rather than in the laws.

Effect of the omnipotence of the majority on the arbitrary power of American public officials.

The freedom which American law leaves to functionaries within the sphere marked out for them. Their power.

It is important to make the distinction between arbitrary power and tyranny. Tyranny can use even the law as its instrument, and then it is no longer arbitrary; arbitrary power may be used in the interest of the ruled, and then it is not tyrannical.

Tyranny ordinarily makes use of arbitrariness, but it can at need do without it.

In the United States that omnipotence of the majority which favors the legal despotism of the legislator also smiles on the arbitrary power of the magistrate. The majority, being in absolute command both of lawmaking and of the execution of the laws, and equally controlling both rulers and ruled, regards public functionaries as its passive agents and is glad to leave them the trouble of carrying out its plans. It therefore does not enter by anticipation into the details of their duties and hardly takes the trouble to define their rights. It treats them as a master might treat his servants if, always seeing them act under his eyes, he could direct or correct them at any moment.

In general, the law leaves American officials much freer than ours within the sphere marked out for them. Sometimes the majority may even allow them to go beyond that. Assured of the views and strengthened by the support of the greatest number, they then dare to do things which astonish a European, accustomed though he be to the spectacle of arbitrary power. Thus habits form in freedom that may one day become fatal to that freedom.

The power exercised by the majority in America over thought

In the United States, when the majority has irrevocably decided about any question, it is no longer discussed. Why? Moral authority exercised by the majority over thought. Democratic republics have turned despotism into something immaterial.

It is when one comes to look into the use made of thought in the United States that one most clearly sees how far the power of the majority goes beyond all powers known to us in Europe.

Thought is an invisible power and one almost impossible to lay hands on, which makes sport of all tyrannies. In our day the most absolute sovereigns in Europe cannot prevent certain thoughts hostile to their power from silently circulating in their states and even in their own courts. It is not like that in America; while the majority is in doubt, one talks; but when it has irrevocably pronounced, everyone is silent, and friends and enemies alike seem to make for its bandwagon. The reason is simple: no monarch is so absolute that he can hold all the forces of society in his hands, and overcome all resistance, as a majority invested with the right to make the laws and to execute them, can do.

Moreover a king's power is physical only, controlling actions but not influencing desires, whereas the majority is invested with both physical and moral authority, which acts as much upon the will as upon behavior and at the same moment prevents both the act and the desire to do it.

I know no country in which, speaking generally, there is less independence of mind and true freedom of discussion than in America.

There is no religious or political theory which one cannot preach freely in the constitutional states of Europe or which does not penetrate into the others, for there is no country in Europe so subject to a single power that he who wishes to speak the truth cannot find support enough to protect him against the consequences of his independence. If he is unlucky enough to live under an absolute government, he often has the people with him; if he lives in a free country, he may at need find shelter behind the royal authority. In democratic countries the aristocracy may support him, and in other lands the democracy. But in a democracy organized on the model of the United States there is only one authority, one source of strength and of success, and nothing outside it.

In America the majority has enclosed thought within a formidable fence. A writer is free inside that area, but woe to the man who goes beyond it. Not that he stands in fear of an *auto-da-fé*, but he must face all kinds of unpleasantness and everyday persecution. A career in politics is closed to him, for he has offended the only power that holds the keys. He is denied everything, including renown. Before he goes into print, he believes he has supporters; but he feels that he has them no more once he stands revealed to all, for those who condemn him express their views loudly, while those who think as he does, but without his courage, retreat into silence as if ashamed of having told the truth.

Formerly tyranny used the clumsy weapons of chains and hangmen; nowadays even despotism, though it seemed to have nothing more to learn, has been perfected by civilization.

Princes made violence a physical thing, but our contemporary democratic republics have turned it into something as intellectual as the human will it is intended to constrain. Under the absolute government of a single man, despotism, to reach the soul, clumsily struck at the body, and the soul, escaping from such blows, rose gloriously above it; but in democratic republics that is not at all how tyranny behaves; it leaves the body alone and goes straight for the soul. The master no longer says: "Think like me or you die." He does say: "You are free not to think as I do; you can keep your life and property and all; but from this day you are a stranger among us. You can keep your privileges in the township, but they will be useless to you, for if you solicit your fellow citizens' votes, they will not give them to you, and if you only ask for their esteem, they will make excuses for refusing that. You will remain among men, but you will lose your rights to count as one. When you approach your fellows, they will shun you as an impure being, and even those who believe in your innocence will abandon you too, lest they in turn be shunned. Go in peace. I have given you your life, but it is a life worse than death."

Absolute monarchies brought despotism into dishonor; we must beware lest democratic republics rehabilitate it, and that while they make it more oppressive toward some, they do not rid it of its detestable and degrading character in the eyes of the greatest number.

In the proudest nations of the Old World works were published which faithfully portrayed the vices and absurdities of contemporaries; La Bruyère lived in Louis XIV's palace while he wrote his chapter o the great, and Molière criticized the court in plays acted before the courtiers. But the power which dominates in the United States does not understand being mocked like that. The least reproach offends it, and the slightest sting of truth turns it fierce; and one must praise everything, from the turn of its phrases to its most robust virtues. No writer, no matter how famous, can escape from this obligation to sprinkle incense over his fellow citizens. Hence the majority lives in a state of perpetual self-adoration; only strangers or experience may be able to bring certain truths to the Americans' attention.

We need seek no other reason for the absence of great writers in America so far; literary genius cannot exist without freedom of the spirit, and there is no freedom of the spirit in America.

In Spain the Inquisition was never able to prevent the circulation of books contrary to the majority religion. The American majority's sway extends further and has rid itself even of the thought of publishing such books. One finds unbelievers in America, but unbelief has, so to say, no organ.

One finds governments striving to protect mores by condemning the authors of licentious books. No one in the United States is condemned for works of that sort, but no one is tempted to write them. Not that all the citizens are chaste in their mores, but those of the majority are regular.

In this, no doubt, power is well used, but my point is the nature of the power in itself. This irresistible power is a continuous fact and its good use only an accident.

Effects of the majority's tyranny on American national character; the courtier spirit in the United States

Up to now the tyranny of the majority has had more effect on the mores than on the behavior of society. The growth of great characters is halted. Democratic republics organized on American lines put the courtier spirit within the reach of great numbers. Evidence of this spirit in the United States. Why the people are more patriotic than those who govern.

The influence of what I have been talking about is as yet only weakly felt in political society, but its ill effects on the national character are already apparent. I think that the rareness now of outstanding men on the political scene is due to the ever-increasing despotism of the American majority.

When the Revolution broke out, a crowd of them appeared; at that time public opinion gave direction to men's wills but did not tyrannize over them. The famous men of that time, while they freely took part in the intellectual movement of the age, had a greatness all their own; their renown brought honor to the nation, not vice versa.

The great men close to the throne of an absolute monarch flatter their master's passions and willingly bow to his caprices. But the mass of the nation does not countenance servitude; its submission is often from weakness, habit, or ignorance and sometimes from love of the throne or of the king. Some nations have taken a kind of pleasure and pride in sacrificing their wills to that of the prince, and by this means introducing a sort of independence of mind into the very heart of obedience. In such nations there is much less degradation than misery. Moreover, there is a great difference between doing something of which you do not approve and pretending to approve of what you are doing; the first is the part of a weak man, but the second fits only the manner of a valet.

In free countries, where everyone is more or less called on to give his opinion about affairs of state, and in democratic republics, where there is a constant mingling of public with private life and where the sovereign is approachable from every side, to raise one's voice being enough to attract his attention, one finds many more people seeking to gamble on his weaknesses and live off his passions than would be found under absolute monarchies. It is not that men are naturally worse there than elsewhere, but the temptation is greater and offered to more men at the same time. Consequently there is a much more general lowering of standards.

Democratic republics put the spirit of a court within reach of the multitude and let it penetrate through all classes at once. That is one of the main reproaches to be made against them.

This is particularly true of democratic states organized after the fashion of the American republics, where the majority has such absolute and irresistible sway that one must in a sense renounce one's rights as a citizen and, so to say, one's status as a man when one wants to diverge from the path it has marked out.

Among the immense thrusting crowd of American political aspirants I saw very few men who showed that virile candor and manly independence of thought which often marked the Americans of an earlier generation and which, wherever found, is the most salient feature in men of great character. At first glance one might suppose that all American minds had been fashioned after the same model, so exactly do they follow along the same paths. A foreigner does, it is true, sometimes meet Americans who are not strict slaves of slogans; such men may deplore the defects of the laws and the unenlightened mutability of democracy; often they even go as far as to point out the defects which this tendency could be corrected, but no one, except yourself, listens to them, and you, to whom they confide these secret thoughts, are only a stranger and will pass on. To you they will disclose trusts that have no use for you, but when they go down into the marketplace they use quite different language.

If these lines ever come to be read in America, I am sure of two things; first, that all readers will raise their voices to condemn me; secondly, that in the depths of their conscience many will hold me innocent.

I have heard talk of the motherland in the United States, and I have come across real patriotism among the people but have often looked in vain for any such thing among their rulers. An analogy will make this easily understandable: despotism corrupts the man who submits to it much more than the man who imposes it. In absolute monarchies the king may often have great virtues, but the courtiers are always vile.

It is true that American courtiers never say "Sire" or "Your Majesty," as if the difference mattered; but they are constantly talking of their master's natural brilliance; they do not raise the question which of all the prince's virtues is most to be admired, for they assure him that he possess all virtues, without having acquired them and, so to say, without desiring them; they do not give him their wives or their daughters hoping that he will raise them to the rank of his mistresses, but they do sacrifice their opinions to him and so prostitute themselves.

American moralists and philosophers are not obliged to wrap their views in veils of allegory, but before hazarding an unpleasant truth they say: "We know that we are addressing a people so far above human weaknesses that they will always be masters of themselves. We would not use such language unless we knew that we were speaking to men whose virtues and enlightenment make them alone among all others worthy to remain free."

How could the flatterers of Louis XIV improve on that?

For my part, I think that in all governments whatsoever meanness will cling to strength, and flattery to power. And I now of only one way of preventing men from degrading themselves, namely, not to give anybody that omnipotence which carries with it sovereign power to debase them.

The greatest danger to the American republics comes from the omnipotence of the majority

It is not impotence but the ill use of power that threatens the existence of democratic republics. The government of the American republics is more centralized and more energetic than that of European monarchies. Consequential dangers. Views of Madison and Jefferson on the matter.

Governments ordinarily break down either through impotence or through tyranny. In the first case power slips from their grasp, whereas in the second it is taken from them.

Many people, seeing democratic states fall into anarchy, have supposed that government in such states was by nature weak and impotent. The truth is that once war has broken out between the parties, government influence over society ceases. But I do not think a lack of strength or resources is part of the nature of democratic authority; on the contrary, I believe that it is almost always the abuse of that strength and the ill use of those resources which bring it down. Anarchy is almost always a consequence either of the tyranny or of the inability of democracy, but not of its impotence.

One must not confuse stability with strength or a thing's size with its duration. In democratic republics the power directing[7] society is not stable, for both its personnel and its aims change often. But wherever it is brought to bear, its strength is almost irresistible.

The government of the American republics seems to me as centralized and more energetic than the absolute monarchies of Europe. So I do not think that it will collapse from weakness.[8]

If ever freedom is lost in America, that will be due to the omnipotence of the majority driving the minorities to desperation and forcing them to appeal to physical force. We may then see anarchy, but it will have come as the result of despotism.

President James Madison has given expression to just these thoughts. (*The Federalist*, No. 51.)

"It is of great importance in a republic not only to guard the society against the oppression of its rulers, but to guard one part of the society against the injustice of the other part. . . . Justice is the end of government. It is the end of civil society. It ever has been and ever will be pursued until it be obtained, or until liberty be lost in the pursuit. In a society under the forms of which the stronger faction can readily unite and oppress the weaker, anarchy may as truly be said to reign as in a state of nature, where the weaker individual is not secured against the violence of the stronger; and as, in the latter state, even the stronger individuals are prompted, by the uncertainty of their condition, to submit to a government which may protect the weak as well as themselves; so, in the former state, will the more powerful factions or parties be gradually induced, by a like motive, to wish for a government which will protect all parties, the weaker as well as the more powerful. It can be little doubted that if the state of Rhode Island was separated from the Confederacy and left to itself, the insecurity of rights under the popular form of government within such narrow limits would be displayed by such reiterated oppressions of factious majorities that some power altogether independent of the people would soon be called for by the voice of the very factions whose misrule had proved the necessity of it."

Jefferson also said: "The executive, in our government is not the sole, it is scarcely the principal, object of my jealousy. The tyranny of the legislature is the most formidable dread at present and will be for many years. That of the executive will come in its turn, but it will be at a remote period."[9]

I prefer to quote Jefferson rather than anybody else on this topic, regarding him as the most powerful apostle of democracy there has ever been.

Notes

1. Temperance societies are associations whose members undertake to abstain from strong drink. At the time of my visit temperance societies already counted more than 270,000 members, and consequently, in the state of Pennsylvania alone the consumption of strong liquors had fallen by 500,000 gallons a year.

2. The same fact was already noted at Rome under the first Caesars. Montesquieu remarks somewhere that nothing equals the despair of certain Roman citizens who after the excitements of a political existence suddenly return to the calm of private life.

3. In examining the federal Constitution we have seen that the lawgivers of the Union strove in the opposite direction. The result of their efforts has been to make the federal government more independent in its sphere than are the states in theirs. But the federal government is hardly concerned with anything except foreign affairs; it is the state governments which really control American society.

4. The legislative acts promulgated by the state of Massachusetts alone between 1780 and the present day already fill three large volumes. Moreover, one must note that the collection to which I refer was revised in 1823, and that many outdated laws and those that had become irrelevant were omitted. Now, the state of Massachusetts, which has a population no greater than one of our departments, might be taken as the most stable in the whole union and the one which shows most continuity and wisdom in its undertakings.

5. No one would wish to maintain that a nation cannot abuse its power against another nation. But parties form something like little nations within the nation, and the relations between them are like those of strangers.

If it is agreed that a nation can be tyrannical toward another nation, how can one deny that a party can be so toward another party?

6. At Baltimore during the War of 1812 there was a striking example of the excesses to which despotism of the majority may lead. At that time the war was very popular at Baltimore. A newspaper which came out in strong opposition to it aroused the indignation of the inhabitants. The people assembled, broke the presses, and attacked the house of the editors. An attempt was made to summon the militia, but it did not answer the appeal. Finally, to save the lives of these wretched men threatened by the fury of the public, they were taken to prison like criminals. This precaution was useless. During the night the people assembled again; the magistrates having failed to bring up the militia, the prison was broken open; one of the journalists was killed on the spot and the others left for dead; the guilty were brought before a jury and acquitted.

I once said to a Pennsylvanian: "Please explain to me why in a state founded by Quakers and renowned for its tolerance, freed Negroes are not allowed to use their rights as citizens? They pay taxes; is it not right that they should vote?"

"Do not insult us," he replied, "by supposing that our legislators would commit an act of such gross injustice and intolerance."

"So, with you, Negroes do have the right to vote?"

"Certainly."

"Then how was it that at the electoral college this morning I did not see a single one of them in the meeting?"

"That is not the fault of the law," said the American. "It is true that Negroes have the right to be present at elections, but they voluntarily abstain from appearing."

"That is extraordinarily modest of them."

"Oh! It is not that they are reluctant to go there, but they are afraid they may be maltreated. With us it sometimes happens that the law lacks force when the majority does not support it. Now, the majority is filled with the strongest prejudices against Negroes, and the magistrates do not feel strong enough to guarantee the rights granted to them by the lawmakers."

"What! The majority, privileged to make the law, wishes also to have the privilege of disobeying the law?"

7. Authority may be centralized in an assembly, and in that case it is strong but not stable. Or it may be centralized in one man, and in that case it is less strong but more stable.

8. There is no need to remind the reader that here, and throughout this chapter, I am speaking not of the federal government but of the governments of each state, where a despotic majority is in control.

9. Letter from Jefferson to Madison, March 15, 1789.

GEORG WILHELM
FRIEDRICH HEGEL

Georg Wilhelm Friedrich Hegel (1770–1831), son of a senior financial official, was born in the city of Stuttgart, capital of Württemberg, a duchy in southwest Germany. Hegel received his university education at the Tübingen *Stift,* where he became friends with Hölderlin and Schelling. He entered the Lutheran theological seminary in 1788, received his *Magister* (master's degree) in philosophy in 1790, and completed his training in 1793 with a *Magister* in theology. For the next six years, Hegel earned his living as a house tutor, first in Bern (1793–1796), then in Frankfurt (1797–1800), and engaged in a series of social and religious studies. His father's death in 1799 left him a small legacy that enabled him to begin a career as a professional philosopher. Under Schelling's sponsorship, he moved to Jena in the beginning of 1801, where, on the basis of his dissertation, *De Orbitis Planetarum,* he became a *Privatdozent* (unsalaried lecturer). In Jena, Hegel met Goethe and Schiller, wrote *The Difference between Fichte's and Schelling's Systems of Philosophy* (1801), collaborated with Schelling on the *Critical Journal of Philosophy,* and wrote *The Phenomenology of Spirit* (1807), the text that established his position as a central figure in philosophy. During his time in Jena, Hegel also became involved with Christiana Burkhart, a chambermaid, who gave birth to his first child. Napoleon's defeat of the Prussian army in October 1806 at the battle of Jena, the subsequent closing of the university, and Hegel's own private financial difficulties led to a ten-year interruption of his university career. Between March 1807 and November 1808, he worked as the editor of a pro-French daily paper in Bamberg, Bavaria. He then assumed the position of *Rektor* (schoolmaster) of the *Gymnasium* (secondary school) in Nuremberg, where he married the aristocratic Marie von Tucher (1811) and wrote the *Science of Logic* (Book I, 1812; Book II, 1813; Book III, 1816). In October 1816, Hegel finally resumed his university career, becoming professor of philosophy in Heidelberg, where he elaborated his philosophical system in a series of lectures on such topics as the philosophy of art, religion, history, and right, and published the first edition of the *Encyclopedia of Philosophical Sciences* (1817). Hegel's final move took place in 1818 when he became professor of philosophy in Berlin. While there he continued his cycle of lectures and published the *Philosophy of Right* (1821) and the expanded second edition of his *Encyclopedia* (1827). He became *Rektor* of the University in 1829.

The Philosophy of Right or, to give the work its full title, *Natural Law and Political Science in Outline; Elements of the Philosophy of Right* represents the most comprehensive statement of Hegel's social and political philosophy published in his lifetime. Written as a textbook to accompany his lectures on moral and political philosophy, the *Philosophy of Right* has the role within Hegel's philosophical system of providing an account of objective *Geist,* the form of mind or spirit that is realized within human society and history.

As such it represents a more extensive and systematic treatment of the material presented in Part III, Section II (Objective Spirit) of his *Encyclopedia*.

Within the history of philosophy, the significance of the *Philosophy of Right* is commonly attributed to its radical critique of, and sharp break with, the social-contract tradition of Hobbes, Locke, Kant, and Rousseau. Inasmuch as Hegel denies the contractualist thesis that social and political relations are or ought to be contractual in character and rejects the contractualist project of using the notion of contract to explain the legitimacy of the state, this view is correct. Nonetheless, Hegel's actual relation to the social-contract tradition is more complex than the standard view suggests. First of all, Hegel recognizes and celebrates the fact that the modern social world contains a sphere of contractual relations: the sphere he calls *civil society*. He contends that this sphere provides an essential form of freedom: the freedom of the burgher, or member of civil society, the freedom expressed in individual choice. More important, Hegel retains the contractualist insight that the justification of social institutions must take the form of showing that they can be rationally willed and that social institutions can be rationally willed only if they are free. His fundamental disagreement with the social-contract tradition turns on two points: the standpoint from which institutions are to be assessed and the nature of freedom. The social-contract theorists maintained that the legitimacy of social institutions is to be assessed from the standpoint of the state of nature. Hegel argues that this individualistic standpoint fails to recognize the social nature of human beings. In its place, Hegel offers the standpoint of modern ethical life (*Sittlichkeit*), which acknowledges both the social nature of modern human beings and their particularity or subjectivity. The contractualist conception of freedom is deficient because it fails to recognize the highest form of practical freedom: the freedom of the citizen, the freedom that consists in willing "the universal," or participating in a politically organized community. Hegel's account of the modern political state (and his celebrated distinction between civil society and the state) is designed to explain what the freedom of the citizen comes to. It is additionally meant to show how the modern political state makes both the freedom of the citizen and the freedom of the burgher possible. That it does so is what Hegel means by saying:

> The principle of modern states has prodigious strength and depth because it allows the principle of subjectivity to progress to its culmination in the extreme of self-subsistent personal particularity, and yet at the same time brings it back to the substantive unity and so maintains this unity in the principle of subjectivity itself (Sec. 260).

In this volume, the Introduction and Section III of the *Philosophy of Right* are reproduced. The Introduction provides an account of the basic notions of Hegel's social and political philosophy, the most central being the notion of right (*Recht*) itself (Sec. 1). In Hegel's expansive sense of the term, law, rights, morality, and the forms of "ethical life" embodied in the family, civil society, and state all count as shapes of "right." In his view, law, ethics, and social and political philosophy all form a single domain called *right*, and the philosophy of *right* is the philosophy of this domain. Hegel's central philosophical claim about the right is that the "idea" of right (the concept of right and its various actualizations) is properly explained in terms of "the will." (In speaking of *the* will, Hegel means to abstract from the question Whose will? and refer to willing in general.) More specifically, the will is the basic principle of the right,

and the basic fact about the will is that it is free. Freedom is thus "both the substance of right and its goal," and the right is properly defined as the actualization, or embodiment, of freedom (Sec. 4). Thus, for Hegel, every genuine
configuration of the right (be it one of abstract right, morality, or ethical life) is
an actualization of the free will, and every actualization of the free will is a
configuration of right. Hence, in order to attain a more concrete understanding of the right, we must come to a clearer understanding of the structure of
the will: We must know what the free will must *will* in order to be free. Hegel's
answer is that it must will the free will. The free will, for Hegel, is the will
"which wills the free will" (Sec. 27). This suggests that, from the perspective of
the philosophy of right, the key questions concerning the social world are:
What configuration of social institutions makes it possible for the free will to
will the free will? And, more radically: What configuration of social institutions
itself actualizes the free will's willing of itself?

The third part of the *Philosophy of Right* (Ethical Life) is meant to provide
an answer to these two questions. It contains Hegel's account of the concept
of ethical life (Secs. 142–156) and his analysis of the rational form of the family (Secs. 158–180), civil society (Secs. 182–255), and the state (Secs.
257–360). The modern family, for Hegel, is nuclear, bourgeois, and patriarchal. It is *nuclear* in that the basic family unit consists of the mother, father,
and their biological children; *bourgeois* in that it is a unit of consumption
rather than production and fosters the form of sentimental personal relations
characteristic of bourgeois life; and *patriarchal* in that the head of the household and the family's legal representative is the father. The family is also in
Hegel's view, an "immediate" unity. In a well-ordered family, family members
regard themselves as members of the family unit rather than as individuals
(separate bearers of right), and all property is communally owned. The family's
function within the modern social world is to provide human beings with an
institutional structure within which they can realize and find acceptance of the
emotional aspects of their particularity. Civil society, as Hegel represents it,
consists of the "system of needs," the modern marketplace; the "administration
of justice," a legal and political system; the "police," a public authority responsible for social and economic regulation; and the "corporations," a group of
voluntary associations including professional and trade organizations,
churches, and municipal governments. Civil society represents the stage "of
difference" of ethical life (Sec. 182A): It is the institutional sphere within which
human beings pursue their separate and particular interests. As such, it is a
sphere of private activity. But Hegel's account is also meant to show that the
rational form of civil society includes institutions that make it a civic community, a community that protects the rights and welfare of individuals and within
which individuals form associations to pursue a good larger than their own.
The modern political state, in Hegel's view, consists of a constitutional monarchy, containing three branches: the crown or princely power, the executive,
and the legislature. Its proper function is to promote "the universal" (the common good); to unify the common good with the particular good of individuals,
families, and private associations; and to organize the nation as whole into a
politically organized community. It is this politically organized community, the
state in the larger sense, which constitutes the concrete actualization of ethical
life, in Hegel's view. It is within this national community, which includes civil
society and the family, that, Hegel tells us, the free will is able to will the free
will and individuals are able to find reconciliation.

For an excellent discussion of Hegel's philosophical development, see H. S. Harris, *Hegel's Development: Towards the Sunlight 1770–1801* (Oxford: Oxford University Press, 1976) and *Hegel's Development: Night Thought (Jena 1801–1806)* (Oxford: Oxford University Press, 1983). Laurence Dickey's insightful *Religion, Economics, and the Politics of Spirit, 1770–1807* (Cambridge: Cambridge University Press, 1987) sets Hegel's political philosophy in the context of the religious and political culture of old Württemburg. J. N. Findlay's *Hegel: a Reexamination* (Oxford: Oxford University Press, 1958), Charles Taylor's Hegel (Cambridge: Cambridge University Press, 1975), and Frederick C. Beiser's edited collection, *The Cambridge Companion to Hegel* (Cambridge: Cambridge University Press, 1993), all provide good introductions to Hegel's philosophy. Michael Inwood's *A Hegel Dictionary* (Cambridge: Blackwell Publishers, 1992) is an extremely helpful guide to Hegel's technical vocabulary. A good introduction to Hegel's political philosophy can be found in Shlomo Avineri's *Hegel's Theory of the Modern State* (Cambridge: Cambridge University Press, 1972). Raymond Plant's Hegel (Bloomington: Indiana University Press, 1973) gives a very good analysis of Hegel's social and political philosophy. Michael Hardimon's *Hegel's Social Philosophy: The Project of Reconciliation* (Cambridge: Cambridge University Press, 1994) approaches Hegel's social and political philosophy from the standpoint of reconciliation. In addition to providing an excellent treatment of Hegel's contribution to ethics, Allen Wood's *Hegel's Ethical Theory* (Cambridge: Cambridge University Press, 1990) also provides a first-rate discussion of his social and political philosophy.

M. O. H.

PHILOSOPHY OF RIGHT

INTRODUCTION

1. The subject-matter of the philosophical science of right is the Idea of right, i.e. the concept of right together with the actualization of that concept.

Philosophy has to do with Ideas, and therefore not with what are commonly dubbed 'mere concepts'. On the contrary, it exposes such concepts as one-sided and false, while showing at the same time that it is the concept alone (not the mere abstract category of the understanding which we often hear called by the name) which has actuality, and further that it gives this actuality to itself. All else, apart from this actuality established through the working of the concept itself, is ephemeral existence, external contingency, opinion, unsubstantial appearance, falsity, illusion, and so forth. The shapes which the concept assumes in the course of its actualization are indispensable for the knowledge of the concept itself. They are the second essential moment of the Idea, in distinction from the first, i.e. from its form, from its mode of being as concept alone.

Reprinted from *Hegel's Philosophy of Right,* translated by T. M. Knox (1942), by permission of Oxford University Press. Some footnotes omitted.

2. The science of right is a section of philosophy. Consequently, its task is to develop the Idea—the Idea being the rational factor in any object of study—out of the concept, or, what is the same thing, to look on at the proper immanent development of the thing itself. As a section, it has a definite starting-point, i.e. the result and the truth of what has preceded, and it is what has preceded which constitutes the so-called 'proof' of the starting-point. Hence the concept of right, so far as its coming to be is concerned, falls outside the science of right; it is to be taken up here as given and its deduction is presupposed.

According to the abstract, non-philosophical, method of the sciences, the first thing sought and demanded is a definition, or at any rate this demand is made for the sake of preserving the external form of scientific procedure. (But the science of positive law at least cannot be very intimately concerned with definitions since it begins in the first place by stating what is legal, i.e. what the particular legal provisions are, and for this reason the warning has been given: *omnis definitio in jure civili periculosa*. In fact, the more disconnected and inherently contradictory are the provisions giving determinate character to a right, the less are any definitions in its field possible, for definitions should be stated in universal terms, while to use these immediately exposes in all its nakedness what contradicts them—the wrong in this instance. Thus in Roman law, for example, there could be no definition of 'man', since 'slave' could not be brought under it—the very status of slave indeed is an outrage on the conception of man; it would appear just as hazardous to attempt a definition of 'property' and 'proprietor' in many cases.) But the deduction of the definition is derived, it may be, from etymology, or especially by abstraction from particular cases, so that it is based on human feelings and ideas. The correctness of the definition is then made to lie in its correspondence with current ideas. This method neglects what is all-essential for science—i.e. in respect of content, the absolute necessity of the thing (right, in this instance), and, in respect of form, the nature of the concept.

The truth is that in philosophical knowledge the necessity of a concept is the principal thing; and the process of its production as a result is its proof and deduction. Then, once its content has been shown in this way to be necessary on its own account, the second step is to look round for what corresponds to it in our ideas and language. But this concept as it actually is in its truth not only may be different from our common idea of it, but in fact must be different from it in form and outline. If, however, the common idea of it is not false in content also, the concept may be exhibited as implied in it and as essentially present in it. In other words, the common idea may be raised to assume the form of the concept. But the common idea is so far from being the standard or criterion of the concept (which is necessary and true on its own account) that it must rather derive its truth from the latter, adjust itself to it, and recognize its own nature by its aid.

But while the above-mentioned abstract way of knowing with its formal definitions, syllogisms, proofs, and the like, is more or less a thing of the past, still it is a poor substitute which a different artifice has provided, namely to adopt and uphold Ideas in general (and in particular the Idea of right and its further specifications) as immediate 'facts of consciousness' and to make into the source of right our natural or our worked up feelings and the inspirations of our own hearts. This method may be the handiest of all, but it is also the most unphilosophical—not to mention here other aspects of such an outlook, which has a direct bearing on action and not simply on knowledge. While the old method, abstract as it is, does at least insist on the *form* of the concept in its definition and the *form* of necessary knowledge in its demonstration, the artifice of feeling and immediate awareness elevates into a guiding principle the subjectivity, contingency, and arbitrariness of sapience. What constitutes scientific procedure in philosophy is expounded in philosophical logic and is here presupposed.

3. Right is positive in general (a) when it has the *form* of being valid in particular state, and this legal authority is the guiding principle for the knowledge of right in this positive form, i.e., for the science of positive law. (b) Right in this positive form acquires a positive element in its *content*

 (α) through the particular national character of a people, its stage of historical development, and the whole complex of relations connected with the necessities of nature;

 (β) because a system of positive law must necessarily involve the application of the universal concept to particular, externally given, characteristics of objects and cases. This application lies outside speculative thought and the development of the concept, and is the subsumption by the Understanding [of the particular under the universal];

 (γ) through the finally detailed provisions requisite for actually pronouncing judgement in court.

If inclination caprice, and the sentiments of the heart are set up in opposition to positive right and the laws, philosophy at least cannot recognize authorities of that sort.— That force and tyranny may be an element in law is accidental to law and has nothing to do with its nature. Later on in this book, in Paragraphs 211-14, it will be shown at what point right must become positive. The details to be expounded there are being mentioned here only to indicate the limits of the philosophical study of law and to obviate at once any possible supposition, let alone demand, that the outcome of its systematic development should be a code of positive law, i.e. a code like the one an actual state requires.

Natural law, or law from the philosophical point of view, is distinct from positive law; but to pervert their difference into an opposition and a contradiction would be a gross misunderstanding. The relation between them is much more like that between Institutes and Pandects.

As for the historical element in positive law, mentioned above in Paragraph 3, Montesquieu proclaimed the true historical view, the genuinely philosophical position, namely that legislation both in general and in its particular provisions is to be treated not as something isolated and abstract but rather as a subordinate moment in a whole, interconnected with all the other features which make up the character of a nation and an epoch. It is in being so connected that the various laws acquire their true meaning and therewith their justification. To consider particular laws as they appear and develop in time is a purely historical task. Like acquaintance with what can be logically deduced from a comparison of these laws with previously existing legal principles, this task is appreciated and rewarded in its own sphere and has no relation whatever to the philosophical study of the subject—unless of course the derivation of particular laws from historical events is confused with their derivation from the concept, and the historical explanation and justification is stretched to become an absolutely valid justification. This difference, which is very important and should be firmly adhered to, is also very obvious. A particular law may be shown to be wholly grounded in and consistent with the circumstances and with existing legally established institutions, and yet it may be wrong and irrational in its essential character, like a number of provisions in Roman private law which followed quite logically from such institutions as Roman matrimony and Roman *patria potestas*. But even if particular laws *are* both right and reasonable, still it is one thing to *prove* that they have that character—which cannot be truly done except by means of the concept—and quite another to describe their appearance in history or the circumstances, contingencies, needs, and events which brought about their enactment. That kind of exposition and (pragmatic) knowledge, based on proximate or remote historical causes, is frequently called 'explanation' or preferably 'comprehension' by those who think that to expound history in this way is the only thing, or rather the essential thing, the only important thing, to be done in order to comprehend law or an established institution; whereas what is really essential, the concept of the thing, they have not discussed at all. From the same point of view, reference is commonly made also to the Roman or the German 'concepts' of law, i.e. concepts of law as they might be defined in this or that legal code, whereas what is meant is not concepts but only general legal principles, propositions of the Understanding, maxims, positive laws, and the like.

By dint of obscuring the difference between the historical and the philosophical study of law, it becomes possible to shift the point of view and slip over from the problem of the true justification of a thing to a justification by appeal to circumstances, to deductions from presupposed conditions which in themselves may have no higher validity, and so forth. To generalize, by this means the relative is put in place of the absolute and the external appearance in place of the true nature of the thing. When those who try to justify things on historical grounds confound an origin in external circumstances with one in the concept, they unconsciously achieve the very opposite of what they intend. Once the origination of an institution has been shown to be wholly to the purpose and necessary in the circumstances of the time, the demands of history have been fulfilled. But if this is supposed to pass for a general justification of the thing itself, it turns out to be the opposite, because, since those circumstances are no longer present, the institution so far from being justified has by their disappearance lost its meaning and its right. Suppose, for example, that we accept as a vindication of the monasteries their service in cultivating wildernesses and populating them, in keeping learning alive by transcribing manuscripts and giving instruction, &c., and suppose further that this service has been deemed to be the ground and the purpose of their continued existence, then what really follows from considering this past service is that, since circumstances have now entirely altered, the monasteries are at least in this respect superfluous and inappropriate.

Now that the historical meaning of coming to be—the historical method of portraying it and making it comprehensible—is at home in a different sphere from the philosophical survey of the concept of the thing and of a thing's coming to be too, philosophy and history are able to that extent to preserve an attitude of mutual indifference. But they are not always at peace in this way, even in scientific circles, and so I quote something, relevant to their contact, which appears in Herr Hugo's *Lehrbuch der Geschichte des römischen Rechts,* and which will at the same time cast further light on the affectation that they are opposed. Herr Hugo says that 'Cicero praises the Twelve Tables with a side glance at the philosophers . . . but the philosopher Favorinus treats them exactly as many a great philosopher since his day has treated positive law'. In the same context Herr Hugo makes the final retort to a treatment of the subject like Favorinus' when he gives as the reason for it that 'Favorinus understood the Twelve Tables just as little as these philosophers have understood positive law.

The correction of the philosopher Favorinus by the jurist Sextus Caecilius in Aulus Gellius is primarily an expression of the permanent and true principle for justifying what is purely positive in its intrinsic worth. *Non . . . ignoras,* Caecilius happily retorts to Favorinus, *legum opportunitates et medelas pro temporum moribus et pro rerum publicarum generibus, ac pro utilitatum praesentium rationibus, proque vitiorum, quibus medendum est, fervoribus, mutari ac flecti, neque uno statu consistere, quin, ut facies coeli et maris, ita rerum atque fortunae tempestatibus varientur. Quid salubrius visum est rogatione illa Stolonis . . ., quid utilius plebiscito Voconio . . . ? Quid tam necessarium existimatum est . . . quam Lex Licinia . . . ? Omnia tamen haec obliterata et operta sunt civitatis opulentia.* These laws are positive in so far as they have their meaning and appropriateness in contemporary conditions, and therefore their sole value is historical and they are of a transitory nature. The wisdom of what legislators and administrators did in their day or settled to meet the needs of the hour is a separate matter and one properly to be assessed by history. History's recognition of it will be all the deeper the more its assessment is supported by a philosophical outlook.

Of Caecilius's further arguments in justification of the Twelve Tables against Favorinus, however, I will give an example, because he introduces in them the eternally deceptive method and argumentation of the Understanding, I mean the production of a good reason for a bad thing and the supposition that the bad thing has thereby been justified. Caecilius is discussing the horrible law that gave a creditor the right after a fixed period of time to kill his debtor or sell him into slavery, or, if there were several creditors, to cut pieces off their debtor and divide him up amongst themselves; and there was even a further proviso that if one of them cut off too much or too little, no action was for that reason to lie against him—a clause which would have benefited Shakespeare's Shylock in the *Merchant of Venice* and of which he would most gratefully have availed himself. For this law Caecilius adduces the good reason that it rendered trust and credit all the more secure and that because of its horrible character there was never to have been any question of its application. In his thoughtlessness not only does the reflection escape him that if the law could never have been applied, then the aim of securing trust and credit by it was frustrated, but he even goes on directly afterwards to give an example of how the law concerning false witness was made ineffective owing to its immoderate penalties.

There is no knowing, however, what Herr Hugo means when he says that Favorinus did not understand the law. Any schoolboy is perfectly capable of understanding it, and Shylock would have understood better than anyone else the clause, cited above, which would have been so advantageous to him. By 'understand' Herr Hugo must have meant only that level of understanding which in the case of such a law is content if it can find a good reason for it.

Still, another misunderstanding of which Favorinus was convicted by Caecilius in the same context is one to which a philosopher may surely confess without exactly blushing; I mean the failure to understand that *jumentum* (which 'as distinct from *arcera*' is, according to the law, the only conveyance to be provided for a sick man who has to appear in court) is to be interpreted to mean not only a horse but also a carriage or wagon. From this legal proviso Caecilius was able to derive a further proof of the excellence and precision of the old laws by pointing out that, in fixing the terms of a summons to a sick man to appear in court, they even carried precision so far as to distinguish not only between a horse and a wagon, but even between one wagon and another, between one covered in and 'upholstered', according to Caecilius' interpretation, and one not so comfortable. Here we would have the choice between the severity of the original law and the triviality of such distinctions, but to describe such things, and still more their learned interpretation, as 'trivial' would be one of the worst of insults to erudition of this kind and others!

But in the same *Lehrbuch* Herr Hugo goes on to speak of rationality in connexion with Roman law, and what has struck me in his remarks is the following. In his treatment of the 'period from the origin of the state to the Twelve Tables' he says that (in Rome) 'men had many wants and were compelled to work and hence needed assistance of draught and pack animals, such as we are familiar with ourselves; that in Roman territory hills and valleys alternated and that the city was built on a hill' and so forth—disquisitions which were perhaps intended to carry out Montesquieu's ideas, but in which one will hardly find that his spirit has been caught. Then he goes on to say that 'the legal position was still very far from satisfying the highest demands of reason'. That is quite right, Roman law in respect of the family, slavery, &c., fails even to satisfy reason's most modest demands. But in dealing with later periods of Roman history, Herr Hugo forgets to tell us whether in any of them, and if so in which, Roman law did 'satisfy the highest demands of reason'. However, of the classical jurists in the period of the 'highest maturity of Roman law as a science', Herr Hugo writes: 'It has long since been observed that the classical jurists were educated through philosophy', yet 'few know' (though more know now, thanks to the numerous editions of Herr Hugo's *Lehrbuch*) 'that no class of writers is so well entitled as these same Roman jurists to be compared with mathematicians in respect of the rigorous logic of their deductive reasoning or with the new founder of metaphysics in respect of their quite strikingly distinctive method of developing their concepts—a contention supported by the curious fact that nowhere are there to be found so many trichotomies as there are in the classical jurists and in Kant'. Logical deduction, a method commended by Leibniz, is certainly an essential characteristic of the study of positive law, as of mathematics and any other science of the Understanding, but this deductive method of the Understanding has nothing whatever to do with the satisfaction of the demands of reason or with philosophical science. But apart from that it is the *il*logicality of the Roman jurists and praetors that must be regarded as one of their chief virtues, for by dint of being illogical they evaded unjust and detestable laws, though in the process they found themselves compelled *callide* to devise empty verbal distinctions (e.g. to call *bonorum possessio* what was nevertheless *hereditas*) and downright foolish subterfuges (and folly also is illogicality) in order to preserve the letter of the Twelve Tables (e.g. by the *fictio ὑπόκρισις*, that a *filia* was a *filius*). It is ludicrous though to see the classical jurists compared with Kant because of a few trichotomous divisions, especially those cited as examples in the fifth note to Herr Hugo's paragraph, and to see that kind of thing called 'development of concepts'.

4. The basis of right is, in general, mind; its precise place and point of origin is the will. The will is free, so that freedom is both the substance of right and its goal, while the system of right is the realm of freedom made actual, the world of mind brought forth out of itself like a second nature.

In considering the freedom of the will, we may recall the old method of cognition. The procedure was to presuppose the idea of the will and to attempt to establish a definition of the will by deriving it from that idea; then the so-called 'proof' of the will's freedom was extracted, in the manner of the old empirical psychology, from the various feelings and phenomena of the ordinary consciousness, such as remorse, guilt, and the like, by maintaining that they were to be explained only in the light of a will that was free. But it is more convenient of course to arrive at the same point by taking the short cut of supposing that freedom is given as a 'fact of consciousness' and that we must simply *believe* in it!

The proof that the will is free and the proof of the nature of the will and freedom can be established (as has already been pointed out in Paragraph 2) only as a link in the whole chain [of philosophy]. The fundamental premisses of this proof are that mind to start with is intelligence, that the phases through which it passes in its development from feeling, through representative thinking, to thinking proper, are the road along which it produces itself as will, and that will, as practical mind in general, is the truth of intelligence, the stage next above it. These premisses I have expounded in my *Encyclopaedia of the Philosophical Sciences* and I hope by and by to be able to elaborate them still further. There is all the more need for me by so doing to make my contribution to what I hope is the deeper knowledge of the nature of mind in that, as I have said in the *Encyclopedia*, scarcely any philosophical science is so neglected and so ill off as the theory of mind, usually called 'psychology'. The moments in the concept of the will which are dealt with in this and the following Paragraphs of the Introduction result from the premises to which I have just referred, but in addition anyone may find help towards forming an idea of them by calling on his own self-consciousness. In the first place, anyone can discover in himself ability to abstract from everything whatever, and in the same way to determine himself, to posit any content in himself by his own effort; and similarly the other specific characteristics of the will are exemplified for him in his own consciousness.

5. The will contains (α) the element of pure indeterminacy or that pure reflection of the ego into itself which involves the dissipation of every restriction and every content either immediately presented by nature, by needs, desires, and impulses, or given and determined by any means whatever. This is the unrestricted infinity of absolute abstraction or universality, the pure thought of oneself.

Those who regard thinking as one special faculty, distinct from the will as another special faculty, and who even proceed to contend that thinking is prejudicial to the will, especially the good will, reveal at the very outset their complete ignorance of the nature of the will—a remark we shall have to make rather often when dealing with this same subject.

In Paragraph 5, it is only one side of the will which is described, namely this unrestricted possibility of abstraction from every determinate state of mind which I may find in myself or which I may have set up in myself, my flight from every content as from a restriction. When the will's self-determination consists in this alone, or when representative thinking regards this side by itself as freedom and clings fast to it, then we have negative freedom or freedom as the Understanding conceives it. This is the freedom of the void which rises to a passion and takes shape in the world; while still remaining theoretical, it takes shape in religion as the Hindu fanaticism of pure contemplation, but when it turns to actual practice, it takes shape in religion and politics alike as the fanaticism of destruction—the destruction of the whole subsisting social order—as the elimination of individuals who are objects of suspicion to any social order, and the annihilation of any organization which tries to rise anew from the ruins. Only in destroying something does this negative will possess the feeling of itself as existent. Of course it imagines that it is willing some positive state of affairs, such as universal equality or universal religious life, but in fact it does not will that this shall be positively actualized, and for this reason: such actuality leads at once to some sort of order, to a particularization of organizations and individuals alike; while it is precisely out of the annihilation of particularity and objective characterization that the self-consciousness of this negative freedom proceeds. Consequently, what negative freedom intends to will can never be anything in itself but an abstract idea, and giving effect to this idea can only be the fury of destruction.

6. (β) At the same time, the ego is also the transition from undifferentiated indeterminacy to the differentiation, determination, and positing of a determinacy as a content and object. Now further, this content may either be given by nature or engendered by the concept of mind. Through this positing itself as something determinate, the ego steps in principle into determinate existence. This is the absolute moment, the finitude or particularization of the ego.

This second moment—determination—is negativity and cancellation like the first, i.e., it cancels the abstract negativity of the first. Since it is the general rule that the particular is contained in the universal, it follows that this second moment is already contained in the first and is simply an explicit positing of what the first already was implicitly. The first moment, I mean—because by itself it is only the first—is not true infinity or concrete universality, not the concept, but only something determinate, one-sided; i.e., being abstraction from all determinacy, it is itself not without determinacy; and to be something abstract and one-sided constitutes its determinacy, its defectiveness, and its finitude.

The determination and differentiation of the two moments which have been mentioned is to be found in the philosophies of Fichte, Kant, and others; only, in Fichte—to confine ourselves to his exposition—the ego, as that which is without limitation, is taken (in the first proposition of his *Science of Knowledge*) purely and simply as something positive and so as the universality and identity of the Understanding. The result is that this abstract ego by itself is supposed to be the whole truth, and therefore the restriction—the negative in general, whether as a given external barrier or as an activity of the ego itself—appears (in the second proposition) as an addition merely.

To apprehend the negativity immanent in the universal or self-identical, e.g., in the ego, was the next step which speculative philosophy had to take—a step of whose necessity they have no inkling who hold to the dualism of infinite and finite and do not even grasp it in that immanence and abstraction in which Fichte did.

7. (γ) The will is the unity of both these moments. It is particularity reflected into itself and so brought back to universality, i.e. it is individuality. It is the *self*-determination of the ego, which means that at one and the same time the ego posits itself as its own negative, i.e., as restricted and determinate, and yet remains by itself, i.e., in its self-identity and universality. It determines itself and yet at the same time binds itself together with itself. The ego determines itself in so far as it is the relating of negativity to itself. As this self-relation, it is indifferent to this determinacy; it knows it as something which is its own, something which is only ideal, a mere possibility by which it is not constrained and in which it is confined only because it has put itself in it.—This is the freedom of the will and it constitutes the concept or substantiality of the will, its weight, so to speak, just as weight constitutes the substantiality of a body.

Every self-consciousness knows itself (i) as universal, as the potentiality of abstracting from everything determinate, and (ii) as particular, with a determinate object, content, and aim. Still, both these moments are only abstractions; what is concrete and true (and everything true is concrete) is the universality which has the particular as its opposite, but the particular which by its reflection into itself has been equalized with the universal. This unity is individuality, not individuality in its immediacy as a unit, our first idea of individuality, but individuality in accordance with its concept; indeed, individuality in this sense is just precisely the concept itself. The first two moments—(i) that the will can abstract from everything, and (ii) that it is also determined in some specific way either by itself or by something else—are readily admitted and grasped because, taken independently, they are false and moments of the Understanding. But the third moment, which is true and speculative (and everything true must be thought speculatively if it is to be comprehended) is the one into which the Understanding declines to advance, for it is precisely the concept which it persists in calling the inconceivable. It is the task of logic as purely speculative philosophy to prove and explain further this innermost secret of speculation, of infinity as negativity relating itself to itself, this ultimate spring of all activity, life, and consciousness. Here attention can only be drawn to the fact that if you say 'the will is universal, the will determines itself', the words you use to describe the will presuppose it to be a subject or substratum from the start. But the will is not something complete and universal prior to its determining itself and prior to its superseding and idealizing this determination. The will is not a will until it is this self-mediating activity, this return into itself.

8. The more detailed process of particularization (see Paragraph 6) constitutes the difference between the forms of the will: (*a*) If the will's determinate character lies in the abstract opposition of its subjectivity to the objectivity of external immediate existence, then this is the formal will of mere self-consciousness which finds an external world confronting it. As individuality returning in its determinacy into itself, it is the process of translating the subjective purpose into objectivity through the use of its own activity and some external means. Once mind has developed its potentialities to actuality (*wie er an und für sich ist*), its determinate character is true and simply its own. At that stage, the relation of consciousness constitutes only the *appearance* of the will, an aspect which is not separately considered any further here. [A.]

9. (*b*) In so far as the specific determinations of the will are its own or, in general, its particularization reflected into itself, they are its content. This content, as content of the will, is, in accordance with the form of will described in (*a*), its purpose, either its inward or subjective purpose when the will merely images its object, or else its purpose actualized and achieved by means of its activity of translating its subjective purpose into objectivity.

10. This content, or the will's determination on something specific, is in the first place immediate. Consequently the will is then free only *in* itself or *for* an external observer, or, to speak generally, it is the will in its concept. It is not until it has itself as its object that the will is for *itself* what it is in itself.

Finitude consists therefore in this, that what something is *in* itself or in accordance with its concept is one phenomenon or exists in one way, while what it is for itself is a different phenomenon or exists in another way; so, for example, *in* itself the abstract reciprocal externality characteristic of nature is space, but *for* itself it is time. In this connexion, two things are to be noticed: (i) The true is the Idea and the Idea alone, and hence if you take an object or a category only as it is in itself or in its concept, you have not yet grasped it in its truth. (ii) A thing which is in itself or as concept is also existent in some way and its existence in such a way is a shape proper to the thing itself (as space is in the example just given). The gulf present in the sphere of the finite between 'in-itself-ness' and 'for-itself-ness' constitutes at the same time that sphere's mere existential or phenomenal character. (Examples of this—the natural will and then formal rights, &c.—will be forthcoming directly.)

The Understanding goes no further than the purely implicit character of a thing and consequently calls the freedom which accords with this implicit character a 'potency', because if freedom is only implicit it is indeed mere potentiality. But the Understanding looks upon this implicit character as absolute and perennial; and it takes the relation of freedom to what it wills, or in general to the object in which it is realized, as merely a matter of its application to a given material, not belonging to the essence of freedom itself. Thus it has to do with the abstract only, not with its Idea and its truth.

11. The will which is but implicitly free is the immediate or natural will. The specific characteristics of the difference which the self-determining concept sets up within the will appear in the natural will as an immediately existing content, i.e. as the impulses, desires, inclinations, whereby the will finds itself determined in the course of nature. This content, together with the specific differences developed within it, arises from the

rationality of the will and so is implicitly rational; but, poured out in this way into the mould of immediacy, it still lacks the form of rationality. It is true that this content has for me the general character of being mine; but this form is still different from the content, and hence the will is still a will finite in character.

Empirical psychology details and describes these impulses and inclinations, and the needs arising from them, as it finds them, or presumes it finds them, in experience, and it proceeds in the usual way to classify this given material. Consideration is given below to the objective element in these impulses, both to its true character stripped of the form of irrationality which it possesses as impulse and also to the manner in which at the same time it is shaped externally.

12. The whole of this content, as we light upon it in its immediacy in the will, is there only as a medley and multiplicity of impulses, each of which is merely 'my desire' but exists alongside other desires which are likewise all 'mine', and each of which is at the same time something universal and indeterminate, aimed at all kinds of objects and satiable in all kinds of ways. When, in this twofold indeterminacy, the will gives itself the form of individuality (see Paragraph 7), this constitutes the resolution of the will, and it is only in so far as it resolves that the will is an actual will at all.

To resolve on something is to cancel the state of indeterminacy in which one content is prima facie just as much of a possibility as any other. As an alternative to *etwas beschliessen* (to resolve on something) the German language also contains the expression *sich entschliessen*. This expresses the fact that the indeterminate character of the will itself, as itself neutral yet infinitely prolific, the original seed of all determinate existence, contains its determinations and aims within itself and simply brings them forth out of itself.

13. By resolving, the will posits itself as the will of a specific individual and as a will separating itself off against another individual. But apart from this finitude as consciousness (see Paragraph 8), the immediate will is on account of the difference between its form and its content (see Paragraph 11) a will only in form. The decision which belongs to it as such is only abstract and its content is not yet the content and product of its freedom.

In so far as intelligence thinks, its object and content remains something universal, while its own behaviour consists of a universal activity. In the will, 'the universal' also means in essence 'mine', 'individuality'; and in the immediate will—the will which is will in form only—it means abstract individuality, individuality not yet filled with its free universality. Hence it is in the will that the intrinsic finitude of intelligence has its beginning; and it is only by raising itself to become thought again, and endowing its aims with immanent universality, that the will cancels the difference of form and content and makes itself the objective, infinite, will. Thus they understand little of the nature of thinking and willing who suppose that while, in willing as such, man is infinite, in thinking, he, or even reason itself, is restricted. In so far as thinking and willing are still distinguished, the opposite is rather the truth, and will is thinking reason resolving itself to finitude.

14. The finite will as, in respect of its form, though only its form, the self-reflecting, independent, and infinite ego (see Paragraph 5), stands over its content, i.e. its various impulses, and also over the further separate ways in which these are actualized and satisfied. At the same time, since it is infinite in form only, it is tied to this content (see Paragraphs 6 and 11) as to the specific determinations of its nature and its external actuality; though since it is indeterminate, it is not tied to this or that specific content. From

the point of view of the ego reflected into itself, this content is only a possible one, i.e. it may be mine or it may not; and the ego similarly is the possibility of determining myself to this or to something else, of *choosing* between these specific determinations, which at this point I regard as external to me.

15. At this stage, the freedom of the will is arbitrariness (*Willkür*) and this involves two factors: (*a*) free reflection, abstracting from everything, and (*b*) dependence on a content and material given either from within or from without. Because this content, implicitly necessary as purpose, is at the same time qualified in the face of free reflection as possible, it follows that arbitrariness is contingency manifesting itself as will.

The idea which people most commonly have of freedom is that it is arbitrariness—the mean, chosen by abstract reflection, between the will wholly determined by natural impulses, and the will free absolutely. If we hear it said that the definition of freedom is ability to do what we please, such an idea can only be taken to reveal an utter immaturity of thought, for it contains not even an inkling of the absolutely free will, of right, ethical life, and so forth. Reflection, the formal universality and unity of self-consciousness, is the will's abstract certainty of its freedom, but it is not yet the truth of freedom, because it has not yet got *itself* as its content and aim, and consequently the subjective side is still other than the objective; the content of this self-determination, therefore, also remains purely and simply finite. Instead of being the will in its truth, arbitrariness is more like the will as contradiction.

In the controversy carried on especially at the time of Wolff's metaphysic as to whether the will were really free or whether the conviction of its freedom were only a delusion, it was arbitrariness which was in view. In opposition to the certitude of this abstract self-determination, determinism has rightly pointed to the content which, as something met with, is not contained in that certitude and so comes to it from outside, although 'outside' in this case means impulses, ideas, or, in general, consciousness so filled in one way or another that its content is not intrinsic to its self-determining activity as such. Since, then, arbitrariness has immanent in it only the formal element in willing, i.e. free self-determination, while the other element is something given to it, we may readily allow that, if it is arbitrariness which is supposed to be freedom, it may indeed be called an illusion. In every philosophy of reflection, like Kant's, and Kant's deprived of all its depth by Fries, freedom is nothing else but this empty self-activity.

16. What the will has decided to choose (see Paragraph 14) it can equally easily renounce (see Paragraph 5). But its ability to go beyond any other choice which it may substitute, and so on *ad infinitum* never enables it to get beyond its own finitude, because the content of every such choice is something other than the form of the will and therefore something finite, while the opposite of determinacy, namely indeterminacy, i.e. indecision or abstraction from any content, is only the other, equally one-sided, moment of the will.

17. The contradiction which the arbitrary will is (see Paragraph 15), comes into appearance as a dialectic of impulses and inclinations; each of them is in the way of every other—the satisfaction of one is unavoidably subordinated or sacrificed to the satisfaction of another, and so on. An impulse is simply a uni-directional urge and thus has no measuring-rod in itself, and so this determination of its subordination or sacrifice is the contingent decision of the arbitrary will which, in deciding, may proceed either by using intelligence to calculate which impulse will give most satisfaction, or else in accordance with any other optional consideration.

18. In connexion with the *judgment* of impulses, this dialectic appears in the following form: (*a*) As immanent and so positive, the determinations of the immediate will are good; thus man is said to be by nature good. (*b*) But, in so far as these determinations are natural and thus are in general opposed to freedom and the concept of mind, and hence negative, they must be uprooted, and so man is said to be by nature evil.—At this point a decision in favour of either thesis depends equally on subjective arbitrariness. [A.]

19. In the demand for the *purification* of impulses there lies the general notion that they should be freed both from their form as immediate and natural determinations, and also from the subjectivity and contingency of their content, and so brought back to their substantial essence. The truth behind this vague demand is that the impulses should become the rational system of the will's volitions. To grasp them like that, proceeding out of the concept of the will, is the content of the philosophical science of right.

The content of this science through every single one of its moments, e.g. right, property, morality, family, state, and so forth, may be expounded in the form: man has by nature the impulse towards right, also the impulse to property and morality, also the impulse of love between the sexes, the impulse to sociability, &c. This form is to be found in empirical psychology. But if in its stead the greater dignity of a philosophical dress is desired, then according to what, as was remarked before, has passed in recent times, and still passes, for philosophy, this dress may be had cheap by the simple device of saying that man discovers within himself as a 'fact of his consciousness' that right, property, the state, &c., are objects of his volition. Later in the text, this same subject-matter, which appears here in the shape of impulses, will come on the scene in another form, i.e. in the shape of duties.

20. When reflection is brought to bear on impulses, they are imaged, estimated, compared with one another, with their means of satisfaction and their consequences, &c., and with a sum of satisfaction (i.e., with happiness). In this way reflection invests this material with abstract universality and in this external manner purifies it from its crudity and barbarity. This growth of the universality of thought is the absolute value in education (compare Paragraph 187).

21. The truth, however, of this abstract universality, which is indeterminate in itself and finds its determinacy in the material mentioned in Paragraph 20, is self-determining universality, the will, freedom. In having universality, or itself *qua* infinite form, for its object, content, and aim, the will is free not only *in* itself but *for* itself also; it is the Idea in its truth.

(i) When the will's self-consciousness takes the form of desire and impulse, this consciousness is sense-consciousness, just as sensation in general denotes externality and therefore the condition in which self-consciousness is self-external. (ii) When the will is reflective, it contains two elements—this sense-consciousness and the universality of thought. (iii) When the will's potentialities have become fully explicit, then it has for its object the will itself as such, and so the will in its sheer universality—a universality which is what it is simply because it has absorbed in itself the immediacy of instinctive desire and the particularity which is produced by reflection and with which such desire *eo ipso* becomes imbued. But this process of absorption in or elevation to universality is what is called the activity of thought. The self-consciousness which purifies its object, content, and aim, and raises them to this universality effects this as thinking getting its own way in the will. Here is the point at which it becomes clear that it is only as thinking intelligence that the will is genuinely a will and free. The slave does not know his essence, his infinity, his freedom; he does not know himself as human in essence, and he lacks this knowledge of himself because he does not think himself. This self-consciousness which apprehends itself through thinking as essentially human, and thereby frees itself from the contingent and the false, is the principle of right, morality, and all ethical life. Philosophic utterances about right, morality, and ethical life from those who would banish thought and have recourse instead to feeling, enthusiasm, the heart and the breast, are expressive of the utterly contemptible position into which thought and philosophic science have fallen, because what this amounts to is that even philosophic science itself, plunged in self-despair and extreme exhaustion, is taking as its principle barbarity and absence of thought, and would do its best to rob mankind of all truth, worth, and dignity.

22. It is the will whose potentialities have become fully explicit which is truly infinite, because its object is itself and so is not in its eyes an 'other' or a barrier; on the contrary, in its object this will has simply turned backward into itself. Further this will is not mere potentiality, capacity, potency (*potentia*), but the infinite in actuality (*infinitum actu*), since the concept's existence or its objective externality is inwardness itself.

Thus, if anyone speaks simply of the 'free will' as such, without specifically referring to the will which is free absolutely, he is speaking only of the capacity for freedom, or of the natural and finite will (see Paragraph 11), and not by any means therefore of the free will, despite his intention and the words he uses.

Since the Understanding takes the infinite only as something negative and so as something 'beyond', it supposes that it is doing all the more honour to the infinite, the more it pushes it into the distance away from itself and removes it from itself as something alien. In the free will, the truly infinite becomes actual and present; the free will itself is this Idea whose nature it is to be present here and now.

23. Only in freedom of this kind is the will by itself without qualification, because then it is related to nothing except itself and so is released from every tie of dependence on anything else. The will is then true, or rather truth itself, because its self-determination consists in a correspondence between what it is in its existence (i.e., what it is as objective to itself) and its concept; or in other words, the pure concept of the will has the intuition of itself for its goal and its reality.

24. The will is then universal, because all restriction and all particular individuality have been absorbed within it. These lie only in the difference between the concept and its content or object, or, to put it otherwise, in the difference between its implicit character and its subjective awareness of itself, or between its universality and its exclusive individuality, the individuality which resolves.

The various types of universality develop in logic. In connexion with this word 'universality', what strikes representative thinking first is the idea of abstract and external universality; but in connexion with absolute universality—and the universality here in question is of this character—we have to think neither of the universality of reflection, i.e. 'all-ness' or the universal as a common characteristic, nor of the abstract universality which stands outside and over against the individual, the abstract identity of the Understanding (see Remark to Paragraph 6). It is the universality concrete in character and so explicitly universal which is the substance of self-consciousness, its immanent generic essence, or its immanent Idea. This—the concept of the free will—is the universal which overlaps its object, penetrates its particular determination through and through and therein remains identical with itself. The absolutely universal is definable as what is called the 'rational', and it can be apprehended only in this speculative way.

25. The subjective, in relation to the will in general, means the will's self-conscious side, its individuality (see Paragraph 7) in distinction from its implicit concept. The subjectivity of the will means therefore

(α) the pure form of the will, the absolute unity of self-consciousness with itself (a unity in which self-consciousness, as I = I, is purely and simply inward and abstractly self-dependent), the pure certainty, as distinguished from the truth, of individuality;

(β) the particular will as the arbitrary will and the contingent content of optional aims;

(γ) in general, the one-sided form of the will (see Paragraph 8) for which the thing willed, whatever its content, is but a content belonging to self-consciousness and an aim unfulfilled.

26. (α) The will is purely and simply objective in so far as it has itself for its determination and so is in correspondence with its concept and genuinely a will;

(β) but the objective will, being without the infinite form of self-consciousness, is the will absorbed in its object or condition, whatever the content of these may be; it is the will of the child, the ethical will, also the will of the slave, the superstitious man, &c;

(γ) objectivity, finally, is the one-sided form opposed to the subjective volition, and hence it is the immediacy of existence as external reality; the will first becomes objective to itself in this sense through the fulfillment of its aims.

These logical categories—subjectivity and objectivity—have been set forth in detail here primarily with a view to pointing out expressly in relation to them, since they are often used in the sequel, that they, like other distinctions and opposed categories of reflection, pass over into their opposites as a result of their finitude and their dialectical character. In other cases of opposition between two categories, each opposite retains a hard and fast meaning for representative thinking and the Understanding, because the identity of the opposites is still only something inward. In the will, on the other hand, these opposed aspects are supposed to be at one and the same time abstractions and yet determinations of the *will*, which can be known only as something concrete and they lead automatically to their identity and to the confusion of their meanings—a confusion into which the Understanding slips quite unconsciously. Thus, for example, the will as inward freedom is subjectivity itself; subjectivity therefore is the concept of the will and so its objectivity. But it is its subjectivity, contrasted with objectivity, which is finitude, and yet, because of this very contrast, the will is not by itself but is entangled with its object, and so its finitude consists quite as much in the fact that it is not subjective—and so on. Hence the meaning to be attributed in what follows to 'subjective' or 'objective' in respect of the will must each time appear from the context, which supplies the data for inferring their position in relation to the will as a whole.

27. The absolute goal, or, if you like, the absolute impulse, of free mind (see Paragraph 21) is to make its freedom its object, i.e. to make freedom objective as much in the sense that freedom shall be the rational system of mind, as in the sense that this system shall be the world of immediate actuality (see Paragraph 26). In making freedom its object, mind's purpose is to be explicitly, as Idea, what the will is implicitly. The definition of the concept of the will in abstraction from the Idea of the will is 'the free will which wills the free will'.

28. The will's activity consists in annulling the contradiction between subjectivity and objectivity and giving its aims an objective instead of a subjective character, while at the same time remaining by itself even in objectivity. Outside the formal mode of willing (i.e. consciousness, see Paragraph 8) where objectivity is present only as immediate actuality, this activity is in essence the development of the substantive content of the Idea (see Paragraph 21—a development through which the concept determines the Idea, itself at first abstract, until it becomes a systematized whole. This whole, as what is substantive, is independent of the opposition between a merely subjective aim and its realization and is the same in both despite their difference in form.

29. An existent of any sort embodying the free will, this is what right is. Right therefore is by definition freedom as Idea.

The crucial point in both the Kantian and the generally accepted definition of right (see the Introduction to Kant's *Philosophy of Law*) is the '*restriction* which makes it possible for my freedom or self-will to co-exist with the self-will of each and all according to a universal law'. On the one hand, this definition contains only a negative category, restriction, while on the other hand the positive factor—the universal law or the so-called 'law of reason', the correspondence of the self-will of one individual with that of another—is tantamount to the principle of contradiction and the familiar notion of abstract identity. The definition of right which I have quoted involves that way of looking at the matter, especially popular since Rousseau, according to which what is fundamental, substantive, and primary is supposed to be the will of a single person in his own private self-will, not the absolute or rational will, and mind as a particular individual, not mind as it is in its truth. Once this principle is adopted, of course the rational can come on the scene only as a restriction on the type of freedom which this principle involves, and so also not as something immanently rational but only as an external abstract universal. This view is devoid of any speculative thinking and is repudiated by the philosophic concept. And the phenomena which it has produced both in men's heads and in the world are of a frightfulness parallel only to the superficiality of the thoughts on which they are based.

30. It is only because right is the embodiment of the absolute concept or of self-conscious freedom that it is something sacrosanct. But the exclusively formal character of right (and duty also, as we shall see) arises at a distinct stage in the development of the concept of freedom. By contrast with the right which is comparatively formal (i.e. abstract) and so comparatively restricted, a higher right belongs to the sphere and stage of mind in which mind has determined and actualized within itself the further moments contained in its Idea; and it belongs to this sphere as the sphere which is concreter, intrinsically richer, and more genuinely universal.

Every stage in the development of the Idea of freedom has its own special right, since it is the embodiment of freedom in one of its proper specific forms. When there is said to be a clash between the moral or the ethical and the right, the right in question is only the elementary, formal, right of abstract personality. Morality, ethical life, the interest of the state, each of these is a right of a special character because each of them is a specific form and embodiment of freedom. They can come into collision with each other only in so far as they are all on the same footing as rights. If mind's moral attitude were not also a right, or freedom in one of its forms, it could not possibly come into collision with the right of personality or with any other right, because any right whatever has inherent in it the concept of freedom, i.e. the highest category of mind, in contrast with which any other thing is without substance. Yet at the same time collision involves another moment, namely the fact that it is restrictive, and so if two rights collide one is subordinated to the other. It is only the right of the world-mind which is absolute without qualification.

31. The method whereby, in philosophic science, the concept develops itself out of itself is expounded in logic and is here likewise presupposed. Its development is a purely immanent progress, the engendering of its determinations. Its advance is not effected by the assertion that various things exist and then by the application of the universal to extraneous material of that sort culled from elsewhere.

The concept's moving principle, which alike engenders and dissolves the particularizations of the universal, I call 'dialectic', though I do not mean that dialectic which takes an object, proposition, &c., given to feeling or, in general, to immediate consciousness, and explains it away, confuses it, pursues it this way and that, and has as its sole task the deduction of the contrary of that with which it starts—a negative type of dialectic commonly appearing even in Plato. Dialectic of this kind may regard as its final result either the contrary of the idea with which it begins, or, if it is as incisive as the skepticism of the ancients, the contradictory of this idea, or again, it may be feeble enough to be content with an 'approximation' to the truth, a modern half-measure. The loftier dialectic of the concept consists not simply in producing the determination as a contrary and a restriction, but in producing and seizing upon the positive content and outcome of the determination, because it is this which makes it solely a development and an immanent progress. Moreover, this dialectic is not an activity of subjective thinking applied to some matter externally, but is rather the matter's very soul putting forth its branches and fruit organically. This development of the Idea is the proper activity of its rationality, and thinking, as something subjective, merely looks on at it without for its part adding to it any ingredient of its own. To consider a thing rationally means not to bring reason to bear on the object from the outside and so to tamper with it, but to find that the object is rational on its own account; here it is mind in its freedom, the culmination of self-conscious reason, which gives itself actuality and engenders itself as an existing world. The sole task of philosophic science is to bring into consciousness this proper work of the reason of the thing itself.

32. The determinations of the concept in the course of its development are from one point of view themselves concepts, but from another they take the form of existents, since the concept is in essence Idea. The series of concepts which this development yields is therefore at the same time a series of shapes of experience, and philosophic science must treat them accordingly.

In a more speculative sense, a concept's determinacy and its mode of existence are one and the same thing. But it is to be noticed that the moments, whose result is a further determined form of the concept, precede it in the philosophical development of the Idea as determinations of the concept, but they do not go in advance of it in the temporal development as shapes of experience. Thus, for instance, the Idea determined as the family, presupposes the determinations of the concept from which the family will later on in this work be shown to result. But the explicit existence of these inner presuppositions as shapes of experience also, e.g. as the right of property, contract, morality, and so forth, is the other aspect of the development, and it is only in a higher and more complete civilization that the development has gone so far as to endow its moments with this appropriately shaped existence.

Division of the Subject

33. In correspondence with the stages in the development of the Idea of the absolutely free will, the will is

A. immediate; its concept therefore is abstract, namely personality, and its embodiment is an immediate external thing—the sphere of *Abstract or Formal Right*;

B. reflected from its external embodiment into itself—it is then characterized as subjective individuality in opposition to the universal. The universal here is characterized as something inward, the good, and also as something outward, a world presented to the will; both these sides of the Idea are here mediated only by each other. This is the Idea in its division or in its existence as particular; and here we have the right of the subjective will in relation to the right of the world and the right of the Idea, though only the Idea implicit—the sphere of *Morality;*

C. the unity and truth of both these abstract moments—the Idea of the good not only apprehended in thought but so realized both in the will reflected into itself and in the external world that freedom exists as substance, as actuality and necessity, no less than as subjective will; this is the Idea in its absolutely universal existence—*Ethical Life*.

But on the same principle ethical substance is

(a) natural mind, the *Family;*

(b) in its division and appearance, *Civil Society;*

(c) the *State* as freedom, freedom universal and objective even in the free self-subsistence of the particular will. This actual and organic mind (α) of a single nation (β) reveals and actualizes itself through the inter-relation of the particular national minds until (λ) in the process of world-history it reveals and actualizes itself as the universal world-mind whose right is supreme.

The fact that when a thing or a content is posited first of all in accordance with its concept or as it is implicitly, it then has the form of immediacy or pure being, is the doctrine of speculative logic, here presupposed; the concept which confronts itself in the form of the concept is a different thing and no longer something immediate.

The principle which determines the division of the subject is likewise here presupposed. The division may also be looked upon as a pre-declaration in historical form of the parts of the book, since the various stages must engender themselves out of the subject-matter itself as moments in the development of the Idea. A philosophical division is far from being an external one, i.e. it is not an external classification of a given material in accordance with one or more borrowed bases of division, but, on the contrary, is the immanent self-differentiation of the concept.

'Morality' and 'ethical life', which perhaps usually pass current as synonyms, are taken here in essentially different senses. Yet even commonplace thinking seems to be distinguishing them; Kant generally prefers to use the word 'morality' and, since the principles of action in his philosophy are always limited to this conception, they make the standpoint of ethical life completely impossible, in fact they explicitly nullify and spurn it. But even if 'moral' and 'ethical' meant the same thing by derivation, that would in no way hinder them, once they had become different words, from being used for different conceptions.

THIRD PART

Ethical Life

142. Ethical life is the Idea of freedom in that on the one hand it is the good become alive—the good endowed in self-consciousness with knowing and willing and actualized by self-conscious action—while on the other hand self-consciousness has in the ethical realm its absolute foundation and the end which actuates its effort. Thus ethical life is the concept of freedom developed into the existing world and the nature of self-consciousness.

143. Since this unity of the concept of the will with its embodiment—i.e., the particular will—is knowing, consciousness of the distinction between these two moments of the Idea is present, but present in such a way that now each of these moments is in its own eyes the totality of the Idea and has that totality as its foundation and content.

144. (α) The objective ethical order, which comes on the scene in place of good in the abstract, is substance made concrete by subjectivity as infinite form. Hence it posits within itself distinctions whose specific character is thereby determined by the concept, and which endow the ethical order with a stable content independently necessary and subsistent in exaltation above subjective opinion and caprice. These distinctions are absolutely valid laws and institutions.

145. It is the fact that the ethical order is the system of these specific determinations of the Idea which constitutes its rationality. Hence the ethical order is freedom or the absolute will as what is objective, a circle of necessity whose moments are the ethical powers which regulate the life of individuals. To these powers individuals are related as accidents to substance, and it is in individuals that these powers are represented, have the shape of appearance, and become actualized.

146. (β) The substantial order, in the self-consciousness which it has thus actually attained in individuals, knows itself and so is an object of knowledge. This ethical substance and its laws and powers are on the one hand an object over against the subject, and from his point of view they *are*—'are' in the highest sense of self-subsistent being. This is an absolute authority and power infinitely more firmly established than the being of nature.

The sun, the moon, mountains, rivers, and the natural objects of all kinds by which we are surrounded, *are.* For consciousness they have the authority not only of mere being but also of possessing a particular nature which it accepts and to which it adjusts itself in dealing with them, using them, or in being otherwise concerned with them. The authority of ethical laws is infinitely higher, because natural objects conceal rationality under the cloak of contingency and exhibit it only in their utterly external and disconnected way.

147. On the other hand, they are not something alien to the subject. On the contrary, his spirit bears witness to them as to its own essence, the essence in which he has a feeling of his selfhood, and in which he lives as in his own element which is not distinguished from himself. The subject is thus directly linked to the ethical order by a relation which is more like an identity than even the relation of faith or trust.

Faith and trust emerge along with reflection; they presuppose the power of forming ideas and making distinctions. For example, it is one thing to be a pagan, a different thing to believe in a pagan religion. This relation or rather this absence of relation, this identity in which the ethical order is the actual living soul of self-consciousness, can no doubt pass over into a relation of faith and conviction and into a relation produced by means of further refection, i.e. into an *insight* due to reasoning starting perhaps from some particular purposes interests, and considerations from fear or hope, or from historical conditions. But adequate *knowledge* of this identity depends on thinking in terms of the concept.

148. As substantive in character, these laws and institutions are duties binding on the will of the individual, because as subjective, as inherently undetermined, or determined as particular, he distinguishes himself from them and hence stands related to them as to the substance of his own being.

The 'doctrine of duties' in moral philosophy (I mean the objective doctrine, not that which is supposed to be contained in the empty principle of moral subjectivity, because that principle determines nothing—see Paragraph 134) is therefore comprised in the systematic development of the circle of ethical necessity which follows in this Third Part. The difference between the exposition in this book and the form of a 'doctrine of duties' lies solely in the fact that, in what follows, the specific types of ethical life turn up as necessary relationships; there the exposition ends, without being supplemented in each case by the addition that 'therefore men have a duty to conform to this institution'.

A 'doctrine of duties' which is other than a philosophical science takes its material from existing relationships and shows its connexion with the moralist's personal notions or with principles and thoughts, purposes, impulses, feelings, &c., that are forthcoming everywhere; and as reasons for accepting each duty in turn, it may tack on its further consequences in their bearing on the other ethical relationships or on welfare and opinion. But an immanent and logical 'doctrine of duties' can be nothing except the serial exposition of the relationships which are necessitated by the Idea of freedom and are therefore actual in their entirety, to wit in the state.

149. The bond of duty can appear as a restriction only on indeterminate subjectivity or abstract freedom, and on the impulses either of the natural will or of the moral will which determines its indeterminate good arbitrarily. The truth is, however, that in duty the individual finds his liberation; first, liberation from dependence on mere natural impulse and from the depression which as a particular subject he cannot escape in his moral reflections on what ought to be and what might be; secondly, liberation from the indeterminate subjectivity which, never reaching reality or the objective determinacy of action, remains self-enclosed and devoid of actuality. In duty the individual acquires his substantive freedom.

150. Virtue is the ethical order reflected in the individual character so far as that character is determined by its natural endowment. When virtue displays itself solely as the individual's simple conformity with the duties of the station to which he belongs, it is rectitude.

In an *ethical* community, it is easy to say what man must do, what are the duties he has to fulfil in order to be virtuous: he has simply to follow the well-known and explicit rules of his own situation. Rectitude is the general character which may be demanded of him by law or custom. But from the standpoint of *morality*, rectitude often seems to be something comparatively inferior, something beyond which still higher demands must be made on oneself and others, because the craving to be something special is not satisfied with what is absolute and universal; it finds consciousness of peculiarity only in what is exceptional.

The various facets of rectitude may equally well be called virtues, since they are also properties of the individual, although not specially of him in contrast with others. Talk about virtue, however, readily borders on empty rhetoric, because it is only about something abstract and indeterminate; and furthermore, argumentative and expository talk of the sort is addressed to the individual as to a being of caprice and subjective inclination. In an existing ethical order in which a complete system of ethical relations has been developed and actualized, virtue in the strict sense of the word is in place and actually appears only in exceptional circumstances or when one obligation clashes with another. The clash, however, must be a genuine one, because moral reflection can manufacture clashes of all sorts to suit its purpose and give itself a consciousness of being something special and having made sacrifices. It is for this reason that the phenomenon of virtue proper is commoner when societies and communities are uncivilized, since in those circumstances ethical conditions and their actualization are more a matter of private choice or the natural genius of an exceptional individual. For instance, it was especially to Hercules that the ancients ascribed virtue. In the states of antiquity, ethical life had not grown into this free system of an objective order self-subsistently developed, and consequently it was by the personal genius of individuals that this defect had to be made good. It follows that if a 'doctrine of virtues' is not a mere 'doctrine of duties', and if therefore it embraces the particular facet of character, the facet grounded in natural endowment, it will be a natural history of mind.

Since virtues are ethical principles applied to the particular, and since in this their subjective aspect they are something indeterminate, there turns up here for determining them the quantitative principle of more or less. The result is that consideration of them introduces their corresponding defects or vices, as in Aristotle, who defined each particular virtue as strictly a mean between an excess and a deficiency.

The content which assumes the form of duties and then virtues is the same as that which also has the form of impulses (see Remark to Paragraph 19). Impulses have the same basic content as duties and virtues, but in impulses this content still belongs to the immediate will and to instinctive feeling; it has not been developed to the point of becoming ethical. Consequently, impulses have in common with the content of duties and virtues only the abstract object on which they are directed, an object indeterminate in itself, and so devoid of anything to discriminate them as good or evil. Or in other words, impulses, considered abstractly in their positive aspect alone, are good, while, considered abstractly in their negative aspect alone, they are evil (see Paragraph 18).

151. But when individuals are simply identified with the actual order, ethical life (*das Sittliche*) appears as their general mode of conduct, i.e., as custom (*Sitte*), while the habitual practice of ethical living appears as a second nature which, put in the place of the initial, purely natural will, is the soul of custom permeating it through and through, the significance and the actuality of its existence. It is mind living and present as a world, and the substance of mind thus exists now for the first time as mind.

152. In this way the ethical substantial order has attained its right, and its right its validity. That is to say, the self-will of the individual has vanished together with his private conscience which had claimed independence and opposed itself to the ethical substance. For, when his character is ethical, he recognizes as the end which moves him to act the universal which is itself unmoved but is disclosed in its specific determinations as rationality actualized. He knows that his own dignity and the whole stability of his particular ends are grounded in this same universal, and it is therein that he actually attains these. Subjectivity is itself the absolute form and existent actuality of the substantial order, and the distinction between subject on the one hand and substance on the other, as the object, end, and controlling power of the subject, is the same as, and has vanished directly along with, the distinction between them in form.

Subjectivity is the ground wherein the concept of freedom is realized (see Paragraph 106). At the level of morality, subjectivity is still distinct from freedom, the concept of subjectivity; but at the level of ethical life it is the realization of the concept in a way adequate to the concept itself.

153. The right of individuals to be subjectively destined to freedom is fulfilled when they belong to an actual ethical order, because their conviction of their freedom finds its truth in such an objective order, and it is in an ethical order that they are actually in possession of their own essence or their own inner universality (see Paragraph 147).

When a father inquired about the best method of educating his son in ethical conduct, a Pythagorean replied: 'Make him a citizen of a state with good laws.' (The phrase has also been attributed to others.)

154. The right of individuals to their *particular* satisfaction is also contained in the ethical substantial order, since particularity is the outward appearance of the ethical order—a mode in which that order is existent.

155. Hence in this identity of the universal will with the particular will, right and duty coalesce, and by being in the ethical order a man has rights in so far as he has duties, and duties in so far as he has rights. In the sphere of abstract right, I have the right and another has the corresponding duty. In the moral sphere, the right of my private judgment and will, as well as of my happiness, has not, but only ought to have, coalesced with duties and become objective.

156. The ethical substance, as containing independent self-consciousness united with its concept, is the actual mind of a family and a nation.

157. The concept of this Idea has being only as mind, as something knowing itself and actual, because it is the objectification of itself, the movement running through the form of its moments. It is therefore

(A) ethical mind in its natural or immediate phase—the *Family*. This substantiality loses its unity, passes over into division, and into the phase of relation, i.e. into

(B) *Civil Society*-an association of members as self-subsistent individuals in a universality which, because of their self-subsistence, is only abstract. Their association is brought about by their needs, by the legal system—the means to security of person and property—and by an external organization for attaining their particular and common interests. This external state

(C) is brought back to and welded into unity in the *Constitution of the State* which is the end and actuality of both the substantial universal order and the public life devoted thereto.

SUB-SECTION I

The Family

158. The family, as the immediate substantiality of mind, is specifically characterized by love, which is mind's feeling of its own unity. Hence in a family, one's frame of mind is to have self-consciousness of one's individuality within this unity as the absolute essence of oneself, with the result that one is in it not as an independent person but as a member.

159. The right which the individual enjoys on the strength of the family unity and which is in the first place simply the individual's life within this unity, takes on the *form* of right (as the abstract moment of determinate individuality) only when the family begins to dissolve. At that point those who should be family-members both in their inclination and in actuality begin to be self-subsistent persons, and whereas they formerly constituted one specific moment within the whole, they now receive their share separately and so only in an external fashion by way of money, food, educational expenses, and the like.

160. The family is completed in these three phases:

(a) *Marriage*, the form assumed by the concept of the family in its immediate phase;

(b) *Family Property and Capital* (the external embodiment of the concept) and attention to these;

(c) *The Education of Children and the Dissolution of the Family.*

A. Marriage

161. Marriage, as the immediate type of ethical relationship, contains first, the moment of physical life; and since marriage is a *substantial* tie, the life involved in it is life in its totality, i.e. as the actuality of the race and its life-process. But, secondly, in self-consciousness the natural sexual union—a union purely inward or implicit and for that very reason *existent* as purely external—is changed into a union on the level of mind, into self-conscious love.

162. On the subjective side, marriage may have a more obvious source in the particular inclination of the two persons who are entering upon the marriage tie, or in the foresight and contrivance of the parents, and so forth. But its objective source lies in the free consent of the persons, especially in their consent to make themselves one person, to renounce their natural and individual personality to this unity of one with the other. From this point of view, their union is a self-restriction, but in fact it is their liberation, because in it they attain their substantive self-consciousness.

Our objectively appointed end and so our ethical duty is to enter the married state. The external origin of any *particular* marriage is in the nature of the case contingent, and it depends principally on the extent to which reflective thought has been developed. At one extreme, the first step is that the marriage is arranged by the contrivance of benevolent parents; the appointed end of the parties is a union of mutual love, and their inclination to marry arises from the fact that each grows acquainted with the other from the first as a destined partner. At the other extreme, it is the inclination of the parties which comes first, appearing in them as *these* two infinitely particularized individuals. The more ethical way to matrimony may be taken to be the former extreme or any way at all whereby the decision to marry comes first and the inclination to do so follows, so that in the actual wedding both decision and inclination coalesce. In the latter extreme, it is the uniqueness of the infinitely particularized which makes good its claims in accordance with the subjective principle of the modern world (see Remark to Paragraph 124).

But those works of modern art, dramatic and other, in which the love of the sexes is the main interest, are pervaded by a chill despite the heat of passion they portray, for they associate the passion with accident throughout and represent the entire dramatic interest as if it rested solely on the characters as *these individuals*; what rests on them may indeed be of infinite importance to *them*, but is of none whatever in itself.

163. The ethical aspect of marriage consists in the parties' consciousness of this unity as their substantive aim, and so in their love, trust, and common sharing of their entire existence as individuals. When the parties are in this frame of mind and their union is actual, their physical passion sinks to the level of a physical moment, destined to vanish in its very satisfaction. On the other hand, the spiritual bond of union secures its rights as the substance of marriage and thus rises, inherently indissoluble, to a plane above the contingency of passion and the transience of particular caprice.

It was noted above (in Paragraph 75) that marriage, so far as its essential basis is concerned, is not a contractual relation. On the contrary, though marriage begins in contract, it is precisely a contract to transcend the standpoint of contract, the standpoint from which persons are regarded in their individuality as self-subsistent units. The identification of personalities, whereby the family becomes one person and its members become its accidents (though substance is in essence the relation of accidents to itself), is the ethical mind. Taken by itself and stripped of the manifold externals of which it is possessed owing to its embodiment in *these* individuals and the interests of the phenomenal realm, interests limited in time and numerous other ways, this mind emerges in a shape for representative thinking and has been revered as *Penates,* &c.; and in general it is in this mind that the religious character of marriage and the family, or *pietas*, is grounded. It is a further abstraction still to separate the divine, or the substantive, from its body, and then to stamp it, together with the feeling and consciousness of mental unity, as what is falsely called 'Platonic' love. This separation is in keeping with the monastic doctrine which characterizes the moment of physical life as purely negative and which, precisely by thus separating the physical from the mental, endows the former by itself with infinite importance.

164. Mere agreement to the stipulated terms of a contract in itself involves the genuine transfer of the property in question (see Paragraph 79). Similarly, the solemn declaration by the parties of their consent to enter the ethical bond of marriage, and its corresponding recognition and confirmation by their family and community,[1] constitutes the formal completion and actuality of marriage. The knot is tied and made ethical only after this ceremony, whereby through the use of signs, i.e. of language (the most mental embodiment of mind—see Paragraph 78), the substantial thing in the marriage is brought completely into being. As a result, the sensuous moment, the one proper to physical life, is put into its ethical place as something only consequential and accidental, belonging to the external embodiment of the ethical bond, which indeed can subsist exclusively in reciprocal love and support.

If with a view to framing or criticizing legal enactments, the question is asked: what should be regarded as the chief end of marriage?, the question may be taken to mean: which single facet of marriage in its actuality is to be regarded as the most essential one? No one facet by itself, however, makes up the whole range of its implicit and explicit content, i.e. of its ethical character, and one or other of its facets may be lacking in an existing marriage without detriment to the essence of marriage itself.

It is in the actual conclusion of a marriage, i.e. in the wedding, that the essence of the tie is expressed and established beyond dispute as something ethical, raised above the contingency of feeling and private inclination. If this ceremony is taken as an external formality, a mere so-called 'civil requirement', it is thereby stripped of all significance except perhaps that of serving the purpose of edification and attesting the civil relation of the parties. It is reduced indeed to a mere *fiat* of a civil or ecclesiastical authority. As such it appears as something not merely indifferent to the true nature of marriage, but actually alien to it. The heart is constrained by the law to attach a value to the formal ceremony and the latter is looked upon merely as a condition which must precede the complete mutual surrender of the parties to one another. As such it appears to bring disunion into their loving disposition and, like an alien intruder, to thwart the inwardness of their union. Such a doctrine pretentiously claims to afford the highest conception of the freedom, inwardness, and perfection of love; but in fact it is a travesty of the ethical aspect of love, the higher aspect which restrains purely sensual impulse and puts it in the background. Such restraint is already present at the instinctive level in shame, and it rises to chastity and modesty as consciousness becomes more specifically intelligent. In particular the view just criticized casts aside marriage's specifically ethical character, which consists in this, that the consciousness of the parties is crystallized out of its physical and subjective mode and lifted to the thought of what is substantive; instead of continually reserving to itself the contingency and caprice of bodily desire, it removes the marriage bond from the province of this caprice, surrenders to the substantive, and swears allegiance to the *Penates*; the physical moment it subordinates until it becomes something wholly conditioned by the true and ethical character of the marriage relation and by the recognition of the bond as an ethical one. It is effrontery and its buttress, the Understanding, which cannot apprehend the speculative character of the substantial tie; nevertheless, with this speculative character there correspond both ethical purity of heart and the legislation of Christian peoples.

165. The difference in the physical characteristics of the two sexes has a rational basis and consequently acquires an intellectual and ethical significance. This significance is determined by the difference into which the ethical substantiality, as the concept, internally sunders itself in order that its vitality may become a concrete unity consequent upon this difference.

166. Thus one sex is mind in its self-diremption into explicit personal self-subsistence and the knowledge and volition of free universality, i.e. the self-consciousness of conceptual thought and the volition of the objective final end. The other sex is mind maintaining itself in unity as knowledge and volition of the substantive, but knowledge and volition in the form of concrete individuality and feeling. In relation to externality, the former is powerful and active, the latter passive and subjective. It follows that man has his actual substantive life in the state, in learning, and so forth, as well as in labour and struggle with the external world and with himself so that it is only out of his diremption that he fights his way to self-subsistent unity with himself. In the family he has a tranquil intuition of this unity, and there he lives a subjective ethical life on the plane of feeling. Woman, on the other hand, has her substantive destiny in the family, and to be imbued with family piety is her ethical frame of mind.

For this reason, family piety is expounded in Sophocles' *Antigone*—one of the most sublime presentations of this virtue—as principally the law of woman, and as the law of a substantiality at once subjective and on the plane of feeling, the law of the inward life, a life which has not yet attained its full actualization; as the law of the ancient gods, 'the gods of the underworld'; as 'an everlasting law, and no man knows at what time it was first put forth'. This law is there displayed as a law opposed to public law, to the law of the land. This is the supreme opposition in ethics and therefore in tragedy; and it is individualized in the same play in the opposing natures of man and woman.

167. In essence marriage is monogamy because it is personality—immediate exclusive individuality—which enters into this tie and surrenders itself to it; and hence the tie's truth and inwardness (i.e. the subjective form of its substantiality) proceeds only from the

mutual, whole-hearted, surrender of this personality. Personality attains its right of being conscious of itself in another only in so far as the other is in this identical relationship as a person, i.e. as an atomic individual.

Marriage, and especially monogamy, is one of the absolute principles on which the ethical life of a community depends. Hence marriage comes to be recorded as one of the moments in the founding of states by gods or heroes.

168. Further, marriage results from the free surrender by both sexes of their personality— a personality in every possible way unique in each of the parties. Consequently, it ought not to be entered by two people identical in stock who are already acquainted and perfectly known to one another; for individuals in the same circle of relationship have no special personality of their own in contrast with that of others in the same circle. On the contrary, the parties should be drawn from separate families and their personalities should be different in origin. Since the very conception of marriage is that it is a freely undertaken ethical transaction, not a tie directly grounded in the physical organism and its desires, it follows that the marriage of blood-relations runs counter to this conception and so also to genuine natural feeling.

Marriage itself is sometimes said to be grounded not in natural rights but simply in instinctive sexual impulses; or again it is treated as a contract with an arbitrary basis. External arguments in support of monogamy have been drawn from physical considerations such as the number of men and women. Dark feelings of repulsion are advanced as the sole ground for prohibiting consanguineous marriage. The basis of all these views is the fashionable idea of a state of nature and a natural origin for rights, and the lack of the concept of rationality and freedom.

169. The family, as person, has its real external existence in property; and it is only when this property takes the form of capital that it becomes the embodiment of the substantial personality of the family.

B. The Family Capital

170. It is not merely property which a family possesses; as a universal and enduring person, it requires possessions specifically determined as permanent and secure, i.e. it requires capital. The arbitrariness of a single owner's particular needs is one moment in property taken abstractly; but this moment, together with the selfishness of desire, is here transformed into something ethical, into labour and care for a common possession.

In the sagas of the founding of states, or at least of a social and orderly life, the introduction of permanent property is linked with the introduction of marriage. The nature of this capital, however, and the proper means of its consolidation will appear in the section on civil society.

171. The family as a legal entity in relation to others must be represented by the husband as its head. Further, it is his prerogative to go out and work for its living, to attend to its needs, and to control and administer its capital. This capital is common property so that, while no member of the family has property of his own, each has his right in the common stock. This right, however, may come into collision with the head of the family's right of administration owing to the fact that the ethical temper of the family is still only at the level of immediacy (see Paragraph 158) and so is exposed to partition and contingency.

172. A marriage brings into being a new family which is self-subsistent and independent of the clans or 'houses' from which its members have been drawn. The tie between these and the new family has a natural basis—consanguinity, but the new family is based on love of an ethical type. Thus an individual's property too has an essential connexion with his conjugal relationship and only a comparatively remote one with his relation to his clan or 'house'.

The significance of marriage settlements which impose a restriction on the couple's common ownership of their goods, of arrangements to secure continued legal assistance for the woman, and so forth, lies in their being provisions in case of the dissolution of the marriage, either naturally by death, or by divorce, &c. They are also safeguards for securing that in such an eventuality the different members of the family shall secure their share of the common stock.

C. The Education of Children and the Dissolution of the Family

173. In substance marriage is a unity, though only a unity of inwardness or disposition; in outward existence, however, the unity is sundered in the two parties. It is only in the children that the unity itself exists externally, objectively, and explicitly as a unity, because the parents love the children as their love, as the embodiment of their own substance. From the physical point of view, the presupposition—persons immediately existent (as parents)—here becomes a result, a process which runs away into the infinite series of generations, each producing the next and presupposing the one before. This is the mode in which the single mind of the *Penates* reveals its existence in the finite sphere of nature as a race.

174. Children have the right to maintenance and education at the expense of the family's common capital. The right of the parents to the service as service of their children is based upon and is restricted by the common task of looking after the family generally. Similarly, the right of the parents over the wishes of their children is determined by the object in view—discipline and education. The punishment of children does not aim at justice as such; the aim is more subjective and moral in character, i.e. to deter them from exercising a freedom still in the toils of nature and to lift the universal into their consciousness and will.

175. Children are potentially free and their life directly embodies nothing save potential freedom. Consequently they are not things and cannot be the property either of their parents or others. In respect of his relation to the family, the child's education has the positive aim of instilling ethical principles into him in the form of an immediate feeling for which differences are not yet explicit, so that thus equipped with the foundation of an ethical life, his heart may live its early years in love, trust, and obedience. In respect of the same relation, this education has the negative aim of raising children out of the instinctive, physical, level on which they are originally, to self-subsistence and freedom of personality and so to the level on which they have power to leave the natural unity of the family.

One of the blackest marks against Roman legislation is the law whereby children were treated by their fathers as slaves. This gangrene of the ethical order at the tenderest point of its innermost life is one of the most important clues for understanding the place of the Romans in the history of the world and their tendency towards legal formalism.

The necessity for education is present in children as their own feeling of dissatisfaction with themselves as they are, as the desire to belong to the adult world whose superiority they divine, as the longing to grow up. The play theory of education assumes that what is childish is itself already something of inherent worth and presents it as such to the children; in their eyes it lowers serious pursuits, and education itself, to a form of childishness for which the children themselves have scant respect. The advocates of this method represent the child, in the immaturity in which he feels himself to be, as really mature and they struggle to make him satisfied with himself as he is. But they corrupt and distort his genuine and proper need for something better, and create in him a blind indifference to the substantial ties of the intellectual world, a contempt of his elders because they have thus posed before him, a child, in a contemptible and childish fashion, and finally a vanity and conceit which feeds on the notion of its own superiority.

176. Marriage is but the ethical Idea in its *immediacy* and so has its objective actuality only in the inwardness of subjective feeling and disposition. In this fact is rooted the fundamental contingency of marriage in the world of existence. There can be no compulsion on people to marry; and, on the other hand, there is no merely legal or positive bond which can hold the parties together once their dispositions and actions have become hostile and contrary. A third ethical authority, however, is called for to maintain the right of marriage—an ethical substantiality—against the mere whims of hostile disposition or the accident of a purely passing mood, and so forth. Such an authority distinguishes these from the total estrangement of the two parties and may not grant divorce until it is satisfied that the estrangement is total.

177. The ethical dissolution of the family consists in this, that once the children have been educated to freedom of personality, and have come of age, they become recognized as persons in the eyes of the law and as capable of holding free property of their own and founding families of their own, the sons as heads of new families, the daughters as wives. They now have their substantive destiny in the new family; the old family on the other hand falls into the background as merely their ultimate basis and origin, while *a fortiori* the clan is an abstraction, devoid of rights.

178. The natural dissolution of the family by the death of the parents, particularly the father, has inheritance as its consequence so far as the family capital is concerned. The essence of inheritance is the transfer to private ownership of property which is in principle common. When comparatively remote degrees of kinship are in question, and when persons and families are so dispersed in civil society that they have begun to gain self-subsistence, this transfer becomes the less hard and fast as the sense of family unity fades away and as every marriage becomes the surrender of previous family relationships and the founding of a new self-subsistent family.

It has been suggested that the basis of inheritance lies in the fact that, by a man's death, his property becomes wealth without an owner, and as such falls to the first person who takes possession of it, because of course it is the relatives who are normally nearest a man's death-bed and so they are generally the first to take possession. Hence it is supposed that this customary occurrence is made a rule by positive legislation in the interests of orderliness. This ingenious idea disregards the nature of family relationship.

179. The result of this disintegration of the family is that a man may at will either squander his capital altogether, mainly in accordance with his private caprices, opinions, and ends, or else look upon a circle of friends and acquaintances, &c., as if they were his family and make a will embodying a declaration to that effect, with the result that they become his legal heirs.

The ethical justification of freedom to dispose of one's property by will to a circle of friends would depend on the formation of such a circle; but there goes to its formation so much accident, arbitrariness, and shrewd self-seeking, &c.—especially since testamentary hopes have a bearing on readiness to enter it—that the ethical moment in it is only something very vague. Further, the recognition of a man's competence to bequeath his property arbitrarily is much more likely to be an occasion for breach of ethical obligations and for mean exertions and equally mean subservience; and it also provides opportunity and justification for the folly, caprice, and malice of attaching to professed benefactions and gifts vain, tyrannical, and vexatious conditions operative after the testator's death and so in any case after his property ceases to be his.

180. The principle that the members of the family grow up to be self-subsistent persons in the eyes of the law (see Paragraph 177) lets into the circle of the family something of the same arbitrariness and discrimination among the natural heirs, though its exercise there must be restricted to a minimum in order to prevent injury to the basic family relationship.

The mere downright arbitrariness of the deceased cannot be made the principle underlying the right to make a will, especially if it runs counter to the substantive right of the family. For after all no respect would be forthcoming for his wishes after his death, if not from the family's love and veneration for its deceased fellow-member. Such arbitrariness by itself contains nothing worthy of higher respect than the right of the family as such—on the contrary.

The other ground for the validity of testamentary disposition would consist simply in its arbitrary recognition by others. But such an argument may prima facie be admitted only when family ties, to which testamentary disposition is intrinsic, become remoter and more ineffective. If they are actually present, however, without being effective, the situation is unethical; and to give extended validity to arbitrary dispositions at the expense of family ties *eo ipso* weakens the ethical character of the latter.

To make the father's arbitrary will within the family the main principle of inheritance was part of the harsh and unethical legal system of Rome to which reference has been made already. That system even gave a father power to sell his son, and if the son was manumitted by a third party, he came under his father's *potestas* once more. Not until he was manumitted a third time was he actually and finally free. The son never attained his majority *de jure* nor did he become a person in law; the only property he could hold was booty won in war (*peculium castrense*). If he passed out of his father's *potestas* after being thrice sold and manumitted, he did not inherit along with those who had continued in bondage to the head of the family, unless the will specifically so provided. Similarly, a wife[2] remained attached to her family of origin rather than to the new family which by her marriage she had helped to found, and which was now properly her own, and she was therefore precluded from inheriting any share of the goods of what was properly her own family, for neither wife nor mother shared in the distribution of an estate.

Later, with the growing feeling for rationality, the unethical provisions of laws such as these and others were evaded in the course of their administration, for example with the help of the expression *bonorum possessio*[3] instead of *hereditas*, and through the fiction of nicknaming a *filia* a *filius*. This was referred to above (see Remark to Paragraph 3) as the sad necessity to which the judge was reduced in the face of bad laws—the necessity of smuggling reason into them on the sly, or at least into some of their consequences. Connected with this were the terrible instability of the chief political institutions and a riot of legislation to stem the outbreak of resulting evils.

From Roman history and the writings of Lucian and others, we are sufficiently familiar with the unethical consequences of giving the head of a Roman family the right to name whom he pleased as his heir.

Marriage is ethical life at the level of immediacy; in the very nature of the case, therefore, it must be a mixture of a substantial tie with natural contingency and inner arbitrariness. Now when by the slave-status of children, by legal provisions such as those
mentioned above as well as others consequential upon them, and in addition by the ease
of Roman divorce, pride of place is given to arbitrariness instead of to the right of the
substantial (so that even Cicero—and what fine writing about the *Honestum* and *Decorum*
there is in his *De Officiis* and in all sorts of other places!—even Cicero divorced his wife as
a business speculation in order to pay his debts with his new wife's dowry), then a legal
road is paved to the corruption of manners, or rather the laws themselves necessitate such
corruption.

The institution of heirs-at-law with a view to preserving the family and its *splendor* by
means of *fideicommissa* and *substitutiones* (in order to favour sons by excluding daughters
from inheriting, or to favour the eldest son by excluding the other children) is an infringement of the principle of the freedom of property (see Paragraph 62), like the admission of
any other inequality in the treatment of heirs. And besides, such an institution depends
on an arbitrariness which in and by itself has no right to recognition, or more precisely on
the thought of wishing to preserve intact not so much *this* family but rather *this* clan or
'house'. Yet it is not this clan or 'house', but the family proper which is the Idea and
which therefore possesses the right to recognition, and both the ethical disposition and
family trees are much more likely to be preserved by freedom of property and equality of
inheritance than by the reverse of these.

Institutions of this kind, like the Roman, wholly ignore the right due to marriage,
because by a marriage the foundation of a unique actual family is *eo ipso* completed (see
Paragraph 172), and because what is called, in contrast with the new family, the family in
the wide sense, i.e., the *stirps* or *gens*, becomes only an abstraction (see Paragraph 177)
growing less and less actual the further it recedes into the background as one generation
succeeds another. Love, the ethical moment in marriage, is by its very nature a feeling for
actual living individuals, not for an abstraction. This abstraction of the Understanding
[the *gens*] appears in history as the principle underlying the contribution of the Roman
Empire to world history (see Paragraph 357). In the higher sphere of the state, a right of
primogeniture arises together with estates rigidly entailed; it arises, however, not arbitrarily but as the inevitable outcome of the Idea of the state. On this point see below,
Paragraph 306.

Transition of the Family into Civil Society

181. The family disintegrates (both essentially, through the working of the principle of
personality, and also in the course of nature) into a plurality of families, each of which conducts itself as in principle a self-subsistent concrete person and therefore as externally
related to its neighbours. In other words, the moments bound together in the unity of the
family, since the family is the ethical Idea still in its concept, must be released from the
concept to self-subsistent objective reality. This is the stage of difference. This gives us, to
use abstract language in the first place, the determination of particularity which is related
to universality but in such a way that universality is its basic principle, though still only
an inward principle; for that reason, the universal merely shows in the particular as its
form. Hence this relation of reflection prima facie portrays the disappearance of ethical life
or, since this life as the essence necessarily shows itself, this relation constitutes the world
of ethical appearance—civil society.

The expansion of the family, as its transition into a new principle, is in the external world sometimes its peaceful expansion until it becomes a people, i.e. a nation, which thus has a common natural origin, or sometimes the federation of scattered groups of families under the influence of an overlord's power or as a result of a voluntary association produced by the tie of needs and the reciprocity of their satisfaction.

SUB-SECTION 2

Civil Society

182. The concrete person, who is himself the object of his particular aims, is, as a totality of wants and a mixture of caprice and physical necessity, one principle of civil society. But the particular person is essentially so related to other particular persons that each establishes himself and finds satisfaction by means of the others, and at the same time purely and simply by means of the form of universality, the second principle here.

183. In the course of the actual attainment of selfish ends—an attainment conditioned in this way by universality—there is formed a system of complete interdependence, wherein the livelihood, happiness, and legal status of one man is interwoven with the livelihood, happiness, and rights of all. On this system, individual happiness, &c., depend, and only in this connected system are they actualized and secured. This system may be prima facie regarded as the external state, the state based on need, the state as the Understanding envisages it.

184. The Idea in this its stage of division imparts to each of its moments a characteristic embodiment; to particularity it gives the right to develop and launch forth in all directions; and to universality the right to prove itself not only the ground and necessary form of particularity, but also the authority standing over it and its final end. It is the system of the ethical order, split into its extremes and lost, which constitutes the Idea's abstract moment, its moment of reality. Here the Idea is present only as a relative totality and as the inner necessity behind this outward appearance.

185. Particularity by itself, given free rein in every direction to satisfy its needs, accidental caprices, and subjective desires, destroys itself and its substantive concept in this process of gratification. At the same time, the satisfaction of need, necessary and accidental alike, is accidental because it breeds new desires without end, is in thoroughgoing dependence on caprice and external accident, and is held in check by the power of universality. In these contrasts and their complexity, civil society affords a spectacle of extravagance and want as well as of the physical and ethical degeneration common to them both.

The development of particularity to self-subsistence (compare Remark to Paragraph 124) is the moment which appeared in the ancient world as an invasion of ethical corruption and as the ultimate cause of that world's downfall. Some of these ancient states were built on the patriarchal and religious principle, others on the principle of an ethical order which was more explicitly intellectual, though still comparatively simple; in either case they rested on primitive unsophisticated intuition. Hence they could not withstand the disruption of this state of mind when self-consciousness was infinitely reflected into itself; when this reflection began to emerge, they succumbed to it, first in spirit and then in substance, because the simple principle underlying them lacked the truly infinite power to be found only in that unity which allows both sides of the antithesis of reason to develop themselves separately in all their strength and which has so overcome the antithesis that it maintains itself in it and integrates it in itself.

In his *Republic,* Plato displays the substance of ethical life in its ideal beauty and truth; but he could only cope with the principle of self-subsistent particularity, which in his day had forced its way into Greek ethical life, by setting up in opposition to it his purely substantial state. He absolutely excluded it from his state, even in its very beginnings in private property (see Remark to Paragraph 46) and the family, as well as in its more mature form as the subjective will, the choice of a social position, and so forth. It is this defect which is responsible both for the misunderstanding of the deep and substantial truth of Plato's state and also for the usual view of it as a dream of abstract thinking, as what is often called a 'mere ideal'. The principle of the self-subsistent inherently infinite personality of the individual, the principle of subjective freedom, is denied its right in the purely substantial form which Plato gave to mind in its actuality. This principle dawned in an inward form in the Christian religion and in an external form (and therefore in one linked with abstract universality) in the Roman world. It is historically subsequent to the Greek world, and the philosophic reflection which descends to its depth is likewise subsequent to the substantial Idea of Greek philosophy.

186. But in developing itself independently to totality, the principle of particularity passes over into universality, and only there does it attain its truth and the right to which its positive actuality is entitled. This unity is not the identity which the ethical order requires, because at this level, that of division (see Paragraph 184), both principles are self-subsistent. It follows that this unity is present here not as freedom but as necessity, since it is by compulsion that the particular rises to the form of universality and seeks and gains its stability in that form.

187. Individuals in their capacity as burghers in this state are private persons whose end is their own interest. This end *mediated* through the universal which thus *appears* as a *means* to its realization. Consequently, individuals can attain their ends only in so far as they themselves determine their knowing, willing, and acting in a universal way and make themselves links in this chain of social connexions. In these circumstances, the interest of the Idea—an interest of which these members of civil society are as such unconscious— lies in the process whereby their singularity and their natural condition are raised, as a result of the necessities imposed by nature as well as of arbitrary needs, to formal freedom and formal universality of knowing and willing—the process whereby their particularity is educated up to subjectivity.

The idea that the state of nature is one of innocence and that there is a simplicity of manners in uncivilized (*ungebildeter*) peoples, implies treating education (*Bildung*) as something purely external, the ally of corruption. Similarly, the feeling that needs, their satisfaction, the pleasures and comforts of private life, and so forth, are absolute ends, implies treating education as a mere means to these ends. Both these views display lack of acquaintance with the nature of mind and the end of reason. Mind attains its actuality only by creating a dualism within itself, by submitting itself to physical needs and the chain of these external necessities, and so imposing on itself this barrier and this finitude, and finally by maturing (*bildet*) itself inwardly even when under this barrier until it overcomes it and attains its objective reality in the finite. The end of reason, therefore, is neither the manners of an unsophisticated state of nature, nor, as particularity develops, the pleasure for pleasure's sake which education procures. On the contrary, its end is to banish natural simplicity, whether the passivity which is the absence of the self, or the crude type of knowing and willing, i.e. immediacy and singularity, in which mind is absorbed. It aims in the first instance at securing for this, its external condition, the rationality of which it is capable, i.e. the form of universality or the Understanding (*Verständigkeit*). By this means alone does mind become at home with itself within this pure externality. There, then, mind's freedom is existent and mind becomes objective to itself in this element which is implicitly inimical to mind's appointed end, freedom; it has to do there only with what it has itself produced and stamped with its seal. It is in this way then that the form of universality comes explicitly into existence in thought, and this form is the only worthy element for the existence of the Idea. The final purpose of education, therefore, is liberation and the struggle for a higher liberation still; education is the absolute transition from an ethical substantiality which is immediate and natural to the one which is intellectual and so both infinitely subjective and lofty enough to have attained universality of form. In the individual subject, this liberation is the hard struggle against pure subjectivity of demeanour, against the immediacy of desire, against the empty subjectivity of feeling and the caprice of inclination. The disfavour showered on education is due in part to its being this hard struggle; but it is through this educational struggle that the subjective will itself attains objectivity within, an objectivity in which alone it is for its part capable and worthy of being the actuality of the Idea.

Moreover, this form of universality—the Understanding, to which particularity has worked its way and developed itself, brings it about at the same time that particularity becomes individuality genuinely existent in its own eyes. And since it is from this particularity that the universal derives the content which fills it as well as its character as infinite self-determination, particularity itself is present in ethical life as infinitely independent free subjectivity. This is the position which reveals education as a moment immanent in the Absolute and which makes plain its infinite value.

188. Civil society contains three moments:

- (A) The mediation of need and one man's satisfaction through his work and the satisfaction of the needs of all others—the *System of Needs*.
- (B) The actuality of the universal principle of freedom therein contained—the protection of property through the *Administration of Justice*.
- (C) Provision against contingencies still lurking in systems (A) and (B), and care for particular interests as a common interest, by means of the *Police* and the *Corporation*.

A. The System of Needs

189. Particularity is in the first instance characterized in general by its contrast with the universal principle of the will and thus is subjective need (see Paragraph 59). This attains its objectivity, i.e. its satisfaction, by means of (α) external things, which at this stage are likewise the property and product of the needs and wills of others, and (β) work and effort, the middle term between the subjective and the objective. The aim here is the satisfaction of subjective particularity, but the universal asserts itself in the bearing which this satisfaction has on the needs of others and their free arbitrary wills. The show of rationality thus produced in this sphere of finitude is the Understanding, and this is the aspect which is of most importance in considering this sphere and which itself constitutes the reconciling element within it.

Political economy is the science which starts from this view of needs and labour but then has the task of explaining mass-relationships and mass-movements in their complexity and their qualitative and quantitative character. This is one of the sciences which have arisen out of the conditions of the modern world. Its development affords the interesting spectacle (as in Smith, Say, and Ricardo) of thought working upon the endless mass of details which confront it at the outset and extracting therefrom the simple principles of the thing, the Understanding effective in the thing and directing it. It is to find reconciliation here to discover in the sphere of needs this show of rationality lying in the thing and effective there; but if we look at it from the opposite point of view, this is the field in which the Understanding with its subjective aims and moral fancies vents its discontent and moral frustration.

(a) The Kind of Need and Satisfaction {typical of civil society}

190. An animal's needs and its ways and means of satisfying them are both alike restricted in scope. Though man is subject to this restriction too, yet at the same time he evinces his transcendence of it and his universality, first by the multiplication of needs and means of satisfying them, and secondly by the differentiation and division of concrete need into single parts and aspects which in turn become different needs, particularized and so more abstract.

In [abstract] right, what we had before us was the person; in the sphere of morality, the subject; in the family, the family-member; in civil society as a whole, the burgher or bourgeois. Here at the standpoint of needs (compare Remark to Paragraph 123) what we have before us is the composite idea which we call man. Thus this is the first time, and indeed properly the only time, to speak of man in this sense.

191. Similarly, the means to particularized needs and all the various ways of satisfying these are themselves divided and multiplied and so in turn become proximate ends and abstract needs. This multiplication goes on *ad infinitum*; taken as a whole, it is refinement, i.e. a discrimination between these multiplied needs, and judgement on the suitability of means to their ends.

192. Needs and means, as things existent *realiter*, become something which has being for others by whose needs and work satisfaction for all alike is conditioned. When needs and means become abstract in quality (see Paragraph 191), abstraction is also a character of the reciprocal relation of individuals to one another. This abstract character, universality, is the character of being recognized and is the moment which makes concrete, i.e. social, the isolated and abstract needs and their ways and means of satisfaction.

193. This social moment thus becomes a particular end-determinant for means in themselves and their acquisition, as well as for the manner in which needs are satisfied. Further, it directly involves the demand for equality of satisfaction with others. The need for this equality and for emulation, which is the equalizing of oneself with others, as well as the other need also present here, the need of the particular to assert itself in some distinctive way, become themselves a fruitful source of the multiplication of needs and their expansion.

194. Since in social needs, as the conjunction of immediate or natural needs with mental needs arising from ideas, it is needs of the latter type which because of their universality make themselves preponderant, this social moment has in it the aspect of liberation, i.e., the strict natural necessity of need is obscured and man is concerned with his own opinion, indeed with an opinion which is universal, and with a necessity of his own making alone, instead of with an external necessity, an inner contingency, and mere caprice.

The idea has been advanced that in respect of his needs man lived in freedom in the so-called 'state of nature' when his needs were supposed to be confined to what are known as the simple necessities of nature, and when he required for their satisfaction only the means which the accidents of nature directly assured to him. This view takes no account of the moment of liberation intrinsic to work, on which see the following Paragraphs. And apart from this, it is false, because to be confined to mere physical needs as such and their direct satisfaction would simply be the condition in which the mental is plunged in the natural and so would be one of savagery and unfreedom, while freedom itself is to be found only in the reflection of mind into itself, in mind's distinction from nature, and in the reflex of mind in nature.

195. This liberation is abstract since the particularity of the ends remains their basic content. When social conditions tend to multiply and subdivide needs, means, and enjoyments indefinitely—a process which, like the distinction between natural and refined needs, has no qualitative limits—this is luxury. In this same process, however, dependence and want increase *ad infinitum*, and the material to meet these is permanently barred to the needy man because it consists of external objects with the special character of being property, the embodiment of the free will of others, and hence from his point of view its recalcitrance is absolute.

(b) The Kind of Work {typical of civil society}

196. The means of acquiring and preparing the particularized means appropriate to our similarly particularized needs is work. Through work the raw material directly supplied by nature is specifically adapted to these numerous ends by all sorts of different processes. Now this formative change confers value on means and gives them their utility, and hence man in what he consumes is mainly concerned with the products of men. It is the products of human effort which man consumes.

197. The multiplicity of objects and situations which excite interest is the stage on which theoretical education develops. This education consists in possessing not simply a multiplicity of ideas and facts, but also a flexibility and rapidity of mind, ability to pass from one idea to another, to grasp complex and general relations, and so on. It is the education of the understanding in every way, and so also the building up of language. Practical education, acquired through working, consists first in the automatically recurrent need for something to do and the habit of simply being busy; next, in the strict adaptation of one's activity according not only to the nature of the material worked on, but also, and especially, to the pleasure of other workers; and finally, in a habit, produced by this discipline, of objective activity and universally recognized aptitudes.

198. The universal and objective element in work, on the other hand, lies in the abstracting process which effects the subdivision of needs and means and thereby *eo ipso* subdivides production and brings about the division of labour. By this division, the work of the individual becomes less complex, and consequently his skill at his section of the job increases, like his output. At the same time, this abstraction of one man's skill and means of production from another's completes and makes necessary everywhere the dependence of men on one another and their reciprocal relation in the satisfaction of their other needs. Further, the abstraction of one man's production from another's makes work more and more mechanical, until finally man is able to step aside and install machines in his place.

(c) Capital {and class-divisions}

199. When men are thus dependent on one another and reciprocally related to one another in their work and the satisfaction of their needs, subjective self-seeking turns into a contribution to the satisfaction of the needs of everyone else. That is to say, by a dialectical advance, subjective self-seeking turns into the mediation of the particular through the universal, with the result that each man in earning, producing, and enjoying on his own account is *eo ipso* producing and earning for the enjoyment of everyone else. The compulsion which brings this about is rooted in the complex interdependence of each on all, and it now presents itself to each as the universal permanent capital (see Paragraph 170) which gives each the opportunity, by the exercise of his education and skill, to draw a share from it and so be assured of his livelihood, while what he thus earns by means of his work maintains and increases the general capital.

200. A particular man's resources, or in other words his opportunity of sharing in the general resources, are conditioned, however, partly by his own unearned principal (his capital), and partly by his skill; this in turn is itself dependent not only on his capital, but also on accidental circumstances whose multiplicity introduces differences in the development of natural, bodily, and mental characteristics, which were already in themselves dissimilar. In this sphere of particularity, these differences are conspicuous in every direction and on every level, and, together with the arbitrariness and accident which this sphere contains as well, they have as their inevitable consequence disparities of individual resources and ability.

The objective right of the particularity of mind is contained in the Idea. Men are made unequal by nature, where inequality is in its element, and in civil society the right of particularity is so far from annulling this natural inequality that it produces it out of mind and raises it to an inequality of skill and resources, and even to one of moral and intellectual attainment. To oppose to this right a demand for equality is a folly of the Understanding which takes as real and rational its abstract equality and its 'ought-to-be'.

This sphere of particularity, which fancies itself the universal, is still only relatively identical with the universal, and consequently it still retains in itself the particularity of nature, i.e. arbitrariness, or in other words the relics of the state of nature. Further, it is reason, immanent in the restless system of human needs, which articulates it into an organic whole with different members (see the following Paragraph).

201. The infinitely complex, criss-cross, movements of reciprocal production and exchange, and the equally infinite multiplicity of means therein employed, become crystallized, owing to the universality inherent in their content, and distinguished into general groups. As a result, the entire complex is built up into particular systems of needs, means, and types of work relative to these needs, modes of satisfaction and of theoretical and practical education, i.e., into systems, to one or other of which individuals are assigned—in other words, into class-divisions.

202. The classes are specifically determined in accordance with the concept as (*a*) the *substantial* or immediate [or agricultural] class; (*b*) the reflecting or *formal* [or business] class; and finally, (*c*) the *universal* class [the class of civil servants].

203. (*a*) The substantial [or agricultural] class has its capital in the natural products of the soil which it cultivates—soil which is capable of exclusively private ownership and which demands formation in an objective way and not mere haphazard exploitation. In face of the connexion of [agricultural] work and its fruits with separate and fixed times of the year, and the dependence of harvests on the variability of natural processes, the aim of need in this class turns into provision for the future; but owing to the conditions here, the agricultural mode of subsistence remains one which owes comparatively little to reflection and independence of will, and this mode of life is in general such that this class has the substantial disposition of an ethical life which is immediate, resting on family relationship and trust.

The real beginning and original foundation of states has been rightly ascribed to the introduction of agriculture along with marriage, because the principle of agriculture brings with it the formation of the land and consequentially exclusively private property (compare Remark to Paragraph 170); the nomadic life of savages, who seek their livelihood from place to place, it brings back to the tranquillity of private rights and the assured satisfaction of their needs. Along with these changes, sexual love is restricted to marriage, and this bond in turn grows into an enduring league, inherently universal, while needs expand into care for a family, and personal possessions into family goods. Security, consolidation, lasting satisfaction of needs, and so forth—things which are the most obvious recommendations of marriage and agriculture—are nothing but forms of universality, modes in which rationality, the final end and aim, asserts itself in these spheres.

In this matter, nothing is of more interest than the ingenious and learned explanations which my distinguished friend, Herr Creuzer, has given of the agrarian festivals, images, and sanctuaries of the ancients. He shows that it was because the ancients themselves had become conscious of the divine origin of agriculture and other institutions associated with it that they held them in such religious veneration.

In course of time, the character of this class as 'substantial' undergoes modifications through the working of the civil law, in particular the administration of justice, as well as through the working of education, instruction, and religion. These modifications, which occur in the other classes also, do not affect the substantial content of the class but only its form and the development of its power of reflection.

204. (b) The business class has for its task the adaptation of raw materials, and for its means of livelihood it is thrown back on its work, on reflection and intelligence, and essentially on the mediation of one man's needs and work with those of others. For what this class produces and enjoys, it has mainly itself, its own industry, to thank. The task of this class is subdivided into

(α) work to satisfy single needs in a comparatively concrete way and to supply single orders—craftsmanship;

(β) work of a more abstract kind, mass-production to satisfy single needs, but needs in more universal demand—manufacture;

(γ) the business of exchange, whereby separate utilities are exchanged the one for the other, principally through the use of the universal medium of exchange, money, which actualizes the abstract value of all commodities—trade.

205. (c) The universal class [the class of civil servants] has for its task the universal interests of the community. It must therefore be relieved from direct labour to supply its needs, either by having private means or by receiving an allowance from the state which claims its industry, with the result that private interest finds its satisfaction in its work for the universal.

206. It is in accordance with the concept that class-organization, as particularity become objective to itself, is split in this way into its general divisions. But the question of the particular class to which an individual is to belong is one on which natural capacity, birth,

and other circumstances have their influence, though the essential and final determining factors are subjective opinion and the individual's arbitrary will, which win in this sphere their right, their merit, and their dignity. Hence what happens here by inner necessity occurs at the same time by the mediation of the arbitrary will, and to the conscious subject it has the shape of being the work of his own will.

In this respect too there is a conspicuous difference, in relation to the principle of particularity and the subject's arbitrary will, between the political life of the east and the west, and also between that of the ancient and the modern world. In the former, the division of the whole into classes came about objectively of itself, because it is inherently rational; but the principle of subjective particularity was at the same time denied its rights, in that, for example, the allotment of individuals to classes was left to the ruling class, as in Plato's *Republic*,[4] or to the accident of birth, as in the Indian caste-system. Thus subjective particularity was not incorporated into the organization of society as a whole; it was not reconciled in the whole, and therefore—since as an essential moment it emerges there in any event—it shows itself there as something hostile, as a corruption of the social order (see Remark to Paragraph 185). Either it overthrows society, as happened in the Greek states and in the Roman Republic; or else, should society preserve itself in being as a force or as a religious authority, for instance, it appears as inner corruption and complete degeneration, as was the case to some extent in Sparta and is now altogether the case in India.

But when subjective particularity is upheld by the objective order in conformity with it and is at the same time allowed its rights, then it becomes the animating principle of the entire civil society, of the development alike of mental activity, merit, and dignity. The recognition and the right that what is brought about by reason of necessity in civil society and the state shall at the same time be effected by the mediation of the arbitrary will is the more precise definition of what is primarily meant by freedom in common parlance (see Paragraph 121).

207. A man actualizes himself only in becoming something definite, i.e. something specifically particularized; this means restricting himself exclusively to one of the particular spheres of need. In this class-system, the ethical frame of mind therefore is rectitude and *esprit de corps*, i.e., the disposition to make oneself a member of one of the moments of civil society by one's own act, through one's energy, industry, and skill, to maintain oneself in this position, and to fend for oneself only through this process of mediating oneself with the universal, while in this way gaining recognition both in one's own eyes and in the eyes of others. Morality has its proper place in this sphere where the paramount thing is reflection on one's doings, and the quest of happiness and private wants, and where the contingency in satisfying these makes into a duty even a single and contingent act of assistance.

At first (i.e., especially in youth) a man chafes at the idea of resolving on a particular social position, and looks upon this as a restriction on his universal character and as a necessity imposed on him purely *ab extra*. This is because his thinking is still of that abstract kind which refuses to move beyond the universal and so never reaches the actual. It does not realize that if the concept is to be determinate, it must first of all advance into the distinction between the concept and its real existence and thereby into determinacy and particularity (see Paragraph 7). It is only thus that the concept can win actuality and ethical objectivity.

208. As the private particularity of knowing and willing, the principle of this system of needs contains absolute universality, the universality of freedom, only abstractly and therefore as the right of property. At this point, however, this right is no longer merely

implicit but has attained its recognized actuality as the protection of property through the administration of justice.

B. The Administration of Justice

209. The relatedness arising from the reciprocal bearing on one another of needs and work to satisfy these is first of all reflected into itself as infinite personality, as abstract right. But it is this very sphere of relatedness—a sphere of education—which gives abstract right the determinate existence of being something universally recognized, known, and willed, and having a validity and an objective actuality mediated by this known and willed character.

It is part of education, of thinking as the consciousness of the single in the form of universality, that the ego comes to be apprehended as a universal person in which all are identical. A man counts as a man in virtue of his manhood alone, not because he is a Jew, Catholic, Protestant, German, Italian, &c. This is an assertion which thinking ratifies and to be conscious of it is of infinite importance. It is defective only when it is crystallized, e.g. as a cosmopolitanism in opposition to the concrete life of the state.

210. The objective actuality of the right consists, first, in its existence for consciousness, in its being known in some way or other; secondly, in its possessing the power which the actual possesses, in its being valid, and so also in its becoming known as universally valid.

(a) Right as Law

211. The principle of rightness becomes the law (*Gesetz*) when, in its objective existence, it is posited (*gesetzt*), i.e., when thinking makes it determinate for consciousness and makes it known as what is right and valid; and in acquiring this determinate character, the right becomes positive law in general.

To posit something as universal, i.e. to bring it before consciousness as universal, is, I need hardly say, to think (compare Remarks to Paragraphs 13 and 21). Thereby its content is reduced to its simplest form and so is given its final determinacy. In becoming law, what is right acquires for the first time not only the form proper to its universality, but also its true determinacy. Hence making a law is not to be represented as merely the expression of a rule of behaviour valid for everyone, though that is one moment in legislation; the more important moment, the inner essence of the matter, is knowledge of the content of the law in its determinate universality.

Since it is only animals which have their law as instinct, while it is man alone who has law as custom, even systems of customary law contain the moment of being thoughts and being known. Their difference from positive law consists solely in this, that they are known only in a subjective and accidental way, with the result that in themselves they are less determinate and the universality of thought is less clear in them. (And apart from this, knowledge of a system of law either in general or in its details, is the accidental possession of a few.) The supposition that it is customary law, on the strength of its character as custom, which possesses the privilege of having become part of life is a delusion, since the valid laws of a nation do not cease to be its customs by being written and codified— and besides, it is as a rule precisely those versed in the deadest of topics and the deadest of thoughts who talk nowadays of 'life' and of 'becoming part of life'. When a nation begins to acquire even a little culture, its customary law must soon come to be collected and put together. Such a collection is a legal code, but one which, as a mere collection, is markedly formless, indeterminate, and fragmentary. The main difference between it and a code properly so-called is that in the latter the principles of jurisprudence in their universality, and so in their determinacy, have been apprehended in terms of thought and expressed. English national law or municipal law is contained, as is well known, in statutes (written laws) and in so-called 'unwritten' laws. This unwritten law, however, is as good as written, and knowledge of it may, and indeed must, be acquired simply by reading the numerous quartos which it fills. The monstrous confusion, however, which prevails both in English law and its administration is graphically portrayed by those acquainted with the matter. In particular, they comment on the fact that, since this unwritten law is contained in court verdicts and judgements, the judges are continually legislators. The authority of precedent is binding on them, since their predecessors have done nothing but give expression to the unwritten law; and yet they are just as much exempt from its authority, because they are themselves repositories of the unwritten law and so have the right to criticize previous judgements and pronounce whether they accorded with the unwritten law or not.

A similar confusion might have arisen in the legal system of the later Roman Empire owing to the different but authoritative judgements of all the famous jurists. An Emperor met the situation, however, by a sensible expedient when, by what was called the Law of Citations, he set up a kind of College of the jurists who were longest deceased. There was a President, and the majority vote was accepted.

No greater insult could be offered to a civilized people or to its lawyers than to deny them ability to codify their law; for such ability cannot be that of constructing a legal system with a novel content, but only that of apprehending, i.e. grasping in thought, the content of existing laws in its determinate universality and then applying them to particular cases.

212. It is only because of this identity between its implicit and its posited character that positive law has obligatory force in virtue of its rightness. In being posited in positive law, the right acquires determinate existence. Into such existence there may enter the contingency of self-will and other particular circumstances and hence there may be a discrepancy between the content of the law and the principle of rightness.

In positive law, therefore, it is the legal which is the source of our knowledge of what is right, or, more exactly, of our legal rights (*Rechtens*). Thus the science of positive law is to that extent an historical science with authority as its guiding principle. Anything over and above this historical study is matter for the Understanding and concerns the collection of laws, their classification on external principles, deductions from them, their application to fresh details, &c. When the Understanding meddles with the nature of the thing itself, its theories, e.g. of criminal law, show what its deductive argumentation can concoct.

The science of positive law has not only the right, but even the inescapable duty, to study given laws, to deduce from its positive data their progress in history, their applications and subdivisions, down to the last detail, and to exhibit their implications. On the other hand, if, after all these deductions have been proved, the further question about the rationality of a specific law is still raised, the question may seem perverse to those who are busied with these pursuits, but their astonishment at it should at least stop short of dismay.

With this Remark, compare what was said in the Remark to Paragraph 3 about 'understanding' the law.

213. Right becomes determinate in the first place when it has the form of being posited as positive law; it also becomes determinate in content by being applied both to the ma-

terial of civil society (i.e. to the endlessly growing complexity and subdivision of social ties and the different species of property and contract within the society) and also to ethical ties based on the heart, on love and trust, though only in so far as these involve abstract right as one of their aspects (see Paragraph 159). Morality and moral commands concern the will on its most private, subjective, and particular side, and so cannot be a matter for positive legislation. Further material for the determinate content of law is provided by the rights and duties which have their source in the administration of justice itself, in the state, and so forth.

214. But apart from being applied to particular instances, right by being embodied in positive law becomes applicable to the single case. Hence it enters the sphere where quantity, not the concept, is the principle of determination. This is the sphere of the quantitative as such, of the quantitative as that which determines the relative value in exchange of *qualia*. In this sphere, the concept merely lays down a general limit, within which vacillation is still allowed. This vacillation must be terminated, however, in the interest of getting something done, and for this reason there is a place within that limit for contingent and arbitrary decisions.

The purely positive side of law lies chiefly in this focusing of the universal not merely on a particular instance, but on an isolated case, i.e., in its *direct* application. Reason cannot determine, nor can the concept provide any principle whose application could decide whether justice requires for an offence (i) a corporal punishment of forty lashes or thirty-nine, or (ii) a fine of five dollars or four dollars ninety-three, four, &c., cents, or (iii) imprisonment of a year or three hundred and sixty-four, three, &c., days, or a year and one, two, or three days. And yet injustice is done at once if there is one lash too many, or one dollar or one cent, one week in prison or one day, too many or too few.

Reason itself requires us to recognize that contingency, contradiction, and show have a sphere and a right of their own, restricted though it be, and it is irrational to strive to resolve and rectify contradictions within that sphere. Here the only interest present is that something be actually done, that the matter be settled and decided somehow, no matter how (within a certain limit). This decision pertains to abstract subjectivity, to formal self-certainty, which may decide either by simply holding to its power (within that limit) of settling the matter by merely terminating deliberation and thereby dismissing it out of hand, or else by adopting some reason for decision such as keeping to round numbers or always adopting, say thirty-nine.

It is true that the law does not settle these ultimate decisions required by actual life; it leaves them instead to the judge's discretion, merely limiting him by a maximum and minimum. But this does not affect the point at issue, because the maximum and minimum are themselves in every instance only round numbers once more. To fix them, therefore, does not exempt the judge from making a finite, purely positive, decision, since on the contrary such a decision is still left to him by the necessities of the case.

(b) Law determinately existent

215. If laws are to have a binding force, it follows that, in view of the right of self-consciousness (see Paragraph 132 and the Remark thereto) they must be made universally known.

To hang the laws so high that no citizen could read them (as Dionysius the Tyrant did) is injustice of one and the same kind as to bury them in row upon row of learned tomes, collections of dissenting judgements and opinions, records of customs, &c., and in a dead language—too, so that knowledge of the law of the land is accessible only to those who

have made it their professional study. Rulers who have given a national law to their peoples in the form of a well-arranged and clear-cut legal code—or even a mere formless collection of laws, like Justinian's—have been the greatest benefactors of their peoples and
have received thanks and praise for their beneficence. But the truth is that their work was
at the same time a great act of justice.

216. For a public legal code, simple general laws are required, and yet the nature of the
finite material to which law is applied leads to the further determining of general laws *ad
infinitum*. On the one hand, the law ought to be a comprehensive whole, closed and complete; and yet, on the other hand, the need for further determinations is continual. But
since this antinomy arises only when universal principles, which remain fixed and
unchanged, are applied to particular types of case, the right to a complete legal code
remains unimpaired, like the right that these simple general principles should be capable
of being laid down and understood apart and in distinction from their application to such
particular types.

A fruitful source of complexity in legislation is the gradual intrusion of reason, of what
is inherently and actually right, into primitive institutions which have something wrong
at their roots and so are purely historical survivals. This occurred in Roman law, as was
remarked above (see Remark to Paragraph 180), in medieval feudal law, &c. It is essential
to notice, however, that the very nature of the finite material to which law is applied necessarily entails an infinite progress in the application to it of principles universal in themselves and inherently and actually rational.

It is misunderstanding which has given rise alike to the demand—a morbid craving of
German scholars chiefly—that a legal code should be something absolutely complete,
incapable of any fresh determination in detail, and also to the argument that because a
code is incapable of such completion, therefore we ought not to produce something
'incomplete', i.e. we ought not to produce a code at all. The misunderstanding rests in
both cases on a misconception of the nature of a finite subject-matter like private law,
whose so-called 'completeness' is a perennial approximation to completeness, on a misconception of the difference between the universal of reason and the universal of the
Understanding, and also on the application of the latter to the material of finitude and
atomicity which goes on for ever.—*Le plus grand ennemi du Bien, c'est le Meilleur* is the
utterance of true common sense against the common sense of idle argumentation and
abstract reflection.

217. The principle of rightness passes over in civil society into law. My individual right,
whose embodiment has hitherto been immediate and abstract, now similarly becomes
embodied in the existent will and knowledge of everyone, in the sense that it becomes recognized. Hence property acquisitions and transfers must now be undertaken and concluded
only in the form which that embodiment gives to them. In civil society, property rests on
contract and on the formalities which make ownership capable of proof and valid in law.

Original, i.e., direct, titles and means of acquisition (see Paragraphs 54 ff.) are simply
discarded in civil society and appear only as isolated accidents or as subordinated factors
of property transactions. It is either feeling, refusing to move beyond the subjective, or
reflection, clinging to its abstract essences, which casts formalities aside, while the dry-as-
dust Understanding may for its part cling to formalities instead of the real thing and multiply them indefinitely.

Apart from this, however, the march of mental development is the long and hard
struggle to free a content from its sensuous and immediate form, endow it with its appro-

priate form of thought, and thereby give it simple and adequate expression. It is because this is the case that when the development of law is just beginning, ceremonies and formalities are more circumstantial and count rather as the thing itself than as its symbol. Thus even in Roman law, a number of forms and especially phrases were retained from old-fashioned ceremonial usages, instead of being replaced by intelligible forms and phrases adequately expressing them.

218. Since property and personality have legal recognition and validity in civil society, wrongdoing now becomes an infringement, not merely of what is subjectively infinite, but of the universal thing which is existent with inherent stability and strength. Hence a new attitude arises: the action is seen as a danger to society and thereby the magnitude of the wrongdoing is increased. On the other hand, however, the fact that society has become strong and sure of itself diminishes the external importance of the injury and so leads to a mitigation of its punishment.

The fact that an injury to one member of society is an injury to all others does not alter the conception of wrongdoing, but it does alter it in respect of its outward existence as an injury done, an injury which now affects the mind and consciousness of civil society as a whole, not merely the external embodiment of the person directly injured. In heroic times, as we see in the tragedy of the ancients, the citizens did not feel themselves injured by wrongs which members of the royal houses did to one another.

Implicitly, crime is an infinite injury; but as an existent fact it must be measured in quantity and quality (see Paragraph 96), and since its field of existence here has the essential character of affecting an idea and consciousness of the validity of the laws, its danger to civil society is a determinant of the magnitude of a crime, or even *one* of its qualitative characteristics.

Now this quality or magnitude varies with the state of civil society; and this is the justification for sometimes attaching the penalty of death to a theft of a few pence or a turnip, and at other times a light penalty to a theft of a hundred or more times that amount. If we consider its danger to society, this seems at first sight to aggravate the crime; but in fact it is just this which has been the prime cause of the mitigation of its punishment. A penal code, then, is primarily the child of its age and the state of civil society at the time.

(c) The Court of Justice

219. By taking the form of law, right steps into a determinate mode of being. It is then something on its own account, and in contrast with particular willing and opining of the right, it is self-subsistent and has to vindicate itself as something universal. This is achieved by recognizing it and making it actual in a particular case without the subjective feeling of private interest; and this is the business of a public authority—the court of justice.

The historical origin of the judge and his court may have had the form of a patriarch's gift to his people or of force or free choice; but this makes no difference to the concept of the thing. To regard the introduction of a legal system as no more than an optional act of grace or favour on the part of monarchs and governments (as Herr von Haller does in his *Restauration der Staatswissenschaft*) is a piece of the mere thoughtlessness which has no inkling of the point at issue in a discussion of law and the state. The point is that legal and political institutions are rational in principle and therefore absolutely necessary, and the question of the form in which they arose or were introduced is entirely irrelevant to a consideration of their rational basis.

At the other extreme from Herr von Haller's point of view is the barbarous notion that the administration of justice is now, as it was in the days when might was right, an improper exercise of force, a suppression of freedom, and a despotism. The administration of justice must be regarded as the fulfilment of a duty by the public authority, no less than as the exercise of a right; and so far as it is a right, it does not depend upon an optional delegation to one authority by the individual members of society.

220. When the right against crime has the form of revenge (see Paragraph 102), it is only right implicit, not right in the form of right, i.e. no *act* of revenge is justified. Instead of the injured party, the injured *universal* now comes on the scene, and this has its proper actuality in the court of law. It takes over the pursuit and the avenging of crime, and this pursuit consequently ceases to be the subjective and contingent retribution of revenge and is transformed into the genuine reconciliation of right with itself, i.e. into punishment. Objectively, this is the reconciliation of the law with itself; by the annulment of the crime, the law is restored and its authority is thereby actualized. Subjectively, it is the reconciliation of the criminal with himself, i.e. with the law known by him as his own and as valid for him and his protection; when this law is executed upon him, he himself finds in this process the satisfaction of justice and nothing save his own act.

221. A member of civil society has the right in *judicio stare* and, correspondingly, the duty of acknowledging the jurisdiction of the court and accepting its decision as final when his own rights are in dispute.

222. In court the specific character which rightness acquires is that it must be demonstrable. When parties go to law, they are put in the position of having to make good their evidence and their claims and to make the judge acquainted with the facts. These steps in a legal process are themselves rights, and their course must therefore be fixed by law. They also constitute an essential part of jurisprudence.

223. These steps in a legal process are subdivided continually within no fixed limits into more and more actions, each being distinct in itself and a right. Hence a legal process, in itself in any case a means, now begins to be something external to its end and contrasted with it. This long course of formalities is a right of the parties at law and they have the right to traverse it from beginning to end. Still, it may be turned into an evil, and even an instrument of wrong, and for this reason it is by law made the duty of the parties to submit themselves to the simple process of arbitration (before a tribunal of arbitrators) and to the attempt to reconcile their differences out of court, in order that they—and right itself, as the substance of the thing and so the thing really at issue—may be protected against legal processes and their misuse.

Equity involves a departure from formal rights owing to moral or other considerations and is concerned primarily with the content of the lawsuit. A court of equity, however, comes to mean a court which decides in a single case without insisting on the formalities of a legal process or, in particular, on the objective evidence which the letter of the law may require. Further, it decides on the merits of the single case as a unique one, not with a view to disposing of it in such a way as to create a binding legal precedent for the future.

224. Amongst the rights of the subjective consciousness are not only the publication of the laws (see Paragraph 215) but also the possibility of ascertaining the actualization of the law in a particular case (the course of the proceedings, the legal argument, &c.)—i.e. the publicity of judicial proceedings. The reason for this is that a trial is implicitly an event of universal validity, and although the particular content of the action affects the interests of the parties alone, its universal content, i.e. the right at issue and the judgement thereon, affects the interests of everybody.

If the members of the bench deliberate amongst themselves about the judgement which they are to deliver, such deliberations express opinions and views still personal and so naturally are not public.

225. By the judgment of the court, the law is applied to a single case, and the work of judgement has two distinct aspects: first, ascertainment of the nature of the case as a unique, single, occurrence (e.g. whether a contract, &c., &c., has been made, whether a trespass has been committed, and if so by whom) and, in criminal cases, reflection to determine the essential, criminal, character of the deed (see Remark to Paragraph 119); secondly, the subsumption of the case under the law that right must be restored. Punishment in criminal cases is a conception falling under this law. Decisions on these two different aspects are given by different functionaries.

In the Roman judicial system, this distinction of functions appeared in that the Praetor pronounced judgement on the assumption that the facts were so and so, and then appointed a special *judex* to inquire into the facts.

In English law, it is left to the insight or option of the prosecutor to determine the precise character of a criminal act (e.g., whether it is murder or manslaughter) and the court is powerless to alter the indictment if it finds the prosecutor's choice wrong.

226. First, the conduct of the entire process of inquiry, secondly, the detailed stages of the action between the parties (these stages themselves being rights—see Paragraph 222), and then also the second of the aspects of the work of judgement mentioned in the previous Paragraph, are all a task which properly belongs to the judge at law. He is the organ of the law, and the case must be prepared for him in such a way as to make possible its subsumption under some principle; that is to say, it must be stripped of its apparent, empirical, character and exalted into a recognized fact of a general type.

227. The first aspect of the work of judgment, i.e. the knowledge of the facts of the case as a unique, single, occurrence, and the description of its general character, involves in itself no pronouncement on points of law. This is knowledge attainable by any educated man. In settling the character of an action, the subjective moment, i.e., the agent's insight and intention (see the Second Part), is the essential thing; and apart from this, the proof depends not on objects of reason or abstractions of the Understanding, but only on single details and circumstances, objects of sensuous intuition and subjective certainty, and therefore does not contain in itself any absolute, objective, probative factor. It follows that judgement on the facts lies in the last resort with subjective conviction and conscience (*animi sententia*), while the proof, resting as it does on the statements and affidavits of others, receives its final though purely subjective verification from the oath.

In this matter it is of the first importance to fix our eyes on the type of proof here in question and to distinguish it from knowledge and proof of another sort. To establish by proof a rational category, like the concept of right itself, means to apprehend its necessity, and so demands a method other than that requisite for the proof of a geometrical theorem. Further, in this latter case, the figure is determined by the Understanding and made abstract in advance according to a rule. But in the case of something empirical in content, like a fact, the material of knowledge is a given sensuous intuition and subjective sense-certainty, and statements and affidavits about such material. It is then a question of drawing conclusions and putting two and two together out of depositions of that kind, attestations and other details, &c. The objective truth which emerges from material of this kind and the method appropriate to it leads, when attempts are made to determine it rigidly and objectively, to half-proofs and then, by further sincere deductions from these—deductions which at the same time involve formal illogicality—to extraordinary punishments. But such objective truth means something quite different from the truth of a rational category or a proposition whose content the Understanding has determined for itself abstractly in advance. To show that, since the strictly legal character of a court covers competence to ascertain this sort of truth about empirical events, it thereby properly qualifies a court for this task and so gives it an inherent exclusive right to perform it and lays on it the necessity of performing it—that is the best approach to settling the question of how far decisions on points of fact, as well as on points of law, should be ascribed to courts as strictly juristic bodies.

228. When judgement is pronounced—so far as the function of judgement is the subsumption under the law of the case whose nature has been settled—the right due to the parties on the score of their self-consciousness is preserved in relation to the *law* because the law is known and so is the law of the parties themselves, and in relation to the *subsumption*, because the trial is public. But when a verdict is given on the particular, subjective, and external facts of the case (knowledge of which falls under the first of the aspects described in Paragraph 225), this right is satisfied by the confidence which the parties feel in the subjectivity of those who give the verdict. This confidence is based primarily on the similarity between them and the parties in respect of their particularity, i.e. their social position, &c.

The right of self-consciousness, the moment of subjective freedom, may be regarded as the fundamental thing to keep before us in considering the necessity for publicity in legal proceedings and for the so-called jury-courts, and this in the last resort is the essence of whatever may be advanced in favour of these institutions on the score of their utility. Other points of view and reasoning about their several advantages and disadvantages may give rise to an argumentative exchange, but reasoning of this kind, like all deductive reasoning, is either secondary and inconclusive, or else drawn from other and perhaps higher spheres than that of advantage. It may be the case that if the administration of justice were entirely in the hands of professional lawyers, and there were no lay institutions like juries, it would in theory be managed just as well, if not better. It may be so, but even if this possibility rises by general consent to probability, or even certainty, it still does not matter, for on the other side there is always the right of self-consciousness, insisting on its claims and dissatisfied if laymen play no part.

Owing to the character of the entire body of the laws, knowledge both of what is right and also of the course of legal proceedings may become, together with the capacity to prosecute an action at law, the property of a class which makes itself an exclusive clique by the use of a terminology like a foreign tongue to those whose rights are at issue. If this happens, the members of civil society, who depend for their livelihood on their industry, on their own knowledge and will, are kept strangers to the law, not only to those parts of it affecting their most personal and intimate affairs, but also to its substantive and rational basis, the right itself, and the result is that they become the wards, or even in a sense the bondsmen, of the legal profession. They may indeed have the right to appear in court in person and to 'stand' there (*in judicio stare*), but their bodily presence is a trifle if their minds are not to be there also, if they are not to follow the proceedings with their own knowledge, and if the justice they receive remains in their eyes a doom pronounced *ab extra*.

229. In civil society, the Idea is lost in particularity and has fallen asunder with the separation of inward and outward. In the administration of justice, however, civil society returns to its concept, to the unity of the implicit universal with the subjective particular, although here the latter is only that present in single cases and the universality in question is that of *abstract* right. The actualization of this unity through its extension to the whole ambit of particularity is (i) the specific function of the Police, though the unification which it effects is only relative; (ii) it is the Corporation which actualizes the unity completely, though only in a whole which, while concrete, is restricted.

C. *The Police and the Corporation*

230. In the system of needs, the livelihood and welfare of every single person is a possibility whose actual attainment is just as much conditioned by his caprices and particular endowment as by the objective system of needs. Through the administration of justice, offences against property or personality are annulled. But the right actually present in the particular requires, first, that accidental hindrances to one aim or another be removed, and undisturbed safety of person and property be attained; and secondly, that the securing of every single person's livelihood and welfare be treated and actualized as a right, i.e. that particular welfare as such be so treated.

(a) Police {or the public authority}

231. Inasmuch as it is still the particular will which governs the choice of this or that end, the universal authority by which security is ensured remains in the first instance, (*a*) restricted to the sphere of contingencies, and (*b*) an external organization.

232. Crime is contingency as subjective willing of evil, and this is what the universal authority must prevent or bring to justice. But, crime apart, the subjective willing which is permissible in actions lawful *per se* and in the private use of property, also comes into external relation with other single persons, as well as with public institutions, other than law-courts, established for realizing a common end. This universal aspect makes private actions a matter of contingency which escapes the agent's control and which either does or may injure others and wrong them.

233. There is here only a possibility of injury; but the actual non-occurrence of injury is at this stage not just another contingency. The point is that the actions of individuals may always be wrongful, and this is the ultimate reason for police control and penal justice.

234. The relations between external existents fall into the infinite of the Understanding; there is, therefore, no inherent line of distinction between what is and what is not injurious, even where crime is concerned, or between what is and what is not suspicious, or between what is to be forbidden or subjected to supervision and what is to be exempt from prohibition, from surveillance and suspicion, from inquiry and the demand to render an account of itself. These details are determined by custom, the spirit of the rest of the constitution, contemporary conditions, the crisis of the hour, and so forth.

235. In the indefinite multiplication and interconnexion of day-to-day needs, (*a*) the acquisition and exchange of the means to their satisfaction—a satisfaction which everyone confidently expects to be possible of attainment without hindrance, and (*b*) the endeavours made and the transactions carried out in order to shorten the process of attainment as much as possible, give rise to factors which are a common interest, and when one man

occupies himself with these his work is at the same time done for all. The situation is productive too of contrivances and organizations which may be of use to the community as a
whole. These universal activities and organizations of general utility call for the oversight
and care of the public authority.

236. The differing interests of producers and consumers may come into collision with
each other; and although a fair balance between them on the whole may be brought about
automatically, still their adjustment also requires a control which stands above both and
is consciously undertaken. The right to the exercise of such control in a single case (e.g.
in the fixing of the prices of the commonest necessaries of life) depends on the fact that,
by being publicly exposed for sale, goods in absolutely universal daily demand are offered
not so much to an individual as such but rather to a universal purchaser, the public; and
thus both the defence of the public's right not to be defrauded, and also the management
of goods inspection, may lie, as a common concern, with a public authority. But public
care and direction are most of all necessary in the case of the larger branches of industry,
because these are dependent on conditions abroad and on combinations of distant circumstances which cannot be grasped as a whole by the individuals tied to these industries
for their living.

   At the other extreme to freedom of trade and commerce in civil society is public organization to provide for everything and determine everyone's labour—take for example in
ancient times the labour on the pyramids and the other huge monuments in Egypt and
Asia which were constructed for public ends, and the worker's task was not mediated
through his private choice and particular interest. This interest invokes freedom of trade
and commerce against control from above; but the more blindly it sinks into self-seeking
aims, the more it requires such control to bring it back to the universal. Control is also
necessary to diminish the danger of upheavals arising from clashing interests and to
abbreviate the period in which their tension should be eased through the working of a
necessity of which they themselves know nothing.

237. Now while the possibility of sharing in the general wealth is open to individuals and
is assured to them by the public authority, still it is subject to contingencies on the subjective side (quite apart from the fact that this assurance must remain incomplete), and
the more it presupposes skill, health, capital, and so forth as its conditions, the more is it
so subject.

238. Originally the family is the substantive whole whose function it is to provide for the
individual on his particular side by giving him either the means and the skill necessary to
enable him to earn his living out of the resources of society, or else subsistence and maintenance in the event of his suffering a disability. But civil society tears the individual from
his family ties, estranges the members of the family from one another, and recognizes
them as self-subsistent persons. Further, for the paternal soil and the external inorganic
resources of nature from which the individual formerly derived his livelihood, it substitutes its own soil and subjects the permanent existence of even the entire family to dependence on itself and to contingency. Thus the individual becomes a son of civil society
which has as many claims upon him as he has rights against it.

239. In its character as a universal family, civil society has the right and duty of superintending and influencing education, inasmuch as education bears upon the child's capacity
to become a member of society. Society's right here is paramount over the arbitrary and
contingent preferences of parents, particularly in cases where education is to be completed

not by the parents but by others. To the same end, society must provide public educational facilities so far as is practicable.

240. Similarly, society has the right and duty of acting as trustee to those whose extravagance destroys the security of their own subsistence or their families'. It must substitute for extravagance the pursuit of the ends of society and the individuals concerned.

241. Not only caprice, however, but also contingencies, physical conditions, and factors grounded in external circumstances (see Paragraph 200) may reduce men to poverty. The poor still have the needs common to civil society, and yet since society has withdrawn from them the natural means of acquisition (see Paragraph 217) and broken the bond of the family—in the wider sense of the clan (see Paragraph 181)—their poverty leaves them more or less deprived of all the advantages of society, of the opportunity of acquiring skill or education of any kind, as well as of the administration of justice, the public health services, and often even of the consolations of religion, and so forth. The public authority takes the place of the family where the poor are concerned in respect not only of their immediate want but also of laziness of disposition, malignity, and the other vices which arise out of their plight and their sense of wrong.

242. Poverty and, in general, the distress of every kind to which every individual is exposed from the start in the cycle of his natural life has a subjective side which demands similarly subjective aid, arising both from the special circumstances of a particular case and also from love and sympathy. This is the place where morality finds plenty to do despite all public organization. Subjective aid, however, both in itself and in its operation, is dependent on contingency and consequently society struggles to make it less necessary, by discovering the general causes of penury and general means of its relief, and by organizing relief accordingly.

Casual almsgiving and casual endowments, e.g., for the burning of lamps before holy images, &c., are supplemented by public almshouses, hospitals, street-lighting, and so forth. There is still quite enough left over and above these things for charity to do on its own account. A false view is implied both when charity insists on having this poor relief reserved solely to private sympathy and the accidental occurrence of knowledge and a charitable disposition, and also when it feels injured or mortified by universal regulations and ordinances which are *obligatory*. Public social conditions are on the contrary to be regarded as all the more perfect the less (in comparison with what is arranged publicly) is left for an individual to do by himself as his private inclination directs.

243. When civil society is in a state of unimpeded activity, it is engaged in expanding internally in population and industry. The amassing of wealth is intensified by generalizing (*a*) the linkage of men by their needs, and (*b*) the methods of preparing and distributing the means to satisfy these needs, because it is from this double process of generalization that the largest profits are derived. That is one side of the picture. The other side is the subdivision and restriction of particular jobs. This results in the dependence and distress of the class tied to work of that sort, and these again entail inability to feel and enjoy the broader freedoms and especially the intellectual benefits of civil society.

244. When the standard of living of a large mass of people falls below a certain subsistence level—a level regulated automatically as the one necessary for a member of the society—and when there is a consequent loss of the sense of right and wrong, of honesty and the self-respect which makes a man insist on maintaining himself by his own work and effort,

the result is the creation of a rabble of paupers. At the same time this brings with it, at the other end of the social scale, conditions which greatly facilitate the concentration of disproportionate wealth in a few hands.

245. When the masses begin to decline into poverty, (a) the burden of maintaining them at their ordinary standard of living might be directly laid on the wealthier classes, or they might receive the means of livelihood directly from other public sources of wealth (e.g., from the endowments of rich hospitals, monasteries, and other foundations). In either case, however, the needy would receive subsistence directly, not by means of their work, and this would violate the principle of civil society and the feeling of individual independence and self-respect in its individual members. (b) As an alternative, they might be given subsistence indirectly through being given work, i.e., the opportunity to work. In this event the volume of production would be increased, but the evil consists precisely in an excess of production and in the lack of a proportionate number of consumers who are themselves also producers, and thus it is simply intensified by both of the methods (a) and (b) by which it is sought to alleviate it. It hence becomes apparent that despite an excess of wealth civil society is not rich enough, i.e. its own resources are insufficient to check excessive poverty and the creation of a penurious rabble.

   In the example of England we may study these phenomena on a large scale and also in particular the results of poor-rates, immense foundations, unlimited private beneficence, and above all the abolition of the Guild Corporations. In Britain, particularly in Scotland, the most direct measure against poverty and especially against the loss of shame and self-respect—the subjective bases of society—as well as against laziness and extravagance, &c., the begetters of the rabble, has turned out to be to leave the poor to their fate and instruct them to beg in the streets.

246. This inner dialectic of civil society thus drives it—or at any rate drives a specific civil society—to push beyond its own limits and seek markets, and so its necessary means of subsistence, in other lands which are either deficient in the goods it has overproduced, or else generally backward in industry, &c.

247. The principle of family life is dependence on the soil, on land, *terra firma*. Similarly, the natural element for industry, animating its outward movement, is the sea. Since the passion for gain involves risk, industry though bent on gain yet lifts itself above it; instead of remaining rooted to the soil and the limited circle of civil life with its pleasures and desires, it embraces the element of flux, danger, and destruction. Further, the sea is the greatest means of communication, and trade by sea creates commercial connexions between distant countries and so relations involving contractual rights. At the same time, commerce of this kind is the most potent instrument of culture, and through it trade acquires its significance in the history of the world.

   Rivers are not natural boundaries of separation, which is what they have been accounted to be in modern times. On the contrary, it is truer to say that they, and the sea likewise, link men together. Horace is wrong when he says:

>   *deus abscidit*
> *prudens Oceano dissociabili*
> *terras.*

The proof of this lies not merely in the fact that the basins of rivers are inhabited by a single clan or tribe, but also, for example, in the ancient bonds between Greece, Ionia, and Magna Graecia, between Brittany and Britain, between Denmark and Norway, Sweden, Finland, Livonia, &c., bonds, further, which are especially striking in contrast with the comparatively slight intercourse between the inhabitants of the littoral and those of the hinterland. To realize what an instrument of culture lies in the link with the sea, consider countries where industry flourishes and contrast their relation to the sea with that of countries which have eschewed sea-faring and which, like Egypt and India, have become stagnant and sunk in the most frightful and scandalous superstition. Notice also how all great progressive peoples press onward to the sea.

248. This far-flung connecting link affords the means for the colonizing activity—sporadic or systematic—to which the mature civil society is driven and by which it supplies to a part of its population a return to life on the family basis in a new land and so also supplies itself with a new demand and field for its industry.

249. While the public authority must also undertake the higher directive function of providing for the interests which lead beyond the borders of its society (see Paragraph 246), its primary purpose is to actualize and maintain the universal contained within the particularity of civil society, and its control takes the form of an external system and organization for the protection and security of particular ends and interests *en masse,* inasmuch as these interests subsist only in this universal. This universal is immanent in the interests of particularity itself and, in accordance with the Idea, particularity makes it the end and object of its own willing and activity. In this way ethical principles circle back and appear in civil society as a factor immanent in it; this constitutes the specific character of the Corporation.

(b) The Corporation

250. In virtue of the substantiality of its natural and family life, the agricultural class has directly within itself the concrete universal in which it lives. The class of civil servants is universal in character and so has the universal explicitly as its ground and as the aim of its activity. The class between them, the business class, is essentially concentrated on the particular, and hence it is to it that Corporations are specially appropriate.

251. The labour organization of civil society is split, in accordance with the nature of its particulars, into different branches. The implicit likeness of such particulars to one another becomes really existent in an association, as something common to its members. Hence a selfish purpose, directed towards its particular self-interest, apprehends and evinces itself at the same time as universal; and a member of civil society is in virtue of his own particular skill a member of a Corporation, whose universal purpose is thus wholly concrete and no wider in scope than the purpose involved in business, its proper task and interest.

252. In accordance with this definition of its functions, a Corporation has the right, under the surveillance of the public authority, (*a*) to look after its own interests within its own sphere, (*b*) to co-opt members, qualified objectively by the requisite skill and rectitude, to a number fixed by the general structure of society, (*c*) to protect its members against particular contingencies, (*d*) to provide the education requisite to fit others to become members. In short, its right is to come on the scene like a second family for its members, while civil society can only be an indeterminate sort of family because it comprises everyone and so is farther removed from individuals and their special exigencies.

The Corporation member is to be distinguished from a day labourer or from a man who is prepared to undertake casual employment on a single occasion. The former who is, or will become, master of his craft, is a member of the association not for casual gain on single occasions but for the whole range, the universality, of his personal livelihood.

Privileges, in the sense of the rights of a branch of civil society organized into a Corporation, are distinct in meaning from privileges proper in the etymological sense. The latter are casual exceptions to universal rules; the former, however, are only the crystallization, as regulations, of characteristics inherent in an essential branch of society itself owing to its nature as particular.

253. In the Corporation, the family has its stable basis in the sense that its livelihood is assumed there, conditionally upon capability, i.e., it has a stable capital (see Paragraph 170). In addition, this nexus of capability and livelihood is a *recognized* fact, with the result that the Corporation member needs no external marks beyond his own membership as evidence of his skill and his regular income and subsistence, i.e. as evidence that he is a somebody. It is also recognized that he belongs to a whole which is itself an organ of the entire society, and that he is actively concerned in promoting the comparatively disinterested end of this whole. Thus he commands the respect due to one in his social position.

The institution of Corporations corresponds, on account of its assurance of capital, to the introduction of agriculture and private property in another sphere (see Remark to Paragraph 203).

When complaints are made about the luxury of the business classes and their passion for extravagance—which have as their concomitant the creation of a rabble of paupers (see Paragraph 244)—we must not forget that besides its other causes (e.g., increasing mechanization of labour) this phenomenon has an ethical ground, as was indicated above. Unless he is a member of an authorized Corporation (and it is only by being authorized that an association becomes a Corporation), an individual is without rank or dignity, his isolation reduces his business to mere self-seeking, and his livelihood and satisfaction become insecure. Consequently, he has to try to gain recognition for himself by giving external proofs of success in his business, and to these proofs no limits can be set. He cannot live in the manner of his class, for no class really exists for him, since in civil society it is only something common to particular persons which really exists, i.e. something legally constituted and recognized. Hence he cannot achieve for himself a way of life proper to his class and less idiosyncratic.

Within the Corporation the help which poverty receives loses its accidental character and the humiliation wrongfully associated with it. The wealthy perform their duties to their fellow associates and thus riches cease to inspire either pride or envy, pride in their owners, envy in others. In these conditions rectitude obtains its proper recognition and respect.

254. The so-called 'natural' right of exercising one's skill and thereby earning what there is to be earned is restricted within the Corporation only in so far as it is therein made rational instead of natural. That is to say, it becomes freed from personal opinion and contingency, saved from endangering either the individual workman or others, recognized, guaranteed, and at the same time elevated to conscious effort for a common end.

255. As the family was the first, so the Corporation is the second ethical root of the state, the one planted in civil society. The former contains the moments of subjective particularity and objective universality in a substantial unity. But these moments are sundered in civil society to begin with; on the one side there is the particularity of need and satisfaction, reflected into itself, and on the other side the universality of abstract rights. In the Corporation these moments are united in an inward fashion, so that in this union particular welfare is present as a right and is actualized.

The sanctity of marriage and the dignity of Corporation membership are the two fixed points round which the unorganized atoms of civil society revolve.

256. The end of the Corporation is restricted and finite, while the public authority was an external organization involving a separation and a merely relative identity of controller and controlled. The end of the former and the externality and relative identity of the latter find their truth in the absolutely universal end and its absolute actuality. Hence the sphere of civil society passes over into the state.

The town is the seat of the civil life of business. There reflection arises, turns in upon itself, and pursues its atomizing task; each man maintains himself in and through his relation to others who, like himself, are persons possessed of rights. The country, on the other hand, is the seat of an ethical life resting on nature and the family. Town and country thus constitute the two moments, still ideal moments, whose true ground is the state, although it is from them that the state springs.

The philosophic proof of the concept of the state is this development of ethical life from its immediate phase through civil society, the phase of division, to the state, which then reveals itself as the true ground of these phases. A proof in philosophic science can only be a development of this kind.

Since the state appears as a result in the advance of the philosophic concept through displaying itself as the true ground [of the earlier phases], that show of mediation is now cancelled and the state has become directly present before us. Actually, therefore, the state as such is not so much the result as the beginning. It is within the state that the family is first developed into civil society, and it is the Idea of the state itself which disrupts itself into these two moments. Through the development of civil society, the substance of ethical life acquires its infinite form, which contains in itself these two moments: (1) infinite differentiation down to the inward experience of independent self-consciousness, and (2) the form of universality involved in education, the form of thought whereby mind is objective and actual to itself as an organic totality in laws and institutions which are its will in terms of thought.

SUB-SECTION 3

The State

257. The state is the actuality of the ethical Idea. It is ethical mind *qua* the substantial will manifest and revealed to itself, knowing and thinking itself, accomplishing what it knows and in so far as it knows it. The state exists immediately in custom, mediately in individual self-consciousness, knowledge, and activity, while self-consciousness in virtue of its sentiment towards the state finds in the state, as its essence and the end and product of its activity, its substantive freedom.

The *Penates* are inward gods, gods of the underworld; the mind of a nation (Athene for instance) is the divine, knowing and willing itself. Family piety is feeling, ethical behaviour directed by feeling; political virtue is the willing of the absolute end in terms of thought.

258. The state is absolutely rational inasmuch as it is the actuality of the substantial will which it possesses in the particular self-consciousness once that consciousness has been raised to consciousness of its universality. This substantial unity is an absolute unmoved end in itself, in which freedom comes into its supreme right. On the other hand this final end has supreme right against the individual, whose supreme duty is to be a member of the state.

If the state is confused with civil society, and if its specific end is laid down as the security and protection of property and personal freedom, then the interest of the individuals as such becomes the ultimate end of their association, and it follows that membership of the state is something optional. But the state's relation to the individual is quite different from this. Since the state is mind objectified, it is only as one of its members that the individual himself has objectivity, genuine individuality, and an ethical life. Unification pure and simple is the true content and aim of the individual, and the individual's destiny is the living of a universal life. His further particular satisfaction, activity, and mode of conduct have this substantive and universally valid life as their starting point and their result.

Rationality, taken generally and in the abstract, consists in the thorough-going unity of the universal and the single. Rationality, concrete in the state, consists (*a*) so far as its content is concerned, in the unity of objective freedom (i.e. freedom of the universal or substantial will) and subjective freedom (i.e. freedom of everyone in his knowing and in his volition of particular ends); and consequently, (*b*) so far as its form is concerned, in self-determining action on laws and principles which are thoughts and so universal. This Idea is the absolutely eternal and necessary being of mind.

But if we ask what is or has been the historical origin of the state in general, still more if we ask about the origin of any particular state, of its rights and institutions, or again if we inquire whether the state originally arose out of patriarchal conditions or out of fear or trust, or out of Corporations, &c., or finally if we ask in what light the basis of the state's rights has been conceived and consciously established, whether this basis has been supposed to be positive divine right, or contract, custom, &c.—all these questions are no concern of the Idea of the state. We are here dealing exclusively with the philosophic science of the state, and from that point of view all these things are mere appearance and therefore matters for history. So far as the authority of any existing state has anything to do with reasons, these reasons are culled from the forms of the law authoritative within it.

The philosophical treatment of these topics is concerned only with their inward side, with the thought of their concept. The merit of Rousseau's contribution to the search for this concept is that, by adducing the will as the principle of the state, he is adducing a principle which has thought both for its form and its content, a principle indeed which is thinking itself, not a principle, like gregarious instinct, for instance, or divine authority, which has thought as its form only. Unfortunately, however, as Fichte did later, he takes the will only in a determinate form as the individual will, and he regards the universal will not as the absolutely rational element in the will, but only as a 'general' will which proceeds out of this individual will as out of a conscious will. The result is that he reduces the union of individuals in the state to a contract and therefore to something based on their arbitrary wills, their opinion, and their capriciously given express consent; and abstract reasoning proceeds to draw the logical inferences which destroy the absolutely divine principle of the state, together with its majesty and absolute authority. For this reason, when these abstract conclusions came into power, they afforded for the first time in human history the prodigious spectacle of the overthrow of the constitution of a great actual state and its complete reconstruction *ab initio* on the basis of pure thought alone, after the destruction of all existing and given material. The will of its re-founders was to give it what they alleged was a purely rational basis, but it was only abstractions that were being used; the Idea was lacking; and the experiment ended in the maximum of frightfulness and terror.

Confronted with the claims made for the individual will, we must remember the fundamental conception that the objective will is rationality implicit or in conception, whether it be recognized or not by individuals, whether their whims be deliberately for it or not. We must remember that its opposite, i.e. knowing and willing, or subjective freedom (the *only* thing contained in the principle of the individual will) comprises only one moment, and therefore a one-sided moment, of the Idea of the rational will, i.e. of the will which is rational solely because what it is implicitly, that it also is explicitly.

The opposite to thinking of the state as something to be known and apprehended as explicitly rational is taking external appearances—i.e. contingencies such as distress, need for protection, force, riches, &c.—not as moments in the state's historical development, but as its substance. Here again what constitutes the guiding thread of discovery is the individual in isolation—not, however, even so much as the *thought* of this individuality, but instead only empirical individuals, with attention focused on their accidental characteristics, their strength and weakness, riches and poverty, &c. This ingenious idea of ignoring the absolute infinity and rationality in the state and excluding thought from apprehension of its inward nature has assuredly never been put forward in such an unadulterated form as in Herr von Haller's *Restauration der Staatswissenschaft*. I say 'unadulterated', because in all other attempts to grasp the essence of the state, no matter on what one-sided or superficial principles, this very intention of comprehending the state rationally has brought with it thoughts, i.e. universal determinations. Herr von Haller, however, with his eyes open, has not merely renounced the rational material of which the state consists, as well as the form of thought, but he has even gone on with passionate fervour to inveigh against the form and the material so set aside. Part of what Herr von Haller assures us is the 'wide-spread' effect of his principles, this *Restauration* undoubtedly owes to the fact that, in his exposition, he has deliberately dispensed with thought altogether, and has deliberately kept his whole book all of a piece with its lack of thought. For in this way he has eliminated the confusion and disorder which lessen the force of an exposition where the accidental is treated along with hints of the substantial, where the purely empirical and external are mixed with a reminiscence of the universal and rational, and where in the midst of wretched inanities the reader is now and again reminded of the loftier sphere of the infinite. For the same reason again his exposition is consistent. He takes as the essence of the state, not what is substantive but the sphere of accident, and consistency in dealing with a sphere of that kind amounts to the complete inconsistency of utter thoughtlessness which jogs along without looking behind, and is just as much at home now with the exact opposite of what it approved a moment ago.[5]

259. The Idea of the state

  (a) has immediate actuality and is the individual state as a self-dependent organism—the *Constitution* or *Constitutional Law;*

  (b) passes over into the relation of state to other states—*International Law;*

  (c) is the universal Idea as a genus and as an absolute power over individual states—the mind which gives itself its actuality in the process of *World-History.*

A. Constitutional Law

260. The state is the actuality of concrete freedom. But concrete freedom consists in this, that personal individuality and its particular interests not only achieve their complete development and gain explicit recognition for their right (as they do in the sphere of the family and civil society) but, for one thing, they also pass over of their own accord into the interest of the universal, and, for another thing, they know and will the universal; they even recognize it as their own substantive mind; they take it as their end and aim and are active in its pursuit. The result is that the universal does not prevail or achieve completion except along with particular interests and through the co-operation of particular knowing and willing; and individuals likewise do not live as private persons for their own ends alone, but in the very act of willing these they will the universal in the light of the universal, and their activity is consciously aimed at none but the universal end. The principle of modern states has prodigious strength and depth because it allows the principle of subjectivity to progress to its culmination in the extreme of self-subsistent personal particularity, and yet at the same time brings it back to the substantive unity and so maintains this unity in the principle of subjectivity itself.

261. In contrast with the spheres of private rights and private welfare (the family and civil society), the state is from one point of view an external necessity and their higher authority; its nature is such that their laws and interests are subordinate to it and dependent on it. On the other hand, however, it is the end immanent within them, and its strength lies in the unity of its own universal end and aim with the particular interest of individuals, in the fact that individuals have duties to the state in proportion as they have rights against it (see Paragraph 155).

In the Remark to Paragraph 3 above, reference was made to the fact that it was Montesquieu above all who, in his famous work *L'Esprit des Lois*, kept in sight and tried to work out in detail both the thought of the dependence of laws—in particular, laws concerning the rights of persons—on the specific character of the state, and also the philosophic notion of always treating the part in its relation to the whole.

Duty is primarily a relation to something which from my point of view is substantive, absolutely universal. A right, on the other hand, is simply the embodiment of this substance and thus is the particular aspect of it and enshrines my particular freedom. Hence at abstract levels, right and duty appear parcelled out on different sides or in different persons. In the state, as something ethical, as the inter-penetration of the substantive and the particular, my obligation to what is substantive is at the same time the embodiment of my particular freedom. This means that in the state duty and right are united in one and the same relation. But further, since none the less the distinct moments acquire in the state the shape and reality peculiar to each, and since therefore the distinction between right and duty enters here once again, it follows that while implicitly, i.e. in form, identical, they at the same time differ in content. In the spheres of personal rights and morality, the necessary bearing of right and duty on one another falls short of actualization; and hence there is at that point only an abstract similarity of content between them, i.e. in those abstract spheres, what is one man's right ought also to be another's, and what is one man's duty ought also to be another's. The absolute identity of right and duty in the state is present in these spheres not as a genuine identity but only as a similarity of content, because in them this content is determined as quite general and is simply the fundamental principle of both right and duty, i.e., the principle that men, as persons, are free. Slaves, therefore, have no duties because they have no rights, and vice versa. (Religious duties are not here in point.)

In the course of the inward development of the concrete Idea, however, its moments become distinguished and their specific determinacy becomes at the same time a difference of content. In the family, the content of a son's duties to his father differs from the content of his rights against him; the content of the rights of a member of civil society is not the same as the content of his duties to his prince and government.

This concept of the union of duty and right is a point of vital importance and in it the inner strength of states is contained.

Duty on its abstract side goes no farther than the persistent neglect and proscription of a man's particular interest, on the ground that it is the inessential, even the discreditable, moment in his life. Duty, taken concretely as Idea, reveals the moment of particularity as itself essential and so regards its satisfaction as indisputably necessary. In whatever way an individual may fulfil his duty, he must at the same time find his account therein and attain his personal interest and satisfaction. Out of his position in the state, a right must accrue to him whereby public affairs shall be his own particular affair. Particular interests should in fact not be set aside or completely suppressed; instead, they should be put in correspondence with the universal, and thereby both they and the universal are upheld. The *isolated* individual, so far as his duties are concerned, is in subjection; but as a member of *civil society* he finds in fulfilling his duties to it protection of his person property, regard for his private welfare, the satisfaction of the depths of his being, the consciousness and feeling of himself as a member of the whole; and, in so far as he completely fulfills his duties by performing tasks and services for the *state*, he is upheld and preserved. Take duty abstractly, and the universal's interest would consist simply in the completion as duties of the tasks and services which it exacts.

262. The actual Idea is mind, which, sundering itself into the two ideal spheres of its concept, family and civil society, enters upon its finite phase, but it does so only in order to rise above its ideality and become explicit as infinite actual mind. It is therefore to these ideal spheres that the actual Idea assigns the material of this its finite actuality, viz. human beings as a mass, in such a way that the function assigned to any given individual is visibly mediated by circumstances, his caprice and his personal choice of his station in life (see Paragraph 185 and the Remark thereto).

263. In these spheres in which its moments, particularity and individuality, have their immediate and reflected reality, mind is present as their objective universality glimmering in them as the power of reason in necessity (see Paragraph 184), i.e., the institutions considered above.

264. Mind is the nature of human beings *en masse* and their nature is therefore twofold: (i) at one extreme, explicit individuality of consciousness and will, and (ii) at the other extreme, universality which knows and wills what is substantive. Hence they attain their right in both these respects only in so far as both their private personality and its substantive basis are actualized. Now in the family and civil society they acquire their right in the first of these respects directly and in the second indirectly, in that (i) they find their substantive self-consciousness in social institutions which are the universal implicit in their particular interests, and (ii) the Corporation supplies them with an occupation and an activity directed on a universal end.

265. These institutions are the components of the constitution (i.e. of rationality developed and actualized) in the sphere of particularity. They are, therefore, the firm foundation not only of the state but also of the citizen's trust in it and sentiment towards it. They are the pillars of public freedom since in them particular freedom is realized and rational, and therefore there is *implicitly* present even in them the union of freedom and necessity.

266. But mind is objective and actual to itself not merely as this necessity and as a realm of appearance, but also as the ideality and the heart of this necessity. Only in this way is this substantive universality *aware* of itself as its own object and end, with the result that the necessity appears to itself in the shape of freedom as well.

267. This necessity in ideality is the inner self-development of the Idea. As the substance of the individual subject, it is his political sentiment [patriotism]; in distinction therefrom, as the substance of the objective world, it is the organism of the state, i.e. it is the strictly political state and its constitution.

268. The political sentiment, patriotism pure and simple, is assured conviction with truth as its basis—mere subjective assurance is not the outcome of truth but is only opinion—and a volition which has become habitual. In this sense it is simply a product of the institutions subsisting in the state, since rationality is *actually* present in the state, while action in conformity with these institutions gives rationality its practical proof. This sentiment is, in general, trust (which may pass over into a greater or lesser degree of educated insight), or the consciousness that my interest, both substantive and particular, is contained and preserved in another's (i.e. in the state's) interest and end, i.e. in the other's relation to me as an individual. In this way, this very other is immediately not an other in my eyes, and in being conscious of this fact, I am free.

Patriotism is often understood to mean only a readiness for exceptional sacrifices and actions. Essentially, however, it is the sentiment which, in the relationships of our daily life and under ordinary conditions, habitually recognizes that the community is one's substantive groundwork and end. It is out of this consciousness, which during life's daily round stands the test in all circumstances, that there subsequently also arises the readiness for extraordinary exertions. But since men would often rather be magnanimous than law-abiding, they readily persuade themselves that they possess this exceptional patriotism in order to be sparing in the expression of a genuine patriotic sentiment or to excuse their lack of it. If again this genuine patriotism is looked upon as that which may begin of itself and arise from subjective ideas and thoughts, it is being confused with opinion, because so regarded patriotism is deprived of its true ground, objective reality.

269. The patriotic sentiment acquires its specifically determined content from the various members of the organism of the state. This organism is the development of the Idea to its differences and their objective actuality. Hence these different members are the various powers of the state with their functions and spheres of action, by means of which the universal continually engenders itself, and engenders itself in a necessary way because their specific character is fixed by the nature of the concept. Throughout this process the universal maintains its identity, since it is itself the presupposition of its own production. This organism is the constitution of the state.

270. (1) The abstract actuality or the substantiality of the state consists in the fact that its end is the universal interest as such and the conservation therein of particular interests since the universal interest is the substance of these. (2) But this substantiality of the state is also its *necessity*, since its substantiality is divided into the distinct spheres of its activity which correspond to the moments of its concept, and these spheres, owing to this substantiality, are thus actually fixed determinate characteristics of the state, i.e. its *powers*. (3) But this very substantiality of the state is mind knowing and willing itself after passing through the forming process of education. The state, therefore, knows what it wills and knows it in its universality, i.e., as something thought. Hence it works and acts by reference to consciously adopted ends, known principles, and laws which are not merely implicit but are actually present to consciousness; and further, it acts with precise knowledge of existing conditions and circumstances, inasmuch as its actions have a bearing on these.

This is the place to allude to the relation of the state to religion, because it is often reiterated nowadays that religion is the basis of the state, and because those who make this assertion even have the impertinence to suggest that, once it is made, political science has said its last word. No doctrine is more fitted to produce so much confusion, more fitted indeed to exalt confusion itself to be the constitution of the state and the proper form of knowledge.

In the first place, it may seem suspicious that religion is principally sought and recommended for times of public calamity, disorder, and oppression, and that people are referred to it as a solace in face of wrong or as a hope in compensation for loss. Then further, while the state is mind on earth (*der Geist der in der Welt steht*), religion may sometimes be looked upon as commanding downright indifference to earthly interests, the march of events, and current affairs, and so to turn men's attention to religion does not seem to be the way to exalt the interest and business of the state into the fundamental and serious aim of life. On the contrary, this suggestion seems to assert that politics is wholly a matter of caprice and indifference, either because this way of talking merely amounts to saying that it is only the aims of passion and lawless force, &c., which bear sway in the state, or because this recommendation of religion is supposed to be of self-sufficient validity, and religion is to claim to decide the law and administer it. While it might seem a bitter jest to stifle all animus against tyranny by asserting that the oppressed find their consolation in religion, it still must not be forgotten that religion may take a form leading to the harshest bondage in the fetters of superstition and man's degraded subservience to animals. (The Egyptians and the Hindus, for instance, revere animals as beings higher than themselves.) This phenomenon may at least make it evident that we ought not to speak of religion at all in general terms and that we really need a power to protect us from it in some of its forms and to espouse against them the rights of reason and self-consciousness.

The essence of the relation between religion and the state can be determined, however, only if we recall the concept of religion. The content of religion is absolute truth, and consequently the religious is the most sublime of all dispositions. As intuition, feeling, representative knowledge, its task is concentrated upon God as the unrestricted principle and cause on which everything hangs. It thus involves the demand that everything else shall be seen in this light and depend on it for corroboration, justification, and verification. It is in being thus related to religion that state, laws, and duties all alike acquire for consciousness their supreme confirmation and their supreme obligatoriness, because even the state, laws, and duties are in their actuality something determinate which passes over into a higher sphere and so into that on which it is grounded. It is for this reason that in religion there lies the place where man is always assured of finding a consciousness of the unchangeable, of the highest freedom and satisfaction, even within all the mutability of the world and despite the frustration of his aims and the loss of his interests and possessions.[6] Now if religion is in this way the groundwork which includes the ethical realm in general, and the state's fundamental nature—the divine will—in particular, it is at the same time only a groundwork; and it is at this point that state and religion begin to diverge. The state is the divine will, in the sense that it is mind present on earth, unfolding itself to be the actual shape and organization of a world. Those who insist on stopping at the form of *religion*, as opposed to the state, are acting like those logicians who think they are right if they continually stop at the essence and refuse to advance beyond that abstraction to existence, or like those moralists (see Remark to Paragraph 140) who will only good in the abstract and leave it to caprice to decide what is good. Religion is a relation to the Absolute, a relation which takes the form of feeling, representative thinking, faith; and, brought within its all-embracing circumference, everything becomes only accidental and transient. Now if, in relation to the state, we cling to this form of experience and make it the authority for the state and its essential determinant, the state must become a prey to weakness, insecurity, and disorder, because it is an organism in which firmly fixed distinct powers, laws, and institutions have been developed. In contrast with the form of religion, a form which draws a veil over everything determinate, and so comes to be purely subjective, the objective and universal element in the state, i.e. the laws, acquires a negative instead of a stable and authoritative character, and the result is the production of maxims of conduct like the following: 'To the righteous man no law is given; only be pious, and for the rest, practice what thou wilt; yield to thine own caprice and passion, and if thereby others suffer wrong, commend them to the consolations and hopes of religion, or better still, call them irreligious and condemn them to perdition.' This negative attitude, however, may not confine itself to an inner disposition and attitude of mind; it may turn instead to the outside world and assert its authority there, and then there is an outbreak of the religious fanaticism which, like fanaticism in politics, discards all government and legal order as barriers cramping the inner life of the heart and incompatible with its infinity, and at the same time proscribes private property, marriage, the ties and work involved in civil society, &c., &c., as degrading to love and the freedom of feeling. But since even then decisions must somehow be made for everyday life and practice, the same doctrine which we had before (see Remark to Paragraph 140, where we dealt generally with the subjectivity of the will which knows itself to be absolute) turns up again here, namely that subjective ideas, i.e. opinion and capricious inclination, are to do the deciding.

   In contrast with the truth thus veiled behind subjective ideas and feelings, the genuine truth is the prodigious transfer of the inner into the outer, the building of reason into the real world, and this has been the task of the world during the whole course of its history. It is by working at this task that civilized man has actually given reason an embodiment in law and government and achieved consciousness of the fact. Those who 'seek guidance from the Lord' and are assured that the whole truth is directly present in their unschooled opinions, fail to apply themselves to the task of exalting their subjectivity to consciousness of the truth and to knowledge of duty and objective right. The only possible fruits of their attitude are folly, abomination, and the demolition of the whole ethical order, and these fruits must inevitably be reaped if the religious disposition holds firmly and exclusively to its intuitive form and so turns against the real world and the truth present in it in the form of the universal, i.e. of the laws. Still, there is no necessity for this disposition to turn outward and actualize itself in this way. With its negative standpoint, it is of course also open to it to remain something inward, to accommodate itself to government and law, and to acquiesce in these with sneers and idle longings, or with a sigh of resignation. It is not strength but weakness which has turned religious feeling nowadays into piety of a polemical kind, whether the polemic be connected with some genuine need or simply with unsatisfied vanity. Instead of subduing one's opinions by the labour of study, and subjecting one's will to discipline and so elevating it to free obedience, the line of least resistance is to renounce knowledge of objective truth. Along this line we may preserve a feeling of abject humility and so also of self-conceit, and claim to have ready to hand in godliness everything requisite for seeing into the heart of law and government, for passing sentence on them, and laying down what their character should and must be; and of course if we take this line, the source of our claims is a pious heart, and they are therefore infallible and unimpeachable, and the upshot is that since we make religion the basis of our intentions and assertions, they cannot be criticized on the score of their shallowness or their immorality.

But if religion be religion of a genuine kind, it does not run counter to the state in a negative or polemical way like the kind just described. It rather recognizes the state and upholds it, and furthermore it has a position and an external organization of its own. The practice of its worship consists in ritual and doctrinal instruction, and for this purpose possessions and property are required, as well as individuals dedicated to the service of the flock. There thus arises a relation between the state and the church. To determine this relation is a simple matter. In the nature of the case, the state discharges a duty by affording every assistance and protection to the church in the furtherance of its religious ends; and, in addition, since religion is an integrating factor in the state, implanting a sense of unity in the depths of men's minds, the state should even require all its citizens to belong to a church—*a* church is all that can be said, because since the content of a man's faith depends on his private ideas, the state cannot interfere with it. A state which is strong because its organization is mature may be all the more liberal in this matter; it may entirely overlook details of religious practice which affect it, and may even tolerate a sect (though, of course, all depends on its numbers) which on religious grounds declines to recognize even its direct duties to the state. The reason for the state's liberal attitude here is that it makes over the members of such sects to civil society and its laws, and is content if they fulfill their direct duties to the state passively, for instance by such means as commutation or the performance of a different service.[7]

But since the church owns property and carries on besides the practice of worship, and since therefore it must have people in its service, it forsakes the inner for the worldly life and therefore enters the domain of the state, and *eo ipso* comes under its laws. The oath and ethical ties generally, like the marriage bond, entail that inner permeation and elevation of *sentiment* which acquires its deepest confirmation through religion. But since ethical ties are in essence ties within the actual *rational* order, the first thing is to affirm within that order the rights which it involves. Confirmation of these rights by the church is secondary and is only the inward, comparatively abstract, side of the matter.

As for the other ways in which an ecclesiastical communion gives expression to itself, so far as doctrine is concerned the inward preponderates over the outward to a greater extent than is the case with acts of worship and other lines of conduct connected with these, in which the legal side at least seems at once to be a matter for the state. (It is true, of course, that churches have managed to exempt their ministers and property from the power and jurisdiction of the state, and they have even arrogated to themselves jurisdiction over laymen as well in matters in which religion co-operates, such as divorce and the taking of the oath, &c.) Public control of actions of this kind is indeterminate in extent, but this is due to the nature of public control itself and obtains similarly in purely civil transactions (see Paragraph 234). When individuals, holding religious views in common, form themselves into a church, a Corporation, they fall under the general control and oversight of the higher state officials. Doctrine as such, however, has its domain in conscience and falls within the right of the subjective freedom of self-consciousness, the sphere of the inner life, which as such is not the domain of the state. Yet the state, too, has a doctrine, since its organization and whatever rights and constitution are authoritative within it exist essentially in the form of thought as law. And since the state is not a mechanism but the rational life of self-conscious freedom, the system of the ethical world, it follows that an essential moment in the actual state is the mental attitude of the citizens, and so their consciousness of the *principles* which this attitude implies. On the other hand, the doctrine of the church is not purely and simply an inward concern of conscience. As doctrine it is rather the expression of something, in fact the expression of a subject-matter which is most closely linked, or even directly concerned, with ethical principles and the law of the land. Hence at this point the paths of church and state either coincide or diverge at right angles. The difference of their two domains may be pushed by the church into sheer antagonism since, by regarding itself as enshrining the content of religion—a content which is absolute—it may claim as its portion mind in general and so the whole ethical sphere, and conceive the state as a mere mechanical scaffolding for the attainment of external, non-mental, ends. It may take itself to be the Kingdom of God, or at least as the road to it or its vestibule, while it regards the state as the kingdom of this world, i.e. of the transient and the finite. In a word, it may think that it is an end in itself, while the state is a mere means. These claims produce the demand, in connexion with doctrinal instruction, that the state should not only allow the church to do as it likes with complete freedom, but that it should pay unconditional respect to the church's doctrines as doctrines, whatever their character, because their determination is supposed to be the task of the church alone. The church bases this claim on the wide ground that the whole domain of mind (*Geist*) is its property. But science and all types of knowledge also have a footing in that domain and, like a church, they build themselves into a whole with a guiding principle of its own, and, with even better justification, may regard themselves as occupying the position which the church claims. Hence science also may in the same way demand to be independent of the state, which is then supposed to be a mere means with the task of providing for science as though science were an end in itself.

Further, for determining the relation between church and state, it makes no difference whether the leaders of congregations or individuals ordained to the service of the church feel impelled to withdraw from the state and lead a sort of secluded life of their own, so that only the other church members are subject to the state's control, or whether they remain within the state except in their capacity as ecclesiastics, a capacity which they take to be but one side of their life. The most striking thing about such a conception of the church's relation to the state is that it implies the idea that the state's specific function consists in protecting and securing everyone's life, property, and caprice, in so far as these do not encroach upon the life, property, and caprice of others. The state from this point of view is treated simply as an organization to satisfy men's necessities. In this way the element of absolute truth, of mind in its higher development, is placed, as subjective religious feeling or theoretical science, beyond the reach of the state. The state, as the laity pure and simple, is confined to paying its respects to this element and so is entirely deprived of any strictly ethical character. Now it is, of course, a matter of history that in times and under conditions of barbarism, all higher forms of intellectual life had their seat only in the church, while the state was a mere mundane rule of force, caprice, and passion. At such times it was the abstract opposition of state and church which was the main underlying principle of history (see Paragraph 359). But it is far too blind and shallow a proceeding to declare that this situation is the one which truly corresponds with the Idea. The development of this Idea has proved this rather to be the truth, that mind, as free and rational, is implicitly ethical, while the Idea in its truth is rationality actualized; and this it is which exists as the state. Further, this Idea has made it no less clearly evident that the ethical truth in it is present to conscious thought as a content worked up into the form of universality, i.e. as law—in short, that the state *knows* its aims, apprehends and gives practical proof of them with a clear-cut consciousness and in accordance with principles.

Now, as I said earlier, religion has the truth as its universal subject-matter, but it possesses it only as a *given* content which has not been apprehended in its fundamental characteristics as a result of thinking and the use of concepts. Similarly, the relation of the individual to this subject-matter is an obligation grounded on authority, while the 'witness of his own spirit and heart', i.e., that wherein the moment of freedom resides, is faith and feeling. It is philosophic insight which sees that while church and state differ in form, they do not stand opposed in content, for truth and rationality are the content of both. Thus when the church begins to teach doctrines (though there are and have been some churches with a ritual only, and others in which ritual is the chief thing, while doctrine and a more educated consciousness are only secondary), and when these doctrines touch on objective principles, on thoughts of the ethical and the rational, then their expression *eo ipso* brings the church into the domain of the state. In contrast with the church's faith and authority in matters affecting ethical principles, rightness, laws, institutions, in contrast with the church's subjective conviction, the state is that which knows. Its principle is such that its content is in essence no longer clothed with the form of feeling and faith but is determinate thought.

If the content of absolute truth appears in the form of religion as a particular content, i.e. as the doctrines peculiar to the church as a religious community, then these doctrines remain out of the reach of the state (in Protestantism they are out of the reach of priests too because, as there is no laity there, so there is no priesthood to be an exclusive depository of church doctrine). Since ethical principles and the organization of the state in general are drawn into the domain of religion and not only may, but also should, be established by reference thereto, this reference gives religious credentials to the state itself. On the other hand, however, the state retains the right and the form of self-conscious, objective, rationality, the right to make this form count and to maintain it against pretensions springing from truth in a subjective dress, no matter how such truth may girdle itself with certitude and authority.

The state is universal in form, a form whose essential principle is thought. This explains why it was in the state that freedom of thought and science had their origin. It was a church, on the other hand, which burnt Giordano Bruno, forced Galileo to recant on his knees his exposition of the Copernican view of the solar system, and so forth.[8] Science too, therefore, has its place on the side of the state since it has one element, its form, in common with the state, and its aim is knowledge, knowledge of objective truth and rationality in terms of thought. Such knowledge may, of course, fall from the heights of science into opinion and deductive argumentation, and, turning its attention to ethical matters and the organization of the state, set itself against their basic principles. And it may perhaps do this while making for this opining—as if it were reason and the right of subjective self-consciousness—the same pretentious claim as the church makes for its own sphere, the claim, namely, to be free from restraint in its opinions and convictions.

This principle of the subjectivity of knowing has been dealt with above (see Remark to Paragraph 140). It is here only necessary to add a note on the twofold attitude of the state to this opining. On the one hand, in so far as opining is mere opining, a purely subjective matter, it is without any genuine inherent force or power, plume itself as it may; and from this point of view the state may be as totally indifferent to it as the painter who sticks to the three primary colours on his palette is indifferent to the academic wisdom which tells him there are seven. On the other hand, however, when this opining of bad principles embodies itself in a general organization corrosive of the actual order, the state has to set its face against it and protect objective truth and the principles of ethical life (and it must do the same in face of the formulae of unconditioned subjectivity if these have proposed to take the starting point of science as their basis, and turn state educational institutions against the state by encouraging them to make against it claims as pretentious as those of a church); while, vice versa, in face of a church claiming unrestricted and unconditional authority, the state has in general to make good the formal right of self-consciousness to its own insight, its own conviction, and, in short, its own thought of what is to hold good as objective truth.

Mention may also be made of the 'unity of state and church'—a favourite topic of modern discussion and held up by some as the highest of ideals. While state and church are essentially one in truth of principle and disposition, it is no less essential that, despite this unity, the distinction between their forms of consciousness should be externalized as a distinction between their special modes of existence. This often desired unity of church and state is found under oriental despotisms, but an oriental despotism is not a state, or at any rate not the self-conscious form of state which is alone worthy of mind, the form which is organically developed and where there are rights and a free ethical life. Further, if the state is to come into existence as the self-*knowing* ethical actuality of mind, it is essential that its form should be distinct from that of authority and faith. But this distinction emerges only in so far as the church is subjected to inward divisions. It is only thereafter that the state, in contrast with the particular sects, has attained to universality of thought—its formal principle—and is bringing this universality into existence. (In order to understand this, it is necessary to know not only what universality is in itself, but also what its existence is.) Hence so far from its being or its having been a misfortune for the state that the church is disunited, it is only as a result of that disunion that the state has been able to reach its appointed end as a self-consciously rational and ethical organization. Moreover, this disunion is the best piece of good fortune which could have befallen either the church or thought so far as the freedom and rationality of either is concerned.

271. The constitution of the state is, in the first place, the organization of the state and the self-related process of its organic life, a process whereby it differentiates its moments within itself and develops them to self-subsistence. Secondly, the state is an individual, unique and exclusive, and therefore related to others. Thus it turns its differentiating activity outward and accordingly establishes within itself the ideality of its subsisting inward differentiations.

I. The Constitution (on its internal side only)

272. The constitution is rational in so far as the state inwardly differentiates and determines its activity in accordance with the nature of the concept. The result of this is that each of these powers is in itself the totality of the constitution, because each contains the other moments and has them effective in itself, and because the moments, being expressions of the differentiation of the concept, simply abide in their ideality and constitute nothing but a single individual whole.

In our day there has come before the public an endless amount of babble about the constitution, as about reason itself, and the stalest babble of all has been produced in Germany, thanks to those who have persuaded themselves that they have the best, or even the sole, understanding of what a constitution is. Elsewhere, particularly in governments, misunderstanding is supposed to reign. And these gentlemen are convinced that they have an unassailable justification for what they say because they claim that religion and piety are the basis of all this shallow thinking of theirs. It is no wonder that this babble has made reasonable men just as sick of the words 'reason', 'enlightenment', 'right', &c., as of the words 'constitution' and 'freedom', and a man might well be ashamed now to go on discussing the constitution of the state at all! However, we may at least hope that this surfeit will be effective in producing the general conviction that philosophical *knowledge* of such topics cannot arise from argumentation, deduction, calculations of purpose and utility, still less from the heart, love, and inspiration, but only from the concept. We may also hope that those who hold that the divine is inconceivable and the knowledge of truth a wild-goose chase will feel themselves bound to refrain from taking part in the discussion. The products of their hearts and their inspirations are either undigested chatter or mere edification, and whatever the worth of these neither can pretend to notice from philosophy.

Amongst current ideas, mention may be made (in connexion with Paragraph 269) of the necessity for a division of powers within the state. This point is of the highest importance and, if taken in its true sense, may rightly be regarded as the guarantee of public freedom. It is an idea, however, with which the very people who pretend to talk out of their inspiration and love neither have, nor desire to have, any acquaintance, since it is precisely there that the moment of rational determinacy lies. That is to say, the principle of the division of powers contains the essential moment of difference, of rationality *realized*. But when the abstract Understanding handles it, it reads into it the false doctrine of the absolute self-subsistence of each of the powers against the others, and then, one-sidedly interprets their relation to each other as negative, as a mutual restriction. This view implies that the attitude adopted by each power to the others is hostile and apprehensive, as if the others were evils, and that their function is to oppose one another and as a result of this counterpoise to effect an equilibrium on the whole, but never a living unity. It is only the inner self-determination of the concept, not any other consideration, whether of purpose or advantage, that is the absolute source of the division of powers, and in virtue of this alone is the organization of the state something inherently rational and the image of eternal reason.

How the concept and then, more concretely, how the Idea, determining themselves inwardly and so posit their moments—universality, particularity, and individuality—in abstraction from one another, is discoverable from my logic, though not of course from the logic current elsewhere. To take the merely negative as a starting-point and to exalt to the first place the volition of evil and the mistrust of this volition, and then on the basis of this presupposition slyly to construct dikes whose efficiency simply necessitates corresponding dikes over against them, is characteristic in thought of the negative Understanding and in sentiment of the outlook of the rabble (see Paragraph 244).

If the powers (e.g., what are called the 'Executive' and the 'Legislature') become self-subsistent, then as we have recently seen on a grand scale, the destruction of the state is forthwith a *fait accompli*. Alternatively, if the state is maintained in essentials, it is strife which through the subjection by one power of the others, produces unity at least, however defective, and so secures the bare essential, the maintenance of the state.

273. The state as a political entity is thus cleft into three substantive divisions:

(a) the power to determine and establish the universal—the Legislature;
(b) the power to subsume single cases and the spheres of particularity under the universal-the Executive;
(c) the power of subjectivity, as the will with the power of ultimate decision—the Crown. In the crown, the different powers are bound into an individual unity which is thus at once the apex and basis of the whole, i.e., of constitutional monarchy.

The development of the state to constitutional monarchy is the achievement of the modern world, a world in which the substantial Idea has won the infinite form [of subjectivity—see Paragraph 144]. The history of this inner deepening of the world mind—or in other words this free maturation in course of which the Idea, realizing rationality in the external, releases its moments (and they are only its moments) from itself as totalities, and just for that reason still retains them in the ideal unity of the concept—the history of this genuine formation of ethical life is the content of the whole course of world-history.

The ancient division of constitutions into monarchy, aristocracy, and democracy, is based upon the notion of substantial, still undivided, unity, a unity which has not yet come to its inner differentiation (to a matured, internal organization) and which therefore has not yet attained depth or concrete rationality. From the standpoint of the ancient world, therefore, this division is the true and correct one, since for a unity of that still substantial type, a unity inwardly too immature to have attained its absolutely complete development, difference is essentially an external difference and appears at first as a difference in the number of those in whom that substantial unity is supposed to be immanent. These forms, which on this principle belong to different wholes, are given in limited monarchy the humbler position of moments in a whole. The monarch is a *single* person; the *few* come on the scene with the executive, and the *many* en masse with the legislative. But, as has been indicated, purely quantitative distinctions like these are only superficial and do not afford the concept of the thing. Equally inadequate is the mass of contemporary talk about the democratic and aristocratic elements in monarchy, because when the elements specified in such talk are found in a monarchy there is no longer anything democratic or aristocratic about them. There are notions of constitutions in which the state is portrayed from top to bottom as an abstraction which is supposed to rule and command, and how many individuals are at the head of such a state, whether one or a few or all, is a question left undecided and regarded as a matter of indifference. [E.g.:] 'All these forms', says Fichte, '. . . are justified, provided there be an ephorate' (a scheme devised by Fichte to be a counterpoise to the chief power in the state) 'and may . . . be the means of introducing universal rights into the state and maintaining them there.' A view of this kind—and the device of the ephorate also—is begotten by the superficial conception of the state to which reference has just been made. It is true enough that in quite simple social conditions these differences of constitutional form have little or no meaning. For instance, in the course of his legislation Moses prescribed that, in the event of his people's desiring a king, its institutions should remain unchanged except for the new requirement that the king should not 'multiply horses to himself . . . nor wives . . . nor silver and gold'.[9] Besides, in a sense one may of course say that the Idea too is indifferent to these forms (including monarchy, but only when it is restricted in meaning by being defined as an *alternative* on a parity with aristocracy and democracy). But the Idea is indifferent to them, not in Fichte's but in the opposite sense, because every one of them is inadequate to it in its rational development (see Paragraph 272) and in none of them, taken singly, could the Idea attain its right and its actuality. Consequently, it is quite idle to inquire which of the three is most to be preferred. Such forms must be discussed historically or not at all.

Still, here again, as in so many other places, we must recognize the depth of Montesquieu's insight in his now famous treatment of the basic principles of these forms of government. To recognize the accuracy of his account, however, we must not misunderstand it. As is well known, he held that 'virtue' was the principle of democracy [and rightly], since it is in fact the case that that type of constitution rests on sentiment, i.e. on the purely substantial form in which the rationality of the absolute will still exists in democracy. But Montesquieu goes on to say that in the seventeenth century England provided 'a fine spectacle of the way in which efforts to found a democracy were rendered ineffective by a lack of virtue in the leaders'. And again he adds 'when virtue vanishes from the republic, ambition enters hearts which are capable of it and greed masters everyone . . . so that the state becomes everyone's booty and its strength now consists only in the power of a few citizens and the licence of all alike'. These quotations call for the comment that in more mature social conditions and when the powers of particularity have developed and become free, a form of rational law other than the form of sentiment is required, because virtue in the heads of the state is not enough if the state as a whole is to gain the power to resist disruption and to bestow on the powers of particularity, now become mature, both their positive and their negative rights. Similarly, we must remove the misunderstanding of supposing that because the sentiment of virtue is the substantial form of a democratic republic, it is evidently superfluous in monarchy or even absent from it altogether, and, finally, we may not suppose that there is an opposition and an incompatibility between virtue and the legally determinate agency of a state whose organization is fully articulated.

The fact that 'moderation' is cited as the principle of aristocracy implies the beginning at this point of a divorce between public authority and private interest. And yet at the same time these touch each other so directly that this constitution by its very nature stands on the verge of lapsing forthwith into tyranny or anarchy—the harshest of political conditions—and so into self-annihilation. See Roman history, for example.

The fact that Montesquieu discerns 'honour' as the principle of monarchy at once makes it clear that by 'monarchy' he understands, not the patriarchal or any ancient type, nor, on the other hand, the type organized into an objective constitution, but only feudal monarchy, the type in which the relationships recognized in its constitutional law are crystallized into the rights of private property and the privileges of individuals and Corporations. In this type of constitution, political life rests on privileged persons and a great part of what must be done for the maintenance of the state is settled at their pleasure. The result is that their services are the objects not of duty but only of ideas and opinions. Thus it is not duty but only honour which holds the state together.

Another question readily presents itself here: 'Who is to frame the constitution?' This question seems clear, but closer inspection shows at once that it is meaningless, for it presupposes that there is no constitution there, but only an agglomeration of atomic individuals. How an agglomeration of individuals could acquire a constitution, whether automatically or by someone's aid, whether as a present or by force or by thought, it would have to be allowed to settle for itself, since with an agglomeration the concept has nothing to do. But if the question presupposes an already existent constitution, then it is not about framing, but only about altering the constitution, and the very presupposition of a constitution directly implies that its alteration may come about only by constitutional means. In any case, however, it is absolutely essential that the constitution should not be regarded as something made, even though it has come into being in time. It must be treated rather as something simply existent in and by itself, as divine therefore, and constant, and so as exalted above the sphere of things that are made.

274. Mind is actual only as that which it knows itself to be, and the state, as the mind of a nation, is both the law permeating all relationships within the state and also at the same time the manners and consciousness of its citizens. It follows, therefore, that the constitution of any given nation depends in general on the character and development of its self-consciousness. In its self-consciousness its subjective freedom is rooted and so, therefore, is the actuality of its constitution.

The proposal to give a constitution—even one more or less rational in content—to a nation *a priori* would be a happy thought overlooking precisely that factor in a constitution which makes it more than an *ens rationis*. Hence every nation has the constitution appropriate to it and suitable for it.

(a) The Crown

275.The power of the crown contains in itself the three moments of the whole (see Paragraph 272), viz. (α) the *universality* of the constitution and the laws; (β) counsel, which refers the *particular* to the universal; and (γ) the moment of ultimate decision, as the *self-determination* to which everything else reverts and from which everything else derives the beginning of its actuality. This absolute self-determination constitutes the distinctive principle of the power of the crown as such, and with this principle our exposition is to begin.

276. (I) The fundamental characteristic of the state as a political entity is the substantial unity, i.e. the ideality, of its moments. (α) In this unity, the particular powers and their activities arc dissolved and vet retained. They are retained, however, only in the sense that their authority is no independent one but only one of the order and breadth determined by the Idea of the whole; from its might they originate, and they are its flexible limbs while it is their single self.

277. (β) The particular activities and agencies of the state are its essential moments and therefore are proper to *it*. The individual functionaries and agents are attached to their office not on the strength of their immediate personality, but only on the strength of their universal and objective qualities. Hence it is in an external and contingent way that these offices are linked with particular persons, and therefore the functions and powers of the state cannot be private property.

278. These two points (α) and (β) constitute the sovereignty of the state. That is to say, sovereignty depends on the fact that the particular functions and powers of the state are not self-subsistent or firmly grounded either on their own account or in the particular will of the individual functionaries, but have their roots ultimately in the unity of the state as their single self.

This is the sovereignty of the state at home. Sovereignty has another side, i.e. sovereignty *vis-à-vis* foreign states, on which see below.

In feudal times, the state was certainly sovereign *vis-à-vis* other states; at home however, not only was the monarch not sovereign at all, but the state itself was not sovereign either. For one thing, the particular functions and powers of the state and civil society were arranged (compare Remark to Paragraph 273) into independent Corporations and societies, so that the state as a whole was rather an aggregate than an organism; and, for another thing, office was the private property of individuals, and hence what they were to do in their public capacity was left to their own opinion and caprice.

The idealism which constitutes sovereignty is the same characteristic as that in accordance with which the so-called 'parts' of an animal organism are not parts but members, moments in an organic whole, whose isolation and independence spell disease. The principle here is the same as that which came before us (see Paragraph 7) in the abstract concept of the will (see Remark to Paragraph 279) as self-related negativity, and therefore as the universality of the will determining itself to individuality and so cancelling all particularity and determinacy, as the absolute self-determining ground of all volition. To understand this, one must have mastered the whole conception of the substance and genuine subjectivity of the concept.

The fact that the sovereignty of the state is the ideality of all particular authorities within it gives rise to the easy and also very common misunderstanding that this ideality is only might and pure arbitrariness while 'sovereignty' is a synonym for 'despotism'. But despotism means any state of affairs where law has disappeared and where the particular will as such, whether of a monarch or a mob (ochlocracy), counts as law or rather takes the place of law; while it is precisely in legal, constitutional, government that sovereignty is to be found as the moment of ideality—the ideality of the particular spheres and functions. That is to say, sovereignty brings it about that each of these spheres is not something independent, self-subsistent in its aims and modes of working, something immersed solely in itself, but that instead, even in these aims and modes of working, each is determined by and dependent on the aim of the whole (the aim which has been denominated in general terms by the rather vague expression 'welfare of the state').

This ideality manifests itself in a twofold way:

(i) In times of peace, the particular spheres and functions pursue the path of satisfying their particular aims and minding their own business, and it is in part only by way of the unconscious necessity of the thing that their self-seeking is turned into a contribution to reciprocal support and to the support of the whole (see Paragraph 183). In part, however, it is by the direct influence of higher authority that they are not only continually brought back to the aims of the whole and restricted accordingly (see Paragraph 289), but are also constrained to perform direct services for the support of the whole.

(ii) In a situation of exigency, however, whether in home or foreign affairs, the organism of which these particular spheres are members fuses into the single concept of sovereignty. The sovereign is entrusted with the salvation of the state at the sacrifice of these particular authorities whose powers are valid at other times, and it is then that that ideality comes into its proper actuality (see Paragraph 321).

279. (2) Sovereignty, at first simply the universal *thought* of this ideality, comes into *existence* only as subjectivity sure of itself, as the will's abstract and to that extent ungrounded self-determination in which finality of decision is rooted. This is the strictly individual aspect of the state, and in virtue of this alone is the state *one*. The truth of subjectivity, however, is attained only in a subject, and the truth of personality only in a person; and in a constitution which has become mature as a realization of rationality, each of the three moments of the concept has its explicitly actual and separate formation. Hence this absolutely decisive moment of the whole is not individuality in general, but a single individual, the monarch.

The immanent development of a science, the derivation of its entire content from the concept in its simplicity (a science otherwise derived, whatever its merit, does not deserve the name of a philosophical science) exhibits this peculiarity, that one and the same concept—the will in this instance—which begins by being abstract (because it is at the beginning), maintains its identity even while it consolidates its specific determinations, and that too solely by its own activity, and in this way gains a concrete content. Hence it is the basic moment of personality, abstract at the start in immediate rights, which has matured itself through its various forms of subjectivity, and now—at the stage of absolute rights, of the state, of the completely concrete objectivity of the will—has become the personality of the state, its certainty of itself. This last reabsorbs all particularity into its single self, cuts short the weighing of pros and cons between which it lets itself oscillate perpetually now this way and now that, and by saying 'I will' makes its decision and so inaugurates all activity and actuality.

Further, however, personality, like subjectivity in general, as infinitely self-related, has its truth (to be precise, its most elementary, immediate, truth) only in a person, in a subject existing 'for' himself, and what exists 'for' itself is just simply a unit. It is only as a person, the monarch, that the personality of the state is actual. Personality expresses the concept as such; but the person enshrines the actuality of the concept, and only when the concept is determined as person is it the Idea or truth. A so-called 'artificial person', be it a society, a community, or a family, however inherently concrete it may be, contains personality only abstractly, as one moment of itself. In an 'artificial person', personality has not achieved its true mode of existence. The state, however, is precisely this totality in which the moments of the concept have attained the actuality correspondent to their degree of truth. All these categories, both in themselves and in their external formations, have been discussed in the whole course of this treatise. They are repeated here, however, because while their existence in their particular external formations is readily granted, it does not follow at all that they are recognized and apprehended again when they appear in their true place, not isolated, but in their truth as moments of the Idea.

The conception of the monarch is therefore of all conceptions the hardest for ratiocination, i.e. for the method of reflection employed by the Understanding. This method refuses to move beyond isolated categories and hence here again knows only *raisonnement*, finite points of view, and deductive argumentation. Consequently it exhibits the dignity of the monarch as something deduced, not only in its form, but in its essence. The truth is, however, that to be something not deduced but purely self-originating is precisely the conception of monarchy. Akin, then, to this reasoning is the idea of treating the monarch's right as grounded in the authority of God, since it is in its divinity that its unconditional character is contained. We are familiar, however, with the misunderstandings connected with this idea, and it is precisely this 'divine' element which it is the task of a philosophic treatment to comprehend.

We may speak of the 'sovereignty of the people' in the sense that any people whatever is self-subsistent *vis-à-vis* other peoples, and constitutes a state of its own, like the British people for instance. But the peoples of England, Scotland, or Ireland, or the peoples of Venice, Genoa, Ceylon, &c., are not sovereign peoples at all now that they have ceased to have rulers or supreme governments of their own.

We may also speak of sovereignty in home affairs residing in the people, provided that we are speaking generally about the whole state and meaning only what was shown above (see Paragraphs 277, 278), namely that it is to the state that sovereignty belongs.

The usual sense, however, in which men have recently begun to speak of the 'sovereignty of the people' is that it is something opposed to the sovereignty existent in the monarch. So opposed to the sovereignty of the monarch, the sovereignty of the people is one of the confused notions based on the wild idea of the 'people'. Taken without its monarch and the articulation of the whole which is the indispensable and direct concomitant of monarchy, the people is a formless mass and no longer a state. It lacks every one of those determinate characteristics—sovereignty, government, judges, magistrates, class-divisions, &c.,—which are to be found only in a whole which is inwardly organized. By the very emergence into a people's life of moments of this kind which have a bearing on an organization, on political life, a people ceases to be that indeterminate abstraction which, when represented in a quite general way, is called the 'people'.

If by 'sovereignty of the people' is understood a republican form of government, or to speak more specifically (since under 'republic' are comprised all sorts of other mixed forms of government, which are purely empirical, let alone irrelevant in a philosophical treatise) a democratic form, then all that is needed in reply has been said already (in the Remark to Paragraph 273); and besides, such a notion cannot be further discussed in face of the Idea of the state in its full development.

If the 'people' is represented neither as a patriarchal clan, nor as living under the simple conditions which make democracy or aristocracy possible as forms of government (see Remark to Paragraph 273), nor as living under some other unorganized and haphazard conditions, but instead as an inwardly developed, genuinely organic, totality, then sovereignty is there as the personality of the whole, and this personality is there, in the real existence adequate to its concept, as the person of the monarch.

At the stage at which constitutions are divided, as above mentioned, into democracy, aristocracy, and monarchy, the point of view taken is that of a still substantial unity, abiding in itself, without having yet embarked on its infinite differentiation and the plumbing of its own depths. At that stage, the moment of the final, self-determining, decision of the will does not come on the scene explicitly in its own proper actuality as an organic moment immanent in the state. None the less, even in those comparatively immature constitutional forms, there must always be individuals at the head. Leaders must either be available already, as they are in monarchies of that type, or, as happens in aristocracies, but more particularly in democracies, they may rise to the top, as statesmen or generals, by chance and in accordance with the particular needs of the hour. This must happen, since everything done and everything actual is inaugurated and brought to completion by the single decisive act of a leader. But comprised in a union of powers which remains undifferentiated, this subjectivity of decision is inevitably either contingent in its origin and appearance, or else is in one way or another subordinate to something else. Hence in such states, the power of the leaders was conditioned, and only in something beyond them could there be found a pure unambiguous decision, a *fatum*, determining affairs from without. As a moment of the Idea, this decision had to come into existence, though rooted in something outside the circle of human freedom with which the state is concerned. Herein lies the origin of the need for deriving the last word on great events and important affairs of state from oracles, a 'divine sign' (in the case of Socrates), the entrails of animals, the feeding and flight of birds, &c. It was when men had not yet plumbed the depths of self-consciousness or risen out of their undifferentiated unity of substance to their independence that they lacked strength to look within their own being for the final word.

In the 'divine sign' of Socrates (compare Remark to Paragraph 138) we see the will which formerly had simply transferred itself beyond itself now beginning to apply itself to itself and so to recognize its own inward nature. This is the beginning of a self-knowing and so of a genuine freedom. This realized freedom of the Idea consists precisely in giving to each of the moments of rationality its own self-conscious actuality here and now. Hence it is this freedom which makes the ultimate self-determining certitude—the culmination of the concept of the will—the function of a single consciousness. This ultimate self-determination, however, can fall within the sphere of human freedom only in so far as it has the position of a pinnacle, explicitly distinct from, and raised above, all that is particular and conditional, for only so is it actual in a way adequate to its concept.

280. (3) This ultimate self in which the will of the state is concentrated is, when thus taken in abstraction, a single self and therefore is *immediate* individuality. Hence its 'natural' character is implied in its very conception. The monarch, therefore, is essentially characterized as *this* individual, in abstraction from all his other characteristics, and *this*

individual is raised to the dignity of monarchy in an immediate, natural, fashion, i.e., through his birth in the course of nature.

This transition of the concept of pure self-determination into the immediacy of being and so into the realm of nature is of a purely speculative character, and apprehension of it therefore belongs to logic. Moreover, this transition is on the whole the same as that familiar to us in the nature of willing, and there the process is to translate something from subjectivity (i.e., some purpose held before the mind) into existence (see Paragraph 8). But the proper form of the Idea and of the transition here under consideration is the immediate conversion of the pure self-determination of the will (i.e. of the simple concept itself) into a single and natural existent without the mediation of a particular content (like a purpose in the case of action).

In the so-called 'ontological' proof of the existence of God, we have the same conversion of the absolute concept into existence. This conversion has constituted the depth of the Idea in the modern world, although recently it has been declared inconceivable, with the result that knowledge of truth has been renounced, since truth is simply the unity of concept and existence (see Paragraph 23). Since the Understanding has no inner consciousness of this unity and refuses to move beyond the separation of these two moments of the truth, it may perhaps, as far as God is concerned, still permit a 'faith' in this unity. But since the idea of the monarch is regarded as being quite familiar to ordinary consciousness, the Understanding clings here all the more tenaciously to its separatism and the conclusions which its astute ratiocination deduces therefrom. As a result, it denies that the moment of ultimate decision in the state is linked implicitly and actually (i.e. in the rational concept) with the immediate birthright of the monarch. Consequently it infers, first, that this link is a matter of accident, and further—since it has claimed that the absolute diversity of these moments is the rational thing—that such a link is irrational, and then there follow the other deductions disruptive of the Idea of the state.

281. Both moments in their undivided unity—(a) the will's ultimate ungrounded self, and (b) therefore its similarly ungrounded objective existence (existence being the category which is at home in nature—constitute the Idea of something against which caprice is powerless, the 'majesty' of the monarch. In this unity lies the actual unity of the state, and it is only through this, its inward and outward immediacy, that the unity of the state is saved from the risk of being drawn down into the sphere of particularity and its caprices, ends, and opinions, and saved too from the war of factions round the throne and from the enfeeblement and overthrow of the power of the state.

The rights of birth and inheritance constitute the basis of legitimacy, the basis of a right not purely positive but contained in the Idea.

If succession to the throne is rigidly determined, i.e. if it is hereditary, then faction is obviated at a demise of the crown; this is one aspect of hereditary succession and it has long been rightly stressed as a point in its favour. This aspect, however, is only consequential, and to make it the reason for hereditary succession is to drag down the majesty of the throne into the sphere of argumentation, to ignore its true character as ungrounded immediacy and ultimate inwardness, and to base it not on the Idea of the state immanent within it, but on something external to itself, on some extraneous notion such as the 'welfare of the state' or the 'welfare of the people'. Once it has been so based, its hereditary character may of course be deduced by the use of *medii termini*. But other *medii termini* are equally available, and so therefore are different conclusions, and it is only too well known what conclusions have in fact been drawn from this 'welfare of the people' (*salut du peu-*

ple). Hence the majesty of the monarch is a topic for thoughtful treatment by philosophy alone, since every method of inquiry, other than the speculative method of the infinite Idea which is purely self-grounded, annuls the nature of majesty altogether.

An elective monarchy seems of course to be the most natural idea, i.e. the idea which superficial thinking finds handiest. Because it is the concerns and interests of his people for which a monarch has to provide, so the argument runs, it must be left to the people to entrust with its welfare whomsoever it pleases, and only with the grant of this trust does his right to rule arise. This view, like the notion of the monarch as the highest executive official in the state, or the notion of a contractual relation between him and his people, &c., &c., is grounded on the will interpreted as the whim, opinion, and caprice of the Many. A will of this character counts as the first thing in civil society (as was pointed out long ago) or rather it tries to count as the only thing there, but it is not the guiding principle of the family, still less of the state, and in short it stands opposed to the Idea of ethical life.

It is truer to say that elective monarchy is the worst of institutions, and its results suffice to reveal this to ratiocination. To ratiocination, however, these results have the appearance of something merely possible and probable, though they are in fact inherent in the very essence of this institution. In an elective monarchy, I mean, the nature of the relation between king and people implies that the ultimate decision is left with the particular will, and hence the constitution becomes a Compact of Election, i.e., surrender of the power of the state at the discretion of the particular will. The result of this is that the particular offices of state turn into private property, the sovereignty of the state is enfeebled and lost, and finally the state disintegrates within and is overthrown from without.

282. The right to pardon criminals arises from the sovereignty of the monarch, since it is this alone which is empowered to actualize mind's power of making undone what has been done and wiping out a crime by forgiving and forgetting it.

The right of pardon is one of the highest recognitions of the majesty of mind. Moreover it is one of those cases where a category which belongs to a higher sphere is applied to or reflected in the sphere below. Applications of higher categories to a lower sphere, however, concern the particular science which has to handle its subject-matter in all its empirical details (see [the second] footnote to the Remark to Paragraph 270). Another instance of the same kind of thing is the subsumption under the concept of crime (which came before us earlier—see Paragraphs 95-102) of injuries against the state in general, or against the sovereignty, majesty, and person of the prince. In fact these acquire the character of crime of the worst kind, requiring a special procedure, &c.

283. The second moment in the power of the crown is the moment of particularity, or the moment of a determinate content and its subsumption under the universal. When this acquires a special objective existence, it becomes the supreme council and the individuals who compose it. They bring before the monarch for his decision the content of current affairs of state or the legal provisions required to meet existing needs, together with their objective aspects, i.e. the grounds on which decision is to be based, the relative laws, circumstances, &c. The individuals who discharge these duties are in direct contact with the person of the monarch and therefore their choice and dismissal alike rest with his unrestricted caprice.

284. It is only for the *objective* side of decision, i.e., for knowledge of the problem and the attendant circumstances, and for the legal and other reasons which determine its solution,

that men are answerable; in other words, it is these alone which are capable of objective proof. It is for this reason that these may fall within the province of a council which is distinct from the personal will of the monarch as such. Hence it is only councils or their individual members that are made answerable. The personal majesty of the monarch, on the other hand, as the final *subjectivity* of decision, is above all answerability for acts of government.

285. The third moment in the power of the crown concerns the absolute universality which subsists subjectively in the conscience of the monarch and objectively in the whole of the constitution and the laws. Hence the power of the crown presupposes the other moments in the state just as it is presupposed by each of them.

286. The *objective* guarantee of the power of the crown, of the hereditary right of succession to the throne, and so forth, consists in the fact that just as monarchy has its own actuality in distinction from that of the other rationally determined moments in the state, so these others explicitly possess the rights and duties appropriate to their own character. In the rational organism of the state, each member, by maintaining itself in its own position, *eo ipso* maintains the others in theirs.

One of the results of more recent history is the development of a monarchical constitution with succession to the throne finally fixed on hereditary principles in accordance with primogeniture. With this development, monarchy has been brought back to the patriarchal principle in which it had its historical origin, but its determinate character is now higher, because the monarch is the absolute apex of an organically developed state. This historical result is of the utmost importance for public freedom and for rationality in the constitution, but, as was remarked above, it is often grossly misunderstood despite the respect paid to it.

The history of despotisms, as of the now obsolete, purely feudal, monarchies, is a tale of the vicissitudes of revolt, monarchical tyranny, civil war, the ruin of princes of the blood and whole dynasties, and, consequentially, the general devastation and overthrow of the state in both its home and foreign concerns. This is all due to the fact that, in monarchies of that type, the division of the business of the state is purely mechanical, the various sections being merely handed over to pashas, vassals, &c. The difference between the departments is simply one of greater or lesser power instead of being one of form and specific character. Hence each department maintains itself and in doing so is productive only of itself and not of the others at the same time; each is independent and autonomous and completely incorporates in itself all the moments of the concept. When there is an *organic* relation subsisting between members, not parts, then each member by fulfilling the functions of its own sphere is *eo ipso* maintaining the others; what each fundamentally aims at and achieves in maintaining itself is the maintenance of the others.

The guarantees in question here for the maintenance of the succession to the throne or for the power of the crown generally, or for justice, public freedom, &c., are modes of securing these things by means of institutions. For *subjective* guarantees we may look to the affection of the people, to character, oaths of allegiance, power, and so forth, but, when the constitution is being discussed, it is only objective guarantees that are relevant. And such guarantees are institutions, i.e. mutually conditioning moments, organically interconnected. Hence public freedom in general and an hereditary monarchy guarantee each other; they stand or fall together of necessity, because public freedom means a rational constitution, while the hereditary character of the power of the crown is, as has been shown, the moment lying in the concept of that power.

(b) The Executive

287. There is a distinction between the monarch's decisions and their execution and application, or in general between his decisions and the continued execution or maintenance of
past decisions, existing laws, regulations, organizations for the securing of common ends,
and so forth. This task of merely subsuming the particular under the universal is comprised in the executive power, which also includes the powers of the judiciary and the
police. The latter have a more immediate bearing on the particular concerns of civil society and they make the universal interest authoritative over its particular aims.

288. Particular interests which are common to everyone fall within civil society and lie
outside the absolutely universal interest of the state proper (see Paragraph 256). The
administration of these is in the hands of Corporations (see Paragraph 251), commercial
and professional as well as municipal, and their officials, directors, managers, and the like.
It is the business of these officials to manage the private property and interests of these
particular spheres and, from that point of view, their authority rests on the confidence of
their commonalties and professional equals. On the other hand, however, these circles of
particular interests must be subordinated to the higher interests of the state, and hence
the filling of positions of responsibility in Corporations, &c., will generally be effected by
a mixture of popular election by those interested with appointment and ratification by
higher authority.

289. The maintenance of the state's universal interest, and of legality, in this sphere of particular rights, and the work of bringing these rights back to the universal, require to be
superintended by holders of the executive power, by (*a*) the executive civil servants, and
(*b*) the higher advisory officials (who are organized into committees). These converge in
their supreme heads who are in direct contact with the monarch.

Just as civil society is the battlefield where everyone's individual private interest meets
everyone else's, so here we have the struggle (*a*) of private interests against particular matters of common concern and (*b*) of both of these together against the organization of the
state and its higher outlook. At the same time the corporation mind, engendered when
the particular spheres gain their title to rights, is now inwardly converted into the mind
of the state, since it finds in the state the means of maintaining its particular ends. This
is the secret of the patriotism of the citizens in the sense that they know the state as their
substance, because it is the state that maintains their particular spheres of interest
together with the title, authority, and welfare of these. In the corporation mind the rooting of the particular in the universal is directly entailed, and for this reason it is in that
mind that the depth and strength which the state possesses in sentiment is seated.

The administration of a Corporation's business by its own officials is frequently clumsy,
because although they keep before their minds and are acquainted with its special interests
and affairs, they have a far less complete appreciation of the connexion of those affairs with
more remote conditions and the outlook of the state. In addition, other circumstances contribute to the same result, e.g. close private relationships and other factors putting officials
on a footing of equality with those who should be their subordinates, the rather numerous
ways in which officials lack independence, and so on. This sphere of private interests, however, may be regarded as the one left to the moment of formal freedom, the one which
affords a playground for personal knowledge, personal decisions and their execution, petty
passions and conceits. This is all the more permissible, the more trivial, from the point of
view of the more universal affairs of state, is the intrinsic worth of the business which in

this way comes to ruin or is managed less well or more laboriously, &c. And further, it is all the more permissible, the more this laborious or foolish management of such trivial affairs stands in direct relation with the self-satisfaction and vanity derived therefrom.

290. Division of labour (see Paragraph 198) occurs in the business of the executive also. For this reason, the organization of officials has the abstract though difficult task of so arranging that (*a*) civil life shall be governed in a concrete manner from below where it is concrete, but that (*b*) none the less the business of government shall be divided into its abstract branches manned by special officials as different centres of administration, and further that (*c*) the operations of these various departments shall converge again when they are directed on civil life from above, in the same way as they converge into a general supervision in the supreme executive.

291. The nature of the executive functions is that they are objective and that in their substance they have been explicitly fixed by previous decisions (see Paragraph 287); these functions have to be fulfilled and carried out by individuals. Between an individual and his office there is no immediate natural link. Hence individuals are not appointed to office on account of their birth or native personal gifts. The *objective* factor in their appointment is knowledge and proof of ability. Such proof guarantees that the state will get what it requires; and since it is the sole condition of appointment, it also guarantees to every citizen the chance of joining the class of civil servants.

292. Since the objective qualification for the civil service is not genius (as it is for work as an artist, for example), there is of necessity an indefinite plurality of eligible candidates whose relative excellence is not determinable with absolute precision. The selection of one of the candidates, his nomination to office, and the grant to him of full authority to transact public business—all this, as the linking of two things, a man and his office, which in relation to each other must always be fortuitous, is the *subjective* aspect of election to office, and it must lie with the crown as the power in the state which is sovereign and has the last word.

293. The particular public functions which the monarch entrusts to officials constitute one part of the objective aspect of the sovereignty residing in the crown. Their specific discrimination is therefore given in the nature of the thing. And while the actions of the officials are the fulfillment of their duty, their office is also a right exempt from contingency.

294. Once an individual has been appointed to his official position by the sovereign's act (see Paragraph 292), the tenure of his post is conditional on his fulfilling its duties. Such fulfilment is the very essence of his appointment, and it is only consequential that he finds in his office his livelihood and the assured satisfaction of his particular interests (see Paragraph 264), and further that his external circumstances and his official work are freed from other kinds of subjective dependence and influence.

   The state does not count on optional, discretionary, services (e.g. on justice administered by knights errant). It is just because such services are optional and discretionary that the state cannot rely on them, for casual servants may fail for private reasons to fulfil their duties completely, or they may arbitrarily decide not to fulfill them at all but pursue their private ends instead. The opposite extreme to a knight errant, so far as the service of the state goes, would be an official who clung to his office purely and simply to make a living without any real sense of duty and so without any real right to go on holding it.

What the service of the state really requires is that men shall forgo the selfish and capricious satisfaction of their subjective ends; by this very sacrifice, they acquire the right to find their satisfaction in, but only in, the dutiful discharge of their public functions. In this fact, so far as public business is concerned, there lies the link between universal and particular interests which constitutes both the concept of the state and its inner stability (see Paragraph 260).

It follows that a man's tenure of his civil service post is not contractual (see Paragraph 75), although his appointment involves a consent and an undertaking on both sides. A civil servant is not appointed, like an agent, to perform a single casual act of service; on the contrary, he concentrates his main interests (not only his particular interests but his mental interests also) on his relation to his work. Similarly, the work imposed upon him and entrusted to him is not merely a particular thing, external in character; the value of such a thing is something inward and therefore distinct from its outward character, so that it is in no way impaired if what has been stipulated is not fulfilled (see Paragraph 77). The work of a civil servant, however, is as such a value in and for itself. Hence the wrong committed through its non-performance, or positive mis-performance (i.e., through an action contrary to official duty, and both of these are of that type), is an infringement of the universal content itself (i.e., is a negatively infinite judgement—see Paragraph 95) and so is a trespass or even a crime.

The assured satisfaction of particular needs removes the external compulsion which may tempt a man to seek ways and means of satisfying them at the expense of his official duties. Those who are entrusted with affairs of state find in its universal power the protection they need against another subjective phenomenon, namely the personal passions of the governed, whose private interests, &c., suffer injury as the interest of the state is made to prevail against them.

295. The security of the state and its subjects against the misuse of power by ministers and their officials lies directly in their hierarchical organization and their answerability; but it lies too in the authority given to societies and Corporations, because in itself this is a barrier against the intrusion of subjective caprice into the power entrusted to a civil servant, and it completes from below the state control which does not reach down as far as the conduct of individuals.

The conduct and culture of officials is the sphere where the laws and the government's decisions come into contact with individuals and are actually made good. Hence it is on the conduct of officials that there depend not only the contentment of citizens and their confidence in the government, but also the execution—or alternatively the distortion and frustration—of state projects; at any rate, this is the case in the sense that feeling and sentiment may easily rate the manner of execution as highly as the very content of the command to be executed, even though the content may in fact be the imposition of a tax. Owing to the direct and personal nature of this contact with individuals, control from above can attain its ends in this respect only to a rather incomplete extent. Moreover, its ends may also be hindered by interests common to officials who form a clique over against their inferiors on one side and their superiors on the other. In states whose institutions may perhaps be imperfectly developed in other respects also, the removal of hindrances like these requires and justifies the higher intervention of the sovereign (as for example of Frederick the Great in the notorious affair of Arnold the miller).

296. But the fact that a dispassionate, upright, and polite demeanour becomes customary [in civil servants] is (i) partly a result of direct education in thought and ethical conduct.

Such an education is a mental counterpoise to the mechanical and semimechanical activity involved in acquiring the so-called 'sciences' of matters connected with administration, in the requisite business training, in the actual work done, &c. (ii) The size of the state, however, is an important factor in producing this result, since it diminishes the stress of family and other personal ties, and also makes less potent and so less keen such passions as hatred, revenge, &c. In those who are busy with the important questions arising in a great state, these subjective interests automatically disappear, and the habit is generated of adopting universal interests, points of view, and activities.

297. Civil servants and the members of the executive constitute the greater part of the middle class, the class in which the consciousness of right and the developed intelligence of the mass of the people is found. The sovereign working on the middle class at the top, and Corporation-rights working on it at the bottom, are the institutions which effectually prevent it from acquiring the isolated position of an aristocracy and using its education and skill as means to an arbitrary tyranny.

At one time the administration of justice, which is concerned with the private interests of all members of the state, was in this way turned into an instrument of profit and tyranny, when the knowledge of the law was buried in pedantry and a foreign tongue, and knowledge of legal processes was similarly buried in involved formalities.

(c) The Legislature

298. The legislature is concerned (*a*) with the laws as such in so far as they require fresh and extended determination; and (*b*) with the content of home affairs affecting the entire state. The legislature is itself a part of the constitution which is presupposed by it and to that extent lies absolutely outside the sphere directly determined by it; none the less, the constitution becomes progressively more mature in the course of the further elaboration of the laws and the advancing character of the universal business of government.

299. Legislative business is more precisely determined, in relation to private individuals, under these two heads: (*α*) provision by the state for their well-being and happiness, and (*β*) the exaction of services from them. The former comprises the laws dealing with all sorts of private rights, the rights of communities, Corporations, and organizations affecting the entire state, and further it indirectly (see Paragraph 298) comprises the whole of the constitution. As for the services to be exacted, it is only if these are reduced to terms of money, the really existent and universal value of both things and services, that they can be fixed justly and at the same time in such a way that any particular tasks and services which an individual may perform come to be mediated through his own arbitrary will.

The proper object of universal legislation may be distinguished in a general way from the proper function of administrative officials or of some kind of state regulation, in that the content of the former is wholly universal, i.e. determinate laws, while it is what is particular in content which falls to the latter, together with ways and means of enforcing the law. This distinction, however, is not a hard and fast one, because a law, by being a law, is *ab initio* something more than a mere command in general terms (such as 'Thou shalt not kill'—compare Remark (*d*) to Paragraph 140). A law must in itself be something determinate, but the more determinate it is, the more readily are its terms capable of being carried out as they stand. At the same time, however, to give to laws such a fully detailed determinacy would give them empirical features subject inevitably to alteration in the course of their being actually carried out, and this would contravene their character as laws. The organic unity of the powers of the state itself implies that it is one single mind which both firmly establishes the universal and also brings it into its determinate actuality and carries it out.

In the state it may happen, to begin with, that the numerous aptitudes, possessions, pursuits, and talents of its members, together with the infinitely varied richness of life intrinsic to these—all of which are at the same time linked with their owner's mentality—are not subject to direct levy by the state. It lays claim only to a single form of riches, namely money. (Services requisitioned for the defence of the state in war arise for the first time in connexion with the duty considered in the next subdivision of this book.) In fact, however, money is not one particular type of wealth amongst others, but the universal form of all types so far as they are expressed in an external embodiment and so can be taken as 'things'. Only by being translated into terms of this extreme culmination of externality can services exacted by the state be fixed quantitatively and so justly and equitably.

In Plato's *Republic*, the Guardians are left to allot individuals to their particular classes and impose on them their particular tasks (compare Remark to Paragraph 185). Under the feudal monarchies the services required from vassals were equally indeterminate, but they had also to serve in their *particular* capacity, e.g., as judges. The same particular character pertains to tasks imposed in the East and in Egypt in connexion with colossal architectural undertakings, and so forth. In these circumstances the principle of subjective freedom is lacking, i.e. the principle that the individual's substantive activity—which in any case becomes something particular in content in services like those mentioned—shall be mediated through his particular volition. This is a right which can be secured only when the demand for service takes the form of a demand for something of universal value, and it is this right which has brought with it this conversion of the state's demands into demands for cash.

300. In the legislature as a whole the other powers are the first two moments which are effective, (i) the monarchy as that to which ultimate decisions belong; (ii) the executive as the advisory body since it is the moment possessed of (α) a concrete knowledge and oversight of the whole state in its numerous facets and the actual principles firmly established within it, and (β) a knowledge in particular of what the state's power needs. The last moment in the legislature is the Estates.

301. The Estates have the function of bringing public affairs into existence not only implicitly, but also actually, i.e. of bringing into existence the moment of subjective formal freedom, the public consciousness as an empirical universal, of which the thoughts and opinions of the Many are particulars.

The phrase 'the Many' ($o\dot{\iota}\ \pi o\lambda\lambda o\dot{\iota}$) denotes empirical universality more strictly than 'All', which is in current use. If it is said to be obvious that this 'all' prima facie excludes at least children, women, &c., then it is surely still more obvious that the quite definite word 'all' should not be used when something quite indefinite is meant.

Current opinion has put into general circulation such a host of perverse and false ideas and ways of speaking about 'People', 'Constitution', and 'Estates' that it would be a waste of energy to try to specify, expound, and correct them. The idea uppermost in men's minds when they speak about the necessity or the expediency of 'summoning the Estates' is generally something of this sort: (i) The deputies of the people, or even the people themselves, must know best what is in their best interest, and (ii) their will for its promotion is undoubtedly the most disinterested. So far as the first of these points is concerned, however, the truth is that if 'people' means a particular section of the citizens, then it means precisely that section which does *not* know what it wills. To know what one wills, and still more to know what the absolute will, Reason, wills, is the fruit of profound apprehension and insight, precisely the things which are *not* popular.

The Estates are a guarantee of the general welfare and public freedom. A little reflection will show that this guarantee does not lie in their particular power of insight, because the highest civil servants necessarily have a deeper and more comprehensive insight into the nature of the state's organization and requirements. They are also more habituated to the business of government and have greater skill in it, so that even without the Estates they are *able* to do what is best, just as they also continually *have* to do while the Estates are in session. No, the guarantee lies on the contrary (α) in the *additional* insight of the deputies, insight in the first place into the activity of such officials as are not immediately under the eye of the higher functionaries of state, and in particular into the more pressing and more specialized needs and deficiencies which are directly in their view; (β) in the fact that the anticipation of criticism from the Many, particularly of public criticism, has the effect of inducing officials to devote their best attention beforehand to their duties and the schemes under consideration, and to deal with these only in accordance with the purest motives. This same compulsion is effective also on the members of the Estates themselves.

As for the conspicuously good will for the general welfare which the Estates are supposed to possess, it has been pointed out already (in the Remark to Paragraph 272) that to regard the will of the executive as bad, or as less good [than that of the ruled] is a presupposition characteristic of the rabble or of the negative outlook generally. This presupposition might at once be answered on its own ground by the counter-charge that the Estates start from isolated individuals, from a private point of view, from particular interests, and so are inclined to devote their activities to these at the expense of the general interests, while *per contra* the other moments in the power of the state explicitly take up the standpoint of the state from the start and devote themselves to the universal end.

As for the general guarantee which is supposed to lie peculiarly in the Estates, each of the other political institutions shares with the Estates in being a guarantee of public welfare and rational freedom, and some of these institutions, as for instance the sovereignty of the monarch, hereditary succession to the throne, the judicial system, &c., guarantee these things far more effectively than the Estates can.

Hence the specific function which the concept assigns to the Estates is to be sought in the fact that in them the subjective moment in universal freedom—the private judgement and private will of the sphere called 'civil society' in this book—comes into existence integrally related to the state. This moment is a determination of the Idea once the Idea has developed to totality, a moment arising as a result of an inner necessity not to be confused with external necessities and expediencies. The proof of this follows, like all the rest of our account of the state, from adopting the philosophical point of view.

302. Regarded as a mediating organ, the Estates stand between the government in general on the one hand and the nation broken up into particulars (people and associations) on the other. Their function requires them to possess a political and administrative sense and temper, no less than a sense for the interests of individuals and particular groups. At the same time the significance of their position is that, in common with the organized executive, they are a middle term preventing both the extreme isolation of the power of the crown, which otherwise might seem a mere arbitrary tyranny, and also the isolation of the particular interests of persons, societies, and Corporations. Further, and more important, they prevent individuals from having the appearance of a mass or an aggregate and so from acquiring an unorganized opinion and volition and from crystallizing into a powerful *bloc* in opposition to the organized state.

It is one of the most important discoveries of logic that a specific moment which, by standing in an opposition, has the position of an extreme, ceases to be such and is a moment in an organic whole by being at the same time a mean. In connexion with our present topic it is all the more important to emphasize this aspect of the matter because of the popular, but most dangerous, prejudice which regards the Estates principally from the point of view of their opposition to the executive, as if that were their essential attitude. If the Estates become an organ in the whole by being taken up into the state, they evince themselves solely through their mediating function. In this way their opposition to the executive is reduced to a show. There may indeed be an appearance of opposition between them, but if they were opposed, not merely superficially, but actually and in substance, then the state would be in the throes of destruction. That the clash is not of this kind is evident in the nature of the thing, because the Estates have to deal, not with the essential elements in the organism of the state, but only with rather specialized and trifling matters, while the passion which even these arouse spends itself in party cravings in connexion with purely subjective interests such as appointments to the higher offices of state.

303. The universal class, or, more precisely, the class of civil servants, must, purely in virtue of its character as universal, have the universal as the end of its essential activity. In the Estates, as an element in the legislative power, the unofficial class acquires its political significance and efficacy; it appears, therefore, in the Estates neither as a mere indiscriminate multitude nor as an aggregate dispersed into its atoms, but as what it already is, namely a class subdivided into two, one sub-class [the agricultural class] being based on a tie of substance between its members, and the other [the business class] on particular needs and the work whereby these are met (see Paragraph 201 ff.). It is only in this way that there is a genuine link between the particular which is effective in the state and the universal.

This runs counter to another prevalent idea, the idea that since it is in the legislature that the unofficial class rises to the level of participating in matters of state, it must appear there in the form of individuals, whether individuals are to choose representatives for this purpose, or whether every single individual is to have a vote in the legislature himself. This atomistic and abstract point of view vanishes at the stage of the family, as well as that of civil society where the individual is in evidence only as a member of a general group. The state, however, is essentially an organization each of whose members is in itself a group of this kind, and hence no one of its moments should appear as an unorganized aggregate. The Many, as units—a congenial interpretation of 'people', are of course something connected, but they are connected only as an aggregate, a formless mass whose commotion and activity could therefore only be elementary, irrational, barbarous, and frightful. When we hear speakers on the constitution expatiating about the 'people'—this unorganized collection—we know from the start that we have nothing to expect but generalities and perverse declamations.

The circles of association in civil society are already communities. To picture these communities as once more breaking up into a mere conglomeration of individuals as soon as they enter the field of politics, i.e. the field of the highest concrete universality, is *eo ipso* to hold civil and political life apart from one another and as it were to hang the latter in the air, because its basis could then only be the abstract individuality of caprice and opinion, and hence it would be grounded on chance and not on what is absolutely stable and justified.

So-called 'theories' of this kind involve the idea that the classes (*Stände*) of civil society and the Estates (*Stände*), which are the 'classes' given a political significance, stand wide apart from each other. But the German language, by calling them both *Stände* has still maintained the unity which in any case they actually possessed in former times.

304. The Estates, as an element in political life, still retain in their own function the class distinctions already present in the lower spheres of civil life. The position of the classes is abstract to begin with, i.e. in contrast with the whole principle of monarchy or the crown, their position is that of an extreme—empirical universality. This extreme opposition implies the possibility, though no more, of harmonization, and the equally likely possibility of set hostility. This abstract position changes into a rational relation (into a syllogism, see Remark to Paragraph 302) only if the middle term between the opposites comes into existence. From the point of view of the crown, the executive already has this character (see Paragraph 300). So, from the point of view of the classes, one moment in them must be adapted to the task of existing as in essence the moment of mediation.

305. The principle of one of the classes of civil society is in itself capable of adaptation to this political position. The class in question is the one whose ethical life is natural, whose basis is family life, and, so far as its livelihood is concerned, the possession of land. Its particular members attain their position by birth, just as the monarch does, and, in common with him, they possess a will which rests on itself alone.

306. This class is more particularly fitted for political position and significance in that its capital is independent alike of the state's capital, the uncertainty of business, the quest for profit, and any sort of fluctuation in possessions. It is likewise independent of favour, whether from the executive or the mob. It is even fortified against its own wilfulness, because those members of this class who are called to political life are not entitled, as other citizens are, either to dispose of their entire property at will, or to the assurance that it will pass to their children, whom they love equally, in similarly equal divisions. Hence their wealth becomes inalienable, entailed, and burdened by primogeniture.

307. The right of this section of the agricultural class is thus based in a way on the natural principle of the family. But this principle is at the same time reversed owing to hard sacrifices made for political ends, and thereby the activity of this class is essentially directed to those ends. As a consequence of this, this class is summoned and entitled to its political vocation by birth without the hazards of election. It therefore has the fixed, substantive position between the subjective wilfulness or contingency of both extremes; and while it mirrors in itself (see Paragraph 305) the moment of the monarchical power, it also shares in other respects the needs and rights of the other extreme [i.e. civil society] and hence it becomes a support at once of the throne and society.

308. The second section of the Estates comprises the fluctuating element in civil society. This element can enter politics only through its deputies; the multiplicity of its members is an external reason for this, but the essential reason is the specific character of this element and its activity. Since these deputies are the deputies of civil society, it follows as a direct consequence that their appointment is made by the society as a society. That is to say, in making the appointment, society is not dispersed into atomic units, collected to perform only a single and temporary act, and kept together for a moment and no longer. On the contrary, it makes the appointment as a society, articulated into associations, communities, and Corporations, which although constituted already for other purposes, acquire in this way a connexion with politics. The existence of the Estates and their assembly finds a constitutional guarantee of its own in the fact that this class is entitled to send deputies at the summons of the crown, while members of the former class are entitled to present themselves in person in the Estates (see Paragraph 307).

To hold that every single person should share in deliberating and deciding on political matters of general concern on the ground that all individuals are members of the state, that its concerns are their concerns, and that it is their right that what is done should be done with their knowledge and volition, is tantamount to a proposal to put the democratic element without any rational form into the organism of the state, although it is only in virtue of the possession of such a form that the state is an organism at all. This idea comes readily to mind because it does not go beyond the abstraction of 'being a member of the state', and it is superficial thinking which clings to abstractions. The rational consideration of a topic, the consciousness of the Idea, is concrete, and to that extent coincides with a genuine practical sense. Such a sense is itself nothing but the sense of rationality or the Idea, though it is not to be confused with mere business routine or the horizon of a restricted sphere. The concrete state is the whole, articulated into its particular groups. The member of a state is a member of such a group, i.e. of a social class, and it is only as characterized in this objective way that he comes under consideration when we are dealing with the state. His mere character as universal implies that he is at one and the same time both a private person and also a thinking consciousness, a will which wills the universal. This consciousness and will, however, lose their emptiness and acquire a content and a living actuality only when they are filled with particularity, and particularity means determinacy as particular and a particular class-status; or, to put the matter otherwise, abstract individuality is a generic essence, but has its immanent universal actuality as the generic essence next higher in the scale. Hence the single person attains his actual and living destiny for universality only when he becomes a member of a Corporation, a society, &c. (see Paragraph 251), and thereby it becomes open to him, on the strength of his skill, to enter any class for which he is qualified, the class of civil servants included.

Another presupposition of the idea that all should participate in the business of the state is that everyone is at home in this business—a ridiculous notion, however commonly we may hear it sponsored. Still, in public opinion (see Paragraph 316) a field is open to everyone where he can express his purely personal political opinions and make them count.

309. Since deputies are elected to deliberate and decide on *public* affairs, the point about their election is that it is a choice of individuals on the strength of confidence felt in them, i.e. a choice of such individuals as have a better understanding of these affairs than their electors have and such also as essentially vindicate the universal interest, not the particular interest of a society or a Corporation in preference to that interest. Hence their relation to their electors is not that of agents with a commission or specific instructions. A further bar to their being so is the fact that their assembly is meant to be a living body in which all members deliberate in common and reciprocally instruct and convince each other.

310. The guarantee that deputies will have the qualifications and disposition that accord with this end—since independent means attains its right in the first section of the Estates is to be found so far as the second section is concerned—the section drawn from the fluctuating and changeable element in civil society above all in the knowledge (of the organization and interests of the state and civil society), the temperament, and the skill which a deputy acquires as a result of the actual transaction of business in managerial or official positions, and then evinces in his actions. As a result, he also acquires and develops a managerial and political sense, tested by his experience, and this is a further guarantee of his suitability as a deputy.

Subjective opinion, naturally enough, finds superfluous and even perhaps offensive the demand for such guarantees, if the demand is made with reference to what is called the 'people'. The state, however, is characterized by objectivity, not by a subjective opinion and its self-confidence. Hence it can recognize in individuals only their objectively recognizable and tested character, and it must be all the more careful on this point in connexion with the second section of the Estates, since this section is rooted in interests and activities directed towards the particular, i.e. in the sphere where chance, mutability, and caprice enjoy their right of free play.

The external guarantee, a property qualification, is, if taken by itself, evidently just as one-sided in its externality as, at the other extreme, are purely subjective confidence and the opinion of the electorate. Both alike are abstractions in contrast with the concrete qualifications requisite for deliberation on affairs of state and comprised in the points indicated in Paragraph 302. This apart, however, a property qualification has a sphere, where it may work effectively, in the choice of the heads and other officers of the associations and societies, especially if many of these posts are honorary, and in direct reference to Estates business if the members draw no salary.

311. A further point about the election of deputies is that, since civil society is the electorate, the deputies should themselves be conversant with and participate in its special needs, difficulties, and particular interests. Owing to the nature of civil society, its deputies are the deputies of the various Corporations (see Paragraph 308), and this simple mode of appointment obviates any confusion due to conceiving the electorate abstractly and as an agglomeration of atoms. Hence the deputies *eo ipso* adopt the point of view of society, and their actual election is therefore either something wholly superfluous or else reduced to a trivial play of opinion and caprice.

It is obviously of advantage that the deputies should include representatives of each particular main branch of society (e.g., trade, manufactures, &c., &c.)—representatives who are thoroughly conversant with it and who themselves belong to it. The idea of free unrestricted election leaves this important consideration entirely at the mercy of chance. All such branches of society, however, have equal rights of representation. Deputies are sometimes regarded as 'representatives'; but they are representatives in an organic, rational sense only if they are representatives not of individuals or a conglomeration of them, but of one of the essential spheres of society and its large-scale interests. Hence representation cannot now be taken to mean simply the substitution of one man for another; the point is rather that the interest itself is actually present in its representative, while he himself is there to represent the objective element of his own being.

As for popular suffrage, it may be further remarked that especially in large states it leads inevitably to electoral indifference, since the casting of a single vote is of no significance where there is a multitude of electors. Even if a voting qualification is highly valued and esteemed by those who are entitled to it, they still do not enter the polling booth. Thus the result of an institution of this kind is more likely to be the opposite of what was intended; election actually falls into the power of a few, of a caucus, and so of the particular and contingent interest which is precisely what was to have been neutralized.

312. Each class in the Estates (see Paragraphs 305-8) contributes something peculiarly its own to the work of deliberation. Further, one moment in the class-element has in the sphere of politics the special function of mediation, mediation between two existing things. Hence this moment must likewise acquire a separate existence of its own. For this reason the assembly of the Estates is divided into two houses.

313. This division, by providing chambers of the first and second instance, is a surer guarantee for ripeness of decision and it obviates the accidental character which a snap-division has and which a numerical majority may acquire. But the principal advantage of this arrangement is that there is less chance of the Estates being in direct opposition to the executive; or that, if the mediating element is at the same time on the side of the lower house, the weight of the lower house's opinion is all the stronger, because it appears less partisan and its opposition appears neutralized.

314. The purpose of the Estates as an institution is not to be an inherent *sine qua non* of maximum efficiency in the consideration and dispatch of state business, since in fact it is only an *added* efficiency that they can supply (see Paragraph 301). Their distinctive purpose is that in their pooled political knowledge, deliberations, and decisions, the moment of formal freedom shall come into its right in respect of those members of civil society who are without any share in the executive. Consequently, it is knowledge of public business above all which is extended by the publicity of Estates debates.

315. The opening of this opportunity to know has a more universal aspect because by this means public opinion first reaches thoughts that are true and attains insight into the situation and concept of the state and its affairs, and so first acquires ability to estimate these more rationally. By this means also, it becomes acquainted with and learns to respect the work, abilities, virtues, and dexterity of ministers and officials. While such publicity provides these abilities with a potent means of development and a theatre of higher distinction, it is at the same time another antidote to the self-conceit of individuals singly and *en masse*, and another means—indeed one of the chief means—of their education.

316. The formal subjective freedom of individuals consists in their having and expressing their own private judgements, opinions, and recommendations on affairs of state. This freedom is collectively manifested as what is called 'public opinion', in which what is absolutely universal, the substantive and the true, is linked with its opposite, the purely particular and private opinions of the Many. Public opinion as it exists is thus a standing self-contradiction, knowledge as appearance, the essential just as directly present as the inessential.

317. Public opinion, therefore, is a repository not only of the genuine needs and correct tendencies of common life, but also, in the form of common sense (i.e., all-pervasive fundamental ethical principles disguised as prejudices), of the eternal, substantive principles of justice, the true content and result of legislation, the whole constitution, and the general position of the state. At the same time, when this inner truth emerges into consciousness and, embodied in general maxims, enters representative thinking—whether it be there on its own account or in support of concrete arguments about felt wants, public affairs, the organization of the state, and relations of parties within it—it becomes infected by all the accidents of opinion, by its ignorance and perversity, by its mistakes and falsity of judgment. Since in considering such opinion we have to do with the consciousness of an insight and conviction peculiarly one's own, the more peculiarly one's own an opinion may be the worse its content is, because the bad is that which is wholly private and personal in its content; the rational, on the other hand, is the absolutely universal, while it is on peculiarity that opining prides itself.

Hence it is not simply due to a subjective difference of view that we find it said the *vox populi, vox Dei*, and on the other hand, as Ariosto has it,

> Che 'l volgare ignorante ogn' un riprenda
> E parli più di quel che meno intenda

or, as Goethe puts it, 'the masses are respectable hands at fighting, but miserable hands at judging'.

Both types of assertion are true at one and the same time of public opinion, and since it is such a hotch-potch of truth and endless error, it cannot be genuinely serious about both of these. But about which *is* it serious? The question may seem hard to answer, and it will actually be hard if we cling simply to the words in which public opinion is directly expressed. The substantial, however, is the heart of public opinion, and therefore it is with that alone that it is truly serious. What the substantial is, though, is not discoverable from public opinion, because its very substantiality implies that it is known in and from itself alone. The passion with which an opinion is urged or the seriousness with which it is maintained or attacked and disputed is no criterion of its real content; and yet the last thing which opinion could be made to see is that its seriousness is nothing serious.

A great genius propounded as a problem for a public essay competition the question 'whether it be permissible to deceive a people'. The answer must have been that a people does not allow itself to be deceived about its substantive basis, the essence and specific character of its mind. On the other hand, it is *self*-deceived about the manner of its knowledge of these things and about its corresponding judgement of its actions, experiences, &c.

318. Public opinion therefore deserves to be as much respected as despised—despised for its concrete expression and for the concrete consciousness it expresses, respected for its essential basis, a basis which only glimmers more or less dimly in that concrete expression. But in itself it has no criterion of discrimination, nor has it the ability to extract the substantive element it contains and raise it to precise knowledge. Thus to be independent of public opinion is the first formal condition of achieving anything great or rational whether in life or in science. Great achievement is assured, however, of subsequent recognition and grateful acceptance by public opinion, which in due course will make it one of its own prejudices.

319. Freedom of public communication—of the two modes of communication, the press and the spoken word, the first exceeds the second in range of contact but lags behind it in vivacity—satisfaction of the goading desire to say one's say and to have said it, is directly assured by the laws and by-laws which control or punish its excesses. But it is assured indirectly by the innocuous character which it acquires as a result principally of the rationality of the constitution, the stability of government, and secondly of the publicity of Estates Assemblies. The reason why the latter makes free speech harmless is that what is voiced in these Assemblies is a sound and mature insight into the concerns of the state, with the result that members of the general public are left with nothing of much importance to say, and above all are deprived of the opinion that what they say is of peculiar importance and efficacy. A further safeguard of free speech is the indifference and contempt speedily and necessarily visited on shallow and cantankerous talking.

To define freedom of the press as freedom to say and write whatever we please is parallel to the assertion that freedom as such means freedom to do as we please. Talk of this kind is due to wholly uneducated, crude, and superficial ideas. Moreover, it is in the very nature of the thing that abstract thinking should nowhere be so stubborn, so unintelligent, as in this matter of free speech, because what it is considering is the most fleeting, the most contingent, and the most personal side of opinion in its infinite diversity of content and tergiversation. Beyond the direct incitation to theft, murder, rebellion, &c., there lies its artfully constructed expression—an expression which seems in itself quite general and vague, while all the time it conceals a meaning anything but vague or else is compatible with inferences which are not actually expressed, and it is impossible to determine whether they rightly follow from it, or whether they were meant to be inferred from it. This vagueness of matter and form precludes laws on these topics from attaining the requisite determinacy of law, and since the trespass, wrong, and injury here are so extremely personal and subjective in form, judgement on them is reduced equally to a wholly subjective verdict. Such an injury is directed against the thoughts, opinions, and wills of others, but apart from that, these form the element in which alone it is actually anything. But this element is the sphere of the freedom of others, and it therefore depends on them whether the injurious expression of opinion is or is not actually an effective act.

Laws then [against libel, &c.] may be criticized by exhibiting their indeterminacy as well as by arguing that they leave it open to the speaker or writer to devise turns of phrase or tricks of expression, and so evade the laws or claim that judicial decisions are mere subjective verdicts. Further, however, against the view that the expression of opinion is an act with injurious effects, it may be maintained that it is not an act at all, but only opining and thinking, or only talking. And so we have before us a claim that mere opining and talking is to go unpunished because it is of a purely subjective character both in form and content, because it does not mean anything and is of no importance. And yet in the same breath we have the claim that this same opining and talking should be held in high esteem and respect—the opining because it is personal property and in fact pre-eminently the property of mind; the talking because it is only this same property being expressed and used.

But the substance of the matter is and remains that traducing the honour of anyone, slander, abuse, the contemptuous caricature of government, its ministers, officials, and in particular the person of the monarch, defiance of the laws, incitement to rebellion, &c., &c., are all crimes or misdemeanours in one or other of their numerous gradations. The rather high degree of indeterminability which such actions acquire on account of the element in which they are expressed does not annul this fundamental character of theirs. Its only effect is that the subjective field in which they are committed also determines the nature and form of the reaction to the offence. It is the field in which the offence was committed which itself necessitates subjectivity of view, contingency, &c., in the reaction to the offence, whether the reaction takes the form of punishment proper or of police action to prevent crimes. Here, as always, abstract thinking sets itself to explain away the fundamental and concrete nature of the thing by concentrating on isolated aspects of its external appearance and on abstractions drawn therefrom.

The sciences, however, are not to be found anywhere in the field of opinion and subjective views, provided of course that they be sciences in other respects. Their exposition is not a matter of clever turns of phrase, allusiveness, half-utterances, and semi-reticences, but consists in the unambiguous, determinate, and open expression of their

meaning and purport. It follows that they do not fall under the category of public opinion (see Paragraph 316). Apart from this, however, as I said just now, the element in
which views and their expression become actions in the full sense and exist effectively,
consists of the intelligence, principles, and opinions of others. Hence this aspect of these
actions, i.e. their effectiveness proper and their danger to individuals, society, and the
state (compare Paragraph 218), depends on the character of the ground on which they
fall, just as a spark falling on a heap of gunpowder is more dangerous than if it falls on
hard ground where it vanishes without trace. Thus, just as the right of science to express
itself depends on and is safeguarded by its subject-matter and content, so an illegitimate
expression may also acquire a measure of security, or at least sufferance, in the scorn
which it has brought upon itself. An offence of this sort is punishable on its own account
too, but part of it may be accounted that kind of nemesis which inner impotence, feeling itself oppressed by the preponderating abilities and virtues of others, is impelled to
vent in order to come to itself again in face of such superiority, and to restore some self-
consciousness to its own nullity. It was a nemesis of a more harmless type which Roman
soldiers vented against their generals when they sang scurrilous songs about them in triumphal processions in order in a way to get even with them for all the hard service and
discipline they had undergone, and especially for the omission of their names from the
triumphal honours. The former type of nemesis, the bad and hateful type, is deprived of
its effect by being treated with scorn, and hence, like the public, which perhaps forms a
circle of spectators of scurrility, it is restricted to futile malice and to the self-condemnation which it implicitly contains.

320. Subjectivity is manifested in its most external form as the undermining of the established life of the state by opinion and ratiocination when they endeavour to assert the
authority of their own fortuitous character and so bring about their own destruction. But
its true actuality is attained in the opposite of this, i.e. in the subjectivity identical with
the substantial will of the state, the subjectivity which constitutes the concept of the
power of the crown and which, as the ideality of the whole state, has not up to this point
attained its right or its existence.

2. *Sovereignty* vis-à-vis *foreign States*

321. Sovereignty at home (see Paragraph 278) is this ideality in the sense that the
moments of mind and its actuality, the state, have become developed in their necessity
and subsist as the organs of the state. Mind in its freedom is an infinitely negative relation
to itself and hence its essential character from its own point of view is its singleness, a singleness which has incorporated these subsistent differences into itself and so is a unit,
exclusive of other units. So characterized, the state has individuality, and individuality is
in essence an individual, and in the sovereign an actual, immediate individual (see
Paragraph 279).

322. Individuality is awareness of one's existence as a unit in sharp distinction from others. It manifests itself here in the state as a relation to other states, each of which is
autonomous *vis-à-vis* the others. This autonomy embodies mind's actual awareness of itself
as a unit and hence it is the most fundamental freedom which a people possesses as well
as its highest dignity.

Those who talk of the 'wishes' of a collection of people constituting a more or less
autonomous state with its own centre, of its 'wishes' to renounce this centre and its

autonomy in order to unite with others to form a new whole, have very little knowledge of the nature of a collection or of the feeling of selfhood which a nation possesses in its independence.

Thus the dominion which a state has at its first entry into history is this bare autonomy, even if it be quite abstract and without further inner development. For this reason, to have an individual at its head—a patriarch, a chieftain, &c.—is appropriate to this original appearance of the state.

323. This negative relation of the state to itself is embodied in the world as the relation of one state to another and as if the negative were something external. In the world of existence, therefore, this negative relation has the shape of a happening and an entanglement with chance events coming from without. But in fact this negative relation is that moment in the state which is most supremely its own, the state's actual infinity as the ideality of everything finite within it. It is the moment wherein the substance of the state— i.e., its absolute power against everything individual and particular, against life, property, and their rights, even against societies and associations—makes the nullity of these finite things an accomplished fact and brings it home to consciousness.

324. This destiny whereby the rights and interests of individuals are established as a passing phase, is at the same time the positive moment, i.e. the positing of their absolute, not their contingent and unstable, individuality. This relation and the recognition of it is therefore the individual's substantive duty, the duty to maintain this substantive individuality, i.e. the independence and sovereignty of the state, at the risk and the sacrifice of property and life, as well as of opinion and everything else naturally comprised in the compass of life.

An entirely distorted account of the demand for this sacrifice results from regarding the state as a mere civil society and from regarding its final end as only the security of individual life and property. This security cannot possibly be obtained by the sacrifice of what is to be secured—on the contrary.

The ethical moment in war is implied in what has been said in this Paragraph. War is not to be regarded as an absolute evil and as a purely external accident, which itself therefore has some accidental cause, be it injustices, the passions of nations or the holders of power, &c., or in short, something or other which ought not to be. It is to what is by nature accidental that accidents happen, and the fate whereby they happen is thus a necessity. Here as elsewhere, the point of view from which things seem pure accidents vanishes if we look at them in the light of the concept and philosophy, because philosophy knows accident for a show and sees in it its essence, necessity. It is necessary that the finite— property and life—should be definitely established as accidental, because accidentality is the concept of the finite. From one point of view this necessity appears in the form of the power of nature, and everything is mortal and transient. But in the ethical substance, the state, nature is robbed of this power, and the necessity is exalted to be the work of freedom, to be something ethical. The transience of the finite becomes a willed passing away, and the negativity lying at the roots of the finite becomes the substantive individuality proper to the ethical substance.

War is the state of affairs which deals in earnest with the vanity of temporal goods and concerns—a vanity at other times a common theme of edifying sermonizing. This is what makes it the moment in which the ideality of the particular attains its right and is actualized. War has the higher significance that by its agency, as I have remarked elsewhere, 'the ethical health of peoples is preserved in their indifference to the stabilization of finite institutions; just as the blowing of the winds preserves the sea from the foulness which would be the result of a prolonged calm, so also corruption in nations would be the product of prolonged, let alone 'perpetual', peace.' This, however, is said to be only a philosophic idea, or, to use another common expression, a 'justification of Providence', and it is maintained that actual wars require some other justification. On this point, see below.

The ideality which is in evidence in war, i.e., in an accidental relation of a state to a foreign state, is the same as the ideality in accordance with which the domestic powers of the state are organic moments in a whole. This fact appears in history in various forms, e.g., successful wars have checked domestic unrest and consolidated the power of the state at home. Other phenomena illustrate the same point: e.g. peoples unwilling or afraid to tolerate sovereignty at home have been subjugated from abroad, and they have struggled for their independence with the less glory and success the less they have been able previously to organize the powers of the state in home affairs—their freedom has died from the fear of dying; states whose autonomy has been guaranteed not by their armed forces but in other ways (e.g., by their disproportionate smallness in comparison with their neighbours) have been able to subsist with a constitution of their own which by itself would not have assured peace in either home or foreign affairs.

325. Sacrifice on behalf of the individuality of the state is the substantial tie between the state and all its members and so is a universal duty. Since this tie is a *single* aspect of the ideality, as contrasted with the reality, of subsistent particulars, it becomes at the same time a *particular* tie, and those who are in it form a class of their own with the characteristic of courage.

326. The matter at issue in disputes between states may be only one particular aspect of their relation to each other, and it is for such disputes that the particular class devoted to the state's defence is principally appointed. But if the state as such, if its autonomy, is in jeopardy, all its citizens are in duty bound to answer the summons to its defence. If in such circumstances the entire state is under arms and is torn from its domestic life at home to fight abroad, the war of defense turns into a war of conquest.

The armed force of the state becomes a standing army, while its appointment to the particular task of state defence makes it a class. This happens from the same necessity as compels other particular moments, interests, and activities in the state to crystallize into a given status or class, e.g. into the status of marriage or into the business or civil servant class, or into the Estates of the Realm. Ratiocination, running hither and thither from ground to consequent, launches forth into reflections about the relative advantages and disadvantages of standing armies. Opinion readily decides that the latter preponderate, partly because the concept of a thing is harder to grasp than its single and external aspects, but also because particular interests and ends (the expense of a standing army, and its result, higher taxation, &c.) are rated in the consciousness of civil society more highly than what is necessary in and by itself. In this way the latter comes to count only as a means to particular ends.

327. In itself, courage is a *formal* virtue, because (i) it is a display of freedom by radical abstraction from all particular ends, possessions, pleasure, and life; but (ii) this negation is a negation of externalities, and their alienation, the culmination of courage, is not intrinsically of a spiritual (*geistiger*) character; (iii) the courageous man's inner motive need only be some particular reason or other, and even the actual result of what he does need be present solely to the minds of others and not to his own.

328. The intrinsic worth of courage as a disposition of mind is to be found in the genuine, absolute, final end, the sovereignty of the state. The work of courage is to actualize this final end, and the means to this end is the sacrifice of personal actuality. This form of experience thus contains the harshness of extreme contradictions: a self-sacrifice which yet is the real existence of one's freedom; the maximum self-subsistence of individuality, yet only as a cog playing its part in the mechanism of an external organization; absolute obedience, renunciation of personal opinions and reasonings, in fact complete *absence* of mind, coupled with the most intense and comprehensive *presence* of mind and decision in the moment of acting; the most hostile and so most personal action against individuals, coupled with an attitude of complete indifference or even liking toward them as individuals.

To risk one's life is better than merely fearing death, but is still purely negative and so indeterminate and without value in itself. It is the positive aspect, the end and content, which first gives significance to this spiritedness. Robbers and murderers bent on crime as their end, adventurers pursuing ends planned to suit their own whims, &c., these too have spirit enough to risk their lives.

The principle of the modern world—thought and the universal—has given courage a higher form, because its display now seems to be more mechanical, the act not of this particular person, but of a member of a whole. Moreover, it seems to be turned not against single persons, but against a hostile group, and hence personal bravery appears impersonal. It is for this reason that thought has invented the gun, and the invention of this weapon, which has changed the purely personal form of bravery into a more abstract one, is no accident.

329. The state's tendency to look abroad lies in the fact that it is an individual subject. Its relation to other states therefore falls to the power of the crown. Hence it directly devolves on the monarch, and on him alone, to command the armed forces, to conduct foreign affairs through ambassadors &c., to make war and peace, and to conclude treaties of all kinds.

B. International Law

330. International law springs from the relations between autonomous states. It is for this reason that what is absolute in it retains the form of an ought-to-be, since its actuality depends on different wills each of which is sovereign.

331. The nation state is mind in its substantive rationality and immediate actuality and is therefore the absolute power on earth. It follows that every state is sovereign and autonomous against its neighbours. It is entitled in the first place and without qualification to be sovereign from their point of view, i.e. to be recognized by them as sovereign. At the same time, however, this title is purely formal, and the demand for this recognition of the state, merely on the ground that it is a state, is abstract. Whether a state is in fact something absolute depends on its content, i.e. on its constitution and general situation; and recognition, implying as it does an identity of both form and content, is conditional on the neighbouring state's judgement and will.

A state is as little an actual individual without relations to other states (see Paragraph 322) as an individual is actually a person without *rapport* with other persons (see Paragraph 71 and elsewhere). The legitimate authority of a state and, more particularly, so far as its foreign relations are concerned, of its monarch also, is partly a purely domestic matter (one state should not meddle with the domestic affairs of another). On the other hand, however, it is no less essential that this authority should receive its full and final legitimation through its recognition by other states, although this recognition requires to be safeguarded by the proviso that where a state is to be recognized by others, it shall likewise recognize them, i.e. respect their autonomy; and so it comes about that they cannot be indifferent to each other's domestic affairs.

The question arises how far a nomadic people, for instance, or any people on a low level of civilization, can be regarded as a state. As once was the case with the Jews and the Mohammedan peoples, religious views may entail an opposition at a higher level between one people and its neighbours and so preclude the general identity which is requisite for recognition.

332. The immediate actuality which any state possesses from the point of view of other states is particularized into a multiplicity of relations which are determined by the arbitrary will of both autonomous parties and which therefore possess the formal nature of contracts pure and simple. The subject-matter of these contracts, however, is infinitely less varied than it is in civil society, because in civil society individuals are reciprocally interdependent in the most numerous respects, while autonomous states are principally wholes whose needs are met within their own borders.

333. The fundamental proposition of international law (i.e. the universal law which ought to be absolutely valid between states, as distinguished from the particular content of positive treaties) is that treaties, as the ground of obligations between states, ought to be kept. But since the sovereignty of a state is the principle of its relations to others, states are to that extent in a state of nature in relation to each other. Their rights are actualized only in their particular wills and not in a universal will with constitutional powers over them. This universal proviso of international law therefore does not go beyond an ought-to-be, and what really happens is that international relations in accordance with treaty alternate with the severance of these relations.

There is no Praetor to judge between states; at best there may be an arbitrator or a mediator, and even he exercises his functions contingently only, i.e. in dependence on the particular wills of the disputants. Kant had an idea for securing 'perpetual peace' by a League of Nations to adjust every dispute. It was to be a power recognized by each individual state, and was to arbitrate in all of dissension in order to make it impossible for disputants to resort to war in order to settle them. This idea presupposes an accord between states; this would rest on moral or religious or other grounds and considerations, but in any case would always depend ultimately on a particular sovereign will and for that reason would remain infected with contingency.

334. It follows that if states disagree and their particular wills cannot be harmonized, the matter can only be settled by war. A state through its subjects has widespread connexions and many-sided interests, and these may be readily and considerably injured; but it remains inherently indeterminable which of these injuries is to be regarded as a specific breach of treaty or as an injury to the honour and autonomy of the state. The reason for this is that a state may regard its infinity and honour as at stake in each of its concerns, however minute, and it is all the more inclined to susceptibility to injury the more its strong individuality is impelled as a result of long domestic peace to seek and create a sphere of activity abroad.

335. Apart from this, the state is in essence mind and therefore cannot be prepared to stop at just taking notice of an injury *after* it has actually occurred. On the contrary, there arises in addition as a cause of strife the *idea* of such an injury as the idea of a danger *threatening* from another state, together with calculations of degrees probability on this side and that, guessing at intentions, &c., &c.

336. Since states are related to one another as autonomous entities and so as particular wills on which the very validity of treaties depends, and since the particular will of the whole is in content a will for its own welfare pure and simple, it follows that welfare is the highest law governing the relation of one state to another. This is all the more the case since the Idea of the state is precisely the supersession of the clash between right (i.e. empty abstract freedom) and welfare (i.e., the particular content which fills that void), and it is when states become *concrete* wholes that they first attain recognition (see Paragraph 331.)

337. The substantial welfare of the state is its welfare as a particular state in its specific interest and situation and its no less special foreign affairs, including its particular treaty relations. Its government therefore is a matter of particular wisdom, not of universal Providence (compare Remark to Paragraph 324). Similarly, its aim in relation to other states and its principle for justifying wars and treaties is not a universal thought (the thought of philanthropy) but only its actually injured or threatened welfare as something specific and peculiar to itself.

At one time the opposition between morals and politics, and the demand that the latter should conform to the former, were much canvassed. On this point only a general remark is required here. The welfare of a state has claims to recognition totally different from those of the welfare of the individual. The ethical substance, the state, has its determinate being, i.e., its right, directly embodied in something existent, something not abstract but concrete, and the principle of its conduct and behaviour can only be this concrete existent and not one of the many universal thoughts supposed to be moral commands. When politics is alleged to clash with morals and so to be always wrong, the doctrine propounded rests on superficial ideas about morality, the nature of the state, and the state's relation to the moral point of view.

338. The fact that states reciprocally recognize each other as states remains, even in war— the state of affairs when rights disappear and force and chance hold sway—a bond wherein each counts to the rest as something absolute. Hence in war, war itself is characterized as something which ought to pass away. It implies therefore the proviso of the *jus gentium* that the possibility of peace be retained (and so, for example, that envoys must be respected), and, in general, that war be not waged against domestic institutions, against the peace of family and private life, or against persons in their private capacity.

339. Apart from this, relations between states (e.g., in war-time, reciprocal agreements about taking prisoners; in peace-time, concessions of rights to subjects of other states for the purpose of private trade and intercourse, &c.) depend principally upon the customs of nations, custom being the inner universality of behaviour maintained in all circumstances.

340. It is as particular entities that states enter into relations with one another. Hence their relations are on the largest scale a maelstrom of external contingency and the inner particularity of passions, private interests and selfish ends, abilities and virtues, vices, force, and wrong. All these whirl together, and in their vortex the ethical whole itself, the autonomy of the state, is exposed to contingency. The principles of the national minds are wholly restricted on account of their particularity, for it is in this particularity that, as existent individuals, they have their objective actuality and their self-consciousness. Their deeds and destinies in their reciprocal relations to one another are the dialectic of the finitude of these minds, and out of it arises the universal mind, the mind of the world, free from all restriction, producing itself as that which exercises its right—and its right is the highest right of all—over these finite minds in the 'history of the world which is the world's court of judgement.'

C. World History

341. The element in which the universal mind exists in art is intuition and imagery, in religion feeling and representative thinking, in philosophy pure freedom of thought. In world history this element is the actuality of mind in its whole compass of internality and externality alike. World history is a court of judgement because in its absolute universality, the particular—i.e. the *Penates*, civil society, and the national minds in their variegated actuality—is present as only ideal, and the movement of mind in this element is the exhibition of that fact.

342. Further, world history is not the verdict of mere might, i.e. the abstract and non-rational inevitability of a blind destiny. On the contrary, since mind is implicitly and actually reason, and reason is explicit to itself in mind as knowledge, world history is the necessary development, out of the concept of mind's freedom alone, of the moments of reason and so of the self-consciousness and freedom of mind. This development is the interpretation and actualization of the universal mind.

343. The history of mind is its own act. Mind is only what it does, and its act is to make itself the object of its own consciousness. In history its act is to gain consciousness of itself as mind, to apprehend itself in its interpretation of itself to itself. This apprehension is its being and its principle, and the completion of apprehension at one stage is at the same time the rejection of that stage and its transition to a higher. To use abstract phraseology, the mind apprehending this apprehension anew, or in other words returning to itself again out of its rejection of this lower stage of apprehension, is the mind of the stage higher than that on which it stood in its earlier apprehension.

   The question of the perfectibility and *Education of the Human Race* arises here. Those who have maintained this perfectibility have divined something of the nature of mind, something of the fact that it is its nature to have γνῶθι σεαυτόν as the law of its being, and, since it apprehends that which it is, to have a form higher than that which constituted its mere being. But to those who reject this doctrine, mind has remained an empty word, and history a superficial play of casual, so called 'merely human', strivings and passions. Even if, in connexion with history, they speak of Providence and the plan of Providence, and so express a faith in a higher power, their ideas remain empty because they expressly declare that for them the plan of Providence is inscrutable and incomprehensible.

344. In the course of this work of the world mind, states, nations, and individuals arise animated by their particular determinate principle which has its interpretation and actuality in their constitutions and in the whole range of their life and condition. While their consciousness is limited to these and they are absorbed in their mundane interests, they are all the time the unconscious tools and organs of the world mind at work within them. The shapes which they take pass away, while the absolute mind prepares and works out its transition to its next higher stage.

345. Justice and virtue, wrongdoing, power and vice, talents and their achievements, passions strong and weak, guilt and innocence, grandeur in individual and national life, autonomy, fortune and misfortune of states and individuals, all these have their specific significance and worth in the field of known actuality; therein they are judged and therein they have their partial, though only partial justification. World-history, however, is above the point of view from which these things matter. Each of its stages is the presence of a necessary moment in the Idea of the world mind, and that moment attains its absolute right in that stage. The nation whose life embodies this moment secures its good fortune and fame, and its deeds are brought to fruition.

346. History is mind clothing itself with the form of events or the immediate actuality of nature. The stages of its development are therefore presented as immediate natural principles. These, because they are natural, are a plurality external to one another, and they are present therefore in such a way that each of them is assigned to one nation in the external form of its geographical and anthropological conditions.

347. The nation to which is ascribed a moment of the Idea in the form of a natural principle is entrusted with giving complete effect to it in the advance of the self-developing self-consciousness of the world mind. This nation is dominant in world history during this one epoch, and it is only once (see Paragraph 345) that it can make its hour strike. In contrast with this its absolute right of being the vehicle of this present stage in the world mind's development, the minds of the other nations are without rights, and they, along with those whose hour has struck already, count no longer in world history.

The history of a single world-historical nation contains (a) the development of its principle from its latent embryonic stage until it blossoms into the self-conscious freedom of ethical life and presses in upon world history; and (b) the period of its decline and fall, since it is it decline and fall that signalizes the emergence in it of a higher principle as the pure negative of its own. When this happens, mind passes over into the new principle and so marks out another nation for world-historical significance. After this period, the declining nation has lost the interest of the absolute; it may indeed absorb the higher principle positively and begin building its life on it, but the principle is only like an adopted child, not like a relative to whom its ties are immanently vital and vigorous. Perhaps it loses its autonomy, or it may still exist, or drag out its existence, as a particular state or a group of states and involve itself without rhyme or reason in manifold enterprises at home and battles abroad.

348. All actions, including world-historical actions, culminate with individuals as subjects giving actuality to the substantial (see Remark to Paragraph 279). They are the living instruments of what is in substance the deed of the world mind and they are therefore directly at one with that deed though it is concealed from them and is not their aim and object (see Paragraph 344). For the deeds of the world mind, therefore, they receive no honour or thanks either from their contemporaries (see Paragraph 344) or from public opinion in later ages. All that is vouchsafed to them by such opinion is undying fame in respect of the subjective form of their acts.

349. A nation does not begin by being a state. The transition from a family, a horde, a clan, a multitude, &c., to political conditions is the realization of the Idea in the form of that nation. Without this form, a nation, as an ethical substance—which is what it is implicitly, lacks the objectivity of possessing in its own eyes and in the eyes of others, a universal and universally valid embodiment in laws, i.e., in determinate thoughts, and as a result it fails to secure recognition from others. So long as it lacks objective law and an explicitly established rational constitution, its autonomy is formal only and is not sovereignty.

It would be contrary even to commonplace ideas to call patriarchal conditions a 'constitution' or a people under patriarchal government a 'state' or its independence 'sovereignty'. Hence, before history actually begins, we have on the one hand dull innocence, devoid of interest, and, on the other, the courage of revenge and of the struggle for formal recognition (see Paragraph 331 and Remark to Paragraph 57).

350. It is the absolute right of the Idea to step into existence in clear-cut laws and objective institutions, beginning with marriage and agriculture (see Remark to Paragraph 203), whether this right be actualized in the form of divine legislation and favour, or in the form of force and wrong. This right is the right of heroes to found states.

351. The same consideration justifies civilized nations in regarding and treating as barbarians those who lag behind them in institutions which are the essential moments of the state. Thus a pastoral people may treat hunters as barbarians, and both of these are barbarians from the point of view of agriculturists, &c. The civilized nation is conscious that the rights of barbarians are unequal to its own and treats their autonomy as only a formality.

When wars and disputes arise in such circumstances, the trait which gives them a significance for world history is the fact that they are struggles for recognition in connexion with something of specific intrinsic worth.

352. The concrete Ideas, the minds of the nations, have their truth and their destiny in the concrete Idea which is absolute universality, i.e., in the world mind. Around its throne they stand as the executors of its actualization and as signs and ornaments of its grandeur. As mind, it is nothing but its active movement towards absolute knowledge of itself and therefore towards freeing its consciousness from the form of natural immediacy and so coming to itself. Therefore the principles of the formations of this self-consciousness in the course of its liberation—the world-historical realms—are four in number.

353. In its *first* and immediate revelation, mind has as its principle the shape of the substantial mind, i.e. the shape of the identity in which individuality is absorbed in its essence and its claims are not explicitly recognized.

The *second* principle is this substantial mind endowed with knowledge so that mind is both the positive content and filling of mind and also the individual self-awareness which is the living form of mind. This principle is ethical individuality as beauty.

The *third* principle is the inward deepening of this individual self-awareness and knowledge until it reaches abstract universality and therefore infinite opposition to the objective world which in the same process has become mind-forsaken.

The principle of the *fourth* formation is the conversion of this opposition so that mind receives in its inner life its truth and concrete essence, while in objectivity it is at home and reconciled with itself. The mind which has thus reverted to the substantiality with which it began is the mind which has returned out of the infinite opposition, and which consequently engenders and knows this its truth as thought and as a world of actual laws.

354. In accordance with these four principles, the world-historical realms are the following: (1) the Oriental, (2) the Greek, (3) the Roman, (4) the Germanic.

355. (1) The Oriental realm.

The world-view of this first realm is substantial, without inward division, and it arises in natural communities patriarchically governed. According to this view, the mundane form of government is theocratic, the ruler is also a high priest or God himself; constitution and legislation are at the same time religion, while religious and moral commands, or usages rather, are at the same time natural and positive law. In the magnificence of this regime as a whole, individual personality loses its rights and perishes; the external world of nature is either directly divine or else God's ornament, and the history of the actual is poetry. Distinctions are developed in customs, government, and state on their many sides, and in default of laws and amidst the simplicity of manners, they become unwieldy, diffuse, and superstitious ceremonies, the accidents of personal power and arbitrary rule, and class differences become crystallized into hereditary castes. Hence in the Oriental state nothing is fixed, and what is stable is fossilized; it lives therefore only in an outward movement which becomes in the end an elemental fury and desolation. Its inner calm is merely the calm of non-political life and immersion in feebleness and exhaustion.

A still substantial, natural, mentality is a moment in the development of the state, and the point at which any state takes this form is the absolute beginning of its history. This has been emphasized and demonstrated with learning and profound insight in connexion with the history of particular states by Dr. Stuhr in his book *Der Untergang der Naturstaaten*—a work in which he leads the way to a rational treatment of constitutional history and of history generally. The principle of subjectivity and self-conscious freedom is there too shown to be the principle of the Germanic people, but the book goes no further than the decline of natural states, and consequently the principle is only brought to the point where it appears either as a restless mobility, as human caprice and corruption, or in its particular form as emotion, and where it has not yet developed to the objectivity of the self-conscious substantiality or to an organized legal system.

356. (2) The Greek realm.

This realm possesses this substantial unity of finite and infinite, but only as a mysterious background, suppressed in dim recesses of the memory, in caves and traditional imagery. This background, reborn out of the mind which differentiates itself to individual mentality, emerges into the daylight of knowing and is tempered and transfigured into beauty and a free and unruffled ethical life. Hence it is in a world of this character that the principle of personal individuality arises, though it is still not self-enclosed but kept in its ideal unity. The result is that the whole is divided into a group of particular national minds; ultimate decision is ascribed not to the subjectivity of explicitly independent self-consciousness but to a power standing above and outside it (see Remark to Paragraph 279); on the other hand, the due satisfaction of particular needs is not yet comprised in the sphere of freedom but is relegated exclusively to a class of slaves.

357. (3) The Roman realm.

In this realm, differentiation is carried to its conclusion, and ethical life is sundered without end into the extremes of the private self-consciousness of persons on the one hand, and abstract universality on the other. This opposition begins in the clash between the substantial intuition of an aristocracy and the principle of free personality in democratic form. As the opposition grows, the first of these opponents develops into superstition and the maintenance of heartless self-seeking power, while the second becomes more and more corrupt until it sinks into a rabble. Finally, the whole is dissolved and the result is universal misfortune and the destruction of ethical life. National heroes die away into the unity of a Pantheon, all individuals are degraded to the level of private persons equal with one another, possessed of formal rights, and the only bond left to hold them together is abstract insatiable self-will.

358. (4) The Germanic realm.
    Mind and its world are thus both alike lost and plunged in the infinite grief of that fate for which a people, the Jewish people, was held in readiness. Mind is here pressed back upon itself in the extreme of its absolute negativity. This is the absolute turning point; mind rises out of this situation and grasps the infinite positivity of this its inward character, i.e., it grasps the principle of the unity of the divine nature and the human, the reconciliation of objective truth and freedom as the truth and freedom appearing within self-consciousness and subjectivity, a reconciliation with the fulfilment of which the principle of the north, the principle of the Germanic peoples, has been entrusted.

359. This principle is first of all inward and abstract; it exists in feeling as faith, love, and hope, the reconciliation and resolution of all contradiction. It then discloses its content, raising it to become actuality and self-conscious rationality, to become a mundane realm proceeding from the heart, fidelity, and comradeship of free men, a realm which in this its subjectivity is equally a realm of crude individual caprice and barbarous manners. This realm it sets over against a world of beyond, an intellectual realm, whose content is indeed the truth of its (the principle's) mind, but a truth not yet thought and so still veiled in barbarous imagery. This world of beyond, as the power of mind over the mundane heart, acts against the latter as a compulsive and frightful force.

360. These two realms stand distinguished from one another though at the same time they are rooted in a single unity and Idea. Here their distinction is intensified to absolute opposition and a stern struggle ensues in the course of which the realm of mind lowers the place of its heaven to an earthly here and now, to a common worldliness of fact and idea. The mundane realm, on the other hand, builds up its abstract independence into thought and the principle of rational being and knowing, i.e., into the rationality of right and law. In this way their opposition implicitly loses its marrow and disappears. The realm of fact has discarded its barbarity and unrighteous caprice, while the realm of truth has abandoned the world of beyond and its arbitrary force, so that the true reconciliation which discloses the state as the image and actuality of reason has become objective. In the state, self-consciousness finds in an organic development the actuality of its substantive knowing and willing; in religion, it finds the feeling and the representation of this its own truth as an ideal essentiality; while in philosophic science, it finds the free comprehension and knowledge of this truth as one and the same in its mutually complementary manifestations, i.e. in the state, in nature, and in the ideal world.

Notes

1. The fact that the church comes in in this connexion is a further point, but not one for discussion here.
2. i.e., a *matrona*, not a wife who *in manum convenit*, *in mancipio est*, and whose marriage was a slavery to her husband.

3. The fact that there is a further distinction between this and *possessio bonorum* is a piece of the erudition which constitutes the juristic expert.
4. Book iii [415 *a-d*].
5. I have described the book sufficiently to show that it is of an original kind. There might be something noble in the author's indignation by itself, since it was kindled by the false theories, mentioned above, emanating principally from Rousseau, and especially by the attempt to realize them in practice. But to save himself from these theories, Herr von Haller has gone to the other extreme by dispensing with thought altogether and consequently it cannot be said that there is anything of intrinsic value in his virulent hatred of all laws and legislation, of all expressly and legally determinate rights. The hatred of law, of right made determinate in law, is the shibboleth whereby fanaticism, flabby-mindedness, and the hypocrisy of good intentions are clearly and infallibly recognized for what they are, disguise themselves as they may.

Originality like Herr von Haller's is always a curious phenomenon, and for those of my readers who are not yet acquainted with his book I will quote a few specimen passages. This is how he lays down (vol. i, pp. 342 ff. [pp. 361 ff.]) his most important basic proposition: 'Just as, in the inorganic world, the greater dislodges the less and the mighty the weak . . . , so in the animal kingdom, and then amongst human beings, the same law appears in nobler' (often, too, surely in ignobler?) 'forms', and [p. 375] 'this, therefore, is the eternal, unalterable, ordinance of God, that the mightier rules, must rule, and will always rule'. It is clear enough from this, let alone from what follows, in what sense 'might' is taken here. It is not the might of justice and ethics, but only the irrational power of brute force. Herr von Haller then goes on (ibid., pp. 365 ff. [pp. 380 ff.]) to support this doctrine on various grounds, amongst them that 'nature with amazing wisdom has so ordered it that the mere sense of personal superiority irresistibly ennobles the character and encourages the development of just those virtues which are most necessary for dealing with subordinates'. He asks with a great elaboration of undergraduate rhetoric [ibid.] 'whether it is the strong or the weak in the kingdom of science who more misuse their trust and their authority in order to achieve their petty selfish ends and the ruin of the credulous; whether to be a past master in legal learning is not to be a pettifogger, a *leguleius*, one who cheats the hopes of unsuspecting clients, who makes white black and black white, who misapplies the law and makes it a vehicle for wrongdoing, who brings to beggary those who need his assistance and rends them as the hungry vulture rends the innocent lamb', &c., &c. Herr von Haller forgets here that the point of this rhetoric is to support his proposition that the rule of the mightier is an everlasting ordinance of God; so presumably it is by the same ordinance that the vulture rends the innocent lamb, and that hence the mighty are quite right to treat their unsuspecting clients as the weak and to make use of knowledge of the law to *empty* their pockets. It would be too much, however, to ask that two thoughts should be put together where there is really not a single one.

It goes without saying that Herr von Haller is an enemy of codes of law. In his view, the laws of the land, are on the one hand, in principle 'unnecessary, because they spring self-explanatory from the laws of nature'. If men had remained satisfied with 'self-explanatory' as the basis of their thinking, then they would have been spared the endless labour devoted, since ever there were states, to legislation and legal codes, and which is still devoted thereto and to the study of positive law. 'On the other hand, laws are not exactly promulgated for private individuals, but as instructions to puisne judges, acquainting them with the will of the high court' [vol. ii, part i, chap. 32]. Apart from that, the provision of law-courts is (vol. i, p. 297 [pp. 309 ff.], vol. ii, part i, p. 254 [pp. 264-9] and all over the place) not a state duty, but a favour, help rendered by the authorities, and 'quite supererogatory'; it is not the most perfect method of guaranteeing men's rights; on the contrary, it is an insecure and uncertain method, 'the only one left to us by our modern lawyers. They have reft us of the other three methods, of just those which lead most swiftly and surely to the goal, those which, unlike law-courts, friendly nature has given to man for the safeguarding of his rightful freedom'. And these three methods are—what do you suppose?—'(1) Personal acceptance and inculcation of the law of nature; (2) Resistance to wrong; (3) Flight, when there is no other remedy'. Lawyers are unfriendly indeed, it appears, in comparison with the friendliness of nature! 'But' (vol. i, p. 292 [p. 305]) 'the natural, divine, law, given to everyone by nature the all bountiful, is: Honour everyone as thine equal' (on the author's principles this should read 'Honour not the man who is thine equal, but the one who is mightier'); 'hurt no man who hurts thee not; demand from him nothing but what he owes' (but what does he owe?); 'nay more, love thy neighbour and serve him when thou canst'. The 'implanting of this law' is to make a legislator and a constitution superfluous. It would be curious to see how Herr von Haller makes it intelligible why legislators and constitutions have appeared in the world despite this 'implanting'.

In vol. iii, pp. 362 [361] ff., the author comes to the 'so-called national liberties', by which he means the laws and constitutions of nation states. Every legally constituted right is in this wide sense of the word a 'liberty'. Of these laws he says, *inter alia*, that 'their content is usually very insignificant, although in books a high value may be placed on documentary liberties of that kind'. When we then realize that the author is speaking here of the national liberties of the German Estates, of the English people (e.g. Magna Carta [p.367] 'which is little read, and on account of its archaic phraseology still less understood', the Bill of Rights, and so forth), of the people of Hungary, &c., we are surprised to find that these possessions, formerly so highly prized, are only insignificant; and no less surprised to learn that it is only in books that these nations place a value on laws whose co-operation has entered into every coat that is worn and every crust that is eaten, and still enters into every day and hour of the lives of everyone.

To carry quotation further, Herr von Haller speaks particularly ill (vol. i, pp. 185 ff. [pp. 192-3]) of the Prussian General Legal Code, because of the 'incredible' influence on it of the errors of false philosophy (though in this instance at any rate the fault cannot be ascribed to Kant's philosophy, a topic on which Herr von Haller is at his angriest), especially where it speaks of the state, the resources of the state, the end of the state, the head of the state, his duties, and those of civil servants, and so forth. Herr von Haller finds particularly mischievous [vol. i, pp. 198-9] 'the right of defraying the expenses of the state by levying taxes on the private wealth of individuals, on their businesses, on goods produced or consumed. Under those circumstances, neither the king himself (since the resources of the state belong to the state and are not the private property of the king), nor the Prussian citizens can call anything their own, neither their person nor their property; and all subjects are bondslaves to the law, since they may not withdraw themselves from the service of the state.'

In this welter of incredible crudity, what is perhaps most comical of all is the emotion with which Herr von Haller describes his unspeakable pleasure in his discoveries (vol. i, Preface [pp. xxv-xxvii])—'a joy such as only the friend of truth can feel when after honest search he has become confident that he has found as it were' (yes indeed! 'as it were' is right!) 'the voice of nature, the very word of God'. (The truth is that the word of God very clearly distinguishes its revelations from the voices of nature and unregenerate man.) 'The author could have sunk to the ground in open amazement, a stream of joyful tears burst from his eyes, and living religious feeling sprang up in him there and then.' Herr von Haller might have discovered by his 'religious feeling' that he should rather bewail his condition as the hardest chastisement of God. For the hardest thing which man can experience is to be so far excluded from thought and reason, from respect for the laws, and from knowing how infinitely important and divine it is that the duties of the state and the rights of the citizens, as well as the rights of the state and the duties of the citizens, should be defined by law—to be so far excluded from all this that absurdity can foist itself upon him as the word of God.

6. Religion, knowledge, and science have as their principle a form peculiar to each and different from that of the state. They therefore enter the state partly as *means*—means to education and [a higher] mentality—partly in so far as they are in essence *ends* in themselves, for the reason that they are embodied in existent institutions. In both these respects the principles of the state have, in their application, a bearing on them. A comprehensive, concrete treatise on the state would also have to deal with those spheres of life as well as with art and such things as mere geographical matters, and to consider their place in the state and their bearing on it. In this book, however, it is the principle of the state in its own special sphere which is being fully expounded in accordance with the Idea, and it is only in passing that reference can be made to the principles of religion, &c., and to the application of the right of the state to them.

7. Quakers, Anabaptists, &c., may be said to be active members only of civil society, and they may be regarded as private persons standing in merely private relations to others. Even when this position has been allowed them, they have been exempted from taking the oath. They fulfil their direct duties to the state in a passive way; one of the most important of these duties, the defence of the state against its enemies, they refuse outright to fulfil, and their refusal may perhaps be admitted provided they perform some other service instead. To sects of this kind, the state's attitude is toleration in the strict sense of the word, because since they decline to recognize their duty to the state,

they may not claim the rights of citizenship. On one occasion when the abolition of the slave-trade was being pressed with great vigour in the American Congress, a member from one of the Southern States made the striking retort: 'Give us our slaves, and you may keep your Quakers.' Only if the state is otherwise strong can it overlook and suffer such anomalies, because it can then rely principally on the strength of custom and the inner rationality of its institutions to diminish and close the gap between the existence of anomalies and the full assertion of its own strict rights. Thus technically it may have been right to refuse a grant of even civil rights to the Jews on the ground that they should be regarded as belonging not merely to a religious sect but to a foreign race. But the fierce outcry raised against the Jews, from that point of view and others, ignores the fact that they are, above all, *men;* and manhood, so far from being a mere superficial, abstract quality (see Remark to Paragraph 209), is on the contrary itself the basis of the fact that what civil rights rouse in their possessors is the feeling of oneself as counting in civil society as a person with rights, and this feeling of self-hood, infinite and free from all restrictions, is the root from which the desired similarity in disposition and ways of thinking comes into being. To exclude the Jews from civil rights, on the other hand, would rather be to confirm the isolation with which they have been reproached—a result for which the state refusing them rights would be blamable and reproachable, because by so refusing, it would have misunderstood its own basic principle, its nature as an objective and powerful institution (compare the end of the Remark to Paragraph 268). The exclusion of the Jews from civil rights may be supposed to be a right of the highest kind and may be demanded on that ground; but experience has shown that so to exclude them is the silliest folly, and the way in which governments now treat them has proved itself to be both prudent and dignified.

8. 'When Galileo published the discoveries' about the phases of Venus, &c., which he had made with the aid of the telescope, 'he showed that they incontestably proved the motion of the earth. But this idea of the motion of the earth was declared heretical by an assembly of Cardinals, and Galileo, its most famous advocate, was haled before the Inquisition and compelled to recant it, under pain of severe imprisonment. One of the strongest of passions is the love of truth in a man of genius. . . . Convinced of the motion of the earth as a result of his own observations, Galileo meditated a long while on a new work in which he had resolved to develop all the proofs in its favour. But in order at the same time to escape from the persecution of which otherwise he would inevitably have been the victim, he hit upon the device of expounding them in the form of dialogues between three speakers. . . . It is obvious enough in them that the advantage lies with the advocate of the Copernican system; but since Galileo did not decide between the speakers, and gave as much weight as possible to the objections raised by the partisans of Ptolemy, he might well have expected to be left to enjoy undisturbed the peace to which his advanced age and his labours had entitled him. . . . In his seventieth year he was haled once more before the tribunal of the Inquisition. . . . He was imprisoned and required to recant his opinions a second time under threat of the penalty fixed for a relapse into heresy. . . . He was made to sign an abjuration in the following terms: "I, Galileo, appearing in person before the court in my seventieth year, kneeling, and with my eyes on the holy Gospels which I hold in my hands, abjure, damn, and execrate with my whole heart and true belief the absurd, false, and heretical doctrine of the motion of the earth. . . ." What a spectacle! An aged, venerable man, famous throughout a long life exclusively devoted to the study of nature, abjuring on his knees, against the witness of his own conscience, the truth which he had demonstrated so convincingly! By the judgement of the Inquisition he was condemned to perpetual imprisonment. A year later he was set at liberty through the intercession of the Grand Duke of Florence. . . . He died in 1642. . . . Europe mourned his loss. It had been enlightened by his labours and was exasperated by the judgement passed by a defeated tribunal on a man of his greatness.' (Laplace: *Exposition du système du monde*, Book V, chap. 4.)

9. Deut. xvii. 16 ff.

KARL MARX AND FRIEDRICH ENGELS

Karl Marx (1818–1883) was born in Trier, in a Prussian province along the Rhine. His family was upper middle class, nominally Protestant, and ethnically Jewish. From 1835 to 1841, Marx pursued his university studies, first at Bonn, then at Berlin, Hegel's old university, where his tenuous interest in the law shifted to a commitment to philosophy. Marx became one of the "Young Hegelians" who followed Hegel in viewing history as the rational development of the idea of freedom through the generation and resolution of contradictions, and, much more than Hegel, criticized received traditions and institutions as obstacles to this progress.

Although Marx earned a doctorate in philosophy in 1841, he turned to journalism as his most effective means of social criticism. But Prussian repression intervened. His newspaper was shut down in 1843, largely in response to Marx's investigations of poverty among the Rhenish peasantry.

Marx moved to Paris, where he combined more journalism with intensive study of English economists, French political historians, and "Communists," i.e., advocates of communal ownership and the leveling of economic differences who had begun to attract a working-class following in France and Germany. The source of our first selection, a series of rough drafts now known as the "*Economic and Philosophical Manuscripts* of 1844," was the most important product of this diverse ferment. First published in 1927, the *Manuscripts* mark a large step away from the rationalist reformism of the Young Hegelians and have served, since their publication, as an epitome of Marx's abiding spiritual concerns.

Often, Marx's project in these manuscripts is to use his experience and reading concerning economic life to transform certain diagnoses of psychological impoverishment that he had encountered in Hegel and in the atheist, materialist philosopher Ludwig Feuerbach (1804–1872). Both philosophers were concerned with processes of "alienation," in which aspects of human life through which people could potentially express themselves or their common humanity are instead confronted as external phenomena, opposed to self-expression. Marx's predecessors locate the roots of this self-estrangement in confused thinking: the self's overly rigid conceptualization of its relation to objective reality (Hegel), or humans' conversion of "species-being," our appreciation of our common humanity, into awe at an imagined God embodying our common strivings (Feuerbach). Marx accepts the devastating effect of estrangement from oneself and others but traces it to a specific feature of economic life under capitalism: the necessity that wage earners face of selling their life activity as a commodity in order to survive. Unrestrained economic competition leads more and more people to lose control of means of production, forcing them to submit to the labor market. So the cure for alienation is not mere removal of political restrictions but the creation of a new kind of

economy, based on common control of production in the interest of reciprocity, expressive work, and the satisfaction of the needs characteristic of cooper-
ating human beings.

In 1845, the French government, under pressure from the Prussian
monarchy, expelled Marx, who moved to Brussels. There, Marx began his lifelong collaboration with Friedrich Engels, with whom he had become friends in
Paris. One of their first coauthored works, *The German Ideology* (finished
in 1846, but unpublished until 1932) is the source of our second reading. As in
the 1844 *Manuscripts*, the project is sometimes the economic explanation of
spiritual ills, both alienation and the one-sided personal development that
Marx and Engels trace to the division of labor. A new theme is the explanation
of how social systems develop. In a vague outline that would be filled in and
revised in much future work, Marx and Engels propose that the pursuit of
enhanced powers of material production has the unintended consequence
of creating new social relations of production, which, in turn, mold the political
and cultural features of an era.

Along with this theoretical work, Marx and Engels were getting to know
working-class radicals, especially members of the League of the Just, a con-
spiratorial Communist group with branches throughout western Europe. As
they moved the League closer to their own views, they joined it. In a congress
in London, the League renamed itself "the Communist League" and adopted
guiding principles that Marx and Engels were asked to elaborate in a manifesto. The result, *Manifesto of the Communist Party*, our next selection, came
off the presses in February 1848, just as a continental wave of revolutions
began with the overthrow of the French monarchy.

The *Manifesto's* astounding mixture of advocacy, theorizing, and historical narration centers on a conception of capitalist society as based on an
antagonistic relation that will, inevitably, destroy it, the relation between the
proletariat and the bourgeoisie. Broadly speaking, the proletariat are those who
control no significant means of production and must make a living by selling
the use of their labor power to others who do. The bourgeoisie are these others,
people exercising significant control over means of production and mainly
deriving their income from the sale of what proletarians working these means
produce. The two classes are "two great hostile camps," since the competitive
bourgeois drive for profits creates relentless pressure to reduce wages and to
eliminate individualized ways of working that conflict with industrial routines.
Marx and Engels take political and cultural institutions (including "the modern
representative state") to advance the long-term interests of the bourgeoisie in
this conflict. Yet, in the face of this "ruling class" dominance, the bourgeoisie
"produces . . . , above all, its own grave-diggers." Economic interdependence,
the reduced importance of mastercraftsmen's expertise, mass literacy, and ease
of communication are features of modern proletarian life due to the bourgeois
drive to expand production. Yet their utterly unintended result is increased unity
in resistance to the burdens of capitalist production, ultimately progressing to
full-scale revolution and the creation of a proletarian ruling class. Marx and
Engels see this as the basis for yet further transformations, ultimately including
a stateless society in which work is motivated by a desire for mutual benefit.

Responding to the revolutionary fervor that coincided with the appearance of the *Manifesto*, Marx and Engels returned to Germany—Marx as organizer and main writer of a revolutionary newspaper, Engels both as journalist
and officer in a revolutionary army. The failure of the revolutions brought Marx's

final exile. He was expelled from Prussia in 1850 on account of the "dangerous tendencies" of his newspaper, soon settling in London, where he spent the rest of his life. The Marx family was desperately poor at the start, and, for the next two decades (after which Engels provided a stipend), Marx's struggle to make ends meet as a freelance journalist never kept them far from poverty.

Most of Marx's theoretical work in this second half of his life was devoted to the description of the economic "laws of motion" of capitalism, which eventually took the form of his multivolume treatise, *Capital*. Only the first volume appeared in Marx's lifetime, in 1867. Marx's most important political activity in London was his leading role in the International Workingmen's Association (1864–1876), an international group of predominantly working-class activists, which led demonstrations of English workers in favor of Irish independence, organized international strike support, and outraged the respectable classes of Europe by supporting the Paris Commune, a revolutionary government, including members of the International, which controlled Paris for two months at the end of the Franco-Prussian War.

Our next selection is the celebrated Preface to an otherwise little-read work that prefigured parts of *Capital* I—*A Contribution to a Critique of Political Economy* (1859). Its fame rests on part of a paragraph in a brief autobiographical sketch, a few lines that contain Marx's most detailed statement of his general conception of social stability and social change. With the help of other writings by Marx and the many thousands of pages of commentary inspired by these few lines, some features of Marx's meaning here have become fairly well established. As in his analysis of capitalist society in the *Manifesto*, Marx takes relations of control that dominate material production to be the foundation on which political and cultural institutions rest: i.e., the most important features of these "superstructural" institutions are as they are because this helps to maintain the "economic structure" consisting of those "relations of production." Despite these stabilizing institutions, Marx thinks that there are processes internal to some social systems that make change inevitable. The ultimate origin of such internal change lies in the mode of production, i.e., the ensemble of relations of control, work relations, and technological capacities through which material goods are produced. In particular, people's locations in an initially stable economic structure may lead them to increase the productive capacity of resources they control until further productive improvement is inhibited by the old relations of production. Marx's paradigm is the inhibition of productive capitalist investment by guild rules, traditional overlord-tenant ties, and economically arbitrary grants of royal monopolies in late-feudal England. Eventually, the enhanced productive forces, together with their fettering, provide resources and motivations for an effective social revolution, so that the chains are broken and a new structure established, facilitating the growth of productive power.

The development of Marx's theory of capitalism in his London years, which led to our next selection, was sustained by countless hours of reading in the British Museum library. At the same time, the evolution of Marx's thinking reflected his personal contact with British trades unionism. While the *Manifesto* had emphasized spontaneous tendencies of capitalism to dissolve divisions among workers based on ethnicity, religion, or nation, Marx came to see the antagonism between ethnically English and ethnically Irish workers as "the secret of the impotence of the English working class," a division maintained by the mass media of the time, requiring organized opposition by groups such as the International. While the *Manifesto* had described a down-ward trend of wages and working conditions to the threshold of bare physical survival, Marx became acutely aware of the sustained upward trend in real wages in Britain and the benefits of the shortened working day.

Value, Price and Profit, the basis for talks Marx gave in the General Council of the International in 1865, reflects this combination of theoretical work and concrete experience. The first six chapters, omitted here, argue against a position advanced in Council discussions that trades union activity could do nothing to improve the economic situation of workers under capital-ism. In our selection, Marx, in effect, gives a preview of aspects of Volume I of *Capital* in order to shed light on the actual limits of the capitalist labor market.

For purposes of economic theorizing, Marx measures the value of a com-modity by the total time needed to produce it (both at the final stage and in the provision of equipment and raw materials) when work is done with current techniques at typical intensity. Under average conditions, then, the value that a worker adds to what a firm owns in the course of a working day will be the length of this working day. But the value of the use of a worker's labor power for that time will be the labor time needed to provide for the worker's exis-tence for the day—a smaller magnitude in any firm with a hope of surviving. Marx calls the difference between these magnitudes *surplus value*. He takes it to be the most important source of all the various forms of profit on capital (interest included), while the values of commodities are the basic determinants of prices, including the wage paid for labor.

Marx's identification of the value of labor power with what is necessary to maintain and reproduce it suggests his earlier view that capitalism forces wages down to the minimum needed for physical subsistence. But in fact, Marx adds a further "historical or social element." It, too, comprises "neces-sities" for workers, but this is because people's needs are themselves deter-mined, in part, by their social conditions. Marx does think that reduction to the physical minimum is "the tendency of *things* under capitalism." If workers only advance their interests as competing individuals in the labor market, they are bound to succumb to the superior bargaining power of cap-italist employers—a superiority based, for example, on the desperation of a reserve army of the unemployed replenished by capitalists' recourse to labor-saving, capital-intensive innovations. But, Marx insists, workers can combine to resist the tendency of things, through militant trades union struggles and the forcing of favorable legislation such as the Ten Hours' Act. Indeed, his judgment of the balance of forces, in *Capital*, is that workers will succeed in cashing in a constant proportionate share of gains from technological improvement when fluctuations in the business cycle are discounted. This gain in material possessions entails no increase in the value of labor power, because value is a matter of labor time expended with current techniques, regardless of their productivity.

The last selection is our only one solely written by Friedrich Engels. Engels (1820–1895) was born to a wealthy, devoutly Pietist family in Barmen, about 100 miles north of Marx's Trier, also in Prussian territory near the Rhine. The family business was an international textile-manufacturing firm, with a branch in Manchester, England. As he became part of the family business, Engels was increasingly appalled by the conditions he encountered among factory workers. This experience, together with his readings in philosophy and political economy, led him through the same phases as the young Marx, culminating in a widely read indictment of the most advanced capitalism of the time, *The Condition of the Working Class in England* (1845).

From his joining the Manchester branch of the family firm in 1843 until his death, Engels' home was in England, apart from his fateful travels in Continental radical circles in the mid-1840s and his participation in the revolutions of 1848 to 1849. Until 1869, Engels played an active role in the financial (though not the managerial) affairs of his firm, quite painfully aware of the irony, which was made all the more sardonic by his common law marriage to an Irish immigrant whom he met when she was a factory worker. Having saved enough to retire on (despite giving away much of his income as a one-man foundation helping Marx and other radicals), Engels left the firm at 48, with vast relief. In many of his later writings, he extends his and Marx's perspective to anthropology, the natural sciences, and the philosophical description of knowledge and reality.

Engels is not as complex and suggestive a writer as Marx, whose rich narratives and flashing metaphors yield fresh insights after many readings. But if what is there in a work of Engels' is largely what first meets the eye, this is a tribute to great expository powers at the service of very wide-ranging thoughts. These skills served Engels well when he distilled parts of a long and frequently abstract work, *Herr Eugen Duehring's Revolution in Science* (1878), into the widely read popularization that is our last selection, *Socialism: Utopian and Scientific* (1880). Of special interest is Engels' argument that capitalism gives rise to industrial crises of increasing severity: Capitalism has already begun to socialize production, through worldwide interdependence and the concentration of control; but production still depends on the anarchic decisions of profit-seeking firms, whose efforts to expand at one another's expense lead to periodic crises in which swollen inventories trigger a downward spiral of cutbacks in employment and production. As the scope and interdependence of production grows, so, too does the severity of the crises. This thesis was one important substitute for the earlier claim that real wages decline to the margin of physical subsistence. In Marx's writings, tendencies toward wars of increasing violence and toward increasingly repressive regimes also play a role in eventually motivating proletarian revolution.

Some of the most important works by Marx and Engels that have not been cited are Marx, *The Eighteenth Brumaire of Louis Napoleon* (1852), his most detailed political history; Marx, *The Civil War in France* (1871), notable for his response to political innovations of the Paris Commune; Marx, "Critique of the Gotha Program" (1875), which includes his most detailed vision of postcapitalist institutions; and Engels, *The Origin of the Family, Private Property and the State* (1884).

Among the many questions about Marx's and Engels' meanings, some have proved especially apt to shed light on large issues in political and social theory. The Preface to *A Contribution to the Critique of Political Economy* seems to many readers to make technological innovation the ultimate source of social change, but Marx's specific historical explanations, including the economic histories in *Capital*, rarely give technology the leading role. Is there an underlying theory that fits both general statements and concrete practice? In the *Manifesto* and elsewhere, Marx and Engels seem to reject appeals to justice and even to morality as part of their "radical rupture with traditional ideas." Is there any sense in which the rejections are genuine, and, if so, what replaces justice and morality? Marx and Engels treat politics and culture as "superstructural," yet political goals and religious beliefs have obviously motivated conduct of socially important kinds. Can they admit that social processes are based on individual conduct that often has these motives, without watering down their intriguing claims into banalities about the need to eat and the presence of economic and technological processes as some of the many important sources of change? Recent work exploring these questions includes Gerald Cohen, *Karl Marx's Theory of History* (Princeton: Princeton University Press, 1978), a defense of a technological determinist interpretation; Jon Elster, *Making Sense of Marx* (Cambridge: Cambridge University Press, 1985), which defends a "methodological individualist" view of Marx; Alan Gilbert, *Marx's Politics* (Rutgers: Rutgers University Press, 1981), which questions economic deterministic understandings of Marx; Richard W. Miller, *Analyzing Marx* (Princeton: Princeton University Press, 1984), with discussions of morality, the nature of the state, and (from an antitechnological-determinist perspective) history; Allen Wood, *Karl Marx* (London: Routledge & Kegan Paul, 1981), including discussions of morality and alienation.

R. M.

ECONOMIC AND PHILOSOPHIC MANUSCRIPTS OF 1844

ESTRANGED LABOR

We have proceeded from the premises of political economy. We have accepted its language and its laws. We presupposed private property, the separation of labor, capital and land, and of wages, profit of capital and rent of land—likewise division of labor, competition, the concept of exchange-value, etc. On the basis of political economy itself, in its own words, we have shown that the worker sinks to the level of a commodity and becomes indeed the most wretched of commodities; that the wretchedness of the worker is in inverse proportion to the power and magnitude of his production; that the necessary result of competition is the accumulation of capital in a few hands, and thus the restoration of monopoly in a more terrible form; and that finally the distinction between capitalist and land rentier, like that between the tiller of the soil and the factory worker, disappears and that the whole of society must fall apart into the two classes—the property *owners* and the propertyless *workers*.

Political economy starts with the fact of private property, but it does not explain it to us. It expresses in general, abstract formulas the *material* process through which private property actually passes, and these formulas it then takes for *laws*. It does not *comprehend* these laws, i.e., it does not demonstrate how they arise from the very nature of private property. Political economy does not disclose the source of the division between labor and capital, and between capital and land. When, for example, it defines the relationship of

Translated by Martin Milligan. Reprinted by permission of International Publishers.

wages to profit, it takes the interest of the capitalists to be the ultimate cause, i.e., it takes for granted what it is supposed to explain. Similarly, competition comes in everywhere. It is explained from external circumstances. As to how far these external and apparently accidental circumstances are but the expression of a necessary course of development, political economy teaches us nothing. We have seen how exchange itself appears to it as an accidental fact. The only wheels which political economy sets in motion are *greed* and the war *amongst the greedy—competition.*

Precisely because political economy does not grasp the way the movement is connected, it was possible to oppose, for instance, the doctrine of competition to the doctrine of monopoly, the doctrine of the freedom of the crafts to the doctrine of the guild, the doctrine of the division of landed property to the doctrine of the big estate——for competition, freedom of the crafts and the division of landed property were explained and comprehended only as accidental, premeditated and violent consequences of monopoly, of the guild system, and of feudal property, not as their necessary, inevitable and natural consequences.

Now, therefore, we have to grasp the essential connection between private property; greed, and the separation of labor, capital and landed property; between exchange and competition, value and the devaluation of men, monopoly and competition, etc.—the connection between this whole estrangement and the *money* system.

Do not let us go back to a fictitious primordial condition as the political economist does, when he tries to explain. Such a primordial condition explains nothing; it merely pushes the question away into a gray nebulous distance. It assumes in the form of a fact, of an event, what the economist is supposed to deduce—namely, the necessary relationship between two things—between, for example, division of labor and exchange. Theology in the same way explains the origin of evil by the fall of man; that is, it assumes as a fact, in historical form, what has to be explained.

We proceed from an economic fact *of the present.*

The worker becomes all the poorer the more wealth he produces, the more his production increases in power and size. The worker becomes an ever cheaper commodity the more commodities he creates. With the *increasing value* of the world of things proceeds in direct proportion the *devaluation* of the world of men. Labor produces not only commodities: it produces itself and the worker as a *commodity*—and this in the same general proportion in which it produces commodities.

This fact expresses merely that the object which labor produces—labor's product—confronts it as *something alien*, as a *power independent* of the producer. The product of labor is labor which has been embodied in an object, which has become material: it is the objectification of labor. Labor's realization is its objectification. In the sphere of political economy this realization of labor appears as loss of *realization* for the workers; objectification as loss of the *object* and *bondage to it*; appropriation as *estrangement*, as *alienation*.

So much does labor's realization appear as loss of realization that the worker loses realization to the point of starving to death. So much does objectification appear as loss of the object that the worker is robbed of the objects most necessary not only for his life but for his work. Indeed, labor itself becomes an object which he can obtain only with the greatest effort and with the most irregular interruptions. So much does the appropriation of the object appear as estrangement that the more objects the worker produces the less he can possess and the more he falls under the sway of his product, capital.

All these consequences result from the fact that the worker is related to the *product of his labor* as to an *alien* object. For on this premise it is clear that the more the worker spends himself, the more powerful becomes the alien world of objects which he creates over and against himself, the poorer he himself—his inner world—becomes, the less belongs to him as his own. It is the same in religion. The more man puts into God, the less he retains in himself. The worker puts his life into the object; but now his life no longer belongs to him but to the object. Hence, the greater this activity, the greater is the worker's lack of objects. Whatever the product of his labor is, he is not. Therefore the greater this product, the less is he himself. The *alienation* of the worker in his product means not only that his labor becomes an object, an *external* existence, but that it exists *outside* him, independently, as something alien to him, and that it becomes a power on its own confronting him. It means that the life which he has conferred on the object confronts him as something hostile and alien.

Let us now look more closely at the *objectification,* at the production of the worker; and in it as the *estrangement,* the *loss* of the object, of his product.

The worker can create nothing without *nature,* without the *sensuous external world.* It is the material on which his labor is realized, in which it is active, from which and by means of which it produces.

But just as nature provides labor with the *means of life* in the sense that labor cannot live without objects on which to operate, on the other hand, it also provides the *means of life* in the more restricted sense, i.e., the means for the physical subsistence of the *worker* himself.

Thus the more the worker by his labor *appropriates* the external world, hence sensuous nature, the more he deprives himself of *means of life* in double manner: first, in that the sensuous external world more and more ceases to be an object belonging to his labor—to be his labor's *means of life;* and secondly, in that it more and more ceases to be *means of life* in the immediate sense, means for the physical subsistence of the worker.

In both respects, therefore, the worker becomes a slave of his object, first, in that he receives an *object of labor,* i.e., in that he receives *work;* and secondly, in that he receives *means of subsistence.* Therefore, it enables him to exist, first, as a *worker;* and, second as a *physical subject.* The height of this bondage is that it is only as a *worker* that he continues to maintain himself as a *physical subject,* and that is only as a *physical subject* that he is a *worker.*

(The laws of political economy express the estrangement of the worker in his object thus: the more the worker produces, the less he has to consume; the more values he creates, the more valueless, the more unworthy he becomes; the better formed his product, the more deformed becomes the worker; the more civilized his object, the more barbarous becomes the worker; the more powerful labor becomes, the more powerless becomes the worker; the more ingenious labor becomes, the less ingenious becomes the worker and the more he becomes nature's bondsman.)

Political economy conceals the estrangement inherent in the nature of labor by not considering the direct relationship between the worker (labor) *and production.* It is true that labor produces for the rich wonderful things—but for the worker it produces privation. It produces palaces—but for the worker, hovels. It produces beauty—but for the worker, deformity. It replaces labor by machines, but it throws a section of the workers back to a barbarous type of labor, and turns the other workers into machines. It produces intelligence—but for the worker stupidity, cretinism.

The direct relationship of labor to its products is the relationship of the worker to the objects of his production. The relationship of the man of means to the objects of production and to production itself is only a *consequence* of this first relationship—and confirms it. We shall consider this other aspect later.

When we ask, then, what is the essential relationship of labor we are asking about the relationship of the *worker* to production.

Till now we have been considering the estrangement, the alienation of the worker only in one of its aspects, i.e., the worker's *relationship to the products of his labor.* But the estrangement is manifested not only in the result but in the *act of production,* within the *producing activity,* itself. How could the worker come to face the product of his activity as a stranger, were it not that in the very act of production he was estranging himself from himself? The product is after all but the summary of the activity, of production. If then the product of labor is alienation, production itself must be active alienation, the alienation of activity, the activity of alienation. In the estrangement of the object of labor is merely summarized the estrangement, the alienation, in the activity of labor itself.

What, then, constitutes the alienation of labor?

First, the fact that labor is *external* to the worker, i.e., it does not belong to his essential being; that in his work, therefore, he does not affirm himself but denies himself, does not feel content but unhappy, does not develop freely his physical and mental energy but mortifies his body and ruins his mind. The worker therefore only feels himself outside his work, and in his work feels outside himself. He is at home when he is not working, and when he is working he is not at home. His labor is therefore not voluntary, but coerced; it is *forced labor.* It is therefore not the satisfaction of a need; it is merely a *means* to satisfy needs external to it. Its alien character emerges clearly in the fact that as soon as no physical or other compulsion exists, labor is shunned like the plague. External labor, labor in which man alienates himself, is a labor of self-sacrifice, of mortification. Lastly, the external character of labor for the worker appears in the fact that it is not his own, but someone else's, that it does not belong to him, that in it he belongs, not to himself, but to another. Just as in religion the spontaneous activity of the human imagination, of the human brain and the human heart, operates independently of the individual—that is, operates on him as an alien, divine or diabolical activity—so is the worker's activity not his spontaneous activity. It belongs to another; it is the loss of his self.

As a result, therefore, man (the worker) only feels himself freely active in his animal functions—eating, drinking, procreating, or at most in his dwelling and in dressing-up, etc.; and in his human functions he no longer feels himself to be anything but an animal. What is animal becomes human and what is human becomes animal.

Certainly eating, drinking, procreating, etc., are also genuinely human functions. But abstractly taken, separated from the sphere of all other human activity and turned into sole and ultimate ends, they are animal functions.

We have considered the act of estranging practical human activity, labor, in two of its aspects. (1) The relation of the worker to the *product of labor* as an alien object exercising power over him. This relation is at the same time the relation to the sensuous external world, to the objects of nature, as an alien world inimically opposed to him. (2) The relation of labor to the *act of production* within the *labor* process. This relation is the relation of the worker to his own activity as an alien activity not belonging to him; it is activity as suffering, strength as weakness, begetting as emasculating, the worker's *own* physical and mental energy, his personal life indeed, what is life but activity?—as an activity which is turned against him, independent of him and not belonging to him. Here we have *self-estrangement,* as previously we had the estrangement of the *thing.*

We have still a third aspect of *estranged labor* to deduce from the two already considered.

Man is a species being, not only because in practice and in theory he adopts the species as his object (his own as well as those of other things), but—and this is only another way of expressing it—also because he treats himself as the actual, living species; because he treats himself as a *universal* and therefore a free being.

The life of the species, both in man and in animals, consists physically in the fact that man (like the animal) lives on inorganic nature; and the more universal man is compared with an animal, the more universal is the sphere of inorganic nature on which he lives.

Just as plants, animals, stones, air, light, etc., constitute theoretically a part of human consciousness, partly as objects of natural science, partly as objects of art—his spiritual inorganic nature, spiritual nourishment which he must first prepare to make palatable and digestible—so also in the realm of practice they constitute a part of human life and human activity. Physically man lives only on these products of nature, whether they appear in the form of food, heating, clothes, a dwelling, etc. The universality of man appears in practice precisely in the universality which makes all nature his *inorganic body*—both inasmuch as nature is (1) his direct means of life, and (2) the material, the object, and the instrument of his life activity. Nature is man's *inorganic body*—nature, that is, in so far as it is not itself the human body. Man *lives* on nature—means that nature is his body, with which he must remain in continuous interchange if he is not to die. That man's physical and spiritual life is linked to nature means simply that nature is linked to itself, for man is a part of nature.

In estranging from man (1) nature, and (2) himself, his own active functions, his life activity, estranged labor estranges the *species* from man. It changes for him the *life of the species* into a means of individual life, and secondly it makes individual life in its abstract form the purpose of the life of the species, likewise in its abstract and estranged form.

Indeed, labor, *life-activity, productive life* itself, appears in the first place merely as a means of satisfying a need—the need to maintain physical existence. Yet the productive life is the life of the species. It is life-engendering life. The whole character of a species— its species character—is contained in the character of its life activity; and free, conscious activity is man's species character. Life itself appears only as a *means to life*.

The animal is immediately one with its life activity. It does not distinguish itself from it. It is *its life activity*. Man makes his life activity itself the object of his will and of his consciousness. He has conscious life activity. It is not a determination with which he directly merges. Conscious life activity distinguishes man immediately from animal life activity. It is just because of this that he is a species being. Or rather, it is only because he is a species being that he is a conscious being, i.e., that his own life is an object for him. Only because of that is his activity free activity. Estranged labor reverses this relationship, so that it is just because man is a conscious being that he makes his life activity, his *essential* being, a mere means to his *existence*.

In creating a *world of objects* by his practical activity, in *his work upon* inorganic nature, man proves himself a conscious species being, i.e., as a being that treats the species as its own essential being, or that treats itself as a species being. Admittedly animals also produce. They build themselves nests, dwellings, like the bees, beavers, ants, etc. But an animal only produces what it immediately needs for itself or its young. It produces one-sidedly, whilst man produces universally. It produces only under the dominion of immediate physical need, whilst man produces even when he is free from physical need and only truly produces in freedom therefrom. An animal produces only itself, whilst man reproduces the whole of nature. An animal's product belongs immediately to its physical body, whilst man freely confronts his product. An animal forms things in accordance with the standard and the need of the species to which it belongs, whilst man knows how to produce in accordance with the standard of every species, and knows how to apply everywhere the inherent standard to the object. Man therefore also forms things in accordance with the laws of beauty.

It is just in his work upon the objective world, therefore, that man first really proves himself to be a *species being*. This production is his active species life. Through and because of this production, nature appears as his work and his reality. The object of labor is, therefore, the *objectification of man's species life*: for he duplicates himself not only, as in consciousness, intellectually, but also actively, in reality, and therefore he contemplates himself in a world that he has created. In tearing away from man the object of his production, therefore, estranged labor tears from him his *species life,* his real objectivity as a member of the species and transforms his advantage over animals into the disadvantage that his inorganic body, nature, is taken away from him.

Similarly, in degrading spontaneous, free, activity, to a means, estranged labor makes man's species life a means to his physical existence.

The consciousness which man has of his species is thus transformed by estrangement in such a way that species life becomes for him a means.

Estranged labor turns thus:

(3) *Man's species being,* both nature and his spiritual species property, into a being *alien* to him, into a *means* to his *individual existence.* It estranges from man his own body, as well as external nature and his spiritual essence, his *human* being.

(4) An immediate consequence of the fact that man is estranged from the product of his labor, from his life activity, from his species being is the *estrangement of man* from *man.* When man confronts himself, he confronts the *other* man. What applies to a man's relation to his work, to the product of his labor and to himself, also holds of a man's relation to the other man, and to the other man's labor and object of labor.

In fact, the proposition that man's species nature is estranged from him means that one man is estranged from the other, as each of them is from man's essential nature.

The estrangement of man, and in fact every relationship in which man stands to himself, is first realized and expressed in the relationship in which a man stands to other men.

Hence within the relationship of estranged labor each man views the other in accordance with the standard and the relationship in which he finds himself as a worker.

We took our departure from a fact of political economy—the estrangement of the worker and his production. We have formulated this fact in conceptual terms as *estranged, alienated* labor. We have analyzed this concept—hence analyzing merely a fact of political economy.

Let us now see, further, how the concept of estranged, alienated labor must express and present itself in real life.

If the product of labor is alien to me, if it confronts me as an alien power, to whom, then, does it belong?

If my own activity does not belong to me, if it is an alien, a coerced activity, to whom, then, does it belong?

To a being *other* than myself.

Who is this being?

The *gods?* To be sure, in the earliest times the principal production (for example, the building of temples, etc., in Egypt, India and Mexico) appears to be in the service of the gods, and the product belongs to the gods. However, the gods on their own were never the lords of labor. No more was *nature.* And what a contradiction it would be if, the more man subjugated nature by his labor and the more the miracles of the gods were rendered superfluous by the miracles of industry, the more man were to renounce the joy of production and the enjoyment of the product in favor of these powers.

The *alien* being, to whom labor and the product of labor belongs, in whose service labor is done and for whose benefit the product of labor is provided, can only be *man* himself.

If the product of labor does not belong to the worker, if it confronts him as an alien power, then this can only be because it belongs to some *other man than the worker.* If the worker's activity is a torment to him, to another it must be *delight* and his life's joy. Not the gods, not nature, but only man himself can be this alien power over man.

We must bear in mind the previous proposition that man's relation to himself only becomes for him *objective* and *actual* through his relation to the other man. Thus, if the product of his labor, his labor *objectified,* is for him an *alien,* hostile, powerful object independent of him, then his position towards it is such that someone else is master of this object, someone who is alien, hostile, powerful, and independent of him. If his own activity is to him related as an unfree activity, then he is related to it as an activity performed in the service, under the dominion, the coercion, and the yoke of another man.

Every self-estrangement of man, from himself and from nature, appears in the relation in which he places himself and nature to men other than and differentiated from himself. For this reason religious self-estrangement necessarily appears in the relationship of the layman to the priest, or again to a mediator, etc., since we are here dealing with the intellectual world. In the real practical world self-estrangement can only become manifest through the real practical relationship to other men. The medium through with estrangement takes place is itself *practical.* Thus through estranged labor man not only creates his relationship to the object and to the act of production as to men that are alien and hostile to him; he also creates the relationship in which other men stand to his production and to his product, and the relationship in which he stands to these other men. Just as he creates his own production as the loss of his reality, as his punishment; his own product as a loss, as a product not belonging to him; so he creates the domination of the person who does not produce over production and over the product. Just as he estranges his own activity from himself, so he confers to the stranger an activity which is not his own.

We have until now only considered this relationship from the standpoint of the worker and later we shall be considering it also from the standpoint of the non-worker.

Through *estranged, alienated* labor, then, the worker produces the relationship to this labor of a man alien to labor and standing outside it. The relationship of the worker to labor creates the relation to it of the capitalist (or whatever one chooses to call the master of labor). *Private property* is thus the product, the result, the necessary consequence, of *alienated labor,* of the external relation of the worker to nature and to himself.

Private property thus results by analysis from the concept of *alienated labor,* of *alienated man,* of estranged labor, of estranged life, of estranged man.

True, it as a result of the *movement of private property* that we have obtained the concept of *alienated labor (of alienated life)* from political economy. But on analysis of this concept it becomes clear that though private property appears to be the source, the cause of alienated labor, it is rather its consequence, just as the gods are *originally* not the cause but the effect of man's intellectual confusion. Later this relationship becomes reciprocal.

Only at the last culmination of the development of private property does this, its secret, appear again, namely, that on the one hand it is the *product* of alienated labor, and that on the other it is the *means* by which labor alienates itself, the *realization of this alienation.*

This exposition immediately sheds light on various hitherto unsolved conflicts.

(1) Political economy starts from labor as the real soul of production; yet to labor it gives nothing, and to private property everything. Confronting this contradiction, Proudhon has decided in favor of labor it gives nothing, and to private property everything. Confronting this contradiction, Proudhon has decided in favor of labor against private property. We understand, however, that this apparent contradiction is the contradiction of *estranged labor* with itself, and that political economy has merely formulated the laws of estranged labor.

We also understand, therefore, that *wages* and *private property* are identical: since the product, as the object of labor pays for labor itself, therefore the wage is but a necessary consequence of labor's estrangement. After all, in the wage of labor, labor does not appear as an end in itself but as the servant of the wage. We shall develop this point later, and meanwhile will only derive some conclusions.

An enforced increase of wages (disregarding all other difficulties, including the fact that it would only be by force, too, that higher wages, being an anomaly, could be maintained) would therefore be nothing but *better payment for the slave,* and would not win either for the worker or for labor their human status and dignity.

Indeed, even the *equality of wages* demanded by Proudhon only transforms the relationship of the present-day worker to his labor into the relationship of all men to labor. Society is then conceived as an abstract capitalist.

Wages are a direct consequence of estranged labor, and estranged labor is the direct cause of private property. The downfall of the one must involve the downfall of the other.

(2) From the relationship of estranged labor to private property it follows further that the emancipation of society from private property, etc., from servitude, is expressed in the *political* form of the *emancipation of the workers;* not that *their* emancipation alone is at stake, but because the emancipation of the workers contains universal human emancipation— and it contains this, because the whole of human servitude is involved in the relation of the worker to production, and every relation of servitude is but a modification and consequence of this relation.

Just as we have derived the concept of *private property* from the concept of *estranged, alienated labor* by *analysis,* so we can develop every *category* of political economy with the help of these two factors; and we shall find again in each category, e.g., trade, competition, capital, money, only a *definite* and *developed expression* of these first elements.

Before considering this aspect, however, let us try to solve two problems.

(1) To define the general *nature of private property,* as it has arisen as a result of estranged labor, in its relation to *truly human* and *social property.*

(2) We have accepted the *estrangement of labor,* its *alienation,* as a fact, and we have analyzed this fact. How, we now ask, does *man* come to *alienate,* to estrange, *his labor?* How is this estrangement rooted in the nature of human development? We have already gone a long way to the solution of this problem by *transforming* the question of the *origin of private property* into the question of the relation of *alienated labor* to the course of humanity's development. For when one speaks of *private property,* one thinks of dealing with something external to man. When one speaks of labor, one is directly dealing with man himself. This new formulation of the question already contains its solution.

As to (1): The general nature of private property and its relation to truly human property.

Alienated labor has resolved itself for us into two elements which mutually condition one another, or which are but different expressions of one and the same relationship. *Appropriation* appears as *estrangement,* as *alienation;* and *alienation* appears as *appropriation, estrangement* as true introduction into society.

We have considered the one side—*alienated* labor in relation to the *worker* himself, i.e., *the relation of alienated labor to itself.* The *property relation of the non-worker to the worker and to labor* we have found as the product, the necessary outcome of this relationship. *Private property,* as the material, summary expression of alienated labor, embraces both relations— *the relation of the worker to work and to the product of his labor and to the non-worker,* and the relation of the *non-worker to the worker and to the product of his labor.*

Having seen that in relation to the worker who *appropriates* nature by means of his labor, this appropriation appears as estrangement, his own spontaneous activity as activity for another and as activity of another, vitality as a sacrifice of life, production of the object as loss of the object to an alien power, to an *alien* person—we shall now consider the relation to the worker, to labor and its object of this person who is *alien* to labor and the worker.

First it has to be noted that everything which appears in the worker as an *activity of alienation, of estrangement,* appears in the non-worker as a *state of alienation, of estrangement.*

Secondly, that the worker's *real, practical attitude* in production and to the product (as a state of mind) appears in the non-worker confronting him as a *theoretical* attitude.

Thirdly, the non-worker does everything against the worker which the worker does against himself; but he does not do against himself what he does against the worker.

Let us look more closely at these three relations.

{At this point the manuscript breaks off unfinished.}

PRIVATE PROPERTY AND COMMUNISM

The antithesis between *lack of property* and *property,* so long as it is not comprehended as the antithesis of *labor* and *capital,* still remains an indifferent antithesis, not grasped in its *active connection,* with its *internal* relation—an antithesis not yet grasped as a *contradiction.* It can find expression in this *first* form even without the advanced development of private property (as in ancient Rome, Turkey, etc.). It does not yet *appear* as having been established by private property itself. But labor, the subjective essence of private property as exclusion of property, and capital, objective labor as exclusion of labor, constitute *private property* as its developed state of contradiction—hence a dynamic relationship moving to its resolution.

The transcendence of self-estrangement follows the same course as self-estrangement. *Private property* is first considered only in its objective aspect—but nevertheless with labor as its essence. Its form of existence is therefore *capital,* which is to be annulled "as such" (Proudhon). Or a *particular form* of labor—labor leveled, parceled, and therefore unfree— is conceived as the source of private property's *perniciousness* and of its existence in estrangement from men. For instance, *Fourier,* who, like the physiocrats, also conceived *agricultural labor* to be at least the *exemplary* type, whilst *Saint-Simon* declares in contrast that *industrial labor* as such is the essence, and only aspires to the *exclusive* rule of the industrialists and the improvement of the workers' condition. Finally, *communism* is the *positive* expression of annulled private property—at first as *universal* private property. By embracing this relation as a *whole,* communism is:

(1) In its first form only a *generalization* and *consummation* of this relationship. As such it appears in a twofold form: on the one hand, the dominion of *material* property bulks so large that it wants to destroy *everything* which is not capable of being possessed by all as *private property.* It wants to do away *by force* with talent, etc. For it the sole purpose of life and existence is direct, physical *possession.* The task of the *laborer* is not done away with, but extended to all men. The relationship of private property persists as the relationship of the community to the world of things.

Finally, this movement of opposing universal private property to private property finds expression in the animal form of opposing to *marriage* (certainly a *form of exclusive private property*) the *community of women* in which a woman becomes a piece of *communal* and *common* property. It may be said that this idea of the *community of women* gives away the *secret* of this as yet completely crude and thoughtless communism. Just as woman passes from marriage to general prostitution,[1] so the entire world of wealth (that is, of man's objective substance) passes from the relationship of exclusive marriage with the owner of private property to a state of universal prostitution with the community. In negating the *personality* of man in every sphere, this type of communism is really nothing but the logical expression of private property, which is its negation. General *envy* constituting itself as a power is the disguise in which *greed* reestablishes itself and satisfies itself, only in *another* way. The thought of every piece of private property—inherent in each piece as such—is *at least* turned against all *wealthier* private property in the form of envy and the urge to reduce things to a common level, so that this envy and urge even constitute the essence of competition. The crude communism is only the culmination of this envy and of this leveling-down proceeding from the *preconceived* minimum. It has a *definite, limited* standard, How little this annulment of private property is really an appropriation is in fact proved by the abstract negation of the entire world of culture and civilization, the regression to the *unnatural* simplicity of the *poor and undemanding* man who has not only failed to go beyond private property, but has not yet even reached it.

The community is only a community of *labor*, and of equality of *wages* paid out by communal capital—the *community* as the universal capitalist. Both sides of the relationship are raised to an *imagined* universality—*labor* as a state in which every person is placed, and *capital* as the acknowledged universality and power of the community.

In the approach to *woman* as the spoil and handmaid of communal lust is expressed the infinite degradation in which man exists for himself, for the secret of this approach has its *unambiguous*, decisive, *plain* and undisguised expression in the relation of *man* to *woman* and in the manner in which the *direct* and *natural* species relationship is conceived. This direct, natural, and necessary relation of person to person is the *relation of man to woman*. In this *natural* species relationship man's relation to nature is immediately his relation to man, just as his relation to man is immediately his relation to nature—his own *natural* destination. In this relationship, therefore, is *sensuously manifested*, reduced to an observable *fact*, the extent to which the human essence has become nature to man, or to which nature to him has become the human essence of man. From this relationship one can therefore judge man's whole level of development. From the character of this relationship follows how much *man* as a *species being*, as *man*, has come to be himself and to comprehend himself; the relation of man to woman is *the most natural* relation of human being to human being. It therefore reveals the extent to which man's *natural* behavior has become *human*, or the extent to which the *human* essence in him has become a *natural* essence— the extent to which his *human nature* has come to be *nature to him*. In this relationship is revealed, too, the extent to which man's *need* has become a *human* need; the extent to which, therefore, the *other* person as a person has become for him a need—the extent to which he in his individual existence is at the same time a social being.

The first positive annulment of private property—*crude* communism—is thus merely one *form* in which the vileness of private property, which wants to set itself up as the *positive community, comes to the surface.*

(2) Communism (*a*) still political in nature—democratic or despotic; (*b*) with the abolition of the state, yet still incomplete, and being still affected by private property (i.e., by the estrangement of man). In both forms communism already is aware of being reintegration or return of man to himself, the transcendence of human self-estrangement; but since it has not yet grasped the positive essence of private property, and just as little the *human* nature of need, it remains captive to it and infected by it. It has, indeed, grasped its concept, but not its essence.

(3) Communism as the *positive* transcendence of *private property*, as *human self-estrangement*, and therefore as the real *appropriation of the human* essence by and for man; communism therefore as the complete return of man to himself as a *social* (i.e., human) being—a return become conscious, and accomplished within the entire wealth of previous development. This communism, as fully developed naturalism, equals humanism, and as fully devel-

oped humanism equals naturalism; it is the *genuine* resolution of the conflict between man and nature and between man and man—the true resolution of the strife between existence and essence, between objectification and self-confirmation, between freedom and necessity, between the individual and the species. Communism is the riddle of history solved, and it knows itself to be this solution.

The entire movement of history is, therefore, both its *actual* act of genesis (the birth act of its empirical existence) and also for its thinking consciousness the *comprehended* and *known* process of its *becoming*. That other, still immature communism, meanwhile, seeks an *historical* proof for itself—a proof in the realm of what already exists—among disconnected historical phenomena opposed to private property, tearing single phases from the historical process and focusing attention on them as proofs of its historical pedigree (a hobbyhorse ridden hard especially by Cabet, Villegardelle, etc.). By so doing it simply makes clear that by far the greater part of this process contradicts its own claim, and that, it has ever existed, precisely its being in the *past* refutes its pretension to being *essential being*.

It is easy to see that the entire revolutionary movement necessarily finds both its empirical and its theoretical basis in the movement of *private property*—more precisely, in that of the economy.

This *material*, immediately perceptible private property is the material perceptible expression of *estranged human* life. Its movement—production and consumption—is the *perceptible* revelation of the movement of all production until now, i.e., the realization or the reality of man. Religion, family, state, law, morality, science, art, etc., are only *particular* modes of production, and fall under its general law. The positive transcendence of *private property*, as the appropriation of *human* life, is therefore the positive transcendence of all estrangement—that is to say, the return of man from religion, family, state, etc., to his *human*, i.e., *social* existence. Religious estrangement as such occurs only in the realm of *consciousness*, of man's inner life, but economic estrangement is that of *real life*; its transcendence therefore embraces both aspects. It is evident that the *initial* stage of the movement amongst the various peoples depends on whether the true and *authentic* life of the people manifests itself more in consciousness or in the external world—is more ideal or real. Communism begins from the outset (*Owen*) with atheism; but atheism is at first far from being *communism;* indeed, it is still mostly an abstraction.

The philanthropy of atheism is therefore at first only *philosophical,* abstract, philanthropy, and that of communism is at once *real* and directly bent on *action*.

We have seen how on the assumption of positively annulled private property man produces man—himself and the other man; how the object, being the direct embodiment of his individuality, is simultaneously his own existence for the other man, the existence of the other man, and that existence for him. Likewise, however, both the material of labor and man as the subject, are the point of departure as well as the result of the movement (and precisely in this fact, that they must constitute the *point of departure*, lies the historical *necessity* of private property). Thus the *social* character is the general character of the whole movement: *just as* society itself produces *man as man*, so is society *produced* by him. Activity and mind, both in their content and in their *mode of existence,* are *social: social* activity and *social* mind. The *human* essence of nature first exists only for *social* man; for only here does nature exist for him as a *bond* with *man*—as his existence for the other and the other's existence for him—as the life-element of human reality. Only here does nature exist as the *foundation* of his own *human* existence. Only here has what is to him his *natural* existence become his *human* existence, and nature become man for him. Thus *society* is the unity of being of man with nature—the true resurrection of nature—the naturalism of man and the humanism of nature both brought to fulfillment.

Social activity and social mind exist by no means *only* in the form of some *directly* communal activity and directly *communal* mind, although *communal* activity and *communal* mind—i.e., activity and mind which are manifested and directly revealed in *real association* with other men—will occur wherever such a *direct* expression of sociability stems from the true character of the activity's content and is adequate to its nature.

But also when I am active *scientifically,* etc.,—when I am engaged in activity which I can seldom perform in direct community with others—then I am *social,* because I am active as a *man.* Not only is the material of my activity given to me as a social product (as is even the language in which the thinker is active): my *own* existence *is* social activity, and therefore that which I make of myself, I make of myself for society and with the consciousness of myself as a social being.

My *general* consciousness is only the *theoretical* shape of that which the *living* shape is the *real* community, the social fabric, although at the present day *general* consciousness is an abstraction from real life and as such confronts it with hostility. The *activity* of my general consciousness, as an activity, is therefore also my *theoretical* existence as a social being.

Above all we must avoid postulating "Society" again as an abstraction *vis-à-vis* the individual. The individual *is the social being.* His life, even if it may not appear in the direct form of a *communal* life in association with others—is therefore an expression and confirmation of *social life.* Man's individual and species life are not *different,* however much—and this is inevitable—the mode of existence of the individual is a more *particular,* or more *general* mode of the life of the species, or the life of the species is a more *particular* or more *general* individual life.

In his *consciousness of species* man confirms his real *social life* and simply repeats his real existence in thought, just as conversely the being of the species confirms itself in species-consciousness and exists for *itself* in its generality as a thinking being.

Man, much as he may therefore be a *particular* individual (and it is precisely his particularity which makes him an individual, and a real *individual* social being), is just as much the *totality*—the subjective existence of thought and experienced society for itself; just as he exists also in the real world as the awareness and the real mind of social existence, and as a totality of human manifestation of life.

Thinking and being are thus no doubt *distinct,* but at the same time they are in *unity* with each other.

Death seems to be a harsh victory of the species over the *definite* individual and to contradict their unity. But the particular individual is only a *particular species being,* and as such mortal.

(4) Just as *private property* is only the perceptible expression of the fact that man becomes *objective* for himself and at the same time becomes to himself a strange and inhuman object; just as it expresses the fact that the assertion of his life is the alienation of his life, that his realization is his loss of reality, is an *alien* reality: so, the positive transcendence of private property—i.e., the *perceptible* appropriation for and by man of the human essence and of human life, of objective man, of human *achievements*—should not to be conceived merely in the sense of *immediate,* one-sided *gratification*—merely in the sense of *possessing,* of *having.* Man appropriates his total essence in a total manner, that is to say, as a whole man. Each of his *human* relations to the world—seeing, hearing, smelling, tasting, feeling, thinking, observing, experiencing, wanting, acting, loving—in short, all the organs of his individual being, like those organs which are directly social in their form, are in their *objective* orientation or in their *orientation to the object,* the appropriation of that object. The appropriation of *human* reality,[2] its orientation to the object is the *manifestation of the human reality,* it is human *activity* and human *suffering,* for suffering, humanly considered, is a self-indulgence of man.

Private property has made us so stupid and one-sided that an object is only *ours* when we have it—when it exists for us as capital, or when it is directly possessed, eaten, drunk, worn, inhabited, etc.,—in short, when it is *used* by us. Although private property itself again conceives all these direct realizations of possession only as *means of life* and the life which they serve as means is the *life of private property*—labor and conversion into capital.

All these physical and mental senses have therefore—the sheer estrangement of *all* these senses—the sense of *having*. The human being had to be reduced to this absolute poverty in order that he might yield his inner wealth to the outer world. (On the category of *"having,"* see Hess in the *Twenty-One Sheets.*)

The transcendence of private property is therefore the complete *emancipation* of all human senses and qualities, but it is this emancipation precisely because these senses and attributes have become, subjectively and objectively, *human*. The eye has become a *human* eye, just as its *object* has become a social, *human* object—an object made by man for man. The *senses* have therefore become directly in their practice *theoreticians*. They relate themselves to the *thing* for the sake of the thing, but the thing itself is an *objective human* relation to itself and to man[3] and vice versa. Need or enjoyment have consequently lost their *egotistical* nature, and nature has lost its mere utility by use becoming *human* use.

In the same way, the senses and minds of other men have become my *own* appropriation. Besides these organs, therefore, *social* organs develop in the *form* of society; thus, for instance, activity in direct association with others, etc., has become an organ for *expressing* my own *life,* and a mode of appropriating *human* life.

It is obvious that the human eye enjoys things in a way different from the crude, non-human eye; the human ear different from the crude ear, etc.

To recapitulate: man is not lost in his object only when the object becomes for him a *human* object or objective man. This is possible only when the object becomes for him a *social* object, he himself for himself a social being, just as society becomes a being for him in this object.

On the one hand, therefore, it is only when the objective world becomes everywhere for man in society the world of man's essential powers—human reality, and for that reason the reality of his *own* essential powers—that all *objects* become for him the *objectification of himself,* become *his* objects: that is, *man himself* becomes the object. The manner in which they become *his* depends on the *nature of the objects* and on the nature of the *essential power* corresponding *to it;* for it is precisely the *determinate nature* of this relationship which shapes the particular, real mode of affirmation. To the *eye* an object comes to be other than it is to the *ear,* and the object of the eye is another object than the object of the *ear.* The specific character of each essential power is precisely its *specific essence,* and therefore also the specific mode of its objectification, of its *objectively actual* living *being.* Thus man is affirmed in the objective world not only in the act of thinking, but with *all* his senses.

On the other hand, let us look at this in its subjective aspect. Just as music alone awakens in man the sense of music, and just as the most beautiful music has *no* sense for the unmusical ear—is no object for it, because my object an only be the confirmation of one of my essential powers. It can therefore only be so for me as my essential power exists for itself as a subjective capacity, because the meaning of an object for me goes only so far as *my* senses go (has only a meaning for a sense corresponding to that object)—for this reason the *senses* of the social man are *other* senses than those of the non-social man. Only through the objectively unfolded richness of man's essential being is the richness of subjective *human sensibility* (a musical ear, an eye for beauty of form—in short, *senses* capable of human gratification, senses affirming themselves as essential powers of *man*) either cultivated or brought into being. For not only the five senses but also the so-called mental senses—the practical senses (will, love, etc.)—in a word, *human* sense—the human nature of the senses—comes to be by virtue of its object, by virtue of *humanized* nature. The *form-ing* of the five senses is a labor of the entire history of the world down to the present.

The *sense* caught up in crude practical need has only a restricted sense. For the starving man, it is not the human form of food that exists, but only its abstract being as food. It could just as well be there in its crudest form, and it would be impossible to say wherein this feeding activity differs from that of *animals.* The care-burdened man in need has no sense for the finest play; the dealer in minerals sees only the commercial value but not the beauty and the unique nature of the mineral: he has no mineralogical sense. Thus, the objectification of the human essence, both in its theoretical and practical aspects, is required to make man's *sense human,* as well as to create the *human sense* corresponding to the entire wealth of human and natural substance.

Just as through the movement of *private property,* of its wealth as well as its poverty—or of its material and spiritual wealth and poverty—the budding society finds at hand all the material for this *development,* so *established* society produces man in this entire rich-ness of his being—produces the *rich* man *profoundly endowed with all the senses*—as its enduring reality.

We see how subjectivism and objectivism, spiritualism and materialism, activity and suffering, only lose their antithetical character, and thus their existence as such antitheses in social centers; we see how the resolution of the *theoretical* antitheses is *only* possible *in a practical* way, by virtue of the practical energy of man. Their resolution is therefore by no means merely a problem of understanding, but a *real* problem of life, which *philosophy* could not solve precisely because it conceived this problem as *merely* a theoretical one.

We see how the history of *industry* and the established *objective* existence of industry are the *open book* of *man's essential powers,* the exposure to the senses of human *psychology.* Hitherto this was not conceived in its inseparable connection with man's *essential being,* but only in an external relation of utility, because, moving in the realm of estrangement, people could only think of man's general mode of being—religion or history in its abstract-general character as politics, art, literature, etc.—as the reality of man's essential powers and *man's species activity.* We have before us the *objectified essential powers* of man in the form of *sensuous, alien, useful objects,* in the form of estrangement, displayed in *ordinary material industry* (which can be conceived as well as a part of that general movement, just as that movement can be conceived as *particular* part of industry, since all human activity hitherto has been labor—that is, industry—activity estranged from itself).

A *psychology* for which this, the part of history most contemporary and accessible to sense, remains a closed book, cannot become a genuine, comprehensive and *real* science. What indeed are we to think of a science which *airily* abstracts from this large part of human labor and which fails to feel its own incompleteness, while such a wealth of human endeavor, unfolded before it, means nothing more to it than, perhaps, what can be expressed in one word—*"need," "vulgar need"*?

The *natural sciences* have developed an enormous activity and have accumulated an ever-growing mass of material. Philosophy, however, has remained just as alien to them as they remain to philosophy. Their momentary unity was only a *chimerical illusion.* The will was there, but the means were lacking. Even historiography pays regard to natural science only occasionally, as a factor of enlightenment, utility, and of some special great discover-ies. But natural science has invaded and transformed human life all the more *practically* through the medium of industry; and has prepared human emancipation, although its immediate effect had to be the furthering of the dehumanization of man. *Industry* is the *actual,* historical relationship of nature, and therefore of natural science, to man. If, there-fore, industry is conceived as the *exoteric* revelation of man's *essential powers,* we also gain an

understanding of the *human* essense of nature or the *natural* essence of man. In consequence, natural science will lose its abstractly material—or rather, its idealistic—tendency, and will become the basis of *human* science, as it has already become the basis of
actual human life, albeit in an estranged form. *One* basis for life and another basis for *science*
is *a priori* a lie. The nature which develops in human history—the genesis of human society—is man's *real* nature; hence nature as it develops through industry, even though in an
estranged form, is true *anthropological* nature.

Sense-perception (see Feuerbach) must be the basis of all science. Only when it proceeds
from sense-perception in the two-fold form both of *sensuous* consciousness and of *sensuous*
need—that is, only when science proceeds from nature—is it *true* science. All history is
the preparation for *"man"* to become the object of *sensuous* consciousness, and for the needs
of "man as man" to become [natural, sensuous] needs. History itself is a *real* part of *natural history*—of nature developing into man. Natural science will in time incorporate into
itself the science of man, just as the science of man will incorporate into itself natural science: there will be *one* science.

Man is the immediate object of natural science; for immediate, *sensuous nature* for man
is, immediately, human sensuousness (the expressions are identical)—presented immediately in the form of the *other* man sensuously present for him. Indeed, his own sensuousness first exists as human sensuousness for himself through the other man. But *nature* is
the immediate object of the *science of man*: the first object of man—man—is nature,
sensuousness; and the particular sensuous human essential powers can only find their self-
understanding in the science of the natural world in general, since they can find their
objective realization in *natural* objects only. The element of thought itself—the element
of thought's living expression—*language*—is of a sensuous nature. The *social* reality of
nature, and *human* natural science, or the *natural science about man,* are identical terms.

It will be seen how in place of the *wealth* and *poverty* of political economy comes the *rich
human being* and the rich *human* need. The *rich* human being is simultaneously the human
being *in need of* a totality of human manifestations of life—the man in whom his own realization exists as in inner necessity, as *need.* Not only *wealth,* but likewise the *poverty* of
man—under the assumption of socialism—receives in equal measure a *human* and therefore social significance. Poverty is the passive bond which causes the human being to
experience the need of the greatest wealth—the *other* human being. The dominion of the
objective being in me, the sensuous outburst of my life activity, is *passion,* which thus
becomes here the *activity* of my being.

(5) A *being* only considers himself independent when he stands on his own feet; and he
only stands on his own feet when he owes his *existence* to himself. A man who lives by the
grace of another regards himself as a dependent being. But I live completely by the grace
of another if I owe him not only the maintenance of my life, but if he has, moreover, *created*
my *life*—if he is the *source* of my life. When it is not of my own creation, my life has necessarily a source of this kind outside of it. The *Creation* is therefore an idea very difficult to
dislodge from popular consciousness. The fact that nature and man exist in their own
account is *incomprehensible* to it, because is contradicts everything *tangible* in practical life.

The creation of the *earth* has received a mighty blow from geogeny—i.e., from the
science which presents the formation of the earth, the further development of the earth,
as a process, as a self-generation. *Generatio aequivoca* is the only practical refutation of the
theory of creation.

Now it is certainly easy to say to the single individual what Aristotle has already said:
You have been begotten by your father and your mother; therefore in you the mating of
two human beings—a species-act of human beings—has produced the human being. You

see, therefore, that even physically, man owes his existence to man. Therefore you must not only keep sight of *one* aspect—the *infinite* progression which leads you further to enquire: "Who begot my father? Who his grandfather?," etc. You must also hold on to the *circular movement* sensuously perceptible in that progression, by which man repeats himself in procreation, *man* thus always remaining the subject. You will reply, however: I grant you this circular movement; now grant me the progression which drives me ever further until I ask: Who begot the first man, the nature as a whole? I can only answer you: Your question is itself a product of abstraction. Ask yourself how you arrived at that question. Ask yourself whether your question is not posed from a standpoint to which I cannot reply, because it is wrongly put. Ask yourself whether that progression as such exists for a reasonable mind. When you ask about the creation of nature and man, you are abstracting, in so doing, from man and nature. You postulate them as *non-existent,* and yet you want me to prove them to you as *existing.* Now I say to you: Give up your abstraction and you will also give up your question. Or if you want to hold on to your abstraction, then be consistent, and if you think of man and nature as *non-existent,* then think of yourself as non-existent, for you too are surely nature and man. Don't think, don't ask me, for as soon as you think and ask, your *abstraction* from the existence of nature and man has no meaning. Or are you such an egotist that you conceive everything as nothing, and yet want yourself to exist?

You can reply: I do not want to conceive the nothingness of nature, etc. I ask you about *its genesis,* just as I ask the anatomist about the formation of bones, etc.

But since for the socialist man the *entire so-called history of the world* is nothing but the creation of man through human labor, nothing but the emergence of nature for man, so he has the visible, irrefutable proof of his *birth* through himself, of the *process of his creation.* Since the real *existence* of man and nature—since man has become for man as the being of nature, and nature for man as the being of man has become practical, sensuous, perceptible—the question about an *alien* being, about a being above nature and man—a question which implies the admission of the unreality of nature and of man—has become impossible in practice. *Atheism,* as the denial of this unreality, has no longer any meaning, for atheism is a *negation of God,* and postulates the *existence of man* through this negation; but socialism as socialism no longer stands in any need of such a mediation. It proceeds from the *practically and theoretically sensuous consciousness* of man and of nature as the *essence.* Socialism is man's *positive self-consciousness,* no longer mediated through the annulment of religion, just as *real life* is man's positive reality, no longer mediated through the annulment of private property, through *communism.* Communism is the position as the negation of the negation, and is hence the *actual* phase necessary for the next stage of historical development in the process of human emancipation and rehabilitation. *Communism* is the necessary pattern and the dynamic principle of the immediate future, but communism as such is not the goal of human development—which goal is the structure of human society.

Notes

1. Prostitution is only a *specific* expression of the *general* prostitution of the *laborer,* and since it is a relationship in which falls not the prostitute alone, but also the one who prostitutes—and the latter's abomination is still greater—the capitalist, etc., also comes under this head.
2. For this reason it is just as highly varied as the *determinations* of human *essence* and *activities.*
3. In practice I can relate myself to a thing humanly only if the thing relates itself humanly to the human being.

THE GERMAN IDEOLOGY

PREFACE

Hitherto men have constantly made up for themselves false conceptions about themselves, about what they are and what they ought to be. They have arranged their relationships according to their ideas of God, of normal man, etc. The phantoms of their brains have got out of their hands. They, the creators, have bowed down before their creations. Let us liberate them from the chimeras, the ideas, dogmas, imaginary beings under the yoke of which they are pining away. Let us revolt against the rule of thoughts. Let us teach men, says one, to exchange these imaginations for thoughts which correspond to the essence of man; says the second, to take up a critical attitude to them; says the third, to knock them out of their heads; and—existing reality will collapse.

These innocent and childlike fancies are the kernel of the modern Young-Hegelian philosophy, which not only is received by the German public with horror and awe, but is announced by our philosophic heroes with the solemn consciousness of its cataclysmic dangerousness and criminal ruthlessness. The first volume of the present publication has the aim of uncloaking these sheep, who take themselves and are taken for wolves of show-ing how their bleating merely imitates in a philosophic form the conceptions of the German middle class; how the boasting of these philosophic commentators only mirrors the wretchedness of the real conditions in Germany. It is its aim to debunk and discredit the philosophic struggle with the shadows of reality, which appeals to the dreamy and muddled German nation.

Once upon a time a valiant fellow had the idea that men were drowned in water only because they were possessed with the idea of gravity. If they were to knock this notion out of their heads, say by stating it to be a superstition, a religious concept, they would be sublimely proof against any danger from water. His whole life long he fought against the illusion of gravity, of whose harmful results all statistics brought him new and manifold evidence. This honest fellow was the type of the new revolutionary philosophers in Germany.

FEUERBACH

A. Idealism and Materialism

First Premises of Materialist Method

The premises from which we begin are not arbitrary ones, not dogmas, but real premises from which abstraction can only be made in the imagination. They are the real individuals, their activity and the material conditions under which they live, both those which they find already existing and those produced by their activity. These premises can thus be verified in a purely empirical way.

Edited by C. J. Arthur. Reprinted by permission of International Publishers.

The first premise of all human history is, of course, the existence of living human individuals. Thus the first fact to be established is the physical organisation of these individuals and their consequent relation to the rest of nature. Of course, we cannot here go either into the actual physical nature of man, or into the natural conditions in which man finds himself—geological, oreohydrographical, climatic and so on. The writing of history must always set out from these natural bases and their modification in the course of history through the action of men.

Men can be distinguished from animals by consciousness, by religion or anything else you like. They themselves begin to distinguish themselves from animals as soon as they begin to *produce* their means of subsistence, a step which is conditioned by their physical organisation. By producing their means of subsistence men are indirectly producing their actual material life.

The way in which men produce their means of subsistence depends first of all on the nature of the actual means of subsistence they find in existence and have to reproduce. This mode of production must not be considered simply as being the production of the physical existence of the individuals. Rather it is a definite form of activity of these individuals, a definite form of expressing their life, a definite *mode of life* on their part. As individuals express their life, so they are. What they are, therefore, coincides with their production, both with *what* they produce and with *how* they produce. The nature of individuals thus depends on the material conditions determining their production.

This production only makes its appearance with the *increase of population*. In its turn this presupposes the *intercourse* [*Verkehr*] of individuals with one another. The form of this intercourse is again determined by production.

The relations of different nations among themselves depend upon the extent to which each has developed its productive forces, the division of labour and internal intercourse. This statement is generally recognised. But not only the relation of one nation to others, but also the whole internal structure of the nation itself depends on the stage of development reached by its production and its internal and external intercourse. How far the productive forces of a nation are developed is shown most manifestly by the degree to which the division of labour has been carried. Each new productive force, insofar as it is not merely a quantitative extension of productive forces already known (for instance the bringing into cultivation of fresh land), causes a further development of the division of labour.

The division of labour inside a nation leads at first to the separation of industrial and commercial from agricultural labour, and hence to the separation of *town* and *country* and to the conflict of their interests. Its further development leads to the separation of commercial from industrial labour. At the same time through the division of labour inside these various branches there develop various divisions among the individuals co-operating in definite kinds of labour. The relative position of these individual groups is determined by the methods employed in agriculture, industry and commerce (patriarchalism, slavery, estates, classes). These same conditions are to be seen (given a more developed intercourse) in the relations of different nations to one another.

The various stages of development in the division of labour are just so many different forms of ownership, i.e. the existing stage in the division of labour determines also the relations of individuals to one another with reference to the material, instrument, and product of labour.

The first form of ownership is tribal [*Stammeigentum*] ownership. It corresponds to the undeveloped stage of production, at which a people lives by hunting and fishing, by the rearing of beasts or, the highest stage, agriculture. In the latter case it presupposes a great mass of uncultivated stretches of land. The division of labour is at this stage still very elementary and is confined to a further extension of the natural division of labour existing in the family. The social structure is, therefore, limited to an extension of the family; patriarchal family chieftains, below them the members of the tribe, finally slaves. The slavery latent in the family only develops gradually with the increase of population, the growth of wants, and with the extension of external relations, both of war and of barter.

The second form is the ancient communal and State ownership which proceeds especially from the union of several tribes into a *city* by agreement or by conquest, and which is still accompanied by slavery. Beside communal ownership we already find movable, and later also immovable, private property developing, but as an abnormal form subordinate to communal ownership. The citizens hold power over their labouring slaves only in their community, and on this account alone, therefore, they are bound to the form of communal ownership. It is the communal private property which compels the active citizens to remain in this spontaneously derived form of association over against their slaves. For this reason the whole structure of society based on this communal ownership, and with it the power of the people, decays in the same measure as, in particular, immovable private property evolves. The division of labour is already more developed. We already find the antagonism of town and country; later the antagonism between those states which represent town interests and those which represent country interests, and inside the towns themselves the antagonism between industry and maritime commerce. The class relation between citizens and slaves is now completely developed.

With the development of private property, we find here for the first time the same conditions which we shall find again, only on a more extensive scale, with modern private property. On the one hand, the concentration of private property, which began very early in Rome (as the Licinian agrarian law proves[1]) and proceeded very rapidly from the time of the civil wars and especially under the Emperors; on the other hand, coupled with this, the transformation of the plebeian small peasantry into a proletariat, which, however, owing to its intermediate position between propertied citizens and slaves, never achieved an independent development.

The third form of ownership is feudal or estate property. If antiquity started out from the *town* and its little territory, the Middle Ages started out from the *country*. This different starting-point was determined by the sparseness of the population at that time, which was scattered over a large area and which received no large increase from the conquerors. In contrast to Greece and Rome, feudal development at the outset, therefore, extends over a much wider territory, prepared by the Roman conquests and the spread of agriculture at first associated with it. The last centuries of the declining Roman Empire and its conquest by the barbarians destroyed a number of productive forces; agriculture had declined, industry had decayed for wane of a market, trade had died out or been violently suspended, the rural and urban population had decreased. From these conditions and the mode of organisation of the conquest determined by them, feudal property developed under the influence of the Germanic military constitution. Like tribal and communal ownership, it is based again on a community; but the directly producing class standing over against it is not, as in the case of the ancient community, the slaves, but the enserfed small peasantry. As soon as feudalism is fully developed, there also arises antagonism to the towns. The hierarchical structure of landownership, and the armed bodies of retainers associated with it, gave the nobility power over the serfs. This feudal organisation was, just as much as the ancient communal ownership, an association against a subjected producing class; but the form of association and the relation to the direct producers were different because of the different conditions of production.

This feudal system of landownership had its counterpart in the *towns* in the shape of corporative property, the feudal organisation of trades. Here property consisted chiefly in the labour of each individual person. The necessity for association against the organised robber-nobility, the need for communal covered markets in an age when the industrialist was at the same time a merchant, the growing competition of the escaped serfs swarming into the rising towns, the feudal structure of the whole country: these combined to bring about the *guilds*. The gradually accumulated small capital of individual craftsmen and their stable numbers, as against the growing population, evolved the relation of journeyman and apprentice, which brought into being in the towns a hierarchy similar to that in the country.

Thus the chief form of property during the feudal epoch consisted on the one hand of landed property with serf labour chained to it, and on the other of the labour of the individual with small capital commanding the labour of journeymen. The organisation of both was determined by the restricted conditions of production—the small-scale and primitive cultivation of the land, and the craft type of industry. There was little division of labour in the heyday of feudalism. Each country bore in itself the antithesis of town and country; the division into estates was certainly strongly marked; but apart from the differentiation of princes, nobility, clergy and peasants in the country, and masters, journeymen, apprentices and soon also the rabble of casual labourers in the towns, no division of importance took place. In agriculture it was rendered difficult by the strip-system, beside which the cottage industry of the peasants themselves emerged. In industry there was no division of labour at all in the individual trades themselves, and very little between them. The separation of industry and commerce was found already in existence in older towns; in the newer it only developed later, when the towns entered into mutual relations.

The grouping of larger territories into feudal kingdoms was a necessity for the landed nobility as for the towns. The organisation of the ruling class, the nobility, had, therefore, everywhere a monarch at its head.

The fact is, therefore, that definite individuals who are productively active in a definite way enter into these definite social and political relations. Empirical observation must in each separate instance bring out empirically, and without any mystification and speculation, the connection of the social and political structure with production. The social structure and the State are continually evolving out of the life-process of definite individuals, but of individuals, not as they may appear in their own or other people's imagination, but as they *really* are; i.e. as they operate, produce materially, and hence as they work under definite material limits, presuppositions and conditions independent of their will.

The production of ideas, of conceptions, of consciousness, is at first directly interwoven with the material activity and the material intercourse of men, the language of real life. Conceiving, thinking, the mental intercourse of men, appear at this stage as the direct efflux of their material behavior. The same applies to mental production as expressed in the language of politics, laws, morality, religion, metaphysics, etc. of a people. Men are the producers of their conceptions, ideas, etc.—real, active men, as they are conditioned by a definite development of their productive forces and of the intercourse corresponding to these, up to its furthest forms. Consciousness can never be anything else than conscious existence, and the existence of men is their actual life-process. If in all ideology men and their circumstances appear upside own as in a *camera obscura*, this phenomenon arises just as much from their historical life-process as the inversion of objects on the retina does from their physical life-process.

In direct contrast to German philosophy which descends from heaven to earth, here we ascend from earth to heaven. That is to say, we do not set out from what men say, imagine, conceive, nor from men as narrated, thought of, imagined, conceived, in order to arrive at men in the flesh. We set out from real, active men, and on the basis of their real life-process we demonstrate the development of the ideological reflexes and echoes of this life-process. The phantoms formed in the human brain are also, necessarily, sublimates of their material life-process, which is empirically verifiable and bound to material premises. Morality, religion, metaphysics, all the rest of ideology and their corresponding forms of consciousness, thus no longer retain the semblance of independence. They have no history, no development; but men, developing their material production and their material inter-course, alter, along with this their real existence, their thinking and the products of their thinking. Life is not determined by consciousness, but consciousness by life. In the first method of approach the starting-point is consciousness taken as the living individual; in the second method, which conforms to real life, it is the real living individuals themselves, and consciousness is considered solely as *their* consciousness.

This method of approach is not devoid of premises. It starts out from the real premises and does not abandon them for a moment. Its premises are men, not in any fantastic iso-lation and rigidity, but in their actual, empirically perceptible process of development under definite conditions. As soon as this active life-process is described, history ceases to be a collection of dead facts as it is with the empiricists (themselves still abstract), or an imagine activity of imagine subjects, as with the idealists.

Where speculation ends—in real life—there real, positive science begins: the repre-sentation of the practical activity, of the practical process of development of men. Empty talk about consciousness ceases, and real knowledge has to take its place. When reality is depicted, philosophy as an independent branch of knowledge loses its medium of exis-tence. At the best its place can only be taken by a summing-up of the most general results, abstractions which arise from the observation of the historical development of men. Viewed apart from real history, these abstractions have in themselves no value whatsoever. They can only serve to facilitate the arrangements of historical materials, to indicate the sequence of its separate strata. But they by no means afford a recipe or schema, as does philosophy, for neatly trimming the epochs of history. On the contrary, our difficulties begin only when we set about the observation and the arrangement—the real depiction—of our historical material, whether of a past epoch or of the present. The removal of these difficulties is governed by premises which it is quite impossible to state here, but which only the study of the actual life-process and the activity of the individuals of each epoch will make evident. We shall select here some of these abstractions, which we use in constradistinction to the ideologists, and shall illustrate them by historical examples.

History: Fundamental Conditions

Since we are dealing with the Germans, who are devoid of premises, we must begin by stating the first premise of all human existence and, therefore, of all history, the premise, namely, that men must be in a position to live in order to be able to "make history". But life involves before everything else eating and drinking, a habitation, clothing and many other things. The first historical act is thus the production of the means to satisfy these needs, the production of material life itself. And indeed this is an historical act, a funda-mental condition of all history, which today, as thousands of years ago, must daily and hourly be fulfilled merely in order to sustain human life. Even when the sensuous world is reduced to a minimum, to a stick as with Saint Bruno [Bauer], it presupposes the action of producing the stick. Therefore in any interpretation of history one has first of all to observe this fundamental fact in all its significance and all its implications and to accord it its due importance. It is well known that the Germans have never done this, and they have never, therefore, had an *earthly* basis for history and consequently never an historian. The French and the English, even if they have conceived the relation of this fact with so-called history only in an extremely one-sided fashion, particularly as long as they remained in the toils of political ideology, have nevertheless made the first attempts to give the writing of history a materialistic basis by being the first to write histories of civil society, of the commerce and industry.

The second point is that the satisfaction of the first need (the action of satisfying, and the instrument of satisfaction which has been acquired) leads to new needs; and this production of new needs is the first historical act. Here we recognise immediately the spiritual ancestry of the great historical wisdom of the Germans who, when they run out of positive material and when they can serve up neither theological nor political nor literary rubbish, assert that this is not history at all, but the "prehistoric era". They do not, however, enlighten us as to how we proceed from this nonsensical "prehistory" to history proper; although, on the other hand, in their historical speculation they seize upon this "prehistory" with especial eagerness because they imagine themselves safe there from interference on the part of "crude facts", and, at the same time, because there they can give full rein to their speculative impulse and set up and knock down hypotheses by the thousand.

The third circumstance which, from the very outset, enters into historical development, is that men, who daily remake their own life, begin to make other men, to propagate their kind: the relation between man and woman, parents and children, the *family*. The family, which to begin with is the only social relationship, becomes later, when increased needs create a new social relations and the increased population new needs, a subordinate one (except in Germany), and must then be treated and analysed according to the existing empirical data, not according to "the concept of the family", as is the custom in Germany. These three aspects of social activity are not of course to be taken as three different stages, but just as three aspects or, to make it clear to the Germans, three "moments", which have existed simultaneously since the dawn of history and the first men, and which still assert themselves in history today.

The production of life, both of one's own labour and of fresh life in procreation, now appears as a double relationship; on the one hand as a natural, on the other as a social relationship. By social we understand the co-operation of several individuals, no matter under what conditions, in what manner and to what end. It follows from this that a certain mode of production, or industrial stage, is always combined with a certain mode of co-operation, or social stage, and this mode of co-operation is itself a "productive force". Further, that the multitude of productive forces accessible to men determines the nature of society, hence, that the "history of humanity" must always be studied and treated in relation to the history of humanity and exchange. But it is also clear how in Germany it is impossible to write this sort of history, because the Germans lack not only the necessary power of comprehension and the material but also the "evidence of their senses", for across the Rhine you cannot have any experience of these things since history has stopped happening. Thus it is quite obvious from the start that there exists a materialistic connection of men with one another, which is determined by their needs and their mode of production, and which is as old as men themselves. This connection is ever taking on new forms, and thus presents a "history" independently of the existence of any political or religious nonsense which in addition may hold men together.

Only now, after having considered four moments, four aspects of the primary historical relationships, do we find that man also possesses "consciousness", but, even so, not inherent, not "pure" consciousness. From the start the "spirit" is afflicted with the curse of being "burdened" with matter, which here makes its appearance in the form of agitated layers of air, sounds, in short, of language. Language is as old as consciousness, language *is* practical consciousness that exists also for other men, and for that reason alone it really exists for me personally as well; language, like consciousness, only arises from the need, the necessity, of intercourse with other men. Where there exists a relationship, it exists for me: the animal does not enter into *"relations"* with anything, it does not enter into any relation at all. For the animal, its relation to others does not exist as a relation. Consciousness is, therefore, from the very beginning a social product, and remains so as long as men exist at all. Consciousness is at first, of course, merely consciousness concerning the *immediate* sensuous environment and consciousness of the limited connection with other persons and things outside the individual who is growing self-conscious. At the same time it is consciousness of nature, which first appears to men as a completely alien, all-powerful and unassailable force, with which men's relations are purely animal and by which they are overawed like beasts; it is thus a purely animal consciousness of nature (natural religion) just because nature is as yet hardly modified historically. (We see here immediately: this natural religion or this particular relation of men to nature is determined by the form of society and vice versa. Here, as everywhere, the identity of nature and man appears in such a way that the restricted relation of men to nature determines their restricted relation to one another, and their restricted relation to one another determines men's restricted relation to nature.) On the other hand, man's consciousness of the necessity of associating with the individuals around him is the beginning of the consciousness that he is living in society at all. This beginning is as animal as social life itself at this stage. It is mere herd-consciousness, and at this point man is only distinguished from sheep by the fact that with him consciousness takes the place of instinct or that his instinct is a conscious one. This sheep-like or tribal consciousness receives its further development and extension through increased productivity, the increase of needs, and, what is fundamental to both of these, the increase of population. With these there develops the division of labour, which was originally nothing but the division of labour in the sexual act, then that division of labour which develops spontaneously or "naturally" by virtue of natural predisposition (e.g. physical strength), needs, accidents, etc. etc. Division of labour only becomes truly such from the moment when a division of material and mental labour appears. (The first form of ideologists, *priests*, is concurrent.) From this moment onwards consciousness *can* really flatter itself that it is something other than consciousness of existing practice, that it *really* represents something without representing something real; from now on consciousness is in a position to emancipate itself from the world and to proceed to the formation of "pure" theory, theology, philosophy, ethics, etc. But even if this theory, theology, philosophy, ethics, etc. comes into contradiction with the existing relations, this can only occur because existing social relations have come into contradiction with existing forces of production; this, moreover, can also occur in a particular national sphere of relations through the appearance of the contradiction, not within the national orbit, but between this national consciousness and the practice of other nations, i.e. between the national and the general consciousness of a nation (as we see it now in Germany).

Moreover, it is quite immaterial what consciousness starts to do on its own: out of all such muck we get only the one inference that these three moments, the forces of production, the state of society, and consciousness, can and must come into contradiction with one another, because the *division of labour* implies the possibility, nay the fact that intellectual and material activity—enjoyment and labour, production and consumption—devolve on different individuals, and that the only possibility of their not coming into contradiction lies in the negation in its turn of the division of labour. It is self-evident, moreover, that "spectres", "bonds", "the higher being", "concept", "scruple", are merely the idealistic, spiritual expression, the conception apparently of the isolated individual, the image of very empirical fetters and limitations, within which the mode of production of life and the form of intercourse coupled with it move.

Private Property and Communism

With the division of labour, in which all these contradictions are implicit, and which in its turn is based on the natural division of labour in the family and the separation of society into individual families opposed to one another, is given simultaneously the *distribution*, and indeed the *unequal* distribution, both quantitative and qualitative, of labour and its products, hence property: the nucleus, the first form, of which lies in the family, where wife and children are the slaves of the husband. This latent slavery in the family, though still very crude, is the first property, but even at this early stage it corresponds perfectly to the definition of modern economists who call it the power of disposing of the labour-power of others. Division of labour and private property are, moreover, identical expressions: in the one the same thing is affirmed with reference to activity as is affirmed in the other with reference to the product of the activity.

Further, the division of labour implies the contradiction between the interest of the separate individual or the individual family and the communal interest of all individuals who have intercourse with one another. And indeed, this communal interest does not exist merely in the imagination, as the "general interest", but first of all in reality, as the mutual interdependence of the individuals among whom the labour is divided. And finally, the division of labour offers us the first example of how, as long as man remains in natural society, that is, as long as a cleavage exists between the particular and the common interest, as long, therefore, as activity is not voluntarily, but naturally, divided, man's own deed becomes an alien power opposed to him, which enslaves him instead of being controlled by him. For as soon as the distribution of labour comes into being, each man has a particular, exclusive sphere of activity, which is forced upon him and from which he cannot escape. He is a hunter, a fisherman, a shepherd, or a critical critic, and must remain so if he does not want to lose his means of livelihood; while in communist society, where nobody has one exclusive sphere of activity but each can become accomplished in any branch he wishes, society regulates the general production and thus makes it possible for me to do one thing today and another tomorrow, to hunt in the morning, fish in the afternoon, rear cattle in the evening, criticise after dinner, just as I have a mind, without ever becoming hunter, fisherman, shepherd or critic. This fixation of a social activity, this consolidation of what we ourselves produce into an objective power above us, growing out of our control, thwarting our expectations, bringing to naught our calculations, is one of the chief factors in historical development up till now.

(And out of this very contradiction between the interest of the individual and that of the community the latter takes an independent form as the *State*, divorced from the real interests of individual and community, and at the same time as an illusory communal life, always based, however, on the real ties existing in every family and tribal conglomeration—such as flesh and blood, language, division of labour on a larger scale, and other interests—and especially, as we shall enlarge upon later, on the classes, already determined by the division of labour, which in every such mass of men separate out, and of which one dominates all the others. It follows from this that all struggles within the State, the struggle between democracy, aristocracy, and monarchy, the struggle for the franchise, etc. etc.

are merely the illusory forms in which the real struggles of the different classes are fought out among one another. Of this the German theoreticians have not the faintest inkling, although they have received a sufficient introduction to the subject in the *Deutsch-Französische Jahrbücher* and *Die heilige Familie*. Further, it follows that every class which is struggling for mastery, even when its domination, as is the case with the proletariat, postulates the abolition of the old form of society in its entirety and of domination itself, must first conquer for itself political power in order to represent its interest in turn as the general interest, which immediately it is forced to do. Just because individuals seek *only* their particular interest, which for them does not coincide with their communal interest, the latter will be imposed on them as an interest "alien" to them, and "independent" of them, as in its turn a particular, peculiar "general" interest; or they themselves must remain within this discord, as in democracy. On the other hand, too, the *practical* struggle of these particular interests, which constancy *really* run counter to the communal and illusory communal interests, makes *practical* intervention and control necessary through the illusory "general" interest in the form of the State.)

The social power, i.e. the multiplied productive force, which arises through the cooperation of different individuals as it is determined by the division of labour, appears to these individuals, since their cooperation is not voluntary but has come about naturally, not as their own united power, but as an alien force existing outside them, of the origin and goal of which they are ignorant, which they thus cannot control, which on the contrary passes through a peculiar series of phases and stages independent of the will and the action of man, nay even being the prime governor of these.

How otherwise could for instance property have had a history at all, have taken on different forms, and landed property, for example, according to the different premises given, have proceeded in France from parcellation to centralisation in the hands of a few, in England from centralisation in the hands of a few to parcellation, as is actually the case today? Or how does it happen that trade, which after all is nothing more than the exchange of products of various individuals and countries, rules the whole world through the relation of supply and demand—a relation which, as an English economist says, hovers over the earth like the fate of the ancients, and with invisible hand allots fortune and misfortune to men, sets up empires and overthrows empires, causes nations to rise and to disappear—while with the abolition of the basis of private property, with the communistic regulation of production (and, implicit in this, the destruction of the alien relation between men and what they themselves produce), the power of the relation of supply and demand is dissolved into nothing, and men get exchange, production, the mode of their mutual relation, under their own control again?

In history up to the present it is certainly an empirical fact that separate individuals have, with the broadening of their activity into world-historical activity, become more and more enslaved under a power alien to them (a pressure which they have conceived of as a dirty trick on the part of the so-called universal spirit, etc.), a power which has become more and more enormous and, in the last instance, turns out to be the *world market*. But it is just as empirically established that, by the overthrow of the existing state of society by the communist revolution (of which more below) and the abolition of private property which is identical with it, this power, which so baffles the German theoreticians, will be dissolved; and that then the liberation of each single individual will be accomplished in the measure in which history becomes transformed into world history. From the above it is clear that the real intellectual wealth of the individual depends entirely on the wealth of his real connections. Only then will the separate individuals be liberated from the various national and local barriers, be brought into practical connection with the material and intellectual production of the whole world and be put in a position to acquire the capacity of enjoy this all-sided production of the whole earth (the creations of man). *All-round* dependence, this natural form of the *world-historical* co-operation of individuals, will be transformed by this communist revolution into the control and conscious mastery of these powers, which, born of the action of men on one another, have till now overawed and governed men as powers completely alien to them. Now this view can be expressed again in speculative-idealistic, i.e. fantastic, terms as "self-generation of the species" ("society as the subject"), and thereby the consecutive series of interrelated individuals connected with each other can be conceived as a single individual, which accomplishes the mystery of generating itself. It is clear here that individuals certainly make *one another*, physically and mentally, but do not make themselves.

This "alienation" (to use a term which will be comprehensible to the philosophers) can, of course, only be abolished given two *practical* premises. For it to become an "intolerable" power, i.e. a power against which men make a revolution, it must necessarily have rendered the great mass of humanity "propertyless", and produced, at the same time, the contradiction of an existing world of wealth and culture, both of which conditions presuppose a great increase in productive power, a high degree of its development. And, on the other hand, this development of productive forces (which itself implies the actual empirical existence of men in their *world-historical*, instead of local, being) is an absolutely necessary practical premise because without it *want* is merely made general, and with *destitution* the struggle for necessities and all the old filthy business would necessarily be produced; and furthermore, because only with this universal development of productive forced is a *universal* intercourse between men established, which produces in all nations simultaneously the phenomenon of the "propertyless" mass (universal competition), makes each nation dependent on the revolutions of the others, and finally has put *world-historical*, empirically universal individuals in the place of local ones. Without this, (1) communism could only exist as a local event; (2) the *forces* of intercourse themselves could not have developed as *universal*, hence intolerable powers: they would have remained home-bred conditions surrounded by superstition; and (3) each extension of intercourse would abolish local communism. Empirically, communism is only possible as the act of the dominant peoples "all at once" and simultaneously, which presupposes the universal development of productive forces and the world intercourse bound up with communism. Moreover, the mass of *propertyless* workers—the utterly precarious position of labour-power on a mass scale cut off from capital or from even a limited satisfaction and, therefore, no longer merely temporarily deprived of work itself as a secure source of life—presupposes the *world market* through competition. The proletariat can thus only exist *world-historically*, just as communism, its activity, can only have a "world-historical" existence. World-historical existence of individuals means, existence of individuals which is directly linked up with world history.

Communism is for us not a *state of affairs* which is to be established, an *ideal* to which reality [will] have to adjust itself. We call communism the *real* movement which abolishes the present state of things. The conditions of this movement result from the premises now in existence.

Notes

1. The building of houses. With savages each family has as a matter of course its own cave or hut like the separate family tent of the nomads. This separate domestic economy is made only the more necessary by the further development of private property. With the agricultural peoples a communal

domestic economy is just as impossible as a communal cultivation of the soil. A great advance was the building of towns. In all previous periods, however, the abolition of individual economy, which is inseparable from the abolition of private property, was impossible for the simple reason that the material conditions governing it were not present. The setting-up of a communal domestic economy presupposes the development of machinery, of the use of natural forces and of many other productive forces—e.g. of water-supplies, of gas-lighting, steam-heating, etc., the removal [of the antagonism] of town and country. Without these conditions a communal economy would not in itself form a new productive force; lacking any material basis and resting on a purely theoretical foundation, it would be a mere freak and would end in nothing more than a monastic economy—What was possible can be seen in the towns brought about by condensation and the erection of communal buildings for various definite purposes (prisons, barracks, etc.). That the abolition of individual economy is inseparable from the abolition of the family is self-evident.

MANIFESTO OF THE COMMUNIST PARTY

PREFACE TO THE ENGLISH EDITION OF 1888

Friedrich Engels

The Manifesto was published as the platform of the Communist League, a workingmen's association, first exclusively German, later on international, and, under the political conditions of the Continent before 1848, unavoidably a secret society. At a Congress of the League, held in London in November 1847, Marx and Engles were commissioned to prepare for publication a complete theoretical and practical party program. Drawn up in German, in January 1848, the manuscript was sent to the printer in London a few weeks before the French Revolution of February 24. A French translation was brought out in Paris shortly before the insurrection of June 1848. The first English translation, by Miss Helen Macfarlane, appeared in George Julian Harney's *Red Republican*, London, 1850. A Danish and a Polish edition had also been published.

The defeat of the Parisian insurrection of June 1848—the first great battle between proletariat and bourgeoisie—drove again into the background, for a time, the social and political aspirations of the European working class. Thenceforth the struggle for supremacy was again, as it had been before the revolution of February, solely between different sections of the propertied class; the working class was reduced to a fight for political elbowroom, and to the position of extreme wing of the middle-class radicals. Wherever independent proletarian movements continued to show signs of life they were ruthlessly hunted down. Thus the Prussian police hunted out the Central Board of the Communist League, then located in Cologne. The members were arrested and, after eighteen months' imprisonment, they were tried in October 1852. This celebrated "Cologne Communist trial" lasted from October 4 till November 12; seven of the prisoners were sentenced to terms of imprisonment in a fortress, varying from three to six years. Immediately after the sentence the League was formally dissolved by the remaining members. As to the Manifesto, it seemed thenceforth to be doomed to oblivion.

When the European working class had recovered sufficient strength for another attack on the ruling classes, the International Workingmen's Association sprang up. But this

Association, formed with the express aim of welding into one body the whole militant proletariat of Europe and America, could not at once proclaim the principles laid down in the Manifesto. The International was bound to have a program broad enough to be acceptable to the English trade unions, to the followers of Proudhon of France, Belgium, Italy, and Spain, and to the Lassalleans[1] in Germany. Marx, who drew up this program to the satisfaction of all parties, entirely trusted to the intellectual development of the working class, which was sure to result from combined action and mutual discussion. The very events and vicissitudes of the struggle against capital, the defeats even more than the victories, could not help bringing home to men's minds the insufficiency of their various favorite nostrums and preparing the way for a more complete insight into the true conditions of working-class emancipation. And Marx was right. The International, on its breaking up in 1874, left the workers quite different men from what it had found them in 1864. Proudhonism in France, Lassalleanism in Germany were dying out, and even the conservative English trade unions, though most of them had long since severed their connection with the International, were gradually advancing towards that point at which, last year at Swansea, their president could say in their name: "Continental socialism has lost its terrors for us." In fact, the principles of the Manifesto had made considerable headway among the workingmen of all countries.

The Manifesto itself thus came to the front again. The German text had been, since 1850, reprinted several times in Switzerland, England, and America. In 1872 it was translated into English in New York, where the translation was published in *Woodhull and Claflin's Weekly*. From this English version a French one was made in *Le Socialiste* of New York. Since then at least two more English translations, more or less mutilated, have been brought out in America, and one of them has been reprinted in England. The first Russian translation, made by Bakounine, was published at Herzen's *Kolokol* office in Geneva, about 1863; a second one, by the heroic Vera Zasulich, also in Geneva, 1881. A new Danish edition is to be found in *Socialdemokratisk Bibliothek*, Copenhagen, 1885; a fresh French translation in *Le Socialiste*, Paris, 1885. From this latter a Spanish version was prepared and published in Madrid, 1986. The German reprints are not to be counted; there have been twelve altogether at the least. An Armenian translation, which was to be published in Constantinople some months ago, did not see the light, I am told, because the publisher was afraid of bringing out a book with the name of Marx on it, while the translator declined to call it his own production. Of further translations into other languages I have heard, but have not seen them. Thus the history of the Manifesto reflects, to a great extent, the history of modern working-class movement; at present it is undoubtedly the most widespread, the most international production of all socialist literature, the common platform acknowledged by millions of workingmen from Siberia to California.

Yet, when it was written, we could not have called it a *Socialist* Manifesto. By socialists, in 1847, were understood, on the one hand, the adherents of the various utopian systems: Owenites in England, Fourierists in France, both of them already reduced to the position of mere sects, and gradually dying out; on the other hand, the most multi-farious social quacks, who, by all manners of tinkering, professed to redress, without any danger to capital and profit, all sorts of social grievances, in both cases men outside the working-class movement and looking rather to the "educated" classes for support. Whatever portion of the working class had become convinced of the insufficiency of mere political revolutions and had proclaimed the necessity of a total social change, that portion then called itself communist. It was a crude, rough-hewn, purely instinctive sort of communism; still, it touched the cardinal point and was powerful enough among the working class to produce the utopian communism, in France, of Cabet and, in Germany, of

Weitling. Thus socialism was, in 1847, a middle-class movement, communism a working-class movement. Socialism was, on the Continent at least, "respectable"; communism was the very opposite. And as our notion, from the very beginning, was that "the emancipation of the working class must be the the act of the working class itself," there could be no doubt as to which of the two names we must take. Moreover, we have, ever since, been far from repudiating it.

The Manifesto being our joint production, I consider myself bound to state that the fundamental proposition, which forms its nucleus, belongs to Marx. That proposition is that in every historical epoch the prevailing mode of economic production and exchange and the social organization necessarily following from it form the basis upon which is built up, and from which alone can be explained, the political and intellectual history of that epoch; that consequently the whole history of mankind (since the dissolution of primitive tribal society, holding land in common ownership) has been a history of class struggles, contests between exploiting and exploited, ruling and oppressed classes; that the history of these class struggles forms a series of evolutions in which, nowadays, a stage has been reached where the exploited and oppressed class—the proletariat—cannot attain its emancipation from the sway of the exploiting and ruling class—the bourgeoisie—without, at the same time, and once and for all, emancipating society at large from all exploitation, oppression, class distinctions, and class struggles.

This proposition, which, in my opinion, is destined to do for history what Darwin's theory has done for biology, we, both of us, had been gradually approaching for some years before 1845. How far I had independently progressed towards it is best shown by my *Condition of the Working Class* in England. But when I again met Marx at Brussels, in spring 1845, he had it already worked out, and put it before me, in terms almost as clear as those in which I have stated it here.

From our joint preface to the German edition of 1872, I quote the following:

"However much the state of things may have altered during the last twenty-five years, the general principles laid down in this Manifesto are, on the whole, as correct today as ever. Here and there some detail might be improved. The practical application of the principles will depend, as the Manifesto itself states, everywhere and at all times, on the historical conditions for the time being existing, and for that reason no special stress is laid on the revolutionary measures proposed at the end of Section II. That passage would, in many respects, be very differently worded today. In view of the gigantic strides of modern industry since 1848, and of the accompanying improved and extended organization of the working class, in view of the practical experience gained, first in the February revolution, and then, still more, in the Paris Commune, where the proletariat for the first time held political power for two whole months, this program has in some details become antiquated. One thing especially was proved by the Commune, viz., 'that the working class cannot simply lay hold of the ready-made state machinery and wield it for its own purposes.' (See *The Civil War in France; Address of the General Council of the International Workingmen's Association*, London, Truelove, 1871, page 15, where this point is further developed.) Further, it is self-evident that the criticism of socialist literature is deficient in relation to the present time, because it comes down only to 1847; also, that the remarks on the relation of the communists to the various opposition parties (Section IV), although in principle still correct, yet in practice are antiquated, because the political situation has been entirely changed and the progress of history has swept from off the earth the greater portion of the political parties there enumerated.

"But then, the Manifesto has become a historical document which we have no longer any right to alter."

The present translation is by Mr. Samuel Moore, the translator of the greater portion of Marx's *Capital*. We have revised it in common, and I have added a few notes explanatory of historical allusions.

MANIFESTO OF THE COMMUNIST PARTY

A specter is haunting Europe—the specter of communism. All the powers of old Europe have entered into a holy alliance to exorcise this specter: Pope and Czar, Metternich and Guizot, French radicals and German police spies.

Where is the party in opposition that has not been decried as communistic by its opponents in power? Where the opposition that has not hurled back the branding reproach of communism against the more advanced opposition parties, as well as against its reactionary adversaries?

Two things result from this fact:

I. Communism is already acknowledged by all European powers to be itself a power.

II. It is high time that communists should openly, in the face of the whole world, publish their views, their aims, their tendencies, and meet this nursery tale of the specter of communism with a Manifesto of the party itself.

To this end, communists of various nationalities have assembled in London and sketched the following Manifesto, to be published in the English, French, German, Italian, Flemish, and Danish languages.

I. Bourgeois and Proletarians[2]

The history of all hitherto existing society[3] is the history of class struggles.

Free man and slave, patrician and plebeian, lord and serf, guild master[4] and journeyman, in a word, oppressor and oppressed, stood in constant opposition to one another, carried on an uninterrupted, now hidden, now open fight, a fight that each time ended either in a revolutionary reconstitution of society at large or in the common ruin of the contending classes.

In the earlier epochs of history we find almost everywhere a complicated arrangement of society into various orders, a manifold gradation of social rank. In ancient Rome we have patricians, knights, plebeians, slaves; in the Middle Ages, feudal lords, vassals, guild masters, journeymen, apprentices, serfs; in almost all of these classes, again, subordinate gradations.

The modern bourgeois society that has sprouted from the ruins of feudal society has not done away with class antagonisms. It has but established new classes, new conditions of oppression, new forms of struggle in place of the old ones.

Our epoch, the epoch of the bourgeoisie, possesses, however, this distinctive feature: it has simplified the class antagonisms. Society as a whole is more and more splitting up into two great hostile camps, into two great classes directly facing each other: bourgeoisie end proletariat.

From the serfs of the Middle Ages sprang the chartered burghers of the earliest towns. From these burgesses the first elements of the bourgeoisie were developed.

The discovery of America, the rounding of the Cape opened up fresh ground for the rising bourgeoisie. The East Indian and Chinese markets, the colonization of America, trade with the colonies, the increase in the means of exchange and in commodities generally, gave to commerce, to navigation, to industry an impulse never before known, and thereby, to the revolutionary element in the tottering feudal society, a rapid development.

The feudal system of industry, under which industrial production was monopolized by closed guilds, now no longer sufficed for the growing wants of the new markets. The manufacturing system took its place. The guild masters were pushed on one side by the manufacturing middle class; division of labor between the different corporate guilds vanished in the face of division of labor in each single workshop.

Meantime the markets kept ever growing, the demand ever rising. Even manufacture no longer sufficed. Thereupon steam and machinery revolutionized industrial production. The place of manufacture was taken by the giant, modern industry, the place of the industrial middle class by industrial millionaires, the leaders of whole industrial armies, the modern bourgeois.

Modern industry has established the world market, for which the discovery of America paved the way. This market has given an immense development to commerce, to navigation, to communication by land. This development has, in its turn, reacted on the extension of industry; and in proportion as industry, commerce, navigation, railways extended, in the same proportion the bourgeoisie developed, increased its capital, and pushed into the background every class handed down from the Middle Ages.

We see, therefore, how the modern bourgeoisie is itself the product of a long course of development, of a series of revolutions in the modes of production and of exchange.

Each step in the development of the bourgeoisie was accompanied by a corresponding political advance of that class. An oppressed class under the sway of the feudal nobility, an armed and self-governing association in the medieval commune,[5] here independent urban republic (as in Italy and Germany), there taxable "third estate" of the monarchy (as in France), afterwards, in the period of manufacture proper, serving either the semi-feudal or the absolute monarchy as a counterpoise against the nobility, and, in fact, cornerstone of the great monarchies in general, the bourgeoisie has at last, since the establishment of modern industry and of the world market, conquered for itself, in the modern representative state, exclusive political sway. The executive of the modern state is but a committee for managing the common affairs of the whole bourgeoisie.

The bourgeoisie, historically, has played a most revolutionary part.

The bourgeoisie, wherever it has got the upper hand, has put an end to all feudal, patriarchal, idyllic relations. It has pitilessly torn asunder the motley feudal ties that bound man to his "natural superiors," and has left remaining no other nexus between man and man than naked self-interest, than callous "cash payment." It has drowned the most heavenly ecstasies of religious fervor, of chivalrous enthusiasm, of Philistine sentimentalism in the icy water of egotistical calculation. It has resolved personal worth into exchange value and, in place of the numberless indefeasible chartered freedoms, has set up that single, unconscionable freedom— free trade. In one word, for exploitation, veiled by religious and political illusions, it has substituted naked, shameless, direct, brutal exploitation.

The bourgeoisie has stripped of its halo every occupation hitherto honored and looked up to with reverent awe. It has converted the physician, the lawyer, the priest, the poet, the man of science into its paid wage laborers.

The bourgeoisie has torn away from the family its sentimental veil, and has reduced the family relation to a mere money relation.

The bourgeoisie has disclosed how it came to pass that the brutal display of vigor in the Middle Ages, which reactionists so much admire, found its fitting complement in the most slothful indolence. It has been the first to show what man's activity can bring about.

It has accomplished wonders far surpassing Egyptian pyramids, Roman aqueducts, and Gothic cathedrals; it has conducted expeditions that put in the shade all former exoduses of nations and crusades.

The bourgeoisie cannot exist without constantly revolutionizing the instruments of production, and thereby the relations of production, and with them the whole relations of society. Conservation of the old modes of production in unaltered form was, on the contrary, the first condition of existence for all earlier industrial classes. Constant revolutionizing of production, uninterrupted disturbance of all social conditions, everlasting uncertainty and agitation distinguish the bourgeois epoch from all earlier ones. All fixed, fast-frozen relations, with their train of ancient and venerable prejudices and opinions, are swept away, all newformed ones become antiquated before they can ossify. All that is solid melts into air, all that is holy is profaned, and man is at last compelled to face with sober senses his real conditions of life and his relations with his kind.

The need of a constantly expanding market for its products chases the bourgeoisie over the whole surface of the globe. It must nestle everywhere, settle everywhere, establish connections everywhere.

The bourgeoisie has through its exploitation of the world market given a cosmopolitan character to production and consumption in every country. To the great chagrin of reactionists, it has drawn from under the feet of industry the national ground on which it stood. All old-established national industries have been destroyed or are daily being destroyed. They are dislodged by new industries, whose introduction becomes a life and death question for all civilized nations, by industries that no longer work up indigenous raw material, but raw material drawn from the remotest zones; industries whose products are consumed not only at home, but in every quarter of the globe. In place of the old wants, satisfied by the productions of the country, we find new wants, requiring for their satisfaction the products of distant lands and climes. In place of the old local and national seclusion and self-sufficiency we have intercourse in every direction, universal interdependence of nations. And as in material, so also in intellectual production. The intellectual creations of individual nations become common property. National one-sidedness and narrow-mindedness become more and more impossible, and from the numerous national and local literatures there, arises a world literature.

The bourgeoisie, by the rapid improvement of all instruments of production, by the immensely facilitated means of communication, draws all, even the most barbarian, nations into civilization. The cheap prices of its commodities are the heavy artillery with which it batters down all Chinese walls, with which it forces the barbarians' intensely obstinate hatred of foreigners to capitulate. It compels all nations, on pain of extinction, to adopt the bourgeois mode of production; it compels them to introduce what it calls civilization into their midst, i.e., to become bourgeois themselves. In one word, it creates a world after its own image.

The bourgeoisie has subjected the country to the rule of the towns. It has created enormous cities, has greatly increased the urban population as compared with the rural, and has thus rescued a considerable part of the population from the idiocy of rural life. Just as it has made the country dependent on the towns, so it has made barbarian and semi-barbarian countries dependent on the civilized ones, nations of peasants on nations of bourgeois, the East on the West.

The bourgeoisie keeps more and more doing away with the scattered state of the population, of the means of production, and of property. It has agglomerated population, centralized means of production, and has concentrated property in a few hands. The necessary consequence of this was political centralization. Independent, or but loosely connected provinces, with separate interests, laws, governments and systems of taxation, became lumped together into one nation, with one government, one code of laws, one national class interest, one frontier, and one customs tariff.

The bourgeoisie, during its rule of scarce one hundred years, has created more massive and more colossal productive forces than have all preceding generations together. Subjection of nature's forces to man, machinery, application of chemistry to industry and agriculture, steam navigation, railways, electric telegraphs, clearing of whole continents for cultivation, canalization of rivers, whole populations conjured out of the ground—what earlier century had even a presentiment that such productive forces slumbered in the lap of social labor?

We see then: the means of production and of exchange, on whose foundation the bourgeoisie built itself up, were generated in feudal society. At a certain stage in the development of these means of production and of exchange, the conditions under which feudal society produced and exchanged, the feudal organization of agriculture and manufacturing industry, in one word, the feudal relations of property, became no longer compatible with the already developed productive forces; they became so many fetters. They had to be burst asunder; they were burst asunder.

Into their place stepped free competition, accompanied by a social and political constitution adapted to it, and by the economic and political sway of the bourgeois class.

A similar movement is going on before our own eyes. Modem bourgeois society with its relations of production, of exchange, and of property, a society that has conjured up such gigantic means of production and of exchange, is like the sorcerer who is no longer able to control the powers of the nether world whom he has called up by his spells. For many a decade past, the history of industry and commerce is but the history of the revolt of modern productive forces against modern conditions of production, against the property relations that are the conditions for the existence of the bourgeoisie and of its rule. It is enough to mention the commercial crises that by their periodic return put on its trial, each time more threatening, the existence of the entire bourgeois society. In these crises a great part not only of the existing products but also of the previously created productive forces are periodically destroyed. In these crises there breaks out an epidemic that in all earlier epochs would have seemed an absurdity—the epidemic of overproduction. Society suddenly finds itself put back into a state of momentary barbarism; it appears as if a famine, a universal war of devastation had cut off the supply of every means of subsistence; industry and commerce seem to be destroyed; and why? Because there is too much civilization, too much means of subsistence, too much industry, too much commerce. The productive forces at the disposal of society no longer tend to further the development of the conditions of bourgeois property; on the contrary, they have become too powerful for these conditions, by which they are fettered, and as soon as they overcome these fetters they bring disorder into the whole of bourgeois society, endanger the existence of bourgeois property. The conditions of bourgeois society are too narrow to comprise the wealth created by them. And how does the bourgeoisie get over these crises? On the one hand, by enforced destruction of a mass of productive forces; on the other, by the conquest of new markets, and by the more thorough exploitation of the old ones. That is to say, by paving the way of more extensive and more destructive crises, and by diminishing the means whereby crises are prevented.

The weapons with which the bourgeoisie felled feudalism to the ground are now turned against the bourgeoisie itself.

But not only has the bourgeoisie forged the weapons that bring death to itself; it has also called into existence the men who are to wield those weapons—the modern working class—the proletarians.

In proportion as the bourgeoisie, i.e., capital, is developed, in the same proportion is the proletariat, the modern working class, developed—a class of laborers, who live only so long as they find work, and who find work only so long as their labor increases capital. These laborers, who must sell themselves piecemeal, are a commodity, like every other article of commerce, and are consequently exposed to all the vicissitudes of competition, to all the fluctuations of the market.

Owing to the extensive use of machinery and to division of labor, the work of the proletarians has lost all individual character and, consequently, all charm for the workman. He becomes an appendage of the machine, and it is only the simplest, most monotonous, and most easily acquired knack that is required of him. Hence the cost of production of a workman is restricted, almost entirely, to the means of subsistence that he requires for his maintenance and for the propagation of his race. But the price of a commodity, and therefore also of labor, is equal to its cost of production. In proportion, therefore, as the repulsiveness of the work increases, the wage decreases. Nay, more, in proportion as the use of machinery and division of labor increases, in the same proportion the burden of toil also increases, whether by prolongation of the working hours, by increase of the work exacted in a given time, or by increased speed of the machinery, etc.

Modern industry has converted the little workshop of the patriarchal master into the great factory of the industrial capitalist. Masses of laborers, crowded into the factory, are organized like soldiers. As privates of the industrial army they are placed under the command of a perfect hierarchy of officers and sergeants. Not only are they slaves of the bourgeois class, and of the bourgeois state; they are daily and hourly enslaved by the machine, by the overlooker, and, above all, by the individual bourgeois manufacturer himself. The more openly this despotism proclaims gain to be its end and aim, the more petty, the more hateful, and the more embittering it is.

The less the skill and exertion of strength implied in manual labor, in other words, the more modern industry becomes developed, the more is the labor of men superseded by that of women. Differences of age and sex have no longer any distinctive social validity for the working class. All are instruments of labor, more or less expensive to use, according to their age and sex.

No sooner is the exploitation of the laborer by the manufacturer over, to the extent that he receives his wages in cash, than he is set upon by the other portions of the bourgeoisie, the landlord, the shopkeeper, the pawnbroker, etc.

The lower strata of the middle class—the small tradespeople, shopkeepers, and retired tradesman generally, the handicraftsmen and peasants—all these sink gradually into the proletariat, partly because their diminutive capital does not suffice for the scale on which modern industry is carried on, and is swamped in the competition with the large capitalists, partly because their specialized skill is rendered worthless by new methods of production. Thus the proletariat is recruited from all classes of the population.

The proletariat goes through various stages of development. With its birth begins its struggle with the bourgeoisie. At first the contest is carried on by individual laborers, then by the workpeople of a factory, then by the operatives of one trade, in one locality, against the individual bourgeois who directly exploits them. They direct their attacks not against the bourgeois conditions of production, but against the instruments of production themselves; they destroy imported wares that compete with their labor, they smash to pieces machinery, they set factories ablaze, they seek to restore by force the vanished status of the workman of the Middle Ages.

At this stage the laborers still form an incoherent mass scattered over the whole country and broken up by their mutual competition. If anywhere they unite to form more compact bodies, this is not yet the consequence of their own active union, but of the union of the bourgeoise, which class, in order to attain its own political ends, is compelled to set the whole proletariat in motion, and is moreover yet, for a time, able to do so. At this stage, therefore, the proletarians do not fight their enemies, but the enemies of their enemies, the remnants of absolute monarchy, the landowners, the non-industrial bourgeois, the petty bourgeoisie. Thus the whole historical movement is concentrated in the hands of the bourgeoisie; every victory so obtained is a victory for the bourgeoisie.

But with the development of industry the proletariat not only increases in number; it becomes concentrated in greater masses, its strength grows, and it feels that strength more. The various interests and conditions of life within the ranks of the proletariat are more and more equalized, in proportion as machinery obliterates all distinctions of labor and nearly everywhere reduces wages to the same low level. The growing competition among the bourgeois and the resulting commercial crises make the wages of the workers ever more fluctuating. The unceasing improvement of machinery, ever more rapidly developing, makes their livelihood more and more precarious; the collisions between individual workmen and individual bourgeois take more and more the character of collisions between two classes. Thereupon the workers begin to form combinations (trade unions) against the bourgeois; they club together in order to keep up the rate of wages; they found permanent associations in order to make provision beforehand for these occasional revolts. Here and there the contest breaks out into riots.

Now and then the workers are victorious, but only for a time. The real fruit of their battles lies not in the immediate result, but in the ever expanding union of the workers. This union is helped on by the improved means of communication that are created by modern industry and that place the workers of different localities in contact with one another. It was just this contact that was needed to centralize the numerous local struggles, all of the same character, into one national struggle between classes. But every class struggle is a political struggle. And that union, to attain which the burghers of the Middle Ages, with their miserable highways, required centuries, the modern proletarians, thanks to railways, achieve in a few years.

This organization of the proletarians into a class, and consequently into a political party, is continually being upset again by the competition between the workers themselves. But it ever rises up again, stronger, firmer, mightier. It compels legislative recognition of particular interests of the workers by taking advantage of the divisions among the bourgeoisie itself. Thus the ten-hour bill in England was carried.

Altogether collisions between the classes of the old society further, in many ways, the course of development of the proletariat. The bourgeoisie finds itself involved in a constant battle. At first with the aristocracy, later on with those portions of the bourgeoisie itself whose interests have become antagonistic to the progress of industry; at all times, with the bourgeoisie of foreign countries. In all these battles it sees itself compelled to appeal to the proletariat, to ask for is help, and thus to drag it into the political arena. The bourgeoisie itself, therefore, supplies the proletariat with its own elements of political and general education: in other words, it furnishes the proletariat with weapons for fighting the bourgeoisie.

Further, as we have already seen, entire sections of the ruling classes are, by the advance of industry, precipitated into the proletariat, or are at least threatened in their conditions of existence. These also supply the proletariat with fresh elements of enlightenment and progress.

Finally, in times when the class struggle nears the decisive hour, the process of dissolution going on within the ruling class, in fact within the whole range of old society, assumes such a violent, glaring character that a small section of the ruling class cuts itself adrift and joins the revolutionary class, the class that holds the future in its hands. Just as, therefore, at an earlier period, a section of the nobility went over to the bourgeoisie, so now a portion of the bourgeoisie goes over to the proletariat, and in particular a portion of the bourgeois ideologists, who have raised themselves to the level of comprehending theoretically the historical movement as a whole.

Of all the classes that stand face to face with the bourgeoisie today, the proletariat alone is a really revolutionary class. The other classes decay and finally disappear in the face of modern industry, the proletariat is its special and essential product.

The lower-middle class, the small manufacturer, the shopkeeper, the artisan, the peasant, all these fight against the bourgeoisie, to save from extinction their existence as fractions of the middle class. They are therefore not revolutionary, but conservative. Nay, more, they are reactionary, for they try to roll back the wheel of history. If by chance they are revolutionary they are so only in view of their impending transfer into the proletariat; they thus defend not their present but their future interests, they desert their own standpoint to place themselves at that of the proletariat.

The "dangerous class," the social scum, that passively rotting mass thrown off by the lowest layers of old society, may, here and there, be swept into the movement by a proletarian revolution; its conditions of life, however, prepare it far more for the part of a bribed tool of reactionary intrigue.

In the conditions of the proletariat those of old society at large are already virtually swamped. The proletarian is without property; his relation to his wife and children has no longer anything in common with the bourgeois family relations; modern industrial labor, modern subjection to capital, the same in England as in France, in America as in Germany, has stripped him of every trace of national character. Law, morality, religion are to him so many bourgeois prejudices, behind which lurk in ambush just as many bourgeois interests.

All the preceding classes that got the upper hand sought to *fortify* their already acquired status by subjecting society at large to their conditions of appropriation. The proletarians cannot become masters of the productive forces of society, except by abolishing their own previous mode of appropriation, and thereby also every other previous mode of appropriation. They have nothing of their own to secure and to fortify; their mission is to destroy all previous securities for, and insurances of, individual property.

All previous historical movements were movements of minorities, or in the interest of minorities. The proletarian movement is the self-conscious, independent movement of the immense majority, in the interests of the immense majority. The proletariat, the lowest stratum of our present society, cannot stir, cannot raise itself up, without the whole superincumbent strata of official society being sprung into the air.

Though not in substance, yet in form, the struggle of the proletariat with the bourgeoisie is at first a national struggle. The proletariat of each country must, of course, first of all settle matters with its own bourgeoisie.

In depicting the most general phases of the development of the proletariat, we traced the more or less veiled civil war, raging within existing society, up to the point where that war breaks out into open revolution, and where the violent overthrow of the bourgeoisie lays the foundation for the sway of the proletariat.

Hitherto every form of society has been based, as we have already seen, on the antagonism of oppressing and oppressed classes. But in order to oppress a class certain conditions must be assured to it under which it can, at least, continue its slavish existence. The serf, in the period of serfdom, raised himself to membership in the commune just as the petty bourgeois, under the yoke of feudal absolutism, managed to develop into a bourgeois. The modern laborer, on the contrary, instead of rising with the progress of industry, sinks deeper and deeper below the conditions of existence of his own class. He becomes a pauper, and pauperism develops more rapidly than population and wealth. And here it becomes evident that the bourgeoisie is unfit any longer to be the ruling class in society, and to impose its conditions of existence upon society as an overriding law. It is unfit to rule because it is incompetent to assure an existence to its slave within his slavery, because it cannot help letting him sink into such a state that it has to feed him instead of being fed by him. Society can no longer live under this bourgeoisie: in other words, its existence is no longer compatible with society.

The essential condition for the existence, and for the sway of the bourgeois class, is the formation and augmentation of capital; the condition for capital is wage labor. Wage labor rests exclusively on competition between the laborers. The advance of industry, whose involuntary promoter is the bourgeoisie, replaces the isolation of the laborers, due to competition, by their revolutionary combination, due to association. The development of modern industry, therefore, cuts from under its feet the very foundation on which the bourgeoisie produces and appropriates products. What the bourgeoisie, therefore, produces, above all, is its own gravediggers. Its fall and the victory of the proletariat are equally inevitable.

II. Proletarians and Communists

In what relation do the communists stand to the proletarians as a whole?

The communists do not form a separate party opposed to other working-class parties.

They have no interests separate and apart from those of the proletariat as a whole.

They do not set up any sectarian principles of their own, by which to shape and mold the proletarian movement.

The communists are distinguished from the other working-class parties by this only: 1. In the national struggles of the proletarians of the different countries they point out and bring to the front the common interests of the entire proletariat, independent of all nationality. 2. In the various stages of development which the struggle of the working class against the bourgeoisie has to pass through, they always and everywhere represent the interests of the movement as a whole.

The communists, therefore, are on the one hand, practically, the most advanced and resolute section of the working-class parties of every country, that section which pushes forward all others; on the other hand, theoretically, they have over the great mass of the proletariat the advantage of clearly understanding the line of march, the conditions, and the ultimate general results of the proletarian movement.

The immediate aim of the communists is the same as that of all the other proletarian parties: formation of the proletariat into a class, overthrow of the bourgeois supremacy, conquest of political power by the proletariat.

The theoretical conclusions of the communists are in no way based on ideas or principles that have been invented, or discovered, by this or that would-be universal reformer.

They merely express, in general terms, actual relations springing from an existing class struggle, from a historical movement going on under our very eyes. The abolition of existing property relations is not at all a distinctive feature of communism.

All property relations in the past have continually been subject to historical change consequent upon the change in historical conditions.

The French Revolution, for example, abolished feudal property in favor of bourgeois property.

The distinguishing feature of communism is not the abolition of property generally, but the abolition of bourgeois property. But modern bourgeois private property is the final and most complete expression of the system of producing and appropriating products that is based on antagonisms, on the exploitation of the many by the few.

In this sense the theory of the communists may be summed up in the single sentence: Abolition of private property.

We communists have been reproached with the desire of abolishing the right of personally acquiring property as the fruit of a man's own labor, which property is alleged to be the groundwork of all personal freedom, activity, and dependence.

Hard-won, self-acquired, self-earned property! Do you mean the property of the petty artisan and of the small peasant, a form of property that preceded the bourgeois form? There is no need to abolish that; the development of industry has to a great extent already destroyed it and is still destroying it daily.

Or do you mean modern bourgeois private property?

But does wage labor create any property for the laborer? Not a bit. It creates capital, i.e., that kind of property which exploits wage labor, and which cannot increase except upon condition of begetting a new supply of wage labor for fresh exploitation. Property, in its present form, is based on the antagonism of capital and wage labor. Let us examine both sides of this antagonism.

To be a capitalist is to have not only a purely personal but a social *status* in production. Capital is a collective product, and only by the united action of many members, nay, in the last resort only by the united action of all members of society, can it be set in motion.

Capital is, therefore, not a personal, it is a social power.

When, therefore, capital is converted into common property, into the property of all members of society, personal property is not thereby transformed into social property. It is only the social character of the property that is changed. It loses its class character.

Let us now take wage labor.

The average price of wage labor is the minimum wage, i.e., that quantum of the means of subsistence which is absolutely requisite to keep the laborer in bare existence as a laborer. What, therefore, the wage laborer appropriates by means of his labor merely suffices to prolong and reproduce a bare existence. We by no means intend to abolish this personal appropriation of the products of labor, an appropriation that is made for the maintenance and reproduction of human life, and that leaves no surplus wherewith to command the labor of others. All that we want to do away with is the miserable character of this appropriation, under which the laborer lives merely to increase capital, and is allowed to live only in so far as the interest of the ruling class requires it.

In bourgeois society living labor is but a means to increase accumulated labor. In communist society accumulated labor is but a means to widen, to enrich, to promote the existence of the laborer.

In bourgeois society, therefore, the past dominates the present; in communist society the present dominates the past. In bourgeois society capital is independent and has individuality, while the living person is dependent and has no individuality.

And the abolition of this state of things is called by the bourgeois abolition of individuality and freedom! And rightly so. The abolition of bourgeois individuality, bourgeois independence, and bourgeois freedom is undoubtedly aimed at.

By freedom is meant, under the present bourgeois conditions of production, free trade, free selling and buying.

But if selling and buying disappear, free selling and buying disappear also. This talk about free selling and buying, and all the other "brave words" of our bourgeoisie about freedom in general, have a meaning, if any, only in contrast with restricted selling and buying, with the fettered traders of the Middle Ages, but have no meaning when opposed to the communistic abolition of buying and selling, of the bourgeois conditions of production, and of the bourgeoisie itself.

You are horrified at our intending to do away with private property. But in your existing society private property is already done away with for nine tenths of the population; its existence for the few is solely due to its nonexistence in the hands of those nine tenths. You reproach us, therefore, with intending to do away with a form of property the necessary condition for whose existence is the non-existence of any property for the immense majority of society.

In one word, you reproach us with intending to do away with your property. Precisely so; that is just what we intend.

From the moment when labor can no longer be converted into capital, money, or rent, into a social power capable of being monopolized, i.e., from the moment when individual property can no longer be transformed into bourgeois property, into capital, from that moment, you say, individuality vanishes.

You must, therefore, confess that by "individual" you mean no other person than the bourgeois, than the middle-class owner of property. This person must, indeed, be swept out of the way and made impossible.

Communism deprives no man of the power to appropriate the products of society; all that it does is to deprive him of the power to subjugate the labor of others by means of such appropriation.

It has been objected that upon the abolition of private property all work will cease and universal laziness will overtake us.

According to this, bourgeois society ought long ago have gone to the dogs through sheer idleness, for those of its members who work acquire nothing and those who acquire anything do not work. The whole of this objection is but another expression of the tautology that there can no longer be any wage labor when there is no longer any capital.

All objections urged against the communistic mode of producing and appropriating material products have, in the same way, been urged against the communistic modes of producing and appropriating intellectual products. Just as, to the bourgeois, the disappearance of class property is the disappearance of production itself, so the disappearance of class culture is to him identical with the disappearance of all culture.

That culture, the loss of which he laments, is, for the enormous majority, a mere training to act as a machine.

But don't wrangle with us so long as you apply, to our intended abolition of bourgeois property, the standard of your bourgeois notions of freedom, culture, law, etc. Your very ideas are but the outgrowth of the conditions of your bourgeois production and bourgeois property, just as your jurisprudence is but the will of your class made into a law for all, a well whose essential character and direction are determined by the economic conditions of existence of your class.

The selfish misconception that induces you to transform into eternal laws of nature and of reason the social forms springing from your present mode of production and form of property—historical relations that rise and disappear in the progress of production—this misconception you share with every ruling class that has preceded you. What you see clearly in the case of ancient property, what you admit in the case of feudal property you are of course forbidden to admit in the case of your own bourgeois form of property.

Abolition of the family! Even the most radical flare up at this infamous proposal of the communists.

On what foundation is the present family, the bourgeois family, based? On capital, on private gain. In its completely developed form this family exists only among the bourgeoisie. But this state of things finds its complement in the practical absence of the family among the proletarians, and in public prostitution.

The bourgeois family will vanish as a matter of course when its complement vanishes, and both will vanish with the vanishing of capital.

Do you charge us with wanting to stop the exploitation of children by their parents? To this crime we plead guilty.

But, you will say, we destroy the most hallowed of relations when we replace home education by social.

And your education! Is not that also social, and determined by the social conditions under which you educate, by the intervention, direct or indirect, of society, by means of schools, etc.? The communists have not invented the intervention of society in education; they do but seek to alter the character of that intervention, and to rescue education from the influence of the ruling class.

The bourgeois claptrap about the family and education, about the hallowed co-relation of parent and child, becomes all the more disgusting, the more, by the action of modern industry, all family ties among the proletarians are torn asunder and their children transformed into simple articles of commerce and instruments of labor.

"But you communists would introduce community of women," screams the whole bourgeoisie in chorus.

The bourgeois sees in his wife a mere instrument of production. He hears that the instruments of production are to be exploited in common and, naturally, can come to no other conclusion than that the lot of being common to all will likewise fall to the women.

He has not even a suspicion that the real point aimed at is to do away with the status of women as mere instruments of production.

For the rest, nothing is more ridiculous than the virtuous indignation of our bourgeois at the community of women which, they pretend, is to be openly and officially established by the communists. The communists have no need to introduce community of women; it has existed almost from time immemorial.

Our bourgeois, not content with having the wives and daughters of their proletarians at their disposal, not to speak of common prostitutes, take the greatest pleasure in seducing each other's wives.

Bourgeois marriage is in reality a system of wives in common and thus, at the most, what the communists might possibly be reproached with is that they desire to introduce, in substitution for a hypocritically concealed, an openly legalized community of women. For the rest, it is self-evident that the abolition of the present system of production must bring with it the abolition of the community of women springing from that system, i.e., of prostitution, both public and private.

The communists are further reproached with desiring to abolish countries and nationality.

The workingmen have no country. We cannot take from them what they have not got. Since the proletariat must first of all acquire political supremacy, must rise to be the leading class of the nation, must constitute itself *the* nation, it is, so far, itself national, though not in the bourgeois sense of the word.

National differences and antagonisms between peoples are daily more and more vanishing, owing to the development of the bourgeoisie, to freedom of commerce, to the world market, to uniformity in the mode of production and in the conditions of life corresponding thereto.

The supremacy of the proletariat will cause them to vanish still faster. United action, of the leading civilized countries at least, is one of the first conditions for the emancipation of the proletariat.

In proportion as the exploitation of one individual by another is put to an end, the exploitation of one nation by another will also be put to an end. In proportion as the antagonism between classes within the nation vanishes, the hostility of one nation to another will come to an end.

The charges against communism made from a religious, a philosophical, and, generally, from an ideological standpoint are not deserving of serious examination.

Does it require deep intuition to comprehend that man's ideas, views, and conceptions, in one word, man's consciousness, change with every change in the conditions of his material existence, in his social relations, and in his social life?

What else does the history of ideas prove than that intellectual production changes its character in proportion as material production is changed? The ruling ideas of each age have ever been the ideas of its ruling class.

When people speak of ideas that revolutionize society they do but express the fact that within the old society the elements of a new one have been created, and that the dissolution of the old ideas keeps even pace with the dissolution of the old conditions of existence.

When the ancient world was in its last throes, the ancient religions were overcome by Christianity. When Christian ideas succumbed in the eighteenth century to rationalist ideas, feudal society fought its death battle with the then revolutionary bourgeoisie. The ideas of religious liberty and freedom of conscience merely gave expression to the sway of free competition within the domain of knowledge.

"Undoubtedly," it will be said, "religious, moral, philosophical, and juridical ideas have been modified in the course of historical development. But religion, morality, philosophy, political science, and law constantly survived this change.

There are, besides, eternal truths, such as freedom, justice, etc., that are common to all states of society. But communism abolishes eternal truths, it abolishes all religion, and all morality, instead of constituting them on a new basis; it therefore acts in contradiction to all past historical experience."

What does this accusation reduce itself to? The history of all past society has consisted in the development of class antagonisms, antagonisms that assumed different forms at different epochs.

But whatever form they may have taken, one fact is common to all past ages, viz., the exploitation of one part of society by the other. No wonder then that the social consciousness of past ages, despite all the multiplicity and variety it displays, moves within certain common forms, or general ideas, which cannot completely vanish except with the total disappearance of class antagonisms.

The communist revolution is the most radical rupture with traditional property relations; no wonder that its development involves the most radical rupture with traditional ideas.

But let us have done with the bourgeois objections to communism.

We have seen above that the first step in the revolution by the working class to raise the proletariat to the position of ruling class, to win the battle of democracy.

The proletariat will use its political supremacy to wrest, by degrees, all capital from the bourgeoisie, to centralize all instruments of production in the hands of the state, i.e., of the proletariat organized as the ruling class, and to increase the total of productive forces as rapidly as possible.

Of course, in the beginning this cannot be effected except by means of despotic inroads on the rights of property and on the conditions of bourgeois production; by means of measures, therefore, which appear economically insufficient and untenable, but which, in the course of the movement, outstrip themselves, necessitate further inroads upon the old social order, and are unavoidable as a means of entirely revolutionizing the mode of production.

These measures will of course be different in different countries.

Nevertheless, in the most advanced countries the following will be pretty generally applicable:

1. Abolition of property in land and application of all rents of land to public purposes.
2. A heavy progressive or graduated income tax.
3. Abolition of all right of inheritance.
4. Confiscation of the property of all emigrants and rebels.
5. Centralization of credit in the hands of the state, by means of a national bank with state capital and an exclusive monopoly.
6. Centralization of the means of communication and transport in the hands of the state.
7. Extension of factories and instruments of production owned by the state; the bringing into cultivation of wastelands, and the improvement of the soil generally in accordance with a common plan.
8. Equal liability of all to labor. Establishment of industrial armies, especially for agriculture.
9. Combination of agriculture with manufacturing industries; gradual abolition of the distinction between town and country, by a more equable distribution of the population over the country.
10. Free education for all children in public schools. Abolition of children's factory labor in its present form. Combination of education with industrial production, etc.

When, in the course of development, class distinctions have disappeared and all production has been concentrated in the hands of a vast association of the whole nation, the public power will lose its political character. Political power, properly so called, is merely the organized power of one class for oppressing another. If the proletariat during its contest with the bourgeoisie is compelled, by the force of circumstances, to organize itself as a class, if by means of a revolution, it makes itself the ruling class and, as such, sweeps away by force the old conditions of production, then it will, along with these conditions, have swept away the conditions for the existence of class antagonisms and of classes generally, and will thereby have abolished its own supremacy as a class.

In place of the old bourgeois society, with its classes and class antagonisms, we shall have an association in which the free development of each is the condition for the free development of all.

III. Socialist and Communist Literature

1. Reactionary Socialism

a. Feudal socialism

Owing to their historical position, it became the vocation of the aristocracies of France and England to write pamphlets against modern bourgeois society. In the French Revolution of July 1830, and in the English reform agitation, these aristocracies again succumbed to the hateful upstart. Thenceforth a serious political contest was altogether out of question. A literary battle alone remained possible. But even in the domain of literature the old cries of the Restoration period[6] had become impossible.

In order to arouse sympathy, the aristocracy were obliged to lose sight, apparently, of their own interests, and to formulate their indictment against the bourgeoisie in the interest of the exploited working class alone. Thus the aristocracy took their revenge by singing lampoons on their new master, and whispering in his ears sinister prophecies of coming catastrophe.

In this way arose feudal socialism: half lamentation, half lampoon; half echo of the past, half menace of the future; at times, by its bitter, witty, and incisive criticism, striking the bourgeoisie to the very heart's core, but always ludicrous in its effect, through total incapacity to comprehend the march of modern history.

The aristocracy, in order to rally the people to them, waved the proletarian alms bag in front for a banner. But the people, as often as it joined them, saw on their hindquarters the old feudal coats of arms, and deserted with loud and irreverent laughter.

One section of the French Legitimists and "Young England" exhibited this spectacle.

In pointing out that their mode of exploitation was different from that of the bourgeoisie, the feudalists forget that they exploited under circumstances and conditions that were quite different and that are now antiquated. In showing that, under their rule, the modern proletariat never existed, they forget that the modern bourgeoisie is the necessary offspring of their own form of society.

For the rest, so little do they conceal the reactionary character of their criticism that their chief accusation against the bourgeoisie amounts to this, that under the bourgeois regime a class is being developed which is destined to cut up root and branch the old order of society.

What they upbraid the bourgeoisie with is not so much that it creates a proletariat as that it creates a *revolutionary* proletariat.

In political practice, therefore, they join in all coercive measures against the working class; and in ordinary life, despite their highfalutin phrases, they stoop to pick up the golden apples dropped from the tree of industry, and to barter truth, love, and honor for traffic in wool, beetroot sugar, and potato spirits.[7]

As the parson has ever gone hand in hand with the landlord, so has clerical socialism with feudal socialism.

Nothing is easier than to give Christian asceticism a socialist tinge. Has not Christianity declaimed against private property, against marriage, against the state? Has it not preached, in the place of these, charity and poverty, celibacy and mortification of the flesh, monastic life and Mother Church? Christian socialism is but the holy water with which the priest consecrates the heartburnings of the aristocrat.

b. Petty-bourgeois socialism

The feudal aristocracy was not the only class that was ruined by the bourgeoisie, not the only class whose conditions of existence pined and perished in the atmosphere of modern bourgeoisie society. The medieval burgesses and the small peasant proprietors were the precursors of the modern bourgeoisie. In those countries which are but little developed, industrially and commercially, these two classes still vegetate side by side with the rising bourgeoisie.

In countries where modern civilization has become fully developed, a new class of petty bourgeois has been formed, fluctuating between proletariat and bourgeoisie and ever renewing itself as a supplementary part of bourgeois society. The individual members of this class, however, are being constantly hurled down into the proletariat by the action of competition, and as modern industry develops they even see the moment approaching when they will completely disappear as an independent section of modern society, to be replaced, in manufactures, agriculture, and commerce, by overlookers, bailiffs, and shopmen.

In countries like France, where the peasants constitute far more than half of the population, it was natural that writers who sided with the proletariat against the bourgeoisie should use, in their criticism of the bourgeois regime, the standard of the peasant and petty bourgeois, and from the standpoint of these intermediate classes should take up the cudgels for the working class. Thus arose petty–bourgeois socialism. Sismondi was the head of this school, not only in France but also in England.

This school of socialism dissected with great acuteness the contradictions in the conditions of modern production. It laid bare the hypocritical apologies of economists. It proved, incontrovertibly, the disastrous effects of machinery and division of labor, the concentration of capital and land in a few hands, overproduction and crises; it pointed out the inevitable ruin of the petty bourgeois and peasant, the misery of the proletariat, the anarchy in production, the crying inequalities in the distribution of wealth, the industrial war of extermination between nations, the dissolution of old moral bonds, of the old family relations, of the old nationalities.

In its positive aims, however, this form of socialism aspires either to restoring the old means of production and of exchange, and with them the old property relations and the old society, or to cramping the modern means of production and of exchange within the framework of the old property relations that have been, and were bound to be, exploded by those means. In either case it is both reactionary and utopian.

Its last words are: corporate guilds for manufacture; patriarchal relations in agriculture.

Ultimately, when stubborn historical facts had dispersed all intoxicating effects of self-deception, this form of socialism ended in a miserable fit of the blues.

c. German, or "true," socialism

The socialist and communist literature of France, a literature that originated under the pressure of a bourgeoisie in power, and that was the expression of the struggle against this power, was introduced into Germany at a time when the bourgeoisie in that country had just begun its contest with feudal absolutism.

German philosophers, would-be philosophers, and *beaux esprits* eagerly seized on this literature, only forgetting that when these writings immigrated from France into Germany, French social conditions had not immigrated along with them. In contact with German social conditions, this French literature lost all its immediate practiced significance, and assumed a purely literary aspect. Thus, to the German philosophers of the eighteenth century, the demands of the first French Revolution were nothing more than the demands of "practical reason" in general, and the utterance of the will of the revolutionary French bourgeoisie signified in their eyes the laws of pure will, of will as it was bound to be, of true human will generally.

The work of the German literati consisted solely in bringing the new French ideas into harmony with their ancient philosophical conscience, or rather, in annexing the French ideas without deserting their own philosophic point of view.

This annexation took place in the same way in which a foreign language is appropriated, namely, by translation.

It is well known how the monks wrote silly lives of Catholic saints *over* the manuscripts on which the classical works of ancient heathendom had been written. The German literati reversed this process with the profane French literature. They wrote their philosophical nonsense beneath the French original. For instance, beneath the French criticism of the economic functions of money they wrote *Alienation of Humanity* and beneath the French criticism of the bourgeois state they wrote, *Dethronement of the Category of the General*, and so forth.

The introduction of these philosophical phrases at the back of the French historical criticisms they dubbed, "philosophy of action," "true socialism," "German science of socialism," "philosophical foundation of socialism," and so on.

The French socialist and communist literature was thus completely emasculated. And since it ceased in the hands of the German to express the struggle of one class with the other he felt conscious of having overcome "French one-sidedness" and of representing not true requirements, but the requirements of truth; not the interests of the proletariat, but the interests of human nature, of man in general, who belongs to no class, has no reality, who exists only in the misty realm of philosophical fantasy.

This German socialism, which took its schoolboy task so seriously and solemnly, and extolled its poor stock in trade in such mountebank fashion, meanwhile gradually lost its pedantic innocence.

The fight of the German, and especially of the Prussian, bourgeoisie against feudal aristocracy and absolute monarchy, in other words, the liberal movement, became more earnest.

By this, the long-wished-for opportunity was offered to "true" socialism of confronting the political movement with the socialist demands, of hurling the traditional anathemas against liberalism, against representative government, against bourgeois competition, bourgeois freedom of the press, bourgeois legislation, bourgeois liberty and equality, and of preaching to the masses that they had nothing to gain, and everything to lose, by this bourgeois movement. German socialism forgot, in the nick of time, that the French criticism, whose silly echo it was, presupposed the existence of modern bourgeois society, with its corresponding economic conditions of existence, and the political constitution adapted thereto, the very things whose attainment was the object of the pending struggle in Germany.

To the absolute governments, with their following of parsons, professors, country squires, and officials, it served as a welcome scarecrow against the threatening bourgeoisie.

It was a sweet finish after the bitter pills of floggings and bullets with which these same governments, just at that time, dosed the German working-class risings.

While this "true" socialism thus served the governments as a weapon for fighting the German bourgeoisie, it, at the same time, directly represented a reactionary interest, the interest of the German Philistines. In Germany the petty–bourgeois class, a relic of the sixteenth century, and since then constantly cropping up again under various forms, is the real social basis of the existing state of things.

To preserve this class is to preserve the existing state of things in Germany. The industrial and political supremacy of the bourgeoisie threatens it with certain destruction: on the one hand, from the concentration of capital; on the other, from the rise of a revolutionary proletariat. "True" socialism appeared to kill these two birds with one stone. It spread like an epidemic.

The robe of speculative cobwebs, embroidered with flowers of rhetoric, steeped in the dew of sickly sentiment, this transcendental robe in which the German socialists wrapped their sorry "eternal truths," all skin and bone, served to wonderfully increase the sale of their goods among such a public.

And on its part, German socialism recognized more and more its own calling as the bombastic representative of the petty-bourgeois Philistine.

It proclaimed the German nation to be the model nation and the German petty Philistine to be the typical man. To every villainous meanness of this model man it gave a hidden, higher, socialistic interpretation, the exact contrary of its real character. It went to the extreme length of directly opposing the "brutally destructive" tendency of communism, and of proclaiming its supreme and impartial contempt of all class struggles. With very few exceptions, all the so-called socialist and communist publications that now (1847) circulate in Germany belong to the domain of this foul and enervating literature.

2. *Conservative, or Bourgeois, Socialism*

A part of the bourgeoisie is desirous of redressing social grievances, in order to secure the continued existence of bourgeois society.

To this section belong economists, philanthropists, humanitarians, improvers of the condition of the working class, organizers of charity, members of societies for the prevention of cruelty to animals, temperance fanatics, hole-and-corner reformers of every imaginable kind. This form of socialism has, moreover, been worked out into complete systems.

We may cite Proudhon's *Philosophie de la Misère* [*Philosophy of Poverty*] as an example of this form.

The socialistic bourgeois want all the advantages of modern social conditions without the struggles and dangers necessarily resulting therefrom. They desire the existing state of society minus its revolutionary and disintegrating elements. They wish for a bourgeoisie without a proletariat. The bourgeoisie naturally conceives the world in which it is supreme to be the best; and bourgeois socialism develops this comfortable conception into various more or less complete systems. In requiring the proletariat to carry out such a system, and thereby to march straightway into the social New Jerusalem, it but requires in reality that the proletariat should remain within the bounds of existing society, but should cast away all its hateful ideas concerning the bourgeoisie.

A second and more practical, but less systematic, form of this socialism sought to depreciate every revolutionary movement in the eyes of the working class, by showing that no mere political reform, but only a change in the material conditions of existence, in economic relations, could be of any advantage to them. By changes in the material conditions of existence, this form of socialism, however, by no means understands abolition of the bourgeois relations of production, an abolition that can be effected only by a revolution, but administrative reforms, based on the continued existence of these relations; reforms, therefore, that in no respect affect the relations between capital and labor, but, at the best, lessen the cost and simplify the administrative work of bourgeois government.

Bourgeois socialism attains adequate expression when, and only when, it becomes a mere figure of speech.

Free trade: for the benefit of the working class. Protective duties: for the benefit of the working class. Prison reform: for the benefit of the working class. This is the last word and the only seriously meant word of bourgeois socialism.

The socialism of the bourgeoisie simply consists of the assertion that the bourgeois are bourgeois—for the benefit of the working class.

3. *Critical Utopian Socialism and Communism*

We do not here refer to that literature which, in every great modern revolution, has always given voice to the demands of the proletariat, such as the writings of Babeuf and others.

The first direct attempts of the proletariat to attain its own ends, made in times of universal excitement when feudal society was being overthrown, these attempts necessarily failed, owing to the then undeveloped state of the proletariat, as well as to the absence of the economic conditions for its emancipation, conditions that had yet to be produced, and could be produced by the impending bourgeois epoch alone. The revolutionary literature that accompanied these first movements of the proletariat had necessarily a reactionary character. It inculcated universal asceticism and social leveling in its crudest form.

The socialist and communist systems properly so called, those of St. Simon, Fourier, Owen, and others, spring into existence in the early undeveloped period, described above, of the struggle between proletariat and bourgeoisie (see Section I, Bourgeois and Proletarians).

The founders of these systems see, indeed, the class antagonisms as well as the action of the decomposing elements in the prevailing form of society. But the proletariat, as yet in its infancy, offers to them the spectacle of a class without any historical initiative or any independent political movement.

Since the development of class antagonism keeps even pace with the development of industry, the economic situation, as they find it, does not as yet offer to them the material conditions for the emancipation of the proletariat. They therefore search after a new social science, after new social laws that are to create these conditions.

Historical action is to yield to their personal inventive action, historically created conditions of emancipation to fantastic ones, and the gradual, spontaneous class organization of the proletariat to an organization of society specially contrived by these inventors. Future history resolves itself, in their eyes, into the propaganda and the practical carrying out of their social plans.

In the formation of their plans they are conscious of caring chiefly for the interests of the working class as being the most suffering class. Only from the point of view of being the most suffering class does the proletariat exist for them.

The undeveloped state of the class struggle, as well as their own surroundings, causes socialists of this kind to consider themselves far superior to all class antagonisms. They want to improve the condition of every member of society, even that of the most favored. Hence they habitually appeal to society at large, without distinction of class; nay, by preference, to the ruling class. For how can people, when once they understand their system, fail to see in it the best possible plan of the best possible state of society?

Hence they reject all political, and especially all revolutionary, action; they wish to attain their ends by peaceful means, and endeavor, by small experiments, necessarily doomed to failure, and by the force of example, to pave the way for the new social gospel.

Such fantastic pictures of future society, painted at a time when the proletariat is still in a very undeveloped state and has but a fantastic conception of its own position, correspond with the first instinctive yearnings of that class for a general reconstruction of society.

But these socialist and communist publications contain also a critical element. They attack every principle of existing society. Hence they are full of the most valuable materials for the enlightenment of the working class. The practical measures proposed in them—such as the abolition of the distinction between town and country, of the family, of the carrying on of industries for the account of private individuals, and of the wage system, the proclamation of social harmony, the conversion of the functions of the state into a mere superintendence of production—all these proposals point solely to the disappearance of class antagonisms which were, at that time, only just cropping up, and which, in these publications, are recognized in their earliest, indistinct and undefined forms only. These proposals, therefore, are of a purely utopian character.

The significance of critical utopian socialism and communism bears an inverse relation to historical development. In proportion as the modern class struggle develops
and takes definite shape, this fantastic standing apart from the contest, these fantastic
attacks on it lose all practical value and all theoretical justification. Therefore,
although the originators of these systems were, in many respects, revolutionary, their
disciples have, in every case, formed mere reactionary sects. They hold fast by the original views of their masters, in opposition to the progressive historical development of
the proletariat. They, therefore, endeavor, and that consistently, to deaden the class
struggle and to reconcile the class antagonisms. They still dream of experimental realization of their social utopias, of founding isolated *"phalanstères,"* of establishing
"home colonies," of setting up a "Little Icaria"[8] duodecimo editions of the New
Jerusalem—and to realize all these castles in the air they are compelled to appeal to
the feelings and purses of the bourgeois. By degrees they sink into the category of the
reactionary conservative socialists depicted above, differing from these only by more
systematic pedantry, and by their fanatical and superstitious belief in the miraculous
effects of their social science.

They, therefore, violently oppose all political action on the part of the working class;
such action, according to them, can only result from blind unbelief in the new gospel.

The Owenites in England and the Fourierists in France, respectively, oppose the Chartists and the Réformistes.

IV. Position of the Communists in Relation to the
Various Existing Opposition Parties

Section II has made clear the relations of the communists to the existing working-class
parties, such as the Chartists in England and the agrarian reformers in America.

The communists fight for the attainment of the immediate aims, for the enforcement
of the momentary interests of the working class, but in the movement of the present they
also represent and take care of the future of that movement. In France the communists ally
themselves with the social democrats,[9] against the conservative and radical bourgeoisie,
reserving, however, the right to take up a critical position in regard to phrases and illusions traditionally handed down from the Great Revolution.

In Switzerland they support the radicals, without losing sight of the fact that this party
consists of antagonistic elements, partly of democratic socialists, in the French sense,
partly of radical bourgeois.

In Poland they support the party that insists on an agrarian revolution as the prime
condition for national emancipation, that party which fomented the insurrection of
Cracow in 1846.

In Germany they fight with the bourgeoisie whenever it acts in a revolutionary way,
against the absolute monarchy, the feudal squirearchy, and the petty bourgeoisie.

But they never cease, for a single instant, to instill into the working class the clearest
possible recognition of the hostile antagonism between bourgeoisie and proletariat, in
order that the German workers may straightway use, as so many weapons against the
bourgeoisie, the social and political conditions that the bourgeoisie must necessarily
introduce along with its supremacy, and in order that, after the fall of the reactionary
classes in Germany, the fight against the bourgeoisie itself may immediately begin.

The communists turn their attention chiefly to Germany, because that country is on the eve of a bourgeois revolution that is bound to be carried out under more advanced conditions of European civilization, and with a much more developed proletariat, than that of England was in the seventeenth and of France in the eighteenth century, and because the bourgeois revolution in Germany will be but the prelude to an immediately following proletarian revolution.

In short, the communists everywhere support every revolutionary movement against the existing social and political order of things.

In all these movements they bring to the front, as the leading question in each, the property question, no matter what its degree of development at the time.

Finally, they labor everywhere for the union and agreement of the democratic parties of all countries.

The communists disdain to conceal their views and aims. They openly declare that their ends can be attained only by the forcible overthrow of all existing social conditions. Let the ruling classes tremble at a communistic revolution. The proletarians have nothing to lose but their chains. They have a world to win.

WORKINGMEN OF ALL COUNTRIES, UNITE!

Notes

1. Lassalle personally, to us, always acknowledged himself to be a disciple of Marx and, as such, stood on the ground of the Manifesto. But in his public agitation, 1862–64, be did not go beyond demanding co-operative workshops supported by state credit.
2. By "bourgeoisie" is meant the class of modern capitalists, owners of the means of social production and employers of wage labor. By proletariat, the class of modern wage laborers who, having no means of production of their own, are reduced to selling their labor power in order to live.
3. That is, all *written* history. In 1847 the pre-history of society, the social organization existing previous to recorded history, was all but unknown. Since then Haxthausen discovered common ownership of land in Russia, Maurer proved it to be the social foundation from which all Teutonic races started in history, and by and by village communities were found to be, or to have been the primitive form of society everywhere from India to Ireland. The inner organization of this primitive communistic society was laid bare, in its typical form, by Morgan's crowning discovery of the true nature of the *gens* and its relation to the *tribe*. With the dissolution of these primeval communities society begins to be differentiated into separate and finally antagonistic classes. I have attempted to retrace this process of dissolution in *Der Ursprung der Familie des Privateigenthums und des Staats* [*The Origin of the Family, Private Property and the State*], second edition, Stuttgart, 1886.
4. Guild master, that is, a full member of a guild, a master within, not a head of a guild.
5. "Commune" was the name taken, in France, by the nascent towns even before they had conquered from their feudal lords and masters local self-government and political rights as the "third estate." Generally speaking, for the economic development of the bourgeoisie, England is here taken as the typical country; for its political development, France.
6. Not the English Restoration, 1660 to 1689, but the French Restoration, 1814 to 1830.
7. This applies chiefly to Germany, where the landed aristocracy and squirearchy have large portions of their estates cultivated for their own account by stewards, and are, moreover extensive beetroot sugar manufacturers and distillers of potato spirits. The wealthier British aristocracy are, as yet, rather above that; but they, too, know how to make up for declining rents by lending their names to floaters of more or less shady joint-stock companies.
8. *Phalanstères* were socialist colonies on the plan of Charles Fourier; "Icaria" was the name given by Cabet to his utopia and, later on, to his American communist colony.
9. The party then represented in Parliament by Ledru-Rollin, in literature by Louis Blanc, in the daily press by the *Réforme*. The name of social democracy signified, with these its inventors, a section of the democratic or republican party more or less tinged with socialism.

A CONTRIBUTION TO THE CRITIQUE
OF POLITICAL ECONOMY

PREFACE

I examine the system of bourgeois economy in the following order: *capital, landed property, wage-labour; the State, foreign trade, world market*. The economic conditions of "existence of the three great classes into which modern bourgeois society is divided are analysed under the first three headings; the interconnection of the other three headings is self-evident. The first part of the first book, dealing with Capital, comprises the following chapters: 1. The commodity; 2. Money or simple circulation; 3. Capital in general. The present part consists of the first two chapters. The entire material lies before me in the form of monographs, which were written not for publication but for self-clarification at widely separated periods; their remoulding into an integrated whole according to the plan I have indicated will depend upon circumstances.

A general introduction, which I had drafted, is omitted, since on further consideration it seems to me confusing to anticipate results which still have to be substantiated, and the reader who really wishes to follow me will have to decide to advance from the particular to the general. A few brief remarks regarding the course of my study of political economy may, however, be appropriate here.

Although I studied jurisprudence, I pursued it as a subject subordinated to philosophy and history. In the year 1842–43, as editor of the *Rheinische Zeitung,* I first found myself in the embarrassing position of having to discuss what is known as material interests. The deliberations of the Rhenish Landtag on forest thefts and the division of landed property; the official polemic started by Herr von Schaper,, then Oberpräsident of the Rhine Province, against the *Rheinische Zeitung* about the condition of the Moselle peasantry, and finally the debates on free trade and protective tariffs caused me in the first instance to turn my attention to economic questions. On the other hand, at that time when good intentions "to push forward" often took the place of factual knowledge, an echo of French socialism and communism, slightly tinged by philosophy, was noticeable in the *Rheinische Zeitung*. I objected to this dilettantism, but at the same time frankly admitted in a controversy with the *Allgemeine Augsburger Zeitung* that my previous studies did not allow me to express any opinion on the content of the French theories. When the publishers of the *Rheinische Zeitung* conceived the illusion that by a more compliant policy on the part of the paper it might be possible to secure the abrogation of the death sentence passed upon it, I eagerly grasped the opportunity to withdraw from the public stage to my study.

The first work which I undertook to dispel the doubts assailing me was a critical re-examination of the Hegelian philosophy of law; the introduction to this work being published in the *Deutsch-Französische Jahrbücher* issued in Paris in 1844. My inquiry led me to the conclusion that neither legal relations nor political forms could be comprehended whether by themselves or on the basis of a so-called general development of the human mind, but that on the contrary they originate in the material conditions of life, the totality of which Hegel, following the example of English and French thinkers of the eighteenth century, embraces within the term "civil society"; that the anatomy of this civil

Translated by S. W. Ryazanskaya. Reprinted with permission of International Publishers.

society, however, has to be sought in political economy. The study of this, which I began in Paris, I continued in Brussels, where I moved owing to an expulsion order issued by M. Guizot. The general conclusion at which I arrived and which, once reached, became the guiding principle of my studies can be summarised as follows. In the social production of their existence, men inevitably enter into definite relations, which are independent of their will, namely relations of production appropriate to a given stage in the development of their material forces of production. The totality of these relations of production constitutes the economic structure of society, the real foundation, on which arises a legal and political superstructure and to which correspond definite forms of social consciousness. The mode of production of material life conditions the general process of social, political and intellectual life. It is not the consciousness of men that determines their existence, but their social existence that determines their consciousness. At a certain stage of development, the material productive forces of society come into conflict with the existing relations of production or—this merely expresses the same thing in legal terms—with the property relations within the framework of which they have operated hitherto. From forms of development of the productive forces these relations turn into their fetters. Then begins an era of social revolution. The changes in the economic foundation lead sooner or later to the transformation of the whole immense superstructure. In studying such transformations it is always necessary to distinguish between the material transformation of the economic conditions of production, which can be determined with the precision of natural science, and the legal, political, religious, artistic or philosophic—in short, ideological forms in which men become conscious of this conflict and fight it out. Just as one does not judge an individual by what he thinks about himself, so one cannot judge such a period of transformation by its consciousness, but, on the contrary, this consciousness must be explained from the contradictions of material life, from the conflict existing between the social forces of production and the relations of production. No social order is ever destroyed before all the productive forces for which it is sufficient have been developed, and new superior relations of production never replace older ones before the material conditions for their existence have matured within the framework of the old society. Mankind thus inevitably sets itself only such tasks as it is able to solve, since closer examination will always show that the problem itself arises only when the material conditions for its solution are already present or at least in the course of formation. In broad outline, the Asiatic, ancient, feudal and modern bourgeois modes of production may be designated as epochs marking progress in the economic development of society. The bourgeois mode of production is the last antagonistic form of the social process of production—antagonistic not in the sense of individual antagonism but of an antagonism that emanates from the individuals' social conditions of existence—but the productive forces developing within bourgeois society create also the material conditions for a solution of this antagonism. The prehistory of human society accordingly closes with this social formation.

Frederick Engels, with whom I maintained a constant exchange of ideas by correspondence since the publication of his brilliant essay on the critique of economic categories (printed in the *Deutsch-Französische Jahrbücher*), arrived by another road (compare his *Lage der arbeitenden Klasse in England*) at the same result as I, and when in the spring of 1845 he too came to live in Brussels, we decided to set forth together our conception as opposed to the ideological one of German philosophy, in fact to settle accounts with our former philosophical conscience. The intention was carried out in the form of a critique of post-Hegelian philosophy. The manuscript, two large octavo volumes, had long ago reached the publishers in Westphalia when we were informed that owing to changed circumstances it could not be printed. We abandoned the manuscript to the gnawing criticism of the mice all the more willingly since we had achieved our main purpose—self-clarification. Of the scattered works in which at that time we presented one or another aspect of our views to the public, I shall mention only the *Manifesto of the Communist Party,* jointly written by Engels and myself, and a *Discours sur le libre échange,* which I myself published. The salient points of our conception were first outlined in an academic, although polemical, form in my *Misère de la philosophie . . . ,* this book which was aimed at Proudhon appeared in 1847. The publication of an essay on *Wage-Labour* written in German in which I combined the lectures I had held on this subject at the German Workers' Association in Brussels, was interrupted by the February Revolution and my forcible removal from Belgium in consequence.

The publication of the *Neue Rheinische Zeitung* in 1848 and 1849 and subsequent events cut short my economic studies, which I could only resume in London in 1850. The enormous amount of material relating to the history of political economy assembled in the British Museum, the fact that London is a convenient vantage point for the observation of bourgeois society, and finally the new stage of development which this society seemed to have entered with the discovery of gold in California and Australia, induced me to start again from the very beginning and to work carefully through the new material. These studies led partly of their own accord to apparently quite remote subjects on which I had to spend a certain amount of time. But it was in particular the imperative necessity of earning my living which reduced the time at my disposal. My collaboration, continued now for eight years, with the *New York Tribune,* the leading Anglo-American newspaper, necessitated an excessive fragmentation of my studies, for I wrote only exceptionally newspaper correspondence in the strict sense. Since a considerable part of my contributions consisted of articles dealing with important economic events in Britain and on the Continent, I was compelled to become conversant with practical detail which, strictly speaking, lie outside the sphere of political economy.

This sketch of the course of my studies in the domain of political economy is intended merely to show that my views—no matter how they may be judged and how little they conform to the interested prejudices of the ruling classes—are the outcome of conscientious research carried on over many years. At the entrance to science, as at the entrance to hell, the demand must be made:

> *Qui si convien lasciare ogni sospetto*
> *Ogni viltà convien che qui sia morta.*

VALUE, PRICE AND PROFIT

VI

Value and Labour

Citizens, I have now arrived at a point where I must enter upon the real development of the question. I cannot promise to do this in a very satisfactory way because to do so I should be obliged to go over the whole field of political economy. I can, as the French would say, but *effleurer la question*, touch upon the main points.

The first question we have to put is: What is the *value* of a commodity? How is it determined?

At first sight it would seem that the value of a commodity is a thing quite *relative*, and not to be settled without considering one commodity in its relations to all other commodities. In fact, in speaking of the value, the value in exchange of a commodity, we mean the proportional quantities in which it exchanges with all other commodities. But then arises the question: How are the proportions in which commodities exchange with each other regulated?

We know from experience that these proportions vary infinitely. Taking one single commodity, wheat, for instance, we shall find that a quarter of wheat exchanges in almost countless variations of proportion with different commodities. Yet, *its value remaining always the same,* whether expressed in silk, gold, or any other commodity, it must be something distinct from, and independent of, these *different rates of exchange* with different articles. It must be possible to express, in a very different form, these various equations with various commodities.

Besides, if I say a quarter of wheat exchanges with iron in a certain proportion, or the value of a quarter of wheat is expressed in a certain amount of iron, I say that the value of wheat and its equivalent in iron are equal to *some third thing,* which is neither wheat nor iron, because I suppose them to express the same magnitude in two different shapes. Either of them, the wheat or the iron, must, therefore, independently of the other, be reducible to this third thing which is their common measure.

To elucidate this point I shall recur to a very simple geometrical illustration. In comparing the areas of triangles of all possible forms and magnitudes, or comparing triangles with rectangles, or any other rectilinear figure, how do we proceed? We reduce the area of any triangle whatever to an expression quite different from its visible form. Having found from the nature of the triangle that its area is equal to half the product of its base by its height, we can then compare the different values of all sorts of triangles, and of all rectilinear figures whatever, because all of them may be resolved into a certain number of triangles.

The same mode of procedure must obtain with the values of commodities. We must be able to reduce all of them to an expression common to all, and distinguishing them only by the proportions in which they contain that same and identical measure.

As the *exchangeable values* of commodities are only *social functions* of those things, and have nothing at all to do with the *natural* qualities, we must first ask: What is the common *social substance* of all commodities? It is *labour*. To produce a commodity a certain amount of labour must be bestowed upon it, or worked up in it. And I say not only *labour,* but *social labour*. A man who produces an article for his own immediate use, to consume it himself,

Reprinted by permission of International Publishers.

creates a *product,* but not a *commodity.* As a self-sustaining producer he has nothing to do with society. But to produce a *commodity,* a man must not only produce an article satisfying some *social* want, but his labour itself must form part and parcel of the total sum of labour expended by society. It must be subordinate to the *division of labour within society.* It is nothing without the other division of labour, and on its part is required to *integrate* them.

If we consider *commodities as values,* we consider them exclusively under the single aspect of *realised, fixed,* or, if you like, *crystallised social labour.* In this respect they can *differ* only by representing greater or smaller quantities of labour, as, for example, a greater amount of labour may be worked up in a silken handkerchief than in a brick. But how does one measure *quantities of labour?* By the *time the labour lasts,* in measuring the labour by the hour, the day, etc. Of course, to apply this measure, all sorts of labour are reduced to average or simple labour as their unit.

We arrive, therefore, at this conclusion. A commodity has a *value,* because it is a *crystallisation of social labour.* The greatness of its value, or its *relative* value, depends upon the greater or less amount of that social substance contained in it; that is to say, on the relative mass of labour necessary for its production. The *relative values of commodities* are, therefore, determined by the *respective quantities or amounts of labour, worked up, realised, fixed in them.* The *correlative* quantities of commodities which can be produced in the *same time of labour* are *equal.* Or the value of one commodity is to the value of another commodity as the quantity of labour fixed in the one is to the quantity of labour fixed in the other.

I suspect that many of you will ask: Does then, indeed, there exist such a vast, or any difference whatever, between determining of values of commodities by *wages,* and determining them by the *relative quantities of labour* necessary for their production? You must, however, be aware that the *reward* for labour, and *quantity* of labour, are quite disparate things. Suppose, for example, *equal quantities of labour* to be fixed in one quarter of wheat and one ounce of gold. I resort to the example because it was used by Benjamin Franklin in his first essay published in 1721, and entitled: *A Modest Enquiry into the Nature and Necessity of a Paper Currency,* where he, one of the first, hit upon the true nature of value. Well. We suppose, then, that one quarter of wheat and one ounce of gold are *equal values* or *equivalents,* because they are *crystallisations of equal amounts of average labour,* of so many days' or so many weeks' labour respectively fixed in them. In thus determining the relative values of gold and corn, do we refer in any way whatever to the *wages* of the agricultural labourer and the miner? Not a bit. We leave it quite *indeterminate how* their day's or week's labour was paid, or even whether wages labour was employed at all. If it was, wages may have been very unequal. The labourer whose labour is realised in the quarter of wheat may receive two bushels only, and the labourer employed in mining may receive one half of the ounce of gold. Or, supposing their wages to be equal, they may deviate in all possible proportions from the values of the commodities produced by them. They may amount to one half, one third, one fourth, one fifth, or any other proportional part of the one quarter of corn or the one ounce of gold. Their *wages* can, of course, not *exceed,* not be more than the values of the commodities they produced, but they can be *less* in every possible degree. Their *wages* will be *limited* by the *values* of the products, but the *values of their products* will not be limited by the wages. And above all, the values, the relative values of corn and gold, for example, will have been settled without any regard whatever to the value of the labour employed, that is to say, to *wages.* To determine the values of commodities by the *relative quantities of labour fixed in them,* is, therefore, a thing quite different from the tautological method of determining the values of commodities by the value of labour, or by wages. This point, however, will be further elucidated in the progress of our inquiry.

In calculating the exchangeable value of a commodity we must add to the quantity of labour *last* employed the quantity of labour *previously* worked up in the raw material of the commodity, and the labour bestowed on the implements, tools, machinery, and buildings, with which such labour is assisted. For example, the value of a certain amount of cotton yarn is the crystallisation of the quantity of labour added to the cotton during the spinning process, the quantity of labour previously realised in the cotton, itself, the quantity of labour realised in the coal, oil, and other auxiliary matter used, the quantity of labour fixed in the steam-engine, the spindles, the factory building, and so forth. Instruments of production properly so-called such as tools, machinery, buildings, serve again and again for a longer or shorter period during repeated processes of production. If they were used up at once, like the raw material, their whole value would at once be transferred to the commodities they assist in producing. But as a spindle, for example, is but gradually used up, an average calculation is made, based upon the average time it lasts, and its average waste or wear and tear during a certain period, say a day. In this way we calculate how much of the value of the spindle is transferred to the yarn daily spun, and how much, therefore, of the total amount of labour realised in a pound of yarn, for example, is due to the quantity of labour previously realised in the spindle. For our present purpose it is not necessary to dwell any longer upon this point.

It might seem that if the value of a commodity is determined by the *quantity of labour bestowed upon its production,* the lazier a man, or the clumsier a man, the more valuable his commodity, because the greater the time of labour required for finishing the commodity. This, however, would be a sad mistake. You will recollect that I used the word "*social* labour," and many points are involved in this qualification of "*social.*" In saying that the value of a commodity is determined by the *quantity of labour* worked up or crystallised in it, we mean *the quantity of labour necessary* for its production in a given state of society, under certain social average conditions of production, with a given social average intensity, and average skill of the labour employed. When, in England, the power-loom came to compete with the hand-loom, only one-half the former time of labour was wanted to convert a given amount of yarn into a yard of cotton or cloth. The poor hand-loom weaver now worked seventeen and eighteen hours daily, instead of the nine or ten hours he had worked before. Still the product of twenty hours of his labour represented now only ten social hours of labour, or ten hours of labour socially necessary for the conversion of a certain amount of yarn into textile stuffs. His product of twenty hours had, therefore, no more value than his former product of ten hours.

If then the quantity of socially necessary labour realised in commodities regulates their exchangeable values, every increase in the quantity of labour wanted for the production of a commodity must augment its value, as every diminution must lower it.

If the respective quantities of labour necessary for the production of the respective commodities remained constant, their relative values also would be constant. But such is not the case. The quantity of labour necessary for the production of a commodity changes continuously with the changes in the productive powers of the labour employed. The greater the productive powers of labour, the more produce is finished in a given time of labour; and the smaller the productive powers of labour, the less produce is finished in the same time. If, for example, in the progress of population it should become necessary to cultivate less fertile soils, the same amount of produce would be only attainable by a greater amount of labour spent, and the value of agricultural produce would consequently rise. On the other hand, if with the modern means of production, a single spinner converts into yarn, during one working day, many thousand times the amount of cotton which he could have spun during the same time with the spinning wheel, it is evident that every single pound of cotton will absorb many thousand times less of spinning labour than it did before, and, consequently, the value added by spinning to every single pound of cotton will be a thousand times less than before. The value of yarn will sink accordingly.

Apart from the different natural energies and acquired working abilities of different peoples, the productive powers of labour must principally depend:

Firstly. Upon the *natural* conditions of labour, such as fertility of soil, mines, and so forth.

Secondly. Upon the progressive improvement of the *social powers of labour,* such as are derived from production on a grand scale, concentration of capital and combination of labour, subdivision of labour, machinery, improved methods, appliance of chemical and other natural agencies, shortening of time and space by means of communication and transport, and every other contrivance by which science presses natural agencies into the service of labour, and by which the social or co-operative character of labour is developed. The greater the productive powers of labour, the less labour is bestowed upon a given amount of produce; hence the smaller the value of this produce The smaller the productive powers of labour, the more labour is bestowed upon the same amount of produce; hence the greater its value. As a general law we may, therefore, set it down that:

The values of commodities are directly as the times of labour employed in their production, and are inversely as the productive powers of the labour employed.

Having till now only spoken of *value,* I shall add a few words about *price,* which is a peculiar form assumed by value.

Price, taken by itself, is nothing but the *monetary expression of value.* The values of all commodities of this country, for example, are expressed in gold prices, while on the Continent they are mainly expressed in silver prices. The value of gold or silver, like that of all other commodities, is regulated by the quantity of labour necessary for getting them. You exchange a certain amount of your national products, in which a certain amount of your national labour is crystallised, for the produce of the gold and silver producing countries, in which a certain quantity of *their* labour is crystallised. It is in this way, in fact by barter, that you learn to express in gold and silver the values of all commodities, that is the respective quantities of labour bestowed upon them. Looking somewhat closer into *the monetary expression of value,* or what comes to the same, the *conversion of value into price,* you will find that it is a process by which you give to the *values* of all commodities an *independent* and *homogeneous form,* or by which you express them as quantities of *equal* social labour. So far as it is but the monetary expression of value, price has been called *natural price* by Adam Smith, *prix nécessaire* by the French physiocrats.

What then is the relation between *value* and *market prices,* or between *natural prices* and *market prices?* You all know that the *market price* is the *same* for all commodities of the same kind, however the conditions of production may differ for the individual producers. The market price expresses only the *average amount of social labour* necessary, under the average conditions of production, to supply the market with a certain mass of a certain article. It is calculated upon the whole lot of a commodity of a certain description.

So far the *market price* of a commodity coincides with its *value.* On the other hand, the oscillations of market prices, rising now over, sinking now under the value or natural price, depend upon the fluctuations of supply and demand. The deviations of market prices from values are continual, but as Adam Smith says: "The natural price is the central price to which the prices of commodities are continually gravitating. Different accidents may sometimes keep them suspended a good deal above it, and sometimes force them down even somewhat below it. But whatever may be the obstacles which hinder them from settling in this centre of repose and continuance, they are constantly tending towards it."

I cannot now sift this matter. It suffices to say that if supply and demand equilibrate each other, the market prices of commodities will correspond with their natural prices, that is to say with their values, as determined by the respective quantities of labour required for their production. But supply and demand *must* constantly tend to equilibrate each other, although they do so only by compensating one fluctuation by another, a rise by a fall, and *vice versa*. If instead of considering only the daily fluctuations you analyse the movement of market prices for longer periods, as Mr. Tooke, for example, has done in his *History of Prices*, you will find that the fluctuations of market prices, their deviations from values, their ups and downs, paralyse and compensate each other; so that apart from the effect of monopolies and some other modifications I must now pass by, all descriptions of commodities are, on the average, sold at their respective *values* or natural prices. The average periods during which the fluctuations of market prices compensate each other are different for different kinds of commodities, because with one kind it is easier to adapt supply to demand than with the other.

If then, speaking broadly, and embracing somewhat longer periods, all descriptions of commodities sell at their respective values, it is nonsense to suppose that profit, not in individual cases, but that the constant and usual profits of different trades spring from surcharging the prices of commodities or selling them at a price over and above their *value*. The absurdity of this notion becomes evident if it is generalised. What a man would constantly win as a seller he would as constantly lose as a purchaser. It would not do to say that there are men who are buyers without being sellers, or consumers without being producers. What these people pay to the producers, they must first get from them for nothing. If a man first takes your money and afterwards returns that money in buying your commodities, you will never enrich yourselves by selling your commodities too dear to that same man. This sort of transaction might diminish a loss, but would never help in realising a profit.

To explain, therefore, the *general nature of profits*, you must start from the theorem that, on an average, commodities are *sold at their real values*, and that *profits are derived from selling them at their values*, that is, in proportion to the quantity of labour realised in them. If you cannot explain profit upon this supposition, you cannot explain it at all. This seems paradox and contrary to everyday observation. It is also paradox that the earth moves round the sun, and that water consists of two highly inflammable gases. Scientific truth is always paradox, if judged by everyday experience, which catches only the delusive appearance of things.

VII

Labouring Power

Having now, as far as it could be done in such a cursory manner, analysed the nature of *Value*, of the *Value of any commodity whatever*, we must turn our attention to the specific *Value of Labour*. And here, again, I must startle you by a seeming paradox. All of you feel sure that what they daily sell is their Labour; that, therefore, Labour has a Price, and that, the price of a commodity being only the monetary expression of its value, there must certainly exist such a thing as the *Value of Labour*. However, there exists no such thing as the *Value of Labour* in the common acceptance of the word. We have seen that the amount of necessary labour crystallised in a commodity constitutes its value. Now, applying this notion of value, how could we define, say, the value of a ten hours' working day? How much labour is contained in that day? Ten hours' labour. To say that the value of a ten hours' working day is equal to ten hours' labour, or the quantity of labour contained in it, would be a tautological and, moreover, a nonsensical expression. Of course, having once found out the true but hidden sense of the expression *"Value of Labour,"* we shall be able to interpret this irrational, and seemingly impossible application of value, in the same way that, having once made sure of the real movement of the celestial bodies, we shall be able to explain their apparent or merely phenomenal movements.

What the working man sells is not directly his *Labour,* but his *Labouring Power,* the temporary disposal of which he makes over to the capitalist. This is so much the case that I do not know whether by the English laws, but certainly by some Continental laws, the *maximum time* is fixed for which a man is allowed to sell his labouring power. If allowed to do so for any indefinite period whatever, slavery would be immediately restored. Such a sale, if it comprised his lifetime, for example, would make him at once the lifelong slave of his employer.

One of the oldest economists and most original philosophers of England—Thomas Hobbes—has already, in his *Leviathan,* instinctively hit upon this point overlooked by all his successors. He says: *"The value or worth of a man* is, as in all other things, his price: that is so much as would be given for the *Use of his Power."*

Proceeding from this basis, we shall be able to determine the *Value of Labour* as that of all other commodities.

But before doing so, we might ask, how does this strange phenomenon arise, that we find on the market a set of buyers, possessed of land, machinery, raw material, and the means of life, all of them, save land in its crude state, the *products of labour,* and on the other hand, a set of sellers who have nothing to sell except their labouring power, their working arms and brains? That the one set buys continually in order to make a profit and enrich themselves, while the other set continually sells in order to earn their livelihood? The inquiry into this question would be an inquiry into what the economists call *"Previous, or Original Accumulation,"* but which ought to be called *Original Expropriation.* We should find that this so-called *Original Accumulation* means nothing but a series of historical processes, resulting in a *Decomposition of the Original Union* existing between the Labouring Man and his Means of Labour. Such an inquiry, however, lies beyond the pale of my present subject. The *Separation* between the Man of Labour and the Means of Labour once established, such a state of things will maintain itself and reproduce itself upon a constantly increasing scale, until a new and fundamental revolution in the mode of production should again overturn it, and restore the original union in a new historical form.

What, then, is the *Value of Labouring Power?*

Like that of every other commodity, its value is determined by the quantity of labour necessary to produce it. The labouring power of a man exists only in his living individuality. A certain mass of necessaries must be consumed by a man to grow up and maintain his life. But the man, like the machine, will wear out, and must be replaced by another man. Beside the mass of necessaries required for *his own* maintenance, he wants another amount of necessaries to bring up a certain quota of children that are to replace him on the labour market and to perpetuate the race of labourers. Moreover, to develop his labouring power, and acquire a given skill, another amount of values must be spent. For our purpose it suffices to consider only average labour, the costs of whose education and development are vanishing magnitudes. Still I must seize upon this occasion to state that, as the costs of producing labouring powers of different quality do differ, so must differ the values of the labouring powers employed in different trades. The cry for an *equality of wages* rests, therefore, upon a mistake, is an inane wish never to be fulfilled. It is an offspring of that false and superficial radicalism that accepts premises and tries to evade conclusions. Upon the basis of the wages system the value of labouring power is settled like that of every other commodity; and as different kinds of labouring power have different values, or require different quantities of labour for their production, they *must* fetch different prices in the labour market. To clamour for *equal or even equitable retribution* on the basis of the wages system is the same as to clamour for *freedom* on the basis of the slavery system. What you think just or equitable is out of the question. The question is: What is necessary and unavoidable with a given system of production?

After what has been said, the *value of labouring power* is determined by the *value of the necessaries* required to produce, develop, maintain, and perpetuate the labouring power.

VIII

Production of Surplus Value

Now suppose that the average amount of the daily necessaries of a labouring man require *six hours of average labour* for their production. Suppose, moreover, six hours of average labour to be also realised in a quantity of gold equal to 3*s*. Then 3*s*. would be the *Price*, or the monetary expression of the *Daily Value* of that man's *Labouring Power*. If he worked daily six hours he would daily produce a value sufficient to buy the average amount of his daily necessaries, or to maintain himself as a labouring man.

But our man is a wages labourer. He must, therefore, sell his labouring power to a capitalist. If he sells it at 3*s*. daily, or 18*s*. weekly, he sells it at its value. Suppose him to be a spinner. If he works six hours daily he will add to the cotton a value of 3*s*. daily. This value, daily added by him, would be an exact equivalent for the wages, or the price of his labouring power, received daily. But in that case no *surplus value* or *surplus produce* whatever would go to the capitalist. Here, then, we come to the rub.

In buying the labouring power of the workman, and paying its value, the capitalist, like every other purchaser, has acquired the right to consume or use the commodity bought. You consume or use the labouring power of a man by making him work, as you consume or use a machine by making it run. By paying the daily or weekly value of the labouring power of the workman, the capitalist has, therefore, acquired the right to use or make that labouring power work during the *whole day or week*. The working day or the working week has, of course, certain limits, but those we shall afterwards look more closely at.

For the present I want to turn your attention to one decisive point.

The *value* of the labouring power is determined by the quantity of labour necessary to maintain or reproduce it, but the *use* of that labouring power is only limited by the active energies and physical strength of the labourer. The daily or weekly value of the labouring power is quite distinct from the daily or weekly exercise of that power, the same as the food a horse wants and the time it can carry the horseman are quite distinct. The quantity of labour by which the *value* of the workman's labouring power is limited forms by no means a limit to the quantity of labour which his labouring power is apt to perform. Take the example of our spinner. We have seen that, to daily reproduce his labouring power, he must daily reproduce a value of three shillings, which he will do by working six hours daily. But this does not disable him from working ten or twelve or more hours a day. But by paying the daily or weekly *value* of the spinner's labouring power the capitalist has acquired the right of using that labouring power during *the whole day or week*. He will, therefore, make him work daily, say, twelve hours. *Over and above* the six hours required to replace his wages, or the value of his labouring power, he will, therefore, have to work *six other hours*, which I shall call hours of *surplus labour,* which surplus labour will realise itself in a *surplus value* and a *surplus produce.* If our spinner, for example, by his daily labour of six hours, added three shillings' value to the cotton, a value forming an exact equivalent to his wages, he will, in twelve hours, add six shillings' worth to the cotton, and produce a *proportional surplus of yarn.* As he has sold his labouring power to the capitalist, the whole value or produce created by him belongs to the capitalist, the owner *pro tem.* of his labouring power. By advancing three shillings, the capitalist will, therefore, realise a value of six shillings, because, advancing a value in which six hours of labour are crystallised, he will receive in return a value in which twelve hours of labour are crystallised. By repeating this same process daily, the capitalist will daily advance three shillings and daily pocket six shillings, one half of which will go to pay wages anew, and the other half of which will form the *surplus value,* for which the capitalist pays no equivalent. It is this *sort of exchange between capital and labour* upon which capitalistic production, or the wages system, is founded, and which must constantly result in reproducing the working man as a working man, and the capitalist as a capitalist.

The rate of surplus value, all other circumstances remaining the same, will depend on the proportion between that part of the working day necessary to reproduce the value of the labouring power and the *surplus time or surplus labour* performed for the capitalist. It will, therefore, depend on the *ratio in which the working day is prolonged over and above* that extent, by working which the working man would only reproduce the value of his labouring power, or replace his wages.

IX

Value of Labour

We must now return to the expression, *"Value, or Price of Labour."*

We have seen that, in fact, it is only the value of the labouring power, measured by the values of commodities necessary for its maintenance. But since the workman receives his wages *after* his labour is performed, and knows, moreover, that what he actually gives to the capitalist is his labour, the value or price of his labouring power necessarily appears to him as the *price* or *value of his labour itself.* If the price of his labouring power is three shillings, in which six hours of labour are realised, and if he works twelve hours, he necessarily considers these three shillings as the value or price of twelve hours of labour, although these twelve hours of labour realise themselves in a value of six shillings. A double consequence flows from this.

Firstly. *The value or price of the labouring power* takes the semblance of the *price or value of labour itself,* although, strictly speaking, value and price of labour are senseless terms.

Secondly. Although one part only of the workman's daily labour is *paid,* while the other part is *unpaid,* and while that unpaid or surplus labour constitutes exactly the fund out of which *surplus value* or *profit* is formed, it seems as if the aggregate labour was paid labour.

This false appearance distinguishes *wages labour* from other *historical* forms of labour. On the basis of the wages system even the *unpaid* labour seems to be *paid* labour. With the *slave,* on the contrary, even that part of his labour which is paid appears to be unpaid. Of course, in order to work the slave must live, and one part of his working day goes to replace the value of his own maintenance. But since no bargain is struck between him and his master, and no acts of selling and buying are going on between the two parties, all his labour seems to be given away for nothing.

Take, on the other hand, the peasant serf, such as he, I might say, until yesterday existed in the whole east of Europe. This peasant worked, for example, three days for himself on his own field or the field allotted to him, and the three subsequent days he performed compulsory and gratuitous labour on the estate of his lord. Here, then, the paid and unpaid parts of labour were visibly separated, separated in time and space; and our Liberals overflowed with moral indignation at the preposterous notion of making a man work for nothing.

In point of fact, however, whether a man works three days of the week for himself on his own field and three days for nothing on the estate of his lord, or whether he works in the factory or the workshop six hours daily for himself and six for his employer, comes to the same, although in the latter case the paid and unpaid portions of labour are inseparably mixed up with each other, and the nature of the whole transaction is completely masked by the *intervention of a contract* and the *pay* received at the end of the week. The gratuitous labour appears to be voluntarily given in the one instance, and to be compulsory in the other. That makes all the difference.

In using the word *"value of labour,"* I shall only use it as a popular slang term for *"value of labouring power."*

X

Profit is Made by Selling a Commodity at Its Value

Suppose an average hour of labour to be realised in a value equal to sixpence, or twelve average hours of labour to be realised in six shillings. Suppose, further, the value of labour to be three shillings or the produce of six hours' labour. If, then, in the raw material, machinery, and so forth, used up in a commodity, twenty-four average hours of labour were realised, its value would amount to twelve shillings. If, moreover, the workman employed by the capitalist added twelve hours of labour to those means of production, these twelve hours would be realised in an additional value of six shillings. The *total value of the product* would, therefore, amount to thirty-six hours of realised labour, and be equal to eighteen shillings. But as the value of labour, or the wages paid to the workman, would be three shillings only, no equivalent would have been paid by the capitalist for the six hours of surplus labour worked by the workman, and realised in the value of the commodity. By selling this commodity at its value for eighteen shillings, the capitalist would, therefore, realise a value of three shillings, for which he had paid no equivalent. These three shillings would constitute the surplus value or profit pocketed by him. The capitalist would consequently realise the profit of three shillings, not by selling his commodity at a price *over and above* its value, but by selling it *at its real value*.

The value of a commodity is determined by the *total quantity of labour* contained in it. But part of that quantity of labour is realised in a value, for which an equivalent has been paid in the form of wages; part of it is realised in a value for which *no* equivalent has been paid. Part of the labour contained in the commodity is *paid* labour; part is *unpaid* labour. By selling, therefore, the commodity *at its value,* that is, as the crystallisation of the *total quantity of labour* bestowed upon it, the capitalist must necessarily sell it at a profit. He sells not only what has cost him an equivalent, but he sells also what has cost him nothing, although it has cost the labour of his workman. The cost of the commodity to the capitalist and its real cost are different things. I repeat, therefore, that normal and average profits are made by selling commodities not *above,* but *at their real values.*

XI

The Different Parts into which Surplus Value is Decomposed

The *surplus value,* or that part of the total value of the commodity in which the *surplus labour* or *unpaid labour* the working man is realised, I call *Profit.* The whole of that profit is not pocketed by the employing capitalist. The monopoly of land enables the landlord to take one part of that *surplus value,* under the name of *rent,* whether the land is used for agriculture or buildings or railways, or for any other productive purpose. On the other hand, the very fact that the possession of the *means of labour* enables the employing capitalist to produce a *surplus value,* or, what comes to the same, to *appropriate to himself a certain amount of unpaid labour,* enables the owner of the means of labour, which he lends wholly or partly to the employing capitalist—enables, in one word, the *money-lending capitalist* to claim for himself under the name of interest another part of that surplus value, so that there remains to the employing capitalist *as such* only what is called *industrial* or *commercial profit.*

By what laws this division of the total amount of surplus value amongst the three categories of people is regulated is a question quite foreign to our subject. This much, however, results from what has been stated.

Rent, Interest, and Industrial Profit are only *different names for different parts of the surplus value* of the commodity or the *unpaid labour realised in it,* and they are *equally derived from this source, and from this source alone.* They are not derived from *land* as such nor from *capital* as such, but land and capital enable their owners to get their respective shares out of the surplus value extracted by the employing capitalist from the labourer. For the labourer himself it is a matter of subordinate importance whether that surplus value, the result of his surplus labour, or unpaid labour, is altogether pocketed by the employing capitalist, or whether the latter is obliged to pay portions of it, under the names of rent and interest, away to third parties. Suppose the employing capitalist to use only his own capital and to be his own landlord, then the whole surplus value would go into his pocket.

It is the employing capitalist who immediately extracts from the labourer this surplus value, whatever part of it he may ultimately, be able to keep for himself. Upon this relation, therefore, between the employing capitalist and the wages labourer the whole wages system and the whole present system of production hinge. Some of the citizens who took part in our debate were, therefore, wrong in trying to mince matters, and to treat this fundamental relation between the employing capitalist and the working man as a secondary question, although they were right in stating that, under given circumstances, a rise of prices might affect in very unequal degrees the employing capitalist, the landlord, the moneyed capitalist, and, if you please, the tax-gatherer.

Another consequence follows from what has been stated.

That part of the value of the commodity which represents only the value of the raw materials, the machinery, in one word, the value of the means of production used up, forms *no revenue* at all, but replaces *only capital.* But, apart from this, it is false that the other part of the value of the commodity *which forms revenue,* or may be spent in the form of wages, profits, rent, interest, is *constituted* by the value of wages, the value of rent, the value of profit, and so forth. We shall, in the first instance, discard wages, and only treat industrial profits, interest, and rent. We have just seen that the *surplus value* contained in the commodity, or that part of its value in which *unpaid labour* is realised, resolves itself into different fractions, bearing three different names. But it would be quite the reverse of the truth to say that its value is *composed* of, or *formed* by, the *addition of the independent values of the three constituents*.

If one hour of labour realises itself in a value of sixpence, if the working day of the labourer comprises twelve hours, if half of this time is unpaid labour, that surplus labour will add to the commodity a *surplus value* of three shillings, that is of value for which no equivalent has been paid. This surplus value of three shillings constitutes the *whole fund* which the employing capitalist may divide, in whatever proportions, with the landlord and the money-lender. The value of these three shillings constitutes the limit of the value they have to divide amongst them. But it is not the employing capitalist who adds to the value of the commodity an arbitrary value for his profit, to which another value is added for the landlord, and so forth, so that the addition of these arbitrarily fixed values would constitute the total value. You see, therefore, the fallacy of the popular notion, which confounds the *decomposition* of a *given value* into three parts, with the *formation* of that value by the addition of three *independent values,* thus converting the aggregate value, from which rent, profit, and interest are derived, into an arbitrary magnitude.

If the total profit realised by a capitalist be equal to £100, we call this sum, considered as absolute magnitude, the *amount of profit*. But if we calculate the ratio which those £100 bear to the capital advanced, we call this *relative* magnitude, the *rate of profit*. It is evident that this rate of profit may be expressed in a double way.

Suppose £100 to be the capital *advanced in wages*. If the surplus value created is also £100—and this would show us that half the working day of the labourer consists of unpaid labour—and if we measured this profit by the value of the capital advanced in wages, we should say that the *rate of profit* amounted to one hundred per cent, because the value advanced would be one hundred and the value realised would be two hundred.

If, on the other hand, we should not only consider the *capital advanced in wages,* but the *total capital* advanced, say, for example, £500, of which £400 represented the value of raw materials, machinery, and so forth, we should say that the *rate of profit* amounted only to twenty per cent, because the profit of one hundred would be but the fifth part of the total capital advanced.

The first mode of expressing the rate of profit is the only one which shows you the real ratio between paid and unpaid labour, the real degree of the *exploitation* (you must allow me this French word) *of labour*. The other mode of expression is that in common use, and is, indeed, appropriate for certain purposes. At all events, it is very useful for concealing the degree in which the capitalist extracts gratuitous labour from the workman.

In the remarks I have still to make I shall use the word *Profit* for the whole amount of the surplus value extracted by the capitalist without any regard to the division of that surplus value between different parties, and in using the words *Rate of Profit,* I shall always measure profits by the value of the capital advanced in wages.

SOCIALISM: UTOPIAN AND SCIENTIFIC

I

Modern socialism is, in its essence, the direct product of the recognition, on the one hand, of the class antagonisms existing in the society of today between proprietors and non-proprietors, between capitalists and wage workers; on the other hand, of the anarchy existing in production. But in its theoretical form modern socialism originally appears ostensibly as a more logical extension of the principles laid down by the great French philosophers of the eighteenth century. Like every new theory, modern socialism had, at first, to connect itself with the intellectual stock in trade ready to its hand, however deeply its roots lay in material economic facts.

The great men, who in France prepared men's minds for the coming revolution, were themselves extreme revolutionists. They recognized no external authority of any kind whatever. Religion, natural science, society, political institutions—everything was subjected to the most unsparing criticism: everything must justify its existence before the judgment seat of reason or give up existence. Reason became the sole measure of everything. It was the time when, as Hegel says, the world stood upon its head[1], first in the sense that the human head, and the principles arrived at by its thought, claimed to be the basis of all human action and association; but by and by, also, in the wider sense that the reality which was in contradiction to these principles had, in fact, to be turned upside down. Every form of society and government then existing, every old traditional notion was flung into the lumber room as irrational; the world had hitherto allowed itself to be led solely by prejudices; everything in the past deserved only pity and contempt. Now, for the first time, appeared the light of day, the kingdom of reason; henceforth superstition, injustice, privilege, oppression were to be superseded by eternal truth, eternal right, equality based on nature and the inalienable rights of man.

We know today that this kingdom of reason was nothing more than the idealized kingdom of the bourgeoisie; that this eternal right found its realization in bourgeois justice; that this equality reduced itself to bourgeois equality before the law; that bourgeois property was proclaimed as one of the essential rights of man; and that the government of reason, the *contrat social* of Rousseau, came into being, and only could come into being, as a democratic bourgeois republic. The great thinkers of the eighteenth century could, no more than their predecessors, go beyond the limits imposed upon them by their epoch.

But, side by side with the antagonism of the feudal nobility and the burghers, who claimed to represent all the rest of society, was the general antagonism of exploiters and exploited, of rich idlers and poor workers. It was this very circumstance that made it possible for the representatives of the bourgeoisie to put themselves forward as representing not one special class, but the whole of suffering humanity. Still further. From its origin the bourgeoisie was saddled with its antithesis: capitalists cannot exist without wage workers, and, in the same proportion as the medieval burgher of the guild developed into the modern bourgeois, the guild journeyman and the day laborer, outside the guilds, developed into the proletarian. And although, upon the whole, the bourgeoisie, in their struggle with the nobility, could claim to represent at the same time the interests of the different working classes of that period, yet in every great bourgeois movement there were independent outbursts of that class which was the forerunner, more or less developed, of

Translated by Edward Aveling.

the modern proletariat. For example, at the time of the German Reformation and the Peasants' War, the Anabaptists and Thomas Münzer; in the great English Revolution, the Levelers; in the great French Revolution, Babeuf.

There were theoretical enunciations corresponding with these revolutionary uprisings of a class not yet developed: in the sixteenth and seventeenth centuries, utopian pictures of ideal social conditions; in the eighteenth, actual communistic theories (Morelly and Mably). The demand for equality was no longer limited to political rights; it was extended also to the social conditions of individuals. It was not simply class privileges that were to be abolished, but class distinctions themselves. A communism, ascetic, denouncing all the pleasures of life, Spartan, was the first form of the new teaching. Then came the three great Utopians: St. Simon, to whom the middle-class movement, side by side with the proletarian, still had a certain significance; Fourier; and Owen, who in the country where capitalist production was most developed, and under the influence of the antagonisms begotten of this, worked out his proposals for the removal of class distinction systematically and in direct relation to French materialism.

One thing is common to all three. Not one of them appears as a representative of the interests of that proletariat which historical development had, in the meantime, produced. Like the French philosophers, they to not claim to emancipate a particular class to begin with, but all humanity at once. Like them, they wish to bring in the kingdom of reason and eternal justice, but this kingdom, as they see it, is as far as heaven from earth from that of the French philosophers.

For, to our three social reformers, the bourgeois world, based upon the principles of these philosophers, is quite as irrational and unjust and, therefore, finds its way to the dust hole quite as readily as feudalism and all the earlier stages of society. If pure reason and justice have not hitherto ruled the world, this has been the case only because men have not rightly understood them. What was wanted was the individual man of genius, who has now arisen and who understands the truth. That he has now arisen, that the truth has now been clearly understood, is not an inevitable event, following of necessity in the chain of historical development, but a mere happy accident. He might just as well have been born five hundred years earlier, and might then have spared humanity five hundred years of error, strife, and suffering.

We saw how the French philosophers of the eighteenth century, the forerunners of the Revolution, appealed to reason as the sole judge of all that is. A rational government, rational society were to be founded; everything that ran counter to eternal reason was to be remorselessly done away with. We saw also that this eternal reason was in reality nothing but the idealized understanding of the eighteenth-century citizen, just then evolving into the bourgeois. The French Revolution had realized this rational society and government.

But the new order of things, rational enough as compared with earlier conditions, turned out to be by no means absolutely rational. The state based upon reason completely collapsed. Rousseau's *contrat social* had found its realization in the Reign of Terror, from which the bourgeoisie, who had lost confidence in their own political capacity, had taken refuge first in the corruption of the Directorate, and, finally, under the wing of the Napoleonic despotism. The promised eternal peace was turned into an endless war of conquest. The society based upon reason had fared no better. The antagonism between rich and poor, instead of dissolving into general prosperity, had become intensified by the removal of the guild and other privileges, which had to some extent bridged it, and by the removal of the charitable institutions of the Church. The "freedom of property" from feudal fetters, now veritably accomplished, turned out to be, for the small capitalists and small proprietors, the freedom to sell their small property, crushed under the overmastering competition of the large capitalists and landlords, to these great lords, and thus, as far as the small capitalists and peasant proprietors were concerned, became "freedom *from* property." The development of industry upon a capitalistic basis made poverty and misery of the working masses conditions of existence of society. Cash payment became more and more, in Carlyle's phrase, "the sole nexus between man and man." The number of crimes increased from year to year. Formerly the feudal vices had openly stalked about in broad daylight; though not eradicated, they were now at any rate thrust into the background. In their stead the bourgeois vices, hitherto practiced in secret, began to blossom all the more luxuriantly. Trade became to a greater and greater extent cheating. The "fraternity" of the revolutionary motto was realized in the chicanery and rivalries of the battle of competition. Oppression by force was replaced by corruption; the sword, as the first social lever, by gold. The right of the first night was transferred from the feudal lords to the bourgeois manufacturers. Prostitution increased to an extent never heard of. Marriage itself remained, as before, the legally recognized form, the official cloak of prostitution, and, moreover, was supplemented by rich crops of adultery.

In a word, compared with the splendid promises of the philosophers, the social and political institutions born of the "triumph of reason" were bitterly disappointing caricatures. All that was wanting was the men to formulate this disappointment, and they came with the turn of the century. In 1802, St. Simon's Geneva letters appeared; in 1808 appeared Fourier's first work, although the ground work of his theory dated from 1799; on January 1, 1800, Robert Owen undertook the direction of New Lanark.

At this time, however, the capitalist mode of production, and with it the antagonism between the bourgeoisie and the proletariat, was still very incompletely developed. Modern industry, which had just arisen in England, was still unknown in France. But modern industry develops, on the one hand, the conflicts which make absolutely necessary a revolution in the mode of production and the doing away with its capitalistic character—conflicts not only between the classes begotten of it, but also between the very productive forces and the forms of exchange created by it. And, on the other hand, it develops, in these very gigantic productive forces, the means of ending these conflicts. If, therefore, about the year 1800 the conflicts arising from the new social order were only just beginning to take shape, this holds still more fully as to the means of ending them. The "have-nothing" masses of Paris, during the Reign of Terror, were able for a moment to gain the mastery, and thus to lead the bourgeois revolution to victory in spite of the bourgeoisie themselves. But in doing so they only proved how impossible it was for their domination to last under the conditions then obtaining. The proletariat, which then for the first time evolved from these "have-nothing" masses as the nucleus of a new class, as yet quite incapable of independent political action, appeared as an oppressed, suffering order, to which, in its incapacity to help itself, help could, at best, be brought in from without or down from above.

This historical situation also dominated the founders of socialism. To the crude conditions of capitalistic production and the crude class conditions corresponded crude theories. The solution of the social problems, which as yet lay hidden in undeveloped economic conditions, the Utopians attempted to evolve out of the human brain. Society presented nothing but wrongs; to remove these was the task of reason. It was necessary, then, to discover a new and more perfect system of social order and to impose this upon society from without by propaganda, wherever it was possible, by the example of model experiments. These new social systems were foredoomed as utopian; the more completely they were worked out in detail, the more they could not avoid drifting off into pure fantasies.

These facts once established, we need not dwell a moment longer upon this side of the question, now wholly belonging to the past. We can leave it to the literary small fry to solemnly quibble over these fantasies, which today only make us smile, and to crow over the superiority of their own bald reasoning as compared with such "insanity." For ourselves, we delight in the stupendously grand thoughts and germs of thought that everywhere break out through their fantastic covering, and to which these Philistines are blind.

St. Simon was a son of the great French Revolution, at the outbreak of which he was not yet thirty. The Revolution was the victory of the third estate, i.e., of the great masses of the nation, *working* in production and in trade, over the privileged *idle* classes, the nobles and the priests. But the victory of the third estate soon revealed itself as exclusively the victory of a small part of this "estate," as the conquest of political power by the socially privileged section of it, i.e., the propertied bourgeoisie. And the bourgeoisie had certainly developed rapidly during the Revolution, partly by speculation in the lands of the nobility and of the Church, confiscated and afterwards put up for sale, and partly by frauds upon the nation by means of army contracts. It was the domination of these swindlers that, under the Directorate, brought France to the verge of ruin, and thus gave Napoleon the pretext for his *coup d'etat*.

Hence to St. Simon the antagonism between the third estate and the privileged classes took the form of an antagonism between "workers" and "idlers." The idlers were not merely the old privileged classes, but also all who, without taking any part in production or distribution, lived on their incomes. And the workers were not only the wage workers, but also the manufacturers, the merchants, the bankers. That the idlers had lost the capacity for intellectual leadership and political supremacy had been proved, and was by the Revolution finally settled. That the non-possessing classes had not this capacity seemed to St. Simon proved by the experiences of the Reign of Terror. Then who was to lead and command? According to St. Simon, science and industry, both united by a new religious bond, destined to restore that unity of religious ideas which had been lost since the time of the Reformation—a necessarily mystic and rigidly hierarchic "new Christianity." But science, that was the scholars; and industry, that was, in the first place, the working bourgeois, manufacturers, merchants, bankers. These bourgeois were certainly intended by St. Simon to transform themselves into a class of public officials, of social trustees; but they were still to hold, vis-a-vis the workers, a commanding and economically privileged position. The bankers especially were to be called upon to direct the whole of social production by the regulation of credit. This conception was in exact keeping with a time in which modern industry in France and, with it, the chasm between bourgeoisie and proletariat was only just coming into existence. But what St. Simon especially lays stress upon is this: what interests him first, and above all other things, is the lot of the class that is the most numerous and the poorest (*"la classe la plus nombreuse et la plus pauvre"*).

Already in his Geneva letters St. Simon lays down the proposition that "all men ought to work." In the same work he recognizes also that the Reign of Terror was the reign of the non-possessing masses. "See," says he to them, "what happened in France at the time when your comrades held sway there; they brought about a famine." But to recognize the French Revolution as a class war, and not simply one between nobility and bourgeoisie, but between nobility, bourgeoisie, and the non-possessors, was, in the year 1802, a most pregnant discovery. In 1816 he declares that politics is the science of production, and foretells the complete absorption of politics by economics. The knowledge that economic conditions are the basis of political institutions appears here only in embryo. Yet what is here already very plainly expressed is the idea of the future conversion of political rule over men into an administration of things and a direction of processes of production—that is to say, the "abolition of the state," about which recently there has been so much noise.

St. Simon shows the same superiority over his contemporaries, when in 1814, immediately after the entry of the allies into Paris, and again in 1815, during the Hundred
Days' War, he proclaims the alliance of France with England, and then of both these countries with Germany, as the only guarantee for the prosperous development and peace of
Europe. To preach to the French in 1815 an alliance with the victors of Waterloo required
as much courage as historical foresight.

If in St. Simon we find a comprehensive breadth of view, by virtue of which almost all
the ideas of later socialists that are not strictly economic are found in him in embryo, we
find in Fourier a criticism of the existing conditions of society, genuinely French and
witty, but not upon that account any the less thorough. Fourier takes the bourgeoisie,
their inspired prophets before the Revolution, and their interested eulogists after it at
their own word. He remorselessly lays bare the material and moral misery of the bourgeois
world. He confronts it with the earlier philosophers' dazzling promises of a society in
which reason alone should reign, of a civilization in which happiness should be universal,
of an illimitable human perfectibility, and with the rose-colored phraseology of the bourgeois ideologists of his time. He points out how everywhere the most pitiful reality corresponds with the most high-sounding phrases, and he overwhelms this hopeless fiasco of
phrases with his mordant sarcasm.

Fourier is not only a critic; his imperturbably serene nature makes him a satirist, and
assuredly one of the greatest satirists of all time. He depicts with equal power and charm
the swindling speculations that blossomed out upon the downfall of the Revolution and
the shopkeeping spirit prevalent in, and characteristic of, French commerce at that time.
Still more masterly is his criticism of the bourgeois form of the relations between the sexes
and the position of woman in bourgeois society. He was the first to declare that in any
given society the degree of woman's emancipation is the natural measure of the general
emancipation.

But Fourier is at his greatest in his conception of the history of society. He divides its
whole course, thus far, into four stages of evolution—savagery, barbarism, the patriar-
chate, civilization. This last is identical with the so-called civil, or bourgeois, society of
today—i.e., with the social order that came in with the sixteenth century. He proves "that
the civilized stage raises every vice practiced by barbarism in a simple fashion into a form
of existence, complex, ambiguous, equivocal, hypocritical"—that civilization moves in
"a vicious circle," in contradictions which it constantly reproduces without being able
to solve them; hence it constantly arrives at the very opposite to that which it wants to
attain, or pretends to want to attain, so that, e.g., "under civilization poverty is born of
superabundance itself."

Fourier, as we see, uses the dialectic method in the same masterly way as his contemporary, Hegel. Using these same dialectics, he argues against the talk about illimitable
human perfectibility, that every historical phase has its period of ascent and also its period
of descent, and he applies this observation to the future of the whole human race. As Kant
introduced into natural science the idea of the ultimate destruction of the earth, Fourier
introduced into historical science that of the ultimate destruction of the human race.

While in France the hurricane of the Revolution swept over the land, in England a qui-
eter, but not on that account less tremendous, revolution was going on. Steam and the
new tool-making machinery were transforming manufacture into modern industry, and
thus revolutionizing the whole foundation of bourgeois society. The sluggish march of
development of the manufacturing period changed into a veritable storm-and-stress
period of production. With constantly increasing swiftness the splitting up of society into
large capitalists and non-possessing proletarians went on. Between these, instead of the

former stable middle class, an unstable mass of artisans and small shopkeepers, the most fluctuating portion of the population, now led a precarious existence.

The new mode of production was, as yet, only at the beginning of its period of ascent; as yet it was the normal, regular method of production—the only one possible under existing conditions. Nevertheless, even then it was producing crying social abuses—the herding together of a homeless population in the worst quarters of the large towns; the loosening of all traditional moral bonds, of patriarchal subordination, of family relations; overwork, especially of women and children, to a frightful extent; complete demoralization of the working class, suddenly flung into altogether new conditions, from the country into the town, from agriculture into modern industry, from stable conditions of existence into insecure ones that changed from day to day.

At this juncture there came forward as a reformer a manufacturer twenty-nine years old—a man of almost sublime, childlike simplicity of character, and at the same time one of the few born leaders of men. Robert Owen had adopted the teaching of the materialistic philosophers: that man's character is the product, on the one hand, of heredity; on the other, of the environment of the individual during his lifetime, and especially during his period of development. In the industrial revolution most of his class saw only chaos and confusion, and the opportunity of fishing in these troubled waters and making large fortunes quickly. He saw in it the opportunity of putting into practice his favorite theory, and so of bringing order out of chaos. He had already tried it with success, as superintendent of more than five hundred men in a Manchester factory. From 1800 to 1829 he directed the great cotton mill at New Lanark, in Scotland, as managing partner, along the same lines, but with greater freedom of action and with a success that made him a European reputation. A population, originally consisting of the most diverse and, for the most part, very demoralized elements, a population that gradually grew to twenty-five hundred, he turned into a model colony, in which drunkenness, police, magistrates, lawsuits, poor laws, charity were unknown. And all this simply by placing the people in conditions worthy of human beings, and especially by carefully bringing up the rising generation. He was the founder of infant schools, and introduced them first at New Lanark. At the age of two the children came to school, where they enjoyed themselves so much that they could scarcely be got home again. While his competitors worked their people thirteen or fourteen hours a day, in New Lanark the working day was only ten and a half hours. When a crisis in cotton stopped work for four months, his workers received their full wages all the time. And with all this the business more than doubled in value, and to the last yielded large profits to its proprietors.

In spite of all this Owen was not content. The existence which he secured for his workers was, in his eyes, still far from being worthy of human beings. "The people were slaves at my mercy." The relatively favorable conditions in which he had placed them were still far from allowing a rational development of the character and of the intellect in all directions, much less of the free exercise of all their faculties. "And yet, the working part of this population of twenty-five hundred persons was daily producing as much real wealth for society as, less than half a century before, it would have required the working part of a population of six hundred thousand to create. I asked myself, what became of the difference between the wealth consumed by twenty-five hundred persons and that which would have been consumed by six hundred thousand?"[2]

The answer was clear. It had been used to pay the proprietors of the establishment 5 per cent on the capital they had laid out, in addition to over three hundred thousand pounds' clear profit. And that which held for New Lanark held to a still greater extent for all the factories in England. "If this new wealth had not been created by machinery, imperfectly as it has been applied, the wars of Europe, in opposition to Napoleon, and to support the aristocratic principles of society, could not have been maintained. And yet this new power was the creation of the working class."[3] To them, therefore, the fruits of this new power belonged. The newly created gigantic productive forces, hitherto used only to enrich individuals and to enslave the masses, offered to Owen the foundations for a reconstruction of society; they were destined, as the common property of all, to be worked for the common good of all.

Owen's communism was based upon this purely business foundation, the outcome, so to say, of commercial calculation. Throughout it maintained this practical character. Thus in 1823 Owen proposed the relief of the distress in Ireland by communist colonies, and drew up complete estimates of costs of founding them, yearly expenditure, and probable revenue. And in his definite plan for the future the technical working out of details is managed with such practical knowledge—ground plan, front and side and bird's-eye views all included—that, the Owen method of social reform once accepted, there is from the practical point of view little to be said against the actual arrangement of details.

His advance in the direction of communism was the turning point in Owen's life. As long as he was simply a philanthropist he was rewarded with nothing but wealth, applause, honor, and glory. He was the most popular man in Europe. Not only men of his own class, but statesmen and princes listened to him approvingly. But when he came out with his communist theories, that was quite another thing. Three great obstacles seemed to him especially to block the path to social reform: private property, religion, the present form of marriage. He knew what confronted him if he attacked these—outlawry, excommunication from official society, the loss of his whole social position. But nothing of this prevented him from attacking them without fear of consequences, and what he had foreseen happened. Banished from official society, with a conspiracy of silence against him in the press, ruined by his unsuccessful communist experiments in America, in which he sacrificed all his fortune, he turned directly to the working class and continued working in their midst for thirty years. Every social movement, every real advance in England on behalf of the workers links itself to the name of Robert Owen. He forced through in 1819, after five years' fighting the first law limiting the hours of labor of women and children in factories. He was president of the first congress at which all the trade unions of England united in a single great trade association. He introduced as transition measures to the complete communistic organization of society, on the one hand, co-operative societies for retail trade and production. These have since that time, at least, given practical proof that the merchant and the manufacturer are socially quite unnecessary. On the other hand, he introduced labor bazaars for the exchange of the products of labor through the medium of labor notes, whose unit was a single hour of work; institutions necessarily doomed to failure, but completely anticipating Proudhon's bank of exchange of a much later period, and differing entirely from this in that it did not claim to be the panacea for all social ills, but only a first step towards a much more radical revolution of society.

The Utopians' mode of thought has for a long time governed the socialist ideas of the nineteenth century, and still governs some of them. Until very recently all French and English socialists did homage to it. The earlier German communism, including that of Weitling, was of the same school. To all these socialism is the expression of absolute truth, reason, and justice, and has only to be discovered to conquer all the world by virtue of its own power. And as absolute truth is independent of time, space, and of the historical development of man, it is a mere accident when and where it is discovered. With all this, absolute truth, reason, and justice are different with the founder of each different school. And as each one's special kind of absolute truth, reason, and justice is again conditioned by his subjective understanding, his conditions of existence, the measure of his knowledge, and his intellectual training, there—is no other ending possible in this conflict of absolute truths than that they shall be mutually exclusive one of the other. Hence from this nothing could come but a kind of eclectic, average socialism, which, as a matter of fact, has up to the present time dominated the minds of most of the socialist workers in France and England. Hence a mishmash allowing of the most manifold shades of opinion; a mishmash of such critical statements, economic theories, pictures of future society by the founders of different sects as excite a minimum of opposition; a mishmash which is the more easily brewed the more the definite sharp edges of the individual constituents are rubbed down in the stream of debate, like rounded pebbles in a brook.

To make a science of socialism it had first to be placed upon a real basis.

II

In the meantime, along with and after the French philosophy of the eighteenth century, had arisen the new German philosophy, culminating in Hegel. Its greatest merit was the taking up again of dialectics as the highest form of reasoning. The old Greek philosophers were all born natural dialecticians, and Aristotle, the most encyclopedic intellect of them, had already analyzed the most essential forms of dialectic thought. The newer philosophy, on the other hand, although in it, also, dialectics had brilliant exponents (e.g., Descartes and Spinoza), had, especially through English influence, become more and more rigidly fixed in the so-called metaphysical mode of reasoning, by which also the French of the eighteenth century were almost wholly dominated, at all events in their special philosophical work. Outside of philosophy in the restricted sense the French, nevertheless, produced masterpieces of dialectics. We need only call to mind Diderot's *Le Neveu de Rameau,* and Rousseau's *Discours sur l'origine et les fondements de l'inegalite parmi les hommes.* We give here, in brief, the essential character of these two modes of thought.

When we consider and reflect upon nature at large or the history of mankind or our own intellectual activity, at first we see the picture of an endless entanglement of relations and reactions, permutations and combinations, in which nothing remains what, where, and as it was, but everything moves, changes, comes into being, and passes away. We see, therefore, at first the picture as a whole, with its individual parts still more or less kept in the background; we observe the movements, transitions, connections rather than the things that move, combine, and are connected. This primitive, naive but intrinsically correct conception of the world is that of ancient Greek philosophy, and was first clearly formulated by Heraclitus: everything is and is not, for everything is fluid, is constantly changing, constantly coming into being and passing away.

But this conception, correctly as it expresses the general character of the picture of appearances as a whole, does not suffice to explain the details of which this picture is made up, and so long as we do not understand these we have not a clear idea of the whole picture. In order to understand these details we must detach them from their natural or historical connection and examine each one separately, its nature, special causes, effects, etc. This is primarily the task of natural science and historical research: branches of science which the Greeks of classical times, on very good grounds, relegated to a subordinate position, because they had, first of all, to collect materials for these sciences to work upon. A certain amount of natural and historical material must be collected before there can be any critical analysis, comparison, and arrangement in classes, orders, and species. The foundations of the exact natural sciences were, therefore, first worked out by the

Greeks of the Alexandrian period, and later on, in the Middle Ages, by the Arabs. Real natural science dates from the second half of the fifteenth century, and thence onward it had advanced with constantly increasing rapidity. The analysis of nature into its individual parts, the grouping of the different natural processes and objects in definite classes, the study of the internal anatomy of organic bodies in their manifold forms— these were the fundamental conditions of the gigantic strides in our knowledge of nature that have been made during the last four hundred years. But this method of work has also left us as legacy the habit of observing natural objects and processes in isolation, apart from their connection with the vast whole; of observing them in repose, not in motion; as constants, not as essentially variables; in their death, not in their life. And when this way of looking at things was transferred by Bacon and Locke from natural science to philosophy, it begot the narrow, metaphysical mode of thought peculiar to the last century.

To the metaphysician things and their mental reflexes, ideas, are isolated, are to be considered one after the other and apart from each other, are objects of investigation fixed, rigid, given once for all. He thinks in absolutely irreconcilable antitheses. "His communication is 'yea, yea; nay, nay'; for whatsoever is more than these cometh of evil." For him a thing either exists or does not exist; a thing cannot at the same time be itself and something else. Positive and negative absolutely exclude one another; cause and effect stand in a rigid antithesis one to the other.

At first sight this mode of thinking seems to us very luminous, because it is that of so-called sound common sense. Only sound common sense, respectable fellow that he is, in the homely realm of his own four walls, has very wonderful adventures directly he ventures out into the wide world of research. And the metaphysical mode of thought, justifiable and necessary as it is in a number of domains whose extent varies according to the nature of the particular object of investigation, sooner or later reaches a limit beyond which it becomes one-sided, restricted, abstract, lost in insoluble contradictions. In the contemplation of individual things it forgets the connection between them; in the contemplation of their existence it forgets the beginning and end of that existence; of their repose, it forgets their motion. It cannot see the wood for the trees.

For everyday purposes we know and can say, e.g., whether an animal is alive or not. But upon closer inquiry, we find that this is, in many cases, a very complex question, as the jurists know very well. They have cudgeled their brains in vain to discover a rational limit beyond which the killing of the child in its mother's womb is murder. It is just as impossible to determine absolutely the moment of death, for physiology proves that death is not an instantaneous, momentary phenomenon, but a very protracted process.

In like manner every organic being is every moment the same and not the same; every moment it assimilates matter supplied from without and gets rid of other matter; every moment some cells of its body die and others build themselves anew; in a longer or shorter time the matter of its body is completely renewed, and is replaced by other molecules of matter, so that every organic being is always itself and yet something other than itself.

Further, we find upon closer investigation that the two poles of an antithesis, positive and negative, e.g., are as inseparable as they are opposed, and that despite all their opposition they mutually interpenetrate. And we find, in like manner, that cause and effect are conceptions which hold good only in their application to individual cases; but as soon as we consider the individual cases in their general connection with the universe as a whole they run into each other, and they become confounded when we contemplate that universal action and reaction in which causes and effects are eternally changing places, so that what is effect here and now will be cause there and then, and vice versa.

None of these processes and modes of thought enters into the framework of metaphysical reasoning. Dialectics, on the other hand, comprehends things and their representations, ideas, in their essential connection, concatenation, motion, origin, and ending. Such processes as those mentioned above are, therefore, so many corroborations of its own method of procedure.

Nature is the proof of dialectics, and it must be said for modern science that it has furnished this proof with very rich materials, increasing daily, and thus has shown that, in the last resort, nature works dialectically and not metaphysically; that she does not move in the eternal oneness of a perpetually recurring circle, but goes through a real historical evolution. In this connection Darwin must be named before all others. He dealt the metaphysical conception of nature the heaviest blow by his proof that all organic beings, plants, animals, and man himself are the products of a process of evolution going on through millions of years. But the naturalists who have learned to think dialectically are few and far between, and this conflict of the results of discovery with preconceived modes of thinking explains the endless confusion now reigning in theoretical natural science, the despair of teachers as well as learners, of authors and readers alike.

An exact representation of the universe, of its evolution, of the development of mankind, and of the reflection of this evolution in the minds of men can therefore be obtained only by the methods of dialectics, with its constant regard to the innumerable actions and reactions of life and death, of progressive or retrogressive changes. And in this spirit the new German philosophy has worked. Kant began his career by resolving the stable solar system of Newton and its eternal duration, after the famous initial impulse had once been given, into the result of a historic process, the formation of the sun and all the planets out of a rotating nebulous mass. From this he at the same time drew the conclusion that, given this origin of the solar system, its future death followed of necessity. His theory half a century later was established mathematically by Laplace, and half a century after that the spectroscope proved the existence in space of such incandescent masses of gas in various stages of condensation.

This new German philosophy culminated in the Hegelian system. In this system—and herein is its great merit—for the first time the whole world, natural, historical, intellectual, is represented as a process, i.e., as in constant motion, change, transformation, development; and the attempt is made to trace out the internal connection that makes a continuous whole of all this movement and development. From this point of view the history of mankind no longer appeared as a wild whirl of senseless deeds of violence, all equally condemnable at the judgment seat of mature philosophic reason and best forgotten as quickly as possible, but as the process of evolution of man himself. It was now the task of the intellect to follow the gradual march of this process through all its devious ways, and to trace out the inner law running through all its apparently accidental phenomena.

That the Hegelian system did not solve the problem it propounded is here immaterial. Its epoch-making merit was that it propounded the problem. This problem is one that no single individual will ever be able to solve. Although Hegel was—with St. Simon—the most encyclopedic mind of his time, yet he was limited, first, by the necessarily limited extant of his own knowledge and, second, by the limited extent and depth of the knowledge and conceptions of his age. To these limits a third must be added. Hegel was an idealist. To him the thoughts within his brain were not the more or less abstract pictures of actual things and processes, but, conversely, things and their evolution were only the realized pictures of the "Idea," existing somewhere from eternity before the world was. This way of thinking turned everything upside down, and completely reversed the actual connection of things in the world. Correctly and ingeniously as many individual groups of facts were grasped by Hegel, yet, for the reasons just given, there is much that is botched, artificial, labored—in a word, wrong—in point of detail. The Hegelian system, in itself, was a collosal miscarriage—but it was also the last of its kind. It was suffering, in fact, from an internal and incurable contradiction. Upon the one hand, its essential proposition was the conception that human history is a process of evolution, which, by its very nature, cannot find its intellectual final term in the discovery of any so-called absolute truth. But, on the other hand, it laid claim to being the very essence of this absolute truth. A system of natural and historical knowledge, embracing everything, and final for all time, is a contradiction to the fundamental law of dialectic reasoning. This law, indeed, by no means excludes, but, on the contrary, includes the idea that the systematic knowledge of the external universe can make giant strides from age to age.

The perception of the fundamental contradiction in German idealism led necessarily back to materialism, but, *nota bene,* not to the simply metaphysical, exclusively mechanical materialism of the eighteenth century. Old materialism looked upon all previous history as a crude heap of irrationality and violence; modern materialism sees in it the process of evolution of humanity, and aims at discovering the laws thereof. With the French of the eighteenth century, and even with Hegel, the conception obtained of nature as a whole, moving in narrow circles and forever immutable, with its eternal celestial bodies, as Newton, and unalterable organic species, as Linnaeus, taught. Modern materialism embraces the more recent discoveries of natural science, according to which nature also has its history in time, the celestial bodies, like the organic species that under favorable conditions people them, being born and perishing. And even if nature as a whole must still be said to move in recurrent cycles, these cycles assume infinitely larger dimensions. In both aspects modern materialism is essentially dialectic, and no longer requires the assistance of that sort of philosophy which, queenlike, pretended to rule the remaining mob of sciences. As soon as each special science is bound to make clear its position in the great totality of things and of our knowledge of things, a special science dealing with this totality is superfluous or unnecessary. That which still survives of all earlier philosophy is the science of thought and its laws—formal logic and dialectics. Everything else is subsumed in the positive science of nature and history.

While, however, the revolution in the conception of nature could be made only in proportion to the corresponding positive materials furnished by research, already much earlier certain historical facts had occurred which led to a decisive change in the conception of history. In 1831 the first working-class rising took place in Lyons; between 1838 and 1842 the first national working-class movement, that of the English Chartists, reached its height. The class struggle between proletariat and bourgeoisie came to the front in the history of the most advanced countries in Europe, in proportion to the development, upon the one hand, of modern industry; upon the other, of the newly acquired political supremacy of the bourgeoisie. Facts more and more strenuously gave the lie to the teachings of bourgeois economy as to the identity of the interests of capital and labor, as to the universal harmony and universal prosperity that would be the consequence of unbridled competition. All these things could no longer be ignored, any more than the French and English socialism, which was their theoretical, though very imperfect, expression. But the old idealist conception of history, which was not yet dislodged, knew nothing of class struggles based upon economic interests, knew nothing of economic interests; production and all economic relations appeared in it only as incidental, subordinate elements in the "history of civilization."

The new facts made imperative a new examination of all past history. Then it was seen that *all* past history, with the exception of its primitive stages, was the history of class struggles; that these warring classes of society are always the products of the modes of production and of exchange—in a word, of the *economic* conditions of their time; that the economic structure of society always furnishes the real basis, starting from which we can alone work out the ultimate explanation of the whole superstructure of juridical and political institutions as well as of the religious, philosophical, and other ideas of a given historical period. Hegel had freed history from metaphysics-he had made it dialectic; but his conception of history was essentially idealistic. But now idealism was driven from its last refuge, the philosophy of history, now a materialistic treatment of history was propounded, and a method found of explaining man's "knowing" by his "being" instead of, as heretofore, his "being" by his "knowing."

From that time forward socialism was no longer an accidental discovery of this or that ingenious brain, but the necessary outcome of the struggle between two historically developed classes—the proletariat and the bourgeoisie. Its task was no longer to manufacture a system of society as perfect as possible, but to examine the historico-economic succession of events from which these classes and their antagonism had of necessity sprung, and to discover in the economic conditions thus created the means of ending the conflict. But the socialism of earlier days was as incompatible with this materialistic conception as the conception of nature of the French materialists was with dialectics and modern natural science. The socialism of earlier days certainly criticized the existing capitalistic mode of production and its consequences. But it could not explain them, and, therefore, could not get the mastery of them. It could only simply reject them as bad. The more strongly this earlier socialism denounced the exploitation of the working class, inevitable under capitalism, the less able was it clearly to show in what this exploitation consisted and how it arose. But for this it was necessary (1) to present the capitalistic method of production in its historical connection and its inevitableness during a particular historical period, and therefore, also, to present its inevitable downfall; and (2) to lay bare its essential character, which was still a secret. This was done by the discovery of *surplus value*. It was shown that the appropriation of unpaid labor is the basis of the capitalist mode of production, and of the exploitation of the worker that occurs under it; that even if the capitalist buys the labor power of his laborer at its full value as a commodity on the market he yet extracts more value from it than he paid for, and that in the ultimate analysis this surplus value forms those sums of value from which are heaped up the constantly increasing masses of capital in the hands of the possessing classes. The genesis of capitalist production and the production of capital were both explained.

These two great discoveries, the materialistic conception of history and the revelation of the secret of capitalistic production through surplus value, we owe to Marx. With these discoveries socialism became a science. The next thing was to work out all its details and relations.

III

The materialist conception of history starts from the proposition that the production of the means to support human life—and, next to production, the exchange of things produced—is the basis of all social structure; that in every society that has appeared in history, the manner in which wealth is distributed and society divided into classes or orders is dependent upon what is produced, how it is produced, and how the products are exchanged. From this point of view the final causes of all social changes and political revolutions are to be sought not in men's brains, not in man's better insight into eternal truth and justice, but in changes in the modes of production and exchange. They are to be sought not in the *philosophy,* but in the *economics* of each particular epoch. The growing perception that existing social institutions are unreasonable and unjust, that reason has become unreason and right wrong, is only proof that in the modes of production and exchange changes have silently taken place with which the social order, adapted to earlier economic conditions, is no longer in keeping. From this it also follows that the means of getting rid of the incongruities that have been brought to light must also be present, in a more or less developed condition, within the changed modes of production themselves. These means are not to be invented by deduction from fundamental principles, but are to be discovered in the stubborn facts of the existing system of production.

What is, then, the position of modern socialism in this connection?

The present structure of society—this is now pretty generally conceded—is the creation of the ruling class of today, of the bourgeoisie. The mode of production peculiar to the bourgeoisie, known, since Marx, as the capitalist mode of production, was incompatible with the feudal system, with the privileges it conferred upon individuals, entire social ranks, and local corporations, as well as with the hereditary ties of subordination which constituted the framework of its social organization. The bourgeoisie broke up the feudal system and built upon its ruins the capitalist order of society, the kingdom of free competition, of personal liberty, of the equality, before the law, of all commodity owners, of all the rest of the capitalist blessings. Thenceforward the capitalist mode of production could develop in freedom. Since steam, machinery, and the making of machines by machinery transformed the older manufacture into modern industry, the productive forces evolved under the guidance of the bourgeoisie developed with a rapidity and in a degree unheard of before. But just as the older manufacture, in its time, and handicraft, becoming more developed under its influence, had come into collision with the feudal trammels of the guilds, so now modern industry, in its more complete development, comes into collision with the bounds within which the capitalistic mode of production holds it confined. The new productive forces have already outgrown the capitalistic mode of using them. And this conflict between productive forces and modes of production is not a conflict engendered in the mind of man, like that between original sin and divine justice. It exists, in fact, objectively, outside us, independently of the will and actions even of the men who have brought it on. Modern socialism is nothing but the reflex in thought of this conflict in fact; its ideal reflection in the minds, first, of the class directly suffering under it, the working class.

Now in what does this conflict consist?

Before capitalistic production, i.e., in the Middle Ages, the system of petty industry obtained generally, based upon the private property of the laborers in their means of production; in the country, the agriculture of the small peasant, free man, or serf; in the towns, the handicrafts organized in guilds. The instruments of labor—land, agricultural implements, the workshop, the tool—were the instruments of labor of single individuals, adapted for the use of one worker, and, therefore, of necessity, small, dwarfish, circumscribed. But for this very reason they belonged, as a rule, to the producer himself. To concentrate these scattered, limited means of production, to enlarge them, to turn them into the powerful levers of production of the present day—this was precisely the historic role of capitalist production and of its upholder, the bourgeoisie. In the fourth section of *Capital,* Marx has explained in detail how since the fifteenth century this has been historically worked out through the three phases of simple cooperation, manufacture, and modern industry. But the bourgeoisie, as is also shown there, could not transform these puny means of production into mighty productive forces without transforming them, at the same time, from means of production of the individual into *social* means of production workable only by a collectivity of men. The spinning wheel, the hand loom, the blacksmith's hammer were replaced by the spinning machine, the power loom, the steam hammer; the individual workshop, by the factory, implying the co-operation of hundreds and thousands of workmen. In like manner production itself changed from a series of individual into a series of social acts, and the products from individual to social products. The yarn, the cloth, the metal articles that now came out of the factory were the joint product of many workers, through whose hands they successively had to pass before they were ready. No one person could say of them: "I made that; this is *my* product."

But where, in a given society, the fundamental form of production is that spontaneous division of labor which creeps in gradually and not upon any preconceived plan, there the products take on the form of *commodities,* whose mutual exchange, buying and selling, enable the individual producers to satisfy their manifold wants. And this was the case in the Middle Ages. The peasant, e.g., sold to the artisan agricultural products and bought from him the products of handicraft. Into this society of individual producers, of commodity producers, the new mode of production thrust itself. In the midst of the old division of labor, grown up spontaneously and upon *no definite plan,* which had governed the whole of society, now arose division of labor upon a *definite plan,* as organized in the factory; side by side with *individual* production appeared *social* production. The products of both were sold in the same market, and, therefore, at prices at least approximately equal. But organization upon a definite plan was stronger than spontaneous division of labor. The factories working with the combined social forces of a collectivity of individuals produced their commodities far more cheaply than the individual small producers. Individual production succumbed in one department after another. Socialized production revolutionized all the old methods of production. But its revolutionary character was, at the same time, so little recognized that it was, on the contrary, introduced as a means of increasing and developing the production of commodities. When it arose it found ready-made, and made liberal use of, certain machinery for the production and exchange of commodities: merchants' capital, handicraft, wage labor. Socialized production thus introducing itself as a new form of the production of commodities, it was a matter of course that under it the old forms of appropriation remained in full swing and were applied to its products as well.

In the medieval stage of evolution of the production of commodities the question as to the owner of the product of labor could not arise. The individual producer, as a rule, had, from raw material belonging to himself and generally his own handiwork, produced it with his own tools, by the labor of his own hands or of his family. There was no need for him to appropriate the new product. It belonged wholly to him, as a matter of course. His property in the product was, therefore, based *upon his own labor.* Even where external help was used, this was, as a rule, of little importance, and very generally was compensated by something other than wages. The apprentices and journeymen of the guilds worked less for board and wages than for education, in order that they might become master craftsmen themselves.

Then came the concentration of the means of production and of the producers in large workshops and manufactories, their transformation into actual socialized means of production and socialized producers. But the socialized producers and means of production and their products was still treated, after this change, just as they had been before, i.e., as the means of production and the products of individuals. Hitherto the owner of the instruments of labor had himself appropriated the product because, as a rule, it was his own product and the assistance of others was the exception. Now the owner of the instruments of labor always appropriated to himself the product, although it was no longer his product, but exclusively the product of the *labor of others*. Thus the products now produced socially were not appropriated by those who had actually set in motion the means of production and actually produced the commodities, but by the *capitalists*. The means of production, and production itself, had become in essence socialized. But they were subjected to a form of appropriation which presupposes the private production of individuals, under which, therefore, everyone owns his own product and brings it to market. The mode of production is subjected to this form of appropriation, although it abolishes the conditions upon which the latter rests.[4]

This contradiction, which gives to the new mode of production its capitalistic character, *contains the germ of the whole of the social antagonisms of today*. The greater the mastery obtained by the new mode of production over all important fields of production and in all manufacturing countries, the more it reduced individual production to an insignificant residuum, *the more clearly was brought out the incompatibility of socialized production with capitalistic appropriation*.

The first capitalists found, as we have said, alongside of other forms of labor, wage labor ready-made for them on the market. But it was exceptional, complementary, accessory, transitory wage labor. The agricultural laborer, though upon occasion he hired himself out by the day, had a few acres of his own land on which he could at all events live in a pinch. The guilds were so organized that the journeyman of today became the master of tomorrow. But all this changed as soon as the means of production became socialized and concentrated in the hands of capitalists. The means of production, as well as the product, of the individual producer became more and more worthless; there is nothing left for him but to turn wage worker under the capitalist. Wage labor, aforetime the exception and accessory, now became the rule and basis of all production; aforetime complementary, it now became the sole remaining function of the worker. The wage worker for a time became a wage worker for life. The number of these permanent wage workers was further enormously increased by the breaking up of the feudal system that occurred at the same time, by the disbanding of the retainers of the feudal lords, the eviction of the peasants from their homesteads, etc. The separation was made complete between the means of production, concentrated in the hands of the capitalists, on the one side, and the producers, possessing nothing but their labor power, on the other. *The contradiction between socialized production and capitalistic appropriation manifested itself as the antagonism of proletariat and bourgeoisie.*

We have seen that the capitalistic mode of production thrust its way into a society of commodity producers, of individual producers, whose social bond was the exchange of their products. But every society based upon the production of commodities has this peculiarity: that the producers have lost control over their own social interrelations. Each man produces for himself with such means of production as he may happen to have, and for such exchange as he may require to satisfy his remaining wants. No one knows how much of his particular article is coming on the market, nor how much of it will be wanted. No one knows whether his individual product will meet an actual demand, whether he will be able to make good his costs of production or even to sell his commodity at all. Anarchy reigns in socialized production.

But the production of commodities, like every other form of production, has its peculiar, inherent laws inseparable from it; and these laws work, despite anarchy, in and through anarchy. They reveal themselves in the only persistent form of social interrelations, i.e., in exchange, and here they affect the individual producers as compulsory laws of competition. They are, at first, unknown to these producers themselves, and have to be discovered by them gradually and as the result of experience. They work themselves out, therefore, independently of the producers, and in antagonism to them, as inexorable natural laws of their particular form of production. The product governs the producers.

In medieval society, especially in the earlier centuries, production was essentially directed towards satisfying the wants of the individual. It satisfied, in the main, only the wants of the producer and his family. Where relations of personal dependence existed, as in the country, it also helped to satisfy the wants of the feudal lord. In all this there was, therefore, no exchange; the products, consequently, did not assume the character of commodities. The family of the peasant produced almost everything it wanted: clothes and furniture, as well as means of subsistence. Only when it began to produce more than was sufficient to supply its own wants and the payments in kind to the feudal lord, only than did it also produce commodities. This surplus, thrown into socialized exchange and offered for sale, became commodities.

The artisans of the towns, it is true, had from the first to produce for exchange. But they, also, themselves supplied the greatest part of their own individual wants. They had gardens and plots of land. They turned their cattle out into the communal forest, which, also, yielded them timber and firing. The women spun flax, wool, and so forth. Production for the purpose of exchange, production of commodities, was only in its infancy. Hence exchange was restricted, the market narrow, the methods of production stable; there was local exclusiveness without, local unity within; the mark in the country; in the town, the guild.

But with the extension of the production of commodities, and especially with the introduction of the capitalist mode of production, the laws of commodity production, hitherto latent, came into action more openly and with greater force. The old bonds were loosened, the old exclusive limits broken through, the producers were more and more turned into independent, isolated producers of commodities. It became apparent that the production of society at large was ruled by absence of plan, by accident, by anarchy; and this anarchy grew to greater and greater height. But the chief means by aid of which the capitalist mode of production intensified this anarchy of socialized production was the exact opposite of anarchy. It was the increasing organization of production, upon a social basis, in every individual productive establishment. By this the old, peaceful, stable condition of things was ended. Whatever this organization of production was introduced into a branch of industry, it brooked no other method of production by its side. The field of labor became a battleground. The great geographical discoveries, and the colonization following upon them, multiplied markets and quickened the transformation of handicraft into manufacture. The war did not break out simply between the individual producers of particular localities. The local struggles begot in their turn national conflicts, the commercial wars of the seventeenth and the eighteenth centuries.

Finally, modern industry and the opening of the world market made the struggle universal, and at the same time gave it an unheard-of virulence. Advantages in natural or artificial conditions of production now decide the existence or non existence of individual capitalists, as well as of whole industries and countries. He that falls is remorselessly cast aside. It is the Darwinian struggle of the individual for existence transferred from nature to society with intensified violence. The conditions of existence natural to the animal appear as the final term of human development. The contradiction between socialized production and capitalistic appropriation now presents itself as *an antagonism between the organization of production in the individual workshop and the anarchy of production in society generally*.

The capitalistic mode of production moves in these two forms of the antagonism immanent to it from its very origin. It is never able to get out of that "vicious circle" which Fourier had already discovered. What Fourier could not, indeed, see in his time is that this circle is gradually narrowing; that the movement becomes more and more a spiral, and must come to an end, like the movement of the planets, by collision with the center. It is the compelling force of anarchy in the production of society at large that more and more completely turns the great majority of men into proletarians, and it is the masses of the proletariat again who will finally put an end to anarchy in production. It is the compelling force of anarchy in social production that turns the limitless perfectibility of machinery under modern industry into a compulsory law by which every individual industrial capitalist must perfect his machinery more and more, under penalty of ruin.

But the perfecting of machinery is making human labor superfluous. If the introduction and increase of machinery means the displacement of millions of manual by a few machine workers, improvement in machinery means the displacement of more and more of the machine workers themselves. It means, in the last instance, the production of a number of available wage workers in excess of the average needs of capital, the formation of a complete industrial reserve army, as I called it in 1845,[5] available at the times when industry is working at high pressure, to be cast out upon the street when the inevitable crash comes, a constant dead weight upon the limbs of the working class in its struggle for existence with capital, a regulator for the keeping of wages down to the low level that suits the interests of capital. Thus it comes about, to quote Marx, that machinery becomes the most powerful weapon in the war of capital against the working class; that the instruments of labor constantly tear the means of subsistence out of the hands of the laborer; that the very product of the worker is turned into an instrument for his subjugation. Thus it comes about that the economizing of the instruments of labor becomes at the same time, from the outset, the most reckless waste of labor power, and robbery based upon the normal conditions under which labor functions; that machinery, "the most powerful instrument for shortening labor time, becomes the most unfailing means for placing every moment of the laborer's time and that of his family at the disposal of the capitalist for the purpose of expanding the value of his capital." (*Capital*, American edition, page 445.) Thus it comes about that the overwork of some becomes the preliminary condition for the idleness of others, and that modern industry, which hunts after new consumers over the whole world, forces the consumption of the masses at home down to a starvation minimum, and in doing thus destroys its own home market. "The law that always equilibrates the relative surplus population, or industrial reserve army, to the extent and energy of accumulation, this law rivets the laborer to capital more firmly than the wedges of Vulcan did Prometheus to the rock. It establishes an accumulation of misery corresponding with accumulation of capital. Accumulation of wealth at one pole is, therefore, at the same time accumulation of misery, agony of toil, slavery, ignorance, brutality, mental degradation at the opposite pole, i.e., on the side of the class that produces *its own product in the form of capital.*" (Marx's *Capital,* American edition, page 661.) And to expect any other division of the products from the capitalistic mode of production is the same as expecting the electrodes of a battery not to decompose acidulated water, not to liberate oxygen at the positive, hydrogen at the negative pole, so long as they are connected with the battery.

We have seen that the ever increasing perfectibility of modern machinery is, by the anarchy of social production, turned into a compulsory law that forces the individual industrial capitalist always to improve his machinery, always to increase its protective force. The bare possibility of extending the field of protection is transformed for him into a similar compulsory law. The enormous expansive force of modern industry, compared with which that of gases is mere child's play, appears to us now as a *necessity* for expansion, both qualitative and quantitative, that laughs at all resistance. Such resistance is offered by consumption, by sales, by the markets for the products of modern industry. But the capacity for expansion, extensive and intensive, of the markets is primarily governed by quite different laws that work much less energetically. The expansion of the markets can- not keep pace with the extension of production. The collision becomes inevitable, and as this cannot produce any real solution so long as it does not break into pieces the capital- ist mode of production, the collisions become periodic. Capitalist production has begot- ten another "vicious circle."

As a matter of fact, since 1825, when the first general crisis broke out, the whole industrial and commercial world, production and exchange among an civilized peoples and their more or less barbaric hangers-on, are thrown out of joint about once every ten years. Commerce is at a standstill, the markets are glutted, products accumulate, as mul- titudinous as they are unstable, hard cash disappears, credit vanishes, factories are closed, the mass of the workers are in want of the means of subsistence because they have pro- duced too much of the means of subsistence; bankruptcy follows upon bankruptcy, execu- tion upon execution. The stagnation lasts for years; productive forces and products are wasted and destroyed wholesale, until the accumulated mass of commodities finally filters off, more or less depreciated in value, until production and exchange gradually begin to move again. Little by little the pace quickens. It becomes a trot. The industrial trot breaks into a canter, the canter in turn grows into the headlong gallop of a perfect steeplechase of industry, commercial credit, and speculation, which finally, after breakneck leaps, ends where it began—in the ditch of a crisis. And so over and over again. We have now, since the year 1825, gone through this five times, and at the present moment (1877) we are going through it for the sixth time. And the character of these crises is so clearly defined that Fourier hit all of them off when he described the first as *"crise plethorique,"* a crisis from plethora.

In these crises the contradiction between socialized production and capitalist appropri- ation ends in a violent explosion. The circulation of commodities is, for the time being, stopped. Money, the means of circulation, becomes a hindrance to circulation. All the laws of production and circulation of commodities are turned upside down. The economic col- lision has reached its apogee. *The mode of production is in rebellion against the mode of exchange.*

The fact that the socialized organization of production within the factory has devel- oped so far that it has become incompatible with the anarchy of production in society, which exists side by side with and dominates it, is brought home to the capitalists them- selves by the violent concentration of capital that occurs during crises, through the ruin of many large, and a skill greater number of small, capitalists. The whole mechanism of the capitalist mode of production breaks down under the pressure of the productive forces, its own creations. It is no longer able to turn all this mass of means of production into capital. They lie fallow, and for that very reason the industrial reserve army must also lie fallow. Means of production, means of subsistence, available laborers, all the elements of production and of general wealth, are present in abundance. But "abundance becomes the source of distress and want" (Fourier), because it is the very thing that prevents the trans- formation of the means of production and subsistence into capital. For in capitalistic soci- ety the means of production can function only when they have undergone a preliminary transformation into capital, into the means of exploiting human labor power. The neces- sity of this transformation into capital of the means of production and subsistence stands like a ghost between these and the workers. It alone prevents the coming together of the material and personal levers of production; it alone forbids the means of production to function, the workers to work and live. On the one hand, therefore, the capitalistic mode of production stands convicted of its own incapacity to further direct these productive forces. On the other, these productive forces themselves, with increasing energy, press forward to the removal of the existing contradiction, to the abolition of their quality as capital, to the *practical recognition of their character as social productive forces.*

This rebellion of the productive forces, as they grow more and more powerful, against their quality as capital, this stronger and stronger command that their social character shall be recognized, forces the capitalist class itself to treat them more and more as social productive forces, so far as this is possible under capitalist conditions. The period of industrial high pressure, with its unbounded inflation of credit, not less than the crash itself, by the collapse of great capitalist establishments, tends to bring about that form of the socialization of great masses of means of production which we meet with in the different kinds of joint-stock companies. Many of these means of production and of distribution are, from the outset, so colossal that, like the railways, they exclude all other forms of capitalistic exploitation. At a further stage of evolution this form also becomes insufficient. The producers on a large scale in a particular branch of industry in a particular country unite in a "trust," a union for the purpose of regulating production. They determine the total amount to be produced, parcel it out among themselves, and thus enforce the selling price fixed beforehand. But trusts of this kind, as soon as business becomes bad, are generally liable to break up, and on this very account compel a yet greater concentration of association. The whole of the particular industry is turned into one gigantic joint-stock company; internal competition gives place to the internal monopoly of this one company. This has happened in 1890 with the English *alkali* production, which is now, after the fusion of forty-eight large works, in the hands of one company, conducted upon a single plan and with a capital of six million pounds.

In the trusts freedom of competition changes into its very opposite—into monopoly; and the production without any definite plan of capitalistic society capitulates to the production upon a definite plan of the invading socialistic society. Certainly this is so far still to the benefit and advantage of the capitalists. But in this case the exploitation is so palpable that it must break down. No nation will put up with production conducted by trusts, with so barefaced an exploitation of the community by a small band of dividend-mongers.

In any case, with trusts or without, the official representative of capitalist society—the state—will, ultimately have to undertake the direction of production. This necessity for conversion into state property is felt first in the great institutions for intercourse and communication—the post office, the telegraphs, the railways.

If the crises demonstrate the incapacity of the bourgeoisie for managing any longer modern productive forces, the transformation of the great establishments for production and distribution into joint-stock companies, trusts, and state property show how unnecessary the bourgeoisie are for that purpose. All the social functions of the capitalist are now performed by salaried employees. The capitalist has no further social function than that of pocketing dividends, tearing off coupons, and gambling on the stock exchange, where the different capitalists despoil one another of their capital. At first the capitalistic mode of production forces out the workers. Now it forces out the capitalists, and reduces them, just as it reduced the workers, to the ranks of the surplus population, although not immediately into those of the industrial reserve army.

But the transformation either into joint-stock companies and trusts or into state ownership, does not do away with the capitalistic nature of the productive forces. In the joint-stock companies and trusts this is obvious. And the modern state, again, is only the organization that bourgeois society takes on in order to support the external conditions of the capitalist mode of production against the encroachments as well of the workers as of individual capitalists. The modern state, no matter what its form, is essentially a capitalist machine, the state of the capitalists, the ideal personification of the total national capital. The more it proceeds to the taking over of productive forces, the more does it actually become the national capitalist, the more citizens does it exploit. The workers remain wage workers—proletarians. The capitalist relation is not done away with. It is rather brought to a head. But, brought to a head, it topples over. State ownership of the productive forces is not the solution of the conflict, but concealed within it are the technical conditions that form the elements of that solution.

This solution can consist only in the practical recognition of the social nature of the modern forces of production, and therefore in the harmonizing of the modes of production, appropriation, and exchange with the socialized character of the means of production. And this can come about only by society openly and directly taking possession of the productive forces which have outgrown all control except that of society as a whole. The social character of the means of production and of the products today reacts against the producers, periodically disrupts all production and exchange, acts only like a law of nature working blindly, forcibly, destructively. But with the taking over by society of the productive forces, the social character of the means of production and of the products will be utilized by the producers with a perfect understanding of its nature, and instead of being a source of disturbance and periodic collapse will become the most powerful lever of production itself.

Active social forces work exactly like natural forces: blindly, forcibly, destructively, so long as we do not understand, and reckon with, them. But when once we understand them, when once we grasp their action, their direction, their effects, it depends only upon ourselves to subject them more and more to our own will, and by means of them to reach our own ends. And this holds quite especially of the mighty productive forces of today. As long as we obstinately refuse to understand the nature and the character of these social means of action—and this understanding goes against the grain of the capitalist mode of production and its defenders—so long as these forces are at work in spite of us, in opposition to us, so long do they master us, as we have shown above in detail.

But when once their nature is understood, they can, in the hands of the producers working together, be transformed from master demons into willing servants. The difference is as that between the destructive force of electricity in the lightning of the storm and electricity under command in the telegraph and the voltaic arc, the difference between a conflagration and fire working in the service of man. With this recognition, at last, of the real nature of the productive forces of today, the social anarchy of production gives place to a social regulation of production upon a definite plan, according to the needs of the community and of each individual. Then the capitalist mode of appropriation, in which the product enslaves first the producer and then the appropriator, is replaced by the mode of appropriation of the products that is based upon the nature of the modern means of production: upon the one hand, direct social appropriation as means to the maintenance and extension of production; on the other, direct individual appropriation as means of subsistence and of enjoyment.

While the capitalist mode of production more and more completely transforms the great majority of the population into proletarians, it creates the power which, under penalty of its own destruction, is forced to accomplish this revolution. While it forces on more and more the transformation of the vast means of production, already socialized, into state property, it shows itself the way to accomplishing this revolution. *The proletariat seizes political power and turns the means of production into state property.*

But in doing this it abolishes itself as proletariat, abolishes all class distinctions and class antagonisms, abolishes also the state as state. Society thus far, based upon class antagonisms, has had need of the state. That is, of an organization of the particular class which

was *pro tempore* the exploiting class, an organization for the purpose of preventing any interference from without with the existing conditions of production, and, therefore, especially
for the purpose of forcibly keeping the exploited classes in the condition of oppression corresponding with the given mode of production (slavery, serfdom, wage labor). The state
was the official representative of society as a whole; the gathering of it together into a visible embodiment. But it was this only in so far as it was the state of that class which itself
represented, for the time being, society as a whole: in ancient times, the state of slave-own-
ing citizens; in the Middle Ages, the feudal lords; in our own time, the bourgeoisie. When
at last it becomes the real representative of the whole of society it renders itself unnecessary. As soon as there is no longer any social class to be held in subjection, as soon as class
rule and the individual struggle for existence based upon our present anarchy in production, with the collisions and excesses arising from these, are removed, nothing more
remains to be repressed, and a special repressive force, a state, is no longer necessary. The
first act by virtue of which the state really constitutes itself the representative of the whole
of society—the taking possession of the means of production in the name of society—this
is, at the same time, its last independent act as a state. State interference in social relations
becomes, in one domain after another, superfluous, and then dies out of itself; the government of persons is replaced by the administration of things, and by the conduct of processes
of production. The state is not "abolished." *It dies out.* This gives the measure of the value
of the phrase *"a free state,"* both as to its justifiable use at times by agitators and as to its
ultimate scientific insufficiency, and also of the demands of the so-called anarchists for the
abolition of the state out of hand.

Since the historical appearance of the capitalist production, the appropriation by society
of all the means of production has often been dreamed of, more or less vaguely, by individuals as well as by sects, as the ideal of the future. But it could become possible, could
become a historical necessity, only when the actual conditions for its realization were there.
Like every other social advance, it becomes practicable not by men understanding that the
existence of classes is in contradiction to justice, equality, etc., not by the mere willingness
to abolish these classes, but by virtue of certain new economic conditions. The separation
of society into an exploiting and an exploited class, a ruling and an oppressed class, was the
necessary consequence of the deficient and restricted development of production in former
times. So long as the total social labor yields only a produce which but slightly exceeds that
barely necessary for the existence of all; so long, therefore, as labor engages all or almost all
the time of the great majority of the members of society—so long, of necessity, this society
is divided into classes. Side by side with the great majority, exclusively bond slaves to labor,
arises a class freed from directly productive labor, which looks after the general affairs of
society: the direction of labor, state business, law, science, art, etc. It is, therefore, the law
of division of labor that lies at the basis of the division into classes. But this does not prevent this division into classes from being carried out by means of violence and robbery,
trickery and fraud. It does not prevent the ruling class, once having the upper hand, from
consolidating its power at the expense of the working class, from turning its social leadership into an intensified exploitation of the masses.

But if, upon this showing, division into classes has a certain historical justification, it
has this only for a given period, only under given social conditions. It was based upon the
insufficiency of production. It will be swept away by the complete development of modern productive forces. And, in fact, the abolition of classes in society presupposes a degree
of historical evolution at which the existence not simply of this—or that particular ruling
class, but of any ruling class at all, and, therefore, the existence of class distinction itself,
has become an anachronism. It presupposes, therefore, the development of production

carried out to a degree at which appropriation of the means of production and of the products, and, with this, of political domination, of the monopoly of culture, and of intellectual leadership by a particular class of society, has become not only superfluous but economically, politically, intellectually a hindrance to development.

This point is now reached. Their political and intellectual bankruptcy is scarcely any longer a secret to the bourgeoisie themselves. Their economic bankruptcy recurs regularly every ten years. In every crisis society is suffocated beneath the weight of its own productive forces and products, which it cannot use, and stands helpless, face to face with the absurd contradiction that the producers have nothing to consume because consumers are wanting. The expansive force of the means of production bursts the bonds that the capitalist mode of production imposed upon them. Their deliverance from these bonds is the one pre-condition for an unbroken, constantly accelerated development of the productive forces, and therewith for a practically unlimited increase of production itself. Nor is this all. The socialized appropriation of the means of production does away not only with the present artificial restrictions upon production, but also with the positive waste and devastation of productive forces and products that are at the present time the inevitable concomitants of production, and that reach their height in the crises. Further, it sets free for the community at large a mass of means of production and of products by doing away with the senseless extravagance of the ruling classes of today and their political representatives. The possibility of securing for every member of society, by means of socialized production, an existence not only fully sufficient materially, and becoming day by day fuller, but an existence guaranteeing to all the free development and exercise of their physical and mental faculties—this possibility is now for the first time here, but *it is here*.

With the seizing of the means of production by society, production of commodities is done away with, and, simultaneously, the mastery of the product over the producer. Anarchy in social production is replaced by systematic, definite organization. The struggle for individual existence disappears. Then for the first time man, in a certain sense, is finally marked off from the rest of the animal kingdom and emerges from mere animal conditions of existence into really human ones. The whole sphere of the conditions of life which environ man, and which have hitherto ruled man, now comes under the dominion and control of man, who for the first time becomes the real, conscious lord of nature because he has now become master of his own social organization. The laws of his own social action, hitherto standing face to face with man as laws of nature foreign to and dominating him, will now be used with full understanding, and so mastered by him. Man's own social organization, hitherto confronting him as a necessity imposed by nature and history, now becomes the result of his own free action. The extraneous objective forces that have hitherto governed history pass under the control of man himself. Only from that time will man himself, more and more consciously, make his own history— only from that time will the social causes set in movement by him have, in the main and in a constantly growing measure, the results intended by him. It is the ascent of man from the kingdom of necessity to the kingdom of freedom.

Let us briefly sum up our sketch of historical evolution.

I. Medieval Society—Individual production on a small scale. Means of production adapted for individual use; hence primitive, ungainly, petty, dwarfed in action. Production for immediate consumption, either of the producer himself or of his feudal lord. Only where an excess of production over this consumption occurs is such excess offered for sale, enters into exchange. Production of commodities, therefore, only in its infancy. But already it contains within itself, in embryo, *anarchy in the production of society at large*.

II. Capitalist Revolution—Transformation of industry, at first by means of simple co-operation and manufacture. Concentration of the means of production, hitherto scattered, into great workshops. As a consequence their transformation from individual to social means of production—a transformation which does not, on the whole, affect the form of exchange. The old forms of appropriation remain in force. The capitalist appears. In his capacity as owner of the means of production he also appropriates the products and turns them into commodities. Production has become a *social* act. Exchange and appropriation continue to be *individual* acts, the acts of individuals. *The social product is appropriated by the individual capitalist.* Fundamental contradiction, whence arise all the contradictions in which our present-day society moves, and which modern industry brings to light.

A. Severance of the producer from the means of production. Condemnation of the worker to wage labor for life. *Antagonism between the proletariat and the bourgeoisie.*

B. Growing predominance and increasing effectiveness of the laws governing the production of commodities. Unbridled competition. *Contradiction between socialized organization in the individual factory and social anarchy in production as a whole.*

C. On the one hand, perfecting of machinery, made by competition compulsory for each individual manufacturer, and complemented by a constantly growing displacement of laborers. *Industrial reserve army.* On the other hand, unlimited extension of production, also compulsory under competition, for every manufacturer. On both sides, unheard-of development of productive forces, excess of supply and demand, overproduction, glutting of the markets, crises every ten years, the vicious circle: excess here of means of production and products—excess there of laborers, without employment and without means of existence. But these two levers of production and of social well-being are unable to work together because the capitalist form of production prevents the productive forces from working and the products from circulating, unless they are first turned into capital—which their very superabundance prevents. The contradiction has grown into an absurdity. *The mode of production rises in rebellion against the form of exchange.* The bourgeoisie are convicted of incapacity further to manage their own social productive forces.

D. Partial recognition of the social character of the productive forces forced upon the capitalists themselves. Taking over of the great institutions for production and communication, first by joint-stock companies, later on by trusts, then by the state. The bourgeoisie demonstrated to be a superfluous class. All its social functions are now performed by salaried employees.

III. Proletarian Revolution—Solution of the contradictions. The proletariat seizes the public power, and by means of this transforms the socialized means of production, slipping from the hands of the bourgeoisie, into public property. By this act the proletariat frees the means of production from the character of capital they have thus far borne and gives their socialized character complete freedom to work itself out. Socialized production upon a predetermined plan becomes henceforth possible. The development of production makes the existence of different classes of society thenceforth an anachronism. In proportion as anarchy in social production vanishes, the political authority of the state dies out. Man, at last the master of his own form of social organization, becomes at the same time the lord over nature, his own master—free.

To accomplish this act of universal emancipation is the historical mission of the modern proletariat. To thoroughly comprehend the historical conditions and thus the very nature of this act, to impart to the now oppressed proletarian class a full knowledge of the conditions and of the meaning of the momentous act it is called upon to accomplish, this is the task of the theoretical expression of the proletarian movement, scientific socialism.

Notes

1. This is the passage on the French Revolution: "Thought, the concept of law, all at once made itself felt, and against this the old scaffolding of wrong could make no stand. In this conception of law, therefore, a constitution has now been established, and henceforth everything must be based upon this. Since the sun had been in the firmament, and the planets circled round him, the sight had never been seen of man standing upon his head—i.e., on the Idea—and building reality after this image. Anaxagoras first said that the nous, reason, rules the world; but now, for the first time, had man come to recognize that the Idea must rule the mental reality. And this was a magnificent sunrise. All thinking beings have participated in celebrating this holy day. A sublime emotion swayed men at that time, an enthusiasm of reason pervaded the world, as if now had come the reconciliation of the Divine Principle with the world." Is it not high time to set the anti-socialist law in action against such teachings, subversive and to the common danger, by the late Professor Hegel?
2. From *The Revolution in Mind and Practice*, p. 21, a memorial addressed to all the "red Republicans, Communists and Socialists of Europe," and sent to the provisional government of France, 1848, and also "to Queen Victoria and her responsible advisers."
3. *Ibid.* p. 22.
4. It is hardly necessary in this connection to point out that, even if the form of appropriation remains the same, the *character* of the appropriation is just as much revolutionized as production is by the changes described above. It is, of course, a very different matter whether I appropriate to myself my own product or that of another. Note in passing that wage labor, which contains the whole capitalistic mode of production in embryo, is very ancient; in a sporadic, scattered form it existed for centuries alongside of slave labor. But the embryo could duly develop into the capitalistic mode of production only when the necessary historical preconditions had been furnished.
5. *The Condition of the Working Class in England.*

JOHN STUART MILL

John Stuart Mill (1806–1873) was born in London and educated privately by his father, James Mill, a utilitarian, a friend and follower of Jeremy Bentham, and a considerable political thinker in his own right.

The story of Mill's peculiar education is notorious, largely through his own account of it in the *Autobiography* published shortly after his death. Under Bentham's guidance and (as the boy grew older) in the company of such distinguished thinkers as the economist David Ricardo and the jurist John Austin, Mill senior set out to cultivate in his son the perfect Utilitarian mind—an intellect equipped with the material and analytical skills that would enable it to focus without distraction on the Benthamite political agenda.

"Without distraction" turned out to mean without the benefit of any religion, art, poetry, or philosophy (besides the basic empiricism that Bentham's system required or presupposed), or more generally without any sense of the proper place the emotions should occupy in a healthy view of the world. These deficiencies surfaced in a mental crisis that beset the young man in 1826 to 1827, and Mill's realization that they *were* deficiencies meant that his own outlook and (because of the eventual importance of his work) utilitarian philosophy were never the same again. The young man who had worked so assiduously for social improvement—who among other things had been arrested in 1823 for distributing leaflets about birth control in London—became convinced that a Benthamite calculus of cost and benefit, pain and pleasure, was too crude to be deployed as a tool of social change. In its place, Mill sought to reconstruct utilitarianism, so that it incorporated elements of Romantic thought and embodied a sense that while happiness in general was good, certain experiences and enjoyments were qualitatively, not just quantitatively, better than others.

The distinction between the "higher" and "lower" pleasures elaborated in Mill's book, *Utilitarianism* (1861)—"Better to be a human being dissatisfied than a pig satisfied"—can easily be made to sound elitist, or indulgently aestheticist. Three points are worth bearing in mind in assessing its influence in Mill's political theory. First, the higher pleasures were not understood as languid or effete enjoyments. What counted most for Mill was the cultivation and employment of our *active* faculties: our curiosity, our questioning, and our ability to make something of our lives and of the world we experience. Second, Mill was convinced—rightly or wrongly—that true happiness, even on his elevated definition, was not just the birthright of the few. Mill was an optimist: He believed that a life "of few and transitory pains, many and various pleasures, with a decided predominance of the active over the passive," was already the lot of many and that "the present wretched education, and wretched social arrangements, are the only real hindrance to its being available to all."

And so—thirdly—though he repudiated Bentham's psychology and theory of value, Mill never abandoned his commitment to forward-looking social reform in a broadly utilitarian spirit. On the contrary, the three works excerpted here represent a sustained effort to alter the "wretched social arrangements"—such as the subordination of women, the tyranny of mass culture, and the exclusion of the great majority of working people from participation in politics—which stood in the way of human happiness.

In each of these instances, a case was made by supporters of the status quo that people were often better off submitting to others' ideas of how to live their lives or letting others look after their interests. In each case, Mill responded: "What sort of human beings can be formed under such a regimen? What development can either their thinking or their active faculties attain under it?" And in each case he did his best, through his writings, to swing the spirit of reform in England away from paternalism and towards the cultivation of freedom and individuality of which he thought all men and women were capable. As he said at the beginning of *On Liberty*, he continued to "regard utility as the ultimate appeal on all ethical questions"—he remained Benthamite enough not to be interested in abstract theories of natural right—but it must, he said, be "utility in the largest sense, grounded on the permanent interests of man as a progressive being."

Thus, after his mental crisis, Mill did not retreat,—under the influence of Schiller or Coleridge, into the indulgent life of a Victorian romantic, concerned only to protect beauty and feeling from the ravages of Gradgrind utilitarianism. His whole career was one of public service, whether in the pages of the *London and Westminster Review*, which he founded in 1836 along with other young Benthamite radicals, or in the offices of the East India Company, where he worked from 1823 to 1858, or in Parliament where he served one term as M.P. for Westminster in the mid-1860s.

His political career in and out of Parliament was notable for his principled stands in favor of the rights of workers, the rights of political prisoners, and the rights of colonial peoples to a just and decent administration, stands that made him, in Isaiah Berlin's words, "the most passionate and best-known champion of the insulted and the oppressed" of his day. In 1862, he published an article entitled "The Contest in America" in which he attempted to influence public opinion in Britain against the Southern states and to impress on them that the issue was slavery, not just the right to secession—by no means an easy task even in the liberal circles in which he moved. In the House of Commons, Mill spoke against capital punishment and against the suspension of habeas corpus in Ireland, and in favor of proportional representation, municipal reform, and women's suffrage.

In particular, his position on women's rights is a striking exception to the casual indifference of most liberal philosophers to the issue. It is explained in part by his association from 1830 with Harriet Taylor, a woman he described in the dedication to *On Liberty* as "the inspirer, and in part the author of all that is best in my writings." But though *The Subjection of Women* was written and published after her death in 1858, there is no reason to doubt the assertion in the opening lines of that tract that opposition to "the legal subordination of one sex to the other" was an opinion he had held from the earliest period of his moral and political thinking.

Harriet Taylor's influence is discernible in other areas of Mill's writing. There is no doubt that he was more favorably inclined to socialism than he would have been without her presence (though he believed that in an ideal world, capitalist arrangements were better, provided something could be done to mitigate the sources of inherited inequality). There is no doubt, either, that Mill's experience of an open and committed friendship with a married woman—for the two were wed only after the death of Harriet Taylor's husband in 1849—laid an important experiential foundation for the loathing of the repressive, moralistic, and, as Isaiah Berlin put it, "uniformitarian despotism" of contemporary public opinion expressed in *On Liberty*.

The works represented here—*On Liberty*, the *Considerations on Representative Government*, and *The Subjection of Women*, along with his essay in moral philosophy, *Utilitarianism*—were all composed during a period of Mill's life (1854–1861) in which, as John Gray has pointed out, he thought that his life might be short, following a grave illness, and that he should say what he had to say on the issues he judged central in his time. But Mill's earlier writings are important too. *A System of Logic* (1843) and *Principles of Political Economy* (1848) quickly became standard texts in their respective subjects, and the essays collected in Mill's *Dissertations and Discussions*, including a long review of Alexis de Tocqueville's *Democracy in America*, add a dimension of sociological and cultural insight that often eludes those who confine themselves to his better-known works. In particular, the affinity with de Tocqueville helps us understand that Mill's primary concerns in *On Liberty* are to do with social not just legal repression, and with the threat to individuality from mass society even more than majoritarian legislation.

There is an immense and growing literature on Mill's moral and political theory. Isaiah Berlin's essay, "John Stuart Mill and the Ends of Life," in his collection *Four Essays on Liberty* (Oxford: Oxford University Press, 1969), is an excellent starting point, while Alan Ryan's book, *The Philosophy of John Stuart Mill* (London: Macmillan, 1970), provides an authoritative overview of Mill's arguments. Much of the modern literature focuses on the essay *On Liberty*. Two good book-length studies are C. L. Ten, *Mill on Liberty* (Oxford: Clarendon Press, 1980), and John Gray, *Mill on Liberty—A Defence* (London: Routledge, 1983)—the latter arguing for the consistency of *On Liberty* and *Utilitarianism*. P. Radcliff has put together a useful collection of articles in *Limits of Liberty: Studies of Mill's On Liberty* (Belmont, CA: Wadsworth, 1966). D. F. Thompson, *John Stuart Mill and Representative Government* (Princeton: Princeton University Press, 1976), is a useful study of Mill's democratic theory, and there is a fine discussion of Mill's feminism in Susan Moller Okin, *Women in Western Political Thought* (Princeton: Princeton University Press, 1979).

J. W.

ON LIBERTY

The grand, leading principle, towards which every argument unfolded in these pages directly converges, is the absolute and essential importance of human development in its richest diversity.—Wilhelm von Humboldt: *Sphere and Duties of Government*.

To the beloved and deplored memory of her who was the inspirer, and in part the author, of all that is best in my writings—the friend and wife whose exalted sense of truth and right was my strongest incitement, and whose approbation was my chief reward—I dedicate this volume. Like all that I have written for many years, it belongs as much to her as to me; but the work as it stands has had, in a very insufficient degree, the inestimable advantage of her revision; some of the most important portions having been reserved for a more careful re-examination, which they are now never destined to receive. Were I but capable of interpreting to the world one half the great thoughts and noble feelings which are buried in her grave, I should be the medium of a greater benefit to it, than is ever likely to arise from anything that I can write, unprompted and unassisted by her all but unrivaled wisdom.

CHAPTER I

Introductory

The subject of this essay is not the so-called "liberty of the will," so unfortunately opposed to the misnamed doctrine of philosophical necessity; but civil, or social liberty: the nature and limits of the power which can be legitimately exercised by society over the individual. A question seldom stated, and hardly ever discussed in general terms, but which profoundly influences the practical controversies of the age by its latent presence, and is likely soon to make itself recognized as the vital question of the future. It is so far from being new that, in a certain sense, it has divided mankind almost from the remotest ages; but in the stage of progress into which the more civilized portions of the species have now entered, it presents itself under new conditions and requires a different and more fundamental treatment.

The struggle between liberty and authority is the most conspicuous feature in the portions of history with which we are earliest familiar, particularly in that of Greece, Rome, and England. But in old times this contest was between subjects, or some classes of subjects, and the government. By liberty was meant protection against the tyranny of the political rulers. The rulers were conceived (except in some of the popular governments of Greece) as in a necessarily antagonistic position to the people whom they ruled. They consisted of a governing One, or a governing tribe or caste, who derived their authority from inheritance or conquest, who, at all events, did not hold it at the pleasure of the governed, and whose supremacy men did not venture, perhaps did not desire, to contest, whatever precautions might be taken against its oppressive exercise. Their power was regarded as necessary, but also as highly dangerous; as a weapon which they would attempt to use against their subjects, no less than against external enemies. To prevent the weaker members of the community from being preyed upon by innumerable vultures, it was needful that there should be an animal of prey stronger than the rest, commissioned to keep them down. But as the king of the vultures would be no less bent upon preying on the flock than any of the minor harpies, it was indispensable to be in a perpetual attitude of defense against his beak and claws. The aim, therefore, of patriots was to set limits to the power which the ruler should be suffered to exercise over the community; and this limitation was what they meant by liberty. It was attempted in two ways. First, by obtaining a recognition of certain immunities, called political liberties or rights, which it was to be regarded as a breach of duty in the ruler to infringe, and which if he did infringe, specific resistance or general rebellion was held to be justifiable. A second, and generally a later, expedient was the establishment of constitutional checks by which the consent of the community, or of a body of some sort, supposed to represent its interests, was made a necessary condition to some of the more important acts of the governing power. To the first of these modes of limitation, the ruling power, in most European countries, was compelled, more or less, to submit. It was not so with the second; and, to attain this, or, when already in some degree possessed, to attain it more completely, became everywhere the principal object of the lovers of liberty. And so long as mankind were content to combat one enemy by another, and to be ruled by a master on condition of being guaranteed more or less efficaciously against his tyranny, they did not carry their aspirations beyond this point.

A time, however, came, in the progress of human affairs, when men ceased to think it a necessity of nature that their governors should be an independent power opposed in interest to themselves. It appeared to them much better that the various magistrates of the state should be their tenants or delegates, revocable at their pleasure. In that way alone, it seemed, could they have complete security that the powers of government would never be abused to their disadvantage. By degrees this new demand for elective and temporary rulers became the prominent object of the exertions of the popular party wherever any such party existed, and superseded, to a considerable extent, the previous efforts to limit the power of rulers. As the struggle proceeded for making the ruling power emanate from the periodical choice of the ruled, some persons began to think that too much importance had been attached to the limitation of the power itself. *That* (it might seem) was a resource against rulers whose interests were habitually opposed to those of the people. What was now wanted was that the rulers should be identified with the people, that their interest and will should be the interest and will of the nation. The nation did not need to be protected against its own will. There was no fear of its tyrannizing over itself. Let the rulers be effectually responsible to it, promptly removable by it, and it could afford to trust them with power of which it could itself dictate the use to be made. Their power was but the nation's own power, concentrated and in a form convenient for exercise. This mode of thought, or rather perhaps of feeling, was common among the last generation of European liberalism, in the Continental section of which it still apparently predominates. Those who admit any limit to what a government may do, except in the case of such governments as they think ought not to exist, stand out as brilliant exceptions among the political thinkers of the Continent. A similar tone of sentiment might by this time have been prevalent in our country if the circumstances which for a time encouraged it had continued unaltered.

But, in political and philosophical theories as well as in persons, success discloses faults and infirmities which failure might have concealed from observation. The notion that the people have no need to limit their power over themselves might seem axiomatic, when popular government was a thing only dreamed about, or read of as having existed at some distant period of the past. Neither was that notion necessarily disturbed by such temporary aberrations as those of the French Revolution, the worst of which were the work of a usurping few, and which, in any case, belonged, not to the permanent working of popular institutions, but to a sudden and convulsive outbreak against monarchical and aristocratic despotism. In time, however, a democratic republic came to occupy a large portion of the earth's surface and made itself felt as one of the most powerful members of the community of nations, and elective and responsible government became subject to the observations and criticisms which wait upon a great existing fact. It was now perceived that such phrases as "self-government," and "the power of the people over themselves," do not express the true state of the case. The "people" who exercise the power are not always the same people with those over whom it is exercised; and the "self-government" spoken of is not the government of each by himself, but of each by all the rest. The will of the people, moreover, practically means the will of the most numerous or the most active *part* of the people—the majority, or those who succeed in making themselves accepted as the majority; the people, consequently, *may* desire to oppress a part of their number, and precautions are as much needed against this as against any other abuse of power. The limitation, therefore, of the power of government over individuals loses none of its importance when the holders of power are regularly accountable to the community, that is, to the strongest party therein. This view of things, recommending itself equally to the intelligence of thinkers and to the inclination of those important classes in European society to whose real or supposed interests democracy is adverse, has had no difficulty in establishing itself; and in political speculations "the tyranny of the majority" is now generally included among the evils against which society requires to be on its guard.

Like other tyrannies, the tyranny of the majority was at first, and is still vulgarly, held in dread, chiefly as operating through the acts of the public authorities. But reflecting persons perceived that when society is itself the tyrant—society collectively over the separate individuals who compose it—its means of tyrannizing are not restricted to the acts which it may do by the hands of its political functionaries. Society can and does execute its own mandates; and if it issues wrong mandates instead of right, or any mandates at all in things with which it ought not to meddle, it practices a social tyranny more formidable—than many kinds of political oppression, since, though not usually upheld by such extreme penalties, it leaves fewer means of escape, penetrating much more deeply into the details of life, and enslaving the soul itself. Protection, therefore, against the tyranny of the magistrate is not enough; there needs protection also against the tyranny of the prevailing opinion and feeling, against the tendency of society to impose, by other means than civil penalties, its own ideas and practices as rules of conduct on those who dissent from them; to fetter the development and, if possible, prevent the formation of any individuality not in harmony with its ways, and compel all characters to fashion themselves upon the model of its own. There is a limit to the legitimate interference of collective opinion with individual independence; and to find that limit, and maintain it against encroachment, is as indispensable to a good condition of human affairs as protection against political despotism.

But though this proposition is not likely to be contested in general terms, the practical question where to place the limit—how to make the fitting adjustment between individual independence and social control—is a subject on which nearly everything remains to be done. All that makes existence valuable to anyone depends on the enforcement of restraints upon the actions of other people. Some rules of conduct, therefore, must be imposed—by law in the first place, and by opinion on many things which are not fit subjects for the operation of law. What these rules should be is the principal question in human affairs; but if we except a few of the most obvious cases, it is one of those which least progress has been made in resolving. No two ages, and scarcely any two countries, have decided it alike; and the decision of one age or country is a wonder to another. Yet the people of any given age and country no more suspect any difficulty in it than if it were a subject on which mankind had always been agreed. The rules which obtain among themselves appear to them self-evident and self-justifying. This all but universal illusion is one of the examples of the magical influence of custom, which is not only, as the proverb says, a second nature but is continually mistaken for the first. The effect of custom, in preventing any misgiving respecting the rules of conduct which mankind impose on one another, is all the more complete because the subject is one on which it is not generally considered necessary that reasons should be given, either by one person to others or by each to himself. People are accustomed to believe, and have been encouraged in the belief by some who aspire to the character of philosophers, that their feelings on subjects of this nature are better than reasons and render reasons unnecessary. The practical principle which guides them to their opinions on the regulation of human conduct is the feeling in each person's mind that everybody should be required to act as he, and those with whom he sympathizes, would like them to act. No one, indeed, acknowledges to himself that his standard of judgment is his own liking; but an opinion on a point of conduct, not supported by reasons, can only count as one person's preference; and if the reasons, when given, are a mere appeal to a similar preference felt by other people, it is still only many people's liking instead of one. To an ordinary man, however, his own preference, thus supported, is not only a perfectly satisfactory reason but the only one he generally has for any of his notions of morality, taste, or propriety, which are not expressly written in his religious creed, and his chief guide in the interpretation even of that. Men's opinions, accordingly, on what is laudable or blamable are affected by all the multifarious causes which influence their wishes in regard to the conduct of others, and which are as numerous as those which determine their wishes on any other subject. Sometimes their reason; at other times their prejudices or superstitions; often their social affections, not seldom their antisocial ones, their envy or jealousy, their arrogance or contemptuousness; but most commonly their desires or fear for themselves—their legitimate or illegitimate self-interest. Wherever there is an ascendant class, a large portion of the morality of the country emanates from its class interests and its feelings of class superiority. The morality between Spartans and Helots, between planters and Negroes, between princes and subjects, between nobles and roturiers, between men and women has been for the most part the creation of these class interests and feelings; and the sentiments thus generated react in turn upon the moral feelings of the members of the ascendant class, in their relations among themselves. Where, on the other hand, a class, formerly ascendant, has lost its ascendancy, or where its ascendancy is unpopular, the prevailing moral sentiments frequently bear the impress of an impatient dislike of superiority. Another grand determining principle of the rules of conduct, both in act and forbearance, which have been enforced by law or opinion, has been the servility of mankind toward the supposed preferences or aversions of their temporal masters or of their gods. This servility, though essentially selfish, is not hypocrisy; it gives rise to perfectly genuine sentiments of abhorrence; it made men burn magicians and heretics. Among so many baser influences, the general and obvious interests of society have, of course, had a share, and a large one, in the direction of the moral sentiments; less, however, as a matter of reason, and on their own account, than as a consequence of the sympathies and antipathies which grew out of them; and sympathies and antipathies which had little or nothing to do with the interests of society have made themselves felt in the establishment of moralities with quite as great force.

The likings and dislikings of society, or of some powerful portion of it, are thus the main thing which has practically determined the rules laid down for general observance, under the penalties of law or opinion. And in general, those who have been in advance of society in thought and feeling have left this condition of things unassailed in principle, however they may have come into conflict with it in some of its details. They have occupied themselves rather in inquiring what things society ought to like or dislike than in questioning whether its likings or dislikings should be a law to individuals. They preferred endeavoring to alter the feelings of mankind on the particular points on which they were themselves heretical rather than make common cause in defense of freedom with heretics generally. The only case in which the higher ground has been taken on principle and maintained with consistency, by any but an individual here and there, is that of religious belief: a case instructive in many ways, and not least so as forming a most striking instance of the fallibility of what is called the moral sense; for the *odium theologicum,* in a sincere bigot, is one of the most unequivocal cases of moral feeling. Those who first broke the yoke of what called itself the Universal Church were in general as little willing to permit difference of religious opinion as that church itself. But when the heat of the conflict was over, without giving a complete victory to any party, and each church or sect was reduced to limit its hopes to retaining possession of the ground it already occupied, minorities, seeing that they had no chance of becoming majorities, were under the necessity of pleading to those whom they could not convert for permission to differ. It is accordingly on this battlefield, almost solely, that the rights of the individual against society have been asserted on broad grounds of principle, and the claim of society to exercise authority over dissentients openly controverted. The great writers to whom the world owes what religious liberty it possesses have mostly asserted freedom of conscience as an indefeasible right, and denied absolutely that a human being is accountable to others for his religious belief. Yet so natural to mankind is intolerance in whatever they really care about that religious freedom has hardly anywhere been practically realized, except where religious indifference, which dislikes to have its peace disturbed by theological quarrels, has added its weight to the scale. In the minds of almost all religious persons, even in the most tolerant countries, the duty of toleration is admitted with tacit reserves. One person will bear with dissent in matters of church government, but not of dogma; another can tolerate everybody, short of a Papist or a Unitarian; another, everyone who believes in revealed religion; a few extend their charity a little further, but stop at the belief in a God and in a future state. Wherever the sentiment of the majority is still genuine and intense, it is found to have abated little of its claim to be obeyed.

In England, from the peculiar circumstances of our political history, though the yoke of opinion is perhaps heavier, that of law is lighter than in most other countries of Europe; and there is considerable jealousy of direct interference by the legislative or the executive power with private conduct, not so much from any just regard for the independence of the individual as from the still subsisting habit of looking on the government as representing an opposite interest to the public. The majority have not yet learned to feel the power of the government their power, or its opinions their opinions. When they do so, individual liberty will probably be as much exposed to invasion from the government as it already is from public opinion. But, as yet, there is a considerable amount of feeling ready to be called forth against any attempt of the law to control individuals in things in which they have not hitherto been accustomed to be controlled by it; and this with very little discrimination as to whether the matter is, or is not, within the legitimate sphere of legal control; insomuch that the feeling, highly salutary on the whole, is perhaps quite as often misplaced as well grounded in the particular instances of its application. There is, in fact, no recognized principle by which the propriety or impropriety of government interference is customarily tested. People decide according to their personal preferences. Some, whenever they see any good to be done, or evil to be remedied, would willingly instigate the government to undertake the business, while others prefer to bear almost any amount of social evil rather than add one to the departments of human interests amenable to governmental control. And men range themselves on one or the other side in any particular case, according to this general direction of their sentiments, or according to the degree of interest which they feel in the particular thing which it is proposed that the government should do, or according to the belief they entertain that the government would, or would not, do it in the manner they prefer; but very rarely on account of any opinion to which they consistently adhere, as to what things are fit to be done by a government. And it seems to me that in consequence of this absence of rule or principle, one side is at present as often wrong as the other; the interference of government is, with about equal frequency, improperly invoked and improperly condemned.

The object of this essay is to assert one very simple principle, as entitled to govern absolutely the dealings of society with the individual in the way of compulsion and control, whether the means used be physical force in the form of legal penalties or the moral coercion of public opinion. That principle is that the sole end for which mankind are warranted, individually or collectively, in interfering with the liberty of action of any of their number is self-protection. That the only purpose for which power can be rightfully exercised over any member of a civilized community, against his will, is to prevent harm to others. His own good, either physical or moral, is not a sufficient warrant. He cannot rightfully be compelled to do or forbear because it will be better for him to do so, because it will make him happier, because, in the opinions of others, to do so would be wise or even right. These are good reasons for remonstrating with him, or reasoning with him, or persuading him, or entreating him, but not for compelling him or visiting him with any evil in case he do otherwise. To justify that, the conduct from which it is desired to deter him must be calculated to produce evil to someone else. The only part of the conduct of anyone for which he is amenable to society is that which concerns others. In the part which merely concerns himself, his independence is, of right, absolute. Over himself, over his own body and mind, the individual is sovereign.

It is, perhaps, hardly necessary to say that this doctrine is meant to apply only to human beings in the maturity of their faculties. We are not speaking of children or of young persons below the age which the law may fix as that of manhood or womanhood. Those who are still in a state to require being taken care of by others must be protected against their own actions as well as against external injury. For the same reason we may leave out of consideration those backward states of society in which the race itself may be considered as in its nonage. The early difficulties in the way of spontaneous progress are so great that there is seldom any choice of means for overcoming them; and a ruler full of the spirit of improvement is warranted in the use of any expedients that will attain an end perhaps otherwise unattainable. Despotism is a legitimate mode of government in dealing with barbarians, provided the end be their improvement and the means justified by actually effecting that end. Liberty, as a principle, has no application to any state of things anterior to the time when mankind have become capable of being improved by free and equal discussion. Until then, there is nothing for them but implicit obedience to an Akbar or a Charlemagne if they are so fortunate as to find one. But as soon as mankind have attained the capacity of being guided to their own improvement by conviction or persuasion (a period long since reached in all nations with whom we need here concern ourselves), compulsion, either in the direct form or in that of pains and penalties for non-compliance, is no longer admissible as a means to their own good, and justifiable only for the security of others.

It is proper to state that I forego any advantage which could be derived to my argument from the idea of abstract right as a thing independent of utility. I regard utility as the ultimate appeal on all ethical questions; but it must be utility in the largest sense, grounded on the permanent interests of man as a progressive being. Those interests, I contend, authorize the subjection of individual spontaneity to external control only in respect to those actions of each which concern the interest of other people. If anyone does an act hurtful to others, there is a *prima facie* case for punishing him by law or, where legal penalties are not safely applicable, by general disapprobation. There are also many positive acts for the benefit of others which he may rightfully be compelled to perform, such as to give evidence in a court of justice, to bear his fair share in the common defense or in any other joint work necessary to the interest of the society of which he enjoys the protection, and to perform certain acts of individual beneficence, such as saving a fellow creature's life or interposing to protect the defenseless against ill usage—things which whenever it is obviously a man's duty to do he may rightfully be made responsible to society for not doing.

A person may cause evil to others not only by his actions but by his inaction, and in either case he is justly accountable to them for the injury. The latter case, it is true, requires a much more cautious exercise of compulsion than the former. To make anyone answerable for doing evil to others is the rule; to make him answerable for not preventing evil is, comparatively speaking, the exception. Yet there are many cases clear enough and grave enough to justify that exception. In all things which regard the external relations of the individual, he is *de jure* amenable to those whose interests are concerned, and, if need be, to society as their protector. There are often good reasons for not holding him to the responsibility; but these reasons must arise from the special expediencies of the case: either because it is a kind of case in which he is on the whole likely to act better when left to his own discretion than when controlled in any way in which society have it in their power to control him; or because the attempt to exercise control would produce other evils, greater than those which it would prevent. When such reasons as these preclude the enforcement of responsibility, the conscience of the agent himself should step into the vacant judgment seat and protect those interests of others which have no external protection; judging himself all the more rigidly, because the case does not admit of his being made accountable to the judgment of his fellow creatures.

But there is a sphere of action in which society, as distinguished from the individual, has, if any, only an indirect interest: comprehending all that portion of a person's life and conduct which affects only himself or, if it also affects others, only with their free, voluntary, and undeceived consent and participation. When I say only himself, I mean directly and in the first instance; for whatever affects himself may affect others through himself: and the objection which may be grounded on this contingency will receive consideration in the sequel. This, then, is the appropriate region of human liberty. It comprises, first, the inward domain of consciousness, demanding liberty of conscience in the most comprehensive sense, liberty of thought and feeling, absolute freedom of opinion and sentiment on all subjects, practical or speculative, scientific, moral, or theological. The liberty of expressing and publishing opinions may seem to fall under a different principle, since it belongs to that part of the conduct of an individual which concerns other people, but, being almost of as much importance as the liberty of thought itself and resting in great part on the same reasons, is practically inseparable from it. Secondly, the principle requires liberty of tastes and pursuits, of framing the plan of our life to suit our own character, of doing as we like, subject to such consequences as may follow, without impediment from our fellow creatures, so long as what we do does not harm them, even though they should think our conduct foolish, perverse, or wrong. Thirdly, from this liberty of each individual follows the liberty, within the same limits, of combination among individuals; freedom to unite for any purpose not involving harm to others: the persons combining being supposed to be of full age and not forced or deceived.

No society in which these liberties are not, on the whole, respected is free, whatever may be its form of government; and none is completely free in which they do not exist absolute and unqualified. The only freedom which deserves the name is that of pursuing our own good in our own way, so long as we do not attempt to deprive others of theirs or impede their efforts to obtain it. Each is the proper guardian of his own health, whether bodily *or* mental and spiritual. Mankind are greater gainers by suffering each other to live as seems good to themselves than by compelling each to live as seems good to the rest.

Though this doctrine is anything but new and, to some persons, may have the air of a truism, there is no doctrine which stands more directly opposed to the general tendency of existing opinion and practice. Society has expended fully as much effort in the attempt (according to its lights) to compel people to conform to its notions of personal as of social excellence. The ancient commonwealths thought themselves entitled to practice, and the ancient philosophers countenanced, the regulation of every part of private conduct by public authority, on the ground that the State had a deep interest in the whole bodily and mental discipline of every one of its citizens—a mode of thinking which may have been admissible in small republics surrounded by powerful enemies, in constant peril of being subverted by foreign attack or internal commotion, and to which even a short interval of relaxed energy and self-command might so easily be fatal that they could not afford to wait for the salutary permanent effects of freedom. In the modern world, the greater size of political communities and, above all, the separation between spiritual and temporal authority (which placed the direction of men's consciences in other hands than those which controlled their worldly affairs) prevented so great an interference by law in the details of private life; but the engines of moral repression have been wielded more strenuously against divergence from the reigning opinion in self-regarding than even in social matters; religion, the most powerful of the elements which have entered into the formation of moral feeling, having almost always been governed either by the ambition of a hierarchy seeking control over every department of human conduct, or by the spirit of Puritanism. And some of those modern reformers who have placed themselves in strongest opposition to the religions of the past have been noway behind either churches or sects in their assertion of the right of spiritual domination: M. Comte, in particular, whose social system, as unfolded in his *Système de Politique Positive*, aims at establishing (though by moral more than by legal appliances) a despotism of society over the individual surpassing anything contemplated in the political ideal of the most rigid disciplinarian among the ancient philosophers.

Apart from the peculiar tenets of individual thinkers, there is also in the world at large an increasing inclination to stretch unduly the powers of society over the individual both by force of opinion and even by that of legislation; and as the tendency of all the changes taking place in the world is to strengthen society and diminish the power of the individual, this encroachment is not one of the evils which tend spontaneously to disappear, but, on the contrary, to grow more and more formidable. The disposition of mankind, whether as rulers or as fellow citizens, to impose their own opinions and inclinations as a rule of conduct on others is so energetically supported by some of the best and by some of the worst feelings incident to human nature that it is hardly ever kept under restraint by anything but want of power; and as the power is not declining, but growing, unless a strong barrier of moral conviction can be raised against the mischief, we must expect, in the present circumstances of the world, to see it increase.

It will be convenient for the argument if, instead of at once entering upon the general thesis, we confine ourselves in the first instance to a single branch of it on which the principle here stated is, if not fully, yet to a certain point, recognized by the current opinions. This one branch is the Liberty of Thought, from which it is impossible to separate the cognate liberty of speaking and of writing. Although these liberties, to some considerable amount, form part of the political morality of all countries which profess religious toleration and free institutions, the grounds, both philosophical and practical, on which they rest are perhaps not so familiar to the general mind, nor so thoroughly appreciated by many, even of the leaders of opinion, as might have been expected. Those grounds, when rightly understood, are of much wider application than to only one division of the subject, and a thorough consideration of this part of the question will be found the best introduction to the remainder. Those to whom nothing which I am about to say will be new may therefore, I hope, excuse me if on a subject which for now three centuries has been so often discussed I venture on one discussion more.

CHAPTER II

Of the Liberty of Thought and Discussion

The time, it is hoped, is gone by when any defense would be necessary of the "liberty of the press" as one of the securities against corrupt or tyrannical government. No argument, we may suppose, can now be needed against permitting a legislature or an executive, not identified in interest with the people, to prescribe opinions to them and determine what doctrines or what arguments they shall be allowed to hear. This aspect of the question, besides, has been so often and so triumphantly enforced by preceding writers that it needs not be specially insisted on in this place. Though the law of England, on the subject of the press, is as servile to this day as it was in the time of the Tudors, there is little danger of its being actually put in force against political discussion except during some temporary panic when fear of insurrection drives ministers and judges from their propriety;[1] and, speaking generally, it is not, in constitutional countries, to be apprehended that the government, whether completely responsible to the people or not, will often attempt to control the expression of opinion, except when in doing so it makes itself the organ of the general intolerance of the public. Let us suppose, therefore, that the government is entirely at one with the people, and never thinks of exerting any power of coercion unless in agreement with what it conceives to be their voice. But I deny the right of the people to exercise such coercion, either by themselves or by their government. The power itself is illegitimate. The best government has no more title to it than the worst. It is as noxious, or more noxious, when exerted in accordance with public opinion than when in opposition to it. If all mankind minus one were of one opinion, mankind would be no more justified in silencing that one person than he, if he had the power, would be justified in silencing mankind. Were an opinion a personal possession of no value except to the owner, if to be obstructed in the enjoyment of it were simply a private injury, it would make some difference whether the injury was inflicted only on a few persons or on many. But the peculiar evil of silencing the expression of an opinion is that it is robbing the human race, posterity as well as the existing generation—those who dissent from the opinion, still more than those who hold it. If the opinion is right, they are deprived of the opportunity of exchanging error for truth; if wrong, they lose, what is almost as great a benefit, the clearer perception and livelier impression of truth produced by its collision with error.

It is necessary to consider separately these two hypotheses, each of which has a distinct branch of the argument corresponding to it. We can never be sure that the opinion we are endeavoring to stifle is a false opinion; and if we were sure, stifling it would be an evil still.

First, the opinion which it is attempted to suppress by authority may possibly be true. Those who desire to suppress it, of course, deny its truth; but they are not infallible. They have no authority to decide the question for all mankind and exclude every other person from the means of judging. To refuse a hearing to an opinion because they are sure that it is false is to assume that *their* certainty is the same thing as *absolute* certainty. All silencing of discussion is an assumption of infallibility. Its condemnation may be allowed to rest on this common argument, not the worse for being common.

Unfortunately for the good sense of mankind, the fact of their fallibility is far from carrying the weight in their practical judgment which is always allowed to it in theory; for while everyone well knows himself to be fallible, few think it necessary to take any precautions against their own fallibility, or admit the supposition that any opinion of which they feel very certain may be one of the examples of the error to which they acknowledge themselves to be liable. Absolute princes, or others who are accustomed to unlimited deference, usually feel this complete confidence in their own opinions on nearly all subjects. People more happily situated, who sometimes hear their opinions disputed and are not wholly unused to be set right when they are wrong, place the same unbounded reliance only on such of their opinions as are shared by all who surround them, or to whom they habitually defer; for in proportion to a man's want of confidence in his own solitary judgment does he usually repose, with implicit trust, on the infallibility of "the world" in general. And the world, to each individual, means the part of it with which he comes in contact: his party, his sect, his church, his class of society; the man may be called, by comparison, almost liberal and large-minded to whom it means anything so comprehensive as his own country or his own age. Nor is his faith in this collective authority at all shaken by his being aware that other ages, countries, sects, churches, classes, and parties have thought, and even now think, the exact reverse. He devolves upon his own world the responsibility of being in the right against the dissentient worlds of other people; and it never troubles him that mere accident has decided which of these numerous worlds is the object of his reliance, and that the same causes which make him a churchman in London would have made him a Buddhist or a Confucian in Peking. Yet it is as evident in itself, as any amount of argument can make it, that ages are no more infallible than individuals—every age having held many opinions which subsequent ages have deemed not only false but absurd; and it is as certain that many opinions, now general, will be rejected by future ages, as it is that many, once general, are rejected by the present.

The objection likely to be made to this argument would probably take some such form as the following. There is no greater assumption of infallibility in forbidding the propagation of error than in any other thing which is done by public authority on its own judgment and responsibility. Judgment is given to men that they may use it. Because it may be used erroneously, are men to be told that they ought not to use it at all? To prohibit what they think pernicious is not claiming exemption from error, but fulfilling the duty incumbent on them, although fallible, of acting on their conscientious conviction. If we were never to act on our opinions, because those opinions may be wrong, we should leave all our interests uncared for, and all our duties unperformed. An objection which applies to all conduct can be no valid objection to any conduct in particular. It is the duty of governments, and of individuals, to form the truest opinions they can; to form them carefully, and never impose them upon others unless they are quite sure of being right. But when they are sure (such reasoners may say), it is not conscientiousness but cowardice to shrink from acting on their opinions and allow doctrines which they honestly think dangerous to the welfare of mankind, either in this life or in another, to be scattered abroad without restraint, because other people, in less enlightened times, have persecuted opinions now believed to be true. Let us take care, it may be said, not to make the same mistake; but governments and nations have made mistakes in other things which are not denied to be fit subjects for the exercise of authority: they have laid on bad taxes, made unjust wars. Ought we therefore to lay on no taxes and, under whatever provocation, make no wars? Men and governments must act to the best of their ability. There is no such thing as absolute certainty, but there is assurance sufficient for the purposes of human life. We may, and must, assume our opinion to be true for the guidance of our own conduct; and it is assuming no more when we forbid bad men to pervert society by the propagation of opinions which we regard as false and pernicious.

I answer, that it is assuming very much more. There is the greatest difference between presuming an opinion to be true because, with every opportunity for contesting it, it has not been refuted, and assuming its truth for the purpose of not permitting its refutation.

Complete liberty of contradicting and disproving our opinion is the very condition which justifies us in assuming its truth for purposes of action; and on no other terms can a being with human faculties have any rational assurance of being right.

When we consider either the history of opinion or the ordinary conduct of human life, to what is it to be ascribed that the one and the other are no worse than they are? Not certainly to the inherent force of the human understanding, for on any matter not self-evident there are ninety-nine persons totally incapable of judging of it for one who is capable; and the capacity of the hundredth person is only comparative, for the majority of the eminent men of every past generation held many opinions now known to be erroneous, and did or approved numerous things which no one will now justify. Why is it, then, that there is on the whole a preponderance among mankind of rational opinions and rational conduct? If there really is this preponderance—which there must be unless human affairs are, and have always been, in an almost desperate state—it is owing to a quality of the human mind, the source of everything respectable in man either as an intellectual or as a moral being, namely, that his errors are corrigible. He is capable of rectifying his mistakes by discussion and experience. Not by experience alone. There must be discussion to show how experience is to be interpreted. Wrong opinions and practices gradually yield to fact and argument; but facts and arguments, to produce any effect on the mind, must be brought before it. Very few facts are able to tell their own story, without comments to bring out their meaning. The whole strength and value, then, of human judgment depending on the one property, that it can be set right when it is wrong, reliance can be placed on it only when the means of setting it right are kept constantly at hand. In the case of any person whose judgment is really deserving of confidence, how has it become so? Because he has kept his mind open to criticism of his opinions and conduct. Because it has been his practice to listen to all that could be said against him; to profit by as much of it as was just, and to expound to himself, and upon occasion to others, the fallacy of what was fallacious. Because he has felt that the only way in which a human being can make some approach to knowing the whole of a subject is by hearing what can be said about it by persons of every variety of opinion, and studying all modes in which it can be looked at by every character of mind. No wise man ever acquired his wisdom in any mode but this; nor is it in the nature of human intellect to become wise in any other manner. The steady habit of correcting and completing his own opinion by collating it with those of others, so far from causing doubt and hesitation in carrying it into practice, is the only stable foundation for a just reliance on it; for, being cognizant of all that can, at least obviously, be said against him, and having taken up his position against gainsayers—knowing that he has sought for objections and difficulties instead of avoiding them, and has shut out no light which can be thrown upon the subject from any quarter—he has a right to think his judgment better than that of any person, or any multitude, who have not gone through a similar process.

It is not too much to require that what the wisest of mankind, those who are best entitled to trust their own judgment, find necessary to warrant their relying on it, should be submitted to by that miscellaneous collection of a few wise and many foolish individuals called the public. The most intolerant of churches, the Roman Catholic Church, even at the canonization of a saint admits, and listens patiently to, a "devil's advocate." The holiest of men, it appears, cannot be admitted to posthumous honors until all that the devil could say against him is known and weighed. If even the Newtonian philosophy were not permitted to be questioned, mankind could not feel as complete assurance of its truth as they now do. The beliefs which we have most warrant for have no safeguard to rest on but a standing invitation to the whole world to prove them unfounded. If the challenge is not accepted, or is accepted and the attempt fails, we are far enough from certainty still, but we have done the best that the existing state of human reason admits of: we have neglected nothing that could give the truth a chance of reaching us; if the lists are kept open, we may hope that, if there be a better truth, it will be found when the human mind is capable of receiving it; and in the meantime we may rely on having attained such approach to truth as is possible in our own day. This is the amount of certainty attainable by a fallible being, and this the sole way of attaining it.

Strange it is that men should admit the validity of the arguments for free discussion, but object to their being "pushed to an extreme," not seeing that unless the reasons are good for an extreme case, they are not good for any case. Strange that they should imagine that they are not assuming infallibility when they acknowledge that there should be free discussion on all subjects which can possibly be *doubtful*, but think that some particular principle or doctrine should be forbidden to be questioned because it is so *certain*, that is, because *they are certain* that it is certain. To call any proposition certain, while there is anyone who would deny its certainty if permitted, but who is not permitted, is to assume that we ourselves, and those who agree with us, are the judges of certainty, and judges without hearing the other side.

In the present age—which has been described as "destitute of faith, but terrified at skepticism"—in which people feel sure, not so much that their opinions are true as that they should not know what to do with them—the claims of an opinion to be protected from public attack are rested not so much on its truth as on its importance to society. There are, it is alleged, certain beliefs so useful, not to say indispensable, to well-being that it is as much the duty of governments to uphold those beliefs as to protect any other of the interests of society. In a case of such necessity, and so directly in the line of their duty, something less than infallibility may, it is maintained, warrant, and even bind, governments to act on their own opinion confirmed by the general opinion of mankind. It is also often argued, and still oftener thought, that none but bad men would desire to weaken these salutary beliefs; and there can be nothing wrong, it is thought, in restraining bad men and prohibiting what only such men would wish to practice. This mode of thinking makes the justification of restraints on discussion not a question of the truth of doctrines but of their usefulness, and flatters itself by that means to escape the responsibility of claiming to be an infallible judge of opinions. But those who thus satisfy themselves do not perceive that the assumption of infallibility is merely shifted from one point to another. The usefulness of an opinion is itself matter of opinion—as disputable, as open to discussion, and requiring discussion as much as the opinion itself. There is the same need of an infallible judge of opinions to decide an opinion to be noxious as to decide it to be false, unless the opinion condemned has full opportunity of defending itself. And it will not do to say that the heretic may be allowed to maintain the utility or harmlessness of his opinion, though forbidden to maintain its truth. The truth of an opinion is part of its utility. If we would know whether or not it is desirable that a proposition should be believed, is it possible to exclude the consideration of whether or not it is true? In the opinion, not of bad men, but of the best men, no belief which is contrary to truth can be really useful; and can you prevent such men from urging that plea when they are charged with culpability for denying some doctrine which they are told is useful, but which they believe to be false? Those who are on the side of received opinions never fail to take all possible advantage of this plea; you do not find *them* handling the question of ability as if it could be completely abstracted from that of truth; on the contrary, it is, above all, because their doctrine is "the truth" that the knowledge or the belief of it is held to be so indispensable. There can be no fair discussion of the question of usefulness when an argument so vital may be employed on one side, but not on the other. And in point of fact, when law or public feeling do not permit the truth of an opinion to be disputed, they are just as little tolerant of a denial of its usefulness. The utmost they allow is an extenuation of its absolute necessity, or of the positive guilt of rejecting it.

In order more fully to illustrate the mischief of denying a hearing to opinions because we, in our own judgment, have condemned them, it will be desirable to fix down the discussion to a concrete case; and I choose, by preference, the cases which are least favorable to me—in which the argument against freedom of opinion, both on the score of truth and on that of utility, is considered the strongest. Let the opinions impugned be the belief in a God and in a future state, or any of the commonly received doctrines of morality. To fight the battle on such ground gives a great advantage to an unfair antagonist, since he will be sure to say (and many who have no desire to be unfair will say it internally), Are these the doctrines which you do not deem sufficiently certain to be taken under the protection of law? Is the belief in a God one of the opinions to feel sure of which you hold to be assuming infallibility? But I must be permitted to observe that it is not the feeling sure of a doctrine (be it what it may) which I call an assumption of infallibility. It is the undertaking to decide that question *for others*, without allowing them to hear what can be said on the contrary side. And I denounce and reprobate this pretension not the less if put forth on the side of my most solemn convictions. However positive anyone's persuasion may be, not only of the falsity but of the pernicious consequences—not only of the pernicious consequences, but (to adopt expressions which I altogether condemn) the immorality and impiety of an opinion—yet if, in pursuance of that private judgment, though backed by the public judgment of his country or his contemporaries, he prevents the opinion from being heard in its defense, he assumes infallibility. And so far from the assumption being less objectionable or less dangerous because the opinion is called immoral or impious, this is the case of all others in which it is most fatal. These are exactly the occasions on which the men of one generation commit those dreadful mistakes which excite the astonishment and horror of posterity. It is among such that we find the instances memorable in history, when the arm of the law has been employed to root out the best men and the noblest doctrines; with deplorable success as to the men, though some of the doctrines have survived to be (as if in mockery) invoked in defense of similar conduct toward those who dissent from *them*, or from their received interpretation.

Mankind can hardly be too often reminded that there was once a man called Socrates, between whom and the legal authorities and public opinion of his time there took place a memorable collision. Born in an age and country abounding in individual greatness, this man has been handed down to us by those who best knew both him and the age as the most virtuous man in it; while *we* know him as the head and prototype of all subsequent teachers of virtue, the source equally of the lofty inspiration of Plato and the judicious utilitarianism of Aristotle, *"i maestri di color che sanno,"* the two headsprings of ethical as of all other philosophy. This acknowledged master of all the eminent thinkers who have since lived—whose fame, still growing after more than two thousand years, all but outweighs the whole remainder of the names which make his native city illustrious—was put to death by his countrymen, after a judicial conviction, for impiety and immorality. Impiety, in denying the gods recognized by the State; indeed, his accuser asserted (see the *Apologia*) that he believed in no gods at all. Immorality, in being, by his doctrines and instructions, a "corruptor of youth." Of these charges the tribunal, there is every ground for believing, honestly found him guilty, and condemned the man who probably of all then born had deserved best of mankind to be put to death as a criminal.

To pass from this to the only other instance of judicial iniquity, the mention of which, after the condemnation of Socrates, would not be an anticlimax: the event which took place on Calvary rather more than eighteen hundred years ago. The man who left on the memory of those who witnessed his life and conversation such an impression of his moral grandeur that eighteen subsequent centuries have done homage to him as the Almighty in person, was ignominiously put to death, as what? As a blasphemer. Men did not merely mistake their benefactor, they mistook him for the exact contrary of what he was and treated him as that prodigy of impiety which they themselves are now held to be for their treatment of him. The feelings with which mankind now regard these lamentable transactions, especially the later of the two, render them extremely unjust in their judgment of the unhappy actors. These were, to all appearance, not bad men—not worse than men commonly are, but rather the contrary; men who possessed in a full, or somewhat more than a full measure, the religious, moral, and patriotic feelings of their time and people: the very kind of men who, in all times, our own included, have every chance of passing through life blameless and respected. The high priest who rent his garments when the words were pronounced, which, according to all the ideas of his country, constituted the blackest guilt, was in all probability quite as sincere in his horror and indignation as the generality of respectable and pious men now are in the religious and moral sentiments they profess; and most of those who now shudder at his conduct, if they had lived in his time, and been born Jews, would have acted precisely as he did. Orthodox Christians who are tempted to think that those who stoned to death the first martyrs must have been worse men than they themselves are ought to remember that one of those persecutors was Saint Paul.

Let us add one more example, the most striking of all, if the impressiveness of an error is measured by the wisdom and virtue of him who falls into it. If ever anyone possessed of power had grounds for thinking himself the best and most enlightened among his contemporaries, it was the Emperor Marcus Aurelius. Absolute monarch of the whole civilized world, he preserved through life not only the most unblemished justice, but what was less to be expected from his Stoical breeding, the tenderest heart. The few failings which are attributed to him were all on the side of indulgence, while his writings, the highest ethical product of the ancient mind, differ scarcely perceptibly, if they differ at all, from the most characteristic teachings of Christ. This man, a better Christian in all but the dogmatic sense of the word than almost any of the ostensibly Christian sovereigns who have since reigned, persecuted Christianity. Placed at the summit of all the previous attainments of humanity, with an open, unfettered intellect, and a character which led him of himself to embody in his moral writings the Christian ideal, he yet failed to see that Christianity was to be a good and not an evil to the world, with his duties to which he was so deeply penetrated. Existing society he knew to be in a deplorable state. But such as it was, he saw, or thought he saw, that it was held together, and prevented from being worse, by belief and reverence of the received divinities. As a ruler of mankind, he deemed it his duty not to suffer society to fall in pieces; and saw not how, if its existing ties were removed, any others could be formed which could again knit it together. The new religion openly aimed at dissolving these ties; unless, therefore, it was his duty to adopt that religion, it seemed to be his duty to put it down. Inasmuch then as the theology of Christianity did not appear to him true or of divine origin, inasmuch as this strange history of a crucified God was not credible to him, and a system which purported to rest entirely upon a foundation to him so wholly unbelievable, could not be foreseen by him to be that renovating agency which, after all abatements, it has in fact proved to be; the gentlest and most amiable of philosophers and rulers, under a solemn sense of duty, authorized the persecution of Christianity. To my mind this is one of the most tragical facts in all history. It is a bitter thought how different a thing the Christianity of the world might have been if the Christian faith had been adopted as the religion of the empire under the auspices of Marcus Aurelius instead of those of Constantine. But it would be equally unjust to him and false to truth to deny that no one plea which can be urged for punishing anti-Christian teaching was wanting to Marcus Aurelius for punishing, as he did, the propagation of Christianity. No Christian more firmly believes that atheism is false and tends to the dissolution of society than Marcus Aurelius believed the same things of Christianity; he who, of all men then living, might have been thought the most capable of appreciating it. Unless anyone who approves of punishment for the promulgation of opinions flatters himself that he is a wiser and better man than Marcus Aurelius—more deeply versed in the wisdom of his time, more elevated in his intellect above it, more earnest in his search for truth, or more single-minded in his devotion to it when found—let him abstain from that assumption of the joint infallibility of himself and the multitude which the great Antoninus made with so unfortunate a result.

Aware of the impossibility of defending the use of punishment for restraining irreligious opinions by any argument which will not justify Marcus Antoninus, the enemies of religious freedom, when hard pressed, occasionally accept this consequence and say, with Dr. Johnson, that the persecutors of Christianity were in the right, that persecution is an ordeal through which truth ought to pass, and always passes successfully, legal penalties being, in the end, powerless against truth, though sometimes beneficially effective against mischievous errors. This is a form of the argument for religious intolerance sufficiently remarkable not to be passed without notice.

A theory which maintains that truth may justifiably be persecuted because persecution cannot possibly do it any harm cannot be charged with being intentionally hostile to the reception of new truths; but we cannot commend the generosity of its dealing with the persons to whom mankind are indebted for them. To discover to the world something which deeply concerns it, and of which it was previously ignorant, to prove to it that it had been mistaken on some vital point of temporal or spiritual interest, is as important a service as a human being can render to his follow creatures, and in certain cases, as in those of the early Christians and of the Reformers, those who think with Dr. Johnson believe it to have been the most precious gift which could be bestowed on mankind. That the authors of such splendid benefits should be requited by martyrdom, that their reward should be to be dealt with as the vilest of criminals, is not, upon this theory, a deplorable error and misfortune for which humanity should mourn in sackcloth and ashes, but the normal and justifiable state of things. The propounder of a new truth, according to this doctrine, should stand, as stood, in the legislation of the Locrians, the proposer of a new law, with a halter round his neck, to be instantly tightened if the public assembly did not, on hearing his reasons, then and there adopt his proposition. People who defend this mode of treating benefactors cannot be supposed to set much value on the benefit; and I believe this view of the subject is mostly confined to the sort of persons who think that new truths may have been desirable once, but that we have had enough of them now.

But, indeed, the dictum that truth always triumphs over persecution is one of those pleasant falsehoods which men repeat after one another till they pass into commonplaces, but which all experience refutes. History teems with instances of truth put down by persecution. If not suppressed forever, it may be thrown back for centuries. To speak only of religious opinions: the Reformation broke out at least twenty times before Luther, and was put down. Arnold of Brescia was put down. Fra Dolcino was put down. Savonarola was put down. The Albigeois were put down. The Vaudois were put down. The Lollards were put down. The Hussites were put down. Even after the era of Luther, wherever persecution was persisted in, it was successful. In Spain, Italy, Flanders, the Austrian empire, Protestantism was rooted out; and, most likely, would have been so in England had Queen

Mary lived or Queen Elizabeth died. Persecution has always succeeded save where the heretics were too strong a party to be effectually persecuted. No reasonable person can doubt that Christianity might have been extirpated in the Roman Empire. It spread and became predominant because the persecutions were only occasional, lasting but a short time, and separated by long intervals of almost undisturbed propagandism. It is a piece of idle sentimentality that truth, merely as truth, has any inherent power denied to error of prevailing against the dungeon and the stake. Men are not more zealous for truth than they often are for error, and a sufficient application of legal or even of social penalties will generally succeed in stopping the propagation of either. The real advantage which truth has consists in this, that when an opinion is true, it may be extinguished once, twice, or many times, but in the course of ages there will generally be found persons to rediscover it, until some one of its reappearances falls on a time when from favorable circumstances it escapes persecution until it has made such head as to withstand all subsequent attempts to suppress it.

It will be said that we do not now put to death the introducers of new opinions: we are not like our fathers who slew the prophets; we even build sepulchers to them. It is true we no longer put heretics to death; and the amount of penal infliction which modern feeling would probably tolerate, even against the most obnoxious opinions, is not sufficient to extirpate them. But let us not flatter ourselves that we are yet free from the stain even of legal persecution. Penalties for opinion, or at least for its expression, still exist by law; and their enforcement is not, even in these times, so unexampled as to make it at all incredible that they may some day be revived in full force. In the year 1857, at the summer assizes of the county of Cornwall, an unfortunate man,[2] said to be of unexceptionable conduct in all relations of life, was sentenced to twenty-one months' imprisonment for uttering, and writing on a gate, some offensive words concerning Christianity. Within a month of the same time, at the Old Bailey, two persons,[3] on two separate occasions, were rejected as jurymen, and one of them grossly insulted by the judge and by one of the counsel, because they honestly declared that they had no theological belief; and a third, a foreigner,[4] for the same reason, was denied justice against a thief. This refusal of redress took place in virtue of the legal doctrine that no person can be allowed to give evidence in a court of justice who does not profess belief in a God (any god is sufficient) and in a future state, which is equivalent to declaring such persons to be outlaws, excluded from the protection of the tribunals; who may not only be robbed or assaulted with impunity, if no one but themselves, or persons of similar opinions, be present, but anyone else may be robbed or assaulted with impunity, if the proof of the fact depends on their evidence. The assumption on which this is grounded is that the oath is worthless of a person who does not believe in a future state—a proposition which betokens much ignorance of history in those who assent to it (since it is historically true that a large proportion of infidels in all ages have been persons of distinguished integrity and honor), and would be maintained by no one who had the smallest conception how many of the persons in greatest repute with the world, both for virtues and attainments, are well known, at least to their intimates, to be unbelievers. The rule, besides, is suicidal and cuts away its own foundation. Under pretense that atheists must be liars, it admits the testimony of all atheists who are willing to lie, and rejects only those who brave the obloquy of publicly confessing a detested creed rather than affirm a falsehood. A rule thus self-convicted of absurdity so far as regards its professed purpose can be kept in force only as a badge of hatred, a relic of persecution—a persecution, too, having the peculiarity that the qualification for undergoing it is the being clearly proved not to deserve it. The rule and the theory it implies are hardly less insulting to believers than to infidels. For if he who does not believe in a future state necessarily lies, it follows that they who do believe are only prevented from lying, if prevented they are, by the fear of hell. We will not do the authors and abettors of the rule the injury of supposing that the conception which they have formed of Christian virtue is drawn from their own consciousness.

These, indeed, are but rags and remnants of persecution, and may be thought to be not so much an indication of the wish to persecute, as an example of that very frequent infirmity of English minds, which makes them take a preposterous pleasure in the assertion of a bad principle, when they are no longer bad enough to desire to carry it really into practice. But unhappily there is no security in the state of the public mind that the suspension of worse forms of legal persecution, which has lasted for about the space of a generation, will continue. In this age the quiet surface of routine is as often ruffled by attempts to resuscitate past evils as to introduce new benefits. What is boasted of at the present time as the revival of religion is always, in narrow and uncultivated minds, at least as much the revival of bigotry; and where there is the strong permanent leaven of intolerance in the feelings of a people, which at all times abides in the middle classes of this country, it needs but little to provoke them into actively persecuting those whom they have never ceased to think proper objects of persecution.[5] For it is this—it is the opinions men entertain, and the feelings they cherish, respecting those who disown the beliefs they deem important which makes this country not a place of mental freedom. For a long time past, the chief mischief of the legal penalties is that they strengthen the social stigma. It is that stigma which is really effective, and so effective is it that the profession of opinions which are under the ban of society is much less common in England than is, in many other countries, the avowal of those which incur risk of judicial punishment. In respect to all persons but those whose pecuniary circumstances make them independent of the good will of other people, opinion, on this subject, is as efficacious as law; men might as well be imprisoned as excluded from the means of earning their bread. Those whose bread is already secured, and who desire no favors from men in power, or from bodies of men, or from the public, have nothing to fear from the open avowal of any opinions but to be ill-thought of and ill-spoken of, and this it ought not to require a very heroic mold to enable them to bear. There is no room for any appeal *ad misericordiam* in behalf of such persons. But though we do not now inflict so much evil on those who think differently from us as it was formerly our custom to do, it may be that we do ourselves as much evil as ever by our treatment of them. Socrates was put to death, but the Socratic philosophy rose like the sun in heaven and spread its illumination over the whole intellectual firmament. Christians were cast to the lions, but the Christian church grew up a stately and spreading tree, overtopping the older and less vigorous growths, and stifling them by its shade. Our merely social intolerance kills no one, roots out no opinions, but induces men to disguise them or to abstain from any active effort for their diffusion. With us, heretical opinions do not perceptibly gain, or even lose, ground in each decade or generation; they never blaze out far and wide, but continue to smolder in the narrow circles of thinking and studious persons among whom they originate, without ever lighting up the general affairs of mankind with either a true or a deceptive light. And thus is kept up a state of things very satisfactory to some minds, because, without the unpleasant process of fining or imprisoning anybody, it maintains all prevailing opinions outwardly undisturbed, while it does not absolutely interdict the exercise of reason by dissenients afflicted with the malady of thought. A convenient plan for having peace in the intellectual world, and keeping all things going on therein very much as they do already. But the price paid for this sort of intellectual pacification is the sacrifice of the entire moral courage of the human mind. A state of things in which a large portion of the most active and inquiring intellects find it advisable to keep the general principles and grounds of their convictions within their own breasts, and attempt, in what they address to the public, to fit as much as they can of their own conclusions to premises which they have internally renounced, cannot send forth the open, fearless characters and logical, consistent intellects who once adorned the thinking world. The sort of men who can be looked for under it are either mere conformers to commonplace, or timeservers for truth, whose arguments on all great subjects are meant for their hearers, and are not those which have convinced themselves. Those who avoid this alternative do so by narrowing their thoughts and interest to things which can be spoken of without venturing within the region of principles, that is, to small practical matters which would come right of themselves, if but the minds of mankind were strengthened and enlarged, and which will never be made effectually right until then, while that which would strengthen and enlarge men's minds—free and daring speculation on the highest subjects—is abandoned.

Those in whose eyes this reticence on the part of heretics is no evil should consider, in the first place, that in consequence of it there is never any fair and thorough discussion of heretical opinions; and that such of them as could not stand such a discussion, though they may be prevented from spreading, do not disappear. But it is not the minds of heretics that are deteriorated most by the ban placed on all inquiry which does not end in the orthodox conclusions. The greatest harm done is to those who are not heretics, and whose whole mental development is cramped and their reason cowed by the fear of heresy. Who can compute what the world loses in the multitude of promising intellects combined with timid characters, who dare not follow out any bold, vigorous, independent train of thought, lest it should land them in something which would admit of being considered irreligious or immoral? Among them we may occasionally see some man of deep conscientiousness and subtle and refined understanding, who spends a life in sophisticating with an intellect which he cannot silence, and exhausts the resources of ingenuity in attempting to reconcile the promptings of his conscience and reason with orthodoxy, which yet he does not, perhaps, to the end succeed in doing. No one can be a great thinker who does not recognize that as a thinker it is his first duty to follow his intellect to whatever conclusions it may lead. Truth gains more even by the errors of one who, with due study and preparation, thinks for himself than by the true opinions of those who only hold them because they do not suffer themselves to think. Not that it is solely, or chiefly, to form great thinkers that freedom of thinking is required. On the contrary, it is as much and even more indispensable to enable average human beings to attain the mental stature which they are capable of. There have been, and may again be, great individual thinkers in a general atmosphere of mental slavery. But there never has been, nor ever will be, in that atmosphere an intellectually active people. Where any people has made a temporary approach to such a character, it has been because the dread of heterodox speculation was for a time suspended. Where there is a tacit convention that principles are not to be disputed, where the discussion of the greatest questions which can occupy humanity is considered to be closed, we cannot hope to find that generally high scale of mental activity which has made some periods of history so remarkable. Never when controversy avoided the subjects which are large and important enough to kindle enthusiasm was the mind of a people stirred up from its foundations, and the impulse given which raised even persons of the most ordinary intellect to something of the dignity of thinking beings. Of such we have had an example in the condition of Europe during the times immediately following the Reformation; another, though limited to the Continent and to a more cultivated class, in the speculative movement of the latter half of the eighteenth century; and a third, of still briefer duration, in the intellectual fermentation of Germany during the Goethian and Fichtean period. These periods differed widely in the particular opinions which they developed, but were alike in this, that during all three the yoke of authority was broken. In each, an old mental despotism had been thrown off, and no new one had yet taken its place. The impulse given at these three periods has made Europe what it now is. Every single improvement which has taken place either in the human mind or in institutions may be traced distinctly to one or other of them. Appearances have for some time indicated that all three impulses are well-nigh spent; and we can expect no fresh start until we again assert our mental freedom.

Let us now pass to the second division of the argument, and dismissing the supposition that any of the received opinions may be false, let us assume them to be true and examine into the worth of the manner in which they are likely to be held when their truth is not freely and openly canvassed. However unwillingly a person who has a strong opinion may admit the possibility that his opinion may be false, he ought to be moved by the consideration that, however true it may be, if it is not fully, frequently, and fearlessly discussed, it will be held as a dead dogma, not a living truth.

There is a class of persons (happily not quite so numerous as formerly) who think it enough if a person assents undoubtingly to what they think true, though he has no knowledge whatever of the grounds of the opinion and could not make a tenable defense of it against the most superficial objections. Such persons, if they can once get their creed taught from authority, naturally think that no good, and some harm, comes of its being allowed to be questioned. Where their influence prevails, they make it nearly impossible for the received opinion to be rejected wisely and considerately, though it may still be rejected rashly and ignorantly; for to shut out discussion entirely is seldom possible, and when it once gets in, beliefs not grounded on conviction are apt to give way before the slightest semblance of an argument. Waiving, however, this possibility—assuming that the true opinion abides in the mind, but abides as a prejudice, a belief independent of, and proof against, argument—this is not the way in which truth ought to be held by a rational being. This is not knowing the truth. Truth, thus held, is but one superstition the more, accidentally clinging to the words which enunciate a truth.

If the intellect and judgment of mankind ought to be cultivated, a thing which Protestants at least do not deny, on what can these faculties be more appropriately exercised by anyone than on the things which concern him so much that is it considered necessary for him to hold opinions on them? If the cultivation of the understanding consists in one thing more than in another, it is surely in learning the grounds of one's own opinions. Whatever people believe, on subjects on which it is of the first importance to believe rightly, they ought to be able to defend against at least the common objections. But, someone may say, "Let them be *taught* the grounds of their opinions. It does not follow that opinions must be merely parroted because they are never heard controverted. Persons who learn geometry do not simply commit the theorems to memory, but understand and learn likewise the demonstrations; and it would be absurd to say that they remain ignorant of the grounds of geometrical truths because they never hear anyone deny and attempt to disprove them." Undoubtedly: and such teaching suffices on a subject like mathematics, where there is nothing at all to be said on the wrong side of the question. The peculiarity of the evidence of mathematical truths is that all the argument is on one side. There are no objections, and no answers to objections. But on every subject on which difference of opinion is possible, the truth depends on a balance to be struck between two sets of conflicting reasons. Even in natural philosophy, there is always some other explanation possible of the same facts; some geocentric theory instead of heliocentric, some phlogiston instead of oxygen; and it has to be shown why that other theory cannot be the true one; and until this is shown, and until we know how it is shown, we do not understand the grounds of our opinion. But when we turn to subjects infinitely more complicated, to morals, religion, politics, social relations, and the business of life, three-fourths of the arguments for every disputed opinion consist in dispelling the appearances which favor some opinion different from it. The greatest orator, save one, of antiquity, has left it on record that he always studied his adversary's case with as great, if not still greater, intensity than even his own. What Cicero practiced as the means of forensic success requires to be imitated by all who study any subject in order to arrive at the truth. He who knows only his own side of the case knows little of that. His reasons may be good, and no one may have been able to refute them. But if he is equally unable to refute the reasons on the opposite side, if he does not so much as know what they are, he has no ground for preferring either opinion. The rational position for him would be suspension of judgment, and unless he contents himself with that, he is either led by authority or adopts, like the generality of the world, the side to which he feels most inclination. Nor is it enough that he should hear the arguments of adversaries from his own teachers, presented as they state them, and accompanied by what they offer as refutations. That is not the way to do justice to the arguments or bring them into real contact with his own mind. He must be able to hear them from persons who actually believe them, who defend them in earnest and do their very utmost for them. He must know them in their most plausible and persuasive form; he must feel the whole force of the difficulty which the true view of the subject has to encounter and dispose of, else he will never really possess himself of the portion of truth which meets and removes that difficulty. Ninety-nine in a hundred of what are called educated men are in this condition, even of those who can argue fluently for their opinions. Their conclusion may be true, but it might be false for anything they know; they have never thrown themselves into the mental position of those who think differently from them, and considered what such persons may have to say; and, consequently, they do not, in any proper sense of the word, know the doctrine which they themselves profess. They do not know those parts of it which explain and justify the remainder—the considerations which show that a fact which seemingly conflicts with another is reconcilable with it, or that, of two apparently strong reasons, one and not the other ought to be preferred. All that part of the truth which turns the scale and decides the judgment of a completely informed mind, they are strangers to; nor is it ever really known but to those who have attended equally and impartially to both sides and endeavored to see the reasons of both in the strongest light. So essential is this discipline to a real understanding of moral and human subjects that, if opponents of all-important truths do not exist, it is indispensable to imagine them and supply them with the strongest arguments which the most skillful devil's advocate can conjure up.

To abate the force of these considerations, an enemy of free discussion may be supposed to say that there is no necessity for mankind in general to know and understand all that can be said against or for their opinions by philosophers and theologians. That it is not needful for common men to be able to expose all the misstatements or fallacies of an ingenious opponent. That it is enough if there is always somebody capable of answering them, so that nothing likely to mislead uninstructed persons remains unrefuted. That simple minds, having been taught the obvious grounds of the truths inculcated in them, may trust to authority for the rest and, being aware that they have neither knowledge nor talent to resolve every difficulty which can be raised, may repose in the assurance that all those which have been raised have been or can be answered by those who are specially trained to the task.

Conceding to this view of the subject the utmost that can be claimed for it by those most easily satisfied with the amount of understanding of truth which ought to accompany the belief of it, even so, the argument for free discussion is noway weakened. For even this doctrine acknowledges that mankind ought to have a rational assurance that all objections have been satisfactorily answered; and how are they to be answered if that which requires to be answered is not spoken? Or how can the answer be known to be satisfactory if the objectors have no opportunity of showing that it is unsatisfactory? If not the public, at least the philosophers and theologians who are to resolve the difficulties must make themselves familiar with those difficulties in their most puzzling form; and this cannot be accomplished unless they are freely stated and placed in the most advantageous light which they admit of. The Catholic Church has its own way of dealing with this embarrassing problem. It makes a broad separation between those who can be permitted to receive its doctrines on conviction and those who must accept them on trust. Neither, indeed, are allowed any choice as to what they will accept; but the clergy, such at least as can be fully confided in, may admissibly and meritoriously make themselves acquainted with the arguments of opponents, in order to answer them, and may, therefore, read heretical books; the laity, not unless by special permission, hard to be obtained. This discipline recognizes a knowledge of the enemy's case as beneficial to the teachers, but finds means, consistent with this, of denying it to the rest of the world, thus giving to the *élite* more mental culture, though not more mental freedom, than it allows to the mass. By this device it succeeds in obtaining the kind of mental superiority which its purposes require; for though culture without freedom never made a large and liberal mind, it can make a clever *nisi prius* advocate of a cause. But in countries professing Protestantism, this resource is denied, since Protestants hold, at least in theory, that the responsibility for the choice of a religion must be borne by each for himself and cannot be thrown off upon teachers. Besides, in the present state of the world, it is practically impossible that writings which are read by the instructed can be kept from the uninstructed. If the teachers of mankind are to be cognizant of all that they ought to know, everything must be free to be written and published without restraint.

If, however, the mischievous operation of the absence of free discussion, when the received opinions are true, were confined to leaving men ignorant of the grounds of those opinions, it might be thought that this, if an intellectual, is no moral evil and does not affect the worth of the opinions, regarded in their influence on the character. The fact, however, is that not only the grounds of the opinion are forgotten in the absence of discussion, but too often the meaning of the opinion itself. The words which convey it cease to suggest ideas, or suggest only a small portion of those they were originally employed to communicate. Instead of a vivid conception and a living belief, there remain only a few phrases retained by rote; or, if any part, the shell and husk only of the meaning is retained, the finer essence being lost. The great chapter in human history which this fact occupies and fills cannot be too earnestly studied and meditated on.

It is illustrated in the experience of almost all ethical doctrines and religious creeds. They are all full of meaning and vitality to those who originate them, and to the direct disciples of the originators. Their meaning continues to be felt in undiminished strength, and is perhaps brought out into even fuller consciousness, so long as the struggle lasts to give the doctrine or creed an ascendancy over other creeds. At last it either prevails and becomes the general opinion, or its progress stops; it keeps possession of the ground it has gained, but ceases to spread further. When either of these results has become apparent, controversy on the subject flags, and gradually dies away. The doctrine has taken its place, if not as a received opinion, as one of the admitted sects or divisions of opinion; those who hold it have generally inherited, not adopted it; and conversion from one of these doctrines to another, being now an exceptional fact, occupies little place in the thoughts of their professors. Instead of being, as at first, constantly on the alert either to defend themselves against the world or to bring the world over to them, they have subsided into acquiescence and neither listen, when they can help it, to arguments against their creed, nor trouble dissentients (if there be such) with arguments in its favor. From this time may usually be dated the decline in the living power of the doctrine. We often hear the teachers of all creeds lamenting the difficulty of keeping up in the minds of believers a lively apprehension of the truth which they nominally recognize, so that it may penetrate the feelings and acquire a real mastery over the conduct. No such difficulty is complained of while the creed is still fighting for its existence; even the weaker combatants then know and feel what they are fighting for, and the difference between it and other doctrines; and in that period of every creed's existence not a few persons may be found who have realized its fundamental principles in all the forms of thought, have weighed and considered them in all their important bearings, and have experienced the full effect on the character which belief in that creed ought to produce in a mind thoroughly imbued with it. But when it has come to be an hereditary creed, and to be received passively, not actively—when the mind is no longer compelled, in the same degree as at first, to exercise its vital powers on the questions which its belief presents to it, there is a progressive tendency to forget all of the belief except the formularies, or to give it a dull and torpid assent, as if accepting it on trust dispensed with the necessity of realizing it in consciousness, or testing it by personal experience, until it almost ceases to connect itself at all with the inner life of the human being. Then are seen the cases, so frequent in this age of the world as almost to form the majority, in which the creed remains as it were outside the mind, incrusting and petrifying it against all other influences addressed to the higher parts of our nature; manifesting its power by not suffering any fresh and living conviction to get in, but itself doing nothing for the mind or heart except standing sentinel over them to keep them vacant.

To what an extent doctrines intrinsically fitted to make the deepest impression upon the mind may remain in it as dead beliefs, without being ever realized in the imagination, the feelings, or the understanding, is exemplified by the manner in which the majority of believers hold the doctrines of Christianity. By Christianity, I here mean what is accounted such by all churches and sects—the maxims and precepts contained in the New Testament. These are considered sacred, and accepted as laws, by all professing Christians. Yet it is scarcely too much to say that not one Christian in a thousand guides or tests his individual conduct by reference to those laws. The standard to which he does refer it is the custom of his nation, his class, or his religious profession. He has thus, on the one hand, a collection of ethical maxims which he believes to have been vouchsafed to him by infallible wisdom as rules for his government; and, on the other, a set of everyday judgments and practices which go a certain length with some of those maxims, not so great a length with others, stand in direct opposition to some, and are, on the whole, a compromise between the Christian creed and the interests and suggestions of worldly life. To the first of these standards he gives his homage; to the other his real allegiance. All Christians believe that the blessed are the poor and humble, and those who are ill-used by the world; that it is easier for a camel to pass through the eye of a needle than for a rich man to enter the kingdom of heaven; that they should judge not, lest they be judged; that they should swear not at all; that they should love their neighbor as themselves; that if one take their cloak, they should give him their coat also; that they should take no thought for the morrow; that if they would be perfect they should sell all that they have and give it to the poor. They are not insincere when they say that they believe these things. They do believe them, as people believe what they have always heard lauded and never discussed. But in the sense of that living belief which regulates conduct, they believe these doctrines just up to the point to which it is usual to act upon them. The doctrines in their integrity are serviceable to pelt adversaries with; and it is understood that they are to be put forward (when possible) as the reasons for whatever people do that they think laudable. But anyone who reminded them that the maxims require an infinity of things which they never even think of doing would gain nothing but to be classed among those very unpopular characters who affect to be better than other people. The doctrines have no hold on ordinary believers—are not a power in their minds. They have an habitual respect for the sound of them, but no feeling which spreads from the words to the things signified and forces the mind to take *them* in and make them conform to the formula. Whenever conduct is concerned, they look round for Mr. A and B to direct them how far to go in obeying Christ.

Now we may be well assured that the case was not thus, but far otherwise, with the early Christians. Had it been thus, Christianity never would have expanded from an obscure sect of the despised Hebrews into the religion of the Roman empire. When their enemies said, "See how these Christians love one another" (a remark not likely to be made by anybody now), they assuredly had a much livelier feeling of the meaning of their creed than they have ever had since. And to this cause, probably, it is chiefly owing that Christianity now makes so little progress in extending its domain, and after eighteen centuries is still nearly confined to Europeans and the descendants of Europeans. Even with the strictly religious, who are much in earnest about their doctrines and attach a greater amount of meaning to many of them than people in general, it commonly happens that the part which is thus comparatively active in their minds is that which was made by Calvin, or Knox, or some such person much nearer in character to themselves. The sayings of Christ coexist passively in their minds, producing hardly any effect beyond what is caused by mere listening to words so amiable and bland. There are many reasons, doubtless, why doctrines which are the badge of a sect retain more of their vitality than those common to all recognized sects, and why more pains are taken by teachers to keep their meaning alive; but one reason certainly is that the peculiar doctrines are more questioned and have to be oftener defended against open gainsayers. Both teachers and learners go to sleep at their post as soon as there is no enemy in the field.

The same thing holds true, generally speaking, of all traditional doctrines—those of prudence and knowledge of life as well as of morals or religion. All languages and literatures are full of general observations on life, both as to what it is and how to conduct oneself in it—observations which everybody knows, which everybody repeats or hears with acquiescence, which are received as truisms, yet of which most people first truly learn the meaning when experience, generally of a painful kind, has made it a reality to them. How often, when smarting under some unforeseen misfortune or disappointment, does a person call to mind some proverb or common saying, familiar to him all his life, the meaning of which, if he had ever before felt it as he does now, would have saved him from the calamity. There are indeed reasons for this, other than the absence of discussion; there are many truths of which the full meaning *cannot* be realized until personal experience has brought it home. But much more of the meaning even of these would have been understood, and what was understood would have been far more deeply impressed on the mind, if the man had been accustomed to hear it argued *pro* and *con* by people who did understand it. The fatal tendency of mankind to leave off thinking about a thing when it is no longer doubtful is the cause of half their errors. A contemporary author has well spoken of "the deep slumber of a decided opinion."

But what! (it may be asked), Is the absence of unanimity an indispensable condition of true knowledge? Is it necessary that some part of mankind should persist in error to enable any to realize the truth? Does a belief cease to be real and vital as soon as it is generally received—and is a proposition never thoroughly understood and felt unless some doubt of it remains? As soon as mankind have unanimously accepted a truth, does the truth perish within them? The highest aim and best result of improved intelligence, it has hitherto been thought, is to unite mankind more and more in the acknowledgment of all important truths; and does the intelligence only last as long as it has not achieved its object? Do the fruits of conquest perish by the very completeness of the victory?

I affirm no such thing. As mankind improve, the number of doctrines which are no longer disputed or doubted will be constantly on the increase; and the well-being of mankind may almost be measured by the number and gravity of the truths which have reached the point of being uncontested. The cessation, on one question after another, of serious controversy is one of the necessary incidents of the consolidation of opinion—a consolidation as salutary in the case of true opinions as it is dangerous and noxious when the opinions are erroneous. But though this gradual narrowing of the bounds of diversity of opinion is necessary in both senses of the term, being at once inevitable and indispensable, we are not therefore obliged to conclude that all its consequences must be beneficial. The loss of so important an aid to the intelligent and living apprehension of a truth as is afforded by the necessity of explaining it to, or defending it against, opponents, though not sufficient to outweigh, is no trifling drawback from the benefit of its universal recognition. Where this advantage can no longer be had, I confess I should like to see the teachers of mankind endeavoring to provide a substitute for it—some contrivance for making the difficulties of the question as present to the learner's consciousness as if they were pressed upon him by a dissentient champion, eager for his conversion.

But instead of seeking contrivances for this purpose, they have lost those they formerly had. The Socratic dialectics, so magnificently exemplified in the dialogues of Plato, were a contrivance of this description. They were essentially a negative discussion of the great questions of philosophy and life, directed with consummate skill to the purpose of convincing anyone who had merely adopted the commonplaces of received opinion that he did not understand the subject that he as yet attached no definite meaning to the doctrines he professed; in order that, becoming aware of his ignorance, he might be put in the way to obtain a stable belief, resting on a clear apprehension both of the meaning of doctrines and of their evidence. The school disputations of the Middle Ages had a somewhat similar object. They were intended to make sure that the pupil understood his own opinion, and (by necessary correlation) the opinion opposed to it, and could enforce the grounds of the one and confute those of the other. These last-mentioned contests had indeed the incurable defect that the premises appealed to were taken from authority, not from reason; and, as a discipline to the mind, they were in every respect inferior to the powerful dialectics which formed the intellects of the *"Socratici viri"*; but the modern mind owes far more to both than it is generally willing to admit, and the present modes of education contain nothing which in the smallest degree supplies the place either of the one or of the other. A person who derives all his instruction from teachers or books, even if he escape the besetting temptation of contenting himself with cram, is under no compulsion to hear both sides; accordingly it is far from a frequent accomplishment, even among thinkers, to know both sides; and the weakest part of what everybody says in defense of his opinion is what he intends as a reply to antagonists. It is the fashion of the present time to disparage negative logic—that which points out weaknesses in theory or errors in practice without establishing positive truths. Such negative criticism would indeed be poor enough as an ultimate result, but as a means to attaining any positive knowledge or conviction worthy the name it cannot be valued too highly; and until people are again systematically trained to it, there will be few great thinkers and a low general average of intellect in any but the mathematical and physical departments of speculation. On any other subject no one's opinions deserve the name of knowledge, except so far as he has either had forced upon him by others or gone through of himself the same mental process which would have been required of him in carrying on an active controversy with opponents. That, therefore, which, when absent, it is so indispensable, but so difficult, to create, how worse than absurd it is to forego when spontaneously offering itself! If there are any persons who contest a received opinion, or who will do so if law or opinion will let them, let us thank them for it, open our minds to listen to them, and rejoice that there is someone to do for us what we otherwise ought, if we have any regard for either the certainty or the vitality of our convictions, to do with much greater labor for ourselves.

It still remains to speak of one of the principal causes which make diversity of opinion advantageous, and will continue to do so until mankind shall have entered a stage of intellectual advancement which at present seems at an incalculable distance. We have hitherto considered only two possibilities: that the received opinion may be false, and some other opinion, consequently, true; or that, the received opinion being true, a conflict with the opposite error is essential to a clear apprehension and deep feeling of its truth. But there is a commoner case than either of these: when the conflicting doctrines, instead of being one true and the other false, share the truth between them, and the nonconforming opinion is needed to supply the remainder of the truth of which the received doctrine embodies only a part. Popular opinions, on subjects not palpable to sense, are often true, but seldom or never the whole truth. They are a part of the truth, sometimes a greater, sometimes a smaller part, but exaggerated, distorted, and disjointed from the truths by which they ought to be accompanied and limited. Heretical opinions, on the other hand, are generally some of these suppressed and neglected truths, bursting the bonds which kept them down, and either seeking reconciliation with the truth contained in the common opinion, or fronting it as enemies, and setting themselves up, with similar exclusiveness, as the whole truth. The latter case is hitherto the most frequent, as, in the human mind, one-sidedness has always been the rule, and many-sidedness the exception. Hence, even in revolutions of opinion, one part of the truth usually sets while another rises. Even progress, which ought to superadd, for the most part only substitutes one partial and incomplete truth for another; improvement consisting chiefly in this, that the new fragment of truth is more wanted, more adapted to the needs of the time than that which it displaces. Such being the partial character of prevailing opinions, even when resting on a true foundation, every opinion which embodies somewhat of the portion of truth which the common opinion omits ought to be considered precious, with whatever amount of error and confusion that truth may be blended. No sober judge of human affairs will feel bound to be indignant because those who force on our notice truths which we should otherwise have overlooked, overlook some of those which we see. Rather, he will think that so long as popular truth is one-sided, it is more desirable than otherwise that unpopular truth should have one-sided assertors, too, such being usually the most energetic and the most likely to compel reluctant attention to the fragment of wisdom which they proclaim as if it were the whole.

Thus, in the eighteenth century, when nearly all the instructed, and all those of the uninstructed who were led by them, were lost in admiration of what is called civilization, and of the marvels of modern science, literature, and philosophy, and while greatly overrating the amount of unlikeness between the men of modern and those of ancient times, indulged the belief that the whole of the difference was in their own favor; with what a salutary shock did the paradoxes of Rousseau explode like bombshells in the midst, dislocating the compact mass of one-sided opinion and forcing its elements to recombine in a better form and with additional ingredients. Not that the current opinions were on the whole farther from the truth than Rousseau's were; on the contrary, they were nearer to it; they contained more of positive truth, and very much less of error. Nevertheless there lay in Rousseau's doctrine, and has floated down the stream of opinion along with it, a considerable amount of exactly those truths which the popular opinion wanted; and these are the deposit which was left behind them when the flood subsided. The superior worth of simplicity of life, the enervating and demoralizing effect of the trammels and hypocrisies of artificial society are ideas which have never been entirely absent from cultivated minds since Rousseau wrote; and they will in time produce their due effect, though at present needing to be asserted as much as ever, and to be asserted by deeds; for words, on this subject, have nearly exhausted their power.

In politics, again, it is almost a commonplace that a party of order or stability and a party of progress or reform are both necessary elements of a healthy state of political life, until the one or the other shall have so enlarged its mental grasp as to be a party equally of order and of progress, knowing and distinguishing what is fit to be preserved from what ought to be swept away. Each of these modes of thinking derives its utility from the deficiencies of the other; but it is in a great measure the opposition of the other that keeps each within the limits of reason and sanity. Unless opinions favorable to democracy and to aristocracy, to property and to equality, to co-operation and to competition, to luxury and to abstinence, to sociality and individuality, to liberty and discipline, and all the other standing antagonisms of practical life, are expressed with equal freedom and enforced and defended with equal talent and energy, there is no chance of both elements obtaining their due; one scale is sure to go up, and the other down. Truth, in the great practical concerns of life, is so much a question of the reconciling and combining of opposites that very few have minds sufficiently capacious and impartial to make the adjustment with an approach to correctness, and it has to be made by the rough process of a struggle between combatants fighting under hostile banners. On any of the great open questions just enumerated, if either of the two opinions has a better claim than the other, not merely to be tolerated, but to be encouraged and countenanced, it is the one which happens at the particular time and place to be in a minority. That is the opinion which, for the time being, represents the neglected interests, the side of human well-being which is in danger of obtaining less than its share. I am aware that there is not, in this country, any intolerance of differences of opinion on most of these topics. They are adduced to show, by admitted and multiplied examples, the universality of the fact that only through diversity of opinion is there, in the existing state of human intellect, a chance of fair play to all sides of the truth. When there are persons to be found who form an exception to the apparent unanimity of the world on any subject, even if the world is in the right, it is always probable that dissentients have something worth hearing to say for themselves, and that truth would lose something by their silence.

It may be objected, "But *some* received principles, especially on the highest and most vital subjects, are more than half-truths. The Christian morality, for instance, is the whole truth on that subject, and if anyone teaches a morality which varies from it, he is wholly in error." As this is of all cases the most important in practice, none can be fitter to test the general maxim. But before pronouncing what Christian morality is or is not, it would be desirable to decide what is meant by Christian morality. If it means the morality of the New Testament, I wonder that any one who derives his knowledge of this from the book itself can suppose that it was announced, or intended, as a complete doctrine of morals. The Gospel always refers to a preexisting morality and confines its precepts to the particulars in which that morality was to be corrected or superseded by a wider and higher, expressing itself, moreover, in terms most general, often impossible to be interpreted literally, and possessing rather the impressiveness of poetry or eloquence than the precision of legislation. To extract from it a body of ethical doctrine has never been possible without eking it out from the Old Testament, that is, from a system elaborate indeed, but in many respects barbarous, and intended only for a barbarous people. St. Paul, a declared enemy to this Judaical mode of interpreting the doctrine and filling up the scheme of his Master, equally assumes a pre-existing morality, namely that of the Greeks and Romans; and his advice to Christians is in a great measure a system of accommodation to that, even to the extent of giving an apparent sanction to slavery. What is called Christian, but should rather be termed theological, morality was not the work of Christ or the Apostles, but is of much later origin, having been gradually built up by the Catholic Church of the first five centuries, and though not implicitly adopted by moderns and Protestants, has been much less modified by them than might have been expected. For the most part, indeed, they have contented themselves with cutting off the additions which had been made to it in the Middle Ages, each sect supplying the place by fresh additions, adapted to its own character and tendencies. That mankind owe a great debt to this morality, and to its early teachers, I should be the last person to deny, but I do not scruple to say of it that it is, in many important points, incomplete and one-sided, and that, unless ideas and feelings not sanctioned by it had contributed to the formation of European life and character, human affairs would have been in a worse condition than they now are. Christian morality (so called) has all the characters of a reaction; it is, in great part, a protest against paganism. Its ideal is negative rather than positive; passive rather than active; innocence rather than nobleness; abstinence from evil rather than energetic pursuit of good; in its precepts (as has been well said) "thou shalt not" predominates unduly over "though shalt." In its horror of sensuality, it made an idol of asceticism which has been gradually compromised away into one of legality. It holds out the hope of heaven and the threat of hell as the appointed and appropriate motives to a virtuous life: in this falling far below the best of the ancients, and doing what lies in it to give to human morality an essentially selfish character, by disconnecting each man's feelings of duty from the interests of his fellow creatures, except so far as a self-interested inducement is offered to him for consulting them. It is essentially a doctrine of passive obedience; it inculcates submission to all authorities found established; who indeed are not to be actively obeyed when they command what religion forbids, but who are not to be resisted, far less rebelled against, for any amount of wrong to ourselves. And while, in the morality of the best pagan nations, duty to the State holds even a disproportionate place, infringing on the just liberty of the individual, in purely Christian ethics that grand department of duty is scarcely noticed or acknowledged. It is in the Koran, not the New Testament, that we read the maxim: "A ruler who appoints any man to an office, when there is in his dominions another man better qualified for it, sins against God and against the State." What little recognition the idea of obligation to the public obtains in modern morality is derived from Greek and Roman sources, not from Christian; as, even in the morality of private life, whatever exists of magnanimity, highmindedness, personal dignity, even the sense of honor, is derived from the purely human, not the religious part of our education, and never could have grown out of a standard of ethics in which the only worth, professedly recognized, is that of obedience.

I am as far as anyone from pretending that these defects are necessarily inherent in the Christian ethics in every manner in which it can be conceived, or that the many requisites of a complete moral doctrine which it does not contain do not admit of being reconciled with it. Far less would I insinuate this out of the doctrines and precepts of

Christ himself. I believe that the sayings of Christ are all that I can see any evidence of their having been intended to be; that they are irreconcilable with nothing which a comprehensive morality requires; that everything which is excellent in ethics may be brought within them, with no greater violence to their language than has been done to it by all who have attempted to deduce from them any practical system of conduct whatever. But it is quite consistent with this to believe that they contain, and were meant to contain, only a part of the truth; that many essential elements of the highest morality are among the things which are not provided for, nor intended to be provided for, in the recorded deliverances of the Founder of Christianity, and which have been entirely thrown aside in the system of ethics erected on the basis of those deliverances by the Christian Church. And this being so, I think it a great error to persist in attempting to find in the Christian doctrine that complete rule for our guidance which its Author intended it to sanction and enforce, but only partially to provide. I believe, too, that this narrow theory is becoming a grave practical evil, detracting greatly from the moral training and instruction which so many well-meaning persons are now at length exerting themselves to promote. I much fear that by attempting to form the mind and feelings on an exclusively religious type, and discarding those secular standards (as for want of a better name they may be called) which heretofore coexisted with and supplemented the Christian ethics, receiving some of its spirits, and infusing into it some of theirs, there will result, and is even now resulting, a low, abject, servile type of character which, submit itself as it may to what it deems the Supreme Will, is incapable of rising to or sympathizing in the conception of Supreme Goodness. I believe that other ethics than any which can be evolved from exclusively Christian sources must exist side by side with Christian ethics to produce the moral regeneration of mankind; and that the Christian system is no exception to the rule that in an imperfect state of the human mind the interests of truth require a diversity of opinions. It is not necessary that in ceasing to ignore the moral truths not contained in Christianity men should ignore any of those which it does contain. Such prejudice or oversight, when it occurs, is altogether an evil, but it is one from which we cannot hope to be always exempt, and must be regarded as the price paid for an inestimable good. The exclusive pretension made by a part of the truth to be the whole must and ought to be protested against; and if a reactionary impulse should make the protestors unjust in their turn, this one-sidedness, like the other, may be lamented but must be tolerated. If Christians would teach infidels to be just to Christianity, they should themselves be just to infidelity. It can do truth no service to blink the fact, known to all who have the most ordinary acquaintance with literary history, that a large portion of the noblest and most valuable moral teaching has been the work, not only of men who did not know, but of men who knew and rejected, the Christian faith.

I do not pretend that the most unlimited use of the freedom of enunciating all possible opinions would put an end to the evils of religious or philosophical sectarianism. Every truth which men of narrow capacity are in earnest about is sure to be asserted, inculcated, and in many ways even acted on, as if no other truth existed in the world, or at all events none that could limit or qualify the first. I acknowledge that the tendency of all opinions to become sectarian is not cured by the freest discussion, but is often heightened and exacerbated thereby; the truth which ought to have been, but was not, seen, being rejected all the more violently because proclaimed by persons regarded as opponents. But it is not on the impassioned partisan, it is on the calmer and more disinterested bystander, that this collision of opinions works its salutary effect. Not the violent conflict between parts of the truth, but the quiet suppression of half of it, is the formidable evil; there is always hope when people are forced to listen to both sides; it is when they attend only to one that errors harden into prejudices, and truth itself ceases to have the effect of truth by being exaggerated into falsehood. And since there are few mental attributes more rare than that judicial faculty which can sit in intelligent judgment between two sides of a question, of which only one is represented by an advocate before it, truth has no chance but in proportion as every side of it, every opinion which embodies any fraction of the truth, not only finds advocates, but is so advocated as to be listened to.

We have now recognized the necessity to the mental well-being of mankind (on which all their other well-being depends) of freedom of opinion, and freedom of the expression of opinion, on four distinct grounds, which we will now briefly recapitulate:

First, if any opinion is compelled to silence, that opinion may, for aught we can certainly know, be true. To deny this is to assume our own infallibility.

Secondly, though the silenced opinion be an error, it may, and very commonly does, contain a portion of truth; and since the general or prevailing opinion on any subject is rarely or never the whole truth, it is only by the collision of adverse opinions that the remainder of the truth has any chance of being supplied.

Thirdly, even if the received opinion be not only true, but the whole truth; unless it is suffered to be, and actually is, vigorously and earnestly contested, it will, by most of those who receive it, be held in the manner of a prejudice, with little comprehension or feeling of its rational grounds. And not only this, but, fourthly, the meaning of the doctrine itself will be in danger of being lost or enfeebled, and deprived of its vital effect on the character and conduct: the dogma becoming a mere formal profession, inefficacious for good, but cumbering the ground and preventing the growth of any real and heartfelt conviction from reason or personal experience.

Before quitting the subject of freedom of opinion, it is fit to take some notice of those who say that the free expression of all opinions should be permitted on condition that the manner be temperate, and do not pass the bounds of fair discussion. Much might be said on the impossibility of fixing where these supposed bounds are to be placed; for if the test be offense to those whose opinions are attacked, I think experience testifies that this offense is given whenever the attack is telling and powerful, and that every opponent who pushes them hard, and whom they find it difficult to answer, appears to them, if he shows any strong feeling on the subject, an intemperate opponent. But this, though an important consideration in a practical point of view, merges in a more fundamental objection. Undoubtedly, the manner of asserting an opinion, even though it be a true one, may be very objectionable and may justly incur severe censure. But the principal offenses of the kind are such as it is mostly impossible, unless by accidental self-betrayal, to bring home to conviction. The gravest of them is, to argue sophistically, to suppress facts or arguments, to misstate the elements of the case, or misrepresent the opposite opinion. But all this, even to the most aggravated degree, is so continually done in perfect good faith by persons who are not considered, and in many other respects may not deserve to be considered, ignorant or incompetent, that it is rarely possible, on adequate grounds, conscientiously to stamp the misrepresentation as morally culpable, and still less could law presume to interfere with this kind of controversial misconduct. With regard to what is commonly meant by intemperate discussion, namely invective, sarcasm, personality, and the like, the denunciation of these weapons would deserve more sympathy if it were ever proposed to interdict them equally to both sides; but it is only desired to restrain the employment of them against the prevailing opinion; against the unprevailing they may not only be used without general disapproval, but will be likely to obtain for him who uses them the praise of honest zeal and righteous indignation. Yet whatever mischief arises from their use is greatest when they are employed against the comparatively defenseless; and whatever unfair advantage can be derived by any opinion from this mode of asserting it accrues almost exclusively to received opinions. The worst offense of this kind which can be committed by a polemic is to stigmatize those who hold the contrary opinion as bad and immoral men. To calumny of this sort, those who hold any unpopular opinion are peculiarly exposed, because they are in general few and uninfluential, and nobody but themselves feels much interested in seeing justice done them; but this weapon is, from the nature of the case, denied to those who attack a prevailing opinion: they can neither use it with safety to themselves, nor, if they could, would it do anything but recoil on their own cause. In general, opinions contrary to those commonly received can only obtain a hearing by studied moderation of language and the most cautious avoidance of unnecessary offense, from which they hardly ever deviate even in a slight degree without losing ground, while unmeasured vituperation employed on the side of the prevailing opinion really does deter people from professing contrary opinions and from listening to those who profess them. For the interest, therefore, of truth and justice it is far more important to restrain this employment of vituperative language than the other; and, for example, if it were necessary to choose, there would be much more need to discourage offensive attacks on infidelity than on religion. It is, however, obvious that law and authority have no business with restraining either, while opinion ought, in every instance, to determine its verdict by the circumstances of the individual case—condemning everyone, on whichever side of the argument he places himself, in whose mode of advocacy either want of candor, or malignity, bigotry, or intolerance of feeling manifest themselves; but not inferring these vices from the side which a person takes, though it be the contrary side of the question to our own; and giving merited honor to everyone, whatever opinion he may hold, who has calmness to see and honesty to state what his opponents and their opinions really are, exaggerating nothing to their discredit, keeping nothing back which tells, or can be supposed to tell, in their favor. This is the real morality of public discussion; and if often violated, I am happy to think that there are many controversialists who to a great extent observe it, and a still greater number who conscientiously strive toward it.

CHAPTER III

Of Individuality, as One of the Elements of Well-being

Such being the reasons which make it imperative that human beings should be free to form opinions and to express their opinions without reserve; and such the baneful consequences to the intellectual, and through that to the moral nature of man, unless this liberty is either conceded or asserted in spite of prohibition; let us next examine whether the same reasons do not require that men should be free to act upon their opinions—to carry these out in their lives without hindrance, either physical or moral, from their fellow men, so long as it is at their own risk and peril. This last proviso is of course indispensable. No one pretends that actions should be as free as opinions. On the contrary, even opinions lose their immunity when the circumstances in which they are expressed are such as to constitute their expression a positive instigation to some mischievous act. An opinion that corn dealers are starvers of the poor, or that private property is robbery, ought to be unmolested when simply circulated through the press, but may justly incur punishment when delivered orally to an excited mob assembled before the house of a corn dealer, or when handed about among the same mob in the form of a placard. Acts, of whatever kind, which without justifiable cause do harm to others may be, and in the more important cases absolutely require to be, controlled by the unfavorable sentiments, and, when needful, by the active interference of mankind. The liberty of the individual must be thus far limited; he must not make himself a nuisance to other people. But if he refrains from molesting others in what concerns them, and merely acts according to his own inclination and judgment in things which concern himself, the same reasons which show that opinion should be free prove also that he should be allowed, without molestation, to carry his opinions into practice at his own cost. That mankind are not infallible; that their truths, for the most part, are only half-truths; that unity of opinion, unless resulting from the fullest and freest comparison of opposite opinions, is not desirable, and diversity not an evil, but a good, until mankind are much more capable than at present of recognizing all sides of the truth, are principles applicable to men's modes of action not less than to their opinions. As it is useful that while mankind are imperfect there should be different opinions, so it is that there should be different experiments of living; that free scope should be given to varieties of character, short of injury to others; and that the worth of different modes of life should be proved practically, when anyone thinks fit to try them. It is desirable, in short, that in things which do not primarily concern others individuality should assert itself. Where not the person's own character but the traditions or customs of other people are the rule of conduct, there is wanting one of the principal ingredients of human happiness, and quite the chief ingredient of individual and social progress.

In maintaining this principle, the greatest difficulty to be encountered does not lie in the appreciation of means toward an acknowledged end, but in the indifference of persons in general to the end itself. If it were felt that the free development of individuality is one of the leading essentials of well-being; that it is not only a co-ordinate element with all that is designated by the terms civilization, instruction, education, culture, but is itself a necessary part and condition of all those things, there would be no danger that liberty should be undervalued, and the adjustment of the boundaries between it and social control would present no extraordinary difficulty. But the evil is that individual spontaneity is hardly recognized by the common modes of thinking as having any intrinsic worth, or deserving any regard on its own account. The majority, being satisfied with the ways of mankind as they now are (for it is they who make them what they are), cannot comprehend why those ways should not be good enough for everybody; and what is more, spontaneity forms no part of the ideal of the majority of moral and social reformers, but is rather looked on with jealousy, as a troublesome and perhaps rebellious obstruction to the general acceptance of what these reformers, in their own judgment, think would be best for mankind. Few persons, out of Germany, even comprehend the meaning of the doctrine which Wilhelm von Humboldt, so eminent both as a *savant* and as a politician, made the text of a treatise—that "the end of man, or that which is prescribed by the eternal or immutable dictates of reason, and not suggested by vague and transient desires, is the highest and most harmonious development of his powers to a complete and consistent whole"; that, therefore, the object "toward which every human being must ceaselessly direct his efforts, and on which especially those who design to influence their fellow men must ever keep their eyes, is the individuality of power and development"; that for this there are two requisites, "freedom, and variety of situations"; and that from the union of these arise "individual vigor and manifold diversity," which combine themselves in "originality."[6]

Little, however, as people are accustomed to a doctrine like that of von Humboldt, and surprising as it may be to them to find so high a value attached to individuality, the question, one must nevertheless think, can only be one of degree. No one's idea of excellence in conduct is that people should do absolutely nothing but copy one another. No one would assert that people ought not to put into their mode of life, and into the conduct of their concerns, any impress whatever of their own judgment or of their own individual character. On the other hand, it would be absurd to pretend that people ought to live as if nothing whatever had been known in the world before they came into it; as if experience had as yet done nothing toward showing that one mode of existence, or of conduct, is preferable to another. Nobody denies that people should be so taught and trained in youth as to know and benefit by the ascertained results of human experience. But it is the privilege and proper condition of a human being, arrived at the maturity of his faculties, to use and interpret experience in his own way. It is for him to find out what part of recorded experience is properly applicable to his own circumstances and character. The traditions and customs of other people are, to a certain extent, evidence of what their experience has taught *them*—presumptive evidence, and as such, have a claim to his deference: but, in the first place, their experience may be too narrow, or they may have not interpreted it rightly. Secondly, their interpretation of experience may be correct, but unsuitable to him. Customs are made for customary circumstances and customary characters; and his circumstances or his character may be uncustomary. Thirdly, though the customs be both good as customs and suitable to him, yet to conform to custom merely as custom does not educate or develop in him any of the qualities which are the distinctive endowment of a human being. The human faculties of perception, judgment, discriminative feeling, mental activity, and even moral preference are exercised only in making a choice. He who does anything because it is the custom makes no choice. He gains no practice either in discerning or in desiring what is best. The mental and moral, like the muscular, powers are improved only by being used. The faculties are called into no exercise by doing a thing merely because others do it, no more than by believing a thing only because others believe it. If the grounds of an opinion are not conclusive to the person's own reason, his reason cannot be strengthened, but is likely to be weakened, by his adopting it: and if the inducements to an act are not such as are consentaneous to his own feelings and character (where affection, or the rights of others, are not concerned), it is so much done toward rendering his feelings and character inert and torpid instead of active and energetic.

He who lets the world, or his own portion of it, choose his plan of life for him has no need of any other faculty than the ape-like one of imitation. He who chooses his plan for himself employs all his faculties. He must use observation to see, reasoning and judgment to foresee, activity to gather materials for decision, discrimination to decide, and when he has decided, firmness and self-control to hold to his deliberate decision. And these qualities he requires and exercises exactly in proportion as the part of his conduct which he determines according to his own judgment and feelings is a large one. It is possible that he might be guided in some good path, and kept out of harm's way, without any of these things. But what will be his comparative worth as a human being? It really is of importance, not only what men do, but also what manner of men they are that do it. Among the works of man which human life is rightly employed in perfecting and beautifying, the first in importance surely is man himself. Supposing it were possible to get houses built, corn grown, battles fought, causes tried, and even churches erected and prayers said by machinery—by automatons in human form—it would be a considerable loss to exchange for these automatons even the men and women who at present inhabit the more civilized parts of the world, and who assuredly are but starved specimens of what nature can and will produce. Human nature is not a machine to be built after a model, and set to do exactly the work prescribed for it, but a tree, which requires to grow and develop itself on all sides, according to the tendency of the inward forces which make it a living thing.

It will probably be conceded that it is desirable people should exercise their understandings, and that an intelligent following of custom, or even occasionally an intelligent deviation from custom, is better than a blind and simply mechanical adhesion to it. To a certain extent it is admitted that our understanding should be our own; but there is not the same willingness to admit that our desires and impulses should be our own likewise, or that to possess impulses of our own, and of any strength, is anything but a peril and a snare. Yet desires and impulses are as much a part of a perfect human being as beliefs and restraints; and strong impulses are only perilous when not properly balanced, when one set of aims and inclinations is developed into strength, while others, which ought to coexist with them, remain weak and inactive. It is not because men's desires are strong that they act ill; it is because their consciences are weak. There is no natural connection between strong impulses and a weak conscience. The natural connection is the other way. To say that one person's desires and feelings are stronger and more various than those of another is merely to say that he has more of the raw material of human nature and is therefore capable, perhaps of more evil, but certainly of more good. Strong impulses are but another name for energy. Energy may be turned to bad uses; but more good may always be made of an energetic nature than of an indolent and impassive one. Those who have most natural feeling are always those whose cultivated feelings may be made the strongest. The same strong susceptibilities which make the personal impulses vivid and powerful are also the source from whence are generated the most passionate love of virtue and the sternest self-control. It is through the cultivation of these that society both does its duty and protects its interests, not by rejecting the stuff of which heroes are made, because it knows not how to make them. A person whose desires and impulses are his own—are the expression of his own nature, as it has been developed and modified by his own culture—is said to have a character. One whose desires and impulses are not his own has no character, no more than a steam engine has a character. If, in addition to being his own, his impulses are strong and are under the government of a strong will, he has an energetic character. Whoever thinks that individuality of desires and impulses should not be encouraged to unfold itself must maintain that society has no need of strong natures—is not the better for containing many persons who have much character—and that a high general average of energy is not desirable.

In some early states of society, these forces might be, and were, too much ahead of the power which society then possessed of disciplining and controlling them. There has been a time when the element of spontaneity and individuality was in excess, and the social principle had a hard struggle with it. The difficulty then was to induce men of strong bodies or minds to pay obedience to any rules which required them to control their impulses. To overcome this difficulty, law and discipline, like the Popes struggling against the Emperors, asserted a power over the whole man, claiming to control all his life in order to control his character—which society had not found any other sufficient means of binding. But society has now fairly got the better of individuality; and the danger which threatens human nature is not the excess, but the deficiency, of personal impulses and preferences. Things are vastly changed since the passions of those who were strong by station or by personal endowment were in a state of habitual rebellion against laws and ordinances, and required to be rigorously chained up to enable the persons within their reach to enjoy any particle of security. In our times, from the highest class of society down to the lowest, everyone lives as under the eye of a hostile and dreaded censorship. Not only in what concerns others, but in what concerns only themselves, the individual or the family do not ask themselves, what do I prefer? or, what would suit my character and disposition? or, what would allow the best and highest in me to have fair play and enable it to grow and thrive? They ask themselves, what is suitable to my position? What is usually done by persons of my station and pecuniary circumstances? or (worse still) what is usually done by persons of a station and circumstances superior to mine? I do not mean that they choose what is customary in preference to what suits their own inclination. It does not occur to them to have any inclination except for what is customary. Thus the mind itself is bowed to the yoke: even in what people do for pleasure, conformity is the first thing thought of; they like in crowds; they exercise choice only among things commonly done; peculiarity of taste, eccentricity of conduct are shunned equally with crimes, until by dint of not following their own nature they have no nature to follow: their human capacities are withered and starved; they become incapable of any strong wishes or native pleasures, and are generally without either opinions or feelings of home growth, or properly their own. Now is this, or is it not, the desirable condition of human nature?

It is so, on the Calvinistic theory. According to that, the one great offense of man is self-will. All the good of which humanity is capable is comprised in obedience. You have no choice; thus you must do, and no otherwise: "Whatever is not a duty is a sin." Human nature being radically corrupt, there is no redemption for anyone until human nature is killed within him. To one holding this theory of life, crushing out any of the human faculties, capacities, and susceptibilities is no evil: man needs no capacity but that of surrendering himself to the will of God; and if he uses any of his faculties for any other purpose but to do that supposed will more effectually, he is better without them. This is the theory of Calvinism; and it is held, in a mitigated form, by many who do not consider themselves Calvinists; the mitigation consisting in giving a less ascetic interpretation to the alleged will of God, asserting it to be his will that mankind should gratify some of their inclinations, of course not in the manner they themselves prefer, but in the way of obedience, that is, in a way prescribed to them by authority, and, therefore, by the necessary condition of the case, the same for all.

In some such insidious form there is at present a strong tendency to this narrow theory of life, and to the pinched and hidebound type of human character which it patronizes. Many persons, no doubt, sincerely think that human beings thus cramped and dwarfed are as their Maker designed them to be, just as many have thought that trees are a much finer thing when clipped into pollards, or cut out into figures of animals, than as nature made them. But if it be any part of religion to believe that man was made by a good Being, it is more consistent with that faith to believe that this Being gave all human faculties that they might be cultivated and unfolded, not rooted out and consumed, and that he takes delight in every nearer approach made by his creatures to the ideal conception embodied in them, every increase in any of their capabilities of comprehension, of action, or of enjoyment. There is a different type of human excellence from the Calvinistic: a conception of humanity as having its nature bestowed on it for other purposes than merely to be abnegated. "Pagan self-assertion" is one of the elements of human worth, as well as "Christian self-denial."[7] There is a Greek ideal of self-development, which the Platonic and Christian ideal of self-government blends with, but does not supersede. It may be better to be a John Knox than an Alcibiades, but it is better to be a Pericles than either; nor would a Pericles, if we had one in these days, be without anything good which belonged to John Knox.

It is not by wearing down into uniformity all that is individual in themselves, but by cultivating it and calling it forth, within the limits imposed by the rights and interests of others, that human beings become a noble and beautiful object of contemplation; and as the works partake the character of those who do them, by the same process human life also becomes rich, diversified, and animating, furnishing more abundant aliment to high thoughts and elevating feelings, and strengthening the tie which binds every individual to the race, by making the race infinitely better worth belonging to. In proportion to the development of his individuality, each person becomes more valuable to himself, and is, therefore, capable of being more valuable to others. There is a greater fullness of life about his own existence, and when there is more life in the units there is more in the mass which is composed of them. As much compression as is necessary to prevent the stronger specimens of human nature from encroaching on the rights of others cannot be dispensed with; but for this there is ample compensation even in the point of view of human development. The means of development which the individual loses by being prevented from gratifying his inclinations to the injury of others are chiefly obtained at the expense of the development of other people. And even to himself there is a full equivalent in the better development of the social part of his nature, rendered possible by the restraint put upon the selfish part. To be held to rigid rules of justice for the sake of others develops the feelings and capacities which have the good of others for their object. But to be restrained in things not affecting their good, by their mere displeasure, develops nothing valuable except such force of character as may unfold itself in resisting the restraint. If acquiesced in, it dulls and blunts the whole nature. To give any fair play to the nature of each, it is essential that different persons should be allowed to lead different lives. In proportion as this latitude has been exercised in any age has that age been noteworthy to posterity. Even despotism does not produce its worst effects so long as individuality exists under it; and whatever crushes individuality is despotism, by whatever name it may be called and whether it professes to be enforcing the will of God or the injunctions of men.

Having said that the individuality is the same thing with development, and that it is only the cultivation of individuality which produces, or can produce, well-developed human beings, I might here close the argument; for what more or better can be said of any condition of human affairs than that it brings human beings themselves nearer to the best thing they can be? Or what worse can be said of any obstruction to good than that it prevents this? Doubtless, however, these considerations will not suffice to convince those who most need convincing; and it is necessary further to show that these developed human beings are of some use to the undeveloped—to point out to those who do not desire liberty, and would not avail themselves of it, that they may be in some intelligible manner rewarded for allowing other people to make use of it without hindrance.

In the first place, then, I would suggest that they might possibly learn something from them. It will not be denied by anybody that originality is a valuable element in human affairs. There is always need of persons not only to discover new truths and point out when what were once truths are true no longer, but also to commence new practices and set the example of more enlightened conduct and better taste and sense in human life. This cannot well be gainsaid by anybody who does not believe that the world has already attained perfection in all its ways and practices. It is true that this benefit is not capable of being rendered by everybody alike; there are but few persons, in comparison with the whole of mankind, whose experiments, if adopted by others, would be likely to be any improvement on established practice. But these few are the salt of the earth; without them, human life would become a stagnant pool. Not only is it they who introduce good things which did not before exist; it is they who keep the life in those which already exist. If there were nothing new to be done, would human intellect cease to be necessary? Would it be a reason why those who do the old things should forget why they are done, and do them like cattle, not like human beings? There is only too great a tendency in the best beliefs and practices to degenerate into the mechanical; and unless there were a succession of persons whose ever-recurring originality prevents the grounds of those beliefs and practices from becoming merely traditional, such dead matter would not resist the smallest shock from anything really alive, and there would be no reason why civilization should not die out, as in the Byzantine Empire. Persons of genius, it is true, are, and are always likely to be, a small minority; but in order to have them, it is necessary to preserve the soil in which they grow. Genius can only breathe freely in an *atmosphere* of freedom. Persons of genius are, *ex vi termini*, more individual than any other people—less capable, consequently, of fitting themselves, without hurtful compression, into any of the small number of molds which society provides in order to save its members the trouble of forming their own character. If from timidity they consent to be forced into one of these molds, and to let all that part of themselves which cannot expand under the pressure remain unexpanded, society will be little the better for their genius. If they are of a strong character and break their fetters, they become a mark for the society which has not succeeded in reducing them to commonplace, to point out with solemn warnings as "wild," "erratic," and the like—much as if one should complain of the Niagara river for not flowing smoothly between its banks like a Dutch canal.

I insist thus emphatically on the importance of genius and the necessity of allowing it to unfold itself freely both in thought and in practice, being well aware that no one will deny the position in theory, but knowing also that almost everyone, in reality, is totally indifferent to it. People think a genius a fine thing if it enables a man to write an exciting poem or paint a picture. But in its true sense, that of originality in thought and action, though no one says that it is not a thing to be admired, nearly all, at heart, think that they can do very well without it. Unhappily this is too natural to be wondered at. Originality is the one thing which unoriginal minds cannot feel the use of. They cannot see what it is to do for them: how should they? If they could see what it would do for them, it would not be originality. The first service which originality has to render them is that of opening their eyes: which being once fully done, they would have a chance of being themselves original. Meanwhile, recollecting that nothing was ever done which someone was not the first to do, and that all good things which exist are the fruits of originality, let them be modest enough to believe that there is something still left for it to accomplish, and assure themselves that they are more in need of originality, the less they are conscious of the want.

In sober truth, whatever homage may be professed, or even paid, to real or supposed mental superiority, the general tendency of things throughout the world is to render mediocrity the ascendant power among mankind. In ancient history, in the Middle Ages, and in a diminishing degree through the long transition from feudality to the present time, the individual was a power in himself; and if he had either great talents or a high social position, he was a considerable power. At present individuals are lost in the crowd. In politics it is almost a triviality to say that public opinion now rules the world. The only power deserving the name is that of masses, and of governments while they make themselves the organ of the tendencies and instincts of masses. This is as true in the moral and social relations of private life as in public transactions. Those whose opinions go by the name of public opinion are not always the same sort of public: in America, they are the whole white population; in England, chiefly the middle class. But they are always a mass, that is to say, collective mediocrity. And what is a still greater novelty, the mass do not now take their opinions from dignitaries in Church or State, from ostensible leaders, or from books. Their thinking is done for them by men much like themselves, addressing them or speaking in their name, on the spur of the moment, through the newspapers. I am not complaining of all this. I do not assert that anything better is compatible, as a general rule, with the present low state of the human mind. But that does not hinder the government of mediocrity from being mediocre government. No government by a democracy or a numerous aristocracy, either in its political acts or in the opinions, qualities, and tone of mind which it fosters, ever did or could rise above mediocrity except in so far as the sovereign. Many have let themselves be guided (which in their best times they always have done) by the counsels and influence of a more highly gifted and instructed *one or few*. The initiation of all wise or noble things comes and must come from individuals; generally at first from some one individual. The honor and glory of the average man is that he is capable of following that initiative; that he can respond internally to wise and noble things, and be led to them with his eyes open. I am not countenancing the sort of "hero-worship" which applauds the strong man of genius for forcibly seizing on the government of the world and making it do his bidding in spite of itself. All he can claim is freedom to point out the way. The power of compelling others into it is not only inconsistent with the freedom and development of all the rest, but corrupting to the strong man himself. It does seem, however, that when the opinions of masses of merely average men are everywhere become or becoming the dominant power, the counterpoise and corrective to that tendency would be the more and more pronounced individuality of those who stand on the higher eminences of thought. It is in these circumstances most especially that exceptional individuals, instead of being deterred, should be encouraged in acting differently from the mass. In other times there was no advantage in their doing so, unless they acted not only differently but better. In this age, the mere example of nonconformity, the mere refusal to bend the knee to custom, is itself a service. Precisely because the tyranny of opinion is such as to make eccentricity a reproach, it is desirable, in order to break through that tyranny, that people should be eccentric. Eccentricity has always abounded when and where strength of character has abounded; and the amount of eccentricity in a society has generally been proportional to the amount of genius, mental vigor, and moral courage it contained. That so few now dare to be eccentric marks the chief danger of the time.

I have said that it is important to give the freest scope possible to uncustomary things, in order that it may in time appear which of these are fit to be converted into customs. But independence of action and disregard of custom are not solely deserving of encouragement for the chance they afford that better modes of action, and customs more worthy of general adoption, may be struck out; nor is it only persons of decided mental superiority who have a just claim to carry on their lives in their own way. There is no reason that all human existence should be constructed on some one or some small number of patterns. If a person possesses any tolerable amount of common sense and experience, his own mode of laying out his existence is the best, not because it is the best in itself, but because it is his own mode. Human beings are not like sheep; and even sheep are not undistinguishably alike. A man cannot get a coat or a pair of boots to fit him unless they are either made to his measure or he has a whole warehouseful to choose from; and is it easier to fit him with a life than with a coat, or are human beings more like one another in their whole physical and spiritual conformation than in the shape of their feet? If it were only that people have diversities of taste, that is reason enough for not attempting to shape them all after one model. But different persons also require different conditions for their spiritual development; and can no more exist healthily in the same moral than all the variety of plants can in the same physical, atmosphere and climate. The same things which are helps to one person toward the cultivation of his higher nature are hindrances to another. The same mode of life is a healthy excitement to one, keeping all his faculties of action and enjoyment in their best order, while to another it is a distracting burden which suspends or crushes all internal life. Such are the differences among human beings in their sources of pleasure, their susceptibilities of pain, and the operation on them of different physical and moral agencies that, unless there is a corresponding diversity in their modes of life, they neither obtain their fair share of happiness, nor grow up to the mental, moral, and aesthetic stature of which their nature is capable. Why then should tolerance, as far as the public sentiment is concerned, extend only to tastes and modes of life which extort acquiescence by the multitude of their adherents? Nowhere (except in some monastic institutions) is diversity of taste entirely unrecognized; a person may, without blame, either like or dislike rowing, or smoking, or music, or athletic exercises, or chess, or cards, or study, because both those who like each of these things and those who dislike them are too numerous to be put down. But the man, and still more the woman, who can be accused either of doing "what nobody does," or of not doing "what everybody does," is the subject of as much depreciatory remark as if he or she had committed some grave moral delinquency. Persons require to possess a title, or some other badge of rank, or of the consideration of people of rank, to be able to indulge somewhat in the luxury of doing as they like without detriment to their estimation. To indulge somewhat, I repeat: for whoever allow themselves much of that indulgence incur the risk of something worse than disparaging speeches—they are in peril of a commission *de lunatico* and of having their property taken from them and given to their relations.[8]

There is one characteristic of the present direction of public opinion peculiarly calculated to make it intolerant of any marked demonstrations of individuality The general average of mankind are not only moderate in intellect, but also moderate in inclinations; they have no tastes or wishes strong enough to incline them to do anything unusual, and they consequently do not understand those who have, and class all such with the wild and intemperate whom they are accustomed to look down upon. Now, in addition to this fact which is general, we have only to suppose that a strong movement has set in toward the improvement of morals, and it is evident what we have to expect. In these days such a movement has set in; much has actually been effected in the way of increased regularity of conduct and discouragement of excesses; and there is a philanthropic spirit abroad for the exercise of which there is no more inviting field than the moral and prudential improvement of our fellow creatures. These tendencies of the times cause the public to be more disposed than at most former periods to prescribe general rules of conduct and endeavor to make everyone conform to the approved standard. And that standard, express or tacit, is to desire nothing strongly. Its ideal of character is to be without any marked character—to maim by compression, like a Chinese lady's foot, every part of human nature which stands out prominently and tends to make the person markedly dissimilar in outline to commonplace humanity.

As is usually the case with ideals which exclude one-half of what is desirable, the present standard of approbation produces only an inferior imitation of the other half. Instead of great energies guided by vigorous reason and strong feelings strongly controlled by a conscientious will, its result is weak feelings and weak energies, which therefore can be kept in outward conformity to rule without any strength either of will or of reason. Already energetic characters on any large scale are becoming merely traditional. There is now scarcely any outlet for energy in this country except business. The energy expended in this may still be regarded as considerable. What little is left from that employment is expended on some hobby, which may be a useful, even a philanthropic, hobby, but is always some one thing, and generally a thing of small dimensions. The greatness of England is now all collective; individually small, we only appear capable of anything great by our habit of combining; and with this our moral and religious philanthropists are perfectly contented. But it was men of another stamp than this that made England what it has been; and men of another stamp will be needed to prevent its decline.

The despotism of custom is everywhere the standing hindrance to human advancement, being in unceasing antagonism to that disposition to aim at something better than customary, which is called, according to circumstances, the spirit of liberty, or that of progress or improvement. The spirit of improvement is not always a spirit of liberty, for it may aim at forcing improvements on an unwilling people; and the spirit of liberty, in so far as it resists such attempts, may ally itself locally and temporarily with the opponents of improvement; but the only unfailing and permanent source of improvement is liberty, since by it there are as many possible independent centers of improvement as there are individuals. The progressive principle, however, in either shape, whether as the love of liberty or of improvement, is antagonistic to the sway of custom, involving at least emancipation from that yoke; and the contest between the two constitutes the chief interest of the history of mankind. The greater part of the world has, properly speaking, no history, because the despotism of Custom is complete. This is the case over the whole East. Custom is there, in all things, the final appeal; justice and right mean conformity to custom; the argument of custom no one, unless some tyrant intoxicated with power, thinks of resisting. And we see the result. Those nations must once have had originality; they did not start out of the ground populous, lettered, and versed in many of the arts of life; they made themselves all this, and were then the greatest and most powerful nations of the world. What are they now? The subjects or dependents of tribes whose forefathers wandered in the forests when theirs had magnificent palaces and gorgeous temples, but over whom custom exercised only a divided rule with liberty and progress. A people, it appears, may be progressive for a certain length of time, and then stop: when does it stop? When it ceases to possess individuality. If a similar change should befall the nations of Europe, it will not be in exactly the same shape: the despotism of custom with which these nations are threatened is not precisely stationariness. It proscribes singularity, but it dogs not preclude change, provided all change together. We have discarded the fixed costumes of our forefathers; everyone must still dress like other people, but the fashion may change once or twice a year. We thus take care that when there is a change, it shall be for change's sake, and not from any idea of beauty or convenience; for the same idea of beauty or convenience would not strike all the world at the same moment, and be simultaneously thrown aside by all at another moment. But we are progressive as well as changeable: we continually make new inventions in mechanical things, and keep them until they are again superseded by better; we are eager for improvement in politics, in education, even in morals, though in this last our idea of improvement chiefly consists in persuading or forcing other people to be as good as ourselves. It is not progress that we object to; on the contrary, we flatter ourselves that we are the most progressive people who ever lived. It is individuality that we war against: we should think we had done wonders if we had made ourselves all alike, forgetting that the unlikeness of one person to another is generally the first thing which draws the attention of either to the imperfection of his own type and the superiority of another, or the possibility, by combining the advantages of both, of producing something better than either. We have a warning example in China—a nation of much talent and, in some respects, even wisdom, owing to the rare good fortune of having been provided at an early period with a particularly good set of customs, the work, in some measure, of men to whom even the most enlightened European must accord, under certain limitations, the title of sages and philosophers. They are remarkable, too, in the excellence of their apparatus for impressing, as far as possible, the best wisdom they possess upon every mind in the community, and securing that those who have appropriated most of it shall occupy the posts of honor and power. Surely the people who did this have discovered the secret of human progressiveness and must have kept themselves steadily at the head of the movement of the world. On the contrary, they have become stationary—have remained so for thousands of years; and if they are ever to be further improved, it must be by foreigners. They have succeeded beyond all hope in what English

philanthropists are so industriously working at—in making a people all alike, all governing their thoughts and conduct by the same maxims and rules; and these are the fruits.
The modern *régime* of public opinion is, in an unorganized form, what the Chinese educational and political systems are in an organized; and unless individuality shall be able successfully to assert itself against this yoke, Europe, notwithstanding its noble antecedents
and its professed Christianity, will tend to become another China.

What is it that has hitherto preserved Europe from this lot? What has made the
European family of nations an improving, instead of a stationary, portion of mankind?
Not any superior excellence in them, which, when it exists, exists as the effect, not as the
cause, but their remarkable diversity of character and culture. Individuals, classes, nations
have been extremely unlike one another: they have struck out a great variety of paths, each
leading to something valuable; and although at every period those who traveled in different paths have been intolerant of one another, and each would have thought it an excellent thing if all the rest could have been compelled to travel his road, their attempts to
thwart each other's development have rarely had any permanent success, and each has in
time endured to receive the good which the others have offered. Europe is, in my judgment, wholly indebted to this plurality of paths for its progressive and many-sided development. But it already begins to possess this benefit in a considerably less degree. It is
decidedly advancing toward the Chinese idea of making all people alike. M. de
Tocqueville, in his last important work, remarks how much more the Frenchmen of the
present day resemble one another than did those even of the last generation. The same
remark might be made of Englishmen in a far greater degree. In a passage already quoted
from Wilhelm von Humboldt, he points out two things as necessary conditions of human
development—because necessary to render people unlike one another—namely, freedom
and variety of situations. The second of these two conditions is in this country every day
diminishing. The circumstances which surround different classes and individuals, and
shape their characters, are daily becoming more assimilated. Formerly, different ranks,
different neighborhoods, different trades and professions lived in what might be called
different worlds; at present, to a great degree in the same. Comparatively speaking, they
now read the same things, listen to the same things, see the same things, go to the same
places, have their hopes and fears directed to the same objects, have the same rights and
liberties, and the same means of asserting them. Great as are the differences of position
which remain, they are nothing to those which have ceased. And the assimilation is still
proceeding. All the political changes of the age promote it, since they all tend to raise the
low and to lower the high. Every extension of education promotes it, because education
brings people under common influences and gives them access to the general stock of facts
and sentiments. Improvement in the means of communication promotes it, by bringing
the inhabitants of distant places into personal contact, and keeping up a rapid flow of
changes of residence between one place and another. The increase of commerce and manufactures promotes it, by diffusing more widely the advantages of easy circumstances and
opening all objects of ambition, even the highest, to general competition, whereby the
desire of rising becomes no longer the character of a particular class, but of all classes. A
more powerful agency than even all these, in bringing about a general similarity among
mankind, is the complete establishment, in this and other free countries, of the ascendancy of public opinion in the State. As the various social eminences which enabled persons entrenched on them to disregard the opinion of the multitude gradually become
leveled; as the very idea of resisting the will of the public, when it is positively known
that they have a will, disappears more and more from the minds of practical politicians,
there ceases to be any social support for nonconformity—any substantive power in society

which, itself opposed to the ascendancy of numbers, is interested in taking under its protection opinions and tendencies at variance with those of the public.

The combination of all these causes forms so great a mass of influences hostile to individuality that it is not easy to see how it can stand its ground. It will do so with increasing difficulty unless the intelligent part of the public can be made to feel its value—to see that it is good there should be differences, even though not for the better, even though, as it may appear to them, some should be for the worse. If the claims of individuality are ever to be asserted, the time is now while much is still wanting to complete the enforced assimilation. It is only in the earlier stages that any stand can be successfully made against the encroachment. The demand that all other people shall resemble ourselves grows by what it feeds on. If resistance waits till life is reduced *nearly* to one uniform type, all deviations from that type will come to be considered impious, immoral, even monstrous and contrary to nature. Mankind speedily become unable to conceive diversity when they have been for some time unaccustomed to see it.

CHAPTER IV

Of The Limits to the Authority of Society Over the Individual

What, then, is the rightful limit to the sovereignty of the individual over himself? Where does the authority of society begin? How much of human life should be assigned to individuality, and how much to society?

Each will receive its proper share if each has that which more particularly concerns it. To individuality should belong the part of life in which it is chiefly the individual that is interested; to society, the part which chiefly interests society.

Though society is not founded on a contract, and though no good purpose is answered by inventing a contract in order to deduce social obligations from it, everyone who receives the protection of society owes a return for the benefit, and the fact of living in society renders it indispensable that each should be bound to observe a certain line of conduct toward the rest. This conduct consists, first, in not injuring the interests of one another, or rather certain interests which, either by express legal provision or by tacit understanding, ought to be considered as rights; and secondly, in each person's bearing his share (to be fixed on some equitable principle) of the labors and sacrifices incurred for defending the society or its members from injury and molestation. These conditions society is justified in enforcing at all costs to those who endeavor to withhold fulfillment. Nor is this all that society may do. The acts of an individual may be hurtful to others or wanting in due consideration for their welfare, without going to the length of violating any of their constituted rights. The offender may then be justly punished by opinion, though not by law. As soon as any part of a person's conduct affects prejudicially the interests of others, society has jurisdiction over it, and the question whether the general welfare will or will not be promoted by interfering with it becomes open to discussion. But there is no room for entertaining any such question when a person's conduct affects the interests of no persons besides himself, or needs not affect them unless they like (all the persons concerned being of full age and the ordinary amount of understanding). In all such cases, there should be perfect freedom, legal and social, to do the action and stand the consequences.

It would be a great misunderstanding of this doctrine to suppose that it is one of selfish indifference which pretends that human beings have no business with each other's conduct in life, and that they should not concern themselves about the well-doing or well-being of one another, unless their own interest is involved. Instead of any diminution, there is need of a great increase of disinterested exertion to promote the good of others. But disinterested benevolence can find other instruments to persuade people to their good than whips and scourges, either of the literal or the metaphorical sort. I am the last person to undervalue the self-regarding virtues; they are only second in importance, if even second, to the social. It is equally the business of education to cultivate both. But even education works by conviction and persuasion as well as by compulsion, and it is by the former only that, when the period of education is passed, the self-regarding virtues should be inculcated. Human beings owe to each other help to distinguish the better from the worse, and encouragement to choose the former and avoid the latter. They should be forever stimulating each other to increased exercise of their higher faculties and increased direction of their feelings and aims toward wise instead of foolish, elevating instead of degrading, objects and contemplations. But neither one person, nor any number of persons, is warranted in saying to another human creature of ripe years that he shall not do with his life for his own benefit what he chooses to do with it. He is the person most interested in his own well-being: the interest which any other person, except in cases of strong personal attachment, can have in it is trifling compared with that which he himself has; the interest which society has in him individually (except as to his conduct to others) is fractional and altogether indirect, while with respect to his own feelings and circumstances the most ordinary man or woman has means of knowledge immeasurably surpassing those that can be possessed by anyone else. The interference of society to overrule his judgment and purposes in what only regards himself must be grounded on general presumptions which may be altogether wrong and, even if right, are as likely as not to be misapplied to individual cases, by persons no better acquainted with the circumstances of such cases than those are who look at them merely from without. In this department, therefore, of human affairs, individuality has its proper field of action. In the conduct of human beings toward one another it is necessary that general rules should for the most part be observed in order that people may know what they have to expect; but in each person's own concerns his individual spontaneity is entitled to free exercise. Considerations to aid his judgment, exhortations to strengthen his will may be offered to him, even obtruded on him, by others; but he himself is the final judge. All errors which he is likely to commit against advice and warning are far outweighed by the evil of allowing others to constrain him to what they deem his good.

. I do not mean that the feelings with which a person is regarded by others ought not to be in any way affected by his self-regarding qualities or deficiencies. This is neither possible nor desirable. If he is eminent in any of the qualities which conduce to his own good, he is, so far, a proper object of admiration. He is so much the nearer to the ideal perfection of human nature. If he is grossly deficient in those qualities, a sentiment the opposite of admiration will follow. There is a degree of folly, and a degree of what may be called (though the phrase is not unobjectionable) lowness or depravation of taste, which, though it cannot justify doing harm to the person who manifests it, renders him necessarily and properly a subject of distaste, or, in extreme cases, even of contempt: a person could not have the opposite qualities in due strength without entertaining these feelings. Though doing no wrong to anyone, a person may so act as to compel us to judge him, and feel to him, as a fool or as a being of an inferior order; and since this judgment and feeling are a fact which he would prefer to avoid, it is doing him a service to warn him of it beforehand, as of any other disagreeable consequence to which he exposes himself. It would be well, indeed, if this good office were much more freely rendered than the common notions of politeness at present permit, and if one person could honestly point out to another that he thinks him in fault, without being considered unmannerly or presuming. We have a right, also, in various ways, to act upon our unfavorable opinion of anyone, not to the oppression of his individuality, but in the exercise of ours. We are not bound, for example, to seek his society; we have a right to avoid it (though not to parade the avoidance), for we have a right to choose the society most acceptable to us. We have a right, and it may be our duty, to caution others against him if we think his example or conversation likely to have a pernicious effect on those with whom he associates. We may give others a preference over him in optional good offices, except those which tend to his improvement. In these various modes a person may suffer very severe penalties at the hands of others for faults which directly concern only himself; but he suffers these penalties only in so far as they are the natural and, as it were, the spontaneous consequences of the faults themselves, not because they are purposely inflicted on him for the sake of punishment. A person who shows rashness, obstinacy, self-conceit—who cannot live within moderate means; who cannot restrain himself from hurtful indulgence; who pursues animal pleasures at the expense of those of feeling and intellect—must expect to be lowered in the opinion of others, and to have a less share of their favorable sentiments; but of this he has no right to complain unless he has merited their favor by special excellence in his social relations and has thus established a title to their good offices, which is not affected by his demerits toward himself.

What I contend for is that the inconveniences which are strictly inseparable from the unfavorable judgment of others are the only ones to which a person should ever be subjected for that portion of his conduct and character which concerns his own good, but which does not affect the interest of others in their relations with him. Acts injurious to others require a totally different treatment. Encroachment on their rights; infliction on them of any loss or damage not justified by his own rights; falsehood or duplicity in dealing with them; unfair or ungenerous use of advantages over them; even selfish abstinence from defending them against injury—these are fit objects of moral reprobation and, in grave cases, of moral retribution and punishment. And not only these acts, but the dispositions which lead to them, are properly immoral and fit subjects of disapprobation which may rise to abhorrence. Cruelty of disposition; malice and ill-nature; that most antisocial and odious of all passions, envy; dissimulation and insincerity, irascibility on insufficient cause, and resentment disproportioned to the provocation; the love of domineering over others; the desire to engross more than one's share of advantages (the *pleonexia* of the Greeks); the pride which derives gratification from the abasement of others; the egotism which thinks self and its concerns more important than everything else, and decides all doubtful questions in its own favor—these are moral vices and constitute a bad and odious moral character; unlike the self-regarding faults previously mentioned, which are not properly immoralities and, to whatever pitch they may be carried, do not constitute wickedness. They may be proofs of any amount of folly or want of personal dignity and self-respect, but they are only a subject of moral reprobation when they involve a breach of duty to others, for whose sake the individual is bound to have care for himself. What are called duties to ourselves are not socially obligatory unless circumstances render them at the same time duties to others. The term duty to oneself, when it means anything more than prudence, means self-respect or self-development, and for none of these is anyone accountable to his fellow creatures, because for none of them is it for the good of mankind that he be held accountable to them.

The distinction between the loss of consideration which a person may rightly incur by defect of prudence or of personal dignity, and the reprobation which is due to him for an offense against the rights of others, is not a merely nominal distinction. It makes a vast difference both in our feelings and in our conduct toward him whether he displeases us in things in which we think we have a right to control him or in things in which we know that we have not. If he displeases us, we may express our distaste, and we may stand aloof from a person as well as from a thing that displeases us; but we shall not therefore feel called on to make his life uncomfortable. We shall reflect that he already bears, or will bear, the whole penalty of his error; if he spoils his life by mismanagement, we shall not, for that reason, desire to spoil it still further; instead of wishing to punish him, we shall rather endeavor to alleviate his punishment by showing him how he may avoid or cure the evils his conduct tends to bring upon him. He may be to us an object of pity, perhaps of dislike, but not of anger or resentment; we shall not treat him like an enemy of society; the worst we shall think ourselves justified in doing is leaving him to himself, if we do not interfere benevolently by showing interest or concern for him. It is far otherwise if he has infringed the rules necessary for the protection of his fellow creatures, individually or collectively. The evil consequences of his acts do not then fall on himself, but on others; and society, as the protector of all its members, must retaliate on him, must inflict pain on him for the express purpose of punishment, and must take care that it be sufficiently severe. In the one case, he is an offender at our bar, and we are called on not only to sit in judgment on him, but, in one shape or another, to execute our own sentence; in the other case, it is not our part to inflict any suffering on him, except what may incidentally follow from our using the same liberty in the regulation of our own affairs which we allow to him in his.

The distinction here pointed out between the part of a person's life which concerns only himself and that which concerns others, many persons will refuse to admit. How (it may be asked) can any part of the conduct of a member of society be a matter of indifference to the other members? No person is an entirely isolated being; it is impossible for a person to do anything seriously or permanently hurtful to himself without mischief reaching at least to his near connections, and often far beyond them. If he injures his property, he does harm to those who directly or indirectly derived support from it, and usually diminishes, by a greater or less amount, the general resources of the community. If he deteriorates his bodily or mental faculties, he not only brings evil upon all who depended upon him for any portion of their happiness, but disqualifies himself for rendering the services which he owes to his fellow creatures generally, perhaps becomes a burden on their affection or benevolence; and if such conduct were very frequent hardly any offense that is committed would detract more from the general sum of good. Finally, if by his vices or follies a person does no direct harm to others, he is nevertheless (it may be said) injurious by his example, and ought to be compelled to control himself for the sake of those whom the sight or knowledge of his conduct might corrupt or mislead.

And even (it will be added) if the consequences of misconduct could be confined to the vicious or thoughtless individual, ought society to abandon to their own guidance those who are manifestly unfit for it? If protection against themselves is confessedly due to children and persons under age, is not society equally bound to afford it to persons of mature years who are equally incapable of self-government? If gambling, or drunkenness, or incontinence, or idleness, or uncleanliness are as injurious to happiness, and as great a hindrance to improvement, as many or most of the acts prohibited by law, why (it may be asked) should not law, so far as is consistent with practicability and social convenience, endeavor to repress these also? And as a supplement to the unavoidable imperfections of law, ought not opinion at least to organize a powerful police against these vices and visit rigidly with social penalties those who are known to practice them? There is no question here (it may be said) about restricting individuality, or impeding the trial of new and original experiments in living. The only things it is sought to prevent are things which have been tried and condemned from the beginning of the world until now—things which experience has shown not to be useful or suitable to any person's individuality. There must be some length of time and amount of experience after which a moral or prudential truth may be regarded as established; and it is merely desired to prevent generation after generation from falling over the same precipice which has been fatal to their predecessors.

I fully admit that the mischief which a person does to himself may seriously affect, both through their sympathies and their interests, those nearly connected with him and, in a minor degree, society at large. When, by conduct of this sort, a person is led to violate a distinct and assignable obligation to any other person or persons, the case is taken out of the self-regarding class and becomes amenable to moral disapprobation in the proper sense of the term. If, for example, a man, through intemperance or extravagance, becomes unable to pay his debts, or, having undertaken the moral responsibility of a family, becomes from the same cause incapable of supporting or educating them, he is deservedly reprobated and might be justly punished; but it is for the breach of duty to his family or creditors, not for the extravagance. If the resources which ought to have been devoted to them had been diverted from them for the most prudent investment, the moral culpability would have been the same. George Barnwell murdered his uncle to get money for his mistress, but if he had done it to set himself up in business, he would equally have been hanged. Again, in the frequent case of a man who causes grief to his family by addiction to bad habits, he deserves reproach for his unkindness or ingratitude; but so he may for cultivating habits not in themselves vicious, if they are painful to those with whom he passes his life, or who from personal ties are dependent on him for their comfort. Whoever fails in the consideration generally due to the interests and feelings of others, not being compelled by some more imperative duty, or justified by allowable self-preference, is a subject of moral disapprobation for that failure, but not for the cause of it, nor for the errors, merely personal to himself, which may have remotely led to it. In like manner, when a person disables himself by conduct purely self-regarding, from the performance of some definite duty incumbent on him to the public, he is guilty of a social offense. No person ought to be punished simply for being drunk; but a soldier or policeman should be punished for being drunk on duty. Whenever, in short, there is a definite damage, or a definite risk of damage, either to an individual or to the public, the case is taken out of the province of liberty and placed in that of morality or law.

But with regard to the merely contingent or, as it may be called, constructive injury which a person causes to society by conduct which neither violates any specific duty to the public, nor occasions perceptible hurt to any assignable individual except himself, the inconvenience is one which society can afford to bear, for the sake of the greater good of human freedom. If grown persons are to be punished for not taking proper care of themselves, I would rather it were for their own sake than under pretense of preventing them from impairing their capacity or rendering to society benefits which society does not pretend it has a right to exact. But I cannot consent to argue the point as if society had no means of bringing its weaker members up to its ordinary standard of rational conduct, except waiting till they do something irrational, and then punishing them, legally or morally, for it. Society has had absolute power over them during all the early portion of their existence; it has had the whole period of childhood and nonage in which to try whether it could make them capable of rational conduct in life. The existing generation is master both of the training and the entire circumstances of the generation to come; it cannot indeed make them perfectly wise and good, because it is itself so lamentably deficient in goodness and wisdom; and its best efforts are not always, in individual cases, its most successful ones; but it is perfectly well able to make the rising generation, as a whole, as good as, and a little better than, itself. If society lets any considerable number of its members grow up mere children, incapable of being acted on by rational consideration of distant motives, society has itself to blame for the consequences. Armed not only with all the powers of education, but with the ascendency which the authority of a received opinion always exercises over the minds who are least fitted to judge for themselves, and aided by the *natural* penalties which cannot be prevented from falling on those who incur the distaste or the contempt of those who know them—let not society pretend that it needs, besides all this, the power to issue commands and enforce obedience in the personal concerns of individuals in which, on all principles of justice and policy, the decision ought to rest with those who are to abide the consequences. Nor is there anything which tends more to discredit and frustrate the better means of influencing conduct than a resort to the worse. If there be among those whom it is attempted to coerce into prudence or temperance any of the material of which vigorous and independent characters are made, they will infallibly rebel against the yoke. No such person will ever feel that others have a right to control him in his concerns, such as they have to prevent him from injuring them in theirs; and it easily comes to be considered a mark of spirit and courage to fly in the face of such usurped authority and do with ostentation the exact opposite of what it enjoins, as in the fashion of grossness which succeeded, in the time of Charles II, to the fanatical moral intolerance of the Puritans. With respect to what is said of the necessity of protecting society from the bad example set to others by the vicious or the self-indulgent, it is true that bad example may have a pernicious effect, especially the example of doing wrong to others with impunity to the wrongdoer. But we are now speaking of conduct which, while it does no wrong to others, is supposed to do great harm to the agent himself; and I do not see how those who believe this can think otherwise than that the example, on the whole, must be more salutary than hurtful, since, if it displays the misconduct, it displays also the painful or degrading consequences which, if the conduct is justly censured, must be supposed to be in all or most cases attendant on it.

But the strongest of all the arguments against the interference of the public with purely personal conduct is that, when it does interfere, the odds are that it interferes wrongly and in the wrong place. On questions of social morality, of duty to others, the opinion of the public, that is, of an overruling majority, though often wrong, is likely to be still oftener right, because on such questions they are only required to judge of their own interests, of the manner in which some mode of conduct, if allowed to be practiced, would affect themselves. But the opinion of a similar majority, imposed as a law on the minority, on questions of self-regarding conduct is quite as likely to be wrong as right, for in these cases public opinion means, at the best, some people's opinion of what is good or bad for other people, while very often it does not even mean that—the public, with the most perfect indifference, passing over the pleasure or convenience of those whose conduct they censure and considering only their own preference. There are many who consider as an injury to themselves any conduct which they have a distaste for, and resent it as an outrage to their feelings; as a religious bigot, when charged with disregarding the religious feelings of others, has been known to retort that they disregard his feelings by persisting in their abominable worship or creed. But there is no parity between the feeling of a person for his own opinion and the feeling of another who is offended at his holding it, no more than between the desire of a thief to take a purse and the desire of the right owner to keep it. And a person's taste is as much his own peculiar concern as his opinion or his purse. It is easy for anyone to imagine an ideal public which leaves the freedom and choice of individuals in all uncertain matters undisturbed and only requires them to abstain from modes of conduct which universal experience has condemned. But where has there been seen a public which set any such limit to its censorship? Or when does the public trouble itself about universal experience? In its interferences with personal conduct it is seldom thinking of anything but the enormity of acting or feeling differently from itself; and this standard of judgment, thinly disguised, is held up to mankind as the dictate of religion and philosophy by nine-tenths of all moralists and speculative writers. These teach that things are right because they are right; because we feel them to be so. They tell us to search in our own minds and hearts for laws of conduct binding on ourselves and on all others. What can the poor public do but apply these instructions and make their own personal feelings of good and evil, if they are tolerably unanimous in them, obligatory on all the world?

The evil here pointed out is not one which exists only in theory; and it may perhaps be expected that I should specify the instances in which the public of this age and country improperly invests its own preferences with the character of moral laws. I am not writing an essay on the aberrations of existing moral feeling. That is too weighty a subject to be discussed parenthetically, and by way of illustration. Yet examples are necessary to show that the principle I maintain is of serious and practical moment, and that I am not endeavoring to erect a barrier against imaginary evils. And it is not difficult to show, by abundant instances, that to extend the bounds of what may be called moral police until it encroaches on the most unquestionably legitimate liberty of the individual is one of the most universal of all human propensities.

As a first instance, consider the antipathies which men cherish on no better grounds than that persons whose religious opinions are different from theirs do not practice their religious observances, especially their religious abstinences. To cite a rather trivial example, nothing in the creed or practice of Christians does more to envenom the hatred of Mohammedans against them than the fact of their eating pork. There are few acts which Christians and Europeans regard with more unaffected disgust than Mussulmans regard this particular mode of satisfying hunger. It is in the first place, an offense against their religion; but this circumstance by no means explains either the degree or the kind of their repugnance; for wine also is forbidden by their religion, and to partake of it is by all Mussulmans accounted wrong, but not disgusting. Their aversion to the flesh of the "unclean beast" is, on the contrary, of that peculiar character, resembling an instinctive antipathy, which the idea of uncleanness, when once it thoroughly sinks into the feelings, seems always to excite even in those whose personal habits are anything but scrupulously cleanly, and of which the sentiment of religious impurity, so intense in the Hindus, is a remarkable example. Suppose now that in a people of whom the majority were Mussulmans, that majority should insist upon not permitting pork to be eaten within the limits of the country. This would be nothing new in Mohammedan countries.[9] Would it be a legitimate exercise of the moral authority of public opinion, and if not, why not? The practice is really revolting to such a public. They also sincerely think that it is forbidden and abhorred by the Deity. Neither could the prohibition be censured as religious persecution. It might be religious in its origin, but it would not be persecution for religion, since nobody's religion makes it a duty to eat pork. The only tenable ground of condemnation would be that with the personal tastes and self-regarding concerns of individuals the public has no business to interfere.

To come somewhat nearer home: the majority of Spaniards consider it a gross impiety, offensive in the highest degree to the Supreme Being, to worship him in any other manner than the Roman Catholic; and no other public worship is lawful on Spanish soil. The people of all southern Europe look upon a married clergy as not only irreligious, but unchaste, indecent, gross, disgusting. What do Protestants think of these perfectly sincere feelings, and of the attempt to enforce them against non-Catholics? Yet, if mankind are justified in interfering with each other's liberty in things which do not concern the interests of others, on what principle is it possible consistently to exclude these cases? Or who can blame people for desiring to suppress what they regard as a scandal in the sight of God and man? No stronger case can be shown for prohibiting anything which is regarded as a personal immorality than is made out for suppressing these practices in the eyes of those who regard them as impieties; and unless we are willing to adopt the logic of persecutors, and to say that we may persecute others because we are right, and that they must not persecute us because they are wrong, we must beware of admitting a principle of which we should resent as a gross injustice the application to ourselves.

The preceding instances may be objected to, although unreasonably, as drawn from contingencies impossible among us—opinion, in this country, not being likely to enforce abstinence from meats or to interfere with people for worshiping and for either marrying or not marrying, according to their creed or inclination. The next example, however, shall be taken from an interference with liberty which we have by no means passed all danger of Wherever the Puritans have been sufficiently powerful, as in New England, and in Great Britain at the time of the Commonwealth, they have endeavored, with considerable success, to put down all public, and nearly all private, amusements: especially music, dancing, public games, or other assemblages for purposes of diversion, and the theater. There are still in this country large bodies of persons by whose notions of morality and religion these recreations are condemned; and those persons belonging chiefly to the middle class, who are the ascendant power in the present social and political condition of the kingdom, it is by no means impossible that persons of these sentiments may at some time or other command a majority in Parliament. How will the remaining portion of the community like to have the amusements that shall be permitted to them regulated by the religious and moral sentiments of the stricter Calvinists and Methodists? Would they not, with considerable peremptoriness, desire these intrusively pious members of society to mind their own business? This is precisely what should be said to every government and every public who have the pretension that no person shall enjoy any pleasure which they think wrong. But if the principle of the pretension be admitted, no one can reasonably object to its being acted on in the sense of the majority, or other preponderating power in the country; and all persons must be ready to conform to the idea of a Christian commonwealth as understood by the early settlers in New England, if a religious profession similar to theirs should ever succeed in regaining its lost ground, as religions supposed to be declining have so often been known to do.

To imagine another contingency, perhaps more likely to be realized than the one last mentioned. There is confessedly a strong tendency in the modern world toward a democratic constitution of society, accompanied or not by popular political institutions. It is affirmed that in the country where this tendency is most completely realized—where both society and the government are most democratic: the United States—the feeling of the majority, to whom any appearance of a more showy or costly style of living than they can hope to rival is disagreeable, operates as a tolerably effectual sumptuary law, and that in many parts of the Union it is really difficult for a person possessing a very large income to find any mode of spending it which will not incur popular disapprobation. Though such statements as these are doubtless much exaggerated as a representation of existing facts, the state of things they describe is not only a conceivable and possible, but a probable result of democratic feeling combined with the notion that the public has a right to veto on the manner in which individuals shall spend their incomes. We have only further to suppose a considerable diffusion of Socialist opinions, and it may become infamous in the eyes of the majority to possess more property than some very small amount, or any income not earned by manual labor. Opinions similar in principle to these already prevail widely among the artisan class and weigh oppressively on those who are amenable to the opinion chiefly of that class, namely, its own members. It is known that the bad workmen who form the majority of the operatives in many branches of industry are decidedly of opinion that bad workmen ought to receive the same wages as good, and that no one ought to be allowed, through piecework or otherwise, to earn by superior skill or industry more than others can without it. And they employ a moral police, which occasionally becomes a physical one, to deter skillful workmen from receiving, and employers from giving, a larger remuneration for a more useful service. If the public have any jurisdiction over private concerns, I cannot see that these people are in fault, or that any individual's particular public can be blamed for asserting the same authority over his individual conduct which the general public asserts over people in general.

But, without dwelling upon supposititious cases, there are, in our own day, gross usurpations upon the liberty of private life actually practiced, and still greater ones threatened with some expectation of success, and opinions propounded which assert an unlimited right in the public not only to prohibit by law everything which it thinks wrong, but, in order to get at what it thinks wrong, to prohibit a number of things which it admits to be innocent.

Under the name of preventing intemperance, the people of one English colony, and of nearly half the United States, have been interdicted by law from making any use whatever of fermented drinks, except for medical purposes, for prohibition of their sale is in fact, as it is intended to be, prohibition of their use. And though the impracticability of executing the law has caused its repeal in several of the States which had adopted it, including the one from which it derives its name, an attempt has notwithstanding been commenced, and is prosecuted with considerable zeal by many of the professed philanthropists, to agitate for a similar law in the country. The association, or "Alliance," as it terms itself, which has been formed for this purpose, has acquired some notoriety through the publicity given to a correspondence between its secretary and one of the very few English public men who hold that a politican's opinions ought to be founded on principles. Lord Stanley's share in this correspondence is calculated to strengthen the hopes already built on him by those who know how rare such qualities as are manifested in some of his public appearances unhappily are among those who figure in political life. The organ of the Alliance, who would "deeply deplore the recognition of any principle which could be wrested to justify bigotry and persecution," undertakes to point out the "broad and impassable barrier" which divides such principles from those of the association. "All matters relating to thought, opinion, conscience, appear to me," he says, "to be without the sphere of legislation; all pertaining to social act, habit, relation, subject only to a discretionary power vested in the State itself, and not in the individual, to be within it." No mention is made of a third class, different from either of these, viz., acts and habits which are not social, but individual; although it is to this class, surely that the act of drinking fermented liquors belongs. Selling fermented liquors, however, is trading, and trading is a social act. But the infringement complained of is not on the liberty of the seller, but on that of the buyer and consumer; since the State might just as well forbid him to drink wine as purposely make it impossible for him to obtain it. The secretary, however, says, "I claim, as a citizen, a right to legislate whenever my social rights are invaded by the social act of another." And now for the definition of these "social rights": "If anything invades my social rights, certainly the traffic in strong drink does. It destroys my primary right of security by constantly creating and stimulating social disorder. It invades my right of equality by deriving a profit from the creation of a misery I am taxed to support. It impedes my right to free moral and intellectual development by surrounding my path with dangers and by weakening and demoralizing society, from which I have a right to claim mutual aid and intercourse." A theory of "social rights" the like of which probably never before found its way into distinct language: being nothing short of this—that it is the absolute social right of every individual that every other individual shall act in every respect exactly as he ought; that whosoever fails thereof in the smallest particular violates my social right and entitles me to demand from the legislature the removal of the grievance. So monstrous a principle is far more dangerous than any single interference with liberty; there is no violation of liberty which it would not justify; it acknowledges no right to any freedom whatever, except perhaps to that of holding opinions in secret, without ever disclosing them; for the moment an opinion which I consider noxious passes anyone's lips, it invades all the "social rights" attributed to me by the Alliance. The doctrine ascribes to all mankind a vested interest in each other's moral, intellectual, and even physical perfection, to be defined by each claimant according to his own standard.

Another important example of illegitimate interference with the rightful liberty of the individual, not simply threatened, but long since carried into triumphant effect, is Sabbatarian legislation. Without doubt, abstinence on one day in the week, so far as the exigencies of life permit, from the usual daily occupation, though in no respect religiously binding on any except Jews, is a highly beneficial custom. And inasmuch as this custom cannot be observed without a general consent to that effect among the industrious classes, therefore, in so far as some persons by working may impose the same necessity on others, it may be allowable and right that the law should guarantee to each the observance by others of the custom, by suspending the greater operations of industry on a particular day. But this justification, grounded on the direct interest which others have in each individual's observance of the practice, does not apply to the self-chosen occupations in which a person may think fit to employ his leisure, nor does it hold good, in the smallest degree, for legal restrictions on amusements. It is true that the amusement of some is the day's work of others; but the pleasure, not to say the useful recreation, of many is worth the labor of a few, provided the occupation is freely chosen and can be freely resigned. The operatives are perfectly right in thinking that if all worked on Sunday, seven days' work would have to be given for six days' wages; but so long as the great mass of employments are suspended, the small number who for the enjoyment of others must still work obtain a proportional increase of earnings; and they are not obliged to follow those occupations if they prefer leisure to emolument. If a further remedy is sought, it might be found in the establishment by custom of a holiday on some other day of the week for those particular classes of persons. The only ground, therefore, on which restrictions on Sunday amusements can be defended must be that they are religiously wrong—a motive of legislation which can never be too earnestly protested against. "*Deorum injuriae Dus curae.*" It remains to be proved that society or any of its officers holds a commission from on high to avenge any supposed offense to Omnipotence which is not also a wrong to our fellow creatures. The notion that it is one man's duty that another should be religious was the foundation of all the religious persecutions ever perpetrated, and, if admitted, would fully justify them. Though the feeling which breaks out in the repeated attempts to stop railway traveling on Sunday, in the resistance to the opening of museums, and the like, has not the cruelty of the old persecutors, the state of mind indicated by it is fundamentally the same. It is a determination not to tolerate others in doing what is permitted by their religion, because it is not permitted by the persecutor's religion. It is a belief that God not only abominates the act of the misbeliever, but will not hold us guiltless if we leave him unmolested.

I cannot refrain from adding to these examples of the little account commonly made of human liberty the language of downright persecution which breaks out from the press of this country whenever it feels called on to notice the remarkable phenomenon of Mormonism. Much might be said on the unexpected and instructive fact that an alleged new revelation and a religion founded on it—the product of palpable imposture, not even supported by the *prestige* of extraordinary qualities in its founder—is believed by hundreds of thousands, and has been made the foundation of a society in the age of newspapers, railways, and the electric telegraph. What here concerns us is that this religion, like other and better religions, has its martyrs: that its prophet and founder was, for his teaching, put to death by a mob; that others of its adherents lost their lives by the same lawless violence; that they were forcibly expelled, in a body, from the country in which they first grew up, while, now that they have been chased into a solitary recess in the midst of a desert, many in this country openly declare that it would be right (only that it is not convenient) to send an expedition against them and compel them by force to conform to the opinions of other people. The article of the Mormonite doctrine which is the chief provocative to the antipathy which thus breaks through the ordinary restraints of religious tolerance is its sanction of polygamy; which, though permitted to Mohammedans, and Hindus, and Chinese, seems to excite unquenchable animosity when practiced by persons who speak English and profess to be a kind of Christians. No one has a deeper disapprobation than I have of this Mormon institution; both for other reasons and because, far from being in any way countenanced by the principle of liberty, it is a direct infraction of that principle, being a mere riveting of the chains of one half of the community, and an emancipation of the other from reciprocity of obligation toward them. Still, it must be remembered that this relation is as much voluntary on the part of the women concerned in it, and who may be deemed the sufferers by it, as is the case with any other form of the marriage institution; and however surprising this fact may appear, it has its explanation in the common ideas and customs of the world, which, teaching women to think marriage the one thing needful, make it intelligible that many a woman should prefer being one of several wives to not being a wife at all. Other countries are not asked to recognize such unions, or release any portion of their inhabitants from their own laws on the score of Mormonite opinions. But when the dissentients have conceded to the hostile sentiments of others far more than could justly be demanded; when they have left the countries to which their doctrines were unacceptable and established themselves in a remote corner of the earth, which they have been the first to render habitable to human beings, it is difficult to see on what principles but those of tyranny they can be prevented from living there under what laws they please, provided they commit no aggression on other nations and allow perfect freedom of departure to those who are dissatisfied with their ways. A recent writer, in some respects of considerable merit, proposes (to use his own words) not a crusade, but a *civilizade*, against this polygamous community, to put an end to what seems to him a retrograde step in civilization. It also appears so to me, but I am not aware that any community has a right to force another to be civilized. So long as the sufferers by the bad law do not invoke assistance from other communities, I cannot admit that persons entirely unconnected with them ought to step in and require that a condition of things with which all who are directly interested appear to be satisfied should be put an end to because it is a scandal to persons some thousands of miles distant who have no part or concern in it. Let them send missionaries, if they please, to preach against it; and let them, by any fair means (of which silencing the teachers is not one), oppose the progress of similar doctrines among their own people. If civilization has got the better of barbarism when barbarism had the world to itself, it is too much to profess to be afraid lest barbarism, after having been fairly got under, should revive and conquer civilization. A civilization that can thus succumb to its vanquished enemy must first have become so degenerate that neither its appointed priests and teachers, nor anybody else, has the capacity, or will take the trouble, to stand up for it. If this be so, the sooner such a civilization receives notice to quit, the better. It can only go on from bad to worse until destroyed and regenerated (like the Western Empire) by energetic barbarians.

CHAPTER V

Applications

The principles asserted in these pages must be more generally admitted as the basis for discussion of details before a consistent application of them to all the various departments of government and morals can be attempted with any prospect of advantage. The few observations I propose to make on questions of detail are designed to illustrate the principles rather than to follow them out to their consequences. I offer not so much applications as specimens of application, which may serve to bring into greater clearness the meaning and limits of the two maxims which together form the entire doctrine of this essay, and to assist the judgment in holding the balance between them in the cases where it appears doubtful which of them is applicable to the case.

The maxims are, first, that the individual is not accountable to society for his actions in so far as these concern the interests of no person but himself. Advice, instruction, persuasion, and avoidance by other people, if thought necessary by them for their own good, are the only measures by which society can justifiably express its dislike or disapprobation of his conduct. Secondly, that for such actions as are prejudicial to the interests of others, the individual is accountable and may be subjected either to social or to legal punishment if society is of opinion that the one or the other is requisite for its protection.

In the first place, it must by no means be supposed, because damage, or probability of damage, to the interests of others can alone justify the interference of society, that therefore it always does justify such interference. In many cases an individual, in pursuing a legitimate object, necessarily and therefore legitimately causes pain or loss to others, or intercepts a good which they had a reasonable hope of obtaining. Such oppositions of interest between individuals often arise from bad social institutions, but are unavoidable while those institutions last; and some would be unavoidable under any institutions. Whoever succeeds in an overcrowded profession or in a competitive examination, whoever is preferred to another in any contest for an object which both desire, reaps benefit from the loss of others, from their wasted exertion and their disappointment. But it is, by common admission, better for the general interest of mankind that persons should pursue their objects undeterred by this sort of consequences. In other words, society admits no right, either legal or moral, in the disappointed competitors to immunity from this kind of suffering, and feels called on to interfere only when means of success have been employed which it is contrary to the general interest to permit—namely, fraud or treachery, and force.

Again, trade is a social act. Whoever undertakes to sell any description of goods to the public does what affects the interest of other persons, and of society in general; and thus his conduct, in principle, comes within the jurisdiction of society; accordingly, it was once held to be the duty of governments, in all cases which were considered of importance, to fix prices and regulate the process of manufacture. But it is now recognized, though not till after a long struggle, that both the cheapness and the good quality of commodities are most effectually provided for by leaving the producers and sellers perfectly free, under the sole check of equal freedom to the buyers for supplying themselves elsewhere. This is the so-called doctrine of "free trade," which rests on grounds different from, though equally solid with, the principle of individual liberty asserted in this essay. Restrictions on trade, or on production for purposes of trade, are indeed restraints; and all restraint, *qua* restraint, is an evil; but the restraints in question affect only that part of conduct which society is competent to restrain, and are wrong solely because they do not really produce the results which it is desired to produce by them. As the principle of individual liberty is not involved in the doctrine of free trade, so neither is it in most of the questions which arise respecting the limits of that doctrine, as, for example, what amount of public control is admissible for the prevention of fraud by adulteration; how far sanitary precautions, or arrangements to protect workpeople employed in dangerous occupations, should be enforced on employers. Such questions involve considerations of liberty only in so far as leaving people to themselves is always better, *caeteris paribus,* than controlling them; but that they may be legitimately controlled for these ends is in principle undeniable. On the other hand, there are questions relating to interference with trade which are essentially questions of liberty, such as the Maine Law, already touched upon; the prohibition of the importation of opium into China; the restriction of the sale of poisons—all cases, in short, where the object of the interference is to make it impossible or difficult to obtain a particular commodity. These interferences are objectionable, not as infringements on the liberty of the producer or seller, but on that of the buyer.

One of these examples, that of the sale of poisons, opens a new question: the proper limits of what may be called the functions of police; how far liberty may legitimately be invaded for the prevention of crime, or of accident. It is one of the undisputed functions of government to take precautions against crime before it has been committed, as well as to detect and punish it afterwards. The preventive function of government, however, is far more liable to be abused, to the prejudice of liberty, than the punitory function; for there is hardly any part of the legitimate freedom of action of a human being which would not admit of being represented, and fairly, too, as increasing the facilities for some form or other of delinquency. Nevertheless, if a public authority, or even a private person, sees anyone evidently preparing to commit a crime, they are not bound to look on inactive until the crime is committed, but may interfere to prevent it. If poisons were never bought or used for any purpose except the commission of murder, it would be right to prohibit their manufacture and sale. They may, however, be wanted not only for innocent but for useful purposes, and restrictions cannot be imposed in the one case without operating in the other. Again, it is a proper office of public authority to guard against accidents. If either a public officer or anyone else saw a person attempting to cross a bridge which had been ascertained to be unsafe, and there were no time to warn him of his danger, they might seize him and turn him back, without any real infringement of his liberty; for liberty consists in doing what one desires, and he does not desire to fall into the river. Nevertheless, when there is not a certainty, but only a danger of mischief, no one but the person himself can judge of the sufficiency of the motive which may prompt him to incur the risk; in this case, therefore (unless he is a child, or delirious, or in some state of excitement or absorption incompatible with the full use of the reflecting faculty), he ought, I conceive, to be only warned of the danger; not forcibly prevented from exposing himself to it. Similar considerations, applied to such a question as the sale of poisons, may enable us to decide which among the possible modes of regulation are or are not contrary to principle. Such a precaution, for example, as that of labeling the drug with some word expressive of its dangerous character may be enforced without violation of liberty: the buyer cannot wish not to know that the thing he possesses has poisonous qualities. But to require in all cases the certificate of a medical practitioner would make it sometimes impossible, always expensive, to obtain the article for legitimate uses. The only mode apparent to me, in which difficulties may be thrown in the way of crime committed through this means, without any infringement worth taking into account upon the liberty of those who desire the poisonous substance for other purposes, consists in providing what, in the apt language of Bentham, is called "preappointed evidence." This provision is familiar to everyone in the case of contracts. It is usual and right that the law, when a contract is entered into, should require as the condition of its enforcing performance that certain formalities should be observed, such as signatures, attestation of witnesses, and the like, in order that in case of subsequent dispute there may be evidence to prove that the contract was really entered into, and that there was nothing in the circumstances to render it legally invalid, the effect being to throw great obstacles in the way of fictitious contracts, or contracts made in circumstances which, if known, would destroy their validity. Precautions of a similar nature might be enforced in the sale of articles adapted to be instruments of crime. The seller, for example, might be required to enter in a register the exact time of the transaction, the name and address of the buyer, the precise quality and quantity sold; to ask the purpose for which it was wanted, and record the answer he received. When there was no medical prescription, the presence of some third person might be required to bring home the fact to the purchaser, in case there should afterwards be reason to believe that the article had been applied to criminal purposes. Such regulations would in general be no material impediment to obtaining the article, but a very considerable one to making an improper use of it without detection.

The right inherent in society to ward off crimes against itself by antecedent precautions suggests the obvious limitations to the maxim that purely self-regarding misconduct cannot properly be meddled with in the way of prevention or punishment. Drunkenness, for example, in ordinary cases, is not a fit subject for legislative interference, but I should deem it perfectly legitimate that a person who had once been convicted of any act of violence to others under the influence of drink should be placed under a special legal restriction, personal to himself; that if he were afterwards found drunk, he should be liable to a penalty, and that if, when in that state, he committed another offense, the punishment to which he would be liable for that other offense should be increased in severity. The making himself drunk, in a person whom drunkenness excites to do harm to others, is a crime against others. So, again, idleness, except in a person receiving support from the public, or except when it constitutes a breach of contract, cannot without tyranny be made a subject of legal punishment; but if, either from idleness or from any other avoidable cause, a man fails to perform his legal duties to others, as for instance to support his children, it is no tyranny to force him to fulfill that obligation by compulsory labor if no other means are available.

Again, there are many acts which, being directly injurious only to the agents themselves, ought not to be legally interdicted, but which, if done publicly, are a violation of good manners and, coming thus within the category of offenses against others, may rightly be prohibited. Of this kind are offenses against decency; on which it is unnecessary to dwell, the rather as they are only connected indirectly with our subject, the objection to publicity being equally strong in the case of many actions not in themselves condemnable, nor supposed to be so.

There is another question to which an answer must be found, consistent with the principles which have been laid down. In cases of personal conduct supposed to be blamable, but which respect for liberty precludes society from preventing or punishing because the evil directly resulting falls wholly on the agent; what the agent is free to do, ought other persons to be equally free to counsel or instigate? This question is not free from difficulty. The case of a person who solicits another to do an act is not strictly a case of self-regarding conduct. To give advice or offer inducements to anyone is a social act and may, therefore, like actions in general which affect others, be supposed amenable to social control. But a little reflection corrects the first impression, by showing that if the case is not strictly within the definition of individual liberty, yet the reasons on which the principle of individual liberty is grounded are applicable to it. If people must be allowed, in whatever concerns only themselves, to act as seems best to themselves, at their own peril, they must equally be free to consult with one another about what is fit to be so done; to exchange opinions, and give and receive suggestions. Whatever it is permitted to do, it must be permitted to advise to do. The question is doubtful only when the instigator derives a personal benefit from his advice, when he makes it his occupation, for subsistence or pecuniary gain, to promote what society and the State consider to be an evil. Then, indeed, a new element of complication is introduced—namely, the existence of classes of persons with an interest opposed to what is considered as the public weal, and whose mode of living is grounded on the counteraction of it. Ought this to be interfered with, or not? Fornication, for example, must be tolerated, and so must gambling; but should a person be free to be a pimp, or to keep a gambling house? The case is one of those which lie on the exact boundary line between two principles, and it is not at once apparent to which of the two it properly belongs. There are arguments on both sides. On the side of toleration it may be said that the fact of following anything as an occupation, and living or profiting by the practice of it, cannot make that criminal which would otherwise be admissible; that the act should either be consistently permitted or consistently prohibited; that if the principles which we have hitherto defended are true, society has no business, *as* society, to decide anything to be wrong which concerns only the individual; that it cannot go beyond dissuasion, and that one person should be as free to persuade as another to dissuade. In opposition to this it may be contended that, although the public, or the State, are not warranted in authoritatively deciding, for purposes of repression or punishment, that such or such conduct affecting only the interests of the individual is good or bad, they are fully justified in assuming, if they regard it as bad, that its being so or not is at least a disputable question: that, this being supposed, they cannot be acting wrongly in endeavoring to exclude the influence of solicitations which are not disinterested, of instigators who cannot possibly be impartial—who have a direct personal interest on one side, and that side the one which the State believes to be wrong, and who confessedly promote it for personal objects only. There can surely, it may be urged, be nothing lost, no sacrifice of good, by so ordering matters that persons shall make their election, either wisely or foolishly, on their own prompting, as free as possible from the arts of persons who stimulate their inclinations for interested purposes of their own. Thus (it may be said), though the statutes respecting unlawful games are utterly indefensible—though all persons should be free to gamble in their own or each other's houses, or in any place of meeting established by their own subscriptions and open only to the members and their visitors—yet public gambling houses should not be permitted. It is true that the prohibition is never effectual, and that, whatever amount of tyrannical power may be given to the police, gambling houses can always be maintained under other pretenses; but they may be compelled to conduct their operations with a certain degree of secrecy and mystery, so that nobody knows anything about them but those who seek them; and more than this society ought not to aim at. There is considerable force in these arguments. I will not venture to decide whether they are sufficient to justify the moral anomaly of punishing the accessory when the principal is (and must be) allowed to go free; of fining or imprisoning the procurer, but not the fornicator—the gambling-house keeper, but not the gambler. Still less ought the common operations of buying and selling to be interfered with on analogous grounds. Almost every article which is bought and sold may be used in excess, and the sellers have a pecuniary interest in encouraging that excess; but no argument can be founded on this in favor, for instance, of the Maine Law; because the class of dealers in strong drinks, though interested in their abuse, are indispensably required for the sake of their legitimate use. The interest, however, of these dealers in promoting intemperance is a real evil and justifies the State in imposing restrictions and requiring guarantees which, but for that justification, would be infringements of legitimate liberty.

A further question is whether the State, while it permits, should nevertheless indirectly discourage conduct which it deems contrary to the best interests of the agent; whether, for example, it should take measures to render the means of drunkenness more costly, or add to the difficulty of procuring them by limiting the number of the places of sale. On this, as on most other practical questions, many distinctions require to be made. To tax stimulants for the sole purpose of making them more difficult to be obtained is a measure differing only in degree from their entire prohibition, and would be justifiable only if that were justifiable. Every increase of cost is a prohibition to those whose means do not come up to the augmented price; and to those who do, it is a penalty laid on them for gratifying a particular taste. Their choice of pleasures and their mode of expending their income, after satisfying their legal and moral obligations to the State and to individuals, are their own concern and must rest with their own judgment. These considerations may seem at first sight to condemn the selection of stimulants as special subjects of taxation for purposes of revenue. But it must be remembered that taxation for fiscal purposes is absolutely inevitable; that in most countries it is necessary that a considerable part of that taxation should be indirect; that the State, therefore, cannot help imposing penalties, which to some persons may be prohibitory, on the use of some articles of consumption. It is hence the duty of the State to consider, in the imposition of taxes, what commodities the consumers can best spare; and *a fortiori*, to select in preference those of which it deems the use, beyond a very moderate quantity, to be positively injurious. Taxation, therefore, of stimulants up to the point which produces the largest amount of revenue (supposing that the State needs all the revenue which it yields) is not only admissible, but to be approved of.

The question of making the sale of these commodities a more or less exclusive privilege must be answered differently, according to the purposes to which the restriction is intended to be subservient. All places of public resort require the restraint of a police, and places of this kind peculiarly, because offenses against society are especially apt to originate there. It is, therefore, fit to confine the power of selling these commodities (at least for consumption on the spot) to persons of known or vouched-for respectability of conduct; to make such regulations respecting hours of opening and closing as may be requisite for public surveillance, and to withdraw the license if breaches of the peace repeatedly take place through the connivance or incapacity of the keeper of the house, or if it becomes a rendezvous for concocting and preparing offenses against the law. Any further restriction I do not conceive to be, in principle, justifiable. The limitation in number, for instance, of beer and spirit houses, for the express purpose of rendering them more difficult of access and diminishing the occasions of temptation, not only exposes all to an inconvenience because there are some by whom the facility would be abused, but is suited only to a state of society in which the laboring classes are avowedly treated as children or savages, and placed under an education of restraint, to fit them for future admission to the privileges of freedom. This is not the principle on which the laboring classes are professedly governed in any free country; and no person who sets due value on freedom will give his adhesion to their being so governed, unless after all efforts have been exhausted to educate them for freedom and govern them as freemen, and it has been definitively proved that they can only be governed as children. The bare statement of the alternative shows the absurdity of supposing that such efforts have been made in any case which needs be considered here. It is only because the institutions of this country are a mass of inconsistencies, that things find admittance into our practice which belong to the system of despotic, or what is called paternal, government, while the general freedom of our institutions precludes the exercise of the amount of control necessary to render the restraint of any real efficacy as a moral education.

It was pointed out in an early part of this essay that the liberty of the individual, in things wherein the individual is alone concerned, implies a corresponding liberty in any number of individuals to regulate by mutual agreement such things as regard them jointly, and regard no persons but themselves. This question presents no difficulty so long as the will of all the persons implicated remains unaltered; but since that will may change it is often necessary, even in things in which they alone are concerned, that they should enter into engagements with one another; and when they do, it is fit, as a general rule, that those engagements should be kept. Yet, in the laws, probably, of every country, this general rule has some exceptions. Not only persons are not held to engagements which violate the rights of third parties, but it is sometimes considered a sufficient reason for releasing them from an engagement that it is injurious to themselves. In this and most other civilized countries, for example, an engagement by which a person should sell himself, or allow himself to be sold, as a slave would be null and void, neither enforced by law nor by opinion. The ground for thus limiting his power of voluntarily disposing of his own lot in life is apparent, and is very clearly seen in this extreme case. The reason for not interfering, unless for the sake of others, with a person's voluntary acts is consideration for his liberty. His voluntary choice is evidence that what he so chooses is desirable, or at least endurable, to him, and his good is on the whole best provided for by allowing him to take his own means of pursuing it. But by selling himself for a slave, he abdicates his liberty; he foregoes any future use of it beyond that single act. He therefore defeats, in his own case, the very purpose which is the justification of allowing him to dispose of himself. He is no longer free, but is thenceforth in a position which has no longer the presumption in its favor that would be afforded by his voluntarily remaining in it. The principle of freedom cannot require that he should be free not to be free. It is not freedom to be allowed to alienate his freedom. These reasons, the force of which is so conspicuous in this peculiar case, are evidently of far wider application, yet a limit is everywhere set to them by the necessities of life, which continually require, not indeed that we should resign our freedom, but that we should consent to this and the other limitation of it. The principle, however, which demands uncontrolled freedom of action in all that concerns only the agents themselves requires that those who have become bound to one another, in things which concern no third party, should be able to release one another from the engagement; and even without such voluntary release there are perhaps no contracts or engagements, except those that relate to money or money's worth, of which one can venture to say that there ought to be no liberty whatever of retraction. Baron Wilhelm von Humboldt, in the excellent essay from which I have already quoted, states it as his conviction that engagements which involve personal relations or services should never be legally binding beyond a limited duration of time; and that the most important of these engagements, marriage, having the peculiarity that its objects are frustrated unless the feelings of both the parties are in harmony with it, should require nothing more than the declared will of either party to dissolve it. This subject is too important and too complicated to be discussed in a parenthesis, and I touch on it only so far as is necessary for purposes of illustration. If the conciseness and generality of Baron Humboldt's dissertation had not obliged him in this instance to content himself with enunciating his conclusion without discussing the premises, he would doubtless have recognized that the question cannot be decided on grounds so simple as those to which he confines himself. When a person, either by express promise or by conduct, has encouraged another to rely upon his continuing to act in a certain way—to build expectations and calculations, and stake any part of his plan of life upon that supposition—a new series of moral obligations arises on his part toward that person, which may possibly be overruled, but cannot be ignored. And again, if the relation between two contracting parties has been followed by consequences to others; if it has placed third parties in any peculiar position, or, as in the case of marriage, has even called third parties into existence, obligations arise on the part of both the contracting parties toward those third persons, the fulfillment of which, or at all events the mode of fulfillment, must be greatly affected by the continuance or disruption of the relation between the original parties to the contract. It does not follow, nor can I admit, that these obligations extend to requiring the fulfillment of the contract at all costs to the happiness of the reluctant party; but they are a necessary element in the question; and, even if, as von Humboldt maintains, they ought to make no difference in the *legal* freedom of the parties to release themselves from the engagement (and I also hold that they ought not to make *much* difference), they necessarily make a great difference in the *moral* freedom. A person is bound to take all these circumstances into account before resolving on a step which may affect such important interests of others; and if he does not allow proper weight to those interests, he is morally responsible for the wrong. I have made these obvious remarks for the better illustration of the general principle of liberty, and not because they are at all needed on the particular question, which, on the contrary, is usually discussed as if the interest of children was everything, and that of grown persons nothing.

I have already observed that, owing to the absence of any recognized general principles, liberty is often granted where it should be withheld, as well as withheld where it should be granted; and one of the cases in which, in the modern European world, the sentiment of liberty is the strongest is a case where, in my view, it is altogether misplaced. A person should be free to do as he likes in his own concerns, but he ought not to be free to do as he likes in acting for another, under the pretext that the affairs of the other are his own affairs. The State, while it respects the liberty of each in what specially regards himself, is bound to maintain a vigilant control over his exercise of any power which it allows him to possess over others. This obligation is almost entirely disregarded in the case of the family relations—a case, in its direct influence on human happiness, more important than all others taken together. The almost despotic power of husbands over wives needs not be enlarged upon here, because nothing more is needed for the complete removal of the evil than that wives should have the same rights and should receive the protection of law in the same manner as all other persons; and because, on this subject, the defenders of established injustice do not avail themselves of the plea of liberty but stand forth openly as the champions of power. It is in the case of children that misapplied notions of liberty are a real obstacle to the fulfillment by the State of its duties. One would almost think that a man's children were supposed to be literally, and not metaphorically, a part of himself, so jealous is opinion of the smallest interference of law with his absolute and exclusive control over them, more jealous than of almost any interference with his own freedom of action: so much less do the generality of mankind value liberty than power. Consider, for example, the case of education. Is it not almost a self-evident axiom that the State should require and compel the education, up to a certain standard, of every human being who is born its citizen? Yet who is there that is not afraid to recognize and assert this truth? Hardly anyone, indeed, will deny that it is one of the most sacred duties of the parents (or, as law and usage now stand, the father), after summoning a human being into the world, to give to that being an education fitting him to perform his part well in life toward others and toward himself. But while this is unanimously declared to be the father's duty, scarcely anybody, in this country, will bear to hear of obliging him to perform it. Instead of his being required to make any exertion or sacrifice for securing education to his child, it is left to his choice to accept it or not when it is provided gratis! It still remains unrecognized that to bring a child into existence without a fair prospect of being able, not only to provide food for its body, but instruction and training for its mind is a moral crime, both against the unfortunate offspring and against society; and that if the parent does not fulfill this obligation, the State ought to see it fulfilled at the charge, as far as possible, of the parent.

Were the duty of enforcing universal education once admitted there would be an end to the difficulties about what the State should teach, and how it should teach, which now convert the subject into a mere battlefield for sects and parties, causing the time and labor which should have been spent in educating to be wasted in quarreling about education. If the government would make up its mind to require for every child a good education, it might save itself the trouble of providing one. It might leave to parents to obtain the education where and how they pleased, and content itself with helping to pay the school fees of the poorer classes of children, and defraying the entire school expenses of those who have no one else to pay for them. The objections which are urged with reason against State education do not apply to the enforcement of education by the State, but to the State's taking upon itself to direct that education; which is a totally different thing. That the whole or any large part of the education of the people should be in State hands, I go as far as anyone in deprecating. All that has been said of the importance of individuality of character, and diversity in opinions and modes of conduct, involves, as of the same unspeakable importance, diversity of education. A general State education is a mere contrivance for molding people to be exactly like one another; and as the mold in which it casts them is that which pleases the predominant power in the government—whether this be a monarch, a priesthood, an aristocracy, or the majority of the existing generation—in proportion as it is efficient and successful, it establishes a despotism over the mind, leading by natural tendency to one over the body. An education established and controlled by the State should only exist, if it exist at all, as one among many competing experiments, carried on for the purpose of example and stimulus to keep the others up to a certain standard of excellence. Unless, indeed, when society in general is in so backward a state that it could not or would not provide for itself any proper institutions of education unless the government undertook the task, then, indeed, the government may, as the less of two great evils, take upon itself the business of schools and universities, as it may that of joint stock companies when private enterprise in a shape fitted for undertaking great works of industry does not exist in the country. But in general, if the country contains a sufficient number of persons qualified to provide education under government auspices, the same persons would be able and willing to give an equally good education on the voluntary principle, under the assurance of remuneration afforded by a law rendering education compulsory, combined with State aid to those unable to defray the expense.

The instrument for enforcing the law could be no other than public examinations, extending to all children and beginning at an early age. An age might be fixed at which every child must be examined, to ascertain if he (or she) is able to read. If a child proves unable, the father, unless he has some sufficient ground of excuse, might be subjected to a moderate fine, to be worked out, if necessary, by his labor, and the child might be put to school at his expense. Once in every year the examination should be renewed, with a gradually extending range of subjects, so as to make the universal acquisition and, what is more, retention of a certain minimum of general knowledge virtually compulsory. Beyond that minimum there should be voluntary examinations on all subjects, at which all who come up to a certain standard of proficiency might claim a certificate. To prevent the State from exercising, through these arrangements, an improper influence over opinion, the knowledge required for passing an examination (beyond the merely instrumental parts of knowledge, such as languages and their use) should, even in the higher classes of examinations, be confined to facts and positive science exclusively. The examinations on religion, politics, or other disputed topics should not turn on the truth or falsehood of opinions, but on the matter of fact that such and such an opinion is held, on such grounds, by such authors, or schools, or churches. Under this system, the rising generation would be no worse off in regard to all disputed truths than they are at present; they would be brought up either churchmen or dissenters as they now are, the State merely taking care that they should be instructed churchmen, or instructed dissenters. There would be nothing to hinder them from being taught religion, if their parents chose, at the same schools where they were taught other things. All attempts by the State to bias the conclusions of its citizens on disputed subjects are evil; but it may very properly offer to ascertain and certify that a person possesses the knowledge requisite to make his conclusions on any given subject worth attending to. A student of philosophy would be the better for being able to stand an examination both in Locke and in Kant, whichever of the two he takes up with, or even if with neither: and there is no reasonable objection to examining an atheist in the evidences of Christianity, provided he is not required to profess a belief in them. The examinations, however, in the higher branches of knowledge should, I conceive, be entirely voluntary. It would be giving too dangerous a power to governments were they allowed to exclude anyone from professions, even from the profession of teacher, for alleged deficiency of qualifications; and I think, with Wilhelm von Humboldt, that degrees or other public certificates of scientific or professional acquirements should be given to all who present themselves for examination and stand the test, but that such certificates should confer no advantage over competitors other than the weight which may be attached to their testimony by public opinion.

It is not in the matter of education only that misplaced notions of liberty prevent moral obligations on the part of parents from being recognized, and legal obligations from being imposed, where there are the strongest grounds for the former always, and in many cases for the latter also. The fact itself, of causing the existence of a human being, is one of the most responsible actions in the range of human life. To undertake this responsibility—to bestow a life which may be either a curse or a blessing—unless the being on whom it is to be bestowed will have at least the ordinary chances of a desirable existence, is a crime against that being. And in a country, either overpeopled or threatened with being so, to produce children, beyond a very small number, with the effect of reducing the reward of labor by their competition is a serious offense against all who live by the remuneration of their labor. The laws which, in many countries on the Continent, forbid marriage unless the parties can show that they have the means of supporting a family do not exceed the legitimate powers of the State; and whether such laws be expedient or not (a question mainly dependent on local circumstances and feelings), they are not objectionable as violations of liberty. Such laws are interferences of the State to prohibit a mischievous act—an act injurious to others, which ought to be a subject of reprobation and social stigma, even when it is not deemed expedient to superadd legal punishment. Yet the current ideas of liberty, which bend so easily to real infringements of the freedom of the individual in things which concern only himself, would repel the attempt to put any restraint upon his inclinations when the consequence of their indulgence is a life or lives of wretchedness and depravity to the offspring, with manifold evils to those sufficiently within reach to be in any way affected by their actions. When we compare the strange respect of mankind for liberty with their strange want of respect for it, we might imagine that a man had an indispensable right to do harm to others, and no right at all to please himself without giving pain to anyone.

I have reserved for the last place a large class of questions respecting the limits of government interference, which, though closely connected with the subject of this essay, do not, in strictness, belong to it. These are cases in which the reasons against interference do not turn upon the principle of liberty: the question is not about restraining the actions of individuals, but about helping them; it is asked whether the government should do, or cause to be done, something for their benefit instead of leaving it to be done by themselves, individually or in voluntary combination.

The objections to government interference, when it is not such as to involve infringement of liberty, may be of three kinds:

The first is when the thing to be done is likely to be better done by individuals than by the government. Speaking generally, there is no one so fit to conduct any business, or to determine how or by whom it shall be conducted, as those who are personally interested in it. This principle condemns the interferences, once so common, of the legislature, or the officers of government, with the ordinary processes of industry. But this part of the subject has been sufficiently enlarged upon by political economists, and is not particularly related to the principles of this essay.

The second objection is more nearly allied to our subject. In many cases, though individuals may not do the particular thing so well, on the average, as the officers of government, it is nevertheless desirable that it should be done by them, rather than by the government, as a means to their own mental education—a mode of strengthening their active faculties, exercising their judgment, and giving them a familiar knowledge of the subjects with which they are thus left to deal. This is a principal, though not the sole, recommendation of jury trial (in cases not political); of free and popular local and municipal institutions; of the conduct of industrial and philanthropic enterprises by voluntary associations. These are not questions of liberty, and are connected with that subject only by remote tendencies, but they are questions of development. It belongs to a different occasion from the present to dwell on these things as parts of national education, as being, in truth, the peculiar training of a citizen, the practical part of the political education of a free people, taking them out of the narrow circle of personal and family selfishness, and accustoming them to the comprehension of joint interests, the management of joint concerns—habituating them to act from public or semi-public motives, and guide their conduct by aims which unite instead of isolating them from one another. Without these habits and powers, a free constitution can neither be worked nor preserved, as is exemplified by the too often transitory nature of political freedom in countries where it does not rest upon a sufficient basis of local liberties. The management of purely local business by the localities, and of the great enterprises of industry by the union of those who voluntarily supply the pecuniary means, is further recommended by all the advantages which have been set forth in this essay as belonging to individuality of development and diversity of modes of action. Government operations tend to be everywhere alike. With individuals and voluntary associations, on the contrary, there are varied experiments and endless diversity of experience. What the State can usefully do is to make itself a central depository, and active circulator and diffuser, of the experience resulting from many trials. Its business is to enable each experimentalist to benefit by the experiments of others, instead of tolerating no experiments but its own.

The third and most cogent reason for restricting the interference of government is the great evil of adding unnecessarily to its power.

Every function superadded to those already exercised by the government causes its influence over hopes and fears to be more widely diffused, and converts, more and more, the active and ambitious part of the public into hangers-on of the government, or of some party which aims at becoming the government. If the roads, the railways, the banks, the insurance offices, the great joint-stock companies, the universities, and the public charities were all of them branches of the government; if, in addition, the municipal corporations and local boards, with all that now devolves on them, became departments of the central administration; if the employees of all these different enterprises were appointed and paid by the government and looked to the government for every rise in life, not all the freedom of the press and popular constitution of the legislature would make this or any other country free otherwise than in name. And the evil would be greater, the more efficiently and scientifically the administrative machinery was constructed—the more skillful the arrangements for obtaining the best qualified hands and heads with which to work it. In England it has of late been proposed that all the members of the civil service of government should be selected by competitive examination, to obtain for these employments the most intelligent and instructed persons procurable; and much has been said and written for and against this proposal. One of the arguments most insisted on by its opponents is that the occupation of a permanent official servant of the State does not hold out sufficient prospects of emolument and importance to attract the highest talents, which will always be able to find a more inviting career in the professions or in the service of companies and other public bodies. One would not have been surprised if this argument had been used by the friends of the proposition as an answer to its principal difficulty. Coming from the opponents it is strange enough. What is urged as an objection is the safety valve of the proposed system. If, indeed, all the high talent of the country could be drawn into the service of the government, a proposal tending to bring about that result might well inspire uneasiness. If every part of the business of society which required organized concert, or large and comprehensive views, were in the hands of the government, and if government offices were universally filled by the ablest men, all the enlarged culture and practiced intelligence in the country, except the purely speculative, would be concentrated in a numerous bureaucracy, to whom alone the rest of the community would look for all things—the multitude for direction and dictation in all they had to do; the able and aspiring for personal advancement. To be admitted into the ranks of this bureaucracy, and when admitted, to rise therein, would be the sole objects of ambition. Under this *régime* not only is the outside public ill-qualified, for want of practical experience, to criticize or check the mode of operation of the bureaucracy, but even if the accidents of despotic or the natural working of popular institutions occasionally raise to the summit a ruler or rulers of reforming inclinations, no reform can be effected which is contrary to the interest of the bureaucracy. Such is the melancholy condition of the Russian empire, as shown in the accounts of those who have had sufficient opportunity of observation. The Czar himself is powerless against the bureaucratic body; he can send any one of them to Siberia, but he cannot govern without them, or against their will. On every decree of his they have a tacit veto, by merely refraining from carrying it into effect. In countries of more advanced civilization and of a more insurrectionary spirit, the public, accustomed to expect everything to be done for them by the State, or at least to do nothing for themselves without asking from the State not only leave to do it, but even how it is to be done, naturally hold the State responsible for all evil which befalls them, and when the evil exceeds their amount of patience, they rise against the government and make what is called a revolution; whereupon somebody else, with or without legitimate authority from the nation, vaults into the seat, issues his orders to the bureaucracy, and everything goes on much as it did before; the bureaucracy being unchanged, and nobody else being capable of taking their place.

A very different spectacle is exhibited among a people accustomed to transact their own business. In France, a large part of the people, having been engaged in military service, many of whom have held at least the rank of noncommissioned officers, there are in every popular insurrection several persons competent to take the lead and improvise some tolerable plan of action. What the French are in military affairs, the Americans are in every kind of civil business; let them be left without a government, every body of Americans is able to improvise one and to carry on that or any other public business with a sufficient amount of intelligence, order, and decision. This is what every free people ought to be; and a people capable of this is certain to be free; it will never let itself be enslaved by any man or body of men because these are able to seize and pull the reins of the central administration. No bureaucracy can hope to make such a people as this do or undergo anything that they do not like. But where everything is done through the bureaucracy, nothing to which the bureaucracy is really adverse can be done at all. The constitution of such countries is an organization of the experience and practical ability of the nation into a disciplined body for the purpose of governing the rest; and the more perfect that organization is in itself, the more successful in drawing to itself and educating for itself the persons of greatest capacity from all ranks of the community, the more complete is the bondage of all, the members of the bureaucracy included. For the governors are as much the slaves of their organization and discipline as the governed are of the governors. A Chinese mandarin is as much the tool and creature of a despotism as the humblest cultivator. An individual Jesuit is to the utmost degree of abasement the slave of his order, though the order itself exists for the collective power and importance of its members.

It is not, also, to be forgotten that the absorption of all the principal ability of the country into the governing body is fatal, sooner or later, to the mental activity and progressiveness of the body itself. Banded together as they are—working a system which, like all systems, necessarily proceeds in a great measure by fixed rules—the official body are under the constant temptation of sinking into indolent routine, or, if they now and then desert that mill-horse round, of rushing into some half-examined crudity which has struck the fancy of some leading member of the corps; and the sole check to these closely allied, though seemingly opposite, tendencies, the only stimulus which can keep the ability of the body itself up to a high standard, is liability to the watchful criticism of equal ability outside the body. It is indispensable, therefore, that the means should exist, independently of the government, of forming such ability and furnishing it with the opportunities and experience necessary for a correct judgment of great practical affairs. If we would possess permanently a skillful and efficient body of functionaries—above all a body able to originate and willing to adopt improvements—if we would not have our bureaucracy degenerate into a pedantocracy, this body must not engross all the occupations which form and cultivate the faculties required for the government of mankind.

To determine the point at which evils, so formidable to human freedom and advancement, begin, or rather at which they begin to predominate over the benefits attending the collective application of the force of society, under its recognized chiefs, for the removal of the obstacles which stand in the way of its well-being; to secure as much of the advantages of centralized power and intelligence as can be had without turning into governmental channels too great a proportion of the general activity—is one of the most difficult and complicated questions in the art of government. It is, in a great measure, a question of detail in which many and various considerations must be kept in view, and no absolute rule can be laid down. But I believe that the practical principle in which safety resides, the ideal to be kept in view, the standard by which to test all arrangements intended for overcoming the difficulty, may be conveyed in these words: the greatest dissemination of power consistent with efficiency; but the greatest possible centralization of information and diffusion of it from the center. Thus, in municipal administration, there would be, as in the New England states, a very minute division among separate officers, chosen by the localities, of all business which is not better left to the persons directly interested; but besides this, there would be, in each department of local affairs, a central superintendence, forming a branch of the general government. The organ of this superintendence would concentrate, as in a focus, the variety of information and experience derived from the conduct of that branch of public business in all the localities, from everything analogous which is done in foreign countries, and from the general principles of political science. This central organ should have a right to know all that is done, and its special duty should be that of making the knowledge acquired in one place available for others. Emancipated from the petty prejudices and narrow views of a locality by its elevated position and comprehensive sphere of observation, its advice would naturally carry much authority; but its actual power, as a permanent institution, should, I conceive, be limited to compelling the local officers to obey the laws laid down for their guidance. In all things not provided for by general rules, those officers should be left to their own judgment, under responsibility to their constituents. For the violation of rules, they should be responsible to law, and the rules themselves should be laid down by the legislature; the central administrative authority only watching over their execution and, if they were not properly carried into effect, appealing, according to the nature of the case, to the tribunals to enforce the law, or to the constituencies to dismiss the functionaries who had not executed it according to its spirit. Such, in its general conception, is the central superintendence which the Poor Law Board is intended to exercise over the administrators of the Poor Rate throughout the country. Whatever powers the Board exercises beyond this limit were right and necessary in that peculiar case, for the cure of rooted habits of maladministration in matters deeply affecting not the localities merely, but the whole community; since no locality has a moral right to make itself by mismanagement a nest of pauperism, necessarily overflowing into other localities and impairing the moral and physical condition of the whole laboring community. The powers of administrative coercion and subordinate legislation possessed by the Poor Law Board (but which, owing to the state of opinion on the subject, are very scantily exercised by them), though perfectly justifiable in a case of first-rate national interest, would be wholly out of place in the superintendence of interests purely local. But a central organ of information and instruction for all the localities would be equally valuable in all departments of administration. A government cannot have too much of the kind of activity which does not impede but aids and stimulates, individual exertion and development. The mischief begins when, instead of calling forth the activity and powers of individuals and bodies, it substitutes its own activity for theirs; when, instead of informing, advising, and, upon occasion, denouncing, it makes them work in fetters, or bids them stand aside and does their work instead of them. The worth of a State, in the long run, is the worth of the individuals composing it; and a State which postpones the interests of their mental expansion and elevation to a little more of administrative skill, or of that semblance of it which practice gives in the details of business; a State which dwarfs its men, in order that they may be more docile instruments in its hands even for beneficial purposes—will find that with small men no great thing can really be accomplished; and that the perfection of machinery to which it has sacrificed everything will in the end avail it nothing, for want of the vital power which, in order that the machine might work more smoothly, it has preferred to banish.

Notes

1. These words had scarcely been written when, as if to give them an emphatic contradiction, occurred the Government Press Prosecutions of 1858. That ill-judged interference with the liberty of public discussion has not, however, induced me to alter a single word in the text, nor has it at all weakened my conviction that, moments of panic excepted, the era of pains and penalties for political discussion has, in our own country, passed away. For, in the first place, the prosecutions were not persisted in; and, in the second, they were never, properly speaking, political prosecutions. The offense charged was not that of criticizing institutions or the acts or persons of rulers, but of circulating what was deemed an immoral doctrine, the lawfulness of tyrannicide.

   If the arguments of the present chapter are of any validity, there ought to exist the fullest liberty of professing and discussing, as a matter of ethical conviction, any doctrine, however immoral it may be considered. It would, therefore, be irrelevant and out of place to examine here whether the doctrine of tyrannicide deserves that title. I shall content myself with saying that the subject has been at all times one of the open questions of morals; that the act of a private citizen in striking down a criminal who, by raising himself above the law, has placed himself beyond the reach of legal punishment or control has been accounted by whole nations, and by some of the best and wisest of men, not a crime but an act of exalted virtue; and that, right or wrong, it is not of the nature of assassination, but of civil war. As such, I hold that the instigation to it, in a specific case, may be a proper subject of punishment, but only if an overt act has followed, and at least a probable connection can be established between the act and the instigation. Even then it is not a foreign government but the very government assailed which alone, in the exercise of self-defense, can legitimately punish attacks directed against its own existence.

2. Thomas Pooley, Bodmin Assizes, July 31, 1857. In December following, he received a free pardon from the Crown.

3. George Jacob Holyoake, August 17, 1857; Edward Truelove, July 1857.

4. Baron de Gleichen, Marlborough-street Police Court, August 4, 1857.

5. Ample warning may be drawn from the large infusion of the passions of a persecutor, which mingled with the general display of the worst parts of our national character on the occasion of the Sepoy insurrection. The ravings of fanatics or charlatans from the pulpit may be unworthy of notice; but the heads of the Evangelical party have announced as their principle for the government of Hindus and Mohammedans that no schools be supported by public money in which the Bible is not taught, and by necessary consequence that no public employment be given to any but real or pretended Christians. An Undersecretary of State, in a speech delivered to his constituents on the 12th of November, 1857, is reported to have said: "Toleration of their faith" (the faith of a hundred millions of British subjects), "the superstition which they called religion, by the British Government, had had the effect of retarding the ascendancy of the British name, and preventing the salutary growth of Christianity. . . . Toleration was the great cornerstone of the religious liberties of this country; but do not let them abuse that precious word 'toleration.' As he understood it, it means the complete liberty to all, freedom of worship, *among Christians, who worshiped upon the same foundation.* It meant toleration of all sects and denominations of *Christians who believed in the one mediation.*" I desire to call attention to the fact that a man who has been deemed fit to fill a high office in the government of this country under a liberal ministry maintains the doctrine that all who do not believe in the divinity of Christ are beyond the pale of toleration. Who, after this imbecile display, can indulge the illusion that religious persecution has passed away, never to return?

6. *The Spheres and Duties of Government*, from the German of Baron Wilhelm von Humboldt, pages 11 to 13.
7. Stirling's *Essays*.
8. There is something both contemptible and frightful in the sort of evidence on which, of late years, any person can be judicially declared unfit for the management of his affairs; and after his death, his disposal of his property can be set aside if there is enough of it to pay the expenses of litigation— which are charged on the property itself. All the minute details of his daily life are pried into, and whatever is found which, seen through the medium of the perceiving and describing faculties of the lowest of the low, bears an appearance unlike absolute commonplace, is laid before the jury as evidence of insanity, and often with success; the jurors being little, if at all, less vulgar and ignorant than the witnesses, while the judges, with that extraordinary want of knowledge of human nature and life which continually astonishes us in English lawyers, often help to mislead them. These trials speak volumes as to the state of feeling and opinion among the vulgar with regard to human liberty. So far from setting any value on individuality—so far from respecting the right of each individual to act, in things indifferent, as seems good to his own judgment and inclinations, judges and juries cannot even conceive that a person in a state of sanity can desire such freedom. In former days, when it was proposed to burn atheists, charitable people used to suggest putting them in a madhouse instead; it would be nothing surprising nowadays were we to see this done, and the doers applauding themselves because, instead of persecuting for religion, they had adopted so humane and Christian a mode of treating these unfortunates, not without a silent satisfaction at their having thereby obtained their deserts.
9. The case of the Bombay Parsees is a curious instance in point. When this industrious and enterprising tribe, the descendants of the Persian fire-worshipers, flying from their native country before the Caliphs, arrived in western India, they were admitted to toleration by the Hindu sovereigns, on condition of not eating beef. When those regions afterward fell under the dominion of Mohammedan conquerors, the Parsees obtained from them a continuance of indulgence, on condition of refraining from pork. What was at first obedience to authority became a second nature, and the Parsees to this day abstain both from beef and pork. Though not required by their religion, the double abstinence has had time to grow into a custom of their tribe; and custom, in the East, is a religion.

CONSIDERATIONS ON REPRESENTATIVE GOVERNMENT

CHAPTER 3

That the Ideally Best Form of Government Is Representative Government

It has long (perhaps throughout the entire duration of British freedom) been a common form of speech, that if a good despot could be insured, despotic monarchy would be the best form of government. I look upon this as a radical and most pernicious misconception of what good government is, which, until it can be got rid of, will fatally vitiate all our speculations on government.

The supposition is, that absolute power, in the hands of an eminent individual, would insure a virtuous and intelligent performance of all the duties of government. Good laws would be established and enforced, bad laws would be reformed; the best men would be placed in all situations of trust; justice would be as well administered, the public burdens would be as light and as judiciously imposed, every branch of administration would be as purely and as intelligently conducted as the circumstances of the country and its degree of intellectual and moral cultivation would admit. I am willing, for the sake of the argument, to concede all this, but I must point out how great the concession is, how much more is needed to produce even an approximation to these results than is conveyed in the simple expression, a good despot. Their realization would in fact imply, not merely a good monarch, but an all-seeing one. He must be at all times informed correctly, in considerable detail, of the conduct and working of every branch of administration, in every district of the country, and must be able, in the twenty-four hours per day, which are all that is granted to a king as to the humblest laborer, to give an effective share of attention and superintendence to all parts of this vast field; or he must at least be capable of discerning and choosing out, from among the mass of his subjects, not only a large abundance of honest and able men, fit to conduct every branch of public administration under supervision and control, but also the small number of men of eminent virtues and talents who can be trusted not only to do without that supervision, but to exercise it themselves over others. So extraordinary are the faculties and energies required for performing this task in any supportable manner, that the good despot whom we are supposing can hardly be imagined as consenting to undertake it unless as a refuge from intolerable evils, and a transitional preparation for something beyond. But the argument can do without even this immense item in the account. Suppose the difficulty vanished. What should we then have? One man of superhuman mental activity managing the entire affairs of a mentally passive people. Their passivity is implied in the very idea of absolute power. The nation as a whole, and every individual composing it, are without any potential voice in their own destiny. They exercise no will in respect to their collective interests. All is decided for them by a will not their own, which it is legally a crime for them to disobey. What sort of human beings can be formed under such a regimen? What development can either their thinking or their active faculties attain under it? On matters of pure theory they might perhaps be allowed to speculate, so long as their speculations either did not approach politics, or had not the remotest connection with its practice. On practical affairs they could at most be only suffered to suggest; and even under the most moderate of despots, none but persons of already admitted or reputed superiority could hope that their suggestions would be known to, much less regarded by, those who had the management of affairs. A person must have a very unusual taste for intellectual exercise in and for itself who will put himself to the trouble of thought when it is to have no outward effect, or qualify himself for functions which he has no chance of being allowed to exercise. The only sufficient incitement to mental exertion, in any but a few minds in a generation, is the prospect of some practical use to be made of its results. It does not follow that the nation will be wholly destitute of intellectual power. The common business of life, which must necessarily be performed by each individual or family for themselves, will call forth some amount of intelligence and practical ability within a certain narrow range of ideas. There may be a select class of *savants* who cultivate science with a view to its physical uses or for the pleasure of the pursuit. There will be a bureaucracy, and persons in training for the bureaucracy, who will be taught at least some empirical maxims of government and public administration. There may be, and often has been, a systematic organization of the best mental power in the country in some special direction (commonly military) to promote the grandeur of the despot. But the public at large remain without information and without interest on all the greater matters of practice; or, if they have any knowledge of them, it is but a *dilettante* knowledge, like that which people have of the mechanical arts who have never handled a tool. Nor is it only in their intelligence that they suffer. Their moral capacities are equally stunted. Wherever the sphere of action of human beings is artificially circumscribed, their sentiments are narrowed and dwarfed in the same proportion. The food of feeling is action; even domestic affection lives upon voluntary good offices. Let a person have nothing to do for his country, and he will not care for it. It has been said of old that in a despotism there is at most but one patriot, the despot himself; and the saying rests on a just appreciation of the effects of absolute subjection even to a good and wise master. Religion remains; and here, at least, it may be thought, is an agency that may be relied on for lifting men's eyes and minds above the dust at their feet. But religion, even supposing it to escape perversion for the purposes of despotism, ceases in these circumstances to be a social concern, and narrows into a personal affair between an individual and his Maker, in which the issue at stake is but his private salvation. Religion in this shape is quite consistent with the most selfish and contracted egoism, and identifies the votary as little in feeling with the rest of his kind as sensuality itself.

A good despotism means a government in which, so far as depends on the despot, there is no positive oppression by officers of state, but in which all the collective interests of the people are managed for them, all the thinking that has relation to collective interests done for them, and in which their minds are formed by, and consenting to, this abdication of their own energies. Leaving things to the government, like leaving them to Providence, is synonymous with caring, nothing about them, and accepting their results, when disagreeable, as visitations of Nature. With the exception, therefore, of a few studious men who take an intellectual interest in speculation for its own sake, the intelligence and sentiments of the whole people are given up to the material interests, and when these are provided for, to the amusement and ornamentation of private life. But to say this is to say, if the whole testimony of history is worth any thing, that the era of national decline has arrived; that is, if the nation had ever attained any thing to decline from. If it has never risen above the condition of an Oriental people, in that condition it continues to stagnate; but if, like Greece or Rome, it had realized any thing higher, through the energy, patriotism, and enlargement of mind, which, as national qualities, are the fruits solely of freedom, it relapses in a few generations into the Oriental state. And that state does not mean stupid tranquillity, with security against change for the worse; it often means being overrun, conquered, and reduced to domestic slavery either by a stronger despot, or by the nearest barbarous people who retain along with their savage rudeness the energies of freedom.

Such are not merely the natural tendencies, but the inherent necessities of despotic government, from which there is no outlet, unless is so far as the despotism consents not to be despotism; in so far as the supposed good despot abstains from exercising his power, and, though holding it in reserve, allows the general business of government to go on as if the people really governed themselves. However little probable it may be, we may imagine a despot observing many of the rules and restraints of constitutional government. He might allow such freedom of the press and of discussion as would enable a public opinion to form and express itself on national affairs. He might suffer local interests to be managed, without the interference of authority, by the people themselves. He might even surround himself with a council or councils of government, freely chosen by the whole or some portion of the nation, retaining in his own hands the power of taxation, and the supreme legislative as well as executive authority. Were he to act thus, and so far abdicate as a despot, he would do away with a considerable part of the evils characteristic of despotism. Political activity and capacity for public affairs would no longer be prevented from growing up in the body of the nation, and a public opinion would form itself, not the mere echo of the government. But such improvement would be the beginning of new difficulties. This public opinion, independent of the monarch's dictation, must be either with him or against him; if not the one, it will be the other. All governments must displease many persons, and these having now regular organs, and being able to express their sentiments, opinions adverse to the measures of government would often be expressed. What is the monarch to do when these unfavorable opinions happen to be in the majority? Is he to alter his course? Is he to defer to the nation? If so, he is no longer a despot, but a constitutional king; an organ or first minister of the people, distinguished only by being irremovable. If not, he must either put down opposition by his despotic power, or there will arise a permanent antagonism between the people and one man, which can have but one possible ending. Not even a religious principle of passive obedience and "right divine" would long ward off the natural consequences of such a position. The monarch would have to succumb, and conform to the conditions of constitutional royalty or give place to some one who would. The despotism, being thus chiefly nominal, would possess few of the advantages supposed to belong to absolute monarchy, while it would realize in a very imperfect degree those of a free government, since, however great an amount of liberty the citizens might practically enjoy, they could never forget that they held it on sufferance, and by a concession which, under the existing constitution of the state, might at any moment be resumed: that they were legally slaves, though of a prudent or indulgent master.

It is not much to be wondered at if impatient or disappointed reformers, groaning under the impediments opposed to the most salutary public improvements by the ignorance, the indifference, the untractableness, the perverse obstinacy of a people, and the corrupt combinations of selfish private interests, armed with the powerful weapons afforded by free institutions, should at times sigh for a strong hand to bear down all these obstacles, and compel a recalcitrant people to be better governed. But (setting aside the fact that for one despot who now and then reforms an abuse, there are ninety-nine who do nothing but create them) those who look in any such direction for the realization of their hopes leave out of the idea of good government its principal element, the improvement of the people themselves. One of the benefits of freedom is that under it the ruler can not pass by the people's minds and amend their affairs for them without amending *them*. If it were possible for a people to be well governed in spite of themselves, their good government would last no longer than the freedom of a people usually lasts who have been liberated by foreign arms without their own co-operation. It is true, a despot may educate the people, and to do so really would be the best apology for his despotism. But any education which aims at making human beings other than machines, in the long run makes them claim to have the control of their own actions. The leaders of French philosophy in the eighteenth century had been educated by the Jesuits. Even Jesuit education, it seems, was sufficiently real to call forth the appetite for freedom. Whatever invigorates the faculties, in however small a measure, creates an increased desire for their more unimpeded exercise; and a popular education is a failure if it educates the people for any state but that which it will certainly induce them to desire, and most probably to demand.

I am far from condemning, in cases of extreme exigency, the assumption of absolute power in the form of temporary dictatorship. Free nations have, in times of old, conferred such power by their own choice, as a necessary medicine for diseases of the body politic which could not be got rid of by less violent means. But its acceptance, even for a time strictly limited, can only be excused, if, like Solon or Pittacus, the dictator employs the whole power he assumes in removing the obstacles which debar the nation from the enjoyment of freedom. A good despotism is an altogether false ideal, which practically (except as a means to some temporary purpose) becomes the most senseless and dangerous of chimeras. Evil for evil, a good despotism, in a country at all advanced in civilization, is more noxious than a bad one, for it is far more relaxing and enervating to the thoughts, feelings, and energies of the people. The despotism of Augustus prepared the Romans for Tiberius. If the whole tone of their character had not first been prostrated by nearly two generations of that mild slavery, they would probably have had spirit enough left to rebel against the more odious one.

There is no difficulty in showing that the ideally best form of government is that in which the sovereignty, or supreme controlling power in the last resort, is vested in the entire aggregate of the community, every citizen not only having a voice in the exercise of that ultimate sovereignty, but being, at least occasionally, called on to take an actual part in the government by the personal discharge of some public function, local or general.

To test this proposition, it has to be examined in reference to the two branches into which, as pointed out in the last chapter, the inquiry into the goodness of a government conveniently divides itself, namely, how far it promotes the good management of the affairs of society by means of the existing faculties, moral, intellectual, and active, of its various members, and what is its effect in improving or deteriorating those faculties.

The ideally best form of government, it is scarcely necessary to say, does not mean one which is practicable or eligible in all states of civilization, but the one which, in the circumstances in which it is practicable and eligible, is attended with the greatest amount of beneficial consequences, immediate and prospective. A completely popular government is the only polity which can make out any claim to this character. It is pre-eminent in both the departments between which the excellence of a political Constitution is divided. It is both more favorable to present good government, and promotes a better and higher form of national character than any other polity whatsoever.

Its superiority in reference to present well-being rests upon two principles, of as universal truth and applicability as any general propositions which can be laid down respecting human affairs. The first is, that the rights and interests of every or any person are only secure from being disregarded when the person interested is himself able, and habitually disposed to stand up for them. The second is, that the general prosperity attains a greater height, and is more widely diffused, in proportion to the amount and variety of the personal energies enlisted in promoting it.

Putting these two propositions into a shape more special to their present application—human beings are only secure from evil at the hands of others in proportion as they have the power of being, and are *self-protecting;* and they only achieve a high degree of success in their struggle with Nature in proportion as they are *self-dependent,* relying on what they themselves can do, either separately or in concert, rather than on what others can do for them.

The former proposition—that each is the only safe guardian of his own rights and interests—is one of those elementary maxims of prudence which every person capable of conducting his own affairs implicitly acts upon wherever he himself is interested. Many, indeed, have a great dislike to it as a political doctrine, and are fond of holding it up to obloquy as a doctrine of universal selfishness. To which we may answer, that whenever it ceases to be true that mankind, as a rule, prefer themselves to others, and those nearest to them to those more remote, from that moment Communism is not only practicable, but the only defensible form of society, and will, when that time arrives, be assuredly carried into effect. For my own part, not believing in universal selfishness, I have no difficulty in admitting that Communism would even now be practicable among the *élite* of mankind, and may become so among the rest. But as this opinion is any thing but popular with those defenders of existing institutions who find fault with the doctrine of the general predominance of self interest, I am inclined to think they do in reality believe that most men consider themselves before other people. It is not, however, necessary to affirm even thus much in order to support the claim of all to participate in the sovereign power. We need not suppose that when power resides in an exclusive class, that class will knowingly and deliberately sacrifice the other classes to themselves: it suffices that, in the absence of its natural defenders, the interest of the excluded is always in danger of being overlooked; and, when looked at, is seen with very different eyes from those of the persons whom it directly concerns. In this country, for example, what are called the working-classes may be considered as excluded from all direct participation in the government. I do not believe that the classes who do participate in it have in general any intention of sacrificing the working classes to themselves. They once had that intention; witness the persevering attempts so long made to keep down wages by law. But in the present day, their ordinary disposition is the very opposite: they willingly make considerable sacrifices, especially of their pecuniary interest, for the benefit of the working classes, and err rather by too lavish and indiscriminating beneficence; nor do I believe that any rulers in history have been actuated by a more sincere desire to do their duty toward the poorer portion of their countrymen. Yet does Parliament, or almost any of the members composing it, ever for an instant look at any question with the eyes of a working man? When a subject arises in which the laborers as such have an interest, is it regarded from any point of view but that of the employers of labor? I do not say that the working men's view of these questions is in general nearer to truth than the other, but it is sometimes quite as near; and in any case it ought to be respectfully listened to, instead of being, as it is, not merely turned away from, but ignored. On the question of strikes, for instance, it is doubtful if there is so much as one among the leading members of either House who is not firmly convinced that the reason of the matter is unqualifiedly on the side of the masters, and that the men's view of it is simply absurd. Those who have studied the question know well how far this is from being the case, and in how different, and how infinitely less superficial a manner the point would have to be argued if the classes who strike were able to make themselves heard in Parliament.

It is an inherent condition of human affairs that no intention, however sincere, of protecting the interests of others can make it safe or salutary to tie up their own hands. Still more obviously true is it that by their own hands only can any positive and durable improvement of their circumstances in life be worked out. Through the joint influence of these two principles, all free communities have both been more exempt from social injustice and crime, and have attained more brilliant prosperity than any others, or than they themselves after they lost their freedom. Contrast the free states of the world, while their freedom lasted, with the contemporary subjects of monarchical or oligarchical despotism: the Greek cities with the Persian satrapies; the Italian republics, and the free towns of Flanders and Germany, with the feudal monarchies of Europe; Switzerland, Holland, and England with Austria or ante-revolutionary France. Their superior prosperity was too obvious ever to have been gainsaid; while their superiority in good government and social relations is proved by the prosperity, and is manifest besides in every page of history. If we compare, not one age with another, but the different governments which coexisted in the same age, no amount of disorder which exaggeration itself can pretend to have existed amid the publicity of the free states can be compared for a moment with the contemptuous trampling upon the mass of the people which pervaded the whole life of the monarchical countries, or the disgusting individual tyranny which was of more than daily occurrence under the systems of plunder which they called fiscal arrangements, and in the secrecy of their frightful courts of justice.

It must be acknowledged that the benefits of freedom, so far as they have hitherto been enjoyed, were obtained by the extension of its privileges to a part only of the community, and that a government in which they are extended impartially to all is a desideratum still unrealized. But, though every approach to this has an independent value, and in many cases more than an approach could not, in the existing state of general improvement, be made, the participation of all in these benefits is the ideally perfect conception of free government. In proportion as any, no matter who, are excluded from it, the interests of the excluded are left without the guaranty accorded to the rest, and they themselves have less scope and encouragement than they might otherwise have to that exertion of their energies for the good of themselves and of the community to which the general prosperity is always proportioned.

Thus stands the case as regards present well-being—the good management of the affairs of the existing generation. If we now pass to the influence of the form of government upon character, we shall find the superiority of popular government over every other to be, if possible, still more decided and indisputable.

This question really depends upon a still more fundamental one, viz., which of two common types of character, for the general good of humanity, it is most desirable should predominate—the active or the passive type; that which struggles against evils, or that which endures them, that which bends to circumstances, or that which endeavors to bend circumstances to itself.

The commonplaces of moralists and the general sympathies of mankind are in favor of the passive type. Energetic characters may be admired, but the acquiescent and submissive are those which most men personally prefer. The passiveness of our neighbors increases our own sense of security and plays into the hands of our willfulness. Passive characters, if we do not happen to need their activity, seem an obstruction the less in our own path. A contented character is not a dangerous rival. Yet nothing is more certain than that improvement in human affairs is wholly the work of the uncontented characters; and, moreover, that it is much easier for an active mind to acquire the virtues of patience than for a passive one to assume those of energy.

Of the three varieties of mental excellence, intellectual, practical, and moral, there never could be any doubt, in regard to the first two, which side had the advantage. All intellectual superiority is the fruit of active effort. Enterprise, the desire to keep moving, to be trying and accomplishing new things for our own benefit or that of others, is the parent even of speculative, and much more of practical talent. The intellectual culture compatible with the other type is of that feeble and vague description which belongs to a mind that stops at amusement or at simple contemplation. The test of real and vigorous thinking, the thinking which ascertains truths instead of dreaming dreams, is successful application to practice. Where that purpose does not exist, to give definiteness, precision, and an intelligible meaning to thought, it generates nothing better than the mystical metaphysics of the Pythagoreans or the Veds. With respect to practical improvement, the case is still more evident. The character which improves human life is that which struggles with natural powers and tendencies, not that which gives way to them. The self-benefiting qualities are all on the side of the active and energetic character, and the habits and conduct which promote the advantage of each individual member of the community must be at least a part of those which conduce most in the end to the advancement of the community as a whole.

But, on the point of moral preferability, there seems at first sight to be room for doubt. I am not referring to the religious feeling which has so generally existed in favor of the inactive character, as being more in harmony with the submission due to the divine will. Christianity, as well as other religions, has fostered this sentiment; but it is the prerogative of Christianity, as regards this and many other perversions, that it is able to throw them off. Abstractedly from religious considerations, a passive character, which yields to obstacles instead of striving to overcome them, may not indeed be very useful to others, no more than to itself, but it might be expected to be at least inoffensive. Contentment is always counted among the moral virtues. But it is a complete error to suppose that contentment is necessarily or naturally attendant on passivity of character; and unless it is, the moral consequences are mischievous. Where there exists a desire for advantages not possessed, the mind which does not potentially possess them by means of its own energies is apt to look with hatred and malice on those who do. The person bestirring himself with hopeful prospects to improve his circumstances is the one who feels good-will toward others engaged in, or who have succeeded in the same pursuit. And where the majority are so engaged, those who do not attain the object have had the tone given to their feelings by the general habit of the country, and ascribe their failure to want of effort or opportunity, or to their personal ill luck. But those who, while desiring what others possess, put no energy into striving for it, are either incessantly grumbling that fortune does not do for them what they do not attempt to do for themselves, or overflowing with envy and ill-will toward those who possess what they would like to have.

In proportion as success in life is seen or believed to be the fruit of fatality or accident and not of exertion, in that same ratio does envy develop itself as a point of national character. The most envious of all mankind are the Orientals. In Oriental moralists, in Oriental tales, the envious man is markedly prominent. In real life, he is the terror of all who possess any thing desirable, be it a palace, a handsome child, or even good health and spirits: the supposed effect of his mere look constitutes the all-pervading superstition of the evil eye. Next to Orientals in envy, as in inactivity, are some of the Southern Europeans. The Spaniards pursued all their great men with it, embittered their lives, and generally succeeded in putting an early stop to their successes.[1] With the French, who are essentially a Southern people, the double education of despotism and Catholicism has, in spite of their impulsive temperament, made submission and endurance the common character of the people, and their most received notion of wisdom and excellence; and if envy of one another, and of all superiority, is not more rife among them than it is, the circumstance must be ascribed to the many valuable counteracting elements in the French character, and most of all to the great individual energy which, though less persistent and more intermittent than in the self-helping and struggling Anglo-Saxons, has nevertheless manifested itself among the French in nearly every direction in which the operation of their institutions has been favorable to it.

There are, no doubt, in all countries, really contented characters, who not merely do not seek, but do not desire what they do not already possess, and these naturally bear no ill-will toward such as have apparently a more favored lot. But the great mass of seeming contentment is real discontent, combined with indolence or self-indulgence, which, taking no legitimate means of raising itself, delights in bringing others down to its own level. And if we look narrowly even at the cases of innocent contentment, we perceive that they only win our admiration when the indifference is solely to improvement in outward circumstances, and there is a striving for perpetual advancement in spiritual worth, or at least a disinterested zeal to benefit others. The contented man, or the contented family, who have no ambition to make any one else happier, to promote the good of their country or their neighborhood, or to improve themselves in moral excellence, excite in us neither admiration nor approval. We rightly ascribe this sort of contentment to mere unmanliness and want of spirit. The content which we approve is an ability to do cheerfully without what can not be had, a just appreciation of the comparative value of different objects of desire, and a willing renunciation of the less when incompatible with the greater. These, however, are excellences more natural to the character, in proportion as it is actively engaged in the attempt to improve its own or some other lot. He who is continually measuring his energy against difficulties, learns what are the difficulties insuperable to him, and what are those which, though he might overcome, the success is not worth the cost. He whose thoughts and activities are all needed for, and habitually employed in, practicable and useful enterprises, is the person of all others least likely to let his mind dwell with brooding discontent upon things either not worth attaining, or which are not so to him. Thus the active, self-helping character is not only intrinsically the best, but is the likeliest to acquire all that is really excellent or desirable in the opposite type.

The striving, go-ahead character of England and the United States is only a fit subject of disapproving criticism on account of the very secondary objects on which it commonly expends its strength. In itself it is the foundation of the best hopes for the general improvement of mankind. It has been acutely remarked, that whenever any thing goes amiss, the habitual impulse of French people is to say, "Il faut de la patience;" and of English people, "What a shame!" The people who think it a shame when any thing goes wrong—who rush to the conclusion that the evil could and ought to have been prevented, are those who, in the long run, do most to make the world better. If the desires are low placed, if they extend to little beyond physical comfort and the show of riches, the immediate results of the energy will not be much more than the continual extension of man's power over material objects; but even this makes room, and prepares the mechanical appliances for the greatest intellectual and social achievements; and while the energy is there, some persons will apply it, and it will be applied more and more, to the perfecting, not of outward circumstances alone, but of man's inward nature. Inactivity, unaspiringness, absence of desire, is a more fatal hinderance to improvement than any misdirection of energy, and is that through which alone, when existing in the mass, any very formidable misdirection by an energetic few becomes possible. It is this, mainly which retains in a savage or semi-savage state the great majority of the human race.

Now there can be no kind of doubt that the passive type of character is favored by the government of one or a few, and the active self-helping type by that of the many. Irresponsible rulers need the quiescence of the ruled more than they need any activity but that which they can compel. Submissiveness to the prescriptions of men as necessities of nature is the lesson inculcated by all governments upon those who are wholly without participation in them. The will of superiors, and the law as the will of superiors, must be passively yielded to. But no men are mere instruments or materials in the hands of their rulers who have will, or spirit, or a spring of internal activity in the rest of their proceedings, and any manifestation of these qualities, instead of receiving encouragement from despots, has to get itself forgiven by them. Even when irresponsible rulers are not sufficiently conscious of danger from the mental activity of their subjects to be desirous of repressing it, the position itself is a repression. Endeavor is even more effectually restrained by the certainty of its impotence than by any positive discouragement. Between subjection to the will of others and the virtues of self-help and self-government there is a natural incompatibility. This is more or less complete according as the bondage is strained or relaxed. Rulers differ very much in the length to which they carry the control of the free agency of their subjects, or the suppression of it by managing their business for them. But the difference is in degree, not in principle; and the best despots often go the greatest lengths in chaining up the free agency of their subjects. A bad despot, when his own personal indulgences have been provided for, may sometimes be willing to let the people alone; but a good despot insists on doing them good by making them do their own business in a better way than they themselves know of. The regulations which restricted to fixed processes all the leading branches of French manufactures were the work of the great Colbert.

Very different is the state of the human faculties where a human being feels himself under no other external restraint than the necessities of nature, or mandates of society which he has his share in imposing, and which it is open to him, if he thinks them wrong, publicly to dissent from, and exert himself actively to get altered. No doubt, under a government partially popular, this freedom may be exercised even by those who are not partakers in the full privileges of citizenship; but it is a great additional stimulus to any one's self-help and self-reliance when he starts from an even ground, and has not to feel that his success depends on the impression he can make upon the sentiments and dispositions of a body of whom he is not one. It is a great discouragement to an individual, and a still greater one to a class, to be left out of the constitution; to be reduced to plead from outside the door to the arbiters of their destiny, not taken into the consultation within. The maximum of the invigorating effect of freedom upon the character is only obtained when the person acted on either is, or is looking forward to become, a citizen as fully privileged as any other. What is still more important than even this matter of feeling is the practical discipline which the character obtains from the occasional demand made upon the citizens to exercise, for a time and in their turn, some social function. It is not sufficiently considered how little there is in most men's ordinary life to give any largeness either to their conceptions or to their sentiments. Their work is a routine; not a labor of love, but of self-interest in the most elementary form, the satisfaction of daily wants; neither the thing done, nor the process of doing it, introduces the mind to thoughts or feelings extending beyond individuals; if instructive books are within their reach, there is no stimulus to read them; and, in most cases, the individual has no access to any person of cultivation much superior to his own. Giving him something to do for the public supplies, in a measure, all these deficiencies. If circumstances allow the amount of public duty assigned him to be considerable, it makes him an educated man. Notwithstanding the defects of the social system and moral ideas of antiquity, the practice of the dicastery and the ecclesia raised the intellectual standard of an average Athenian citizen far beyond any thing of which there is yet an example in any other mass of men, ancient or modern. The proofs of this are apparent in every page of our great historian of Greece; but we need scarcely look farther than to the high quality of the addresses which their great orators deemed best calculated to act with effect on their understanding and will. A benefit of the same kind, though far less in degree, is produced on Englishmen of the lower middle class by their liability to be placed on juries and to serve parish offices, which, though it does not occur to so many, nor is so continuous, nor introduces them to so great a variety of elevated considerations as to admit of comparison with the public education which every citizen of Athens obtained from her democratic institutions, makes them nevertheless very different beings, in range of ideas and development of faculties, from those who have done nothing in their lives but drive a quill, or sell goods over a counter. Still more salutary is the moral part of the instruction afforded by the participation of the private citizen, if even rarely, in public functions. He is called upon, while so engaged, to weigh interests not his own; to be guided, in case of conflicting claims, by another rule than his private partialities; to apply, at every turn, principles and maxims which have for their reason of existence the general good; and he usually finds associated with him in the same work minds more familiarized than his own with these ideas and operations, whose study it will be to supply reasons to his understanding, and stimulation to his feeling for the general good. He is made to feel himself one of the public, and whatever is their interest to be his interest. Where this school of public spirit does not exist, scarcely any sense is entertained that private persons, in no eminent social situation, owe any duties to society except to obey the laws and submit to the government. There is no unselfish sentiment of identification with the public. Every thought and feeling, either of interest or of duty, is absorbed in the individual and in the family. The man never thinks of any collective interest, of any objects to be pursued jointly with others, but only in competition with them, and in some measure at their expense. A neighbor, not being an ally or an associate, since he is never engaged in any common undertaking for the joint benefit, is therefore only a rival. Thus even private morality suffers, while public is actually extinct. Were this the universal and only possible state of things, the utmost aspirations of the lawgiver or the moralist could only stretch to making the bulk of the community a flock of sheep innocently nibbling the grass side by side.

From these accumulated considerations, it is evident that the only government which can fully satisfy all the exigencies of the social state is one in which the whole people participate; that any participation, even in the smallest public function, is useful; that the participation should every where be as great as the general degree of improvement of the community will allow; and that nothing less can be ultimately desirable than the admission of all to a share in the sovereign power of the state. But since all can not, in a community exceeding a single small town, participate personally in any but some very minor portions of the public business, it follows that the ideal type of a perfect government must be representative.

Notes

1. I limit the expression to past time, because I would say nothing derogatory of a great, and now at last a free people, who are entering into the general movement of European progress with a vigor which bids fair to make up rapidly the ground they have lost. No one can doubt what Spanish intellect and energy are capable of; and their faults as a people are chiefly those for which freedom and industrial ardor are a real specific.

THE SUBJECTION OF WOMEN

I

The object of this Essay is to explain, as clearly as I am able, the grounds of an opinion which I have held from the very earliest period when I had formed any opinions at all on social or political matters, and which, instead of being weakened or modified, has been constantly growing stronger by the progress of reflection and the experience of life: That the principle which regulates the existing social relations between the two sexes—the legal subordination of one sex to the other—is wrong in itself, and now one of the chief hindrances to human improvement; and that it ought to be replaced by a principle of perfect equality, admitting no power or privilege on the one side, nor disability on the other.

The very words necessary to express the task I have undertaken, show how arduous it is. But it would be a mistake to suppose that the difficulty of the case must lie in the insufficiency or obscurity of the grounds of reason on which my conviction rests. The difficulty is that which exists in all cases in which there is a mass of feeling to be contended against. So long as an opinion is strongly rooted in the feelings, it gains rather than loses in stability by having a preponderating weight of argument against it. For if it were accepted as a result of argument, the refutation of the argument might shake the solidity of the conviction; but when it rests solely on feeling, the worse it fares in argumentative contest, the more persuaded its adherents are that their feeling must have some deeper ground, which the arguments do not reach; and while the feeling remains, it is always throwing up fresh entrenchments of argument to repair any breach made in the old. And there are so many causes tending to make the feelings connected with this subject the most intense and most deeply-rooted of all those which gather round and protect old institutions and customs, that we need not wonder to find them as yet less undermined and loosed than any of the rest by the progress of the great modern spiritual and social transition; nor suppose that the barbarisms to which men cling longest must be less barbarisms than those which they earlier shake off.

In every respect the burthen is hard on those who attack an almost universal opinion. They must be very fortunate as well as unusually capable if they obtain a hearing at all. They have more difficulty in obtaining a trial, than any other litigants have in getting a verdict. If they do extort a hearing, they are subjected to a set of logical requirements totally different from those exacted from other people. In all other cases, the burthen of proof is supposed to lie with the affirmative. If a person is charged with a murder, it rests with those who accuse him to give proof of his guilt, not with himself to prove his innocence. If there is a difference of opinion about the reality of any alleged historical event, in which the feelings of men in general are not much interested, as the Siege of Troy for example, those who maintain that the event took place are expected to produce their proofs, before those who take the other side can be required to say anything; and at no time are these required to do more than show that the evidence produced by the others is of no value. Again, in practical matters, the burthen of proof is supposed to be with those who are against liberty; who contend for any restriction or prohibition; either any limitation of the general freedom of human action, or any disqualification or disparity of privilege affecting one person or kind of persons, as compared with others. The *a priori* presumption is in favour of freedom and impartiality. It is held that there should be no restraint not required by the general good, and that the law should be no respecter of persons, but should treat all alike, save where dissimilarity of treatment is required by positive reasons, either of justice or of policy. But of none of these rules of evidence will the benefit be allowed to those who maintain the opinion I profess. It is useless for me to say that those who maintain the doctrine that men have a right to command and women are under an obligation to obey, or that men are fit for government and women unfit, are on the affirmative side of the question, and that they are bound to show positive evidence for the assertions, or submit to their rejection. It is equally unavailing for me to say that those who deny to women any freedom or privilege rightly allowed to men, having the double presumption against them that they are opposing freedom and recommending partiality, must be held to the strictest proof of their case, and unless their success be such as to exclude all doubt, the judgement ought to go against them. These would be thought good pleas in any common case; but will not be thought so in this instance. Before I could hope to make any impression, I should be expected not only to answer all that has ever been said by those who take the other side of the question, but to imagine all that could be said by them—to find them in reasons, as well as answer all I find: and besides refuting all arguments for the affirmative, I shall be called upon for invincible positive arguments to prove a negative. And even if I could do all this, and leave the opposite party with a host of unanswered arguments against them, and not a single unrefuted one on their side, I should be thought to have done little; for a cause supported on the one hand by universal usage, and on the other by so great a preponderance of popular sentiment, is supposed to have a presumption in its favour, superior to any conviction which an appeal to reason has power to produce in any intellects but those of a high class.

I do not mention these difficulties to complain of them; first, because it would be useless; they are inseparable from having to contend through people's understandings against the hostility of their feelings and practical tendencies: and truly the understandings of the majority of mankind would need to be much better cultivated than has ever yet been the case, before they can be asked to place such reliance in their own power of estimating arguments, as to give up practical principals in which they have been born and bred, and which are the basis of much of the existing order of the world, at the first argumentative attack which they are not capable of logically resisting. I do not therefore quarrel with them for having too little faith in argument, but for having too much faith in custom and the general feeling. It is one of the characteristic prejudices of the reaction of the nineteenth century against the eighteenth, to accord to the unreasoning elements in human nature the infallibility which the eighteenth century is supposed to have ascribed to the reasoning elements. For the apotheosis of Reason we have substituted that of Instinct; and we call everything instinct which we find in ourselves and for which we cannot trace any rational foundation. This idolatry, infinitely more degrading than the other, and the most pernicious of the false worships of the present day, of all of which it is now the main support, will probably hold its ground until it gives way before a sound psychology, laying bare the real root of much that is bowed down to as the intention of Nature and the ordinance of God. As regards the present question, I am willing to accept the unfavourable conditions which the prejudice assigns to me. I consent that established custom, and the general feeling, should be deemed conclusive against me, unless that custom and feeling from age to age can be shown to have owed their existence to other causes than their soundness, and to have derived their power from the worse rather than the better parts of human nature. I am willing that judgement should go against me, unless I can show that my judge has been tampered with. The concession is not so great as it might appear; for to prove this, is by far the easiest portion of my task.

The generality of a practice is in some cases a strong presumption that it is, or at all events once was, conducive to laudable ends. This is the case, when the practice was first adopted, or afterwards kept up, as a means to such ends, and was grounded on experience of the mode in which they could be most effectually attained. If the authority of men over women, when first established, had been the result of a conscientious comparison between different modes of constituting the government of society; if, after trying various other modes of social organization—the government of women over men, equality between the two, and such mixed and divided modes of government as might be invented—it had been decided, on the testimony of experience, that the mode in which women are wholly under the rule of men, having no share at all in public concerns, and each in private being under the legal obligation of obedience to the man with whom she has associated her destiny, was the arrangement most conducive to the happiness and well-being of both; its general adoption might then be fairly thought to be some evidence that, at the time when it was adopted, it was the best: though even then the considerations which recommended it may, like so many other primeval social facts of the greatest importance, have subsequently, in the course of ages, ceased to exist. But the state of the case is in every respect the reverse of this. In the first place, the opinion in favour of the present system, which entirely subordinates the weaker sex to the stronger, rests upon theory only; for there never has been trial made of any other: so that experience, in the sense in which it is vulgarly opposed to theory, cannot be pretended to have pronounced any verdict. And in the second place, the adoption of this system of inequality never was the result of deliberation, or forethought, or any social ideas, or any notion whatever of what conduced to the benefit of humanity or the good order of society. It arose simply from the fact that from the very earliest twilight of human society, every woman (owing to the value attached to her by men, combined with her inferiority in muscular strength) was found in a state of bondage to some man. Laws and systems of polity always begin by recognizing the relations they find already existing between individuals. They convert what was a mere physical fact into a legal right, give it the sanction of society, and principally aim at the substitution of public and organized means of asserting and protecting these rights, instead of the irregular and lawless conflict of physical strength. Those who had already been compelled to obedience became in this manner legally bound to it. Slavery, from being a mere affair of force between the master and the slave, became regularized and a matter of compact among the masters, who, binding themselves to one another for common protection, guaranteed by their collective strength the private possessions of each, including his slaves. In early times, the great majority of the male sex were slaves, as well as the whole of the female. And many ages elapsed, some of them ages of high cultivation, before any thinker was bold enough to question the rightfulness, and the absolute social necessity, either of the one slavery or of the other. By degrees such thinkers did arise: and (the general progress of society assisting) the slavery of the male sex has, in all the countries of Christian Europe at least (though, in one of them, only within the last few years) been at length abolished, and that of the female sex has been gradually changed into a milder form of dependence. But this dependence, as it exists at present, is not an original institution, taking a fresh start from considerations of justice and social expediency—it is the primitive state of slavery lasting on, through successive mitigations and modifications occasioned by the same causes which have softened the general manners, and brought all human relations more under the control of justice and the influence of humanity. It has not lost the taint of its brutal origin. No presumption in its favour, therefore, can be drawn from the fact of its existence. The only such presumption which it could be supposed to have, must be grounded on its having lasted till now, when so many other things which came down from the same odious source have been done away with. And this, indeed, is what makes it strange to ordinary ears, to hear it asserted that the inequality of rights between men and women has no other source than the law of the strongest.

That this statement should have the effect of a paradox, is in some respects creditable to the progress of civilization, and the improvement of the moral sentiments of mankind. We now live—that is to say, one or two of the most advanced nations of the world now live—in a state in which the law of the strongest seems to be entirely abandoned as the regulating principle of the world's affairs: nobody professes it, and, as regards most of the relations between human beings, nobody is permitted to practice it. When any one succeeds in doing so, it is under cover of some pretext which gives him the semblance of having some general social interest on his side. This being the ostensible state of things, people flatter themselves that the rule of mere force is ended; that the law of the strongest cannot be the reason of existence of anything which has remained in full operation down to the present time. However any of our present institutions may have begun, it can only, they think, have been preserved to this period of advanced civilization by a well-grounded feeling of its adaptation to human nature, and conduciveness to the general good. They do not understand the great vitality and durability of institutions which place right on the side of might; how intensely they are clung to; how the good as well as the bad propensities and sentiments of those who have power in their hands, become identified with retaining it; how slowly these bad institutions give way, one at a time, the weakest first, beginning with those which are least interwoven with the daily habits of life; and how very rarely those who have obtained legal power because they first had physical, have ever lost their hold of it until the physical power had passed over to the other side. Such shifting of the physical force not having taken place in the case of women; this fact, combined with all the peculiar and characteristic features of the particular case, made it certain from the first that this branch of the system of right founded on might, though softened in its most atrocious features at an earlier period than several of the others, would be the very last to disappear. It was inevitable that this one case of a social relation grounded on force would survive through generations of institutions grounded on equal justice, an almost solitary exception to the general character of their laws and customs; but which, so long as it does not proclaim its own origin, and as discussion has not brought out its true character, is not felt to jar with modern civilization, any more than domestic slavery among the Greeks jarred with their notion of themselves as a free people.

The truth is, that people of the present and the last two or three generations have lost all practical sense of the primitive condition of humanity; and only the few who have studied history accurately, or have much frequented the parts of the world occupied by the living representatives of ages long past, are able to form any mental picture of what society then was. People are not aware how entirely, in former ages, the law of superior strength was the rule of life; how publicly and openly it was avowed, I do not say cynically or shamelessly—for these words imply a feeling that there was something in it to be ashamed of, and no such notion could find a place in the faculties of any person in those ages, except a philosopher or a saint. History gives a cruel experience of human nature, in showing how exactly the regard due to the life, possessions, and entire earthly happiness of any class of persons was measured by what they had the power of enforcing; how all who made any resistance to authorities that had arms in their hands, however dreadful might be the provocation, had not only the law of force but all other laws, and all the notions of social obligation against them; and, in the eyes of those whom they resisted, were not only guilty of crime, but the worst of all crimes, deserving the most cruel chastisement which human beings could inflict. The first small vestige of a feeling of obligation in a superior to acknowledge any right in inferiors, began when he had been induced, for convenience, to make some promise to them. Though these promises, even when sanctioned by the most solemn oaths, were for many ages revoked or violated on the most trifling provocation or temptation, it is probable that this, except by persons of still worse than the average morality, was seldom done without some twinges of conscience. The ancient republics, being mostly grounded from the first upon some kind of mutual compact, or at any rate formed by an union of persons not very unequal in strength, afforded, in consequence, the first instance of a portion of human relations fenced round, and placed under the dominion of another law than that of force. And though the original law of force remained in full operation between them and their slaves, and also (except so far as limited by express compact) between a commonwealth and its subjects, or other independent commonwealths; the banishment of that primitive law, even from so narrow a field, commenced the regeneration of human nature, by giving birth to sentiments of which experience soon demonstrated the immense value even for material interests, and which thenceforward only required to be enlarged, not created. Though slaves were no part of the commonwealth, it was in the free states that slaves were first felt to have rights as human beings. The Stoics were, I believe, the first (except so far as the Jewish law constitutes an exception) who taught as a part of morality that men were bound by moral obligations to their slaves. No one, after Christianity became ascendant, could ever again have been a stranger to this belief, in theory; nor, after the rise of the Catholic Church, was it ever without persons to stand up for it. Yet to enforce it was the most arduous task which Christianity ever had to perform. For more than a thousand years the Church kept up the contest, with hardly any perceptible success. It was not for want of power over men's minds. Its power was prodigious. It could make kings and nobles resign their most valued possessions to enrich the Church. It could make thousands, in the prime of life and the height of worldly advantages, shut themselves up in convents to work out their salvation by poverty, fasting and prayer. It could send hundreds of thousands across land and sea, Europe and Asia, to give their lives for the deliverance of the Holy Sepulchre. It could make kings relinquish wives who were the objects of their passionate attachment, because the Church declared that they were within the seventh (by our calculation the fourteenth) degree of relationship. All this it did; but it could not make men fight less with one another, nor tyrannize less cruelly over the serfs, and, when they were able, over burgesses. It could not make them renounce either of the applications of force; force militant, or force triumphant. This they could never be induced to do until they were themselves in their turn compelled by superior force. Only by the growing power of kings was an end put to fighting except between kings, or competitors for kingship; only by the growth of a wealthy and warlike bourgeoisie in the fortified towns, and of a plebeian infantry which proved more powerful in the field than the undisciplined chivalry, was the insolent tyranny of the nobles over the bourgeoisie and peasantry brought within some bounds. It was persisted in not only until, but long after, the oppressed had obtained a power enabling them often to take conspicuous vengeance; and on the Continent much of it continued to the time of the French Revolution, though in England the earlier and better organization of the democratic classes put an end to it sooner, by establishing equal laws and free national institutions.

If people are mostly so little aware how completely, during the greater part of the duration of our species, the law of force was the avowed rule of general conduct, any other being only a special and exceptional consequence of peculiar ties—and from how very recent a date it is that the affairs of society in general have been even pretended to be regulated according to any moral law; as little do people remember or consider, how institutions and customs which never had any ground but the law of force, last on into ages and states of general opinion which never would have permitted their first establishment. Less than forty years ago, Englishmen might still by law hold human beings in bondage as saleable property: within the present century they might kidnap them and carry them off, and work them literally to death. This absolutely extreme case of the law of force, condemned by those who can tolerate almost every other form of arbitrary power, and which, of all others, presents features the most revolting to the feelings of all who look at it from an impartial position, was the law of civilized and Christian England within the memory of persons now living: and in one half of Anglo-Saxon America three or four years ago, not only did slavery exist, but the slave trade, and the breeding of slaves expressly for it, was a general practice between slave states. Yet not only was there a greater strength of sentiment against it, but, in England at least, a less amount either of feeling or of interest in favour of it, than of any other of the customary abuses of force: for its motive was the love of gain, unmixed and undisguised; and those who profited by it were a very small numerical fraction of the country, while the natural feeling of all who were not personally interested in it, was unmitigated abhorrence. So extreme an instance makes it almost superfluous to refer to any other: but consider the long duration of absolute monarchy. In England at present it is the almost universal conviction that military despotism is a case of the law of force, having no other origin or justification. Yet in all the great nations of Europe except England it either still exists, or has only just ceased to exist, and has even now a strong party favourable to it in all ranks of the people, especially among persons of station and consequence. Such is the power of an established system, even when far from universal; when not only in almost every period of history there have been great and well-known examples of the contrary system, but these have almost invariable been afforded by the most illustrious and most prosperous communities. In this case, too, the possessor of the undue power, the person directly interested in it, is only one person, while those who are subject to it and suffer from it are literally all the rest. The yoke is naturally and necessarily humiliating to all persons, except the one who is on the throne, together with, at most, the one who expects to succeed to it. How different are these cases from that of the power of men over women! I am not now prejudging the question of its justifiableness. I am showing how vastly more permanent it could not but be, even if not justifiable, than these other dominations which have nevertheless lasted down to our own time. Whatever gratification of pride there is in the possession of power, and whatever personal interest in its exercise, is in this case not confined to a limited class, but common to the whole male sex. Instead of being, to most of its supporters, a thing desirable chiefly in the abstract, or, like the political ends usually contended for by factions, of little private importance to any but the leaders; it comes home to the person and hearth of every male head of a family, and of every one who looks forward to being so. The clodhopper exercises, or is to exercise, his share of the power equally with the highest nobleman. And the case is that in which the desire of power is the strongest: for every one who desires power, desires it most over those who are nearest to him, with whom his life is passed, with whom he has most concerns in common, and in whom any independence of his authority is oftenest likely to interfere with his individual preferences. If, in the other cases specified, powers manifestly grounded only on force, and having so much less to support them, are so slowly and with so much difficulty got rid of, much more must it be so with this, even if it rests on no better foundation than those. We must consider, too, that the possessors of the power have facilities in this case, greater than in any other, to prevent any uprising against it. Every one of the subjects lives under the very eye, and almost, it may be said, in the hands, of one of the masters—in closer intimacy with him than with any of her fellow subjects; with no means of combining against him, no power of even locally overmastering him, and, on the other hand, with the strongest motives for seeking his favour and avoiding to give him offence. In struggles for political emancipation, everybody knows how often its champions are bought off by bribes, or daunted by terrors. In the case of women, each individual of the subject-class is in a chronic state of bribery and intimidation combined. In setting up the standard of resistance, a large number of the leaders, and still more of the followers, must make an almost complete sacrifice of the pleasures or the alleviations of their own individual lot. If ever any system of privilege and enforced subjection had its yoke tightly riveted on the necks of those who are kept down by it, this has. I have not yet shown that it is a wrong system: but every one who is capable of thinking on the subject must see that even if it is, it was certain to outlast all other forms of unjust authority. And when some of the grossest of the other forms still exist in many civilized countries, and have only recently been got rid of in others, it would be strange if that which is so much the deepest-rooted had yet been perceptibly shaken anywhere. There is more reason to wonder that the protests and testimonies against it should have been so numerous and so weighty as they are.

Some will object, that a comparison cannot fairly be made between the government of the male sex and the forms of unjust power which I have adduced in illustration of it, since these are arbitrary, and the effect of mere usurpation, while it on the contrary is natural. But was there ever any domination which did not appear natural to those who possessed it? There was a time when the division of mankind into two classes, a small one of masters and a numerous one of slaves, appeared, even to the most cultivated minds, to be a natural, and the only natural, condition of the human race. No less an intellect, and one which contributed no less to the progress of human thought, than Aristotole, held this opinion without doubt or misgiving; and rested it on the same premises on which the same assertion in regard to the dominion of men over women is usually based, namely that there are different natures among mankind, free natures, and slave natures: that the Greeks were of a free nature, the barbarian races of Thracians and Asiatics of a slave nature. But why need I go back to Aristotle? Did not the slave-owners of the Southern United States maintain the same doctrine, with all the fanaticism with which men cling to the theories that justify their passions and legitimate their personal interests? Did they not call heaven and earth to witness that the dominion of the white man over the black is natural, that the black race is by nature incapable of freedom, and marked out for slavery?—some even going so far as to say that the freedom of manual labourers is an unnatural order of things anywhere. Again, the theorists of absolute monarchy have always affirmed it to be the only natural form of government; issuing from the patriarchal, which was the primitive and spontaneous form of society, framed on the model of the paternal, which is anterior to society itself, and, as they contend, the most natural authority of all. Nay, for that matter, the law of force itself, to those who could not plead any other, has always seemed the most natural of all grounds for the exercise of authority. Conquering races hold it to be Nature's own dictate that the conquered should obey the conquerors, or, as they euphoniously paraphrase it, that the feebler and more unwarlike races should submit to the braver and manlier. The smallest acquaintance with human life in the Middle Ages shows how supremely natural the dominion of the feudal nobility over men of low condition appeared to the nobility themselves, and how unnatural the conception seemed, of a person of the inferior class claiming equality with them, or exercising authority over them. It hardly seemed less so to the class held in subjection. The emancipated serfs and burgesses, even in their most vigorous struggles, never made any pretension to a share of authority; they only demanded more or less of limitation to the power of tyrannizing over them. So true is it that unnatural generally means only uncustomary, and that everything which is usual appears natural. The subjection of women to men being a universal custom, any departure from it quite naturally appears unnatural. But how entirely, even in this case, the feeling is dependent on custom, appears by ample experience. Nothing so much astonishes the people of distant parts of the world, when they first learn anything about England, as to be told that it is under a queen: the thing seems to them so unnatural as to be almost incredible. To Englishmen this does not seem in the least degree unnatural, because they are used to it; but they do feel it unnatural that women should be soldiers or members of Parliament. In the feudal ages, on the contrary, war and politics were not thought unnatural to women, because not unusual; it seemed natural that women of the privileged classes should be of manly character, inferior in nothing but bodily strength to their husbands and fathers. The independence of women seemed rather less unnatural to the Greeks than to other ancients, on account of the fabulous Amazons (whom they believed to be historical), and the partial example afforded by the Spartan women; who, though no less subordinate by law than in other Greek states, were more free in fact, and being trained to bodily exercises in the same manner with men, gave ample proof that they were not naturally disqualified for them. There can be little doubt that Spartan experience suggested to Plato, among many other of his doctrines, that of the social and political equality of the two sexes.

But, it will be said, the rule of men over women differs from all these others in not being a rule of force: it is accepted voluntarily; women make no complaint, and are consenting parties to it. In the first place, a great number of women do not accept it. Ever since there have been women able to make their sentiments known by their writings (the only mode of publicity which society permits to them), an increasing number of them have recorded protests against their present social condition: and recently many thousands of them, headed by the most eminent women known to the public, have petitioned Parliament for their admission to the Parliamentary Suffrage. The claim of women to be educated as solidly, and in the same branches of knowledge, as men, is urged with growing intensity, and with a great prospect of success; while the demand for their admission into professions and occupations hitherto closed against them, becomes every year more urgent. Though there are not in this country, as there are in the United States, periodical Conventions and an organized party to agitate for the Rights of Women, there is a numerous and active Society organized and managed by women, for the more limited object of obtaining the political franchise. Nor is it only in our own country and in America that women are beginning to protest, more or less collectively, against the disabilities under which they labour. France, and Italy, and Switzerland, and Russia now afford examples of the same thing. How many more women there are who silently cherish similar aspirations, no one can possibly know; but there are abundant tokens how many *would* cherish them, were they not so strenuously taught to repress them as contrary to the proprieties of their sex. It must be remembered, also, that no enslaved class ever asked for complete liberty at once. When Simon de Montfort called the deputies of the commons to sit for the first time in Parliament, did any of them dream of demanding that an assembly, elected by their constituents, should make and destroy ministries, and dictate to the king in affairs of State? No such thought entered into the imagination of the most ambitious of them. The nobility had already these pretensions; the commons pretended to nothing but to be exempt from arbitrary taxation, and from the gross individual oppression of the king's officers. It is a political law of nature that those who are under any power of ancient origin never begin by complaining of the power itself, but only of its oppressive exercise. There is never any want of women who complain of ill usage by their husbands. There would be infinitely more, if complaint were not the greatest of all provocatives to a repetition and increase of the ill usage. It is this which frustrates all attempts to maintain the power but protect the woman against its abuses. In no other case (except that of a child) is the person who has been proved judicially to have suffered an injury, replaced under the physical power of the culprit who inflicted it. Accordingly wives, even in the most extreme and protracted cases of bodily ill usage, hardly ever dare avail themselves of the laws made for their protection: and if, in a moment of irrepressible indignation, or by the interference of neighbours, they are induced to do so, their whole effort afterwards is to disclose as little as they can, and to beg off their tyrant from his merited chastisement.

All causes, social and natural, combine to make it unlikely that women should be collectively rebellious to the power of men. They are so far in a position different from all other subject classes, that their masters require something more from them than actual service. Men do not want solely the obedience of women, they want their sentiments. All men, except the most brutish, desire to have, in the woman most nearly connected with them, not a forced slave but a willing one; not a slave merely, but a favourite. They have therefore put everything in practice to enslave their minds. The masters of all other slaves rely, for maintaining obedience, on fear; either fear of themselves, or religious fears. The masters of women wanted more than simple obedience, and they turned the whole force of education to effect their purpose. All women are brought up from the very earliest years in the belief that their ideal of character is the very opposite to that of men; not self-will, and government by self-control, but submission, and yielding to the control of others. All the moralities tell them that it is the duty of women, and all the current sentimentalities that it is their nature, to live for others; to make complete abnegation of themselves, and to have no life but in their affections. And by their affections are meant the only ones they are allowed to have—those to the men with whom they are connected, or to the children who constitute an additional and indefeasible tie between them and a man. When we put together three things—first, the natural attraction between opposite sexes; secondly, the wife's entire dependence on the husband, every privilege or pleasure she has being either his gift, or depending entirely on his will; and lastly, that the principal object of human pursuit, consideration, and all objects of social ambition, can in general be sought or obtained by her only through him—it would be a miracle if the object of being attractive to men had not become the polar star of feminine education and formation of character. And, this great means of influence over the minds of women having been acquired, an instinct of selfishness made man avail themselves of it to the utmost as a means of holding women in subjection, by representing to them meekness, submissiveness, and resignation of all individual will into the hands of a man, as an essential part of sexual attractiveness. Can it be doubted that any of the other yokes which mankind have succeeded in breaking, would have subsisted till now if the same means had existed, and had been as sedulously used, to bow down their minds to it? If it had been made the object of the life of every young plebeian to find personal favour in the eyes of some patrician, of every young serf with some seigneur; if domestication with him, and a share of his personal affections, had been held out as the prize which they all should look out for, the most gifted and aspiring being able to reckon on the most desirable prizes; and if, when this prize had been obtained, they had been shut out by a wall of brass from all interests not centring in him, all feelings and desires but those which he shared or inculcated; would not serfs and seigneurs, plebeians and patricians, have been as broadly distinguished at this day as men and women are? and would not all but a thinker here and there have believed the distinction to be a fundamental and unalterable fact in human nature?

The preceding considerations are amply sufficient to show that custom, however universal it may be, affords in this case no presumption, and ought not to create any prejudice, in favour of the arrangements which place women in social and political subjection to men. But I may go farther, and maintain that the course of history, and the tendencies of progressive human society, afford not only no presumption in favour of this system of inequality of rights, but a strong one against it; and that, so far as the whole course of human improvement up to this time, the whole stream of modern tendencies, warrants any inference on the subject, it is, that this relic of the past is discordant with the future, and must necessarily disappear.

For what is the peculiar character of the modern world—the difference which chiefly distinguishes modern institutions, modern social ideas, modern life itself, from those of times long past? It is, that human beings are no longer born to their place in life, and chained down by an inexorable bond to the place they are born to, but are free to employ their faculties, and such favourable chances as offer, to achieve the lot which may appear to them most desirable. Human society of old was constituted on a very different principle. All were born to a fixed social position, and were mostly kept in it by law, or interdicted from any means by which they could emerge from it. As some men are born white and others black, so some were born slaves and others freemen and citizens; some were born patricians, others plebeians; some were born feudal nobles, others commoners and *roturiers*. A slave or serf could never make himself free, nor, except by the will of his master, become so. In most European countries it was not till towards the close of the Middle Ages, and as a consequence of the growth of regal power, that commoners could be enobled. Even among nobles, the eldest son was born the exclusive heir to the paternal possessions, and a long time elapsed before it was fully established that the father could disinherit him. Among the industrious classes, only those who were born members of a guild, or were admitted into it by its members, could lawfully practice their calling within its local limits; and nobody could practice any calling deemed important, in any but the legal manner—by processes authoritatively prescribed. Manufacturers have stood in the pillory for presuming to carry on their business by new and improved methods. In modern Europe, and most in those parts of it which have participated most largely in all other modern improvements, diametrically opposite doctrines now prevail. Law and government do not undertake to prescribe by whom any social or industrial operation shall or shall not be conducted, or what modes of conducting them shall be lawful. These things are left to the unfettered choice of individuals. Even the laws which required that workmen should serve an apprenticeship, have in this country been repealed: there being ample assurance that in all cases in which an apprenticeship is necessary, its necessity will suffice to enforce it. The old theory was, that the least possible should be left to the choice of the individual agent; that all he had to do should, as far as practicable, be laid down for him by superior wisdom. Left to himself he was sure to go wrong. The modern conviction, the fruit of a thousand years of experience, is, that things in which the individual is the person directly interested, never go right but as they are left to his own discretion; and that any regulation of them by authority, except to protect the rights of others, is sure to be mischievous. This conclusion, slowly arrived at, and not adopted until almost every possible application of the contrary theory had been made with disastrous result, now (in the industrial department) prevails universally in the most advanced countries, almost universally in all that have pretensions to any sort of advancement. It is not that all processes are supposed to be equally good, or all persons to be equally qualified for everything; but that freedom of individual choice is now known to be the only thing which procures the adoption of the best processes, and throws each operation into the hands of those who are best qualified for it. Nobody thinks it necessary to make a law that only a strong-armed man shall be a blacksmith. Freedom and competition suffice to make blacksmiths strong-armed men, because the weak-armed can earn more by engaging in occupations for which they are more fit. In consonance with this doctrine, it is felt to be an overstepping of the proper bounds of authority to fix beforehand, on some general presumption, that certain persons are not fit to do certain things. It is now thoroughly known and admitted that if some such presumptions exist, no such presumption is infallible. Even if it be well grounded in a majority of cases, which it is very likely not to be, there will be a minority of exceptional cases in which it does not hold: and in those it is both an injustice to the individuals, and a detriment to society, to place barriers in the way of their using their faculties for their own benefit and for that of others. In the cases, on the other hand, in which the unfitness is real, the ordinary motives of human conduct will on the whole suffice to prevent the incompetent person from making, or from persisting in, the attempt.

If this general principle of social and economical science is not true; if individuals, with such help as they can derive from the opinion of those who know them, are not better judges that the law and the government, of their own capabilities and vocation; the world cannot too soon abandon this principle, and return to the old system of regulations and disabilities. But if the principle is true, we ought to act as if we believed it, and not to ordain that to be born a girl instead of a boy, any more than to be born black instead of white, or a commoner instead of a nobleman, shall decide the person's position through all life—shall interdict people from all the more elevated social positions, and from all, except a few, respectable occupations. Even were we to admit the utmost that is ever pretended as to the superior fitness of men for all the functions now reserved to them, the same argument applies which forbids a legal qualification for members of Parliament. If only once in a dozen years the conditions of eligibility exclude a fit person, there is a real loss, while the exclusion of thousands of unfit persons is no gain; for if the constitution of the electoral body disposes them to choose unfit persons, there are always plenty of such persons to choose from. In all things of any difficulty and importance, those who can do them well are fewer than the need, even with the most unrestricted latitude of choice: and any limitation of the field of selection deprives society of some chances of being served by the competent, without ever saving it from the incompetent.

At present, in the more improved countries, the disabilities of women are the only case, save one, in which laws and institutions take persons at their birth, and ordain that they shall never in all their lives be allowed to compete for certain things. The one exception is that of royalty. Persons still are born to the throne; no one, not of the reigning family, can ever occupy it, and no one even of that family can, by any means but the course of hereditary succession, attain it. All other dignities and social advantages are open to the whole male sex: many indeed are only attainable by wealth, but wealth may be striven for by any one, and is actually obtained by many men of the very humblest origin. The difficulties, to the majority, are indeed insuperable without the aid of fortunate accidents; but no male human being is under any legal ban: neither law nor opinion superadd artificial obstacles to the natural ones. Royalty, as I have said, is excepted; but in this case every one feels it to be an exception—an anomaly in the modern world, in marked opposition to its customs and principles, and to be justified only by extraordinary special expediencies, which though individuals and nations differ in estimating their weight, unquestionably do in fact exist. But in this exceptional case, in which a high social function is, for important reasons, bestowed on birth instead of being put up to competition, all free nations contrive to adhere in substance to the principle from which they nominally derogate; for they circumscribe this high function by conditions avowedly intended to prevent the person to whom it ostensibly belongs from really performing it; while the person by whom it is performed, the responsible minister, does obtain the post by a competition from which no full-grown citizen of the male sex is legally excluded. The disabilities, therefore, to which women are subject from the mere fact of their birth, are the solitary examples of the kind in modern legislation. In no instance except this, which comprehends half the human race, are the higher social functions closed against any one by a fatality of birth which no exertions, and no change of circumstances, can overcome; for even religious disabilities (besides that in England and in Europe they have practically almost ceased to exist) do not close any career to the disqualified person in case of conversion.

The social subordination of women thus stands out an isolated fact in modern social institutions; a solitary breach of what has become their fundamental law; a single relic of an old world of thought and practice exploded in everything else, but retained in the one thing of most universal interest; as if a gigantic dolmen, or a vast temple of Jupiter Olympus, occupied the site of St. Paul's and received daily worship, while the surrounding Christian churches were only resorted to on fasts and festivals. The entire discrepancy between one social fact and all those which accompany it, and the radical opposition between its nature and the progressive movement which is the boast of the modern world, and which has successively swept away everything else of an analogous character, surely affords, to a conscientious observer of human tendencies, serious matter for reflection. It raises a prima facie presumption on the unfavourable side, far outweighing any which custom and usage could in such circumstances create on the favourable; and should at least suffice to make this, like the choice between republicanism and royalty, a balanced question.

The least that can be demanded is, that the question should not be considered as pre-judged by existing fact and existing opinion, but open to discussion on its merits, as a question of justice and expediency: the decision on this, as on any of the other social arrangements of mankind, depending on what an enlightened estimate of tendencies and consequences may show to be most advantageous to humanity in general, without dis-tinction of sex. And the discussion must be a real discussion, descending to foundations, and not resting satisfied with vague and general assertions. It will not do, for instance, to assert in general terms, that the experience of mankind has pronounced in favour of the existing system. Experience cannot possibly have decided between two courses, so long as there has only been experience of one. If it be said that the doctrine of the equality of the sexes rests only on theory, it must be remembered that the contrary doctrine also has only theory to rest upon. All that is proved in its favour by direct experience, is that mankind have been able to exist under it, and to attain the degree of improvement and prosperity which we now see; but whether that prosperity has been attained sooner, or is now greater, than it would have been under the other system, experience does not say. On the other hand, experience does say, that every step in improvement has been so invariable accom-panied by a step made in raising the social position of women, that historians and philosophers have been led to adopt their elevation or debasement as on the whole the surest test and most correct measure of the civilization of a people or an age. Through all the progressive period of human history, the condition of women has been approaching nearer to equality with men. This does not of itself prove that the assimilation must go on to complete equality; but it assuredly affords some presumption that such is the case.

Neither does it avail anything to say that the *nature* of the two sexes adapts them to their present functions and position, and renders these appropriate to them. Standing on the ground of common sense and the constitution of the human mind, I deny that any one knows, or can know, the nature of the two sexes, as long as they have only been seen in their present relation to one another. If men had ever been found in society without women, or women without men, or if there had been a society of men and women in which the women were not under the control of the men, something might have been positively known about the mental and moral differences which may be inherent in the nature of each. What is now called the nature of women is an eminently artificial thing—the result of forced repression in some directions, unnatural stimulation in others. It may be asserted without scruple, that no other class of dependents have had their character so entirely distorted from its natural proportions by their relation with their masters; for, if conquered and slave races have been, in some respects, more forcibly repressed, whatever in them has not been crushed down by an iron heel has generally been let alone, and if left with any liberty of development, it has developed itself according to its own laws; but in the case of women, a hothouse and stove cultivation has always been carried on of some of the capabilities of their nature, for the benefit and pleasure of their masters. Then, because certain products of the general vital force sprout luxuriantly and reach a great development in this heated atmosphere and under this active nurture and watering, while other shoots from the same root, which are left outside in the wintry air, with ice purposely heaped all round them, have a stunted growth, and some are burnt off with fire and disappear; men, with that inability to recognize their own work which distinguishes the unanalytic mind, indolently believe that the tree grows of itself in the way they have made it grow, and that it would die if one half of it were not kept in a vapour bath and the other half in the snow.

Of all difficulties which impede the progress of thought, and the formation of well-grounded opinions on life and social arrangements, the greatest is now the unspeakable ignorance and inattention of mankind in respect to the influences which form human character. Whatever any portion of the human species now are, or seem to be, such, it is supposed, they have a natural tendency to be: even when the most elementary knowledge of the circumstances in which they have been placed, clearly points out the causes that made them what they are. Because a cottier deeply in arrears to his landlord is not industrious, there are people who think that the Irish are naturally idle. Because constitutions can be overthrown when the authorities appointed to execute them turn their arms against them, there are people who think the French incapable of free government. Because the Greeks cheated the Turks, and the Turks only plundered the Greeks, there are persons who think that the Turks are naturally more sincere: and because women, as is often said, care nothing about politics except their personalities, it is supposed that the general good is naturally less interesting to women than to men. History, which is now so much better understood than formerly, teaches another lesson: if only by showing the extraordinary susceptibility of human nature to external influences, and the extreme variableness of those of its manifestations which are supposed to be most universal and uniform. But in history, as in travelling, men usually see only what they already had in their own minds, and few learn much from history, who do not bring much with them to its study.

Hence, in regard to that most difficult question, what are the natural differences between the two sexes—a subject on which it is impossible in the present state of society to obtain complete and correct knowledge—while almost everybody dogmatizes upon it, almost all neglect and make light of the only means by which any partial insight can be obtained into it. This is, an analytic study of the most important department of psychology, the laws of the influence of circumstances on character. For, however great and apparently ineradicable the moral and intellectual differences between men and women might be, the evidence of their being natural differences could only be negative. Those only could be inferred to be natural which could not possibly be artificial—the residuum, after deducting every characteristic of either sex which can admit of being explained from education or external circumstances. The profoundest knowledge of the laws of the formation of character is indispensable to entitle any one to affirm even that there is any difference, much more what the difference is, between the two sexes considered as moral and rational beings; and since no one, as yet, has that knowledge (for there is hardly any subject which, in proportion to its importance, has been so little studied), no one is thus far entitled to any positive opinion on the subject. Conjectures are all that can at present be made; conjectures more or less probable, according as more or less authorized by such knowledge as we yet have of the laws of psychology, as applied to the formation of character.

Even the preliminary knowledge, what the differences between the sexes now are, apart from all question as to how they are made and what they are, is still in the crudest and most incomplete state. Medical practitioners and psychologists have ascertained, to some extent, the differences in bodily constitution; and this is an important element to the psychologist; but hardly any medical practitioner is a psychologist. Respecting the mental characteristics of women; their observations are of no more worth than those of common men. It is a subject on which nothing final can be known, so long as those who alone can really know it, women themselves, have given but little testimony, and that little, mostly suborned. It is easy to know stupid women. Stupidity is much the same all the world over. A stupid person's notions and feelings may confidently be inferred from those which prevail in the circle by which the person is surrounded. Not so with those whose opinions and feelings are an emanation from their own nature and faculties. It is only a man here and there who has any tolerable knowledge of the character even of the women of his own family. I do not mean, of their capabilities; these nobody knows, not even themselves, because most of them have never been called out. I mean their actually existing thoughts and feelings. Many a man thinks he perfectly understands women, because he has had amatory relations with several, perhaps with many of them. If he is a good observer, and his experience extends to quality as well as quantity, he may have learnt something of one narrow department of their nature—an important department, no doubt. But of all the rest of it, few persons are generally more ignorant, because there are few from whom it is so carefully hidden. The most favourable case which a man can generally have for study- ing the character of a woman, is that of his own wife: for the opportunities are greater, and the cases of complete sympathy not so unspeakably rare. And in fact, this is the source from which any knowledge worth having on the subject has, I believe, generally come. But most men have not had the opportunity of studying in this way more than a single case: accordingly one can, to an almost laughable degree, infer what a man's wife is like, from his opinions about women in general. To make even this one case yield any result, the woman must be worth knowing, and the man not only a competent judge, but of a character so sympathetic in itself, and so well adapted to hers, that he can either read her mind by sympathetic intuition, or has nothing in himself which makes her shy of dis- closing it. Hardly anything, I believe, can be more rare, than this conjunction. It often happens that there is the most complete unity of feeling and community of interests as to all external things, yet the one has as little admission into the internal life of the other as if they were common acquaintance. Even with true affection, authority on the one side and subordination on the other prevent perfect confidence. Though nothing may be inten- tionally withheld, much is not shown. In the analogous relation of parent and child, the corresponding phenomenon must have been in the observation of every one. As between father and son, how many are the cases in which the father, in spite of real affection on both sides, obviously to all the world does not know, nor suspect, parts of the son's char- acter familiar to his companions and equals. The truth is, that the position of looking up to another is extremely unpropitious to complete sincerity and openness with him. The fear of losing ground in his opinion or in his feelings is so strong, that even in an upright character, there is an unconscious tendency to show only the best side, or the side which, though not the best, is that which he most likes to see: and it may be confidently said that thorough knowledge of one another hardly ever exists, but between persons who, besides being intimates, are equals. How much more true, then, must all this be, when the one is not only under the authority of the other, but has it inculcated on her as a duty to reckon everything else subordinate to his comfort and pleasure, and to let him neither see nor feel anything coming from her, except what is agreeable to him. All these difficulties stand in the way of a man's obtaining any thorough knowledge even of the one woman whom alone, in general, he has sufficient opportunity of studying. When we further consider that to understand one woman is not necessarily to understand any other woman; that even if he could study many women of one rank, or of one country, he would not thereby understand women of other ranks or countries; and even if he did, they are still only the women of a single period of history; we may safely assert that the knowledge which men can acquire of women, even as they have been and are, without reference to what they might be, is wretchedly imperfect and superficial, and always will be so, until women themselves have told all that they have to tell.

And this time has not come; nor will it come otherwise than gradually. It is but of yes- terday that women have either been qualified by literary accomplishments, or permitted by society, to tell anything to the general public. As yet very few of them dare tell any- thing, which men, on whom their literary success depends, are unwilling to hear. Let us remember in what manner, up to a very recent time, the expression, even by a male author, of uncustomary opinions, or what are deemed eccentric feelings, usually was, and in some degree still is, received; and we may form some faint conception under what impediments a woman, who is brought up to think custom and opinion her sovereign rule, attempts to express in books anything drawn from the depths of her own nature. The greatest woman who has left writings behind her sufficient to give her an eminent rank in the literature of her country, thought it necessary to prefix as a motto to her boldest work, 'Un homme peut braver l'opinion; une femme doit s'y soumettre.'[1] The greater part of what women write about women is mere sycophancy to men. In the case of unmarried women, much of it seems only intended to increase their chance of a husband. Many, both married and unmarried, over-step the mark, and inculcate a servility beyond what is desired or relished by any man, except the very vulgarest. But this is not so often the case as, even at quite a late period, it still was. Literary women are becoming more freespoken, and more willing to express their real sentiments. Unfortunately, in this country especially, they are themselves such artificial products, that their sentiments are compounded of a small element of individual observation and consciousness, and a very large one of acquired associations. This will be less and less the case, but it will remain true to a great extent, as long as social institutions do not admit the same free development of originality in women which is possible to men. When that time comes, and not before, we shall see, and not merely hear, as much as it is necessary to know of the nature of women, and the adaptation of other things to it.

I have dwelt so much on the difficulties which at present obstruct any real knowledge by men of the true nature of women, because in this as in so many other things 'opinio copiae inter maximas causas inopiae est'; and there is little chance of reasonable thinking on the matter, while people flatter themselves that they perfectly understand a subject of which most men know absolutely nothing, and of which it is at present impossible that any man, or all men taken together, should have knowledge which can qualify them to lay down the law to women as to what is, or is not, their vocation. Happily, no such knowledge is necessary for any practical purpose connected with the position of women in relation to society and life. For, according to all the principles involved in modern society, the question rests with women themselves—to be decided by their own experience, and by the use of their own faculties. There are no means of finding what either one person or many can do, but by trying—and no means by which any one else can discover for them what it is for their happiness to do or leave undone.

One thing we may be certain of—that what is contrary to women's nature to do, they never will be made to do by simply giving their nature free play. The anxiety of mankind to interfere in behalf of nature, for fear lest nature should not succeed in effecting its purpose, is an altogether unnecessary solicitude. What women by nature cannot do, it is quite superfluous to forbid them from doing. What they can do, but not so well as the men who are their competitors, competition suffices to exclude them from; since nobody asks for protective duties and bounties in favour of women; it is only asked that the present bounties and protective duties in favour of men should be recalled. If women have a greater natural inclination for some things than for others, there is no need of laws or social inculcation to make the majority of them do the former in preference to the latter. Whatever women's services are most wanted for, the free play of competition will hold out the strongest inducements to them to undertake. And, as the words imply, they are most wanted for the things for which they are most fit; by the apportionment of which to them, the collective faculties of the two sexes can be applied on the whole with the greatest sum of valuable result.

The general opinion of men is supposed to be, that the natural vocation of a woman is that of a wife and mother. I say, is supposed to be, because, judging from acts—from the whole of the present constitution of society—one might infer that their opinion was the direct contrary. They might be supposed to think that the alleged natural vocation of women was of all things the most repugnant to their nature; insomuch that if they are free to do anything else—if any other means of living, or occupation of their time and faculties, is open, which has any chance of appearing desirable to them—there will not be enough of them who will be willing to accept the condition said to be natural to them. If this is the real opinion of men in general, it would be well that it should be spoken out. I should like to hear somebody openly enunciating the doctrine (it is already implied in much that is written on the subject)— 'It is necessary to society that women should marry and produce children. They will not do so unless they are compelled. Therefore it is necessary to compel them.' The merits of the case would then be clearly defined. It would be exactly that of the slaveholders of South Carolina and Louisiana. 'It is necessary that cotton and sugar should be grown. White men cannot produce them. Negroes will not, for any wages which we choose to give. *Ergo* they must be compelled.' An illustration still closer to the point is that of impressment. Sailors must absolutely be had to defend the country. It often happens that they will not voluntarily enlist. Therefore there must be the power of forcing them. How often has this logic been used! and, but for one flaw in it, without doubt it would have been successful up to this day. But it is open to retort—First pay the sailors the honest value of their labour. When you have made it as well worth their while to serve you, as to work for other employers, you will have no more difficulty than others have in obtaining their services. To this there is no logical answer except 'I will not': and as people are now not only ashamed, but are not desirous, to rob the labourer of his hire, impressment is no longer advocated. Those who attempt to force women into marriage by closing all other doors against them, lay themselves open to a similar retort. If they mean what they say, their opinion must evidently be, that men do not render the married condition so desirable to women, as to induce them to accept it for its own recommendations. It is not a sign of one's thinking the boon one offers very attractive, when one allows only Hobson's choice, 'that or none.' And here, I believe, is the clue to the feelings of those men, who have a real antipathy to the equal freedom of women. I believe they are afraid, nor lest women should be unwilling to marry, for I do not think that any one in reality has that apprehension; but lest they should insist that marriage should be on equal conditions; lest all women of spirit and capacity should prefer doing almost anything else, not in their own eyes degrading, rather than marry, when marrying is giving themselves a master, and a master too of all their earthly possessions. And truly, if this consequence were necessarily incident to marriage, I think that the apprehension would be very well founded. I agree in thinking it probable that few women, capable of anything else, would, unless under an irresistible *entraînement,* rendering them for the time insensible to anything but itself, choose such a lot, when any other means were open to them of filling a conventionally honourable place in life: and if men are determined that the law of marriage shall be a law of despotism, they are quite right, in point of mere policy, in leaving to women only Hobson's choice. But, in that case, all that has been done in the modern world to relax the chain on the minds of women, has been a mistake. They never should have been allowed to receive a literary education. Women who read, much more women who write, are, in the existing constitution of things, a contradiction and a disturbing element: and it was wrong to bring women up with any acquirements but those of an odalisque, or of a domestic servant.

Note

1. Title page of Mme de Staël's *Delphine.*